The World Book Encyclopedia

N·O   Volume 14

Field Enterprises Educational Corporation
Chicago   London   Rome   Sydney   Toronto

1972 Edition

The World Book Encyclopedia

Copyright © 1971, U.S.A.
by
Field Enterprises Educational Corporation

Nn

is the 14th letter in our alphabet. It was also the fourteenth letter in the alphabet used by the Semitic peoples, who once lived in Syria and Palestine. They called the letter *nun*, their word for fish. But its symbol apparently came from the Egyptian hieroglyphic (or picture writing) for snake, which began with the same sound. The Greeks took over the letter from the Phoenicians and called it *nu*. See ALPHABET.

Uses. *N* or *n* is about the fifth most frequently used letter in books, newspapers, and other printed material in English. In mathematics, *n* represents an indefinite number. As an abbreviation, *n* may stand for *noun, neuter, noon, name,* or *not. N,* in chemical formulas, means *nitrogen;* in geographic descriptions, *north* or *northern.* As a printer's term, *en* means a medium blank space, half the width of the em (see MM [Uses]). In medieval Roman numerals, *N* represented 90 and *N̄*, 90,000.

Pronunciation. In English, a person pronounces *n* by placing the tip of his tongue against the gums behind his front teeth and making the sound through his nose. In such words as *hymn*, the final *n* is silent. But in such words as *gnostic* or *mnemonic*, the first *n* is pronounced, and the letter before it is silent. Double *n*, in words such as *manner*, is pronounced like *n*. In words like *pen-name*, each *n* is pronounced. The letter has much the same sound in classical Greek and Latin, and in French and German. In Spanish, when written with a tilde, *ñ*, it has a *ny* sound, as in the English word *canyon*. See PRONUNCIATION. I. J. GELB and J. M. WELLS

The fourteenth letter took its shape from a symbol used in ancient Egypt to represent a snake, but its sound came from a Semitic word meaning *fish*.

The Romans, about A.D. 114, used straight lines for the N.

The Greeks, about 600 B.C., called the thirteenth letter *nu*.

The Phoenicians, about 1000 B.C., simplified the Semitic symbol.

The Small Letter n developed from Roman writing about A.D. 500. Monks modified the letter in the 800's. By about 1500, it had its present shape.

n   *n*   TODAY

A.D. 500   A.D. 800   n n

The Egyptians, about 3000 B.C., drew this symbol of a snake.

The Semites, about 1500 B.C., made a letter that stood for a fish and gave it the sound *nun*.

EUROPE
Atlantic Ocean
ROME
GREECE
ASIA
Mediterranean Sea
PHOENICIA
EGYPT SINAI
AFRICA

NAA. See NATIONAL AERONAUTIC ASSOCIATION OF THE U.S.A.

NAACP. See NATIONAL ASSOCIATION FOR THE ADVANCEMENT OF COLORED PEOPLE.

NABATAEAN. See JORDAN (Early Days); PETRA.

NABOKOV, *NAH boh kawf,* **VLADIMIR** (1899-   ), is a Russian-born author. His novels are noted for their complicated plots and the complex attitudes they express toward their subjects. Critics have praised Nabokov's novels for their wit, intricate use of words, and rich language. His novels include *Invitation to a Beheading* (published in Russia, 1938; United States, 1959), *The Real Life of Sebastian Knight* (1941), *Lolita* (published in France, 1955; United States, 1958), *Pnin* (1957), *Pale Fire* (1962), and *Ada* (1969). Nabokov also has published collections of stories and poetry and has translated several Russian literary classics into English. *Speak, Memory* (1951, expanded 1966) is his autobiography.

Nabokov was born in St. Petersburg (now Leningrad). His father was a wealthy landowner and a famous jurist and statesman. The family fled to Western Europe in 1919 because of the Bolshevik revolution. Nabokov attended Cambridge University in England from 1919 to 1922. From 1922 to 1940, he lived in Berlin and Paris among other Russians who had left their country because of the revolution. He wrote his novels in Russian, and most were later translated into English. In 1940, Nabokov settled in the United States and began to write in English. He became a U.S. citizen in 1945. Nabokov returned to Europe to live in 1959.   MARCUS KLEIN

NABONIDUS. See BELSHAZZAR; CYRUS THE GREAT.

NABOPOLASSAR, *NAB oh poh LAS ahr,* reigned as king of Babylonia from 625 to 605 B.C. About 612 B.C., he joined with the Medes to defeat the Assyrians who had ruled Babylonia for more than 100 years. He founded the New Babylonian Empire and started Babylonia on its last rise to greatness. The empire reached its peak under his son and successor, Nebuchadnezzar II. It is sometimes called the *Chaldean* Empire, because Nabopolassar belonged to one of the Chaldean tribes of southern Babylonia.   JACOB J. FINKELSTEIN

NABRIT, JAMES MADISON, JR. (1900-   ), won fame as a lawyer, university president, and diplomat. From 1960 to 1969, he was president of Howard University. He was the first Negro to become deputy U.S. representative to the United Nations (UN). He held the post in 1966 and 1967, while on leave from Howard.

Nabrit was born in Atlanta, Ga. He graduated from Morehouse College and Northwestern University Law School. In 1936, he joined the faculty of Howard University. At his suggestion, the university established—and he taught—the first civil rights course in an American law school. Nabrit was secretary of the university from 1939 to 1960, and dean of its law school from 1958 to 1960. As president of Howard, he encouraged greater student involvement in the operation of the university. As a lawyer, Nabrit specialized in civil rights cases, especially school desegregation cases.   EDGAR ALLAN TOPPIN

NACELLE. See AIRPLANE (Engines).

NACRE. See MOTHER-OF-PEARL.

NADER, RALPH (1934-   ), an American lawyer, became famous for fighting business and government prac-

Newsweek
Ralph Nader

tices that he felt endangered public health and safety. In his book *Unsafe at Any Speed* (1965), Nader argued that the U.S. automobile industry emphasized profits and style over safety. The National Traffic and Motor Vehicle Safety Act of 1966, which established safety standards for new cars, resulted largely from his work.

Nader's studies of the meat and poultry industries, coal mines, and natural gas pipelines also resulted in stricter health and safety laws. He publicized what he felt were the dangers of pesticides, various food additives, radiation from color television sets, and excessive use of X rays. He said the government was not strict enough in enforcing antipollution and consumer protection laws. He also charged that various government agencies denied the people their right to information about the activities of those agencies.

Nader was born in Winsted, Conn., the son of Lebanese immigrants. He graduated from Princeton University and Harvard Law School. Nader's operating funds come mainly from his writings and speeches and from foundation grants. He often relies on college students and young lawyers, nicknamed "Nader's Raiders," to help him gather data.   LEONARD S. SILK

NADIR, *NAY der,* is the point in space directly below where one stands. To an observer on earth, the sky appears to be a half-dome whose edge forms a great circle resting on the flat surface of the earth. Imagine a plumb line suspended from the center of this dome, directly above your head, and passing through the center of the earth and into space as far as the central point of the invisible half-dome beneath the earth. The two points marking the ends of our imaginary plumb line are, respectively, the *zenith* and the *nadir*. They are the poles of the horizon, and each is 90° from the horizon. See also ZENITH.   OLIVER J. LEE

NADIR SHAH. See IRAN (Conquests of Nadir Shah).

NAGANA. See TSETSE FLY.

NAGASAKI, *NAH guh SAH kee* (pop. 420,000; alt. 200 ft.), is the Japanese city with which Westerners have had the longest contact. Its harbor was opened to foreign trade in 1568, and Portuguese ships occasionally called. After 1637, it was the only Japanese port where foreigners were allowed to trade. Dutch traders were permitted to set up a trading post on an island in the harbor, and one Dutch ship each year was allowed to call at the post. In 1857, it was one of the six Japanese ports opened to foreign trade.

Nagasaki is on the west coast of the island of Kyushu. It is important as the Japanese port city closest to the mainland of China. Nearby coal fields provide a source of soft coal for export. Nagasaki is on a landlocked bay, which is deep and large enough to hold many ships. The city itself is built on hills around the harbor. For location, see JAPAN (political map).

Because Nagasaki has a large steel rolling mill, it is one of Japan's most important shipbuilding centers. Many of the factories in Nagasaki were destroyed on

August 9, 1945, by the second atomic bomb used in warfare. The blast destroyed 1.8 square miles in the heart of the city. Forty thousand persons were injured and 40,000 were killed or missing. Since the war, most of Nagasaki has been rebuilt.   Hugh Borton

See also Atomic Bomb (pictures).

NÄGELI, *neh JELL ee*, **KARL WILHELM** (1817-1891), a Swiss botanist and philosopher, studied the growth of roots, stems, and pollen grains. He discovered the nitrogenous nature of protoplasm, and described cell division in the formation of pollen and in simple algae. His philosophical views led him to scorn Gregor Mendel's proof of heredity (see Mendel, Gregor J.).

Nägeli was born in Kilchberg, Switzerland. He was professor of botany at the universities of Freiburg, Zurich, and Munich.

NAGOYA, *nah GO yah* (pop. 1,990,227; alt. 50 ft.), is the third largest city of Japan. It is the capital of Aichi prefecture on the island of Honshu. It stands on Nobi plain, facing Ise Bay (see Japan [political map]).

Nagoya was once the seat of the powerful *daimio* (baron) of Owari, a province of early Japan. In 1610, a great five-story castle was built in Nagoya. The castle was destroyed during World War II.

Nagoya is famous as a manufacturing center. It has an important textile industry. It also manufactures many types of machines, and is noted for its pottery, porcelain, lacquer ware, clocks, fans, and embroidery. Nagoya's industries and its population are crowded into a closely packed area.   Hugh Borton

NAGPUR, *NAHG poor* (pop. 745,847; met. area 820,161; alt. 1,020 ft.), India, is a city in the state of Mahārāshtra. For location, see India (political map). Nagpur is a railroad center. Cotton from nearby farms is made into cloth in Nagpur, and shipped to other parts of India. The city also has oil mills and a large fruit-canning industry. Hislop College and Nagpur University are there.   Robert I. Crane

NAGUIB, *nah GEEB*, **MOHAMMED** (1901-   ), was a leader in the Egyptian revolution of 1952 that forced King Faruk to abdicate. Naguib became prime minister in the new government. But in 1954, Gamal Abdel Nasser replaced Naguib and forced him into retirement.

Naguib was born in Khartoum in the Sudan. He entered the army, and attended Fuad University and the Royal Military Academy in Cairo. He fought against Israel in 1948, and later became a major general. During the fighting, he realized how corruption in government had crippled the Egyptian army. He emerged from the war as a hero, and became a reformist. Naguib formed a secret group known as the Free Officers. This group led the revolution in 1952 that forced Faruk to leave Egypt.   T. Walter Wallbank

NAHUATL. See Aztec (Life of the Aztec); Indian, American (Latin-American Indian Languages).

NAHUM, *NAY hum*, was one of the Hebrew "minor prophets" in the Bible. The Old Testament book bearing his name contains poems he wrote. The book opens with a poem believed to be the work of another author. The second and third chapters are Nahum's description of the fall of Nineveh, Assyria, in 612 B.C. Some scholars believe Nahum described the actual fall of the city. Others say the poems are his prophecy written before the capture of Nineveh.   Walter A. Williams

NAIAD. See Nymph.

NAIL. When a carpenter wants to fasten two pieces of wood or composition building board together cheaply and securely, he uses a nail. The sharp point at one end of a nail forms an opening wedge for the body of the nail when it is driven into the wood with a hammer. At the other end is a flattened head that covers the hole the nail has made.

Kinds of Nails. The United States produces about a half million tons of nails a year, in as many as 1,200 different shapes and sizes. The biggest nail is the boat spike, which weighs about 2 pounds and is about 15 inches long. The smallest nail is the needle nail. It takes 95,000 needle nails to weigh a pound.

Most nails are classified in two ways, by use and by the shape of the head. Nails classified by use include roofing, deck, railroad, boat, shoe, and general carpentry nails. Carpenters use four chief kinds of nails:

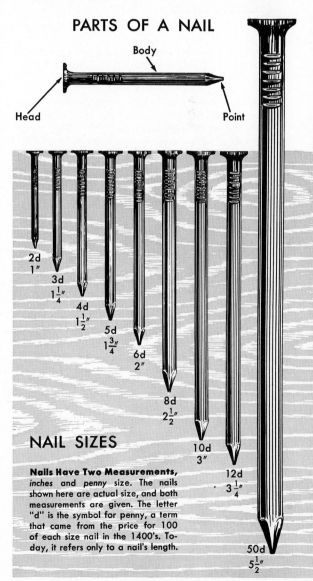

PARTS OF A NAIL

Body

Head

Point

NAIL SIZES

2d
1"

3d
1¼"

4d
1½"

5d
1¾"

6d
2"

8d
2½"

10d
3"

12d
3¼"

50d
5½"

Nails Have Two Measurements, *inches* and *penny* size. The nails shown here are actual size, and both measurements are given. The letter "d" is the symbol for penny, a term that came from the price for 100 of each size nail in the 1400's. Today, it refers only to a nail's length.

TYPES OF NAILS

Nails Have Various Shapes, depending on how they are to be used.

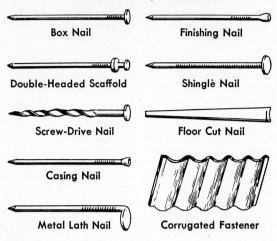

Box Nail

Finishing Nail

Double-Headed Scaffold

Shingle Nail

Screw-Drive Nail

Floor Cut Nail

Casing Nail

Metal Lath Nail

Corrugated Fastener

(1) *common wire nails* for most wood framing projects such as window frames, (2) *smooth and barbed box nails* for box-type wood construction such as cabinet drawers, (3) *flooring brads* for the laying of hardwood floors, and (4) finishing nails and casing nails, which are used when the nail must be hard to see in the finished product.

The shapes of nailheads include the clasp, clinch, double-headed, countersunk, diamond, and rose.

How to Select and Drive a Nail. Carpenters determine the length of the nail they need by the thicknesses of the two pieces of wood that must be fastened together. The nail should be long enough to pierce one of the pieces of wood and a little more than half the second piece.

For most purposes, a rounded nail is satisfactory. But a square-cut nail is best for attaching shingles. This type of nail is cut with squared corners from sheets of metal. Square-cut nails, although stronger than round nails, are harder to drive in and tend to split the wood. The grooved nail stays tightly in place. The shoe and automobile industries use this type of nail extensively.

The best way to drive a nail is to hit it squarely on the head with quick, sharp strokes of the hammer. If the stroke is a little to one side of the head, the nail may be bent or broken and the head pounded out of shape. Many carpenters believe that nails driven into the wood at a slight angle hold better than nails that are driven straight. Carpenters often moisten nails in their mouths to make them drive more easily.

How Nails Are Made. The modern nail-manufacturing machine developed from a machine invented in 1786 by Ezekiel Reed of Massachusetts. The three main parts of a nail machine are the nippers, the pliers, and the hammer. Wire is drawn into the machine from reels. As it passes the nippers, it is cut into the proper lengths. The pliers point one end of each section. The hammer flattens out the blunt ends to make the finished nail. Most nail machines make from 100 to 1,000 nails a minute, the amount depending on the size of the nails being manufactured. Most nails are made from steel or aluminum wire. Aluminum nails will not rust. Stainless steel nails and nails made from titanium will not corrode even when used with powerful chemicals. Nails are also available in copper and bronze.

Sizes of Nails. Nails are usually classified according to their length, a 2½-inch nail being called a "2½." Nails may also be classified as sixpenny, eightpenny, and so on. The "penny" increases with the length of the nail. For example, an eightpenny nail is 2½ inches long, and a twelvepenny nail is 3¼ inches long. The term *penny* originally referred to the weight of the nail. There once were about a thousand penny nails to the pound, and 400 fourpenny nails to the pound.

Nails are sold by the pound or in kegs of 100 pounds. Wire nails are quite cheap, and square-cut nails are expensive by comparison. Nails increase in price as they become smaller than the standard four-inch length that is commonly used.   WALTER R. WILLIAMS, JR.

NAIL. The horns, claws, talons, and hoofs of birds and animals are made up of the same materials as the nails on the fingers and toes of the human body. Deer antlers are another kind of growth. Horns, nails, claws, talons, and hoofs are special growths of the outer skin, or epidermis. They are made up of hardened skin cells.

The skin below the nail, from which it grows, is called the *matrix*. Near the root of the nail, the cells are smaller and carry less blood. The white, crescent-shaped spot indicating these cells is the *lunula* (from *luna*, meaning *moon*). If a nail is torn off, it will grow again, provided the matrix has not been severely injured. White spots on the nail are due to bruises or other minor injuries. They will grow out as the nail grows.

The state of a person's health is often indicated by the nails. A serious illness often affects the growth of the nail.   W. B. YOUMANS

CARE OF THE NAILS

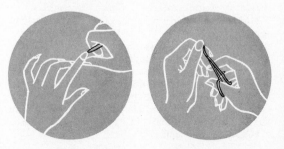

Shaping and Cleaning. Use a file to shape the nails to rounded points, *above*. Cleaning under the nails should be carefully done with an orangewood stick, *below*. Do not use a knife or other metal tool.

Removing the Cuticle. Soften the cuticle with a little Vaseline or oil. Then loosen it gently with an orangewood stick, *above*. Remove the loose cuticle carefully with manicure scissors, *below*.

NAINSOOK, *NAYN sook*, is a fine white cotton fabric often used for making women's blouses, baby dresses, and lingerie. It is like cambric, except that nainsook has a shiny finish. Nainsook is usually bleached white, but may be dyed.

See also CAMBRIC.

NAIROBI, *ny RO bih* (pop. 266,800; alt. 5,542 ft.), is the capital of Kenya, in East Africa. The city stands on the Athi plains at the foot of Kikuyu Hills, about 330 miles northwest of Mombasa (see KENYA [map]). Bantus, a Negro group, make up a large part of the population. More than one-third of the European and Indian settlers of Kenya live in Nairobi. Most of the Europeans live in the hills above the city. Nairobi is the starting point for many big-game safaris.   HIBBERD V. B. KLINE, JR.

See also BANTU; KENYA.

NAISMITH, JAMES A. (1861-1939), invented the game of basketball in 1891 (see BASKETBALL). He wanted to develop a game that could be played indoors during the winter months. He tacked up two peach baskets, and used a soccer ball for the first game. He invented the game when he was a physical-education teacher at the Young Men's Christian Association College in Springfield, Mass.

Naismith was graduated from McGill University in Montreal, Canada, in 1887. He was one of Canada's greatest rugby and lacrosse players. He studied for the ministry, but became a physical-education teacher. He became director of physical education at the University of Kansas in 1898. Naismith was born in Almonte, Ontario, Canada.   RICHARD G. HACKENBERG

NAME, PERSONAL. Practically everyone since the beginning of history has had a name. Some explorers have reported discovering primitive tribes where people had no names. In these cases, tribesmen were probably reluctant to disclose their names to a stranger. A superstition, widespread among primitive peoples throughout the world, held that if a person knew your name, he could acquire power over you and bring harm to you. Some peoples have kept their real names secret, being known only by nicknames.

Almost all names have meanings. Early peoples bestowed a name with a definite consciousness of its meaning. This was especially true among primitive peoples. In the Bible, a widow exclaims, "Call me not Naomi (pleasant), call me Mara (bitter): for the Almighty hath dealt very bitterly with me" (Ruth 1: 20). But today we give little thought to the meanings.

Most people have a given name and a family name. Many also have a middle name or a nickname.

Given, or First, Names

Most of our common *given*, or *first*, names (often called *Christian* names) come from Hebrew, Greek, Latin, or Teutonic tongues.

Hebrew Names taken from the Bible have provided the most important source of Christian names. The most common boy's name is *John* (gracious gift of Yahveh), and the most common girl's name is *Mary* (bitter). Other common Hebrew names include *David* (beloved), *Elizabeth* (oath of God), *James* (may God protect), *Joseph* (He shall add), *Hannah* (God has favored me), and *Samuel* (name of God). These Biblical names occur in various forms among all Christian nations.

Greek and Latin Names often refer to abstract qualities. Common Greek names include *Alexander* (helper of mankind), *Barbara* (stranger), *George* (farmer), *Helen* (light), *Margaret* (pearl), *Philip* (lover of horses), and *Stephen* (crown or garland). Common Latin names include *Clarence* (famous), *Emily* (industrious), *Patricia* (noble), *Victor* (conqueror), and *Virginia* (pertaining to spring).

Teutonic Names are widely used and are among the most popular Christian names, especially boys' names. They usually consist of two elements joined together without regard to their relationship. For example, *William* is composed of two name elements, *Wille* (will, or resolution), and *helm* (helmet). But the name *William* does not mean "helmet of will" or "resolute helmet." It means "will, helmet." Some of these name elements are found at the beginning, as *ead* (rich) in *Edwin* and *Edmund*. They may also occur at the end, as *weard* (guardian) in *Howard* and *Edward*.

Family Names. In England and America, family names may often be used as Christian names. Names like Percy, Sydney, and Lincoln are now recognized Christian names. Some of the outstanding leaders in the United States, including Washington Irving, Hamilton Fish, Franklin Delano Roosevelt, and Jefferson Davis, had such names.

Saints' Names. The Roman Catholic Church, since the Council of Trent (1545-1563), has insisted that Catholic parents give a saint's name to each child. This is not difficult, because most common Christian names have now been borne by one or more saints.

Family, or Last, Names

Beginnings. The Chinese were the first known people to acquire more than one name. The Emperor Fushi is said to have decreed the use of family names, or *surnames*, about 2852 B.C. The Chinese customarily have three names. The family name, placed first, comes from one of the 438 words in the Chinese sacred poem *Po-Chia-Hsing*. It is followed by a *generation name*, taken from a poem of 20 or 30 characters adopted by each family; and a *milk name*, corresponding to our Christian name. In America, the Chinese often follow Western practice and put the family name last.

In early times, the Romans had only one name, but later they also used three names. The *praenomen* stood first as the person's given name. Next came the *nomen*, which indicated the *gens*, or clan. The last name, the *cognomen*, designated the family. For example, Caesar's full name was *Gaius Julius Caesar*. A person sometimes added a fourth name, the *agnomen*, to commemorate an illustrious action or remarkable event. Family names became confused by the fall of the Roman Empire, and single names once again became customary.

The Middle Ages. Family names came into use again in northern Italy about the late A.D. 900's, and became common about the 1200's. Nobles first adopted family names to set them apart from the common people. The nobles made these family names hereditary, and they descended from father to children. The nobility called attention to their ancestors in this way. A family name became the mark of a gentleman, so the common people began to adopt the practice too.

The Crusaders carried the custom of family names

from Italy to the other countries of Western Europe. Throughout Europe, wealthy and noble families first adopted family names. At first, these were not hereditary, but merely described one person. For example, the son of Robert Johnson might be known as Henry Robertson, or Henry, son of Robert.

Origin of Family Names

It is difficult to work out a simple classification of family names, because of corruption and changes in spelling and pronunciation. Many old words are now obsolete or have obsolete meanings. For many years, spelling depended on the discretion of the writer. The same name might be spelled in different ways even in the same document. Some names appear to come from recognizable English words, but they are actually from another language. Foreign names are often altered into more familiar words. The Dutch *Roggenfelder* (dweller in or near a rye field) became the American *Rockefeller*.

Family names have come down to us in various ways. They may have grown out of a person's surroundings, his job, or his ancestor's name.

Place Names came from a man's place of residence. For example, if he lived on or near a hill or mountain, he might be Mr. *Maki*, if from Finland, Mr. *Dumont* or Mr. *Depew* in France; Mr. *Zola* in Italy; Mr. *Jurek* in Poland; and of course, Mr. *Hill* in England. In England, people might be known as *Wood*, *Lake*, *Brook*, *Stone*, or *Ford* because of their location. During the Middle Ages, few people could read. Signboards often exhibited the picture of an animal or object to designate a shop or inn. A person working or living at the place might be called *Bell*, *Star*, or *Swan*. A person might also be named after the town he came from, such as *Middleton* or *Kronenberg*. Many English place names may be recognized by the endings -*ham*, -*thorp*, -*ton*, -*wic*, and -*worth*, meaning a homestead or dwelling.

Occupation. Family names also come from a person's job. Names like *Baker*, *Carpenter*, *Clarke* (the English pronunciation of clerk), *Cook*, *Miller* and *Taylor* are quite common.

The most common surname in the English language is Smith, a shortened form of blacksmith. It is also common in many other countries. It takes the form of *Schmidt* in Germany, *Lefevre* in France, *Ferraro* in Italy, and *Kuznetzvo* in Russia. In the Middle Ages, there was generally only one blacksmith in every village. Because he was respected for his skill, he easily acquired the surname of *Smith*.

Ancestor's Name. Many people took surnames from their father's given name. Practically every language has a suffix or prefix meaning "son of." Some names that include the term "son of" include Irish names beginning with *O'*, German names ending in -*sohn* or -*son*, and Scandinavian names ending in -*sen* or -*son*. Russian and Serbian names ending in -*ovitch* and Romanian names ending in -*escu* have the same meaning. Those describing the bearer of the name as the *son of John* include *Johnson* and *Jackson* in England; *Johns* and *Jones* in Wales; *Jensen*, *Jansen*, and *Hansen* in Denmark; *Jonsson* and *Johanson* in Sweden; *Janowicz* in Poland; *Ivanov* in Russia and Bulgaria; *Janosfi* in Hungary; and *MacEoin* in Ireland. Less common

names indicating relationships include *Brothers*, *Eames* (uncle), and *Watmought* (Wat's brother-in-law).

Many surnames came from terms that described an ancestor. In the Middle Ages, most Europeans lived in small villages, and needed only a single name. When the village clerk had to note in his records that a villager had paid a tax, he often had to identify just which Robert was meant. The clerk would then add some descriptive word without consulting the man involved. For example, he might call a man *Robert, the small*. *Gross* and *Groth* come from the German, and indicate a fat, or large person. Names like *Reid*, *Reed*, and *Read* are early spellings of "red" and refer to a man with red hair. These red-haired men probably received the nickname of "Red" in the same way that boys of today with red hair acquire the name.

Other Family Names may have more than one origin. For example, the common English surname *Bell* may designate one who lived or worked at the sign of the bell, or it may refer to the bellmaker or bellringer. It may also indicate the descendant of *Bel*, a pet form of *Isabel*, or it may be a nickname for *the handsome one*, from the Old French word *bel*, or beautiful.

Jewish family names were the last to develop in most countries. In Europe, Jews usually lived apart from others in secluded communities. Many did not feel the need for family names. Laws passed in the early 1800's compelled them to adopt surnames. Many then chose pleasant combinations of various words like gold, silver, rose *(rosen)*, mountain *(berg)*, stone *(stein)*, and valley *(thal)*, to form such names as *Goldberg*, *Silverstein*, and *Rosenthal*. Others adopted place names of cities where they were born, such as *London* and *Modena*. Some took names with religious connotations. *Katz* is an abbreviation of *kohen tzedek*, Hebrew for *priest of righteousness*. Others took surnames from given names, such as *Benjamin* and *Levy*.

Other Names

Middle Names, or second Christian names, occur frequently today. Many people have as their middle name the *maiden name* of the mother, that is, the surname the mother had before her marriage. In France and Spain, double Christian names appeared in the Middle Ages. The Germans in Pennsylvania used several forenames in colonial times. But middle names did not become common in the United States until after the Revolutionary War.

Nicknames may be either descriptive terms or pet names. Descriptive terms, such as *Schnozzola* and *Gabby*, usually express a person's prominent characteristics. Physical characteristics account for the largest group of nicknames. Sometimes they go by contraries, as when a husky football player is called *Tiny*.

Sometimes a nickname results from a child's attempt to pronounce a word or name, as *Lilibet* for Elizabeth. In other instances, a nickname is a translation of the person's real name. Many persons called New York City's mayor, Fiorello H. La Guardia, *The Little Flower*, a literal translation of his Italian first name. In many other cases, a person's nickname may consist of the initials of his other names, such as *F.D.R.* for Franklin Delano Roosevelt.

Pet, or nursery, names often consist of abbreviations of Christian names, such as Bob, Jimmie, and Debbie.

WHAT'S IN A NAME

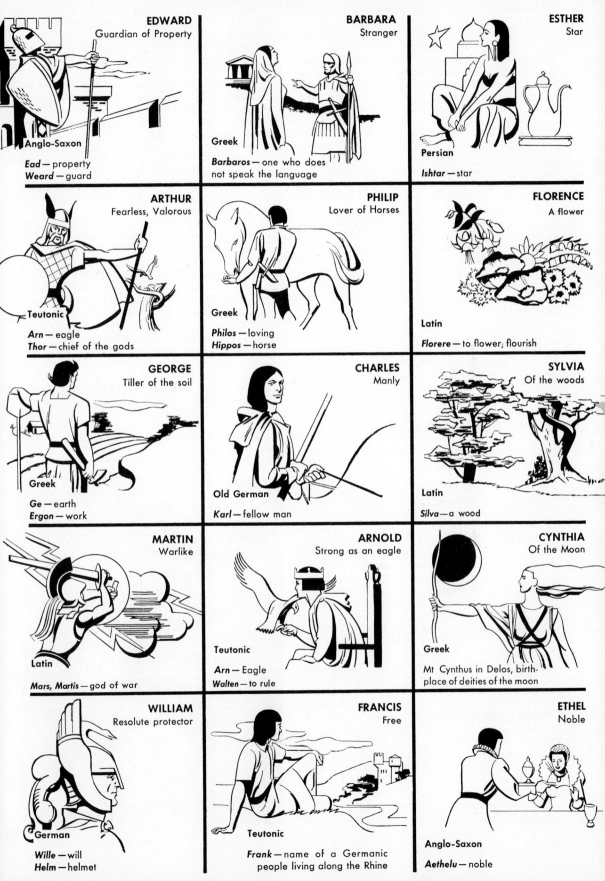

EDWARD
Guardian of Property

Anglo-Saxon

Ead — property
Weard — guard

BARBARA
Stranger

Greek

Barbaros — one who does
not speak the language

ESTHER
Star

Persian

Ishtar — star

ARTHUR
Fearless, Valorous

Teutonic

Arn — eagle
Thor — chief of the gods

PHILIP
Lover of Horses

Greek

Philos — loving
Hippos — horse

FLORENCE
A flower

Latin

Florere — to flower; flourish

GEORGE
Tiller of the soil

Greek

Ge — earth
Ergon — work

CHARLES
Manly

Old German

Karl — fellow man

SYLVIA
Of the woods

Latin

Silva — a wood

MARTIN
Warlike

Latin

Mars, Martis — god of war

ARNOLD
Strong as an eagle

Teutonic

Arn — Eagle
Walten — to rule

CYNTHIA
Of the Moon

Greek

Mt Cynthus in Delos, birthplace of deities of the moon

WILLIAM
Resolute protector

German

Wille — will
Helm — helmet

FRANCIS
Free

Teutonic

Frank — name of a Germanic
people living along the Rhine

ETHEL
Noble

Anglo-Saxon

Aethelu — noble

They may be terms of endearment, or represent surnames, such as *Smitty* for Smith.

Pseudonyms are fictitious names assumed for anonymity or for effect. A *nom de plume* (pen name) is the pseudonym of a writer. Many prominent authors have assumed pen names. For example, *Voltaire* was the pen name of François Marie Arouet. Amantine Dudevant, a French writer, wrote under the nom de plume of *George Sand*. See PSEUDONYM; PEN NAME.

An *alias* usually refers to the name taken by a criminal to disguise his identity (see ALIAS). *Incognito* is a fictitious name temporarily assumed by a person, usually a celebrity, to avoid being recognized.

Stage Names are names that some entertainers assume in their professions. The French actress *Sarah Bernhardt*'s original name was Rosine Bernard. Most motion-picture actors have changed their names. Harry Lillis Crosby is better known as *Bing Crosby*.

The Legal Name of a person in the United States is the name by which he is known. This generally consists of a given name and a family name. Some states require that if a man does business under a name other than his own, he must register it. A title such as *Mr.* or a suffix like *Jr.* is not part of one's legal name. In many countries, names can be changed only by governmental permission. In the United States, a person can change his name without any court order. But it is usually advisable to obtain a court order. See SIGNATURE, LEGAL.   ELSDON C. SMITH

NAMIBIA. See SOUTH WEST AFRICA.

NAMUR, *nah MOOR* (pop. 32,574; alt. 215 ft.), is an industrial city in Belgium. It is located where the Sambre and Meuse rivers join. For location, see BELGIUM (color map). Its factories use the coal and iron mined nearby. Industries also include leather tanneries and machine factories.

In the 1600's and 1700's, the French captured the city three times, and the British seized it once. During both world wars, the Germans captured the forts that surrounded Namur.   DANIEL H. THOMAS

NANAIMO, *nuh NYE moh*, British Columbia (pop. 15,188; alt. 130 ft.), lies in the center of a forestry and farming district on Vancouver Island. It is on the southeast coast of the island and serves as a supply and transport center. Ferry service connects Nanaimo with Vancouver, 40 miles east. For location, see BRITISH COLUMBIA (political map).

Nanaimo ships lumber and pulp products to overseas markets, and is the center of a fishing industry. Its mild climate and good beaches make it a popular tourist resort. The Hudson's Bay Company founded Nanaimo in 1851, calling it Colvilletown until 1860. The city was incorporated in 1874. It has a mayor-council government.   RODERICK HAIG-BROWN

NANAK, GURU, founder of Sikhism. See SIKHISM.

NANCY, *NAN see,* or *NAHN SEE* (pop. 123,428; met. area 257,829; alt. 675 ft.), lies 175 miles east of Paris. For location, see FRANCE (political map). Nancy is the commercial center of Lorraine because it is on the Eastern and Marne-Rhine canals and on the Meurthe River, 6 miles above its junction with the Moselle River. Factories there make furniture, glassware, and electrical equipment. The city has a university, founded in 1572, and a school of forestry and mining.   EDWARD W. FOX

NANGA PARBAT. See HIMALAYA; KASHMIR.

NANKING, *NAN KING* (pop. 1,419 000; alt. 90 ft.), is one of the largest cities of China. It was the capital of the Republic of China from 1928 until 1937, and from 1946 until 1949. It is on the south bank of the Yangtze River. For location, see CHINA (political map).

Railroads connect Nanking with Peking and Shanghai. River steamers stop at Nanking. Seagoing vessels can also come up the river to the city. The chief articles of trade include animal hides, eggs, and meat. A few small factories in Nanking manufacture brocade, cement, porcelain, and silks.

For many years, governmental activities formed the chief industry in Nanking. Most of the government buildings were constructed after Nanking became the capital of the Chinese republic. Many buildings combine Chinese and Western styles. The buildings stand on wide streets amid parks in the northern part of the city.

Two beautiful tombs are dug into the slopes of Purple Mountain, just outside Nanking. One is the tomb of a Ming emperor. Sun Yat-sen, the founder and first president of the republic, is buried in the other tomb.

During the Taiping Rebellion, the rebels held Nanking between 1853 and 1864 and destroyed the famous Porcelain Tower, an octagonal pagoda built in the 1400's. Japanese troops ravaged the city in World War II. In 1949, the Nationalist government moved its capital to Taipei, Formosa. The Communists established their capital at Peking.   THEODORE H. E. CHEN

The Memorial Tower for the Revolutionary Martyrs stands in Nanking, China. Visitors may climb a spiral staircase in the middle of the nine-story pagoda to view the park.

CNS Photos, Rapho-Guillumette

NANSEN, *NAN sun,* or *NAHN sen,* **FRIDTJOF,** *FRIT yawf* (1861-1930), was a famous Norwegian polar explorer. He was also a humanitarian, a statesman, a marine zoologist, and a pioneer oceanographer.

He made his first Arctic cruise in 1882 as a zoological collector aboard a whaler. In the summer of 1888, he and five other men crossed Greenland from east to west, a feat that experts had declared impossible.

Nansen hoped to obtain valuable scientific information by exploring the North Polar Basin. For this expedition, he had a ship specially built to withstand the grinding ice floes. This ship was named the *Fram* (Forward). Nansen left Norway in the *Fram* on June 24, 1893. After two years aboard ship, he and Hjalmar Johansen tried to reach the North Pole with kayaks and sleds. They came within 272 miles of the pole, nearer than anyone before them. After meeting many dangers, they reached Franz Josef Land. They boarded a British ship there in 1896, and sailed back to Norway.

U&U
Fridtjof Nansen

Nansen played a prominent part in the separation of Norway from Sweden in 1905. From 1906 to 1908, he served as Norwegian minister to Great Britain. On his return to Norway, he became a professor of marine zoology (later oceanography) at the University of Christiania. He went on ocean voyages in 1910, 1912, 1913, and 1914, and published his results in many books. His writings include *Farthest North* (1897) and *In Northern Mists* (1911), a history of Arctic exploration.

After World War I, Nansen served as Norwegian delegate to the League of Nations. He aided Russian refugees in Asia Minor, and directed the return of German and Russian war prisoners to their homelands. He devised an identification certificate for refugees, called the *Nansen passport.* He received the 1922 Nobel peace prize for his services. Franz Josef Land in the Arctic Ocean is often called Fridtjof Nansen Land. Oceanographers use a metal container, called a *Nansen bottle* in honor of him, to trap seawater. Nansen was born in Christiania (now Oslo).   JOHN EDWARDS CASWELL

NANTAHALA GORGE. See NORTH CAROLINA (Places to Visit).

NANTES, *nants,* or *nahnt* (pop. 259,208; metropolitan area 393,737; alt. 100 ft.), a port near the mouth of the Loire River, lies 215 miles southwest of Paris (see FRANCE [political map]). A ship canal connects the city with the port of Saint Nazaire, nearer the mouth of the Loire, increasing the importance of Nantes as a trading center. The major industry in Nantes is shipbuilding. Other industries include the preparation of sardines for canning, and the manufacture of sugar, fishing nets, sailcloth, soap, and machinery.

Nantes has many fine buildings, including the ducal castle where Henry IV of France signed the Edict of Nantes.   EDWARD W. FOX

NANTES, *nants,* **EDICT OF.** The Edict of Nantes is one of the most famous royal decrees in history. It was the first official recognition of religious toleration by a great European country. King Henry IV of France signed the edict in the city of Nantes, on April 13, 1598. By the decree, the French Protestants, or Huguenots, were allowed complete freedom of worship in about 75 towns. They were also given equal rights with the Catholics as citizens. The intolerant King Louis XIV abolished the edict in 1685, and thousands of Huguenots left France.   J. SALWYN SCHAPIRO

See also HENRY (IV) of France; HUGUENOTS; LOUIS (XIV); REFORMATION.

NANTUCKET, *nan TUK et,* Mass. (pop. 2,461; alt. 10 ft.), is a summer resort on Nantucket Island, off the coast of Massachusetts. The name was taken from the Indian word, *Nanticut,* meaning *The Far Away Land.* Nantucket is 18 miles south of Cape Cod and about 50 miles southeast of New Bedford. There are many summer homes there because of the scenery and mild climate. For location, see MASSACHUSETTS (political map).

During the late 1700's, Nantucket became one of the greatest whaling centers in the world. As many as 125 whaling ships had their home port there. James I of England granted Nantucket Island to the Plymouth Company in 1621. The island belonged to the province of New York from 1660 to 1692, when it became a part of Massachusetts.   WALTER F. DOWNEY

NAOMI. See RUTH.

NAPALM is a jellied gasoline used in war. A napalm bomb dropped from the air bursts, ignites, and splatters burning napalm over a wide area. The jellied gasoline clings to everything it touches, and burns violently. Napalm causes death from burns or suffocation. Napalm is also used in flame throwers that are carried by ground troops (see FLAME THROWER). Napalm was used in World War II, the Korean War, and in the Vietnam War.

The word *napalm* comes from the two basic ingredients of the white, grainy powder used in the gasoline. *Na* stands for the naphthenic acids, and *palm* for the coconut fatty acids.   HAROLD C. KINNE, JR.

NAPHTHA, *NAP thuh,* or *NAF thuh,* is a liquid that is obtained when petroleum is evaporated during the refining process. Some types of naphtha are used to dissolve rubber and to thin paints and varnish. Others are used as a cleaning agent and as an ingredient in the manufacture of artificial gas.

Naphtha can also be made when coal tar, a sticky substance made from soft coal, is evaporated. Coal tar naphtha is used as a dissolving agent. It is also used in the manufacture of *synthetic* (artificial) resins. Pure naphtha is highly explosive when exposed to an open flame.   CLARENCE KARR, JR.

NAPHTHALENE. See HYDROCARBON (Aromatics).

NAPIER, *NAY pih er,* or *nah PEER,* **JOHN** (1550-1617), LAIRD OF MERCHISTON, a Scottish mathematician, became famous for his discovery of *logarithms* (see LOGARITHMS). He published his first statement of this system in his *Canonis Descriptio* (1614). He also invented "bones" or "rods" for multiplying and dividing, and for extracting square and cube roots. He originated formulas used in spherical trigonometry. He was born in Merchiston, near Edinburgh, Scotland.   PHILLIP S. JONES

Santa Lucia Bay in Naples, *above,* has an old fort which protected the city in Roman times. Sailing boats and small craft now anchor in the quiet harbor. *Porta Capuana, below,* an ancient triumphal arch, was built by the Romans outside the city.

The City of Naples and Its Harbor Lie in the Shadow of Volcanic Mount Vesuvius, *Background.*

NAPLES, or in Italian, Napoli (pop. 1,220,639; alt. 33 ft.), is the third largest city in Italy. It is a major manufacturing center and one of Italy's busiest ports. It is also the capital of Campania, a political region of Italy. Naples lies on the north shore of the Bay of Naples, at the foot of a gentle slope of hills. For location, see ITALY (political map). The city's location is one of the most scenic in Europe, and many artists go there to paint. Mount Vesuvius rises high above a plain 10 miles to the southeast. The famous isle of Capri lies to the south across the Bay of Naples. Vineyards and groves surround the villages on the bay's eastern shores.

Naples is one of the most overcrowded cities in Europe. Beauty and ugliness exist side by side. In the eastern section of the city, picturesque church spires overlook old tenement buildings and factory chimneys. The newer western section of the city lies along the famous *Riviera di Chiaia,* which is a scenic drive that extends 3 miles along the Bay of Naples.

Naples contains many interesting public buildings. The National Museum contains valuable art collections and many relics from Pompeii. The San Carlo Opera House is one of the largest in all Europe. An ancient Gothic cathedral is one of more than 300 churches in Naples. Many old castles help to bring back memories of the Middle Ages. One of the most interesting is the egg-shaped *Castello dell' Ovo.*

The city has several schools and colleges. The best-known of these is the University of Naples. It was founded in 1224 by Emperor Frederick II. Other interesting places in Naples include a national library, a royal conservatory of music, and a botanical garden. A famous aquarium in National Park contains specimens of the plant and animal life in the Mediterranean Sea.

Greek colonists from Cumae founded Naples several hundred years before the birth of Christ. In the Middle Ages, the city became the capital of the Kingdom of the Two Sicilies (see SICILIES, KINGDOM OF THE TWO). The tomb of the Roman poet, Virgil, lies not far from Naples. The ruins of the ancient cities of Herculaneum and Pompeii also are nearby.

Naples is important for the manufacture of ships, locomotives, textiles, gloves, glass, wine, and machinery. Shipping these manufactured products helps make Naples one of the busiest ports in Italy.

Bay of Naples is an inlet of the Tyrrhenian Sea, an arm of the Mediterranean Sea. It is famous for the beautiful scenery along its shores, and for the deep blue color of its waters. The bay cuts into the southwest coast of Italy. It is about 20 miles wide between Cape Miseno and Point Campanella, and cuts inland about 10 miles. Two picturesque islands, Ischia and Capri, lie at the entrance to the bay. BENJAMIN WEBB WHEELER

See also CAMORRA; CAPRI; HERCULANEUM; POMPEII; VESUVIUS.

Face and Reverse Side of the French Napoleon

NAPOLEON was a French gold coin worth 20 francs. It was named for Emperor Napoleon I. The coin went out of general circulation during World War I.

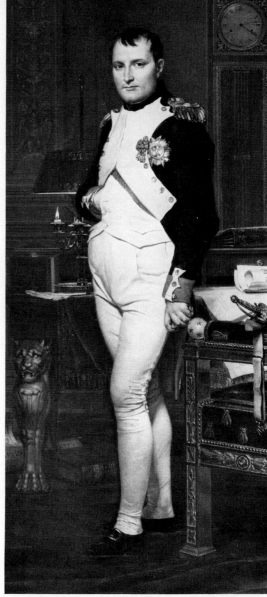

Napoleon I posed in his study for Jacques Louis David in 1810, *above*. David served as the court painter to the Emperor of the French. Napoleon's Great Seal, *upper left*, pictured him on his throne. The reverse side of the seal showed the imperial coat of arms.

NAPOLEON I (1769-1821) crowned himself Emperor of the French and created an empire that covered most of western and central Europe. He was the greatest military genius of his time. Napoleon's armies crushed one foe after another until he seemed invincible. For nearly 20 years, many European nations fought him.

Napoleon had an unimpressive appearance, but he carried himself well. He stood slightly below average height. His courage and short stature led to his early nickname of *le Petit Caporal*, or "the little corporal." He had heavy eyebrows and a weak mouth, but his powerful personality shone in his eyes.

His mother encouraged and helped him in his rise to the height of power. His soldiers adored him. He personally directed complicated military maneuvers and at the same time controlled France's press, its police system, its foreign policy, and its home government. He pioneered new strategy and tactics, and became one of the great military commanders in history. He proved himself a talented administrator. He supervised the work of preparing the system of laws called the *Code Napoléon*. He also founded the Bank of France, reorganized the French educational system, and established a strong centralized government. He created and juggled kingdoms at will. He placed his relatives and friends on the thrones of Europe. And, finally, he brought about his own downfall. His collapse came partly because his pride and stubbornness forced him to go ahead with doubtful plans, and partly because he betrayed the faith of many persons.

Early Years

Boyhood. Napoleon was born on Aug. 15, 1769, at Ajaccio, on the island of Corsica in the Mediterranean Sea. He was the fourth child and second son of Carlo Maria de Buonaparte (later given the French spelling *Bonaparte*) and Letizia Ramolino. His parents belonged to noble Italian families, and his father practiced law. Genoa had ceded Corsica to France in 1768, after a series of revolts on the island. During these troubled times, Napoleon's father skillfully followed a policy most likely to benefit himself and his family. He obtained for Napoleon an appointment to the military school at Brienne. The boy spent a few months learning French, then entered the school at the age of 10.

Napoleon soon transferred to the royal military school at Paris. He found the discipline here stern and the teaching more skillful. Napoleon did not have a brilliant scholastic career, but he showed a special aptitude for mathematics and history. He had great confidence in his own judgment and displayed persistence in carrying out decisions.

At 16, Napoleon received a commission as a second lieutenant of artillery in January, 1786. He had joined an artillery regiment, and within three months had gone through the grades of private, corporal, and sergeant. Napoleon tried to master all the details of his new profession, and devoted much time to study. At first, his chief aim as a soldier seemed to be to free Corsica from French control. He spent many months of leave in Corsica, where the patriot Pasquale Paoli led an independence movement. Napoleon took part in the movement, but never got along with its leader.

The French Revolution broke out in 1789 (see FRENCH REVOLUTION). In 1792, when the mob attacked the royal palace called the Tuileries, Napoleon was again in Paris. He became an artillery captain that year. After Napoleon returned to Corsica, he quarreled with Paoli and abandoned his party. He joined the French revolutionaries on Corsica, and Paoli drove him from the island.

Napoleon rejoined the army and helped revolutionary forces occupy Marseille. His men also helped surround Toulon, which was strongly defended by English troops. The fall of Toulon was generally credited to Napoleon's strategy and organization. Now a major, he had handled his artillery command with such skill that he received a prompt promotion to brigadier general.

Napoleon's real military career began at this time. He developed a principle of war that formed the basis of his future campaigns. He learned to seek a weak point in the enemy's line and throw all his strength against it at the decisive hour of battle. With that point broken or weakened, the enemy collapsed.

In 1794, Robespierre fell from power in the new French government. The army suspended Napoleon and put him briefly under arrest, as a reaction to the violent reign of Robespierre (see ROBESPIERRE).

Fame at 26. A poorly-clad, ill-fed Napoleon waited in Paris for a change in his fortunes. The Convention that governed France grew steadily weaker, and many persons began to long for the monarchy again. In October, nearly 30,000 national guardsmen massed against the Convention, which was protected by 4,500 troops under Vicomte de Barras. Barras had seen Napoleon in action at Toulon, and now sent for him. The Convention appointed Napoleon as Barras' assistant. He showed superb resourcefulness by placing his artillery so that he cleared the streets of Paris "with a whiff of grapeshot."

Oct. 5, 1795, became a red-letter date in the history of Europe. Royalism had been crushed, and Napoleon had paved his own road to power. Barras appointed Napoleon his second in command in the army of the interior. The Directory succeeded the Convention as the government of France. But, in time, Napoleon would crush democracy and monarchy alike, concentrating supreme power in one person—himself.

Marriage. On March 9, 1796, Napoleon married Josephine de Beauharnais, a beautiful Creole from the West Indies (see JOSEPHINE). Her first husband had been guillotined two years earlier because he opposed Robespierre's revolutionary government. Napoleon first met Josephine at the home of Vicomte de Barras. She had become one of the society leaders of Paris. The young general fell violently in love with her. She was six years older than he, and Napoleon had no money. But he determined to marry her.

Two days after his wedding, Napoleon left Paris for Italy. He had prepared a plan to drive out the Austrians.

RED-LETTER DATES IN NAPOLEON'S LIFE

1769 (Aug. 15)	Born at Ajaccio, Corsica.
1796 (Mar. 9)	Married Josephine de Beauharnais.
1799 (Nov. 9)	Seized power in France.
1804 (Dec. 2)	Crowned himself Emperor of the French.
1805 (Dec. 2)	Crushed the allied armies at Austerlitz.
1806 (July 12)	Set up the Confederation of the Rhine.
1806 (Oct. 14)	Defeated the Prussians at Jena and Auerstädt.
1807 (June 14)	Overwhelmed the Russians at Friedland.
1810 (Apr. 2)	Married Marie Louise of Austria.
1812 (Sept. 14)	Occupied Moscow.
1814 (Apr. 11)	Abdicated his throne.
1814 (May 4)	Exiled and arrived on Elba.
1815 (Mar. 20)	Returned to power in France.
1815 (June 18)	Defeated in the Battle of Waterloo.
1815 (Oct. 16)	Exiled to Saint Helena.
1821 (May 5)	Died at Longwood in Saint Helena.

The Directory ordered Gen. Barthélemy Schérer, then in command in Italy, to carry out the plan. But Schérer thought the man who had prepared the plan should carry it out. The Directory agreed, and named Napoleon to command the French Army of Italy.

First Victories

Triumphs in Italy. Napoleon arrived in Nice, France, in March, 1796. He found his army there poorly fed and clothed. He promised his men everything, and they believed him. After a few weeks in Italy, he had conquered

The Austrian Surrender at Austerlitz in 1805 Marked One of Napoleon's Greatest Military Triumphs.

Culver

Brown Bros.

Napoleon Retreated from Moscow after the Disastrous Russian Campaign. Jean Meissonier Painted This Scene.

Milan. Later he confessed that he had a vision of a great future for himself. "When I see an empty throne," he said, "I feel the urge to sit on it."

Napoleon began to hear rumors about his wife's infidelity. In his almost unreadable handwriting, he wrote passionate letters to her, filled with mingled love and hate. But Josephine continued to enjoy herself in Paris.

The Austrians had occupied large parts of northern Italy. After a series of battlefield triumphs, Napoleon forced Naples, Parma, and Modena to seek peace. His armies then crushed the Austrians. In 1797, Austria made peace in the Treaty of Campo Formio. Napoleon, now a national hero, returned in glory to Paris.

Egypt Invaded. Some men in the Directory feared, envied, and distrusted the young hero. Napoleon had great prestige in the army, and his men idolized him. Members of the Directory decided to get Napoleon out of the country. Great Britain had become France's greatest enemy, but Napoleon advised against an invasion of the British Isles. The Directory then ordered him to invade Egypt, a Turkish province, to avenge supposed insults to French merchants.

Napoleon's 35,000-man expedition reached Alexandria in July, 1798. He defeated the Mamelukes within sight of the Egyptian pyramids (see MAMELUKE). But Lord Nelson's British fleet followed Napoleon to Egypt and destroyed the anchored French fleet in the Battle of Aboukir Bay. A tight blockade cut Napoleon's supply lines. The Turks declared war on France, and Great Britain and Russia formed an alliance with Turkey. Austria then reentered the war. The French forces marooned in Egypt advanced in 1799 into Palestine, and then into Syria. The Turks and British checked Napoleon in Syria. He retreated to Egypt and routed the Turkish army there. Napoleon learned that the Second Coalition, which included Austria, Britain, and Russia, had defeated the French in Italy. He also heard that Josephine had again been unfaithful to him.

First Consul of France. Napoleon gave the command of his army to Gen. Jean Kléber and sailed for Paris. He crossed the Mediterranean Sea in a small boat and avoided the British Blockade. In Paris, he and his followers seized power in a bold move called *the Coup d'État of*

Eighteenth Brumaire on Nov. 9, 1799. Napoleon abolished the Directory and set up a new government of three members called *the Consulate*. He became First Consul. "The little corporal" now ruled as dictator of France.

The French people soon discovered that Napoleon had great gifts as a statesman. His government codified and revised the laws of France so well that today the *Code Napoléon* remains the basis of French law (see CODE NAPOLÉON). In 1800, Napoleon set up the Bank of France. He negotiated the Concordat of 1801 with Pope Pius VII, ending the confused church-state relations caused by the French Revolution. He also founded the Legion of Honor in 1802 to honor soldiers and civilians who had made contributions to France.

The Napoleonic Empire

Wars Against Austria. Napoleon ruled France with wisdom and vigor. But he found it difficult to settle down to peacetime government. His thoughts drifted to plans of conquests. Austria still controlled parts of northern Italy. Napoleon planned to strike a quick blow at his old enemy. In 1800, he led a famous march across the Alps, through the Saint Bernard Pass, into the Po Valley. His army clashed with the Austrians at Marengo in June. Napoleon's troops would have been cut to pieces if reinforcements had not arrived. A near defeat was turned into a victory. Austria agreed to sign a peace treaty on Feb. 9, 1801, at Lunéville.

Only Great Britain remained as France's major active enemy. The British and Turks drove the French from Egypt in 1801. This defeat shattered Napoleon's dreams of an empire in the Middle East and India. On March 27, 1802, after long negotiations, Great Britain kept Ceylon and Trinidad, but gave up its other colonial conquests to France and its allies in the Treaty of Amiens. France enjoyed its first real peace in 10 years. But the peace proved short-lived.

Napoleon felt that as long as Britain opposed him, his gains were not secure. But he needed more money to carry on any new wars. In 1803, he sold the Louisiana Territory to the United States (see LOUISIANA PURCHASE). On May 16, Britain declared war on France. Napoleon prepared to invade the British Isles.

Crowned Emperor. The French people in 1802 had voted Napoleon the title of First Consul for life. But the restless Napoleon was not satisfied. He began to whittle away all powers of the government that he did not control, and to strengthen his own authority. In May, 1804, the French senate voted him the title of Emperor. The coronation ceremonies took place at Notre Dame Cathedral on December 2. As the pope prepared to crown him, Napoleon snatched the crown from the pontiff's hands and placed it on his own head, to show that he had personally won the right to wear it. Napoleon then crowned Josephine Empress.

Napoleon is probably most famous for his military achievements. But he guided the internal affairs of France as closely as he directed its armies. He set up a strong central government and appointed prefects to head the territorial areas, called *departments*. He reorganized the education system and founded the Imperial University. His measures later caused a break between the government and the Roman Catholic Church.

Dominates Europe. In 1805, Austria, Russia, and Sweden joined Britain in a new coalition against France and Spain. Emperor Napoleon I abandoned plans to invade Britain, and prepared to fight on the continent. On December 2, he smashed the Austrian and Russian armies at Austerlitz in one of his most brilliant victories. Later that month, Austria signed the Peace of Pressburg, and Russia stopped fighting. But off the southern coast of Spain, Lord Nelson had defeated the French and Spanish fleets at Trafalgar on October 21.

Napoleon now began to change the map of Europe. He believed that "the object of war is victory. The object of victory is conquest. And the object of conquest is occupation." He made his brother Joseph king of Naples, and another brother, Louis, king of Holland. Even his sisters became sovereign rulers in Naples and Tuscany. He carved provinces of Germany and Italy into principalities and dukedoms, and awarded them to his favorite generals and marshals. Napoleon abolished the Holy Roman Empire. He set up a Confederation of the Rhine, made up of western German states under his protection. This action brought about a new war with Prussia. On Oct. 14, 1806, his armies overwhelmed the Prussians at Jena and Auerstädt. Napoleon made a conqueror's entry into Berlin. Here he issued the Berlin Decree that barred British goods from Europe.

Next, Napoleon turned to Russia. The Russian and French armies met at Eylau in February, 1807, but fought to a draw. On June 14, 1807, Napoleon routed the Russian armies at Friedland, and forced Czar Alexander I to seek peace. Napoleon met the czar on a raft anchored in the Neman River near Tilsit, while Frederick William III of Prussia waited on the bank. Russia agreed to close its ports to all British trade. Prussia had to give up about half its territory to France. Napoleon's brother Jerome became king of Westphalia. Later that year, Napoleon issued the Milan Decree, stressing the ban on British goods in Europe.

Portugal had been friendly with Britain for hundreds of years, and had refused to obey Napoleon's Berlin Decree. In 1807, the French occupied Portugal. The following year, Marshal Joachim Murat's French forces invaded Spain. Napoleon removed Ferdinand VII from the throne, and appointed his brother Joseph as king of Spain. Murat took Joseph's place as king of Naples.

Great Britain finally felt strong enough to strike at Napoleon on land. The British invaded Spain and began the bloody Peninsular War, which lasted five years. Austria also declared war on France. At the end of the four-month campaign in 1809, the Austrians were completely defeated. The Peninsular War raged on.

Fall From Power

Divorce and Remarriage. Napoleon left the battlefield and returned to Paris. He had begun to develop a growing concern about the future of his vast empire after his death. Josephine had no children by Napoleon, and he had no heirs to his empire. He wanted a dynasty to rule France. Napoleon decided to divorce Josephine and marry a younger woman. On April 2, 1810, he married Archduchess Marie Louise, the daughter of Emperor Francis I (see MARIE LOUISE). She bore him a son in 1811. The son received the title of king of Rome (see NAPOLEON II). A revolt against French rule erupted in Spain in 1808. The French had to fight the British army and Spanish guerrillas. Finally, in 1812, the British forced Joseph Bonaparte to flee from Madrid.

Disaster in Russia. Napoleon had signed an alliance with Czar Alexander I of Russia in 1807. But the Russians did not fully carry out the Berlin Decree to close their ports to British trade. In 1812, Napoleon decided to teach the Russians a lesson. Long years of war had weakened France, but he raised an army of 600,000 men. His allies and subject nations furnished many of these conscripted soldiers. The Napoleonic Empire now stretched from Spain to the fringes of Russia, and from Norway, an ally of France, to Italy.

Napoleon's army swept across the Neman River in the spring of 1812 and marched eastward. The Russians retreated slowly and destroyed everything of value. At Borodino, the French overwhelmed the czar's troops, but the main Russian force escaped eastward.

Napoleon pushed on to Moscow, where one of the greatest disappointments of his life awaited him. Most of the people had left the city. Those who remained set fire to it, and Napoleon soon found himself surrounded by ruins. The freezing Russian winter was approaching. The Russians rejected a French offer for a truce. Napoleon had no choice but to turn back and begin the long retreat from Moscow. His troops struggled homeward against snowstorms and terrible cold. They became weak because they had so little food. Swarms of Cossacks attacked the suffering French as they trudged through snow and tried to cross rivers. Hunger and the piercing cold accomplished what enemy armies had not been able to do—defeat the Grand Army. Of the 600,000 men in Napoleon's forces, about 500,000 were killed, were captured, deserted, or died of illness in the campaign and in the retreat from Russia.

The disaster proved to be the beginning of the end for Napoleon. He left Murat in command and hurried back to Paris to organize a new army before the news from Russia could reach his enemies. But the news swept across Europe like wildfire. Napoleon's reputation as a military genius suffered a fatal blow. New hope sprang up in countries that had long been under his heel.

The Enemy Alliance. Great Britain, Prussia, Russia, Spain, and Sweden allied themselves against Napoleon.

15

NAPOLEON'S EMPIRE

UNITED KINGDOM
OF GREAT BRITAIN
AND IRELAND

NORTH SEA

ATLANTIC OCEAN

KINGDOM OF DENMARK AND NORWAY

SWEDEN

BALTIC SEA

Battle of Moscow 1812
Battle of Borodino 1812

Battle of Friedland 1807

Battle of Leipzig 1813
PRUSSIA

Battle of
Waterloo
1815

Battle of
Jena
1806

GRAND DUCHY
OF WARSAW

CONFEDERATION OF THE RHINE

RUSSIAN
EMPIRE

FRENCH
EMPIRE

• Paris

SWITZERLAND

ITALY

Battle of Austerlitz 1805
• Vienna
AUSTRIAN
EMPIRE

Battle of Marengo 1800

ILLYRIAN PROVINCES

BLACK SEA

PORTUGAL

Spanish Campaign 1808
• Madrid

SPAIN

ELBA

CORSICA

SARDINIA

NAPLES

OTTOMAN
EMPIRE

Battle of Trafalgar

1805

MEDITERRANEAN SEA

SICILY

Battle of Aboukir Bay 1798

A F R I C A

Battle of the Pyramids 1798 •
EGYPT

▓	French Empire
░	Regions controlled by Napoleon I
▒	Countries allied with Napoleon I

Napoleon Dominated All Europe in 1812, When He Attacked Russia. In Three Years, His Empire Collapsed.

With great effort, Napoleon raised another army. He battled with his old brilliance and defeated the allied armies at Lützen, Bautzen, and Dresden. But Napoleon could not match the strength of his enemies.

In October, 1813, he fought them at Leipzig in the Battle of the Nations and met disaster. Returning again to France, he organized another army and held off the onrushing enemy forces. The Duke of Wellington's army headed for Paris from the south. Napoleon had nothing left but an army of old men and boys. Many trusted veterans of his great triumphs lay buried in the snows of Russia.

Rising nationalism had flared throughout Europe as a result of Napoleon's dictatorial rule. It now turned against Napoleon. He had aroused the anger of the German states, and, under Prussian leadership, the war became a conflict to liberate the Rhineland.

Exile to Elba. One by one, Napoleon's friends and allies began to desert him. By April, 1814, he had decided that his cause was hopeless. The French senate called for a return of a Bourbon king to the French throne. Napoleon's commanders insisted that he give up the throne. On April 11, he abdicated at Fontainebleau. The French called upon Louis XVIII and crowned him king. Napoleon was made ruler of the tiny island of Elba off the coast of Italy, supposedly exiled from France forever.

Europe heaved a sigh of relief. Its diplomats met in the Congress of Vienna to undo many of Napoleon's many changes (see VIENNA, CONGRESS OF). But Napoleon's exile lasted less than a year. In February, 1815, he escaped from Elba. He landed in France with a handful of followers on March 1, and began marching to Paris. Troops under Marshal Michel Ney sped from Paris to arrest him. But when they saw their old leader, the men joyfully joined him and hailed him as their emperor. Louis XVIII fled Paris as Napoleon approached. Once again, allied armies took the field against Napoleon.

The Hundred Days. The period from Napoleon's escape from Elba to his final defeat at Waterloo has been called *the Hundred Days.* Napoleon ruled once again.

On June 12, he left Paris to take personal command of his troops. The Duke of Wellington and Marshal Gebhard von Blücher led separate armies against the French. Napoleon defeated Von Blücher at Ligny on June 16. Ney forced Wellington back to the Belgian village of Waterloo. On June 18, Napoleon attacked Wellington in one of history's most decisive battles. Wellington counted on the arrival of either nightfall or Von Blücher's reinforcements. At the decisive moment, Von Blücher's troops were seen approaching. The British and their allies fought with renewed courage, and Napoleon suffered a crushing defeat (see WATERLOO, BATTLE OF).

Napoleon fled to Paris, abdicated, and tried to escape to the United States. But he failed, and surrendered to the captain of a British warship at Rochefort on July 15. The allied nations made him a prisoner of war. They took him to England, then exiled him to the barren island of Saint Helena, off the west coast of Africa.

Napoleon spent his last days under the care of a stern British governor. He died of cancer on May 5, 1821, and was buried on the island. In 1840, the French government took his body to Paris. There, beneath the dome of the Hôtel des Invalides, a hospital for sick and aged soldiers, the body of Napoleon Bonaparte was laid to rest.

Napoleon's Place in History

History would have given Napoleon Bonaparte a high place even if he had followed only one career. His military campaigns inspired many commanders, who sought the secret of his success. Napoleon's genius at making war lay in an ability to exploit an enemy's weakness.

Napoleon's achievements in government influenced both dictators and liberators of the 1800's and 1900's. His contributions to French law, embodied in the Code Napoléon, survive today. He also made major developments in education and banking.   VERNON J. PURYEAR

Related Articles in WORLD BOOK include:

Outline

I. Early Years
    A. Boyhood   B. Fame at 26   C. Marriage

II. First Victories
    A. Triumph in Italy
    B. Egypt Invaded
    C. First Consul of France

III. The Napoleonic Empire
    A. Wars Against Austria   C. Dominates Europe
    B. Crowned Emperor

IV. Fall From Power
    A. Divorce and Remarriage   D. Exile to Elba
    B. Disaster in Russia   E. The Hundred Days
    C. The Enemy Alliance

V. Napoleon's Place in History

Questions

What military exploit started Napoleon on his great career?

What important civil reforms did Napoleon bring about?

What dealings did Napoleon promote with the United States?

Why did Napoleon's plans to invade Great Britain fail?

Why did Napoleon divorce Josephine and marry again?

When and why did Napoleon first abdicate?

In what battle was Napoleon decisively defeated? By whom?

What were *the Hundred Days?*

What was unusual about Napoleon's coronation as Emperor?

Why did Oct. 5, 1795, become a red-letter date in the history of Europe?

Books to Read

CORLEY, ANTHONY. *The True Story of Napoleon, Emperor of France*. Children's Press, 1964.

HORIZON. *The Horizon Book of the Age of Napoleon*. American Heritage, 1963.

KOMROFF, MANUEL. *Napoleon*. Messner, 1954. The author describes events in Napoleon's boyhood and youth that influenced his character.

LUDWIG, EMIL. *Napoleon*. Liveright, 1926. This famous book on Napoleon is still in print.

ROBBINS, RUTH. *The Emperor and the Drummer Boy*. Parnassus, 1962.

WINWAR, FRANCES. *Napoleon and the Battle of Waterloo*. Random House, 1953. A biography for young people.

Napoleon's Tomb stands in the Hôtel des Invalides in Paris. A single block of red granite, 13 feet long, 6½ feet wide, and 14½ feet high, contains the remains of France's "Little Corporal."
Ewing Galloway

NAPOLEON II

NAPOLEON II (1811-1832), DUKE OF REICHSTADT, *RYKE shtaht*, was the son of Napoleon I and Marie Louise of Austria. Napoleon I had long hoped for a son to inherit his empire, and greeted his son's birth with joy. He gave him the title of the King of Rome.

When Napoleon I was overthrown in 1814, he abdicated in favor of his young son. The senate did not recognize the title, and called Louis XVIII to the throne. Marie Louise took her son to live at the court of her father, Francis I of Austria. When Napoleon I was defeated at Waterloo in 1815, he proclaimed his son Napoleon II. But the French again ignored him and Napoleon II remained in Austria. His mother's family gave him the title of Duke of Reichstadt in 1818.

Culver

Napoleon II

He was never strong, and grew into a tall, slender youth. He died of tuberculosis at the age of 21 and was buried in the Hapsburg family's church tomb in Vienna. The French government later requested that his body be returned to France, but the request was refused for many years. Adolf Hitler ordered the body removed to Paris in 1940. It was placed beside that of Napoleon I in the Hôtel des Invalides. Napoleon II was born in Paris. Edmond Rostand based a play, *L'Aiglon* (The Eaglet), on his life.   VERNON J. PURYEAR

NAPOLEON III (1808-1873) ruled as Emperor of France from 1852 to 1870, and was closely associated with major European political changes.

Early Life. He was born in Paris, the son of Louis Bonaparte, King of Holland and brother of Napoleon I. A French law of 1816 exiled the Bonapartes from France, and Louis Napoleon spent his youth in Italy, Germany, and Switzerland. He became the head of his family in 1832. He was connected with such revolutionary groups as the *Carbonari* in Italy. He tried to overthrow the monarchy of Louis Philippe in 1836 at Strasbourg and again in 1840 at Boulogne (see LOUIS PHILIPPE). He was imprisoned in the fortress of Ham following the 1840 attempt. He escaped to England in 1846. During these years, he wrote his *Napoleonic Ideas* (1839), idealizing the career of his famous uncle, and *The Extinction of Poverty* (1844), proposing in vague terms that the government act to end poverty and suffering.

Becomes Emperor. When the Revolution of 1848 led to the Second Republic in France, Louis Napoleon returned and was elected to the Assembly. In December, benefiting by the glamour of his name, he was elected President, winning 5,500,000 votes out of 7,500,000 cast. He swore an oath to the republic, but in December, 1851, he managed to concentrate all power in his hands. He proclaimed himself emperor in 1852.

Napoleon's domestic policies were conflicting. He ruled as a dictator and was surrounded by dishonest adventurers. Although all men could vote, the legislature was powerless and the press could not publish

Chicago Historical Society

Napoleon III was the last member of the Bonaparte family to rule France. He lost his throne after Von Moltke's Prussian army defeated the French forces in 1870 at Sedan.

legislative debates. Critics such as Victor Hugo were exiled. When, after 1860, Napoleon moved in the direction of a liberal empire, it was too late. Léon Gambetta published *Belleville Manifesto* in 1869, demanding radical democracy. Yet Napoleon keenly realized the problems of the industrial age. He has been called a "socialist on horseback." He favored state help for industries, banks, and railroads, and state action to end poverty.

Foreign Affairs. Napoleon was one of the first to propose general disarmament. He tried to settle disputes through international conferences, and he sympathized with claims of nationalism. He helped with independence for Romania, unification for Italy, and, unwittingly, unification for Germany.

He announced when he became emperor, "The Empire means peace," yet he led France into a long series of unfortunate adventures in other countries. In 1849, he helped overthrow the Roman Republic and restore the Pope. He joined England and Turkey in 1854 in the Crimean War against Russia. He secretly promised in 1859 to help the Count di Cavour drive the Austrians from Italy, in return for the promise of Nice and Savoy (see CAVOUR, COUNT DI). But he withdrew from the war when he saw that Italy, instead of forming a weak confederation, would be united. He tried unsuccessfully to help the Polish people in their 1863 revolt against Russia. He supported a scheme making Maximilian Emperor of Mexico in 1864 (see MAXIMILIAN). He hoped to increase French prestige, but

American pressure in 1867 forced Napoleon to withdraw his troops and leave Maximilian to be shot.

His Defeat. Otto von Bismarck, the Prussian Prime Minister and Secretary of Foreign Affairs, sought a common cause to unite the scattered German states. Napoleon gave Bismarck his chance by secret attempts to annex the Rhineland, Luxembourg, or Belgium. When these moves became known, they caused great indignation in Germany. Bismarck mobilized German opinion, maneuvered France into the Franco-Prussian War of 1870, and made the German Empire.

Napoleon surrendered at Sedan on Sept. 2, 1870, with 80,000 troops. Revolutionists overthrew the Empire on Sept. 4, 1870. Napoleon III died in Chislehurst, England, only three years after the downfall of his empire. E. J. KNAPTON

See also FRANCO-PRUSSIAN WAR; EUGÉNIE MARIE DE MONTIJO; BONAPARTE.

NAPOLEON OF THE STUMP. See POLK, JAMES KNOX (Lawyer and Legislator).

NAPOLEONIC CODE. See CIVIL CODE.

NAPRAPATHY, *nuh PRAP uh thee*, is a system of drugless healing that attributes human ailments to a disorder in the ligaments, or bands of connective tissue. It attempts to correct these ailments by locating and treating the diseased ligaments. The word *naprapathy* comes from the Czech word *napravit*, meaning *to correct*, and the Greek word *pathos*, meaning *suffering*.

The naprapathic method is based upon the theory that strained or contracted ligaments in the spine, thorax, or pelvis cause irritation of the nerves which pass through ligamentous tissue. These irritated nerves then cause symptoms in the organs which they supply. Instead of treating the symptoms, the naprapath treats the diseased ligaments by special manipulation such as massage. Naprapathy is said to be different from both chiropractic and osteopathy. The system was originated in 1905 by Oakley Smith, a Chicago doctor.

NARCISSUS, *nahr SIS us*, is the name of a large group of early spring flowers with lovely blossoms. They grow from brown-coated bulbs. They were named for the legendary Greek youth Narcissus. Narcissuses are native to Europe and Asia, but many are cultivated in America. People love them because they have fragrant and delicately fashioned blossoms of yellow or white. The narcissus is a special flower of December. In Europe, in the springtime, fragrant masses of wild narcissuses cover the Alpine meadows.

The Poet's Narcissus

N.Y. Botanical Garden

There are various types of narcissuses. All of them send up tall shoots from a group of sword-shaped leaves. They have six petals surrounding a trumpet-shaped tube which may be long or short. In one division, the trumpet in the center is the same length as the petals. *Daffodils* are long-trumpet narcissuses. *Jonquils* are short-trumpet narcissuses. Gardeners usually plant the bulbs in the fall. The flowers are perennial.

Another short-trumpet species is the *poet's narcissus*. It produces a single, wide-open blossom on each stalk. White petals surround a short, yellowish cup with a crinkled red edge.

The *paper white* and *polyanthus* narcissus, of the same group, can be grown indoors in winter from bulbs placed in water. They bear large clusters of pure white flowers that are very heavily scented. When cultivators cross these forms with the poet's narcissus, they get improved varieties. Florists value these beautiful hybrids.

Scientific Classification. Narcissuses belong to the amaryllis family, *Amaryllidaceae*. The daffodil is genus *Narcissus*, species *N. pseudo-narcissus*. The poet's narcissus is *N. poeticus;* the paper white is *N. tazetta*. MARCUS MAXON

See also BULB; DAFFODIL; JONQUIL.

NARCISSUS was the son of the river god Cephisus in ancient Greek mythology. He was a handsome youth, and very proud of his own beauty. Many girls loved him, but he paid no attention to them. The nymph Echo, one of those who loved Narcissus, was so hurt by his coldness that all but her voice faded away.

The gods were angered at this, and they punished Narcissus by making him fall in love with his own reflection in a pool of clear water. He was so much in love with himself that he could not leave the pool. At last

Narcissus was forced to fall in love with his own reflection in a pool as punishment for failing to return Echo's love.

Narcissus, a painting (1630?) by Nicolas Poussin, The Louvre, Paris

he died and was changed into the flower called *narcissus*. The Roman poet Ovid told the story of Narcissus in his *Metamorphoses*, a collection of mythological tales in verse. VAN JOHNSON

NARCOLEPSY. See CATAPLEXY; AMPHETAMINE.

NARCOSYNTHESIS. See PENTOTHAL SODIUM.

NARCOTIC, *nahr KAHT ik*, is a substance that has a strong *depressant effect* (lessens activity) upon the human nervous system. Narcotic substances cause insensibility to pain, stupor, sleep, or coma, according to the dose. The term *narcotic* comes from a Greek word meaning *to make numb*.

NARCOTICS AND DANGEROUS DRUGS

Opium is one of the most commonly used narcotics. Others include Indian hemp (hashish), chloral hydrate, codeine, morphine, and heroin. When a narcotic is given in doses large enough to cause sleep or coma, the drug is called a *hypnotic*. The term *anodyne* is applied to a drug that relieves pain by numbing the nerves. Therefore, a narcotic may be both an anodyne and a hypnotic. In one sense, the general anesthetics, ether and chloroform, are narcotics.

Narcotic drugs are extremely useful in medicine, but they also have dangerous possibilities. Large doses of narcotics may cause death. The careless use of opium and substances made from it to relieve pain has often caused the formation of a drug habit. For these reasons, no one should use these drugs except under the direction of a physician.

The United States carefully regulates the importation of narcotics as well as the manufacture and distribution of narcotic by-products. Physicians must state certain facts on narcotic prescriptions, and druggists must keep records of them. The Bureau of Narcotics and Dangerous Drugs in the U.S. Department of Justice oversees all narcotics laws.   A. K. REYNOLDS

Related Articles in WORLD BOOK include:

Analgesic	Cocaine	Heroin
Anodyne	Drug Addiction	Marijuana
Barbiturate	Hallucinatory Drug	Morphine
Belladonna	Hashish	Opium
Chloral Hydrate		

NARCOTICS AND DANGEROUS DRUGS, BUREAU OF, is an agency in the U.S. Department of Justice. It enforces and administers federal laws regarding the sale and use of narcotics and dangerous drugs. The bureau works with state and local governments in preventing illegal trade in drugs and narcotics, and helps to train local agents and investigators. It works closely with other nations to stop the international trade in forbidden narcotics and drugs. The bureau controls the amount of drugs that may be imported into the United States for medical and scientific needs. Founded in 1968, the bureau absorbed the Bureau of Narcotics and the Bureau of Drug Abuse Control.

Critically reviewed by the BUREAU OF NARCOTICS AND DANGEROUS DRUGS

NARD. See SPIKENARD.

NARMADA RIVER, *nur MUD uh*, a large waterway in central India, has been sacred to Hindus for ages. Both banks of the 800-mile river are lined with shrines and temples. The Narmada rises in the state of Madhya Pradesh in central India. For location, see INDIA (physical map). It flows westward and empties into the Gulf of Cambay, about 200 miles from Bombay. Large boats can sail 80 miles up the river.   ROBERT I. CRANE

NARRAGANSET INDIANS, *NAR uh GAN set*, is the name of a tribe that lived in the Narragansett Bay region of Rhode Island in early colonial times. The Narraganset were of Algonkian stock. They were friendly to the colonists at first, but in 1675 they joined forces with Indian chief King Philip and made war on the whites. Only a few members of the tribe survive today.

NARRAGANSETT BAY is a narrow arm of the Atlantic Ocean. It extends 28 miles northward into the state of Rhode Island. The bay is about 20 miles across at its widest point. Its long irregular coastline provides har-

bors which greatly aid the trade and transportation of the state. Newport, a famous resort, lies on Aquidneck Island, the largest island in Narragansett Bay. Providence, the capital of the state, lies on the western shore of the bay.   BOSTWICK H. KETCHUM

NARROWS, THE. See NEW YORK CITY (Location).

NARVÁEZ, *nahr VAH ayth*, **PÁNFILO DE** (1478?-1528), was a Spanish soldier, explorer, and Indian fighter. He helped conquer Cuba in 1511, and lost an eye trying to arrest Hernando Cortes in Mexico in 1521. King Charles V of Spain granted him the unexplored land of Florida in 1526, and he led an expedition there in 1528.

He marched inland, and lost many of his men in storms and Indian attacks. While exploring, he was cut off from his ships, and they returned without him. Attacked by Indians, he and his men built five crude barges. They sailed along the coast to what is now south Texas. Narváez's boat was forced out into the Gulf of Mexico by winds and currents, and he was drowned. He was born in Valladolid.   FRANK GOODWYN

NARWHAL, *NAHR hwul*, is an unusual whale of the Arctic. The male has a spiral ivory tusk about 8 feet long jutting out of the left side of its head. The tusk is really the narwhal's only tooth. A few narwhals,

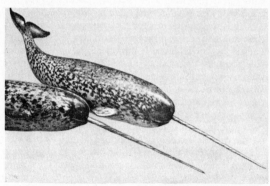

Field Museum of Natural History

Male Narwhals look like most other whales, but they have long, spiral tusks growing forward from the left sides of their heads.

mostly females, have two tusks. The female ordinarily has no tusk. Young narwhals use their tusks in playfighting. So far as is known, the adult makes no use of its tusk. However, the tusks of most adult narwhals are worn at the tip. Perhaps the animal stirs up sand or mud with its tusk while feeding.

Narwhals grow about 18 feet long, not including the tusk, and weigh up to 2 tons. They are gray-white, and have dark gray or black spots. The Eskimos of Greenland hunt narwhals. They eat the skin, which they call *muktuk*, and use the ivory to make tools.

Scientific Classification. The narwhal belongs to the whale order, *Cetacea*. It is genus *Monodon*, species *M. monoceros*.   RAYMOND M. GILMORE

NASA. See NATIONAL AERONAUTICS AND SPACE ADMINISTRATION.

NASBY, PETROLEUM V. See LOCKE, DAVID ROSS.

NASH, CHARLES WILLIAM (1864-1948), was a pioneer in the United States automobile industry. He became president of the Buick Motor Company in 1910, reorganized the company, and made it financially successful. He was elected president of General Motors Corporation in 1912 when it was near bankruptcy. It also prospered under Nash's leadership.

Nash resigned from General Motors in 1916. He then bought an automobile firm from which he formed Nash Motors Company. He was president of the company until 1932, and board chairman until he died. The Nash firm merged with Hudson Motors in 1954, and became American Motors.

Born in De Kalb County, Illinois, Nash had a sixth-grade education. He worked on farms until he was 27, then joined the Flint Road Cart Company (later the Durant-Dort Carriage Company).   Smith Hempstone Oliver

NASH, OGDEN (1902-1971), was a gifted American writer of light, humorous verse. He is one of the most quoted American poets. He used mannerisms that add greatly to the amusing effect of his poems, such as long, loose lines, parenthetical asides, strange puns, and unexpected lines and rhymes. Nash's work is occasionally bitter in its satire, but ordinarily it has a mellow, easygoing tone. His first book of verse, *Hard Lines*, appeared in 1931. His many other books of verse include *I'm a Stranger Here Myself* (1938), *Many Long Years Ago* (1945), *Versus* (1949), *Family Reunion* (1950), *Parents Keep Out* (1951), *The Private Dining Room* (1953), and *Everyone But Thee and Me* (1962).

Kay Bell

Ogden Nash

Nash was born in Rye, N.Y., and attended Harvard University for a year. He taught at St. George's School, in Newport, R.I., for a year, and spent several years in the editing and publishing departments of the Doubleday, Doran & Co. publishing firm. Nash, Kurt Weill, and S. J. Perelman wrote *One Touch of Venus*, a musical comedy, in 1943. Nash wrote the lyrics for *Two's Company* (1952).   William Van O'Connor

NASH, THOMAS (1567-1601?), was an English writer of the Elizabethan period whose works reflect his rowdy nature. He was involved in many disputes, and attacked his opponents in skillfully written pamphlets. Nash is probably best known today for *The Unfortunate Traveller* (1594), an example of Elizabethan prose fiction at its best. This book's narrative structure, realistic detail, and references to actual events and persons make it an important forerunner of the modern novel.

Nash was born in Lowestoft, Suffolk. He studied at Cambridge University, and belonged to a group of popular writers often called the *University Wits*. In 1589, Nash joined in the "Martin Marprelate" controversy between the Puritans and the Church of England. He wrote several pamphlets that attacked the Puritans. Nash and the poet Gabriel Harvey carried on a bitter feud through pamphlets. One of Nash's attacks is contained in *Pierce Penniless* (1592), which also satirizes Elizabethan society.   Frank W. Wadsworth

NASHUA, *NASH yoo uh,* N.H. (pop. 55,820; met. area 66,458; alt. 150 ft.), is the second largest city in the state. It lies on the west bank of the Merrimack River

(see New Hampshire [political map]). Factories there make sheets, asbestos products, shoes, furniture, and blankets. The first permanent settlement was made there in 1656. A town charter was granted in 1673 under the name of Dunstable. Renamed for the Nashua Indians who once lived in the area, Nashua was incorporated as a city in 1853. It has a mayor-council government.   J. Duane Squires

NASHVILLE, Tenn. (pop. 447,877; met. area 541,108; alt. 450 ft.), is the state's capital and second largest city. Only Memphis is larger. Nashville is a commercial and educational center. It occupies hilly ground along the Cumberland River in north-central Tennessee (see Tennessee [political map]).

Products of Nashville include aircraft parts, barges, cellophane, clothing, foods, footwear, heating apparatus, hosiery, plastics, rayon, and textiles. The city has about 60 printing firms, including large religious publishing establishments. Several highways serve the city. Nashville has air, rail, and bus service. It is connected with ports on the Cumberland River.

Nashville's universities and colleges include David Lipscomb College, Fisk University, George Peabody College for Teachers, Scarritt College for Christian Workers, Tennessee State University, and Vanderbilt University. Nashville has a symphony orchestra and the state museum. The Tennessee Centennial of 1897 was held in Nashville's Centennial Park. A replica of the Athenian Parthenon stands in the park. The Parthenon helps account for the city's nickname, *Athens of the South.*

Settlers came to the Nashville area in 1779, and built Fort Nashborough the following year. A replica of the fort now stands in the area. The name was changed to Nashville when the town was incorporated in 1784. The pioneers drew up the Cumberland Compact soon after settlement began, providing the community with a written constitutional government. Nashville received its city charter in 1806. It became the official capital of Tennessee in 1843, and the State Capitol was completed there in 1855. Union troops occupied the city during the Civil War. General John Bell Hood's Confederate army suffered a disastrous defeat at Nashville in 1864. In 1962, Nashville and Davidson County adopted a metropolitan form of government.

For the rainfall and monthly temperatures in Nashville, see Tennessee (Climate).   Jewell A. Phelps

The Parthenon at Nashville, Tenn., a replica of the ancient Greek temple, was built for the Tennessee Centennial in 1897.

Nashville Chamber of Commerce

NASKAPI INDIANS

NASKAPI INDIANS, *NAS kuh pee*, live on the interior plateau of Labrador, in eastern Canada. They are called Montagnais (pronounced *mawn tah NYEH*) in southern Quebec. They number about 500.

Life is very difficult in the harsh climate and barren surroundings of the Naskapi. They live in small, widely scattered family groups. These groups seldom meet one another, and they have no organized tribal government. The Naskapi roam their hunting grounds from fall to spring, and in summer they go to the seacoast to barter furs at trading posts. They use snowshoes and sleds in winter, and travel in canoes in summer. Caribou is the chief game, but the Naskapi also eat bear and fish. Like other Indians of the northern forests, the Naskapi live in tepees covered with birchbark or caribou skins.

The Naskapi rely greatly on magic and *divination* (foretelling the future). They often plan their hunting and fishing according to signs that they read in the cracks of animal bones. The Naskapi Indians decorate their caribou-skin clothing with designs that appear in their dreams. ELMER HARP, JR.

NASMYTH, JAMES (1808-1890), a Scottish engineer, invented the steam hammer. He also developed the *self-acting principle* in machine-tool design, by which a mechanical hand moving along a slide holds a tool. Using this principle, Nasmyth invented a planing mill and a nut-shaping machine.

Nasmyth was born in Edinburgh, the son of a noted artist. In 1829, he became assistant to Henry Maudslay, a tool designer and manufacturer. In 1834, Nasmyth started the Bridgewater Foundry at Manchester, which became famous for machine-tool and steam-engine construction. Nasmyth invented the steam hammer in 1839. He retired in 1856 and devoted his time to studying astronomy. ROBERT E. SCHOFIELD

NASSAU, *NAS aw* (pop. 80,907; alt. 10 ft.), is the capital of the Bahama Islands, a British colony in the West Indies, southeast of Florida. Nassau lies on the northeast coast of New Providence Island, the most important island in the group. For location, see BAHAMAS (map). It has a fine harbor and airport. The city is popular with winter vacationers, to whom it offers fine hotels and restaurants, fishing, yachting, and many other sports. Nassau is clean and bright, with houses of many different colors. The British founded Nassau in the mid-1600's. W. L. BURN

NASSER, *NAH sur*, **GAMAL ABDEL** (1918-1970), led the revolt that overthrew King Faruk in 1952 and established Egypt as a republic. He served as prime minister from 1954 until he was elected president of Egypt in 1956. Later that year, a world crisis occurred after Egypt seized the Suez Canal, then under international control. Nasser wanted to use the tolls collected from users of the canal to build the Aswan High Dam. When Syria and Egypt formed the United Arab Republic (U.A.R.) in 1958, Nasser became its president. Syria withdrew from the U.A.R. in 1961.

Nasser resigned after Egypt lost the six-day Arab-Israeli war of 1967. But the Egyptian National Assembly refused to accept his resignation, and massive demonstrations of public support led him to stay in office. He became both president and prime minister of Egypt. Fighting between Israel and the Arab na-

tions continued into the 1970's. Nasser relied heavily on Russian military aid. In August, 1970, he agreed to a 90-day cease-fire with Israel. His sudden death in September, 1970, threatened the chances for a lasting peace.

Wide World
Gamal Abdel Nasser

Nasser's book, *Egypt's Liberation: The Philosophy of the Revolution* (1955), stated his aim to unite all Arabs under Egyptian leadership. Although his efforts toward this goal failed, he became one of the most influential men in the Arab world. Nasser claimed to follow a neutral foreign policy. His guiding principles were nationalism and economic reform. He redistributed land to farmers and also advanced education.

Born in Alexandria, Nasser graduated from the Royal Military Academy in Cairo. He fought in the Arab war against Israel in 1948 and 1949. T. WALTER WALLBANK

NASSON COLLEGE. See UNIVERSITIES AND COLLEGES (table).

NAST, THOMAS (1840-1902), was an American political cartoonist. He popularized the famous political symbols of the Democratic donkey, and originated the Republican elephant and the Tammany Tiger (see pictures with DEMOCRATIC PARTY; REPUBLICAN PARTY). His caricatures of the Tammany Tiger helped break up the notorious political organization headed by William "Boss" Tweed in New York City (see TWEED, WILLIAM MARCY).

Nast's cartoons began appearing in the popular magazine *Harper's Weekly* during the 1860's. He did his

Chicago Historical Society
Nast Drew the Tammany Tiger to symbolize the corrupt Tammany political machine in New York City. This cartoon appeared after the machine had defeated its Republican opponents in 1871.

22

best work during the Civil War, when his political cartoons influenced public opinion in favor of the North. In the presidential campaign of 1872, Nast's barbed cartoons helped bring about the defeat of Horace Greeley (see GREELEY, HORACE). Nast is also credited with starting the present-day idea of Santa Claus in sketches that appeared in *Harper's Weekly* in the 1860's.

Nast was an excellent draftsman and designer as well as cartoonist. His black-and-white drawings have been exhibited in many museums and galleries.

Nast was born in Landau, Bavaria, on Sept. 27, 1840, and came with his mother to the United States in 1846. He worked as a draftsman on *Frank Leslie's Illustrated Newspaper*, and sketched warfare in Italy for New York, London, and Paris newspapers. He published *Nast's Almanac* for many years. He was consul general in Ecuador when he died.   DICK SPENCER III

See also CARPETBAGGER (picture); RECONSTRUCTION (picture: The Problems of Peace).

NASTURTIUM, *nuhs TUR shum*, is the common name of a group of perennial plants native to tropical America. Nasturtium is a favorite garden flower of North America. There, it is a trailing or climbing annual that may climb to a height of about 10 feet. Its brightly colored blossoms, in yellow, orange, or red, are attractive in flower beds or as cut flowers. Dwarf nasturtiums are also grown.

The nasturtium flower has an interesting structure. There are five small *sepals* (outer "petals"). The three upper ones form a long spur that holds the nectar. There are also five petals. The three lower petals are a little apart from the upper two and have long, fringed claws. The long-stalked leaves are shaped like an umbrella. They have a spicy taste and are sometimes used in salads. The leaves also make an attractive light green background for the bright flowers.

W. Atlee Burpee
The Fragrant Nasturtium grows well in soil that is dry, sandy, or gravelly.

Nasturtiums grow well from seeds sown outdoors in spring. They can also be potted in the early spring and transplanted in May. They cannot stand frost, but may be grown indoors in winter. Nasturtiums are easy to grow. They thrive best in bright sunlight. Small insects, called black aphids, often attack the plants and live on the underside of the leaves. They will destroy the plant unless they are controlled with insecticide.

The name *nasturtium* is also given to the genus of the water cress (see CRESS).

Scientific Classification. Nasturtiums belong to the tropaeolum family, *Tropaeolaceae*. The garden flower is genus *Tropaeolum*, species *T. majus*.   ROBERT W. SCHERY

NATAL, *nuh TAL*, is the smallest province in South Africa. Natal has an area of 33,578 square miles, and lies between the Indian Ocean on the east and the high Drakensberg (mountains) on the west on the southeastern coast of Africa (see SOUTH AFRICA [color map]).

Warm, moist lowlands along the coast produce sugar cane and tropical fruits. Livestock and grain are raised farther inland. Coal is the chief mineral.

Natal has a population of 2,979,920. About three-fourths of the people are Bantus, a Negro group. Pietermaritzburg is the capital of Natal, and the seaport of Durban is the largest city in the province. See DURBAN; PIETERMARITZBURG.

The Portuguese navigator Vasco da Gama sighted Natal on Christmas Day, 1497. Dutch settlers moved into Natal in the 1830's. The British annexed Natal in 1843. In 1844, Natal became a province of Britain's nearby Cape Colony. It was made a separate crown colony in 1856. Zululand was annexed to Natal in 1897. The British annexed part of Transvaal to Natal in 1902, after the Boer War had ended. Natal became a self-governing province in the new Union of South Africa (now South Africa) in 1910. HIBBERD V. B. KLINE, JR.

See also BANTU; ZULULAND.

NATCHEZ, *NATCH ez*, Miss. (pop. 19,704; alt. 215 ft.), is the oldest city along the Mississippi River. It lies on the southwestern border of the state (see MISSISSIPPI [political map]). Products include automobile tires, lumber, oil, rayon pulp, and pecans.

Jean Baptiste le Moyne, Sieur de Bienville, a French governor of Louisiana, built Fort Rosalie on the site in 1716. In 1729, the Natchez Indians destroyed it. Settlers from the East re-established Natchez in 1771. The growth of the cotton industry made Natchez the center of wealth and culture in Mississippi before the Civil War. Natchez has a mayor-council government. It is the seat of Adams County.   CHARLOTTE CAPERS

See also NATCHEZ INDIANS.

NATCHEZ INDIANS, *NATCH ehz*, were one of the few tribes in North America whose chiefs had complete power over the lives and property of their subjects. The Natchez once lived near the city in Mississippi that was named after them.

They were farmers, and made excellent fabrics and pottery. Each member of the tribe inherited his place in a society of rigid class distinctions. There were three classes of nobility, as well as a large group of common people. The Natchez had a highly developed religious life based on sun worship. They believed that their chief was descended from the sun. Servants carried him about in a special litter, so that his feet would not touch the ground. When a chief died, his wives were strangled. Some other tribe members sacrificed their children.

The name of the Natchez first occurs in the reports of La Salle's descent of the Mississippi River in 1682. The Natchez, which probably included about 6,000 persons, were the largest and strongest tribe on the lower Mississippi at that time. They fought many wars with the French, but were so severely beaten in 1729 that they did not fight again. Only a few survivors remain today among the Cherokee and Creek Indians of Oklahoma.   WILLIAM H. GILBERT

NATCHEZ TRACE was an important commercial and military route between Nashville, Tenn., and Natchez, Miss. Frontiersmen who floated their goods on flatboats down the Mississippi River to New Orleans often returned on horseback along this route. Settlers moving into the Gulf States frequently traveled south on the trace. In 1800, Congress designated it as a post road, and the U.S. Army improved it. The trace was important in the early 1800's. In 1938, the Natchez Trace National Parkway was established. W. TURRENTINE JACKSON

NATCHITOCHES, *NACK uh tahsh,* La. (pop. 15,974; alt. 105 ft.), is the oldest town in Louisiana, and the trading center of a rich cotton-growing region (see LOUISIANA [political map]). It houses Northwestern State University of Louisiana. During the town's Christmas festival, it is lighted by over 140,000 light bulbs.

Natchitoches was founded as Fort St. Jean Baptiste by Louis Juchereau de St. Denis in 1714. It served as a French military and trading post on the Red River. The town was later named after the Natchitoches Indians. It was the most important trading center of northwestern Louisiana until 1832, when the Red River moved its channel about 5 miles eastward. Natchitoches has a commission form of government. It is the seat of Natchitoches Parish.

NATHAN. See PARABLE.

NATHAN, ROBERT (1894-), is an American novelist and poet. He has written more than 25 successful novels, and many have been made into motion pictures. His first novel, *Peter Kindred,* was published in 1919. Others that became well-known include *The Bishop's Wife* (1928) and *Portrait of Jennie* (1940). Nathan's war ballad, *Dunkirk* (1942), was widely hailed as effective propaganda. He is a skilled craftsman in poetry, and his sonnets are especially memorable. His books of poetry include *Youth Grows Old* (1922), and *The Green Leaf: Collected Poems* (1950). Nathan's work is touched with irony, and he has a gift for fantasy.

He was born in New York City, and was graduated from Harvard University. He worked for two years in an advertising agency. JOHN HOLMES

NATHANAEL. See BARTHOLOMEW, SAINT.

NATION is a large group of people that unite for mutual safety and welfare. A common language, origin, history, and culture usually characterize a nation. *Nation* is a vague term, and nationhood exists largely because a group considers itself to be a nation. Nations that govern themselves independently may form states. The Serbians, Croatians, and Montenegrins form distinct ethnic groups in Yugoslavia, and consider themselves nations. But they are not states, because they are governed, with some other groups, by the Yugoslav government. ROBERT G. NEUMANN

NATION, CARRY AMELIA MOORE (1846-1911), became well-known for her violent efforts to stop the sale of alcoholic liquors. Although she was arrested often for disturbing the peace, she impressed many people with her sincerity and courage. Others considered her intolerant. She carried the temperance crusade from the level of education and organization to that of action, and helped bring on national prohibition in 1919 (see PROHIBITION).

She was born on Nov. 25, 1846, in Garrard County, Kentucky. In 1867, she was married to Dr. Charles Gloyd, a drunkard who died soon after their marriage. She then taught school and rented rooms. In 1877, she married David Nation, a lawyer and minister. Her strong religious interests became more intense, and she began to see visions. Her belief that she was divinely protected increased in 1889, when a fire in her town left her hotel untouched. She thought, too, that her name (Carry A. Nation) had been preordained.

The Nations settled in Kansas in 1889. An 1880 state law banned liquor sales there. But it was not enforced. Mrs. Nation began in 1890 to pray outside saloons. Later she began to smash them. Nearly 6 feet tall and strong, she did much damage, first with stones and other implements, and later with hatchets. She closed the saloons of her own town, Medicine Lodge, then moved on to neighboring towns. She finally conducted sensational campaigns, destroying saloons in the chief Kansas cities. When she entered states where liquor sales were legal, she was often arrested for disturbing the peace.

Carry Nation opposed tobacco, and immodesty in women's dress. She spoke eloquently, and inspired others to imitate her. Her husband divorced her for desertion in 1901. LOUIS FILLER

NATIONAL. Many organizations are listed in THE WORLD BOOK ENCYCLOPEDIA under the key word in the name of the organization. Example: BUSINESS AND PROFESSIONAL WOMEN'S CLUBS, NATIONAL FEDERATION OF.

NATIONAL ACADEMY OF DESIGN is the oldest organization in the United States with a membership composed exclusively of artists. It was established in 1825, and incorporated in 1828, to cultivate and extend the fine arts. Its present membership is made up of painters, sculptors, architects, workers in the graphic arts, and aquarellists. The membership is divided into two groups known as the associates and academicians. When an artist is elected an associate of the academy, he presents the organization with a diploma portrait. When an associate becomes an academician, he gives the academy one of his own works of art. Through this procedure the academy has accumulated a valuable art collection. Membership is limited to professional artists.

The National Academy acts as trustee of the Ranger and Abbey funds, which finance scholarships, awards, and the purchase of works of art. It maintains a school where painting, sculpture, drawing, and graphic arts are taught. Its galleries are used for exhibition of contemporary art. Headquarters are at 1083 Fifth Avenue, New York, N.Y. 10028. ALICE G. MELROSE

NATIONAL ACADEMY OF EDUCATION is a society devoted to furthering research in education. The acad-

Carry Nation holds the weapons which she used in her crusade against alcoholic beverages in the early 1900's. The Bible was her text for many lectures. She used the hatchet often in her violent saloon-wrecking campaign.

Brown Bros.

emy consists of 50 scholars whose writings have contributed to educational history, practice, or theory. The academy is divided into four categories of membership: (1) history and philosophy; (2) anthropology, economics, politics, and sociology; (3) psychology; and (4) practices. Its purpose is to provide "a forum which will set the highest standards for educational inquiry and discussion." The academy is a private organization and has no connection with the United States government. The National Academy of Education was founded by noted scholars in the United States in 1965.

Critically reviewed by the NATIONAL ACADEMY OF EDUCATION

NATIONAL ACADEMY OF ENGINEERING. See NATIONAL ACADEMY OF SCIENCES.

NATIONAL ACADEMY OF SCIENCES is a nongovernmental organization that serves as a scientific adviser to the United States government. The academy also works to encourage research in the physical and biological sciences and promotes the use of these sciences for the general welfare. The National Research Council is an important part of the National Academy of Sciences. The National Academy of Engineering works with the National Academy of Sciences in advising the government on technological problems.

The National Academy of Sciences consists of about 800 scientists elected to the organization in recognition of their research accomplishments. Scientists from other countries may also be elected to the academy as foreign associates. A maximum of 50 Americans and 10 foreign associates may be elected each year.

The National Research Council enables other scientists to work with members of the academy. The council has about 300 members who are appointed by the president of the academy. They include representatives of major scientific and technological societies, and of the United States government.

The National Academy of Engineering consists of engineers who are elected because of their professional achievements. In 1964, the academy had only 25 members. But it is expected to grow to over 300 members. The academy is independent of the National Academy of Sciences, but cooperates closely with it.

More than 3,000 scientists and engineers take part in committees and other groups established by these three organizations. They devote their time without pay. Their work is financed by funds from both government and private sources.

The National Academy of Sciences was established in 1863 by an act of Congress signed by President Abraham Lincoln. The charter requires that the academy act as an adviser to the government on scientific matters as well as engaging in other scientific activities. The National Research Council was established by the academy in 1916 at the request of President Woodrow Wilson. The National Academy of Engineering was established in 1964 under the charter of the National Academy of Sciences. All three organizations have headquarters at 2101 Constitution Avenue NW, Washington, D.C. 20418.

Critically reviewed by the NATIONAL ACADEMY OF SCIENCES

NATIONAL AERONAUTIC ASSOCIATION OF THE U.S.A. (NAA) promotes the advancement of aviation and space flight in the United States. It is the U.S. representative to the worldwide Fédération Aeronautique Internationale. The NAA documents and certifies

flight records by U.S. aircraft and spacecraft. Groups associated with the NAA include the Academy of Model Aeronautics, the Balloon Federation of America, the Parachute Club of America, the National Pilots Association, and the Soaring Society of America. NAA annually presents four awards for achievements in flight. The NAA was chartered in 1922. Headquarters are at 806 15th Street NW, Washington, D.C. 20005.

Critically reviewed by the NATIONAL AERONAUTIC ASSOCIATION

NATIONAL AERONAUTICS AND SPACE ADMINISTRATION (NASA) and COUNCIL conducts and coordinates United States nonmilitary research into problems of flight within and beyond the earth's atmosphere. The NASA has about 15,000 scientists, engineers, and technicians. Its installations include the John F. Kennedy Space Center at Cape Kennedy, Fla.; the Manned Spacecraft Center, near Houston, Tex.; the Langley Research Center, Hampton, Va.; Wallops Station, Va.; Goddard Space Flight Center, Greenbelt, Md.; Lewis Research Center, Cleveland; George C. Marshall Space Flight Center, Huntsville, Ala.; Flight Research Center, Edwards, Calif.; Ames Research Center, Moffett Field, Calif.; and Jet Propulsion Laboratory, Pasadena, Calif.

The NASA was established in 1958 as an independent agency, with headquarters in Washington, D.C. It absorbed the National Advisory Committee for Aeronautics (NACA). The administrator of the NASA is a member of the National Aeronautics and Space Council headed by the Vice-President. Critically reviewed by the NASA

See also MANNED SPACECRAFT CENTER.

NATIONAL AGRICULTURAL LIBRARY. See LIBRARY (U.S. Government Libraries).

NATIONAL AIR AND SPACE MUSEUM, in Washington, D.C., features exhibits of aviation and space materials. The museum is supported by the United States government and by private funds. Exhibits include the Wright brothers' first airplane; Charles A. Lindbergh's *Spirit of St. Louis;* Wiley Post's *Winnie Mae;* the X-1, the first supersonic airplane; the X-15 rocket-propelled airplane, which set a new altitude record in 1963; and the Mercury, Gemini, and Apollo spacecraft.

Congress created the National Air Museum in 1946 as a bureau of the Smithsonian Institution. The museum was renamed in 1966.

Critically reviewed by the NATIONAL AIR AND SPACE MUSEUM

NATIONAL ALLIANCE OF BUSINESSMEN (NAB) is an organization through which the United States government and industry cooperate to find jobs for the hard-core unemployed—people who have the most difficult time finding jobs. Through the NAB, the government's resources for locating the unemployed are linked with industry's resources for hiring and training them. Many hard-core jobless require special training and counseling because of poor education or lack of skills. Congress provides funds to pay back industry for the cost of hiring and training these persons.

The NAB was established in 1968. It started its program, called JOBS (*Job Opportunities in the Business Sector*), in the nation's 50 largest metropolitan areas. In 1969, the program was expanded to 125 areas. The NAB has headquarters at 726 Jackson Place NW, Washington, D.C. 20506.

Critically reviewed by the NATIONAL ALLIANCE OF BUSINESSMEN

NATIONAL ANTHEMS

NATIONAL ANTHEMS are the official patriotic songs or hymns that are always played at ceremonious occasions or public gatherings. Sometimes they are songs inspired by a great crisis through which a nation has passed. Such a song is France's "La Marseillaise." National anthems, or national hymns, usually express the ideals that a country stands for. They also are used to stimulate patriotism and loyalty to one's country.

Following are national anthems of various nations.

COUNTRY	NATIONAL ANTHEM
Argentina	"Himno Nacional Argentino"
Brazil	"Hino Nacional"
Chile	"Himno Nacional de Chile"
China (Mainland)	"The March of the Volunteers"
Formosa	"Kuo-ko"
France	"La Marseillaise"
Germany (East)	"Auferstanden aus Ruinen"
Germany (West)	(unofficial) "Deutschlandlied"
Great Britain	"God Save the Queen" or "King"
Greece	"Imnos pros tin Eleftherian"
India	"Jana-gana-mana"
Indonesia	"Indonesia Raya"
Ireland	"The Soldier's Song"
Israel	"Hatikva"
Italy	"Inno di Mameli"
Japan	"Kimigayo"
Mexico	"Himno Nacional de México"
Philippines	"Lupang Hinirang"
Russia	"Gosudarstveny Gimn Sovetskogo Soyusa"
Spain	"Himno Nacional"
United States	"The Star-Spangled Banner"

The following are popular songs and hymns used upon patriotic occasions in the United States: "America"; "Battle Hymn of the Republic"; "Dixie"; "God Bless America"; "Semper Fidelis"; and "Yankee Doodle."

Canada does not have an official national anthem. However, both "God Save the Queen" or "King" and "O Canada" are sung as national anthems. In Australia and New Zealand, the national anthem is "God Save the Queen" or "King." RAYMOND KENDALL

Related Articles: See Facts in Brief sections of country articles, such as NETHERLANDS (Facts in Brief). See also:

America	Hail Columbia
Battle Hymn of the Republic	Hail to the Chief
Deutschland Über Alles	Horst Wessel
Dixie	Maple Leaf Forever
God Bless America	Marseillaise
God Save the Queen or King	Star-Spangled Banner
	Yankee Doodle

NATIONAL ARCHIVES. See ARCHIVES, NATIONAL.

NATIONAL ASSEMBLY. See FRENCH REVOLUTION.

NATIONAL ASSOCIATION FOR THE ADVANCEMENT OF COLORED PEOPLE (NAACP) is a civil rights organization in the United States. It works to end discrimination against Negroes and other minority groups.

The NAACP achieves many of its goals through legal action. It played an important part in the 1954 ruling of the Supreme Court of the United States that compulsory segregation in public schools is unconstitutional. Thurgood Marshall, an NAACP lawyer, presented the legal argument that resulted in the decision. Marshall later became a Supreme Court justice.

NAACP legal action has helped enforce antilynching laws and helped enact laws that ban discrimination in education, employment, housing, public accommodations, and the administration of justice. NAACP legal activity has also helped protect the right of Negroes to vote and to serve on juries.

The NAACP conducts a continuous voter education and voter registration program. It works for desegregation in public schools. It urges book publishers to produce textbooks that include Negroes in text and illustrations and that provide an accurate account of Negroes in the United States. The NAACP also works to reduce poverty and hunger. For example, in 1968 it established the Mississippi Emergency Relief Fund to help feed poverty-stricken Negroes in the Mississippi Delta region.

The NAACP was founded in New York City in 1909 by 60 Negro and white citizens. It now has more than 460,000 members. Funds for NAACP programs come from membership fees and from donations by private groups and individuals. National headquarters are at 1790 Broadway, New York, N.Y. 10019. M. CARL HOLMAN

See also EVERS; MARSHALL, THURGOOD; WHITE, WALTER F.; WILKENS, ROY.

NATIONAL ASSOCIATION OF MANUFACTURERS (NAM) is an organization of American manufacturing companies. It serves as a policy-making body for the manufacturing industry on industrial and economic problems. It also interprets industry's policies to the federal government and the public. Many kinds of companies belong to the NAM. Most members are companies that employ 500 or fewer persons.

About 3,000 representatives of member companies form policy-making committees that make recommendations to the NAM's Board of Directors. The board and an Executive Committee meet several times a year to settle policies. The NAM was founded in 1895. It has headquarters at 277 Park Avenue, New York, N.Y. 10017. It also has several branch offices.

Critically reviewed by the NATIONAL ASSOCIATION OF MANUFACTURERS

NATIONAL ASSOCIATION OF SOCIAL WORKERS. See SOCIAL WORKERS, NATIONAL ASSOCIATION OF.

NATIONAL BANK. See BANKS AND BANKING (Commercial Banks).

NATIONAL BANK ACT. See BANKS AND BANKING (Federal Regulations; The Wildcat Period).

NATIONAL BAPTIST CONVENTION OF AMERICA is an organization of Negro Baptists. It traces its history to the founding of the Foreign Mission Baptist Convention in 1880. The group merged in 1895 with the American National Baptist Educational Convention to form the National Baptist Convention of America. In 1915, this group split into the National Baptist Convention of America, commonly called the "unincorporated convention," and the National Baptist Convention, U.S.A.

The National Baptist Convention of America operates the National Baptist Publishing Board in Nashville, Tenn., and does missionary work in Jamaica, Panama, and Liberia. The convention also provides financial support for 10 colleges. For membership in the United States, see RELIGION (table).

Critically reviewed by the NATIONAL BAPTIST CONVENTION OF AMERICA

See also BAPTISTS.

NATIONAL BAPTIST CONVENTION, U.S.A., INC., is one of the largest religious organizations among American Negroes. The convention has 30,000 churches and ranks as the second largest Baptist organization in the world, after the Southern Baptist Convention.

The convention was organized in 1880 to spread the gospel of Christ to other countries. Its founders stressed preaching the gospel to all men as an answer to what they considered the shortcomings of a segregating church. During 1967 and 1968, the convention reaffirmed its faith in civil rights through law and order by adopting the principles set forth in the book *Unholy Shadows and Freedom's Holy Light* by the convention's president, J. H. Jackson. For U.S. membership, see RELIGION (table).

Critically reviewed by the NATIONAL BAPTIST CONVENTION, U.S.A., INC.

NATIONAL BASEBALL HALL OF FAME. See BASEBALL (History; table).

NATIONAL BASEBALL LEAGUE. See BASEBALL (Professional Baseball; History).

NATIONAL BASKETBALL ASSOCIATION. See BASKETBALL (Professional Basketball).

NATIONAL BATTLEFIELD. See NATIONAL PARK SYSTEM.

NATIONAL BOOK AWARD. See AMERICAN LITERATURE (Literary Awards).

NATIONAL BROADCASTING COMPANY (NBC) is one of the largest radio and television networks in the United States. NBC has nearly 400 stations in its radio-television networks. It provides a national program service for these stations, including comedy and drama shows, news broadcasts, and descriptions of sports events.

Almost all the stations that belong to the NBC radio and television networks are independently owned and operated. However, NBC owns and operates seven radio stations and six TV stations in the United States.

NBC organized the first radio network in the United States in 1926 with 25 radio stations. It also pioneered in television, introducing it as a regular service in 1939. In 1951, NBC inaugurated its coast-to-coast television network. It began televising programs in color soon after the federal government approved color television in 1953.

NBC is owned by the Radio Corporation of America and has headquarters in New York City. In 1955, it built in Burbank, Calif., a West Coast headquarters, "Color City," designed for color television. JOSEPH A. RYAN

See also RADIO CORPORATION OF AMERICA.

NATIONAL BUDGET is the financial plan for a nation's government. The budget forecasts the government's income and expenditures for one *fiscal year* (from July 1 to June 30 in the United States). It forecasts how much money the government will collect from taxes and other sources, and suggests how much money each government department should spend.

The U.S. budget is prepared for the President by the Office of Management and Budget. The office receives estimates of government income from the Department of the Treasury and spending estimates from all government departments. Congress must approve the budget before any money can be spent. The President presents the budget to Congress, usually in January. Congressional committees make recommendations to Congress concerning various parts of the budget. The committees may recommend approval or suggest changes. Congress then passes *appropriation bills*, which determine how much each government department can spend.

The government gets most of its income from individual income taxes, corporation income taxes, and employment taxes. Most government expenditures are

NATIONAL CATHOLIC EDUCATIONAL ASSN.

for national defense and for such welfare purposes as education, health, job training, veterans' benefits, public housing, and social security benefits.

The national budget has grown in size and importance as the role of the federal government has grown. The U.S. budget is over 60 times larger today than in the early 1900's, after allowing for price changes. In the late 1960's, the national budget exceeded $180 billion a year and amounted to over 20 per cent of the country's gross national product. The Canadian budget has grown from about 5 per cent of the gross national product in 1900 to about 15 per cent today.

Economists once favored a *balanced budget*, in which income equaled spending. But many fiscal experts now favor a *budget deficit* (expenditures exceeding income) when the economy needs stimulating, and a *planned surplus* (income exceeding expenditures) in boom times to control inflation. PETER WAGNER

See also BUDGET, BUREAU OF THE.

NATIONAL BUREAU OF STANDARDS is a federal agency in the Department of Commerce that establishes accurate measurement standards for science, industry, and commerce in the United States. All measurements made in the United States, from the thrust of a rocket engine to the weight of a load of grain, depend upon the national standards kept at the bureau.

Bureau scientists develop precise measurement standards that control the size, color, electrical resistance, and other critical properties of manufactured products. The bureau measures the properties of materials, such as metals and ceramics, so they may be used to better advantage in new products. The bureau also provides scientists and engineers with accurate values of basic constants, such as the speed of light.

To meet these responsibilities, the bureau conducts a broad research and development program in physics, chemistry, mathematics, and some branches of engineering. Results of this research are published through the Government Printing Office. The bureau, created in 1901, became part of the Department of Commerce in 1903.

Critically reviewed by the NATIONAL BUREAU OF STANDARDS

See also CONSUMER EDUCATION.

NATIONAL CANCER INSTITUTE. See NATIONAL INSTITUTES OF HEALTH.

NATIONAL CATHEDRAL. See WASHINGTON CATHEDRAL.

NATIONAL CATHOLIC EDUCATIONAL ASSOCIATION is an organization to encourage cooperation and mutual helpfulness among Catholic educators, and to promote, by study, conference, and discussion, Catholic educational work in the United States. The organization was founded as the Catholic Educational Association in 1904 in St. Louis, Mo., and, in 1927, became the National Catholic Educational Association. Its work is carried on by the departments of Major Seminary, Minor Seminary, College and University, Secondary School, School Superintendents, Elementary School, and Special Education. Headquarters are at 1785 Massachusetts Avenue NW, Washington, D.C. 20036. The National Catholic Educational Association has about 16,000 members.

Critically reviewed by the NATIONAL CATHOLIC EDUCATIONAL ASSOCIATION

NATIONAL CEMETERY is a burial place for persons who served honorably in the armed forces of the United States. The federal government maintains 131 cemeteries and similar installations in various parts of the United States. Servicemen or former servicemen may still be buried in most of them, but 28 of the cemeteries are inactive, with no space for future burials.

Two government agencies operate national cemeteries. The National Park Service, a part of the Department of the Interior, operates 10 cemeteries. The Department of the Army, through the chief of support services, operates 85 cemeteries. In addition, the chief of support services has charge of 21 soldiers' lots, 7 Confederate cemeteries and plots, 2 Confederate monuments, a prison park, and 2 other activities.

The cemeteries operated by the National Park Service lie in or next to historical units of the park system, and are now perpetuated as historical shrines. They were originally set up by the Army. In 1933, they were transferred to the Department of the Interior along with national military parks and battlefield sites.

In all national burial installations, authorization for interment, erection of headstones and monuments, and maintenance of burial records continue to be the responsibility of the chief of support services. Regulations governing burials are the same under both systems. The chief of support services is authorized to furnish headstones and markers for unmarked graves of all military personnel. These include graves of soldiers who served in the Union and Confederate armies in the

Ollie Atkins

Arlington National Cemetery in Arlington, Va., *left,* is across the Potomac River from Washington, D.C. The Custis-Lee Mansion, home of General Robert E. Lee, overlooks the cemetery.

National Cemetery at the Presidio of San Francisco, *below,* stands on a hillside overlooking San Francisco Bay and the Golden Gate Bridge. The Presidio was once a Spanish Army post.

U.S. Army

Civil War, and all other members of the armed forces who died in service. The authorization also extends to certain other graves. The federal government has provided more than 2 million headstones and markers under its national cemetery systems.

Legislative authority to establish national cemeteries dates back to 1862. During the Civil War, Congress gave President Abraham Lincoln permission to establish cemeteries to provide for the burial of Union veterans.

One of the best-known national cemeteries is in Gettysburg, Pa. President Abraham Lincoln delivered his famous Gettysburg Address there on Nov. 19, 1863. Other cemeteries under the National Park Service are: Antietam, Md.; Battleground, Washington, D.C.; Fort Donelson, Tenn.; Fredericksburg, Va.; Poplar Grove, Va.; Shiloh, Tenn.; Stones River, Tenn.; Vicksburg, Miss.; and Yorktown, Va.

The American Battle Monuments Commission administers and maintains all American military cemeteries outside the United States and its possessions.

Critically reviewed by the DEPARTMENT OF THE ARMY

See also ARLINGTON NATIONAL CEMETERY; HAWAII (World War II).

NATIONAL CITY BANK, FIRST. See FIRST NATIONAL CITY BANK.

NATIONAL COLLECTION OF FINE ARTS is a bureau of the Smithsonian Institution that preserves and displays certain works of art belonging to the United States government. The bureau also presents a continuing series of special exhibitions. The collection includes paintings, sculptures, prints, drawings, and decorative art works. Most items in the collection are by American artists. The bureau's Traveling Exhibition Service presents art exhibits throughout the United States and in other countries. The bureau lends works of art to federal agencies and provides facilities for art education and research. The collection is the oldest federal government art collection in the United States.

Critically reviewed by the SMITHSONIAN INSTITUTION

NATIONAL COLLEGE OF EDUCATION. See UNIVERSITIES AND COLLEGES (table).

NATIONAL COLLEGIATE ATHLETIC ASSOCIATION (NCAA) establishes athletic standards and official playing rules for college sports. It conducts National Collegiate Championship events in 13 sports and keeps the official national statistics and records of college sports. It also conducts studies on athletic problems and maintains a large film library covering play in National Collegiate Championship events. It sponsors an extensive postgraduate scholarship program and controls the televising of college football games.

The NCAA was founded in 1906. Its membership has grown from 13 schools to over 700, including colleges and universities, athletic conferences, and coaches' associations. Its headquarters are at 1221 Baltimore Avenue, Kansas City, Mo. 64105.

Critically reviewed by the NATIONAL COLLEGIATE ATHLETIC ASSOCIATION

NATIONAL CONFERENCE OF CHRISTIANS AND JEWS fights prejudice, intolerance, and bigotry. It has programs to improve intergroup relations in factories, oppose intolerance with the aid of fraternal, civic, labor, and other groups, and promote understanding among Jews, Protestants, and Roman Catholics.

The conference was founded in 1928. It has 65 regional offices, and committees in hundreds of communities. In 1950, it helped organize World Brotherhood to reduce hostilities created by religious, racial, national, and cultural differences. The conference sponsors Brotherhood Week in the United States (see BROTHERHOOD WEEK). Headquarters are at 43 W. 57th Street, New York N.Y. 10019.   STERLING W. BROWN

NATIONAL CONGRESS OF PARENTS AND TEACHERS. See PARENTS AND TEACHERS, NATIONAL CONGRESS OF.

NATIONAL CONSUMERS LEAGUE is an educational movement founded in 1899 to awaken interest in the conditions under which goods are made and distributed, and to show consumers their responsibility for these conditions. The league worked for child labor laws, the 8-hour day for women, minimum wage laws, social insurance, and national health insurance for the elderly under social security. It prepared legal briefs to defend these laws in court. It now works to improve the conditions of migratory farmworkers, extend the Fair Labor Standards Act, and extend consumer protection. The National Consumers League has national headquarters at 1029 Vermont Avenue NW, Washington, D.C. 20005.

Critically reviewed by the NATIONAL CONSUMERS LEAGUE

NATIONAL COUNCIL OF CATHOLIC YOUTH (NCCY), established in 1951, promotes and provides many services for Roman Catholic youth groups in the United States. The council has two sections. The college and university section consists of the National Newman Apostolate and the National Federation of Catholic College Students. The diocesan section includes national organizations and the local Catholic Youth Organizations (CYO). The Division of Youth Activities of the United States Catholic Conference sponsors the NCCY. Headquarters are at 1312 Massachusetts Avenue NW, Washington, D.C. 20005.

Critically reviewed by the NATIONAL COUNCIL OF CATHOLIC YOUTH

See also NEWMAN APOSTOLATE.

NATIONAL COUNCIL OF CHURCHES is an agency through which churches work together to promote social justice and understanding among people in the United States and overseas. Its work includes community development, education, evangelism, medical aid, missions, relief, research, and social welfare programs. Each year, the council spends more than $11 million in overseas programs. It represents 33 Protestant and Orthodox denominations with about 42 million members.

A General Assembly of about 800 delegates appointed by member churches governs the council. It meets every three years. A General Board of about 250 General Assembly members governs the council between assembly meetings. It meets three times a year.

The council was formed in 1950 by the merger of 11 interdenominational agencies. Its full name is NATIONAL COUNCIL OF THE CHURCHES OF CHRIST IN THE UNITED STATES OF AMERICA. It publishes a newspaper called *Tempo* every two weeks. Headquarters are at 475 Riverside Drive, New York, N.Y. 10027.

Critically reviewed by the NATIONAL COUNCIL OF CHURCHES

NATIONAL COUNCIL ON MARINE RESOURCES AND ENGINEERING DEVELOPMENT. See PRESIDENT OF THE UNITED STATES (Executive Office of the President).

NATIONAL COVENANT. See COVENANTERS.

NATIONAL DEBT

NATIONAL DEBT is the total amount that the federal government owes because of money it has borrowed by selling bonds and certificates of indebtedness. The national debt exists because the government's expenses often exceed its income from taxes. In such situations, the government sells bonds to get the extra money it needs. It must repay the bondholders the original amount of the bonds on a specified date, and it must also pay interest on this indebtedness.

Government debt differs from private debt because the government is not required to post any *collateral* (pledge of security) in order to guarantee payment. However, the United States government has always repaid its loans in full.

UNITED STATES GROSS NATIONAL DEBT COMPARED WITH GROSS NATIONAL PRODUCT SINCE THE CIVIL WAR

The gross national debt of the United States is over 140 times as large today as it was 100 years ago. But the U.S. population is only 5 times as large. As a result, the debt per person is about 27 times as great as it was 100 years ago. In 1945, the national debt exceeded the U.S. gross national product (GNP). The GNP is the total value of the goods and services produced during the year. Since the mid-1940's, the GNP has grown faster than the debt. Today, the debt is only about two-fifths of the GNP.

Year	Gross National Debt	Debt per Person	Gross National Debt as Percentage of Gross National Product	Year	Gross National Debt	Debt per Person	Gross National Debt as Percentage of Gross National Product
1865	$2,677,929,000	$75	—	1920	$24,299,321,000	$228	27
1870	$2,436,453,000	$61	30	1930	$16,185,310,000	$132	18
1880	$2,090,909,000	$42	16	1940	$42,967,531,000	$325	43
1890	$1,122,397,000	$18	9	1950	$257,357,352,000	$1,697	90
1900	$1,263,417,000	$17	7	1960	$286,330,761,000	$1,585	57
1910	$1,146,940,000	$12	3	1968	$369,723,000,000	$1,838	43

Sources: Department of the Treasury; Department of Commerce

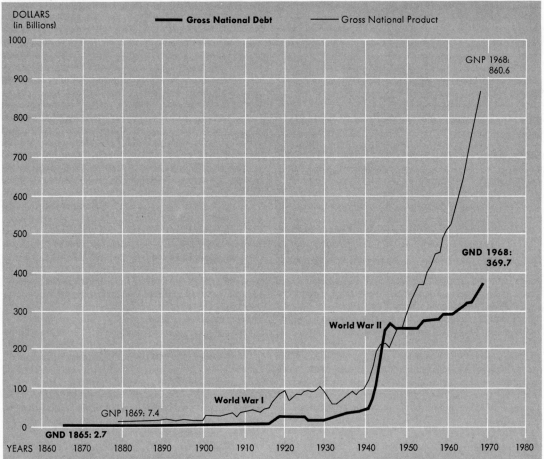

DOLLARS (in Billions) — Gross National Debt — Gross National Product

GNP 1968: 860.6

GND 1968: 369.7

World War II

World War I

GNP 1869: 7.4

GND 1865: 2.7

YEARS 1860 1870 1880 1890 1900 1910 1920 1930 1940 1950 1960 1970 1980

Causes of National Debt. The United States debt originated in the 1790's, when the newly established federal government assumed debts that the individual states had run up during the Revolutionary War. Wars have been by far the most common cause of increases in the U.S. national debt. For example, the federal debt was only $1 billion before World War I (1914-1918). The war raised it to about $25 billion. By the time World War II ended in 1945, the national debt had risen to about $259 billion. The Korean War in the early 1950's and the Vietnam War in the 1960's and early 1970's have caused the debt to rise sharply again.

Wars have also been responsible for high national debts in other countries. In 1867, the newly formed Dominion of Canada assumed the Canadian debt of $93 million. After increases caused chiefly by Canada's participation in two world wars, the debt totaled about $19 billion in the mid-1940's. By the late 1960's, the Canadian national debt had risen to about $33 billion.

Public improvements also increase the national debt. These include such long-lasting improvements as canals, roads and highways, and dams for irrigation and electrical power. Some of these yield enough income to pay the principal and interest on the bonds issued to finance them. Others, such as roads and river navigation improvements, benefit the nation, but generally do not yield money income.

The United States Congress sets a limit or ceiling on how high the national debt may rise. In July, 1970, the ceiling was $380 billion, but Congress provided that the debt could exceed this limit by $15 billion on a temporary basis, if necessary.

Ownership of the Debt. About one-fifth of the national debt is held by various government agencies. However, banks and private individuals are the largest owners of the debt. Banks and insurance companies buy government bonds as a safe investment and to earn interest on funds not used for other purposes. Individuals also buy bonds for family security and for patriotic reasons. During World War II, millions of Americans bought war bonds. Businesses also buy government bonds when they have extra cash which they wish to keep in a safe place while it earns interest. For those who wish to invest for a short time only, the government issues notes or certificates of indebtedness for periods as short as 30 days. At the end of that time, these securities must be repaid out of income from taxes or from sales of new certificates to other investors. Banks and other business firms buy most of the short-term certificates of indebtedness.

Debt Policy. It is important to consider the national debt in relation to the nation's total economic strength. One way of doing this is to compare the national debt to the *gross national product* (GNP). The GNP is the value of a nation's entire production of goods and services in a given year. For example, the United States national debt rose from $259 billion in 1945 to $370 billion in 1968. But the 1945 debt amounted to 122 per cent of that year's GNP, while the 1968 debt was only 43 per cent of the 1968 GNP. The 1968 national debt accounted for only about a fifth of all public (federal, state, and local) and private debts. In 1945, on the other hand, the United States national debt accounted

for over three-fifths of all public and private debts.

Some persons argue that, just as in a family or business, federal government spending should be kept equal to or below its income. Others declare that this comparison is misleading. They point out that, except for the small portion of the debt held by persons in other countries, the size of the debt itself is not as important as the effects that increasing or reducing the debt might have on the economy. Both groups usually agree that taxes in prosperous times should be high enough to cover government spending and even leave a surplus to reduce the debt.

Those who call for a balanced budget would not favor measures that would increase the national debt if a recession occurred or threatened to occur. But members of the second group would urge government borrowing to pay for public improvements as a sound way to prevent or end recession. They believe it is the government's responsibility to take such action to stimulate business activity, thereby creating more jobs to reduce unemployment.   PETER WAGNER

See also NATIONAL BUDGET; GROSS NATIONAL PRODUCT; KEYNES, JOHN MAYNARD; SAVINGS BOND.

CANADA NATIONAL DEBT AND PRODUCT SINCE CONFEDERATION IN 1867

Canada's national debt, like that of the United States, has increased because the government has borrowed huge sums to develop the country and to fight wars. Today, Canada's debt is rising more slowly than its gross national product.

Year	Gross National Debt	Debt per Person	Gross National Debt as Per Cent of Gross National Product
1867	$93,046,000	$27	—
1870	$115,994,000	$32	25
1880	$194,634,000	$46	33
1890	$286,112,000	$60	36
1900	$346,207,000	$65	33
1910	$470,663,000	$67	21
1920	$3,041,530,000	$355	55
1930	$2,544,586,000	$249	44
1940	$4,028,729,000	$354	60
1950	$16,750,756,000	$1,222	93
1960	$20,986,367,000	$1,174	58
1968	$32,924,170,000	$1,587	49

Source: Dominion Bureau of Statistics

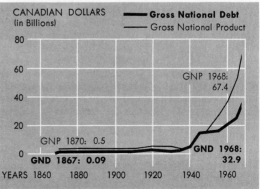

CANADIAN DOLLARS (in Billions) — **Gross National Debt** / Gross National Product
GNP 1968: 67.4
GNP 1870: 0.5
GND 1867: 0.09
GND 1968: 32.9
YEARS 1860 1880 1900 1920 1940 1960

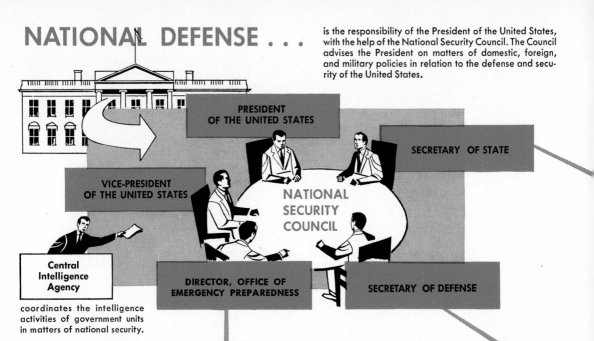

NATIONAL DEFENSE . . .

is the responsibility of the President of the United States, with the help of the National Security Council. The Council advises the President on matters of domestic, foreign, and military policies in relation to the defense and security of the United States.

PRESIDENT OF THE UNITED STATES

SECRETARY OF STATE

VICE-PRESIDENT OF THE UNITED STATES

NATIONAL SECURITY COUNCIL

Central Intelligence Agency coordinates the intelligence activities of government units in matters of national security.

DIRECTOR, OFFICE OF EMERGENCY PREPAREDNESS

SECRETARY OF DEFENSE

NATIONAL DEFENSE. A nation must be able to defend itself if it is attacked. The problem of defense was easy when men lived in small tribes. There were only a few simple weapons, and every man could use them in defending his tribe. As communities grew larger, and weapons more complicated, small armies of professional soldiers took over the job of defense. But today, when men have built weapons that can destroy entire cities, defense has become a matter of concern to everyone.

National defense affects almost every phase of a nation's life. It includes guns and butter, atomic bombs and cattle. The national defense policy of any nation is tied directly to its relationships with other countries. A nation must have the military strength to support its foreign policy. In time of peace, a nation must fit its military strength into the total national picture. It must not spend so much on defense that it bankrupts the rest of its economy.

Planning for Defense

How strong must a nation be? It takes great leadership and planning to answer this question, not only for today, but for tomorrow. A nation, particularly a powerful country such as the United States, must study the other major political powers. It must estimate their strength now, two years from now, and even twenty years from now. Which nation is likely to be an aggressor, and provoke war? Which probably will be friendly? What about the natural resources, industry, and political and social make-up of other nations? All these questions must be considered.

The President of the United States is the head of all national defense activities. He is the commander in chief of the armed forces, and appoints civilian leaders to supervise the government's defense activities.

The National Security Council is the highest defense planning group in the country. The President and the Vice-President meet with the Secretaries of State and Defense, and the Director of the Office of Emergency Preparedness (OEP), to discuss all problems relating to the defense of the nation. These men bring together their knowledge of national and international problems, and decide on a unified policy designed to meet all the problems. They study the objectives and risks involved in any proposed policy.

The Council supervises the work of the Central Intelligence Agency, which has two jobs: (1) It must interpret information about foreign and domestic activities which could be a threat to national security; (2) it also pro-

ECONOMIC STRENGTH Careful planning is necessary on the home front to conserve natural resources, to prepare for emergencies, and to convert to wartime economy.

Ford Motor Co.

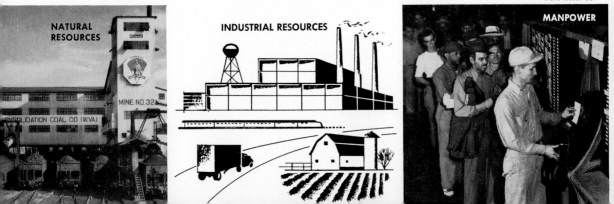

NATURAL RESOURCES

INDUSTRIAL RESOURCES

MANPOWER

vides facts and information to help the Council and other federal agencies in making plans and decisions.

Military Defense Forces

The Secretary of Defense is the President's appointed leader of the military defense activities. He is responsible for the entire military program of the country, including problems of man power, research, and supply.

The Joint Chiefs of Staff (JCS) forms the top strategic planning and military advisory group in the Department of Defense. The JCS is made up of a chairman; the Chief of Staff of the United States Army; the Chief of Naval Operations; and the Chief of Staff of the United States Air Force. On matters relating to the Marine Corps, the Commandant of the corps meets with the JCS as an equal member. The JCS is not a general staff group to exercise military command. It makes recommendations to the Secretary of Defense, the President, or the National Security Council.

Air Defense. Defense experts believe that the first blow in an atomic war probably would come by air. They have planned ways to detect, intercept, and destroy enemy planes and rockets in the air. Air defense of the United States and Canada is the job of the North American Air Defense Command (NORAD), with headquarters in Colorado Springs, Colo. NORAD controls all Canadian and American air defense forces. Bands of radar stations in Canada and off the east and west coasts of the United States watch for attacking planes. Air Force planes equipped with radar patrol the skies over the Arctic and far out over the Atlantic and Pacific oceans. The Ballistic Missile Early Warning System (BMEWS) uses giant radar screens to watch for enemy rockets. All unidentified planes or missiles are reported to a direction center that operates every minute of every day in the year. The center can order interceptor planes or guided missiles into the air. See RADAR.

Sea Defense is designed to protect the United States from possible attack by submarines or surface vessels armed with atomic weapons. Navy patrol planes and ships at sea keep constant watch for potential enemy ships of any kind.

Land Defense is the third line of defense of the United States. Military experts believe that an invasion of the United States would not come until after bombardment from the air and attacks by sea. But the Army's job in defense also includes maintaining defense forces in Europe and in Asia. These forces are ready to repel aggression against Allied nations. Defense planners con-

INTERNATIONAL CO-OPERATION

The government works to promote peace through co-operation with other nations of the world. By means of agreements for economic and military aid, the government builds strong allies.

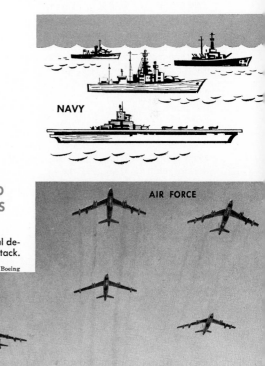

NAVY

AIR FORCE

Boeing

ARMED FORCES

The Army, Navy, and Air Force form the spearhead of national defense. They are kept in constant readiness to repel an enemy attack.

ARMY

sider that the job of defending the United States is also a matter of defending its allies throughout the world.

Mobilizing for Defense

Making preparations to *mobilize,* or gather together, men and materials for war is one of the most important parts of the defense effort. This involves mobilization of all the natural resources, industries, and manpower.

Civil Defense is the responsibility of the Office of Civil Defense (OCD) in the Department of the Army, and the Office of Emergency Preparedness (OEP) in the Executive Office of the President. The OCD is responsible for developing a fallout shelter program; a defense program against chemical, bacteriological, and radiological warfare; warning and communications systems; and programs for aid to state and local governments after an attack. The OEP advises the President on defense matters and coordinates the nation's defense programs. It provides for the operation of the federal government during an emergency.

Natural Resources form the great strength of the country's defenses. The OEP sees to it that critical and strategic materials are not wasted or used in nonessential industries. It also supervises the government's stockpiling of critical materials.

Industries which produce the country's civilian goods would, in case of war, have to be converted to making weapons and military supplies. The OEP must make plans for the government's part in shifting industry from a peacetime to a wartime economy.

Manpower programs are supervised by the OEP. Technicians and skilled workers in vital industries are often far more valuable in their jobs than they would be as soldiers. The government sees that such persons are not drafted into the armed forces. The OEP also has charge of wage problems, labor disputes, and contracts for special defense industries.

The Selective Service System was set up before World War II, and again in 1948, for the purpose of supplying the armed forces with a "draft" of men. In the first six years of operation after World War II, more than 15 million men were registered under the system.

Research goes into the development of every new weapon and means of defense. Government researchers, working with industry and the armed forces, develop and test guided missiles, atomic weapons, atomic-powered ships and airplanes, and new types of jet aircraft.

History

In the early United States, one government department was responsible for the defense of the country. This was the War Department. Henry Knox served as its first secretary. The next addition was a Navy Department, with Benjamin Stoddert as its first secretary. These departments organized the nation's defense forces from the War of 1812 through World War I.

From 1789 to 1800, the government spent about $2,210,000 a year for defense. During the Civil War, this figure had risen to more than $613,000,000 a year. In the four-year period from 1916 to 1920, the average annual cost for defense was $4,095,000,000. During World War II, the government spent an average of $49,817,000,000 a year for the Army, Navy, and Air

Corps alone. By 1970, the government was spending about $80,000,000,000 a year for defense.

The first major change in defense organization came in World War II, when the Joint Chiefs of Staff met to coordinate worldwide land, naval, and air operations. Under the National Security Act of 1947, the War and Navy departments were united with a new Department of the Air Force in the National Military Establishment (NME). Only the head of NME, the Secretary of Defense, was a member of the President's Cabinet. James V. Forrestal was the first secretary. The National Security Council also was created.

In 1949, Congress changed the NME's name to the *Department of Defense.* The department was streamlined and the Secretary of Defense was given greater powers. The Army, the Navy, and the Air Force remained separately administered under the Secretary of Defense.

Two agencies were set up in 1953 to handle all problems of mobilization and foreign aid. The Office of Defense Mobilization (ODM) and the Foreign Operations Administration (FOA) were given centralized authority over problems that had been handled by separate agencies. The departments of State and Defense took over FOA functions in 1955. The ODM was reorganized as the Office of Civil and Defense Mobilization (OCDM) in 1958. In 1961, the Department of Defense took over major civil-defense operations. The OCDM, with its defense coordinating functions, was renamed first the Office of Emergency Planning (OEP), and later the Office of Emergency Preparedness. JOHN H. THOMPSON

Related Articles in WORLD BOOK include:

Air Force, United States	Joint Chiefs of Staff
Antiaircraft Defense	Marine Corps, United
Army, United States	States
Atomic Bomb	National Security Council
Central Intelligence Agency	Navy, United States
Civil Defense	RAND Corporation
Defense, Department of	Selective Service System
Guided Missile	

NATIONAL DEFENSE EDUCATION ACT (NDEA) is a law enacted by the United States Congress in 1958. It was one of the most significant education bills in U.S. history. NDEA provides financial aid to states, educational institutions, and individuals to improve educational programs in the United States.

NDEA provides federal loans to superior students who can show financial need. A student in higher education may borrow a total of $5,000. He has 10 years to repay the loan, beginning one year after completing his course of study. He must repay only one-half the loan if he teaches in any nonprofit public or private institution for five years.

NDEA also provides funds for states, to buy teaching equipment in science, mathematics, language, English, reading, history, civics, and geography. Private schools also can borrow money for this purpose. Other NDEA programs include graduate fellowships, research into the use of communications media for educational purposes, the improvement of counseling and testing programs, expanded teacher-training programs in critical subjects, and the improvement of vocational education. States must match federal funds to get NDEA funds.

The NDEA is administered by the U.S. Department of Health, Education, and Welfare. Congress passed the NDEA on Sept. 2, 1958. JOHN D. MILLETT

The National Education Association Headquarters was completed in 1957. The building stands in Washington, D.C.

NATIONAL EDUCATION ASSOCIATION OF THE UNITED STATES (NEA) is the largest educational organization in the world. It is supported by American teachers, and works to strengthen education in the United States. The association seeks to benefit teachers and American children, and to improve the education of all Americans. It conducts research on school problems and teacher welfare, and works to improve curriculums and instruction. The organization also works with educational groups in other parts of the world. It helped form the World Confederation of Organizations of the Teaching Profession (WCOTP) in 1946. The NEA has about 1¼ million members.

Plans for the organization's work are made by a representative assembly composed of delegates from state, territorial, and local associations. A board of directors and an executive committee help the assembly make plans. The National Education Association has 34 departments, representing almost every professional interest in education.

In 1857, 43 leaders from state teachers' associations organized the National Teachers Association in Philadelphia. In 1870, this organization merged with the National Association of School Superintendents and the American Normal School Association to form the NEA. The association's early program consisted chiefly of holding an annual convention and publishing a report of its proceedings. In 1922, it started research in various teacher-welfare problems. Its headquarters are at 1201 16th Street NW, Washington, D.C. 20036.

The NEA publishes *Today's Education*, the *NEA Reporter*, *Proceedings* of the conventions, and the *Research Bulletin*. It also publishes materials for American Education Week.   Critically reviewed by NATIONAL EDUCATION ASSOCIATION OF THE UNITED STATES

See also EDUCATION WEEK, AMERICAN; FUTURE TEACHERS OF AMERICA.

NATIONAL FARMERS ORGANIZATION. See FARMERS ORGANIZATION, NATIONAL.

NATIONAL FARMERS UNION. See FARMERS UNION, NATIONAL.

NATIONAL FEDERATION OF STATE HIGH-SCHOOL ATHLETIC ASSOCIATIONS. See SPORTS AND SPORTSMANSHIP (High-School Sports).

NATIONAL FIRE PREVENTION WEEK is held to make the public more aware of fire prevention. It always includes October 8, the anniversary of the Great Chicago Fire of 1871. See also FIRE PREVENTION.

NATIONAL FLOWERS. See FLOWER (table).

NATIONAL FOOTBALL LEAGUE. See FOOTBALL (Professional Football).

NATIONAL FOREST is a forest area set aside by the President of the United States to be protected and managed by the federal government. The Forest Service, a part of the Department of Agriculture, manages more than 150 national forests in the United States and Puerto Rico. These forests cover a total area of about 190 million acres, larger than California and Nevada combined. Most national forests are named for Indian tribes or famous men in American history. For location, size, and recreational facilities of these forests, see the *table* on the following pages.

Uses. National forests serve many purposes. Foresters mark groups of full-grown trees, and the government sells them to the highest bidder for cutting into lumber, pulpwood, poles, and other wood products. But the Forest Service makes sure that forest growth exceeds the amount of timber cut or destroyed each year. Controlled grazing by cattle and sheep is permitted on grass-covered sections of the forests. The government also allows private water-power development and mining operations in the forests. National forests safeguard *watersheds* (sources of creeks and rivers), provide a home for wildlife, and are valuable recreational areas.

Administration. A *forest supervisor* administers each national forest. The forests are divided into *ranger districts*, each headed by a *forest ranger*. One ranger may have charge of as much as 400,000 acres of land. His first duty is to prevent and fight forest fires. He is the local manager of all forest uses and services. These include production of wood, forage, wildlife, and resources for outdoor recreation.

National forests in the United States are grouped into 10 regions. The national forest in Puerto

National Forest Symbol

Rico is a separate region called the Institute of Tropical Forestry. Regional foresters head each region. They direct the work of the forest supervisors in their regions. The regional foresters report to the chief of the Forest Service in Washington, D.C.

History. Early settlers in the United States adopted the first conservation laws. In spite of this encouraging start, destruction of forests became widespread during the settlement of the United States. In 1891, Congress established the first national forest-conservation policy. In that year, Congress authorized the President to set aside areas known as *forest reserves*. The first one was established in Wyoming. In 1907, the name was changed to national forests.   ROBERT T. HALL

See also FOREST SERVICE.

FOREST	STATE	AREA (acres)†	CHIEF FEATURES
Allegheny*	Pennsylvania	479,489	Allegheny Mountains, Indian reservation, oil field, fishing, bear, turkey, and deer hunting, scenic drives, swimming, hiking
Angeles*	California	648,873	Old Baldy, San Gabriel Wilderness, riding, hiking, winter sports, fishing, hunting, Devil's Canyon-Bear Canyon Primitive Area
Angelina*	Texas	154,389	Shortleaf, loblolly pine, hardwoods, fishing, hunting, swimming
Apache*	Arizona and New Mexico	1,807,925	Spruce forests, prehistoric cliff dwellings, scenic drives, fishing, hunting, riding, Blue Range and Mt. Baldy Primitive Areas
Apalachicola*	Florida	556,972	Pine-hardwood forests, hardwood swamps, fishing, big-game hunting, boating, swimming
Arapaho*	Colorado	1,003,373	Mt. Evans, ghost towns, fishing, hunting, winter sports, scenic drives, dude ranches, Gore Range-Eagle Nest Primitive Area
Ashley*	Utah	1,271,151	Scenic gorges, fishing, big-game hunting, riding, High Uintas Wilderness, ancient geologic formations
Beaverhead*	Montana	2,111,058	Historic sites, mountains, swimming, fishing, big-game hunting, hot springs, winter sports, Anaconda-Pintlar Primitive Area
Bienville*	Mississippi	175,731	Virgin loblolly pine, fishing, quail hunting
Bighorn*	Wyoming	1,113,769	Bighorn Mountains, glaciers, Indian Medicine Wheel, fishing, hunting, riding, scenic drives, winter sports, Cloud Peak Primitive Area
Bitterroot*	Idaho and Montana	1,575,959	Hot springs, fishing, big-game hunting, Bitterroot Mountains, riding, dude ranches, winter sports, Selway-Bitterroot Wilderness
Black Hills*	South Dakota and Wyoming	1,221,694	Canyons, waterfalls, historic sites, Mt. Rushmore National Memorial, logging, mining, fishing, hunting, swimming, boating, hiking, riding, scenic drives, dude ranches
Boise*	Idaho	2,638,450	Ponderosa pine, mining, ghost towns, historic sites, fishing, big-game hunting, scenic drives, winter sports, Sawtooth Primitive Area
Bridger*	Wyoming	1,700,029	Glaciers, fishing, hunting, scenic drives, winter sports, Bridger Wilderness
Cache*	Idaho and Utah	676,255	Mountains, caves, canyons, winter sports, fishing, big-game hunting, scenic drives, riding, hiking
Calaveras Bigtree	California	380	Special group of big trees (giant sequoias)
Caribbean	Puerto Rico	27,889	Tropical trees, palms, tree ferns, waterfalls, cliffs, swimming, hiking, scenic drives
Caribou*	Idaho, Utah, and Wyoming	977,672	Mountain ranges, historic trails, waterfalls, fishing, big-game hunting, scenic drives, riding, winter sports
Carson*	New Mexico	1,422,402	Historic sites, Indian pueblo, mountains, hot springs, fishing, hunting, scenic drives, riding, winter sports, Pecos Wilderness
Challis*	Idaho	2,447,243	Mt. Borah, fishing, big-game hunting, scenic drives, riding, hiking, boating, Idaho and Sawtooth Primitive Areas
Chattahoochee*	Georgia	691,977	Blue Ridge Mountains, waterfalls, small-game hunting, fishing, swimming, boating, hiking, archery hunting, Appalachian Trail
Chequamegon*	Wisconsin	832,480	Pine, spruce, and balsam forests, lakes, fishing, hunting, canoeing, skiing
Cherokee*	North Carolina and Tennessee	602,308	Mountains, river gorges, fishing, small- and big-game hunting, hiking, boating, swimming
Chippewa*	Minnesota	645,548	Red pine, headwaters of the Mississippi, fishing, hunting, water sports, winter sports, scenic drives
Chugach*	Alaska	4,723,030	Glaciers, mountains, fiords, canneries, fishing, hunting, boating, hiking, mountain climbing, salmon-spawning runs
Cibola*	New Mexico	1,584,577	Mt. Taylor, antelope herds, Pueblo Indian villages, prehistoric ruins, hunting, scenic drives, winter sports, Sandia Crest
Clark*	Missouri	775,469	Ozark Mountains, oak and pine forests, redbud and dogwood, fishing, hunting, float trips, brilliant fall coloring
Clearwater*	Idaho	1,675,562	White pine, fishing, hunting, scenic drives, Selway-Bitterroot Wilderness, Lolo Trail, pack trips
Cleveland*	California	393,220	Palomar Observatory, fishing, hunting, scenic drives, Aqua Tibia Primitive Area, Pacific Crest trail route
Coconino*	Arizona	1,807,761	San Francisco Peaks, canyons, scenic drives, hunting, fishing, riding, boating, winter sports, Sycamore Canyon Primitive Area
Coeur d'Alene	Idaho	723,168	Mining, fishing, deer hunting, Cataldo Mission, winter sports
Colville*	Washington	943,517	Grand Coulee Dam, hunting, fishing, winter sports, huckleberries
Conecuh	Alabama	83,900	Fishing, deer, turkey, and small-game hunting, swimming
Coronado*	Arizona and New Mexico	1,790,503	Mountains, desert, canyons, caves, hunting, scenic drives, dude ranches, winter sports, rare plants and animals, Chiricahua and Galiuro Wilderness, Santa Catalina
Croatan*	North Carolina	152,370	Pine, swamp hardwoods, historic sites, hunting, fishing, boating, swimming
Custer*	Montana and South Dakota	1,185,664	Peaks and alpine plateaus, glaciers, ice caverns, fossil beds, fishing, big-game hunting, riding, winter sports, Beartooth Primitive Area
Daniel Boone*	Kentucky	468,169	Cliffs, rock arches, caves, fishing, hiking, boating

†National forest lands owned by the United States and administered by the Forest Service. *Camping facilities available.

FOREST	STATE	AREA (acres)†	CHIEF FEATURES
Davy Crockett*	Texas	161,479	Shortleaf and loblolly pine, hardwoods, fishing, deer hunting, swimming, Red River Gorge
Deerlodge*	Montana	1,181,276	Fishing, big-game hunting, riding, winter sports, hiking, Anaconda-Pintlar Wilderness, Tobacco Root Mountains
Delta*	Mississippi	58,923	Flooded delta land, bayous, waterfowl preserve, hunting
Deschutes*	Oregon	1,587,692	Mountains, ice caves, waterfalls, lava caves, trout fishing, deer hunting, riding, scenic drives, winter sports, Three Sisters, Diamond Peak, and Mount Jefferson Wildernesses
De Soto*	Mississippi	501,323	Quail hunting, fishing, boating, swimming
Dixie*	Utah	1,884,044	Canyons, peaks, colored cliffs, big-game hunting, fishing
Eldorado*	California and Nevada	652,629	Sierra Nevadas, Lake Tahoe, historic sites, fishing, deer and bear hunting, scenic drives, riding, winter sports, dude ranches, Desolation Valley Primitive Area, Gold Rush Country
Fishlake*	Utah	1,424,774	Petrified forest, fishing, big-game hunting, scenic drives
Flathead*	Montana	2,341,832	Geological formations, glaciers, fishing, hunting, boating, riding, scenic drives, winter sports, wilderness and primitive areas
Francis Marion	South Carolina	246,167	Oaks, yucca, dogwood, holly, historic sites, fishing, boating, bathing, alligator, deer, turkey, and quail hunting
Fremont*	Oregon	1,208,377	Indian paintings, antelope, deer hunting, Gearhart Wilderness
Gallatin*	Montana	1,699,548	Mountains, canyons, waterfalls, fishing, big-game hunting, scenic drives, riding, winter sports, hiking, dude ranches, primitive areas
George Washington	Virginia and West Virginia	1,019,495	Mountains, falls, limestone caverns, fishing, hunting, scenic drives, swimming, hiking, Sherando Lake Recreation Area
Gifford Pinchot*	Washington	1,267,340	Mt. Adams, fishing, scenic drives, riding, mountain climbing, winter sports, hunting, Mt. Adams and Goat Rocks Wilderness
Gila*	New Mexico	2,701,614	Semidesert-to-alpine country, cliff dwellings, Indian reservation, prehistoric ruins, fishing, big-game hunting, scenic drives, riding, hiking, dude ranches, primitive areas
Grand Mesa*	Colorado	346,143	Grand Mesa and Uncompahgre plateau, cliffs, canyons, waterfalls, fishing, big-game hunting, scenic drives, riding, winter sports
Green Mountain*	Vermont	235,558	Historic battlegrounds, fishing, hunting, hiking, winter sports
Gunnison*	Colorado	1,633,020	Mountain peaks, ghost towns, trout fishing, big-game hunting, hiking, riding, winter sports, wild areas, West Elk Wilderness
Helena*	Montana	969,004	Continental Divide, ghost towns, fishing, elk and deer hunting, scenic drives, riding, winter sports, hiking, Gates of the Mountains Wilderness
Hiawatha*	Michigan	846,168	Waterfalls, scenic drives, fishing, hunting, canoeing
Holly Springs	Mississippi	143,892	Erosion gullies, quail and small-game hunting, swimming
Homochitto*	Mississippi	189,023	Eroded loess country, excellent timber sites, fishing, swimming
Hoosier*	Indiana	145,319	Black walnut, dogwood, redbud, buffalo trail, hunting, fishing, scenic drives, swimming, Lost, White, and Ohio Rivers
Humboldt*	Nevada	2,512,184	Mountains, canyons, colorful cliffs, historic mining camps, elk herd, deer hunting, scenic trails, winter sports, Jarbridge Wilderness
Huron*	Michigan	415,773	Trout fishing, hunting, winter sports, swimming, Lake Huron
Inyo*	California and Nevada	1,835,937	Mt. Whitney, Palisade Glacier, fishing, deer hunting, winter sports, wilderness trips, Ancient Bristlecone Pine Forest Botanical Area
Jefferson*	Virginia, West Virginia, and Kentucky	576,381	Blue Ridge Mountains, rhododendron, big-game hunting, swimming, Mount Rogers National Recreation Area
Kaibab*	Arizona	1,719,346	Grand Canyon, game preserve, Kaibab squirrels, big-game hunting, scenic drives, fishing, riding, wild buffalo herd
Kaniksu*	Idaho, Montana, and Washington	1,621,935	Cedars, Chimney Rock, mountains, fishing, big-game and bird hunting, boating, swimming, scenic drives, winter sports
Kisatchie*	Louisiana	593,024	Longleaf, loblolly, and slash pine, bayous and lakes, fishing, hunting, boating, swimming, historic sites
Klamath*	California and Oregon	1,696,959	Mountain lakes and streams, salmon and steelhead trout fishing, deer hunting, riding, Marble Mountain Wilderness Area
Kootenai*	Idaho and Montana	1,819,777	Fishing, big-game hunting, scenic drives, winter sports, dude ranches, Cabinet Mountains Wilderness
Lassen*	California	1,045,587	Volcanic lava flows, tubes, craters, ice caves, hot springs, mud pots, scenic drives, fishing, deer hunting, winter sports, Thousand Lakes and Caribou Peak Wildernesses
Lewis and Clark*	Montana	1,834,652	Limestone canyons, mountains, fishing, big-game hunting, riding, Continental Divide, winter sports, Bob Marshall Wilderness Area
Lincoln*	New Mexico	1,086,379	Ponderosa pine, firs, fishing, big-game hunting, winter sports, scenic drives, riding, White Mountain Wilderness
Lolo*	Montana	2,086,357	Continental Divide, fishing, hunting, riding, scenic drives, hiking
Los Padres*	California	1,724,026	Coast redwood, California condor, peaks, hunting, trout fishing, winter sports, San Rafael Wilderness, Ventana Primitive Areas

†National forest lands owned by the United States and administered by the Forest Service.   *Camping facilities available.

FOREST	STATE	AREA (acres)†	CHIEF FEATURES
Malheur*	Oregon	1,204,973	Ponderosa pine, mountains, fossil beds, fishing, elk and deer hunting, scenic drives, riding, Strawberry Mountain Wilderness
Manistee*	Michigan	471,897	Fishing, deer and small-game hunting, skiing, swimming, canoeing
Manti-LaSal*	Colorado and Utah	1,263,593	Aspens, alpine meadows, cliff dwellings, unique geology, fishing, hunting, scenic drives, riding, hiking, winter sports
Mark Twain*	Missouri	612,324	Ozark Mountains, caves, scenic drives, fishing, quail hunting
Medicine Bow*	Wyoming	1,091,387	Beaver colonies, fishing, deer hunting, riding, winter sports
Mendocino*	California	872,287	Black-tailed deer, hunting, fishing, hiking, riding, wilderness trips
Modoc*	California	1,689,777	Lava flows, historic sites, deer herd, hunting, fishing, scenic drives, winter sports, South Warner Wilderness, bird refuge
Monongahela*	West Virginia	812,795	Cranberry glades, rhododendron, canyons, falls, historic sites, limestone caves, beaver colonies, fishing, hunting, swimming, Spruce Knob-Seneca Rocks National Recreation Area
Mount Baker*	Washington	1,818,348	Douglas fir, peaks, glaciers, trout fishing, deer and bear hunting, winter sports, mountain climbing, North Cascade Primitive Area
Mount Hood*	Oregon	1,117,532	Alpine meadows, hot springs, glacier, scenic drives, fishing, swimming, winter sports, riding, mountain climbing, Mount Hood
Nantahala*	North Carolina	450,082	Azaleas, rhododendrons, falls, man-made lakes, fishing, hunting, swimming, boating, primeval forest, Appalachian Trail
Nebraska	Nebraska	245,414	Planted forest on sand hills, game refuge, fishing, swimming
Nezperce*	Idaho	2,198,094	Canyons, hot springs, big-game hunting, fishing, riding, scenic drives, winter sports, Selway-Bitterroot Wilderness
Nicolet*	Wisconsin	646,235	Pine, spruce-balsam, hardwood, and cedar-spruce swamp forests, fishing, hunting, swimming, boating, hiking, snowshoeing, skiing
Ocala*	Florida	361,497	Palms, hardwoods, sand pine, springs, fishing, deer and bear hunting
Ochoco*	Oregon	845,855	Ponderosa pine, beaver colonies, historic sites, trout fishing, deer hunting, scenic drives, geologic formations
Oconee	Georgia	102,912	Piedmont hills, archaeological remains, Rock Eagle Lake, 4-H center, wildlife refuge, deer and small-game hunting, fishing
Okanogan*	Washington	1,520,448	Alpine meadows, peaks, glaciers, Lake Chelan, fishing, boating, riding, mountain climbing, winter sports, Pacific Crest Trail
Olympic*	Washington	621,756	Dense rain forests, peaks, fishing, hunting, scenic drives, riding
Osceola*	Florida	157,233	Cypress swamps, longleaf pine, fishing, hunting, swimming, boating
Ottawa*	Michigan	887,452	Victoria Dam, falls, fishing, deep-sea trolling, deer and bear hunting, scenic drives, winter sports, Lake Superior
Ouachita*	Arkansas and Oklahoma	1,566,958	Historic sites, caves, falls, medicinal springs, bass fishing, hunting, scenic drives, hiking, swimming
Ozark*	Arkansas	1,093,001	Oaks, fishing, hunting, swimming, scenic drives, rock cliffs and pools
Payette	Idaho	2,307,158	Hells Canyon, fishing, big-game hunting, scenic drives, hiking, winter sports, dude ranches, Idaho Primitive Area, elk
Pike*	Colorado	1,106,127	Pikes Peak, historic sites, mountain sheep, hunting, fishing, riding, hiking, scenic drives, winter sports
Pisgah*	North Carolina	480,014	Rhododendron, falls, fishing, hunting, hiking, riding, scenic drives, Linville Gorge, Mount Mitchell
Plumas*	California	1,146,745	Falls, historic sites, limestone caves, fishing, hunting, scenic drives, riding, hiking, winter sports, canyons, Pacific Crest Trail
Prescott*	Arizona	1,248,454	Hunting, riding, scenic drives, winter sports, dude ranches, Sycamore Canyon and Pine Mountain Primitive Areas, ghost towns
Rio Grande*	Colorado	1,799,393	Rugged mountains, mining camps, trout fishing, hunting, hiking, scenic drives, winter sports, primitive areas
Rogue River*	California and Oregon	621,325	Sugar pine, Douglas fir, Table Rock, waterfalls, trout fishing, hunting, riding, winter sports, Pacific Crest Trail
Roosevelt*	Colorado	776,463	Glaciers, Continental Divide, canyons, trout fishing, big-game hunting, hiking, scenic drives, winter sports, Rawah Wilderness
Routt*	Colorado	1,125,235	Continental Divide, trout fishing, hunting, scenic drives, riding, hiking, winter sports, Mt. Zirkel-Dome Peak Wilderness
Sabine*	Texas	183,830	Southern pine and hardwoods, swimming, fishing, fox hunting
St. Francis*	Arkansas	20,611	Indian burial mounds, wild game, fishing, swimming
St. Joe*	Idaho	862,027	White pine, canyons, big-game hunting, fishing, Bitterroot Range
Salmon*	Idaho	1,767,585	Fishing, big-game hunting, boating, scenic drives, winter sports, dude ranches, Idaho Primitive Area, Lewis and Clark Trail
Sam Houston*	Texas	158,408	Shortleaf and loblolly pine, hardwoods, fishing, swimming
San Bernardino*	California	617,206	Historic sites, fishing, hunting, riding, winter sports
San Isabel*	Colorado	1,106,298	Peaks, mines, alpine lakes, fishing, big-game and bird hunting, scenic drives, riding, winter sports, primitive area
San Juan*	Colorado	1,850,411	Canyons, waterfalls, cataracts, geologic formations, archaeological ruins, historic mines, fishing, hunting, scenic drives, riding, winter sports, primitive areas
Santa Fe*	New Mexico	1,441,569	Peaks, Indian villages, ancient pueblo and Spanish mission ruins, cliff dwellings, fishing, hunting, skiing, Pecos Wilderness

†National forest lands owned by the United States and administered by the Forest Service.

*Camping facilities available.

FOREST	STATE	AREA (acres)†	CHIEF FEATURES
Sawtooth*	Idaho and Utah	1,803,311	Wind- and water-worn rocks, hot springs, fishing, hunting, riding, Sun Valley, bathing, winter sports, Sawtooth Primitive Area
Sequoia*	California	1,115,596	Sequoias, canyons, caves, peaks, fishing, hunting, riding, hiking, swimming, boating, winter sports, High Sierra Primitive Area
Shasta*	California	1,004,266	Glaciers, lava beds, caves, chimneys, limestone caves, fishing, hunting, riding, winter sports, wilderness area, national recreation area
Shawnee*	Illinois	224,487	Prehistoric stone forts and Indian mounds, rock formations, fishing
Shoshone*	Wyoming	2,424,987	Glaciers, peaks, fishing, big-game and bird hunting, riding, scenic drives, winter sports, wilderness and primitive areas
Sierra*	California	1,294,113	Sequoias, falls, mountain climbing, fishing, hunting, boating, swimming, riding, winter sports, primitive areas, John Muir Trail
Siskiyou*	California and Oregon	1,081,412	Port Orford cedar, California laurel, wild lilac, rhododendron, azaleas, pitcher plants, Brewer weeping spruce, Saddler oak, fishing, hunting, boating, riding, Kalmiopsis Wilderness
Sitgreaves*	Arizona	802,782	Pueblo ruins, elk herd, hunting, riding, Mongollon Rim Drive
Siuslaw*	Oregon	618,774	Sitka spruce, western hemlock, cedar, Douglas fir, pitcher plants, dunes, fishing, hunting, swimming, boating, riding, scuba diving
Six Rivers*	California	939,713	Redwood, fir, fishing, riding, scenic drives, hunting, winter sports
Snoqualmie*	Washington	1,208,540	Douglas fir, peaks, falls, big-game hunting, fishing, scenic drives, riding, winter sports, mountain climbing, Goat Rocks Wilderness
Stanislaus*	California	896,292	Canyons, historic sites, fishing, deer and bear hunting, scenic drives, riding, winter sports, Emigrant Basin Primitive Area
Sumter	South Carolina	342,747	Rhododendron and other flowering shrubs, Piedmont Region and Blue Ridge Mountains, fishing, quail hunting, scenic drives
Superior*	Minnesota	2,041,003	Islands, sand beaches, 5,000 lakes, fishing, deer hunting, scenic drives, canoeing, Boundary Waters Canoe Area
Tahoe*	California	697,015	Lake Tahoe, historic sites, winter sports, fishing, deer and bear hunting, riding, hiking, scenic drives, Squaw Valley
Talladega	Alabama	357,627	Hunting, fishing, swimming, scenic drives
Targhee*	Idaho and Wyoming	1,663,383	Grand Tetons, canyons, falls, fishing, big-game hunting, riding, hiking, scenic drives, winter sports, dude ranches, Snake River
Teton*	Wyoming	1,700,820	Tetons, Continental Divide, Jackson Hole, fishing, big-game hunting, scenic drives, swimming, winter sports, Teton Wilderness Area
Toiyabe*	California and Nevada	3,132,994	Lake Tahoe, historic ghost towns, fishing, big-game hunting, riding, skiing, scenic drives, Hoover Wilderness
Tombigbee*	Mississippi	65,261	Indian mounds, Davis and Choctaw lakes, Natchez Trace Parkway, deer and quail hunting, fishing
Tongass*	Alaska	16,011,643	Totems, Indian villages, glaciers, fiords, fishing, big-game hunting, boating, hiking, mountain climbing
Tonto	Arizona	2,886,185	Semidesert to pine-fir forest, prehistoric ruins, fishing, hunting, riding, scenic drives, boating, swimming, wilderness areas
Trinity*	California	1,062,989	Glaciers, lava beds, caves, chimneys, limestone caves, fishing, hunting, riding, scenic drives, winter sports, wilderness areas, national recreation area
Tuskegee	Alabama	10,778	Pine plantation, bream fishing
Uinta*	Utah	795,157	Maple, aspen, oak, canyons, waterfalls, geologic formations, big-game hunting, fishing, hiking, winter sports
Umatilla*	Oregon, Washington	1,389,709	Skyline drives, hot sulfur springs, hunting, riding, winter sports
Umpqua*	Oregon	984,497	Cataracts, falls, fishing, hunting, scenic drives, winter sports
Uncompahgre*	Colorado	943,247	Wild flowers, cliffs, canyons, waterfalls, fishing, big-game hunting, scenic drives, riding, winter sports
Uwharrie	North Carolina	43,826	Uwharrie Mountain Range, deer hunting
Wallowa*	Oregon	981,084	Alpine meadows and rare flowers, peaks, glaciers, canyons, fishing, big-game hunting, riding, scenic drives, dude ranches
Wasatch*	Utah and Wyoming	880,458	Mountains, canyons, skiing, fishing, hunting, boating, swimming, riding, skating, mountain climbing, High Uintas Wilderness
Wayne*	Ohio	127,235	Hardwoods, historic sites, hunting, fishing, hiking, riding, scenic drives
Wenatchee*	Washington	1,733,413	Alpine meadows, rare flowers, peaks, fishing, deer and bear hunting, Lake Chelan, riding, winter sports, Pacific Crest Trail
White Mountain*	Maine and New Hampshire	716,487	Mount Washington, Presidential Range, falls, fishing, deer and bear hunting, scenic drives, skiing, mountain climbing, hiking, swimming, Great Gulf Wilderness
White River*	Colorado	1,960,193	Canyons, falls, hot springs, caves, mines, fishing, hunting, hiking, riding, scenic drives, winter sports, primitive areas
Whitman*	Oregon	1,515,960	Alpine meadows, rare flowers, fishing, hunting, riding
Willamette*	Oregon	1,666,002	Peaks, waterfalls, hot springs, volcanic formations, fishing, hunting, scenic drives, riding, winter sports, wilderness areas
William B. Bankhead	Alabama	178,929	Limestone gorges, falls, natural bridges, hunting, fishing
Winema*	Oregon	909,069	Klamath Indian range lands, boating, winter sports area, Ponderosa pine, Douglas fir, and lodgepole pine, Oregon Cascades

†National forest lands owned by the United States and administered by the Forest Service.   *Camping facilities available.

NATIONAL FOUNDATION

NATIONAL FOUNDATION is a health organization financed by funds gathered in the annual March of Dimes. It supports research, treatment, and professional and public education concerning birth defects. It also supports the Salk Institute for Biological Studies. The organization was founded by President Franklin D. Roosevelt in 1938 as the National Foundation for Infantile Paralysis. It financed the research that produced the Salk and Sabin vaccines, which help prevent poliomyelitis (see POLIOMYELITIS). The present name and goals were adopted in 1958. Headquarters are at 800 Second Ave., New York, N.Y. 10017.

Critically reviewed by the NATIONAL FOUNDATION

NATIONAL FOUNDATION ON THE ARTS AND THE HUMANITIES is an independent agency of the federal government. Its purpose is to develop and promote a broadly conceived national policy of support for the humanities and the arts in the United States.

The foundation is administered by a National Endowment for the Arts and a National Endowment for the Humanities. Each endowment is guided by a council composed of 26 private citizens distinguished for their knowledge and experience in the two allied cultural areas, the arts and the humanities. A Federal Council on the Arts and the Humanities coordinates the foundation's activities with related federal agencies.

The Arts Endowment is authorized to assist individuals and nonprofit organizations in a wide range of artistic endeavors. Additional funds are authorized to aid activities in the arts sponsored by the states.

The Humanities Endowment aids training and research in the humanities through fellowships and grants, and supports the publication of scholarly works.

Each endowment is headed by a chairman, who serves on the federal council, along with representatives of federal agencies whose programs are related to the arts and humanities. The foundation was established in 1965. It is located at 1800 G Street NW, Washington, D.C. 20506.

Critically reviewed by the NATIONAL FOUNDATION ON THE ARTS AND THE HUMANITIES

NATIONAL FREEDOM DAY. See FREEDOM DAY, NATIONAL.

NATIONAL GALLERY OF ART in Washington, D.C., has nationally owned collections of paintings, sculptures, prints, drawings, and items of decorative art. Andrew W. Mellon, an American financier, made the original donation for the gallery in 1937. He gave the United States government his great art collection, and $15 mil-

lion to build the gallery. The gallery opened in 1941.

The paintings and sculptures given by Mellon represent the works of many of the greatest European artists from the 1200's to the 1800's. Among the works are the *Alba Madonna* by Raphael, *The Annunciation* by Van Eyck, 23 paintings by Rembrandt, and 6 by Vermeer. The A. W. Mellon Educational and Charitable Trust also presented a collection of American paintings. Two of the most famous of these are Gilbert Stuart's portrait of Washington and Edward Savage's painting *The Washington Family*.

Samuel H. Kress, an American merchant, gave the gallery a collection of Italian art ranging from the 1200's through the 1700's. It includes works by such masters as Giotto, Raphael, and Bellini. The Samuel H. Kress Foundation has enlarged the gift of Italian art, and added to the collection in many other areas, including a gift of paintings by French artists of the 1700's.

Joseph E. Widener, an American businessman, presented the National Gallery with a famous art collection that he and his father had gathered. The collection includes many works by Raphael, Bellini, Rembrandt, Vermeer, Van Dyck, and others. Lessing J. Rosenwald, another American businessman, gave a collection of over 17,000 prints and drawings. Many other donors have made important gifts to the National Gallery.

The National Gallery of Art is one of the largest marble structures in the world. It is 785 feet long, has more than 500,000 square feet of floor space, and has about 238,000 square feet for exhibits. The building is of classic design, with rose-white marble used for the outside walls. In the center of the building is a rotunda, or round room, covered with a dome. There are sculpture halls on the east and west sides of the rotunda. Each leads to a garden court with fountains and plants. Around the sculpture halls are over 125 galleries or exhibition rooms where the works of art are shown. The gallery has a resident composer-conductor who leads weekly concerts by the National Gallery Orchestra.

Critically reviewed by the NATIONAL GALLERY OF ART

NATIONAL GEOGRAPHIC SOCIETY is the world's largest scientific and educational organization. It was formed in 1888 to gather and spread geographic information throughout the world. It has more than 6 million members in approximately 185 countries. The society has sponsored and supported more than 450 expeditions and research projects that have expanded man's knowledge of the earth, sea, and sky.

The society distributes its information through *Na-*

Ewing Galloway

The National Gallery of Art in Washington, D.C., displays works of some of the world's greatest artists.

tional Geographic Magazine, geographic school bulletins for children, authoritative books, and an information service for the press. It produces atlases, globes, maps, filmstrips, and television programs.

Among the projects the society has sponsored are the historic polar expeditions by Richard E. Byrd and Robert E. Peary. It also sponsored excavations in East Africa that uncovered the fossils of a primitive being called *Homo habilis* that lived about 1,750,000 years ago. In 1963, it helped back the first successful United States expedition to the top of Mount Everest. It also aided in the construction of livable quarters under the ocean, and the Sky Atlas project at Palomar Observatory. In this project, scientists made extensive photographs that expanded man's view of the universe by 25 times.

The society's headquarters are at 17th and M Sts. NW, Washington, D.C. 20036, only a few blocks from the White House. The white marble, 10-story building serves as an office, museum, and laboratory. The society's past presidents include Alexander Graham Bell, and Gilbert Grosvenor, who edited the magazine from 1899 to 1954 (see GROSVENOR, GILBERT H.). Grosvenor's son Melville Bell Grosvenor became president and editor in 1957. In 1967, he became chairman of the board and editor in chief, and Melvin M. Payne was named president of the society.

Critically reviewed by the NATIONAL GEOGRAPHIC SOCIETY

NATIONAL GUARD is one of the organizations of the United States Army and Air Force. An outgrowth of the volunteer militia that was first authorized in 1792, the National Guard of the United States is a reserve group. Other types of civilian reserves, such as the Army, Air Force, and naval reserves, have no connection with the National Guard.

Each state, each territory, and the District of Columbia has its own National Guard. The National Guard Bureau of the Department of the Army directs Army units. The Department of the Air Force supervises Air National Guard units. The two guards have an authorized strength of nearly 700,000, of which the Air National Guard's part is 60,000.

Guardsmen enlist voluntarily, and are formed into distinctive units in the same manner as the active Army and Air Force. These two services supervise training. State funds provide armories and storage facilities. Federal funds provide clothing, weapons, and equipment for the guardsmen.

During peacetime, National Guard men attend 48 weekly drill and training periods a year. They

National Guard Emblem

also receive two weeks of field training every year. The federal government pays members of the National Guard for the time that they spend training.

Guardsmen have a *dual status*, because they take an oath of allegiance to their state, as well as to the federal government. Until 1903, the state controlled the militia units entirely. The President had to call units into federal service through the governors of the states (see MILITIA). The National Defense Acts of 1920 and 1933 further extended federal authority. Since that time, the

President may order National Guard units to active duty during any national emergency. State governors may order the units to active duty during emergencies, such as strikes, riots, and disasters.   CHARLES B. MACDONALD

See also AIR FORCE, UNITED STATES (Air Force Reserves); ARMY, UNITED STATES (Regulars, Reserves, and National Guard Men).

NATIONAL HISTORIC SITE. See NATIONAL PARK SYSTEM.

NATIONAL HOCKEY LEAGUE. See HOCKEY.

NATIONAL HOLIDAY. See HOLIDAY.

NATIONAL HONOR SOCIETY is an organization for high school boys and girls. Members are chosen on the basis of scholarship, leadership, citizenship, service, and character. College scholarships are awarded each year to top-ranking senior members. The society is sponsored by the National Association of Secondary-School Principals, which founded it in 1921. In 1929, the National Junior Honor Society was founded for boys and girls in junior high schools. The senior society has about 14,000 local chapters; the junior society, 3,575. Both have their headquarters at 1201 16th Street NW, Washington, D.C. 20036.

Critically reviewed by NATIONAL HONOR SOCIETY

NATIONAL HYMNS. See NATIONAL ANTHEMS.

NATIONAL INCOME may be computed in two ways. In the method used by most economists, depreciation and capital used in the production of goods are deducted from the *gross national product* (total market value of all the goods and services produced by a country in a single year). The result is the *net national product*. National income is figured by deducting indirect business taxes, such as sales and excise taxes, from the net national product. In the second method, wages, interest, rents, profits, and other business and professional income are totaled to find national income.

Individual Income. We usually define income as the amount of money received for goods and services. But economists define it as the value of the goods and services a person can use up during a year, and still have the same amount of wealth at the end of a year that he had at the beginning. It is not necessarily the amount actually consumed. If a person consumes less than his income, he saves. If he consumes more than his income, either by borrowing or by spending previously acquired wealth, he does not save.

Not all cash receipts are income. In a business, costs must be deducted from gross receipts to compute the net income. In the case of an individual, economists do not include money received from selling a house or stock when they compute national income. If a person spends the money, he will have less wealth at the end of the year than he had at the beginning. For example, a person may spend $100 for stock, and sell it for $200. But, if he spends the entire $200, he actually has less money. He has neither the capital received for the stock, nor the original $100 invested in the stock.

Income can be in forms other than cash. Some employees receive food or lodging as part of their pay. Homeowners can consider the rental value of their houses as a part of their income. Vegetables raised by home gardeners are income. A housewife's services may be considered part of her family's income.

UNITED STATES NATIONAL INCOME

National income has risen sharply since the depression years of the 1930's. This graph shows how it has risen and how much of it comes from the income of employees, the net income of businesses, and interest and rent.

Sources: Office of Business Economics, U.S. Department of Commerce; Center for Economic Projections, National Planning Association

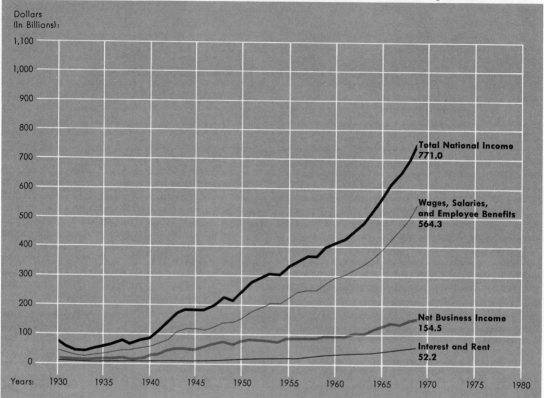

Dollars (In Billions):

Total National Income 771.0

Wages, Salaries, and Employee Benefits 564.3

Net Business Income 154.5

Interest and Rent 52.2

Years: 1930 1935 1940 1945 1950 1955 1960 1965 1970 1975 1980

Real Income is the amount of goods and services that money income will buy. If we have an increase in national money income and at the same time have a 25 per cent increase in prices over the preceding year, we would have to divide the current year's money income by 1.25 to find out how much real income had increased over last year. But, if average prices in the current year are only 80 per cent of last year's prices, we would divide this year's income by .80 and find that real income had increased more than money income.

Real National Income may be increased by four means: (1) by an increase in the quantity of capital, because more machines will make more goods; (2) by an improvement in the quality of capital, as in substituting better machines for old ones; (3) by an increase in employment; or (4) by an increase in labor effort.

Real national income in the United States and Canada has moved up and down since 1900, but generally upward. The declines have been due largely to periods of unemployment. The long-run trend upward is mainly due to increases in the quantity and the quality of capital.   KENNETH E. BOULDING

See also GROSS NATIONAL PRODUCT; INCOME; STANDARD OF LIVING.

NATIONAL INDUSTRIAL RECOVERY ACT. See NEW DEAL (Helping Industry and Labor).

NATIONAL INSTITUTES OF HEALTH (NIH) is an agency of the United States government. It is part of the Public Health Service, a division of the Department of Health, Education, and Welfare (HEW). NIH conducts and supports medical research. It provides funds for training medical researchers, building research facilities, and developing health manpower resources. It also classifies and distributes biological and medical information. In the late 1960's, about a third of all medical research in the United States was financed by NIH.

NIH conducts research at its own laboratories and clinics in Bethesda, Md. There are 10 NIH institutes. They are: (1) allergy and infectious diseases, (2) arthritis and metabolic diseases, (3) cancer, (4) child health and human development, (5) dental research, (6) eye, (7) general medical sciences, (8) heart, (9) neurological diseases and stroke, and (10) environmental health sciences. A research hospital serves the institutes. The Division of Biologics Standards tests the safety and effectiveness of serums, vaccines, and other biological products. The Bureau of Health Manpower and the National Library of Medicine are also part of NIH.

NIH adopted its present name in 1948. It traces its history to 1887, when the Hygienic Laboratory was set up at the U.S. Marine Hospital on Staten Island.

Critically reviewed by the NATIONAL INSTITUTES OF HEALTH

See INVENTION (Inventions for the Future).

NATIONAL LABOR RELATIONS BOARD (NLRB) was created as an independent agency by Congress in 1935 to administer the National Labor Relations Act (Wagner Act). The NLRB has two major functions. It works to correct or prevent unfair labor practices committed by either employers or unions. When asked by a union, an employer, employees, or an individual, it conducts elections to determine the representatives of employees for collective bargaining. The NLRB can ask the federal courts to enforce board rulings.

The President of the United States appoints the five board members and the general counsel, with the consent of the Senate. Each board member serves a five-year term. The general counsel has a four-year term. The NLRB's main offices are at 1717 Pennsylvania Ave. NW, Washington, D.C. 20006. Petitions and charges are normally sent to regional offices.   OGDEN W. FIELDS

See also INDUSTRIAL RELATIONS; UNITED STATES, HISTORY OF (Relief, Recovery, and Reform).

NATIONAL LEAGUE. See BASEBALL (Professional Baseball; History).

NATIONAL LIBRARY OF MEDICINE. See LIBRARY (U.S. Government Libraries).

NATIONAL MEDIATION BOARD is an agency of the U.S. government that works to settle disputes between airline and railroad workers and their employers. The board also supervises elections that determine the proper representative of airline and railroad employees. The National Mediation Board was created in 1934. Its three members are appointed by the President with the consent of the Senate.

In a dispute, either party may apply for the board's services, or the board may act on its own if an emergency exists. Both sides are given solutions to consider. This is called *mediation*. Neither party has to accept the solutions, however. If mediation fails, the board asks the parties to enter into *arbitration*. If the parties agree, the board may appoint a referee, whose decision is binding.   Critically reviewed by the NATIONAL MEDIATION BOARD

NATIONAL MEDICAL ASSOCIATION (NMA) is an organization of medical doctors in the United States. It works to raise medical standards, inform the public on matters concerning health, and eliminate racial and religious discrimination from medical institutions.

A group of Negro doctors founded the NMA in 1895 as an alternative to the American Medical Association (AMA). Doctors could not belong to the AMA unless they also belonged to one of its local associate medical societies. But Negroes were barred from membership in local societies in the South.

The NMA has more than 3,000 members, most of whom are Negroes. It publishes a bimonthly magazine called the *Journal of the National Medical Association.* NMA headquarters are in Washington, D.C.

Critically reviewed by the NATIONAL MEDICAL ASSOCIATION

NATIONAL MONUMENT. See NATIONAL PARK SYSTEM.

NATIONAL MOTTO, UNITED STATES, is *In God We Trust.* Congress made this phrase the official motto of the United States in 1956. It has appeared on coins since 1864, and probably originated from verse 4 of "The Star-Spangled Banner"—"And this be our motto: 'In God is our trust.' " See also E PLURIBUS UNUM.

NATIONAL MUSEUM, UNITED STATES. See UNITED STATES NATIONAL MUSEUM.

NATIONAL MUSIC CAMP is a summer school of music held every year in Interlochen, Mich. Its 1,100-acre campus borders two lakes in the northern part of the state. The school was founded in 1928 to provide a place of instruction for students interested in all branches of music and allied arts. It is a nonprofit corporation affiliated with the University of Michigan, and has a full-time faculty. The National High School Orchestra meets there in summer.   JOSEPH E. MADDY

NATIONAL OCEAN SURVEY is an agency of the United States government that gathers scientific data about the land, seas, and inland waters. It maps the nation's land areas, coastal waters, lakes, and rivers.

The survey prepares and distributes nautical and aeronautical charts to guide navigators on water and in the air. It publishes tables and charts of U.S. coastal tides and currents. The agency also records earthquake activity, and it issues warnings of *tsunamis* (huge sea waves caused by underwater earthquakes) in the Pacific Ocean region.

The National Ocean Survey was created in 1970 as part of the National Oceanic and Atmospheric Administration. The survey performs the functions of the former Coast and Geodetic Survey and the U.S. Lake Survey of the U.S. Army Corps of Engineers.

Critically reviewed by the NATIONAL OCEANIC AND
ATMOSPHERIC ADMINISTRATION

NATIONAL OCEANIC AND ATMOSPHERIC ADMINISTRATION (NOAA) is a United States government agency that works to improve man's understanding and use of his environment and of marine life. The NOAA combines the functions of several agencies that were formerly part of the Department of Commerce or the Department of the Interior. It also administers several programs that were previously run by other government agencies or by the Army or the Navy.

The NOAA has nine major divisions: the National Ocean Survey, National Weather Service, National Marine Fisheries Service, National Environmental Satellite Service, Environmental Research Laboratories, Office of Sea Grant, National Oceanographic Instrumentation Center, Marine Minerals Technology Center, and National Data Buoy Project Office. The NOAA was created in 1970 as part of the Department of Commerce.

Critically reviewed by the NATIONAL OCEANIC AND
ATMOSPHERIC ADMINISTRATION

See also NATIONAL OCEAN SURVEY.

NATIONAL PARK SERVICE is a bureau of the United States Department of the Interior. It manages the more than 270 areas of the National Park System, including the national parks and other park areas. The National Park Service also preserves many historic and archeological sites and structures. It was established in 1916, when the park system consisted of 38 acres. They included Yellowstone National Park, the world's first national park. The U.S. secretary of the interior appoints a director to head the bureau in its Washington, D.C., headquarters. It has six regional offices, three planning and service centers, and two training centers. See NATIONAL PARK SYSTEM.   GEORGE B. HARTZOG, JR.

Everglades National Park has a great variety of wild-life but is especially famous for its many species of birds.

NATIONAL PARK SYSTEM

NATIONAL PARK SYSTEM. The United States is rich in natural wonderlands, famous historic places, and sites for many kinds of outdoor recreation. The government has set aside more than 270 such areas to preserve them for the benefit and enjoyment of the people. All these areas are called *parklands*, and all of them together make up the National Park System. They include parks, monuments, historic sites, memorials, cemeteries, seashores, lakeshores, and battlefields. Even the White House and the Statue of Liberty are part of the National Park System.

The first national park in the world, Yellowstone National Park, was established by the U.S. government in 1872. The National Park System developed with the creation of other parklands. Today, the system's parklands total about 46,000 square miles—an area larger than that of Pennsylvania. Every state except Delaware has at least one national parkland. The District of Columbia, Puerto Rico, and the Virgin Islands also have national parklands.

The magnificent scenery of the national parks attracts more and more visitors every year. Yellowstone is world famous for hot geysers that erupt from the ground, thundering waterfalls that plunge into deep gorges, and sparkling lakes that lie high among snow-capped mountains. Bears, deer, elk, moose, and other wildlife roam Yellowstone's great evergreen forests, free of danger from man. In Carlsbad Caverns, rock formations cover the floors and ceilings of great underground caves. The formations look like Oriental temples, strange beasts, and upside-down forests of icicles. The Olympic rain forests, almost as thick as tropical jungles, lie under rugged, towering peaks. On these mountains are mighty glaciers, and meadows blanketed by wild flowers. The breathtaking Grand Canyon has mile-deep walls of black, brown, lavender, and red. The weirdly beautiful Petrified Forest has rainbow-colored logs and tree trunks that are millions of years old and have turned into stone.

National monuments include the Statue of Liberty, ancient Indian pueblos, and forts dating from colonial or revolutionary times. Among the historical areas are the birthplaces of George Washington, Abraham Lincoln, Franklin D. Roosevelt, and John F. Kennedy.

The manager of the National Park System is the National Park Service, a bureau of the United States Department of the Interior. The director of the service names a superintendent to manage each individual area or a group of areas close together. Park rangers patrol the parklands to protect them from fire and other danger, and to perform various services for visitors. See the separate WORLD BOOK article on NATIONAL PARK SERVICE. See also the separate articles on the various parklands as listed in the tables with this article.

George B. Hartzog, Jr., the contributor of this article, is Director of the National Park Service.

The National Park System consists of three basic kinds of areas: (1) natural, (2) historical, and (3) recreational. Within these three groups, areas are identified by more than 20 types, such as national parks, national monuments, national historic sites, national seashores, and so on. See the table of *Types of Areas*.

Congress must approve nearly all new areas for the National Park System, including any area planned as a national park. The President may establish a national monument if the government owns the land. The secretary of the interior may approve a national historic site.

The National Park Service acquires land for new areas through donations, exchanges, purchases, or reassignment of federal properties. Many parklands include some land that the government does not own. The government is gradually acquiring these sections as well. Twelve areas are owned by state, local, or private agencies. Some of these areas are managed under cooperative agreements.

Natural Areas are preserved chiefly for the outstanding beauty or scientific importance of their natural features. These areas include all the national parks except Mesa Verde, which is preserved for its prehistoric Indian cliff dwellings. They also include almost half the national monuments. Among these are the Agate Fossil Beds, world-famous deposits of ancient animal fossils; and Death Valley, a desert with strange and beautiful rock formations in the earth's crust. Death Valley has the lowest land surface in the Western Hemisphere—282 feet below sea level. Another natural area is the Ice Age National Scientific Reserve. It has many land features that show the effects of the great glaciers that began to plow across much of North America more than 1 million years ago.

The largest natural area, Glacier Bay National Monument, is more than twice as large as the state

TYPES OF AREAS

Name	Number	Acres
International Park	1	2,721.50
National Battlefield Parks	4	9,082.96
National Battlefield Sites	3	785.87
National Battlefields	5	4,229.36
National Capital Park System	1	7,786.85
National Cemeteries	10	220.13
National Historic Sites	50	9,688.13
National Historical Parks	13	44,782.85
National Lakeshores	2	75,721.00
National Memorial Park	1	70,436.00
National Memorials	21	5,747.67
National Military Parks	11	31,720.23
National Monuments	85	10,222,045.51
National Parks	35	14,458,275.59
National Recreation Areas	13	3,809,004.00
National Scenic Riverways	3	145,364.22
National Scientific Reserve	1	32,500.00
National Seashores	7	355,005.23
Parks (Other)	5	25,605.44
National Parkways	5	150,261.03
National Scenic Trail	1	50,000.00
White House	1	18.07
TOTAL	**278**	**29,511,001.64**

Yellowstone National Park features famous Old Faithful geyser. Crowds watch Old Faithful erupt about every 65 minutes.

John Arthur Polky, Tom Stack & Associates

City of Refuge National Historical Park preserves early Hawaiian culture and the history of the Polynesian people.

Werner Stoy, Camera Hawaii

PARKLANDS OF THE NATIONAL PARK SYSTEM

This map shows the location of the more than 270 parklands in the National Park System. Because of space limitations, the parklands within the East Coast area outlined in black are not named on the map. Their names can be found by matching their numbers with those in the tables on the right of the map.

WORLD BOOK map

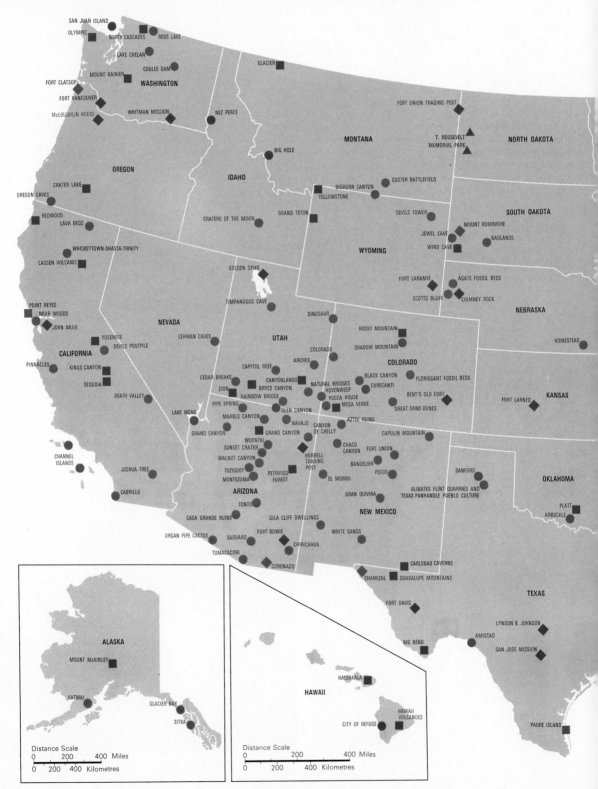

Legend

- ■ NATIONAL PARKS
- ● NATIONAL MONUMENTS
- ◆ NATIONAL HISTORIC SITES
- ● NATIONAL HISTORICAL PARKS
- ◆ NATIONAL MEMORIALS
- ● NATIONAL RECREATION AREAS
- ▲ NATIONAL MILITARY PARKS
- ● NATIONAL BATTLEFIELDS, NATIONAL BATTLEFIELD PARKS, AND NATIONAL BATTLEFIELD SITES.
- ■ NATIONAL LAKESHORES AND NATIONAL SEASHORES
- ● NATIONAL CEMETERIES
- ▲ PARKWAYS AND OTHER NATIONAL PARKLANDS

Distance Scale

0 100 200 300 400 Miles
0 100 200 300 400 Kilometres

Memorials
30 CUSTIS-LEE
31 FEDERAL HALL
32 FORD'S THEATRE
33 F. DOUGLASS
34 GENERAL GRANT
35 HAMILTON GRANGE
36 HOUSE WHERE LINCOLN DIED
37 LINCOLN MEMORIAL
38 R. WILLIAMS
39 THOMAS JEFFERSON
40 WASHINGTON MONUMENT

Recreation Area
41 DELAWARE WATER GAP

Military Parks
42 FREDERICKSBURG AND SPOTSYLVANIA
43 GETTYSBURG

Battlefields, Battlefield Parks, and Battlefield Sites
44 ANTIETAM
45 MANASSAS
46 PETERSBURG
47 RICHMOND

Lakeshores and Seashores
48 ASSATEAGUE ISLAND
49 CAPE COD
50 FIRE ISLAND

Cemeteries
51 ANTIETAM
52 BATTLEGROUND
53 FREDERICKSBURG
54 POPLAR GROVE
55 YORKTOWN

Parkways and other Parklands
56 BALTIMORE-WASHINGTON PARKWAY
57 CATOCTIN MOUNTAIN
58 G. WASHINGTON PARKWAY
59 NATIONAL CAPITAL PARK SYSTEM
60 PISCATAWAY
61 PRINCE WILLIAM
62 SUITLAND
63 THEODORE ROOSEVELT
64 WHITE HOUSE
65 WOLF TRAP FARM

Parks
1 SHENANDOAH

Monuments
2 CASTLE CLINTON
3 CHESAPEAKE AND OHIO CANAL
4 FORT McHENRY
5 G. WASHINGTON BIRTHPLACE
6 STATUE OF LIBERTY

Historic Sites
7 ADAMS
8 DORCHESTER HEIGHTS
9 EDISON
10 EISENHOWER
11 GLORIA DEI
12 HAMPTON
13 HOME OF F. D. ROOSEVELT
14 HOPEWELL
15 JAMESTOWN
16 J. F. KENNEDY
17 PENNSYLVANIA AVE.
18 SAGAMORE HILL
19 SAINT PAUL'S CHURCH
20 SALEM MARITIME
21 SAUGUS IRON WORKS
22 T. ROOSEVELT BIRTHPLACE
23 TOURO SYNAGOGUE
24 VANDERBILT MANSION

Historical Parks
25 APPOMATTOX COURT HOUSE
26 COLONIAL
27 INDEPENDENCE
28 MINUTE MAN
29 MORRISTOWN

Distance Scale

0 50 100 Miles
0 50 100 Kilometres

PUERTO RICO

VIRGIN ISLANDS

of Delaware. It is also the largest area in the National Park System.

To keep the natural areas in their unspoiled condition, the *balance of nature* must be preserved. That is, the plant and animal life is left as undisturbed as possible (see BALANCE OF NATURE). Hunting and lumbering are prohibited, though fishing is allowed. Mining is permitted in only a few areas. Livestock grazing is limited and is steadily being eliminated. In most areas, water resources may not be used for such purposes as irrigation or the production of hydroelectric power.

The National Park Service encourages recreational activities in the natural areas if they do not disturb the surroundings. Many visitors enjoy camping, hiking, horseback riding, mountain climbing, water and winter sports, and other activities. The service tries to enrich people's understanding of the natural processes that have made the land of each area what it is. Park rangers and other staff members are trained to explain natural and scientific features. The National Park Service also encourages scholars and institutions to carry out research and educational activities in all the parklands.

Historical Areas are set aside to preserve their historical or archaeological features. Among these features are ancient Indian ruins, such as the remains of Mound Builders' towns at Ocmulgee National Monument. Others honor important persons or events in the history of the United States. These areas include battle-fields, forts, national cemeteries and memorials, and historic bridges, buildings, dams, canals, and farms. The most famous historical area is probably the White House.

The historical areas are made to look as much as possible as they did when they became important. For example, staff members sometimes restore natural features and man-made structures, raise animals on the farms, and wear clothing styles from the past.

Recreational Areas provide outstanding land and water resources for outdoor activities. Hunting is permitted in some of the areas. Many also have a variety of natural and historical features.

In many recreational areas, including national seashores and lakeshores, visitors use the natural features for recreation. For example, 68 miles of white sand beaches and dunes line the Gulf of Mexico at Padre Island National Seashore. Its fishing, horseback riding, sailing, and swimming attract visitors from all parts of the country. Padre Island is also famous for its wide variety of sea and shore birds.

In other recreation areas, man-made features such as roads, trails, and water reservoirs provide the major recreational opportunities. One of the largest man-made lakes in the world, 254.69-square-mile Lake Mead, is a popular playground for water sports. It is formed by 726-foot-high Hoover Dam, one of the world's tallest dams. The Lake Mead National Recreation Area includes Lake Mohave, formed by Davis Dam. The area also has much desert animal and plant life.

Glen Canyon National Recreation Area is highlighted by Lake Powell, *below,* one of the largest man-made lakes in the world. The 186-mile-long lake was created by Glen Canyon Dam.

Jack Zehrt

Each year, more and more people seek a relaxing change from city life or everyday routine. In the late 1960's, more than 150 million visits were made yearly to the national parklands, compared with about 80 million in 1960.

The Blue Ridge Parkway is the most popular national parkland. It is the only area in the National Park System that has had more than 11 million visits in a year. This highway in the Blue Ridge Mountains winds from Virginia through North Carolina, and connects Shenandoah and Great Smoky Mountain national parks.

Visitors and park rangers share the responsibility of protecting the parklands. Carelessness can start a forest fire that could destroy lives and valuable resources. Visitors are not allowed to remove or damage any natural feature—not even a flower. The National Park Service repeatedly warns the public not to feed, tease, or touch any animals of the parklands.

Planning a Visit. Learning about a parkland beforehand will increase the enjoyment of a visit. Useful information includes the natural or historical features to look for, and why they are important. For an overnight stay, visitors should know whether the area has lodgings or campgrounds that will be open. Other useful information includes available services and recreational activities, traveling routes, and various fees.

The tables with this article show which parklands have overnight lodgings, permit camping, are closed part of the year, or are not yet open to the public. Area superintendents will mail other information upon request. For their addresses, write to Chief, Branch of General Inquiries, Division of Information, National Park Service, Washington, D.C. 20240.

Visitors should stop at a parkland's visitor center for pamphlets and maps that tell about the area's features and activities. At many parklands, staff members are available for campfire talks, guided trips, and amphitheater programs.

Visitors' Costs. At more than 100 parklands, the National Park Service charges an entrance fee of $1 to $2 daily per carload. The fee is 50 cents daily for a person not entering by car. The service also sells Golden Eagle Passports for up to $10 a year. They may be used at all parklands that charge an entrance fee and at certain Bureau of Land Management areas, national forests, and national wildlife refuges. Persons under 16 years of age and organized groups of high school age pay no entrance fee. All visitors pay fees for the use of bathhouses, boat ramps, campgrounds, electrical outlets, and other facilities.

Overnight lodgings vary in price, according to quality. They include cabins, cottages, lodges, motels, hotels, and trailer villages. These lodgings, available in more than 30 areas, are operated privately under contract with the National Park Service. Visitors should make reservations early. The busiest periods, except in warm climates, are from late May to mid-October, and weekends and holidays the rest of the year.

Camping is permitted in more than 80 national parklands—in the wilderness or on campgrounds. A wilderness site may be miles from such conveniences as drinking water and food supplies. Wilderness campers must notify the superintendent or a park ranger of their plans.

Inexperienced campers should camp on the campgrounds. Some of these sites have a few conveniences, and others have a wide variety, including play areas for children. Some campgrounds are designed for individuals or for families or other small groups. Others are for large, organized groups such as Boy Scout troops or school groups. Reservations can be made for group sites. For camping tips, see the WORLD BOOK article on CAMPING.

Problems of Overcrowding. The growing numbers of visitors put more and more pressure on the national parklands. Problems include demands for such basic services as food, water, lodging, and transportation. Only through careful planning and management can these problems be handled without spoiling the parklands. Otherwise, overcrowding could result in too much automobile traffic, air pollution from automobile fumes and campfire smoke, dirty streams, and jammed campgrounds.

The National Park Service has taken many steps to correct early mistakes in parkland development. It has tightened controls on air and water pollution, food supplies, and health care. In Yosemite National Park, for example, public transportation was begun to reduce automobile traffic. The park's "firefall"—a huge bonfire pushed over a cliff every summer night—was eliminated to decrease smoke and traffic jams. The service also cut the number of campers permitted in overcrowded Yosemite Valley.

Redwood National Park, home of the world's tallest known tree, has many scenic sites that are ideal for picnicking.

David Muench, Van Cleve Photography

NATIONAL PARK SYSTEM

NATIONAL PARKS

Name	Acres	Location	Outstanding Features
Acadia*	41,642.41	Maine	Highest land on U.S. Atlantic Coast; rugged coastline
Big Bend*†	708,221.20	Texas	Chisos Mountains and Desert in big bend of Rio Grande
Bryce Canyon*†	36,010.38	Utah	Oddly shaped, beautifully colored rock formations in horseshoe-shaped basins
Canyonlands*	257,640.00	Utah	Canyons, mesas, and sandstone spires; 1,000-year-old Indian rock carvings
Carlsbad Caverns	46,753.07	New Mexico	Huge underground caves with countless strange rock formations
Crater Lake*†	160,290.33	Oregon	Lake in dead volcano; lava walls almost 2,000 feet high
Everglades*†	1,400,533.00	Florida	Subtropical wilderness with plentiful wildlife
Glacier*†	1,013,129.12	Montana	Many glaciers and lakes among towering Rocky Mountains
Grand Canyon*†	673,575.00	Arizona	Mile-deep canyon with brightly colored walls and rock shapes
Grand Teton*†	310,350.18	Wyoming	Rugged Teton peaks; winter feeding ground of large elk herd
Great Smoky Mountains*†	516,626.02	North Carolina, Tennessee	High mountains; large hardwood and evergreen forests
Guadalupe Mountains**	81,077.02	Texas	Fossil limestone reef; evergreen forest overlooking desert
Haleakala*	27,282.78	Hawaii	Inactive volcano with large, colorful crater
Hawaii Volcanoes*†	220,344.84	Hawaii	Two active volcanoes; rare plants and animals
Hot Springs*	3,535.24	Arkansas	Mineral springs at base of Hot Springs Mountain
Isle Royale*†‡	539,341.01	Michigan	Island wilderness with large moose herd and wolves
Kings Canyon*†	460,330.90	California	Mountain wilderness of giant sequoia trees
Lassen Volcanic*†	106,933.78	California	Active volcano; steep domes of lava
Mammoth Cave*†	51,354.40	Kentucky	Huge cave with 150 miles of corridors; underground lakes, rivers, and waterfalls
Mesa Verde*†	52,073.62	Colorado	Prehistoric Indian cliff dwellings
Mount McKinley*†	1,939,492.80	Alaska	Highest mountain in North America; wildlife
Mount Rainier*†	241,992.00	Washington	Greatest single-peak glacier system in United States
North Cascades*	505,000.00	Washington	Mountain wilderness with glaciers, lakes, and jagged peaks
Olympic*†	896,599.10	Washington	Oceanside mountain wilderness with rain forest and elk
Petrified Forest	94,189.33	Arizona	Ancient, rock-hard wood; Indian ruins; Painted Desert
Platt*	911.97	Oklahoma	Cold mineral springs
Redwood	56,984.83	California	World's tallest known tree in coastal redwood forest
Rocky Mountain*	262,324.22	Colorado	More than 100 peaks over 11,000 feet high
Sequoia*†	386,862.97	California	Giant sequoia trees; Mount Whitney
Shenandoah*†	193,536.91	Virginia	Blue Ridge Mountains; hardwood forest; Skyline Drive
Virgin Islands*†	15,150.00	Virgin Islands	White beaches; tropical plants and animals
Wind Cave*	28,059.26	South Dakota	Limestone caverns; prairie wildlife
Yellowstone*†	2,221,772.61	Wyoming, Idaho, Montana	World's greatest geyser area; canyons and waterfalls; wide variety of wildlife
Yosemite*†	761,320.32	California	Mountain scenery with deep gorges and high waterfalls
Zion*†	147,034.97	Utah	Colorful canyons and mesas

Each national park has a separate article in WORLD BOOK.
*Camping permitted.   ‡Closed part of the year.   **Not yet open to the public.   †Has overnight lodging.

NATIONAL CEMETERIES

Name	Acres	Location	Name	Acres	Location
Antietam (Sharpsburg)	11.36	Maryland	Poplar Grove	8.72	Virginia
Battleground*	1.03	District of Columbia	Shiloh (Pittsburg Landing)	10.25	Tennessee
			Stones River (Murfreesboro)	20.09	Tennessee
Fort Donelson (Dover)	15.34	Tennessee	Vicksburg	117.85	Mississippi
Fredericksburg	12.00	Virginia	Yorktown	2.91	Virginia
Gettysburg	20.58	Pennsylvania			

*Has a separate article in WORLD BOOK.

NATIONAL RECREATION AREAS

Name	Acres	Location	Outstanding Features
Amistad*	65,000.00	Texas	U.S. part of Amistad Reservoir on Rio Grande
Arbuckle*	8,851.00	Oklahoma	Arbuckle Reservoir
Bighorn Canyon*	122,623.00	Wyoming, Montana	Reservoir created by Yellowtail Dam
Coulee Dam*	100,059.00	Washington	Franklin D. Roosevelt Lake, formed by Grand Coulee Dam
Curecanti*	41,103.00	Colorado	Blue Mesa, Crystal, and Morrow Point reservoirs
Delaware Water Gap	68,826.00	Pennsylvania, New Jersey	Scenery along Delaware River
Glen Canyon*†	1,196,545.00	Arizona, Utah	Lake Powell, formed by Glen Canyon Dam
Lake Chelan*	62,000.00	Washington	Snow-fed Lake Chelan in forested valley
Lake Mead*†	1,936,978.00	Arizona, Nevada	Lake Mead, formed by Hoover Dam; Lake Mohave, formed by Davis Dam
Ross Lake*	107,000.00	Washington	Lakes and forested valleys among snow-capped peaks
Sanford*	39,792.00	Texas	Sanford Reservoir on Canadian River
Shadow Mountain*	18,240.00	Colorado	Shadow Mountain and Granby lakes on Colorado River
Whiskeytown-Shasta-Trinity*	41,987.00	California	Whiskeytown Reservoir, formed by Whiskeytown Dam

*Camping permitted.
†Has overnight lodging.

Werner Stoy, Camera Hawaii

Yosemite National Park has many spectacular waterfalls, including Yosemite Falls, *above,* one of the world's highest falls.

Fred Bond, Publix

Vicksburg National Military Park includes relics of the famous Civil War battle. Many states whose soldiers fought in the battle have memorials in the park.

David Muench, Van Cleve Photography

Grand Canyon National Monument, near Grand Canyon National Park, offers a breathtaking view of the Inner Gorge of the Grand Canyon, *right,* from Toroweap Point.

E. Carle, Shostal

Bernie Donahue, Publix

Fort Sumter National Monument is on the site where the Civil War began. Confederate guns attacked a Union force there.

George Washington Carver National Monument marks the site where the famous scientist was born a slave.

NATIONAL MONUMENTS

Name	Acres	Location	Outstanding Features
Agate Fossil Beds	2,995.19	Nebraska	Deposits of animal fossils
Alibates Flint Quarries and Texas Panhandle Pueblo Culture**	1,422.00	Texas	Site of quarry used by prehistoric Indians in making tools and weapons
Arches*	82,953.05	Utah	Giant arches, windows, and towers of rock formed by erosion
Aztec Ruins	27.14	New Mexico	Ruins of large Indian town of the 1100's
Badlands*	243,508.41	South Dakota	Rugged ravines, ridges, and cliffs; prehistoric animal fossils
Bandelier*†	29,661.20	New Mexico	Ruins of prehistoric Indian pueblos and cliff dwellings; canyons
Biscayne	95,064.00	Florida	Living coral reef in Atlantic Ocean and Biscayne Bay
Black Canyon of the Gunnison*	13,689.72	Colorado	Narrow, steep-walled canyon with shadowed depths
Booker T. Washington	217.93	Virginia	Birthplace and childhood home of famous Negro leader and educator
Buck Island Reef	850.00	Virgin Islands	Marine garden in Caribbean Sea; underwater trail
Cabrillo	123.25	California	Memorial to Juan Rodríguez Cabrillo, who discovered West Coast
Canyon de Chelly*†	83,840.00	Arizona	Prehistoric Indian ruins at base of cliffs and in caves
Capitol Reef*	254,241.72	Utah	Colorful 20-mile-long ridge with white dome-shaped rock
Capulin Mountain*	775.42	New Mexico	Cinder cone of dead volcano, with trails around rim and into crater
Casa Grande Ruins	472.50	Arizona	Ruins of adobe tower built by Indians 600 years ago
Castillo de San Marcos	20.36	Florida	Fort begun by Spaniards in 1672 to defend St. Augustine
Castle Clinton	1.00	New York	Landing depot for $8\frac{1}{4}$ million immigrants from 1855 to 1890
Cedar Breaks*†‡	6,154.60	Utah	Huge natural amphitheater in colorful Pink Cliff
Chaco Canyon*	21,509.40	New Mexico	Ruins of large pueblos built by prehistoric Indians

Continued

Ray Atkeson

Death Valley National Monument includes the lowest spot in the Western Hemisphere—Bad Water, 282 feet below sea level.

Jack Zehrt, Shostal

Grand Portage National Monument in Minnesota marks the location of a famous fur-trading post of the 1700's.

NATIONAL MONUMENTS

Name	Acres	Location	Outstanding Features
Channel Islands*	18,166.68	California	Large sea lion breeding place; nesting sea birds; animal fossils
Chesapeake and Ohio Canal*	4,647.19	Maryland, West Virginia	One of the United States' oldest and least-changed lock canals for mule-drawn boats
Chiricahua*	10,645.90	Arizona	Strange, rocky landscape formed by nearly a billion years of erosion
Colorado*	17,659.51	Colorado	Canyons and unusual sandstone formations
Craters of the Moon*	53,545.05	Idaho	Lava fields with volcanic caves, cinder cones, craters, and tunnels
Custer Battlefield	765.34	Montana	Site of Battle of Little Bighorn in 1876
Death Valley*†	1,907,760.00	California, Nevada	Great desert famous in Western history; lowest land surface in Western Hemisphere
Devils Postpile*‡	798.46	California	Remains of lava flow forming rock columns up to 60 feet high
Devils Tower*	1,346.91	Wyoming	Volcanic rock tower 865 feet high
Dinosaur*	206,233.55	Colorado, Utah	Fossil deposits of dinosaurs and other prehistoric animals; canyons cut by rivers
Effigy Mounds	1,467.50	Iowa	Indian mounds in shapes of bears and birds
El Morro*	1,278.72	New Mexico	Soft sandstone with prehistoric rock carvings; inscriptions by early explorers and settlers
Florissant Fossil Beds	5,992.32	Colorado	Fossil insects, leaves, and seeds
Fort Frederica	250.00	Georgia	Built in 1736 to protect British colonists from Spaniards
Fort Jefferson*	47,125.00	Florida	Built in 1846 to control Florida Straits; underwater trail
Fort Matanzas	298.51	Florida	Spanish fort built in 1742 to protect St. Augustine from British
Fort McHenry	43.26	Maryland	Defended against British in War of 1812; battle inspired "The Star-Spangled Banner"
Fort Pulaski	5,516.62	Georgia	Captured by Union forces during Civil War
Fort Stanwix**	18.00	New York	Site of treaty with Iroquois Indians in 1768 and Revolutionary War siege in 1777
Fort Sumter	34.27	South Carolina	Site of beginning of Civil War
Fort Union	720.60	New Mexico	Ruins of fort built in 1851 to protect travelers on Santa Fe Trail
George Washington Birthplace	393.68	Virginia	Plantation where Washington was born; memorial mansion and gardens

Continued

Ray Manley, Shostal

Wupatki National Monument in Arizona features pueblos built of red sandstone by prehistoric farming Indians. The Hopi tribe may have descended partially from these Indians.

NATIONAL MONUMENTS

Name	Acres	Location	Outstanding Features
George Washington Carver	210.00	Missouri	Birthplace and boyhood home of famous Negro scientist
Gila Cliff Dwellings	533.13	New Mexico	Prehistoric dwellings in overhanging cliff
Glacier Bay*†	2,803,840.00	Alaska	Glaciers that move down mountainsides and break up into the sea; much wildlife
Gran Quivira	610.94	New Mexico	Ruins of Spanish mission buildings and Indian pueblos
Grand Canyon*	198,280.00	Arizona	Unusual view from Toroweap Point of canyon's Inner Gorge
Grand Portage	709.27	Minnesota	Fur-trading post on portage of canoe route to Northwest
Great Sand Dunes*	36,740.32	Colorado	Some of largest and highest dunes in United States
Homestead	162.73	Nebraska	One of first land claims under Homestead Act of 1862
Hovenweep*	505.43	Colorado, Utah	Prehistoric Indian cliff dwellings, pueblos, and towers
Jewel Cave	1,274.56	South Dakota	Underground limestone chambers connected by narrow corridors
Joshua Tree*	558,183.73	California	Joshua trees; desert plants and animals
Katmai†‡	2,792,137.00	Alaska	Valley of Ten Thousand Smokes, scene of 1912 volcanic eruption
Lava Beds*	46,238.69	California	Unusual caves, cinder cones, and other results of volcanic action
Lehman Caves	640.00	Nevada	Limestone caverns with many tunnels and corridors
Marble Canyon	32,664.69	Arizona	Views of upper Grand Canyon of Colorado River
Montezuma Castle	842.09	Arizona	Prehistoric Indian dwellings in limestone cliff
Mound City Group	67.50	Ohio	Burial mounds built by prehistoric Indians
Muir Woods	502.90	California	Grove of coast redwood trees
Natural Bridges*	7,600.00	Utah	Three gigantic natural bridges of sandstone
Navajo*	360.00	Arizona	Ruins of prehistoric Indian cliff dwellings
Ocmulgee	683.48	Georgia	Remains of Indian mounds and towns, some dating from 8000 B.C.
Oregon Caves†	480.00	Oregon	Limestone caverns with rock formations of beauty and variety

Continued

Bob and Ira Spring

Sitka National Monument marks the site of the fort where, in 1804, the Tlingit Indians fought —and lost—their final battle against Russian settlers in Alaska.

NATIONAL MONUMENTS

Name	Acres	Location	Outstanding Features
Organ Pipe Cactus*	330,874.25	Arizona	Organ pipe cacti and other desert plants found nowhere else in United States
Pecos	340.90	New Mexico	Ruins of Spanish mission of 1600's and Indian pueblos of 1300's
Perry's Victory and International Peace Memorial	21.44	Ohio	Near site of U.S. naval victory in War of 1812; honors peace among United States, Canada, and Great Britain
Pinnacles*	14,497.77	California	Spirelike rock formations from 500 to 1,200 feet high; numerous caves
Pipe Spring	40.00	Arizona	Fort and other structures built by Mormon pioneers
Pipestone	282.31	Minnesota	Quarry where Indians took stone for making peace pipes
Rainbow Bridge	160.00	Utah	World's largest known natural bridge—309 feet high and 278 feet long
Russell Cave	310.45	Alabama	Tools and other evidence of human life from 6500 B.C. to A.D. 1650
Saguaro	78,644.00	Arizona	Cactus forest, including giant saguaro cacti
Saint Croix Island	56.50	Maine	Site of 1604 French settlement
Scotts Bluff	3,084.00	Nebraska	Landmark on Oregon Trail
Sitka	54.33	Alaska	Site of Tlingit Indians' last stand against Russian settlers in 1804
Statue of Liberty	58.38	New York, New Jersey	World's largest statue, gift of France
Sunset Crater	3,040.00	Arizona	Volcanic cinder cone and crater formed about A.D. 1100
Timpanogos Cave*	250.00	Utah	Limestone caverns known for coloring and twig-shaped wall formations
Tonto	1,120.00	Arizona	Indian cliff dwellings dating from 1300's
Tumacacori	10.15	Arizona	Spanish mission building built in 1700's
Tuzigoot	42.67	Arizona	Ruins of prehistoric Indian pueblos
Walnut Canyon	1,879.46	Arizona	Ancient cliff pueblos built in shallow caves under limestone ledges
White Sands	146,535.34	New Mexico	Glistening white dunes of gypsum sand
Wupatki	35,232.84	Arizona	Red sandstone pueblos built by prehistoric farming Indians
Yucca House**	9.60	Colorado	Ruins of large prehistoric Indian pueblo

Each national monument has a separate article in WORLD BOOK.
*Camping permitted.   †Has overnight lodging.   ‡Closed part of the year.   **Not yet open to the public.

——— NATIONAL HISTORIC SITES ———

Name	Acres	Location	Outstanding Features
Abraham Lincoln Birthplace	116.50	Kentucky	Log cabin inside memorial building on site of Lincoln's birthplace
Adams	4.77	Massachusetts	Home of Adams family, including Presidents John Adams and John Quincy Adams
Allegheny Portage Railroad	767.05	Pennsylvania	Honors Pennsylvania Canal and the railroad that carried canal boat passengers and cargoes over Allegheny Mountains
Andrew Johnson	16.68	Tennessee	President Andrew Johnson's home, tailor shop, and grave
Ansley Wilcox House	1.03	New York	House where Theodore Roosevelt was sworn in as President
Bent's Old Fort	178.00	Colorado	Important fur-trading post of Old West
Carl Sandburg Home	246.58	North Carolina	The poet's home and farm
Chicago Portage	91.20	Illinois	Section of important route linking Lake Michigan and Mississippi River
Chimney Rock	83.36	Nebraska	Landmark and campsite on Oregon Trail
Christiansted	27.15	Virgin Islands	Honors Danish colonial development of Virgin Islands
Dorchester Heights	5.43	Massachusetts	Tower on artillery site that forced British to leave Boston in 1776
Edison	19.96	New Jersey	Laboratories and home of inventor Thomas A. Edison
Eisenhower†	493.13	Pennsylvania	Home and farm of Dwight D. Eisenhower during and after his presidency
Fort Bowie	900.00	Arizona	Military headquarters for operations against Geronimo and his Apaches
Fort Davis	460.00	Texas	Major fort in west Texas defense system against Apaches and Comanches
Fort Laramie	546.28	Wyoming	Important post that guarded covered wagons heading west
Fort Larned	681.39	Kansas	Protection of Santa Fe Trail
Fort Raleigh	159.66	North Carolina	Site of first attempted English settlement in what is now United States, in 1585
Fort Smith	18.58	Arkansas	One of first U.S. military posts in Louisiana Territory
Fort Union Trading Post†	380.00	North Dakota, Montana	Major fur-trading post in upper Missouri River region
Fort Vancouver*	220.00	Washington	Western headquarters of Hudson's Bay Company
Gloria Dei Church	3.43	Pennsylvania	Second oldest Swedish church in United States; founded 1677
Golden Spike	2,171.69	Utah	Honors completion in 1869 of first coast-to-coast railroad in United States
Hampton	45.42	Maryland	Great mansion built in late 1700's
Herbert Hoover	148.00	Iowa	Birthplace, boyhood home, and burial place of President Hoover
Home of Franklin D. Roosevelt	187.69	New York	Birthplace, home, "Summer White House," and burial place of President Franklin D. Roosevelt
Hopewell Village	848.06	Pennsylvania	Rural iron-making village of 1800's
Hubbell Trading Post	157.00	Arizona	Shows role of Indian reservation traders in settling West
Jamestown	20.63	Virginia	Honors first permanent English settlement in North America; founded 1607
Jefferson National Expansion Memorial	90.96	Missouri	Museum and 630-foot-high Gateway Arch honor U.S. expansion west of Mississippi River
John Fitzgerald Kennedy	0.09	Massachusetts	Birthplace and early boyhood home of President Kennedy
John Muir	8.90	California	Honors contributions to conservation and literature by explorer-naturalist
Lyndon B. Johnson	7.57	Texas	President Lyndon Johnson's birthplace
Mar-A-Lago, The†	17.17	Florida	Private mansion of 1920's
McLoughlin House	0.63	Oregon	Home of John McLoughlin, leader in early development of Pacific Northwest
Pennsylvania Avenue	——	District of Columbia	Section of avenue between Capitol and White House, including Ford's Theatre, House Where Lincoln Died, and other areas listed separately

Continued

NATIONAL HISTORIC SITES

Name	Acres	Location	Outstanding Features
Sagamore Hill	85.00	New York	Last home of President Theodore Roosevelt
Saint-Gaudens**	86.00	New Hampshire	Home, studio, and gardens of sculptor Augustus Saint-Gaudens
Saint Paul's Church	6.09	New York	Church connected with events leading to first major victory for freedom of press in American colonies
St. Thomas	1.66	Virgin Islands	Fort Christian, completed 1680; oldest standing structure in Virgin Islands
Salem Maritime	10.73	Massachusetts	Derby Wharf and other important structures in New England history
San Jose Mission	4.13	Texas	One of finest Spanish missions in North America; established 1720
San Juan	43.61	Puerto Rico	Spanish fort begun in 1539 to protect Bay of San Juan
Saugus Iron Works**	9.00	Massachusetts	One of first ironworks in North America, built in 1640's
Theodore Roosevelt Birthplace	0.11	New York	Birthplace of 26th President
Touro Synagogue	0.23	Rhode Island	One of finest examples of colonial religious architecture in United States
Vanderbilt Mansion	211.65	New York	Magnificent country home built in 1890's
Whitman Mission*	98.15	Washington	Site where Indians killed missionaries Marcus Whitman and his wife
William Howard Taft	0.78	Ohio	President Taft's birthplace

*Has a separate article in WORLD BOOK.
**Closed part of the year.
†Not yet open to the public.

Jamestown National Historic Site recalls the first permanent English settlement in North America. A reconstruction of old James Fort, *below,* stands in Jamestown Festival Park at the site.

B. & R. Keene, Shostal

─── NATIONAL MEMORIALS ───

Name	Acres	Location	Outstanding Features
Arkansas Post	304.60	Arkansas	First permanent white settlement in lower Mississippi Valley, founded by French 1686
Chamizal†	55.00	Texas	Honors peaceful settlement in 1963 of 99-year-old border dispute with Mexico
Coronado	2,834.16	Arizona	Honors Francisco Coronado's exploration of Southwest in 1540's
Custis-Lee Mansion	3.47	Virginia	Home of Gen. Robert E. Lee, begun in 1802
De Soto*	30.00	Florida	Near site of 1539 landing of explorer Hernando De Soto
Federal Hall	0.45	New York	Site of first U.S. Capitol, 1785-1790
Ford's Theatre (Lincoln Museum)	0.18	District of Columbia	Reconstruction of theater in which Abraham Lincoln was shot; Lincoln Museum
Fort Caroline	128.29	Florida	Stockade overlooking attempted French settlement in 1560's
Fort Clatsop	124.97	Oregon	Winter campsite of Lewis and Clark expedition in 1805-1806
Frederick Douglass Home†	8.00	District of Columbia	Home of Negro leader from 1877 to 1895
General Grant	0.76	New York	Tombs of President and Mrs. Ulysses S. Grant
Hamilton Grange	0.71	New York	Home of Alexander Hamilton, first U.S. secretary of the treasury
House Where Lincoln Died	0.05	District of Columbia	Scene of Lincoln's death, across street from Ford's Theatre
Johnstown Flood	54.18	Pennsylvania	Memorial to more than 2,000 persons killed in Johnstown Flood of 1889
Lincoln Boyhood	200.00	Indiana	Farm site where Lincoln spent most of his boyhood
Lincoln Memorial*	163.63	District of Columbia	Marble building with 19-foot-high statue of Lincoln
Mount Rushmore*	1,278.45	South Dakota	Huge heads of four Presidents carved on face of granite cliff
Roger Williams†	5.00	Rhode Island	Honors founder of Rhode Island colony, a pioneer leader for religious freedom
Thomas Jefferson (Jefferson Memorial*)	18.36	District of Columbia	Circular marble building with 19-foot-high statue of Jefferson
Washington Monument*	106.01	District of Columbia	Four-sided, pyramid-topped pillar 555 feet high honoring George Washington
Wright Brothers	431.40	North Carolina	Site of Wilbur and Orville Wright's first powered airplane flight

*Has a separate article in WORLD BOOK.
†Not yet open to the public.

─── NATIONAL MILITARY PARKS ───

Name	Acres	Location	Outstanding Features
Chickamauga and Chattanooga	8,231.77	Georgia, Tennessee	Civil War battles of 1863—Chickamauga, Lookout Mountain, Missionary Ridge, and Orchard Knob
Fort Donelson	600.00	Tennessee	First major Union victory of Civil War, 1862
Fredericksburg and Spotsylvania County Battlefields Memorial	3,672.15	Virginia	Civil War battles of Chancellorsville, Fredericksburg, Wilderness, and Spotsylvania Court House; 1862-1864
Gettysburg	3,408.64	Pennsylvania	Civil War battle that stopped Confederate invasion, 1863
Guilford Courthouse	233.00	North Carolina	Revolutionary War battle at Yorktown that led to British defeat, 1781
Horseshoe Bend	2,040.00	Alabama	Battle won by Andrew Jackson ending Creek Indian War, 1814
Kings Mountain	3,950.00	South Carolina	Revolutionary War victory of American frontiersmen, 1780
Moores Creek	49.68	North Carolina	Patriots' victory over Loyalists in Revolutionary War, 1776
Pea Ridge	4,278.75	Arkansas	Important Union victory of Civil War, 1862
Shiloh	3,515.46	Tennessee	Civil War battle of 1862 that led to fall of Vicksburg
Vicksburg	1,740.78	Mississippi	Battle that gave Union control of Mississippi River, 1863

— NATIONAL BATTLEFIELDS, NATIONAL BATTLEFIELD PARKS, AND NATIONAL BATTLEFIELD SITES —

Name	Acres	Location	Outstanding Features
Antietam (NBS)	783.63	Maryland	Civil War battle that stopped first Confederate invasion of North, 1862
Big Hole (NB)	666.00	Montana	U.S. defeat of Chief Joseph's forces in Nez Percé Indian War, 1877
Brices Cross Roads (NBS)	1.00	Mississippi	Large Union force defeated by outnumbered Confederate cavalrymen, 1864
Cowpens (NBS)	1.24	South Carolina	American victory of Revolutionary War, 1781
Fort Necessity (NB)*	500.00	Pennsylvania	French defeat of colonial troops led by George Washington; first battle of French and Indian War, 1754
Kennesaw Mountain (NBP)	3,682.62	Georgia	Civil War battle during Gen. William T. Sherman's march to Atlanta, 1864
Manassas (NBP)	2,926.24	Virginia	Two battles of Manassas (Bull Run) in Civil War, 1861 and 1862
Petersburg (NB)	2,731.00	Virginia	Unsuccessful nine-month siege of Confederate railroad center, 1864-1865
Richmond (NBP)	746.56	Virginia	Several Union attempts to capture Richmond, the Confederate capital
Stones River (NB)	330.86	Tennessee	Beginning of Union drive to divide Confederacy into three parts, 1862-1863
Tupelo (NB)	1.50	Mississippi	Battle over Gen. William T. Sherman's supply line during march to Atlanta, 1864
Wilson's Creek (NBP)	1,727.54	Missouri	Defeat of Union militia by Confederate forces, 1861

*Camping permitted.

PARKWAYS AND OTHER NATIONAL PARKLANDS

Name	Acres	Location	Outstanding Features
Appalachian National Scenic Trail†	50,000.00	From Maine to Georgia	Wilderness hiking trail through Appalachian Mountains; about 2,000 miles
Baltimore-Washington Parkway†	2,431.24	Maryland	Pleasant 29-mile drive; Greenbelt Park, a natural woodland
Blue Ridge Parkway†**	94,660.07	Georgia, North Carolina, Virginia	Scenic mountain parkway
Catoctin Mountain Park†	5,768.90	Maryland	Mountain scenery
Fort Scott Historic Area and Other Kansas Historic Areas	7.00	Kansas	Honors various events in Kansas before and during Civil War
George Washington Memorial Parkway	7,141.63	Virginia, Maryland	Potomac River landmarks associated with Washington's life; 49-mile road
Ice Age National Scientific Reserve	32,500.00	Wisconsin	Natural features showing effects of ancient glaciers
Natchez Trace Parkway†	45,297.51	Mississippi, Tennessee, Alabama	Scenic 450-mile road along Indian and frontier trail
National Capital Park System	7,875.17	District of Columbia, Virginia, Maryland	A 724-unit park system in and near Washington, D.C.
Ozark National Scenic Riverways	72,101.00	Missouri	Narrow river park along Current and Jacks Fork rivers; caves and springs
Piscataway Park‡	1,058.81	Maryland	View from Mount Vernon
Prince William Forest Park†	18,571.55	Virginia	Woodland with about 90 kinds of trees
Roosevelt Campobello International Park*§	2,721.50	New Brunswick in Canada	Summer home of President Franklin D. Roosevelt, where he was stricken with polio
Saint Croix National Scenic Riverway	67,746.92	Minnesota, Wisconsin	About 200 miles of Saint Croix River
Suitland Parkway	730.58	District of Columbia, Maryland	Nine-mile landscaped road
Theodore Roosevelt Island	88.32	District of Columbia	Wooded parkland
Theodore Roosevelt National Memorial Park†	70,436.00	North Dakota	Badlands along Little Missouri River and part of President Theodore Roosevelt's ranch
White House*	18.07	District of Columbia	President's home and office
Wolf National Scenic Riverway‡	5,516.30	Wisconsin	Scenic canoeing and fishing
Wolf Trap Farm Park	117.86	Virginia	Park for the performing arts

*Has a separate article in WORLD BOOK.
†Camping permitted.   **Has overnight lodging.   §Closed part of the year.   ‡Not yet open to the public.

NATIONAL HISTORICAL PARKS

Name	Acres	Location	Outstanding Features
Appomattox Court House	937.52	Virginia	Site of Gen. Robert E. Lee's surrender to Gen. Ulysses S. Grant, ending Civil War
Chalmette	142.45	Louisiana	Scene of part of Battle of New Orleans in War of 1812
City of Refuge	180.78	Hawaii	Prehistoric house sites, royal fish ponds, and coconut groves
Colonial	9,430.00	Virginia	Major sites of colonial development—Jamestown, Williamsburg, and Yorktown; Yorktown battlefield
Cumberland Gap*	20,176.49	Kentucky, Tennessee, Virginia	Famous mountain pass of Wilderness Road explored by Daniel Boone and used by pioneers heading west
George Rogers Clark	22.65	Indiana	Honors Revolutionary War victories won by Clark in Northwest Territory
Harpers Ferry	1,530.00	West Virginia, Maryland	Scene of 1859 raid by John Brown, foe of slavery, and his capture
Independence	21.84	Pennsylvania	Independence Hall and other Philadelphia buildings and sites associated with founding of United States
Minute Man	750.00	Massachusetts	Landmarks of battles on first day of Revolutionary War
Morristown	1,339.13	New Jersey	Campsites in Revolutionary War; Washington's headquarters in 1777 and 1779-1780
Nez Perce	3,000.00	Idaho	Honors history and life of Nez Percé Indian region, and Lewis and Clark expedition
San Juan Island	1,751.99	Washington	Honors peaceful settlement of boundary dispute with Canada and Great Britain in 1872
Saratoga	5,500.00	New York	Scene of key U.S. military victory in Revolutionary War

*Camping permitted.

NATIONAL LAKESHORES AND NATIONAL SEASHORES

Name	Acres	Location	Outstanding Features
Assateague Island (NS)*	39,630.00	Maryland, Virginia	Wide, sloping beaches; animal life includes wild Chincoteague ponies
Cape Cod (NS)*†	44,600.00	Massachusetts	Beaches, birdlife, dunes, marshes, woodlands, and freshwater ponds
Cape Hatteras (NS)*	28,500.00	North Carolina	Beaches, dunes, and birdlife; lighthouse overlooks "Grayeyard of the Atlantic," scene of many shipwrecks
Cape Lookout (NS)	24,500.00	North Carolina	Barrier islands with beaches, dunes, salt marshes, and lighthouse
Fire Island (NS)*	19,311.00	New York	Atlantic island with beaches, dunes, marshes, and wildlife
Indiana Dunes (NL)	8,721.00	Indiana	Dunes up to 200 feet high along Lake Michigan; beaches and woodlands
Padre Island (NS)*	133,918.23	Texas	Gulf Coast island with long beaches and bird and marine life
Pictured Rocks (NL)	67,000.00	Michigan	Beaches, dunes, woods, and cliffs along Lake Superior
Point Reyes (NS)*	64,546.00	California	Pacific peninsula with beaches, cliffs, lagoons, and wildlife

*Camping permitted.
†Has overnight lodging.

NATIONAL PARK SYSTEM / History

During the 1800's, a number of hunters and trappers returned from the wild Yellowstone region with glowing reports of strange natural wonders. These stories—of boiling hot springs, spurting geysers, and a mountain of black glass—seemed too fantastic to believe. In 1870, an expedition led by General Henry D. Wash-

burn, surveyor general of the Montana Territory, visited the region to check the reports.

After four weeks of exploring by horseback, the men camped near the Madison River. There, they talked far into the night about the amazing sights they had seen. They discussed developing the land for private resorts, or for lumbering and mining. But then Cornelius Hedges, a Montana judge, proposed that the region be preserved as a national park to benefit all people for all time. The other men agreed enthusiastically.

Members of the expedition promoted the national park idea by writing articles in newspapers and magazines, giving lectures, and meeting with high government officials. Their efforts succeeded in 1872, when Congress established Yellowstone National Park. During the 1890's, four more national parks were established—Yosemite, Sequoia, General Grant (now Kings Canyon), and Mount Rainier.

In 1906, Congress passed the Antiquities Act to stop looting and destruction at prehistoric Indian sites in the Southwest. This law gave the President the power to establish national monuments on land owned or controlled by the government. Later in 1906, Devils Tower National Monument became the first such area. More than 30 national monuments were established during the next 10 years.

In 1916, Congress set up the National Park Service as a bureau of the Department of the Interior. Stephen T. Mather, a Chicago businessman, became its first director. Mather did much to promote and expand the National Park System. In 1916, there were 16 national parks and 21 national monuments, with a total area of 7,426 square miles. When Mather retired in 1929, the system consisted of 25 national parks, 32 national monuments, and a national memorial. It had a total area of more than 16,000 square miles.

In 1933, Congress transferred more than 70 areas from other government agencies to the Department of the Interior. These areas, most of them historical, were added to the National Park System. In 1935, the Historic Sites Act gave the secretary of the interior the power to approve national historic sites.

The Park, Parkway, and Recreation Area Study Act of 1936 led to establishment of recreational areas in the National Park System. The first such area, the Blue Ridge Parkway, was established later that year. An act of 1946 allowed the park service to manage recreational areas under cooperative agreements with other government agencies that controlled the areas.

By 1955, the National Park System had grown to almost 200 areas. About 50 million visits were recorded that year. During the 1960's, the National Park Service added 75 areas. Including boundary changes, over 7,300 square miles—a total area almost as large as that of New Jersey—were added.

Grand Canyon of the Yellowstone was one of the paintings by Thomas Moran that helped persuade Congress to establish Yellowstone National Park in 1872. Easterners had found it hard to believe the reports of hunters and trappers of the region's magnificent beauty and natural wonders.

National Collection of Fine Arts, Smithsonian Institution

Since ancient times, rulers and noblemen throughout the world have set aside parklands to preserve outstanding landscapes and wild animals. But these reserves were not open to the people. The idea of national parks for the public did not take shape until the United States government established Yellowstone National Park in 1872. Since then, about 100 countries have established over 1,200 national parks and similar reserves. Many nations send people to the United States for training in park management by the National Park Service. The service also sends advisers to other countries.

Canada became the second country with a national park. In 1885, the Canadian government set aside 10 square miles in the Canadian Rockies. This land was the start of Banff National Park. Banff, Canada's best-known and most popular national park, has magnificent mountain scenery, glacier-fed lakes, and mineral hot springs. Wood Buffalo National Park, which covers 17,300 square miles, is the largest national park in the world. The largest buffalo herd in North America lives in this park. For information on these and other Canadian parks, see CANADA (National Parks).

In Africa, countless wild animals roam the vast plains, tropical rain forests, and thick bushlands of national parks and reserves. This wildlife includes buffaloes, elephants, giraffes, gorillas, lions, and zebras. Among the leading African national parks are Albert in Congo (Kinshasa), Kafue in Zambia, Kruger in South Africa, and Serengeti in Tanzania.

In Asia, the Indian rhinoceros, largest of the Asian rhinoceroses, lives in the Kaziranga Reserve of India and the Chitawan Sanctuary of Nepal. The small number of lions still in Asia, outside zoos, make their home in the Gir Forest of India. Tigers and the rare Javan rhinoceroses live in Indonesia's Udjung Reserve.

The lakes, hills, and dales of Peak District National Park in England attract many tourists. Lüneburger Heath in West Germany has rolling sandy plains, and forests of birch, oak, and pine trees. Australia's Royal National Park is known for its rare, beautiful wild flowers. Japan's famous Mount Fuji is one of the magnificent natural features preserved in national parks. Another is Iguaçu Falls, more than 2 miles wide, on the Argentine-Brazilian border.

The broadest worldwide park conservation effort is that of the International Union for Conservation of Nature and Natural Resources (IUCN). It was founded in 1948, and has headquarters in Morges, Switzerland. More than 230 national governments and organizations, including the U.S. Department of the Interior, belong to the IUCN. The IUCN points out threats to resources and wildlife in individual countries, and encourages and assists them in park planning. It holds frequent international conferences, and publishes books and reports on conservation.   GEORGE B. HARTZOG, JR.

Tom Myers

Waterton Lakes National Park is famous for its lakes, mountains, waterfalls, and trails. The park is the Canadian portion of Waterton-Glacier International Peace Park.

Norman Myers, Photo Researchers

Serengeti National Park, near the slopes of Kilimanjaro in Tanzania, has one of the world's largest animal reserves.

NATIONAL PARK SYSTEM/*Study Aids*

Related Articles. See the WORLD BOOK articles on the national parklands as listed in the tables with this article. See also NATIONAL PARK SERVICE.

Questions

How does the National Park Service acquire land for new parklands?

What is the largest area in the National Park System?

What was the first national park in the world? When was it established?

How are national parklands established?

Which national park is preserved chiefly for its prehistoric importance?

What is the world's largest national park?

Where is the lowest land surface in the Western Hemisphere?

What is the most popular parkland?

How many types of national parklands are there?

What is probably the most famous historical area in the National Park System?

NATIONAL PRIMITIVE BAPTIST CONVENTION IN THE U.S.A. is a religious organization that has more than 1,800 churches. Each church is independent, controlling its own membership. These Baptists follow three *ordinances* (established religious ceremonies)—baptism, holy communion, and feet-washing rites. They believe that a definite number of the human race were chosen for redemption before the world was created, and these persons will be saved before the final judgment.

The convention was formed in 1907. It consists of state conventions and associations. It operates a publishing house, women's auxiliaries, training unions, and church schools. Headquarters are in Tallahassee, Fla. For the membership of the convention in the United States, see RELIGION (table). Critically reviewed by the NATIONAL PRIMITIVE BAPTIST CONVENTION IN THE U.S.A.

See also BAPTISTS.

NATIONAL RADIO ASTRONOMY OBSERVATORY (NRAO) is an observatory used by scientists throughout the United States. It is financed by the National Science Foundation (NSF). The observatory occupies 2,700 acres of land near Green Bank, W.Va. It has scientific offices in Charlottesville, Va. The NRAO was founded in 1956 by NSF to provide radio telescopes that are too expensive and complex to be built by individual universities. It is operated by Associated Universities, Inc., an association of nine United States universities.

Equipment at the NRAO includes six radio telescopes. Each telescope has a large, dish-shaped metal mirror used to receive radio signals from space. The largest telescope has a mirror 300 feet in diameter. Other telescopes include one with a 140-foot mirror, three with 85-foot mirrors, and one with a 36-foot mirror. Radio signals from the telescopes are amplified and strengthened by electronic equipment. The amplified signals are recorded for study.

Scientists using the NRAO were the first to detect radio signals from the planets Uranus and Neptune. Scientists at NRAO also discovered details about the structure of the Milky Way and other galaxies, and gathered information from radio signals on the behavior of hydrogen atoms and hydroxyl (OH^-) ions in space. Critically reviewed by the NATIONAL RADIO ASTRONOMY OBSERVATORY

See also RADIO TELESCOPE.

NATIONAL RECOVERY ADMINISTRATION (NRA), was a United States government agency in the early 1930's. The President set up the NRA in 1933 under the National Industrial Recovery Act as part of the New Deal program (see NEW DEAL). The NRA prepared and enforced codes of fair competition for businesses and industries. Hugh S. Johnson was the first head of the NRA. Donald R. Richberg succeeded him in 1934. The President abolished the NRA in 1935, after the Supreme Court ruled the recovery act unconstitutional. See also SCHECHTER V. UNITED STATES.

NATIONAL RECREATION AND PARK ASSOCIATION. See RECREATION AND PARK ASSOCIATION, NATIONAL.

NATIONAL RECREATION AREA. See NATIONAL PARK SYSTEM.

NATIONAL REPUBLICAN PARTY was a political party that arose when the Democratic-Republican party split during President John Quincy Adams' administration (1825-1829). Followers of Andrew Jackson opposed the party's conservative leaders, including Adams and Henry Clay. During Jackson's presidency (1829-1837), the National Republicans merged with other groups to form the Whig Party (see WHIG).　　RAY ALLEN BILLINGTON

NATIONAL RESEARCH COUNCIL. See NATIONAL ACADEMY OF SCIENCES.

NATIONAL ROAD. In the early 1800's, many settlers moved west of the Ohio River. They wanted their section to grow rapidly, and began demanding a better route from the East to the West. In 1811, work began on a road that, when completed, led from Cumberland, Md., to Vandalia, Ill. Over $7 million in federal funds was spent on the road. It was known at first as the Great National Pike, but later came to be called the National Road or the Cumberland Road.

For many years, the National Road was the chief road west. As railroads developed, the National Road became less important. Each of the states was finally given control of that part of the road which passed through it.

Now known as the National Old Trail Road, it is paved from Washington, D.C., to St. Louis, Mo. A monument to Henry Clay stands near Wheeling, W.Va. It honors Clay's great services in getting Congress to advance money for the road.　　W. TURRENTINE JACKSON

NATIONAL SAFETY COUNCIL is a nonprofit educational organization that promotes accident prevention. It has about 10,600 members, including individuals, businesses, schools, government agencies, and trade, labor, and civic organizations. The council helps members solve their safety problems. It promotes public safety by carrying on publicity campaigns, cooperating with public officials, and helping to establish safety groups. It makes awards for outstanding safety achievements to cities, states, schools, and organizations. The council's many publications include "Accident Facts," a yearly collection of accident statistics.

The council was founded in 1913, and was chartered by Congress in 1953. It has headquarters at 425 N. Michigan Avenue, Chicago, Ill. 60611.　　HOWARD PYLE

NATIONAL SCIENCE FOUNDATION is an independent agency of the federal government. It supports research in the life, physical, engineering, and social sciences. The foundation also supports efforts to improve the quality of science education through grants to universities and colleges for activities aimed at upgrading science teaching. It also provides financial aid to outstanding students, and supports improvement in the spread of science information.

The foundation conducts studies that help the government formulate its science programs. It also supports such programs as Antarctic research, the use of computers for research and education, and studies of the oceans. It maintains, under contract, the National Radio Astronomy Observatory in Green Bank, W.Va., the Kitt Peak National Observatory in Arizona, and the National Center for Atmospheric Research in Boulder, Colo. It was established by the National Science Foundation Act of 1950. Headquarters are at 1800 G Street NW, Washington, D.C. 20550.

Critically reviewed by the NATIONAL SCIENCE FOUNDATION

See also KITT PEAK NATIONAL OBSERVATORY; NATIONAL RADIO ASTRONOMY OBSERVATORY.

NATIONAL SECURITY ACT OF 1947. See DEFENSE, DEPARTMENT OF (History); NATIONAL DEFENSE (History).

NATIONAL SECURITY AGENCY (NSA) develops security measures for the United States. This government agency also directs certain activities that provide *intelligence* (information) on various other countries. NSA organizes research and operates facilities that obtain such information. President Harry S. Truman created the National Security Agency in 1952 as part of the Department of Defense.

NATIONAL SECURITY COUNCIL (NSC) serves as an interdepartmental defense cabinet of the United States government. It is a part of the Executive Office of the President. Members include the President, the Vice-President, the secretaries of state and defense, and the director of the Office of Emergency Preparedness.

The NSC advises the President on a broad range of security problems. It brings together the departments and agencies most concerned with foreign policy and

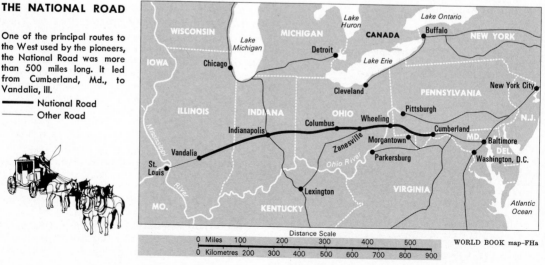

THE NATIONAL ROAD

One of the principal routes to the West used by the pioneers, the National Road was more than 500 miles long. It led from Cumberland, Md., to Vandalia, Ill.

━━━━ National Road
──── Other Road

WORLD BOOK map—FHa

military matters. The council supervises the Central Intelligence Agency (see CENTRAL INTELLIGENCE AGENCY). Ordinarily, the NSC meets once a week. If a serious world crisis develops, the President may summon the group into immediate session.

The NSC is assisted by a staff headed by the assistant to the President for national security affairs. The staff works with the member departments and agencies to prepare studies and policy papers for the council's action. Congress created the council in 1947.

Critically reviewed by the NATIONAL SECURITY COUNCIL

NATIONAL SECURITY MEDAL. See DECORATIONS AND MEDALS (table: U.S. Civilian Decorations).

NATIONAL SOCIALIST PARTY. See NAZISM.

NATIONAL SOCIETY FOR MEDICAL RESEARCH is an organization of more than 670 scientific and civic groups. The society is devoted to a cooperative program of informing the public on medical research. The groups include all medical schools, most veterinary and dental schools, health organizations such as the American Cancer Society, and all special medical societies in the United States. Among the groups are the American Medical Association, the Mayo Foundation, and the Rockefeller University. The society was founded in 1946. Headquarters are at 1330 Massachusetts Avenue NW, Washington, D.C. 20005.

Critically reviewed by NATIONAL SOCIETY FOR MEDICAL RESEARCH

NATIONAL TRAILWAYS BUS SYSTEM. See BUS (Leading Bus Companies).

NATIONAL TUBERCULOSIS AND RESPIRATORY DISEASE ASSOCIATION stimulates study for the prevention of tuberculosis and other respiratory diseases. The association has about 1,500 affiliated organizations in the United States. It serves as a clearinghouse for information and gives advice about respiratory diseases. It publishes literature about tuberculosis and other respiratory diseases, supports research through grants-in-aid, and gives fellowships for medical education. Funds for the national group and its affiliates come from the annual Christmas Seal campaign. It publishes *The American Review of Respiratory Diseases, The Bulletin, Abstracts,* and *Clinical Notes on Respiratory Diseases.* It has headquarters at 1740 Broadway, New York, N.Y. 10019. SOL S. LIFSON

NATIONAL WAR COLLEGE, located in Washington, D.C., is a school for United States government career personnel. It was established in 1946 and placed under the direction of the Joint Chiefs of Staff.

The college prepares personnel to plan national strategy, and to exercise joint high-level policy, command, and staff functions. There are about 130 students in each class. Three-fourths are selected from the Army, Navy, and Air Force, and a fourth from government agencies, particularly the Department of State. A commandant from one of the military services heads the college. He is assisted by deputies, two from the military services and one from the Department of State. The faculty includes military and civilian members. The course lasts 10 months. RICHARD M. SKINNER

NATIONAL WILDLIFE FEDERATION is an organization founded to create interest and promote public education in the conservation, restoration, and protection of forests, lands, waters, and wildlife in the United States. The federation issues several free and inexpensive publications. It also publishes *National Wildlife* for

its adult members and *Ranger Rick's Nature Magazine* for children who are members.

State wildlife federations and conservation leagues, made up of local clubs, are affiliated with the national organization. The federation has about 2 million members, counting members of affiliated organizations. The national group is financed by an annual direct-mail distribution of National Wildlife Conservation poster stamps. The federation began in 1936. It has headquarters at 1412 16th Street NW, Washington, D.C. 20036. Critically reviewed by NATIONAL WILDLIFE FEDERATION

NATIONAL WOMAN SUFFRAGE ASSOCIATION. See WOMAN SUFFRAGE.

NATIONAL YOUTH ADMINISTRATION. See NEW DEAL (Leading New Deal Agencies).

NATIONAL ZOOLOGICAL PARK is a 175-acre zoo maintained by the United States government in Rock Creek Valley in the District of Columbia. The Smithsonian Institution operates the park. The zoo contains about 3,000 animals of all kinds. The park is used for public exhibitions, scientific research, and education. Biologists, artists, photographers, and writers often do research there. The park provides information on buildings for housing animals, and cooperates with other governments in research work. JOHN C. BOLLENS

NATIONALISM is the belief that one's own country is the best country, or that one's own national group is the best nationality in the world. At its best, nationalism may be a healthy pride in one's country or national group. But if it is carried too far, it may cause one nation to try to dominate other nations.

The feeling of nationalism was not common in ancient times. A man usually owed allegiance to a political unit like the Greek city-state that was smaller than his national group, or to one like the Roman Empire that was larger. During the Middle Ages, man's chief loyalty was to his church or social class rather than to his nation. But nationalism began to replace old loyalties as trade and better means of communication brought men closer together, and as the influence of the church declined. The French Revolution of 1789 strengthened nationalism by uniting the masses of the people in the common cause of winning freedom at home and defending their nation against foreign enemies. As a result of growing nationalism, strong leaders in Germany, Italy, and other nations were able to mold their people into independent, unified countries.

During the 1900's, extreme nationalism in such countries as Germany and Japan resulted in racial persecution and aggression against other nations. After World War II, nationalism played a large part in independence movements in Africa and Asia. Many former colonies became independent nations. Some authorities believe that nationalism was also a major cause of the "split" between the Communist nations, Russia and China, during the 1960's. WILLIAM EBENSTEIN

See also FASCISM (Extreme Nationalism); PATRIOTISM.

NATIONALIST CHINA. See FORMOSA.

NATIONALITY. In law, nationality is a person's status as a member of a particular country. Usually, a person's citizenship is the same as his nationality. But the terms do not mean exactly the same thing. For example, before the Philippine Islands became independent, their people were U.S. nationals. They owed allegiance to the United States, but were not U.S. citizens.

Nationality is acquired at birth according to either of two principles. The first is the *jus sanguinis*, or *right of blood*, which gives to a child the nationality of one of his parents, usually the father. The second, called *jus soli*, or *right of the place of one's birth*, makes a person a national of the country in which he is born. Most countries use both principles. Every country has the right to determine who its nationals shall be.

In the British Commonwealth, the difference between nationality and citizenship is extremely important. The people of the Commonwealth and of all British possessions are known as British subjects. This means that they have British nationality. But their citizenship comes from the particular country to which they belong. Thus, a British subject may be a citizen of Canada, of New Zealand, or of the United Kingdom itself.

Nationality Groups. A second meaning of nationality has nothing at all to do with law. It refers to the fact that many people continue the habits, the customs, and even the language of their native land when they go to live elsewhere. Many groups of people in U.S. cities try to keep alive the customs and traditions of other countries. Some of these people were born outside the United States. But in some cases, every member of the group was born in the United States.   HERBERT W. BRIGGS

See also CITIZENSHIP; NATURALIZATION.

NATIONALIZED INDUSTRY. See FASCISM (Suppression of Labor and Industry); GREAT BRITAIN (Government Ownership; The Welfare State); SOCIALISM.

NATIVE SLOTH. See KOALA.

NATIVISM. See LATIN-AMERICAN LITERATURE (Romanticism; After World War I).

NATIVITY. See JESUS CHRIST (The Nativity); CHRISTMAS.

NATO. See NORTH ATLANTIC TREATY ORGANIZATION.

NATTA, GIULIO. See NOBEL PRIZES (table [1963]).

NATURAL BRIDGE. Not only man, but also nature, builds bridges, some of which are hundreds or thousands of years in the making. A natural bridge is often the result of water working its way slowly through loose soil or soft rock. If there is a harder layer of rock on top of the soil or soft rock, it will stay firm and form a bridge. Sometimes, a stream of water or a small valley is left beneath the bridge. See also VIRGINIA (color picture: Natural Bridge near Lexington).

NATURAL BRIDGES NATIONAL MONUMENT is in southeastern Utah. It includes three natural sandstone bridges, among the largest examples of their kind. They are called by their Hopi Indian names: *Sipapu*, *Owachomo*, and *Kachina*. The largest bridge, Sipapu, is 220 feet high and 56 feet thick at the top of the arch. The arch is 37 feet wide and it spans 268 feet. Second in size is Kachina bridge, with a span of 186 feet and a thickness of 107 feet at its smallest part. It arches 205 feet above water. Owachomo, the smallest and oldest bridge, is only 10 feet thick in the center, but is 108 feet high and 194 feet long. Many prehistoric drawings appear on Kachina. The 7,600-acre monument was established in 1908.   C. LANGDON WHITE

NATURAL GAS. See GAS.

NATURAL HISTORY. See NATURE STUDY.

NATURAL KEY is the key of C major in music. It has no sharps or flats and is played on the white keys of a piano keyboard, usually starting with the note of C. See also MUSIC (The Elements of Music).

NATURAL RESOURCES are those products and features of the earth that permit it to support life and satisfy man's needs. Land and water are natural resources. So are biological resources on the land and in the water, such as flowers, trees, birds, wild animals, and fish. Mineral resources include oil, coal, metals, stone, and sand. Other natural resources are air, sunshine, and climate. Natural resources are used for producing (1) food; (2) fuel; and (3) raw materials for the production of finished goods.

This article discusses natural resources in general. For information on the natural resources of specific areas, see the *Natural Resources* section in each state and province article, and in various country articles.

Uses and Importance. Biological resources are the most important natural resources. All the food we eat comes from plants or animals. Since early days, man has used wood from trees for fuel and shelter. Biological resources, in turn, are dependent on other natural resources. Most plants and animals could not live without air, sunshine, soil, and water.

Mineral resources are less important in supporting life, but they are extremely important to modern living. Mineral fuels—including coal, oil, and natural gas—provide heat, light, and power for homes, factories, and vehicles. Minerals serve as raw materials for the production of finished goods, such as automobiles, clocks, dishes, and refrigerators.

The wealth of a nation depends to an important degree on its natural resources. Most wealthy, or *developed*, countries—including Canada, Russia, and the United States—are rich in natural resources. But some well-to-do nations, such as Denmark and Ireland, have few resources. Poor, or *underdeveloped*, countries generally have fewer resources, though some—like Peru and Congo (Kinshasa)—have many natural resources.

Conservation and Development. Since modern civilization—even life itself—is dependent on natural

Conservation Practices, such as the replanting and selective cutting of trees, help to preserve valuable natural resources.

American Forest Institute

resources, many persons have been concerned about whether there will always be enough. They have asked, for example, what will happen if all the world's petroleum, iron, or coal gets used up.

Scientists and economists believe that man can never use up all the mineral raw materials like iron, aluminum, sand, and fertilizer. There are sufficient quantities in the earth and the sea, and most of the materials can be used over and over. For example, scrap iron can be melted down and used again in steelmaking. However, men may have to explore farther and dig deeper to get what they need. Or they may have to substitute one material for another that has become too scarce. For example, aluminum may be used in place of copper for many purposes. While copper is scarce, deposits of bauxite and clay contain more aluminum than the world can ever use.

Mineral fuels are different and can all be used up. The earth contains enough mineral fuels to last only one or two centuries. When these supplies run out, man may depend more on atomic energy to power autos and factories and to heat homes. Even today, uranium and other atomic fuels generate electricity. Such fuels will last for many centuries. Sunlight is already used to run the instruments in space satellites, and may someday be used to provide abundant energy. See ATOMIC ENERGY; SOLAR ENERGY.

Preserving the delicate balance of nature in biological resources appears to be the most difficult and important part of saving our natural resources. Man has often upset this balance. For example, poor farming methods have ruined much fertile farmland and left it barren. Each year, millions of tons of fertile topsoil that could produce good crops are washed away by rains. Chemicals sprayed on crops and washed off by rain sometimes end up in rivers and streams. Some of these chemicals kill the fish in the streams. Some entire species of birds and animals have been killed off by hunters.

Fumes from automobiles and trucks and smoke from factories poison the air. This *air pollution* in many cities kills trees and endangers human health. As more cars and factories are built, the problem gets worse. To correct these conditions, man will have to make big changes in ways of traveling and in ways of generating heat and power. See AIR POLLUTION.

Even if natural resources are conserved and developed, the earth will be unable to provide enough food if the population increases too much. With much effort, the amount of land under cultivation could be doubled, and farms in many underdeveloped countries could produce three or four times as much as they now do. Scientists also believe that man can get much more food from the sea. All this might increase the food supply to 5 or even 10 times what it now is. But at the present rate of increase, the world's population would double in 32 years. If this rate of increase continued, population would be 8 times as large in 100 years, and 64 times as large in 200 years.　　　　NEAL POTTER

Related Articles in WORLD BOOK include:

Air	Industry (Natural	Water
Conservation	Resources)	Wildlife
Forest and	Mineral	Conservation
Forest Products	Soil	World (The
Game	Underdeveloped	Wealth of
	Country	Nations)

NATURAL SELECTION is a process of nature which was first explained by the English naturalist Charles Darwin. He believed it to be an important factor in the origin of new groups of plants and animals.

There is not nearly enough food, space, shelter, and other necessities for all the offspring that living things can produce. Living things, therefore, constantly compete with each other to live. Darwin's theory points out that even animals of the same kind are a little different from each other. In their struggle for existence, some will be a little better suited to live and have young. Others will be a little more likely to die or fail to produce offspring. This process is always going on, so the species lose unfavorable variations and keep the favorable ones. Variations can arise by *mutations*. Mutations are random changes in *genes* caused by radiation and certain chemicals found in the surroundings (see GENE). After thousands of years, the surviving members may be greatly different from their ancestors. The phrase "survival of the fittest" is applied to this process of change by natural selection. J. HERBERT TAYLOR

See also DARWIN (Charles Robert); EVOLUTION.

NATURAL TUNNEL. See VIRGINIA (Places to Visit).

NATURALISM, in literature, is the attempt to apply scientific theory and methods to imaginative writing. Naturalists concentrate on the physical world to the exclusion of the supernatural. Naturalism thrived in the late 1800's and early 1900's, and has been most important in the novel and in drama.

Theory of Naturalism. Naturalists have been the most uncompromising realists. They believe that knowledge is acquired through the senses, and that the function of the writer is to report accurately what he observes. The naturalist tries to be as objective as a laboratory scientist in dealing with his material. In his theory of life, he is more pessimistic than the realist. The realist believes man can make moral choices, but the naturalist believes man cannot. Naturalists believe that everything man does is determined by his heredity, his environment, or both. They try to show man trapped by one or both of these great forces over which he has no control.

In picturing man as trapped, the naturalist usually deals with the more sordid aspects of life. The characters in naturalistic literature are driven by their most basic urges. They are often brutal and usually failures. Their language is often coarse, their view of life hopeless, and their mood depressing. Yet in the best naturalistic works, there is a tone of compassion and even admiration for those who struggle against overwhelming odds.

Naturalism in Fiction. The principles of naturalistic fiction were first stated by the French author Émile Zola in *The Experimental Novel* (1880). Zola argued that the novelist should treat his material as a scientist treats his. Before 1880, psychological and physiological studies such as Zola recommended had appeared in works by Honoré de Balzac, Jules and Edmond de Goncourt, Gustave Flaubert, and other French writers. Zola's books shocked English and American readers, but his theories and novels established naturalism as an important literary movement.

Naturalism never became popular in England, but it has been a major influence in the United States since the 1890's. Stephen Crane, Hamlin Garland, and Frank

NATURALIST

Norris were the first Americans consciously to adopt the style. Most critics, however, consider Theodore Dreiser the best American naturalist. His novel *An American Tragedy* (1925) is a moving account of a young man trapped by circumstance. Later American naturalistic novelists include Nelson Algren, James T. Farrell, and Norman Mailer.

Naturalism in Drama has the same goals as naturalism in fiction. A highly realistic setting provides a sense of environment overwhelming the characters. The staging, acting, and plots are realistic and simple. Everything focuses upon the hopeless, but often admirable, struggle of the characters against fate.

Zola also led the movement in drama with his adaptation of his novel *Thérèse Raquin* into a play in 1873. August Strindberg of Sweden and Gerhart Hauptmann of Germany rank among the best European naturalistic playwrights. Strindberg's *The Father* (1887) and *Miss Julie* (1888) are two violent studies of sex. *The Weavers* (1892) by Hauptmann, a grim portrait of a workers' revolt, set the style for German naturalism. Naturalism also appears in plays by Henrik Ibsen of Norway and Leo Tolstoy and Maxim Gorky of Russia.

In the United States, naturalism became most popular and important in the plays of Eugene O'Neill. Many of O'Neill's plays, especially the trilogy *Mourning Becomes Electra* (1931), have pathetic characters and depressing atmosphere. Other American naturalistic playwrights include Sidney Kingsley, Arthur Miller, Clifford Odets, Elmer Rice, and Tennessee Williams.

Naturalism today has declined in influence, but its methods and its view of life are responsible for much of the imaginative power in today's fiction and drama. Excessive though naturalism may have been in its hopelessness and brutality, modern literature reveals life more honestly because of it.   JOHN C. GERBER

Each person mentioned in this article has a separate biography in WORLD BOOK.

NATURALIST. See NATURE STUDY with its list of Related Articles.

NATURALIZATION is the legal process by which a person changes his citizenship from one country to another. Not all countries have the same naturalization laws. The laws of most countries provide that a naturalized citizen has no further obligations to the land of his birth. He also loses any political rights there. He takes an oath of allegiance pledging loyalty to his adopted country.

In many countries, when a man is naturalized, his wife and minor children automatically become citizens. Unmarried women of legal age become naturalized in the same way that men do. Most countries that have compulsory military service do not allow men to become citizens of other countries until they have served their required time in the armed forces of the country of their birth. Occasionally a man leaves without performing this service. If he ever returns, he may still be forced to serve in the armed forces.

A naturalized citizen of the United States has the same rights as any other citizen, except that he cannot be elected President or Vice-President. He is entitled to full protection by the United States if he travels abroad. But, if he returns to the land of his birth, and

if that country has not honored his withdrawal of allegiance, the United States might have difficulty in protecting him.

Naturalization in the United States

The procedure for naturalization in the United States involves three steps. These are: (1) a petition for naturalization, (2) an investigation and interview, and (3) final hearings in court. The law no longer requires a person to "take out first papers," or file a *declaration of intention* to become an American citizen. Some aliens still file such a declaration, however, because they need it to practice a profession under the laws of some states.

Petition for Naturalization. The Immigration and Nationality Act of 1952 requires an alien to apply for a petition for naturalization. This form may be obtained from any office of the Immigration and Naturalization Service, a division of the Department of Justice, or from any court authorized to naturalize aliens.

Before applying, an alien must be at least 18 years old and must have been lawfully admitted to live permanently in the United States. He must have lived in the United States for five years and for the last six months in the state where he seeks to be naturalized. In some cases, he need only have lived three years in the United States. He must be of good moral character and "attached to the principles of the Constitution." The law states that an alien is not of good moral character if he is a drunkard, has committed adultery, has more than one wife, makes his living by gambling, has lied to the Immigration and Naturalization Service, has been in jail more than 180 days for any reason during his five years in the United States, or is a convicted murderer.

Investigation and Interview. Officers of the Immigration and Naturalization Service investigate and interview the alien. He must appear with two citizen-witnesses who vouch for his qualifications. He must show that he can read, write, and speak simple English, if he is physically able to do so. Aliens who were more than 50 years old on Dec. 24, 1952, and had lived in the United States for at least 20 years, are exempted from this literacy test. The alien must also show that he knows something of the history and the form of government of the United States. The Service then makes its recommendation to the naturalization court.

Final Hearings are held in public sessions of the court after the petition has been filed. If the Immigration and Naturalization Service denies an alien's petition, he may request an examination by the judge. If the court denies his petition, he can appeal to the next higher court.

If the court approves the petition, the alien takes an oath renouncing all foreign titles and allegiance to any other country. He pledges to support and defend the Constitution, and to bear arms on behalf of the United States, unless he can prove that he is a conscientious objector whose beliefs forbid him to bear arms. The court clerk then gives him a certificate of naturalization, and the alien becomes a citizen.

Naturalization in Other Countries

Naturalization procedure differs in every country. In France, Germany, Great Britain, Italy, and Spain, a department in the executive branch of the government supervises naturalization. In Belgium, the legislature grants citizenship. Each Swiss canton (state) has the authority to naturalize an alien.

In Canada, the minister of manpower and immigration issues certificates of citizenship through county and district courts. The Citizenship Act of 1946 recognizes two types of citizens: *natural-born*, and *other than natural-born*, or naturalized. Naturalization of aliens consists of three steps: (1) the petition for citizenship, (2) the hearing in court, and (3) taking the oath of allegiance in a second court hearing.

An alien generally must meet the following requirements for Canadian citizenship. He must be at least 21 years old, and have lived in Canada for a year before applying. He must have been lawfully admitted to live permanently in the country, and such residence must have been established for five years. He must be of good character, have an adequate knowledge of English or French, know the responsibilities of citizenship, and intend to live permanently in Canada.

The alien files his petition at the nearest court. The court posts the petition publicly for three months. At the court hearing, the alien must show evidence that he meets citizenship requirements. If the court approves, it sends the certified copy of the petition to the minister of manpower and immigration. The minister decides whether to issue a certificate of citizenship. If he does, the alien appears in court and takes the oath of allegiance. The court clerk endorses the certificate.

British Dominions and Colonies may naturalize aliens, but these persons do not then become citizens of other British dominions or colonies. All countries, however, recognize a person as a British subject if he is a naturalized citizen of the United Kingdom and its colonies under the British Nationality Act of 1948. This law provides that a citizen of any colony or of any member of the Commonwealth is a British subject, or a Commonwealth citizen.

Denaturalization

A naturalized citizen of the United States may be *denaturalized* or *expatriated*. The government may bring suit to *denaturalize* a person, or cancel his certificate of naturalization, based on his conduct and other circumstances *before* he was granted citizenship. The grounds for such action include the charges that he (1) concealed a fact bearing on his petition, (2) did not intend to live permanently in the United States, (3) took his oath with mental reservation, or (4) refused to testify before a congressional committee about his alleged subversive activities.

A naturalized citizen may also be *expatriated*, or be forced to give up his citizenship, because of acts he committed *after* he became a citizen. Such acts include becoming a citizen of another country, serving in the government or armed forces of another country, voting in another country's elections, formally renouncing United States citizenship, deserting the United States armed forces during time of war, avoiding military service, or committing treason. The Immigration and Nationality Act of 1952 provided that a naturalized citizen would lose his citizenship by living continuously in the country of his origin for more than three years. But the Supreme Court of the United States ruled in 1964 that this provision was unconstitutional.

The term *expatriation* also means voluntarily transferring allegiance from one country to another. See CITIZENSHIP (Expatriation).

History

Before the 1800's, a person always remained a citizen of his native land, no matter where he lived. According to an old saying in English common law, "Once an Englishman, always an Englishman." One of the causes of the War of 1812 was that the British arrested seamen who held American citizenship, but who had been born in Great Britain. In 1870, Britain finally recognized the right of an individual to *expatriate* himself, or leave the country and become the citizen of another country. Most governments have naturalization laws and recognize that their citizens can change citizenship.

United States naturalization laws caused other countries to liberalize their naturalization laws. The relaxed spirit of American laws spread first to the British dominions (in the late 1800's), then to South America, and later to Europe. Some European countries have even less strict laws regarding naturalized citizens than does the United States. In France, for example, a naturalized citizen can be elected president.

Nations usually make treaties concerning the rights of a naturalized citizen who returns to his native land. For example, a treaty between the United States and Italy provides that Italy may not claim naturalized Americans as citizens if they return to Italy during time of peace, but may do so in wartime.

In the United States. Congress passed its first naturalization law in 1790. This law gave certain courts the right to naturalize aliens. An alien could apply for citizenship after being in the country for two years. In 1795, the period of residence became five years, with one of these years spent in the state where the application was filed. An alien had to declare his intention to become a citizen at least three years before applying for citizenship. In 1906, Congress set up a Bureau of Immigration and Naturalization.

Originally, only "free white persons" could be naturalized. Negroes became eligible for naturalization in 1870. American Indians qualified in 1940. A law passed in 1943 allowed Chinese persons to be naturalized. Persons from India and the Philippines became eligible for U.S. citizenship in 1946. The Immigration and Nationality Act of 1952 removed all racial bars to naturalization in the United States. An average of 125,000 persons are naturalized yearly.

Status of Women. Before 1922, a woman's citizenship usually changed with that of her husband. A law passed that year provided that an alien woman does not automatically become a United States citizen through marriage to a citizen. She too must petition for naturalization. The alien wife or husband of a citizen may be naturalized after only three years' residence.

The Immigration and Nationality Act of 1952 combined in a single act all laws affecting naturalization and citizenship.　　　　　　　　ROBERT RIENOW

Related Articles in WORLD BOOK include:

Nature Study

Nature Study includes identifying wild animals and learning their habits. These boys are studying the tracks of a marsh bird in a wildlife refuge.

NATURE STUDY means watching and learning about the things in nature. A student of nature does not merely learn the names of a few birds and flowers and rocks. He observes what is new every time he goes outdoors. Then he finds out why these things happen and when they may occur again.

The nature student learns about every new bird and flower he sees. He knows when certain trees will bud and burst into bloom. He finds out why the white butterflies hover over the cabbages in summer. He watches long lines of ants and learns where they are going and why they are always so busy.

Almost always we associate nature study with the outdoors. Nature lovers like to be out in the fields, in the forest, on the mountains, or along the running streams. Nature lovers in the cities go to the parks or gardens if they cannot get into the open country.

Most persons think nature study is concerned only with living things—birds, wild animals, insects, fishes, frogs, snakes, trees, wild flowers, weeds, shrubs, water plants, and grasses. But nature study really includes any of the things or doings of the natural world about us.

Studying Nature

Activities of Nature Students are followed all year long, both outdoors and in the home. Most students learn the names of unfamiliar plants and animals. But they usually go further than just learning names. They want to be sure that they will know a new bird the next time they see it. The student learns the size, shape, and color of the bird and some of its habits. Sometimes he learns its song or call. He finds out what family, or group of similar birds, it belongs to. Perhaps the observer will watch the new bird for a long time. He will want to know what it eats, where it can be found most often, where it nests, how it cares for its young, and whether it remains all winter or goes south in the fall.

Another common activity of the nature student is collecting. The collection may be an aquarium of fresh-water animals and plants gathered from near-by streams and ponds. It may be a collection of rocks, minerals, leaves, wild flowers, ferns, or shells, or a wild-flower garden. All collectors are careful not to destroy the forms of life from which they take their specimens.

Other common activities of nature students are field trips and excursions, nature hikes, gardening, and caring for pets. Many students make wildlife photographs or take part in wildlife-protection projects. The wildlife-protection projects include such things as feeding birds in winter, providing field cover for birds and animals, winter protection, setting up watering places for animals, and building birdhouses.

The Student's Notebook is an important part of his hobby. He has many questions to ask about the things in nature. To find answers to his questions, he makes careful observations of the plants and animals that interest him. He repeats the observations. In this way he can find out if he always sees the same thing, or if the animal that he is watching always behaves the same way under the same conditions.

People cannot always remember later exactly what they have seen. Thus, it is desirable for nature observers to make notes on what they see. The record is often more complete if it contains sketches made in the field.

Nature notebooks help in comparing observations of other seasons with those made at this season. For example, someone may say, "Robins are back early this year." A bird record kept for several years would show whether or not robins were early in their return.

Equipment for Nature Hobbies will grow as the student becomes more interested in nature. There are, of course, the nature books and pictures. In time the student will want field glasses for observing birds and animals, and a camera for photographs. He may want various magnifiers, and perhaps even a microscope for examining tiny objects. There are also collecting jars, nets, labels, and mounts of all kinds.

Perhaps the best way to get started on a new nature hobby is to find someone who has made a beginning. There are always other naturalists (nature students) with whom to exchange experiences and possibly specimens. Some are young and some are old. But all like to exchange ideas about a nature hobby.

Information about Nature can be obtained from many different sources. The nature student can use them to compare his findings with those of others. He can talk with other workers, read nature books written by specialists, or visit the collections in the great natural-history museums. There are many useful articles about nature in THE WORLD BOOK ENCYCLOPEDIA. The student can use them to check his field observations against those of specialists in science and nature study.

Field Trips are an important part of nature study. Students frequently make large, colorful collections of butterflies that they find in woods and fields near their homes. They use specially designed nets to catch them.

Youth organizations such as the Boy Scouts, Camp Fire Girls, and Girl Scouts all have nature-study programs. The handbooks of these organizations are often useful. Many city parks have interesting trees and flowers, planted and labeled especially for nature students. The great state and national parks offer opportunities for study during vacations. Many of these parks have marked nature trails. Many also have nature directors who work with visitors.

Some cities have zoos and botanical gardens. Some have great natural-history museums with large collections of specimens. Often these specimens are arranged in natural groupings as they are found in nature. Examples of such fine museums are the National Museum in Washington, D.C., the American Museum of Natural History in New York City, and the Field Museum of Natural History in Chicago.

Most states now have state conservation departments to help preserve and build up the wildlife of the state. These departments publish useful bulletins.

There are a great many books on nature-study subjects. Some are stories about animal life and are to be read for the story appeal. Others are stories and records of explorers who have found interesting plants and animals in out-of-the-way places. Besides these, there are books to help in learning animals, insects, trees, birds, wild flowers, rocks, and stars. Often these are beautifully illustrated in colors. Some are expensive sets for fine libraries. Others are inexpensive pocket and field guides that the beginning student can buy for his own use. Every public library has many books about nature.

Nature Study Is a Science. At one time many schools and colleges had classes in nature study. But some

Killing Jar

Tweezers

Setting Board for Drying Specimens

Magnifying Glass

The Butterfly Collector's Equipment includes his net and a killing jar containing poison-soaked cotton. He also needs rustproof pins for mounting butterflies, first on a setting board, and then in boxes. Tweezers and a magnifying glass help him work.

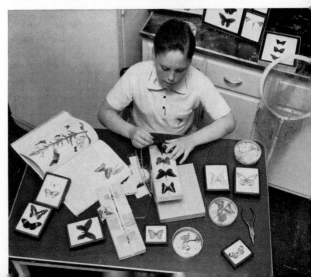

Photos by Lars H. Hedman

Aquariums provide students with an opportunity to study water life. They are glass containers in which fish and water animals are kept in surroundings that resemble those of the sea. Museums that house water plants and animals are also called *aquariums*.

Feathers make an interesting, colorful collection. They can be gathered outdoors and mounted on cardboard with a description of each feather and the bird it comes from. Students also may take photographs of different kinds of birds in their natural settings.

Pressed and Framed Leaves help nature students learn more about trees. Leaves should be dried and placed in a frame with a transparent cover. A description of each leaf should be put on the cover to help students identify various trees.

Insects can be kept in jars for study purposes. Grass and weeds should be planted in the jars to create natural surroundings for the insects. Holes in the tops of the jars will permit the insects to have air, and labels will identify the type in each jar.

science teachers objected. They said that people who are interested in nature study are carried away by their love of the beauties of nature. They said that much of the nature study was not good science. And they accused the nature students of careless work and inaccurate observations. For this reason, nature study is not so popular in schools as it once was. Schools now have classes in elementary science instead. But nature students can get much help from these science classes.

Much of our scientific knowledge has been gathered through careful and repeated observations of students of nature. Famous persons have been both naturalists and scientists. The nature student can read about Roy Chapman Andrews, Liberty Hyde Bailey, William Beebe, Frank M. Chapman, Anna Botsford Comstock, Charles Darwin, Raymond L. Ditmars, Henri Fabre, David Fairchild, William T. Hornaday, and John Muir.

For people who like to be outdoors and who are interested in animals, plants, rocks, or stars, nature study offers worthy and enjoyable hobbies. These can be carried on throughout life and will always provide something new. New material can be found everywhere.

Suggestions for Things to Do

1. Ask your teacher at school, or the librarian of your local public library, for the address of the Audubon Society nearest to you. Write to this address and ask for a price list of the pictures of birds. Buy a set of bird cards for the birds most often found in your region. Learn as many of these birds as you can in a season.

2. With a group of friends, find a path through a neighboring woods that has interesting natural features. If possible, find a path that reaches a stream, pond, or lake. Be sure to ask permission of the owner to use this path. Mark it as a nature trail with names of trees, shrubs, and wild flowers. Show spots where birds, squirrels, and other animals are usually seen. Perhaps you can get help with this project from your science teacher, a Scout leader, or a Camp Fire guardian.

3. If you have a camera, make a collection of photographs of 12 or 15 trees in winter and summer. Mount the photos and label each tree with its correct name.

4. Make three wren houses. Be sure to make the openings just one inch across so that wrens can get in and sparrows cannot. Put these houses up in suitable places about the lawn at home. If you can, also put up a bird bath where the birds can drink and splash about.

5. Set up a winter bird-feeding station outside a south or an east window. Insect-eating birds, such as woodpeckers, chickadees, or jays, will feed on bits of suet tied to the feeder or to the limb of a tree. Seed-eating birds, such as cardinals or juncos, feed on many kinds of small seeds, sunflower seeds, or cracked grain.

6. Make a tree-flowering calendar that shows the

dates when trees in your area bloom in the spring. Mark the dates when fruit trees bloom. You may also record when these trees have seeds or fruit. RALPH K. WATKINS

Related Articles in WORLD BOOK include:

AMERICAN NATURALISTS

Agassiz (family)	Beebe, William	Osborn (Henry F.)
Andrews, Roy	Bessey, Charles E.	Seton, Ernest
Chapman	Burroughs, John	Thompson
Audubon, John J.	Muir, John	Vogt, William
Beard, Daniel C.		

BRITISH NATURALISTS

Bewick, Thomas	Murray, Sir John
Darwin (Charles R.)	Sloane, Sir Hans
Hudson, William H.	Wallace, Alfred R.

OTHER NATURALISTS

Asbjørnsen, Peter C.	De Vries, Hugo
Cohn, Ferdinand J.	Fabre, Jean H. C.
Cuvier, Baron	Lamarck, Chevalier de

SOME NATURE STUDY SUBJECTS

Animal	Earth	Insect	Seed
Astronomy	Fish	Lake	Star
Balance of	Flower	Leaf	Tree
Nature	Forest and	Mountain	Vegetable
Bird	Forest Products	Ocean	Volcano
Botany	Fruit	Plant	Water
Butterfly	Game	River	Waterfall
Conservation	Gardening	Rock	Weather
Constellation	Geology	Season	Zoology
Desert	Hobby		

NATURE STUDY ORGANIZATIONS

Academy of Natural Sciences of Philadelphia	Girl Scouts
	Izaak Walton League
American Forestry Association	of America
Audubon Society, National	Woodcraft League of
Boy Scouts	America
Camp Fire Girls	

OTHER RELATED ARTICLES

Aquarium	National Forest	Planetarium
Arbor Day	National Park System	Telescope
Botanical Garden	Observatory	Terrarium
Museum	Park	Zoo

NATURE WORSHIP has been part of the religion of many lands. It considers the objects and forces of nature sacred. In times past, people have worshiped mountains, springs, rivers, fields, and even the earth itself. Objects in nature were often seen as gods in the mythology of Greece and Rome. The sun, for instance, was a god who drove a flaming chariot across the sky. The moon was believed to be a goddess called Selene. Hindus worshiped the winds, and Persians the rainbow. The Maypole dance is possibly a survival of the worship of the oak tree by the ancient Britons, Vikings, and Slavs. WILSON D. WALLIS

See also ANIMISM; MAY DAY; MOTHER; PANTHEISM.

NAUGATUCK, *NAW guh tuck,* Conn. (pop. 23,034; alt. 195 ft.), lies on the Naugatuck River 4 miles south of Waterbury (see CONNECTICUT [political map]). An old *green* (public square) is in the center of Naugatuck. This industrial city produces candy, chemicals, chewing gum, rubber goods, and safety pins.

Naugatuck received a town charter in 1844, but settlers had lived in the area since 1704. Charles Goodyear built a rubber mill in Naugatuck in 1843. The city was chartered as a borough in 1893. It has a borough form of government. ALBERT E. VAN DUSEN

NAURU

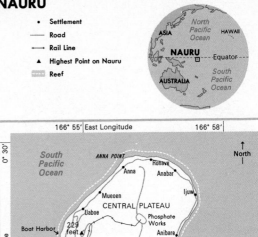

- • Settlement
- — Road
- ←→ Rail Line
- ▲ Highest Point on Nauru
- ▨ Reef

166° 55′ East Longitude   166° 58′

WORLD BOOK map-GJa

NAURU, *NAH roo,* is a small island country in the central Pacific Ocean. It has an area of 8 square miles and a population of about 7,000. Nauru is the third smallest country in the world. Only Vatican City and Monaco are smaller. Nauru is rich in *phosphates*—valuable chemical compounds used in making fertilizers. Phosphate exports earn about $11 million a year for the government of Nauru. The government has used some of the income to build homes, schools, and hospitals. The government has also saved much of the income to help support the Nauruan people after all the phosphates have been mined.

Government. Nauru is a republic. Its government consists of a Parliament, a Council of State, and a Supreme Court. The 18 members of the Parliament are elected by the people. All Nauruans 20 years old or more may vote. Parliament chooses five of its members to serve on the Council of State, which names one of its members as president. The president and the council administer the government.

Land. Nauru, an oval-shaped coral island, lies 33 miles south of the equator. Most of the island is a

───────── FACTS IN BRIEF ─────────

Capital: None.

Official Languages: English, Nauruan.

Area: 8 square miles. *Coastline*—12 miles.

Population: *1966 Census*—6,056; *Estimated 1972 Population*—7,000; density, 875 persons to the square mile. *Estimated 1977 Population*—9,000.

Chief Product: Phosphates.

Flag: A horizontal gold stripe crosses a field of royal blue. Below the stripe is a white 12-pointed star. See FLAG (color picture: Flags of Asia and the Pacific).

Money: Australian dollar. See MONEY (table: Values).

57

The Chambered Nautilus. The shell shown here has been cut lengthwise to expose its many chambers of increasing size. As the nautilus outgrew each chamber, it moved forward in the shell and built a pearly partition behind it.

American Museum of Natural History

200-foot-high plateau containing deposits of phosphates. Near the center of the plateau is a lagoon surrounded by a belt of fertile land. Another belt of fertile land extends around the coast. Most of the people live along the coast. In the past, the people raised their own food. Now, they import most of their food and the other products they need. Nauru has a tropical climate cooled by trade winds. Temperatures range from 76° F. to 93° F. About 80 inches of rain falls yearly.

People. About half of Nauru's population are Nauruans—people of mixed Polynesian, Micronesian, and Melanesian ancestry. They are Christians. Most of them speak both the Nauruan language and English. Most Nauruan men work in the phosphate industry. The rest of Nauru's people are from the Gilbert and Ellice islands, Hong Kong, and Australia. They come for limited periods of time to help mine the phosphates.

The government provides Nauruans with modern homes at low rents, and 2 government hospitals and 11 clinics give them free medical care. The law requires Nauruan children between the ages of 6 and 17 to attend school. Nauru has two elementary schools, a high school, a Roman Catholic mission school, and a teacher training center. The government pays the expenses of students who go to college in other countries.

Economy. Phosphates are Nauru's only important resource and the country's only export. The government is trying to build a shipping industry. It also encourages such local industries as fishing and canoe building. Imported products include food, machinery, automobiles, furniture, shoes, and medicine.

History. John Fearn, an English explorer, was the first European to visit Nauru. He came in 1798. In 1888, Germany took over the island and administered it until 1914 when Australia took control. After World War I, Australia began to administer the island under a League of Nations mandate held also by Great Britain and New Zealand.

Japan seized Nauru during World War II. In 1945, Australian forces retook the island. In 1947, the United Nations provided for Australian control of the island under a trusteeship held also by Great Britain and New Zealand. In 1964, Nauru began to work for independence and control of the phosphate industry. The U.N.

granted Nauru independence in 1968. In 1970, the Nauruan government gained control of the phosphate industry. PETER PIRIE

NAUSEA, *NAW she uh,* or *NAW see uh,* is a disagreeable sensation best described by the familiar phrase "sick to my stomach." The word is strongly associated with seasickness. In fact, the word comes from Greek and Latin roots which mean *pertaining to the sea.* It is closely related in its origin to the words *nautical* and *navigate.*

In nausea the stomach muscle contracts gently in a direction that is the opposite of its normal contraction. A stronger contraction in this direction causes vomiting and the food is brought up into the mouth.

There are many causes of nausea, both physical and mental. Mental causes include revolting sights, disgusting odors, and sudden fright. Physical causes include severe pain arising anywhere in the body, blockage or obstruction of the digestive tract, and the stimulation of our balancing organs, the semicircular canals in the ears. Nausea often accompanies pregnancy, especially during the first three months.

The sensation of nausea may be produced by stimulating certain nerves which have their centers in the part of the brain called the *medulla.* It may come from the digestive tract or other parts of the body, from higher centers in the brain, or as a direct result of outside agents such as the drugs morphine and digitalis.

The tendency to nausea varies widely among different persons. Some can endure the tossing of a ship on the roughest sea without discomfort. Others are nauseated merely by the gentle swaying motion of a swing or hammock.

A tendency to nausea is sometimes a symptom of disease. Anyone who suffers from chronic attacks should consult a physician. E. CLINTON TEXTER, JR.

See also CHLORPROMAZINE.

NAUSICAA, *naw SIK ay uh,* is a character in the famous Greek epic the *Odyssey.* She was the daughter of Alcinous, king of the Phaeacians, and Arete. Nausicaa found Ulysses after he was shipwrecked on the shore of Scheria and conducted him to the court of her father.

NAUTCH. See DANCING (The Far East).

NAUTICAL ALMANAC. See NAVIGATION (Celestial Navigation).

NAUTICAL BELL. See Ship (Nautical Terms [Ship's Bell]).

NAUTICAL MILE. See Knot; Mile.

NAUTICAL TERMS. See Ship.

NAUTILUS. See Submarine (Development).

NAUTILUS, *NAW tuh lus*, is a sea animal whose soft body is partly covered with a coiled shell. The nautilus belongs to the same class of animals as the squid and octopus. A nautilus shell contains about 30 chambers which are lined with a rainbow-colored substance called *mother-of-pearl* or *nacre*. Because of this substance, the animal is often called a *pearly nautilus*. The nautilus lives at depths of from 20 to 1,000 feet in the South Pacific and Indian oceans. It feeds on lobsters and crabs. Only 5 species of nautilus are living today, although at least 2,000 fossil forms are known.

The body of a full-grown nautilus is about the size of a man's fist. Its cone-shaped head is surrounded by about 90 short *tentacles* (feelers). As the animal grows, its shell develops in the form of a spiral. The nautilus adds a new chamber to its shell each time it outgrows its old one. Each new chamber is closed at the rear, so the animal always lives in the outermost chamber of its shell. The closed chambers behind the animal are filled with a gas composed mainly of nitrogen. The *siphuncle*, a coiled, blood-filled tube enclosed in a limy covering, extends through all the chambers.

Scientific Classification. The nautilus is in the phylum *Mollusca*. It belongs to the nautilus family, *Nautiliidae*. The pearly nautilus is genus *Nautilus*, species *N. pompilius*. R. Tucker Abbott

See also Argonaut; Shell (Octopuses and Squids).

NAUVOO. See Illinois (Places to Visit); Mormons (Mormons in the Middle West); Smith, Joseph (Life at Nauvoo).

NAVAHO INDIANS, *NAV uh hoh*, also spelled Navajo, are a tribe in the Southwestern United States related to the Apache. Both groups probably wandered down from Canada into Arizona and New Mexico around A.D. 1000. The Navaho settled near the peaceful Pueblo Indians, who taught them to raise corn and to weave. The Pueblo also taught the Navaho how to make sand paintings (see Sand Painting).

After Spanish and American colonists settled in the Southwest, the Navaho raided their ranches for horses and sheep. Finally, in 1863, Kit Carson rounded up the Indians and marched them to Fort Sumner, N.Mex. (see Indian Wars [Desert Battleground]). Today, most of the more than 80,000 Navaho live on a large reservation in Arizona, New Mexico, and Utah. Many still use the traditional Navaho house, the *hogan* (see Hogan). They make a living as farmers, sheep raisers, and laborers. Many own timber, oil, gas, and uranium enterprises. Skilled craftsmen make silver jewelry, and women weave colorful rugs. Many Navaho artists paint murals and water colors. Bertha P. Dutton

See also Indian, American (Indians of the Southwest; pictures); Arizona (picture).

NAVAJO NATIONAL MONUMENT is in northern Arizona. It contains three of the largest and most elaborate of known cliff dwellings. The Navajo Indian Reservation completely surrounds the 360-acre monument. The monument was established in 1909.

NAVAL ACADEMY, UNITED STATES. See United States Naval Academy.

NAVAL ATTACHÉ. See Attaché.

NAVAL OBSERVATORY, UNITED STATES. Scientists at the United States Naval Observatory in Washington, D.C., study the stars, magnetism, and other facts and events in nature. They conduct studies to make time measurements more accurate throughout the world. The Naval Observatory also supplies official time signals to regulate clocks throughout the United States and its possessions. The Naval Observatory was established by the federal government in 1842. It is under the jurisdiction of the chief of naval operations. See also Newcomb, Simon. Payson S. Wild

NAVAL POSTGRADUATE SCHOOL. See Universities and Colleges (table).

NAVAL RESERVE. See Navy, United States.

NAVAL SHIPYARD is a waterside area where naval vessels are built or where logistic support is provided for the operating fleet. It is responsible for repairing damaged vessels and for overhauling ships after long periods at sea. It also alters or converts ships, and installs new types of gear and equipment. John A. Oudine

Related Articles in World Book include:

Boston Naval Base	Mare Island Naval Shipyard
Charleston Naval Base	Norfolk Naval Base
Key West Naval Base	Philadelphia Naval Base
Los Angeles Naval	Portsmouth Naval Shipyard
Base	Puget Sound Naval Shipyard

NAVAL STORES. In the days of wooden sailing ships, the term *naval stores* referred to tar and pitch. These two materials were essential for shipbuilding. Today, the term includes the rosin, turpentine, pitch, and tar products from pine and other resinous trees.

NAVAL WAR COLLEGE, in Newport, R.I., is the highest educational institution of the United States Navy. It prepares officers for higher command by teaching them the fundamentals of warfare, international relations, and interservice operations. The Navy Electronic Warfare Simulator, which imitates actual combat conditions, aids in the study of combat methods.

The staff and students of the Naval War College represent all the armed services. Since 1956, the college has offered a command course for officers from other countries. Commodore Stephen B. Luce, the college's first president, founded the Naval War College in 1884. The college is also the headquarters for the Institute of Naval Studies. The institute's functions include long-range studies on how to use changes in science and technology. John A. Oudine

NAVAL WEAPONS PLANT, UNITED STATES. See Washington Navy Yard.

NAVARINO, BATTLE OF. See Greece (Independence).

NAVARRE, *nuh VAHR*, was once an independent kingdom which included a small part of southern France. It now forms the modern Spanish province of Navarre and the western part of the French department of Basses-Pyrénées. It covers an area of 4,056 square miles. Its largest city is Pamplona.

Navarre is famous for its orchards and vineyards. Important products include flax, olive oil, hemp, livestock, lumber, fish, and small game. Walter C. Langsam

NAVE. See Basilica; Cathedral.

NAVEL. See Umbilical Cord.

1. A navigator can use the stars to help determine his ship's position on the ocean.

U.S. Lines

NAVIGATION, NAV *ih GAY shun,* is the means of finding your way from one place to another and knowing where you are along the way. To find your way to a friend's house you follow such instructions as, "Go eight blocks north and six blocks east. The house is next to a grocery store. The address is 631 Stewart Street." *You are navigating* when you count the blocks you travel in each direction, look for the grocery store, and check the address of your friend's house. See DIRECTION.

Usually, however, when we speak of navigation we refer to guiding ships or aircraft from one place to another. The word *navigate* comes from two Latin words, *navis,* meaning *ship,* and *agere,* meaning to *direct.*

Methods of Navigation

Principles of Navigation. Navigators on ships and aircraft must work mathematical problems to find where they are in relation to landmarks and stars. To solve these problems, the navigator uses navigational aids and instruments to get information about (1) *time,* (2) *direction,* (3) *distance,* (4) *speed,* and (5) *position.* With this information, the navigator figures out (1) what course he should steer to arrive at his destination, and (2) what speed he should use to arrive there at a certain time. The navigator uses algebra, geometry, and trigonometry in solving his problems.

There are four general methods of navigation. These are (1) *dead reckoning,* (2) *piloting,* (3) *celestial navigation,* and (4) *electronic navigation.* The four methods generally are used in combination with each other.

Dead Reckoning is a means of figuring, or *reckoning,* courses and distances from a known position by marking, or *plotting,* the ship's course and speed on a chart. The navigator figures out the distance traveled by multiplying the speed by the time traveled. Dead reckoning is the basis of all navigation and is used whether or not other methods are available or are used.

Piloting, called *contact flying* by airmen, is a means of navigating by watching for landmarks. The ship navigator uses piloting, when close to land, by watching for lighthouses, buoys, and other landmarks. The air navigator checks his position when contact flying by using such landmarks as rivers, bridges, and highways.

Celestial Navigation is a means of checking a position by observing the sun, moon, planets, and stars. The ship navigator carries with him a book called the *Nautical Almanac.* This book gives the exact position of each heavenly body for exact times and dates. It tells the position of the heavenly body if it were to drop straight to earth at any instant. By observing the direction, or *bearing,* of a star, and by measuring its angle above the horizon, the navigator can figure out how far he is from the earthly position of the star. One observation gives a *circle of position,* but the circle is so large it is considered a straight line. This line is called a *line of position.* By observing several heavenly bodies, the navigator obtains several of these lines of position. The spot where the lines cross on his chart marks a *celestial fix,* or the position of his craft. The time used by a navigator for celestial navigation is *Greenwich Mean Time* (GMT), or the time it is in Greenwich, England. See GREENWICH OBSERVATORY, ROYAL.

Electronic Navigation makes use of such electronic devices as voice and code radio, radio direction finders, loran, shoran, radar, and electronic depth finders.

A Trip with a Ship Navigator

Leaving Port. Before the ship gets under way for the voyage, the navigator makes sure he has all the necessary navigation charts, books, and instruments aboard. Then he stands by on the bridge with the captain while a local pilot familiar with the harbor steers, or *cons,* the ship out into deep water. When the pilot turns the ship over to the captain and gets off to return to port, the navigator determines the position of the ship and the exact time. This position, or *fix,* is known as the *point of departure.* It might be the time when the ship passes close to a buoy. The navigator simply marks a small circle on the chart and notes the time.

Near Land the navigator is a busy but unhurried person. He draws on a large-scale Mercator chart the course the ship is to follow (see MAP [Cylindrical Projections]). He observes lighthouses and other landmarks to get their bearing from the ship. He plots each bearing on the chart. Each bearing line is a line of position. When the navigator obtains two lines of position, the spot where they cross gives the exact location of the ship. He plots the position on the chart and notes its latitude and longitude in the *navigator's notebook.* He also keeps a close check on the depth of the water by taking soundings with the *fathometer.*

At Sea. As the ship steams away from land, the navigator does not need to check the ship's position so frequently. He plots the ship's course and speed on the chart by dead reckoning. During the day he regularly observes the sun and makes lines of position from his observations.

On clear nights, shortly after sunset and shortly

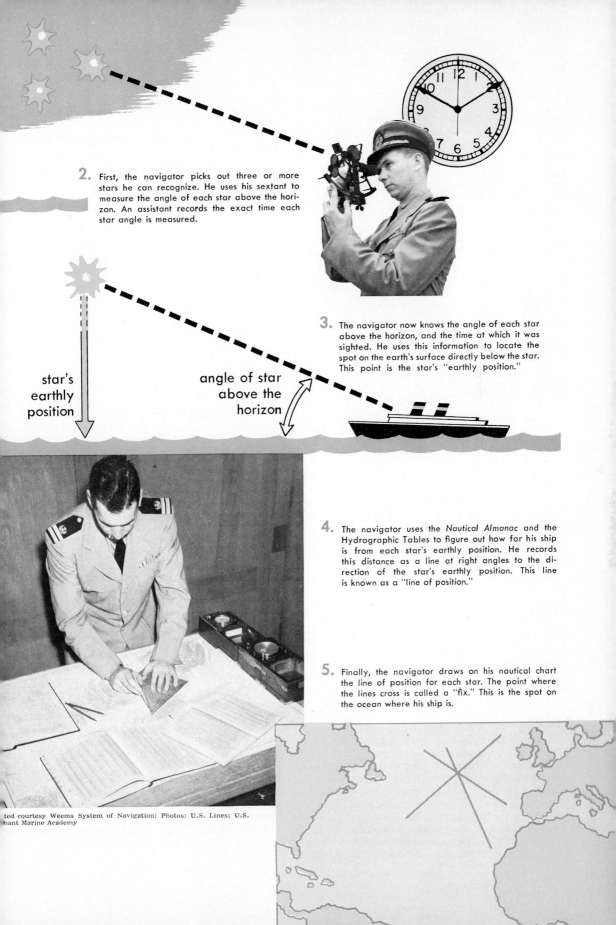

2. First, the navigator picks out three or more stars he can recognize. He uses his sextant to measure the angle of each star above the horizon. An assistant records the exact time each star angle is measured.

star's earthly position

angle of star above the horizon

3. The navigator now knows the angle of each star above the horizon, and the time at which it was sighted. He uses this information to locate the spot on the earth's surface directly below the star. This point is the star's "earthly position."

4. The navigator uses the *Nautical Almanac* and the Hydrographic Tables to figure out how far his ship is from each star's earthly position. He records this distance as a line at right angles to the direction of the star's earthly position. This line is known as a "line of position."

5. Finally, the navigator draws on his nautical chart the line of position for each star. The point where the lines cross is called a "fix." This is the spot on the ocean where his ship is.

...ted courtesy Weems System of Navigation; Photos: U.S. Lines; U.S. ...hant Marine Academy

Azimuth Circle, or **Bearing Circle,** is mounted on a gyro-compass repeater on the wing of a ship's bridge. It is used to determine the direction of objects from the ship.

before sunrise, the navigator figures out his position by observing the stars. He looks up at the sky until he finds a familiar star, such as Betelgeuse in the constellation Orion. The navigator then sights at the star through his *sextant* to measure its angle above the horizon. Meanwhile, one of his assistants measures the direction of Betelgeuse from the ship. A second assistant stands by with a stop watch. When the navigator calls out "Mark!" the second assistant writes down the time, the angle of Betelgeuse above the horizon, and its bearing. The navigator makes such observations on several stars. Then he and his assistants go into the lighted charthouse and figure out the ship's position.

If the sky is cloudy or foggy, the navigator must depend on electronic devices to tell him his position. If he is within a few hundred miles of land, he may use the radio direction finder to give him lines of position on radio beacons. If he is farther out to sea, he may use a loran receiving set to obtain lines of position on loran transmitting stations.

The good navigator also must be a weather forecaster. He must have training in meteorology and be able to read weather instruments.

Approaching Land. The first land sighted after a voyage is called a *landfall*. The navigator checks the landfall on his chart to make sure his navigation has been accurate. If the weather is stormy or foggy, the navigator depends on radar in approaching his destination. A *plan position indicator*, or *p.p.i.*, on the radar continuously provides the navigator with a circular map-picture of the sea and shoreline, with the ship at the center of the map. Ships and buoys also are shown on the radar screen, making it possible to pass safely through heavy traffic in a fog. From the radar operator, the navigator receives accurate distances and bearings on landmarks. The navigator also keeps a close check on the depth of the water by using a fathometer. When the ship arrives at the entrance to the harbor, a local pilot usually comes aboard and takes charge of conning the ship into port.

Air Navigation

The air navigator's work is much the same as that of the ship navigator. However, he has less time in which to do it because aircraft travel much faster than ships. See AIRPLANE (A Trip in an Airliner).

The air navigator is much more concerned with wind than the ship navigator is. This is because wind can change the course and speed of an aircraft more easily. In celestial navigation, the air navigator must use an artificial horizon in measuring the angles of heavenly bodies above the earth. He uses an *Air Almanac* to find the positions of heavenly bodies. The air navigator also has many special electronic instruments and aids to help him. Air navigation is sometimes called *avigation*.

Space Navigation

Scientists who are looking ahead to the building of spaceships for travel from the earth to other planets have worked out the problem of navigating in space, or *astrogation*. The navigator, or *astrogator*, of a space ship would have to have a special almanac with tables giving the positions of planets in relation to the sun at any time. The astrogator would measure the angle between the sun and each of at least two planets, then compute his distance from the sun by simple geometry. See SPACE TRAVEL (Aiming at the Moon).

Navigation Aids and Instruments

Aids. Most aids to navigation, such as buoys and lighthouses, are provided and maintained by the federal government. This is because safe sea and air commerce are vital to our way of life. The most important aid to navigation is an accurate *chart* which covers the area of the trip. Charts are marked in latitude and longitude and provide means of identifying any point on land or in coastal and inland waters. For details on many important aids to navigation, see separate articles listed in the *Related Articles* at the end of this article. Other navigation aids include:

Fog Signals, such as bells, whistles, and sirens, which can be identified easily in fog or darkness at a particular spot on the navigator's chart.

Light Lists, books which contain complete descriptions of each navigation aid maintained by the government, so that navigators can tell one lighthouse from another.

Nautical Almanac, a publication which contains tables of information about the position of stars.

Notices to Mariners, publications which regularly inform navigators of changes in aids to navigation.

Range Lights, two lights located some distance apart and one over the other, to mark the center line of a harbor channel.

Tide and Current Tables, publications which tell the navigator when to expect tides and currents in each locality.

Astrolabe was used by navigators before the invention of the sextant to determine the angle of stars above the horizon.

Press Syndicate

Instruments. These are devices for determining the depth of water, the exact time of day, the direction the ship is traveling, the distance traveled, the ship's speed, and its position. The most important navigation instruments are the *compass*, which tells direction, and the

Gyropilot automatically steers a ship on a course figured out by the navigator. Such equipment as this on a modern ocean liner helps make the navigator's job easier today.

Sperry Gyroscope Co.

chronometer, which tells time. A navigator also uses simple instruments to plot positions on a chart, such as a *geometry compass, dividers, parallel rules,* a *straightedge,* and a *protractor*. Other instruments include:

Azimuth Circle, or *Bearing Circle,* a device like a gunsight mounted on a movable ring on a stand called a *pelorus* which contains a compass. By sighting through the azimuth circle, the navigator can determine the bearing of an object from his craft.

Computer, a device which the navigator uses to work out mathematical problems of time, speed, and distance. It may be a circular slide rule or a complicated electronic machine.

Plotter, a device combining a protractor with a ruler. It is used in plotting positions on a chart.

Plotting Board, or *Maneuvering Board,* a graph with

─────── **RED-LETTER DATES IN NAVIGATION** ───────

1100?-1200? Magnetic compass used by Chinese and Mediterranean sailors.
1519-1522 First circumnavigation of the earth by Ferdinand Magellan's fleet.
1569? Mercator chart invented by Gerhardus Mercator.
1730 Reflecting sextant invented, independently, by John Hadley in England and Thomas Godfrey in America.
1733 Bubble sextant, or artificial horizon sextant, invented by John Hadley. It made long-range air navigation possible 200 years later.
1735 First accurate chronometer made by John Harrison in England.
1767 First nautical almanac published in England by Nevil Maskelyne, an astronomer.
1767 Buoys first used in navigable waters of America, in the Delaware River.
1789 Federal maintenance of lighthouses voted by first Congress of the United States.
1802 *American Practical Navigator* published by Nathaniel Bowditch.
1807 Coast Survey Bureau authorized by the United States Congress.
1837 Line of Position, or the Sumner Line, first discovered and used by Captain Thomas H. Sumner of Massachusetts.
1842 Ocean currents charted by Lieutenant Matthew F. Maury of the United States Navy. Maury helped found the U.S. Naval Observatory and the Hydrographic Office.
1881 First lighted buoy put in service outside New York Harbor. It burned oil gas.
1885 First bell buoy put in service in the United States.
1896 Ship-to-shore radio signals sent by Guglielmo Marconi.
1906 Gyroscopic compass invented by Hermann Anschütz-Kämpfe in Germany.
1910 Plane-to-ground radio messages sent over New York City by J. A. D. McCurdy.
1922 Radar effects first noted by A. Hoyt Taylor at Washington, D.C. This led to the development of radar in World War II.
1928 Second-setting watch for navigators invented by P. V. H. Weems in the United States.
1933 First air almanac prepared by P. V. H. Weems.
1940 Principle of loran discovered by Alfred L. Loomis. This led to the building of the first four loran transmitting stations by the U.S. government in 1942.
1953 Inertial guidance system developed. It navigates automatically without using outside signals, and can be used on ships, airplanes, and missiles.

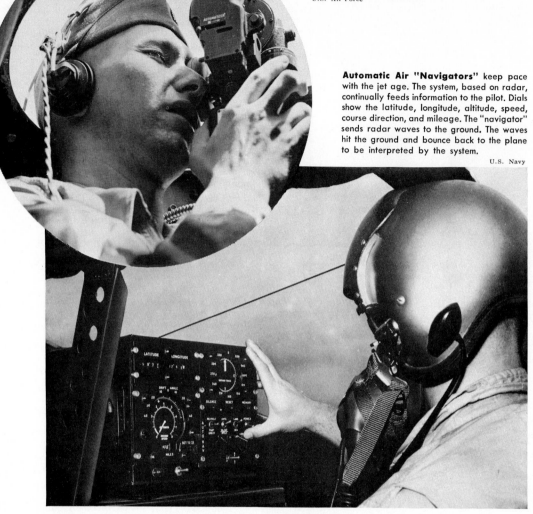

An Air Force Navigator, *left*, takes a "fix" on the sun. His navigational equipment will indicate the exact position of the plane, its speed, direction, and height. These instruments also tell how much the plane is drifting. All this information enables the navigator to direct the course of the plane.
U.S. Air Force

Automatic Air "Navigators" keep pace with the jet age. The system, based on radar, continually feeds information to the pilot. Dials show the latitude, longitude, altitude, speed, course direction, and mileage. The "navigator" sends radar waves to the ground. The waves hit the ground and bounce back to the plane to be interpreted by the system.
U.S. Navy

concentric circles, used in solving triangle problems.

Star Finder, a map of the stars used by the navigator to identify stars used in celestial navigation.

History of Navigation

Early Navigators. For thousands of years man has sailed the seas. Early seafaring men such as the Phoenicians, the Carthaginians, and the Greeks moved chiefly from point to point along the coasts.

Scientific navigation began to develop in the 1100's. Crude magnetic compasses came into use. Prince Henry of Portugal (1394-1460) established an observatory and school in navigation at Sagres, Portugal, and was known as Henry the Navigator. He encouraged Portuguese sailors to sail to remote seas.

Early explorers were aided by the invention of the *astrolabe.* The astrolabe was a graduated circle with sights down which the navigator could roughly measure the angle between the horizon and heavenly bodies.

In the 1700's, the invention of the accurate chronometer and the sextant, which replaced the astrolabe, made it possible for navigators to know exactly where they were, even when far from land.

Modern Navigation. The invention of radio and its use on ships and aircraft at the beginning of the 1900's marked the start of electronic navigation (see RADIO [Navigation]). The development of electronic depth finders made it possible for ships to sail in shallow waters with less danger of going aground. The development of radar during World War II made navigation safer at night and in fog. *Loran* (**LO**ng **RA**nge **N**avigation) was invented in 1940. This system uses fixed radio station signals to determine the exact position of the navigator. After World War II, automatic navigation devices were developed for guided missiles (see GUIDED MISSILE). Other devices automatically computed celestial fixes and measured distances.

The United States Coast Guard today maintains over 36,000 marine-navigation aids along more than 40,000 miles of seacoasts and navigable waters of the United States. The Federal Aviation Administration provides air-navigation aids, such as light beacons and markers painted on the tops of buildings, for over 70,000 miles of airways in the United States.   P. V. H. WEEMS

Related Articles in WORLD BOOK include:

Electronic Navigation Instruments play a vital part in modern aviation. This Air Force navigator uses information from his *loran* equipment to plot his ship's position on a chart. Loran, or **LO**ng **RA**nge **N**avigation, uses signals from fixed radio stations to determine a plane's location.

United Aircraft Corp.

NAVIGATION SATELLITE

Greenwich Observatory, Royal	Longitude	Tide
	Meridian	Time
Knot	North Star	Trade Wind
Latitude	Sailing	

Outline

I. Methods of Navigation
  A. Principles of Navigation
  B. Dead Reckoning
  C. Piloting
  D. Celestial Navigation
  E. Electronic Navigation

II. A Trip with a Ship Navigator
  A. Leaving Port   C. At Sea
  B. Near Land   D. Approaching Land

III. Air Navigation

IV. Space Navigation

V. Navigation Aids and Instruments
  A. Aids   B. Instruments

VI. History of Navigation

Questions

What information is provided by navigational instruments?

What is dead reckoning? Piloting?

How is celestial navigation done?

What is loran?

What is an astrolabe?

How does a sextant help the navigator?

NAVIGATION ACT. Several laws passed in the 1600's by the English Parliament were called the Navigation Acts. The purpose of the laws was to protect English trade. In 1645 a law forbade the importation of whale oil into England in vessels other than English, or in ships which were not manned by English sailors.

The act known officially as the First Navigation Act was passed by Parliament in 1651. This act was aimed against the English colonies and the Dutch, who were enjoying a greater part of the carrying trade between the West Indies and Europe. The act provided that no products from any foreign country might be shipped into England in any but English-built ships manned by English crews. The First Navigation Act was not strictly enforced. The Dutch continued to carry on their trade with the colonies. As a result the English Parliament passed other trade laws in 1660, 1663, and 1672. These acts repeated the former warnings. The act of 1660 required that all the tobacco from the colonies must be brought to England. The act of 1663 (Second Navigation Act) declared that almost all goods imported into the colonies must be landed in England first. In 1672, an act was passed requiring that goods had to be shipped to England before they could pass from one of the American colonies to another.

Before 1761, 29 acts had been passed in restraint of colonial trade. These included one law which prohibited the importation of molasses and sugar. America suffered little from these laws, because of the wholesale smuggling practiced by the colonists. Several provisions of the acts were favorable to American industry, especially shipbuilding, because they encouraged American shipping. But the restrictions on commerce were vigorously opposed by the Americans. This opposition was one of the principal causes of the Revolutionary War. The British Parliament, in 1849, repealed all the Navigation laws.   BASIL D. HENNING

NAVIGATION SATELLITE. See SPACE TRAVEL (Artificial Satellites).

NAVY

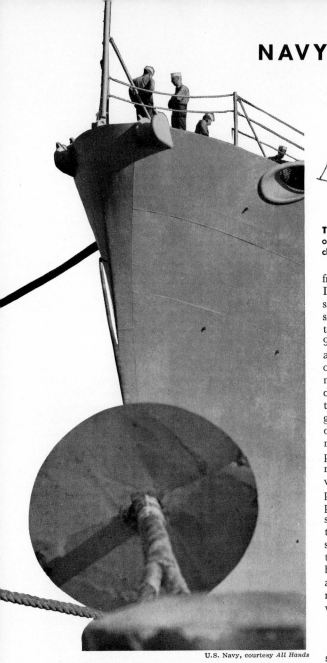

The Story of Navies is the story of men and ships, from oars and sails to atomic power. Metal shields, *left,* keep rats from climbing up ropes onto ships, an age-old problem for navy men.

from the *galleys* (oar-driven ships) of the earliest navies. In early battles, ships rammed each other while the sailors shot arrows at one another. Then men from each ship swarmed aboard the other vessel and fought hand to hand, like soldiers on a floating battlefield. By the 900's, opposing fleets began hurling stones and fireballs at each other by means of catapults. The development of gunpowder to fire projectiles forced navies to adopt new methods of fighting. With cannons, a fleet could destroy enemy ships without coming into actual contact with them. *Galleasses* (galleys mounting heavy guns) took the place of smaller galleys as the backbone of a fleet. In the 1800's, the Industrial Revolution mechanized naval warfare. The development of steam power doomed the sailing warship. Advances in gunnery meant the replacement of wooden warships by armored vessels. Each nation needed far-flung naval bases to provide fuel and supplies for its ships. Navies built powerful battleships. But in World War I, new underseas weapons—submarines, torpedoes, and mines— threatened the supremacy of the battleship and other surface vessels. World War II brought a new dimension to naval warfare. Aircraft carriers launched swarms of bombers and fighters against an enemy many miles away. In the Atomic Age, guided missiles began to replace bombs and cannons as the chief offensive weapons of atomic-powered navies.

Major Navies of the World

A nation's military sea forces are usually divided into separate *fleets*. Fleets may be further divided into task forces, squadrons, flotillas, and other commands. Vessels classified as *warships* include aircraft carriers, battleships, cruisers, destroyers, and submarines. Other vessels, called *service* or *auxiliary ships*, make up the *fleet train* that supports fighting ships. See WARSHIP.

Canada. The navy in Canada is part of one military force called the *Canadian Armed Forces*. Canada had a separate air force, army, and navy until the three services merged in 1967. For a complete discussion of the Canadian Armed Forces, see CANADA, ARMED FORCES OF.

France. The French Navy is administered by a chief of naval staff directly responsible to the minister of defense. It has about 95 warships and about 260 other ships. Most men in the French Navy are volunteers, but it also includes drafted men. The navy controls all

NAVY includes ships, naval aircraft, and the men who operate them. A navy also needs land or shore bases to supply and repair its *fleet* (sea-going forces).

A nation's *sea power* (ability to gain and keep command of the sea) depends on a strong navy and merchant ships that support the navy. Sea power has decided the outcome of many wars. With control of the seas, a nation can send its ships to any part of the world. In time of war, it can extend the fighting to almost any area. A powerful navy can sweep enemy vessels from the seas, and can ensure the safety of a nation's commercial shipping. It can land and support troops as they invade enemy shores in amphibious attacks.

Modern fleets, made up of fast-moving surface warships and submarines, developed over hundreds of years coastal defenses through four naval frontier districts. It maintains fleets in the North and Mediterranean seas.

Great Britain. A minister of state for defence administers the British navy, called the Royal Navy. The minister heads the Admiralty Board that governs the navy. He is responsible to the secretary of state for defence, and is assisted by the navy's chief of staff. The navy has about 160 warships and about 400 other vessels. Principal commands include the Home Fleet, based in England; the Far East Fleet, based in Singapore and Hong Kong; and the Mediterranean Fleet, based in Malta. British naval squadrons also operate in the East Indies, South Atlantic Ocean, and West Indies.

Italy. The Italian Navy guards the country's coastline from four main bases at Naples, La Spezia, Taranto, and Venice. It also has posts at Ancona, Augusta, Brindisi, Genoa, and Leghorn, and bases on Sardinia and Sicily. It numbers about 70 warships and 230 other ships.

Japan. The Japanese Navy was re-established in 1952, when the United States leased seven frigates to Japan. Sea-going forces include the Maritime Self-Defense Force of about 55 warships and 290 other ships, and the Maritime Safety Agency fleet of 280 ships, chiefly patrol vessels that provide navigational aid.

The Netherlands. The Royal Netherlands Navy has bases in The Netherlands and the Netherlands Antilles. A secretary of state for the navy administers the Royal Navy. A chief of naval staff serves as commander in chief of the fleet. The strength of the navy stands at about 45 warships and about 110 other ships. The fleet air arm, or naval air force, includes carrier- and land-based aircraft.

Russia. The Russian Navy ranks second only to the United States Navy in strength. It has the world's largest submarine force, with about 380. Naval strength stands at about 840 warships and about 1,950 other ships.

Principal naval commands include the Baltic, Black Sea, and Pacific fleets. They operate from naval bases in Murmansk on the Barents Sea, Kaliningrad and Tallinn on the Baltic Sea, Sevastopol on the Black Sea, and the Kamchatka Peninsula in Siberia. Komsomol'sk, Leningrad, Molotovsk, Nikolaiev, and Sevastopol have major shipyards. A unified ministry of defense controls the Russian Navy, with an admiral serving as commander in chief of naval forces.

United States. For a description of the United States Navy, see NAVY, UNITED STATES.

The First Navies

Early Sea Battles involved men in ships against other men in ships. Ramming was almost the only way that one ship could damage another. As the enemy approached, men shot arrows. After ramming the opposing ship, they swarmed aboard and fought hand to hand. Often they tried to set fire to the enemy vessel. Early warships also sailed past enemy ships at close range and broke their oars. Then men climbed aboard and attacked the rowers.

The fleets of early civilizations such as Assyria, Egypt, Phoenicia, Greece, Rome, and Carthage protected seacoasts and guarded trade routes. They also fought pirates and unfriendly neighbors. These early peoples built galleys that used sails for cruising in favorable winds. Slaves manned oars to move the galleys in battle or against the wind when it was unfavorable. See GALLEY.

Ancient Navies. In the 700's B.C., King Sennacherib of Assyria organized what was probably the first fleet to carry armed men. The Athenians in 483 B.C. began to build and maintain a large permanent navy under their leader Themistocles. Athens became the leading naval power in the Aegean Sea after it defeated the Persian fleet in the Battle of Salamis in 480 B.C. This battle was the first naval engagement of which there is a complete record. The Athenian navy included hundreds of *triremes* (galleys with three banks or tiers of oars) manned by skillful sailors. The ancient Greeks maneuvered their fleets to outflank the enemy.

Victory in the Battle of Actium in 31 B.C. made Rome the supreme sea power in the Mediterranean. For the next 400 years, Roman rulers considered the Mediterranean *Mare Nostrum* (*our sea*). They set up naval bases in the Bay of Naples and in ports on the Adriatic Sea. Roman fleets operated in the English Channel and in the Black Sea. The Romans invented the *harpago*, a device to grapple the enemy ship and force a narrow, swinging bridge across to it. This kind of fighting continued for almost 1,600 years, until the Battle of Lepanto in 1571.

A new naval power rose in northern Europe during the late 700's, when the vikings began to plunder ships and towns (see VIKING). They built galleys as long as 300 feet. Alfred the Great is often called "the father of the English Navy." He built a great fleet that finally forced the vikings to halt their attacks, which had gone on for more than 200 years. In the 900's, England had a huge fleet guarding its coasts and its overseas trade routes.

European nations fought many naval campaigns, but no decisive ones. Navies found it difficult to blockade the enemy, except by occupying the coasts or harbors. Ships could not stay at sea for long periods of time,

STRENGTH OF MAJOR NAVIES
(including warships not on active duty)

	Personnel	Carriers	Cruisers	Destroyers	Landing Craft	Submarines Conventional	Submarines Nuclear
Canada	19,000	1	0	33	0	3	0
France	71,000	4	2	49	19	21	0
Great Britain	103,000	7	5	87	14	42	3
Italy	39,000	0	3	40	23	6	0
Japan	35,000	0	0	40	10	7	0
The Netherlands	18,000	1	2	31	7	6	0
Russia	500,000	0	20	210	230	340	40
United States	742,000	56	37	694	260	137	70

Source: Jane's Fighting Ships, 1966-1967

FAMOUS SEA BATTLES

Actium (31 B.C.)—A Roman fleet crushed an Egyptian force off the coast of Greece. The victory ended Egyptian influence on the Roman Empire.

Jutland (1916)—The Allies repulsed the German fleet in the North Sea. It was the biggest battle of World War I between battleships.

Spanish Armada (1588)—Lord Howard's fleet destroyed the "Invincible Armada" in the English Channel. England began its rise as a great sea power.

EUROPE

Salamis (480 B.C.)—The Greeks forced the Persians under Xerxes to leave Greece and surrender naval command in the Aegean Sea.

Trafalgar (1805)—The British fleet ended Napoleon's dreams of invading England by destroying a French and Spanish force off southern Spain.

because they depended on land bases for food. Each side found it hard to check on the other's movements.

From Sail to Steam

Sail and Cannon. In the 1100's, shipbuilders began to construct warships with deep hulls. Sails became the chief means of propulsion, and oars were used only to maneuver in harbor. Most navies followed a set pattern in battle. Warships arranged themselves side by side in a straight line. As they advanced toward the enemy fleet, they hurled stones and flaming chemical mixtures, such as Greek fire (see GREEK FIRE). Ships then maneuvered to ram, and men attempted to board the enemy vessels. In the early 1300's, navies adopted cannons. But naval tactics remained unchanged.

Venice reigned as the major sea power of the Mediterranean during the Middle Ages. By 1400, it had

more than 3,000 galleys. The Turks were the chief rivals of the Venetians. Venice allied itself with the Papal States and Spain in defeating the Turks in the Battle of Lepanto. This clash in 1571 was the last great battle of oar-driven galleys.

England, France, Spain, and The Netherlands then began their rise as the world's chief naval powers. During the reign of Henry VIII, in the 1500's, the English began to build their navy around sailing ships instead of galleys. They continued the practice of building warships for the Royal Navy, instead of relying on merchant vessels that could be used to fight in wartime.

In the Battle of the Spanish Armada, only 17 years after the Battle of Lepanto, sails and cannons dominated the fighting. Ships fought in columns with their guns arranged in broadside. In fighting the Spaniards, the English had ships that were easier to maneuver, manned by better seamen. They also had more light naval guns of relatively long range than the Spaniards, who had heavy guns of short range. The English ships stayed close to their bases so they could take on more ammunition as they used it in battle. They kept away from the Spanish warships, and fired at long range. When the Spanish ships ran out of ammunition, they were helpless. The thousands of troops aboard proved useless. English gunfire actually sank few ships of the Armada. Most of the ships were lost in storms.

Spain had been the world's leading naval power for about a hundred years. But England replaced Spain as leader after the defeat of the Armada. It held this lead in sea power for more than 300 years. The Dutch competed with the English in the 1600's for trade and control of the high seas. The two nations fought three naval wars. The first of these clashes brought important advances in naval tactics. Robert Blake commanded the English fleet, opposing Martin Tromp of The Netherlands. Each commander divided his fleets into squadrons, with ships in *line*, or side by side. The squadron commanders had freedom of action, but they all worked together under the fleet commander.

In the late 1600's and early 1700's, this method of

FAMOUS SEA BATTLES OF HISTORY

480 B.C.—Salamis. Themistocles' 360 Greek ships routed a Persian fleet of 1,200 vessels under Xerxes. Persia lost naval command in the Aegean Sea and had to withdraw from Greece. See SALAMIS.

405 B.C.—Aegospotami. Lysander's Spartan sailors in 200 vessels destroyed a superior Athenian fleet of about 180 ships under Conon, along the coast of western Asia. The battle resulted in the final defeat of Athens in the Peloponnesian wars.

31 B.C.—Actium. Octavian (later Emperor Augustus) and Agrippa led a 400-ship Roman fleet that destroyed an Egyptian naval force of equal size under Mark Antony and Cleopatra off the coast of Greece. The victory ended a split in Roman power, and stopped Egyptian influence in Roman affairs.

1571—Lepanto. A fleet of 300 ships from Venice, Spain, and the Papal States, under Don John of Austria, defeated the 273-ship Turkish fleet under Ali Pasha. This was the last great battle of oar-driven ships. The battle, fought near Greece, marked a turning point of Moslem power in Europe.

1588—Spanish Armada. In a struggle in the English Channel, Lord Howard's 197 warships smashed Spain's 130-ship "Invincible Armada" under the Duke of Medina Sidonia. The loss marked the beginning of Spain's decline and England's rise as a dominant sea power. See ARMADA.

1781—Chesapeake Bay. A French fleet of 24 warships under Comte de Grasse forced a British naval force of 19 ships led by Thomas Graves to withdraw to New York Harbor. The battle itself was inconclusive, but it helped force Lord Cornwallis to surrender at Yorktown, ending the Revolutionary War in America.

1805—Trafalgar. Napoleon's dreams of invading England were shattered when Lord Nelson's 27-ship British fleet defeated a force of 33 French and Spanish warships under Pierre de Villeneuve off the coast of southern Spain. The battle ended a 100-year struggle for domination of the seas. See TRAFALGAR.

1905—Tsushima. Japan climaxed the Russo-Japanese War when its 28-ship fleet under Heihachiro Togo overwhelmed the Russian Baltic fleet of 29 vessels under Zinovi Rozhdestvenski in the Korean Strait. Japan began its rise as a great naval power.

1916—Jutland. The 150-ship British Grand Fleet under John Jellicoe repulsed the German High Sea Fleet of 99 ships under Reinhard Scheer in the North Sea. The battle confirmed British command of the seas in World War I, and forced Germany to adopt submarine warfare. See JUTLAND, BATTLE OF.

1942—Midway. American carrier forces of 44 ships under Raymond A. Spruance crippled a 92-vessel Japanese fleet under Isoroku Yamamoto and saved Midway Island from invasion. The battle was a turning point of World War II. See MIDWAY ISLAND.

1944—Leyte Gulf. The United States destroyed Japan's last remaining naval power and assured Allied victory in World War II. American fleets of 296 ships under William F. Halsey, Jr., and Thomas C. Kinkaid clashed off the Philippines with Japanese naval forces of 69 ships under Takeo Kurita, Jisaburo Ozawa, Shoji Nishimura, and Kiyohide Shima.

MIDWAY

PACIFIC OCEAN

HAWAII

Midway Island (1942)—The Pacific Fleet ended Japanese threats to Hawaii by forcing back the enemy fleet off Midway. The battle was one of the turning points of World War II.

NAVY

AUSTRALIAN NAVY INSIGNIA	BRITISH NAVY INSIGNIA	FRENCH NAVY INSIGNIA
Officers	**Officers**	**Officers**
Admiral of the Fleet	Admiral of the Fleet	Admiral
Admiral	Admiral	Squadron Vice Admiral
Vice Admiral	Vice Admiral	Vice Admiral
Rear Admiral	Rear Admiral	Rear Admiral
Commodore 2nd Class	Commodore	Ship's Captain
Captain	Captain	Frigate Captain
Commander	Commander	Corvette Captain
Lieutenant Commander	Lieutenant Commander	Ship's Lieutenant
Lieutenant	Lieutenant	Ship's Ensign (1st Class)
Sub-Lieutenant	Sub-Lieutenant	Ship's Ensign (2nd Class)
Enlisted Men	Midshipman	Midshipman
Chief Petty Officer	Cadet	**Enlisted Men**
Petty Officer	**Enlisted Men**	Chief Petty Officer
Leading Rating	Chief Petty Officer	1st Petty Officer
	Petty Officer	Petty Officer
	Leading Rate	2nd Petty Officer (after 2 years in rank)
		2nd Petty Officer
		Quarter Master (1st Class)
		Quarter Master (2nd Class)
		Certified Seaman

AUSTRALIA

Gunnery

Diver (T.A.S. Branch)

Coxswain

Signal

Engineering Mechanic

Naval Airman

Electrical

Supply and Secretariat

Sick Berth

Artisan

GREAT BRITAIN

Radar Plot

Torpedo Anti-Submarine

Boom Defence

Physical Training

Navigator's Yeoman

Communications

Medical Assistant

P.O. Coxswain

Supply and Secretariat

Bugler

FRANCE

Infantry

Artillery

Storage Vessels

Telegraphists

Administration Officers

Administrative Agents
of the Troop Corps

Administrative Agents
of the Chancellery

Naval Paymasters

Doctors

Administration Officers
C.O.A.C.

fighting underwent important changes. Ships formed in a *column* (one behind the other). The commander directed all ship movements. During this period and in the 1800's, France became England's chief rival on the seas and in the colonial world. After France lost the Battle of Trafalgar in 1805, it could no longer compete with British naval power. Great Britain ruled the waves, and its navy helped make it the greatest colonial power in the world.

Steam and Steel. In 1814, Robert Fulton built the first steam warship. Steam-powered warships did not have to depend on the wind, and they could cruise much faster than sailing warships. But steamships faced a new problem. They needed fuel that they could find only at their own naval bases. A nation's naval power depended on the range of its overseas supply bases.

With the development of steam-powered fleets, the life of a seaman became more comfortable. In the early 1800's, 10 or 20 of every 100 seamen died from disease aboard ship. Sailors had to eat hard biscuits that were usually full of weevils or maggots. The water on ships was often unfit to drink. Crew members included thieves, drunkards, vagrants, and former pirates. With steam, ships could follow more regular schedules between ports, and navy men had a chance to enjoy some home life. Navies adopted more humane methods of treating their men, and discarded the harsh discipline of the cat-o'-nine-tails (beatings with cords studded with lead weights). With improved conditions, a higher quality of men volunteered for naval service.

Another development that affected naval warfare came in the improvement of armor and guns. In the 1820's, inventors developed naval guns that fired explosive shells rather than solid cannon balls. In 1853, during the Crimean War, the Russians fired explosive shells for the first time, tearing enormous holes in Turkish wooden vessels. The Turks fired guns that hurled solid shots. Ship designers began to use iron armor instead of thick wooden plankings. Soon naval guns had become so large and had such a great recoil that even a large ship could only carry a few cannons. Gun turrets were soon developed so cannons could be turned to fire to either side of a ship.

In the 1850's, inventors introduced the rifled gun, which spins projectiles through the air and gives them greater range and accuracy (see RIFLE). Boarding and hand-to-hand combat in sea battles became obsolete. Warships fought each other from a distance. As ship guns grew in size, ever heavier armor became necessary.

In 1862, during the Civil War, the *Monitor* battled the *Merrimack* (then called the *Virginia*) in the first duel between iron-armored ships. It was also the first battle between two ships maneuvering solely under steam. The *Monitor* was the first warship to have its guns in a rotating turret. See MONITOR AND MERRIMACK.

From Cannon to Missiles

The Dreadnought Era. In 1906, the British navy introduced the *Dreadnought* class of battleships. This signaled the wholehearted adoption of the "all-big-gun" theory of building warships. The *Dreadnought* mounted heavier guns than any previous battleship. It could also travel much faster. The vessel had a speed of

21 knots, and displaced 18,000 tons. The next class of British warships, known as *superdreadnoughts*, had even bigger guns. Some ships displaced more than 27,000 tons.

During the 1800's and up to the end of World War I, Great Britain controlled the high seas. In the early 1900's, the German fleet ranked a close second to the British navy, with the United States just behind Germany. Heavily armor-plated battleships, mounting the largest guns ever made, formed the core of the fighting fleets.

The World Wars. Two new weapons—the submarine and the airplane—brought sweeping changes to naval warfare (see AIR FORCE; SUBMARINE). When World War I broke out in 1914, the British navy set up a tight blockade of Germany. At first, the Germans used sea raiders, either single vessels or small groups of surface warships, to attack Allied ships in the Atlantic and Pacific oceans. In 1915, they began widespread submarine warfare. By 1917, Germany was trying to sink all enemy or neutral ships found in European waters. The submarine had had a long and slow development, but it became a great and surprising success in the war. In 1916, the British and German fleets clashed off Jutland. This was the last great battle in which battleships played the leading roles (see WORLD WAR I [The Battle of Jutland]).

World War I eliminated Germany as a major naval power. The United States demanded equal rank with Great Britain in naval strength. These nations and Japan finally agreed to limit naval armaments and avoid a costly and dangerous navy-building race (see DISARMAMENT).

When World War II broke out in 1939, the British fleet again blockaded Germany. As in World War I, the Germans resorted to submarine warfare. The Allies fought submarines with new weapons, including radar, sonar, fast-sinking depth charges, rocket projectiles, and destroyer escorts.

The development of airpower brought the widespread use of a new type of warship, the aircraft carrier. After the battles of the Coral Sea and Midway in 1942, carriers became the backbone of the Allied fleets. Other warships served as escort or auxiliary ships for swift carriers that prowled the Pacific Ocean and launched thousands of bombers and fighters against enemy targets. The United States Navy organized naval carrier task forces, or fleets assigned to specific tasks. It developed the *circular* formation, with carriers in the center and other warships grouped in circles around them.

The Battle of the Coral Sea was the first naval battle in which the opposing fleets did not fire a single shot at each other. Carrier-based airplanes of the United States and Japanese navies did all the actual fighting. The Battle for Leyte Gulf, the largest naval battle of all times in terms of tonnage involved, took place in World War II. The opposing fleets totaled more than 2 million tons. This battle eliminated Japanese naval power as an important factor in the war.

World War II destroyed Japan's naval power. It also knocked out the fleets of France, Germany, and Italy. The United States built so many ships during the war that, except in submarines, its fleet became more powerful than all the navies of the world combined. The British no longer had the resources to compete with the United States on the seas. As a result, the nation that had been "mistress of the seas" for more than 300 years became second to the United States in naval power. By the late 1950's, the British navy had fallen into third place, behind the American and Russian navies.

Nuclear-Age Navies. In the 1950's, nations began building atomic-powered warships and equipping warships with guided missiles. In 1954, the United States Navy launched the submarine *Nautilus*, the first atomic-propelled warship. Many naval experts believe that the atomic submarine will be the chief warship of the future. A submarine's weapons include missiles and torpedoes. Atomic submarines do not require oxygen for their engines, and can cruise submerged for months at a time. Navies also developed atomic submarines which could fire ballistic missiles armed with atomic warheads at targets 1,500 miles away.

New aircraft carriers have decks designed to launch airplanes large enough to deliver atomic bombs. Catapults hurl these planes into the sky. Angled flight decks allow some planes to take off at the same time that others are landing. Rockets and guided missiles began replacing long-range guns and antiaircraft guns on many warships.   BERNARD BRODIE

Related Articles in WORLD BOOK include:

BATTLES

Armada	Midway Island	Salamis
Jutland,	Pearl Harbor Naval Base	Trafalgar
Battle of		

HISTORY

Alabama (ship)	Galleon	Privateer
Constellation (ship)	Galley	Trireme
Constitution (ship)	Maine (ship)	Viking
Frigate		

KINDS OF SHIPS

Aircraft Carrier	Destroyer	PT Boat
Battleship	Landing Craft	Submarine
Corvette	Mine Layer	Torpedo Boat
Cruiser	Mine Sweeper	Warship

WEAPONS

Airship	Depth Charge	Torpedo
Blockade	Guided Missile	Turret
Bomb	Mine, Military	

OTHER RELATED ARTICLES

Admiralty	Desertion	Navy, U.S.
Air Force, U.S.	Dry Dock	Prisoner of War
Amphibious Warfare	Insignia	Recruiting
Army, United States	Logistics	Salute
Canada, Armed	Marine	Task Force
Forces of	Marine Corps,	Underwater
Coast Guard,	United States	Demolition
United States	Military School	Team
Convoy	Military Training	Uniform
Court-Martial	Naval Shipyard	War
Decorations		
and Medals		

Outline

I. Major Navies of the World
  A. Canada.
  B. France.
  C. Great Britain.
  D. Italy.
  E. Japan.
  F. The Netherlands.
  G. Russia.
  H. United States.

II. The First Navies
  A. Early Sea Battles
  B. Ancient Navies

III. From Sail to Steam
  A. Sail and Cannon
  B. Steam and Steel

IV. From Cannon to Missiles
  A. The Dreadnought Era
  B. The World Wars
  C. Nuclear-Age Navies

Questions

What is a *fleet?* A *fleet train?*
What was the last great battle involving oar-driven galley ships and galley tactics?
How did the use of cannon and armor change the design and construction of warships?
How did the use of steam power in warships change naval strategy?
What was the last major battle in which battleships were the chief warships?
What was the first battle between two iron-armored ships?
In what major naval battle did the opposing fleets fire no shots at each other?
What navy has the largest number of submarines?
What great naval battle began England's rise as a dominant sea power?
What naval battle assured the Allies of victory in World War II?

NAVY, DEPARTMENT OF THE, is one of the three military departments within the Department of Defense of the United States government. It serves as headquarters of the U.S. Navy, and is located in Washington, D.C. It includes the U.S. Marine Corps. In wartime, the President may assign the U.S. Coast Guard to the Department of the Navy. The department is responsible for having naval and marine forces ready to defend the nation's interests, guard its commerce, and improve international relations.

The *secretary of the navy* heads the department, under the direction of the secretary of defense. He ranks equally with the secretaries of the army and the air force. He has general responsibility for all naval affairs. The secretary's principal civilian aides include an undersecretary, three assistant secretaries, and a special assistant.

The *chief of naval operations,* an admiral, is the secretary's principal naval adviser. He commands such members and units of the Navy and Marine Corps as are determined by the secretary. His top assistants include the vice chief of naval operations and six deputy chiefs.

The commandant of the marine corps is responsible directly to both the secretary and the chief of naval operations.

Congress set up the Department of the Navy in 1798. The secretary of war had directed naval affairs for nine years before then. Congress reorganized the department in 1862, and created bureaus to manage such activities as construction, navigation, ordnance, medicine, steam engineering, and supplies. It created the office of chief of naval operations in 1915.

The secretary of the navy has not served as a member of the President's Cabinet since 1947. In that year, the Department of the Navy was incorporated in the National Military Establishment. Then it became a military department within the Department of Defense in 1949.   Critically reviewed by the DEPARTMENT OF DEFENSE

Related Articles in WORLD BOOK include:

Coast Guard, United States	National Defense
(Supporting the Navy)	Navy, United States
Defense, Department of	Oceanographic Office,
Marine Corps, U.S.	U.S. Naval

Aircraft Carriers pack the main striking power of the surface fleet. They can launch supersonic jets to any part of the world.

In time of war, the Navy seeks out and destroys the enemy on, under, or above the sea. If attacked, it can return the blow almost anywhere on earth from its warships. Navy task forces can carry naval aircraft to any danger point. Powerful naval amphibious forces can support troop landings against heavy enemy resistance. Nuclear-powered submarines that carry missiles can travel around the world under water. Any enemy that might attack the United States must expect counterblows from these submarines, whose exact locations cannot be pinpointed in advance.

To perform its functions efficiently, the Navy has many types of ships, including aircraft carriers, battleships, cruisers, frigates, destroyers, submarines, and amphibious type ships. These fighting ships depend on the services of ammunition ships, hospital ships, mine layers and mine sweepers, oilers, repair ships, supply ships, and tugs. Both fighting ships and service ships rely on a shore organization, including naval bases, shipyards, docks, naval air stations, and training stations, for supplies, repairs, training, and other services.

Many men choose the Navy as a career because of their love of adventure and the sea. They may have an opportunity to visit many parts of the world.

NAVY, UNITED STATES, is the branch of the armed forces of the United States that acts to maintain command of the sea. In time of peace, the Navy often serves as an instrument of international relations. The very presence of naval vessels may be helpful in keeping a crisis from flaring into war. Navy ships also speed on errands of mercy, such as carrying food and medical supplies to disaster areas. Merchant vessels and passenger ships often call on the Navy for help in emergencies.

Captain Harry A. Seymour, USN, Retired, the contributor of this article, is the Academic Dean of the California Maritime Academy, Vallejo, Calif.

The history of the United States Navy is a colorful story of daring deeds and famous ships at sea. It is the story of growth from a few sailing ships in Revolutionary War days to the greatest fleet ever to sail the seas. It recounts the changes from sails and cannon to nuclear power and guided missiles. It blazes with the achievements of such historic ships as the *Bonhomme Richard*, *Constitution*, *Monitor*, *Olympia*, *Enterprise*, and *Nautilus*.

Naval history tells of John Paul Jones, whose battle cry, "I have not yet begun to fight," established the Navy's fighting traditions. It includes the achievements of James Lawrence, who rallied his men with the historic words: "Don't give up the ship!" It reflects the deeds of David G. Farragut, the Navy's first admiral, who bellowed "Damn the torpedoes! Full steam ahead!" as his forces charged into Mobile Bay. It includes leaders such as Chester W. Nimitz, who directed the Pacific Fleet in its sweep from Pearl Harbor to Tokyo Bay. It shines with the names of famous ships, such as the *Nautilus*, the world's first nuclear-powered warship.

The Navy operates under the Department of the Navy. By 1969, it had a strength of about 790,300 men and about 6,000 women. Its reserve units numbered about 509,000 men and women. The Department of the Navy also maintains the 306,500-man U.S. Marine Corps, and employs 400,000 civilians in all parts of the world.

The Navy emblem was adopted in 1957. "Anchors Aweigh" is the Navy's famous marching song. Blue and gold are the official colors of the Navy.

Life in the Navy

Training a Sailor. The enlisted ranks of the Navy consist of three grades of seaman and six grades of petty officer, from seaman recruit to master chief petty officer.

The Navy recruit first learns discipline and seamanship at a naval training center called a *boot camp*. He is called a "boot" because, in early days, recruits wore leggings that looked like boots. Then he may attend a trade school, such as those for enginemen, cooks, and electricians. Or he may be assigned directly to a ship where he learns his duties and practices his trade. Sailors take competitive examinations for advancement through the *ratings* (ranks) to the highest enlisted grades. Some may be qualified to attend advanced schools. Qualified enlisted men can take examinations for admission to the U.S. Naval Academy at Annapolis, Md., or other officer training programs.

Enlisted women receive basic training at the naval training center in Bainbridge, Md. About half of them are assigned to advanced training schools, and the remainder receive on-the-job training at naval bases.

Training an Officer. Male officers train at the U.S. Naval Academy or in the following naval programs: (1) the Naval Reserve Officer Training Corps (NROTC) for high-school graduates; (2) officer-candidate training for enlisted men and college graduates; (3) the aviation-cadet and aviation-officer candidate programs for men with two or more years of college; and (4) programs to appoint warrant officers and limited-duty officers from the enlisted ranks. Limited-duty officers specialize in certain fields, such as naval ordnance and aeronautical engineering. Doctors, dentists, and ministers may be commissioned without any military training. Women officer candidates train at the Naval Officer Candidate School, Newport, R.I.

Naval officers are assigned to one of three divisions: (1) line, (2) staff, or (3) warrant. *Line* officers usually command ships or aircraft and men. A *restricted line* officer specializes in such duty as engineering or law. *Staff* officers include doctors, dentists, nurses, supply officers, civil engineers, and chaplains. A *warrant* officer is usually appointed from the enlisted ranks as an administrative or technical specialist.

Newly appointed ensigns may apply for surface, submarine, or aviation duty. After about four years, they become eligible for many technical postgraduate programs. Senior-ranking officers may take command and strategy courses at the Naval War College in Newport, R.I., or at one of the joint service colleges, such as the National War College in Washington, D.C.

A Typical Day. A *bluejacket's* (sailor's) life at sea varies with the type of ship he is on. Naval ships range from tugboats with a crew of five men to giant aircraft carriers with a crew of thousands. Cargo ships spend long periods of time at sea. Repair ships usually stay in port. A sailor on a submarine gets to know every member of its crew. But on a carrier, each man does his specialized job and may never see many areas of the ship.

In peacetime aboard a naval ship, a typical day begins with reveille at about 6 A.M. Meals are generally served at 7 A.M., noon, and 5 P.M. These hours may be changed to meet operating requirements. The crew *musters* (assembles) at 8 A.M., after breakfast. Practically every man on a ship *stands watch*, or is at his post of duty, during four-hour periods. Each man has a battle station and a post for emergencies.

Certain days of the week have traditional meanings. For example, Wednesday is usually a half holiday. Friday is "field day," for cleaning the ship and inspections below decks. On Saturday morning, the captain inspects the living spaces and topside areas. He also inspects the crew, and may present awards and commendations. When a ship is in port, men who are not on duty may be granted *liberty* (time off ashore).

The Navy tries to make life aboard ship as comfortable and pleasant as possible for men who may have to live in limited space for weeks or months at a time without seeing land. Every ship has a library for the crew, and many have recreation rooms and hobby shops. Movies are shown every night when possible. Tailor and shoe-repair shops, laundries, and ship's stores provide for the men's everyday needs. Doctors and dentists on the ships care for the men's health.

Careers in the Navy. A sailor has a chance to see much of the world, and many learn to love the sea. A man's first enlistment may prepare him for a civilian job or a naval career. Applicants must be United States citizens between the ages of 17 and 31, and must meet the Navy's physical standards. A man may enlist in the Navy for four to six years. A woman may enlist for three or four years.

A qualified enlisted man usually advances to chief petty officer in 12 to 14 years. He receives a pay increase with each promotion, and extra pay according to length of service. The Navy also pays money for *quarters* (housing) and *subsistence* (food). It gives additional pay for hazardous duty, such as submarine duty, and for sea duty and duty in some other countries. A sailor is eligible for 30 days' *leave* (vacation) a year. He is entitled to free medical and dental care, and free hospital and medical care is available to his family. Men and women in the Navy may retire with pay after 20 years' service. For ranks and pay in the Navy, see RANK IN ARMED SERVICES.

Ships and Weapons of the Navy

Warships. The U.S. Navy's *attack aircraft carriers* are its chief warships. Nuclear-powered carriers displace 85,000 tons and are the world's largest warships. The Navy uses special carriers for antisubmarine warfare and for helicopter amphibious assaults. *Battleships* serve in the Navy's reserve fleets, located along the Atlantic and Pacific coasts. They are particularly useful for shore bombardment. *Cruisers* protect a group of ships against larger enemy ships and provide air defense. Missile cruisers carry medium- and long-range guided missiles. *Frigates* (large destroyers) and *destroyers* detect and attack enemy submarines and aircraft. Newer ships of these types carry guided missiles. *Submarines* operate against surface ships, other submarines, and shore positions. *Tactical command ships* carry elaborate communications and radar equipment. They serve as *command* (headquarters) facilities for the task-force or higher level. The Navy's *amphibious ships* land troops on enemy-held shores. The *landing ship, tank* carries troops, cargo, and vehicles. The *landing ship, dock* carries landing boats in a floodable basin that opens to the rear. It can also carry assault helicopters. The *landing ship, dock* is a combination ship and dry dock. It transports landing boats and dry-docks them for repairs. See NAVY (table: Strength of Major Navies).

Auxiliary and Service Ships. The Navy's *attack transports* and *cargo ships* operate with amphibious forces.

Amphibious command ships serve as communication centers for amphibious operations. The Navy's *oilers*, *supply ships*, and *ammunition ships* furnish supply needs of the fleet at sea. *Tenders* and *repair ships* carry repair parts and have shops for almost any type of repairs. *Floating dry docks* moored in harbors near operating forces dry-dock ships for underwater repairs. *Mine layers* and *mine sweepers* lay or sweep up various types of mines. *Ice-breakers* smash lanes through ice for other ships. Fleet and salvage *tugs* and *submarine-rescue vessels* perform towing and salvage work. Other Navy ships include *net tenders*, *radar pickets*, *research vessels*, and *yard craft*.

The Navy carries troops of all the military services. *Attack transports* land troops under combat conditions. Many small types of transport ships have also been used, and submarines have landed small forces secretly.

Naval Aviation helps the Navy control the seas, takes part in amphibious attacks, and strikes at strategic shore targets. The Navy trains naval and marine pilots and, in wartime, coast-guard aviators. Naval pilots fly light, medium, and heavy attack bombers based on aircraft carriers. They also operate patrol bombers that may be flying boats or shore-based aircraft. The Navy's fighter planes are designed for low-speed landings on and take-offs from carriers. Their wings fold back, so they require less storage space. Navy bombers include the *A-4B Skyhawk* and the *A-3B Skywarrior*. Fighters include the *F-8C Crusader*, *F-3B Demon*, and *F-4B Phantom II*.

Navy planes can carry guided missiles and nuclear weapons. Planes such as the *P-3 Orion* and *P-5 Marlin* have electronic devices to hunt enemy submarines. The Navy also operates helicopters for antisubmarine work and for carrying assault troops ashore.

Naval aircraft are classified by letters and numbers. For example, the F-4B is a fighter plane (F) of design number four (-4). It is the second model of that design (B). Other symbols that indicate the purpose of the

Barrett Gallagher

aircraft are: *A*, attack; *B*, bomber; *C*, cargo/transport; *E*, special electronic installation; *H*, helicopter; *K*, tanker; *O*, observation; *P*, patrol; *S*, antisubmarine; *T*, trainer; *U*, Utility; *V*, vertical or short take-off and landing; *X*, research; *Z*, airship.

Ordnance Weapons include bombs, depth charges, guns, mines, missiles, and torpedoes. Picket-boat depth charges protect harbors and inland waterways. Heavy cruisers, rather than battleships, now carry the Navy's largest guns, 8-inch guns that can hurl shells more than 17 miles. Light cruisers have 6-inch guns. Destroyers mount 5-inch guns in turrets that can drop shells on targets more than 10 miles away. Surface warships also carry 3-inch rapid-fire guns for defense against enemy aircraft.

Naval mines may be fixed, moored, or mobile. Rockets such as Weapon Alfa and *ASROC* combat submarines. The Navy has air-launched, surface-launched, and subsurface-launched torpedoes. They can be used against surface ships or submarines.

Missiles. The Navy's surface-to-air missiles include the *Terrier*, *Tartar*, and *Talos*, with ranges from 10 to more than 65 miles. Air-to-air missiles include the *Sidewinder* and *Sparrow*. Such air-to-surface missiles as the *Bullpup* have a 15,000-foot range. These missiles are used to support ground troops or to hit targets at sea. The *Polaris* can be launched under water to blast targets up to 2,500 miles away. Underwater-to-air-to-underwater missiles are launched from submarines. See GUIDED MISSILE.

Organization of the Navy

The U.S. Navy operates under the Department of the Navy in the Department of Defense. The department is also known as the *naval establishment*. It consists of (1) Navy headquarters, (2) naval operating forces, and (3) the shore establishment.

Navy Headquarters, located in Washington, D.C., include the offices of the secretary of the navy, the chief of naval operations, and the commandant of the Marine Corps, and their assistants and staff organizations. The secretary of the navy, a civilian, heads the entire naval establishment. He is responsible directly to the secretary of defense. The chief of naval operations is the Navy's highest-ranking officer. He serves as the principal naval adviser to the secretary, and represents the Navy on the Joint Chiefs of Staff.

Operating Forces. The principal sea commands include the *Atlantic Fleet*, with headquarters at Norfolk Naval Base, Va., and the *Pacific Fleet*, with headquarters at Pearl Harbor Naval Base, Hawaii. The Navy divides its major commands into smaller *fleets* for operations. These include the First Fleet in the eastern Pacific, the Second Fleet in the western Atlantic, the Sixth Fleet in the Mediterranean, and the Seventh Fleet in the western Pacific. The numbered fleets are divided into *task forces* that perform specific tasks and meet the changing needs of the Navy. Task forces may be divided into *task groups*, *task units*, and *task elements*.

Ships and forces of the same type in the major fleets are grouped for administration and training into *type commands*. For example, the commander of cruisers and destroyers for the Atlantic Fleet has administrative control over all cruisers and destroyers in that fleet. Other commands include amphibious forces, fleet marine forces, mine forces, naval air forces, service forces, submarine forces, and training commands.

The Military Sea Transportation Service provides transportation of troops and military cargo for the Department of Defense. It is the only fleet command with civilian-manned ships and its own supply, medical, and legal services.

◄ **Inspection in the Ranks** is a routine that all naval personnel must often undergo. It may be held ashore or aboard a Navy ship.

U. S. Navy

Schools on ships and ashore train men to operate today's nuclear-powered Navy. They combine classroom and practical work.

Recreational Swimming is no problem for men aboard ships. The oceans provide the world's biggest swimming pools.

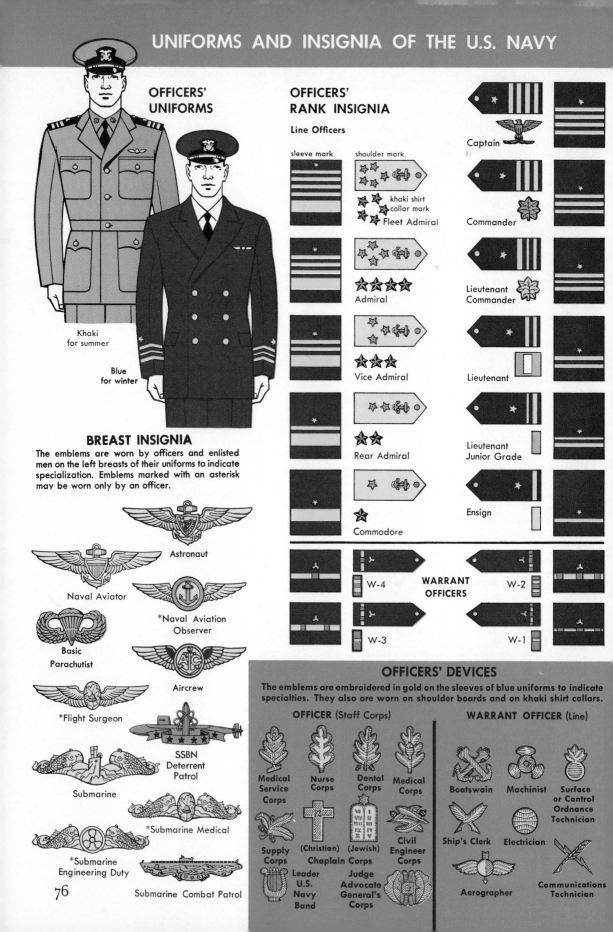

OFFICERS' UNIFORMS

Khaki for summer

Blue for winter

BREAST INSIGNIA

The emblems are worn by officers and enlisted men on the left breasts of their uniforms to indicate specialization. Emblems marked with an asterisk may be worn only by an officer.

Astronaut

Naval Aviator

*Naval Aviation Observer

Basic Parachutist

Aircrew

*Flight Surgeon

SSBN Deterrent Patrol

Submarine

*Submarine Medical

*Submarine Engineering Duty

Submarine Combat Patrol

76

OFFICERS' RANK INSIGNIA

Line Officers

sleeve mark   shoulder mark

khaki shirt collar mark

Fleet Admiral

Admiral

Vice Admiral

Rear Admiral

Commodore

Captain

Commander

Lieutenant Commander

Lieutenant

Lieutenant Junior Grade

Ensign

WARRANT OFFICERS

W-4

W-3

W-2

W-1

OFFICERS' DEVICES

The emblems are embroidered in gold on the sleeves of blue uniforms to indicate specialties. They also are worn on shoulder boards and on khaki shirt collars.

OFFICER (Staff Corps)

Medical Service Corps

Nurse Corps

Dental Corps

Medical Corps

Supply Corps

(Christian) Chaplain Corps

(Jewish)

Civil Engineer Corps

Leader U.S. Navy Band

Judge Advocate General's Corps

WARRANT OFFICER (Line)

Boatswain

Machinist

Surface or Control Ordnance Technician

Ship's Clerk

Electrician

Aerographer

Communications Technician

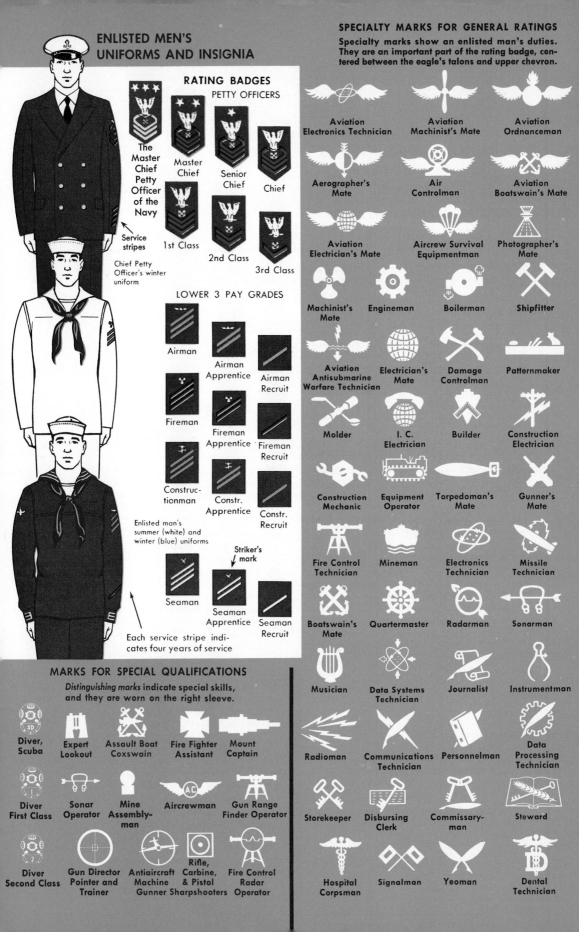

ENLISTED MEN'S UNIFORMS AND INSIGNIA

RATING BADGES
PETTY OFFICERS

The Master Chief Petty Officer of the Navy

Master Chief

Senior Chief

Chief

1st Class

2nd Class

3rd Class

Service stripes

Chief Petty Officer's winter uniform

LOWER 3 PAY GRADES

Airman

Airman Apprentice

Airman Recruit

Fireman

Fireman Apprentice

Fireman Recruit

Construction-man

Constr. Apprentice

Constr. Recruit

Enlisted man's summer (white) and winter (blue) uniforms

Striker's mark

Seaman

Seaman Apprentice

Seaman Recruit

Each service stripe indicates four years of service

MARKS FOR SPECIAL QUALIFICATIONS

Distinguishing marks indicate special skills, and they are worn on the right sleeve.

Diver, Scuba

Expert Lookout

Assault Boat Coxswain

Fire Fighter Assistant

Mount Captain

Diver First Class

Sonar Operator

Mine Assembly-man

Aircrewman

Gun Range Finder Operator

Diver Second Class

Gun Director Pointer and Trainer

Antiaircraft Machine Gunner

Rifle, Carbine, & Pistol Sharpshooters

Fire Control Radar Operator

SPECIALTY MARKS FOR GENERAL RATINGS
Specialty marks show an enlisted man's duties. They are an important part of the rating badge, centered between the eagle's talons and upper chevron.

Aviation Electronics Technician

Aviation Machinist's Mate

Aviation Ordnanceman

Aerographer's Mate

Air Controlman

Aviation Boatswain's Mate

Aviation Electrician's Mate

Aircrew Survival Equipmentman

Photographer's Mate

Machinist's Mate

Engineman

Boilerman

Shipfitter

Aviation Antisubmarine Warfare Technician

Electrician's Mate

Damage Controlman

Patternmaker

Molder

I. C. Electrician

Builder

Construction Electrician

Construction Mechanic

Equipment Operator

Torpedoman's Mate

Gunner's Mate

Fire Control Technician

Mineman

Electronics Technician

Missile Technician

Boatswain's Mate

Quartermaster

Radarman

Sonarman

Musician

Data Systems Technician

Journalist

Instrumentman

Radioman

Communications Technician

Personnelman

Data Processing Technician

Storekeeper

Disbursing Clerk

Commissary-man

Steward

Hospital Corpsman

Signalman

Yeoman

Dental Technician

DEPARTMENT OF THE NAVY

The Department of the Navy is a military agency within the Department of Defense in Washington, D. C. The principal assistants of the secretary of the navy include an undersecretary, the chief of naval operations, and the Marine Corps commandant.

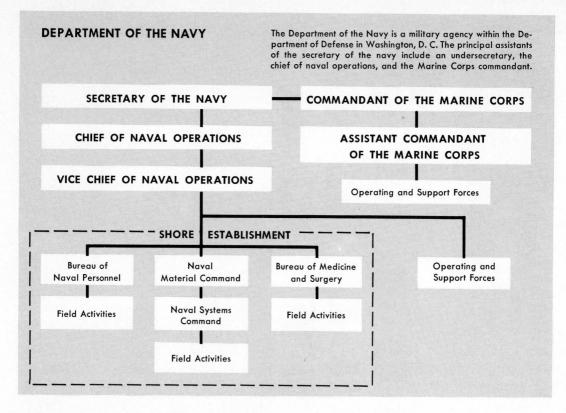

Other operating forces include fleet commands organized for special purposes. For example, the operational test and evaluation force tests newly designed equipment for later use by the Navy. The antisubmarine warfare force develops antisubmarine warfare tactics. The Navy may also organize special task forces for temporary missions, such as expeditions for the exploration of Antarctica.

The Shore Establishment supports the fleets and other operating forces. Its commands provide facilities to overhaul, convert, and berth ships, to train men, and to perform other *logistic* (supply) operations.

Sea Frontiers are naval divisions of United States coasts and adjacent areas. There are five frontier commands: Alaskan, Caribbean, Eastern, Hawaiian, and Western. They handle naval shipping control, harbor defense, and coastal patrol.

Naval Districts. The United States is divided into eight naval districts. The commandant of each naval district coordinates shore activities in his area. The naval districts and their headquarters are: 3rd, New York City; 5th, Norfolk, Va.; 6th, Charleston, S.C.; 8th, New Orleans; 9th, Great Lakes, Ill.; 11th, San Diego; 12th, San Francisco; and the Washington Naval District, Washington, D.C. Shore activities in possessions of the United States are directed by the sea frontier commanders.

Naval Bases are centers for the activities that support the fleet. Most bases include a naval shipyard, a naval air station, or a naval station. Naval stations perform administrative and housekeeping duties. Naval shipyards build and maintain Navy vessels (see NAVAL SHIPYARD). Vessels called *tenders* provide additional support

in areas where the Navy may or may not have shore stations.

Other Naval Commands include laboratories and test centers, such as the Naval Research Laboratory in Washington, D.C. Naval air stations serve as bases for fleet aircraft and aviation training. Naval air-reserve bases are in many major cities. Shore commands also include hospitals, radio stations, and schools. The Navy governs a number of mandated islands in the Pacific Ocean under a United Nations trusteeship. It assigns naval attachés and missions to many countries in all parts of the world.

Regulars and Reserves. The *Regular Navy* is the permanent professional naval force. It consists of men and women who join the Navy as a career.

The *Naval Reserve* has two divisions: (1) the Ready Reserve and (2) the Standby Reserve. The *Ready Reserve* is made up of officers and enlisted men who take annual training and are alert for immediate mobilization in emergencies. The *Standby Reserve* consists of reservists who can be ordered to active duty by Congress only in a national emergency.

Reservists may apply for active duty in the Navy. About half the active-duty naval officers are reservists. The Navy has continuing programs for two- or three-year tours of active duty, and for extensions of active duty. Reservists on active duty have the same promotion and retirement opportunities as regular Navy officers. Reservists on inactive duty may earn points toward retirement by attending drills and by taking correspondence courses in various naval subjects.

Women in the Navy do not form a separate organization or unit, except for those in the Navy Nurse Corps.

They serve as enlisted or commissioned personnel in the Regular Navy or Naval Reserve. Women in the Navy are called *WAVES* as a matter of convenience, from their title during World War II. Women are not assigned to combat units, but may serve at overseas bases and aboard transport ships and aircraft. They are trained in many different specialties. See WAVES.

The Marine Corps is a separate military service within the Department of the Navy. Its commandant is responsible directly to the secretary of the navy. The corps assigns *fleet marine forces* (expeditionary troops) to the Atlantic and Pacific fleets. The Marines have the primary jobs of amphibious warfare and land operations in connection with naval campaigns. They also provide security forces that guard naval stations and ships, and U.S. embassies in other countries. See MARINE CORPS, UNITED STATES.

The Coast Guard operates under the secretary of the navy in wartime. It may then provide air-sea rescue services, carry out antisubmarine patrols, control and guard shipping in United States ports, and prevent waterfront disasters. In peacetime, the Coast Guard

helps enforce American laws and ensures safety at sea. See COAST GUARD, UNITED STATES.

History

The Colonial Navy was born in 1631, when the English colonists of Massachusetts built the first American warship, the 30-ton bark *Blessing of the Bay*. They used it to fight pirates off the Atlantic Coast. By the late 1700's, the colonists had built hundreds of ships, including *privateers*, or privately owned vessels (see PRIVATEER).

The Continental Congress established the Continental Navy in 1775. It set up a naval committee to administer naval affairs, and a marine committee to build and equip warships. Two merchantmen were converted into combat vessels. In 1776, Esek Hopkins, the Navy's first commodore and its first commander in chief, raided Nassau in the Bahama Islands with a fleet of five ships. During the Revolutionary War, 53 vessels served in the Continental Navy. Naval ships and privateers usually operated on independent missions. Captain John Paul Jones' badly damaged *Bonhomme Richard* forced the British vessel *Serapis* to surrender in one of the war's most exciting battles. Jones uttered the Navy's famous watchword: "I have not yet begun to fight!" See REVOLUTIONARY WAR IN AMERICA.

In 1779, Congress organized a five-man Board of Admiralty to administer the Navy. It discontinued the board in 1781, and put Robert Morris, a financier, in charge of naval activities. Congress disbanded the Navy after the war, because it felt the country did not need a permanent naval force. In 1785, it sold the last warship. But the need for a fleet soon arose again. Barbary pirates off North Africa preyed on American merchant ships, and killed or captured American seamen. In 1794, Congress voted to build six frigates to fight the pirates. This sea-going force operated under the secretary of war. The launching of the *United States* in 1797 marked the rebirth of the United States Navy.

Undeclared War with France. In the summer of 1796, relations between the United States and France had reached a state of undeclared war. France and Great Britain were at war with each other at this time. The French treated American merchant seamen like British subjects and, by 1798, had seized more than 300 American merchant ships. That year, Congress created a Navy Department under a secretary of the navy. The 44-gun frigates *Constitution* and *United States* and the 36-gun *Constellation* formed the basis of a new fleet that had grown to 49 ships by 1799. American squadrons operated with the British in the West Indies. Many battles raged between American and French ships. Napoleon Bonaparte ended the undeclared war with the United States after he seized power in France in 1799.

American relations with the Barbary states of Morocco, Algiers, Tunis, and Tripoli became worse. The Barbary rulers demanded more tribute money as the price for not attacking American ships in the Mediterranean. Tripoli declared war on the United States in 1801, and again in 1812. Stephen Decatur commanded a powerful squadron that forced all Moorish forces to surrender and accept his terms in 1815.

The War of 1812. Great Britain declared a blockade of France when war broke out in 1803. It seized Amer-

---

MAJOR U.S. NAVY INSTALLATIONS

Name	Location
Adak Naval Station	Adak, Alaska
Alameda Naval Air Station	Alameda, Calif.
*****Bethesda National Naval Medical Center**	Bethesda, Md.
*****Boston Naval Base**	Boston
*****Charleston Naval Base**	Charleston, S.C.
*****Corpus Christi Naval Air Station**	Corpus Christi, Tex.
*****Glenview Naval Air Station**	Glenview, Ill.
*****Great Lakes Naval Training Center**	Great Lakes, Ill.
Hunter's Point Naval Shipyard	San Francisco
Jacksonville Naval Air Station	Jacksonville, Fla.
Johnsville Naval Air Development Center	Johnsville, Pa.
*****Key West Naval Base**	Key West, Fla.
*****Lakehurst Naval Air Station**	Lakehurst, N.J.
Little Creek Naval Amphibious Base	Little Creek, Va.
*****Los Angeles Naval Base**	Los Angeles
*****Mare Island Naval Shipyard**	Vallejo, Calif.
Monterey Naval Postgraduate School	Monterey, Calif.
*****Naval Observatory, United States**	Washington, D.C.
*****Naval War College**	Newport, R.I.
*****New London Naval Submarine Base**	New London, Conn.
*****Newport Naval Base**	Newport, R.I.
*****Norfolk Naval Base**	Norfolk, Va.
Oakland Naval Supply Center	Oakland, Calif.
*****Oceanographic Office, United States Naval**	Suitland, Md.
*****Pacific Missile Range**	Point Mugu, Calif.
Patuxent River Naval Air Test Center	Patuxent River, Md.
*****Pearl Harbor Naval Base**	Pearl Harbor, Hawaii
*****Pensacola Naval Air Station**	Pensacola, Fla.
Philadelphia Naval Air Engineering Center	Philadelphia
*****Philadelphia Naval Base**	Philadelphia
*****Portsmouth Naval Shipyard**	Kittery, Me.
*****Puget Sound Naval Shipyard**	Bremerton, Wash.
*****Quonset Point Naval Air Station**	Quonset Point, R.I.
*****San Diego Naval Base**	San Diego
*****Treasure Island Naval Station**	Treasure Island, Calif.
*****United States Naval Academy**	Annapolis, Md.
*****Washington Navy Yard**	Washington, D.C.
Whidbey Island Naval Air Station	Oak Harbor, Wash.

*Has a separate article in WORLD BOOK.

79

WARSHIPS
OF THE NAVY

Warships include aircraft carriers, battleships, cruisers, command ships, destroyers, and submarines. Other naval combat vessels are amphibious-landing ships, mine warfare ships, and patrol ships. The Navy has about 70 types of combat ships. Major warships with their symbols are shown in the silhouettes below.

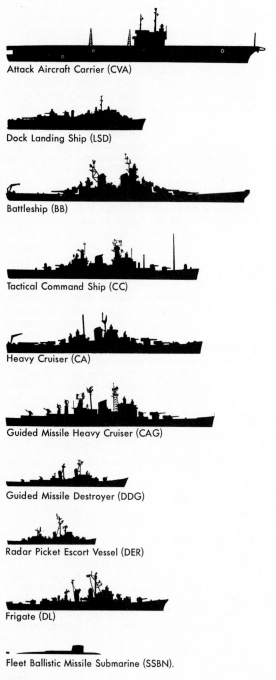

Attack Aircraft Carrier (CVA)

Dock Landing Ship (LSD)

Battleship (BB)

Tactical Command Ship (CC)

Heavy Cruiser (CA)

Guided Missile Heavy Cruiser (CAG)

Guided Missile Destroyer (DDG)

Radar Picket Escort Vessel (DER)

Frigate (DL)

Fleet Ballistic Missile Submarine (SSBN).

ican ships that violated the blockade, and imprisoned their seamen. The U.S. Navy had only 14 warships when the War of 1812 began, but it also had frigates commanded by skilled captains. In early victories, the *Constitution* captured the British ships *Guerrière* and *Java,* and the *United States* captured the *Macedonian.* The British warship *Shannon* destroyed the American ship *Chesapeake.* Captain James Lawrence of the *Chesapeake* issued as his dying command: "Don't give up the ship!"

The Royal Navy clamped a tight blockade on American ports, but American privateers continued to operate. They captured almost 1,000 enemy vessels and damaged British overseas trade. American ships won decisive victories on Lake Erie and Lake Champlain. By the end of the war in 1814, the Navy had established its place in national policy. See WAR OF 1812.

In the Mexican War, from 1846 to 1848, the Navy's work consisted chiefly of landings on the California coast and establishing a blockade along the Gulf of Mexico.

The Civil War found the Union Navy with only 42 ships. Within a month after the war began on Apr. 12, 1861, the Navy had blockaded the Southern States from Virginia to the Rio Grande to keep them from exporting cotton and importing supplies. The Confederate Navy countered with blockade runners and commerce raiders. The Southern ironclad warship *Merrimack* threatened to destroy the unarmored Union fleet that blockaded Hampton Roads in Virginia. In March, 1862, the Union's *Monitor* fought the *Merrimack* to a draw in the first battle between ironclad ships (see MONITOR AND MERRIMACK).

Rear Admiral David G. Farragut led a squadron that seized forts in Mobile Bay, Alabama. As his fleet swept into the bay, he barked the famous command: "Damn the torpedoes! Full steam ahead!" Farragut later became the Navy's first full admiral.

The Navy played a subordinate role throughout the Civil War. But it was essential to the success of the land armies, and showed the powerful effect of control of the

——— NAMES OF NAVAL SHIPS ———
The United States Navy names various types of ships after persons, places, or things, as follows:

Ammunition Ships—Volcanoes *(Mauna Kea)* or explosive terms *(Nitro)*.

Attack Aircraft Carriers—Famous ships *(Ranger)*, battles *(Midway)*, or men *(Forrestal)*.

Battleships—States *(Missouri)*.

Cargo Ships—Stars *(Virgo)*.

Coastal Mine Sweepers—Birds *(Bluebird)*.

Cruisers—Cities *(Boston)*.

Destroyers—Naval heroes *(Forrest Sherman)*, secretaries of the navy *(Frank Knox)*, or congressmen *(Norris)*.

Destroyer Tenders—Geographic regions *(Cascade)*.

Hospital Ships—Words of comfort *(Haven)*.

Landing Ships—Counties *(Suffolk County)* or places of historic interest *(Comstock)*.

Ocean Mine Sweepers—Abstract qualities *(Gallant)*.

Ocean Tugs—Indian tribes *(Sioux)*.

Oilers—Rivers *(Neosho)*.

Repair Ships—Mythological characters *(Vulcan)*.

Submarines—Fish or marine creatures *(Nautilus)*, or, for ballistic missile submarines, famous patriots of the Western Hemisphere *(George Washington)*.

Submarine Tenders—Submarine pioneers *(Holland)*.

Transports—Flag or general officers and other historic figures *(General Alexander M. Patch)*.

seas. The Union Navy came out of the war as the largest and most powerful naval force in the world. It had more than 670 ships and 57,000 men. See CIVIL WAR.

The Spanish-American War started in 1898. The two major naval battles of the war took place half a world apart. On May 1, 1898, Commodore George Dewey's squadron steamed through the entrance to Manila Bay in the Philippines. As his flagship *Olympia* approached the Spanish fleet off Cavite, he gave the historic command: "You may fire when you are ready, Gridley." The battle ended with the 10-ship enemy fleet destroyed or burning. On July 3, Commodore Winfield S. Schley's warships crushed a Spanish fleet outside Santiago harbor in Cuba. After the war, the United States realized that it needed a Navy to guard its possessions. See MAINE (ship); SPANISH-AMERICAN WAR.

"The Great White Fleet." A force of 16 battleships and 4 destroyers of the Atlantic Fleet began a 14-month world cruise in 1907. It was called "the Great White Fleet," because the ships had been painted white. At the end of the 46,000-mile cruise, the Navy had proved that it could easily shift from the Atlantic to the Pacific.

The Navy took two other major steps in the early 1900's. In 1915, it established the office of chief of naval operations. Admiral William S. Benson was the first to fill this position. Naval aviation was born during this same period. In 1911, the Navy purchased its first airplane. Shortly before, on Nov. 14, 1910, Eugene Ely had made the first shipboard take-off from a warship, the cruiser *Birmingham*. By 1914, the Navy had established its first naval air station at Pensacola, Fla., and in 1922, it built its first aircraft carrier, the *Langley*.

World War I began for U.S. combat forces on May 4, 1917, when a destroyer division docked in southern Ireland for duty with Great Britain's Royal Navy. In April, Rear Admiral William S. Sims had arrived in London to command U.S. Naval Forces in European waters. He found the British predicting an Allied defeat in six months unless the German submarine attacks could be stopped. The Allied navies began convoys, and assigned destroyers and submarine chasers to the Atlantic.

The Navy developed new types of mines, and laid a mine *barrage* (field) in the North Sea. It planted 56,000 mines in the largest mining operation in history. During the war, the Navy transported more than 2 million American soldiers across the Atlantic without a single loss of life. See WORLD WAR I.

After World War I, the Navy entered a period of decline. It scrapped, sank, or demilitarized about 2 million tons of ships, including 31 major warships, according to the 1921 Washington Conference that limited naval armament (see DISARMAMENT). By the 1930's, the United States had again started a shipbuilding program. It planned a two-ocean Navy.

World War II. The Japanese attack against the Pacific Fleet at Pearl Harbor, Hawaii, on Dec. 7, 1941, brought the United States into World War II. Nearly four years later, the war ended with surrender ceremonies held aboard the battleship *Missouri* in Tokyo Bay, Japan.

The Navy had been involved in defense activities as early as September, 1939. On Oct. 31, 1941, a German submarine sank the destroyer *Reuben James* west of Iceland. This was the first casualty of the undeclared war in the Atlantic.

The Navy recovered quickly from its losses at Pearl

AUXILIARY AND SERVICE SHIPS OF THE NAVY

Auxiliary and Service Ships support the combat vessels. The Navy's 50 types of auxiliary ships range from large tankers to small tugs. Service ships include about 65 types of yard, harbor, and district craft. Some types of auxiliary and service ships with their naval symbols are shown in the silhouettes below.

Submarine Chaser (PCS)

Ocean Minesweeper (MSO)

Fleet Minelayer (MMF)

Hospital Ship (AH)

Cargo Ship (AK)

Icebreaker (AGB)

Oiler (AO)

Transport (AP)

Repair Ship (AR)

Salvage Ship (ARS)

Auxiliary Ocean Tug (ATA)

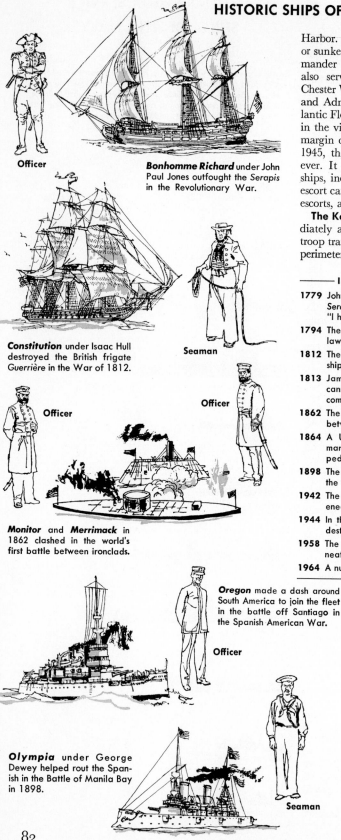

HISTORIC SHIPS OF THE UNITED STATES NAVY

Officer

Bonhomme Richard under John Paul Jones outfought the *Serapis* in the Revolutionary War.

Seaman

Constitution under Isaac Hull destroyed the British frigate *Guerrière* in the War of 1812.

Officer

Officer

Monitor and **Merrimack** in 1862 clashed in the world's first battle between ironclads.

Harbor. It salvaged and repaired many of the damaged or sunken ships. Admiral Ernest J. King became commander in chief of the United States Fleet, and later also served as chief of naval operations. Admiral Chester W. Nimitz took command of the Pacific Fleet, and Admiral Royal E. Ingersoll commanded the Atlantic Fleet. By June, 1942, the Navy's decisive victory in the vital Battle of Midway Island had cut Japan's margin of superiority. When World War II ended in 1945, the Navy had become the most powerful fleet ever. It had 3,400,000 men and women, and 2,500 ships, including 24 battleships, 35 aircraft carriers, 77 escort carriers, 92 cruisers, 501 destroyers, 406 destroyer escorts, and 262 submarines. See WORLD WAR II.

The Korean War involved naval forces almost immediately after the conflict began. Aircraft carriers and troop transports played vital roles in holding the Pusan perimeter during the first three months of the war. On

---
IMPORTANT DATES IN NAVY HISTORY

1779 John Paul Jones' *Bonhomme Richard* outfought the *Serapis*, and gave the Navy its famous watchword: "I have not yet begun to fight."

1794 The United States Navy was formally established in a law providing for ship construction.

1812 The *Constitution* under Isaac Hull overwhelmed the British ship *Guerrière* in the War of 1812.

1813 James Lawrence and the *Chesapeake* fell before the cannons of British warship *Shannon*. The dying Lawrence commanded: "Don't give up the ship!"

1862 The first battle between ironclad warships was fought between the *Monitor* and the *Merrimack*.

1864 A Union fleet stormed into Mobile Bay as its commander, David Farragut, bellowed: "Damn the torpedoes! Full steam ahead!"

1898 The United States fleet under George Dewey crushed the Spanish fleet in Manila Bay.

1942 The Pacific Fleet repulsed a Japanese fleet that threatened Midway Island and Hawaii.

1944 In the biggest naval battle in history, the Pacific Fleet destroyed Japanese sea power off Leyte Gulf.

1958 The world's first nuclear warship, *Nautilus*, cruised beneath the North Pole, the first ship to reach it.

1964 A nuclear-powered task force cruised around the world.

Oregon made a dash around South America to join the fleet in the battle off Santiago in the Spanish American War.

Officer

Transports carried more than 2,000,000 soldiers to fight in France during World War I.

Olympia under George Dewey helped rout the Spanish in the Battle of Manila Bay in 1898.

Seaman

Seaman

82

Sept. 15, 1950, an amphibious landing at Inchon helped reverse the course of the war. A feature of the ground battles was the success of naval and marine close air support, with aircraft and infantry operations closely coordinated. Without command of the sea, the Korean War would have been lost. See KOREAN WAR.

The Nuclear Age Navy. In 1948, the Navy assigned Captain Hyman G. Rickover the job of building a nuclear power plant for submarines. Six years later, the Navy commissioned the first nuclear-powered ship, the submarine *Nautilus*.

By the early 1960's, the Navy had nearly 60 nuclear-powered submarines built or scheduled for construction. These submarines can go over 60,000 miles before refueling, and can dive deeper and stay submerged longer than older types. Some are armed with Polaris missiles and form a major part of the United States defense system. Polaris submarines can cruise so deep, so fast, and so quietly that they are very difficult for an enemy to detect. Each submarine keeps most of its Polaris missiles ready to fire in about 15 minutes.

Such nuclear-powered surface ships as the cruiser U.S.S. *Long Beach* and the aircraft carrier U.S.S. *Enterprise* were also in service in the early 1960's. The U.S.S. *Enterprise* can cover over 150,000 miles at top cruising speed before refueling. In 1964, a nuclear-powered task force, consisting of the U.S.S. *Enterprise*, U.S.S. *Long Beach*, and U.S.S. *Bainbridge*, conducted Operation *Sea Orbit*, a cruise around the world.

The Navy is strengthening its forces in other ways. It has added guided missile frigates and destroyers, and such large attack carriers as the U.S.S. *America* and the U.S.S. *John F. Kennedy*. In 1962, the Navy formed its first destroyer division and its first cruiser-destroyer flotilla of guided missile ships. Amphibious landing force ships, such as the assault helicopter carrier U.S.S. *Okinawa*, have been designed for present-day naval operations. The Navy's construction program includes new aircraft carriers, guided missile frigates and destroyers, and combat support ships.　　　　HARRY A. SEYMOUR

Related Articles. See NAVY with its list of Related Articles, and articles on naval installations listed in the *Table* with this article. See also the following articles:

Outline

I. Life in the Navy
  A. Training a Sailor　　C. A Typical Day
  B. Training an Officer　D. Careers in the Navy

II. Ships and Weapons of the Navy
  A. Warships　　　　　　　　D. Ordnance
  B. Auxiliary and Service Ships　　Weapons
  C. Naval Aviation　　　　　E. Missiles

III. Organization of the Navy
  A. Navy Headquarters　　D. Regulars and Reserves
  B. Operating Forces　　　E. Women in the Navy
  C. The Shore　　　　　　F. The Marine Corps
  　Establishment　　　　　G. The Coast Guard

IV. History

Questions

How does the Navy serve in peacetime emergencies?
What is a *fleet?* A *type command?* A *task force?*
What are the two divisions of the Naval Reserve?
Who was the first full admiral in the U.S. Navy?
When did the Navy reach its peak strength? How many ships and men did it have?
What is the role of naval aviation?
What are the naval operating forces? The shore establishment? Navy headquarters?
What was "the Great White Fleet"?
What was the world's first nuclear-powered warship?
How did the Union Navy rank as a naval force?

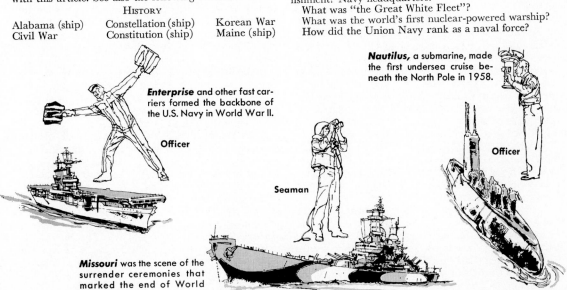

Enterprise and other fast carriers formed the backbone of the U.S. Navy in World War II.

Officer

Nautilus, a submarine, made the first undersea cruise beneath the North Pole in 1958.

Officer

Seaman

Missouri was the scene of the surrender ceremonies that marked the end of World War II.

NAVY AND MARINE CORPS MEDAL. See DECORA-
TIONS AND MEDALS (Military Awards).

NAVY CROSS. See DECORATIONS AND MEDALS (Military Awards).

NAVY DAY was a day set apart each year when
Americans honored the United States Navy. Navy Day,
set on October 27, was first celebrated in 1922. It was
last observed officially in 1948. The military services
now combine in one celebration called *Armed Forces
Day.* See also ARMED FORCES DAY; VETERANS DAY.

NAVY INTELLIGENCE SERVICE. See INTELLIGENCE
SERVICE.

NAVY JACK is a flag of the United States Navy.
It has 50 white stars on a blue background. It looks
like the blue and white corner portion of the flag of
the United States. The Navy Jack is flown from the
bow of a ship from sunrise until sunset when the ship
is in port. See also FLAG (color picture: The Shapes
of Flags).   WHITNEY SMITH, JR.

NAVY LEAGUE OF THE UNITED STATES is a civilian
organization that works for greater understanding of the
importance of the seas to the nation's economy and
security. It promotes a strong, progressive maritime
policy for the United States. The league was founded in
1902, and has headquarters at 818 18th Street NW,
Washington, D.C. 20006.

Critically reviewed by the NAVY LEAGUE OF THE UNITED STATES

NAVY YARD. See NAVAL SHIPYARD.

NAXOS, ISLE OF. See CYCLADES.

NAY is a vertical flute. See FLUTE.

NAYARIT, *nah yah REET,* is a state of Mexico. It
lies along the Pacific Coast in west-central Mexico (see
MEXICO [political map]). Nayarit has a population of
494,858. It covers 10,664 square miles of narrow coastal
lowlands and rugged mountains. Cattle, sheep, goats,
and horses graze on plains in the northwest. Farmers
grow sugar cane, tobacco, peanuts, vegetables, and
cotton. Because of bad treatment by the Spanish
colonists, the Indians of Nayarit fought a series of wars
against the white men between the 1500's and 1800's.
The territory became a state in 1917. Tepic is the
capital.   CHARLES C. CUMBERLAND

NAZARENE, *NAZ uh REEN,* refers to an inhabitant
of Nazareth, an ancient town in Israel. The term is
often applied to Jesus Christ, or to His followers (see
JESUS CHRIST). A Nazarene was a member of an early
Jewish-Christian sect that lived in Palestine until about
the A.D. 300's. A group of German painters in the 1800's
were also called Nazarenes. They moved to Rome and
had the goal of restoring Christian art to its medieval
purity. *Nazarene* also refers to a member of the Church
of the Nazarene (see CHURCH OF THE NAZARENE).

NAZARETH (pop. 29,100; alt. 1,320 ft.), is a town in
northern Israel. For location, see ISRAEL (color map). It
was the home of Jesus Christ during His early youth.
The town of Nazareth was in the Roman province of
Galilee (see GALILEE).

The Old Testament does not mention Nazareth.
Nathanael in the New Testament expressed the attitude
of the times about the village when he said, "Can there
any good thing come out of Nazareth?" (John 1: 46).

Nazareth remained insignificant for many years after
the time of Christ. But pilgrims visited the town about

Russell Wright
Mary's Well in Nazareth, an ancient spring which flowed
in Biblical times, still provides water for many people.

A.D. 600, and a large basilica was built. The Arabs captured the city in the 600's. The Crusaders built several
churches there, but the Ottoman Turks forced Christians to leave in 1517. A new town of Nazareth stands on
the site of the old. Its population is far more than Nazareth had in Biblical times. The Latin Church of the
Annunciation, completed in 1730, now rises where some
persons think the home of Mary, the mother of Jesus,
stood. Since the 1700's, several denominations have
built churches and monasteries. An ancient well, called
Mary's Well, still flows, and people still take water from
it.   SYDNEY N. FISHER and BRUCE M. METZGER

See also ISRAEL (color picture).

NAZARETH COLLEGE. See UNIVERSITIES AND COL-
LEGES (table).

NAZARETH COLLEGE OF KENTUCKY. See UNIVER-
SITIES AND COLLEGES (table).

NAZARETH COLLEGE OF ROCHESTER is a liberal
arts college for women in Rochester, N.Y. It is conducted by a religious congregation of women of the
Roman Catholic Church. Courses at the college lead
to bachelor's degrees. The college was founded in
1924. For enrollment, see UNIVERSITIES AND COLLEGES
(table).

NAZARITE, *NAZ uh rite,* was a name given to a
sacred person by the ancient Hebrews. Such a person
was not allowed to drink wine, cut his hair, or touch a
corpse. Nazarite was also a name once given to members
of the Free Methodist Church.

NAZIMOVA, *nuh ZIM oh vuh,* **ALLA** (1879-1945), a
Russian actress, became famous on the American stage
and in motion pictures. She was one of the first in the
United States to show the psychological approach in
acting. She played leading parts in the stage plays
*Ghosts, Hedda Gabler, The Master Builder, The Cherry
Orchard, The Good Earth,* and *Mourning Becomes Electra.*
She appeared in such motion pictures as *The Bridge of
San Luis Rey, In Our Time,* and *Since You Went Away.*

Alla Nazimova was born in Yalta, in the Crimea. She
performed at the famous Moscow Art Theatre before
she came to the United States in 1906.   RICHARD MOODY

NAZISM, or NAZIISM, was the political and social doctrine of the German dictator Adolf Hitler and his followers. Hitler and the Nazis ruled Germany from 1933 to 1945. *Nazi* stands for the first word in the German name for the *National Socialist German Workers' Party* (*Nationalsozialistische Deutsche Arbeiterpartei*).

Nazism was part of the dictatorial political movement called *fascism*. The Nazis were extreme nationalists who believed in the superiority of the Germans and other members of the so-called "Aryan race." The Nazis worked to strengthen German military might in order to bring the world under German control. They believed in a totalitarian government, where all opposition is ruthlessly put down. See TOTALITARIANISM.

A small group of men started the Nazi Party in Munich, Germany, just after World War I. Hitler joined the group in 1919 and became its leader. Many discontented Germans turned to Nazism after the economic depression of 1930. The movement seemed to promise jobs for them and glory for their country. But the promises proved false. Hitler became chancellor of Germany on Jan. 30, 1933. He made the government a Nazi dictatorship. The Nazis set up concentration camps where they killed thousands of political opponents and members of religious minorities.

In 1939, the Nazi government started World War II by attacking Poland. It soon conquered most of Europe. Great Britain, Russia, and the United States fought against the Nazis and finally defeated them. Hitler committed suicide on April 30, 1945.

Millions of people died in the war the Nazis started. The Nazis murdered about 12 million civilians, including almost all the Jews who lived under German rule. After the war, the Allies prosecuted many Nazi leaders for taking part in these murders and abolished the Nazi Party in Germany.   WILLIAM EBENSTEIN

Related Articles in WORLD BOOK include:

Auschwitz	Goebbels, Paul Joseph
Belsen	Goering, Hermann Wilhelm
Buchenwald	Himmler, Heinrich
Dachau	Hitler, Adolf
Eichmann, Adolf	Horst Wessel
Fascism	Nuremberg
Flag (color picture: Historical Flags of the World)	Nuremberg Trials
	Swastika
Germany (History)	World War II (Causes of Conflict)
Gestapo	

NBC. See NATIONAL BROADCASTING COMPANY.

NCAA. See NATIONAL COLLEGIATE ATHLETIC ASSOCIATION.

NE PLUS ULTRA. See PILLARS OF HERCULES.

NE WIN (1911-   ) became military ruler of Burma in 1962. He seized power when rebel tribesmen threatened to split the country. Ne Win set up a Revolutionary Council, with himself as chairman, and began to make Burma a socialist country.

By 1965, Ne Win had placed all private businesses under government control. But in spite of his socialist goals and the fact that Burma borders Communist China, Ne Win maintained a neutral foreign policy. He also fought Communist rebels in Burma.

Ne Win was born in Paungde, Burma. He became the head of the Burmese Army in 1950. In 1958, Prime Minister U Nu asked him to take over the government because of the threat of civil war. Ne Win headed a caretaker government from 1958 until elections were held in 1960 and U Nu returned to power. Ne Win overthrew U Nu in 1962.   JOHN F. CADY

See also BURMA (Recent Developments).

NEAGH, LOUGH. See LOUGH NEAGH.

NEANDERTHAL MAN, *nee AN der TAHL*, or NEANDERTAL, is the name of a race of prehistoric men who lived in caves in Europe, and western and central Asia. Neanderthal people probably lived between 110,-000 and 30,000 years ago. The name *Neanderthal* comes from the Neander Gorge near Düsseldorf, Germany, where scientists discovered a skullcap in 1856. It was the first remains of this ancient people to be found. Since then, archaeologists have found about 30 skeletons.

Neanderthal people were heavily built, but walked fully erect. They had heavy jaws, powerful teeth, and sloping foreheads. Their brains were as large as those of modern man. Neanderthals made excellent flint tools. They may have practiced a form of religion, because they buried their dead, sometimes with offerings. Scientists believe that they died out or were absorbed by newcomers, or that some of them developed into the white race.   CARLETON S. COON

See also FAMILY (picture); PREHISTORIC MAN (picture).

NEAP TIDE. See TIDE (High Tides and Low Tides).

NEAR EAST is a name sometimes given to a region that includes non-Soviet Asia from the Mediterranean Sea to the eastern boundary of Iran, plus part of northeastern Africa. The British and French first called this region the Near East because it lay nearer to London and Paris than the Far East. Many people refer to the Near East as the Middle East (see MIDDLE EAST).

The United States Department of State recognizes the Near East as being Cyprus; Egypt (officially the United Arab Republic); Syria; Iraq; Jordan; Saudi Arabia; Sudan; Yemen; Southern Yemen; Lebanon; Israel; the Persian Gulf Sheikdoms of Kuwait, Bahrain, and Qatar; the Trucial States; and the Sultanate of Muscat and Oman.   SYDNEY N. FISHER

NEARSIGHTEDNESS is a defect of sight in which distant objects that should be clearly seen are blurred. Doctors call this condition *myopia*. A nearsighted person's eyeballs are too long. When the eye brings distant objects into focus, the image falls too far in front of the retina to produce a sharp picture. To correct this, nearsighted persons often wear glasses with lenses that are thin in the middle and thick at the edges. Contact lenses also produce clear vision in most nearsighted persons.

Very few babies are born nearsighted. The defect usually develops in childhood and adolescence, and sometimes progresses rapidly until about the age of 21. Heredity is the most important cause of myopia.

Nearsightedness cannot be cured. Vision should be kept as near to normal as possible by using properly fitted glasses. Parents should be alert for signs of nearsightedness in their children.   JOHN R. MCWILLIAMS

See also GLASSES; EYE (picture: Nearsightedness).

NEBO, *NAY boh*, the god of wisdom in Babylonian mythology, was said to have invented the art of writing. He was also a god of the sun, and some say he was a god of the water. Nebo was the son of Marduk, who controlled the fates of men. It was Nebo's duty to write down the judgments passed on to the dead souls.

NEBO, MOUNT. See MOUNT NEBO.

NEBRASKA

The Cornhusker State

NEBRASKA is one of the leading farming states in the United States. Yet it was once considered part of the "Great American Desert." The people of Nebraska, with their determined pioneer spirit, made the Nebraska "desert" a land of productive ranches and farms. The hardy Nebraska farmers clung to their land despite dry periods, economic depression, and grasshopper plagues. To grow crops in dry regions, they built irrigation systems and practiced scientific farming. Where crops could not be made to grow, Nebraskans used the land to graze cattle. They learned the value of joining together to sell their products cooperatively.

Today, the sounds of busy tractors and other farm machinery are heard across Nebraska. In the west, waving fields of golden wheat stretch as far as the eye can see. In north-central Nebraska, huge herds of beef cattle graze on enormous ranches. On the fertile farms of the east, farmers grow corn, grain sorghums, and other crops. The farmers there also raise hogs and fatten cattle for market.

Nebraska's chief manufacturing activity is processing the food produced on its ranches and farms. Meat packing is the leading food-processing activity, and Omaha is one of the world's largest meat-packing centers.

Much of the history of Nebraska is the story of the tough, strong-willed Nebraska farmer. Many of the first farm settlers built their homes out of the Nebraska sod because they found few trees on this grassy land. In the 1860's, the first great wave of homesteaders poured into Nebraska to claim free land granted by the federal government. Hard times, insect pests, and droughts discouraged many farmers, and they returned to the East. But most of them refused to give up—and they built a rich, productive state.

The independent, pioneer spirit of the people of Nebraska also led them to adopt a *unicameral* (one-house) state legislature. Nebraska is the only state in the nation with a unicameral legislature. Lincoln is the capital of Nebraska, and Omaha is the largest city.

The name *Nebraska* comes from the Oto Indian word *nebrathka*. The word means *flat water*, and was the Indian name for Nebraska's chief river, the Platte. Nebraska's official nickname is the *Cornhusker State*. This nickname comes from corn, the state's leading crop, and from the cornhusking contests that were once held each fall in many rural communities.

For the relationship of Nebraska to other states in its region, see MIDWESTERN STATES.

The contributors of this article are William O. Dobler, Editor of the Lincoln Star; *Leslie Hewes, Professor of Geography at the University of Nebraska; and James C. Olson, Chancellor of the University of Missouri at Kansas City, and former Chairman of the Department of History at the University of Nebraska.*

Dick Hufnagle, Publix

Stockyards in Omaha

FPG

Herding Cattle in Western Nebraska

Nebraska (blue) ranks 15th in size among all the states, and is the third largest of the Midwestern States (gray).

Autumn on a Nebraska Farm

FACTS IN BRIEF

Capital: Lincoln.

Government: *Congress*—U.S. senators, 2; U.S. representatives, 3. *Electoral Votes*—5. *State Legislature*—members of the unicameral legislature, 49. *Counties*—93. *Voting Age*—20 years (state and local elections); 18 years (national elections).

Area: 77,227 square miles (including 705 square miles of inland water), 15th in size among the states. *Greatest Distances*—(east-west) 415 miles; (north-south) 205 miles.

Elevation: *Highest*—5,424 feet above sea level in southwestern Kimball County; *Lowest*—840 feet above sea level in Richardson County.

Population: *1970 Census*—1,483,791; 35th among the states; density, 19 persons to the square mile; distribution, 62 per cent urban, 38 per cent rural. *1960 Census*—1,411,330.

Chief Products: *Agriculture*—beef cattle, corn, dairy products, grain sorghums, hogs, soybeans, wheat. *Manufacturing*—chemicals; electrical machinery; food products; metal products; nonelectrical machinery; printing and publishing; transportation equipment. *Mining*—natural gas, natural gas liquids, petroleum, sand and gravel, stone.

Statehood: March 1, 1867, the 37th state.

State Motto: *Equality Before the Law.*

State Song: "Beautiful Nebraska." Words by Jim Fras and Guy G. Miller; music by Jim Fras.

Constitution of Nebraska was adopted in 1875. Nebraska had one earlier constitution, adopted in 1866. Amendments may be proposed in the legislature, by a constitutional convention, or by the people. An amendment proposed in the legislature becomes law after approval by three-fifths of the legislature and by a majority of voters casting ballots on the amendment.

A proposal to call a constitutional convention also must be approved by three-fifths of the legislature and by a majority of voters casting ballots on the proposal. Convention proposals become law after they have been approved by a majority of people voting on the proposals. The people of Nebraska may sign a *petition* (formal request) proposing a constitutional amendment. The number of signatures on a petition must equal 10 per cent of the total votes cast for governor in the last general election. The proposed amendment becomes law after a majority of the voters have approved it and the governor has proclaimed it a part of the constitution.

Executive. Nebraska voters elect the governor and lieutenant governor to four-year terms. The governor may serve any number of terms, but not more than two terms in succession. He receives a yearly salary of $25,000. For a list of all the governors of Nebraska, see the *History* section of this article.

In 1964, the voters approved another constitutional amendment, increasing the terms of other top state officials from two to four years, effective in 1967. These officials are the secretary of state, attorney general, treasurer, and auditor. All these officials except the treasurer may serve an unlimited number of successive terms. The treasurer may serve any number of terms, but not more than two in succession.

Legislature. Nebraska is the only state with a *unicameral* (one-house) legislature. The 49 members of the legislature are called *senators*. Voters in each of 49 legislative districts elect one senator. The people elect the senators on a *nonpartisan* ballot—the ballot has no political party labels. Minnesota is the only other state in which the state legislators are chosen in nonpartisan elections. The people approved a constitutional amendment in 1962 increasing the legislators' terms from two years to four years. In the 1964 general election, 24 senators were elected to two-year terms and 25 senators were elected to four-year terms. Since the 1966 election, half the senators have been elected every two years to four-year terms.

The legislature meets every year. Regular sessions begin on the first Tuesday in January. They are limited to 60 days in even-numbered years and 90 days in odd-numbered years. The governor may call special sessions. Between sessions, members of the legislature make up the legislative council. The council studies state problems and recommends new laws to the legislature.

Courts in Nebraska are headed by the state supreme court. It consists of a chief justice and six associate justices. Nebraska also has 21 district courts, with a total of 43 judges. A merit plan for selecting supreme court and district court judges went into effect in 1964. Under the plan, the governor appoints a judge to fill a vacancy in these courts from a list submitted by a nominating committee. Each judge appointed must be approved by the voters at the next general election after holding office for three years. If approved, he serves for six more years. Thereafter, the voters must approve him every six years.

Every Nebraska county has a county court presided over by a judge elected to a four-year term. Omaha and Lincoln each has a municipal court and a juvenile court. Judges of these courts are selected in the same way as are the judges of the supreme court and the district courts. No political party labels are allowed on the ballot for electing or approving any judge in Nebraska.

Local Government. Nebraska has 93 counties. About two-thirds of the counties have the commissioner-precinct form of government, and the rest have the supervisor-township form. Counties with the commissioner-precinct form are governed by a board of commissioners of three or five members. The commissioners are elected to four-year terms. Counties with the supervisor-township form are governed by a seven-man board of supervisors. The supervisors are also elected to four-year terms. Other officials in both kinds of Nebraska counties include the county clerk, treasurer, sheriff, and attorney.

Nebraska has about 540 cities and villages. Most cities have the mayor-council form of government. Nebraska City uses the commission form, and a few cities use the council-manager plan. Each village is governed by a five-man board of trustees. The Nebraska constitution gives *home rule* to all cities with more than 5,000 persons. Such cities may operate under their own charters. Only Lincoln and Omaha have chosen to adopt their own charters.

Taxation. Taxes and licenses bring in about two-thirds of the state government's income. Almost all of the other one-third comes from federal grants and other U.S. government programs. The state collects personal

The Governor's Mansion, completed in 1958, stands south of the Capitol in Lincoln.

The State Seal

Symbols of Nebraska. On the state seal, adopted in 1867, the smith represents the mechanical arts. The settler's cabin, the growing corn, and the shocks of grain stand for agriculture. The steamboat and train symbolize transportation. The state flag, adopted in 1925, bears a silver and gold reproduction of the seal centered on a field of dark blue.

Seal, flag, bird, and flower illustrations, courtesy of Eli Lilly and Company

and corporation income taxes, a 2½ per cent sales and use tax, and taxes on alcoholic beverages, insurance payments, motor fuels, and tobacco. Nebraskans voted out the state property tax in 1966.

Politics. Nebraskans generally vote for Republicans when party labels are on the ballot. However, all members of the legislature, all judges and school officials, and many local officials are elected or approved on non-partisan ballots. This system has weakened party politics in the state. In about two-thirds of the elections for President and governor, most Nebraskans have voted for Republicans. For Nebraska's electoral votes and voting record in presidential elections, see ELECTORAL COLLEGE (table).

Two of Nebraska's most famous citizens were national political leaders. William Jennings Bryan ran for President unsuccessfully three times. George W. Norris won fame as an independent statesman during his 40 years in the U.S. House of Representatives and Senate.

Nebraska's Capitol in Lincoln was completed in 1932. The central tower is 400 feet high. Lincoln was named the capital in 1867. Omaha was the capital from 1855 to 1867.

Nebraska Game Commission

The State Flag

The State Bird
Western Meadow Lark

The State Flower
Goldenrod

The State Tree
American Elm

89

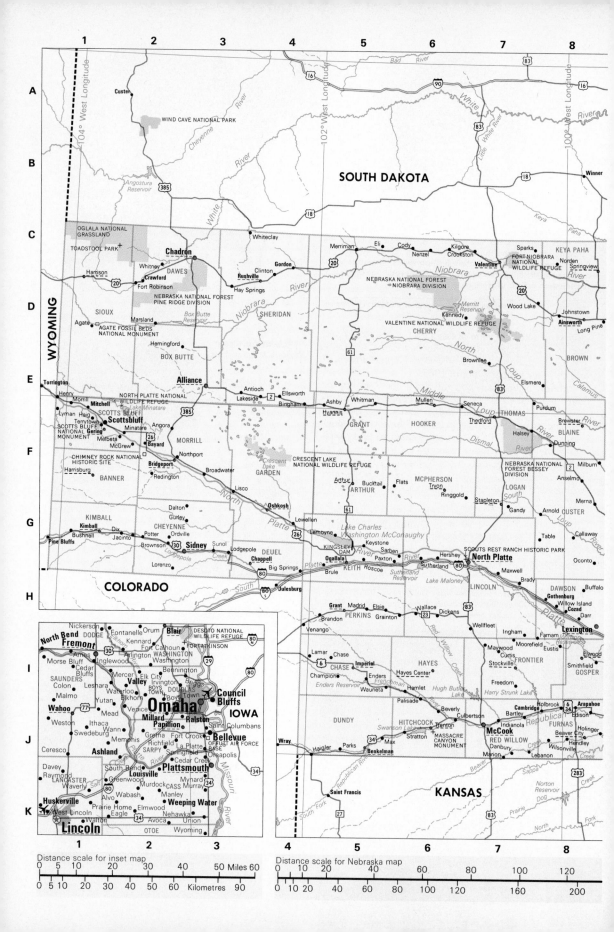

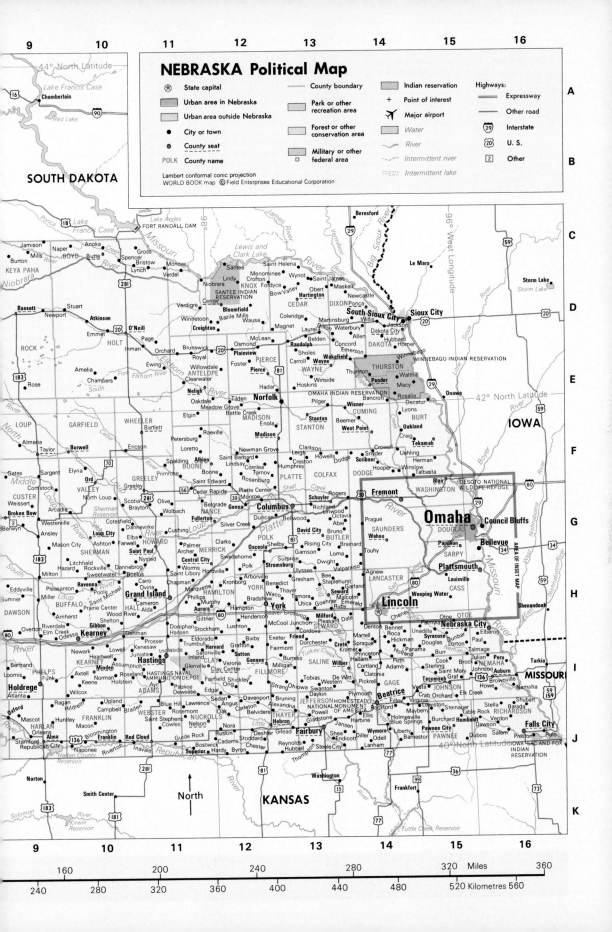

Pleasant Dale .258..H 14	Roseland ....212..I 11	Snyder ....383..F 14	Taylor ......240.°F 9	Washington ...76..I 2
Pleasanton ...261..H 10	Rosemont ....J 11	South Bend ...86..J 2	Tecumseh ..2,058.°I 15	Waterbury ....81..D 14
Plymouth ....424..I 14	Royal ....86..E 11	South	Tekamah ..1,848.°F 15	Waterloo ....455..I 2
Polk ....413..H 12	Ruby ....H 13	Sioux City 7,920..D 14	Terrytown ...747..F 1	Wauneta .....738..I 8
Ponca ....984.°D 14	Rulo ....299..J 16	Spalding ....676..F 11	Thayer ....78..H 12	Wausa ....720..D 12
Poole ....19..H 10	Rushville ..1,137.°D 4	Sparks ....C 7	Thedford ....303.°E 7	Waverly ...1,152..K 1
Potter ....356..G 2	Ruskin ....229..J 12	Spencer .....606..C 10	Thompson ....J 13	Wayne .....5,379.°E 13
Powell ....J 13	St. Bernard ......F 12	Sprague .....119..I 14	Thurston ....117..E 14	Weeping
Prague ....291..G 14	St. Columbans ....J 3	Springfield ..795..J 2	Tilden ......947..E 12	Water ...1,143..H 15
Prairie Home ......K 1	St. Edward ...853..F 12	Springview ..260.°C 8	Tobias ......124..I 13	Weissert ....G 9
Preston ....64..J 16	St. Helena ..102..C 13	Stamford ....207..J 9	Touhy ....G 14	Wellfleet .....51..H 7
Primrose .....88..F 11	St. James ....D 13	Stanton ...1,363.°E 13	Trenton .....770.°J 6	West Lincoln .....K 1
Princeton ......I 14	St. Libory ....H 11	Staplehurst ..227..H 13	Trumbull ....220..I 11	West Point ..3,385.°F 14
Prosser ....70..I 11	St. Mary ....I 15	Stapleton ...311.°G 7	Tryon ....°F 6	Western .....344..I 13
Purdum ....E 7	St. Michael ......H 10	Steele City ..176..J 13	Uehling .....249..F 14	Westerville ....G 9
Raeville ....F 11	St. Paul ...2,026.°G 11	Steinauer ...118..J 15	Ulysses .....312..H 13	Weston ......285..J 1
Ragan ....60..J 9	St. Stephens .....J 11	Stella ....282..I 16	Unadilla ....271..H 15	Whiteclay ....C 3
Ralston ....4,265..J 2	Salem ....214..J 16	Sterling .....476..I 15	Union ....275..K 3	Whitman ....E 5
Randolph ..1,130..D 13	Santee ....C 12	Stockham .....65..H 12	Upland ......205..I 10	Whitney ......82..C 2
Ravenna ...1,356..H 10	Sarben ....G 6	Stockville ....61.°I 7	Utica ....602..H 13	Wilber ....1,483.°H 13
Raymond ....187..K 1	Sargent .....789..F 9	Strang ....47..I 12	Valentine ..2,662.°C 7	Wilcox ......280..I 9
Red Cloud ..2,195.°J 11	Saronville ...74..I 12	Stratton .....481..I 6	Valley .....1,595..I 2	Willow Island ....H 8
Republi-	Schuyler ..3,597.°G 13	Stromsburg .1,215..H 12	Valparaiso ..415..H 14	Wilsonville ..266..J 8
can City ...179..J 9	Scotia ....354..G 10	Stuart ......561..D 9	Venango .....218..H 4	Winnebago ...675..E 14
Reynolds ...115..J 13	Scottsbluff .14,507..F 1	Sumner ......184..H 9	Venice ....J 2	Winnetoon ....84..D 12
Richfield ....J 2	Scribner ..1,031..F 14	Sunol ....G 3	Verdel ....74..C 11	Winside .....453..E 13
Richland ....123..G 13	Sedan ....I 12	Superior ..2,779..J 11	Verdigre ....570..D 11	Winslow .....145..F 14
Rising City ..344..G 13	Seneca ....I I..E 6	Surprise .....77..H 13	Verdon ......265..J 16	Wisner ....1,315..E 13
Riverdale ...155..H 9	Seward ....5,294.°H 13	Sutherland ..840..G 6	Virginia .....83..J 14	Wolbach .....366..G 11
Riverton ....220..J 10	Shelby ....647..G 13	Sutton ....1,361..I 12	Wabash ....K 2	Wood Lake ...117..D 8
Roca ....118..I 14	Shelton ...1,028..H 10	Swanton .....160..I 13	Waco ....214..H 13	Wood
Rockford ....J 14	Shickley ....385..I 12	Swedeburg ....J 1	Wahoo .....3,835.°G 14	River ...1,061..H 10
Rockville ...114..H 10	Sholes ....22..E 13	Syracuse ..1,562..I 15	Wakefield ..1,160..E 14	Worms ....H 11
Rogers ....95..G 14	Shubert .....240..J 16	Table Rock ..429..J 15	Wallace .....241..H 6	Wymore ...1,790..J 14
Rosalie .....204..E 14	Sidney ....6,403.°G 2	Talmage .....285..I 15	Walthill ....897..E 14	Wynot ....226..D 13
Roscoe ....G 5	Silver Creek .483..G 12	Tamora ....93..H 13	Walton ....K 1	York ....6,778.°H 12
Rose ....E 9	Smithfield ...58..I 8	Tarnov ....63..F 12	Wann ....J 2	Yutan ....507..J 1

*Does not appear on map; key shows general location.
°County seat

Source: Latest census figures (1970). Places without population figures are unincorporated areas and are not listed in census reports.

NEBRASKA/People

The 1970 United States census reported that Nebraska had 1,483,791 persons. The population had increased 5 per cent over the 1960 figure, 1,411,330.

About two-thirds of the people live in urban areas. Nebraska has two Standard Metropolitan Statistical Areas (see METROPOLITAN AREA). These are Omaha and Lincoln. The population of the Omaha metropolitan area is 540,142, and that of the Lincoln area is 167,972.

Omaha, the state's largest city, serves as the industrial and trade center of eastern Nebraska and western Iowa. Omaha is one of the nation's chief rail centers. Lincoln, the second largest city, became Nebraska's capital in 1867. The first Capitol stood on the open prairie.

Pioneers planted the trees that still shade many of Lincoln's streets. D Street is famous for its many huge pin oaks.

Lincoln is an educational, governmental, and retail-shopping center. Grand Island, Nebraska's third largest city, has a population of 31,269. It is an important shipping point for farm and manufactured products. Only nine other Nebraska cities have more than 10,000 persons. See the separate articles on the cities of Nebraska listed in the *Related Articles* at the end of this article.

Nearly 97 out of 100 Nebraskans were born in the United States. Persons of German descent make up about a third of Nebraska's population, and Germans make up the largest group of Nebraskans born in other countries.

Protestants make up the chief religious group in Nebraska. The largest Protestant bodies include the Baptists, Disciples of Christ, Episcopalians, Lutherans, Methodists, Presbyterians, and members of the United Church of Christ. Lutherans make up the largest Protestant group in the state. Many Roman Catholics live in Nebraska, especially in cities and towns.

POPULATION

PERSONS PER SQUARE MILE

50 to 1,250
20 to 50
5 to 20
1 to 5

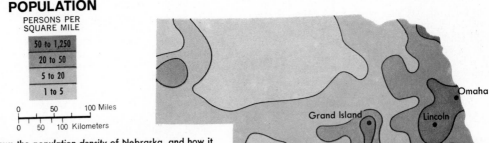

This map shows the *population density* of Nebraska, and how it varies in different parts of the state. Population density means the average number of persons who live on each square mile.

WORLD BOOK map

Schools. In the 1820's, the U.S. Army established Nebraska's first school, at Fort Atkinson (near present-day Fort Calhoun). During the 1830's and 1840's, missionaries of various religious faiths founded schools in many parts of the Nebraska region to teach the Indians. The first legislature of the Nebraska Territory adopted a free-school law in 1855, one year after the territory was opened for settlement. The state constitution, adopted in 1875, provides for the present system of public education. Children must attend school between their 7th and 16th birthdays.

The state department of education supervises the school system. The department consists of a state board of education and a state commissioner of education. The people elect the eight members of the state board to four-year terms. The members of the board appoint the commissioner to a two-year term. For the number of students and teachers in Nebraska, see EDUCATION (table).

Libraries. Nebraska's first library was established in 1820 at the Fort Atkinson military post. The Kansas-Nebraska Act of 1854 provided for a territorial library in Nebraska. In 1871, Omaha established the state's first public library. The legislature passed a law in 1877 providing state funds to support public libraries. The Nebraska public library commission was set up in 1901. It serves as a center for the development of libraries and the coordination of library services in the state.

Nebraska has more than 255 public libraries which are part of 20 developing regional library systems. The state has 33 college and university libraries. The University of Nebraska library in Lincoln is the largest library in the state. It has more than 1 million books. The Nebraska State Historical Society in Lincoln owns the largest collection of historical documents concerning Nebraska. The law section of the Nebraska State Library in Lincoln ranks among the nation's best law libraries.

NEBRASKA /A Visitor's Guide

Every year, thousands of tourists drive along Nebraska highways that follow the historic Oregon and Mormon trails. Ruts left by the pioneers' covered wagons can still be seen along the roadsides. In western Nebraska, the forests and rugged rocks of the Pine Ridge are a camper's and hiker's paradise. Other scenic spots include the valleys of the Platte, Niobrara, Big Blue, Loup, and Republican rivers and the bluffs along the Missouri River. Fishermen delight in the lakes and streams of the Sand Hills area, which teem with bass, pike, and other game fish. On the broad prairies, hunters bag pheasants, quail, and other game birds.

-------- PLACES TO VISIT --------

Following are brief descriptions of some of Nebraska's many interesting places to visit.

Bellevue is the oldest town in Nebraska. It was established about 1823 as a fur-trading center. Some of the town's buildings are more than a hundred years old.

Boys Town, near Omaha, is a home for neglected and homeless boys of all races and creeds.

Brownville was a leading river port of the 1850's. Many colorful reminders of pioneer days still stand.

Fort Atkinson, near Fort Calhoun, was the site of the first U.S. military post west of the Missouri River. A monument marks the site of the old fort, which stood from 1819 to 1827.

Massacre Canyon Monument, near Trenton, marks the site of the last battle between the Sioux and Pawnee Indians.

Scouts Rest Ranch, near North Platte, was the home of Buffalo Bill, the dashing frontiersman. His famous Wild West Show rehearsed there.

Toadstool Park, in the Badlands near Crawford, has huge, oddly shaped rock formations. Many of them resemble giant toadstools.

Union Stockyards, in Omaha, covers about 100 acres. It is one of the world's largest livestock markets.

Buffalo Bill's Home at Scouts Rest Ranch near North Platte
Nebraska Information and Tourism Div.

National Forest, Monuments, and Site. The Nebraska National Forest is the only national forest in the United States which was planted entirely by man. The forest contains a game refuge, and it also has fishing and swimming facilities. The Agate Fossil Beds National Monument contains famous deposits of animal fossils. The Homestead National Monument of America occupies the site of one of the first pieces of land claimed under the Homestead Act of 1862. The Scotts Bluff National Monument marks a landmark 766 feet above the North Platte River on the Oregon Trail. The spire at Chimney Rock National Historic Site rises about 500 feet above the North Platte.

State Parks. Nebraska has five state parks. For information on the state parks of Nebraska, write to Director, Game and Parks Commission, State Capitol, Lincoln, Nebr. 68509.

Museums. The Nebraska State Historical Society museum features exhibits dealing with the history of Nebraska and the West. The Hastings Museum also has displays on Nebraska's history. The Harold Warp Pioneer Village in Minden features thousands of indoor and outdoor exhibits dealing with life in the West from 1830 on. The University of Nebraska State Museum in Lincoln has one of the nation's largest collections of fossils, including an exceptional display of prehistoric mammoth skeletons. The Joslyn Art Museum in Omaha owns many outstanding European and American paintings. The University of Nebraska Art Galleries in Lincoln display a large collection of paintings by modern American artists. These works are housed in the $3½ million Sheldon Memorial Art Gallery, which was completed in 1963. The National Park Service operates museums at Scotts Bluff National Monument near Scottsbluff, and at the Homestead National Monument of America near Beatrice.

UNIVERSITIES AND COLLEGES

Nebraska has 14 universities and colleges accredited by the North Central Association of Colleges and Secondary Schools. For enrollments and further information, see UNIVERSITIES AND COLLEGES (table).

Name	Location	Founded
Chadron State College	Chadron	1911
Concordia Teachers College	Seward	1894
Creighton University	Omaha	1878
Dana College	Blair	1884
Doane College	Crete	1858
Hastings College	Hastings	1882
Kearney State College	Kearney	1905
Midland Lutheran College	Fremont	1887
Nebraska, University of	*	1869
Nebraska Wesleyan University	Lincoln	1887
Peru State College	Peru	1867
Saint Mary, College of	Omaha	1923
Union College	Lincoln	1891
Wayne State College	Wayne	1891

*For campuses, see UNIVERSITIES AND COLLEGES (table).

Father Flanagan Memorial at Boys Town near Omaha
FPG

Chimney Rock National Historic Site near Bayard
Dick Hufnagle, Publix

ANNUAL EVENTS

The Nebraska State Fair and the Ak-Sar-Ben Festival are the state's most important annual events. The fair is held in Lincoln in September. It features exhibits of livestock, crops, farm machinery, and household equipment. Omaha's Ak-Sar-Ben Festival includes a brilliant parade and a ball. The festival takes place in October. The Knights of Ak-Sar-Ben is an organization devoted to promoting good citizenship and economic advancement in Nebraska and western Iowa. The name *Ak-Sar-Ben* is *Nebraska* spelled backwards. Almost every Nebraska county has a fair during the summer, and many communities hold annual fall festivals.

Other annual events held in Nebraska include the following.

March-May: State Day, statewide (March 1); P-F-L (Pasture-Forage-Livestock) Meeting in Omaha (March); Arbor Day, statewide (April 22); Ak-Sar-Ben Ice Follies in Omaha (April); Intercollegiate Rodeo in Chadron (May); State High School Rodeo in Ogallala (May); Spring Festival in Brownville (May).

June-August: Homestead Week Celebration in Beatrice (June); Plum Creek Days in Lexington (June); Oregon Trail Days in Gering (July); Little Britches Rodeo in Chadron (July); Fort Sidney Days in Sidney (July); Ak-Sar-Ben Charity Horse Show in Omaha (July); Burwell Rodeo in Burwell (August); Massacre Canyon Powwow in Trenton and Winnebago (August).

September-October: Fall Frolic in Columbus (September); Ak-Sar-Ben Rodeo and Livestock Show in Omaha (September); Open House Day in Battle Creek (September); Band Day at the University of Nebraska in Lincoln (October).

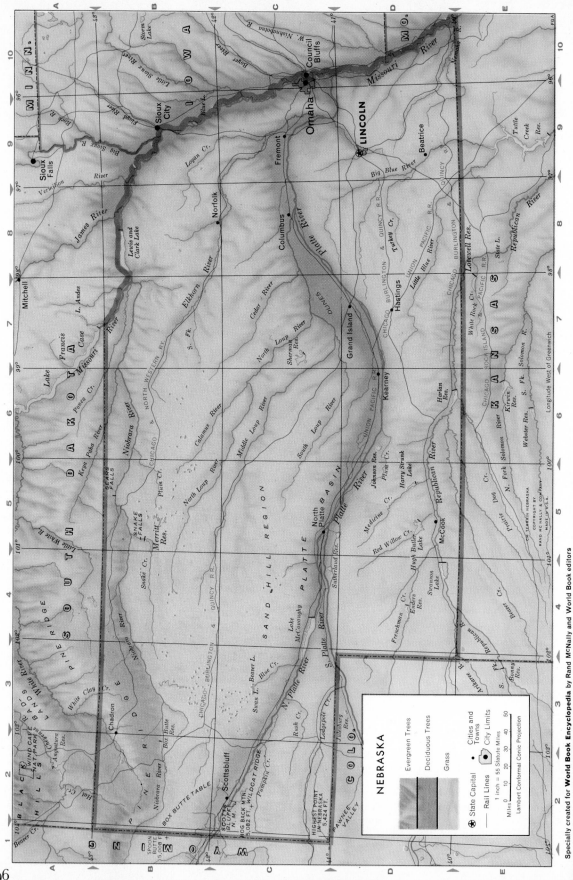

NEBRASKA

State Capital
Cities and Towns
City Limits

Rail Lines

Evergreen Trees
Deciduous Trees
Grass

1 inch = 55 Statute Miles

Miles 0 10 20 30 40 50

Lambert Conformal Conic Projection

Specially created for **World Book Encyclopedia** by Rand McNally and World Book editors

96

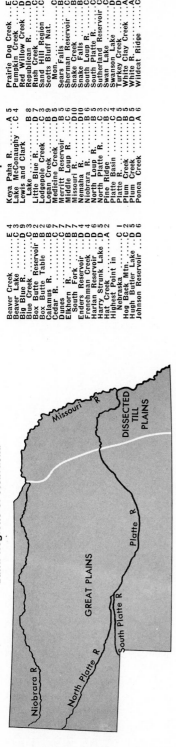

Land Regions of Nebraska

NEBRASKA / The Land

Land Regions. Nebraska rises in a series of rolling plateaus from the southeast to the extreme southwestern border. The elevation increases from about 800 feet above sea level to over 5,400 feet. Nebraska has two major land regions. These are, from east to west: (1) the Dissected Till Plains and (2) the Great Plains.

The Dissected Till Plains cover about the eastern fifth of Nebraska and extend into South Dakota, Iowa, Missouri, and Kansas. Glaciers once covered the Till Plains. The last glacier melted several hundred thousand years ago. It left a thick cover of rich, soil-forming material called *till*. A deep deposit of wind-blown dust called *loess* then settled on the till. Streams have *dissected* (cut up) the region, giving it a rolling surface. In the southeastern section of Nebraska's Till Plains, the action of the streams has exposed glacial materials on the sides of the valleys. The northern section of the Till Plains is known as the *Loess Hills*. Most of the Dissected Till Plains is well suited to farming with modern machinery.

The Great Plains region of Nebraska stretches westward from the Dissected Till Plains and extends into

Wyoming and Colorado. A series of sand hills rises north of the Platte River in the central part of the region. The soil of the *Sand Hills* section consists of fine sand piled up by the wind. The sand was formed into low hills and into ridges many miles long and several hundred feet high. Grasses that now cover the Sand Hills hold most of the sand in place. Sometimes, however, overgrazing by cattle kills the grass cover. The wind then cuts great holes called *blowouts* into the hillsides. Most ranchers take care not to overgraze the land. The Sand Hills make exceptionally fine cattle country because of the area's flowing streams, abundant well water, and excellent grasses. Some of the grass is cut as *wild hay*.

The soil of the Sand Hills acts like a giant sponge. It absorbs and holds most of the area's limited rainfall. The rainfall seeps down and creates vast underground reservoirs of *ground water*. Movements of the ground water make it possible for farmers to pump irrigation water to the surface in areas around the Sand Hills section.

A deep deposit of loess covers the central and south-central parts of the Great Plains. Some of this loess country is rough and hilly. But in the southeast, a vast area of flat loess land covers about 7,000 square miles. This area, called the *Loess Plain*, is farmed even more intensively than the Till Plains.

North and west of the Sand Hills are the *High Plains*, which cover about 12,000 square miles. The High Plains in the west rise more than a mile above sea level along part of the Wyoming border. The High Plains receive little rainfall. Farmers there must use irrigation or practice *dry farming*, methods that make the most of the limited rainfall (see DRY FARMING). Rough parts of the High Plains are used mainly to graze cattle. Some of the rough areas, including the beautiful Wildcat Ridge and Pine Ridge, are covered with evergreen trees. The highest point in Nebraska is 5,424 feet above sea level in southwestern Kimball County.

A small area of *Badlands* is found in northwestern Nebraska. There, the forces of nature have carved weird formations in the sandstone and claylike rocks.

NEBRASKA

Mitchell Pass, at Scotts Bluff National Monument, was part of the Oregon Trail. The pass and bluffs are in the Great Plains Region of western Nebraska.

Rich Farmlands make up most of eastern Nebraska. Farmers use contour plowing on the rolling land. Rows of trees protect the flat areas from the weather.

The Badlands have little economic importance, but ranchers use some of the area to graze cattle.

Rivers and Lakes. The great Missouri River forms Nebraska's eastern and northeastern border. Nebraska's principal river, the Platte, flows into the Missouri at Plattsmouth. The North Platte and South Platte rivers join near the city of North Platte and form the Platte. The North Platte River flows into the state from Wyoming, and the South Platte enters from Colorado. The Platte River winds across central and southern Nebraska. In some places, it is as much as a mile wide. The Platte is one of the shallowest rivers in the United States. Its depth ranges from a few inches to several feet. Nebraskans use the waters of the Platte River and its branches for irrigation and to generate hydroelectric power.

The Loup and Elkhorn rivers are the Platte's most important branches. Both rise in the Sand Hills. The abundant supplies of ground water in the Sand Hills keep these rivers flowing the year around. The Loup River is formed by the North, Middle, and South Loup rivers.

The Republican River enters southwestern Nebraska from Kansas. It flows near the southern edge of Nebraska for about 200 miles, and then turns back into Kansas and empties into the Kansas River. Other branches of the Kansas River in Nebraska include the Big Blue and Little Blue rivers. These three branches of the Kansas River usually flow gently. But heavy rainstorms sometimes cause them to overflow their banks and flood the countryside. This danger has been reduced by flood-control projects and by dams built for irrigation and generating electric power.

The Niobrara River flows into northwestern Nebraska

from Wyoming. It winds across the northern part of the state. This narrow, swift river passes through many scenic spots. It joins the Missouri River in Knox County.

Nebraska has more than 2,000 lakes. None of the natural lakes is very large. Hundreds of small, shallow lakes dot the Sand Hills. Lake McConaughy, Nebraska's largest lake, is man-made. It covers about 55 square miles and has a shoreline of 105 miles. Lake McConaughy was formed on the North Platte River by Kingsley Dam. Other important man-made lakes on the Platte River irrigation and power system include Jeffrey, Johnson, and Sutherland reservoirs. Additional large man-made lakes are Swanson Lake and Harlan Reservoir on the Republican River, and Enders Reservoir and Harry Strunk Lake on branches of the Republican.

NEBRASKA/Climate

Nebraska's climate ranges from extremely hot in summer to extremely cold in winter. The weather changes suddenly—and sometimes violently. Hot, moist breezes from the Gulf of Mexico occasionally make summer nights uncomfortably warm in eastern areas of the state. Nebraska sometimes has violent thunderstorms, tornadoes, blizzards, and hailstorms. The temperature varies only moderately from one section to another. But the humidity decreases average from east to west. July temperatures average about 77° F., and January temperatures average about 25° F. The state's record high temperature of 118° F. was set at Geneva on July 15, 1934; at Hartington on July 17, 1936; and at Minden on July 24, 1936. Camp Clarke, near Northport, recorded the state's lowest temperature, −47° F., on Feb. 12, 1899.

Rainfall also decreases steadily from east to west. The eastern section receives an average of about 27 inches of rain yearly, but less than 18 inches fall in the west. The state has droughts in some years, floods in others. Most of the rain comes between April and September. Nebraska's growing season ranges from about 165 days in the southeast to about 120 days in the northwest. Snowfall averages almost 30 inches yearly in the east. Western Nebraska generally receives less snow.

A Sudden Snowstorm, typical of Nebraska's quick changes in weather, puts a frosty white blanket over this farm near Albion.

George W. Stewart

AVERAGE YEARLY PRECIPITATION
(Rain, Melted Snow, and Other Moisture)

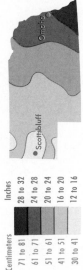

Centimeters	Inches
71 to 81	28 to 32
61 to 71	24 to 28
51 to 61	20 to 24
41 to 51	16 to 20
30 to 41	12 to 16

SEASONAL TEMPERATURES

JANUARY

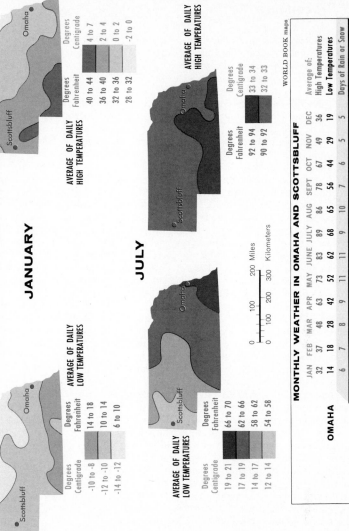

AVERAGE OF DAILY LOW TEMPERATURES

Degrees Fahrenheit	Degrees Centigrade
14 to 18	-10 to -8
10 to 14	-12 to -10
6 to 10	-14 to -12

AVERAGE OF DAILY HIGH TEMPERATURES

Degrees Fahrenheit	Degrees Centigrade
40 to 44	4 to 7
36 to 40	2 to 4
32 to 36	0 to 2
28 to 32	-2 to 0

JULY

AVERAGE OF DAILY LOW TEMPERATURES

Degrees Fahrenheit	Degrees Centigrade
66 to 70	19 to 21
62 to 66	17 to 19
58 to 62	14 to 17
54 to 58	12 to 14

AVERAGE OF DAILY HIGH TEMPERATURES

Degrees Fahrenheit	Degrees Centigrade
92 to 94	33 to 34
90 to 92	32 to 33

WORLD BOOK maps

0   100   200 Miles
0 100 200 300 Kilometers

MONTHLY WEATHER IN OMAHA AND SCOTTSBLUFF

		JAN	FEB	MAR	APR	MAY	JUNE	JULY	AUG	SEPT	OCT	NOV	DEC
OMAHA	Average of: High Temperatures	32	37	48	63	73	83	89	86	78	67	49	36
	Low Temperatures	14	18	28	42	52	62	68	65	56	44	29	19
	Days of Rain or Snow	6	7	8	9	11	11	7	7	6	6	5	5
SCOTTSBLUFF	Days of Rain or Snow	5	4	6	8	12	12	7	7	6	5	4	4
	High Temperatures	37	42	49	61	70	81	90	88	78	66	50	40
	Low Temperatures	10	15	21	32	42	52	59	57	46	35	22	14

Temperatures are given in degrees Fahrenheit.

Source: U.S. Weather Bureau

Natural Resources. Soil and water are Nebraska's most precious natural resources. They must be carefully conserved. Farmers rotate their crops and practice terracing and other soil-saving methods to keep the soil from wearing out or wearing away. Many dams have been built to provide water for livestock and irrigation. The dams are also used to help control the flow of rivers and to produce electric power.

Soil. A fertile silt loam covers eastern Nebraska, the state's best farming area. The soil of the Sand Hills consists of loose sand. It drifts badly if plowed. But if left untouched, it supports grasses on which cattle can graze. The High Plains in the west have a loamy soil. The Badlands have a clay soil.

Minerals. Nebraska has few minerals. Fields of petroleum and natural gas lie chiefly in the western and southeastern sections of the state. Sand and gravel can be found along the Platte and Republican rivers and their branches. Quarries along the Missouri River in the southeast produce limestone. Clay deposits are found in Cass, Douglas, Jefferson, Lancaster, and Otoe counties.

Forests. Trees covered only about 3 of every 100 acres when white men first came to Nebraska. Most of the trees grew along the banks of rivers. There were not enough of them to be called forests. Many early settlers from wooded eastern states became active in programs to plant trees. A Nebraska City editor, J. Sterling Morton, originated the idea of Arbor Day, a special day set aside each year for planting trees. In 1872, Nebraska became the first state to celebrate Arbor Day. Charles E. Bessey, botanist of the University of Nebraska, did much to promote the planting of forests in the state. He was chiefly responsible for the establishment in 1902 of the Nebraska National Forest. This forest of cone-bearing trees is wholly man-made. Common trees in eastern and central Nebraska include ashes, basswoods, box elders, cottonwoods, elms, hackberries, locusts, oaks, walnuts, and willows. Pines and cedars grow in the extreme west.

Other Plant Life. Pioneers in eastern Nebraska found tall prairie grasses, especially bluestem. These grasses still grow in uncultivated parts of the east. Short grasses, such as grama and buffalo grass, cover the land in drier western regions. Eastern shrubs include wild plums and chokecherries. Evening primroses, phloxes, and violets bloom in the east in spring. In summer, blue flags, columbines, larkspurs, poppies, spiderworts, and wild roses thrive throughout the state. Goldenrod and sunflowers brighten roadsides and fields in late summer.

Animal Life consists chiefly of mule deer and small animals such as badgers, coyotes, muskrats, opossums, prairie dogs, rabbits, raccoons, skunks, and squirrels. Sportsmen hunt ducks, geese, pheasants, and quail, which are plentiful in the state. Common fish include bass, carp, catfish, crappies, perch, pike, and trout.

Agriculture accounts for almost two-thirds of the value of all goods produced in Nebraska. The state, with a yearly total of $1,942,000,000, ranks as a leader in farm income. Nebraska has more than 80,000 farms. They average 596 acres in size. Nebraska farms cover a total of about 47,793,000 acres, of which almost 2,200-000 acres are irrigated. Nebraska is a leading state in the amount of its irrigated land. Most of the irrigated farmlands lie in the south-central and far western areas.

Nebraska's largest farms are the cattle ranches of the Sand Hills area. Some of these ranches cover more than 50,000 acres. The smallest farms are in the eastern and south-central sections. These farms produce livestock, and corn, small grains, and other field crops.

Livestock. Beef cattle provide the largest source of agricultural income—about $851 million yearly. Only Texas and Iowa raise more beef cattle than Nebraska. The rich grasses that grow on the Sand Hills and in the west provide fine feed for range beef cattle. Ranchers ship calves and yearlings to farmers in the eastern corn-raising areas. These farmers, called *feeders*, fatten the young cattle on corn and other grains. Then they send the cattle to Omaha or other livestock markets. Nebraska is a leading state in fattening cattle and lambs for market. Some farmers raise dairy cattle.

Hogs rank next to cattle in value of livestock, and usually provide about $212 million in income yearly. Nebraska ranks high among the hog-producing states. Farmers throughout the state raise hogs, but most hogs come from corn-growing areas. Farmers in eastern Nebraska lead the state in poultry and egg production.

Field Crops. Farmers in the east and in irrigated areas raise most of Nebraska's corn, the state's chief crop. Corn provides a yearly income of about $253 million. Wheat,

NEBRASKA'S PRODUCTION IN 1967

Total yearly value of goods produced—$3,163,011,000

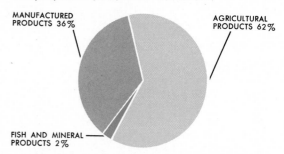

MANUFACTURED PRODUCTS 36%

AGRICULTURAL PRODUCTS 62%

FISH AND MINERAL PRODUCTS 2%

Note: Manufacturing percentage based on value added by manufacture. Other percentages based on value of production. Fish Products are less than 1 per cent.

Sources: U.S. Government statistics

NEBRASKA'S EMPLOYMENT IN 1967

Total number of persons employed in 1967—558,000

		Number of Employees
Agriculture	𝕏 𝕏 𝕏 𝕏 𝕏 𝕏	114,100
Wholesale & Retail Trade	𝕏 𝕏 𝕏 𝕏 𝕏 𝕏 𝕏	109,300
Government	𝕏 𝕏 𝕏 𝕏 𝕏 𝕏	90,400
Manufacturing	𝕏 𝕏 𝕏 𝕏 𝕏	79,800
Services	𝕏 𝕏 𝕏 𝕏 𝕏	72,600
Transportation & Public Utilities	𝕏 𝕏 𝕏	37,300
Construction & Mining	𝕏 𝕏	28,000
Finance, Insurance & Real Estate	𝕏 𝕏	26,500

Source: U.S. Department of Labor

with an annual income of $123,152,000, ranks second to corn. Most wheat farms are in the west, though farmers in central and southeastern Nebraska also grow wheat. Many ranchers of the Sand Hills cut the grasses for hay. Nebraska leads the states in the production of this wild hay. Other important field crops include cultivated hay, grain sorghums, soybeans, and sugar beets. Farmers grow large crops of alfalfa, beans, corn, grain sorghums, potatoes, and sugar beets on the irrigated lands of the Platte River Valley.

Manufacturing accounts for about a third of the value of all goods produced in Nebraska. Goods manufactured in the state have a *value added by manufacture* of about $1 billion yearly. This figure represents the value created in products by Nebraska's industries, not counting such costs as materials, supplies, and fuel. Food processing is by far the leading manufacturing industry, with a yearly value added by manufacture of $427,600,000.

Meat packing, the leading food-processing activity, is centered in Omaha. Omaha is one of the world's largest processors of meat products. Omaha and Lincoln make huge quantities of butter, ice cream, and other dairy products. Large flour mills are in Crete, Fremont, Grand Island, Humboldt, Lincoln, and Omaha. Nebraska City cans great amounts of vegetables and other foods. Beet-sugar refineries are in Bayard, Gering, Mitchell, and Scottsbluff.

Nebraska mills produce large quantities of livestock feed. The biggest feed mills are in Crete, Gering, Humboldt, Lincoln, North Platte, and Omaha. Alfalfa-dehydrating plants operate along the Platte River and in a few other areas. Nebraska ranks first in the United States in the production of dehydrated alfalfa.

Other leading industries in Nebraska produce chemicals, electrical machinery, metal products, nonelectrical machinery, printed materials, and transportation equipment. Omaha is the state's chief industrial center. Factories in Omaha make chemicals, farm implements, machine tools, paper products, telephone equipment, and truck bodies. Plants in Lincoln produce bricks, candy, drugs, motor scooters, railroad cars, and rubber goods.

Mining accounts for only about 2 per cent of the value of goods produced in Nebraska, or about $71 million yearly. More than half this sum comes from petroleum. Most of the state's crude oil and natural gas is produced in Banner, Cheyenne, Kimball, and Red Willow counties. Natural gasoline for fuel comes from the main gas fields. Construction companies use great quantities of sand and gravel from the Platte Valley. Manufacturers use clay from eastern Nebraska for bricks, tiles, and pottery. Limestone is used in construction, in making cement, and in treating soil.

Electric Power in Nebraska is produced and distributed entirely by publicly owned plants and systems. Steam-generating plants provide most of the power. Hydroelectric plants supplement the steam plants in

WORLD BOOK map

FARM AND MINERAL PRODUCTS

This map shows where the state's leading farm and mineral products are produced. The major urban areas (shown on the map in red) are the state's important manufacturing centers.

some areas. The chief hydroelectric projects include the Central Nebraska Public Power and Irrigation District, the Loup River Public Power District, and the Platte Valley Public Power and Irrigation District. More than 30 rural power .districts provide electricity for farm areas. Nuclear power plants at Brownville and Fort Calhoun are scheduled to begin operating in 1972. For Nebraska's kilowatt-hour production, see ELECTRIC POWER (table).

Transportation. In the early days, thousands of pioneers crossed the Nebraska region on their way to the West. The famous Oregon and Mormon trails followed the sweep of Nebraska's Platte River.

Aviation. Five commercial airlines serve Nebraska today. The state has about 260 airports, of which about 80 are public. Most of the rest handle light aircraft only.

Railroads. In 1865, the first transcontinental railroad, the Union Pacific, began laying track westward from Omaha. Today, nine major railroads serve the state. These railroads and other lines operate on about 5,600 miles of track in Nebraska.

Roads and Highways. Nebraska has about 100,000 miles of roads and highways, of which about 70 per cent are surfaced. The state has had difficulty building and maintaining roads. Nebraska is a large state, and its relatively small population must pay for roads that cross vast areas.

Waterways. Shippers use barges to transport huge quantities of grain, steel, and other bulky products on the Missouri River. Omaha and Nebraska City are the state's major river ports.

Communication. Thomas Morton began Nebraska's first newspaper, the *Nebraska Palladium and Platte Valley Advocate*, in Bellevue in 1854. Today, Nebraska publishers issue about 235 newspapers, of which 19 are dailies. Daily newspapers with the largest circulations include the *Lincoln Evening Journal*, the *Lincoln Star*, and the *Omaha World-Herald*. Nebraska publishers also issue about 70 periodicals.

Nebraska has about 60 radio stations and 13 television stations. Nebraska Wesleyan University established Nebraska's first radio station, WCAJ, in Lincoln in 1921. The first commercial station, WOAW (now WOW), began broadcasting from Omaha in 1923. Nebraska's first television stations, KMTV and WOW-TV, started operations in Omaha in 1949. The University of Nebraska established an educational television station, KUON-TV, in Lincoln in 1954. In 1963, the Nebraska legislature provided for a state-wide educational television network.

Chief Crazy Horse surrendered to the U.S. Army at Fort Robinson on May 6, 1877. The Sioux Indians remained on reservations after this time.

Buffalo Bill organized his famous Wild West Show in 1883 at his ranch near North Platte.

HISTORIC NEBRASKA

NEBRASKA/*History*

Indian Days. A prehistoric people probably lived in the Nebraska region between 10,000 and 25,000 years ago. Scientists base this belief on the discovery of tips of stone tools and weapons which were found buried in the Nebraska earth.

During the early 1700's, white explorers found several Indian tribes in the Nebraska region. The Missouri, Omaha, Oto, and Ponca Indians lived peacefully, farming and hunting along the rivers. The Pawnee hunted buffalo on the plains, and grew corn, beans, and squash. They fought fiercely with other tribes, especially with the Sioux who lived to the north. But the Pawnee were friendly with white settlers, and Pawnee scouts helped the U.S. Army in wars against the Sioux. The Arapaho, Cheyenne, Comanche, and Sioux hunted in western Nebraska. These wandering tribes built no villages and did not cultivate the soil. To keep their hunting grounds, the Arapaho, Cheyenne, and Sioux fought the white settlers.

Other Indian tribes moved into the Nebraska region

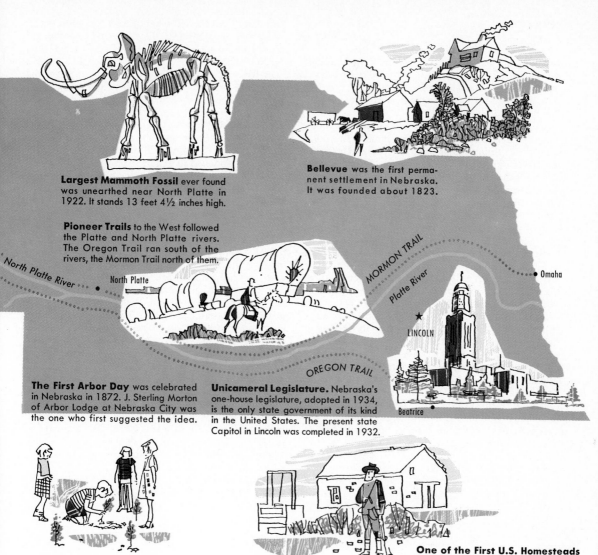

Largest Mammoth Fossil ever found was unearthed near North Platte in 1922. It stands 13 feet 4½ inches high.

Pioneer Trails to the West followed the Platte and North Platte rivers. The Oregon Trail ran south of the rivers, the Mormon Trail north of them.

North Platte River

North Platte

MORMON TRAIL

Platte River

• Omaha

★ LINCOLN

OREGON TRAIL

Beatrice

Bellevue was the first permanent settlement in Nebraska. It was founded about 1823.

The First Arbor Day was celebrated in Nebraska in 1872. J. Sterling Morton of Arbor Lodge at Nebraska City was the one who first suggested the idea.

Unicameral Legislature. Nebraska's one-house legislature, adopted in 1934, is the only state government of its kind in the United States. The present state Capitol in Lincoln was completed in 1932.

One of the First U.S. Homesteads was granted to Daniel Freeman on Jan. 1, 1863. His 162-acre farm near Beatrice became a national monument in 1939.

as white men drove them from their homes in the East. The Fox, Iowa, and Sauk tribes arrived in the late 1830's, and the Santee Sioux came in 1863. The last Indians to settle in Nebraska were the Winnebago, who originally lived in Wisconsin. White men drove the Winnebago first to Iowa and then to Minnesota and South Dakota. In 1863 and 1864, the Winnebago fled into what later became Thurston County. The Omaha and Winnebago now live on reservations in the state. See INDIAN, AMERICAN (table, Indian Tribes).

Exploration. In 1541, Francisco Vásquez de Coronado, a Spanish explorer, led an expedition across the American Southwest and into present-day Kansas. Spain claimed all this territory, including Nebraska, although the Spaniards made no settlements.

In 1682, the French explorer Robert Cavelier, Sieur de la Salle, traveled down the Mississippi River to its mouth. He claimed for France all the land drained by the Mississippi and its branches. La Salle named this vast territory, which included Nebraska, *Louisiana*.

Pony Express Station in Gothenburg stood on the trail to Oregon and California, which followed the Platte River through Nebraska. The station supplied fresh horses for the riders.

A. M. Wettach

NEBRASKA

French traders and trappers moved into the Louisiana region during the 1690's and early 1700's. In 1714, a French explorer and adventurer, Étienne Veniard de Bourgmont, traveled up the Missouri River to the mouth of the Platte River.

Spain objected to French explorers in regions that it claimed, and decided to remove the French. In 1720, a Spanish expedition under Pedro de Villasur marched from Santa Fe into the Nebraska region. But the expedition met a hostile group of Pawnee Indians along the Platte River and withdrew after being badly defeated.

Two French explorers, the brothers Pierre and Paul Mallet, traveled from French forts in Illinois to Santa Fe in 1739. They were probably the first white men to cross what is now the state of Nebraska.

The Louisiana Purchase. In 1762, France gave Louisiana to Spain. But French fur traders and trappers continued to operate in the Nebraska region, and the Spaniards never set up an effective government. In 1800, Napoleon Bonaparte, the ruler of France, forced Spain to return Louisiana to France. Three years later, Napoleon sold the Louisiana Territory to the United States. Nebraska, as part of the Louisiana Purchase, became part of the U.S. (see LOUISIANA PURCHASE).

American Exploration and Settlement. In 1804, President Thomas Jefferson sent an expedition under Meriwether Lewis and William Clark to explore the Louisiana Territory. Lewis and Clark traveled up the Missouri River and explored the eastern edge of Nebraska. Another American explorer, Zebulon M. Pike, visited the south-central part of Nebraska in 1806. Manuel Lisa, a Spanish-American trader, established fur-trading posts along the Missouri River between 1807 and 1820. One of these posts was Fort Lisa, about 10 miles from present-day Omaha.

In 1812, Robert Stuart, a fur agent, set out for New York City from the Astoria fur-trading post in Oregon. Stuart and his party spent the winter in Wyoming, and entered Nebraska early in 1813. They traveled along the North Platte and Platte rivers, and reached the Missouri River in April. Settlers moving to Oregon during the next 50 years followed the route explored by Stuart. This route became known as the Oregon Trail.

The U.S. Army established Fort Atkinson in 1819 on the Missouri River, about 16 miles north of present-day Omaha. The fort became the site of Nebraska's first school, library, sawmill, grist mill, and brickyard. The fort was abandoned in 1827.

In 1820, Major Stephen H. Long led an army expedition across Nebraska through the Platte and North Platte river valleys. Long described the region west of the Missouri River as "almost wholly unfit for farming." He called it the "Great American Desert."

During the 1820's, the American Fur Company and other fur companies set up trading posts at Bellevue and other points along the Missouri River. But until 1854, when Nebraska was made a territory, the federal government maintained Nebraska as Indian country. No white families were allowed to settle there. In 1843, thousands of pioneers began the "Great Migration" to the rich farmlands of Oregon and Washington. They followed the Oregon Trail through Nebraska to the West.

Territorial Days. In 1854, Congress passed the Kansas-Nebraska Act, which created the territories of Kansas and Nebraska. Earlier bills to create the territories had been defeated because Congressmen could not agree on the slavery question. Northerners wanted to forbid slavery in all new territories, but Southerners wanted to permit it. The Kansas-Nebraska Act provided that the people of the new territories could decide for themselves whether to permit slavery. Most Nebraskans opposed slavery. See KANSAS-NEBRASKA ACT.

The Nebraska Territory included what is now Nebraska and parts of Montana, North Dakota, South Dakota, Wyoming, and Colorado. President Franklin

---

IMPORTANT DATES IN NEBRASKA

1682 Robert Cavelier, Sieur de la Salle, claimed the region drained by the Mississippi, including present-day Nebraska, for France.

1714 Étienne Veniard de Bourgmont traveled up the Missouri River to the mouth of the Platte River.

1720 The Pawnee Indians defeated Spanish forces under Pedro de Villasur along the Platte River.

1739 Pierre and Paul Mallet were probably the first white men to cross Nebraska.

1762 France gave the Louisiana Territory to Spain.

1800 Spain returned Louisiana to France.

1803 The United States bought the Louisiana Territory, including Nebraska, from France.

1804 Meriwether Lewis and William Clark traveled up the Missouri River and explored eastern Nebraska.

1806 Zebulon M. Pike visited south-central Nebraska.

1813 Robert Stuart and his party followed the North Platte and Platte rivers across Nebraska.

1819 The U.S. Army established Fort Atkinson.

1843 The "Great Migration" began through Nebraska along the Oregon Trail to the West.

1854 Congress passed the Kansas-Nebraska Act, creating the Nebraska Territory.

1863 One of the first free homesteads was claimed by Daniel Freeman near Beatrice.

1865 The Union Pacific Railroad began building its line west from Omaha.

1867 Nebraska became the 37th state on March 1.

1874-1877 Vast swarms of grasshoppers invaded the Nebraska farmlands and damaged crops badly.

1890 Drought struck the state, and land prices collapsed.

1905 The North Platte River Project was begun to irrigate 165,000 acres in western Nebraska.

1934 Nebraskans voted to adopt a unicameral state legislature.

1937 The unicameral legislature held its first session.

1939 Geologists discovered petroleum in southeastern Nebraska.

1944 Congress authorized the Missouri River Basin Project.

1954 Nebraska celebrated its territorial centennial.

1960-1964 Nebraskans approved a series of constitutional amendments that strengthened the state government by raising salaries and increasing terms of government officials.

1967 Nebraska adopted both a sales and an income tax. It also celebrated its statehood centennial.

Pierce appointed Francis Burt of South Carolina as the first territorial governor. Burt died shortly after he took office, and Secretary of State Thomas B. Cuming became acting governor. Cuming organized the territorial government and took a census so that elections could be held for the legislature. Nebraska had a population of 2,732 in 1854. By 1863, Congress had created several new territories from the region, and the Nebraska Territory was reduced to about the state's present area.

Many early settlers in the Nebraska Territory built their homes of sod, because so few trees grew on the prairies. These pioneers cut out blocks of sod with spades, and piled the blocks on top of each other to form walls Most roofs consisted of sod blocks supported by a mat of branches, brush, and long grasses.

Statehood. By 1860, Nebraska's population had grown to 28,841. In 1862, Congress passed the first Homestead Act. This act granted 160 acres of free land in the western frontier country to settlers. A great rush for land followed. One of the first homesteads was claimed by Daniel Freeman in 1863 near the present city of Beatrice. The 1862 Homestead Act and later similar acts brought many thousands of homesteaders to Nebraska. See HOMESTEAD ACT (picture).

In 1865, the Union Pacific Railroad began building its line west from Omaha. The Union Pacific and the Burlington railroads also started campaigns to bring more settlers to Nebraska. They sent pamphlets describing the Nebraska farmland to people throughout the East, and even to Europe. These advertisements helped the population of Nebraska increase to 122,993 by 1870.

Early in 1867, Congress passed an act admitting Nebraska into the Union. In doing so, Congress overrode President Andrew Johnson's veto. Congress had required Nebraska to make certain changes in its constitution. Johnson believed this action violated the U.S. Constitution. Johnson also did not want Nebraska admitted into the Union because the territory had elected two Republicans to become Senators when statehood would be granted. The Republicans in Congress were trying to impeach Johnson, and the President believed the two new Senators might have been enough to convict him. Nebraska became the 37th state on March 1, 1867. The people elected David Butler, a Republican, as the first governor of the state.

Growth of Agriculture. The settlement of Nebraska slowed down between 1874 and 1877, when vast swarms of grasshoppers invaded the farmlands. The grasshoppers badly damaged oat, barley, wheat, and corn crops. Many settlers left their land and returned East. Farmers in the Midwest saw hundreds of wagons traveling east bearing such signs as "Eaten out by grasshoppers. Going back East to live with wife's folks." But another rush of farmers poured into the state during the 1880's. Prices for land soared higher and higher. In 1890, land prices collapsed because of drought, overuse of credit, and low prices for farm products. Farmers could not pay for land they had bought on credit at high prices.

The farmers blamed the railroads, banks, and other business organizations for their difficulties. Many farmers joined the Populist, or People's party, which sought reforms to help farmers. The party achieved its greatest strength in Nebraska during the 1890's. Many Populists supported William Jennings Bryan, a Democrat and the state's leading political figure of the period. See POPULIST PARTY.

In the 1890's, Nebraska farmers started to use irrigation and dry-farming methods. They also began to learn the value of cooperation in solving their marketing problems. They joined together to sell their products cooperatively and to fight the railroads over shipping rates. Cooperative marketing and purchasing organizations grew rapidly during the early 1900's.

Congress passed the Reclamation Act in 1902, authorizing federal aid for irrigation development. Three years later, construction started on the North Platte Project to irrigate 165,000 acres in western Nebraska. In 1904, Congress passed the Kinkaid Act, which provided for 640-acre homesteads in western Nebraska. Many settlers came to farm, but much of the land proved unsuitable for farming. Cattlemen bought out most of the homesteaders and returned the land to grass.

Economic Depression. A boom in farm prices ended during the early 1920's. Then, in 1929, the stock market crashed and farm prices fell still further. In addition, drought again hit the state. Many farmers faced bankruptcy and the loss of their land. Banks and insurance

Homesteading Families, such as these posing on a farm near Ansley, were often called "sodbusters." They cut *sod* (soil with a thick growth of plants) into blocks and used it to build their houses. In spring, blossoming sod plants decorated the houses with flowers.

Nebraska State Historical Society

companies took over farmers' property because the farmers could not meet their mortgage payments. But so many families were affected that sheriffs often refused to carry out court orders for public sale of the land. During the Great Depression of the 1930's, the federal government provided long-term, low-interest loans and other aid for farmers.

In 1915, a committee of the Nebraska legislature had recommended a unicameral legislature. The committee believed that a one-house legislature would eliminate the delays and the shifting of responsibility that occurs in two-house legislatures. The unicameral legislature would be more economical, because there would be fewer members. The committee also felt that a one-house legislature would attract politicians of higher quality. The committee's recommendation formed the basis of discussions that lasted almost 20 years.

In 1934, U.S. Senator George W. Norris of Nebraska sponsored an amendment to the state constitution for the adoption of a unicameral legislature. The voters approved the amendment in the general elections of November, 1934. The new unicameral legislature held its first meeting in 1937.

The Mid-1900's. Geologists discovered oil in southeastern Nebraska in 1939. Oil companies drilled many wells in the area during the early 1940's, and oil became the state's most important mineral.

During World War II (1939-1945), Nebraska farmers produced millions of tons of corn, oats, potatoes, and wheat to help meet wartime food shortages. The raising of beef cattle also expanded greatly. The state's enormous agricultural output was aided by plentiful rainfall and by the increased use of irrigation and scientific farming methods. By 1947, Nebraska's farm income reached a record of more than $1 billion yearly.

In 1944, Congress approved the Missouri River Basin Project. This huge project calls for construction of flood control dams, hydroelectric plants, and reservoirs in Nebraska and other states drained by the Missouri River. Nebraska has already benefited from the project, though it is far from completion. See MISSOURI RIVER BASIN PROJECT.

In 1948, the Strategic Air Command (SAC) established its headquarters at Offutt Air Force Base near Omaha. The base has been important to the economy of Omaha. In 1949, geologists discovered oil fields in western Nebraska. These fields were larger than those in the southeast.

During the 1950's, Nebraska farms became larger in size but fewer in number. The increased use of machinery lessened the need for farmworkers, and many moved to towns and cities in search of jobs. By 1970, over 60 per cent of Nebraska's people lived in urban areas.

The shift in population made Nebraska aware of the need to expand its industries and to attract new ones. In 1960, the voters approved an amendment to the state constitution allowing cities and counties to acquire and develop property for lease to private businesses. Many new firms moved into Nebraska during the 1960's, partly as a result of the state's campaigns to attract industry. Employment in manufacturing increased 44 per cent in the 1960's.

During the 1960's, the state legislature passed much important legislation. In 1963, it passed the Nebraska

Underground Command Post of the Strategic Air Command is located near Omaha. The center would direct Air Force bombers and missiles against any enemy who might attack the United States.

U.S. Air Force

THE GOVERNORS OF NEBRASKA		
	Party	Term
1. David Butler	Republican	1867-1871
2. W. H. James	Republican	1871-1873
3. Robert W. Furnas	Republican	1873-1875
4. Silas Garber	Republican	1875-1879
5. Albinus Nance	Republican	1879-1883
6. James W. Dawes	Republican	1883-1887
7. John M. Thayer	Republican	1887-1892
8. James E. Boyd	Democratic	1892-1893
9. Lorenzo Crounse	Republican	1893-1895
10. Silas A. Holcomb	Fusion	1895-1899
11. William A. Poynter	Fusion	1899-1901
12. Charles H. Dietrich	Republican	1901
13. Ezra P. Savage	Republican	1901-1903
14. John H. Mickey	Republican	1903-1907
15. George L. Sheldon	Republican	1907-1909
16. Ashton C. Shallenberger	Democratic	1909-1911
17. Chester H. Aldrich	Republican	1911-1913
18. John H. Morehead	Democratic	1913-1917
19. Keith Neville	Democratic	1917-1919
20. Samuel R. McKelvie	Republican	1919-1923
21. Charles W. Bryan	Democratic	1923-1925
22. Adam McMullen	Republican	1925-1929
23. Arthur J. Weaver	Republican	1929-1931
24. Charles W. Bryan	Democratic	1931-1935
25. Robert Leroy Cochran	Democratic	1935-1941
26. Dwight Griswold	Republican	1941-1947
27. Val Peterson	Republican	1947-1953
28. Robert B. Crosby	Republican	1953-1955
29. Victor E. Anderson	Republican	1955-1959
30. Ralph G. Brooks	Democratic	1959-1960
31. Dwight W. Burney	Republican	1960-1961
32. Frank B. Morrison	Democratic	1961-1967
33. Norbert T. Tiemann	Republican	1967-1971
34. J. James Exon	Democratic	1971-

Education Television Act, and Nebraska became one of the first states to cover its entire area with educational television (ETV) broadcasts. In 1967, the legislature adopted sales and income taxes to make up for the revenue lost when the people voted out the state property tax in 1966. The 1969 legislature provided millions of dollars in aid to public elementary and secondary schools and to junior colleges. It also provided for a $30-million bond issue for highway construction.

Nebraska Today still depends heavily on agriculture, in spite of the rapid growth of manufacturing. In the 1970's, the trend toward fewer but larger farms is continuing. Agricultural production is also continuing to increase through the expanding use of machinery and modern farming methods.

The population shift from farms to cities remains one of Nebraska's chief problems. As the shift continues, the state needs more and more industry. In addition, the rising urban population has created great demands on the cities to expand education, transportation, and other services.

WILLIAM O. DOBLER, LESLIE HEWES, and JAMES C. OLSON

NEBRASKA/Study Aids

Related Articles in WORLD BOOK include:

BIOGRAPHIES

Bryan (family)
Cather, Willa
Cudahy, Michael
Flanagan, Edward J.
Morton, Julius Sterling
Norris, George W.
Pound, Roscoe
Red Cloud
Sandoz, Mari S.

CITIES

Boys Town
Grand Island
Hastings
Lincoln
North Platte
Omaha
Scottsbluff

HISTORY

Homestead Act
Kansas-Nebraska Act
Oregon Trail
Railroad (Railroad to the Pacific)
Trails of Early Days
Western Frontier Life

PHYSICAL FEATURES

Badlands
Great Plains
Kingsley Dam
Missouri River
Platte River

PRODUCTS AND INDUSTRY

For Nebraska's rank among the states, see:

Agriculture
Alfalfa
Bean
Cattle
Corn
Hog
Rye
Sugar Beet

OTHER RELATED ARTICLES

Agate Fossil Beds National Monument
Arbor Day
Homestead National Monument
Midwestern States
Offutt Air Force Base
Scotts Bluff National Monument

Outline

I. **Government**
  A. Constitution
  B. Executive
  C. Legislature
  D. Courts
  E. Local Government
  F. Taxation
  G. Politics
II. **People**
III. **Education**
  A. Schools
  B. Libraries
  C. Museums
IV. **A Visitor's Guide**
  A. Places to Visit
  B. Annual Events
V. **The Land**
  A. Land Regions
  B. Rivers and Lakes
VI. **Climate**
VII. **Economy**
  A. Natural Resources
  B. Agriculture
  C. Manufacturing
  D. Mining
  E. Electric Power
  F. Transportation
  G. Communication
VIII. **History**

Questions

What is unusual about the state legislature of Nebraska?

Why did many early settlers in Nebraska build their houses of sod?

Why are the Sand Hills important to Nebraska?

What are the Knights of Ak-Sar-Ben?

Why did President Andrew Johnson oppose Nebraska's admission into the Union?

Nebraska became the first state to celebrate what widely-observed day? Whose idea was it?

How does the Nebraska National Forest differ from all other national forests in the United States?

What famous Nebraskan ran unsuccessfully three times for the presidency of the United States?

Why is road building difficult in Nebraska? What famous pioneer trails crossed Nebraska?

Why did the settlement of Nebraska slow down between 1874 and 1877?

Books for Young Readers

BAILEY, BERNADINE F. *Picture Book of Nebraska.* Whitman, 1956. A combination of history and geography that gives a picture of the state.

BOTHWELL, JEAN. *Tree House at Seven Oaks.* Abelard, 1957. An orphan comes to the Nebraska Territory by way of the Missouri River. His adventures while camping out on an important mission are exciting.

DICK, TRELLA L. *Tornado Jones.* Follett, 1953. The friendship and adventures of two boys in the Nebraska Sand Hills.

NICOLL, BRUCE H., and KELLER, KEN R. *Know Nebraska.* Rev. ed. Johnsen, 1961.

Books for Older Readers

ALDRICH, BESS STREETER. *A Bess Streeter Aldrich Treasury.* Meredith, 1959. Selections from the author's best writing on pioneering and modern Nebraska.

CATHER, WILLA. *My Ántonia.* Houghton, 1918. *O Pioneers!* 1913. These classic American novels about pioneer days in Nebraska are still in print.

FAULKNER, VIRGINIA, ed. *Roundup: A Nebraska Reader.* Univ. of Nebraska Press, 1957. This anthology shows the state at its best and at its worst.

OLSON, JAMES C. *History of Nebraska.* Univ. of Nebraska Press, 1955. An authoritative history of the state.

POUND, LOUISE. *Nebraska Folklore.* University of Nebraska Press, 1959.

SANDOZ, MARI. *Old Jules.* 20th Anniversary ed. Hastings, 1955. A moving story of northwestern Nebraska.

SEARCY, N. D., and LONGWELL, A. R. *Nebraska Atlas.* Kearney, Nebr., 1964. Maps of Nebraska with brief text.

WELSH, ROGER L., ed. *A Treasury of Nebraska Pioneer Folklore.* University of Nebraska Press, 1966.

The University of Nebraska is the largest university in Nebraska. It has campuses in Lincoln and Omaha. Oldfather Hall, *far left background*, stands on the City Campus in Lincoln. It houses faculty offices and some classrooms.

University of Nebraska

NEBRASKA, UNIVERSITY OF, is a state-supported coeducational university. It has two campuses in Lincoln, Nebr., and a campus and medical center in Omaha.

The Lincoln campuses include a teachers college; a graduate college; and colleges of agriculture and home economics, arts and sciences, business administration, dentistry, engineering and architecture, law, and pharmacy. The Lincoln campuses also have schools of architecture, home economics, journalism, and music; and a graduate school of social work.

The University of Nebraska at Omaha has colleges of arts and sciences, business administration, education, engineering and technology, and continuing studies. It also has a graduate college.

The medical center in Omaha includes a college of medicine, a school of nursing, a hospital, a psychiatric institute, and a cancer research institute.

The Lincoln campuses and the college of medicine and the school of nursing in Omaha grant bachelor's, master's, and doctor's degrees. The Omaha campus grants bachelor's and master's degrees.

The university carries on an extensive agricultural research program. It maintains six agricultural experiment stations in the state.

The University of Nebraska was chartered as a land-grant college in 1869. It held its first classes in 1871, in Lincoln. It merged with the Municipal University of Omaha in 1968. The municipal university became the University of Nebraska at Omaha. For enrollment of the University of Nebraska, see UNIVERSITIES AND COLLEGES (table).   GEORGE S. ROUND

NEBRASKA WESLEYAN UNIVERSITY is a coeducational, private liberal arts college in Lincoln, Nebr. It has a school of music and a department of teacher education, and it grants B.A., B.S., and B.F.A. degrees. It was founded in 1887. For enrollment, see UNIVERSITIES AND COLLEGES (table).   VANCE D. ROGERS

NEBUCHADNEZZAR, *NEB yoo kud NEZ er*, was the name of two kings of Babylon.

Nebuchadnezzar I (ruled 1124-1103 B.C.) was the greatest king of the second Isin dynasty, which followed the Kassite kings of Babylonia. He won fame by freeing Babylonia from Elamite control and by extending Babylonian rule over Elam, a country north of the Persian Gulf. Nebuchadnezzar's account of the Elamite battles is a fascinating document of ancient Babylonia.

Nebuchadnezzar II (ruled 605-562 B.C.) was the king of Babylonia about whom both the Old Testament and Babylonian sources have much to tell. He captured Jerusalem in 587 B.C., and destroyed the city. This battle ended the Judean kingdom. Nebuchadnezzar seized some Jews, and sent them to Babylon. The Old Testament tells of Nebuchadnezzar's spells of madness, when he would imagine himself an ox and would go out in the fields and eat grass.

Nebuchadnezzar was the son of Nabopolassar (see NABOPOLASSAR). He became king after his father's death in 605 B.C. Under Nebuchadnezzar's rule, Babylon became one of the most magnificent cities of the ancient world. In his own records, he rarely mentioned his military activities, but wrote of his building projects and his attention to the gods of Babylonia. He probably built the "Hanging Gardens," one of the Seven Wonders of the Ancient World (see SEVEN WONDERS OF THE WORLD [with picture]).   JACOB J. FINKELSTEIN

See also BABYLON; BABYLONIA; DANIEL.

NEBULA, *NEB yoo luh*, is the name astronomers have given certain hazy masses seen among the stars. The term means *mist* in Latin. Generally, a nebula is a huge mass of gaseous or partly gaseous matter, inside the galactic system, or Milky Way, but far from our solar system. Some of these nebulae shine because they reflect light. The energy by which others shine is provided by nearby stars.

Most bright nebulae are close to stars, and their spectra are similar to those of the stars near them. Nebulae which lie outside the Milky Way are great masses of stars, properly called galaxies.

There have been several methods used by astronomers to classify the nebulae. A recent classification divided them into three groups. The first two are inside our galaxy.

Dark Nebulae are vast clouds of dustlike particles. They were named by Edward E. Barnard, who made a detailed study of them for years. These nebulae hide stars in certain parts of the Milky Way, and are responsible for the "dark spots" which puzzled astronomers for a long time.

Bright Nebulae in the Milky Way include gaseous unorganized masses like the Great Nebula in Orion, and rounded forms called planetary nebulae. They are associated with stars and probably get their light from them.

Extragalactic Nebulae lie outside our galactic system, and are more correctly called exterior galaxies. More than half of them appear to be spiral-shaped clouds. The discovery that they were really great groups of stars was a triumph of modern astronomy. The spiral galaxy that appears largest, called the Great Spiral in Andromeda, is about 2 million light-years away, but it can be seen with the naked eye. The faintest spiral nebulae visible through the 200-inch telescope are thought to be 2 billion light-years away.

Not all the galaxies, or extragalactic nebulae, are shaped like spirals. Some are irregular like the Magellanic Clouds, which are the nearest to our galaxy. Others are elliptical. Most of them have flattened forms, which causes astronomers to believe that these galaxies are rotating. The speed of rotation may be about like that of the sun around the center of our galactic system. The sun requires some 200 million years for one revolution. CHARLES ANTHONY FEDERER, JR.

See also MILKY WAY; GALAXY; ASTRONOMY (color pictures: Wonders of the Milky Way).

NEBULAR HYPOTHESIS, *NEB yoo ler*, is a theory advanced by the French astronomer Pierre Simon de Laplace (1749-1827) to explain how our solar system was formed. He said the sun and planets were formed from a *nebula*, or cloud of intensely heated gas. Gravitation caused the nebula to condense and form globes. His theory has been changed and modified by new discoveries and different analyses of known facts. E. C. SLIPHER

See also NEBULA; EARTH; LAPLACE, MARQUIS DE.

NECK. See SKELETON; GIRAFFE (diagram); THROAT.

NECKER, *neh KAIR*, or *NECK er*, **JACQUES** (1732-1804), was a statesman in France under King Louis XVI.

The Ring Nebula of Lyra, photographed at Mt. Wilson Observatory, looks like a smoke ring blown by a smoker.

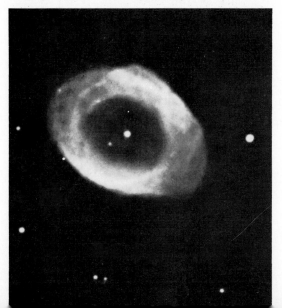

When he was appointed French finance minister in 1777, the nation had an unbalanced treasury. The situation grew worse after France joined the American Revolutionary War. Necker, a noted banker, borrowed heavily, and kept things going without increasing taxes. This only postponed trouble. He angered court circles by publishing, for the first time, a statement showing how taxes were spent and how much money went to court favorites. He resigned in 1781.

Necker was recalled in 1788, after less able successors had brought France close to bankruptcy. He proved too cautious and indecisive to provide the leadership that might have prevented the French Revolution. On July 11, 1789, the king suddenly dismissed Necker, but was forced to take him back, by public demand. Necker again resigned in 1790.

He was born in Geneva, Switzerland. His daughter, Madame de Staël, was a French writer (see STAËL, MADAME DE). RAYMOND O. ROCKWOOD

NECKTIE is a band of material or a bow that a man wears around his neck. The *four-in-hand* and *bow* ties worn today have been about the same style since they were first worn in the 1870's.

Neckties originated in the neck cloths that men folded and wrapped around their necks, with ribbon tied over them to hold the ends in place. In the 1700's, men wore a whalebone *stock*. They fastened it in back with a strap or buckle, and tied it in front with a bow or knot. The *cravats* of the 1600's and 1700's were often frilly and lace-trimmed. By the mid-1800's, narrow string ties, knotted bow ties, and ascot ties had replaced the more elaborate cravat. Around 1870, the wider four-in-hand became popular for general wear, the white bow tie for evening wear, the black string tie for formal wear, and the soft windsor tie for sportswear. In the 1900's, formal black bow ties appeared, and more conservative men usually wore black string ties. Striped neckties also became popular. HAZEL B. STRAHAN

NECROLOGY, *neh KRAHL oh jih*, is a record of deaths, especially one kept by a church. Usually it shows only the day and month, not the year, of the death. A necrology may be a list of persons who have died within a certain time. It also may be an obituary notice.

NECROMANCY, *NECK roh MAN sih*, is a term taken from two Greek words meaning *corpse* and *divination*. It is the belief that the future can be discovered by communication with the spirits of the dead. Necromancy was a common belief in early times.

See also MAGIC.

NECROPOLIS, *neh KRAHP oh lis*, is a Greek word which means *city of the dead*, that is, a cemetery. Archaeologists and historians usually call the cemetery of an ancient city a *necropolis*.

Archaeologists have found large and well-known necropolises in Egypt, at such ancient cities as Memphis and Thebes, and also surrounding the pyramids at El Gîza. Another necropolis, dating from the Bronze Age, is at Hallstatt, Austria. Many necropolises have also been found in America. A necropolis at Paracas, an archaeological site in Peru, dates back to the days before the Inca ruled there.

Ancient peoples often buried tools, weapons, and personal belongings with the dead. Sometimes they also

NECROSIS

carved or painted religious texts, information about the dead, and scenes from everyday life. Archaeologists and historians have learned much about ancient civilizations from necropolises.　　　　GEORGE R. HUGHES

See also TUTANKHAMON; VALLEY OF THE KINGS.

NECROSIS, *neh KROH sis,* is the death of a group of body cells and tissues due to some disease or external cause. *Phosphorus necrosis* is necrosis of the bone caused by exposure to phosphorus fumes (see PHOSPHORUS).

NECTAR, *NECK ter,* is a sugary liquid produced by many flowers. Insects fly from flower to flower feeding on nectar. The nectar glands are usually at the bottom of the flower, and the insect has to brush past the pollen to reach them. It carries this pollen from one plant to another. Bees gather nectar, and change it to honey.

See also BEE (Making Honey).

NECTAR was the drink of the gods in Greek mythology. They drank out of cups brought to them by Hebe and Ganymede. Nectar was probably like sweet red wine. It was drunk with ambrosia, the food of the gods. Nectar and ambrosia gave youth and immortality to those who took them.

See also AMBROSIA; GANYMEDE; HEBE.

A. B. Morse Co.

Nectarines Are Small Fruits Resembling Peaches. They have smooth skins much like those of plums.

NECTARINE, *NECK ter EEN,* or *NECK ter in,* is a fruit much like the peach. The only important difference between the two is that nectarines have smooth skins and peaches are fuzzy. They come from identical trees. Nectarines often originate from peach seeds, and peaches may come from nectarine seeds. Botanists do not know which originated first, nectarine or peach.

Scientific Classification. The nectarine is a member of the rose family, *Rosaceae.* It is classified as genus *Prunus,* species *P. persica.*　　　　REID M. BROOKS

See also PEACH.

NEEDLE is a simple-looking tool, with a fine point at one end and a tiny eye at the other. But needles are not easy to make. Each needle passes through the hands of nearly 20 workers and undergoes at least 20 processes.

Sewing needles are made from coils of steel wire. These coils are cut into pieces long enough for two needles. The pieces are then heated to a dull red and rolled on a flat steel plate to straighten them. The wires are pointed at each end on a grindstone. While they are being ground down to points, they are held in place by a device which makes them turn all the time they are touching the grindstone. This makes the points fine and even. Only one end of the piece of wire is pointed at a time. After the ends are pointed, the center section of the wire pieces is stamped by a machine. This makes a flat place for the eyes. Next, the two eyes are punched in the middle of each piece of wire by another machine. Now each piece of wire has become a double needle. A piece of wire is now run through the eyes. The needles are then cut apart, leaving the needles hanging on the wire. Next, the heads, or eye ends, are rounded and smoothed. Finally, the needles are *tempered* (toughened), and polished, sorted, and packed.

Special needles are made for special uses. Sewing-machine needles are made with the eye near the point. They also have a groove on one side, which acts as a guide for the thread that goes through the eye.

A sewing needle for nearsighted persons has the eye split so that the needle can be threaded through the top. A crochet needle has a hook near the point. The thread is caught in the hook instead of going through an eye. Needles used for sewing shoes and upholstery are curved. Surgeons also use a curved needle for sewing up wounds and incisions.　　　　WALTER R. WILLIAMS, JR.

See also SEWING (Sewing Tools).

NEEDLE LEAVES. See LEAF.

NEEDLE POINT is a type of embroidery made on a coarse background of open-mesh canvas. It is usually worked in woolen yarn, but silk, cotton, and some other materials may also be used.

The *continental* and the *half-cross* are the most common types of stitches used to make needle point. The continental stitch is more widely used, because it fills in the background evenly and fully on both the front and back of the canvas. It is also firmer and more durable than the half-cross

Lee Wards, Elgin, Ill.

Needle-Point Embroidery covers up its canvas backing.

stitch, which is used chiefly for products such as handbags, pictures, and pillows.

Needle point may be worked in *petit point* (fine, small stitches), or in *gros point* (larger stitches). Petit point is a single-yarn canvas. The yarns for it are split into two strands, and worked in the continental stitch. Gros point is a double-yarn mesh, and is usually used for upholstery.　　　　HAZEL B. STRAHAN

See also EMBROIDERY; LACE; PETIT POINT.

NEEDLEFISH. See GAR.

NEEDLEWORK. See CROCHET; EMBROIDERY; KNITTING; LACE; NEEDLE POINT; PETIT POINT; QUILT; SAMPLER; SEWING.

NEFERTITI, *neh fur TEE tee,* was an ancient Egyptian queen, the wife of Akhenaton, a *pharaoh* (king) who ruled from 1367 to 1350 B.C. Akhenaton was the first pharaoh to preach *monotheism* (belief in one god). Nefertiti was a firm supporter of Akhenaton's teachings and assisted him in the new religious ceremonies. The reign of Akhenaton and Nefertiti is called the *Amarna Revolution* because of the many changes in art, religion, and social practices they made.

Nefertiti is the subject of several sculptured portraits. A limestone head of Nefertiti in the Berlin Museum and an unfinished head of the queen kept in the Cairo Museum are among the best known.

The Oriental Institute,
University of Chicago
Nefertiti

RICARDO A. CAMINOS

See also EGYPT, ANCIENT (The Amarna Revolution).

NEGATIVE. See PHOTOGRAPHY (Developing Film).

NEGATIVE INCOME TAX. See POVERTY (Social Welfare Assistance).

NEGATIVE NUMBER. See ALGEBRA (Positive and Negative Numbers).

NEGEV, *NEHG uv,* or *nuh GEHV,* is the triangular southern half of Israel. It extends from Beersheba south to the port of Elath on the Gulf of Aqaba. For location, see ISRAEL (color map). The Negev is a semidesert tableland between 1,000 and 2,000 feet above sea level. It is covered by a thick layer of fertile loam, which must have water to grow crops. The Israelis have farmed part of the Negev by irrigation. They have also mined phosphates and copper. Israel intends to draw water from the River Jordan to irrigate the Negev. But the surrounding Arab countries object to this water-diversion plan. See also WORLD (picture).   SYDNEY N. FISHER

NEGLIGENCE is the legal term for carelessness. The law uses negligence as a test to determine whether a person involved in an accident is responsible for any loss or injury that occurs in the accident.

The law considers negligence the failure to act the way a reasonable man would under the circumstances. But the law does not say what specific conduct is negligent. This decision is made by a judge or a jury after consideration of the circumstances in each case. The basic rule is that a person is responsible in damages for the harm his negligence causes to another person. If the person harmed also has been negligent, he normally cannot recover damages. The law calls such action *contributory negligence.* For example, if a careless motorist hits a pedestrian who is reading a newspaper while he is crossing the street, the pedestrian's carelessness may be considered contributory negligence.

English and American law generally do not regard negligence as a crime. But in cases where someone is killed through negligence, the negligent person may be charged with a crime called *manslaughter* or *negligent homicide.* Most persons convicted of this type of manslaughter are punished seriously, but less severely than someone convicted of murder.

Some experts say the negligence test is no longer a good one for the law, especially in car accidents. Some suggest automobile cases should be handled as claims against some sort of insurance fund.   HARRY KALVEN, JR.

See also DAMAGES; TORT.

NEGOTIABLE INSTRUMENT, *nih GOH shuh buhl,* refers to a type of legal exchange or document that is

either a promise or an order to pay money. Negotiable instruments can be used as evidence of indebtedness or as a substitute for money. A person holding a negotiable instrument is usually in a good legal position to collect from the person who signs the instrument. The signer is called a *maker* or *drawer.* The use of negotiable instruments is regulated by the Uniform Negotiable Instruments Law, which has been adopted by every state.

Negotiable instruments have six essential characteristics: (1) they must be in writing; (2) they must be signed by a maker or drawer, who promises to pay money; (3) they must contain an unconditional promise or order to pay; (4) payment must be in money; (5) instruments must be payable on demand or at a specific date in the future; (6) they must be payable to the bearer or to the order of a person.

Forms. Common forms of negotiable instruments include promissory notes, drafts, and checks. Promissory notes include bonds, certificates of deposits from banks, and real estate mortgage notes. Drafts include bills of exchange, bank drafts, cashier's checks, money orders, and traveler's checks.

Many instruments are not strictly negotiable but have some features of negotiable instruments. For example, instruments calling for the delivery of goods or property instead of money may possess many of the legal qualities of negotiability. Bills of lading and warehouse receipts are examples. A bill of lading is given for goods in transit. A warehouse receipt is given for goods in storage. Each of these instruments can be written so that the promise to pay is negotiable.

Endorsement. Negotiable instruments are usually transferred or handed over to another person by endorsement. Any writing on the back is, in its broadest sense, an endorsement. The word comes from the Latin *in dorso,* meaning *on the back.* The term applies technically to the signature or other writing which indicates or proves that the instrument has been transferred.

An endorsement may be written in different ways. If the holder of the instrument simply signs his name, the endorsement is called *in blank. A special endorsement* or an *endorsement in full* names the person to whom payment is to be made. A *restrictive* endorsement forbids further transfer. A check signed "Pay to First National Bank only" is a restrictive endorsement.

Every endorser of a negotiable instrument is usually liable for its face value, if the maker does not or cannot pay it. The endorser may add the words "without recourse" if he wishes to avoid liability. This form of endorsement does not affect the value of the instrument or prevent further endorsement.   JAMES B. LUDTKE

Related Articles in WORLD BOOK include:

Bill of Exchange	Bond	Draft	Note
Bill of Lading	Check	Money Order	

NEGRILLO. See PYGMY.

NEGRITO is a *pygmy* (small) Negroid person. Negritos live in the Andaman Islands, the central part of the Malay Peninsula and East Sumatra, the Philippine Islands, western New Guinea, and also throughout the islands of Melanesia in the Pacific. Most are less than five feet tall. Their eyes are dark brown or black, and their skin is brown-black. See also PYGMY; PHILIPPINES (The People).   WILTON MARION KROGMAN

The Washington Post, Courtesy of Museum of African Art

The African Heritage. Black Americans develop racial pride through the study of their culturally rich African heritage. A museum lecturer, *above*, tells young school children about the accomplishments of the ancient African civilization that produced these works of art.

NEGRO

NEGRO is a member of an important racial division of man. Most Negroes belong to the African geographical race. This race consists of groups of related peoples in Africa south of the Sahara. Negroes also include descendants of people who moved from those regions of Africa—either voluntarily or against their will. American Negroes are mostly of African origin. Many Negroes prefer to be called *blacks*.

Negroes vary considerably in physical characteristics, but most have dark skin, brown eyes, and dark hair that is woolly or very curly. Many blacks have broad noses and thick lips.

In popular use, the word *Negro* has different meanings in different countries. In the United States, any person known to have a Negro ancestor is usually classed as a Negro, even though his skin may be white. In South Africa, persons who are of mixed racial ancestry are called *Coloureds*. The white people of South Africa often speak of Negroes of unmixed ancestry as *natives* or *blacks*. They are also called *Bantu*, but this term properly refers to the languages they speak, rather than their race. In Latin America and in some other parts of the world, more attention is paid to the social, economic, or educational achievements of people than to the color of their skins or other physical features. A person in Latin America who is of mixed Negro ancestry is sometimes classed as a *mulatto* (a mixture of

Edgar Allan Toppin, the contributor of this article, is Professor of History at Virginia State College.

white and Negro) or a *zambo* (a mixture of Negro and Indian).

The dark-skinned peoples who live in the Melanesian group of the Pacific Islands are sometimes called Negroes. But scholars have determined that these blacks are not closely related to African Negroes. The pygmy Negritos, who live on islands from Australia to the Philippines, are also sometimes called Negroes. But the pygmy Negritos have no known relationship to African blacks.

The slave trade of the 1400's to 1800's carried hundreds of thousands of African Negroes to North and South America. Most Western countries abolished slavery during the 1800's. But many of the economic, social, and political developments that accompanied slavery have continued to the present day.

More than 250 million Negroes live in Africa. About 24 million Negroes live in South America, 22 million in the United States, and 125,000 in Europe. About 32,000 Negroes live in Canada.

THE NEGRO IN AFRICA

Highly developed Negro kingdoms existed in various parts of Africa hundreds of years ago. The Negro kings of the ancient empire of Ghana came to power about the year 700. Their power declined in the 1000's, and their capital was destroyed about 200 years later. Other Negro kingdoms rose and fell, such as Mali and Songhai in the western Sudan, and Kongo at the mouth of the Congo River.

Conditions varied greatly from one part of Africa to

another. Some of the Negro kings and their nobles lived in great wealth and splendor. Their capitals sometimes became centers of culture and trade. Between 1200 and 1600, a Negro-Arabic university flourished at Timbuktu in West Africa and became famous throughout Spain, North Africa, and the Middle East. But most African Negroes lived under primitive tribal conditions, dependent on the animals and crops they could raise.

In some parts of Africa, the people developed great skill in the arts. The Dahomeans of West Africa were noted for their wood carvings of stools, staffs, and statuettes. The Ashanti, in what is now Ghana, were famed for delicate work in gold.

Each tribe had its own language, its own religion, and its own customs. The family was important everywhere in Negro Africa. In some places the people were ruled by chiefs or kings assisted by the tribal elders. In others, councils of elders ruled without chiefs.

Beginning in the late 1500's, white settlers from European nations established colonies in Africa. By 1900, almost all the Negroes in Africa had been brought under colonial rule. Colonialism changed their way of life. It often raised their living standards. But their desire for equality and freedom caused a strong movement for independence after World War II. For the history of the African Negroes, see AFRICA (History).

THE SLAVE TRADE

Slavery existed in Africa from the earliest times. But the nature of African slavery was somewhat different from that of the Western world. Almost nowhere in Africa were slaves used in large numbers on plantations. It also was rare for anyone except the kings to have more than a few slaves. Slaves were persons who had no kinsmen, either because they were captives or because they had been sold into slavery as punishment for crimes. Both masters and slaves were Negroes. A slave usually worked in his master's household and was treated much as a member of the family. In many places, it was considered an insult both to the master and the slave to refer to a person's status as a slave.

From early days, Arab slave traders bought or captured Negroes and sold them in North Africa or the Middle East. A few were sold in southern Europe. The slave trade of the Arabs in East Africa lasted for many years after the European slave trade in West Africa had come to an end.

In the 1400's, European traders began to go to the west coast of Africa for slaves. With the discovery of the Americas, a cheap and plentiful labor supply was needed. As a result, the African slave trade became a profitable business. Portuguese, Dutch, French, and British traders took part in the traffic. Many New England families made fortunes in the slave trade. Treaties made with Portugal forbade Spain to trade in Africa. Therefore, Spanish colonists in the Americas had to have traders of other nations bring in slaves.

Slave traders from Europe and America tapped the human resources of Africa for about 400 years. The Negro kings waged war on each other to capture slaves they could sell or exchange with traders for guns, rum, cloth, and many other items. In all, as many as 10 million African Negroes are believed to have been carried to other parts of the world by the slave merchants.

Aboard ship, the slave captives lived for weeks in filth and horror. Many were chained hand and foot and packed together in the holds so tightly they could hardly move. Thousands died on the slave ships from brutal treatment and from disease. Sometimes slaves killed themselves, preferring death to their ordeal.

The slave trade took various patterns. One of the most familiar developed in the 1700's and 1800's. Traders loaded their ships with New England products. They then sailed to the West Indies and exchanged their cargoes for sugar, molasses, and money. They returned to New England where the molasses was made into rum. Next, they went to Africa and traded the rum for slaves which they took to the West Indies or to the Southern colonies. They traded the slaves for sugar, tobacco, and molasses to be sold in New England. This *triangular trade* with the United States, West Africa, and the West Indies continued well into the 1800's.

SLAVERY IN AMERICA

The Spanish and Portuguese brought the first Negroes to America. Some historians believe that Pedro Alonso Niño, a member of Christopher Columbus's crew, was a Negro. Balboa had Negroes in his expedition when he discovered the Pacific Ocean. Estevanico, a black Moorish slave, took part in Cabeza de Vaca's expedition to what is now New Mexico and Arizona. Other Negroes accompanied Cortes, Pizarro, and De Soto.

In Colonial Times. The first Negroes were brought to the English colonies in America in 1619. In that year, John Rolfe of Jamestown, Virginia, wrote in his *Journal* that a Dutch ship "sold us twenty negars." At first, the colonists thought white indentured servants from England, and Indians, could supply their labor needs. But Southern plantations needed many farm laborers to help raise tobacco and other crops. As a result, by the late 1600's, hundreds of Negro slaves were being brought to the colonies each year.

In the late 1600's and early 1700's, slave uprisings in several colonies caused the colonists to adopt strict laws concerning Negroes. Harsh punishments were ordered for minor offenses. Many laws were directed against free Negroes as well as slaves because the colonists feared that free Negroes might lead revolts.

Between 1700 and 1750, thousands of slaves were brought to the American colonies each year. In some Southern colonies the increase in slaves was so great that they outnumbered white settlers by 2 to 1. But in the Northern colonies the use of slave labor in factories and on small farms was not profitable. As a result, slaves there made up only a small percentage of the population. By the time of the Revolutionary War, Negroes made up nearly 700,000 of the total population of about $2\frac{1}{2}$ million of the American colonies.

About 5,000 Negroes served in the Revolutionary Army, some as freemen, others as slaves. Some historians believe that Crispus Attucks, one of the American patriots killed in the Boston Massacre, was a runaway Negro slave. At the Battle of Bunker Hill, two American Negro soldiers, Peter Salem and Salem Poor, distinguished themselves. The British tried to cause unrest among the slaves by promising freedom to any who would join the British Army. This promise encouraged thousands of slaves to run away.

After the Revolutionary War, many leaders, including Benjamin Franklin, Noah Webster, and John Jay, spoke out against slavery. In 1774, Rhode Island became the first state to prohibit the importation of slaves, and in 1782 Virginia passed legislation encouraging the emancipation of slaves. The legislatures of the Northern States also began enacting laws to end the importation of slaves. When the U.S. Constitution was written in 1787, it included a provision that prohibited Congress from outlawing the importation of slaves at least until 1808. But several Northern States provided for abolition of slavery by gradual means: Pennsylvania (1780), Connecticut (1784), Rhode Island (1784), and New York (1799). Vermont (1777) and Massachusetts (1783) abolished slavery immediately.

One of the best-known Negroes of this period was Phillis Wheatley, a former slave who wrote lyric poetry in the 1770's and 1780's. Another was Benjamin Banneker of Maryland, a mathematician who won praise from Thomas Jefferson for the almanacs he published from 1792 to 1806.

During the 1790's, many slaveowners became fearful of slave revolts as they read reports from Haiti in the West Indies. There, Toussaint L'Ouverture, a Negro slave, led a bloody revolt in which slaves killed their French masters and declared their independence. The slave states placed many restrictions on the Negroes, such as denying slaves the right to own property or to associate with free Negroes or whites. In the following years, these laws were made more and more strict each time a slave revolt occurred.

Growth of Slavery. The invention of the cotton gin in 1793 made it possible to remove the seeds from cotton more economically. The demand for cotton increased and Southern cotton growers expanded their acreage. The cotton plantations needed more slaves as laborers. In addition, large numbers of slaves were needed for the sugar cane plantations of Louisiana, which became a state in 1812. Two new cotton-growing states joined the Union, Mississippi in 1817 and Alabama in 1819. From 1820 to 1840, the number of Negro slaves in the Mississippi-Alabama region increased from about 75,000 to 500,000.

Although Congress had prohibited the importation of slaves after Jan. 1, 1808, the law was poorly enforced. African slaves continued to be brought into the United States. But as it became more difficult to import slaves between 1800 and 1860, the price of slaves nearly doubled. Although the South was the main slave-owning region, less than 5 per cent of the white persons in the South owned slaves. Only about half the slaveholders had more than five slaves.

The Northern States opposed slavery for many reasons. They began to fear that the Southern States would win permanent control of Congress if more Western States were admitted to the Union as slave states. After much debate, Congress passed the Missouri Compromise in 1820. This law provided that Missouri would be admitted as a slave state. But the compromise banned slavery in any other new state north of 36° 30' north latitude, the southern boundary of Missouri.

Friction between the North and South continued. War almost broke out before Congress agreed upon the Compromise of 1850. This compromise settled the issue of slavery in the states to be formed from territory won in the Mexican War, and set up federal laws for the return of runaway slaves. See COMPROMISE OF 1850.

The quarrel over slavery flared again during debates in Congress over the Kansas-Nebraska Act. This act, passed in 1854, voided the Missouri Compromise and enabled the settlers of Kansas and Nebraska to decide the issue of slavery locally. Fighting broke out on the borders of Kansas as slave interests clashed with antislavery groups.

Most Negro slaves worked in the cotton, tobacco, rice, corn, and sugar cane fields. A smaller number of slaves served as house servants. They generally led better lives and picked up some education. Many slaves attended churches or Sunday schools, where a few learned to read and write. Slaves could be sold at any time, and separated from their families. Cruel masters sometimes mistreated their slaves. But many slaveowners showed great concern for the welfare of their slaves.

Free Negroes. Of the 4,441,830 Negroes in the United States in 1860, there were 3,953,760 slaves and 488,070 freemen. Some had bought their own freedom. Others had been freed by their masters or by state legislatures. Many had run away. Increasing numbers were born of free parents. Some of these free Negroes owned slaves themselves. Many free Negroes held relatives or friends as "slaves" to protect them from being taken into slavery by white persons.

Free Negroes often found it difficult to make a living. Every state required that Negroes had to work and be able to show proof they were working. Some free Negroes followed trades, such as carpentry, which they had learned as slaves. But most states restricted the kinds of work in which a Negro could be employed. In the North, white workers often objected to working side by side with Negroes.

The rights of free Negroes were restricted in both the North and the South. Negroes were required to carry

Slavery in America often broke up Negro families, separating children from their parents, and husbands from their wives. This 1859 handbill advertises a man's slaves and other property for sale.

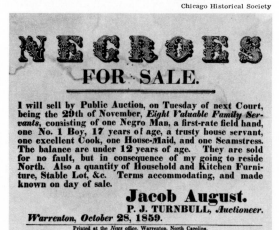

passes, and could not move about as they wished. If found away from home, they might be accused of being runaway slaves. If a white person claimed that a Negro was a runaway slave, the courts usually sent the Negro back to slavery. Courts did not accept testimony from free Negroes in a case involving a white person. For a short time after the Revolutionary War, free Negroes had the right to vote in several Northern States and one Southern State, Tennessee. But by the late 1830's, each of these states abolished voting rights for Negroes or placed restrictions on them. Churches in both the North and the South either did not admit Negroes or required that they sit in separate sections. As a result, some Negroes founded churches of their own, such as the African Methodist Episcopal Church.

In the late 1700's and early 1800's, separate schools were set up in some communities for the education of free Negroes. Some colleges admitted Negro students, including Bowdoin, Oberlin, Franklin, and Rutland colleges, and Harvard University. A few Negro colleges began operating, including Lincoln University in Pennsylvania in 1854 and Wilberforce University in Ohio in 1856. Some free Negroes became writers and editors. The first Negro newspaper, *Freedom's Journal*, was founded in 1827 by Samuel Cornish and John Russwurm.

The American Colonization Society was founded in 1817 to find a place outside the United States where free Negroes could be sent. The society established a colony on the west coast of Africa. In 1847, the colony became the independent country of Liberia, the first self-governing Negro republic in Africa. A few free Negroes were eager to go to Liberia, but many others were indifferent or felt that any colonization plan was just a scheme to get rid of them. Negroes born in the United States felt that Africa was not their home. Even those born in Africa would be strangers in Liberia, and they would not know the language or the customs of the people there. As a result, only about 12,000 went.

CHANGING STATUS OF THE NEGRO

In Canada, the first Negro slave had been sold to a settler in Quebec in 1628. Small numbers of slaves were brought to Canada during the 1600's and 1700's. The Parliament of Upper Canada in 1793 passed a law that no more Negro slaves could be brought into the province, and that every child born of a slave mother would be freed upon reaching the age of 25. A British act of 1797 repealed a law allowing Negroes to be sold along with other property in answer to bankruptcy suits. The courts of Lower Canada interpreted this act as revoking all slavery laws. Thus, by 1800, slavery was becoming a dying institution throughout Canada.

In 1833, Great Britain ordered the abolition of slavery throughout its colonies. The government of Great Britain paid slaveowners for their slaves, and established an apprentice system to help free Negroes to become self-reliant. France abolished slavery in its colonies in 1848.

The United Provinces of Central America in 1824 became the first Latin-American country to abolish slavery. The president of Mexico emancipated slaves in that country in 1829. Other Latin-American countries followed: Bolivia in 1831, Uruguay in 1842, Colombia in 1851, Argentina in 1853, Venezuela in 1854, Peru in 1855, Cuba in 1886, and Brazil in 1888.

The Abolition Movement in the United States had its beginnings as early as 1688 when Quakers in Pennsylvania began to speak out against slavery as a moral wrong. But it was not until the 1830's that the abolition movement became a crusade. William Lloyd Garrison is considered the chief spokesman for the movement. He began publication of his newspaper, the *Liberator*, in 1831. The American Anti-Slavery Society was founded in 1833 with demands for an end to slavery. Abolitionist writings, such as Harriet Beecher Stowe's novel, *Uncle Tom's Cabin*, focused national attention on the slavery issue. Radical abolitionists urged the Negroes to revolt against slavery, but had no plans for providing for the freed slaves. Many persons of both the North and the South opposed the movement. The abolitionists were blamed for such outbreaks as the rebellion in Virginia led by Nat Turner in 1831 (see TURNER, NAT).

Many free Negroes joined the abolitionists. Among the best known was Sojourner Truth, a freed slave who made public talks throughout New England and the West. Another was Frederick Douglass, a fugitive slave who began publication in 1847 of the *North Star*, an abolitionist newspaper. Douglass also made many abolitionist lectures.

The *underground railroad* was an organization established by Quakers and other antislavery groups in the early 1800's. It was a system to help runaway slaves escape from their owners to the Northern States and to Canada. See UNDERGROUND RAILROAD.

John Brown, a radical abolitionist and a worker in the underground railroad, decided to invade the South to free the slaves. To collect arms, he and 18 of his followers in 1859 attacked the federal arsenal at Harpers Ferry in western Virginia (now West Virginia). Brown was quickly captured, was convicted of treason, and was hanged. The abolitionists considered him a martyr. But his act made the South believe that the North would stop at nothing to abolish slavery. Throughout the South, military forces began preparing for war.

Emancipation. When the Civil War broke out in 1861, abolitionists urged the government to free the slaves. President Abraham Lincoln considered various plans to pay slaveowners for slaves they would free. He also studied a plan to settle freed Negroes in the West Indies and elsewhere. He said his primary object was to save the Union, and not to save or destroy slavery.

On Jan. 1, 1863, Lincoln issued the Emancipation Proclamation. This proclamation did not free all the Negro slaves, because it applied only to slaves in the states fighting against the federal government. Four slave states were fighting on the Union side, and their slaves were not affected. In many parts of the Confederacy the slaves did not actually gain their freedom until the war was over. Not until 1865, when the 13th Amendment to the United States Constitution was adopted, were all the slaves freed. The 14th and 15th Amendments were then adopted to guarantee certain rights to the former slaves. No payment was made to the former owners of the slaves, and no plans were made by the federal government to resettle the freedmen or to provide ways for them to make a living.

During the war, many slaves continued to work on the plantations and to look after their masters' families.

Black Soldiers fought in the Union Army during the Civil War. Free Negroes of the 54th Massachusetts Regiment battled Confederate defenders of Fort Wagner, near Charleston, S.C., in 1863.

Some slaves ran away to the Union armies. At first, the slaves were sent back by the Union officers. Later, they were offered their freedom. By the end of the war, about 186,000 Negroes had enlisted in the Union armies. See CIVIL WAR (Negroes in the Civil War).

After the Civil War, the freed Negroes reacted to their new status in various ways. Many Negroes, still dependent on their former masters, continued to live on the plantations. Some, with government help, acquired their own small farms. Others drifted to the cities. This was a period of severe adjustment for the freed slaves. Most of them were untrained and could not read or write. They had never had to rely upon themselves to supply their everyday needs.

Many former slaves turned to education as a means to lead them to a better life. They flocked to new schools set up by state and local governments and by church groups. The Freedmen's Bureau, a federal agency, set up and supervised schools for Negroes throughout the South. When the educational work of the Bureau ended in 1870, there were nearly 250,000 Negro students in more than 4,000 schools. Schools founded with aid from the Freedmen's Bureau included Howard University, Hampton Institute, Atlanta University, and Fisk University.

Local Negro churches sprang up throughout the South. Negro Baptist churches increased their memberships from 150,000 before the Civil War to 500,000 by 1870. The churches gave many Negroes their first opportunities for leadership.

The defeated Southern States with their 4 million newly freed slaves faced huge social and economic prob-lems. President Lincoln seemed to have had in mind to restore state government quickly in the South, and to give voting rights gradually to the Negroes on a basis of educational or property qualifications. After Lincoln was assassinated, President Andrew Johnson tried to follow the same plan. But Congress overrode Johnson's vetoes to set up its own Reconstruction plans.

Immediately after the end of the war, white South-erners who had fought for the Confederacy controlled the state governments in the South and gave little consideration to the voting rights of Negroes. However, under the Reconstruction plans of Congress, many white Southerners lost their vote and newly freed Ne-groes in some states, such as South Carolina, became a majority of the voters. Negroes served in the legislatures of the Southern States and held various state offices. Two, Hiram R. Revels and Blanche K. Bruce, were elected to the U.S. Senate from Mississippi. Altogether, Southern States sent 20 Negroes to serve in the U.S. House of Representatives between 1869 and 1901.

For a more complete description of the Reconstruc-tion era, see the separate article RECONSTRUCTION.

After Reconstruction. Federal troops withdrew from the South in 1877. "King Cotton" ruled the economy of the South, and Negroes were encouraged to con-tinue working in the cotton fields to help both them-selves and the landowners.

Politicians of both the Democratic and Republican parties were competing for the Negro vote. In states with large Negro populations, the whites began to fear that Negroes would gain control of local government. One by one the Southern States withdrew voting rights from the Negroes. The South's pattern of separation of the races gradually developed. The races were separated in schools, railroad stations, trains, hotels, barbershops, theaters, restaurants, and churches. In 1896, the Supreme Court upheld the principle of "separate but equal" facilities for whites and Negroes in the case of *Plessy vs. Ferguson*. This case involved intrastate transportation, but the decision was interpreted as applying to other situations, such as public schools.

Separation of the races was not confined to the South. The Northern States also imposed restraints on the Negro. Negroes who moved to cities in the North found homes only in certain residential areas. These areas were usually overcrowded slums. Most labor organizations would not accept Negro members. Negroes found it almost impossible to find jobs except as servants or as unskilled laborers.

Booker T. Washington became the outstanding Negro leader and educator of the late 1800's and early 1900's. He organized a new school for Negroes, Tuskegee Institute, in Tuskegee, Ala., in 1881. He called on Negroes to respect the laws and to "cultivate friendly relations with Southern white men." He urged Negroes to take vocational training to become farmers, mechanics, and servants. He invited the Negro scientist George Washington Carver to join the staff of Tuskegee Institute in 1896. Carver developed new products from such crops as peanuts and sweet potatoes. These crops helped to diversify agriculture in the South. As time went on, Southern farmers became less dependent on cotton and fewer Negroes were needed to labor in the fields.

The main Negro opponent of Booker T. Washington's views in this period was W. E. B. Du Bois. In 1895, he had become the first Negro to receive a Ph.D. degree from Harvard University. Du Bois believed that Negroes should fight for equal status. When the National Association for the Advancement of Colored People (NAACP) was formed in 1909, Du Bois became its first Negro officer as director of publicity and research. The new organization concentrated on a crusade to end lynching and violence, to obtain voting rights for Negroes, to secure justice in the courts, and to end discrimination in its most glaring forms.

In 1910, the National Urban League was founded. It sought new opportunities for Negroes in industry and tried to help them make the adjustment to city living.

Through the World Wars. World War I gave a new look at the world to the more than 360,000 American Negroes in the military services. They received new educational opportunities, in spite of segregation and friction in the armed forces.

Even more important to the Negro, World War I opened up new job opportunities in manufacturing industries. More than 300,000 Negroes moved to the Northern States between 1910 and 1920. This was the beginning of a continuing migration northward. More than 1,300,000 Negroes went North in the 1920's, 1,500,000 in the 1930's, and 2,500,000 in the 1940's.

Life in the North was also full of difficulties for the Negroes. Race riots occurred in such Northern cities as Detroit and Chicago. Job opportunities for Negroes were restricted. Housing for Negroes was limited mostly to slum areas. Two or three families often crowded into small apartments with relatives, friends, and sometimes strangers. They paid high rents for unsafe and unhealthy quarters. In such crowded conditions, normal family life could not be maintained. Families often had to separate. Social agencies attempting to deal with the resulting problems were overrun with people needing help. Crime rates in such areas increased.

Throughout this period there were Negroes who won distinction in various fields. The development of blues and jazz music was greatly influenced by such Negro musicians as W. C. Handy and Louis Armstrong. In 1928, Chicago Republican Oscar DePriest became the first Northern Negro elected to Congress. Outstanding

The Negro Struggle for Equality in the early 1900's was led by the NAACP. W. E. B. Du Bois, *center,* helped found the organization in 1909, and directed its publications until 1934.

Duke Ellington and His Band gained fame in Harlem in New York City during the late 1920's. Harlem became a black cultural center, and attracted writers, musicians, artists, and entertainers.

From *A Pictorial History of the Negro in America,* by Langston Hughes and Milton Meltzer

Collection of Duncan P. Schiedt

Negro writers included Langston Hughes and Richard Wright. Singer Paul Robeson and dancer Bill Robinson won acclaim. In 1937, Joe Louis became the second Negro heavyweight boxing champion in history, when he won the title that Jack Johnson held before World War I. A. Philip Randolph became an important American labor leader.

Nearly a million Negroes served in all branches of the American armed forces in World War II. Benjamin O. Davis became the first Negro to serve as a brigadier general in the U.S. Army. His son, Benjamin O. Davis, Jr., later became the first Negro to attain the rank of lieutenant general in the U.S. Air Force. Desegregation of the armed forces began on a trial basis during World War II. It was completed soon after President Harry S. Truman issued a 1948 executive order calling for equal treatment for all persons in the armed forces. Hundreds of thousands of Negroes received education and training for jobs in war industries.

After World War II, more and more Negroes won recognition in various fields. In 1947, Jackie Robinson became the first Negro to play modern major league baseball. In 1950, the poet Gwendolyn Brooks became the first Negro to win a Pulitzer prize. Ralph Bunche became the first Negro to win the Nobel peace prize. Marian Anderson in 1955 became the first Negro to sing a leading role in the Metropolitan Opera in New York.

THE CIVIL RIGHTS MOVEMENT

With the end of World War II, Americans showed increasing concern over racial discrimination. In the South, segregation laws separated the races in public schools and prevented Negroes from entering restaurants, theaters, and other public places reserved only for whites. In the North, where no segregation laws existed, Negroes still faced discrimination in buying homes and seeking jobs. Many national leaders, both Negro and white, emphasized the need to end racial discrimination and to guarantee to Negroes their civil rights.

The Legal Battle. The 14th Amendment, adopted after the Civil War, guaranteed equal protection under the law to all citizens. But for many years after the Reconstruction period, proposals for federal legislation to enforce this principle were defeated. Many persons argued that federal civil rights laws would violate states' rights. Some states, most of them in the North and the West, passed state laws against racial discrimination in such fields as housing, education, public accommodations, and employment.

In the mid-1940's, several important Supreme Court decisions attacked the problem of segregation. The Supreme Court ruled in 1946 that a Virginia law requiring segregation on interstate buses was invalid. In 1948, the court held that *restrictive covenants* (agreements to prevent real estate owners from selling their property to members of minority groups) could not be enforced by federal or state courts. In a series of decisions extending over several years, the court ruled that Negro colleges in several states were not equal to white colleges within those states, and that those states should therefore admit Negroes to white state colleges. On May 17, 1954, the court held in *Brown v. Board of Education of Topeka* that compulsory segregation in public schools denies equal protection under the law. This decision, in effect, overturned the 1896 "separate but equal" ruling. The decision applied only to education, but it

The March on Washington on Aug. 28, 1963, brought more than 200,000 civil rights demonstrators to Washington, D.C., to dramatize Negro demands for equal rights and opportunities.

Ebony Magazine

inspired Negroes to seek more rights in other fields. The next year, the court ordered that its 1954 ruling should be carried out "with all deliberate speed."

Partial integration took place in an orderly manner at hundreds of schools during the years that followed. But a few incidents attracted national attention. In 1957, Central High School in Little Rock, Ark., attempted to admit Negro students in accordance with a federal court order. Governor Orval E. Faubus ordered the Arkansas National Guard to surround the school to prevent the Negroes from entering. Integration took place only after President Dwight D. Eisenhower sent federal troops to the school. In 1962, violence broke out when James Meredith enrolled as the first Negro student at the University of Mississippi at Oxford, Miss. Attorney General Robert F. Kennedy sent U.S. marshals to help maintain order, but two persons were killed and several were injured.

The NAACP led the legal battle against segregation. The NAACP worked for federal and state civil rights legislation, and tested hundreds of civil rights cases in the courts.

The Civil Rights Act of 1957 established a six-member commission to investigate denials of civil rights. In 1960, Congress provided measures for helping Negroes overcome efforts to keep them from voting.

The "Negro Revolution." During the 1950's, many Negroes grew impatient with slow progress in achieving the rights promised in laws and court decisions. In 1955, Negroes in Montgomery, Ala., led by Martin Luther King, Jr., a Baptist minister, resorted to direct action. They boycotted a local bus company that practiced segregation. The boycott began as a protest against the arrest of a Negro woman, Mrs. Rosa Parks, who refused to give up her bus seat to a white passenger. But it grew into a mass movement in 1956. The success of the boycott convinced many Negroes that other civil rights goals could be won by direct action.

Beginning in the early 1960's, Negro protests took increasingly active forms. Groups of Negroes and whites conducted "freedom rides" aimed at ending segregation in public facilities in the South. They held "sit-ins" at segregated lunch counters, "pray-ins" at churches, and "wade-ins" at beaches. In the North, civil rights groups protested against discrimination in jobs, housing, and education. One of the major issues was the *de facto* (in fact) segregation of Northern schools that resulted from residential segregation. Many persons felt that such segregation reduced educational opportunities for Negroes.

Several organizations led the civil rights movement. The NAACP, under Roy Wilkins, and the Urban League, under Whitney M. Young, Jr., took part in some civil rights demonstrations. But these older organizations devoted most of their efforts to court cases and educational programs. Newer organizations usually led the more active forms of protest. These organizations included the Southern Christian Leadership Conference (SCLC), led by King; the Congress of Racial Equality (CORE), under James Farmer; and the Student Nonviolent Coordinating Committee (SNCC). In 1969, SNCC changed its name to the Student National Coordinating Committee.

Negro leaders not directly connected with civil rights organizations also influenced the civil rights movement. Author James Baldwin criticized American society for

Wide World

Civil Rights Leaders of the 1960's, shown with President Lyndon B. Johnson, included, *left to right,* Roy Wilkins, NAACP; James Farmer, CORE; Martin Luther King, Jr., Southern Christian Leadership Conference; and Whitney M. Young, Jr., Urban League.

its attitude toward the Negro. Entertainers such as singer Mahalia Jackson and comedian Dick Gregory promoted civil rights causes.

A few *black nationalist* groups such as the Black Muslims favored separation of the races rather than integration. Black nationalist leaders Elijah Muhammad and Malcolm X opposed civil rights activity. They viewed it as a form of cooperation with white society.

The year 1963 marked a turning point in the civil rights movement, as Negro leaders began to organize large demonstrations in all parts of the country. In May, 1963, thousands of Negroes demonstrated against racial segregation in Birmingham, Ala. "Freedom marches" followed in cities throughout the country.

The climax came on Aug. 28, 1963, when more than 200,000 persons, including many whites, took part in a "March on Washington" in Washington, D.C. Millions viewed the march on television, and heard King make a stirring plea for racial justice. King said he had a dream that someday in America a person would be judged by the content of his character, rather than by the color of his skin.

New Civil Rights Acts. In 1963, President John F. Kennedy asked Congress for a civil rights law that would end segregation in public places. Kennedy's bill was still bogged down in Congress when he was assassinated on Nov. 22, 1963.

Kennedy's successor, President Lyndon B. Johnson, asked Congress to make Kennedy's civil rights bill a prime concern. He also raised Negro hopes when he announced plans for a "War on Poverty." Congress passed the Civil Rights Act of 1964 in July. The act (1) required equal access to public accommodations and facilities; (2) forbade discriminatory use of voter registration tests; (3) barred discrimination by employers and unions; and (4) provided for withholding government funds from federally assisted activities that failed to desegregate. As a result of the act, segregation in public places soon crumbled.

In January, 1965, King began a voting rights campaign, concentrating on Selma, Ala. Civil rights workers were bullied, threatened, and arrested there, even though federal court orders directed lawmen not to interfere with orderly demonstrations. The court also ordered voting registrars to stop stalling, using unfair literacy tests, and rejecting applicants for unimportant reasons. King planned a march on the state capitol in Montgomery to inform Governor George Wallace of the barriers to voting.

Wallace banned the march. When 500 Negro marchers tried to set out for Montgomery on March 7, 1965, police used tear gas, nightsticks, and whips to stop them. Many of the marchers were injured. Aroused by this incident, hundreds of persons—including many white clergymen and public figures—rushed to Selma to join the march. About 1,500 persons, white and black, marched one mile beyond Selma, but turned back peacefully when state troopers blocked the road. President Johnson addressed a joint session of Congress, asking for a bill to protect the right to vote. He also announced federal protection for the march from Selma to Montgomery, which took place late in March.

With world attention focused on Alabama, Congress acted. In August, it passed the Voting Rights Act of 1965. The act suspended voter tests in states where fewer than half the adults voted; permitted federal examiners to register voters; and required the federal government to sue to bar poll taxes as a voting requirement in state elections. The 24th Amendment, ratified in 1964, had barred poll taxes for federal elections.

Violence and Racial Tension. Most civil rights demonstrations stressed nonviolence. But the demonstrations sometimes caused tension that resulted in violence. In June, 1963, Medgar Evers, Mississippi field secretary for the NAACP, was shot to death. In September, 1963, four Negro girls were killed when a bomb exploded in a Birmingham church.

Violence increased as the civil rights movement intensified. In 1964 and 1965, electric cattle prods were used on white and black demonstrators in St. Augustine, Fla., and Montgomery. Homes, churches, and cars were dynamited in Mississippi. Three young civil rights workers were murdered during the 1964 "Freedom Summer" campaign to register voters in Mississippi. A Negro school official from Washington, D.C., was slain in Georgia in 1964 while returning from reserve officer training camp. At Selma, two white civil rights workers —a clergyman from Boston and a housewife from Detroit—were murdered. Near Selma, a Negro and a white seminary student were shot to death.

In 1965, Johnson urged Congress to investigate possible Ku Klux Klan involvement in the wave of civil rights murders. Congressional hearings exposed terrorism by Klansmen, but no federal action was taken against the Klan. By the end of 1965, only 3 convictions had been secured in an estimated 34 civil rights murders since 1960. These were on lesser charges of second-degree murder, manslaughter, and conspiracy to deprive persons of their civil rights.

NEGRO MILITANCY

Nonviolence had achieved success with the passage of the Civil Rights Act of 1964 and the Voting Rights Act of 1965. King was awarded the Nobel peace prize for 1964 for his nonviolent leadership. But segregation and voting barriers were easier to overcome than were prejudice, inferior education, and other basic problems. In the middle and late 1960's, many Negroes decided that the civil rights movement had not basically altered their lives. They pushed for more direct action to achieve more rapid change. Their emphasis shifted from legal equality to social and economic equality.

Unrest in the Cities became a major problem in the second half of the 1960's. Negroes became increasingly dissatisfied with life in the city slums. Unrest led to rioting in the Negro ghettos.

During the 1900's, hundreds of thousands of Negroes migrated from the rural South in search of jobs in the manufacturing centers of the North. In 1910, nine of every ten Negroes lived in the South, and most of them were farm laborers. In the late 1960's, only about half lived in the South, and the majority of Negroes lived in the nation's largest metropolitan areas. Most Negroes were poorly prepared by training, education, and cultural background for city life. As Negroes migrated to Northern cities, many whites moved from the cities to the suburbs. As a result, America's large cities became increasingly black.

City ghettos bred unrest. Because of discrimination in the sale and rental of housing, many Negroes were denied the right to live where they chose. They were crowded into all-Negro slums, and paid high rent for inferior housing. Poor schooling limited many Negroes to low-paid, unstable manual labor. In the late 1960's, the median annual income for Negro families was about $4,900, while that of white families was about $8,300. The unemployment rate for Negroes was over twice that for whites. Some merchants sold slum dwellers inferior goods at high prices and high rates of interest.

The riots were often triggered by routine police actions. But ghetto Negroes had come to resent lawmen, both for what they termed "police brutality" and because policemen represented the white power structure.

A riot in the Watts section of Los Angeles in August, 1965, awakened the nation to the explosive conditions in the cities. A traffic arrest there touched off five days of destruction, looting, and arson to chants of "Get Whitey" and "Burn, Baby, Burn." Isolated by lack of public transportation, the Negroes of Watts had an unemployment rate of 14 per cent, more than triple the national rate for whites. As a result of the riot, 34 persons died, over 1,000 were injured, and over 3,000 were arrested. About 200 buildings were destroyed and about 600 were damaged, at a total cost of more than $40 million. Most Negro-owned businesses displaying the words "Soul Brother" were spared. President Johnson condemned the rioting and urged remedying the causes —poverty and frustration. After the Watts riot, jobs were found for half the area's unemployed, bus service was expanded, and a hospital was built there.

During the summer of 1966, other ghettos exploded over minor incidents. In 1967, rioting occurred in about 75 U.S. cities. Detroit suffered one of the worst riots in America in this century. A week of looting and burning there in July, 1967, led to 43 deaths, over 600 injuries, about 7,000 arrests, and property damage of about $45 million. Fires left thousands homeless. Soldiers using tanks, armored cars, and machine guns were called in to stop the riot.

Rock-throwing mobs attacked the open-housing marches King led into white neighborhoods in Chicago in 1966. In 1967, mobs in Milwaukee attacked the housing marches that were staged by the NAACP. The marches were led by a white Roman Catholic priest, James E. Groppi.

Johnson appointed a commission headed by Illinois Governor Otto Kerner to study the causes of the riots. In its 1968 report, the commission put much of the blame on the racial prejudice and discrimination of whites against blacks. It recommended massive programs to improve conditions in the ghettos and to speed efforts toward a truly integrated society.

Black Power. Some civil rights groups grew more militant in 1966 when Floyd McKissick became national director of CORE and Stokely Carmichael was elected chairman of SNCC. Both leaders preached the doctrine of *Black Power.*

Black Power urged Negroes to build power bases by solidifying black communities into political blocs. In this way, Negroes might force improvement as other minority groups in America had done. The doctrine called for black leaders and officeholders to lead black people, and to be directly responsible to the people. White civil rights workers would concentrate on correcting the racist outlook of their fellow whites. Black Power supported separate economic and social institutions in black communities so that black people could gain economic power.

Black Power called for Negroes to meet violence with violence. It held that Americans respected the man defending himself with gun in hand more than the man kneeling helplessly before his oppressors. Black Power also glorified things black, stressing that "black is beautiful." It insisted that Negroes adopt their own standards, such as African clothing and hair styles, rather than the values of white America. Black Power leaders said the term *Negro* was a word applied to blacks by white society. They urged black Americans to refer to themselves as *blacks* or *Afro-Americans.*

Wide World

Black Nationalist Leader Malcolm X became a symbol of black pride and black power after his assassination in 1965. Malcolm drew a large crowd at this Harlem rally in 1963.

At first, Black Power split the civil rights movement. Carmichael's SNCC first gained significant support for the doctrine, and McKissick's CORE adopted it enthusiastically. But the 1966 conventions of King's SCLC and Wilkins' NAACP condemned Black Power. That fall, several civil rights leaders issued a *manifesto* (proclamation) denouncing Black Power. They supported instead democratic methods, nonviolence, integration, and teaming of white and Negro civil rights workers. In 1967, however, Wilkins, King, Young, and their organizations admitted that Black Power had many good points. But they deplored the rash and violent words and deeds of Carmichael and H. Rap Brown, his successor as SNCC chairman.

Black Power was more than a fad. It appealed to idealistic young people who were impatient with gradual gains. It awakened racial pride, and stirred the neglected masses of the rural South and the city ghettos. Supporters of Black Power insisted that integration mainly benefited middle class Negroes with the training and wealth to take advantage of new opportunities.

The King Assassination. In the late 1960's, civil rights groups became increasingly concerned with achieving economic equality for Negroes. Early in 1968, King started to organize a Poor People's March on Washington, D.C., to dramatize the problems of the poor. King also went to Memphis, Tenn., to support striking sanitation workers—most of them Negroes—who were seeking higher pay. There, a hidden rifleman killed him on April 4. Millions mourned King's death, and looting and burning broke out in some black communities. James Earl Ray, an escaped convict, was charged with murdering King. He pleaded guilty to the crime and was sentenced to 99 years in prison.

Since 1966, President Johnson had urged Congress to pass a civil rights law that would extend federal protection to civil rights workers like King, expand equal employment, desegregate Southern juries, and end discrimination in the sale and rental of housing. The Senate passed the bill in March, 1968, but the measure became stalled in the House. Responding to King's death and the riots that followed, the House passed the bill—the Civil Rights Act of 1968—and Johnson signed it into law on April 11. In June, 1968, the Supreme Court went beyond the open housing section of the act. The court banned all housing discrimination, basing its decision on a law passed in 1866.

King's successor as head of the SCLC, Ralph D. Abernathy, carried out the Poor People's March. In May, 1968, thousands of Negroes, American Indians, Spanish-speaking Americans, and poor whites came to Washington, D.C., and set up a shanty town called Resurrection City. But they achieved little.

Student Militancy. In the late 1960's, Negro youth increasingly followed the example of such past black militants as David Walker, Harriet Tubman, Marcus Garvey, and Malcolm X. In the early 1800's, Walker, a free Negro, urged slaves to fight for their freedom. Miss Tubman, an escaped slave, returned South at the risk of her life to lead other slaves to freedom. Garvey, who had a large following in the 1920's, opposed integration. He stressed racial pride and urged Negroes to return to Africa. Malcolm X became a symbol of the black revolution after his assassination in February, 1965.

Many black students argued that traditional education neglected black heroes of the past and did not respond to today's needs. In a number of cities, militants demanded community control of public schools. Violent disorders took place on many university campuses as students demanded separate black studies programs, open admission for disadvantaged minorities, separate dormitories for blacks, and more black professors and administrators. Some schools agreed to these demands or worked out compromises with the students.

The Black Panther Movement. During the late 1960's, the Black Panther Party replaced the Black Muslims as the most feared and publicized extremist group. The party was founded in Oakland, Calif., in October, 1966, by Huey P. Newton and Bobby Seale. Hostility between the Panthers and the police of various cities led to several shoot-outs.

In December, 1969, a police raid on a Panther apartment in Chicago resulted in the deaths of two Panther leaders. A special federal grand jury investigation revealed that the police had riddled the apartment with at least 82 shots, while the Panthers apparently fired only one shot. The action aroused much sympathy for the Panthers. Many blacks believed that the Panthers had given Negroes a needed sense of pride. But the Federal Bureau of Investigation, in its 1970 annual report, called the Black Panther Party the "most dangerous and violence prone of all extremist groups."

In 1971, a Connecticut Supreme Court judge dismissed murder charges against Seale following a mistrial. Authorities in New Haven, Conn., had charged Seale and other Black Panthers in 1969 with killing a suspected informer. The judge declared that the wide

Operation Breadbasket, headed by Jesse L. Jackson, center, a Baptist minister, works to organize black people in urban ghettos so they can achieve greater economic power.

Chicago Daily News

publicity about the case would prevent the selection of an unbiased jury. Another trial that gained widespread publicity in 1970 and 1971 involved Angela Davis, a Black Panther supporter. Miss Davis was accused of buying the guns used in a fatal 1970 shoot-out at the Marin County courthouse in California.

Black Power supporters of the mid-1960's had rejected whites. But in the late 1960's and early 1970's, the Black Panther movement increasingly accepted the help of whites. Many blacks and whites cooperated in Vietnam War protests. Others worked to give blacks a greater say in controlling their affairs and providing community services. See BLACK PANTHER PARTY.

THE NEGRO TODAY

Political Gains. In the late 1960's and early 1970's, more Negroes than ever held important government positions. Negro gains won through democratic processes helped lessen the appeal of extremist groups. In 1966, Robert C. Weaver became the first Negro Cabinet member. President Johnson appointed him secretary of housing and urban development. Andrew F. Brimmer became the first Negro to serve on the Federal Reserve Board of Governors. In 1967, Thurgood Marshall became the first Negro Supreme Court justice.

Also in 1967, Edward W. Brooke of Massachusetts became the first Negro to serve in the U.S. Senate since Reconstruction. Ten Negroes—a new high—were seated in the 91st Congress in 1969. They included Representative Shirley Chisholm of New York City, the first Negro woman in Congress. Thirteen Negroes took seats in Congress in 1971.

Negroes also made gains at the local level. In 1967, blacks for the first time became mayors of major cities— Carl B. Stokes in Cleveland and Walter E. Washington in Washington, D.C. In the same year, Richard G. Hatcher was elected mayor of Gary, Ind., and took office in 1968. In 1969, Howard Lee of Chapel Hill, N.C., became the first Negro to be elected mayor of a predominantly white Southern community. Also in 1969, Charles Evers was elected mayor of Fayette, Miss. He became the first black mayor of a Mississippi town since Reconstruction. In 1970, Kenneth A. Gibson was elected mayor of Newark, N.J. By 1971, blacks held nearly 2,000 of the 522,000 elective offices in the United States.

Unsolved Problems. By the 1970's, most legal barriers to full Negro participation in American life had been broken down. But black Americans still faced many roadblocks.

Although thousands of Negroes had succeeded in many fields, other hundreds of thousands found it impossible to maintain even a comfortable standard of living. About 32 per cent of the nation's poor were nonwhite. But only about 10 per cent of all white persons were poor, compared with about 34 per cent of nonwhites. Discrimination probably accounted for as much Negro joblessness as did lack of training.

Segregation continued to be a major problem as the nation's inner cities became increasingly black. The 1970 census showed that during the 1960's, $2\frac{1}{2}$ million whites left the inner-city areas and that the number of blacks in these areas increased by 3 million.

In the early and mid-1960's, most Negroes had looked to the federal government for leadership in improving race relations. They were encouraged by some government actions. In 1955, the Supreme Court had called for the desegregation of public schools with "all deliberate speed." In 1969, the court ruled that school districts must end segregation "at once." In 1970, President Richard M. Nixon proposed a welfare reform measure to guarantee every family a minimum annual income. His Administration also sought to increase employment of members of minority groups in the construction trades.

During the late 1960's and early 1970's, however, many blacks became confused and disillusioned by what they believed were the shifting policies of the Nixon Administration. They were alarmed at what they considered Nixon's "Southern strategy" of writing off the black and liberal vote while concentrating on winning Southern votes away from the Democratic Party and from third-party leader George C. Wallace. They cited Nixon's unsuccessful attempts to place two Southern conservative judges—Clement F. Haynsworth, Jr., and G. Harrold Carswell—on the Supreme Court. Many blacks feared that Nixon was attempting to change the court to make it less liberal on civil rights.

The Nixon Administration favored neighborhood schools and opposed the busing of pupils from one neighborhood to another to integrate classrooms. Nixon also opposed efforts to force suburban homeowners to accept the building of low-cost houses and low-rent apartments in their communities. But in 1970, a federal

Jack Mitchell

Black Entertainers have excelled in the performing arts, especially in dancing, music, and comedy. The Alvin Ailey Dance Company, above, became famous during the 1960's.

court ordered the Charlotte-Mecklenburg County school system in North Carolina to integrate its schools by means of busing. In April, 1971, the Supreme Court unanimously approved the busing of pupils. A few days later, in a 5 to 3 decision, the Supreme Court approved state laws that gave people the right to vote on whether they wanted low-rent public housing in their community.

In February, 1970, nine black Democrats from the House of Representatives failed in attempts to meet with Nixon. The group boycotted Nixon's State of the Union message in January, 1971. Later that year, they formed a 13-member Black Caucus. In March, the President met with the Black Caucus. The congressmen presented him with 60 demands. Major recommendations included stronger enforcement of civil rights laws and the replacement of the welfare system with a guaranteed annual income of at least $6,500 for a family of four persons.

EDGAR ALLAN TOPPIN

Related Articles in WORLD BOOK include:

ATHLETES AND SPORTS LEADERS

Alcindor, Lew	Clay, Cassius	Owens, Jesse
Ashe, Arthur R., Jr.	Gibson, Althea	Paige, Satchel
Baylor, Elgin	Johnson, Jack	Robertson, Oscar
Brown, Jimmy	Louis, Joe	Robinson, Jackie
Chamberlain, Wilt	Mays, Willie	Russell, Bill

CIVIL RIGHTS LEADERS

Abernathy, Ralph D.	Luthuli, Albert John
Bond, Julian	McKissick, Floyd B.
Carmichael, Stokely	Meredith, James H.
Du Bois, W. E. B.	Randolph, A. Philip
Evers (brothers)	Rustin, Bayard
Farmer, James L.	Terrell, Mary Church
Gregory, Dick	White, Walter F.
Jackson, Jesse L.	Wilkins, Roy
King, Martin Luther, Jr.	Young, Whitney M., Jr.

Chicago Sun-Times

Black-Run Businesses increased in the late 1960's. This shop, above, features African style clothing and accessories.

EDUCATORS AND SCHOLARS

Bethune, Mary McLeod
Clark, Kenneth Bancroft
Franklin, John Hope
Frazier, E. Franklin
Johnson, Charles S.
Locke, Alain L.
Mays, Benjamin E.

Moton, Robert R.
Nabrit, James M., Jr.
Quarles, Benjamin A.
Washington, Booker T.
Weaver, Robert C.
Woodson, Carter G.

JAZZ MUSICIANS AND SINGERS

Armstrong, Louis
Basie, Count
Coltrane, John W.
Davis, Miles D., Jr.
Ellington, Duke
Fitzgerald, Ella
Gillespie, Dizzy
Handy, W. C.
Hawkins, Coleman

Henderson, Fletcher
Holiday, Billie
Joplin, Scott
Lewis, John Aaron
Monk, Thelonious
Parker, Charlie
Smith, Bessie
Tatum, Art
Young, Lester W.

OTHER SINGERS AND ENTERTAINERS

Anderson, Marian
Burleigh, Harry T.
Dunham, Katherine
Hayes, Roland
Maynor, Dorothy

Price, Leontyne
Robeson, Paul
Robinson, Bill
Waters, Ethel

MILITARY FIGURES

Attucks, Crispus
Christophe, Henri
Davis, Benjamin O., Jr.

Delany, Martin R.
Dessalines, Jean J.
Toussaint l'Ouverture

POLITICAL FIGURES

Askia Mohammed
Brooke, Edward W.
Chisholm, Shirley
Duvalier, François
Hastie, William H.
Hatcher, Richard Gordon
Houphouët-Boigny, Félix
Kaunda, Kenneth D.
Kenyatta, Jomo
Mansa Musa
Mobutu, Joseph D.

Nkrumah, Kwame
Nyerere, Julius K.
Nzinga a Nkuwa
Powell, Adam Clayton, Jr.
Senghor, Léopold-Sédar
Stokes, Carl B.
Sundiata Keita
Sunni Ali
Touré, Sékou
Tubman, William V. S.

SCIENTISTS

Banneker, Benjamin
Carver, George W.
Drew, Charles R.

Julian, Percy L.
Lawless, Theodore K.
Williams, Daniel Hale

WRITERS

Baldwin, James A.
Bontemps, Arna
Brooks, Gwendolyn
Cleaver, Eldridge
Cullen, Countee
Dunbar, Paul L.

Ellison, Ralph
Hughes, Langston
Johnson, James W.
McKay, Claude
Wheatley, Phillis
Wright, Richard

OTHER BIOGRAPHIES

Allen, Richard
Beckwourth, James P.
Bunche, Ralph J.
Cuffe, Paul
Douglass, Frederick
Du Sable, Jean Baptiste P.
Estevanico
Garvey, Marcus
Hall, Prince
Henson, Matthew A.
Johnson, John H.

Malcolm X
Marshall, Thurgood
Muhammad, Elijah
Rillieux, Norbert
Rowan, Carl T.
Russwurm, John B.
Smalls, Robert
Truth, Sojourner
Tubman, Harriet
Turner, Nat

HISTORY IN AFRICA

Africa
Benin
Fulani
Gao
Ghana Empire

Ife
Jenne
Kanem
Kongo
Mali Empire

Malinke
Nok
Songhai Empire
Walata
Zimbabwe

HISTORY IN AMERICA

Abolitionist
Black Codes
Carpetbagger
Civil War
Emancipation
  Proclamation
Freedmen's Bureau

Grandfather
  Clause
Jim Crow
Ku Klux Klan
Lynching
Niagara
  Movement

Proslavery
  Movement
Reconstruction
Scalawag
Slavery
Underground
  Railroad

ORGANIZATIONS

Association for the Study
  of Negro Life and History
Black Panther Party
Congress of Racial Equality
National Association for
  the Advancement of
  Colored People
National Medical Association

Rosenwald Fund, Julius
Southern Christian Lead-
  ership Conference
Southern Education
  Foundation
Student National Coor-
  dinating Committee
Urban League

RELIGION

African Methodist Episcopal Church
African Methodist Episcopal Zion Church
Black Muslims
National Baptist Convention of America
National Baptist Convention, U.S.A., Inc.
National Primitive Baptist Convention in the U.S.A.

OTHER RELATED ARTICLES

American Literature (The Negro
  Renaissance; Social and
  Cultural Criticism)
Civil Rights
Henry, John
Jazz
Minority Group

Negrito
Opera (Porgy
  and Bess)
Races of Man
Segregation
Spingarn Medal
Spiritual

Outline

  I. The Negro in Africa
  II. The Slave Trade
  III. Slavery in America
    A. In Colonial Times   C. Growth of Slavery
    B. After the Revolution-   D. Free Negroes
       ary War
  IV. Changing Status of the Negro
    A. The Abolition   C. After Reconstruction
       Movement   D. Through the World Wars
    B. Emancipation
  V. The Civil Rights Movement
    A. The Legal Battle   C. New Civil Rights Acts
    B. The "Negro Revo-   D. Violence and Racial
       lution"   Tension
  VI. Negro Militancy
    A. Unrest in the Cities   D. Student Militancy
    B. Black Power   E. The Black Panther
    C. The King Assassination   Movement
  VII. The Negro Today
    A. Political Gains   B. Unsolved Problems

Questions

How did Negro slavery start in the United States?
What were the achievements of Ralph Bunche, George Washington Carver, and Martin Luther King, Jr.?
Who was the first Negro to attain the rank of brigadier general in the United States Army?
How did the Civil Rights Act of 1964 help Negroes?
What is Black Power?
How did the U.S. help Negroes after the Civil War?
What are some principal causes of Negro joblessness?
What political gains did Negroes make in the 1960's?

NEGRO, RIO. See RIO NEGRO.

NEGROS. See PHILIPPINES (The Islands).

NEHEMIAH, *NEE huh MY uh,* was a Jew who lived in the 400's B.C. His story is told in the book of *Nehemiah* in the Old Testament. He held the highly honored position of cupbearer to King Artaxerxes I in Persia. When a report of bad conditions in Judah reached him, Nehemiah asked the king to help. The king sent Nehemiah to Judah as Persian governor. There, he rebuilt the walls of Jerusalem and reformed the people.   WALTER G. WILLIAMS

NEHRU, *NEH roo,* is the family name of a father and his son, daughter, and granddaughter who became distinguished in Indian public affairs. The father and the son prefixed their names with their caste name, *pandit.* *Pandit* also means *scholar.* The daughter, the first woman president of the UN General Assembly, used Pandit as her last name (see PANDIT, VIJAYA L.). The granddaughter, Indira Gandhi, became the first woman prime minister of India (see GANDHI, INDIRA P.).

Motilal Nehru, *MO tih lahl* (1861-1931), came from a distinguished family in the province of Kashmir. He studied law at Muir College in Allahabad and built up a prosperous legal practice. He was at first a close friend of the English in India, a member of wealthy social groups, and a follower of Western ways. But in the 1920's he was converted to the cause of Indian independence, and became a follower of Mohandas Gandhi (see GANDHI, MOHANDAS K.). Nehru gave up his law practice and began to live in a simple manner.

He wrote the *Nehru Report* in 1928. It outlined a new constitution for India. In 1930, he became active in Gandhi's civil disobedience movement. His energetic efforts on behalf of freedom and several terms in prison weakened Nehru's strength, and he died the next year. Nehru was born in Agra on May 6, 1861.

Jawaharlal Nehru, *juh WAH hur lahl* (1889-1964), the son of Motilal Nehru, was India's first prime minister. He served as prime minister from 1947 until his death. He dominated Indian affairs. He worked to establish a democracy and to increase living standards. He favored a state-controlled economy.

Nehru gained international recognition for opposing alliances with the great powers and for promoting *neutralism* (nonalignment). He advocated nonaggression and ending atomic bomb tests. But he was criticized when Indian forces seized Goa and other Portuguese territories in India in 1961. Nehru acted as a spokesman for nonaligned nations in Asia and Africa. He favored admitting Communist China to the United Nations until the Communist Chinese forces attacked the Indian border in 1962.

Jawaharlal Nehru
Karsh

Nehru and his father were fond and proud of each other, but occasionally disagreed. At one time, the father favored only dominion status for India, while the son demanded complete independence.

Nehru was born on Nov. 14, 1889, in Allahabad. He went to school in England, and was graduated from Harrow School and Cambridge University. He returned to India after his schooling and became active in politics. He supported Mohandas Gandhi's civil disobedience movement in 1920. Nehru served as general secretary of the All India Congress Committee in 1929. That same year, he was elected president of the Indian National Congress. He held that post again in 1936, 1937, and 1946. The British often imprisoned him for his nationalistic activities during this period. Nehru was a master of the English language, and his writings are widely read.   RICHARD L. PARK

See also INDIA (History).

NEIGHBORHOOD. See COMMUNITY.

NEJD. See SAUDI ARABIA (Local Government).

NEKTON. See PLANKTON.

NELEUS. See NESTOR.

NELLIGAN, EMILE. See CANADIAN LITERATURE (Since 1900).

NELSON, British Columbia (pop. 9,504; alt. 1,774 ft.), is called the *Queen City of the Kootenays.* It lies along the west arm of Kootenay Lake (see BRITISH COLUMBIA [political map]). It is a mining, lumbering, and transportation center. Water sports, skiing, and a Summer Curling Bonspiel attract tourists to Nelson. The city was named in 1888 for Hugh Nelson, then lieutenant governor of British Columbia. Nelson was incorporated in 1897. The city has a mayor-council form of government.   RODERICK HAIG-BROWN

NELSON, BYRON. See GOLF (Golf Immortals).

NELSON, HORATIO (1758-1805), VISCOUNT NELSON, was Great Britain's greatest admiral and naval hero. He defeated the combined French and Spanish fleets at Trafalgar in the greatest naval victory in British history. His victory broke the naval power of France, and established Great Britain's rule of the seas for the rest of the 1800's.

Early Life. Nelson was born at Burnham-Thorpe in Norfolk, on Sept. 29, 1758. His father was rector of the local church, and his mother was a member of the famous Walpole family. Nelson was a small, frail child. But he fell in love with the sea early in life, and made up his mind to be a sailor. He spent much time piloting small boats on the river near his home. When he was 12 years old, his uncle, Captain Maurice Suckling, planned a voyage to the Falkland Islands. Nelson begged his family for permission to go along, and was finally allowed to do so. He owed much of his early training to Captain Suckling, who had him transferred from time to time to ships engaged in different types of service. Suckling also encouraged him to study navigation and to practice boat sailing.

Joins the Navy. At the age of 15, Nelson went aboard the *Carcass* as a coxswain. He served on that vessel in an expedition to the Arctic seas. On his return, he was sent to the East Indies on the *Seahorse.* On the East Indies voyage he caught a fever that seriously damaged his health. But he became a lieutenant in the Royal Navy at 18.

In 1779, when not yet 21, he was given command of the frigate *Hinchinbrook.* He was known as a capable officer. His professional ability and his talent for getting along with his men helped him to rise rapidly in the service. A cruise to Central America brought on a second tropical illness and Nelson was sent home in feeble health.

He was given duty on the North Sea as soon as he recovered from the fever. He was then assigned to service in Canadian waters and developed a great fondness for Canada, where the climate strengthened his health. Nelson was given command of the frigate *Boreas*, stationed in the West Indies in 1784. He spent three years on this station.

Nelson married the widow of Josiah Nisbet, an English doctor in the West Indies in 1787. Prince William, who later became King William IV of England, gave the bride away at the wedding. Nelson was recalled from active service soon afterward. He remained on the retired list until soon after the outbreak of war with France in 1793.

Wounded at Calvi. In 1793, he was placed in command of the *Agamemnon* and sailed to join the Mediterranean fleet. This voyage began seven years of almost continual warfare at sea. Nelson was one of the British commanders who blockaded Toulon and captured Corsica. He was wounded at Calvi, on the Corsican coast, and lost the sight of his right eye.

Nelson next distinguished himself at the Battle of Cape St. Vincent in 1797. He served under Admiral Sir John Jervis, who defeated the combined French and Spanish fleets. Nelson was made a Knight of the Bath for his part in this victory. He had become a rear admiral a week before the battle. A few months later, Nelson led a small landing party in an attack on the strongly fortified port of Santa Cruz de Tenerife in the Canary Islands. The attack was a bold gamble, but unlike others, it failed. The British were driven off with heavy losses and Nelson's right arm was badly mangled up to the elbow. The arm had to be cut off in a crude amputation in a pitching boat, and Nelson was invalided home to England in great pain. But he soon returned to duty.

Battle of the Nile. Napoleon, victorious in Europe, began to gather a French fleet for an expedition to con-

Horatio Nelson is the most famous British naval hero.

Brown Bros.

quer Egypt. Nelson was sent to watch the French ships at Toulon. A storm came up, and under its cover the French fleet escaped. Nelson followed it in a long and tiresome pursuit. He finally cornered the French fleet in the Bay of Aboukir, where he attacked and almost destroyed it on Aug. 1, 1798. This engagement is known to history as the Battle of the Nile. It cut off Napoleon's army in Egypt and ruined his Egyptian campaign. He was forced to desert his army in Egypt, and had to sneak across the Mediterranean in a tiny ship. This victory made Nelson world famous. He was made Baron of the Nile and given a large sum of money.

Nelson was wounded again in this battle, and he went to Naples to recover. Lady Emma Hamilton, wife of Sir William Hamilton, the British Ambassador to Naples, fell in love with the battered, one-eyed, one-armed naval hero and became his mistress. Her influence over Nelson became so great that he disobeyed his orders to leave Naples and join a squadron in the Mediterranean. It was Nelson's good fortune that no British defeat resulted from his refusal to leave Naples. Nelson was condemned for his conduct, however, when he returned to England.

Battle of Copenhagen. Nelson became a vice-admiral in 1801, and sailed for Copenhagen in the squadron of Admiral Parker. Great Britain had claimed the right to search neutral ships for contraband of war. Denmark refused to allow its ships to be searched. A council of war chose Nelson to make the attack on the Danish fleet. Admiral Parker later became doubtful of the outcome. He signaled Nelson to retire. Nelson clapped his telescope to his blind eye and studied the signal. "I really do not see the signal," he said to an aide. He ignored the order and turned what might have been a defeat into a great victory.

Victory at Trafalgar. Nelson was made commander-in-chief of the fleet in May, 1803. Sailing on the flagship *Victory*, he once more went in search of the French. He found the fleet at Toulon, but it slipped away from him. Nelson chased the French to the West Indies and back.

Nelson became a naval hero early in the wars against Napoleon. He captured two ships during the battle of Cape Saint Vincent on Feb. 14, 1797. The Spanish admiral commanding the enemy fleet was mortally wounded during the battle. The captain of one of the captured ships surrendered the admiral's sword to Nelson.

Brown Bros.

The Battle of Trafalgar crushed France's naval power. It was fought off the southern coast of Spain on Oct. 21, 1805.

Nelson's Flagship, the *Victory*, led the British fleet at Trafalgar. It is kept in dry dock and is still in good condition.

It was more than two years before he was able to bring the French fleet to battle off Cape Trafalgar on the coast of Spain, on Oct. 21, 1805 (see TRAFALGAR). Nelson hoisted his famous signal, "England expects that every man will do his duty." With only 27 vessels, he attacked the combined French and Spanish fleets. One of the great naval battles of all time followed. Napoleon's fleet, with a total of 33 warships, was destroyed. Nelson was wounded at the height of the battle. He was carried below with a sharpshooter's bullet in his spine. He died during the battle, but he lived long enough to know that the British fleet had defeated the French and Spanish fleets. Nelson's last words were, "Thank God I have done my duty."

One of Nelson's great characteristics as a commander was his willingness to give full credit to his officers and men. After the Battle of Copenhagen, he refused an honor given him by the City of London because he alone was to be honored. Nelson replied, "Never till the City of London thinks justly of the merits of my brave companions of the second of April can I, their commander, receive any attention from the City of London." The poet Robert Southey wrote of Nelson, "England has had many heroes. But never one who so entirely possessed the love of his fellow countrymen. All men knew that his heart was as humane as it was fearless . . . that with perfect and entire devotion he served his country with all his heart, and with all his soul, and with all his strength. And therefore they loved him as truly and fervently as he loved England."

Nelson is perhaps best remembered today by the officers and men of the British Navy. He was a fighter. "I am of the opinion that the boldest measures are the safest," he once said. His frail body housed a great spirit. He had the power to inspire men with his own courage and confidence. Nelson is a symbol of Britain's navy.

Nelson Monument. A great monument to the memory of Nelson stands in Trafalgar Square, in the heart of London. It is one of the great man-made landmarks of the world. It has been said that if you are looking for

an Englishman whose address is unknown, that man will some day pass the Nelson monument in Trafalgar Square. See LONDON (picture). CHARLES F. MULLETT

NELSON, THOMAS (1738-1789), was an American patriot of the Revolutionary War period. He served as a delegate to the Continental Congress from 1775 to 1777 and again in 1779. He was one of the Virginia signers of the Declaration of Independence. During the Revolutionary War, he commanded the Virginia militia. Nelson was born at Yorktown, Va. KENNETH R. ROSSMAN

NELSON, WILLIAM ROCKHILL (1841-1915), founded and built the *Kansas City* (Mo.) *Star*, a crusading newspaper, in 1880. The *Star* campaigned against municipal corruption, and for civic reform and a program of rehabilitation that gave Kansas City green parks, broad boulevards, and an art gallery. Nelson was born in Fort Wayne, Ind. KENNETH N. STEWART

NELSON RIVER is the longest river in Manitoba, Canada. From its outlet at the northern end of Lake Winnipeg, it flows about 400 miles northeastward to empty into Hudson Bay. It is the outlet of Lakes Winnipeg, Winnipegosis, and Manitoba, and the Winnipeg, Red, and Saskatchewan river systems. The watercourse to the head of the Saskatchewan's farthest tributary is 1,600 miles long. Once a transportation link for Hudson's Bay Company, the river is now an important source of hydroelectric power for Manitoba. A power station at Kelsey Rapids supplies power to the nickel mines and refinery at Thompson, Man. Other large power stations are located at Grand Rapids and Squaw Rapids on the Saskatchewan River. D. F. PUTNAM

NEMAN RIVER, sometimes known as the MEMEL or NEMUNAS RIVER, is a water route in Northern Europe. It rises in the Minsk region of Russia and flows northwest. The Neman River crosses Byelorussia and Lithuania before it empties into the Baltic Sea. The river is 580 miles long. The Viliya and Sheshupe streams are its chief branches. A canal connects the Neman, Bober, and Vistula rivers. Ships can sail 450 miles up the Neman River. THEODORE SHABAD

115

NEMATHELMINTHES. See NEMATODA.

NEMATODA, or ROUNDWORMS, is a group of slender, round worms. Individuals in the group are called *nematodes*. Their bodies are usually pointed at the ends. Some are so small they can be seen only through a microscope, and others grow over three feet long. The males are usually smaller than the females.

Some nematodes live in soil and water. Many, such as the eelworm, live as parasites in plants. Others, including hookworms, lungworms, pinworms, trichinella, and filariae, live as parasites in human beings, and such animals as dogs, sheep, and horses.

Scientific Classification. Nematoda is a class of the phylum *Aschelminthes* and is sometimes listed as a separate phylum *Nemathelminthes.* J. A. McLeod

Related Articles in WORLD BOOK include:

Eelworm	Pinworm	Trichina
Hookworm	Roundworm	Vinegar Eel

NEMATOMORPHA. See HAIR SNAKE.

NEMEAN GAMES, *nee ME un*, were one of the four ancient Greek national festivals. The others were the Isthmian Games, the Olympic Games, and the Pythian Games (see the separate articles in WORLD BOOK for each festival). The Nemean games occurred every other year, at the shrine of Zeus (Jupiter) in Nemea, a valley in Argolis. They included athletic and musical contests. The first recorded Nemean games took place in 573 B.C. JOHN H. KENT

NEMERTINEA. See RIBBON WORM.

NEMESIS, *NEM uh sis*, was the goddess of vengeance in Greek mythology. She punished those human beings who angered the gods by becoming too proud of themselves. Nemesis stood for justice in all things.

The word *nemesis* today means a kind of punishing and relentless justice, which is deserved. PADRAIC COLUM

NEMI, LAKE. See LAKE NEMI.

NENE, *nay nay*, known as *Hawaiian Goose*, is a rare bird of Hawaii. It is the official bird of Hawaii. Nenes are dull brown, and have long, pointed, buff-colored neck feathers. They live in open country and feed chiefly on grass.

Scientific Classification. The nene belongs to the water fowl family, *Anatidae.* It is classified as genus *Branta*, and is species *B. sandvicensis.* GEORGE J. WALLACE

See also HAWAII (picture: The State Bird).

NEOCLASSICISM. See CLASSICISM; ENGLISH LITERATURE (The Classical Age); LITERATURE (The Age of Reason); PAINTING (In the 1800's); SCULPTURE (1600-1900).

NEODYMIUM, *NEE oh DIM ih um* (chemical symbol, Nd), is a metallic element belonging to the rare earth group. Its atomic number is 60, and it has an atomic weight of 144.24. C. F. Auer von Welsbach of Germany discovered the element in 1885. He separated the so-called element didymium into neodymium and praseodymium. Neodymium melts at 1024° C., and boils at 3027° C. The metal can be prepared by electrolysis of its halide salts, or by the reduction of these salts by alkaline earth metals in the presence of heat. The ceramic industry uses salts of neodymium to color glass and in glazes. The metal is present in *misch metal*, an alloy with many uses. FRANK H. SPEDDING

See also RARE EARTH.

NEOLITHIC PERIOD. See STONE AGE.

NEO-MALTHUSIANISM. See MALTHUS, THOMAS.

NEON is a chemical element that makes up about 18 parts per million in the earth's atmosphere. The British chemists Sir William Ramsay and Morris W. Travers discovered it in the atmosphere while they were studying liquid air in 1898. Ramsay had predicted the existence of this gas one year earlier. Ramsay and Travers named the gas *neon*, for the Greek word meaning *new*.

Neon is used chiefly for filling lamps and luminous sign tubes. Its usual color in lamps is bright red. The addition of a few drops of mercury makes the light a brilliant blue. Many airplane beacons use neon light because it can penetrate fog. Pilots have reported that neon beacons were visible for 20 miles when it was impossible to see other lights.

Neon lamps are made by removing the air from glass tubes and then filling them with neon gas. When about 15,000 volts of electricity are applied to the tube, an electric discharge occurs and the tube glows fiery red. Instead of a filament, a neon tube has two electrodes sealed within it. The neon forms a luminous band between these electrodes.

Commercially, neon is obtained as a by-product of liquid air manufacture. It liquefies under normal pressure at −246° C. When air is liquefied at about −200° C., neon is left behind as a gas. It is sold in glass tubes that contain a quart of neon under pressure. Neon is

Neon and Electric Advertising Signs Light Up Streets and Make Night Seem Almost Like Day in Downtown Chicago.
John Ingram

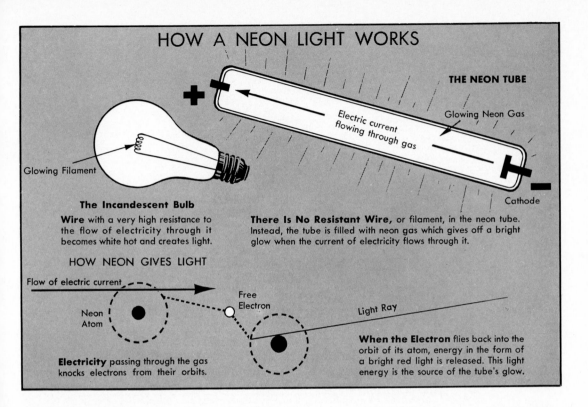

HOW A NEON LIGHT WORKS

THE NEON TUBE

Electric current flowing through gas

Glowing Neon Gas

Glowing Filament

Cathode

The Incandescent Bulb

Wire with a very high resistance to the flow of electricity through it becomes white hot and creates light.

There Is No Resistant Wire, or filament, in the neon tube. Instead, the tube is filled with neon gas which gives off a bright glow when the current of electricity flows through it.

HOW NEON GIVES LIGHT

Flow of electric current

Neon Atom

Free Electron

Light Ray

Electricity passing through the gas knocks electrons from their orbits.

When the Electron flies back into the orbit of its atom, energy in the form of a bright red light is released. This light energy is the source of the tube's glow.

---

expensive but very little is needed for lamps. A quart fills from 200 to 300 feet of the tubing used for signs.

Neon is a colorless, odorless gas. It is called an *inert gas* because it does not react easily with other substances. Its symbol is Ne. It has the atomic number 10, and an atomic weight of 20.183.   FRANK C. ANDREWS

See also ELECTRIC LIGHT (Neon Light).

NEON TETRA. See FISH (color picture: Tropical Fresh-Water Fishes).

NEOPLASM. See TUMOR.

NEOPLATONISM was a dominant school of philosophy from the A.D. 200's to the 500's. Neoplatonism, which means *new Platonism*, developed from the philosophy of Plato. The leading philosophers of the school were Plotinus and Proclus.

The Neoplatonists developed their philosophy from Plato's theory of *forms*. According to this theory, all things owe their identities to unchanging forms in which they share. Our knowledge comes from recognizing the essential form of a thing, rather than from observing its many incidental qualities. The Neoplatonists carried the theory a step further. We are so wholly unreal, they believed, that only forms exist. In addition, the forms exist in a place, or divine mind, beyond the heavens, where our souls can "travel" when they leave our bodies.

In Neoplatonism, there is a single highest form, *The One*, which is completely self-sufficient and alone. It is a mistake even to say that The One *is*, because The One is beyond being. But, without changing, The One emanates or overflows, as light shines through darkness. The first and brightest level of emanation is *divine reason*, in which Plato's forms exist as ideas. The next level, dimmer and less real, is the world of souls. The

lowest order, the realm of bodies and matter, is almost total darkness. The two lower levels feel in themselves a desire, called an *anastrophe*, to turn upward and return. This is the feeling we sometimes have of homesickness or of being in an unreal world.

The Neoplatonists believed that the purpose of philosophy is to escape from the attachment we feel to our bodies and physical environment. In this way, we discover an impersonal immortality by finding our true identity in the world of form. As Plato tells in his myths, impure souls are destined to go from one human life to another. They seek permanent satisfaction, which attachment to their bodies prevents them from finding. Describing this cycle, Plotinus said: "The soul is a traveler, that sleeps every night in another inn."

Neoplatonism was an important philosophical movement. Plotinus influenced Saint Augustine in developing his principles of Christian theology. Proclus' views helped shape Christian *negative theology*, which points out the limits of man's ability to comprehend a supreme being. The Neoplatonic emphasis on spiritual, as opposed to physical, beauty was important to the idea of *platonic love* in the Age of Chivalry during the Middle Ages. Neoplatonic commentaries appeared in the Near East as early as A.D. 529 and were generally accepted as the correct interpretation of both Plato and Aristotle.   ROBERT BRUMBAUGH

See also PLATO; PLOTINUS.

NEOPRENE. See RUBBER (Synthetic Rubber).

NEOPTOLEMUS, *NEE ahp TAHL ee mus,* or PYRRHUS, was the son of Achilles in Greek legend. He killed Priam, the last king of Troy, when Troy was captured by the Greeks. See also HERMIONE.

NEP. See COMMUNISM (Communism Under Lenin).

NEPAL

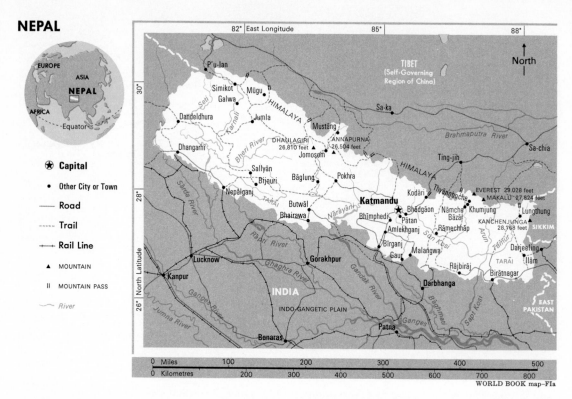

EUROPE
ASIA
NEPAL
AFRICA
Equator

★ Capital

• Other City or Town

——— Road

----- Trail

+—+—+ Rail Line

▲ MOUNTAIN

‖ MOUNTAIN PASS

～～ River

WORLD BOOK map–FIa

NEPAL, *NAY PAHL,* is a mountainous kingdom in southern Asia. The world's highest peak, Mount Everest, stands on the northeastern border of this small, rugged country. Katmandu is the capital of Nepal.

Nepal is a little larger than North Carolina. Most of the people raise crops on the mountain slopes and valleys, or work in the forests on the southern slopes of the great mountain range, the Himalaya.

The people of Nepal were once almost completely isolated from the outside world. Then, in the late 1940's, the government established diplomatic and trade relations with several countries, and began a program to develop the nation's economy.

The Land and Its Resources

Location and Size. Nepal faces Tibet on the north, Sikkim on the northeast, and India on the south and west. Nepal has an area of 54,362 square miles.

Land Regions. The color map with the INDIA article shows how the great Himalaya range covers almost nine-tenths of Nepal. The world's highest mountain, 29,028-foot Mount Everest, stands on the border with Tibet in northeastern Nepal. The world's third highest peak, 28,168-foot Mount Kanchenjunga, rises on the border between Nepal and Sikkim. Three other mountains in the country—Makalu, Dhaulagiri, and Annapurna—tower more than 26,000 feet above sea level. The Himalaya range extends from northern Nepal to a series of low foothills in the south. These hills end in a partly swampy plain called the Tarāi. Many streams rise in the Himalaya and flow through Nepal and into India.

Natural Resources. The fertile soil of the mountain slopes, plains, and valleys is Nepal's chief natural re-

source. Southern Nepal has rich forests of fir, maple, and oak. Mineral deposits include antimony, bauxite, bismuth, coal, copper, iron, mica, salt, and sulfur.

Climate. Nepal's climate varies from the mild temperatures along the border of India to the bitter cold of the Himalaya range. Temperatures on the highest peaks sometimes drop to −40°F. Average temperatures in Katmandu, in central Nepal, range from 50°F. in January to 78°F. in July. About 60 inches of rain falls

---
FACTS IN BRIEF

Form of Government: Constitutional monarchy.

Capital: Katmandu.

Divisions: 14 zones, 75 districts.

Head of State: King.

Parliament: *National Panchayat*—125 members elected for six-year terms.

Official Language: Nepali.

Area: 54,362 square miles. *Greatest Length*—500 miles. *Greatest Width*—150 miles.

Population: *1961 Census*—9,412,996; distribution, 97 per cent rural, 3 per cent urban. *Estimated 1970 Population*—11,110,000; density, 204 persons to the square mile. *Estimated 1975 Population*—12,206,000.

Chief Products: Cattle, corn, rice, wheat, oilseeds.

Flag: The flag has two crimson triangles trimmed in blue, one above the other. The top triangle features a moon, and the lower one a sun, symbols of the long life of Nepal. It is the only nonrectangular flag in the world. See FLAG (picture: Flags of Asia).

National Anthem: Rashtriya Dhun (National Anthem).

National Holiday: National Day, Feb. 18.

Money: *Basic Unit*—rupee. One hundred paisa equal one rupee. For its value in dollars, see MONEY (table).

in the country every year, mostly between June and October. Snow covers the mountain peaks of Nepal throughout the year.

Life of the People

The People. Most Nepalese are farmers. Over 95 of every 100 people live in the country's farm areas.

The people of Nepal are called *Nepalese*. They are related to the people of Tibet, Mongolia, and India. Most of the people belong to a group called the *Gurkhas*. This word comes from the name of a ruling family that conquered the Nepalese in 1768. The warlike Gurkhas rule Nepal and provide most of the country's professional soldiers. Other groups in Nepal include the Newars and the Sherpas. The Newars ruled part of Nepal before the Gurkha conquest. Today, most of the country's craftsmen and government clerks are Newars, because the Gurkhas prefer to earn their living as soldiers. Most of the Sherpas make their living as farmers.

More than half the people are Hindus. Most of the others are Buddhists. Nepal was the birthplace of Gautama Buddha, the founder of the Buddhist religion. Most of the people speak *Nepali*. Many of the people who live in the hills have their own languages.

Family Life. The man is the head of the family, and the women do most of the work in the house. Children receive a great deal of freedom, but they begin helping their parents at an early age.

Shelter. Most Nepalese live in two- or three-room thatch-roofed houses made of sun-dried mud brick. The whole family usually sleeps together in one or two rooms. Well-to-do Nepalese have large, two-story homes made of brick painted with whitewash. The houses usually have tin roofs. Farm animals live in the lower story.

Food. The people squat on the floor while eating their meals from bowls placed on low tables or on the floor. The women do not eat until after the men have eaten. Rice is the chief food. The Nepalese also enjoy *dal*, a split-lentil soup, and vegetables flavored with *curry* powder (see CURRY). Fish and chicken are favorite dishes.

Clothing. Most Nepalese men wear loose, knee-length robes and tight trousers. The women usually wear brightly colored skirts and long-sleeved blouses.

Festivals. The people enjoy folk songs and folk dances. They like to gamble and hunt. Chief holidays are those of the Hindu religion. *Diwali*, The Festival of Lights, is in October. For five days, the people decorate their homes with tiny lamps to honor the Hindu goddess of wealth, Lakshmi. In March, the Nepalese celebrate the coming of spring with a gay holiday called *Holi*.

City Life. Nepal's only large cities are Katmandu and its suburbs, Bhadgaon and Patan. There are a few small towns in southern Nepal. Buddhist and Hindu temples and shrines rise above the two-story houses and mud huts of Nepal's ancient cities and towns.

Country Life. A rural Nepalese village usually consists of thatch-roofed mud huts clustered together in the midst of the fields. A single dirt road generally runs through the village. The villagers keep their houses clean and neat.

Work of the People

About 90 of every 100 persons make their living in farming. Many Gurkhas volunteer for British and Indian army service to make a living and earn retirement pay. Some 60,000 Nepalese are retired Gurkha soldiers who live on pensions paid by the British or Indian governments. This money makes them the wealthiest group in Nepal.

Agriculture and Forestry. Most of the country is mountainous, and farming is possible only along the lower mountain slopes, and in the few valleys and plains of southern Nepal. Most of the farmers raise their crops on terraces that rise like huge steps, one above the other. The farmers cut the terraces in the mountainsides to make more room for crops. During the rainy season, they store rainwater in catch basins built on the slopes above the terraces. Irrigation ditches carry the water to the terraces during the dry season. Rice, wheat, corn, and lentils are the chief terrace crops. Farmers also grow barley, jute, opium poppies, pepper, and tobacco. Many also raise cattle for milk and hides.

Nepal's forests produce fir, maple, oak, other types of lumber, and commercial gums.

Mining, Manufacturing, and Processing. Miners dig small amounts of coal, copper, mica, and graphite. Most of the mines lie in the south.

Nepal has no large-scale manufacturing. Small factories produce jute bags, ceramics, glassware, cotton textiles, paper, and metalware. Nepal's craftsmen have won fame for their decorated objects of wood and bronze.

Trade. Nepal's chief exports include cattle, hides and skins, opium, dyes, gums, jute, wheat, rice, oilseeds, tobacco, timber, and saltpeter. The country imports sheep, goats, salt, sugar, medicines, gasoline, ironware, and cotton and silk textiles. India is Nepal's chief customer and leading source of imports.

Transportation and Communication. Nepal has 64 miles of railways and 237 miles of paved roads. Three airlines serve the country. The elephant and buffalo are still the chief means of transportation. Telephone lines link the capital of Katmandu with a few other areas of the country and with India.

Activities of the People

Education. The country has about 4,000 primary and 900 secondary schools. Most Nepalese children do not attend school because there are not enough teachers and schoolrooms. Only about 9 of every 100 persons can read or write. Tribhuvan University at Katmandu is the country's only university.

In the 1960's, WORLD BOOK ENCYCLOPEDIA sponsored the construction of two schoolhouses at Khumjung and Thyangboche in eastern Nepal. These were the first schools built in the region near Mount Everest.

The Arts. Most of the country's art work is found in the many Buddhist and Hindu temples and shrines. These elaborate buildings are decorated with statues and delicate carvings.

Government

Nepal became a constitutional monarchy in 1959. The king, a hereditary ruler, is the head of state. He appoints a council of ministers from the national legislature to assist him.

In 1962, a new constitution set up four levels of government in Nepal—village, district, zone, and na-

A Katmandu Street Scene, *left,* shows an ornate Buddhist pagoda, so common in Nepal. Merchants set up shop in the street, where people and cattle mill about all day.

Three Gurkha Women, *below,* carry home huge bundles of kindling which they chopped on a wooded mountain slope. Nepalese women do much heavy work around the home.

Pix

tional. Each level has its own *panchayat* (governing council). Each village elects a village council, and the village councils in each of Nepal's 75 districts elect a district council. The district councils elect zone councils which elect the 125 members of the *National Panchayat*, the national legislature. National Panchayat members serve six-year terms.

Each village council elects a man to look after the welfare of the village. District councils elect an administrator to head the district.

The Hindu religious code is the basis of Nepal's laws. The supreme court is the highest court. The king appoints the supreme court judges. There are lower courts in the cities, towns, and villages.

History

Early Days. The Newars and other Mongolian tribes lived in Nepal before the A.D. 1300's. The Gurkhas and other groups from northern India migrated to the area and intermarried with Mongolian tribes. The Indian groups brought the Hindu religion. The Nepalese established several small kingdoms between the 1300's and the 1700's. Most of the kingdoms were in the Nepal Valley in western Nepal. Prithwi Narayan (1730?-1775?), a Gurkha leader, united the country in 1768.

The Rule of the Ranas. The Gurkha army began raiding northern India during the early 1800's, and threatened to conquer the area. The British, who ruled India, declared war on Nepal in 1814. After a hard struggle, the British defeated Nepal's army in 1816 and forced King Girvan-yuddha Vikrama Sah (?-1816) to keep his army within the country's borders.

In 1846, the prime minister of Nepal, a member of the Rana family of Gurkha leaders, seized all political power from the king. Members of the Rana family ruled as hereditary prime ministers and virtual dictators of the country.

Nepal remained isolated until 1947. In that year Nepal established diplomatic and trade relations with several countries, including the United States.

Recent Developments. Various groups revolted against the Ranas in 1950 in an effort to make the country more democratic. King Tribhubana Bir Bikram finally ended the Rana rule in 1951, and tried to establish a constitutional monarchy. He formed a cabinet from members

Black Star

of various political groups. But personal and political rivalries prevented establishment of a stable government. Nepal was opened to tourists in 1951. It had been isolated and closed to all foreigners during the Rana rule.

Tribhubana died in 1955, and his son Mahendra Bir Bikram became king. Nepal became a member of the United Nations in 1955, and started a five-year program to improve its agriculture, education, industry, and transportation.

Mahendra approved a constitution in 1959, and the people voted for the first time. They elected members of the lower house of parliament. B. P. Koirala, Congress party leader, formed a government. But rivalries and political favoritism threatened the country's safety, so Mahendra dismissed the government and dissolved parliament. In 1960, he banned all political parties and took over all powers of government.

In 1962, Mahendra approved a new constitution that called for a one-house parliament. The first parliament was elected in 1963. Mahendra retained control of the government. But he appointed a council of ministers to advise him.   ROBERT I. CRANE

Related Articles in WORLD BOOK include:

Annapurna	Himalaya
Asia	Katmandu
Buddha	Mount Everest
Colombo Plan	Mount Kanchenjunga

NEPHITE. See LEHI.

NEPHRITE. See JADE.

NEPHRITIS, *nee FRY tis*, is the general name for inflammation of the kidneys. The disease may be sudden, not long lasting, and easily relieved. It also may be slow, gradual, and incurable. A common form of nephritis is known as *Bright's disease*. A serious complication of nephritis is poisoning from the waste material which the kidneys have failed to carry off. This disease is known as *uremia*, or *uremic poisoning*. The characteristic symptoms of uremia include drowsiness, stupor, and convulsions. Nephritis may be either the result or the cause of high blood pressure. Any of its forms should have the prompt attention of a physician.   BENJAMIN F. MILLER

See also ARTERIOSCLEROSIS; BRIGHT, RICHARD; KIDNEY; UREMIA.

NEPHRON. See KIDNEY.

NEPOTISM, *NEP oh tiz'm*, is the practice of giving important political or business positions to members of one's family. The word *nepotism* comes from the Latin word for *nephew*.

NEPTUNE was the god of the sea in Roman mythology. He was the son of the Titans Cronus and Rhea (see TITAN). The Greeks called him *Poseidon*. He was Jupiter's brother, and some authorities consider him to have been second in power. Neptune controlled all the water of the earth. Sailors and people who raced horses especially worshiped him. The Isthmian Games were held every second year in Corinth, Greece, in honor of Neptune (see ISTHMIAN GAMES).

Neptune took part in many kinds of contests. The Greeks of Attica wanted to name their chief city after the god or goddess who gave mankind the most useful object. Neptune created the horse, and proudly pointed out its many uses. But Athena (Minerva) made the olive tree, which the judges decided was more valuable. The city was therefore called Athens.

Jupiter at one time punished Neptune because he tried to take more than his share of the world. Neptune was forced to work for Laomedon, the king of Troy. It was his duty to build the walls around the city. Apollo helped Neptune by playing on his lyre, and making the stones leap into place with his music. Laomedon refused to pay them for their work. Neptune fought against the city in the Trojan War.

Neptune is shown in art as a large strong man with a broad chest and well-developed shoulders. He carries a *trident* (three-pronged spear) in his hand. He is often shown in a chariot drawn through the water by dolphins (see DOLPHIN [whale]). His son Triton is usually beside him (see TRITON).   H. LLOYD STOW

See also FOUNTAIN (picture); NEREID.

NEPTUNE is one of the two planets that cannot be seen without a telescope. It is much larger than the earth, but astronomers know little about it. Neptune is about 30 times as far from the sun as is the earth. Pluto is the only planet farther from the sun. Before anyone had ever seen Neptune or Pluto, astronomers "discovered" these planets by the use of mathematics.

The diameter of Neptune is about 27,600 miles, or about $3\frac{1}{2}$ times the earth's diameter. The planet is about 17 times as *massive* (heavy) as the earth, but is not so *dense* as the earth (see MASS; DENSITY).

Neptune travels around the sun in an *elliptical* (oval-shaped) orbit. Its mean distance from the sun is about 2,795,000,000 miles. Neptune goes around the sun once about every 165 earth-years, compared to once a year for the earth. As Neptune orbits the sun, it spins on its *axis*, an imaginary line through its center. Neptune's axis is not *perpendicular* (at an angle of 90°) to the planet's path around the sun. The axis tilts at an angle of about 30° from the perpendicular position. For an illustration of the tilt of Neptune's axis, see PLANET (The Axes of the Planets). Neptune spins around once in about 15 hours and 40 minutes.

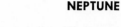
OROC; Culver

Ruins of Temple of Poseidon (Neptune), *above*, which was built by the ancient Greeks at Cape Sounion, stand south of Athens, Greece. According to Roman mythology, the sea god Neptune drove across the water in a sea-shell chariot, *right*. Many drawings show him being drawn by dolphins instead of horses.

NEPTUNE

Surface and Atmosphere. Neptune is so far from the earth that astronomers do not know much about its surface. They believe the portion of Neptune visible from the earth is the top of a thick layer of clouds. These clouds may consist of frozen ammonia, or combinations of crystals of ice, frozen methane, and frozen ammonia.

The atmosphere surrounding Neptune consists chiefly of hydrogen and methane gas, with some helium and ammonia. Astronomers believe this atmosphere is about 2,000 miles thick. The tilt of Neptune's axis causes the sun to heat the planet's northern and southern halves unequally, resulting in seasons and temperature changes. Temperatures on the planet are always much lower than on the earth. The plant and animal life of the earth could not live on Neptune because of the lack of oxygen and the low temperature. Astronomers do not know whether Neptune has any form of life.

Satellites. Two *satellites* (moons) travel around Neptune. One, named Triton, is about 3,000 miles in diameter and about 200,000 miles from Neptune. It is the only large satellite in the solar system that travels in an east-to-west direction. Triton has a circular orbit, and travels around Neptune once every six days.

Neptune's other satellite, called Nereid, is only about 150 miles in diameter. It is about $3\frac{1}{2}$ million miles from the planet, and travels in an extremely elliptical orbit. Nereid goes around Neptune every 360 days.

Discovery. Neptune was discovered by means of mathematics before being seen through a telescope. Astronomers had noticed that Uranus, which they thought was the most distant planet, was not always in the position they predicted for it. The force of gravity of some unknown planet seemed to be influencing Uranus.

In 1843, John C. Adams, a young English astronomer and mathematician, began working to find the location of the unknown planet. Adams predicted that the planet would be about a billion miles farther from the sun than Uranus. He completed his work, which proved to be remarkably accurate, in September, 1845. Adams sent it to Sir George B. Airy, the Astronomer Royal of England. But Airy did not even look for the planet with a telescope. Apparently, he lacked confidence in Adams.

Meanwhile, Urbain J. J. Leverrier, a young French mathematician unknown to Adams, began working on the same project. By the summer of 1846, Leverrier also had predicted the position of Neptune. He sent his predictions, which were similar to those of Adams, to the Urania Observatory in Berlin, Germany. Johann G. Galle, the director of the observatory, had just completed a chart of the fixed stars in the area of the sky where the unknown planet was believed to be. On

NEPTUNE AT A GLANCE

Distance from Sun: *Shortest*—2,771,000,000 miles; *Greatest*—2,819,000,000 miles; *Mean*—2,795,000,000 miles.

Distance from Earth: *Shortest*—2,678,000,000 miles; *Greatest*—2,750,000,000 miles.

Diameter: 27,600 miles.

Length of Year: About 165 earth-years.

Rotation Period: 15 hours and 40 minutes.

Average Temperature: $-280°$ F. ($-173°$ C.)

Atmosphere: Hydrogen, methane, helium, and ammonia.

Number of Satellites: Two.

Sept. 23, 1846, Galle and his assistant, Heinrich L. d' Arrest, searched with a telescope for an object that was not on Galle's chart. They quickly found Neptune close to the position predicted by Leverrier. Today, astronomers credit both Adams and Leverrier with the discovery of Neptune. The planet was named for Neptune, the god of the sea in Roman mythology.   HYRON SPINRAD

See also PLANET; SOLAR SYSTEM.

NEPTUNIUM, *nehp TYOO nih um* (chemical symbol, Np), is a man-made element. Its atomic number is 93. Its most stable isotope has a mass number of 237. In the periodic system of the elements, neptunium follows uranium. Neptunium was discovered by Edwin M. McMillan and P. H. Abelson at the University of California in 1940. It was first produced by bombarding uranium with slow neutrons. Neptunium produced in this way has an atomic weight of 239. This isotope is unstable and decays to form an isotope of plutonium that can be used for nuclear fission, as uranium 235 is used. The longest-lived neptunium isotope, neptunium 237, has a half-life of 2,200,000 years (see RADIOACTIVITY [Half-Life]).   EDWIN M. MCMILLAN

See also PLUTONIUM; U-235.

NEREID, *NEER ee id.* The Nereids were the 50 daughters of Nereus and Doris. They were the lovely and friendly sea nymphs who attended Poseidon (in Latin, Neptune) and his Nereid wife, Amphitrite. They lived under the sea, and came to the surface now and then to dance and play in the waves. Nereids are represented as beautiful maidens, sometimes part fish. See also ANDROMEDA; NYMPH.   PADRAIC COLUM

NEREUS. See OLD MAN OF THE SEA.

NERI, SAINT PHILIP (1515-1595), was the founder of the Oratorians, and a reformer of Rome during the Renaissance. Pope Gregory XIII recognized his group of priests as the Congregation of the Oratory in 1575. Neri, a popular leader, won over cardinals and popes to his unusual methods of reform. He was born in Florence, Italy.   JAMES A. CORBETT and FULTON J. SHEEN

NERNST, *nurnst,* **WALTHER HERMANN** (1864-1941), a German physical chemist, won the 1920 Nobel prize in chemistry for his formulation of the third law of thermodynamics (see THERMODYNAMICS). His measurements of the specific heats of substances at low temperatures proved this law to be valid. Nernst also developed a theory of solutions that explains the voltage of electrochemical batteries (see ELECTROCHEMISTRY). He was born in Briessen, Germany.   SIDNEY ROSEN

NERO, *NEER oh* (A.D. 37-68), was a Roman emperor and the last relative of the Caesars. He is remembered most for his mistreatment of Christians, and his neglect of government affairs while he pursued a musical career.

Nero was born LUCIUS DOMITIUS in Antium at the court of his uncle, Emperor Caligula. Nero's father, Gnaeus Domitius Ahenobarbus, died when Nero was quite young. Caligula sent Nero's mother, Agrippina the Younger, away when the boy was three. Agrippina returned under Emperor Claudius after Caligula's death. Nero studied under Greek teachers, who encouraged his tastes in music, poetry, and sports. Agrippina married Claudius in A.D. 49. Claudius adopted the boy, changed his name to NERO CLAUDIUS DRUSUS GERMANICUS, and designated Nero as his eldest son. Agrippina chose Seneca, the philosopher, and Burrus, a military officer, to serve as Nero's teachers and ad-

Emperor Nero became known as one of the most evil rulers in history. He ordered scores of Christians to be cruelly put to death. In the motion picture *Quo Vadis?*, Peter Ustinov played the role of Nero.

visers. Nero married Claudius' daughter Octavia in 53.

Nero became emperor when Claudius died in 54. Soon afterward, he had Claudius' son Britannicus poisoned, and buried him in haste and secrecy. Tired of his mother's interference, Nero had her murdered in 59. In 62, he had Octavia killed, and married Poppaea Sabina.

In some ways, Nero was a good administrator. Under the guidance of Seneca and Burrus, he brought peace to the province of Britain after a revolt there. He sent a fleet to protect Roman ships on the Black Sea, and chose excellent military commanders for wars in Armenia and Judea.

Nero has been accused of setting a fire that burned part of Rome in 64. This led to the popular saying, "Nero fiddled while Rome burned." Most historians, however, doubt Nero's guilt. Nero blamed the Christians for the fire, and had them put to death cruelly. The apostles Peter and Paul probably died at this time.

Late in his reign, Nero left Rome to sing in festivals in Greece. He returned to find the provinces in revolt and the Senate and his guards in Rome plotting against him. He committed suicide in 68.   MARY FRANCIS GYLES

See also AGRIPPINA THE YOUNGER; SENECA, LUCIUS.

NERUDA, *nay ROO thah,* **PABLO** (1904-   ), is the pen name of NEFTALÍ REYES, a Chilean poet. Many critics consider Neruda the finest Latin-American poet of his time. His use of surrealistic, violent, subconscious imagery and highly personal symbols make his works sometimes difficult to understand. His works communicate a general sense of universal chaos.

Neruda was born in Parral, Chile. Several volumes of his verses had been published by the time he was 20. His best volumes of poetry include *Crepuscular* (1923), *Twenty Poems of Love and One Desperate Song* (1924), *Residence on Earth* (1931; 1935), and *The Furies and the Pains* (1939). Attracted to Communism, Neruda sometimes allows political views to detract from his art in his later works, including *Third Residence* (1947). Pablo Neruda served as Chilean consul to several countries.   MARSHALL R. NASON

NERVAL, GÉRARD DE (1808-1855), was a French poet of the romantic period. His personal charm, odd behavior, periodic mental disorders, and mysterious suicide made him a hero typical of the romantic movement. Critics in the 1900's consider him a major visionary poet.

Nerval believed in *metempsychosis*, the passing of a soul at death from one body to another. In *Les Chimères* (1854), a collection of sonnets, this belief underlies many obscure references to the legendary past which contribute to the haunting beauty of the poems. His search for the eternal feminine ideal is reflected in the short stories of *Les Filles du Feu* (1854), notably in "Sylvie," a tale set in the Valois countryside. *Aurélia* (1855), a prose confession, begins with the phrase "Our dreams are a second life." It describes this "life," including the hallucinations Nerval suffered during his periods of insanity. He was born in Paris.   LEROY C. BREUNIG

NERVE. See NERVOUS SYSTEM.

NERVE GAS. See CHEMICAL-BIOLOGICAL-RADIOLOGICAL WARFARE.

NERVI, PIER L. See ARCHITECTURE (Today; picture: Sports Arenas).

NERVOUS BREAKDOWN is a term often used to refer to anything from fatigue caused by overwork to a severe mental illness. It has no precise medical meaning. Psychiatrists and others who specialize in the study and care of patients with mental illness do not use the term. It is used by people who believe it is an accepted medical term, or by people who want to avoid using the term "mental illness." The original idea behind the term was that mental symptoms were caused by a failure of the nerves to function properly.   CHARLES BRENNER

See also MENTAL ILLNESS (Unhealthy Behavior).

NERVOUS SYSTEM

NERVOUS SYSTEM consists of the brain, the spinal cord, and the nerve cells and fibers that extend throughout the bodies of man and the higher animals. The nervous system keeps us in contact with the world outside our bodies by receiving messages from the sense organs, such as the eyes and ears. It interprets these messages and causes us to react. The nervous system enables all parts of our body, including the internal organs, to work together to keep us alive and well.

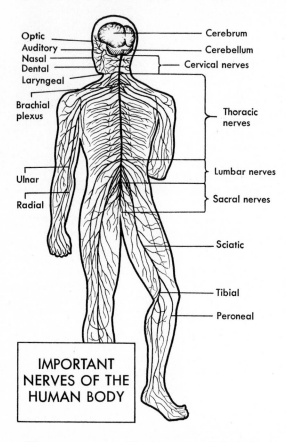

Optic — Cerebrum
Auditory — Cerebellum
Nasal
Dental — Cervical nerves
Laryngeal

Brachial plexus — Thoracic nerves

Ulnar
Radial — Lumbar nerves
— Sacral nerves

— Sciatic

— Tibial
— Peroneal

IMPORTANT NERVES OF THE HUMAN BODY

The nervous system, like other parts of the body, is made up of cells (see CELL). Nerve cells are called *neurons*. Like the other cells of the body, neurons have a nucleus surrounded by cytoplasm. The nucleus and the cytoplasm make up the *cell body*. The cytoplasm surrounding the nucleus of a neuron grows out into one or more fine threads or fibers. Most neurons have a single long fiber called an *axon* and several branched extensions of the cell body called *dendrites*. A *nerve* may be a single nerve fiber or a bundle of nerve fibers. Neurons vary in shape and size depending on their function. Some neurons have short axons and dendrites, and others may have axons that are several feet long.

The sense organs have specialized *nerve endings* (ends of nerve fibers) that respond to stimuli from the world around us. Such sense organs as the eyes and ears allow us to see and hear. Others, including some in the skin, tell us when we are hot or cold. Those in the nose and mouth enable us to smell and to taste. Still other sense organs let us feel what is going on inside our bodies.

Neurons that carry messages from the sense organs to the spinal cord and brain are called *sensory neurons*. Neurons that control the muscles and glands of the body are called *motor neurons*.

The nerve endings in the sense organs respond to special stimuli, including light waves, sound waves, mechanical contacts, and chemicals. Neurons throughout the body—especially in the skin—respond to heat, cold, touch, and changes in posture. The nerve endings send messages to certain parts of the brain, and the brain interprets the messages as various sensations. Neurons respond to strong stimuli, such as extreme heat, with the sensation of pain.

Parts of the nervous system work automatically, without conscious commands from the brain. After a meal, for example, neurons cause the muscles of the intestine to contract and relax automatically, moving the food through the digestive system. Many other body functions are controlled by the *autonomic* (self-controlling) parts of the nervous system.

Nerve Impulses

The human nervous system has several billion neurons, all connected with one another. The dendrites of a neuron receive stimuli from other nerve fibers or from a *receptor organ*, such as a sense organ. The *impulse* (nerve signal) passes from the dendrite through the cell body to the axon. The axon carries impulses to the dendrite or cell body of another neuron, or to an *effector organ*, such as a gland or a muscle.

The place where an axon connects to a nerve cell or dendrite is called a *synapse*. The place where the ends of a motor axon and a muscle meet is called a *neuromuscular junction*. Structures called *end bulbs* and *end plates* are on the ends of axons at synapses or junctions. There, the impulse causes the release of a chemical substance. This substance transmits the message across the synapse, or neuromuscular junction. In some cases, both electrical and chemical transmission occur at synaptic junctions.

An axon and a dendrite are in close contact at a synapse, but they do not grow together. For an impulse to pass from a receptor organ to a neuron, from one neuron to another, or from a neuron to an effector organ, it must cross a synapse. For an impulse to pass from a receptor organ to the brain, or from the brain to an effector organ, it must travel over several neurons, crossing several synapses.

Kinds of Neurons

Neurons that receive impressions from the outside world are called *sensory neurons* or *afferent neurons*. They carry impulses from various sense organs to the brain. Neurons that carry impulses from the brain or other nerve centers to the muscles are called *motor neurons* or *efferent neurons*. *Association neurons* or *internuncial neurons* are in the brain and spinal cord. They carry impulses among the parts of the brain and among the parts of the spinal cord, and between the sensory and motor neurons.

Several nerves bound together by a tough sheet of tissue are called a *nerve trunk*. Some axons are covered by a fat-containing sheath called a *myelin sheath*. When the cell bodies of many neurons are bundled together

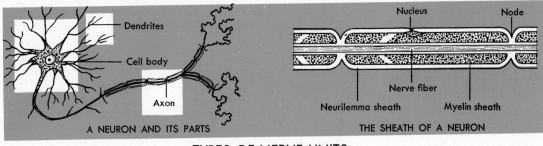

A NEURON AND ITS PARTS — Dendrites, Cell body, Axon

THE SHEATH OF A NEURON — Nucleus, Node, Nerve fiber, Neurilemma sheath, Myelin sheath

TYPES OF NERVE UNITS

outside the brain or spinal cord, they are called a *ganglion*.

Parts of the Nervous System

The nervous system has two basic divisions, the *central nervous system* and the *peripheral nervous system*.

The Central Nervous System consists of the brain and the spinal cord. For a detailed description of the brain and its functions, see the article on BRAIN.

The spinal cord is a long, thick nerve trunk that runs from the base of the brain down through the spinal column, or backbone. The cord is composed of *white matter* (nerve fibers covered with a white myelin sheath), and *gray matter* (cell bodies and dendrites of neurons). A cross sectional view of the spinal cord shows the gray matter as an H-shaped area surrounded by white matter. Thirty-one pair of spinal nerves leave the spinal cord. Each of these nerve trunks is attached to the cord in two places. The root of the nerve that leaves the cord toward the front of the body is called the *ventral root* or *anterior root*. The root that leaves toward the rear of the body is called the *dorsal root* or *posterior root*.

Sensory nerves enter the spinal cord at the dorsal root. Motor nerves leave the spinal cord at the ventral root. If the ventral root of a nerve is cut, the part of the body to which the nerve goes cannot move, but it still has sensation. If the dorsal root is cut, sensation disappears, but the part can still move.

Some nerve impulses entering the spinal cord are directed to the brain. Other impulses are routed directly to nerve centers, and then to the special parts of the body that the nerves control. Responses from sensory impulses that go almost directly to motor nerves are called *spinal reflexes*. See SPINE.

The Peripheral Nervous System consists of 12 pair of cranial nerves, the 31 pair of spinal nerves, and the nerves of the autonomic nervous system.

The Cranial Nerves come from the lower part of the brain. These nerves control many sensations and actions including sight, smell, chewing, and swallowing.

The Spinal Nerves come from the spinal cord and control the muscles of the body. There are 8 pair of *cervical nerves* that leave the spinal column from the first 7 vertebrae. Below them are 12 pair of *thoracic nerves*. The 5 pair of *lumbar nerves* leave the spinal cord at the small of the back. Each of the 5 pair of *sacral nerves* and the 1 pair of *coccygeal nerves* leave the spinal cord between the lowest vertebrae in the spinal cord.

The Autonomic Nervous System regulates the internal organs of the body. The functions it controls are involuntary. For example, you cannot deliberately control the rate of your heart beat, though it may be influenced by your thoughts or emotions.

The nerves of the autonomic nervous system are connected to and regulated by the central nervous system at a subconscious level. Each of these nerves consists

DIVISIONS OF THE NERVOUS SYSTEM

Brain and Spinal Cord

Nerves branching from central system

Nerves Regulating Involuntary Processes

CENTRAL
Main control system to direct and correlate

PERIPHERAL
Carries messages to and from central system

AUTONOMIC
Acts independently of the central nervous system

of a chain of two or more neurons leading from the spinal cord, through a ganglion, and to an organ. The nerve fibers have little or no myelin sheath. Most nerves in the autonomic system are *effectors* (motor nerves), but each trunk also has receptor fibers.

The autonomic nervous system has two main parts—the *sympathetic*, or *thoracolumbar*, *system*, and the *parasympathetic*, or *craniosacral*, *system*. Many organs have nerves coming from both the sympathetic and parasympathetic systems. Such nerves produce opposite reactions in the organs to which they go. For example, a nerve from one system speeds up the heart beat, and a nerve from the other system slows it down.

The nerves of the sympathetic system arise in the thoracic and lumbar portions of the spinal cord. They run from the cord to ganglia that lie along both sides of the spinal column. In the ganglia, the neurons from the cord, called *preganglionic* neurons, form a synapse with the neurons that continue to the various organs. The neurons that run from the ganglia to the organs are called *postganglionic* neurons.

The nerves of the parasympathetic system are divided into *cranial* and *sacral* sections. The cranial section begins with cells in the brain stem, the lowest part of the brain. The sacral section begins with cells in the lowest part, or sacral portion, of the spinal cord. The parasympathetic nerves run from the spinal cord to ganglia that are near, or even on, an organ.

How Nerves Work

Impulses in man's largest nerves travel at a speed of more than 300 feet per second. In the smaller fibers of the autonomic nervous system, impulses may travel as slowly as $1\frac{1}{2}$ to 6 feet per second.

The *membrane theory* is the most commonly accepted theory of how nerves work. The membrane that surrounds each nerve cell or fiber is *polarized*—that is, it has opposite electrical charges on either side. Positive *ions* (positively charged particles) are located outside the membrane. Inside the membrane are negatively charged ions. At the point where the impulse begins, the membrane lets through only certain positively charged ions, such as sodium. These ions rush inside the membrane and cause a local *depolarization* (loss of polarization) of the nerve membrane. This produces a local negative electrical charge called the *action potential*. Depolarization lasts only from .001 to .005 of a second, and the nerve cannot conduct an impulse during this time, which is called the *refractory period*. Polarization is re-established by the movement of positively charged ions, such as potassium, from the inside to the outside of the membrane. This entire process passes down the nerve fiber to a synapse. As soon as the nerve is repolarized, it can conduct another impulse.

When an impulse reaches a synapse, it is passed on to another nerve fiber or to an organ. In most synapses, this occurs by release of a *chemical transmitter*. The chemical acts as a stimulus that starts an impulse along the next nerve fiber, or causes an organ or muscle to react.

The strength and speed of the impulse or action potential in a nerve do not vary, regardless of the strength or nature of the stimulus. A nerve, however,

may send impulses more often when a strong stimulus is applied at the synapse or sense organ. In a nerve trunk, which contains many nerve fibers, a stronger stimulus may produce a stronger response because more fibers are being stimulated, and each may send impulses more rapidly.

After a sensory nerve has been stimulated, the impulses may pass up to the brain. The brain then decides how to respond. For example, you may see a pencil on a table and decide to pick it up. Impulses from the nerves in the eye pass along the sensory nerve to the brain. The brain sends impulses down the motor nerves to the muscles of the hand and arm.

Some impulses do not go to the brain. They are short-circuited more directly to make contact with motor nerves in the spinal cord. The path that the nerve impulse follows is called a *reflex arc*. For example, a pinprick on the skin stimulates a pain receptor. A sensory nerve carries the impulse to the spinal cord, where association nerves transfer it directly to motor nerves, by-passing the brain. The motor nerves send the message of pain to the muscles, which produce an involuntary jerk of the body.

Injuries to the Nervous System

If an axon or dendrite of a neuron is cut by an injury, the cut fiber will be absorbed by the body. If the injury occurs in the peripheral nervous system, the nerve cell may regenerate the fiber. However, if the cell body is damaged, or if the cut nerve fiber is in the central nervous system, the whole neuron will degenerate.

HERBERT H. JASPER

NESS, EVALINE (1911-   ), an illustrator of children's books, won the 1967 Caldecott medal for her illustrations for *Sam, Bangs, & Moonshine* (1966). She also wrote the novel. She previously had been a runner-up three times in the Caldecott competition.

Evaline Ness was born and grew up in Pontiac, Mich. She studied at the Art Institute in Chicago, the Art Students' League in New York City, and the Accademia di belle Arti in Rome.

NESS, LOCH. See LOCH NESS.

NESSUS. See HERCULES (Hercules' Death).

NEST is a place an animal prepares for raising its young. See ANIMAL (Animal Homes); ANT (Nests); BEE (The Nest); BIRD (Building the Nest; picture: Bird Nests); BIRD'S-NEST SOUP; HORNET; WASP.

NESTER. See WESTERN FRONTIER LIFE (The Cattle Boom).

NESTOR was the hero son of Neleus and Chloris, rulers of Pylos, Messenia, in Greek mythology. Late Greek legend said that Hercules killed Nestor's father and brothers. Nestor, a great warrior, fought in the battle between the Centaurs and the Lapiths (see CENTAUR). He helped kill the Calydonian boar, and he went on the voyage of the Argonauts (see ARGONAUTS).

He was over 60 when he took part in the Trojan War, and was outstanding in the Greek councils for his intelligent advice. He appears in Homer's *Iliad* and *Odyssey*. The word *Nestor* is used to describe a wise and clear-sighted person.　　　　　　　　　H. LLOYD STOW

NESTORIAN CHRISTIANS are members of a religious sect that was prominent in the A.D. 400's. They follow the teachings of Nestorius, who was bishop of Constantinople. They believe that Jesus united in Himself two persons: the Word and the man. But these two persons were so closely united that they could almost be regarded as one. Nestorian doctrine does not recognize Mary as the mother of God. It teaches instead that Mary gave birth to a man who was the *instrument* of divinity, but was not divinity itself.

In A.D. 431, a Roman synod condemned Nestorius. He eventually died in exile. The sect continued to flourish in Arabia, Syria, and Palestine, and had missions in China, India, and Egypt. But it split in the 1500's. One group, now known as the Chaldean Christians, transferred its allegiance to the Roman Catholic Church. The other group maintained its old traditions.

NET is a fabric or cloth with an open mesh. It is made by interlacing threads and then knotting or twisting them at the points where they cross each other. The *bobbin threads* (fine cords) cross to the right and to the left. Net may be made of cotton, rayon, nylon, or other fibers. A single twist net is most common, but a double twist is stronger. Narrow widths of net are called *footing*. Wider pieces of net are known as *yardage*, and usually measure 72 inches across.

Crosswise bobbin net resembles Brussels handmade net, and is extremely fine. Its various degrees of fineness are expressed in *points* (the number of holes to a half inch crosswise). Its strength depends on the coarseness of the thread and the number of twists given to the pairs of threads that make up four of the six sides of the mesh. Brussels net washes satisfactorily, but tends to thicken. It should be pulled or stretched into shape, usually on a frame, rather than ironed.

Handmade net has slight irregularities and costs more than machine-made net. *Filet net* has a square mesh that is made by knotting the threads to form corners.

Coarse mesh nets are often used for industrial purposes. They may be made into insect nets, tennis nets, heavy cable nets, and fish nets. Fish nets may be of several types, such as seine, drift, trawl, kettle, and trammel. A trammel net is a set of three nets. According to Norse mythology, Loki, the god of evil, invented fishing nets.　　　　　　　HAZEL B. STRAHAN

See also FISHING INDUSTRY (How Fish Are Caught); LACE.

The Bristol Aeroplane Co., Ltd.

U.S. Navy, Courtesy of Gentex Corp.

Wide World

A Scoop Net, *above left*, is dropped from a helicopter by a sea rescue crew to pick up persons in the water. The net used in water volleyball, *above*, stretches across the pool. A large-mesh cargo net, *below left*, is often used to load and unload ships. A fishing net, *below*, is used by a fisherman in the Caribbean Sea.

Tom Hollyman, Photo Researchers

NETHERLANDS

Bicycle Riding is a popular way to travel in The Netherlands. About half the people own a bike, and many roads throughout the country have special bicycle lanes.

NETHERLANDS is a small kingdom on the North Sea in northwestern Europe. The Netherlands is often called *Holland*, though this name actually refers to only one part of the country. The people of The Netherlands call themselves *Hollanders* or *Nederlanders*, but in English-speaking countries they are known as the *Dutch*.

"God created the world, but the Dutch created Holland," according to an old Dutch saying. More than two-fifths of the country's land was once covered by the sea, or by lakes or swamps. The Dutch "created" this land by pumping out the water. In these drained areas, called *polders*, are the richest farmlands and largest cities of The Netherlands. Amsterdam, the capital and largest city, is on a polder.

To make a polder, the Dutch build a dike around the area to be drained of water. The water is pumped into a series of canals that flow into the North Sea. Windmills were once used to run the pumps, but electric motors have replaced most of them. The polders have no natural drainage because they are below sea level. As a result, the pumping must be continued after the polders are built.

Most of the Zuider Zee, once the largest bay in The Netherlands, is being drained. This project is adding about 860 square miles of farmland to the country. The rest of the Zuider Zee has been changed from salt water to fresh water, and is called IJsselmeer.

The Dutch have great pride in their long battle against the sea. They take extreme care to protect their hard-won land, and are famous for keeping their homes,

towns, and fields clean and neat. Land is especially valuable to the Dutch because The Netherlands is one of the most thickly populated countries in the world. It is less than half the size of Indiana, but it has about 2½ times as many people as that state.

Most of The Netherlands is flat, with some uplands. Many canals cut through the country. They not only drain the land, but also serve as waterways and provide the farmers with extra water. Dairy farming is the most important form of agriculture in The Netherlands. The processing of dairy products is a major branch of Dutch manufacturing, the leading source of income.

--------- FACTS IN BRIEF ---------

Capital: Amsterdam.

Seat of Government: The Hague.

Official Language: Dutch.

Area: 13,961 square miles (including 1,070 square miles of inland water). *Greatest Distances*—(north-south) 196 miles; (east-west) 167 miles. *Coastline*—228 miles.

Elevation: *Highest*—Vaalser Berg, 1,057 feet above sea level. *Lowest*—Koedood Polder, 22 feet below sea level.

Population: *1960 Census*—11,461,964; distribution, 80 per cent urban, 20 per cent rural. *Estimated 1971 Population*—13,246,000; density, 949 persons to the square mile. *Estimated 1976 Population*—14,130,000.

Chief Products: *Agriculture*—barley, dairy products, flower bulbs, oats, potatoes, sugar beets, wheat. *Manufacturing*—clothing, electronic equipment, iron and steel, machinery, petroleum products, processed foods, textiles, transportation equipment. *Mining*—natural gas, petroleum, salt.

National Anthem: "Wilhelmus van Nassouwe" ("William of Nassau").

Money: *Basic Unit*—guilder. One hundred cents equal one guilder. For the value of the guilder in dollars, see MONEY (table: Values). See also GUILDER.

The contributors of this article are Robert W. Adams, Professor of International Business at the University of Michigan; Lewis M. Alexander, Professor of Geography at the University of Rhode Island; and Herbert H. Rowen, Professor of History at Rutgers, The State University.

NETHERLANDS / *Government*

The Netherlands has a democratic government based on the constitution of 1814. The constitution establishes a king or queen as head of state, but gives the ruler little real power. The ruler names all appointed government officials on the advice of various government bodies, and signs all laws passed by the parliament.

A queen has headed The Netherlands since 1890, when King William III died. Queen Juliana became ruler in 1948 in a ceremony called an *inauguration*. Dutch kings and queens, unlike those of other countries, are not crowned. Juliana's oldest daughter, Princess Beatrix, is first in line to inherit the throne. Beatrix' son, Prince William-Alexander, is second in the line of inheritance.

The national government meets in The Hague, though the capital is Amsterdam, 34 miles away. Invading French troops captured Amsterdam in 1795 and made it the capital. The Dutch restored their government in The Hague in 1814.

The Netherlands is part of the Kingdom of The Netherlands. The kingdom also includes two territories—the Netherlands Antilles in the Caribbean Sea, and Surinam in South America. These territories were Dutch colonies until 1954, when they were made equal partners in the kingdom. Each has an appointed governor and cabinet, headed by a prime minister. Each cabinet is responsible to a one-house legislature, whose members are elected by the people to four-year terms.

--------- GOVERNMENT IN BRIEF ---------

Form of Government: Constitutional monarchy.

Political Divisions: 11 provinces.

Head of State: King or queen.

Head of Government: Prime minister, appointed by the ruler. He heads a cabinet, also appointed, which runs the government departments. If the cabinet and the parliament cannot agree, either the cabinet resigns, or the parliament is dissolved and a new election is held.

Parliament (called the States-General): *First Chamber*—75 members, elected by the provincial legislatures to 6-year terms; *Second Chamber*—150 members, elected by the people to 4-year terms. Each house approves or rejects proposed laws, but only the Second Chamber can propose or amend bills. Legislation is also proposed by the ruler on the advice of the cabinet.

Provincial and Municipal Government: Councils elected by the people to 4-year terms. The number of members varies according to population. In the provinces, the chief executive is an appointed commissioner. In the cities and towns, he is an appointed burgomaster. Both are appointed by the ruler.

Courts: All judges are appointed by the ruler for life. They can be removed from office only by the highest court, the High Court of The Netherlands. The High Court has 17 judges and consists of three chambers—for civil, criminal, and tax cases.

Voting Age: 21.

Political Parties: *Largest*—Catholic People's Party, closely followed by the Labor Party. Other major parties include the Anti-Revolutionary Party, the Christian-Historical Union, and the People's Party for Freedom and Democracy (Liberal).

Armed Forces: Army, navy, and air force, with a total of almost 125,000 men. Men are required to serve from 16 to 21 months after reaching the age of 19.

WORLD BOOK photo by Bobbi Jones

Parliament Buildings in The Hague are the home of the two houses of the States-General, the Dutch parliament.

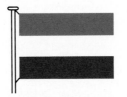

The Dutch Flag dates from about 1630. Until then, an orange stripe was at the top instead of a red one.

The Coat of Arms has old symbols of the Dutch royal family. The sword and arrows represent strength in unity.

Alan Band Associates

Queen Juliana, *second from left,* is the Dutch head of state. Her daughter Beatrix, *second from right,* is the heir to the throne.

The Netherlands, in northwestern Europe, is about 5 per cent as large as the United States, not counting Alaska and Hawaii.

WORLD BOOK map

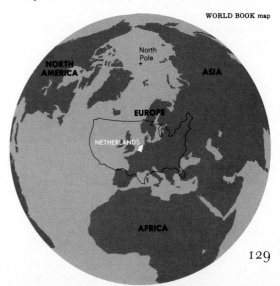

129

The Netherlands is one of the most thickly populated countries in the world. It has over 16 times as many people to the square mile as the United States. But few areas ever seem to be overcrowded. The Dutch keep their tidy homes, busy cities, and small farms as neatly arranged and sparkling clean as possible. Every Saturday, for example, many Dutch housewives scrub the steps and sidewalks in front of their homes.

The Netherlanders are known for their good fellowship, called *gezelligheid*. This cozy friendliness, as well as Dutch orderliness, helps make life pleasant in the thickly populated country. Families welcome friends to drop in uninvited at almost any time. They enjoy making guests feel at home with generous servings of rich Dutch chocolates and pastries. Delicious Dutch cheeses such as Edam and Gouda are also popular. Dairy farmers sell the cheeses at weekly open-air markets.

The Dutch face their continuous battle against the sea—to "create" land and protect it from flooding—with great pride and courage. A famous story tells of a little Dutch boy who noticed water trickling through a dike one evening. There was no one nearby to tell. The boy plugged the hole with his finger, and held back the water until someone finally arrived the next day. A statue near Haarlem is inscribed in honor of this boy "who symbolizes the eternal struggle of Holland against the sea."

Population. In 1971, The Netherlands had about 13,-246,000 people. The following table shows some official census figures for The Netherlands through the years:

1960	11,461,964	1899	5,104,137
1947	9,625,499	1889	4,511,415
1930	7,935,565	1869	3,579,529
1920	6,865,314	1849	3,056,879
1909	5,858,175	1829	2,613,298

More than 40 per cent of the people live in two coastal provinces—Noord-Holland (North Holland) and Zuid-Holland (South Holland). In these provinces are the three Dutch cities with populations of more than 500,000—Amsterdam, Rotterdam, and The Hague. Twelve other cities have populations between 100,000 and 500,000. See the separate articles on the Dutch cities listed in the *Related Articles* at the end of this article.

Religion. Protestants make up a little more than 40 per cent of the Dutch population, and another 40 per cent are Roman Catholics. Traditionally, the two groups have remained as separate as possible. This split in Dutch life has involved separate clubs, labor unions, neighborhoods, newspapers, schools, broadcasting companies, and political parties. Since the 1940's, the split has been slowly breaking down among young people and, because of a housing shortage, in many city neighborhoods.

Of the Protestants, about three-fourths belong to the Dutch Reformed Church. Members of the royal family traditionally belong to this church. Nearly 20 per cent of the Dutch are not church members.

Holidays and Recreation. The Dutch exchange gifts on St. Nicholas' Eve, December 5, instead of on Christmas. The children believe that Saint Nicholas visits their homes with presents for good boys and girls. A man dressed like a bishop represents Saint Nicholas

and rides through the streets. In Amsterdam, he arrives by ship and is greeted by booming cannon, ringing bells, and cheering crowds.

During the 1600's, the Dutch brought the custom of Saint Nicholas' visit with them to America. There, the English settlers changed his Dutch nickname, *Sinter Klaas*, to *Santa Claus* (see SANTA CLAUS).

On Palm Sunday, young people in Dutch villages sing Easter songs and carry lighted lanterns on their way to the market place for music and dancing. On Easter Sunday, children and adults play various games with colored eggs. Many sports events are held on Easter Monday.

The Dutch are famous for raising tulips and other bulb flowers, and they hold many spectacular flower festivals each spring. Long parades of floats covered with blue, pink, red, and yellow blossoms wind through the towns near the bulb fields. Homes and lawns along the way are also decorated with beautiful floral designs.

The canals that carry water from the land are also used for ice skating, an extremely popular sport. But The Netherlands has mild winters, and the people do not have thick ice for skating so often as they would like. When the ice on the canals is hard enough, schools sometimes close to let the children skate. Even many businessmen stop working and take "ice vacations."

Clothing. Most Netherlanders wear clothing similar to that worn in the United States and Canada. People in farm areas and fishing villages sometimes wear the famous wooden shoes called *klompen*. These shoes are noisy, but they protect the feet from damp earth better than leather shoes do. The Dutch rarely wear wooden shoes in their homes. They leave them outside and change to leather shoes.

Dutch national costumes also include full trousers for the men, and full skirts and lace caps for the women. They are still worn in a few regions, including the islands of Zeeland and the West Frisian Islands. See CLOTHING (color picture: Europe).

Language. The Netherlanders are a Germanic people, and the Dutch language is related to German. Many English words have been adapted from Dutch, including *brandy*, *skate*, *skipper*, and *yacht*. Most Netherlanders know English or German in addition to Dutch. The people of the northern province of Friesland also speak Frisian, another Germanic language.

Education. Dutch law requires children from the age of 6 through 14 to go to school. All schools, including religious schools, that meet national educational standards receive government funds. These standards, set by law, include courses of study and the hiring of teachers.

The Netherlands has no general high-school program like that of the United States. Instead, it has several kinds of high schools. Each kind trains students for a special purpose, such as university work, advanced study in various institutes, or jobs in business or industry.

All the universities are supported almost completely by the government. Tuitions are low, and many university students receive some form of government aid. The University of Amsterdam, with about 13,000 students, is the largest university. The State University of Leiden, founded in 1575, is the oldest.

Arts. The Netherlands has produced some of the world's greatest painters. During the 1600's, the country's Golden Age, masterpieces were painted by Pieter de Hooch, Frans Hals, Rembrandt, Jacob van Ruisdael, and Jan Vermeer. At that time, most European artists painted only for churches, nobles, or royalty. But Dutch artists painted ordinary persons and things, and many Dutch businessmen bought these works to beautify their homes. Later Dutch painters included Vincent van Gogh and Piet Mondrian. Paintings by all these artists are shown in the PAINTING article.

Dutch literature is little known outside The Netherlands because few works have been translated. The most important Dutch writer was Joost van den Vondel. Others include Willem Bilderdijk, Herman Gorter, Constantijn Huygens, and "Multatuli" (Eduard Douwes Dekker).

The Netherlands has produced few noted composers. Among the better-known ones were Willem Pijper and Jan Pieterszoon Sweelinck. Several Dutch cities have fine symphony orchestras. The Concertgebouw Orchestra of Amsterdam is world famous, and frequently tours other countries.

Frits Gerritsen, Keystone

Busy Amsterdam, the capital and largest city of The Netherlands, ranks among the chief European commercial centers.

Masterpieces of Dutch Art by such painters as Rembrandt and Jan Vermeer attract visitors to museums in The Netherlands.

Ronny Jaques, Photo Researchers

S. Samelius, Carl Östman

Traditional Clothing of The Netherlands is worn by many of the Dutch people, especially in fishing and farming areas. It includes cap, baggy pants, and wooden shoes.

NETHERLANDS / The Land

Land Regions. The Netherlands has four main land regions: (1) the Dunes, (2) the Polders, (3) the Sand Plains, and (4) the Southern Uplands.

The Dunes rise 15 to 25 feet above sea level. This region curves in a line along the entire North Sea coast of The Netherlands. In the north, the line consists of the West Frisian Islands. The line is unbroken in the center, but is broken in the south by wide river outlets. The sandy Dunes region cannot support farming, and few trees grow there.

The Polders lie below sea level, and are protected from the sea by the sand dunes or by dikes. The Koedood Polder, the lowest point in The Netherlands, lies 22 feet below sea level. The Polders region makes up more than two-fifths of The Netherlands. It consists of flat, fertile areas of clay soils that were once covered by the sea, or by swamps or lakes. It has the country's most productive farmlands and largest cities.

The Sand Plains lie less than 100 feet above sea level in most places. In the southwest, the region rises higher. Some low, sandy ridges cross the plains and create a rolling landscape. The soil is generally dry. Irrigation and fertilizers make farming possible. Pine forests cover much of the region. A broad valley of clay soils marks the courses of the Maas (or Meuse) River and of

LAND REGIONS OF THE NETHERLANDS

Polders

Dunes

Amsterdam

Sand Plains

Rotterdam

Polders

Distance Scale
0 Miles 25 50 75
0 Kilometres 50 75 100

Southern Uplands

WORLD BOOK map

NETHERLANDS MAP INDEX

*Does not appear on map; key shows general location.
★Population of metropolitan area, including suburbs.
Sources: 1968 official estimates for cities over 20,000, which are municipalities that may include rural areas; 1960 census for smaller places.

branches of the Rhine River. These rivers are important waterways, and canals connect them with other rivers and canals to form a transportation network.

The Southern Uplands make up the highest land region of The Netherlands. They rise several hundred feet. The highest point, Vaalser Berg, rises 1,057 feet near Maastricht. The region has naturally fertile soils, and much fruit is grown in orchards there.

Deltas. Much of southwestern Netherlands consists of islands and peninsulas in the North Sea. These marshy areas are deltas of the Maas, Neder Rijn, and Wester Schelde rivers. In 1953, a storm broke through the dikes in the delta region. More than 375,000 acres were flooded by the sea, and over 1,800 persons drowned. In 1958, work began on the Delta Plan, a huge flood-control project, to prevent a similar disaster.

The Delta Plan includes a series of dams that will keep the sea from flooding into four wide outlets of the rivers. The first outlet was dammed in 1961, and a second was closed in 1968. Floodgates in the dams will allow ice in the rivers to flow to sea. Completion of the entire project was scheduled for 1978.

Ray Halin

The Sand Plains of The Netherlands are a low, mostly flat region with some ridges. Dairy cattle graze in pastures there.

THE LONG BATTLE AGAINST THE SEA

For hundreds of years, the Dutch have been "creating" areas of land called *polders* by pumping out the water that covered them. This map shows the development of polders since 1200. The straight line running through Den Helder indicates the areas represented horizontally on the diagram at the bottom of the next page. The diagram shows how dikes keep water from the polders.

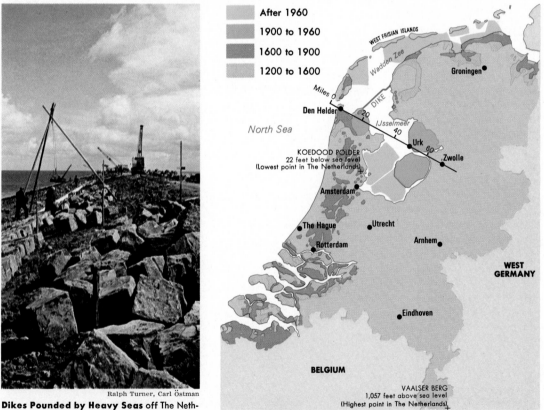

Ralph Turner, Carl Östman

Dikes Pounded by Heavy Seas off The Netherlands must be strengthened from time to time.

WORLD BOOK map-GJa

NETHERLANDS / Climate

The Netherlands has a mild, damp climate, largely because the country is on the sea. In winter, the sea is not so cold as the land. In summer, it is not so warm. As a result, west winds from the sea warm The Netherlands in winter, and cool it in summer. In addition, winds carrying moisture from the sea make the skies over the country extremely cloudy. The clouds shield the land from the heat of the sun. Temperatures average between 60° F. and 65° F. in summer, and a little above 30° F. in winter.

The country has no mountains to block the winds, so there are no great differences of climate from area to area. The extreme southeast, which is the highest part of The Netherlands, is also the wettest. It receives a yearly average of more than 34 inches of *precipitation* (rain, melted snow, and other forms of moisture). An average of 27 inches a year falls on the islands of Zeeland province and along the central Dutch-German border. Summer is the wettest season, but precipitation is fairly evenly distributed throughout the year. Brief showers may fall as often as every 30 minutes.

North Sea storms are heaviest in the coastal areas of The Netherlands. These storms have broken dikes and caused flooding, sometimes with great loss of life. The northern and western regions receive most of the mist that comes from the sea. The mist is heaviest in winter.

Farrell Grehan, Photo Researchers

Strong Sea Winds require vacationers at the beach resort of Scheveningen to have chairs that also serve as shields.

Fred Ward, Black Star

A 20-Mile-Long Dike, the Afsluitdijk, separates the North Sea, *left*, and the IJsselmeer.

Russ Kinne, Photo Researchers

The Polders region has the richest farmland in The Netherlands. Canals that drain away water also irrigate the fertile soil. Tulips and many other flowers grow there.

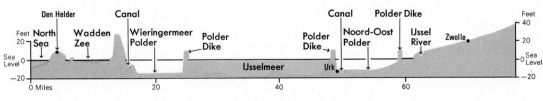

131

NETLANDS / *Economy*

The Netherlands has a thriving economy, even though the country's natural resources are limited. Dutch factories depend heavily on imported raw materials. Much of the total industrial production is exported, but the value of imports is greater than that of exports. The difference is made up by income from Dutch services—including shipping and banking—to other countries, and from tourism.

The great importance of foreign trade to The Netherlands makes the Dutch government and the people strong supporters of international economic cooperation. The Netherlands helped form the European Common Market—now called the European Community—in 1957. This economic union with Belgium, France, Italy, Luxembourg, and West Germany has done much to expand Dutch trade and improve the country's economy. See EUROPEAN COMMUNITY.

Natural Resources. The Netherlands has large deposits of salt and natural gas, and some coal and petroleum. The Polders region has extremely fertile soils.

THE NETHERLANDS' GROSS NATIONAL PRODUCT IN 1967
Total gross national product—$22,878,000,000

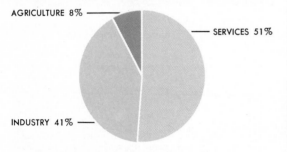

AGRICULTURE 8%

SERVICES 51%

INDUSTRY 41%

The Gross National Product (GNP) is the total value of goods and services produced by a country in a year. The GNP measures a nation's total annual economic performance. It can also be used to compare the economic output and growth of countries.

Production and Workers by Economic Activities

Economic Activities	Per Cent of GDP* Produced	Labor Force† Number of Persons	Labor Force† Per Cent of Total
Manufacturing	31	1,332,000	29
Trade	**19	‡772,000	17
Government	15	382,000	8
Other Services	11	861,000	19
Construction	8	473,000	10
Agriculture, Forestry, & Fishing	7	375,000	8
Transportation & Communication	7	309,000	7
Mining	1	46,000	1
Utilities	1	43,000	1
Total	100	4,593,000	100

*GDP is gross domestic product (gross national product plus net income from abroad).
†1966, latest information available
**Includes Housing
‡Includes Banking, Insurance, & Finance
Sources: Central Bureau of Statistics and Ministry of Economic Affairs, The Netherlands

Forests—most of which are beech, oak, or pine—cover only about 8 per cent of the land.

Many rivers flow through The Netherlands. But the land is so flat that the rivers do not flow with enough force to generate hydroelectricity. As a result, the nation's electric power is produced entirely by fuel-burning power stations. The rivers, together with a connecting network of canals, provide cheap transportation. On these waterways, as well as the nearby sea, The Netherlands imports its industrial needs, exports its products, and carries on valuable shipping services. The coastal waters of the North Sea also have many kinds of fish.

Manufacturing is the most valuable economic activity of The Netherlands. By the mid-1960's, production had reached a level three times that of 1938. This expansion resulted largely from government industrialization programs to rebuild the shattered economy after World War II ended in 1945. The government and organizations of employers and workers have cooperated closely in establishing wages and other job policies. As a result, there have been almost no strikes.

Large iron and steel works operate near Velsen and Utrecht. They use imported ores. Amsterdam, Rotterdam, and other large cities have big shipyards. Eindhoven has one of the world's largest electronics factories. It produces household appliances, radios, and television sets. Various kinds of machinery and transportation equipment also come from many Dutch factories.

Food processing is a major manufacturing industry. Dairy products—especially butter, cheese, and processed milk and eggs—are the chief foods. The Netherlands is one of the world's major cheese manufacturers. Other food products include beet sugar, chocolate, processed meats, and animal feed.

The fast-growing Dutch chemical industry produces drugs, fertilizers, paints, plastics, and synthetic rubber. There are several large oil refineries near Rotterdam. The Netherlands is also a leading clothing manufacturer. Its textile industry produces goods of cotton, linen, wool, and synthetic fibers. Amsterdam has long been a famous center of diamond cutting and polishing. Other important Dutch products include bricks, cement, glassware, leather goods, paper, pottery, rubber products, and tobacco products.

Agriculture. The Dutch cannot afford to waste any land because their country is so thickly populated. The farmers fertilize their land heavily and use modern machinery to get the best results. Dutch farms cover an average of only 25 acres, compared with about 300 acres in the United States. About two-thirds of the total land area is farmland. Almost 60 per cent of the farmland is used for grazing, and crops are grown on the rest.

Dairy farming is the most important branch of agriculture in The Netherlands. Most of the dairy farmers also grow crops, which are used mainly to feed the livestock. Almost 4 million cattle—mainly dairy cattle—graze on the grasslands. About 110,000 tons of butter and 300,000 tons of cheese are produced yearly. Farmers also raise beef cattle, hogs, and poultry.

Crops include barley, fruits, oats, potatoes, rye, sugar

beets, vegetables, and wheat. The Netherlands is a leading flax-producing country. Flower bulbs, especially tulips, are also important. Daffodils, hyacinths, narcissuses, and tulips carpet the countryside between Haarlem and Leiden every April and May. The bulbs of these flowers are shipped to all parts of the world.

Mining. The Dutch produce much natural gas. The world's largest reserve of the fuel—the Slochteren field —lies in Groningen province in the northeastern part of The Netherlands. It contains more than 55 trillion cubic feet of natural gas.

There are thick beds of salt near Hengelo. Miners dissolve the raw salt underground and pump the *brine* (salt water) to the surface, where it is evaporated to get the salt.

Oil wells operate in the northeastern province of Drente and near The Hague. They supply only a small part of the country's needs. The Netherlands has some coal mines in the southeastern province of Limburg. But mining conditions are poor, and almost all the mines are being closed.

Fishing. The Dutch have more than 1,500 commercial fishing boats, and catch about 415,000 tons of fish and other seafood yearly. The catch comes mainly from the North Sea and the English Channel. The most important catch is mussels. Others are flatfish, herring, and haddock. Fishermen also catch eels in IJsselmeer.

Transportation. Boats can travel on about 4,000 miles of rivers and canals in The Netherlands. Many of the canals are important waterways, and ocean-going ships may be seen on the larger ones. Motor barges on the inland waterways carry more than half the nation's total freight. The Netherlands has more than 28,500 miles of paved roads and highways. Over 2,000 miles of government-owned railroads also serve the country.

About half the people have a bicycle, and many roads have special lanes for bicycling. Sturdy motor-driven bicycles called *bromfietsen* (roar bikes) are becoming increasingly popular.

Rotterdam is the largest seaport in Europe. Only the port of New York City handles more cargo yearly. Rotterdam serves as a gateway to and from much of Europe by way of the Rhine River, Europe's busiest inland waterway. Amsterdam, the second largest Dutch port, is linked to the North Sea by the 17-mile-long North Sea Canal, one of the deepest and widest canals in the world. The canal is 49 feet deep and 525 feet wide.

Royal Dutch Airlines (KLM), established in 1919, is the oldest airline in the world still in operation. Its planes fly to about 65 countries.

Communication. The Netherlands has about 90 daily newspapers, with a total daily circulation of more than $3\frac{1}{2}$ million copies. The largest newspaper is *De Telegraaf* of Amsterdam. It has a circulation of about 350,000 copies a day.

The government owns and regulates the nation's two radio networks and two television networks. Five large broadcasting companies prepare programs for them. These broadcasting companies represent religious or political groups. The postal, telephone, and telegraph services are operated by the government.

I. Wimnell, Carl Östman

The Famous Alkmaar Cheese Market is held on Fridays from spring to fall. Porters in colorful hats carry the cheeses.

FARM, MINERAL, AND FOREST PRODUCTS

This map shows where the leading farm, mineral, and forest products of The Netherlands are produced. The map also points out the country's main industrial, pasture, forest, and crop areas. The manufacturing center of each industrial area is named on the map.

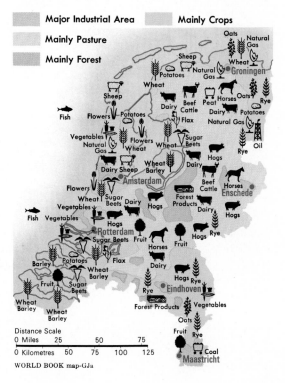

Major Industrial Area   Mainly Crops

Mainly Pasture

Mainly Forest

WORLD BOOK map-GJa

133

Early Days.

In 58 B.C., Roman soldiers under Julius Caesar invaded what are now The Netherlands, Belgium, and Luxembourg. The Romans conquered much of the region, now called the Low Countries. The word *Netherlands* means *Low Countries*, but the Low Countries also include Belgium and Luxembourg.

During the A.D. 400's, Germanic tribesmen called Franks drove the Romans out of the Low Countries. The Frankish kingdom expanded, but broke apart during the 800's. In 870, the Low Countries were divided between the East and West Frankish kingdoms (later Germany and France). The northern part, including what is now The Netherlands, became part of the East Frankish kingdom.

The Rise of Commerce.

At first, the French and German rulers of the Low Countries paid little attention to the region. Local dukes, counts, and bishops became increasingly powerful. But during the 1100's, trade and industry began to expand rapidly in the Low Countries. Fishing, shipbuilding, shipping, and textile manufacturing became especially important. The French and German kings became interested in the Low Countries after the thriving trade developed. The towns, which wanted to stay free, supported the local nobles in struggles against the foreign rulers.

Unification.

Beginning in the 1300's, the French dukes of Burgundy won control of most of the Low Countries through inheritance, marriage, purchase, and war. They promoted central government there, and political and national unity began to develop.

In 1516, Duke Charles of Burgundy also became king of Spain. In this way, the Low Countries came under Spanish control. Charles became archduke of Austria and emperor of the Holy Roman Empire in 1519. Beginning in 1520, Charles further strengthened the central government of the Low Countries.

Freedom from Spain.

During the early 1500's, the Protestant movement called the Reformation spread through the Low Countries. Charles tried to stop this threat to Roman Catholicism by persecuting Protestants. His son, Philip II of Spain, inherited the Low Countries in 1555. Philip stepped up the struggle against Protestants, and tried to take complete power over the Low Countries. In 1568, the nobles there revolted against his harsh rule. They were led by William I (called the Silent), prince of Orange.

The Spanish troops were generally successful in land battles, but the rebels' ships controlled the sea. The Spaniards attacked Leiden in 1573, but the city held out bravely. In 1574, the people opened dikes that held back the sea, and a Dutch fleet sailed over the floodwaters to rescue Leiden from the Spaniards.

By 1579, the revolt had started to break apart. Roman Catholic nobles in the southern provinces of the Low Countries (now Belgium) had become dissatisfied and returned to Spanish control. Protestantism was

William I, Prince of Orange, led nobles of the Low Countries in a revolt against Spain that began in 1568. The Dutch declared their independence in 1581, but fighting continued until 1648.

The Crossing over the River Maas, an etching (1569) by Mathis Zyndt, Rijksmuseum, Amsterdam, The Netherlands

Amsterdam, with Shipping in the River Y, an etching (1663) by Jacob van Meurs,
Nederlandsch Historisch Scheepvaart Museum, Amsterdam, The Netherlands

The Golden Age of The Netherlands was the 1600's. The nation was the leading sea power
and had a colonial empire. Ships bringing goods to Amsterdam made it the world trade center.

strongest in the northern provinces (now The Nether-lands). In 1579, most of the provinces formed the Union of Utrecht and pledged to continue the revolt.

On July 26, 1581, the northern provinces declared their independence from Spain, beginning what later became known as the Dutch Republic or The Nether-lands. The Dutch fought for their freedom until 1648, except for a temporary peace from 1609 to 1621. Spain finally recognized Dutch independence in 1648.

Prosperity and Power. The 1600's were the Golden Age of The Netherlands. The country became the lead-ing sea power. Its merchant fleet tripled in size between 1600 and 1650, and Dutch ships supplied about half the world's shipping. Dutch explorers, including Dirck Hartog and Abel Janszoon Tasman, found new sea routes and fishing grounds. Expanding trade made Amsterdam the world's major commercial city, and gave the Dutch the highest standard of living. There were also outstanding cultural achievements, espe-cially in painting.

During the Golden Age, the Dutch developed a great colonial empire in all parts of the world. In 1602, Dutch firms trading with the East Indies combined to form the Dutch East India Company. The company founded Batavia (now Djakarta, the capital of Indonesia) as its headquarters. The company's forces drove the British, French, Portuguese, and Spanish out of what later be-came the Netherlands Indies (now Indonesia). The company also colonized the southern tip of Africa.

The Dutch West India Company was founded in 1621 to trade in the New World and west Africa. In 1624, the company colonized New Netherland, which consisted of parts of present-day New York, New Jersey, Connecticut, and Delaware. In 1626, Dutch colonists bought Manhattan Island from the Indians for goods worth about $24. They had established New

―――― **IMPORTANT DATES IN THE NETHERLANDS** ――――

58 B.C. Julius Caesar conquered much of the Low Countries, in-cluding what is now The Netherlands.

A.D. 400's-800's The Franks controlled the region.

870 The Netherlands became part of the East Frankish king-dom (now Germany).

1300's-1400's The French dukes of Burgundy united most of the Low Countries.

1516 Duke Charles of Burgundy, ruler of the Low Countries, also became king of Spain.

1581 The Dutch Republic was begun.

1648 Spain recognized Dutch independence.

1600's The Netherlands became the world's major sea power, and developed a great colonial empire.

1652-1674 The Netherlands fought three naval wars with England, and kept leadership of the seas.

1702-1713 The Dutch lost control of the seas to England during a war against France.

1795-1813 France controlled The Netherlands.

1815 The Netherlands became an independent kingdom united with Belgium.

1830 Belgium revolted and became independent.

1914-1918 The Netherlands remained neutral during World War I.

1940-1945 Germany occupied The Netherlands during World War II. Queen Wilhelmina headed the Dutch govern-ment-in-exile in London.

1949 The Netherlands granted independence to the Nether-lands Indies (now Indonesia).

1954 The colonies of Surinam and Netherlands Antilles became equal partners in the Dutch kingdom.

1957 The Netherlands helped form the European Common Market.

1962 The Netherlands gave up control of Netherlands New Guinea (now West Irian) to the United Nations.

1967 Princess Beatrix gave birth to a son, the first male in line to inherit the throne since 1884.

Amsterdam (now New York City) there the year before. In 1634, the Dutch captured what is now the Netherlands Antilles from the Spaniards.

Wars with England and France. The Netherlands fought three great naval wars with England between 1652 and 1674. The English hoped to seize the shipping and trading leadership from the Dutch, but failed. During this period, the Dutch won what is now Surinam from the English, and the English gained New Netherland.

France and England formed a secret alliance against the Dutch Republic in 1670, and attacked it in 1672. The Dutch fleet prevented the English from landing by sea, but French troops seized a number of Dutch towns. William III, prince of Orange, was then elected *stadholder* (governor). He stopped the French by opening some dikes and flooding the land. Spanish and German troops also helped the Dutch. The English suffered major defeats at sea, and made peace with the Dutch in 1674. The French were driven out, and signed a peace treaty in 1678.

William's wife, Mary, was a member of the English royal family. In 1689, he became King William III of England as well as the Dutch stadholder. The Netherlands, England, and other European countries defeated France in two more wars, fought from 1688 to 1697 and from 1702 to 1713.

The 1700's. The long wars against France exhausted The Netherlands. In the war that ended in 1713, The Netherlands lost leadership of the seas to England. Dutch industry and trade stopped expanding.

The Revolutionary War in America began in 1775, and the Dutch aided the Americans against the English. England started a naval war against the Dutch in 1780. The Dutch were severely defeated by 1784.

In 1795, the weakened Netherlands fell to invading French troops. The French renamed the country the Batavian Republic, and set up a new government. England seized most of the Dutch overseas possessions.

Independence. In 1806, Napoleon I of France forced the Dutch to accept his brother, Louis, as their king. The Batavian Republic became the Kingdom of Holland. Napoleon wanted tighter control over the country, and made it a part of France in 1810. The Dutch drove out the French in 1813.

After Napoleon's final defeat in 1815, Europe's political leaders remapped much of the continent at the Congress of Vienna. They united The Netherlands and Belgium into the Kingdom of The Netherlands to strengthen barriers against future French expansion. William VI, prince of Orange, became King William I of The Netherlands and grand duke of Luxembourg.

The customs, economies, languages, and religions of the Dutch and the Belgians differed greatly. Most of the Belgians were Roman Catholics, and the upper classes spoke French. In 1830, Belgium declared its independence. Luxembourg ended its political ties with the Dutch royal family in 1890. That year, 10-year-old Wilhelmina had become queen after the death of her father, William III. But Luxembourg's laws did not permit a female ruler.

The Netherlands remained neutral during World War I (1914-1918). British and German naval operations interfered with Dutch fishing, shipping, and trading.

World War II. On May 10, 1940, German troops invaded The Netherlands. Four days later, German bombers destroyed much of Rotterdam. The Dutch army surrendered. Most of the Dutch navy and merchant fleet escaped capture and supported the Allies.

The Dutch suffered greatly during the German occupation. The Germans killed about 75 per cent of the nation's Jews—about 104,000 persons—mostly in death camps. They also forced thousands of other Netherlanders to work in German factories. Secret Dutch groups fought the Germans, organized strikes, and aided escaped prisoners and Allied fliers who had been shot down. In March, 1942, the Netherlands Indies (Indonesia) fell to Japan, an ally of Germany. By the time Germany surrendered to the Allies in May, 1945, about 270,000 Netherlanders had been killed or starved to death. See WORLD WAR II.

Economic Recovery. World War II left much of The Netherlands in ruins. The destruction included almost half the nation's factories and shipping, and most of its railroads. The great harbors at Amsterdam and Rotterdam were crippled. About a seventh of the land was flooded as a result of war damage to the dikes.

The people dedicated themselves to rebuilding their country, and the government supported close international cooperation to achieve this goal. In 1945, The Netherlands became a charter member of the United Nations. In 1947, it joined the European nations working together for recovery under the Marshall Plan of the United States. The Netherlands received $1 billion in Marshall Plan aid. The Dutch also joined other programs to promote international unity, including Benelux, the Council of Europe, the European Coal and Steel Community, the European Common Market, and the North Atlantic Treaty Organization.

By 1955, Dutch industrial production had increased about 60 per cent over the pre-World War II level. Farm output was almost 20 per cent greater.

Political Changes. In 1948, the aging Wilhelmina gave up the throne to her daughter, Juliana. At that

Hit by German Bombers during World War II, the center of Rotterdam was destroyed. The city was rebuilt after the war.

Wide World

time, a revolt was underway in the Netherlands Indies. The fighting, which had started in 1945, continued until 1949, when The Netherlands recognized Indonesia's independence. See INDONESIA (History).

Surinam and the Netherlands Antilles were made self-governing and equal members of the Dutch kingdom in 1954. In 1962, the Dutch gave up Netherlands New Guinea (now West Irian), their last colony, to United Nations control. Indonesia had claimed the region, and fighting had broken out earlier that year. The UN gave control of West Irian to Indonesia in 1963.

The Netherlands Today has a high standard of living, largely because of its policy of economic cooperation. This cooperation has taken place not only with other countries, but also at home. After World War II, Dutch industry, labor unions, and the government worked together to keep wages and prices low. Their action encouraged the swift expansion of industries. The nation's political parties also cooperated to support the economic program. By the mid-1960's, Dutch prosperity had been re-established. Wage and price levels were then raised to those of other prosperous European countries.

During the 1960's, various protest movements developed in The Netherlands. The leading forces of protest were the *provos* (a Dutch nickname for those who deliberately provoke the police and other authorities). The provos rioted many times, especially over two royal weddings to unpopular foreigners. In 1964, Princess Irene converted to Roman Catholicism and married Prince Carlos Hugo of Spain. In 1966, Princess Beatrix married Claus von Amsberg, a West German diplomat. He had been a German soldier during World War II.

In 1967, royal popularity was largely restored after Beatrix gave birth to a son, William-Alexander, the first male in line to inherit the throne since 1884.

ROBERT W. ADAMS, LEWIS M. ALEXANDER, and HERBERT H. ROWEN

NETHERLANDS / Study Aids

Questions

How do the Netherlanders "make" land?
What is the largest seaport in Europe?
What is the leading branch of Dutch agriculture?
What are the two territories of the Kingdom of The Netherlands in the Western Hemisphere?
What are "ice vacations"?
How did the Dutch lose leadership of the seas to the English? When?
When was the Golden Age of the Netherlands? Who were some great artists of this period?
What does the word *Netherlands* mean?
How did the Dutch come under Spanish control? When did they officially win independence?
What is *gezelligheid*?

Willemstad, Capital of the Netherlands Antilles, *above,* is an important port on Curaçao Island.

NETHERLANDS ANTILLES, also called the Dutch West Indies, consist of two groups of islands in the Caribbean Sea. The main group lies about 50 miles off the coast of Venezuela. The smaller group is about 500 miles northeast of the main islands and about 160 miles east of Puerto Rico.

The islands have a total area of 371 square miles and a population of 222,000. The combined coastline measures 140 miles. The southern group, made up of Aruba, Curaçao, and Bonaire, covers 337 square miles and has over nine-tenths of the population. Curaçao, which covers 172 square miles, is the largest island in the Netherlands Antilles. Willemstad, capital of the Netherlands Antilles, is on Curaçao. The northern group includes Saba and St. Eustatius islands, and the southern part of St. Martin Island. These islands cover only 34 square miles. See ARUBA; SABA; WILLEMSTAD.

Oil refining is the major industry in the Netherlands Antilles. Crude oil is shipped to refineries on Aruba and Curaçao from Venezuela. The land on Aruba and Curaçao is so rocky that little farming is possible. Most of the food must be imported. The people on Aruba and Curaçao speak Dutch, English, Spanish, and a mixture of the three called *Papiamento.* The other islands of the Netherlands Antilles are of little economic importance.

The Spanish first occupied Curaçao in 1527. The Dutch captured the Antilles area in 1634, and soon settled on the other islands.

The several units of the Netherlands Antilles are self-governing, and are equal partners in the Dutch realm. A governor, appointed by the Dutch ruler, serves a four-year term in Willemstad. ISIDORE BLOCH

NETHERLANDS INDIES is the historic name for a group of volcanic islands in the Malay Archipelago, located between Asia and Australia. They were once known as the Dutch East Indies. In 1949 these islands were made into a federation of 16 states called the United States of Indonesia. In August, 1950, these states became the Republic of Indonesia. Its capital is Djakarta. See also INDONESIA. JUSTUS M. VAN DER KROEF

NETHERLANDS NEW GUINEA. See NEW GUINEA.

NETHERLANDS WEST INDIES. See NETHERLANDS ANTILLES.

NETTLE, *NET'l,* is the common name of a group of plants with stinging bristles. They are coarse herbs, found in the north temperate regions. Nettles grow several feet tall. They have toothed leaves that grow in pairs opposite each other on the stem. The small, greenish flowers form in branching clusters.

The bristles of the nettle contain a watery juice that produces an intense itch when it enters a person's skin. This itch does not last long. In places where the skin is very thick, nettle bristles usually have no effect.

Young shoots of nettles can be cooked and eaten. The *great nettle* of Europe, now also found in the United States, has sometimes been cultivated for its fiber, from which a strong, coarse cloth can be made.

Scientific Classification. Nettles belong to the nettle family, *Urticaceae.* The great nettle is genus *Urtica,* species *U. dioica.* ARTHUR CRONQUIST

See also BOEHMERIA.

Wood Nettle Leaves are covered with fine, needle-shaped hairs that produce a stinging irritation on human skin.

NETTLE TREE. See HACKBERRY.

NETWORK. See AMERICAN BROADCASTING COMPANIES, INC.; COLUMBIA BROADCASTING SYSTEM, INC.; MUTUAL BROADCASTING SYSTEM; NATIONAL BROADCASTING COMPANY; RADIO; TELEVISION.

NEUILLY, TREATY OF, ended hostilities between Bulgaria and the Allies after World War I. It was signed on Nov. 27, 1919, at Neuilly-sur-Seine, near Paris. The treaty forced Bulgaria to pay the Allies $450 million in reparations, to limit its army to 20,000 men, and to give up territory to Greece, Romania, and Yugoslavia.

NEUMANN, JOHN NEPOMUCENE (1811-1860), a Roman Catholic priest, was beatified by the church in 1963. Beatification is the last step before sainthood is conferred.

Neumann was the bishop of Philadelphia from 1852 until his death. As bishop, he increased the number of Catholic elementary schools in the city from two to almost 100. He helped bring several sisterhoods from Europe to take charge of the schools. He also founded a Philadelphia branch of the Sisters of St. Francis.

Neumann was born in Prachatitz, Bohemia. He was ordained when he came to the United States in 1836. In 1840, he joined the Redemptorist Fathers, a society of missionary priests. He traveled and preached among the German-speaking people of Pennsylvania and nearby states.   FRANCIS L. FILAS

NEURALGIA, *nyoo RAL jah,* is a severe pain that occurs along a nerve. Its cause is not known. The pain may be limited to one part of the nerve, or it may extend along the nerve's branches. It may occur as repeated stabs of pain in the teeth, sinuses, eyes, face, tongue, or throat.

Neuralgia occurs in only two nerves. One nerve, the *trigeminal,* has three branches that enter the eyes, face, sinuses, and teeth. The other, the *glossopharyngeal,* leads to the back of the tongue and throat.

Neuralgia is sometimes confused with other conditions called *neuritis* and *radiculopathy.* But these occur in many different parts of the body. True neuritis is an inflammation that can permanently damage a nerve. Neuralgia does not harm the nerve.

Tic douloureux is a type of neuralgia that is common among older people. The name is French for *painful twitching.* Tic douloureux affects the trigeminal nerve and causes facial pain. The face muscles may contract each time a stab of pain occurs. The pain occurs very suddenly and then shoots along one side of the face. It usually begins at a specific part of the nerve called the *trigger zone.* It may then spread along various branches of the nerve, but it never involves other nerves. The pain may last only a few hours, or it may last several weeks. It may then disappear for a few months or years, but it usually returns.

Glossopharyngeal neuralgia is a very rare condition. It affects the throat and the back of the tongue.

Temporary relief for both types of neuralgia may be obtained by using drugs, or by numbing the nerve with an injection of alcohol. If the pain does not disappear, the only cure is a surgical operation to remove part of the nerve.   BENJAMIN BOSHES

See also NEURITIS.

NEURASTHENIA, *NYOO rus THEE nih uh,* is a term once used by doctors to describe a chronic mental and physical fatigue and lack of ambition. Such symptoms rarely occur without other physical or mental disturbances. In the past, neurasthenia was used to designate *anxiety reaction,* a form of neurosis (see NEUROSIS). In addition to fatigue and weakness, neurasthenia is characterized by dizziness, chest pain, heart palpitation, trembling, insomnia, and anxiety.   GEORGE A. ULETT

See also MENTAL HEALTH; NERVOUS BREAKDOWN.

NEURITIS, *nyoo RYE tis,* is an inflammation of a nerve caused by disease or injury. It is a painful condition that may affect one or many nerves. Neuritis is sometimes confused with a different disorder called neuralgia (see NEURALGIA).

Bacteria, viruses, and diet and vitamin deficiencies can cause neuritis. Infections such as tuberculosis, syphilis, and *herpes zoster* (shingles) can invade a nerve, resulting in neuritis. Neuritis can also develop when a disease, such as diabetes, changes the activities of the body's cells. Neuritis caused by physical injury to a nerve involves only the injured nerve.

If neuritis continues for a long period of time, a nerve may become so badly damaged that it can no longer function properly. As a result, a person may lose the ability to sense heat, pressure, and touch. The body also may lose control over such automatic activities as sweating. If a nerve no longer can stimulate a muscle, the muscle wastes away and eventually becomes paralyzed. Neuritis is a serious disorder that requires a doctor's care.   BENJAMIN BOSHES

NEUROLOGICAL SURGERY. See MEDICINE (table: Kinds of Medical Specialty Fields).

NEUROLOGY. See MEDICINE (table: Kinds of Medical Specialty Fields [Psychiatry and Neurology]).

NEURON. See NERVOUS SYSTEM.

NEUROPATHOLOGY, *nyoo roh puh THAL oh jih,* is the science that studies alterations in the tissues in diseases of the nervous system. It is concerned with the changes produced in the nerves, brain, and spinal cord. These may be changes in appearance studied with the unaided eye or with the microscope, or they may be changes that occur as a result of the normal chemical reactions of nerve cells.   BENJAMIN BOSHES

See also NERVOUS SYSTEM; PATHOLOGY.

NEUROPTERA, *nyoo RAHP ter uh,* is an order of insects that have thin, transparent wings netted with veins. The name *Neuroptera* means *nerve-winged.* Most members of this order are helpful because they feed on many destructive insects. The adults are delicate and fragile. Most of these insects are poor fliers, although their wings are well developed. See also ANT LION; LACEWING; INSECT (table).

NEUROSIS, *nyoo ROH sis.* Psychiatrists usually divide mental illnesses into two groups—the *psychoses* and the *neuroses.* The neuroses include the less severe illnesses, and the psychoses include the more severe ones.

Neuroses (also called *psychoneuroses*) are caused by mental disturbances rather than by any sort of physical disease or abnormality. These disturbances consist of thoughts, wishes, and emotions that conflict with one another. All persons are aware of such conflicts at times. But the conflicts that give rise to neuroses are special, because the person having them is not aware they exist. For this reason, doctors call them *unconscious conflicts.* Usually these are conflicts over wishes or desires that the patient feared would cause others to hurt or punish him when he was a child. So neuroses have their origins in childhood, although they may not become evident until adult life.

Psychiatrists divide neuroses into several groups, but all doctors do not agree on the same groupings. Most groupings classify the neuroses according to what chiefly troubles the patient. For example, *hysteria* is the name usually given to neuroses in which the patient complains of what seem to be physical ailments (see HYSTERIA). *Anxiety neurosis* is the name often given to neuroses in which the patient complains chiefly of worries and feelings of fear and panic. *Phobia* designates a neurosis in which the patient fears and avoids certain situations, such as riding on trains or in elevators or being alone on the street (see PHOBIA). *Obsessional neurosis* (also called *compulsion neurosis* or *obsessive-compulsive neurosis*) applies to a group of neuroses in which patients complain of troublesome and persistent thoughts. They also feel that something within them forces, or compels, them to perform certain acts.

Doctors usually treat neuroses with psychotherapy (see PSYCHOTHERAPY). Hospital treatment is usually not necessary. However, doctors sometimes use drugs in treatment. In some cases, social workers assist doctors in helping patients.   CHARLES BRENNER

See also MENTAL HEALTH; MENTAL ILLNESS; PSYCHOANALYSIS; PSYCHOSIS.

NEUROSURGERY. See MEDICINE (table: Kinds of Medical Specialty Fields).

NEUTER GENDER. See GENDER.

NEUTRA, *NOY trah,* **RICHARD JOSEPH** (1892-1970), was an Austrian-born architect who worked in California. His best designs show his goal of creating buildings that meet man's biological and psychological needs, as well as artistic and technical considerations. In his book *Survival Through Design* (1954), he stated that man can survive only by controlling his environment through design, architecture, and city planning.

Neutra was born in Vienna. He moved to the United States in 1923 and settled in Los Angeles in 1925. His most famous work is the Lovell "Health" House (1929) in Los Angeles, one of the earliest examples of modern European architecture in the United States. This house is built of concrete and glass on a steel frame. Many of Neutra's later buildings, including the Tremaine House

Neutra's Lovell House in Los Angeles was one of the first homes in America to be constructed of concrete panels and glass.
Julius Shulman

(1948) in Santa Barbara, Calif., suggest a continuous flow of space by the use of vast sheets of glass and thin supports.   STANFORD ANDERSON

NEUTRALITY is the official status of a government that does not take part in a war. The nations that do not take part, either directly or indirectly, are called *neutrals.* The warring countries are called *belligerents* (engaged in fighting). Belligerents want to defeat their enemies and prevent neutrals from trading with them.

Neutrals want to stay out of the war, and expect the belligerents to respect neutral territory, freedom of the seas, and the right to trade. *Neutralization* describes the position of a government that has been recognized as permanently neutral, such as Switzerland.

Since the late 1700's, the rights and duties of neutrals and belligerents have become part of international law. But warring nations have frequently ignored these rights and duties, and in most cases it has been difficult or impossible to enforce them. The rules of neutrality have been developed through both custom and treaty. In 1907, a group of nations at the second Hague Peace Conference set down in two treaties the traditional rules of neutrality on land and sea. These rules were an attempt to balance the differing, and often conflicting, interests of neutrals and belligerents. Individual governments also pass their own laws on neutrality.

Rights and Duties. Traditionally, a neutral must not help either of the belligerents. In return, belligerents must respect the rights of neutrals. They must not fight on neutral territory, or move troops across neutral countries. If belligerent troops enter neutral territory, the neutral has the right to disarm them and *intern* (hold) them until the war is over.

A neutral must not build or arm warships for a belligerent. During the U.S. Civil War, Great Britain failed to prevent the building and departure of the *Alabama* and other British warships for the Confederacy. These ships sank many Union ships. After the war, an international court ruled that Britain had violated its neutrality. Britain had to pay the United States $15½ million in damages (see ALABAMA [ship]).

Belligerent warships may enter a neutral port in an emergency. But if they stay more than 24 hours, they can be interned. Belligerents may not use neutral ports for naval operations.

Neutrals have the right to trade with other neutrals. But belligerents may search neutral ships. If these ships are carrying war materials to the enemy, the belligerent has the right to seize the goods. Belligerents often decide for themselves what to consider as war materials. They may blockade enemy ports and seize neutral vessels that try to *run* (slip through) the blockade.

World War I. In 1914, Germany violated the rules of neutrality by invading Belgium, whose permanent neutrality had been guaranteed by treaty in 1831.

The United States remained neutral in World War I from 1914 to 1917. During this time, the U.S. tried to defend its neutral rights at sea against violation by Great Britain, France, and Germany. Great Britain and France seized cargoes bound for neutral countries such as Denmark and Norway. They argued that such cargoes might eventually reach Germany. The United States insisted that Britain and France could not interfere with neutral rights or blockade neutral ports.

In 1917, the United States declared war against Germany, partly because Germany had violated U.S. neutrality. German submarines had sunk U.S. ships without warning. Under international law, Germany could capture ships carrying war materials to the enemy. But German submarines were unable to take captured ships into port, so they sank them. The loss of lives and property helped turn U.S. public opinion against Germany.

Between Wars. Conflicts over neutral rights had twice been major causes for the United States to go to war, once in 1917 and previously in 1812 (see War of 1812 [Causes of the War]). In the 1930's Congress passed several neutrality acts hoping to keep the U.S. out of another war. These acts placed limits on U.S. neutral rights beyond those required by international law. They forbade the export of war materials and the extension of loans or credits to all belligerent nations. They also provided that other goods could be exported only on a *cash-and-carry* basis. This meant that the belligerent had to pay cash and use its own ships to carry the goods. If the ships were sunk, the United States would not suffer any losses.

World War II. Early in World War II, Germany violated the neutrality of Belgium, Denmark, The Netherlands, Norway, and Yugoslavia. The United States soon shifted from a policy of impartial neutrality to one of preparedness and aid to the Western allies. The laws of the mid-1930's were modified in November, 1939, to permit the export of all materials to belligerents on a cash-and-carry basis.

When German victories threatened Great Britain, the United States violated its neutral obligations by sending 50 destroyers and other war materials to the British. In March, 1941, Congress passed the Lend-Lease Act to aid countries fighting Nazi Germany. After Japan attacked Pearl Harbor in December, 1941, the United States declared war on both Germany and Japan.

Neutrality Today. Total warfare and the growth of world and regional organizations like the United Nations have changed the meaning of neutrality. Total warfare has erased most distinctions between civilian and military activities and materials. This destroys many of the arguments neutrals previously used to support their rights of neutral trade. Also, during a large-scale war, nations find it difficult to remain completely neutral. Most countries now belong to the United Nations. Collective action, such as use of the UN police force against an aggressor, is in many ways in disagreement with earlier practices of impartial neutrality.

Many countries, especially in Asia and Africa, have refused to support either the Communist or non-Communist blocs in the Cold War (see Cold War). These countries have sought security through policies of nonalignment and noninvolvement. They are called *neutralist*, *nonaligned*, or *uncommitted* nations. This group now has so many votes in the UN that neither Communist nor non-Communist powers can get resolutions adopted without support from at least some of the neutralist members. Elton Atwater

See also High Seas; International Law.

NEUTRALIZATION, *NOO trull ih ZAY shun*, is a chemical reaction in which an acid and a base form a salt and water. If the reaction is complete, the final salt solution is usually *neutral* (neither acidic nor basic). Neutralization is one of the most important reactions in chemical analysis, and in many branches of industry. Important processes that go on in the human body include neutralization.

Acids and bases in water solution *ionize* (break down) into positive and negative ions as shown below for hydrochloric acid (HCl) and sodium hydroxide (NaOH).

$$HCl \rightarrow H^+ + Cl^- \quad and \quad NaOH \rightarrow Na^+ + {}^-OH$$

When the acid and base react together, the hydroxyl

(^-OH) ion from the base combines with the hydrogen (H^+) ion from the acid to form water (H_2O).

$$H^+ + Cl^- + Na^+ + {}^-OH \rightarrow Na^+ + Cl^- + H_2O$$

The two remaining ions form a salt that usually stays in solution as ions. If the water is evaporated, the salt can be recovered in crystal form. Neutralization is more specifically defined as the reaction between hydroxyl and hydrogen ions to form water. Chemists can tell when a neutralization reaction is complete by using indicators, such as litmus. Esmarch S. Gilreath

Related Articles in World Book include:

Acid	Ion and	Litmus	Phenolphthalein
Base	Ionization	pH	Salt, Chemical
Hydrolysis			

NEUTRINO. See Atom (Neutrinos); Pauli, Wolfgang.

NEUTRON is one of the basic parts of all matter. It is a subatomic particle with a radius of about one-30,000,000,000,000th of an inch. Neutrons combine with protons to form the nucleus of an atom. Together, they make up 99.9 per cent of the atom's mass. A large cloud of electrons accounts for the rest of the mass. In the nucleus, neutrons and protons are held together by an extremely great force of attraction.

The nucleus of a stable atom contains as many neutrons as protons, or more. A *stable* atom is one that is not naturally radioactive. The number of neutrons in an atom of any element equals the difference between the element's mass number and atomic number. Neutrons have a mass slightly greater than that of protons.

Scientists use neutrons to make ordinary elements radioactive. They bombard such elements as iodine and cobalt with neutrons in an atomic pile or reactor. The nuclei of atoms become radioactive when they absorb neutrons. That is, they decay by giving off some kind of radiation. When the uranium isotope U^{235} absorbs a neutron, it splits into two large parts and several smaller parts. This process, called *fission*, releases a huge amount of energy. It also produces additional neutrons that cause more U^{235} atoms to split in a chain reaction. In this way, neutrons are responsible for atomic energy and the atomic bomb.

The neutron was discovered in 1932 by Sir James Chadwick (1891-), an English physicist. But scientists are just beginning to understand its internal structure. It probably consists of at least two clouds of heavy mesons whose charges cancel each other. As a result, the neutron appears to have no electrical charge. The neutron spins and behaves in some ways like a bar magnet in a magnetic field. When a neutron is removed from a nucleus, it decays quickly into a proton, an electron, and a neutrino. Its half-life is about 12.8 minutes. Robert Hofstadter

See also Atom; Atomic Energy; Chadwick, Sir James; Radioactivity; Baryon.

NEVA RIVER, *NE vuh.* This short stream, only 45 miles long, is an important link in three waterway systems in Russia. It rises at the southern end of Lake Ladoga and flows west into the Gulf of Finland at Leningrad. The Neva River is part of the Ladoga-Volga system that connects the Baltic and Caspian seas. It is also a link in the canal system that connects the Baltic and White seas. Theodore Shabad

NEVADA

THE SILVER STATE

NEVADA, *nuh VAD uh,* or *nuh VAHD uh,* has one of the smallest populations of all the states. But every year Nevada has enough visitors to outnumber the population of any state. Nevada is the only state whose laws allow most kinds of gambling. Large, luxurious gambling casinos attract visitors from all parts of the world to Reno and Las Vegas. Las Vegas is Nevada's largest city and the chief tourist attraction.

Nevada is a land of rugged snow-capped mountains, grassy valleys, and sandy deserts. Pine forests cover many mountain slopes, and crystal-clear streams flow through steep, rocky canyons. Giant trout swim in sparkling valley lakes. In many places, geysers erupt and hot springs gush amid the rocks. In the south, bighorn sheep graze on jagged plateaus that glow red in the brilliant sunshine. Glistening white patches called alkali flats stretch across the deserts. The flowers of cactus, yucca, and sagebrush plants add splashes of color. The gray-green sagebrush gave Nevada one of its nicknames, the SAGEBRUSH STATE. The Atomic Energy Commission maintains a testing center for atomic weapons in the Nevada desert.

The state's most common nickname, the SILVER STATE, comes from the vast amounts of silver once taken from its many mines. Colorful ghost towns and historic mining towns, such as Virginia City, now attract thousands of tourists every year. But mining is still one of Nevada's chief industries. The most important minerals include copper, diatomite, gold, gypsum, iron ore, mercury, sand and gravel, and stone. These resources support the state's growing manufacturing and processing industry.

Less rain falls in Nevada than in any other state. As a result, farming depends on irrigation. The Newlands Irrigation Project, near Reno, was the first system of its kind built by the federal government. Hoover Dam, on the Colorado River, created Lake Mead, one of the world's largest man-made lakes. The dam supplies electricity for Arizona, California, and Nevada.

Nevada's main crops are grain and hay that are fed to livestock in the state. Cattle and sheep graze on vast ranches in central and eastern Nevada. Ranchers also feed their herds on public lands owned by the federal government. Public lands make up more than 85 per cent of the state.

Nevada lies mainly on a broad, rugged highland between the Rocky Mountains and the Sierra Nevada mountain range. In the 1820's and 1830's, the trappers Peter S. Ogden, Jedediah S. Smith, and Joseph Walker explored parts of the region in search of new fur sources. John C. Frémont began the first thorough exploration in 1843. By the 1860's, discoveries of gold and silver had brought thousands of miners to the area.

The name *Nevada* comes from a Spanish word meaning *snow-clad.* Miners and other settlers chose the name Nevada when the region became a territory in 1861. Nevada became a state in 1864 during the Civil War and was nicknamed the BATTLE BORN STATE.

For the relationship of Nevada to the other states in its region, see ROCKY MOUNTAIN STATES.

Desert Land near Las Vegas

Nevada (blue) ranks seventh in size among all the states, and second in size among the Rocky Mountain States (gray).

Downtown Las Vegas at Night

The contributors of this article are James W. Hulse, Associate Professor of History at the University of Nevada; E. R. Larson, Professor of Geology at the University of Nevada; and James M. Leavy, Editor of the Las Vegas Review-Journal.

——————— FACTS IN BRIEF ———————

Capital: Carson City.

Government: Congress—U.S. senators, 2; U.S. representatives, 1. *Electoral Votes*—3. *State Legislature*—senators, 20; assemblymen, 40. *Counties*—16. *Voting Age*—21 years (state and local elections); 18 years (national elections).

Area: 110,540 square miles (including 651 square miles of inland water), 7th in size among the states. *Greatest Distances*—(north-south) 483 miles; (east-west) 320 miles.

Elevation: *Highest*—Boundary Peak, in Esmeralda County, 13,140 feet above sea level. *Lowest*—470 feet above sea level near the Colorado River in Clark County.

Population: *1970 Census*—488,738; 47th among the states; density, 4 persons to the square mile; distribution, 81 per cent urban, 19 per cent rural. *1960 Census*—285,278.

Chief Products: *Agriculture*—alfalfa seed, beef cattle, dairy products, greenhouse and nursery products, hay, sheep, wheat, wool. *Manufacturing and Processing*—food products; lumber and wood products; metal products; primary metals; printing and publishing; stone, clay, and glass products. *Mining*—copper, diatomite, gold, gypsum, iron ore, mercury, sand and gravel, stone.

Statehood: Oct. 31, 1864, the 36th state.

State Motto: *All for Our Country.*

State Song: "Home Means Nevada." Words and music by Bertha Raffetto.

143

Constitution of Nevada was adopted in 1864, when the state entered the Union. Nevada's constitution may be *amended* (changed) by the state legislature or directly by the people. An amendment proposed by the legislature must be approved by a majority of both houses in two successive regular sessions. Then the voters must approve it in the next general election. The people may amend the constitution directly by using the *initiative*. In this procedure, voters who support the amendment first sign a petition. The number of signatures must equal at least 10 per cent of the voters in the last general election in each of three-fourths of the counties, and at least 10 per cent of all the voters in the last general election. The petition states the proposed amendment and calls for a general election to vote on it. If the amendment is approved by a majority of the voters, it becomes part of the constitution.

The Nevada constitution may also be revised by a constitutional convention. To call such a convention, two-thirds of each legislative house must vote for it. Then a majority of voters must approve the convention in the next election.

Executive. The governor of Nevada is elected to a four-year term. He can serve no more than two terms. The governor receives a yearly salary of $30,000. For a list of all the governors of Nevada, see the *History* section of this article.

Key state officials also are elected to four-year terms. They include the lieutenant governor, secretary of state, treasurer, controller, attorney general, and inspector of mines. The governor appoints the members of about a hundred bureaus, commissions, and administrative boards.

Legislature consists of a 20-member senate and a 40-member assembly. Nevada has eight senatorial districts and 11 assembly districts. One senatorial district elects eight senators; one elects six senators; and the other six districts each elect one senator. One assembly district elects 16 assemblymen; one elects 12 assemblymen; and the other nine districts each elect one or two assemblymen, depending on population. Senators serve four-year terms, and assemblymen serve two-year terms.

In 1965, a federal court ordered Nevada to redraw its legislative districts to provide equal representation.

The legislature set up the present districts later in 1965, and the federal court approved them in 1966.

The legislature meets on the third Monday of January in odd-numbered years. Legislators receive their salaries for 60 days, but legislative sessions have no time limit. Regular sessions last about 90 days. The governor can call special sessions.

Courts. The supreme court of Nevada has a chief justice and four associate justices, all elected to six-year terms. One or two justices are elected every two years. The justice who has served the longest acts as chief justice. Nevada has eight district courts, with 18 district judges who serve four-year terms. Court districts with large populations have divisions called departments. Each department is headed by a district judge. Municipal judges serve in city courts, and justices of the peace serve in townships.

Local Government. Three-man boards of county commissioners govern 14 of Nevada's 16 counties. Voters in Clark and Washoe counties elect five-man boards. A five-man board of supervisors governs the independent city of Carson City. County commissioners serve four-year terms. Other elected county officials include the assessor, auditor and recorder, clerk, district attorney, public administrator, and sheriff. Most cities have mayor-council governments.

Taxation provides about 50 per cent of Nevada's income. Almost all the rest comes from federal grants and other U.S. government programs. A 3 per cent sales tax supplies the chief state income, followed by taxes on gambling. Nevada allows many forms of gambling that are not legal in other states. However, Nevada collects less income from gambling taxes than some states that allow fewer kinds of gambling.

Other important sources of state revenue include taxes on alcoholic beverages, motor fuel, and tobacco; and license fees for automobiles, fishing, hunting, and the transportation of passengers and freight. State and local governments share income from a property tax.

To attract industry, Nevada enacted a "free port" tax law in 1949. This law applies to goods being held in Nevada for shipment outside the state. It allows manufacturers to process and store such goods in Nevada without paying property taxes on the goods. In most

Nevada Dept. of Economic Development

The Governor's Mansion in Carson City is a half mile from the state Capitol. Stately white columns give a touch of formality to the mansion, built in 1908.

The State Seal

Symbols of Nevada. On the seal, the plow and the sheaf of wheat represent Nevada's agricultural resources. The quartz mill, mine tunnel, and carload of ore symbolize the mineral wealth of the state. The 36 stars around the outside show that Nevada was the 36th state to enter the Union. The seal was adopted in 1866. On the flag, the words *Battle Born* recall that Nevada gained statehood during the Civil War. The flag was adopted in 1929.

Flag, bird, and flower illustrations, courtesy of Eli Lilly and Company

states, manufacturers must pay taxes on such property. The free port law was written into the Nevada constitution in 1960.

Politics. Nevada has about twice as many registered Democrats as Republicans. The Democratic Party's strength lies mainly in Clark County, where about half of the voters live. Nevadans usually have elected a Democratic majority to the state assembly. But Republicans from rural counties generally have won a majority of seats in the state senate.

In national politics, Nevada Democrats have won more often than Republicans in elections for the United States Senate and House of Representatives. Nevada has voted for the winner of every presidential election since 1912. For Nevada's electoral votes and voting record in presidential elections, see ELECTORAL COLLEGE (table).

The State Capitol in Carson City was built of Nevada stone. Gigantic wooden beams support the roof. The building was first used in 1871. A library annex was built in 1906, and north and south wings were added in 1914. Carson City has been the capital since the Nevada Territory was created in 1861.

Fred Bond, Publix

The State Flag

The State Bird
Mountain Bluebird

The State Flower
Sagebrush

The State Tree
Single-Leaf Piñon

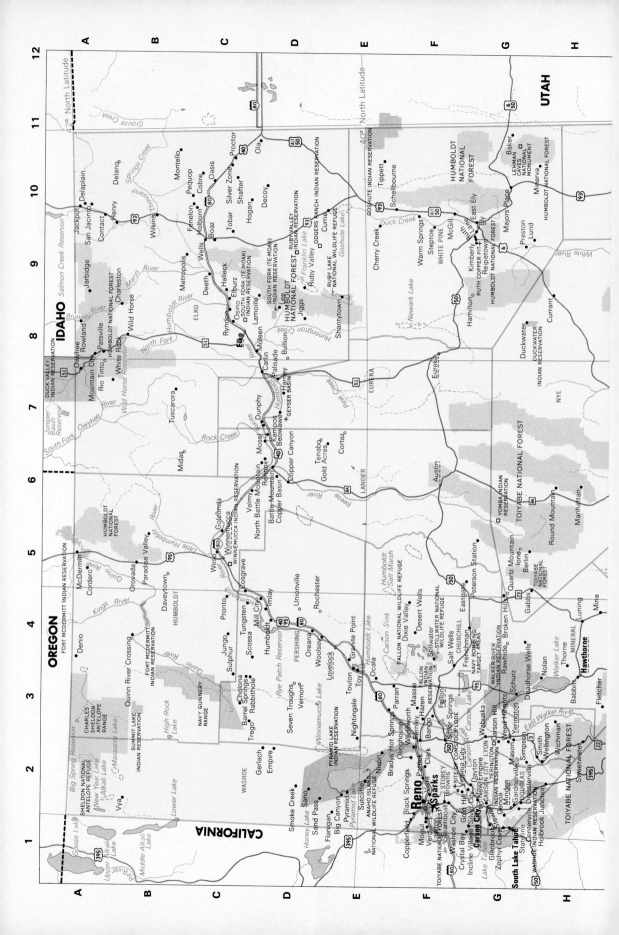

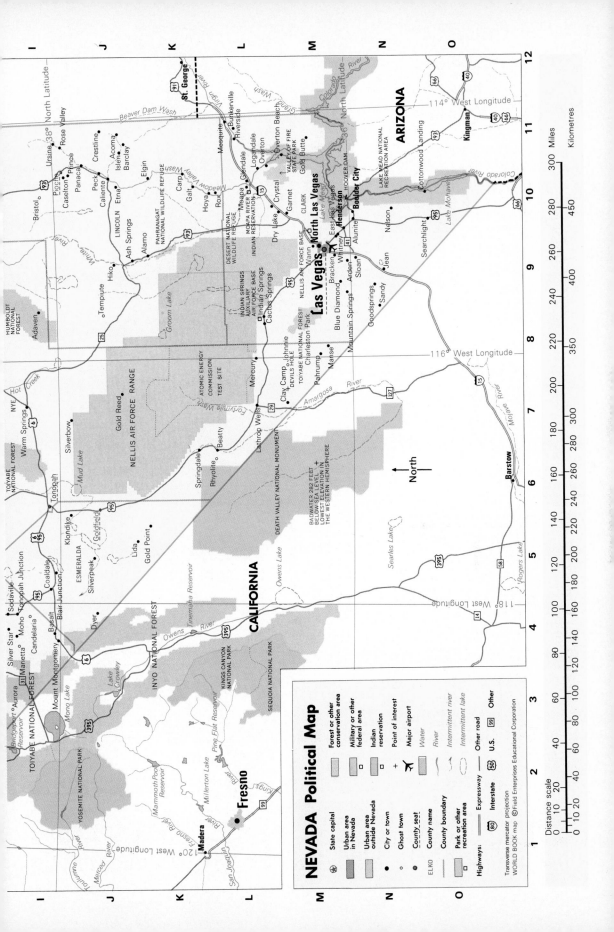

NEVADA Political Map

⊛	State capital
	Urban area in Nevada
	Urban area outside Nevada
	Forest or other conservation area
□	Military or other federal area
□	Indian reservation
+	Point of interest
✈	Major airport
	Water
	River
	Intermittent river
	Intermittent lake
	Park or other recreation area

•	City or town
○	Ghost town
●	County seat
ELKO	County name
	County boundary

Highways:
═══ Expressway
(80) Interstate (50) U.S. (99) Other
═══ Other road

Transverse mercator projection
WORLD BOOK map ©Field Enterprises Educational Corporation

Distance scale
0 10 20   40   60   80
0 10 20 40 60 80 100

North

BADWATER 282 FEET BELOW SEA LEVEL
LOWEST ELEVATION IN THE WESTERN HEMISPHERE

120° West Longitude
118° West Longitude
116° West Longitude
114° West Longitude

38° North Latitude
36° North Latitude

CALIFORNIA
ARIZONA
NEVADA

Miles
0 100 150 200 250 300
Kilometres
0 50 100 150 200 250 300 350 400 450

NEVADA MAP INDEX

Population

488,738 ... Census ... 1970
285,278 ...... " 1960
160,083 ...... " 1950
110,247 ...... " 1940
91,058 ...... " 1930
77,407 ...... " 1920
81,875 ...... " 1910
42,335 ...... " 1900
47,355 ...... " 1890
62,266 ...... " 1880
42,491 ...... " 1870
6,857 ...... " 1860

Metropolitan Areas

Las Vegas 273,288
Reno 121,068

Counties

Churchill ... 10,513 .. F 4
Clark ..... 273,288 .. M 10
Douglas ..... 6,882 .. G 2
Elko .... 13,958 .. C 8
Esmeralda .... 629 .. J 5
Eureka .... 948 .. E 7
Humboldt ... 6,375 .. B 4
Lander ..... 2,666 .. E 6
Lincoln ..... 2,557 .. J 10
Lyon .... 8,221 .. G 2
Mineral ..... 7,051 .. H 4
Nye .... 5,599 .. I 7
Pershing .... 2,670 .. D 4
Storey .... 695 .. F 2
Washoe ... 121,068 .. C 2
White Pine . 10,150 .. F 9

Cities and Towns

Acoma .... J 11
Adaven .... I 8
Alamo .... K 9
Alunite .... N 10
Arden .... N 9
Ash Springs .... J 9
Austin .... °F 6
Babbitt ..... 1,579 .. H 3
Baker .... G 11
Bango .... F 3
Barclay .... J 11
Barrel Springs ...... C 3
Basalt .... I 4
Battle Mountain . 1,856 .. D 6
Beatty .... L 7
Beowawe .... D 7
Berlin .... G 5
Big Canyon .... E 2
Black Springs ...... F 2
Blair Junction ..... I 5
Blue Diamond ..... M 9
Boaz .... C 9
Boulder City 5,223 .. N 10
Bracken .... M 9
Bradys Hot Springs .... F 3
Broken Hills .... G 5
Browns .... F 2
Bunkerville .... L 11
Cactus Springs ..... L 8
Caliente ...... 916 .. J 10
Carlin ...... 1,313 .. D 8
Carp .... K 10
Carson City 15,468†°G 2
Carson Hill .... G 3
Caselton .... I 10
Centerville .... G 2
Charleston .... B 9
Charleston Park .... M 8
Cherry Creek ...... E 10
Cholona .... C 3
Clark .... F 2
Clay Camp .... M 7
Coaldale .... I 5
Cobre .... C 10
Contact .... A 10
Copper Basin ...... D 6
Copper Canyon ..... D 6
Copperfield .... F 1
Cordero .... A 5
Cosgrave .... C 5
Cottonwood Landing .... O 10
Crestline .... J 11
Crystal .... L 10
Crystal Bay .... G 1
Currant .... H 9
Currie .... E 10
Dayton .... G 2
Deadhorse Wells ... G 4
Decoy .... D 10
Deeth .... C 9
Delaplain .... A 10
Denio .... A 4
Desert Wells .... F 4
Dixie Valley .... F 4
Dresslerville .... G 2
Dry Lake .... M 10
Duckwater .... G 8
Dunphy .... D 7
Dyer .... J 4
East Ely .... 1,992 .. G 10
East Las Vegas ..... 6,501 .. M 10
Eastgate .... G 5
Elburz .... C 9
Elgin .... K 10
Elko .... 7,621 .°C 8
Ely .... 4,176 .°G 10
Empire .... D 2
Etna .... J 10
Eureka .... °F 8
Fallon ...... 2,959 .°F 3
Fenelon .... C 10
Fernley .... F 3
Flanigan .... E 2
Fletcher .... I 3
Frenchman .... G 4
Gabbs .... 874 .. G 5
Galt .... K 10
Gardnerville [Minden] . 1,320 .. G 2
Garnet .... M 10
Genoa .... G 2
Gerlach .... D 2
Glenbrook .... G 1
Glendale .... L 10
Golconda .... C 5
Gold Acres .... E 7
Gold Butte .... M 11
Gold Hill .... G 2
Gold Point .... K 6
Gold Reed .... J 7
Goldfield .... °J 6
Goodsprings .... N 9
Granite Point ...... E 4
Halleck .... C 9
Harney .... D 7
Hawthorne .. 3,539 .°H 3
Hazen .... F 3
Henderson . 16,395 .. M 10
Henry .... A 10
Hiko .... J 9
Hogan .... C 10
Holborn .... C 10
Holbrook Junction . H 2
Hoya .... L 10
Humboldt .... D 4
Imlay .... D 4
Incline Village ..... G 1
Indian Springs ..... L 8
Islen .... J 11
Jackpot .... A 10
Jarbridge .... A 9
Jean .... N 9
Jiggs .... D 8
Jungo .... C 4
Kampos .... D 7
Kimberly .... G 9
Klondike .... J 6
Lamoille .... D 9
Lane .... G 10
Las Vegas 125,787 .°M 9
Lathrop Wells ...... L 7
Lawton .... F 1
Lee .... D 9
Lida .... J 5
Logandale .... L 11
Lovelock .... 1,571 .°E 4
Lund .... G 10
Luning .... H 4
Majors Place ...... G 10
Manhattan .... H 6
Manse .... M 8
Mason .... G 3
Massie .... F 3
McDermitt .... A 5
McGill ...... 2,164 .. F 10
Mercury .... L 8
Mesquite .... L 11
Metropolis .... C 9
Mill City .... D 4
Mina .... H 4
Minden .... °G 2
Minerva .... H 11
Moapa .... L 10
Mogul .... F 1
Moho .... I 4

This map shows the *population density* of Nevada, and how it varies in different parts of the state. Population density means the average number of persons who live on each square mile.

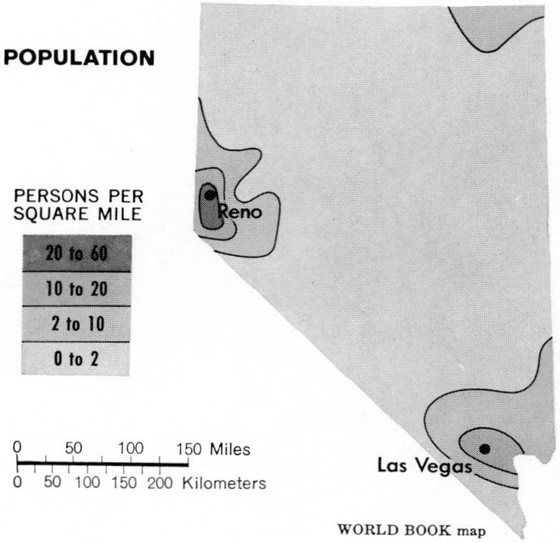
POPULATION
PERSONS PER SQUARE MILE
20 to 60
10 to 20
2 to 10
0 to 2
Reno
Las Vegas
0 50 100 150 Miles
0 50 100 150 200 Kilometers
WORLD BOOK map

NEVADA/*People*

The 1970 United States census reported that Nevada had 488,738 persons. The population had increased 71 per cent over the 1960 figure, 285,278.

About 80 per cent of all Nevadans live in urban areas. But most of Nevada's cities and towns are small. Only 6 have populations greater than 10,000. More than half of the people live within 50 miles of Las Vegas, Nevada's largest city. About a fourth live within 30 miles of Reno, the second largest city. The only other cities with populations greater than 10,000 are North Las Vegas and Henderson, near Las Vegas; Sparks, near Reno; and Carson City, the state capital.

Las Vegas and Reno are population centers for Nevada's two Standard Metropolitan Statistical Areas (see METROPOLITAN AREA). The Las Vegas area includes all of Clark County, and the Reno area includes all of Washoe County.

People living in Las Vegas depend mainly on the tourist and gambling industries for their income. Las Vegas is famous for its gambling casinos and its night clubs. Reno, another tourist favorite, is the center of banking, commerce, and transportation in northern Nevada. See the separate articles on the cities of Nevada listed in the *Related Articles* at the end of this article.

About 95 per cent of the people of Nevada were born in the United States. More than a fifth of the people are Roman Catholics. Members of the Church of Jesus Christ of Latter-day Saints (Mormons) make up almost another fifth of the population. Eastern Nevada has several small Mormon communities. Other religious bodies include Baptists, Episcopalians, Jews, Lutherans, Methodists, and Presbyterians.

University of Nevada's Noble Getchell Library in Reno houses most of the school's library collections.

T. J. (Doc) Kaminski

well as historical relics. This museum also features life-sized mining exhibits built in tunnels beneath the building. The exhibits illustrate blasting, drilling, hoisting, and other mining operations. The Mackay School of Mines Museum in Reno specializes in displays on mining, metallurgy, and geology. The Lost City Museum in Overton has many items found at the Pueblo Grande de Nevada, an ancient Indian settlement. Lake Mead now covers part of the site of the ancient city.

Schools. Nevadans made plans for a tax-supported school system as early as 1861, when Nevada became a territory. In 1865, a year after statehood, the legislature established the first school districts.

Nevada had to overcome unusual problems in developing its public school system. Rural areas were thinly populated. In some places, taxpayers supported schools for as few as three or four school-age children living in a vast area. Some early schools were open only six months of the year because of a lack of funds. Until 1900, the state had only a few high schools. In some parts of Nevada, elementary school students still attend one-room schools.

In 1956, the state legislature made each county a school district. A nine-member board of education supervises Nevada's school system. Board members serve four-year terms. Voters elect three members to the board every two years. The board appoints three members and selects a superintendent of public instruction. Each school district also has its own elected board of education. Children must attend school between their 7th and 17th birthdays. For the number of students and teachers in Nevada, see EDUCATION (table).

The University of Nevada, with campuses in Reno and Las Vegas, is Nevada's only institution of higher learning accredited by the Northwest Association of Secondary and Higher Schools (see NEVADA, UNIVERSITY OF). For the enrollment and further information, see UNIVERSITIES AND COLLEGES (table).

Libraries. The University of Nevada in Reno has the largest library in the state. The Nevada State Library in Carson City acts as the official library for the state government and as the reference and research center for other libraries throughout the state. Nevada has 22 public libraries, including three that provide bookmobile service to both metropolitan and rural areas.

Museums. The museum of the Nevada Historical Society displays many items used by early Nevadans. Its collections include musical instruments, china, embroidery, and lace. The Nevada State Museum in Carson City displays examples of Nevada wildlife as

*Does not appear on map; key shows general location.
†Independent city, not part of any county
○County seat
Source: Latest census figures (1970). Places without population figures are unincorporated areas and are not listed in census reports.

Ruth Copper Pit near Ely

NEVADA / *A Visitor's Guide*

Gambling and the colorful night life in Las Vegas and Reno draw millions of tourists every year. Virginia City and other towns remind travelers of the prospectors who came west seeking gold and silver. Sportsmen hunt mule deer and chukar partridge, and catch cutthroat, brown, and rainbow trout. Skiers race down the slopes of Mount Rose west of Reno, Mount Charleston near Las Vegas, and Ward Mountain near Ely. Vacationers also enjoy swimming and water skiing at Lake Mead, Lake Tahoe, and Pyramid Lake.

PLACES TO VISIT

Following are brief descriptions of some of Nevada's most interesting places to visit.

Atmospherium-Planetarium at the University of Nevada in Reno shows realistic motion pictures of hurricanes, tornadoes, and various weather conditions.

Bowers Mansion, a large Italian-style home near Carson City, was built by "Sandy" Bowers, a silver miner who made a fortune from the Comstock Lode.

Geyser Basin, near Beowawe, has active geysers, hot springs, and pools of bubbling mud. The action of the geysers has built a terrace about half a mile long and a hundred feet wide on the mountainside.

Hamilton, a ghost town between Eureka and Ely, once had a population of nearly 15,000. The city is now completely abandoned.

Hoover Dam, about 25 miles southeast of Las Vegas, is one of the world's largest dams. See HOOVER DAM.

Rhyolite, a ghost town near Beatty, has a museum of desert relics called the Bottle House. The house was built of thousands of bottles cemented together with *adobe* (sun-dried brick).

Ruth Copper Pit, near Ely, is one of the largest open-pit copper mines in the world. It measures about a mile in diameter, and it is nearly a thousand feet deep.

Lehman Caves National Monument near Baker

Bob and Ira Spring
Virginia City, a Famous Western Ghost Town

Fred Ragsdale, Shostal
Elephant Rock in Valley of Fire State Park

Art Marston, Shostal
Admission Day Parade in Carson City

National Forests and Monuments. Humboldt National Forest lies near Elko. Eldorado, Inyo, and Toiyabe national forests are partly in Nevada and partly in California. For the areas and chief features of these forests, see NATIONAL FOREST (table). In September, 1964, Congress set aside part of Nevada's national forests as a national wilderness area. This area is to be preserved in its natural condition. Lehman Caves National Monument, near Baker, is on the eastern slope of Wheeler Peak. The northeast corner of Death Valley National Monument also is in Nevada. See LEHMAN CAVES NATIONAL MONUMENT; DEATH VALLEY NATIONAL MONUMENT. The National Park Service maintains Lake Mead as a national recreation area (see LAKE MEAD).

State Parks. Nevada has a total of nine state parks, monuments, and recreational areas. The largest is the Valley of Fire, near Overton. The rocks in this park have been worn into odd shapes by the weather. For information on Nevada's state parks, write to Director, State Park Commission, State Capitol Building, Carson City, Nev. 89701.

ANNUAL EVENTS

The Helldorado Rodeo in Las Vegas is perhaps Nevada's most exciting event. During this four-day celebration in May, men and women wear Old-West costumes for parades and street dances. Other annual events in Nevada include the following.

January-March: University of Nevada Winter Carnival at Mount Rose (February); Spring Roundup in Ely (March).

April-June: Lake Mead Yacht Club Flotilla (mid-April); Horse Show in Henderson (late April); Pony Express Race in Carson City (May); Silver State Stampede in Elko (June); Reno Rodeo (June).

July-September: July 4th Celebration in Ely; Pony Express Days in Ely (August); Nevada Rodeo in Winnemucca (Labor Day); County Fair in Elko (September); Stampede and '49er Show in Fallon (September).

October-December: Admission Day in Carson City (October 31); National Fast Draw Championship in Las Vegas (November); Lollipop Lane Parade at Lake Tahoe (Christmastime).

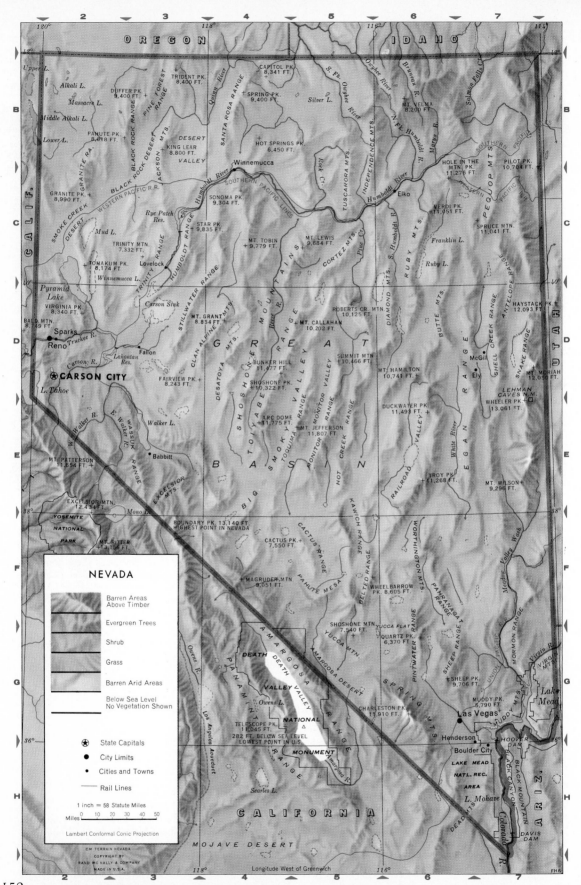

NEVADA

Barren Areas Above Timber

Evergreen Trees

Shrub

Grass

Barren Arid Areas

Below Sea Level No Vegetation Shown

★ State Capitals

● City Limits

• Cities and Towns

Rail Lines

1 inch = 58 Statute Miles

Miles 0 10 20 30 40 50

Lambert Conformal Conic Projection

CM TERRAIN NEVADA
COPYRIGHT BY
RAND McNALLY & COMPANY
MADE IN U.S.A.

Land Regions. Nevada lies almost entirely within the Great Basin, a huge desert area that extends into Oregon, Idaho, Wyoming, California, and Utah (see GREAT BASIN). The state has three main land regions: (1) the Columbia Plateau, (2) the Sierra Nevada, and (3) the Basin and Range Region.

The Columbia Plateau covers a small part of the northeastern corner of Nevada. Deep lava bedrock lies under the entire region. Streams and rivers have cut deep canyons, leaving steep ridges. The land flattens into open prairies near the Idaho border.

The Sierra Nevada, a rugged mountain range, cuts across a corner of the state west and south of Carson City. Lake Tahoe and other mountain lakes in this region attract many vacationers. See SIERRA NEVADA.

The Basin and Range Region covers the remainder of the state. It consists mainly of an upland area broken by more than 30 north-south mountain ranges. The towering Sierra Nevada marks part of the western edge of the region. The Toiyabe and Toquima ranges rise in the center of the state. In the east are the Snake and Toana ranges. Between the mountains lie *buttes* (lone hills) and *mesas* (tablelike mountains), as well as flat valleys with lakes or alkali flats (see BUTTE; MESA).

The elevation of the Basin and Range Region varies from less than 500 feet above sea level near the Colorado River to more than 13,000 feet in the southwest. Boundary Peak, the highest point in Nevada, rises 13,140 feet in Esmeralda County near the California border. Hot springs and geysers in many places show that Nevada is an area of dying volcanoes.

The southeastern tip of the Basin and Range Region is not part of the Great Basin. But the land here closely resembles that of the Great Basin.

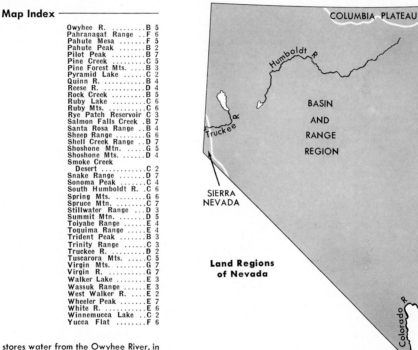

COLUMBIA PLATEAU

Humboldt R.

Truckee R.

BASIN AND RANGE REGION

SIERRA NEVADA

Land Regions of Nevada

Colorado R.

Nevada Highways & Parks Magazine

Wild Horse Reservoir stores water from the Owyhee River, in the lava-covered Columbia Plateau region of northeast Nevada.

Lake Tahoe, center of a famous resort area southwest of Carson City, lies in a valley in the Sierra Nevada Range. The lake is over 6,000 feet above sea level.

Grazing Cattle, such as these on a range in the Ruby Mountains, are a common sight in the Basin and Range Region. This upland region covers most of Nevada.

Rivers and Lakes. Most of Nevada's rivers are small and flow only during the wet season, from December to June. Only a few rivers have outlets to the sea. The Virgin and Muddy rivers join the Colorado in the southeastern tip of the state. The Owyhee (pronounced *oh WYE ee*), Bruneau, and Salmon flow northward across the Columbia Plateau to Idaho's Snake River.

All of Nevada's other rivers empty into the Great Basin. They flow into lakes without outlets or into wide, shallow *sinks* (low spots in the earth). In summer, the water evaporates from the sinks and leaves salty mud flats and dry lakes. The snow-fed Humboldt River is the longest river. It flows westward from the mountains of Elko County for about 300 miles. Then it vanishes into the Humboldt Sink. The Carson River winds northeastward from California and empties into Carson Sink.

The Walker River also rises in California and empties into Walker Lake. The scenic Truckee River flows from Lake Tahoe into Pyramid Lake.

Lake Tahoe, on the Nevada-California border, is one of the nation's loveliest lakes. Lamoille, Liberty, and other beautiful lakes lie among the peaks of the Ruby Range in Elko County. Ruby and Franklin lakes are at the eastern foot of the Ruby Range. Pyramid Lake and Walker Lake are the remains of Lake Lahontan, an ancient lake that gradually dried up. Thousands of years ago, Lake Lahontan covered about a tenth of the present state of Nevada.

Lake Mead, a man-made lake, is the only Nevada lake with an outlet to the sea. Engineers formed this vast reservoir by building Hoover Dam across a canyon of the Colorado River.

Nevada has an unusually dry climate with less rain than any other state. An average of only 7.4 inches of rain falls annually in Nevada. The driest regions include the southeastern tip of the state and the land near Carson Sink. These areas receive only about 4 inches of rain a year.

The rainiest parts of Nevada are in the Sierra Nevada and the eastern foothills of these mountains. As much as 25 inches of rain falls annually in the Lake Tahoe region of the Sierras. Nevada gets most of its rain during the winter. Clouds moving eastward from the Pacific Ocean bring the rain. But the clouds lose most of their moisture in California as they rise over the high Sierra Nevada. Snowfall varies from about 250 inches a year in the highest sections of the Sierra Nevada to about 1 inch in the southeastern part of the state.

Nevada has a wide range of temperatures. The north and the mountains in all sections have cold, long winters and short, hot summers. The west also has short, hot summers, but winters there are only mildly cold. In the south, summers are long and hot, and winters are mild enough to grow some kinds of fruit.

July temperatures average about 70° F. in the north and in the mountains, and 86° F. in the extreme south. January temperatures average 24° F. in the north and 43° F. in the south. The temperature often changes greatly during the day. In Reno, the temperature may change more than 45 degrees on a summer day. The highest temperature recorded in Nevada was 122° F. at Leeland on August 12 and 18, 1914, and at Overton on June 23, 1954. The temperature reached a record low of −50° F. at San Jacinto on January 8, 1937.

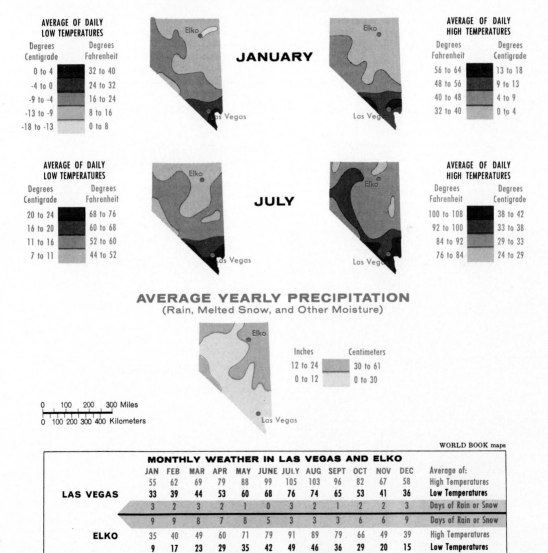

SEASONAL TEMPERATURES

JANUARY

AVERAGE OF DAILY LOW TEMPERATURES

Degrees Centigrade	Degrees Fahrenheit
0 to 4	32 to 40
-4 to 0	24 to 32
-9 to -4	16 to 24
-13 to -9	8 to 16
-18 to -13	0 to 8

AVERAGE OF DAILY HIGH TEMPERATURES

Degrees Fahrenheit	Degrees Centigrade
56 to 64	13 to 18
48 to 56	9 to 13
40 to 48	4 to 9
32 to 40	0 to 4

JULY

AVERAGE OF DAILY LOW TEMPERATURES

Degrees Centigrade	Degrees Fahrenheit
20 to 24	68 to 76
16 to 20	60 to 68
11 to 16	52 to 60
7 to 11	44 to 52

AVERAGE OF DAILY HIGH TEMPERATURES

Degrees Fahrenheit	Degrees Centigrade
100 to 108	38 to 42
92 to 100	33 to 38
84 to 92	29 to 33
76 to 84	24 to 29

AVERAGE YEARLY PRECIPITATION
(Rain, Melted Snow, and Other Moisture)

Inches	Centimeters
12 to 24	30 to 61
0 to 12	0 to 30

0   100   200   300 Miles

0   100 200 300 400 Kilometers

WORLD BOOK maps

MONTHLY WEATHER IN LAS VEGAS AND ELKO	JAN	FEB	MAR	APR	MAY	JUNE	JULY	AUG	SEPT	OCT	NOV	DEC	Average of:
LAS VEGAS	55	62	69	79	88	99	105	103	96	82	67	58	High Temperatures
	33	39	44	53	60	68	76	74	65	53	41	36	Low Temperatures
	3	2	3	2	1	0	3	2	1	2	2	3	Days of Rain or Snow
	9	9	8	7	8	5	3	3	3	6	6	9	Days of Rain or Snow
ELKO	35	40	49	60	71	79	91	89	79	66	49	39	High Temperatures
	9	17	23	29	35	42	49	46	36	29	20	15	Low Temperatures

Temperatures are given in degrees Fahrenheit.

Source: U.S. Weather Bureau

The tourist industry provides the greatest source of income in Nevada. The next highest sources of income are manufacturing, mining, and agriculture. Many of Nevada's mines and factories are controlled by individuals and corporations that have their headquarters in other states.

Natural Resources. Nevada's chief natural resources are its vast mineral deposits and beautiful scenery. In many areas, the poor soil and lack of water make it difficult or impossible to raise field crops. But thick grasses in the valleys provide grazing land for cattle.

Soil. Most of Nevada is covered with a gray soil containing large amounts of sodium carbonate. In most places, the soil has a heavy covering of underbrush. With irrigation, Nevada's soil can grow grain and other field crops. In some valleys, thick layers of sodium carbonate form gleaming white alkali flats, where nothing grows. These flats are sometimes called *dry lakes* because they may be covered with water after a rainstorm. Parts of western Nevada are covered by a reddish soil containing volcanic rocks washed down from the mountains. The northern section of the state has dark soil mixed with powdered lava.

Water. Nevada has a limited water supply because of its light rainfall. Water must be carefully conserved for personal needs and irrigation. Farmers and ranchers pump underground water for their crops and livestock in the Big Smoky, Diamond, Fish Lake, Las Vegas, Pahrump, Ruby, Smith, Spring, Truckee Meadows, and White River valleys. The largest irrigation systems operate along the rivers. The Newlands system includes the Lahontan Reservoir, which stores water from the Carson and Truckee rivers. It provides irrigation water for about 87,000 acres in Churchill and Lyon counties. Other large irrigation projects include Rye Patch Dam on the Humboldt River, Hoover Dam at the southeastern tip of the state, and Wild Horse Dam in the Owyhee River Valley.

Minerals. Huge deposits of copper lie in Lyon and White Pine counties. Mercury deposits, especially in Humboldt County, help make Nevada a national leader in mercury production. Ores containing manganese are found along the eastern edge of the state. Central and northwestern Nevada have large tungsten deposits. Gold and silver have been found in many parts of the state. Other mineral resources include antimony, barite, borax, clays, diatomite, fluorspar, iron ore, lead, magnesite, pumice, salt, and zinc. The state also has valuable deposits of gypsum, limestone, and sand and gravel. Petroleum has been found in some areas near the center of Nevada.

Forests in Nevada grow chiefly on the mountainsides.

Night Clubs in Reno, Las Vegas, and the Lake Tahoe area feature outstanding Broadway and Hollywood entertainers. Actor-singer Frank Sinatra, *left*, introduces baseball personality Leo Durocher during a performance in Las Vegas. Nevada's night life helps attract over 20 million visitors to the state annually.
The Sands Hotel

NEVADA'S PRODUCTION IN 1967

Total value of goods produced—$288,983,000

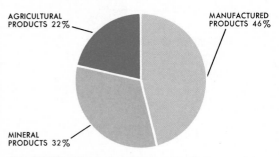

AGRICULTURAL PRODUCTS 22%

MANUFACTURED PRODUCTS 46%

MINERAL PRODUCTS 32%

Note: Manufacturing percentage based on value added by manufacture. Other percentages based on value of production.

Sources: U.S. Government statistics

NEVADA'S EMPLOYMENT IN 1967

Total number of persons employed—177,200

		Number of Employees
Services	🚶🚶🚶🚶🚶🚶	72,600
Government	🚶🚶🚶	31,700
Wholesale & Retail Trade	🚶🚶🚶	31,100
Transportation & Public Utilities	🚶	11,900
Construction	🚶	8,000
Manufacturing	🚶	6,900
Finance, Insurance & Real Estate	🚶	6,600
Agriculture	🚶	4,400
Mining	🚶	4,000

Source: U.S. Department of Labor

Commercially valuable trees include the Englemann spruce, lodgepole pine, mountain hemlock, ponderosa pine, red fir, sugar pine, and white fir. Alder, aspen, cottonwood, and willow trees thrive on the banks of mountain streams. Many juniper trees and piñon pines grow on the mountain slopes and in some valleys. Most of the valleys receive too little rain for trees to grow. Nevada's forests support only a small local lumber industry. But they help conserve water, and they provide wildlife preserves and recreational areas.

Plant Life. Nevada's deserts are dotted with cactus, yucca, and a variety of low brush plants. The most common desert plants include the bitter brush, mesquite, rabbit brush, sagebrush, and shadscale. Grasses grow in mountain and valley meadows. Nevada's meadows bloom in spring with Indian paintbrush, larkspur, shooting stars, and violets. In early spring, blood-red blossoms of the snow plant push through the snow in the pine forests. Wild peach blossoms and desert lilies brighten Nevada's foothills in spring and summer.

Animal Life. Nevada has few large animals, but hundreds of small animals live in the state. Mule deer roam the mountain forests. Pronghorns live mainly in the Charles Sheldon Antelope Refuge in Washoe County. Bighorn sheep climb the steep, rocky slopes of the Sheep Range in Clark County. Nevada's small animals include badgers, coyotes, foxes, minks, marmots, muskrats, porcupines, rabbits, and raccoons. A variety of lizards and snakes live in the desert. Game birds include chukar partridges, ducks, geese, pheasants, quail, and sage hens. Hundreds of white pelicans nest in the Anahoe Island Refuge in Pyramid Lake. Several kinds of trout make the state a favorite spot for fishermen. The *cui-ui* is a large sucker found only in Pyramid Lake. It was once an important food fish among the local Indians. Other fishes that swim in Nevada waters include bass, carp, catfish, and crappies.

Tourist Industry. Every year over 20 million visitors enjoy Nevada's night life, lovely scenery, and exciting sports. The tourist industry earns an annual income of about $732 million. Gambling is legal throughout the state. But about 90 per cent of the large casinos are in Las Vegas, Reno, and in the Lake Tahoe area. Forms of gambling include slot machines, blackjack, keno, poker, roulette, and dice games. Outstanding entertainers from Broadway, Hollywood, and Europe appear in floor shows at casinos and night clubs. Many restaurants and casinos never close. Signs announce "Breakfast Served All Day." Dude ranches, fishing resorts, and hunting lodges operate in many areas.

Manufacturing and Processing. Nevada has few industrial areas. The most important industrial activity is

Manufacturing and Processing Plants make Henderson a major industrial center of southern Nevada. Plants in Henderson refine titanium and produce lime, weedkiller, and other chemicals. Nevada has few large industrial areas. The state's main industrial activity is the processing of minerals and metals from its mines.

Desert Farming. Farmers near Eureka in central Nevada use overhead sprinklers to turn thousands of acres of wasteland into fertile fields of potatoes, grains, and other crops. Irrigated farms operate chiefly in northern, western, and southeastern Nevada.
Photos, Nevada Dept. of Economic Development

FARM AND MINERAL PRODUCTS

This map shows where the leading farm and mineral products are produced. The major urban areas (shown in red) are the important manufacturing centers.

0 25 50 75 100 Miles
0 50 100 150 Kilometers

WORLD BOOK map

Mercury
Gypsum
Tungsten
Beef Cattle
Hay
Gold
Sheep
Sheep
Beef Cattle
Gold
Tungsten
Iron Ore
Sheep
Silver
Lead
Wheat
Mercury
Gold
Beef Cattle
Tungsten
Silver
Copper
Silver
Beef Cattle
Poultry
Hogs
Barley
Silver
Sheep
Beryllium
Reno
Dairy
Gold
Grapes
Diatomite
Beef Cattle
Silver
Tungsten
Copper
Silver
Mercury
Gold
Poultry
Dairy Products
Barite
Gold
Vegetables
Tungsten
Copper
Hay
Potatoes
Sheep
Sheep
Silver
Mercury
Antimony
Oil
Silver
Barley
Gold
Tungsten
Gold
Zinc
Silver
Manganese
Copper
Silver
Gold
Grapes
Zinc
Lead
Magnesium
Manganese
Silver
Magnesium
Sand Gravel
Tungsten
Poultry
Gypsum
Gold
Dairy Products
Las Vegas
Fruit Products
Dairy Products
Vegetables
Cotton
Limestone
Grapes

Hoover Dam, one of the highest dams in the world, towers 726 feet from base to crest. It stands on the Colorado River, near the Arizona-Nevada border. The $120,000,000 dam was completed in 1936.

Fred Bond, Publix

the processing of Nevada's minerals. Nevada's industrial products have a value added by manufacture of about $134 million a year. This figure represents the value created in products by Nevada's industries, not counting such costs as materials, supplies, and fuels.

Copper mills and smelters operate near Yerington and in McGill. Plants in Henderson refine titanium and produce lime, weedkiller, and other chemicals. A kiln southwest of Battle Mountain separates mercury from its ores. Gypsum is crushed and graded near Lovelock. A factory near Las Vegas manufactures plaster and wallboard. Reno is a center of lumber milling, and also has meat-packing houses. Las Vegas and Reno also have large printing and publishing companies.

Mining in Nevada accounts for an income of about $91 million a year. Copper is Nevada's most valuable industrial mineral. Mines near Ely and Yerington produce most of the state's copper. Most of the ore comes from open-pit mines. Nevada's next most valuable mining product is gold. An open-pit gold mine began

operating near Carlin in 1965. Within two years, this mine ranked second only to the Homestake Mine in Lead, S. Dak., in the production of gold in the Western Hemisphere. An open-pit mine near Cortez also ranks among the most productive U.S. gold mines.

Sand and gravel are the third most valuable minerals produced in the state. Nevada ranks second only to California in the production of mercury. Most of the mercury mines are in the western part of the state.

Gypsum, used for insulation materials, plaster, and wallboard, comes from pits in Clark and Pershing counties. Clark County also has a special sand used in making glass. Quarries in many sections produce building stone. Petroleum comes from Nye County. Other minerals include antimony, barite, clays, fluorspar, lead, magnesite, pumice, salt, silver, tungsten, and zinc. Nevada is developing its iron mines and its stores of *diatomite* or *diatomaceous earth* (see DIATOM).

Agriculture provides an annual income of about $64 million in Nevada. Livestock ranching is the chief

154d

agricultural activity. Ranches average 4,650 acres in size, but the largest ones cover as much as 275,000 acres. Farmers must depend on irrigation to raise field crops, but irrigation water reaches less than 2 per cent of the state. Most farms in the irrigated regions cover only about 260 acres.

Livestock and Poultry. Most of Nevada's large cattle and sheep ranches are in Elko, Humboldt, Lander, and White Pine counties. Many ranchers graze their animals for part of the year on public lands that they rent from the federal government. Ranchers sell most of their cattle to farmers in Nevada, California, and the Midwest for fattening. Stockmen also sell sheep and lambs to meat packers, and wool to textile mills. Riding horses are raised in many parts of the state. Churchill County produces turkeys. Milk and butter come from Yerington and the Reno and Las Vegas areas.

Crops. Irrigated farms operate chiefly near the river valleys of northern, western, and southeastern Nevada. Irrigated farming projects are being developed in central and northern Nevada. Water for these projects comes from wells. Nevada's chief crops include alfalfa seed, barley, cotton, hay, oats, and wheat. Nevada ranks fifth among the states in alfalfa seed production. Farmers use about 60 per cent of their hay and grain crops for livestock feed. Cotton, grapes, and melons come from farms in the southeast. Farmers also grow melons in Churchill County. Vegetables grown in Nevada include lettuce, onions, potatoes, radishes, and tomatoes. Greenhouse and nursery products are also chief sources of farm income in Nevada.

Electric Power. Fuel-burning steam plants provide about 60 per cent of Nevada's electric power. Hydroelectric plants generate the rest. The Davis and Hoover dams on the Colorado River provide almost all the electricity for the southern and southeastern sections of the state. Small irrigation dams supply electric power in the north and west. Steam-powered plants operate near Las Vegas and Reno, and in east-central Nevada. For Nevada's kilowatt-hour production, see ELECTRIC POWER (table).

Transportation. Several transcontinental airlines serve Nevada and connect with routes of a local airline. Ranchers and farmers own most of the more than 40 private airfields in the state. Railroads operate on about 1,600 miles of track in Nevada. Three major railroads serve the state. The state has about 48,000 miles of roads and highways, of which about a third are surfaced.

Communication. Nevada's first newspaper, the *Territorial Enterprise*, was established at Genoa in 1858. Mark Twain worked as a reporter on this daily paper from 1862 to 1864, after the paper was moved to Virginia City. The paper is now published weekly in Virginia City as the *Territorial Enterprise and Virginia City News*. More than 25 newspapers are published in Nevada, including 15 weeklies. Daily newspapers with the largest circulations include the *Las Vegas Review-Journal*, the *Las Vegas Sun*, Reno's *Nevada State Journal*, and the *Reno Evening Gazette*.

Nevada has about 25 radio stations and 7 television stations. The state's first radio station, KOH, began broadcasting from Reno in 1928. The first television stations, KOLO-TV in Reno and KLAS-TV in Las Vegas, began operations in 1953.

Indian Days. Some of the earliest American Indians lived in the Nevada region. Bones, ashes, and other remains discovered near Las Vegas indicate that Indians may have lived there more than 20,000 years ago. Cave-dwelling Indians left picture writings on rocks in southern Nevada. Basket Makers once lived at Lovelock Cave, and Pueblo Indians lived around Las Vegas. Explorers of the early 1800's found Mohave, Paiute, Shoshoni, and Washoe Indians in parts of the region.

Exploration. Francisco Garcés, a Spanish missionary, probably was the first white man to enter the Nevada region. He may have traveled through southern Nevada while journeying from New Mexico to California in 1775 or 1776. Fur traders and trappers began to explore the region between 1825 and 1830. Peter S. Ogden explored the Humboldt River valley with a group of trappers of the Hudson's Bay Company (see HUDSON'S BAY COMPANY). Jedediah S. Smith led some trappers across the Las Vegas valley region into California and then back across the Great Basin.

In 1830, William Wolfskill blazed a route, called the Old Spanish Trail, from Santa Fe to Los Angeles. This trail opened Nevada to trade from the southeast. Trapper Joseph Walker blazed a trail along the Humboldt River on his way to California in 1833. Hundreds of wagons rolled westward over this same trail after gold was discovered in California in 1848. Between 1843 and 1845, Lieutenant John C. Frémont explored the Great Basin and Sierra Nevada. Frémont provided the first accurate knowledge of the Nevada region.

Early Settlement. At the end of the Mexican War in 1848, the United States acquired the Nevada region from Mexico. Nevada was then part of a territory that also included California, Utah, and parts of four other states (see MEXICAN WAR [The Peace Treaty]).

In 1849, the Mormon leader Brigham Young organized Utah, most of present-day Nevada, and parts of other present-day states as the State of Deseret. He asked Congress to admit his state to the Union. But in 1850, Congress established the Utah Territory, including Utah and most of present-day Nevada. President Millard Fillmore appointed Young governor of the territory.

In 1851, Mormons from the Great Salt Lake area in Utah built a trading post at Mormon Station (now Genoa) in the Carson Valley. The post supplied provisions for gold seekers heading for California. During the next few years, a few Mormon families came to farm and raise livestock in the Carson Valley and the surrounding region. This section of Utah Territory was organized into Carson County.

Many non-Mormons in Carson County did not want to be governed by Brigham Young. They pleaded unsuccessfully with Congress to make Carson County part of California. The Mormons themselves were troubled by a dispute with the federal government. In 1857, Young recalled the Mormon settlers to Great Salt Lake because he feared that federal troops would attack them. Two years later, the non-Mormons set up a provisional government in an attempt to establish Carson County as a separate territory. But Congress did not authorize the provisional government because only a few hundred persons lived in the Carson County area.

Gridley Sack of Flour. In 1864, R. C. Gridley of Austin collected $275,000 by auctioning a single sack of flour over and over again. He gave all the money to the U.S. Sanitary Commission, forerunner of the American Red Cross.

Trail Blazers. A monk named Francisco Garcés made the first known crossing of Nevada in 1775. Jedediah Smith followed in 1826, and William Wolfskill arrived in 1830.

John C. Frémont mapped Nevada during trips across the region from 1843 to 1845. Kit Carson guided the expeditions.

• Virginia City

★
CARSON CITY

The Comstock Lode, a rich deposit of gold and silver, was discovered at the present site of Virginia City in 1859. Prospectors flocked to the area.

First Federal Irrigation Project, called *The Newlands Project,* was completed in 1907 along Nevada's Carson and Truckee rivers.

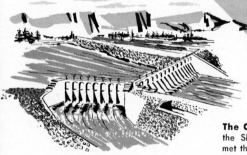

The Central Pacific cut 15 tunnels through the Sierras into Nevada in the 1860's. It met the Union Pacific tracks in Utah, forming the country's first transcontinental railroad.

The Nevada Proving Ground of the Atomic Energy Commission began nuclear tests in 1951 at Yucca and Frenchman flats.

Hoover Dam was completed in 1936. Its 115-mile-long reservoir, Lake Mead, is one of the largest man-made lakes in the world.

HISTORIC NEVADA

The Comstock Lode, a rich deposit of silver ore, was discovered in 1859 at the present site of Virginia City. Henry Comstock, a prospector, took credit for the discovery, although other miners had found the ore. News of the Comstock Lode quickly spread to fortune hunters in California and the East. Hundreds of prospectors rushed to Carson County to "strike it rich." They settled in tents, rough stone huts, and hillside caves. Almost overnight, Virginia City became a thriving mining center.

The settlers led a difficult and dangerous life. They paid unbelievably high prices for provisions that had to be hauled from California over the Sierra Nevada. Some miners became millionaires. But many others found little or no wealth. Many mining camps were lawless, and many miners were rowdies or gunmen.

Nevada Becomes a Territory. By 1860, the booming mining camps of Carson County held more than 6,700 persons. In March, 1861, President James Buchanan signed an act creating the Nevada Territory. President Abraham Lincoln, who took office two days later, appointed James W. Nye, a New York City politician, governor of the territory.

The Civil War (1861-1865) began before Nevada's territorial government could be set up in Carson City. The war gave Nevada's rich mineral resources new importance. Both the North and the South needed silver and gold to pay the costs of the war. President Lincoln wanted Nevada's valuable minerals to help the Union. Also, most Nevadans favored the North. Lincoln needed another "northern" state to support his proposed antislavery amendments. At the time, the Nevada Territory had far less than the 127,381 residents required by law to become a state. But Nevadans held a convention anyway and drew up a state constitution.

Statehood. The convention met in November, 1863, but ended in failure. The voters rejected the proposed constitution because of its provisions for the taxing of mines. Congress then passed an act authorizing a second Nevada convention. In July, 1864, this convention met and completed its work. In September, the revised constitution won the approval of the voters. The people elected Republican Henry G. Blasdel, a mining engineer, their first governor. President Lincoln proclaimed Nevada a state on Oct. 31, 1864.

Mine Failure and Recovery. In the 1870's, mining companies dug the richest silver ore from Nevada's mines. Some of the state's mines produced only "low-grade" ores that contained small amounts of silver. Mine owners made a profit on these ores because silver had a high value.

During the early 1870's, the U.S. government limited the use of silver in its money system. As the government's demand for silver fell, the value of silver also dropped. Many mines closed because they could no longer produce low-grade ores at a profit. Unemployed persons began to leave Nevada by the thousands to find work elsewhere. The state's population dropped from 62,266 in 1880 to 47,355 in 1890. Several thriving communities became ghost towns.

As mining failed, ranching grew in importance. But the ranchers also faced difficult problems. They had to pay the railroad extremely high rates to ship their stock. In addition, severe winters in the late 1880's killed thousands of cattle. Many owners of small herds became bankrupt and had to sell out to operators of large ranches.

Economic recovery began with new mineral discoveries in 1900. Prospectors found huge deposits of silver at Tonopah. They could be mined profitably, although silver still had a low value. Prospectors uncovered copper ores at Ely, Ruth, and Mountain City. In 1902, gold was discovered at Goldfield. Rich deposits discovered the next year brought thousands of miners rushing back to Nevada.

As the mining industry came to life again, the railroads built branch lines to the mining areas. Trains brought equipment to the mines and hauled ore away to processing plants. Cattlemen also used the new branch lines for speedy beef shipments.

Nevada's Newlands Irrigation Project, the country's first federal irrigation project, was completed in 1907. In this project, dams along the Carson and Truckee rivers create irrigation reservoirs and generate electricity. Water from this system supplies an agricultural region that developed near Fallon in west-central Nevada.

The richest of Nevada's gold and silver deposits were running out when the United States entered World War I in 1917. Industries then began to demand copper, tungsten, zinc, and other metals for weapons and wartime supplies. Many new mines opened in Nevada, and mine owners collected top prices for the metals. But prices fell after the war, and many mines closed.

In 1928, Congress authorized the construction of

--- **IMPORTANT DATES IN NEVADA** ---

1775-76 Francisco Garcés, a friar, was probably the first white man to enter the Nevada region.

1825-30 Peter S. Ogden discovered the Humboldt River. Jedediah S. Smith crossed southern Nevada.

1843-45 John C. Frémont and Kit Carson explored the Great Basin and Sierra Nevada.

1848 The United States received Nevada and other lands in the Southwest from Mexico under the Treaty of Guadalupe Hidalgo.

1859 The discovery of silver near Virginia City brought a rush of prospectors to western Nevada.

1861 Congress created the Nevada Territory.

1864 Nevada became the 36th state on October 31.

1877-81 The price of silver fell and caused many Nevada mines to close.

1880-90 Unemployed persons left Nevada and the population dropped by almost 15,000.

1909 The Nevada legislature passed laws making gambling illegal. The laws went into effect in 1910.

1931 The legislature reduced the divorce residence requirement to six weeks. The legislature also made gambling legal in the state.

1936 Boulder (now Hoover) Dam was completed.

1951 The Atomic Energy Commission began testing nuclear weapons in southern Nevada.

1963 The Supreme Court of the United States settled a 40-year dispute by specifying how much water the states of Arizona, California, and Nevada could draw from the Colorado River.

1967 The Nevada legislature changed state gambling laws to allow corporations that sell stock to the public to buy casinos and to hold gambling licenses.

Homes and Schools on the outskirts of Las Vegas serve employees of the Atomic Energy Commission (AEC). During the 1950's, the AEC began testing nuclear weapons near Las Vegas. These research projects have boosted the area's economy.

Boulder (now Hoover) Dam on the Colorado River. Work on the dam began in 1930. The huge project was completed in 1936. Hoover Dam provides power and stores up irrigation water for parts of Nevada, Arizona, and California.

Legal Gambling and Easy Divorce. As early as 1869, Nevada's legislature had permitted gamblers to operate games of chance in the state. By 1910, various groups of citizens had succeeded in having laws passed against gambling. But gamblers continued to operate illegally, and enforcement of the gambling laws required large amounts of money. Finally, the legislature decided it would be better to legalize gambling than to spend money trying to stop it. In 1931, Nevada made gambling legal. Many gambling establishments began to operate during the 1930's.

In the early 1900's, Nevada had passed laws that made it easy to get a divorce. A person had to live in Nevada for only six months to get a divorce there. In 1927, the Nevada legislature passed a law allowing persons to obtain a divorce if they lived in the state for only three months. In 1931, the period was reduced to six weeks. Every year, thousands of persons go to Nevada to get divorces quickly and easily.

The Mid-1900's. World War II (1939-1945) created new business for Nevada's mining industry. Manufacturers of military supplies purchased large amounts of the state's copper, lead, magnesite, manganese, tungsten, and zinc. After the war, mining activities decreased. The industry gradually switched to the production of gypsum, lime, and other nonmetallic minerals.

In the late 1940's, Nevada began a widespread campaign to attract new industry. Although the campaign brought a number of factories into the state, Nevada's economy during the 1950's and 1960's depended chiefly on nuclear research and tourism.

In 1950, the Atomic Energy Commission (AEC) established a testing center about 60 miles northwest of Las Vegas. The next year, the AEC began testing nuclear weapons, and in 1962 it began a program to develop peaceful uses of atomic energy.

Tourism remained Nevada's largest and fastest-growing industry during the 1950's and 1960's. By the late 1960's, the Las Vegas area alone attracted annually about 15 million tourists, who spent about $400 million. Tourists also flocked to the state's two other main resort centers, Reno and the Lake Tahoe area.

In the late 1950's, the Nevada legislature set up strict gambling regulations to prevent cheating and to stop criminals from entering or influencing the gambling industry. The regulations require every gambling house to have a state license, which is issued only after investigation by the Gaming Control Board and final approval by the Gaming Commission. In 1967, the legislature passed a law allowing corporations that sell stock to the public to hold gambling licenses. The new law was a further attempt to keep the underworld out of the gambling industry.

In 1963, the Supreme Court of the United States settled a 40-year dispute between Arizona, California, and Nevada over water supplies from the Colorado River. The court ruled on how much water each state could draw from the river every year.

In 1966, Howard Hughes, an American businessman and one of the world's richest men, moved to Las Vegas. He then bought airports, casinos and hotels, large tracts of land, and a television station in the area.

Nevada Today continues to depend heavily on the tourist industry. In addition, the state is looking forward to and planning for further growth of tourism in the 1970's. Nevada's tourist industry, however, depends on the prosperity of the nation.

With the expected increase in tourism, the Las Vegas and Reno-Lake Tahoe areas will continue their rapid growth. Already, more than four-fifths of the people of Nevada live in the Las Vegas and Reno metropolitan areas. Rural influence in the state legislature is expected

THE GOVERNORS OF NEVADA		
	Party	**Term**
1. Henry G. Blasdel	Republican	1864-1871
2. Lewis R. Bradley	Democratic	1871-1879
3. John H. Kinkead	Republican	1879-1883
4. Jewett W. Adams	Democratic	1883-1887
5. Charles C. Stevenson	Republican	1887-1890
6. Frank Bell	Republican	1890-1891
7. Roswell K. Colcord	Republican	1891-1895
8. John E. Jones	Silver	1895-1896
9. Reinhold Sadler	Silver	1896-1903
10. John Sparks	Silver-Dem.*	1903-1908
11. Denver S. Dickerson	Silver-Dem.	1908-1911
12. Tasker L. Oddie	Republican	1911-1915
13. Emmet D. Boyle	Democratic	1915-1923
14. James G. Scrugham	Democratic	1923-1927
15. Fred B. Balzar	Republican	1927-1934
16. Morley Griswold	Republican	1934-1935
17. Richard Kirman, Sr.	Democratic	1935-1939
18. Edward P. Carville	Democratic	1939-1945
19. Vail M. Pittman	Democratic	1945-1951
20. Charles H. Russell	Republican	1951-1959
21. Grant Sawyer	Democratic	1959-1967
22. Paul Laxalt	Republican	1967-1971
23. Mike O'Callaghan	Democratic	1971-

*Silver-Democratic

to end in the 1970's as Nevada becomes basically a "two-city state."

Las Vegas and Reno are planning better airport and ground transportation facilities to accommodate the increased number of tourists expected to arrive in the 1970's on jumbo jets. In 1967, the Southern Nevada Water Project was created to provide increased water supplies for the expected growth in the Las Vegas area. The $80-million project, which will bring water from Lake Mead, was scheduled for completion in 1971.

Nevada cities face major problems as their populations continue to increase. Many of these problems will require help from the state government. City dwellers are demanding better police and fire protection, improvements in education, better recreational facilities, and other services. Nevada Negroes feel that they do not have equal job opportunities. They also want a state open housing law. Air and water pollution has also become a serious problem in Nevada. In one program to control water pollution, Nevada has joined with California in the Tahoe Regional Planning Compact to fight pollution of Lake Tahoe.

JAMES W. HULSE, E. R. LARSON, and JAMES M. LEAVY

NEVADA/Study Aids

Related Articles in WORLD BOOK include:

BIOGRAPHIES

Beebe, Lucius M.	McCarran, Patrick A.
Carson, Kit	Pittman, Key
Frémont, John C.	Smith, Jedediah S.
Hughes, Howard R.	Wovoka
Mackay (John W.)	Young, Brigham

CITIES AND TOWNS

Carson City	Goldfield	Reno
Elko	Henderson	Tonopah
Ely	Las Vegas	Virginia City

HISTORY

Comstock Lode	Mexican War
Guadalupe Hidalgo,	Mormons
Treaty of	Western Frontier Life

PHYSICAL FEATURES

Boundary Peak	Great Basin	Lake Tahoe
Colorado River	Humboldt River	Sierra Nevada
Desert	Lake Mead	

OTHER RELATED ARTICLES

Copper (table)	Lehman Caves National
Death Valley National	Monument
Monument	Nevada, University of
Gold (table)	Ranching
Hoover Dam	Rocky Mountain States
Irrigation	

Outline

I. Government
  A. Constitution
  B. Executive
  C. Legislature
  D. Courts
  E. Local Government
  F. Taxation
  G. Politics

II. People

III. Education
  A. Schools
  B. Libraries
  C. Museums

IV. A Visitor's Guide
  A. Places to Visit
  B. Annual Events

V. The Land
  A. Land Regions
  B. Rivers and Lakes

VI. Climate

VII. Economy
  A. Natural Resources
  B. Tourist Industry
  C. Manufacturing and Processing

  D. Mining
  E. Agriculture
  F. Electric Power
  G. Transportation
  H. Communication

VIII. History

Questions

Where are about 90 per cent of Nevada's large gambling casinos?

Why did some Nevada mining communities become ghost towns during the 1880's?

How does Nevada's "free port" law attract new industries to the state?

From what country did the United States receive the land that includes the present state of Nevada?

What is Nevada's most valuable mining product?

How many degrees may the temperature change in Reno on a summer day?

Why did President Abraham Lincoln support statehood for Nevada?

What is Nevada's most important industry?

What is the longest river in Nevada? Where does this river stop flowing and disappear?

Why does Nevada enforce strict gambling regulations?

Books for Young Readers

CARPENTER, ALLEN. *Nevada from Its Glorious Past to the Present.* Children's Press, 1964.

MONTGOMERY, RUTHERFORD G. *The Silver Hills.* World Publishing Co., 1958. Virginia City in the 1860's.

UNDERHILL, RUTH. *Antelope Singer.* Coward-McCann, 1961. A family's winter with Paiute Indians.

Books for Older Readers

BEEBE, LUCIUS M. *Comstock Commotion: The Story of The Territorial Enterprise and Virginia City News.* Stanford Univ. Press, 1954. With C. M. CLEGG: *Legends of the Comstock Lode.* 5th ed. 1956; *Steamcars to the Comstock.* 3rd ed. Howell-North, 1960.

BUSHNELL, ELEANORE. *The Nevada Constitution: Origin and Growth.* Univ. of Nevada Press, 1965.

HULSE, JAMES W. *The Nevada Adventure: A History.* Univ. of Nevada Press, 1965.

LEIGH, RUFUS W. *Nevada Place Names—Their Origin and Significance.* Deseret Book Co., Salt Lake City, 1964.

Nevada: A Guide to the Silver State. Binfords, 1940.

THOMPSON, THOMAS H., and WEST, A. A. *History of Nevada.* Howell-North, 1958. A new edition of a book first published in 1881.

TWAIN, MARK (pseud. of SAMUEL L. CLEMENS). *Roughing It.* Rinehart, 1953. A reprint of the book originally published in 1872.

WRIGHT, WILLIAM. *The Big Bonanza.* Knopf, 1947. A reprint of a contemporary account of the Comstock Lode.

NEVADA, UNIVERSITY OF

NEVADA, UNIVERSITY OF, is a state-supported, co-educational institution. It has campuses in Reno and Las Vegas. The Reno campus offers bachelor's, master's, and doctor's degrees. It has colleges of arts and science, business administration, education, and engineering; schools of agriculture, home economics, mines, and nursing; and a graduate school. The Reno campus also has a summer session. Established in 1864, it became a four-year college in 1886. The Las Vegas campus offers bachelor's and master's degrees. It has schools of business, education, fine arts, humanities, social science, and science and mathematics. It was established in 1951, and became a four-year college in 1964. For the university's enrollment, see UNIVERSITIES AND COLLEGES (table). NEIL D. HUMPHREY

NEVADA FALLS is a waterfall in Yosemite National Park, California. This 594-foot drop of the Merced River represents a step in the "Giant's Stairway" as the river descends 2,000 feet in a distance of 1½ miles from Little Yosemite Valley to Yosemite Valley proper. Indians named it *twisted fall*, because a rock ledge spreads the fall's water spray to one side. JOHN W. REITH

NÉVÉ. See GLACIER (Structure).

NEVELSON, LOUISE (1900-), is an American sculptor. She is best known for her *assemblages*, often grouped within boxlike frames. Many of the large black walls of her compartments express a feeling of quiet and majesty. Most of her assemblages are made out of wood that is painted either black or gold or left in the natural color. She also experimented with other materials. Miss Nevelson has constructed "total environments" of everyday "found" objects and utensils, strips of molding, woodwork decorations, or Victorian debris that form powerful unified wholes.

Louise Nevelson was born in Kiev, Russia, and came to the United States in 1905. She studied painting at the Art Students League in New York City. DOUGLAS GEORGE

Louise Nevelson's *Black Zag B* is typical of the complex and mysterious large wooden constructions that have made her famous.

Black Zag B (1968) by Louise Nevelson, Pace Gallery, New York City

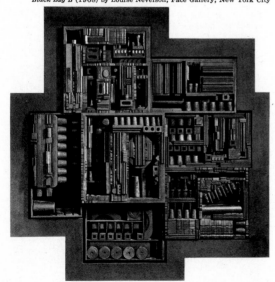

NEVILLE, EMILY CHENEY (1919-), is an American author. She won the 1964 Newbery medal for her first book *It's Like This, Cat* (1963), a story about a boy and a cat in New York City. Emily Neville was born in Manchester, Conn. She was graduated from Bryn Mawr College in 1940.

NEVIN, *NEV in,* **ETHELBERT WOODBRIDGE** (1862-1901), an American composer, was known for his songs and piano pieces. His music is trivial, but charming. He wrote "The Rosary" (1898), one of the most successful songs ever written. He also wrote "Little Boy Blue" (1891), "Venetian Love Song" (1898), and "Mighty Lak' a Rose" (1901). His most popular piano piece is "Narcissus" (1891). He was born in Edgeworth, Pa., and studied music in Europe. GILBERT CHASE

NEVINS, *NEV inz,* **ALLAN** (1890-1971), an American historian and educator, twice was awarded the Pulitzer prize for biography. *Grover Cleveland: A Study in Courage* won the prize in 1933, and *Hamilton Fish: The Inner History of the Grant Administration* received the award in 1937. He won the Bancroft prize and the Scribner Centenary prize for *The Ordeal of the Union* (1947). Nevins' works are noted for being well balanced and thorough, with a distinctive literary style.

His *John D. Rockefeller,* a biography published in 1940, became very popular. It was revised and republished in 1953 as *Study in Power: John D. Rockefeller, Industrialist and Philanthropist.* Nevins and Frank Ernest Hill completed *Ford: the Times, the Man, the Company,* a study of Henry Ford, in 1954.

In addition to his histories and biographies, Nevins also edited collections of the letters of noted historical persons. He published his first book, *Life of Robert Rogers,* in 1914, and followed it with more than 50 other volumes. His other books include *The American States During and After the Revolution* (1924), *Frémont: The West's Greatest Adventurer* (1927), *A Brief History of the United States* (1942), *The Emergence of Lincoln* (1950), and *Herbert H. Lehman and His Era* (1963).

Columbia University
Allan Nevins

Born in Camp Point, Ill., Nevins was graduated from the University of Illinois. He wrote editorials for the *New York Evening Post* from 1913 to 1923. Nevins joined the staff of the *New York Sun* in 1924, and the *New York World* in 1925. He was a professor of history at Cornell University from 1927 to 1928, and at Columbia University from 1931 to 1958. In 1958, he became a senior fellow of research at the Henry E. Huntington Library in San Marino, Calif.

Nevins lectured on American history at several universities in other nations. He served as a special representative for the Office of War Information in Australia and New Zealand in 1943 and 1944, during World War II. MERLE CURTI

NEVIS, BEN. See BEN NEVIS.

NEVUS. See BIRTHMARK.

NEW AMSTERDAM. See NEW YORK CITY (History).

NEW BAHAMA CHANNEL. See FLORIDA, STRAITS OF.

NEW BEDFORD, Mass. (pop. 101,777; met. area pop. 152,642; alt. 15 ft.), once the whaling capital of the world, is a textile center in southeastern Massachusetts. The city lies about 56 miles south of Boston, where the Acushnet River empties into Buzzards Bay. For location, see MASSACHUSETTS (political map).

The city's harbor and mild, damp climate provide favorable conditions for textile manufacturing, and New Bedford ranks high in cotton goods production. Other products include shoes and electrical equipment, glass and rayon fabrics, rubber, and copper products. Many fishing vessels use the port of New Bedford. It is also an important trade and distribution center for southeastern Massachusetts.

The first settlement on the site of New Bedford was made in 1652 on land purchased from Massasoit, chief of the Wampanoag Indians, by a company from Plymouth. It was named in honor of the Duke of Bedford's family. During the Revolutionary War, the New Bedford port harbored privateers that attacked British ships. British troops invaded the town in 1778, burning the homes, business places, and vessels of many American patriots. But the people soon rebuilt New Bedford, and it received its town charter in 1787.

New Bedford launched its whaling industry in the 1760's. Whaling prospered until 1859, when the discovery of petroleum in Pennsylvania ruined the whale oil industry. The Whaling Museum and the New Bedford Public Library exhibit mementos of whaling days in New Bedford. The Wamsutta Mills, the city's first major textile plant, started in 1846. A textile boom in the 1880's established New Bedford as a leading manufacturer of cotton fabrics. New Bedford received its city charter in 1847. It has a mayor-council form of government.   WILLIAM J. REID

NEW BERN, N.C. (pop. 14,660; alt. 15 ft.), is the second oldest city in the state. It lies at the point where the Trent and Neuse rivers meet, about 35 miles from the Atlantic Ocean (see NORTH CAROLINA [political map]). Until 1776, New Bern was the capital of the North Carolina colony, and a leading port. The coming of the railroads, the lack of a deep harbor, and the coastal dangers lessened New Bern's importance.

New Bern was founded in 1710 by Baron Cristoph von Graffenried of Switzerland and German Palatines, who had left their homes to escape religious persecution. Tryon's Palace, the colonial capital, has been restored. Thousands of servicemen were stationed at nearby Camp Lejeune and Cherry Point Marine Corps Air Station during World War II. New Bern, named for Bern, Switzerland, is the seat of Craven County. It has a council-manager government.   HUGH T. LEFLER

NEW BRITAIN is the largest island in the Bismarck Archipelago. The island lies off the northeast coast of New Guinea. New Britain is governed by Australia as part of the United Nations Trust Territory of New Guinea. Rabaul is the administrative center and chief port of New Britain.

New Britain is about 300 miles long, but only about 50 miles wide. It covers an area of 14,100 square miles. A range of volcanic mountains runs the length of the island, rising to 7,546 feet. There are many short rivers.

About 154,000 Melanesians live on the island. They are good fishermen and farmers, and have given up cannibalism. Most of the farming is done along the coasts.

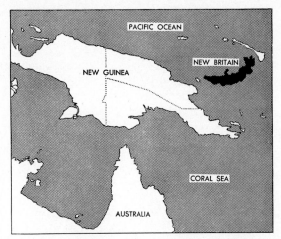

New Britain Island Lies East of New Guinea.

In 1700, the English navigator William Dampier discovered New Britain. In 1884, it became a part of the German Empire under the name of Neu Pommern. British forces took the island from Germany in 1914 during World War I. It was given to Australia as a mandate of the League of Nations in 1920. The Japanese captured Rabaul in 1942, during World War II. They held the Rabaul area until 1945. During this time, Allied forces attacked the Japanese in New Britain. Bombing raids destroyed most of Rabaul, but the city was rebuilt.   EDWIN H. BRYAN, JR.

See also BISMARCK ARCHIPELAGO; SCULPTURE (Pacific Islands; picture: An Owl Mask).

NEW BRITAIN, Conn. (pop. 83,441; met. area pop. 145,269; alt. 200 ft.), often called the *Hardware City*, leads the nation in the production of builders' hardware and carpenters' tools. It lies in central Connecticut, about 10 miles southwest of Hartford. Factories produce ball bearings, automatic machinery, household appliances, electrical tools, and plumbing and heating supplies. For location, see CONNECTICUT (political map).

New Britain has more than 30 parks and public squares. The Art Museum of the New Britain Institute is widely known for its collection of American paintings. New Britain is also the home of Central Connecticut State College. The town was settled in 1687, and became a city in 1870. New Britain has a mayor-council type of government.   ALBERT E. VAN DUSEN

NEW BRUNSWICK, N.J. (pop. 41,885; alt. 45 ft.), is an educational and industrial center on the Raritan River about midway between Newark and Trenton (see NEW JERSEY [political map]). New Brunswick produces medical supplies, pharmaceuticals, machinery, cigars and cigar boxes, and clothing. During World War II, Camp Kilmer, located nearby, processed thousands of soldiers before they were sent to Europe.

In New Brunswick are Rutgers (the state university); Douglass College, which is part of Rutgers; the New Brunswick Theological Seminary; and the State Agricultural Experiment Station. The town became a transportation center early in its history. The Raritan River was part of the land-water route from New York City to Philadelphia. The city was chartered in 1730. It has a commission government. New Brunswick is the seat of Middlesex County.   RICHARD P. MCCORMICK

157

Nick Morant, Miller Services

Wild Flowers Brighten a Meadow at St. Andrews.

Fishermen on the Dock at Letite in Charlotte County
Hodgson, Miller Services

The contributors of this article are J. K. Chapman, Professor of History at the University of New Brunswick; Arnold L. McAllister, Chairman of the Department of Geology at the University of New Brunswick; and Stuart Trueman, editor of The Telegraph-Journal *and* The Evening Times-Globe *of Saint John.*

New Brunswick (blue) is eighth in size among Canada's provinces, and is second largest of the Atlantic, or Maritime, Provinces.

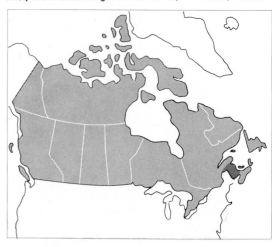

NEW BRUNSWICK

NEW BRUNSWICK is one of the four Atlantic Provinces of Canada. Forests cover about 85 per cent of the land in New Brunswick. The manufacture of lumber, paper, and other forest products ranks as the most important industry of New Brunswick. Saint John is New Brunswick's largest city and its chief industrial and shipping center. Fredericton is the capital.

Clear, swift rivers rush down the many hills and through the steep valleys of New Brunswick. Every spring, these rivers carry millions of logs from lumber camps in the thick forests to great pulp and paper mills. There, the wood is used to make *newsprint* (paper used in printing newspapers) and other paper products.

New Brunswick is in an era of industrial expansion. Prospectors discovered huge deposits of copper, lead, silver, and zinc in northeastern New Brunswick during the 1950's. To develop these resources, a vast industrial program was begun. This program included the construction of new mines, processing plants, shipping facilities, and a steel mill. The provincial government built its greatest hydroelectric plant to generate power for these industries.

New Brunswick has rich farmland in the St. John River Valley and other regions. Farmers produce large crops of potatoes and apples, and dairy farming is extensive. Lobsters are the most important catch in the waters off New Brunswick. Fishing fleets on the Bay of Fundy and the Gulf of St. Lawrence also make large hauls of cod, flounders, and sardines. The rivers and rolling woodlands of New Brunswick are among the best fishing and hunting grounds in North America.

In 1922, Andrew Bonar Law of New Brunswick became the only person born outside the British Isles to serve as prime minister of Great Britain. Richard B. Bennett, another New Brunswicker, became prime minister of Canada in 1930. Other well-known New Brunswickers include Bliss Carman, perhaps Canada's most famous poet; Sir Charles Roberts, an outstanding poet, novelist, and short-story writer; and Francis A. Anglin, chief justice of the supreme court of Canada. Lord Beaverbrook, who became a wealthy newspaper publisher and political power in Great Britain, spent most of his boyhood in New Brunswick.

New Brunswick was named for the British royal family of Brunswick-Lüneburg (the House of Hanover). Most of its early settlers were American colonists who had remained loyal to England during the American Revolutionary War. About 14,000 of these United Empire Loyalists, as they were called, began arriving in 1783. As a result, New Brunswick received the nickname of the *Loyalist Province*. It is also called the *Picture Province* because of its great natural beauty.

New Brunswick, along with Nova Scotia, Ontario, and Quebec, was one of the original provinces of Canada. For the relationship of New Brunswick to the other provinces, see ATLANTIC PROVINCES; CANADA; CANADA, GOVERNMENT OF; CANADA, HISTORY OF.

Hodgson, Miller Services

Falls of the Magaguadavic River at St. George

--------- FACTS IN BRIEF ---------

Capital: Fredericton.

Government: *Parliament*—members of the Senate, 10; members of the House of Commons, 10. *Provincial Legislature*—members of the Legislative Assembly, 58. *Counties*—15. *Voting Age*—18 years.

Area: 28,354 square miles (including 519 square miles of inland water), eighth in size among the provinces. *Greatest Distances*—(north-south) 230 miles; (east-west) 190 miles. *Coastline*—750 miles.

Elevation: *Highest*—Mount Carleton, 2,690 feet above sea level. *Lowest*—sea level, along the Atlantic Coast.

Population: *1966 Census*—616,788, eighth among the provinces; density, 22 persons to the square mile; distribution, 51 per cent urban, 49 per cent rural. *Estimated 1971 Population*—636,000.

Chief Products: *Agriculture*—apples, dairy products, livestock, oats, potatoes. *Manufacturing*—food products, lumber, pulp and paper. *Fishing Industry*—cod, flounders, lobsters, sardines. *Mining*—coal, copper, gypsum, lead, natural gas, peat moss, sand and gravel, silver, stone, zinc.

Entered the Dominion: July 1, 1867; one of the original four provinces.

Lieutenant-Governor of New Brunswick represents Queen Elizabeth in the province. He is appointed by the governor-general-in-council of Canada. The lieutenant-governor's position is largely honorary, like that of the governor-general.

Premier of New Brunswick is the actual head of the provincial government. The province, like the other provinces and Canada itself, has a *parliamentary* form of government. The premier is a member of the legislative assembly, where he is the leader of the majority party. The voters elect him as they do the other members of the assembly. The premier receives a salary of $20,000 a year, plus $12,000 if he heads a provincial department as a cabinet minister. For a list of all the premiers of New Brunswick, see the *History* section of this article.

The premier presides over the executive council, or cabinet. The council also includes ministers chosen by the premier from among his party's members in the legislative assembly. Each minister directs one or more departments of the provincial government. The executive council, like the premier, resigns if it loses the support of a majority of the assembly.

Legislative Assembly of New Brunswick is a one-house legislature that makes the provincial laws. It has 58 members elected from the province's counties and cities. Terms served by the members may last up to five years. However, the lieutenant-governor, on the advice of the premier, may call for an election before the end of the five-year period. If he does so, all members of the assembly, including the premier, must run again for office.

Courts. The highest court in New Brunswick is the supreme court. It is made up of three divisions: (1) appeal, (2) chancery, and (3) queen's bench. The appeal and chancery divisions have the same judges—the chief justice of New Brunswick and three *puisne* (associate) judges. The queen's bench division, which hears criminal cases, has a chief justice and four puisne judges. Each county has a county court.

Judges of the supreme court and county courts are appointed by the governor-general-in-council. They can serve until the age of 75. New Brunswick's minor courts include juvenile and magistrates' courts. Provincial authorities appoint officials of these courts.

Local Government changed throughout the province in 1967. The provincial government now assesses and collects local taxes, and administers all matters relating to education, health, welfare, and justice. City and town councils handle such things as streets, sewers, water service, and fire protection. All cities, towns, and villages have mayors and councils. The mayors and aldermen are elected to two-year terms. Some cities and towns also have managers.

Taxation provides about 40 per cent of the provincial government's income. A sales tax and a gasoline tax account for much of the tax money. New Brunswick also collects taxes on corporations and property. The province receives about 40 per cent of its income from federal-provincial tax-sharing arrangements and federal assistance. About 10 per cent comes from license and permit fees. Most other provincial income comes from the sale of liquor, which is under government control.

Politics. The major political parties of New Brunswick have always been the Liberal and the Progressive Conservative parties, or earlier forms of these groups. The Progressive Conservative party was formerly named the Conservative party, and today its members are

In the Assembly Chamber of New Brunswick's Legislative Building, a high throne symbolizes the British monarch. Sessions of the legislature are opened with a formal speech from the throne by the lieutenant-governor. The paintings next to the throne show King George III and his wife, Queen Charlotte. They were painted by Joshua Reynolds.

The Provincial Coat of Arms

The Provincial Flag

Symbols of New Brunswick. On the coat of arms, the British lion represents New Brunswick's ties with Great Britain. The ancient galley symbolizes the province's early shipbuilding industry. The coat of arms was adopted in 1868. The provincial flag, adopted in 1965, bears the same symbols as the coat of arms.

usually called simply Conservatives. The two parties have controlled the provincial government for about equal periods.

Newer political parties that have become popular in other provinces have received little support in New Brunswick. These groups include the New Democratic and Social Credit parties, which have tried to gain followers in New Brunswick.

The Floral Emblem
Purple Violet

The Legislative Building in Fredericton is built of limestone from nearby quarries. Landscaped grounds surround the stately three-story building. Fredericton has been the capital of New Brunswick since 1785. Some sessions of the legislature before 1788 were held in Saint John (then called Parrtown).

Hodgson, Miller Services

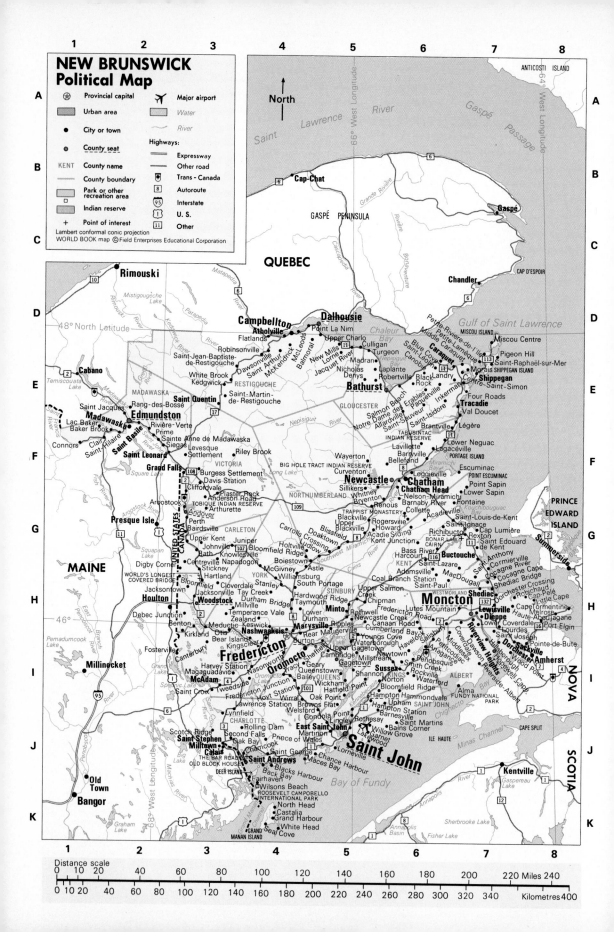

NEW BRUNSWICK MAP INDEX

Population

°County Seat.
*Does not appear on map; key shows general location.
Source: Latest census (1966)

Saint John, New Brunswick's Largest City, lies on the Bay of Fundy. The city's fine harbor is open all year, and ships from many parts of the world dock there. Saint John is the commercial and industrial center of the province.

New Brunswick Travel Bureau

Parade Watchers line a street in Shediac during the Lobster Festival. This annual event attracts visitors from many parts of New Brunswick. Lobstering is an important industry in the province.

NEW BRUNSWICK/*People*

The 1966 Canadian census reported that New Brunswick had 616,788 persons. The population had increased 3 per cent over the 1961 figure of 597,936. By 1971, New Brunswick had an estimated population of 636,000.

About half the people of New Brunswick live in cities and towns. About a sixth—101,192 persons—live in the metropolitan area of Saint John. Saint John has the province's only Census Metropolitan Area as defined by the Dominion Bureau of Statistics.

Besides Saint John, New Brunswick has six cities and towns with populations of more than 10,000. They are, in order of size, Moncton, Fredericton, Bathurst, Oromocto, Edmundston, and Campbellton. See the separate articles on the cities and towns of New Brunswick listed in the *Related Articles* at the end of this article.

More than 95 of every 100 New Brunswickers were born in Canada. Most of the others came from the United States or Great Britain. About 55 per cent of the people have English, Irish, or Scottish ancestors. Many of these persons are descended from *United Empire Loyalists* (persons loyal to England who left the United States after the Revolutionary War). About 40 per cent of the people have French ancestors, and about 10 per cent speak only French. Many New Brunswickers are of Dutch or German descent. The province also has about 4,000 Indians. Most of them live on reservations along the St. John River and its branches.

More than half the people of New Brunswick, and nearly all the French-speaking population, belong to the Roman Catholic Church. Other large religious groups are Baptists and members of the United Church of Canada and the Anglican Church of Canada.

Woodsman Guides Logs into a New Brunswick stream. The large lumber, paper, and wood pulp industries employ many workers to process logs from the province's vast forests.

Photos, New Brunswick Travel Bureau

POPULATION

This map shows the *population density* of New Brunswick, and how it varies in different parts of the province. Population density is the average number of persons who live on each square mile.

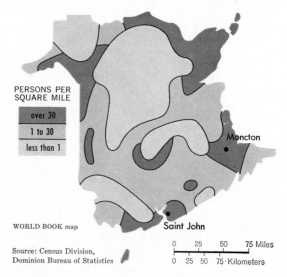

PERSONS PER SQUARE MILE

over 30

1 to 30

less than 1

Moncton

Saint John

WORLD BOOK map

Source: Census Division, Dominion Bureau of Statistics

| 0 | 25 | 50 | 75 Miles |
| 0 | 25 | 50 | 75 Kilometers |

The University of New Brunswick's Old Arts Building was completed in 1828. It is Canada's oldest university building.

NEW BRUNSWICK /*Education*

Schools. During the 1700's, most schooling in the New Brunswick region took place in private homes. Traveling schoolmasters conducted the classes, and school was held only a few months of the year. The first schoolhouses were built of logs. New Brunswick's first *grammar* (high) school was established in Saint John in 1805. In 1816, the colonial legislature provided by law for grammar schools in every county.

During the early 1800's, schools were supported partly by the colonial government and partly by churches and other groups. In 1871, the provincial government established a free public school system and ended all church control. The schools were supported by provincial grants and by county and local taxation. In 1936, the cabinet office of minister of education was created to head the department of education.

New Brunswick law requires children between the ages of 7 and 16 to attend school. The province has about 1,300 public schools. Some of them, in French-speaking areas such as Edmundston, conduct classes in French. For information on the number of students and teachers in New Brunswick, see EDUCATION (table).

Libraries. New Brunswick has seven main public libraries. The provincial legislative library is in Fredericton. Other outstanding libraries include the Bonar Law-Bennett Library of the University of New Brunswick in Fredericton, and the library of Mount Allison University in Sackville.

Museums. The New Brunswick Museum in Saint John is Canada's oldest museum. It was founded as a private museum in 1842, and became the provincial museum in 1930. It has fine cultural, historical, and scientific exhibits. The Miramichi Natural History Museum in Chatham specializes in wildlife. The York-Sunbury Historical Society operates a museum in Fredericton. The Lord Beaverbrook Art Gallery in Fredericton owns works by British and Canadian artists.

UNIVERSITIES

New Brunswick has three degree-granting universities, listed below. See the separate articles in WORLD BOOK on these institutions. For enrollments, see CANADA (table: Universities and Colleges).

Name	Location	Founded
Moncton, University of	Moncton	1963
Mount Allison University	Sackville	1858
New Brunswick, University of	Fredericton	1785

The New Brunswick Museum in Saint John is the oldest museum in Canada. It was founded in 1842. Visitors to the museum can see ship models in the Marine Section.

Annual Lobster Festival in Shediac

NEW BRUNSWICK / A Visitor's Guide

Thousands of visitors come to New Brunswick yearly. They enjoy boating and swimming off the beaches of the Bay of Fundy and the Gulf of St. Lawrence. The province's thick forests offer excellent camping facilities.

Sportsmen find New Brunswick one of the best fishing and hunting grounds in North America. Fishermen cast for fighting Atlantic salmon—the prize catch—and bass, pike, and trout. In autumn, the hunting season, hunters shoot bear, deer, rabbits, and moose. They also hunt various game birds.

PLACES TO VISIT

Following are brief descriptions of some of New Brunswick's many interesting places to visit.

Bonar Law Cairn is in Rexton. This monument honors Andrew Bonar Law, the only British prime minister born outside the British Isles.

Bore View Park, in Moncton, provides a good view of the famous, powerful tidal waves that rush up the Petitcodiac River from the Bay of Fundy.

Covered Bridge, over the St. John River in Hartland, is 1,282 feet long. It is believed to be the longest covered bridge in the world.

Islands in the Bay of Fundy. Campobello, Deer, and Grand Manan islands have excellent beaches, fine harbors for yachting, and colorful fishing villages.

Loyalist House, in Saint John, was built between 1810 and 1817 by David Merritt, a Loyalist from the United States. It was restored and opened in 1960.

Magnetic Hill, near Moncton, offers a remarkable optical illusion. An automobile, left in neutral gear near what appears to be the bottom of the hill, will seemingly roll uphill to the top.

Maliseet Indian Reservation, in Kingsclear, has exhibits of historic relics and Indian handicrafts.

Martello Tower, atop a hill in St. John, is a stone fortress built in 1812.

Mysterious Inscription in French appears on a rock near Albert. Translated, the inscription reads: "1822, May. To the North, 1505." Some persons think the rock marks the way to buried treasure.

Old Block House, in St. Andrews, was built during the War of 1812.

Old Government House, in Fredericton, is the former official residence of the lieutenant-governor of New Brunswick. This historic home was built in 1828.

Reversing Falls are formed at the mouth of the St. John River. High tide from the Bay of Fundy is so strong that it pushes the water backward over the falls.

Ride on the Floor of the Ocean is an automobile road over the ocean sands from St. Andrews to Minister's Island. It can be traveled only at low tide.

Rogersville, in Kent County, has a Trappist monastery. The monks operate a lumber industry and process wool for spinning.

Rocks, at Hopewell Cape in Albert County, rise in fantastic forms, carved by the Bay of Fundy tides.

Roosevelt Campobello International Park was the site of President Franklin D. Roosevelt's summer home. This park is on Campobello Island in the Bay of Fundy. See ROOSEVELT CAMPOBELLO INTERNATIONAL PARK.

National Parks. Fundy National Park, established in 1948, lies near the Bay of Fundy between Saint John and Moncton. Fort Beauséjour National Historic Park was opened in 1926 near Sackville. For the areas and chief features, see CANADA (National Parks).

Provincial Parks. New Brunswick has 54 provincial parks. For information on these parks, write to Director, Parks Branch, New Brunswick Department of Lands and Mines, Fredericton, N.B.

Hodgson, Miller Services

Bedroom in Roosevelt Cottage on Campobello Island

Shostal

Salmon Fishing in the Miramichi River

ANNUAL EVENTS

New Brunswickers celebrate the landing of the American Loyalists in Saint John on May 18. A granite boulder at the harbor marks the site where the Loyalists landed in 1783. A similar stone marks their landing in Fredericton, up the St. John River. Other annual events in New Brunswick include the following.

May-July: Competitive Festival of Music in Saint John (May); Opening of the Reversing Falls Bass Fishing Contest in Saint John (June 15); Danish celebrations in New Denmark (mid-June); Dominion Day, provincewide (July 1); Potato Festivals in Grand Falls and in Hartland (early July); Lumbermen's Festival in Blackville (early July); Lobster Festival in Shediac (mid-July); Fishermen's Festival and Blessing of the Fleet at Cape Bald (end of July).

August-September: Old Home Week in Woodstock (early August); Festival of Crafts in Fundy National Park (early August); Miramichi Folk Song Festival in Newcastle (mid-August); New Brunswick Music Camp in Rothesay (mid-August); Atlantic National Exhibition in Saint John (late August); Fredericton Exhibition and Provincial Livestock Show (early September); Fairs in Chatham, Stanley, and Gagetown (September).

Covered Bridge over the St. John River at Hartland
Hodgson, Miller Services

Hodgson, Miller Services

Reversing Falls of the St. John River, at Low Tide

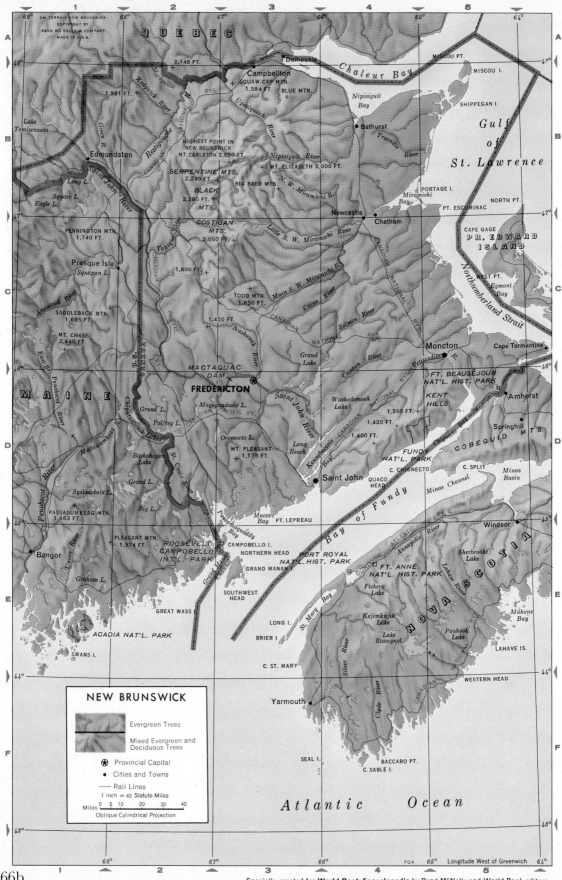

NEW BRUNSWICK

Evergreen Trees

Mixed Evergreen and
Deciduous Trees

⊛ Provincial Capital

• Cities and Towns

— Rail Lines

1 inch = 43 Statute Miles

Miles 0 5 10   20   30   40

Oblique Cylindrical Projection

Specially created for **World Book Encyclopedia** by Rand McNally and World Book editors

New Brunswick Travel Bureau

New Brunswick's Most Important River, the St. John, flows through an area of rolling hills in the Appalachian Region.

NEW BRUNSWICK / *The Land*

Land Regions. New Brunswick is in the northeastern extension of the Appalachian mountain system of the eastern United States. This area is called the Appalachian Region. Most of it consists of wooded highlands with clear, swift rivers in steep valleys. The Coastal Lowlands, also part of the Appalachian Region, make up the rest of the province.

The highlands areas of the Appalachian Region consist of the Central Highlands, the Northern Upland, and the Southern Highlands. The Central Highlands are the highest section of New Brunswick. These rugged hills increase in height from the southwest to the northeast. Many of them rise more than 2,000 feet above sea level. The hills include 2,690-foot-high Mount Carleton, the highest point in New Brunswick. Northwest of the highlands is the flatter Northern Upland, with an elevation of about 1,000 feet. The Southern Highlands,

Villages Dot the Countryside in the Coastal Lowlands region of New Brunswick. These lowlands slope gently down to the east-

ern and southern coasts of the province. Trees, mostly evergreens, cover much of the land, and many rivers flow through the region.

New Brunswick Travel Bureau

NEW BRUNSWICK

along the Bay of Fundy, have long ridges and valleys. Most of the hills are less than 1,000 feet high.

The Coastal Lowlands of the Appalachian Region are sometimes called the Eastern Plains. They slope gently down toward the east from the Central Highlands to the shores of the Gulf of St. Lawrence.

Coastline. New Brunswick has 750 miles of coastline. Deep bays and sharp inlets break the coastline in many places. The Bay of Fundy is the largest bay. Its tides are among the highest in the world. The power of the tides generally keeps the bay's harbors free of ice in winter. However, ice floes close ports on the Gulf of St. Lawrence. Other important bays include Chaleur, Chignecto, Miramichi, and Passamaquoddy.

Heavily wooded islands lie off the coast. Many of these coastal islands are summer resort areas. Numerous islands, many of which are only jagged rocks, lie in the Bay of Fundy. Grand Manan Island is the largest island in the bay. Miscou and Shippegan islands lie off the northeastern coast of the province.

Rivers, Waterfalls, and Lakes. No one in New Brunswick is ever far from a river. The 418-mile-long St. John River, the longest in the province, rises in Maine. It drains the western half of New Brunswick and the lower part of the Coastal Lowlands. The many branches of the St. John River include the Aroostook, Kennebecasis, and Tobique rivers. The St. Croix River forms part of New Brunswick's boundary with Maine. The Restigouche River forms part of the boundary between New Brunswick and Quebec. Other important rivers in New Brunswick include the Miramichi, Nipisiguit, and Petitcodiac.

The great tides of the Bay of Fundy rush into the Petitcodiac River and other rivers in a high wall of water called a *bore*. This bore flows as far inland as Moncton, 20 miles away. The bore is one of the largest in the world, and sometimes rises to about 4 feet. The Bay of Fundy's tides also produce the Reversing Falls at the mouth of the St. John River. At low tide, the water falls toward the sea. But high tide is so strong that it pushes the water backward over the falls. At the city of Grand Falls, the St. John River plunges 75 feet over a cliff.

Grand Lake, the largest lake in New Brunswick, forms a 20-mile-long arm of the St. John River. Other large lakes include Magaguadavic, Oromocto, Washademoak, and the Chiputneticook chain of lakes.

Restigouche River, near Campbellton, forms part of New Brunswick's border with Quebec. New Brunswick has many large rivers.

Fish Ladder beside the falls in St. George helps fish swim upstream. New Brunswick has many waterfalls.

Hodgson, Miller Services

Hopewell Rocks, *left,* on the Bay of Fundy are worn away by strong tides.

NEW BRUNSWICK/*Climate*

New Brunswick's coastal regions have quick changes in temperature, but the seasonal differences are not so great as those inland. The inland regions have cold, crisp winters and warm summers. Saint John, on the coast, has an average temperature of 20° F. in January and 62° F. in July. Inland, the temperature at Fredericton averages 14° F. in January and 67° F. in July.

Sisson Dam had New Brunswick's lowest recorded temperature, −53° F., on Feb. 1, 1955. The highest was 103° F., in Nipisiguit Falls and Woodstock on Aug. 18, 1935, and in Rexton on Aug. 19, 1935.

Northern New Brunswick's *precipitation* (rain, melted snow, and other forms of moisture) averages 38 inches a year. The southern part of the province receives 44 inches a year. Snowfall averages about 96 inches a year.

Malak, Miller Services
Warm New Brunswick Summers Bring Colorful Flowers.

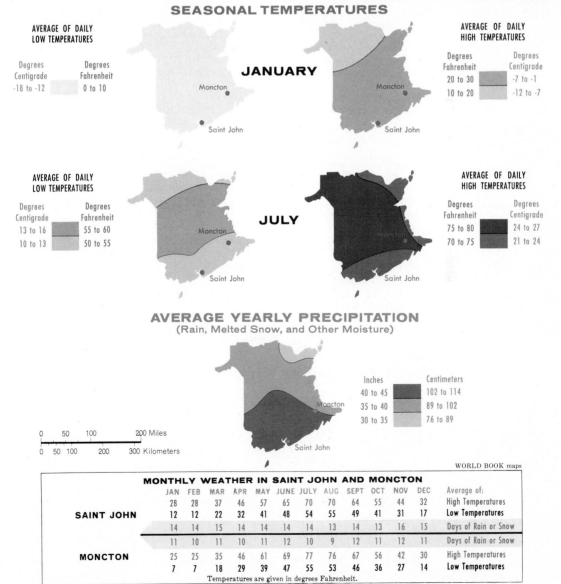

SEASONAL TEMPERATURES

JANUARY

AVERAGE OF DAILY
LOW TEMPERATURES

Degrees Centigrade	Degrees Fahrenheit
-18 to -12	0 to 10

AVERAGE OF DAILY
HIGH TEMPERATURES

Degrees Fahrenheit	Degrees Centigrade
20 to 30	-7 to -1
10 to 20	-12 to -7

JULY

AVERAGE OF DAILY
LOW TEMPERATURES

Degrees Centigrade	Degrees Fahrenheit
13 to 16	55 to 60
10 to 13	50 to 55

AVERAGE OF DAILY
HIGH TEMPERATURES

Degrees Fahrenheit	Degrees Centigrade
75 to 80	24 to 27
70 to 75	21 to 24

AVERAGE YEARLY PRECIPITATION
(Rain, Melted Snow, and Other Moisture)

Inches	Centimeters
40 to 45	102 to 114
35 to 40	89 to 102
30 to 35	76 to 89

WORLD BOOK maps

MONTHLY WEATHER IN SAINT JOHN AND MONCTON		JAN	FEB	MAR	APR	MAY	JUNE	JULY	AUG	SEPT	OCT	NOV	DEC	Average of:
SAINT JOHN		28	28	37	46	57	65	70	70	64	55	44	32	High Temperatures
		12	12	22	32	41	48	54	49	41	31	17		Low Temperatures
		14	14	15	14	14	14	14	13	14	13	16	15	Days of Rain or Snow
		11	10	11	10	11	12	10	9	12	11	12	11	Days of Rain or Snow
MONCTON		25	25	35	46	61	69	77	76	67	56	42	30	High Temperatures
		7	7	18	29	39	47	55	53	46	36	27	14	Low Temperatures

Temperatures are given in degrees Fahrenheit.

Source: Meteorological Branch, Canadian Department of Transport

In the early days, the economy of the New Brunswick region was based chiefly on the fur trade and fishing. Agriculture, forestry, and shipbuilding became important during the 1800's. Today, manufacturing is New Brunswick's chief source of income.

All values given in this section are in Canadian dollars. For the value of Canadian dollars in U.S. money, see MONEY (table).

Natural Resources. Forests are New Brunswick's chief natural resource. Wilderness covers much of the land, and interferes with exploration for other resources.

Forests cover about 85 per cent of the land area of New Brunswick—more than in any other province. Almost unbroken forest covers the central and northern parts of the province, except for a fringe of settlement along the coasts. More than two-thirds of the forest trees are evergreens. Balsam firs and spruces rank highest in commercial importance, followed by beeches, birches, cedars, maples, pines, and poplars.

Soil is not too fertile in most of New Brunswick. The reddish soil that covers most of the province has large amounts of acid. Farmers must use lime and fertilizers to make this soil productive. The flood plains of some rivers have a thin layer of extremely fertile black soil. Marshes and peat bogs cover parts of the east coast.

PRODUCTION IN NEW BRUNSWICK

Total yearly value of goods produced—$234,207,000

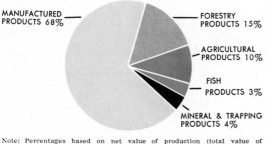

MANUFACTURED PRODUCTS 68%

FORESTRY PRODUCTS 15%

AGRICULTURAL PRODUCTS 10%

FISH PRODUCTS 3%

MINERAL & TRAPPING PRODUCTS 4%

Note: Percentages based on net value of production (total value of shipments less such costs as materials, fuel, electricity, and supplies). Trapping Products are less than 1 per cent.

Source: Dominion Bureau of Statistics

EMPLOYMENT IN NEW BRUNSWICK

Average yearly number of persons employed—152,730

		Number of Employees
Services		30,610
Manufacturing		27,592
Wholesale & Retail Trade		23,862
Transportation, Communications & Utilities		20,595
Government & Defense		17,465
Forestry		9,575
Construction		9,418
Finance, Insurance & Real Estate		3,594
Agriculture		3,547
Mining		1,607
Fishing		1,275
Other		3,590

Source: 1961 Census of Canada.

Minerals. Bituminous (soft) coal lies under the Minto-Chipman area near Grand Lake. The region south of Bathurst has more than 150,000,000 tons of ore that contains copper, lead, silver, and zinc. New Brunswick also has clay, coal, gypsum, manganese, natural gas, peat moss, sand and gravel, and stone.

Plant Life. Purple violets and pink and white mayflowers carpet the forests late in spring. In summer, blackberries, blueberries, raspberries, and strawberries are plentiful. Fiddlehead ferns flourish along the muddy banks of the rivers. When one of these plants breaks through the earth, it looks like the head of a violin.

Animal Life. New Brunswick offers outstanding hunting for sportsmen. Forest animals include beavers, black bears, deer, martens, minks, moose, otters, rabbits, skunks, and squirrels. Game birds include ducks, geese, partridges, pheasants, and woodcocks. New Brunswick's many rivers offer excellent fishing. Anglers especially prize the Atlantic silver salmon, called the *king of game fish.* Other game fish include bass, landlocked salmon (salmon in fresh-water lakes), pike, and trout.

Manufacturing. Goods manufactured in New Brunswick have a *value added by manufacture* of about $159,979,000 yearly. This figure represents the value created in products by New Brunswick's industries, not counting such costs as materials, supplies, and fuel.

The manufacture of lumber, paper, and pulp accounts for about 40 per cent of all the value added, and leads all other industries. Huge paper and pulp mills operate in Bathurst, Campbellton, Dalhousie, Newcastle, and Saint John. The province's sawmills cut about 300,000,000 board feet of lumber a year. About a fifth of the wood is exported as *long lumber* (lumber used in building).

Saint John is the major industrial center of New Brunswick. In addition to pulp and paper mills, the city has an oil refinery, shipyards, a sugar refinery, and metalworking factories. Among the industries of New Brunswick are the manufacture of boots and shoes, cement, chemicals, electrical and heating equipment, processed farm products and seafood, and textiles.

Forestry. Logging started in the New Brunswick region during the 1600's. The French and British navies cut tall white pine trees for masts and spars. *Masting,* as the cutting of such trees was called, employed many workers as late as the 1800's. Today, logs and pulpwood cut in New Brunswick have an annual value of about $34,856,000. Most of the trees cut down are balsam firs and spruces. The forests renew themselves every 20 years. This process provides continual forest growth.

Agriculture. New Brunswick's farm products have an annual value of about $23,775,000. The province has about 8,700 farms. They cover about a tenth of the total land area, and average about 200 acres in size. The best farmland lies in the valleys of the St. John River and its branches, and in southeastern New Brunswick.

Potatoes are the leading cash crop of New Brunswick. Most of the potatoes grow in the St. John River Valley. The province produces thousands of bushels of apples yearly. Milk and other dairy products also rank among the most important farm products of New Brunswick. Farmers raise dairy cattle throughout the province, but

FARM, MINERAL, AND FOREST PRODUCTS

This map shows where the leading farm, mineral, and forest products are produced. The major urban area (shown in red) is the province's important manufacturing center.

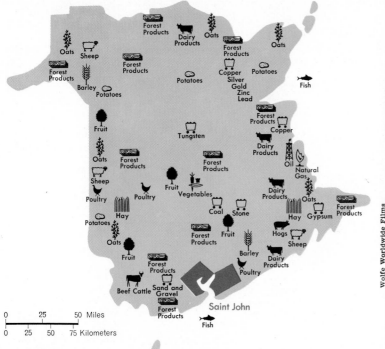

0   25   50 Miles
0   25   50   75 Kilometers

WORLD BOOK map

Wolfe Worldwide Films

Conveyors Stack Logs at a pulp mill near Saint John. Wood is the raw material for New Brunswick's most important industries. Lumber, paper, and pulp are the chief products.

most dairying takes place in the better farming areas. Beef cattle and hogs are also raised in these areas. In addition, the province has poultry farms. Farmers grow hay for livestock feed. They also raise oats and other grains such as barley, buckwheat, and wheat.

Fishing Industry. New Brunswick fishermen catch about $7,730,000 worth of seafood annually. The lobster catch has a yearly value of about $4,000,000, and the sardine catch about $2,000,000. Fishermen also catch alewives, cod, flounders, and pollacks.

Mining production in New Brunswick during 1961 had a value of about $7,725,000. But production increased so rapidly during the early 1960's that the value reached about $92 million in 1967. The greatest expansion took place in the region between Bathurst and Newcastle. Vast deposits of copper, lead, silver, and zinc were discovered there in 1952 and 1953. Although mining began in 1956, production did not boom until 1964. Four mines were in operation in the late 1960's.

Coal is one of New Brunswick's chief mineral products. The largest coal mines are in the Minto-Chipman field near Grand Lake. Mines there produce about 900,000 tons of soft coal yearly. Natural gas and petroleum are produced near Moncton. Gypsum is taken in Albert County, and sand and gravel pits operate throughout the province. Other mining products include manganese, peat moss, and stone.

Electric Power. More than half the electric power generated in New Brunswick is provided by hydroelectric plants. The largest, at Mactaquac Dam on the St. John River near Fredericton, began operating in December, 1967. Other power stations in New Brunswick use steam or diesel power. For the province's kilowatt-hour production, see ELECTRIC POWER (table).

Transportation. Fredericton, Moncton, and Saint John have airports. Airlines link these cities with other cities in eastern Canada and with Boston, Mass.

The province has about 1,800 miles of main railway track. Trains making overnight trips connect Moncton and Saint John with Montreal, Que. An international railroad bridge crosses the St. Croix River from St. Stephen to Calais, Me.

New Brunswick has about 13,000 miles of highways. About 3,500 miles of highway are paved.

Saint John is one of the few seaports of eastern Canada that are ice-free all year around. Transatlantic liners can dock at Saint John during the winter, even when ice shuts the ports on the Gulf of St. Lawrence.

Communication. The first newspaper in New Brunswick, the *Saint John Royal Gazette*, was founded in 1785. Today, the province has more than 20 newspapers, six of which are dailies. The *Telegraph-Journal* and *Times-Globe*, both of Saint John, have the largest daily circulations. *L'Evangeline* of Moncton is the chief French-language newspaper.

The first of New Brunswick's 11 radio stations, CFNB, began broadcasting in Fredericton in 1923. The Canadian Broadcasting Corporation sends programs overseas from its short-wave transmitter in Sackville. New Brunswick's first television station, CHSJ-TV, started in Saint John in 1954. The province now has three major television stations.

Huge Ore Deposits, discovered near Bathurst in the early 1950's, boosted the economy of New Brunswick.

Fur Traders fought for control of the New Brunswick region during the 1600's. The British won complete control in 1763.

HISTORIC NEW BRUNSWICK

Chaleur Bay

Bathurst •

Jacques Cartier explored Chaleur Bay in 1534. He wrote in his journal that the land was ideal for farming.

The Aroostook War began when families from Maine and New Brunswick settled in the Aroostook Valley. A treaty signed in 1842 prevented any fighting.

• Hartland

The 1,282-Foot Covered Bridge over the St. John River at Hartland is probably the longest in the world.

★ FREDERICTON

A Great Forest Fire swept across 6,000 square miles of land in 1825, burning the homes of 15,000 settlers.

Saint John •

Many American Loyalists moved to New Brunswick in 1783, after the United States separated from England.

Samuel de Champlain journeyed up the St. John River in 1604. His party discovered the Reversing Falls.

Indian Days. The first white settlers in what is now New Brunswick found Micmac and Maliseet, or Malecite, Indians living in the region. Both these tribes belonged to the Algonkian Indian family. The Micmac roamed the eastern part of the region, and the Maliseet lived in the St. John River Valley.

The Indians liked to camp downstream from waterfalls or near the farthest reaches of tidewater in rivers. These locations provided the best fishing for salmon and trout. On the coasts, the Indians caught porpoises and gathered clams and oysters. A few Indian groups also farmed, growing chiefly corn and pumpkins.

Exploration and Settlement. In 1534, the French explorer Jacques Cartier arrived in Chaleur Bay. He wrote of the New Brunswick region: "The land along the south side of it is as fine and as good land, as arable and as full of beautiful fields and meadows, as any we have ever seen...."

No further exploration took place until 1604. That year, the French explorers Samuel de Champlain and Pierre du Guast, Sieur de Monts, sailed into the Bay of Fundy. After exploring the coast, they established a settlement on St. Croix Island, near the mouth of the St. Croix River. In 1605, the settlement was moved across the Bay of Fundy to Port Royal, in what is now Nova Scotia. Throughout the 1600's, other Frenchmen arrived and established fur-trading and fishing stations. The French called the region Acadia (see ACADIA).

The Fight for Furs. The French fought among themselves for control of the valuable fur trade. The most famous struggle took place between Charles de la Tour and D'Aulnay de Charnisay. La Tour had a trading post and fort on the site of present-day Saint John. De Charnisay was a fur trader in Port Royal. In 1645, after many years of rivalry, De Charnisay attacked La Tour's fort while La Tour was absent. Marie de la Tour, the trader's wife, led the defense of the fort, but finally surrendered. De Charnisay forced her to watch him hang all members of the garrison except one, who served as executioner.

Competition among the French fur traders gradually gave way to rivalry between the French and the British. To the south, the British colonies were growing rapidly. Many British fishermen and fur traders were attracted to the New Brunswick region. The British conquered Acadia twice during the late 1600's. They returned it to France both times, in the Treaty of Breda (1667) and the Treaty of Ryswick (1697). After Queen Anne's War, France gave Acadia to England in the Peace of Utrecht (1713). The Acadians remained in the New Brunswick region, however. In 1755, during the last of the French and Indian Wars, the British captured the region. They drove out most of the Acadians. The Treaty of Paris (1763) confirmed British ownership of Acadia. See FRENCH AND INDIAN WARS.

English Settlement. Traders from New England arrived in Saint John in 1762. The next year, other New Englanders established the settlement of Maugerville, near what is now Fredericton. Also in 1763, the New Brunswick region became a part of the British province of Nova Scotia. Many Acadians whom the British had driven from the region were allowed to return. The

Acadians received grants of lands in the north and east.

Beginning in 1783, after the American Revolutionary War, about 14,000 persons loyal to England arrived from the United States. These United Empire Loyalists, as they were called, landed in Saint John. Most of them settled in the lower St. John River Valley. They founded Fredericton. Others settled near Passamaquoddy Bay. In 1784, Great Britain established New Brunswick as a separate province. In 1785, Saint John became the first incorporated city in what is now Canada.

The timber trade and shipbuilding flourished during the early 1800's. After 1815, thousands of English, Irish, and Scottish settlers came to New Brunswick because they could not find jobs in Great Britain.

In 1825, a great forest fire blazed through hundreds of square miles in the Miramichi River region. The fire, fanned by a hurricane, destroyed the homes of about 15,000 New Brunswickers. The homeless settlers received clothing, money, and supplies from the other North American provinces, Great Britain, and the United States.

By the 1830's, about four-fifths of New Brunswick was still *crown lands* (lands owned by Great Britain). Timber traders had to pay high fees to operate in the forests. In 1833, the provincial legislature began a movement to acquire the crown lands. The British government gave the lands to New Brunswick in 1837.

The Aroostook War. Settlers from New Brunswick and Maine lived in the valley of the Aroostook River. Great Britain and the United States had never agreed on a boundary in this region, and disputes developed between the settlers. The climax came in 1839 when militiamen from New Brunswick and Maine assembled

---

IMPORTANT DATES IN NEW BRUNSWICK

1534 The French explorer Jacques Cartier arrived in Chaleur Bay.

1604 Samuel de Champlain and Sieur de Monts of France established a settlement on St. Croix Island.

1713 France, in the Peace of Utrecht, gave the New Brunswick region to Great Britain.

1755 The British captured the New Brunswick region and expelled most of the French settlers.

1762 Traders from New England arrived in Saint John.

1763 France, in the Treaty of Paris, confirmed British ownership of the New Brunswick region.

1783 Thousands of Loyalists came from the United States to settle in New Brunswick.

1784 New Brunswick became a separate province.

1825 A great fire swept the Miramichi River region.

1842 The New Brunswick-Maine boundary dispute was settled.

1848 New Brunswick was granted self-government.

1867 New Brunswick became one of the original four provinces of the Dominion of Canada.

1890 Two national railway systems linked New Brunswick cities with Montreal.

1952 and 1953 Vast deposits of copper, lead, silver, and zinc were discovered in the Bathurst-Newcastle region.

1968 A $174-million industrial development program was completed in the Bathurst-Newcastle region and a hydro-electric plant opened at Mactaquac Dam on the St. John River near Fredericton.

Special Dock for Loading Ore towers over the port at Dalhousie. Huge ore discoveries near Bathurst spurred the construction of many mills and smelters in northern New Brunswick.

Ontario, and Quebec. Andrew R. Wetmore, of the Confederation party, became the first premier of New Brunswick after confederation of the provinces.

The province's fishing, lumbering, and mining industries expanded gradually. But the increasing use of iron steamships led to the end of New Brunswick s sailing-ship industry. During the 1870's and 1880's, many New Brunswickers moved to western Canada and the United States. These regions offered better job opportunities than New Brunswick did.

By 1890, two national railway systems linked cities in New Brunswick with Montreal. Saint John ranked with Halifax, N.S., as a chief winter port on Canada's east coast. But Ontario and Quebec controlled manufacturing and trade in Canada. New Brunswick's industries grew during the early 1900's. Public works programs improved communication and transportation.

The Mid-1900's. After World War II (1939-1945), the province's pulp and paper industries expanded greatly, and shipbuilding became important in the Saint John area. Huge deposits of copper, lead, silver, and zinc were discovered in the Bathurst-Newcastle region in 1952 and 1953. In 1953 and 1957, the province completed hydroelectric plants that provided additional power for mining and manufacturing.

A $174-million construction program related to the Bathurst-Newcastle metal discoveries began in 1962 and was completed by 1968. Projects in the program included chemical and fertilizer plants, docking and shipping facilities, milling and manufacturing firms, mines, and pipelines. Mining of the metal ores began to boom in 1964, when the region's largest mine started operations.

In 1968, a $120-million hydroelectric plant opened at Mactaquac Dam on the St. John River near Fredericton. More than half the power from this plant goes to industries in the Bathurst-Newcastle region.

to fight. No fighting took place, however. President Martin Van Buren sent General Winfield Scott to settle the dispute, which was called the Aroostook War. Scott arranged a truce with New Brunswick officials. In 1842, British and American authorities established the New Brunswick-Maine boundary.

As the population of New Brunswick grew, there were increasing demands for less political control by Great Britain. Political power shifted gradually from the British colonial office in London to the provincial legislature located in Fredericton. In 1848, Great Britain granted New Brunswick almost complete control over its own affairs.

Confederation and Progress. In 1864, delegates from New Brunswick, Nova Scotia, and Prince Edward Island met in Charlottetown, P.E.I., to discuss forming a united colony. Delegates from what are now Ontario and Quebec joined them and proposed a confederation of all the British provinces of eastern North America. The delegates met again later in 1864 in Quebec. They drew up a plan for Canadian confederation that led to the creation of the Dominion of Canada.

Many New Brunswickers feared they would lose their political powers in the proposed union. Samuel L. Tilley, a provincial political leader, played a major part in convincing the people that the larger provinces would not control them. On July 1, 1867, New Brunswick became one of the four original provinces of the Dominion of Canada. The others were Nova Scotia,

——— **THE PREMIERS OF NEW BRUNSWICK** ———

	Party	Term
1. Andrew R. Wetmore	Confederation	1867-1870
2. George E. King	Conservative	1870-1871
3. George L. Hatheway	Conservative	1871-1872
4. George E. King	Conservative	1872-1878
5. John J. Fraser	Conservative	1878-1882
6. Daniel L. Hanington	Conservative	1882-1883
7. Andrew G. Blair	Liberal	1883-1896
8. James Mitchell	Liberal	1896-1897
9. Henry R. Emmerson	Liberal	1897-1900
10. Lemuel J. Tweedie	Liberal	1900-1907
11. William Pugsley	Liberal	1907
12. Clifford W. Robinson	Liberal	1907-1908
13. John D. Hazen	Conservative	1908-1911
14. James K. Flemming	Conservative	1911-1914
15. George J. Clarke	Conservative	1914-1917
16. James A. Murray	Conservative	1917
17. Walter E. Foster	Liberal	1917-1923
18. Peter J. Veniot	Liberal	1923-1925
19. John B. M. Baxter	Conservative	1925-1931
20. Charles D. Richards	Conservative	1931-1933
21. Leonard P. de W. Tilley	Conservative	1933-1935
22. A. Allison Dysart	Liberal	1935-1940
23. John B. McNair	Liberal	1940-1952
24. Hugh John Flemming	Progressive Conservative	1952-1960
25. Louis J. Robichaud	Liberal	1960-1970
26. Richard Hatfield	Progressive Conservative	1970-

During the late 1960's, Premier Louis J. Robichaud, a Liberal, led the province in what he called a Program of Equal Opportunity. In this program, the provincial government took over the operation of all courts, schools, and health and welfare institutions. The action was taken to equalize the quality of services provided by such facilities throughout the province.

In 1969, the New Brunswick Legislative Assembly passed a law that made French an official language of equal status with English in the legislature itself and in courts, government offices, and schools. Later that year, the Canadian Parliament passed the Official Languages Act. This law requires federal facilities to provide service in both languages in districts where at least 10 per cent of the people speak French.

New Brunswick Today faces the problem of expanding its industry fast enough to provide jobs for its growing labor force. The province's shipping facilities were enlarged in 1970 when the first deepwater terminal

for oil tankers in North America opened near Saint John. New Brunswick is planning two other projects in the Saint John area as a basis for industrial expansion during the 1970's. One of these projects is the establishment of a *complex* (group) of related industries. The other is the improvement of the port of Saint John.

Plans for the Saint John industrial complex call for 8 to 10 industries in the metals field to be grouped together, along with 17 service industries. Planners expected that the complex would create 8,000 new jobs by 1974. In 1971, a terminal to handle ships that carry cargo in truck trailers or in large metal containers opened at the port of Saint John. New Brunswick's food processing, mining, oil refining, and pulp and paper industries are also planning expansion during the 1970's.

J. K. CHAPMAN, ARNOLD L. MCALLISTER, and STUART TRUEMAN

NEW BRUNSWICK/Study Aids

Related Articles in WORLD BOOK include:

BIOGRAPHIES

Anglin, Francis A.	Foster, Sir George E.
Beaverbrook, Lord	Law, Andrew Bonar
Bennett, Richard B.	Roberts, Sir Charles G. D.
Carman, Bliss	

CITIES AND TOWNS

Bathurst	Moncton	Saint Andrews	Sussex
Fredericton	Sackville	Saint John	

PHYSICAL FEATURES

Bay of Fundy	Passamaquoddy Bay
Campobello Island	Restigouche River
Gulf of St. Lawrence	Reversing Falls of Saint John
Miramichi River	Saint John River

UNIVERSITIES

New Brunswick's universities have separate articles, and are listed in this article's *Education* section.

OTHER RELATED ARTICLES

Acadia	Lead (graph)
Canada	United Empire Loyalist

Outline

I. Government
    A. Lieutenant-Governor   E. Local Government
    B. Premier   F. Taxation
    C. Legislative Assembly   G. Politics
    D. Courts
II. People
III. Education
    A. Schools   B. Libraries   C. Museums
IV. A Visitor's Guide
    A. Places to Visit   B. Annual Events
V. The Land
    A. Land Regions   C. Rivers, Waterfalls,
    B. Coastline   and Lakes
VI. Climate
VII. Economy
    A. Natural Resources   F. Mining
    B. Manufacturing   G. Electric Power
    C. Forestry   H. Transportation
    D. Agriculture   I. Communication
    E. Fishing Industry
VIII. History

Questions

Where is New Brunswick's greatest mining region?
How did New Brunswick get its name?
What percentage of New Brunswickers have French ancestors? What percentage speak only French?
What is Canada's oldest museum? Where is it?
What causes the Reversing Falls?
Who was the only New Brunswicker to become prime minister of Great Britain?
Why do harbors on the Bay of Fundy remain free of ice in the winter?
Who established the first settlement in the New Brunswick region? Where? When?
What caused the Aroostook War? How was it settled?
What is New Brunswick's chief manufacturing activity?

Books to Read

Atlantic Yearbook. Published for the *Atlantic Advocate* by the Brunswick Press (Fredericton).
HANNAY, JAMES. *History of New Brunswick.* 2 vols. John A. Bowes (Saint John), 1909.
LAWSON, JESSIE I., and SWEET, J. M. *This Is New Brunswick.* Ryerson (Toronto), 1951.
MACNUTT, WILLIAM S. *New Brunswick, a History, 1784-1867.* Macmillan (Toronto), 1963. *New Brunswick and Its People: The Biography of a Canadian Province.* New Brunswick Travel Bureau (Fredericton), 1964.
MAXWELL, LILIAN M. *'Round New Brunswick Roads.* Ryerson (Toronto), 1951.
THOMAS, L. J., and BARTON, R. W. *In New Brunswick We'll Find It.* General Publishing Co. (Toronto), 1939.
WRIGHT, ESTHER C. *The Loyalists of New Brunswick.* The author, 407 Island Park Dr., Ottawa 3, 1955.

NEW BRUNSWICK, UNIVERSITY OF, is a coeducational university in Fredericton, N.B. It is supported by the province. It has faculties of arts, science, engineering, forestry, law, nursing, and education. In 1964, the university established a junior college at St. John which offers the first two years in arts and science. The university grants bachelor's, master's, and doctor's degrees. It was established in 1785 as the Provincial Academy of Liberal Arts and Sciences. It assumed its present name in 1859. St. Thomas University became federated with the University of New Brunswick in 1963. For enrollment, see CANADA (table: Universities and Colleges).   COLIN B. MACKAY

NEW CALEDONIA

NEW CALEDONIA, KAL uh DOHN yuh, is an overseas territory of France. It consists of about 25 islands in the South Pacific Ocean. The territory takes its name from New Caledonia, the largest and most important island of the group. This island covers 6,530 square miles. The other islands in the group have a total area of only 806 square miles. They include the Bélep Islands, the Chesterfield Islands, the Isle of Pines, the Loyalty Islands, and Walpole Island. The territory has a population of 104,000. For location, see PACIFIC ISLANDS (map).

Rugged mountains that are rich in mineral resources cover much of the island of New Caledonia. Farmers raise cattle and crops in fertile valleys and on plateaus in the island's interior. Nouméa—the capital, largest city, and leading port of the territory—lies on the southwestern coast.

The original people of New Caledonia were Melanesians. Today, Melanesians make up a little less than half the population. Most of the other people are Europeans of French descent or Polynesians.

Government. The French high commissioner in the Pacific serves as the governor of New Caledonia. A 35-member territorial assembly and a 5-member council assist him. The people elect the members of the assembly, and the assembly elects the council members.

New Caledonians are French citizens. They elect one representative to each house of the French parliament—the Senate and the National Assembly.

Economy. New Caledonia has great mineral wealth. Nickel mining and smelting are the leading industries. Other mineral resources of the territory include chromite, cobalt, iron, and manganese. Farmers raise coffee and copra for export and cattle and vegetables for local use. Mountain forests provide lumber.

Jobs are plentiful in New Caledonia, chiefly because

David Moore, Black Star

Nickel Mining provides New Caledonia with most of its income. Thousands of workers earn their living in the nickel industry.

of the nickel industry. Many workers from other South Pacific islands go there to find work.

History. James Cook, a British navigator, was the first European to visit New Caledonia. He arrived there in 1774. Other Europeans, including explorers, missionaries, and traders, followed. In 1853, France took control of the islands. France made New Caledonia a prison colony in 1864 and sent about 40,000 prisoners there during the next 33 years.

During the early years of French rule, the Melanesians fought to drive out the French. The last uprising took place in 1917. Since then, few New Caledonians have demanded independence. The United States had a military base on New Caledonia during World War II (1939-1945). STUART INDER

See also CHESTERFIELD ISLANDS; LOYALTY ISLANDS.

NEW CASTLE, Pa. (pop. 38,559; alt. 805 ft.), is an industrial center at the meeting point of the Shenango and Neshannock rivers, about 50 miles north of Pittsburgh. Its factories use much of the limestone, bituminous coal, sandstone, clay, and iron ore that are found in the region. Notable products of the city include chemicals, boxes, pottery, fireworks, and machinery.

About 1802, John Carlysle Stewart founded New Castle. It became a city in 1869. New Castle has a commission form of government. Westminster and Geneva colleges are near the city. S. K. STEVENS

NEW COLLEGE. See UNIVERSITIES AND COLLEGES (table).

NEW CONNECTICUT. See VERMONT (History).

NEW CROTON DAM is on the Croton River near New York City. It was built in 1905 to supply water to the city. The dam blocks the Croton River, and creates a lake from which water is piped to the city. The dam is 297 feet high and 2,168 feet long. See also DAM.

Jack Fields, Photo Researchers

Nouméa, the Capital of New Caledonia, is an important port and commercial center.

NEW DEAL was President Franklin D. Roosevelt's program to pull the United States out of the Great Depression in the 1930's. The New Deal did not end the depression. But it relieved much economic hardship and gave Americans faith in the democratic system at a time when other nations hit by the depression turned to dictators. Roosevelt first used the term *new deal* when he accepted the Democratic presidential nomination in 1932. "I pledge you, I pledge myself, to a new deal for the American people," he said.

When Roosevelt became President on March 4, 1933, business was at a standstill and a feeling of panic gripped the nation. The stock market crash in October, 1929, had shattered the prosperity most Americans enjoyed during the 1920's. The depression grew worse during the early 1930's. Banks, small businesses, and factories closed. Workers lost their homes and farmers lost their farms because they could not meet mortgage payments. An estimated 12 to 15 million Americans—1 out of every 4 workers—had no jobs.

In his inaugural address, Roosevelt expressed confidence that the nation could solve its problems. "The only thing we have to fear is fear itself," he said.

The First Hundred Days

Roosevelt called Congress into special session on March 5, 1933. From March 9 to June 16, Congress passed a series of important laws aimed at speeding economic recovery, providing relief for victims of the depression, and making reforms in financial, business, agricultural, and industrial practices. Most of these passed swiftly and with little opposition. Never before had Congress approved so many important laws so quickly. The special session then became known as *The Hundred Days.*

The programs and policies that made up the New Deal did not come from one man. Some were Roosevelt's ideas. Others were proposed by members of the "Brain Trust," a group of unofficial presidential advisers. Congressional leaders suggested others. Some programs conflicted with each other. For example, the Economy Act cut the salaries of federal employees while the Public Works Administration increased government spending. But Roosevelt was willing to experiment and tried the ideas of one group and then another.

Helping Savers and Investors. Roosevelt's first goal was to end the banking crisis. A wave of bank failures in February had frightened the public. Depositors rushed to withdraw their money before their banks failed. Roosevelt declared a "bank holiday," closing all banks on March 6. On March 9, Congress passed the Emergency Banking Act. The new law allowed government inspectors to check each bank's records and to reopen only those banks that were in strong financial condition. Within a few days, half the nation's banks reopened. These banks held 90 per cent of the country's total deposits. This action did much to end the nation's panic.

The Glass-Steagall Banking Act of June, 1933, provided further protection for investors. It gave the Federal Reserve Board more power to regulate loans made by banks and created the Federal Deposit Insurance Corporation (FDIC), which then insured bank deposits up to $2,500.

Congress passed the Truth-in-Securities Act in May, 1933. This law required firms issuing new stocks to give investors full and accurate financial information. Congress created the Securities and Exchange Com-

---

LEADING NEW DEAL AGENCIES

AAA —*Agricultural Adjustment Administration. Founded in 1933 to advise and assist farmers, and to regulate farm production.

CCC — *Civilian Conservation Corps. Founded in 1933 to help unemployed young men obtain work.

CCC — *Commodity Credit Corporation. Founded in 1933 to support the Department of Agriculture.

FCA — *Farm Credit Administration. Founded in 1933 to provide a credit system for farmers by making long-term and short-term credit available.

FCC — *Federal Communications Commission. Founded in 1934 to regulate radio, telephone, and telegraph systems.

FCIC — *Federal Crop Insurance Corporation. Founded in 1938 to provide insurance protection against unavoidable loss of certain crops.

FDIC — *Federal Deposit Insurance Corporation. Founded in 1933 to insure bank deposits.

FERA — Federal Emergency Relief Administration. Founded in 1933 to cooperate with the states in relieving hardships caused by unemployment and drought.

FHA — *Federal Housing Administration. Founded in 1934 to insure private lending companies against loss on home-mortgage loans and on loans for improving small properties.

FSA — Farm Security Administration. Founded in 1937 to help farmers buy needed equipment.

HOLC— *Home Owners Loan Corporation. Founded in 1933 to grant long-term mortgage loans at low cost to homeowners in financial difficulties.

NLRB —*National Labor Relations Board. Founded in 1935 to administer the National Labor Relations Act.

NRA — *National Recovery Administration. Founded in 1933 to carry out the plans that were made by the National Industrial Recovery Act to fight depression.

NYA — National Youth Administration. Founded in 1935 to provide job training for unemployed youths and part-time work for needy students.

PWA — Public Works Administration. Founded in 1933 to increase employment and purchasing power through the construction of useful public works, such as bridges, in the various states.

REA — *Rural Electrification Administration. Founded in 1935 to aid farmers in the electrification of their homes.

SEC — *Securities and Exchange Commission. Founded in 1934 to protect the public from investing in unsafe securities and to regulate stock market practices.

SSB — Social Security Board. Founded in 1935 to secure a sound social security system.

TVA — *Tennessee Valley Authority. Founded in 1933 to help develop the resources of the Tennessee Valley.

USHA— United States Housing Authority. Founded in 1937 to aid in the development of adequate housing throughout the nation.

WPA — Works Progress Administration. Founded in 1935 to provide work for needy persons on public works projects.

*Has a separate article in WORLD BOOK.

mission (SEC) in 1934 to regulate the sale of securities and to curb unfair stock market practices.

Helping the Farmers. The Agricultural Adjustment Administration (AAA), created in May, 1933, tried to raise farm prices by limiting production. The AAA used funds raised through a tax on processors of farm products to pay farmers not to produce as much as they had before. Farmers limited production by not planting crops on part of their land. The plan increased farm income, but critics said farmers should not cut food and cotton production at a time when people were hungry and needed clothing. The Supreme Court of the United States declared the AAA unconstitutional in 1936. The government then paid farmers to leave some land vacant as part of new soil conservation programs.

Helping Industry and Labor. The National Industrial Recovery Act of June, 1933, was one of the most important of the new laws. This act created the National Recovery Administration (NRA) to enforce codes of fair practices for business and industry. Representatives of firms within each industry wrote the codes.

The industrial codes set minimum wages and maximum hours, and supported the right of workers to join unions. The codes primarily aided business. They allowed member firms to set standards of quality and establish the lowest prices that could be charged for goods. The Supreme Court declared the NRA unconstitutional in 1935 (see SCHECHTER V. UNITED STATES).

Helping the Needy. The Civilian Conservation Corps (CCC) launched the New Deal relief program. The CCC put young men from needy families to work at useful conservation projects, such as planting trees and building dams. The Federal Emergency Relief Administration provided the states with money for the needy. The Public Works Administration (PWA) created jobs for large numbers of men. Thousands of schools, courthouses, bridges, dams, and other useful public works projects were built through PWA projects. The Home Owners Loan Corporation (HOLC) provided money at low interest for persons struggling to pay mortgages. The Tennessee Valley Authority (TVA) built many dams to control floods and to provide electricity at low rates for residents of the Tennessee River Valley.

The Second Hundred Days

Congress approved several important relief and reform measures in 1935. These laws became the heart of the New Deal's lasting achievements. Most of the new laws were passed during the summer, and some historians call this period *The Second Hundred Days*. Some of the most important new measures were the Works Progress Administration (WPA), the National Labor Relations Act, and the Social Security Act.

Works Progress Administration provided jobs building highways, streets, bridges, parks, and other projects intended to have long-range value. It also created work for artists, writers, actors, and musicians. The WPA provided some work for about 8½ million persons.

The National Labor Relations Act guaranteed workers the right to organize unions. During the next few years, the American Federation of Labor (AFL) and the new Congress of Industrial Organizations (CIO) enrolled millions of workers in labor unions.

The Social Security Act provided pensions for the aged and insurance for the jobless. The law also provided payments for the blind and disabled and for needy children. See SOCIAL SECURITY.

The Final Measures

Roosevelt proposed a plan to add justices to the Supreme Court in 1937. Critics charged that he was trying to "pack" the court with judges who favored the New Deal. Roosevelt's plan divided the Democrats and cost him his solid support in Congress (see ROOSEVELT, FRANKLIN D. [The Supreme Court]). Congress passed only two other important reform measures after that. The first was the National Housing Act of 1937, which provided money for more federal public housing projects. The second was the Fair Labor Standards Act of 1938, which set a minimum wage of 25 cents an hour and a maximum workweek of 44 hours, with extra pay for extra hours. It also banned children under 16 years of age from working in factories, and during school hours.

The economy faltered late in 1937. Farm prices dropped, and the number of jobless rose from about 5 million in September, 1937, to almost 11 million in May, 1938. The Democrats retained majorities in both houses of Congress in the 1938 elections, but Republicans gained back seats for the first time since 1928. Strong opposition in Congress forced Roosevelt to avoid further reforms, and he soon became occupied primarily with the growing threat of Nazi Germany.

Results of the New Deal

Most scholars agree the New Deal relieved much economic distress and brought about a large measure of recovery. But about 7½ million Americans still had no jobs in 1940. Military spending for World War II, rather than the New Deal, brought back prosperity.

The New Deal tried to spend its way back to prosperity. It spent billions of dollars to create jobs for unemployed persons, so they could buy more and get business going normally. New Deal programs cost more money than the government received through taxes. The government borrowed much of the money it needed by selling bonds, and the federal debt grew from $22½ billion in 1933 to about $40½ billion in 1939.

The New Deal caused important political changes. The Democratic Party, a minority party since the Civil War, became the nation's largest political party. Its main source of strength shifted from the rural South to the urban North. Immigrants, union members, urban intellectuals, and reformers gained a stronger voice in party decisions.

Most scholars also agree that the New Deal preserved the essentials of the American free enterprise system. Profits and competition continued to play a leading part in the system. However, the program added new features. The federal government assumed responsibility for the economic security of the people and the economic growth of the nation. After the New Deal, the government's role in banking and public welfare grew steadily. Also, organized labor became an important force in national affairs.   DAVID A. SHANNON

See the separate articles listed in the table in this article; see also ROOSEVELT, FRANKLIN D.; TRUMAN, HARRY S. (The Fair Deal); LIBERTY LEAGUE.

The Impressive Indian Parliament Building is near the center of New Delhi. The city became the capital of India in 1931, when the seat of government was moved from Delhi. Its site, five miles from Old Delhi, was selected by a commission.

NEW DELHI, *DEL ee* (pop. 324,283), is the capital of India. It lies close to the northern boundary of India, and is about 5 miles south and west of Delhi, the old capital. New Delhi stands on the west bank of the Jumna River. It stands near the edge of the 74,000-square-mile Thar (or Indian) Desert. The Indian government began to irrigate the desert for farming in 1958. See INDIA (political map).

Description. New Delhi is an example of good city planning. Flowering trees line its flat, broad streets. The city is an administrative center. Important structures include Government House, the Parliament Building, the All-India War Memorial in Princes Park, and the great Raisina Court, which is 1,100 feet long and 400 feet wide. The Indian Supreme Court Building and the National Archives Building are also located in New Delhi.

An open-air observatory built by the astronomer-prince, Jai Singh of Jaipur, in the 1700's, still stands in New Delhi. The All-India Radio Station and the National Sports Stadium, holding 30,000 spectators, are located there.

The National Museum of India lies near the President's residence. Built in 1957, the National Museum houses art treasures of India. The city also contains many temples, historic monuments, and national institutes.

History. The seat of the Indian government was moved from Calcutta to Delhi in 1912 because: (1) Delhi had been the capital of the Mogul Empire and it seemed wise to take advantage of the traditional feeling Indians had for Delhi; (2) Calcutta was the center of the Bengal terrorist movement, which was giving the Indian government much trouble.

Later, in 1912, government officials decided to erect the new public buildings away from the crowded conditions in the old city of Delhi. The city of New Delhi was founded for that purpose.

Work on the city continued until 1914, but was suspended during World War I (1914-1918). New Delhi was formally opened in 1931, at which time it became the capital of British India. New Delhi remained the capital after India gained its independence from Great Britain in 1947.

During World War II, New Delhi was headquarters of the Allied forces in southeastern Asia. The city is the center of celebration of India's Republic Day, held on January 26 every year since 1950.   ROBERT I. CRANE

See also DELHI; TEMPLE (picture); UNESCO (Education).

U.S. Embassy in New Delhi was designed by the American architect, Edward Durell Stone. The building is designed to harmonize with the culture and tradition of India.

NEW ENGLAND

NEW ENGLAND forms the northeasternmost section of the United States. Captain John Smith, English explorer, gave the region its name when he explored its shores in 1614. New England includes six states: Maine, New Hampshire, Vermont, Massachusetts, Rhode Island, and Connecticut. These states have a combined area of 66,608 square miles. New England borders Canada on the north, the Atlantic Ocean on the east, Long Island Sound on the south, and New York on the west. All the states except Vermont lie along the Atlantic.

The Pilgrim settlers who came to New England in 1620 found a hilly, forested region with a long, jagged coast line. In general, New England is made up of a low coastal plain and two rocky interior uplands. Several mountain ranges and fertile river valleys separate the boulder-strewn uplands. Early-day farmers had to remove these rocks before they could till the soil. Many of the stone walls they built around their land may still be seen.

Of all the regions in the United States, New England is the most unified in its geography, history, and culture. Although the area consists of six states, it has developed as a unit. From its first settlement until about 1800, New England depended on agriculture, fishing, and shipping for its livelihood. During the early 1800's, the six states built up a profitable shipping trade with foreign countries. Great waves of European immigrants in the late 1800's worked in bustling factories that manufactured textiles, leather goods, and other products. Today, New England ranks as one of the nation's great manufacturing areas. It also is popular as a

Portland Chamber of Commerce
New England's Rocky Coast is dotted by many lighthouses. Portland Head Light, built in 1791, is the oldest lighthouse on the Maine coast. Its tower rises 101 feet above high water.

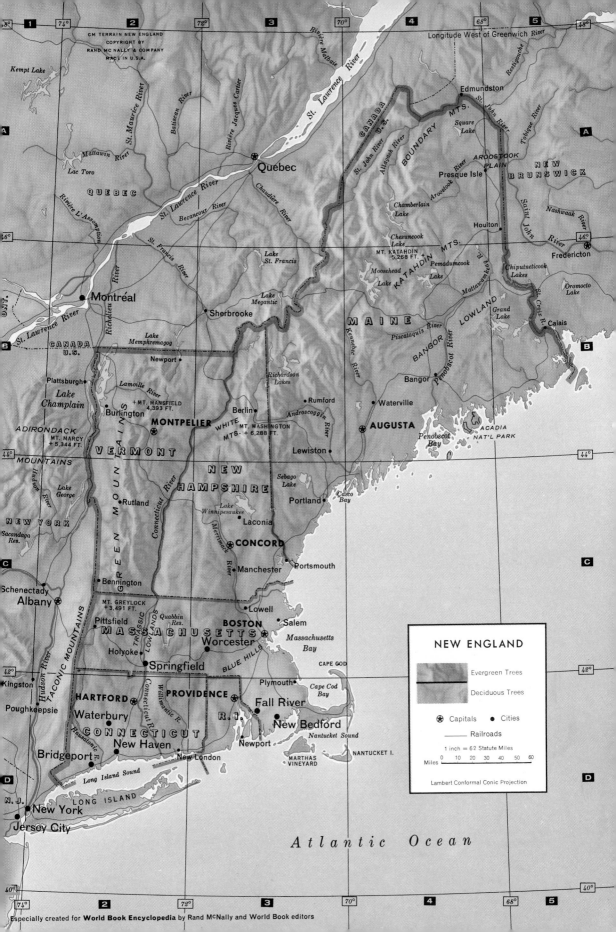

Longitude West of Greenwich River

Atlantic Ocean

NEW ENGLAND

Evergreen Trees

Deciduous Trees

⊛ Capitals   • Cities

—— Railroads

1 inch = 62 Statute Miles

Miles 0 10 20 30 40 50 60

Lambert Conformal Conic Projection

tourist and vacation center. Many interesting old villages add color to the rolling countryside.

The history of the region is rich with contributions to the American way of life. Early settlers in New England showed a strong desire for religious freedom, and for the liberty to speak, think, and write as they pleased. Their statesmen helped make these freedoms basic parts of the Constitution of the United States. New England became known as "the hotbed of the American Revolution." It played a chief part between 1765 and 1777 in defining the issues and hastening the actual hostilities of the Revolutionary War. Its people proudly recall the patriotic debates held in Boston's Faneuil Hall, the Boston Tea Party, and the famous ride of Paul Revere. The first shots of the Revolutionary War were fired at Lexington. General George Washington took command of the Continental Army in Cambridge. New England's statesmen include John Adams, John Quincy Adams, and Daniel Webster.

During the 1800's, New England became famous throughout the country for the products of its Yankee ingenuity. Peddlers sold the output of its many mills and factories, built at the fall line of rivers and streams. Famous Yankee inventions included the cotton gin, the six-shooter, the sewing machine, the telephone, and the Concord stagecoach, used in the opening of the West. The region is also rich in seafaring tradition. It produced the towering masts for the early sailing ships and the famous Yankee clippers. Whaling ships sailing from Nantucket and other ports brought back blubber to light oil lamps in American homes.

New Englanders also established the nation's first newspaper, printing press, and library, and the first college, public secondary school, and general high school. About 13 per cent of the nation's colleges and universities are in New England. These schools include such leading institutions as Amherst College, Bowdoin College, Brown University, Dartmouth College, Harvard University, Massachusetts Institute of Technology, Middlebury College, Wesleyan University, Williams College, and Yale University. New England also has about 16 per cent of the nation's scientific and research organizations.

New England has always been a center of artistic activity. It early became the home of many great libraries and museums. During the 1800's, the region produced such great writers as Emily Dickinson, Ralph Waldo Emerson, Nathaniel Hawthorne, Oliver Wendell Holmes, Henry James, Henry Wadsworth Longfellow, Henry David Thoreau, and John Greenleaf Whittier.

The Land and Its Resources

New England has no natural highway or inland waterway to the West. Its rivers run southward to the Gulf of Maine and Long Island Sound, or northward to Lake Champlain and Canada. A series of north-south mountain ranges rises between the waterways. These mountains discouraged the early settlers from developing commercial traffic with the growing Midwest and West. New England's location helped build a strong unity among its people.

Land Regions. New England has 10 natural land regions: (1) the Coastal Lowlands, (2) the Eastern New England Upland, (3) the Western New England Upland, (4) the White Mountains, (5) the Green Mountains, (6) the Taconic Mountains, (7) the Champlain Valley, (8) the Vermont Valley, (9) the Berkshire Valley, and (10) the Connecticut Valley Lowland.

The Coastal Lowlands stretch along the Atlantic Coast from easternmost Maine to westernmost Connecticut. They extend inland from 10 to 40 miles in Maine, and form the southeastern section of New Hampshire. This region covers the eastern third of Massachusetts, and includes Cape Cod, Nantucket Island, and Martha's Vineyard. The eastern two-thirds of Rhode Island and a narrow belt along the entire Connecticut coast make up the rest of the lowlands. This rolling land has many sandy beaches, rounded hills, glacial deposits, swamps, small lakes and ponds, and shallow rivers. Seaside resorts, state parks, and many cities and towns lie along the coastal plain. Excellent harbors, including those of Portland and Boston, are parts of the deeply indented coast. This area ranks as New England's most populous and industrialized section.

The Eastern New England Upland lies west of the Coastal Lowlands. It extends southward from Maine's northern border in a wide sweep through Maine, the southern half of New Hampshire, central Massachusetts, western Rhode Island, and eastern Connecticut. This rough, hilly region is an extension of the White Mountains of New Hampshire. Its elevation varies between about 200 and 800 feet. Many small rivers cut through the land, separating its wooded hills. It is an area of many lakes, swift-flowing streams, small towns, and farm communities. The most fertile farming areas include the Aroostook Plateau of northern Maine and the New Hampshire section of the Connecticut River Valley. Many upland sections are tourist centers.

The Western New England Upland includes most of eastern Vermont, part of western Massachusetts, and almost all western Connecticut. Generally, this region is more rugged than the Eastern New England Upland. It includes the Granite Hills in Vermont, the Berkshire Hills in Massachusetts, and a section of forested hills and deep valleys in Connecticut. The region's best farmlands lie along the Connecticut River in eastern Vermont, and along the Housatonic River and its tributaries in western Vermont. The Berkshire Hills in Massachusetts are an important tourist area.

The White Mountains region includes western Maine, northern New Hampshire, and a small area of northeastern Vermont. The lofty ranges of the White Mountains include the Franconia and Presidential in New Hampshire. Their peaks usually remain snow-covered from late September to mid-May. The region has many lakes, and is a popular recreation area.

The Green Mountains region runs through the center of Vermont for the state's entire length. The peaks of this range rise more than 4,000 feet above sea level. Important deposits of asbestos, marble, and talc lie throughout the area.

The Taconic Mountains rise along half of Vermont's western border and run southward into Massachusetts. This region has many swift streams and beautiful lakes, and is noted for its scenery. Miners quarry slate and white marble in the Taconics in Vermont.

The Champlain Valley lies along the upper half of Vermont's western border. It is a region of rolling hills and low mountains that merge into fertile plains bordering Lake Champlain. Farmers raise corn, hay, potatoes, and other crops. Dolomite, slate, and red building stone come from the hills.

The Vermont Valley lies in southwestern Vermont between the Green Mountains and the Taconic Mountains. It is made up of the valleys of several small rivers, including the Batten Kill and Otter Creek. Large marble deposits may be found in the region.

The Berkshire Valley, less than 10 miles wide, extends north and south across Massachusetts in the far western part of the state. It also includes a small corner of northwestern Connecticut. The valley, drained by the Hoosic and Housatonic rivers, has many green meadows. Dairy farming is the main industry.

The Connecticut Valley Lowland is a fertile area of central Massachusetts and central Connecticut. Farmers raise onions, tobacco, and other crops on the flat, reddish land that borders the Connecticut River. This area also ranks as an important industrial region, and supplies traprock for roadbuilding.

Cities. New England has about 75 cities with populations of more than 20,000. Boston is by far New England's largest city. It serves as the manufacturing, shipping, financial, and cultural headquarters of the region. About 2,750,000 persons, or about a fourth of New England's entire population, live in Boston and the 77 other towns and cities that make up the Boston metropolitan district.

Providence ranks as New England's second largest city. It is the center of a busy manufacturing and shipping area. Other New England cities with populations of more than 100,000 include Cambridge, New Bedford, Springfield, and Worcester, all in Massachusetts; and Bridgeport, Hartford, New Haven, Stamford, and Waterbury, all in Connecticut.

The northern New England states of Maine, New Hampshire, and Vermont have no urban centers with 100,000 persons. Maine's largest city, Portland, has a population of 65,116. New Hampshire's largest city, Manchester, has 87,754. Burlington, with a population of 38,633, is Vermont's only city with more than 20,000 persons.

Climate. New England has long, cold winters. The average January temperature ranges from 18°F. in Vermont to 34°F. in Massachusetts. In general, the northern interior regions, such as Maine's Aroostook Plateau and Vermont, have colder winter temperatures and receive more snowfall than the coastal and southern regions. Snowfall varies from about 150 inches annually in the White Mountains to about 50 inches along the coast. The brisk air, deep snows, and long winters in New Hampshire and Vermont help make these states popular winter playgrounds.

Summers are short and cool, with few hot days except in the valleys. The mountain regions generally have cooler summer days than the coastal plain. The average temperature varies only slightly among the states, from 67°F. in Maine, New Hampshire, and Vermont to 70°F. in Rhode Island and Connecticut.

White-Spired Churches, many of them built during colonial days, face the village green, or common, in many New England communities. The Congregational Church in the little fishing village and summer resort of East Boothbay, Me., was built in the early 1800's.

Maine Development Commission

Harvard University stands beside the Charles River in Cambridge, Mass. It was founded in 1636.

Small Antique Shops attract many tourists. They feature articles once used by the American settlers.

A New England Potluck Dinner finds the table almost hidden under stacks of hearty, tasty food.

America's Seafaring History is displayed in the Stillman Museum at Mystic Seaport in Connecticut.

A Vermont Farm is blanketed by winter's first snow. In an average winter, parts of northern New England get about 10 feet of snow.

North America's First Successful Ironworks, at Saugus, Mass., was built in 1646. These restored buildings house the stone blast furnace, the forge, and the rolling mill.

Rain falls rather evenly throughout New England. Northern Maine and the Champlain Valley, with about 32 inches of rain annually, receive the least amount. The rest of New England has between 32 and 45 inches of rainfall. Southern Connecticut and the higher mountain regions have the most rain.

New England's growing season ranges between 100 and 200 days. Northern Maine has between 100 and 125 frost-free days, central New England has about 150, and the coastal regions of Massachusetts, Rhode Island, and Connecticut have between 175 and 200.

Activities of the People

The People. Almost half of the people of New England live in Massachusetts, the nation's third most densely populated state. Connecticut, with the second largest share of New England's population, is the fourth most densely populated state.

The earliest settlers were Pilgrims and Puritans, who came to the region from England in the 1600's. Most of these people had a common cultural background. They were deeply religious individualists, and had a special resourcefulness and conservatism that became a strong New England tradition. The early people of New England received the nickname of *Yankees*. This name signifies their frugality, conservatism, and inventiveness. See YANKEE.

Because of New England's economic activities, personal income here exceeds the national average by 10 per cent. The people have 50 per cent more money in savings accounts, carry more life insurance, and own more home appliances than the average American. New England's savings institutions hold 20 per cent of the nation's resources kept in such banks. The region has become nationally famous for its insurance companies. New England's investment assets amount to more than 13 per cent of the country's total, making it the second most important financial center in the United States.

Manufacturing and Processing provides about a third of New England's personal income, and is the largest source of personal income. About 1,500,000 men and women work in the region's 24,000 plants and mills. Manufacturing ranks as the largest source of personal income in each of the six states. Massachusetts earns almost half of New England's personal income, and Connecticut accounts for about a third. This distribution of income-earning activities is one of New England's biggest economic problems. Three-fourths of the manufacturing activities center in the region's 18 largest cities. These cities have two-thirds of New England's popula-

175

tion, and have been hard hit during economic recessions. This is especially true of cities whose economies depend on a single industry, such as textiles.

Raw materials for New England's plants and mills, and markets for its manufactures, lie at great distances. Long-distance hauling adds to the production costs of the various manufactures. The region lost its top rank in the textile industry during the 1930's and 1940's, when the semiskilled labor required became available in the South and in other regions nearer the bulky raw materials. New England helped make up this economic loss by increasing its electronics and metal-fabricating industries. The value of the technical skills required in these industries more than offsets the increased transportation costs.

New England manufactures, in order of economic importance, include machinery, textiles, electrical machinery, transportation equipment; and metal, processed food, pulp and paper, and leather products. Factories in the six states make about 30 per cent of the nation's machine tools, 15 per cent of its electronics equipment, 38 per cent of its shoes, and 56 per cent of its newsprint. North America's largest single producer of newsprint operates at Millinocket and East Millinocket, Me. New England also manufactures 80 per cent of the country's sporting firearms, 80 per cent of its silverware, 50 per cent of its typewriters, 45 per cent of its cutlery, 37 per cent of its ball and roller bearings, 30 per cent of its abrasive products, and 30 per cent of its insulated wire and cable. Steel manufacturing in North America began in Hartford County, Connecticut, in 1728.

Massachusetts ranks first among the states in leather production, and is a leader in the production of clothing, plastics, and textiles, and in printing and publishing. Rhode Island is an important glass maker and textile producer. Maine is an important paper and leather producer.

Tourist Industry provides New England's second largest source of income. Over ten million tourists visit the region every year. Many come for the clean, crisp air, or to be lulled to sleep by the surf pounding against the craggy coast. Leading attractions include Cape Cod, the White and the Green mountains, hundreds of coastal beaches and mountain lakes, yachting harbors, and winter-sports areas. Many tourists visit Plymouth, Lexington, Bunker Hill, Concord, Salem, Boston, and other historic sites. Visitors enjoy displays of colonial and maritime life such as at Old Sturbridge Village, Mystic Seaport, the Shelburne Museum, the Old Dartmouth Whaling Museum, the Adams houses at Quincy, and the Wayside Inn. Along the way, they may visit the beautiful colonial homes that crowd the streets of Bath, Portsmouth, Newburyport, and other towns. The rural New England countryside has many charming old villages built around a common, or green, that faces a white-spired church. Luxurious resorts such as Bar Harbor, Bretton Woods, Chatham, Newport, Lenox, and Great Barrington also attract visitors.

Special New England events include the Berkshire Music Festival, the Jazz Festival at Newport, several winter carnivals, maple-sugar making parties, clambakes, country fairs, fishing derbies, and autumn foliage tours.

Agriculture. Only about 1 per cent of the nation's farmland lies in New England. Most farms are small, because of the generally hilly terrain and rocky soil. Poultry and eggs and dairy products account for almost two-thirds of the farm income. New England farms account for about 5 per cent of the value of the nation's poultry and dairy products. About 15 per cent of the nation's potatoes come from these farms.

Several New England agricultural products are famous throughout the country. Cranberries grow in marshy bogs along the coast in Massachusetts and Maine. Massachusetts ranks as the leading cranberry-producing state. Vermont maple orchards make that state one of the country's leaders in the production of maple syrup and maple sugar. Potatoes from Maine's northern Aroostook Plateau are shipped throughout the country. Maine ranks second to Idaho in potato production. Large crops of tobacco are grown under canvas shades in the fertile Connecticut Valley Lowland of Massachusetts and Connecticut.

Mining. Granite, marble, and other building stones account for most of New England's mineral output. Massachusetts ranks second to Georgia in granite production, and Vermont is third. Other important commercial minerals include sand, gravel, and crushed stone.

Fishing Industry. New England totals about one-seventh of the nation's fish catch. Maine lobstermen take the country's biggest lobster haul. Massachusetts and New Hampshire are also leaders in lobster fishing. Important commercial fish include ocean perch, haddock, scallops, cod, flounder, whiting, pollack, and mackerel. New England plants process about four-fifths of the nation's packaged and frozen sea food.

Forest Products. New England has about 13 per cent of the country's commercial forests. Factories and mills throughout the region make boxes, wood pulp, furniture, and many other wood products.

Transportation. Shipping has been important in New England since early days. In 1786, Samuel Shaw, a New England businessman, established the first American mercantile house in China, at Canton. In 1787, the *Grand Turk* brought to Salem the first of many Oriental cargoes that, for a time, made Salem the third largest city in the nation. Between 1787 and 1790, Captain Robert Gray's *Columbia* carried the American flag around the world for the first time. This voyage laid the foundations for the country's claim to Oregon. It also began a very profitable trade with the northwest coast. New England ships exchanged furs from this region in China for teas and silks.

Today, Boston is New England's busiest port and ranks as the nation's 19th largest in volume of goods handled. About 21 million tons of cargo pass through the port each year. New England's next busiest ports, Portland and Providence, together handle about 25 million tons of freight each year.

Early New England settlers built few roads. Boat service linked the towns along the coast and along rivers. Today, more than 95,000 miles of roads and highways serve the people of the region. About 85,000 miles of these roadways are surfaced. Modern superhighways and toll roads link major centers. The Massachusetts Turnpike stretches westward from near Boston to the New York state line near Albany. The Northern Circumferential Highway swings in a great arc around

Boston and its suburbs from Gloucester to Cohasset. The New Hampshire Turnpike parallels the seacoast for 15 miles, and the Spaulding Turnpike extends the seacoast road from Portsmouth to Rochester. The Everett Turnpike links Concord and the Massachusetts border. The Maine Turnpike extends 106 miles from Kittery to Augusta. The 129-mile Connecticut Turnpike runs from Greenwich to Killingly.

New England has about 6,230 miles of railroads. Boston is the region's main railroad center. Railroads in the area carry mostly freight and commuting passengers.

Logan International Airport, at Boston, is New England's major air center. The region has about 125 public airports, and all important cities have air service.

Regional Cooperation. New England has several regional organizations that study and seek solutions to the area's business and economic problems. The New England Council, established in 1925, is a region-wide association of manufacturers, bankers, business concerns, farmers, and representatives of labor, government, and other groups. Its programs are designed to make full use of New England's resources, and encourage development in industry, agriculture, recreation, and other fields. The New England World Trade Center promotes trade between the region's business firms and those in other countries.   HENRY F. HOWE

Related Articles. See the articles on the New England states with their lists of Related Articles. See also:

Outline

I. **The Land and Its Resources**
    A. Land Regions   B. Cities   C. Climate
II. **Activities of the People**
    A. The People
    B. Manufacturing and
        Processing
    C. Tourist Industry
    D. Agriculture
    E. Mining
    F. Fishing Industry
    G. Forest Products
    H. Transportation
    I. Regional Cooperation

Questions

What states make up New England?
What is the largest source of income in New England?
Why are tourists important to New England?
What is New England's main air center?
What is one of New England's economic problems?
What is a popular nickname for New Englanders?
Who gave New England its name? When?
Why did New England's textile industry decline?
Which of the New England states has the most people?

NEW ENGLAND COLLEGE. See UNIVERSITIES AND COLLEGES (table).

NEW ENGLAND, DOMINION OF, was a group of English colonies in America united in 1686 by King James II of England. The colonies in the dominion were Connecticut, Massachusetts, New Hampshire, New Jersey, New York, Plymouth, and Rhode Island. King James believed the colonies could function best under a single government. But the colonists had no voice in the government, and most of them opposed the dominion. James was overthrown in England in 1688. The dominion broke up the next year, before it had begun to function completely as a government. MARSHALL SMELSER

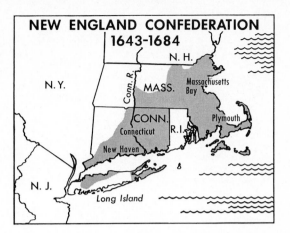

NEW ENGLAND CONFEDERATION 1643-1684

NEW ENGLAND CONFEDERATION was organized in 1643. Four colonies—Massachusetts, Plymouth, Connecticut, and New Haven—formed the UNITED COLONIES OF NEW ENGLAND, as it was called. They worked to solve boundary disputes and to meet the increased danger of attacks by the Dutch, French, and Indians. Maine, New Hampshire, and Rhode Island were excluded from membership for political and religious reasons.

The four colonies agreed to "enter into a firm and perpetual league of friendship and amity, for offence and defence, mutual advice and succor upon all just occasions, both for preserving and propagating the truth and liberties of the gospel, and for their own mutual safety and welfare."

Two commissioners from each member colony met each year to consider problems that were of mutual interest. The confederation had great power in theory, but, in practice, it could only advise. Under confederation regulations, three colonies comprised a decisive majority. A test of the confederation's power came in 1653, when Plymouth, Connecticut, and New Haven favored a war against the Dutch of New Netherland. The fourth colony, Massachusetts, did not agree and absolutely refused to yield. This action lessened the prestige of the organization. After 1664, the commissioners met only every three years, and in 1684 the confederation came to an end.

Despite serious weaknesses, the New England confederation provided valuable experience in discussion and cooperation among the colonies. It also helped prevent the smaller colonies from being totally dominated by Massachusetts.   ALBERT E. VAN DUSEN

NEW ENGLAND CONSERVATORY OF MUSIC, in Boston, Mass., is the oldest music conservatory in the United States. It was founded in 1867. The conservatory grants the degrees of Mus.B. and Mus.M. It also grants the Undergraduate Diploma and Artists' Diploma. For enrollment, see UNIVERSITIES AND COLLEGES (table).   JOHN McKEE

NEW ENGLAND PRIMER. See LITERATURE FOR CHILDREN (The History of Children's Literature).

NEW FRANCE. See CANADA, HISTORY OF.

NEW FRONTIER. See KENNEDY, JOHN FITZGERALD.

NEW GRANADA. See COLOMBIA (History).

NEW GUINEA

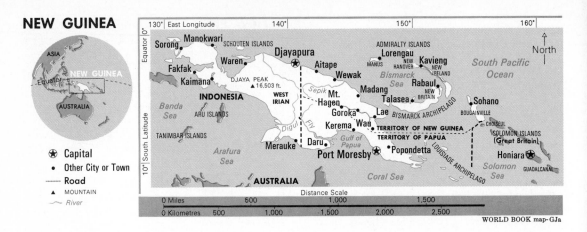

NEW GUINEA is the second largest island in the world. Only Greenland is larger. Some parts of the island have never been explored. New Guinea lies north of Australia, across the Torres Strait.

The Land and Its Resources. The island of New Guinea covers 311,796 square miles. Its greatest length, from northwest to southeast, is about 1,500 miles. Its greatest width, from north to south, is about 430 miles. Many smaller islands lie near the shore.

High mountain ranges run down the center of the island. The important ranges include the Sudirman, Djajawidjaja, Bismarck, and Owen-Stanley mountains. Djaja Peak, in western New Guinea, rises 16,503 feet above sea level. It is the highest point on the island. The coastal plains are often marshy. Important rivers include the Mamberambo, in the west, and the Sepik and the Fly, in the east.

New Guinea's climate generally is hot and humid, except in some parts of the mountain region. The island has an over-all average temperature of 80° F.

Most of New Guinea is covered with tropical jungles. Wild animals on the island, such as the *echidna*, a relative of the duckbill, and the *bandicoot*, a ratlike animal, are related to animals found in Australia.

Other animals include bats, crocodiles, Australian opossums, tree kangaroos, and rodents. Mineral deposits include gold, silver, platinum, and petroleum. New Guinea exports minerals, fibers, copra, lumber and forest products, and rubber.

The People and Their Work. About 2½ million people live on the island of New Guinea. Most of the people are Melanesians. Some Malaysians and Polynesians live on the coast. Pygmies live in the remote highlands. There are also about 10,000 Europeans, Australians, and Chinese on New Guinea. Most of the people supply all their needs by growing their own food, fishing, hunting, and gathering wild fruits and vegetables. Most islanders have only crude tools and weapons made of stone or wood. Many tribes in central New Guinea were once head-hunters. The way of life is generally more modern along the coast than inland.

Government. New Guinea has three political divisions. Indonesia controls the western half of New Guinea. The eastern half is divided into the Territory of Papua in the south, and the UN Trust Territory of New Guinea in the north, both governed by Australia. All three areas include offshore islands.

West Irian, formerly called *West New Guinea,* covers

Australian News and Information Bureau; Photo-Representatives

Technical Training, *left,* helps New Guinea develop an industrial economy. But hand labor, *above,* accounts for most production.

Port Moresby, the capital of the Territory of Papua and New Guinea, is on the southeast coast of New Guinea. Its deep, protected harbor helps make it an important commercial center.

APF

about 162,916 square miles on the western half of New Guinea. It has about 758,400 people. Djajapura (formerly Hollandia) is the capital. Indonesia took control of West Irian in 1963.

The Territory of Papua, formerly called *British New Guinea,* covers 86,100 square miles in the southeastern part of New Guinea. About 685,000 people live there.

The Territory of New Guinea covers the northeastern corner of New Guinea, called *North East New Guinea,* and includes the Bismarck Archipelago and some of the Solomon Islands. The territory has an area of 92,160 square miles, and about 1,663,000 people.

Australia governs both Papua and New Guinea as one area, called the *Territory of Papua and New Guinea.* An Australian administrator controls the combined territory from the capital at Port Moresby, in Papua. He is assisted by a House of Assembly with 10 appointed members and 84 others who are elected to four-year terms. Local councils handle local affairs.

History. Antonio de Abrea, the Portuguese navigator who sighted New Guinea in 1511, was probably the first European to see the island. But the first European to land was Jorge de Meneses, the Portuguese governor of the nearby Molucca Islands. He went ashore in 1526. In 1660, the Sultan of Ternate gave the Dutch East India Company control over most of western New Guinea. In 1828, The Netherlands annexed western New Guinea. Great Britain and The Netherlands agreed on a rough boundary line dividing the island in 1884. German merchants began colonizing the northeastern section of the island, which they called *Kaiser Wilhelms-*

land. The British claimed the southeastern section in 1884 and passed it on to Australia in 1906, calling it *Papua.* Australian forces occupied Kaiser Wilhelmsland during World War I. The League of Nations gave Australia a mandate over the German territory in 1920.

Japanese forces occupied most of the northeastern coastal area early in World War II. But Allied forces pushed up the coast from the south, and other troops landed at Hollandia (now renamed Djajapura). Japanese forces were cut off from their base and surrendered at the end of the war. In 1950, after the Republic of Indonesia was formed, the Dutch refused to give up their part of New Guinea. Indonesia claimed the area on grounds that it is geographically part of Indonesia. But The Netherlands kept control of the region, claiming that the peoples of New Guinea are not racially related to the peoples of Indonesia. In 1962, Indonesia threatened to seize the area by force. The Dutch and Indonesia finally signed an agreement on Aug. 15, 1962, transferring territorial administration to the United Nations until Indonesia took control in May, 1963.   JUSTUS M. VAN DER KROEF

Related Articles in WORLD BOOK include:

Bandicoot	New Britain
Biak Island	Owen-Stanley Mountains
Bird of Paradise	Pacific Islands
Bismarck Archipelago	Papua
Bougainville	Schouten Islands
Coconut Palm (table)	Sculpture (Pacific Islands)
D'Entrecasteaux Islands	Torres Strait
Echidna	World War II (The
Idol (picture)	South Pacific)

179

NEW HAMPSHIRE

THE GRANITE STATE

NEW HAMPSHIRE is a New England state noted for its natural beauty and year-round outdoor activities. In summer, vacationers flock to New Hampshire's rugged mountains, blue lakes, sandy beaches, and quiet villages. In the fall, visitors tour the countryside ablaze with brilliant red, orange, and yellow leaves. In winter, skiers race down snow-covered slopes and then warm themselves near crackling fires in friendly ski lodges. These and other attractions bring millions of tourists to tiny New Hampshire, and give the state a major source of income.

But New Hampshire is more than a vacation wonderland. New Hampshire is the home of freedom-loving, industrious people who built a prosperous state and helped form a nation.

New Hampshire was first settled in 1623, just three years after the Pilgrims landed in Massachusetts. Early New Hampshire settlers carved farms out of a wilderness and worked the land for food. Later, New Hampshirites turned their skills and their state's resources to industrial development. They cut down trees for the giant lumber and papermaking industries. They took minerals from the mountains and hills to start a mining industry. They used the rivers and lakes as sources of power for mills and factories. And they built ships along the state's small Atlantic coastline. In all, the people of New Hampshire changed a wilderness into a farming society, and then turned the farming society into a thriving industrial state.

New Hampshire and its people have played important roles in United States history. On Jan. 5, 1776, New Hampshire became the first of the 13 original colonies to adopt its own constitution. On June 21, 1788, it became the ninth state to ratify the U.S. Constitution. This act put the Constitution into effect. The U.S. Navy's first shipbuilding yard opened at Portsmouth in 1800. One of the country's first tax-supported public libraries was established at Peterborough in 1833. In 1853, Franklin Pierce of New Hampshire became the 14th President of the United States. Daniel Webster, a leading statesman and orator of the 1800's, was born in New Hampshire. So were Mary Baker Eddy, founder of the Christian Science religious movement, and Alan B. Shepard, the first American astronaut to travel in space.

New Hampshire's large granite deposits give it the nickname of the *Granite State*. Concord is the state capital and Manchester is the largest city. For the relationship of New Hampshire to other states in its region, see NEW ENGLAND.

A New Hampshire Village in Autumn

New Hampshire Harvest

New Hampshire (blue) ranks 44th in size among the states, and is the third largest of the New England States (gray).

The contributors of this article are Albert S. Carlson, Professor of Geography at Dartmouth College; Hugh R. O'Neil, Editor of the Manchester Union Leader; *and J. Duane Squires, Chairman of the Department of Social Studies at Colby Junior College, and author of* The Story of New Hampshire.

——————— FACTS IN BRIEF ———————

Capital: Concord.

Government: *Congress*—U.S. senators, 2; U.S. representatives, 2. *Electoral Votes*—4. *State Legislature*—senators, 24; representatives, from 375 to 400. *Counties*—10. *Voting Age*—21 years (state and local elections); 18 years (national elections).

Area: 9,304 square miles (including 271 square miles of inland water), 44th in size among the states. *Greatest Distances*—(north-south) 180 miles; (east-west) 93 miles. *Coastline*—13 miles.

Elevation: *Highest*—Mount Washington, 6,288 feet above sea level; *Lowest*—sea level, along the Atlantic Ocean.

Population: *1970 Census*—737,681; 41st among the states; density, 79 persons to the square mile; distribution, 56 per cent urban, 44 per cent rural. *1960 Census*—606,921.

Chief Products: *Agriculture*—apples, beef cattle, chickens, dairy products, eggs, forest products, greenhouse and nursery products. *Fishing Industry*—cod, haddock, lobsters, smelt. *Manufacturing*—electrical machinery, food products, leather and leather products, lumber and wood products, nonelectrical machinery, paper and paper products, printing and publishing, rubber and plastics products, textiles. *Mining*—clays, feldspar, mica, sand and gravel, stone.

Statehood: June 21, 1788, the ninth state.

State Motto: *Live Free or Die.*

State Songs: "Old New Hampshire." Words by John F. Holmes; music by Maurice Hoffmann. "New Hampshire, My New Hampshire." Words by Julius Richelson; music by Walter P. Smith.

Constitution of New Hampshire was adopted in 1784. It replaced a temporary constitution adopted in 1776. Constitutional amendments may be proposed by a three-fifths vote of each house of the state legislature, or by a constitutional convention. To become law, a proposed amendment needs the approval of two-thirds of the persons voting on the issue in an election.

A majority of the members of both houses of the legislature may propose a constitutional convention. The proposal must be approved by a majority of the citizens voting on it. In the absence of a proposal, the question of holding a convention must be voted on by the people every 10 years.

Executive. The governor of New Hampshire holds office for a two-year term. He may be re-elected any number of times. The governor receives a salary of $30,000 a year. For a list of all the governors of New Hampshire, see the *History* section of this article.

The executive branch of the New Hampshire government is somewhat unusual. The state has no lieutenant governor. But it does have a five-member executive council. Members of the executive council are elected by the people to two-year terms, and serve as advisers to the governor. The major executive officials appointed by the governor must be approved by the council. These officials include the adjutant general, attorney general, commissioner of agriculture, and comptroller. The New Hampshire legislature elects the secretary of state and state treasurer to two-year terms.

Legislature is called the *General Court*. By law, it consists of a 24-member Senate and a House of Representatives of not less than 375 nor more than 400 members. In the late 1960's, the House of Representatives had 400 members. The U.S. House of Representatives is the only legislative body in the country with more members than the New Hampshire house. New Hampshire's towns and *wards* (divisions of cities) send from one to seven legislators to the House of Representatives, depending on their populations. Representatives serve two-year terms. Voters in each of the 24 senatorial districts elect one senator to a two-year term. Senatorial districts are also based on population. In 1965, the legislature *reapportioned* (redivided) all districts to give more equal representation based on population.

The legislature meets on the first Wednesday of January in odd-numbered years. Legislators receive a fixed salary for regular sessions. Their allowance for travel expenses ends after July 1 or 90 business days, whichever comes first. Legislators are paid for 15 business days during special sessions of the General Court. The governor or the General Court can call special sessions.

Courts. The Supreme Court of New Hampshire has a chief justice and four associate justices. The next lower court, the superior court, has a chief justice and nine associates. A probate judge presides over each of the state's 10 probate courts, one in each county. In 1963, New Hampshire began replacing its 85 municipal courts with 37 district courts. The governor, with approval of the executive council, appoints all state and local judges. Judges may serve until they are 70 years old.

Local Government in New Hampshire operates as one of the purest forms of democracy in the world. The state's 222 towns are nicknamed "little republics." They are so named because they have almost complete self-government. Each year, the voters assemble for a town meeting at which they can participate directly in governmental decisions. Voters elect town officials, approve budgets, and decide on other local business. The chief town administrative officials are three *selectmen*. One selectman is chosen each year for a three-year term.

New Hampshire's 13 incorporated cities use either the mayor-council or city-manager form of government. The cities have *home rule*. That is, they are free to write and amend their own charters. Each of the state's 10 counties also has its own government. County officials include the sheriff, attorney, treasurer, register of deeds, register of probate, and county commissioners. These officials are elected to two-year terms.

Taxation provides about two-thirds of the state government's income. The other third comes from the federal government. Taxes on the sale of motor fuels, alcoholic beverages, tobacco products, restaurant meals,

David F. Lawlor, Devaney

Town Meeting, in Dublin, shows one of the purest forms of democracy at work. All New Hampshire towns hold annual meetings at which the townspeople elect officials and vote on local issues. Everyone in the town is invited, and all who attend may express their views.

The State Seal

Symbols of New Hampshire. On the state seal, a reproduction of the Revolutionary War frigate *Raleigh* is surrounded by a laurel wreath to symbolize victory. The date 1776 is the year the state's first constitution was adopted. On the state flag, adopted in 1909, a copy of the state seal is surrounded by nine stars in a laurel wreath. This shows that New Hampshire was the ninth state to ratify the United States Constitution.

Seal, flag, and flower illustrations, courtesy of Eli Lilly and Company

The State Flag

and on motel and hotel room rates bring in a large share of the state's revenue. License fees and horse racing taxes are also important. New Hampshire also has a sweepstakes lottery to help pay public school costs.

Politics. New Hampshire became a Republican state shortly before the Civil War. Until 1850, the state usually voted Democratic. But most New Hampshirites opposed slavery and then became Republicans.

Republicans usually control the state legislature. Since 1856, most New Hampshire governors and U.S. Senators and Representatives have been Republicans. New Hampshire Democrats scored a political breakthrough in 1962. They elected their first Democratic governor in 40 years and their first Democratic U.S. Senator in 30 years. Republican candidates have won New Hampshire's electoral votes in all but six presidential elections since 1856. In 1964, the state voted Democratic in a presidential election for the first time in 20 years. For New Hampshire's electoral votes and voting record in presidential elections, see ELECTORAL COLLEGE (table).

The State Bird
Purple Finch

State Capitol is in Concord, the capital since 1808. The building dates from 1819. Earlier capitals included Portsmouth (1679-1774), Exeter (1775-1781), and Concord (1782-1784).

New Hampshire Division of Economic Development

The State Flower
Purple Lilac

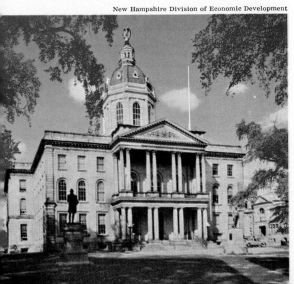

The State Tree
White Birch

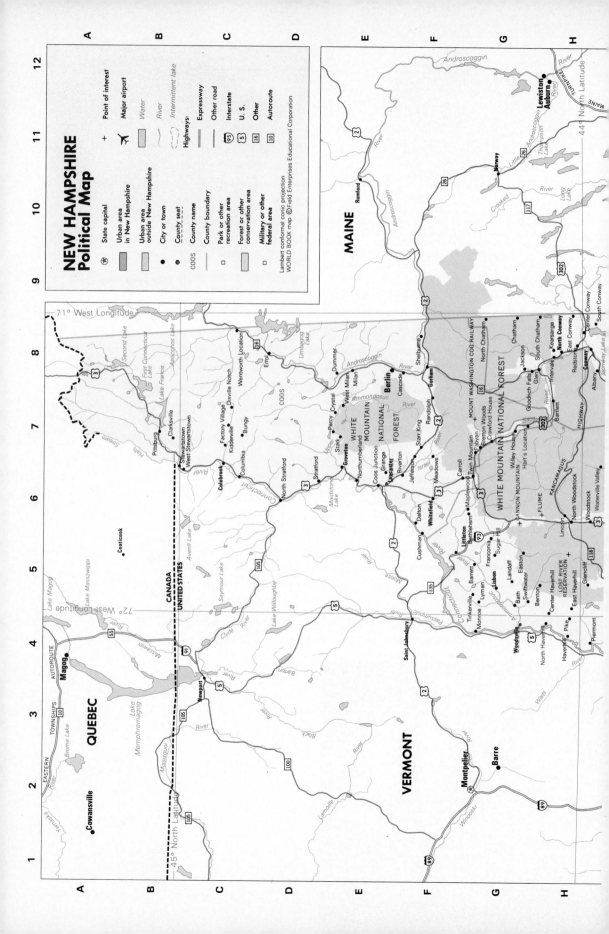

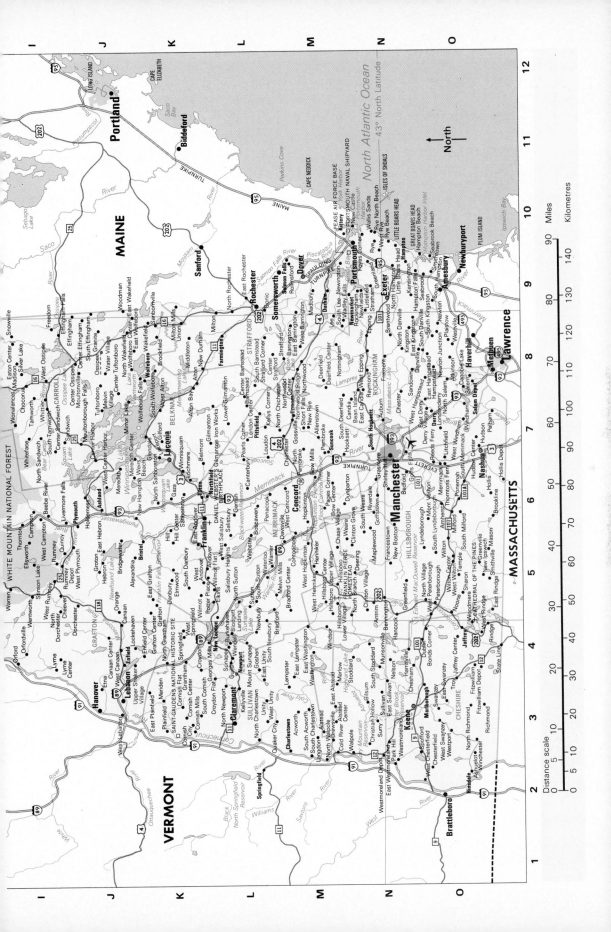

NEW HAMPSHIRE MAP INDEX

Population

737,681		1970
606,921	Census	1960
533,242		1950
491,524		1940
465,293		1930
443,083		1920
430,572		1910
411,588		1900
376,530		1890
346,991		1880
318,300		1870
326,073		1860
317,976		1850
284,574		1840
269,328		1830
244,161		1820
214,460		1810
183,858		1800
141,885		1790

Metropolitan Areas

Manchester	108,461
Nashua	66,458

Counties

Belknap	32,367	K 7
Carroll	18,548	K 6
Cheshire	52,364	D 7
Coos	34,291	O 3
Grafton	54,914	J 4
Hillsborough	223,941	N 5
Merrimack	80,925	L 6
Rockingham	138,951	N 8
Strafford	70,431	L 3
Sullivan	30,949	L 3

Cities and Towns

Acworth 459▲ M 3
Albany 259▲ H 5
Alexandria 466▲ J 5
Allenstown 2,732▲ M 7
Alstead 1,185▲ K 8
Alton 1,647▲ K 8
Alton Bay K 6
Amherst 4,605▲ N 6
Andover 1,138▲ K 6
Antrim 2,122▲ N 5
Ashland 1,391 (1,599▲) J 6
Ashuelot K 7
Atkinson 2,291▲ O 7
Auburn 2,035▲ N 7
Barnstead 1,119▲ L 7
Barrington 1,865▲ M 7
Bartlett 1,098▲ H 4
Bedford 5,859▲ N 6
Beebe River I 4
Belmont 2,493▲ K 7
Bennington 639▲ N 5
Benton 194▲ H 4
Berlin 15,256▲ O 3
Bethlehem 1,142▲ H 3
Boscawen 3,162▲ L 6
Bow* 2,479▲ M 6
Bradford 679▲ L 5
Brentwood 1,468▲ N 7
Bretton Woods H 3
Bridgewater 308▲ J 6
Bristol (1,670▲) 1,080 K 6

Brookfield 198▲ K 8
Brookline 1,167▲ O 6
Canaan 1,171▲ J 4
Candia 1,923▲ N 7
Canobie Lake O 8
Canterbury 895▲ L 6
Carroll 310▲ F 8
Cascade F 8
Center Harbor 540▲ J 7
Center Ossipee J 7
Center Sandwich J 7
Charlestown 1,285 (3,274▲) M 3
Chatham 134▲ G 6
Chester 1,382▲ N 8
Chesterfield (3,274▲) K 3
Chichester 1,817▲ O 2
Chocorua I 3
Christian Hollow 1,083▲ N 3
Claremont 14,221 L 4
Clarksville 166▲ B 7
Colebrook (2,094▲) 1,070 C 6
Columbia 467▲ C 6
Concord 30,022 ○M 6
Contoocook 1,489 M 6
Conway (4,865▲) O 5
Coos Junction E 6
Cornish* 1,268▲ E 6
Crawford House 396▲ G 6
Croydon 425▲ K 4
Danbury 939▲ K 5
Danville 578▲ F 8
Deerfield 1,778▲ M 6
Deering 6,090 M 5
Derry (11,712▲) O 7
Dorchester 141▲ J 5
Dover 20,850 ○M 9
Dublin 837▲ E 4
Dummer 225▲ E 6
Dunbarton 825▲ M 6
Durham 7,221 M 9
East Andover K 6
East Alstead M 5
East Hampstead O 7
East Haverhill H 5
East Kingston 838▲ N 9
East Lempster M 3
East Swanzey L 4
East Wolfeboro J 7
Easton 92▲ G 5
Eaton* 221▲ A 7
Effingham Falls 360▲ J 8
Elkins K 5
Ellsworth 13▲ I 4
Enfield 1,408 J 4
Epping 2,345▲ N 8
Epsom 2,356▲ M 7
Errol 194▲ D 4
Exeter 8,892▲ N 8
Fabyan G 6
Factory Village C 7
Farmington 2,884 M 8
Fitzwilliam 1,362▲ L 3
Fitzwilliam Depot O 4

Francestown 525▲ N 5
Franconia 654▲ K 6
Franklin 7,292 K 6
Freedom 387▲ J 7
Fremont 993▲ N 8
Georges Mills K 5
Gilford 3,219▲ K 7
Gilmanton 1,010▲ L 7
Gilmanton Iron Works L 7
Gilsum 570▲ L 3
Glen H 5
Glencliff I 4
Glendale K 7
Goffstown 9,284▲ N 6
Gonic M 9
Goodrich Falls G 6
Gorham (2,998▲) 2,020 F 5
Goshen 395▲ K 4
Gossville M 7
Grafton 370▲ K 5
Granite B 7
Grasmere 360▲ N 6
Greenfield 1,058▲ N 5
Greenland 1,784▲ N 9
Greenville 1,332 O 5
Groton 120▲ I 5
Groveton 1,597 E 6
Guild K 4
Hampstead 2,401▲ O 8
Hampton 5,407 N 9
Hampton Beach N 9
Hampton Falls 1,254▲ N 9
Hancock 1,909▲ N 4
Hanover (8,494▲) 6,147 I 4
Harrisville 584▲ L 3
Haverhill 3,090▲ H 4
Hebron 234▲ J 5
Henniker 2,348▲ M 5
Hill 450▲ K 5
Hillsboro 1,784 M 5
Hinsdale (3,276▲) 2,775▲ L 3
Hollis 2,616▲ O 6
Holderness 1,048▲ J 6
Hooksett 5,564 ○M 7
Hopkinton 3,007▲ M 6
Hudson 10,638▲ O 7
Hudson Center O 7
Intervale H 5
Jackson 234▲ G 5
Jaffrey 2,348▲ N 4
Jefferson 714▲ F 7
Kearsarge G 6
Keene 20,467 ○L 3
Kellys Corner L 3
Kensington 1,044▲ N 9
Kidderville C 6
Kingston 2,882▲ O 8
Laconia 14,888 ○K 7
Lakeport K 7
Lancaster 2,120 E 6
Landaff 292▲ H 4
Langdon 337▲ M 3
Lebanon (13,166▲) 1,362▲ J 4
Lee 1,481▲ M 9

Lempster 525▲ N 5
Lincoln 1,341▲ H 4
Lisbon (1,480▲) 1,247 G 5
Litchfield 993▲ N 6
Little Boars Head N 9
Littleton (5,290▲) 4,180 G 8
Livermore Falls I 4
Lochmere K 7
Lockhaven K 3
Londonderry 5,346▲ O 7
Loudon 1,707▲ L 7
Lower Gilmanton L 7
Lyman 213▲ H 4
Lynde borough 789▲ N 5
Madbury 704▲ M 9
Madison 572▲ H 6
Manchester 87,754 N 6
Maplewood G 8
Marlborough 1,231 L 3
Marlow 390▲ L 3
Mason 518▲ O 5
Meadows M 3
Melvin Mills L 7
Melvin Village J 7
Meredith (1,587▲) 1,332 J 7
Meredith Center J 7
Meriden 1,597 L 4
Merrimack 8,595▲ N 6
Middleton 430▲ L 8
Milan 713▲ E 4
Milford (6,622▲) 4,997 N 6
Milton 1,254▲ L 8
Milton Mills 1,909▲ L 8
Mirror Lake J 7
Monroe 385▲ G 4
Mont Vernon 906▲ N 6
Moultonborough 1,310▲ J 7
Moultonville J 8
Moultonborough Falls J 7
Mountainview L 4
Mount Sunapee K 5
Munsonville L 4
Nashua 55,820 ○O 6
Nelson 287▲ L 4
New Boston 1,390▲ N 6
New Castle 975▲ N 10
New Durham 583▲ K 8
New Hampton 946▲ J 6
New Ipswich 1,803▲ O 5
New London (2,236▲) 1,347 K 5
New Rye L 5
Newbury 509▲ L 5
Newfields 843▲ N 8
Newington 798▲ M 9
Newmarket (3,361▲) 2,645 N 9
Newport 5,899▲ L 4
Newton 1,920▲ O 8
Newton Junction O 8
Noone N 4
North Branch M 5
North Chatham G 6
North Chichester M 7
North Conway (3,196▲) G 6

North Hampton 3,259▲ N 9
North Haverhill H 4
North Richmond L 3
North Rochester L 9
North Salem O 8
North Sandwich I 7
North Stratford D 6
North Sutton L 5
North Village J 7
North Walpole M 2
North Weare N 6
North Wolfeboro K 8
North Woodstock H 4
Northfield, see Tilton
Northfield* 2,193▲ K 6
Northumberland 2,493▲ E 6
Northwood 1,526▲ M 8
Northwood Ridge M 8
Nottingham 1,227▲ N 8
Orange 103▲ J 5
Orford 793▲ I 4
Orfordville I 4
Ossipee (6,622▲) 1,647▲ J 7
Pages Corner M 3
Park Hill L 3
Pearls Corner N 7
Pelham 5,408▲ O 7
Pembroke 4,261▲ M 7
Penacook L 6
Percy E 5
Peterborough (2,904▲) 2,078 N 5
Piermont (3,807▲) 462▲ I 4
Pike I 4
Pittsburg 724▲ B 7
Pittsfield (2,517▲) 1,662 M 7
Plainfield 1,323▲ L 4
Plaistow 4,712▲ O 8
Plymouth (4,225▲) 3,109 J 6
Ponemah N 6
Portsmouth 25,717 ○N 10
Potter Place L 6
Quaker City L 3
Quincy City J 8
Randolph 169▲ F 5
Raymond 3,003▲ N 8
Redstone H 5
Reeds Ferry 287▲ N 6
Richmond 304▲ L 3
Rindge 1,390▲ O 4
Riverton E 5
Rochester 17,938 L 9
Rockingham N 8
Rollinsford 2,273▲ M 9
Roxbury 161▲ L 3
Rumney 870▲ I 5
Rye 4,083▲ N 10
Rye Beach N 10
Salem 20,142 O 8
Salem Depot O 8
Salisbury 589▲ L 6
Salisbury Heights L 6
Salmon Falls M 9
Sanbornton 1,022▲ K 6
Sanbornville 741▲ K 8
Sandown 666▲ O 8
Sandwich 905▲ I 7
Seabrook 3,053▲ O 9
Sharon 136▲ N 4
Shelburne 199▲ F 5
Shirley Hill N 6
Silver Lake J 7
Smithfield L 3
Smithtown M 7
Snowville H 6

Somersworth 9,026 M 9
South Chatham G 6
South Danbury K 5
South Danville O 8
South Hampton 558▲ O 9
South Hooksett N 7
South Lyndeboro N 5
South Merrimack N 6
South Newbury L 5
South Newmarket, see Newfields N 9
South Sutton L 5
South Weare N 6
South Wolfeboro K 8
Spofford K 3
Springfield 310▲ K 5
Stark 343▲ E 6
Starr King F 7
State Line O 4
Stewartstown 1,008▲ B 6
Stoddard 345▲ L 3
Strafford 945▲ L 8
Stratford 980▲ D 6
Stratham 1,512▲ N 9
Sugar Hill 336▲ G 8
Sullivan 376▲ L 3
Sunapee 1,384▲ K 5
Suncook 4,280 M 7
Surry 507▲ L 3
Sutton 642▲ L 5
Swanzey 4,254▲ L 3
Tamworth 1,054▲ I 7
Temple 441▲ N 5
Thornton 594▲ H 5
Tilton 2,579▲ K 6
Tilton [-Northfield] K 6
Tinkerville L 3
Troy (1,713▲) 2,420 L 3
Tuftonboro 910▲ J 7
Twin Mountain F 5
Union K 8
Unity 709▲ L 3
Upper Shaker Village L 6
Wadleigh Falls N 9
Wakefield 1,420▲ K 8
Wallis Sands N 10
Walpole 2,966▲ M 3
Warner 1,441▲ L 6
Warren 539▲ H 5
Waterloo 248▲ L 6
Waterville H 5
Weare 109▲ N 6
Webster 680▲ L 6
Weirs Beach K 6
Wendell L 5
Wentworth 376▲ I 5
Wentworths Location 37▲ C 4
West Chesterfield K 3
West Epping N 8
West Lebanon J 4
West Milan E 4
West Ossipee J 7
West Peterborough N 5
West Rumney I 5
West Stewartstown B 6
West Swanzey town 1,093 L 3
Westmoreland (1,538▲) L 3
Westport L 3
Westville O 8
Whitefield 1,516▲ F 8
Whittier I 6
Willey House G 6
Wilmot 516▲ K 5
Wilton (2,276▲) 16? I N 5
Winchester 2,869▲ L 3
Windham 3,008▲ O 7
Windsor 43▲ M 5
Winnisquam K 6
Wolfeboro 3,036▲ J 7
Wolfeboro Center J 7
Woodmere M 9
Woodstock 897▲ H 4
Woodsville 1,336 G 8

*Does not appear on the map; key shows general location.
▲Entire town (township), including rural area
○County seat
Source: Latest census figures (1970). Places without population figures are unincorporated areas and are not listed in census reports.

UNIVERSITIES AND COLLEGES

New Hampshire has seven universities and colleges accredited by the New England Association of Colleges and Secondary Schools. For enrollments, see UNIVERSITIES AND COLLEGES (table).

Name	Location	Founded
Dartmouth College	Hanover	1769
Franklin Pierce College	Rindge	1962
Mount Saint Mary College	Hooksett	1934
New England College	Henniker	1946
New Hampshire, University of	*	
Rivier College	Nashua	1933
St. Anselm's College	Manchester	1889

*For the campuses of the University of New Hampshire, see UNIVERSITIES AND COLLEGES (table).

The 1970 United States census reported that New Hampshire had 737,681 persons. The population had increased 22 per cent over the 1960 census figure, 606,921.

About 56 of every 100 New Hampshirites live in urban areas. Almost half the people of New Hampshire live in the state's 13 incorporated cities. Manchester and Nashua form New Hampshire's two Standard Metropolitan Statistical Areas (see METROPOLITAN AREA). Manchester is the state's largest city. Two small portions of the Lawrence-Haverhill, Mass., metropolitan area extend into Rockingham County, New Hampshire.

In addition to Manchester, New Hampshire's 12 other incorporated cities, in order of size, are: Nashua, Concord (the capital), Portsmouth, Dover, Keene, Rochester, Berlin, Laconia, Claremont, Lebanon, Somersworth, and Franklin. See the separate articles on New Hampshire cities that are listed in the *Related Articles* at the end of this article.

Most of the people of New Hampshire were born in the United States. Many New Hampshirites are descendants of settlers who came from Canada and many European countries. The early settlers of New Hampshire came chiefly from the British Isles—England, Ireland, Scotland, and Wales. After the Civil War, thousands of French Canadians and European immigrants came to New Hampshire to work in the state's mills, shops, and factories.

Roman Catholics make up New Hampshire's largest single religious body. But there are more Protestants than Catholics in the state. The largest Protestant groups include Baptists, Episcopalians, Methodists, Unitarian Universalists, and members of the United Church of Christ.

New Hampshirites, like other New Englanders, have long been called *Yankees*. This nickname calls to mind certain traits that are traditionally associated with the people of New England. These traits include business ability, thrift, conservatism, and inventiveness. See YANKEE.

POPULATION

PERSONS PER SQUARE MILE
- 150 to 200
- 70 to 150
- 30 to 70
- 15 to 30

This map shows the population density of New Hampshire, and how it varies in different parts of the state. Population density is the average number of persons who live on each square mile.

0   25   50   50 Miles

0   25   50   75 Kilometers

WORLD BOOK map

Schools. The New Hampshire educational system dates from colonial days, when children of the settlers attended one-room schoolhouses. Some of these early schoolhouses still stand. Today's public schools operate under laws passed in 1789 and broadly revised in 1919. A seven-member state board of education and a commissioner of education govern the state's 42 *school supervisory unions*. A supervisory union is an administrative grouping of the schools in neighboring towns.

The governor and his executive council appoint the board of education members. Members of supervisory unions are elected locally. Profits from the state sweepstakes lottery pay a small part of public school costs.

Children between the ages of 6 and 16 must attend school if they live in a district that has a high school. If their district has no high school, children must attend school until they are 14 years old. For the number of students and teachers in New Hampshire, see EDUCATION (table).

Dartmouth, New Hampshire's oldest college, ranks among the 10 oldest universities and colleges in the United States. It was chartered in 1769.

Libraries. In 1833, Peterborough founded a free, tax-supported, public library. Many historians believe that this was the first library of its kind in the United States. But others claim that a library founded in Salisbury, Conn., was the first. Today, almost every New Hampshire town has a library. The State Library Bookmobile Service is used by many small communities and rural areas. The largest New Hampshire libraries include the Baker Library at Dartmouth College in Hanover; the University of New Hampshire Library in Durham; the State Library in Concord; the Portsmouth Athenaeum; and the public library of Manchester.

Museums. The Morse Museum in Warren exhibits mounted animals from many parts of the world. The state's finest collection of paintings is in Manchester's Currier Gallery of Art. The Manchester Institute of Arts and Sciences has another noted collection of paintings.

NEW HAMPSHIRE / *A Visitor's Guide*

Visitors to New Hampshire enjoy a great variety of recreational activities in six major vacation areas. In the north, the beautiful White Mountains attract skiers, hikers, campers, and sightseers. The state has more than 60 ski lifts, most of them in the White Mountains. The skiing season generally lasts from mid-December to mid-March.

The Lakes area of central New Hampshire provides fun for water-sports enthusiasts. The Seacoast region of the southeast has several beaches along the Atlantic Coast. Also in the southeast is the Merrimack Valley area, where most of New Hampshire's chief cities are located. The Monadnock region, in the southwest, includes many natural beauty spots and some of the state's most interesting towns and villages. Many historic sites and educational institutions are in the Dartmouth-Lake Sunapee area, in the west.

Loran Percy

Profile Mountain at Franconia Notch

Winter Carnival, Dartmouth College

Sanford Photo Associates
Dick Smith

Mount Washington Cog Railway

PLACES TO VISIT

Following are brief descriptions of some of New Hampshire's most interesting places to visit.

Cathedral of the Pines is an interdenominational outdoor place of worship at Rindge. In 1957, Congress made this shrine to the nation's war dead a national memorial.

Daniel Webster's Birthplace, between Salisbury and Franklin, is a two-room cabin set in scenic surroundings. The cabin houses many mementos of the orator.

Flume is an 800-foot-long *chasm* (deep, narrow valley) at Franconia Notch. Visitors can view scenic wilderness on a half-mile tour through the Flume.

Franklin Pierce Homestead, at Hillsboro, is a large two-story house where President Pierce spent his early years. Built in 1804, it has furniture, utensils, and imported wallpaper from the period.

Kancamagus Highway, a 34½-mile road between Lincoln and Conway, offers spectacular views of mountains, forests, and streams.

Lost River Reservation, near North Woodstock, features a waterfall, *potholes* (deep, round holes in the ground), and a garden of New Hampshire plants.

Mount Washington Cog Railway, near Fabyan House, runs to the top of Mount Washington. The 2¾-mile-long railway rises 3,625 feet. Completed in 1869, it was the first cog railway in North America.

Profile Mountain, or CANNON MOUNTAIN, features a rock formation that looks like the side view of an old man's face. The formation, called the *Old Man of the Mountain,* stands about 48 feet high. It was made famous by Nathaniel Hawthorne's short story "The Great Stone Face." See WHITE MOUNTAINS (picture, Profile Mountain).

National Forest. The White Mountain National Forest, established in 1911, lies in north-central New Hampshire. Part of it extends into Maine. For its area and chief features, see NATIONAL FOREST (table).

State Parks and Forests. New Hampshire has 29 state parks and 6 state forests. Many of the parks have lakes and groves of stately trees, especially white birch. For information on the state parks and forests of New Hampshire, write to Director, Division of Parks, Department of Resources and Economic Development, State House Annex, Concord, N.H. 03301.

Ski Lift Near Laconia

Daniel Webster's Birthplace Near Franklin

Flume at Franconia Notch

Eric Sanford

Sanford Photo Associates

Arthur Griffin

--------- ANNUAL EVENTS ---------

Many of New Hampshire's most popular annual events are sports contests. Summer months feature yacht regattas and races. Winter attractions include ski races, dog-sled races, and winter carnivals. The state's best-known annual events include the Winter Carnival held in early February at Dartmouth College in Hanover, and the New Hampshire League of Arts and Crafts Fair held in early August in Newbury. Other annual events include:

January-March: Winter Carnivals in Berlin, Durham, Hanover, Manchester, Newport, and other communities (January and February); Annual World's Sled Dog Derby in Laconia (February).

April-June: Fast Day, statewide legal holiday honoring provincial governor John Cutt (fourth Monday of April); All-State Music Festival (no fixed date or place); Apple Blossom Festival in the Monadnock region (May).

July-October: Regatta races on lakes (July and August); Old Home Week, statewide (August); Annual summer fairs (at various places, August through October 12); Fall Foliage Tours, statewide (late September to mid-October).

189

White Sand Beach in Rye attracts visitors who bathe in the surf and enjoy the brisk, salt-tanged air of New Hampshire's Atlantic Coast.

NEW HAMPSHIRE / The Land

Land Regions. New Hampshire has three main land regions: (1) the Coastal Lowlands, (2) the Eastern New England Upland, and (3) the White Mountains Region.

The Coastal Lowlands cover the extreme southeastern corner of the state. It is part of a larger land region of the same name that covers the entire New England coast. In New Hampshire, the region extends from 15 to 20 miles inland from the Atlantic Ocean. Along the coast, beaches provide popular recreational areas. Rivers winding through the Coastal Lowlands help supply hydroelectric power for the region's many industrial plants.

The Eastern New England Upland covers most of the southern, eastern, and western parts of New Hampshire. The entire Eastern New England Upland stretches from northern Maine to eastern Connecticut. In New Hampshire, the region consists of three areas: (1) the Merrimack Valley, (2) the Hills and Lakes area, and (3) the New Hampshire portion of the Connecticut River Valley.

The Merrimack Valley extends northward from the Massachusetts border to central New Hampshire. It is named for the swift Merrimack River, which winds through the hilly, uneven valley. Large crops of hay and fruits grow in the rich soil between the hills. Many of New Hampshire's chief mill and factory towns are in the Merrimack Valley.

The Hills and Lakes area surrounds the Merrimack Valley on the east, north, and west. It extends in a broad half-circle from Maine almost to the Vermont border. Here, most of New Hampshire's large lakes nestle among forested hills.

The Connecticut River Valley stretches in a long narrow strip down New Hampshire's western border. The Connecticut River flows through the area for 211 miles. Rich farmland lies in the lowlands. Hardwood forests cover the hills. Hydroelectric plants supply

Land Regions of New Hampshire

WHITE

MOUNTAINS

Androscoggin R

EASTERN

NEW ENGLAND

UPLAND

Connecticut R

Merrimack R

COASTAL

LOWLANDS

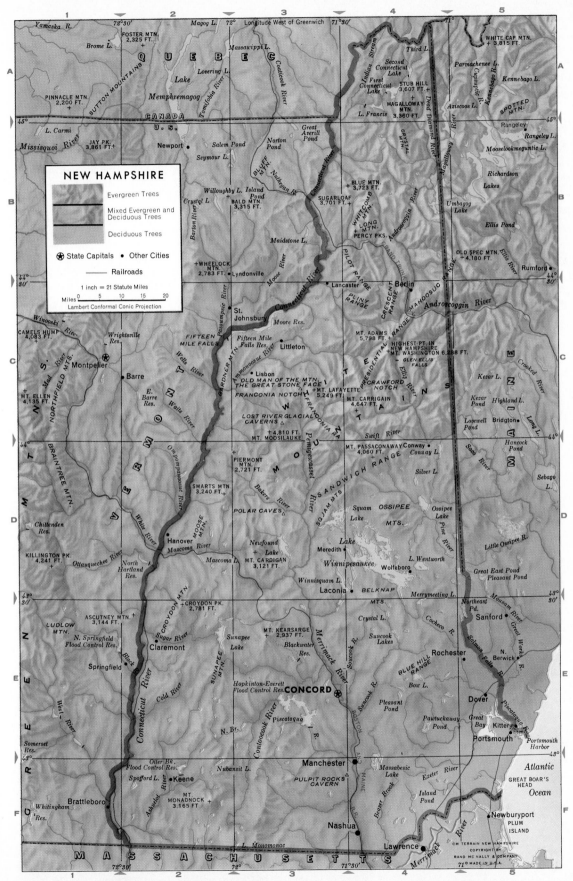

NEW HAMPSHIRE

Evergreen Trees

Mixed Evergreen and Deciduous Trees

Deciduous Trees

⊛ State Capitals • Other Cities

Railroads

1 inch = 21 Statute Miles

Miles 0 5 10 15 20

Lambert Conformal Conic Projection

Franconia Notch, a broad canyon in New Hampshire's White Mountains Region, separates the Kinsman and Franconia ranges. It has many attractions, such as Profile Mountain and the Flume.

power for public utilities. Their dams form long lakes in the valley.

The White Mountains Region lies north of the Eastern New England Upland. Here, rugged mountains rise sharply from wide flat areas that were lakes thousands of years ago. Spruce, fir, and yellow birch provide wood for New Hampshire's paper mills. The towering White Mountains attract summer and winter tourists.

An area of forest-covered hills in Coos County forms the northernmost part of New Hampshire's White Mountains Region. Lumbering and paper manufac-

turing are this area's chief industries. Dairy and potato farms thrive in the west.

Coastline. New Hampshire has only a 13-mile-long general coast along the Atlantic. This is the shortest coastline of any state bordering an ocean. Hampton, Rye, and other beaches lie along the shore. A group of islands called the Isles of Shoals lies nine miles offshore. Four—Lunging, Seavey, Star, and White—belong to New Hampshire. The others are part of Maine.

Mountains. The Presidential Range of the White Mountains has the highest peaks in New England. Mount Washington (6,288 ft.) is the highest mountain in this 86-peak range. Several other peaks in the Presidential Range are more than a mile high. These include Mount Adams (5,798 ft.), Mount Jefferson (5,715 ft.), Mount Clay (5,532 ft.), Mount Monroe (5,385 ft.), and Mount Madison (5,363 ft.). The Franconia Range, also in the White Mountains, includes famous Profile, or Cannon, Mountain. Each year, thousands of sightseers view the remarkable profile of an old man's face caused by a rock formation near the mountaintop.

New Hampshire's mountains include five *monadnocks*. A monadnock is made up of rock that did not wear down when all the land around it was leveled by erosion. The monadnocks are Mount Moosilauke (4,810 ft.), Mount Monadnock (3,165 ft.), Mount Cardigan (3,121 ft.), Mount Kearsarge (2,937 ft.), and Sunapee Mountain (2,743 ft.).

Rivers and Lakes. New Hampshire's chief rivers rise in the mountainous north. The Connecticut River begins near the Canadian border and flows generally southward. It separates New Hampshire and Vermont. After leaving New Hampshire, the 407-mile river cuts across Massachusetts and empties into Long Island Sound. The Pemigewasset River flows south from Franconia Notch. The swift Merrimack River is formed where the Pemigewasset meets the Winnipesaukee River at Franklin. The Merrimack flows south into Massachusetts. The Androscoggin and Saco rivers flow through northeastern New Hampshire, and then cross into Maine. The Piscataqua River, in the southeast, forms part of the New Hampshire-Maine border and empties into Piscataqua Bay.

About 1,300 lakes lie scattered throughout New Hampshire's hills and mountains. The largest, Lake Winnipesaukee, covers about 72 square miles and has many islands. Other lakes include Ossipee, Squam, Sunapee, Umbagog (partly in Maine), and Winnisquam.

Lake Winnipesaukee at Center Harbor nestles in a valley dotted with farms and surrounded by rolling hills. The lake and valley are part of New Hampshire's Hills and Lakes region. The lake, largest in the state, covers about 72 square miles.

NEW HAMPSHIRE / *Climate*

New Hampshire has cool summers with low humidity. In winter, much of the state receives heavy snowfall. January temperatures in northern New Hampshire average about 16° F., or 6° F. lower than in southern New Hampshire. Weathermen recorded the state's lowest temperature, −46° F., at Pittsburg near First Connecticut Lake on Jan. 28, 1925. July temperatures in the north average about 66° F., or 4° F. lower than in the south. The state's highest temperature, 106° F., was recorded at Nashua on July 4, 1911. New Hampshire gets about 42 inches of *precipitation* (rain, melted snow, and other forms of moisture) a year. The state's average yearly snowfall ranges from about 50 inches near the Atlantic Ocean to over 100 inches in the north and west.

Dick Smith

Mount Washington Has Sudden Storms. The strongest winds ever measured at the earth's surface—188 mph—struck Mount Washington on April 12, 1934. One gust reached 231 mph.

SEASONAL TEMPERATURES

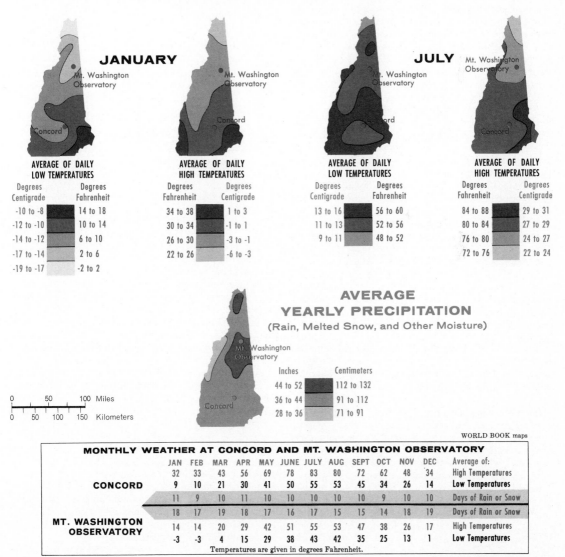

JANUARY

AVERAGE OF DAILY LOW TEMPERATURES

Degrees Centigrade	Degrees Fahrenheit
-10 to -8	14 to 18
-12 to -10	10 to 14
-14 to -12	6 to 10
-17 to -14	2 to 6
-19 to -17	-2 to 2

AVERAGE OF DAILY HIGH TEMPERATURES

Degrees Fahrenheit	Degrees Centigrade
34 to 38	1 to 3
30 to 34	-1 to 1
26 to 30	-3 to -1
22 to 26	-6 to -3

JULY

AVERAGE OF DAILY LOW TEMPERATURES

Degrees Centigrade	Degrees Fahrenheit
13 to 16	56 to 60
11 to 13	52 to 56
9 to 11	48 to 52

AVERAGE OF DAILY HIGH TEMPERATURES

Degrees Fahrenheit	Degrees Centigrade
84 to 88	29 to 31
80 to 84	27 to 29
76 to 80	24 to 27
72 to 76	22 to 24

AVERAGE YEARLY PRECIPITATION
(Rain, Melted Snow, and Other Moisture)

Inches	Centimeters
44 to 52	112 to 132
36 to 44	91 to 112
28 to 36	71 to 91

```
0        50        100  Miles
0     50    100   150  Kilometers
```

WORLD BOOK maps

	JAN	FEB	MAR	APR	MAY	JUNE	JULY	AUG	SEPT	OCT	NOV	DEC	Average of:
CONCORD	32	33	43	56	69	78	83	80	72	62	48	34	High Temperatures
	9	10	21	30	41	50	55	53	45	34	26	14	Low Temperatures
	11	9	10	11	10	10	10	10	10	9	10	10	Days of Rain or Snow
	18	17	19	18	17	16	17	15	15	14	18	19	Days of Rain or Snow
MT. WASHINGTON OBSERVATORY	14	14	20	29	42	51	55	53	47	38	26	17	High Temperatures
	-3	-3	4	15	29	38	43	42	35	25	13	1	Low Temperatures

MONTHLY WEATHER AT CONCORD AND MT. WASHINGTON OBSERVATORY

Temperatures are given in degrees Fahrenheit.

Source: U.S. Weather Bureau

192a

Manufacturing is New Hampshire's most important economic activity. The tourist industry ranks second, followed by agriculture. Manufacturing is centered in the cities of the south and southeast and in Connecticut River Valley communities. The 3 million tourists who visit the state contribute about $250 million a year to the state's economy. Farms thrive in many areas.

Natural Resources. New Hampshire's climate and soils support dense forests and thick grasslands. Many kinds of animals live in the state. Minerals are found in many areas, but mining output is small.

Soil. A mixture of clay and rocks covers most of New Hampshire's hills and mountains. This soil was once farmland, and is now largely covered by trees. The soil in New Hampshire's valleys is chiefly clay and loam, and coarse gravel and sand. The clay and loam support farm crops. The gravel and sand supply low-cost road-building material.

Forests and Plant Life. Forests cover about four-fifths of New Hampshire. Commercially valuable softwood trees include balsam fir, cedar, hemlock, spruce, tamarack, and white pine. Balsam fir, hemlock, pine, and spruce account for about 85 per cent of New Hampshire's lumber. Valuable hardwoods include ash, basswood, beech, birch, elm, maple, and oak. These trees provide about 15 per cent of the state's lumber.

Thick undergrowths of shrubs and flowering plants thrive in New Hampshire forests. The shrubs include American elders, chokeberries, red osiers, and sumacs. Wild flowers, which grow throughout the state, include black-eyed Susans, daisies, fireweed, gentians, goldenrod, purple trillium, violets, and wild asters.

Animal Life. Deer, bears, rabbits, foxes, and raccoons are common in New Hampshire. Minks, beavers, pine martens, otters, squirrels, chipmunks, and lynxes live in the central and northern mountains and forests. Game birds include ruffed grouse, pheasants, and ducks. Robins, bluebirds, purple finches, sparrows, and warblers nest throughout New Hampshire.

Among the state's fresh-water varieties of fish are brook, brown, lake, and rainbow trout; large- and small-mouth black bass; and landlocked salmon, pickerel, perch, whitefish, and bullheads. Salt-water fish include cod, cunners, cusk, flounders, haddock, hake, mackerel, pollack, striped bass, and tuna.

Minerals. New Hampshire's chief mineral resources are its deposits of granite, gravel, sand, mica, feldspar, and quartz. The state's large beds of gray, red, and other kinds of granite give it the nickname of the *Granite State.*

Manufacturing accounts for over 90 per cent of the value of goods produced in New Hampshire. Goods manufactured there have a *value added by manufacture* of about $935 million a year. This figure represents the value created in products by the state's industries, not counting such costs as materials, supplies, and fuel.

New Hampshire has about 1,500 factories, ranging from small plants to giant industrial works. The state's chief manufactured products, in order of value, are electrical machinery, leather and leather products, non-electrical machinery, and paper and paper products. New Hampshire ranks among the leading leather-

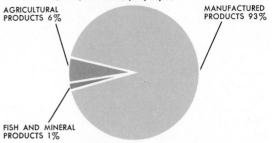

NEW HAMPSHIRE'S PRODUCTION IN 1967

Total value of goods produced—$1,005,200,000

AGRICULTURAL PRODUCTS 6%

MANUFACTURED PRODUCTS 93%

FISH AND MINERAL PRODUCTS 1%

Note: Manufacturing percentage based on value added by manufacture. Other percentages based on value of production.

Sources: U.S. Government statistics

NEW HAMPSHIRE'S EMPLOYMENT IN 1967

Total number of persons employed—261,000

	Number of Employees
Manufacturing	96,700
Services	50,900
Wholesale & Retail Trade	45,800
Government	28,800
Construction	13,400
Transportation & Public Utilities	10,400
Finance, Insurance & Real Estate	9,200
Agriculture & Mining	5,800

Source: U.S. Department of Labor

manufacturing states. Shoes are the most important leather product made in New Hampshire.

Wood from New Hampshire's trees is the raw material for many manufactured products. Paper and pulp are the most important of these products. Factories in the state also use wood to make crutches, floorboards, furniture, railroad ties, shoe heels, skis, and small boats. Many of New Hampshire's fir trees are cut down each year to be used as Christmas trees.

Other manufactured items include chemical products, plastics products, precision instruments, sporting goods, tableware, textiles, and toys. Manchester is New Hampshire's leading manufacturing city.

Agriculture accounts for about 6 per cent of the value of goods produced in New Hampshire. New Hampshire farmers earn about $61,400,000 a year. The state has about 4,600 farms, averaging about 194 acres in size.

Dairy farming is New Hampshire's most important agricultural activity. Milk and other dairy products have a value of about $22 million a year. This is about two-fifths of the state's total farm income. Dairy farms are especially numerous in the west and southeast. Poultry farming ranks next in importance. Eggs—the leading poultry product—and chickens and turkeys account for about 30 per cent of the state's farm income. Most poultry farms are in the south. Beef cattle are another important farm product.

Apples rank as New Hampshire's leading fruit. New

Hampshire farmers also grow peaches, blueberries, and strawberries. Potatoes and sweet corn are the state's most important vegetables. Hay and other forage and greenhouse and nursery products are among the state's other agricultural goods.

Mining. Even though New Hampshire is famous as the *Granite State*, mining is of little importance to its economy. Mining accounts for about $8 million a year, or less than 1 per cent of the value of goods produced in New Hampshire. Granite, quartz, and sand and gravel are the state's chief minerals.

New Hampshire's largest granite quarries are in Carroll, Hillsboro, and Merrimack counties. The Concord quarries, the biggest in the state, have supplied granite for many famous buildings, including the Library of Congress in Washington, D.C. New Hampshire granite was also used as the cornerstone of the main United Nations building in New York City. Most counties produce quartz and sand and gravel. Other minerals include clays, feldspar, and mica.

Fishing Industry is also a relatively minor economic activity in New Hampshire. Hampton, Portsmouth, and Rye are the chief salt-water fishing centers. Fishermen trap lobsters in the coastal waters. The lobster catch totals about 800,000 pounds a year. New Hampshire fishermen also catch some cod, haddock, and smelt.

Electric Power. Over 70 per cent of New Hampshire's power needs are supplied by two large steam generating plants. One plant is near Manchester and the other is in Portsmouth. Large hydroelectric plants on the Connecticut River provide power during the peak periods to the New England Electric System. Chief plants on the river include Comerford Dam near Monroe, Wilder Dam near Hanover, and the Samuel C. Moore Dam near Littleton. For New Hampshire's kilowatt-hour production, see ELECTRIC POWER (table).

Transportation. New Hampshire's industrial growth during the 1800's encouraged the first great expansion of the state's transportation system.

New Hampshire has many small airfields. Larger airports link Berlin, Concord, Keene, Laconia, and Manchester with several major U.S. cities.

Railroads operate on about 900 miles of track in New Hampshire. The Boston and Maine Railroad serves much of the south, and the Grand Trunk Railway operates in the north. New Hampshire's first railroad began operating in the southeast in 1838.

Roads and highways total about 14,000 miles, and most of them are surfaced. The state's highway system includes modern toll roads. The New Hampshire Turnpike parallels the seacoast. The Spaulding Turnpike extends the seacoast turnpike from Portsmouth to Rochester. The Everett Turnpike links Concord and Massachusetts. New Hampshire highways include 120 miles of the federal interstate highway system.

Communication. About 50 daily and weekly newspapers are published in New Hampshire. The leading ones include *Foster's Daily Democrat* of Dover; the *Manchester Union Leader;* the *Nashua Telegraph;* the *New Hampshire Sunday News* of Manchester; and the *Portsmouth Herald. L'Action*, a Manchester weekly, is a leading French-language newspaper.

New Hampshire's first newspaper began publication in 1756 at Portsmouth. It was called the *New Hampshire Gazette*, and is now the weekly supplement of the *Portsmouth Herald*. The state's first radio station, WLNH, was founded at Laconia in 1922. The first television station, WMUR-TV, began operation at Manchester in 1954. New Hampshire now has about 35 radio stations and 2 television stations.

FARM, MINERAL, AND FOREST PRODUCTS

This map shows the areas where the state's leading farm, mineral, and forest products are produced. The major urban area (shown in red) is the state's important manufacturing center.

WORLD BOOK map

Textile Mill in Wilton makes worsted cloth. The yarn comes from another mill in the town. Textiles are among New Hampshire's most important manufactured products.

David F. Lawlor, Devaney

Indian Days. About 5,000 Indians probably lived in what is now New Hampshire before the white man came. Most of them belonged to two branches of the Algonkian Indian family—the Abnaki and the Pennacook. The Abnaki branch included the Ossipee and the Pequawket tribes. The Pennacook included the Amoskeag, Nashua, Piscataqua, Souhegan, and Squamscot tribes. New Hampshire Indians built wigwams of bark and skins. They hunted and fished, and farmed small fields of corn. The tribes lived together in peace, but often warred against their common enemy, the Iroquois.

Exploration. No one knows who was the first white man to reach New Hampshire. But wide-scale exploration of the area began in the early 1600's. In 1603, Martin Pring of England sailed a trading ship up the Piscataqua River. Pring and his men may have landed in Portsmouth. The French explorer Samuel de Champlain landed on the New Hampshire coast in 1605. In 1614, the English captain John Smith reached the Isles of Shoals. He named them *Smith's Islands.*

Settlement. In 1620, King James I of England founded the Council for New England to encourage people to settle in America. The council granted David Thomson land in present-day New Hampshire. In 1623, Thomson and his followers settled at Odiorne's Point (now a part of Rye). Edward Hilton settled Hilton's Point (now Dover) in the 1620's. Some historians believe this settlement began about the same time as Thomson's. Others believe it began a few years later. Other early settlements include Strawbery Banke (now Portsmouth), established in 1630; and Exeter and Hampton, founded in 1638.

In 1622, the Council for New England gave John Mason and Sir Ferdinando Gorges a large tract of land in present-day New Hampshire and Maine. In 1629, the land was divided between the two men. Mason received the part between the Merrimack and Piscataqua rivers. He named the land *New Hampshire,* after his native county—Hampshire, England. New Hampshire was made a part of Massachusetts in 1641. But in 1680, King Charles II again made New Hampshire a separate colony. The king appointed John Cutt as New Hampshire's first provincial governor (then called president).

French and Indian Wars were fought in New Hampshire and the rest of New England off and on from 1689 to 1763. The French and their Indian allies battled to gain control of the area from the British. Guided by Indians, French forces pushed down from Canada. Robert Rogers, the leader of a group of soldiers called Rogers' Rangers, and John Stark, both of New Hampshire, won fame as colonial military leaders during this period. See FRENCH AND INDIAN WARS.

Colonial New Hampshire was a rural society. Most of the people kept busy clearing the wilderness, building houses, and growing food. In 1767, when New Hampshire took its first census, the colony had 52,700 persons. The King of England appointed the governor and governor's council. But the people elected assemblymen to represent them in colonial affairs.

The Revolutionary War. During the 1760's, Great Britain passed a series of laws that caused unrest in New Hampshire and the other American colonies. Most of

---

IMPORTANT DATES IN NEW HAMPSHIRE

1603 Martin Pring of England explored the mouth of the Piscataqua River.

1614 Captain John Smith landed on the Isles of Shoals.

1620's David Thomson and Edward Hilton made the first permanent settlements in New Hampshire.

1629 John Mason named the region *New Hampshire.*

1641 The Massachusetts Colony gained control of New Hampshire.

1680 New Hampshire became a separate royal colony.

1776 New Hampshire broke away from Great Britain and adopted a temporary constitution.

1784 New Hampshire adopted its present constitution.

1788 New Hampshire became the ninth state when it ratified the U.S. Constitution on June 21.

1838 The first railroad in New Hampshire was completed.

1853 Franklin Pierce of Hillsboro became the 14th President of the United States.

1944 The International Monetary Conference was held at Bretton Woods.

1961 Alan B. Shepard, Jr. of East Derry became the first American to travel in space.

1964 The New Hampshire sweepstakes lottery began. It was the first legal U.S. lottery since the 1890's.

---

these laws either imposed severe taxes or restricted colonial trade. In December, 1774, Paul Revere rode to New Hampshire to warn the people of a British military build-up in Massachusetts. A band of New Hampshirites, led by John Sullivan, seized military supplies from a British fort in New Castle. This was one of the first armed actions by colonists against the British.

After the Revolutionary War broke out in Massachusetts in 1775, hundreds of New Hampshire "minutemen" hurried to Boston to fight the British. New Hampshire was the only one of the 13 original colonies in which no actual fighting occurred.

New Hampshire became the first colony to form a government wholly independent of Great Britain. It did so on Jan. 5, 1776, when it adopted a temporary constitution. On July 9, 1778, New Hampshire ratified the Articles of Confederation (the forerunner of the United States Constitution). On June 21, 1788, New Hampshire became the ninth state to ratify the U.S. Constitution. New Hampshire's ratification put the Constitution into effect.

The 1800's. New Hampshire remained an agricultural state from 1800 until the outbreak of the Civil War. But it began an industrial growth that has continued to the present day. Manchester, the largest industrial center, became the state's first incorporated city in 1846. Portsmouth developed as a leading clippership port in the early 1800's, and the first railroad opened in 1838. During the 1850's, businessmen built hosiery plants, woolen mills, and factories that made boots and shoes, machine tools, and wood products.

New Hampshirites who gained national fame during this period included Franklin Pierce, the 14th President of the United States, and Daniel Webster, a leading orator and U.S. senator.

New Hampshire was a leading opponent of slavery. About 34,000 New Hampshirites served with the Union

HISTORIC
NEW HAMPSHIRE

President Franklin Pierce
born at Hillsboro

Concord Wagons and Coaches, first made in 1813 by the Abbot and Downing Co. of Concord, were used during the 1800's to carry passengers and mail.

Bretton Woods Conference delegates in July, 1944, shaped financial and trade policies for the postwar world.

Bretton Woods

Dartmouth College at Hanover was chartered by King George III in 1769 "for the education and instruction of Youth of the Indian Tribes in this Land."

The Textile Industry grew rapidly in New Hampshire after the state's first cotton mill was founded at New Ipswich in 1804. The Amoskeag Mill, established at Manchester in 1809, became one of the world's largest cotton mills.

● Hanover

Daniel Webster's Birthplace stands near Franklin. The famous statesman was born in 1782.

● Franklin

Shoemaking developed into a major industry after Allen Sawyer established the state's first shoe factory at Weare in 1823.

Soldiers at Bunker Hill used gunpowder from 100 barrels captured from the British at Fort William and Mary in New Castle.

CONCORD ★

Hillsboro ●

Weare ●

New Castle ●

Manchester ●

The Library in Peterborough may be the nation's oldest tax-supported free public library. It was founded in 1833.

Peterborough ●

Independence from Great Britain was first achieved by New Hampshire of the 13 colonies. The state adopted a constitution on January 5, 1776, six months before the Declaration of Independence was signed.

New Ipswich

forces during the Civil War, and the Portsmouth Naval Shipyard built ships that blockaded Southern ports.

Industrial development increased greatly after the Civil War. The textile, woodworking, and leather industries were among those that grew at record rates. Thousands of French-Canadian and European immigrants came to New Hampshire to fill the labor needs caused by expansion of mills and factories. At the same time, many farmers left the state to claim free land in the West. Farming activity decreased as industry grew.

The Early 1900's. During World War I (1914-1918), the Portsmouth Naval Shipyard built warships. New Hampshire's cotton and woolen textile industries declined in the 1920's and 1930's. Leather and shoe manufacturing became the state's leading industry. New Hampshire greatly improved its highway system during the 1920's, and private utility companies built hydroelectric plants in the state. The Great Depression of the 1930's slowed the growth of New Hampshire's economy. Conditions improved after the depression eased in the late 1930's.

The Mid-1900's. During World War II (1939-1945), Portsmouth built submarines and repaired warships, and New Hampshire's textile mills supplied materials for military uniforms. In 1944, representatives of 44 nations held the historic International Monetary Conference at Bretton Woods in the White Mountains. They planned postwar world trade and simplified the transfer of money among nations. They also drew up plans for two United Nations agencies—the International Monetary Fund and the International Bank for Reconstruction and Development. See BRETTON WOODS.

New Hampshire became increasingly urban and industrial during the mid-1900's. In the 1950's, the state approved the formation of a Business Development Corporation and established an Industrial Park Authority. These agencies worked to aid new businesses and to attract industry to New Hampshire.

New Hampshire's once important shoe industry declined sharply because of competition from other states and from other countries, especially Italy. But the rapid growth of the state's electronics industry more than made up for shoe industry losses.

In 1961, Alan B. Shepard, Jr. of East Derry became

THE GOVERNORS OF NEW HAMPSHIRE

	Party	Term		Party	Term
Under Articles of Confederation			36. Onslow Stearns	Republican	1869-1871
			37. James A. Weston	Democratic	1871-1872
1. Meshech Weare	None	1776-1785	38. Ezekiel A. Straw	Republican	1872-1874
2. John Langdon	None	1785-1786	39. James A. Weston	Democratic	1874-1875
3. John Sullivan	Federalist	1786-1788	40. Person C. Cheney	Republican	1875-1877
			41. Benjamin F. Prescott	Republican	1877-1879
Under United States Constitution			42. Natt Head	Republican	1879-1881
			43. Charles H. Bell	Republican	1881-1883
1. John Langdon	*Dem.-Rep.	1788-1789	44. Samuel W. Hale	Republican	1883-1885
2. John Sullivan	Federalist	1789-1790	45. Moody Currier	Republican	1885-1887
3. Josiah Bartlett	*Dem.-Rep.	1790-1794	46. Charles H. Sawyer	Republican	1887-1889
4. John T. Gilman	Federalist	1794-1805	47. David H. Goodell	Republican	1889-1891
5. John Langdon	*Dem.-Rep.	1805-1809	48. Hiram A. Tuttle	Republican	1891-1893
6. Jeremiah Smith	Federalist	1809-1810	49. John B. Smith	Republican	1893-1895
7. John Langdon	*Dem.-Rep.	1810-1812	50. Charles A. Busiel	Republican	1895-1897
8. William Plumer	*Dem.-Rep.	1812-1813	51. George A. Ramsdell	Republican	1897-1899
9. John T. Gilman	Federalist	1813-1816	52. Frank W. Rollins	Republican	1899-1901
10. William Plumer	*Dem.-Rep.	1816-1819	53. Chester B. Jordan	Republican	1901-1903
11. Samuel Bell	*Dem.-Rep.	1819-1823	54. Nahum J. Batchelder	Republican	1903-1905
12. Levi Woodbury	*Dem.-Rep.	1823-1824	55. John McLane	Republican	1905-1907
13. David L. Morrill	*Dem.-Rep.	1824-1827	56. Charles M. Floyd	Republican	1907-1909
14. Benjamin Pierce	*Dem.-Rep.	1827-1828	57. Henry B. Quinby	Republican	1909-1911
15. John Bell	National Republican	1828-1829	58. Robert P. Bass	Republican	1911-1913
16. Benjamin Pierce	Democratic	1829-1830	59. Samuel D. Felker	Democratic	1913-1915
17. Matthew Harvey	Democratic	1830-1831	60. Rolland H. Spaulding	Republican	1915-1917
18. Samuel Dinsmoor	Democratic	1831-1834	61. Henry W. Keyes	Republican	1917-1919
19. William Badger	Democratic	1834-1836	62. John H. Bartlett	Republican	1919-1921
20. Isaac Hill	Democratic	1836-1839	63. Albert O. Brown	Republican	1921-1923
21. John Page	Democratic	1839-1842	64. Fred H. Brown	Democratic	1923-1925
22. Henry Hubbard	Democratic	1842-1844	65. John G. Winant	Republican	1925-1927
23. John H. Steele	Democratic	1844-1846	66. Huntley N. Spaulding	Republican	1927-1929
24. Anthony Colby	Whig	1846-1847	67. Charles W. Tobey	Republican	1929-1931
25. Jared W. Williams	Democratic	1847-1849	68. John G. Winant	Republican	1931-1935
26. Samuel Dinsmoor, Jr.	Democratic	1849-1852	69. Styles Bridges	Republican	1935-1937
27. Noah Martin	Democratic	1852-1854	70. Francis P. Murphy	Republican	1937-1941
28. Nathaniel B. Baker	Democratic	1854-1855	71. Robert O. Blood	Republican	1941-1945
29. Ralph Metcalf	†American	1855-1857	72. Charles M. Dale	Republican	1945-1949
30. William Haile	Republican	1857-1859	73. Sherman Adams	Republican	1949-1953
31. Ichabod Goodwin	Republican	1859-1861	74. Hugh Gregg	Republican	1953-1955
32. Nathaniel S. Berry	Republican	1861-1863	75. Lane Dwinell	Republican	1955-1959
33. Joseph A. Gilmore	Republican	1863-1865	76. Wesley Powell	Republican	1959-1963
34. Frederick Smyth	Republican	1865-1867	77. John W. King	Democratic	1963-1969
35. Walter Harriman	Republican	1867-1869	78. Walter R. Peterson, Jr.	Republican	1969-

*Democratic-Republican   †Know-Nothing

the first American to travel in space. In 1962, New Hampshire voters elected a Democrat, John W. King, as governor. King was only the third Democrat since 1875 to serve as governor of the state. The Republicans regained control of the governorship in 1968 with the election of Walter R. Peterson, Jr.

In 1963, New Hampshire adopted the first legal lottery in the United States since the 1890's. Lottery tickets are sold on horse races called *sweepstakes*. The state uses the profits from the lottery to help pay for public education. The first sweepstakes were held in September, 1964.

New Hampshire Today. Manufacturing strengthened its position during the early 1970's as the leading economic producer in the state. Recreational and tourist activities rank second. Agriculture continues to decline as an important economic force in the state.

New Hampshire is one of the few states that does not collect a general sales tax. But many residents are demanding more state programs and services. These demands may force New Hampshire to increase taxes or adopt new taxes to pay for any additional state activities.

Pollution of New Hampshire's rivers and streams is becoming a major problem. The prevention of water pollution is particularly important because recreation has such an important part in the state's economy. Each year, the state's recreational facilities attract thousands of visitors for boating, camping, hiking, and skiing.

ALBERT S. CARLSON, HUGH R. O'NEIL, and J. DUANE SQUIRES

NEW HAMPSHIRE/Study Aids

Related Articles in WORLD BOOK include:

BIOGRAPHIES

Adams, Sherman	Pierce, Franklin
Bartlett, Josiah	Porter, Fitz-John
Bridges, Styles	Shepard, Alan B., Jr.
Dearborn, Henry	Stark, John
Eddy, Mary Baker	Thornton, Matthew
French, Daniel C.	Webster, Daniel
Frost, Robert L.	Wentworth, Benning
Gilman, Nicholas	Whipple, William
Hale, John P.	Winant, John G.
Langdon, John	

CITIES AND TOWNS

Berlin	Manchester
Concord	Nashua
Exeter	Portsmouth
Hanover	Rochester

HISTORY

Colonial Life in America	Dartmouth College Case
French and Indian Wars	

PHYSICAL FEATURES

Connecticut River	Merrimack River
Lake Winnipesaukee	White Mountains

OTHER RELATED ARTICLES

Leather (table)	Portsmouth Naval Shipyard
New England	

Outline

I. Government
  A. Constitution D. Courts F. Taxation
  B. Executive E. Local G. Politics
  C. Legislature Government
II. People
III. Education
  A. Schools B. Libraries C. Museums
IV. A Visitor's Guide
  A. Places to Visit B. Annual Events
V. The Land
  A. Land Regions C. Mountains
  B. Coastline D. Rivers and Lakes
VI. Climate
VII. Economy
  A. Natural Resources E. Fishing Industry
  B. Manufacturing F. Electric Power
  C. Agriculture G. Transportation
  D. Mining H. Communication
VIII. History

Questions

Why was New Hampshire's ratification of the U.S. Constitution especially important?

What record weather condition was recorded at Mount Washington?

What President of the United States was born in New Hampshire?

What is New Hampshire's biggest income-producing activity?

Why are New Hampshire towns called "little republics"?

What important international conference was held in New Hampshire in 1944?

What religious movement was started by a New Hampshirite?

What are the three main land regions of New Hampshire?

What is unique about the coastline of New Hampshire?

What is New Hampshire's oldest college?

Books for Young Readers

BAILEY, CAROLYN S. *The Little Red Schoolhouse.* Viking, 1957.

BUTTERWORTH, OLIVER. *The Enormous Egg.* Little, Brown, 1956. A dinosaur hatches on a New Hampshire farm.

CANDY, ROBERT. *Nature Notebook.* Houghton, 1953.

GREENE, ROSWELL, and CANDY, ROBERT. *Big Jack.* Houghton, 1957. Trout in New Hampshire.

SMITH, BRADFORD. *Rogers' Rangers and the French and Indian War.* Random House, 1956.

STEVENS, LEONARD A. *Old Peppersass: The Locomotive That Climbed Mount Washington.* Dodd, 1959.

Books for Older Readers

CANNON, LEGRAND. *Look to the Mountain.* Holt, 1942.

DUNCAN, JOHN M. *Down the Mast Road.* McGraw, 1956.

FROST, ROBERT. *Complete Poems.* Holt, 1949.

HOLDEN, RAYMOND P. *The Merrimack.* Rinehart, 1958.

LATHROP, WEST. *Black River Captive.* Random House, 1946. A story of the French and Indian War period.

MEADER, STEPHEN W. *King of the Hills.* Harcourt, 1933. A description of a hunting adventure. *Lumberjack,* 1934.

New Hampshire: A Guide to the Granite State. Houghton, 1938.

SQUIRES, J. DUANE. *The Story of New Hampshire.* Van Nostrand, 1964. *New Hampshire: A Students' Guide to Localized History.* Teachers College Press, 1966.

YATES, ELIZABETH. *Patterns on the Wall.* Dutton, 1953. *Amos Fortune, Free Man.* 1950.

193

NEW HAMPSHIRE, UNIVERSITY OF

NEW HAMPSHIRE, UNIVERSITY OF, is a state-supported, coeducational institution with campuses at Durham, Keene, and Plymouth. The Durham campus has colleges of agriculture, liberal arts, and technology; a school of business and economics; a graduate school; and a school of applied science that offers a two-year associate degree. It grants bachelor's, master's, and doctor's degrees. Also on the Durham campus are agricultural and engineering experiment stations. The Keene and Plymouth campuses grant bachelor's and master's degrees. A university extension branch is located in Manchester.

The University of New Hampshire was founded in 1866 as the New Hampshire College of Agriculture and Mechanic Arts. It took its present name in 1923. In 1963, Keene State College and Plymouth State College became part of the university. For enrollments, see UNIVERSITIES AND COLLEGES (table).   JOHN W. McCONNELL

NEW HAMPSHIRE GRANTS. See VERMONT (Land Disputes); ALLEN, ETHAN.

NEW HARMONY, Ind. (pop. 971; alt. 374 ft.), became famous as an educational and cultural center during the 1820's. Today, this quiet town in Posey County is a trading center for a farming region in the lower Wabash River Valley (see INDIANA [map]).

George Rapp (1757-1847), the leader of a religious group called Harmonists, founded the village of Harmonie in 1814. Rapp brought the Harmonists from the kingdom of Württemberg in Germany to escape religious persecution. They spent 10 years in Butler County, Pennsylvania, then migrated to Indiana. The Harmonists practiced celibacy and members could not own property. In 1825, Rapp sold the town to Robert Owen, wealthy social reformer and industrialist from Scotland. The Harmonists returned to Pennsylvania and founded the village of Economy, now Ambridge, where the society died out toward the end of the 1800's.

Owen renamed his town New Harmony. He established a social order based on community ownership and equality of work and profit. His partner was William Maclure, a wealthy scientist from Philadelphia who is sometimes called the "Father of American Geology." In the 1820's, Maclure sent the first seed for the Chinese *golden-rain* trees to Thomas Say, another geologist who had come to New Harmony. These golden-rain, or *gate*, trees now line the streets of the town.

The experiment in community living made New Harmony famous. Scientists and scholars flocked to the town. But few of the 1,000 or more Owenites understood the principles of the experiment, and they split into several factions.

By 1827, it was apparent that Owen's plan had failed. New Harmony remained an educational, scientific, and cultural center until the Civil War. The Minerva Club, the first woman's club to have a constitution and by-laws, was organized at New Harmony in 1859. Some of the buildings erected by the Harmonists and Owenites have been restored.   PAUL E. MILLION, JR.

See also INDIANA (Education; Places to Visit); OWEN (family).

NEW HAVEN, Conn. (pop. 137,707; met. area 355,538; alt. 40 ft.), is the home of Yale University. It is the third largest city in Connecticut and a New England wholesale center.

New Haven is situated on an arm of Long Island Sound about 70 miles northeast of New York City. Three small rivers, the West, the Mill, and the Quinnipiac, meet to form the bay and harbor of New Haven. For location, see CONNECTICUT (political map).

New Haven is partly circled by hills which rise steeply to 350 or 400 feet east and west of the city. It is called the *City of Elms* because of its many elm-lined streets.

Industries. New Haven factories produce clocks, firearms, electrical appliances, automobile radiators, machine tools, rubber products, hardware, toys, and clothing. The city has a wide wholesale trade in oil, gasoline, coal, lumber, paints, and farm products.

Cultural Life. Yale University is one of the oldest schools in the United States (see YALE UNIVERSITY). Other schools there include Albertus Magnus College and Southern Connecticut State College. New Haven has seven public libraries. Its museums and galleries include the Peabody Museum of Natural History, New Haven Colony Historical Society, Yale University Art Gallery and Design Center, and New Haven Art Gallery and Art Lending Library.

Recreation. New Haven has 15 city parks. Judges Cave in West Rock Park is a tourist attraction. In the

Bettmann Archive; Ruohomaa, Black Star

New Harmony Settlers, *below,* lived in a communal society. The restored hedge labyrinth, *right,* was originally designed by George Rapp as entertainment for his followers.

1660's, two English revolutionaries hid for several weeks in the cave to escape capture by forces of King Charles II. Yale Bowl seats 70,896 people. Yale's Payne-Whitney gymnasium, 16 stories high, is one of the world's largest sports buildings. New plays are often presented in New Haven before they open on Broadway in New York City. The city has one of the oldest symphony orchestras in the United States. Other recreational facilities include a city arena, golf courses, a baseball stadium, and a city-owned beach.

History. A company of Puritans, led by Theophilus Eaton and John Davenport, founded New Haven in 1638. The site was once occupied by an Indian village named *Quinnipiac*, which means *Long River Place*. The name was changed to New Haven, after the English city of Newhaven, in 1640. The town was part of New Haven Colony which also included the towns of Branford, Guilford, Milford, Stamford, and Southold. The New Haven Colony became part of the colony of Connecticut in 1665. New Haven was incorporated as a city in 1784. Roger Sherman, one of the committee of five who drafted the Declaration of Independence, was the first mayor. New Haven was one of Connecticut's two capitals from 1701 to 1875. The city is also the burial place of such famous men as Noah Webster and Lyman Beecher. Charles Goodyear, who discovered the process of vulcanizing rubber, was born in New Haven.

New Haven was a busy port during the 1700's and early 1800's. As steam-operated vessels gradually replaced sailing ships, the harbor became less important, and the city turned to manufacturing. Dredging of a deep channel to accommodate ocean-going ships began in 1927. By 1950, New Haven was again an important harbor. New Haven is the seat of New Haven County. It has a mayor-council government. ALBERT E. VAN DUSEN

NEW HAVEN COLLEGE. See UNIVERSITIES AND COLLEGES (table).

NEW HEBRIDES ISLANDS, *HEB ruh deez,* form part of the Pacific region called *Melanesia.* The New Hebrides group lies in the southwest Pacific, about 1,000 miles northeast of the Queensland coast of Australia. The islands stretch across the sea routes between the United States and Australia. This position gave them great importance during World War II. The United States established a large air and naval base at Espiritu Santo during the war. Vila is the New Hebrides capital.

The New Hebrides are made up of 12 principal islands and many smaller ones. Their total area is 5,700

Ewing Galloway

A New Hebrides Tribesman, dressed in a warrior's costume, wears traditional head and nose ornaments. Most New Hebrides tribesmen are Melanesians, but some are Polynesians.

square miles. The islands' total coastline covers 1,300 miles. The climate is damp, hot, and unhealthful. Some of the islands are fertile. The chief products include bananas, cocoa, coffee, copra, pineapples, and timber. The islands also have some cattle.

The New Hebrides have a population of about 90,000. Fewer than 2,800 of these are white people. Most of the inhabitants are dark-skinned Melanesians. European governmental and religious influences have put a stop to their tribal wars and cannibalism. The islanders entertain visitors by diving from the tops of tall trees to the ground. The diver ties a vine to his legs. The other end of the vine is tied to a treetop. The vine breaks his fall just before he reaches the ground.

In 1606, Pedro de Queirós, a Portuguese explorer, became the first white man to see the New Hebrides. The English explorer, Captain James Cook, discovered other islands in the group in 1774, and mapped the entire region. Since 1906, the British and the French have jointly ruled the islands.   EDWIN H. BRYAN, JR.

See also ESPIRITU SANTO.

NEW HOLLAND. See AUSTRALIA (History).

NEW IRELAND is the second largest island of the Bismarck Archipelago, Territory of New Guinea, in the southwest Pacific. New Ireland covers 3,340 square miles, and has a population of about 43,000 persons. It is governed by Australia under United Nations trusteeship. For location, see NEW GUINEA (map).

New Ireland is a volcanic island about 230 miles long. In its center rise the Schleinitz Mountains, which are 2,000 to 4,000 feet high. The island has many coconut plantations. Kavieng is the largest town. NEAL M. BOWERS

The New Hebrides Islands Lie East of Australia.

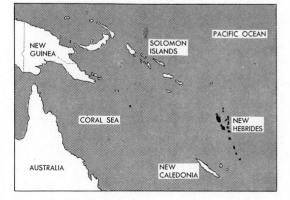

Oil Refinery in Perth Amboy

NEW JERSEY

THE GARDEN STATE

─────── FACTS IN BRIEF ───────

Capital: Trenton.

Government: *Congress*—U.S. senators, 2; U.S. representatives, 15. *Electoral Votes*—17. *State Legislature*—senators, 40; assemblymen, 80. *Counties*—21. *Voting Age*—21 years (state and local elections); 18 years (national elections).

Area: 7,836 square miles (including 304 square miles of inland water), 46th in size among the states. *Greatest Distances*—(north-south) 166 miles; (east-west) 57 miles. *Coastline*—130 miles.

Elevation: *Highest*—High Point, 1,803 feet above sea level; *Lowest*—sea level along the Atlantic Ocean.

Population: *1970 Census*—7,168,164; 8th among the states; density, 915 persons to the square mile; distribution, 89 per cent urban, 11 per cent rural. *1960 Census*—6,066,782.

Chief Products: *Agriculture*—dairy products, eggs, greenhouse and nursery products, tomatoes. *Fishing Industry*—clams, flounders, menhaden, oysters, porgy. *Manufacturing and Processing*—chemicals, clothing, electrical machinery, fabricated metal products, food and food products, nonelectrical machinery, transportation equipment. *Mining*—clays, sand and gravel, stone, zinc.

Statehood: Dec. 18, 1787, the 3rd state.

State Motto: *Liberty and Prosperity.*

196

NEW JERSEY is a state of industrial cities and towns, glistening beaches, and gay summer resorts. It is the fifth smallest state. Only Hawaii, Connecticut, Delaware, and Rhode Island have a smaller area. But New Jersey ranks eighth in population among the states, and few states manufacture more products or attract more vacationers.

About 90 per cent of New Jersey's people live in cities and towns. This is a higher percentage than in any other state. The state's cities include such busy manufacturing centers as Camden, Elizabeth, Jersey City, Newark, Paterson, and Trenton. But New Jersey also has many small, quiet towns. A large number of these are the homes of people who work in New York City and Philadelphia. Both of these giant cities are neighbors of New Jersey.

The thousands of New Jerseyans who work in New York City and Philadelphia commute daily by train, automobile, or bus. The Holland and Lincoln tunnels and the George Washington Bridge link the state with New York City. The Benjamin Franklin Bridge, the Tacony-Palmyra Bridge, and the Walt Whitman Bridge connect New Jersey with Philadelphia.

New Jersey's location gives it great economic importance. The state lies between the Hudson and Delaware rivers, and between New York City and Philadelphia. Miles of wharves stretch along the New Jersey side of the Hudson. Ocean liners, freighters, and other ships from all parts of the world dock there and along the Delaware. Products made in New Jersey are used throughout the United States and in many other countries. They find giant nearby markets in New York City and Philadelphia. New Jersey leads the states in chemical production. It ranks high among producers of machinery, metals, processed foods, and textiles.

The large city populations create a demand for New Jersey farm products. The state is an important supplier of poultry, vegetables, and fruits for many Eastern cities.

New Jersey's vacation areas along the Atlantic Coast contrast sharply with the state's industrial cities. More than 50 resort cities and towns, including Asbury Park and Atlantic City, line the New Jersey coast. They provide a wide variety of recreation activities.

New Jersey and its people have played important roles in United States history. The state earned the nickname *Cockpit of the Revolution* because of the many battles fought on its soil during the Revolutionary War. American patriots and British redcoats clashed nearly a hundred times in New Jersey. People compared these actions with cockfights. General George Washington turned the tide of the war at Trenton in 1776 when he led his tattered army across the Delaware River and surprised the enemy. Trenton and Princeton each served as the nation's capital during the 1780's.

In 1884, Grover Cleveland of New Jersey was elected the 22nd President of the United States. He was elected President again in 1892. Woodrow Wilson served as president of Princeton University and governor of New Jersey before he was elected the 28th President in 1912. Wilson was re-elected in 1916, and led the nation through World War I.

Three of the world's greatest scientists and inventors worked in New Jersey for many years. Thomas Edison invented the electric light and the phonograph in his laboratory in Menlo Park. Albert Einstein worked many years at the Institute for Advanced Study at Princeton University. And Samuel F. B. Morse developed the first successful U.S. electric telegraph near Morristown.

New Jersey's many truck farms, orchards, and flower gardens give it the nickname of the *Garden State*. Trenton is the state capital, and Newark is the largest city. For the relationship of New Jersey to other states in its region, see MIDDLE ATLANTIC STATES.

The contributors of this article are Arthur Getis, Associate Professor of Geography at Rutgers, The State University; Mort Pye, Editor of the Newark Star-Ledger; and Richard P. McCormick, Professor of History and University Historian at Rutgers, The State University, and author of New Jersey from Colony to State.

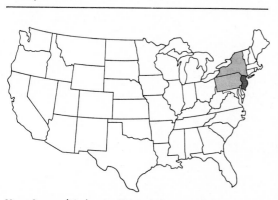

New Jersey (blue) ranks 46th in size among all the states, and is the smallest of the Middle Atlantic States (gray).

High Point, the Highest Peak in New Jersey
Scheller, Three Lions

Constitution of New Jersey was adopted in 1947. New Jersey had two earlier constitutions, adopted in 1776 and 1844. Either house of the state legislature may propose constitutional amendments. Amendments must be approved by three-fifths of the members of both houses, or by a majority vote of both houses in two successive years. To become law, amendments must also be approved by a majority of the voters in a general election. The constitution makes no provision for a constitutional convention that can amend the constitution. But in 1966, the legislature set up a special convention to *reapportion* (redivide) the legislature.

Executive. The governor is the only New Jersey executive official elected by the people. He serves a four-year term and receives a yearly salary of $50,000. The governor may serve any number of terms, but not more than two in succession. For a list of the governors of New Jersey, see the *History* section of this article.

The governor appoints most of the state's key executive officials. These officials include the attorney general; secretary of state; state treasurer; and the commissioners of conservation and economic development, education, health, and labor and industries. The state board of agriculture appoints the secretary of agriculture. The board members are recommended by an agricultural convention and appointed by the governor. All the governor's appointments are subject to approval by the senate. Most of the executive officials serve four-year terms.

Legislature of New Jersey consists of a 40-member senate and an 80-member general assembly. Voters in each of the state's 15 senatorial districts elect from 1 to 6 senators, depending on the district's population. Senators normally serve four-year terms. Voters in the state's assembly districts elect one or two assemblymen. Assemblymen serve two-year terms. The New Jersey legislature meets annually, beginning on the second Tuesday of January. Legislative sessions have no time limit.

Courts. New Jersey's highest court, the state supreme court, hears cases involving constitutional problems, capital punishment, and other major matters. The supreme court has a chief justice and six associate justices. The state superior court is New Jersey's chief trial court. It has three divisions—Appellate, Law, and Chancery. The superior court must have at least 24 judges. It now has 78. The governor, with the senate's approval, appoints the members of both the supreme and superior courts to seven-year terms. If he reappoints them once, they may serve until they are 70 years old.

New Jersey's 21 county courts have from one to eight judges, depending on the population of the county. These judges serve five-year terms. Lower courts include county traffic courts, juvenile and domestic relations courts, single-municipal and multi-municipal courts, and surrogate courts. The governor, with the senate's approval, appoints most lower court judges. Judges of single-municipal courts, called *magistrates*, are appointed by local governments. Voters elect surrogate judges.

Local Government. New Jersey is the only state in which county governments are called *boards of chosen freeholders*. This name comes from colonial days, when only *freeholders* (property owners) could hold public office. Seventeen New Jersey counties have *small boards* of from three to nine members. Small board freeholders represent their entire county. Four counties—Atlantic, Cumberland, Gloucester, and Salem—have *large boards* of 14 to 34 members. Large board freeholders represent a district rather than their entire county. All freeholders are elected to three-year terms.

New Jersey's 567 municipalities include cities, towns, townships, boroughs, and villages. Most of them have the mayor-council, commission, or council-manager form of government. Most of New Jersey's large cities have the mayor-council form. New Jersey municipalities get their charters from the state. They can choose from among a variety of charters. But they cannot write or revise their own charters.

Taxation provides about 85 per cent of the state's income. Almost all the rest comes from federal programs and grants. The state's chief source of revenue is a general sales tax, adopted in 1966. Other sources in-

New Jersey Dept. of Conservation and Economic Development

The Governor's Mansion is a famous historic site in Princeton. The mansion, called *Morven*, was built in 1701 by Richard Stockton, on a plot purchased from William Penn. The buff brick structure consists of a central three-story unit and balancing wings at each end. It was given to the state in 1954 by Walter E. Edge, a former governor of New Jersey.

The State Seal

Symbols of New Jersey. On the seal, the three plows and the goddess Ceres holding a horn of plenty represent the agricultural importance of New Jersey. Liberty stands on the left. A horse's head, which also refers to the state's agriculture, appears above a sovereign's helmet. The date 1776 was the year in which New Jersey signed the Declaration of Independence. The seal was adopted in 1928. New Jersey adopted its state flag in 1896.

clude taxes on motor fuels, cigarettes, motor vehicles, corporation incomes, inheritances, alcoholic beverages, pari-mutuel betting, business personal property, and public utilities.

Politics. During the late 1800's, most New Jersey governors were Democrats. Since 1900, the office has been about equally divided between Democrats and Republicans. The Republicans had a majority in the state senate and general assembly during most of the early 1900's. But the Democrats won increased support in state elections during the late 1950's and early 1960's. In 1958, the Democrats gained control of the general assembly for the first time in almost 20 years. In 1965, they won control of the state senate for the first time in more than 50 years. But the Republicans regained control of both houses in 1967.

Since 1856, New Jersey voters have supported Democratic presidential candidates more often than Republicans. For New Jersey's electoral votes and voting record see ELECTORAL COLLEGE (table).

The State Capitol is in Trenton, New Jersey's capital since 1790. Perth Amboy and Burlington served as twin capitals from 1703 to 1775. There was no definite capital from 1775 to 1790.

The State Flag

The State Bird
Eastern Goldfinch

The State Flower
Violet

The State Tree
Red Oak

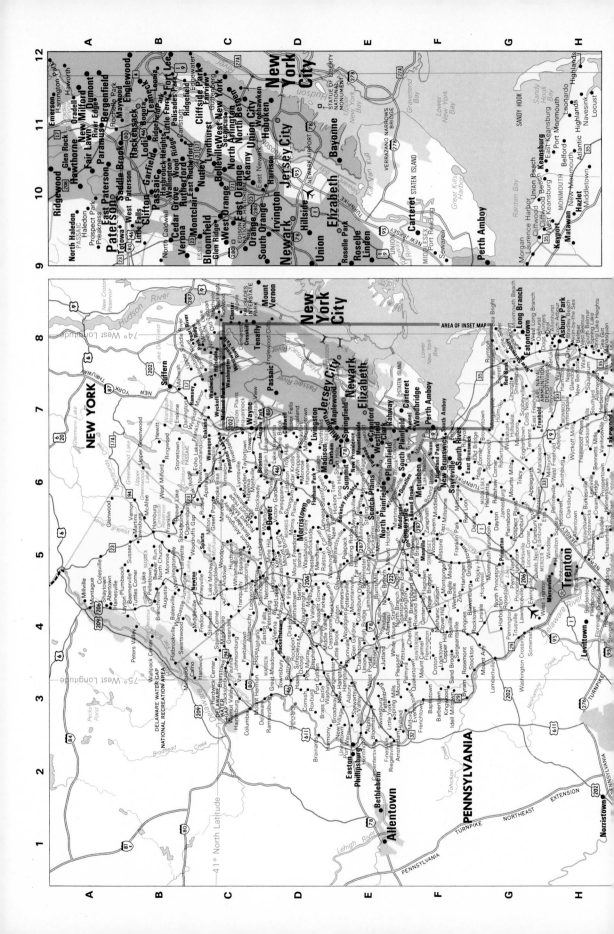

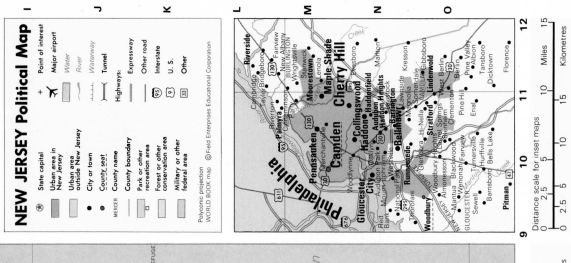
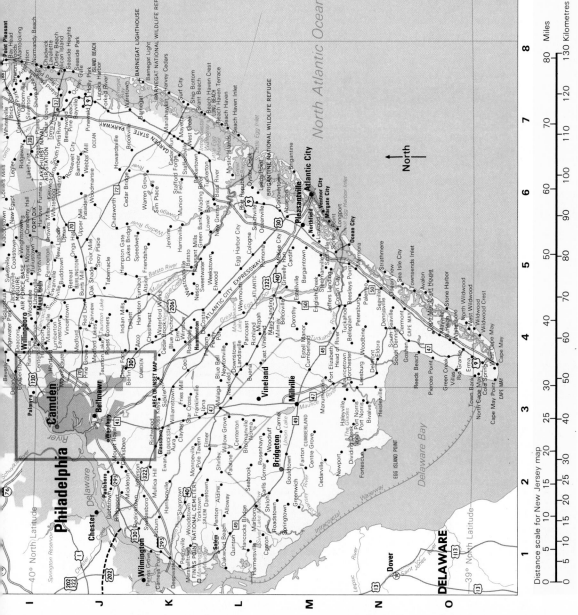

NEW JERSEY MAP INDEX

Population

7,168,164	Census	1970
6,066,782	"	1960
4,835,329	"	1950
4,160,165	"	1940
4,041,334	"	1930
3,155,900	"	1920
2,537,167	"	1910
1,883,669	"	1900
1,444,933	"	1890
1,131,116	"	1880
906,096	"	1870
672,035	"	1860
489,555	"	1850
373,306	"	1840
320,823	"	1830
277,575	"	1820
245,562	"	1810
211,149	"	1800
184,139	"	1790

Metropolitan Areas

Atlantic City ...175,043
Jersey City ...609,266
Newark ...1,856,556
Paterson-Clifton-
  Passaic ...1,358,794
Trenton ...303,968
Vineland-Millville-
  Bridgeton ...121,374

Counties

Atlantic ...175,043..L 5
Bergen ...898,012..C 8
Burlington ...323,132..J 6
Camden ...456,291..K 4
Cape May ...59,554..O 4
Cumber-
  land ...121,374..M 3
Essex ...929,986..D 7
Gloucester ...172,681..K 3
Hudson ...609,266..D 8
Hunterdon ...69,718..F 4
Mercer ...303,968..H 5
Middlesex ...583,813..G 7
Monmouth ...383,454..I 6
Morris ...383,454..D 6
Ocean ...208,470..J 7
Passaic ...460,782..B 6
Salem ...60,346..L 2
Somerset ...198,372..F 5
Sussex ...77,528..B 6
Union ...543,116..E 8
Warren ...73,879..D 3

Madison ...16,710 .D 6
Magnolia ...5,893 .O 1
Mahwah ...10,539▲ .C 4
Malaga ...K 3
Manahawkin ...1,228 .K 8
Manasquan ...4,971 .H 8
Manchester* ...1,913▲ .K 7
...7,550 .J 7
Mannington* ...3,546▲ .A 4
Mansfield ...2,597▲ .H 7
...319 .I 8
Mantoloking ...9,643▲ .D 9
Mantua ...13,029 .F 5
Manville
Maple
Shade ...16,464▲ .M11
Maplewood ...24,932 .E 7
Marcella ...C 6
Margate
City ...10,576 .M 6
Marksboro ...C 4
Marlboro ...10,273▲ .G12
Marlton ...10,180 .N 5
Marmora ...L 7
Martinsville ...E 6
Masonville ...I 6
Matawan* ...17,680▲ .H 9
Matawan ...9,136 .H 9
Maurice
River* ...3,743▲ .N 3
Mauricetown ...N 3
Mays
Landing ...1,272○M .M 5
Mayville ...O 5
Maywood ...11,087 .B11
McAfee ...B 4
McKee City ...10,933 .M 5
Medford ...1,448 .J 4
(8,292▲)
Medford
Lakes ...4,792 .J 4
Mendham* ...3,697▲ .D 5
Mendham ...3,729 .D 5
Mercerville
[-Hamilton
Square] ...24,465 .H 5
Merchant-
ville ...4,425 .M11
Meriden ...B 7
Metuchen ...16,031 .F 6
Meyersville ...E 6
Mickleton ...F 4
Middlebush ...8,725▲ .F 6
Middlesex ...15,038 .F 6
Middletown* ...54,623▲ .H10
Midland
Park ...8,159 .C 7
Milford ...1,230 .E 4
Mill Brook ...C 5
Millburn ...21,307 .E 7
Millington ...2,535 .E 6
Millstone ...630 .G 7
Millville ...21,366 .N 4
Milmay ...M 4
Mine Hill ...3,557▲ .D 5
Mizpah ...M 4
Monmouth
Beach ...2,042 .G 8
Monmouth
Junction ...G 7
Monroe* ...9,138▲ .G 6
Monroe ...14,071▲ .K 3

Monroeville ...131 .K 3
Montague ...A 4
Montclair ...44,043 .C10
Montgomery ...6,353▲ .F 5
Montvale ...7,327 .B11
Montville ...D 5
Moonachie* ...2,937 .B11
Moorestown ...15,577 .M12
[-Lenola] 14,179 .M12
Morganville ...19,414 .D 6
Morris* ...17,662○D .D 6
Morris Plains ...5,540 .D 6
Morristown ...17,662○D .D 6
Mount
Arlington ...3,590 .C 5
Mount Bethel ...E 6
Mount
Ephraim ...5,625 .N10
Mount Fern ...D 5
Mount
Freedom ...1,621 .D 5
Mount
Holly 12,713○I .I 4
Mount Hope ...C 5
Mount
Laurel ...11,221▲ .J 4
Mount Olive ...10,394▲ .D 5
Mount Royal ...F 4
Mountain
Lakes ...4,739 .D 6
Mountainside ...7,520 .L 2
Muttica Hill ...3,394 .L 2
Mystic Islands ...K 6
National
Park ...3,730 .N 9
Navesink ...H 8
Neptune ...27,863▲ .H 8
Neptune City 5,502 .H 8
Nesco ...F 5
Neshanic Station ...F 5
Netcong ...2,858 .H 8
New Bedford ...D 5
New Bruns-
wick ...41,885○F .F 6
New Egypt ...1,769 .I 6
New Gretna ...L 6
New
Hanover* ...27,410▲ .M11
New Lisbon ...I 5
New Milford 20,201 .A12
New Monmouth ...H11
New Provi-
dence 13,796 .E 6
New Shrews-
bury 5,925 .G 8
New Vernon ...E 6
New Village ...D 4
Newark 382,417○E .E 7
Newfield ...1,487 .L 3
Newfoundland ...C 7
Newton ...7,297○C .C10
Newtonville ...L 4
North
Arlington 18,096 .C10
North
Bergen 47,751▲ .C12
North Branch ...E 5
North Bruns-
wick ...16,691▲ .F 6
North
Caldwell ...6,425 .B 9
North Cape
May ...O 6
North
Haledon ...7,614 .A10

North
Hanover* ...9,858▲ .I 5
North
Plainfield 21,796 .E 6
North
Princeton ...5,488 .G 5
North
Wildwood ...3,914 .O 4
Northfield ...8,875 .M 5
Northvale ...5,177 .M 5
Nutley ...32,099 .D11
Oak Ridge ...C 6
Oakhurst ...H 8
Oakland ...14,420 .C 7
Oaklyn ...4,626 .N10
Oakwood
Beach ...18,643 .L 2
Ocean* ...18,222▲ .H 8
Ocean City ...10,575 .N 5
Ocean Gate ...1,081 .K 7
Ocean View ...N 5
Oceanport ...7,503 .G 8
Oceanville ...M 5
Ogdensburg ...2,222 .B 5
Old Bridge 25,176 .G 6
Old Tappan ...3,917 .B12
Oldmans* ...2,088▲ .K 2
Oldwick ...E 5
Oradell ...8,903 .A11
Orange 32,566 .E 7
Ortley Beach ...K 7
Oxford ...1,411 .D 4
Pahaquarry* ...71▲ .A 3
Palisades ...C 3

Park ...13,351 .B12
Palmyra ...6,969 .A11
Paramus ...29,495 .A11
Park Ridge ...8,709 .L 7
Parkertown ...L 7
Parsippany-Troy
Hills* ...55,112▲ .D 6
Parsippany-Troy
Hills ...7,393 .E 7
Passaic ...55,124 .C11
Paterson 144,824○A .A10
Pattenburg ...8,084 .E 5
Peapack [-Glad-
stone] ...1,924 .E 5
Pedricktown ...K 2
Pemberton* 27,547▲ .J 5
Pemberton ...1,344 .I 5
Pennington ...2,151 .H 4
Penns Grove 5,727 .K 2
Penns Neck ...G 5
Pennsauken 36,394▲ .M11
Pennsville ...11,014 .K 1
Penton ...382,417 .H 4
Pequannock 14,350▲ .C 7
Perrineville ...G 7
Perth
Amboy ...38,798 .F 7
Petersburg ...N 5
Phillipsburg 17,849 .D 3
Pilesgrove* ...2,706▲ .K 3
Pine Beach ...1,395 .K 7
Pine Brook ...D 6
Pine Hill ...5,132 .O11
Pine Valley ...23 .O11
Pinewald ...K 7
Pitman ...9,134 .L 3
Pittsgrove* 15,754▲ .L 3
Plainfield ...46,862 .E 6

Plainsboro ...1,648▲ .G 5
Pleasant Plains ...I 7
Pleasant-
ville ...13,778 .M 6
Pluckemin ...4,113▲ .E 5
Plumsted* ...3,924▲ .E 3
Pohatcong*
Point
Pleasant ...15,968▲ .I 8
Point
Pleasant
Beach ...4,882 .I 8
Pomona ...L 5
Pompton
Lakes 11,397 .C 7
Pompton Plains ...C 7
Port Colden ...D 4
Port Elizabeth ...N 4
Port Monmouth ...H11
Port Morris ...D 5
Port Murray ...D 4
Port Norris ...1,955 .N 4
Port Reading ...F 7
Port Republic ...586 .L 6
Pottersville ...E 5
Princeton ...13,651▲ .G 5
Princeton* ...12,311▲ .G 5
Princeton
Junction ...G 5
Prospect
Park ...5,176 .A10
Quakertown ...E 5
Quinton ...2,567▲ .K 2
Rahway ...29,114 .F 7
Ramblewood ...5,556 .M12
Ramsey ...12,571 .B11
Rancocas ...I 4
Randolph* ...13,296▲ .D 5
Raritan ...6,691 .E 5
Readington ...7,688▲ .E 5
Reaville ...F 5
Red Bank 12,847 .G 8
Red Bank ...H 8
Richland ...M 4
Ridgefield ...11,308 .B12
Ridgefield
Park ...14,453 .B11
Ridgeway ...I 7
Ridgewood 27,547 .B11
Riegelsville ...D 3
Ringoes ...F 5
Rio Grande ...O 5
River Edge ...11,204 .B11
River Vale ...9,489▲ .B11
Riverdale ...2,729 .C 7
Riverside ...8,616 .I 4
Riverton ...3,412 .M11
Riviera Beach ...K 7
Robbinsville ...H 5
Rochelle
Park ...6,380▲ .B11
Rockaway ...18,955▲ .C 6
Rockleigh ...308 .B12
Rocky Hill ...917 .G 5
Roebling, see Florence
[-Roebling]
Roosevelt ...814 .H 6
Roseland ...4,453 .D 6
Roselle ...22,585 .E 7
Roselle Park ...14,277 .E 7
Rosenhayn ...L 3
Roxbury* 15,754▲ .D 5
Rumson ...7,421 .G 8
Runnemede 10,475 .O11

Rutherford 20,802 .B11
Saddle
Brook ...15,098▲ .B11
Saddle River 2,437 .K 7
Salem ...7,648○L .L 2
Sandyston* ...2,038▲ .B 4
Sayreville ...32,508 .F 7
Schooleys Mountain ...D 4
Scotch
Plains ...22,279▲ .E 6
Scullville ...M 5
Sea Bright ...1,339 .G 8
Sea Grit ...2,207 .H 8
Sea Isle City 1,712 .N 5
Seabrook ...1,569▲ .L 2
Seaside
Heights ...1,248 .J 8
Seaside Park 1,432 .J 8
Secaucus 13,228 .C11
Sergeantsville ...F 4
Sewaren ...F 7
Sewell ...M12
Shamong* ...1,318▲ .J 5
Shiloh ...573 .L 2
Ship Bottom ...1,079 .K 7
Shore Acres ...J 8
Shore Hills* ...3,064▲ .D 5
Shrewsbury* ...1,164▲ .G 8
Shrewsbury ...3,315 .G 8
Sicklerville ...N11
Silverton ...K 7
Somerdale ...6,510 .O11
Somers Point 7,919 .M 5
Somerset ...13,652 .F 6
Somerville ...13,652○E .E 5
South Amboy ...9,338 .F 7
South Belmar 1,490 .H 8
South Bound
Brook ...4,525 .E 5
South Branch ...E 5
South Bruns-
wick* ...14,058▲ .G 6
South Dennis ...N 5
South Hack-
ensack* ...2,459▲ .B11
South
Harrison* ...1,226▲ .K 2
South
Orange ...16,971 .D 7
South
Plainfield 21,142 .F 6
South River 15,428 .F 6
South Toms
River ...3,981 .J 7
South-
ampton* ...4,982▲ .J 5
Southard ...H 7
Sparta ...10,819▲ .C 5
Spotswood ...7,891 .F 6
Spring Lake 3,896 .H 8
Spring Lake
Heights ...4,602 .H 8
Springfield ...15,740▲ .E 7
Stafford* ...5,684▲ .K 7
Stanhope ...3,040 .C 5
Stanton ...E 5
Steelmanville ...M 5
Stevens ...H 7
Stewartsville ...2,158 .D 3
Stillwater ...B 4
Stirling ...E 6
Stockton ...619 .F 4
Stone Harbor 1,089 .O 5
Stow Creek* ...1,050▲ .L 2
Stratford ...9,801 .O11

Strathmore* 7,674 .F 7
Succasunna ...D 5
Summit ...23,620 .E 7
Surf City ...2,038 .K 8
Sussex ...2,103 .B 4
Swedesboro ...2,287 .K 2
Tabernacle ...2,103▲ .J 5
Tansboro ...N11
Taunton Lake ...J 4
Tavistock ...12 .N11
Taylortown ...D 6
Teaneck ...42,355▲ .B12
Tenafly ...14,827 .B12
Teterboro* ...14 .B11
Tewksbury* ...2,959▲ .E 5
Three Bridges ...E 5
Toms River ...11,580 .J 7
Totowa ...B10
Towaco ...C 6
Town Bank ...O 4
Trenton 104,638○H .H 4
Troy Hills ...D 6
Tuckahoe ...1,926 .N 5
Tuckerton ...2,351▲ .L 6
Turnersville ...O11
Union ...53,077▲ .D 7
Union* ...1,539▲ .K 7
Union
Beach ...6,472 .G 8
Union City 58,537 .C11
Uniontown ...E 3
Upper* ...3,413▲ .N 5
Upper
Deerfield* ...6,648▲ .L 2
Upper
Freehold* ...2,551▲ .H 6
Upper Greenwood
Lake ...1,505 .B 6
Upper Penns
Neck* ...7,016▲ .K 1
Upper Pitts-
grove* ...2,884▲ .L 2
Upper Saddle
River ...7,949 .C 8
Ventnor
City ...10,385 .M 6
Vernon ...6,059▲ .B 6
Verona ...15,067 .D 7
Victory
Gardens ...1,027 .D 6
Vienna ...D 4
Villas ...3,155 .O 4
Vincentown ...I 5
Vineland ...47,399 .L 3
Voorhees* ...6,214▲ .N11
Waldwick ...12,313 .B11
Wall ...16,498▲ .H 8
Wallington ...10,284 .B11
Walpack* ...384▲ .B 3
Wanamassa ...H 8
Wanaque ...8,636 .C 7
Warren* ...4,329▲ .E 6
Warrenville ...E 6
Washington ...8,592 .D 4
Washington ...10,577▲ .K 3
Washington ...3,585▲ .H 7
Washing-
ton ...3,311▲ .H 5
Washington
Crossing ...G 4

Washington
Valley ...D 6
Watchung ...4,750 .E 6
Waterford* ...4,073▲ .K 4
Waterford
Works ...N11
Wayne ...49,141▲ .C 7
Weehawken 13,383 .C12
Wenonah ...2,364 .O10
West
Amwell* ...2,142▲ .G 4
West Belmar ...H 8
West
Caldwell 11,887 .D 7
West
Cape May ...1,005 .O 4
West Creek ...K 7
West
Deptford* 13,928▲ .J 2
West Keansburg ...H10
West Long
Branch ...6,845 .G 8
West Milford 17,304▲ .B 6
West
New York 40,627 .C12
West
Orange ...43,715 .C 9
West
Paterson 11,692 .B10
West
Wildwood ...235 .O 4
West
Windsor* ...6,431▲ .G 5
Westampton* ...2,680▲ .I 5
Westfield ...33,720 .E 6
Westville ...5,170 .N10
Westwood ...11,105 .C 7
Weymouth ...998▲ .M 5
Wharton ...5,535 .D 5
Whippany ...D 6
White* ...2,326▲ .D 3
Whitehouse
see Yardville
White House
Station ...1,019 .E 4
White Meadow
Lake ...8,499 .C 6
Whitesboro ...O 6
Whiting ...K 7
Wickatunk ...G 7
Wildwood ...4,110 .O 4
Wildwood
Crest ...3,483 .O 4
Williams-
town ...4,075 .K 3
Willingboro 43,414▲ .I 4
Windsor ...H 5
Winfield ...2,184 .E 7
Winslow ...11,202▲ .N 4
Wood Ridge 8,311 .B11
Woodbine ...2,625 .N 5
Woodbridge 98,944▲ .F 7
Woodbury ...12,408○J .J 3
Woodbury
Heights ...3,621 .O10
Woodcliff
Lake ...5,506 .C 8
Woodland* ...2,032▲ .J 5
Woodlynne ...3,101 .N10
Woodport ...C 5
Woodruff ...H 5
Woods Tavern ...H 7
Woodstown ...3,137 .K 3
Woolwich* ...1,147▲ .K 2
Wrightstown ...2,719 .I 5
Wyckoff 16,039▲ .C 7
Yardville [-White
Horse] ...18,680 .H 5

*Does not appear on the map; key shows general location.
▲Entire township, including rural area
○County seat

Source: Latest census figures (1970). Places without population figures are unincorporated areas and are not listed in census reports.

Jersey Pictures Inc.

Factory Workers stream from a plant in Jersey City at the end of the day. Many of the city's industrial plants employ more than a thousand workers and operate two or even three shifts a day.

Farm Workers use special scooplike rakes to gather cranberries on a truck farm in southern New Jersey. The state's farmers find nearby markets for their products in several metropolitan centers.

Three Lions

The 1970 United States census reported that New Jersey had 7,168,164 persons. The population had increased by 18 per cent over the 1960 census figure, 6,066,782.

About 90 out of 100 New Jerseyans live in urban areas. This percentage of urban dwellers is the second highest among the states. Only California has a higher percentage. Almost 4½ million persons live in the state's six Standard Metropolitan Statistical Areas (see METROPOLITAN AREA). These areas, which all lie entirely within New Jersey, are Atlantic City, Jersey City, Newark, Paterson-Clifton-Passaic, Trenton, and Vineland-Millville-Bridgeton. For their populations, see the *Index* with the political map in this article. More than 1 million New Jerseyans live in three metropolitan areas that extend into New Jersey from other states. These areas are Allentown-Bethlehem-Easton and Philadelphia, both in Pennsylvania; and Wilmington, in Delaware.

Northeastern New Jersey and the New York City Standard Metropolitan Statistical Area form a Standard Consolidated Metropolitan Area with 16,135,450 persons. The New Jersey part of the area includes the Jersey City, Newark, and Paterson-Clifton-Passaic metropolitan areas, and Middlesex and Somerset counties.

Newark is New Jersey's largest city. Other large cities with more than 100,000 persons, in order of population, include Jersey City, Paterson, Elizabeth, Trenton, and Camden. See the articles on New Jersey cities listed in the *Related Articles* at the end of this article.

About 90 per cent of all New Jerseyans were born in the United States. Of those born in other countries, the largest group came from Italy. Roman Catholics make up New Jersey's largest religious body. Other large groups include Baptists, Episcopalians, Jews, Lutherans, Methodists, and Presbyterians.

POPULATION

This map shows the *population density* of New Jersey, and how it varies in different parts of the state. Population density means the average number of persons who live on each square mile.

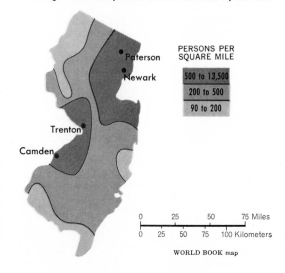

PERSONS PER SQUARE MILE

500 to 13,500
200 to 500
90 to 200

0   25   50   75 Miles
0 25 50 75 100 Kilometers

WORLD BOOK map

Schools. Colonial New Jersey had no public schools. Children attended school only if their parents could afford to pay tuition. New Jersey's public school system began in 1817, when the legislature established a permanent school fund. In 1824, the state added part of its tax income to the fund. But taxes were not used to help support schools until 1829.

A state commissioner of education and a 12-member board of education direct New Jersey's public school system. The governor, with the senate's approval, appoints the commissioner to a five-year term and the board members to six-year terms. Local boards administer local school districts. The chancellor of higher education directs the state's public college system.

New Jersey law requires children between the ages of 6 and 16 to attend school. For the number of students and teachers in New Jersey, see EDUCATION (table).

Two of the oldest U.S. universities and colleges are in New Jersey. They are Princeton University (1746) and Rutgers, The State University (1766).

Libraries. Thomas Cadwalader founded New Jersey's first library at Trenton in 1750. Today, New Jersey has more than a thousand libraries. They include about 300 public libraries, 600 school libraries, and 100 industrial research libraries. The State Library in Trenton has large law and general reference collections that serve state government officials. The Interlibrary Reference and Loan Service loans books to libraries throughout the state. The Harvey S. Firestone Memorial Library of Princeton University is New Jersey's largest school library.

Museums. The New Jersey State Museum in Trenton features outstanding exhibits of archaeology, natural history, and painting. In 1965, a new building was added to house a planetarium and large auditorium.

The Newark Museum includes a planetarium and art, science, and natural history exhibits. The New Jersey Historical Society in Newark has a museum featuring historic items. The Montclair Art Museum displays excellent collections of paintings and sculpture.

UNIVERSITIES AND COLLEGES

New Jersey has 24 universities and colleges accredited by the Middle States Association of Colleges and Secondary Schools. For enrollments and further information, see UNIVERSITIES AND COLLEGES (table).

Name	Location	Founded
Bloomfield College	Bloomfield	1868
Caldwell College	Caldwell	1939
Don Bosco College	Newton	1938
Drew University	Madison	1867
Fairleigh Dickinson University	Rutherford	1941
Georgian Court College	Lakewood	1908
Glassboro State College	Glassboro	1923
Jersey City State College	Jersey City	1921
Monmouth College	West Long Branch	1933
Montclair State College	Montclair	1908
Newark College of Engineering	Newark	1881
Newark State College	Union	1855
Paterson State College	Wayne	1855
Princeton Theological Seminary	Princeton	1812
Princeton University	Princeton	1746
Rider College	Trenton	1865
Rutgers, The State University	New Brunswick	1766
Saint Elizabeth, College of	Convent Station	1899
Saint Peter's College	Jersey City	1872
Seton Hall University	South Orange	1856
Stevens Institute of Technology	Hoboken	1870
Trenton State College	Trenton	1855
Upsala College	East Orange	1893
Westminster Choir College	Princeton	1926

Holder Hall at Princeton University in Princeton

Joseph De Caro, Three Lions

NEW JERSEY / A Visitor's Guide

New Jersey is one of the great coastal playgrounds of the United States. Every year, millions of vacationers flock to the state's seaside resorts. They swim in the Atlantic Ocean, sunbathe on sandy beaches, and stroll along boardwalks lined with shops. Visitors also enjoy dozens of historic sites, chiefly in or near inland cities.

New Jersey attracts many sportsmen. Fishermen can catch a variety of game fish in the ocean. Inland, they can cast for trout in 1,400 miles of stocked streams. Hunters shoot ducks in coastal areas, and deer, pheasants, and rabbits on inland public shooting grounds. Sailing is a popular sport in the state's coastal bays.

WORLD BOOK photo by Three Lions

Convention Hall in Atlantic City

Scheller, Three Lions

The Old Barracks in Trenton

Scheller, Three Lions

The Barn in the Colonial Village of Batsto

PLACES TO VISIT

Following are brief descriptions of some of New Jersey's many interesting places to visit.

Barnegat Lighthouse, near Barnegat Light, is a favorite subject of painters and photographers. The lighthouse is part of a state park that also includes a museum and a sandy beach.

Batsto is a partially restored colonial village in southeastern New Jersey. The community produced cannon balls for General George Washington's troops during the Revolutionary War. Attractions include an ironmaster's house, a blacksmith's shop, a general store, and a glassware exhibition.

Burlington features the birthplaces of novelist James Fenimore Cooper and James Lawrence, the naval officer whose famous dying command was "Don't give up the ship."

Camden includes *Walt Whitman House,* the great poet's home from 1884 until 1892. The house has many mementos of Whitman.

Delaware Water Gap is a deep narrow gorge formed where the Delaware River cuts through the Kittatinny Mountains. This scenic gap separates New Jersey and Pennsylvania north of Columbia, N.J.

Princeton is the home of Princeton University and Princeton Battlefield, the site of an important colonial victory in the Revolutionary War. The university's Nassau Hall served as the U.S. Capitol in 1783.

Seaside Resorts include Asbury Park, Atlantic City, Cape May, North Wildwood, Ocean City, Seaside Heights, Wildwood, and Wildwood Crest. Atlantic City, the most famous resort, has a seven-mile boardwalk and a convention hall that can seat 41,000 persons.

Trenton has many points of interest, including the New Jersey State Museum, the State Capitol, and the Old Barracks, used by British soldiers during the French and Indian Wars.

National Park and Historic Site. Morristown National Historical Park, established in 1933, lies in and near Morristown. It includes Ford Mansion, George Washington's headquarters during the winter of 1779-1780; Fort Nonsense, a restoration of a fort built in 1777; and several camps used by American soldiers during the Revolutionary War. See NATIONAL PARK (National Historical Parks). The Edison National Historic Site in West Orange includes the great inventor's home, library, papers, and models of some of his inventions.

State Parks and Forests. New Jersey has 23 state parks and 12 state forests. For information on these parks and forests, write to Director, Department of Conservation and Economic Development, Division of Research Planning, Bureau of Parks and Recreation, 520 E. State St., Trenton, N.J. 08625.

New Jersey and New York together maintain Palisades Interstate Park. See PALISADES.

Barnegat Lighthouse near Barnegat Light

ANNUAL EVENTS

The Miss America Pageant, held each September in Atlantic City, is New Jersey's best-known annual event. This nationally televised pageant features girls from every state. They compete for the title of Miss America on the basis of beauty, charm, and talent. Other annual events in New Jersey include the following.

January-February: Winter Sports Carnivals in Lakewood, Atlantic City, and Lake Mohawk (no fixed dates).

May-July: Dog Shows in Trenton, Rumson, and Plainfield (May, no fixed dates); New Jersey State Interscholastic Championship, a track and field event in New Brunswick (first week of June); National Marbles Tournament in Wildwood (mid-June); Watchung Horse Show (last weekend of June); Old Home Historical Tour in Cape May (mid-July); Bellwoar Trophy Speedboat Races in Ocean City (each Sunday in July); New Brunswick Horse Show (July, no fixed date).

August-October: Baby Parades in Wildwood and Ocean City (early August); Big Sea Day pageant and parade in Point Pleasant (mid-August); Eastern Lawn Tennis Association Championships in East Orange (late August); Surf Fishing Contest in Atlantic City (third weekend of September); State Fair in Trenton (third week of September); Striped Bass Derby in Ship Bottom (mid-October); Annual Fall Festival in Morristown (third weekend of October).

November-December: Flower Show in Newark (Nov. 1 to 14); Turkey Shoot in Perth Amboy (shortly before Thanksgiving); Memorial honoring Washington's crossing of the Delaware, at Washington Crossing (Dec. 25); Ice Carnival in Morristown (last week of December); Dog Show in Camden (December, no fixed date).

Beach at Ocean City on the Atlantic Coast

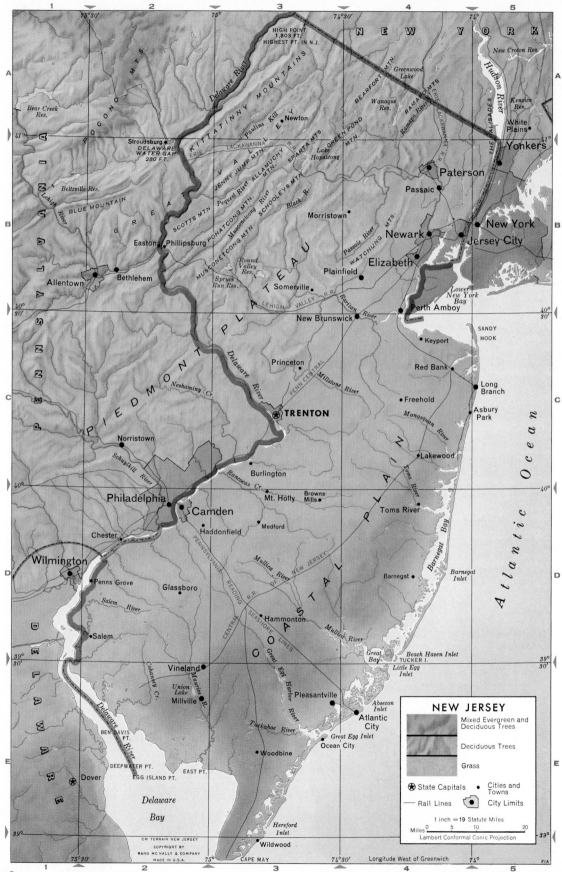

NEW JERSEY

	Mixed Evergreen and Deciduous Trees
	Deciduous Trees
	Grass

✪ State Capitals • Cities and Towns
— Rail Lines   City Limits

1 inch = 19 Statute Miles

Miles 0   5   10   20

Lambert Conformal Conic Projection

CM TERRAIN NEW JERSEY
COPYRIGHT BY
RAND McNALLY & COMPANY
MADE IN U.S.A.

Longitude West of Greenwich

FIA

208

Specially created for **World Book Encyclopedia** by Rand McNally and World Book editors

Land Regions. New Jersey has four main land regions. They are, from northwest to southeast: (1) the Appalachian Ridge and Valley Region, (2) the New England Upland, (3) the Piedmont, and (4) the Atlantic Coastal Plain.

The Appalachian Ridge and Valley Region is a mountainous area in the northwestern corner of the state. It is part of a large region of the same name that runs from New York to Alabama. In New Jersey, it includes the Kittatinny Mountains and several valleys. The Kittatinny Mountains run parallel to New Jersey's northwestern border. The Delaware Water Gap, formed where the Delaware River cuts through the mountains, is one of the most scenic areas in the East. The Appalachian Valley lies southeast of the Kittatinny Mountains. This wide valley is part of the larger Great Valley. The Appalachian Valley is broken by ridges of shale and depressions of limestone. Herds of dairy cattle graze on grassy slopes in the valley, and farmers there raise apples and vegetables.

The New England Upland, usually called the *Highlands,* lies southeast of the Appalachian Ridge and Valley Region. The region extends into New York and Pennsylvania. Flat-topped ridges of hard rock, called *gneiss,* cover much of the New England Upland in New Jersey. Many lakes nestle among the ridges of the New England Upland in New Jersey. These lakes are among the state's most important tourist attractions.

The Piedmont crosses northern New Jersey in a 20-mile-wide belt southeast of the New England Upland. The entire Piedmont covers an area from New York to Alabama. It covers only about a fifth of New Jersey, but almost three-fourths of the state's people live there. The region includes such large industrial cities as Elizabeth, Jersey City, Newark, and Paterson. The cities of the Piedmont region owe much of their industrial importance to the many large rivers in the area. These rivers include the Hudson, the Musconetcong, the Passaic, the Ramapo, and the Raritan.

The Atlantic Coastal Plain is a gently-rolling lowland that covers the southern three-fifths of New Jersey. It is part of a plain with the same name that stretches from New York to Florida. In New Jersey, more than half the plain lies less than a hundred feet above sea level. In the west and southwest, fertile soil supports many truck farms. Camden, Trenton, and other cities lie along the wide Delaware River in the western part of the plain. To the east, forests and salt marshes cover much of the Atlantic Coastal Plain. For this reason, large areas of the region are thinly populated. Salt marshes, shallow lagoons, and meadows lie near New Jersey's Atlantic coast. More than 50 resort cities and towns, including Asbury Park, Atlantic City, and Cape May,

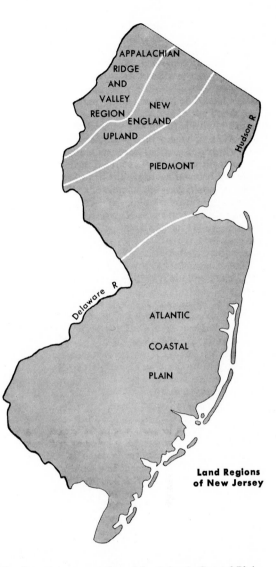

**Land Regions
of New Jersey**

lie along the eastern edge of the Atlantic Coastal Plain.

Coastline. A long, narrow sandbar makes up most of New Jersey's 130-mile coastline. Many inlets break the coast and lead to bays between the sandbar and the mainland. New Jersey's coastal bays include, from south to north, Great Egg Bay, Great Bay, Little Egg Harbor, Barnegat Bay, Sandy Hook Bay, Raritan Bay, and Newark Bay. The sandy beaches along New Jersey's coast make up one of the most popular vacation areas in the United States.

Map Index

NEW JERSEY

Mountains. New Jersey's only mountainous area is in the northwest. High Point, the state's highest peak, rises 1,803 feet in the northwestern corner of the state. High Point is part of the Kittatinny Mountains, New Jersey's chief mountain range. Other ranges include the Sourland and Watchung mountains. They rise about 450 feet in the Piedmont region.

Rivers and Lakes. New Jersey's most important rivers are the Delaware and the Hudson. The Delaware forms the state's western border and empties into Dela-ware Bay. The Hudson separates New Jersey and New York in the northeast and flows into the Atlantic Ocean. The Raritan is the longest river entirely within New Jersey. It flows about 75 miles through the north. Other important rivers in the north include the Hackensack, Millstone, Musconetcong, and Passaic. Southern New Jersey rivers include Great Egg Harbor, Maurice, Mullica, and Toms.

Most of New Jersey's more than 800 lakes and ponds are in the north. Lake Hopatcong is the state's largest lake. Other large lakes include Budd, Culvers, Green Pond, Greenwood (partly in New York), Lake Mohawk, and Swartswood.

Lake Hopatcong, the state's largest lake, nestles among rocky, flat-topped hills in the New England Upland region of northern New Jersey.
Scheller, Three Lions

Grazing Horses feed in a rich green pasture in the gently rolling Piedmont region of north-central New Jersey.
Scheller, Three Lions

WORLD BOOK photo by Three Lions

Fertile Soil supports many truck farms in the Atlantic Coastal Plain region of southern New Jersey. The state is a chief producer of vegetables.

New Jersey has a mild climate. Ocean breezes keep the eastern coast cool in summer and warm in winter. Average July temperatures range from 76° F. in the southwest to 70° F. in the north. On July 10, 1936, Runyon registered New Jersey's highest temperature, 110° F. Average January temperatures range from 34° F. at Cape May to 26° F. in the Appalachian Ridge and Valley Region. On Jan. 5, 1904, River Vale recorded the state's lowest temperature, −34° F.

Snowfall averages about 13 inches a year in the south, and 50 inches in the north. Frost occurs between late September and early May. New Jersey averages about 46 inches of *precipitation* (rain, melted snow, and other forms of moisture) a year. Precipitation is fairly evenly distributed throughout the state. Atlantic and Cape May counties receive a little less than other areas.

Scheller, Three Lions

Gentle Ocean Breezes keep Ship Bottom and other resort areas along the Atlantic Coast cool in summer and warm in winter.

SEASONAL TEMPERATURES

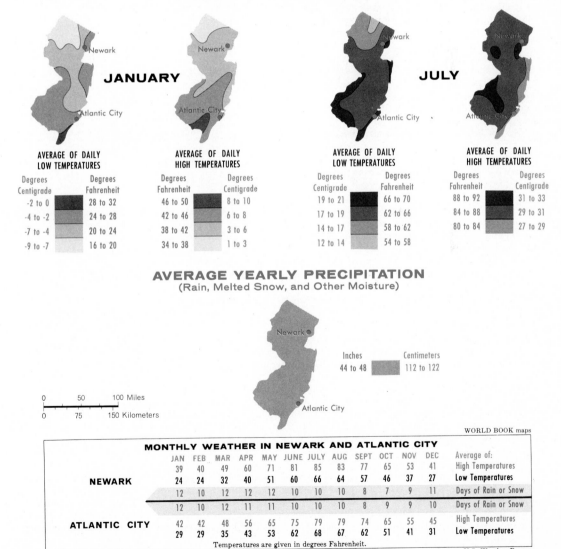

JANUARY

AVERAGE OF DAILY LOW TEMPERATURES

Degrees Centigrade	Degrees Fahrenheit
-2 to 0	28 to 32
-4 to -2	24 to 28
-7 to -4	20 to 24
-9 to -7	16 to 20

AVERAGE OF DAILY HIGH TEMPERATURES

Degrees Fahrenheit	Degrees Centigrade
46 to 50	8 to 10
42 to 46	6 to 8
38 to 42	3 to 6
34 to 38	1 to 3

JULY

AVERAGE OF DAILY LOW TEMPERATURES

Degrees Centigrade	Degrees Fahrenheit
19 to 21	66 to 70
17 to 19	62 to 66
14 to 17	58 to 62
12 to 14	54 to 58

AVERAGE OF DAILY HIGH TEMPERATURES

Degrees Fahrenheit	Degrees Centigrade
88 to 92	31 to 33
84 to 88	29 to 31
80 to 84	27 to 29

AVERAGE YEARLY PRECIPITATION
(Rain, Melted Snow, and Other Moisture)

Inches	Centimeters
44 to 48	112 to 122

0   50   100 Miles

0   75   150 Kilometers

WORLD BOOK maps

MONTHLY WEATHER IN NEWARK AND ATLANTIC CITY													
	JAN	FEB	MAR	APR	MAY	JUNE	JULY	AUG	SEPT	OCT	NOV	DEC	Average of:
NEWARK	39	40	49	60	71	81	85	83	77	65	53	41	High Temperatures
	24	24	32	40	51	60	66	64	57	46	37	27	Low Temperatures
	12	10	12	12	12	10	10	10	8	7	9	11	Days of Rain or Snow
	12	10	12	11	11	10	10	10	8	9	9	10	Days of Rain or Snow
ATLANTIC CITY	42	42	48	56	65	75	79	79	74	65	55	45	High Temperatures
	29	29	35	43	53	62	68	67	62	51	41	31	Low Temperatures

Temperatures are given in degrees Fahrenheit.

Source: U.S. Weather Bureau

Despite its small size, New Jersey ranks among the leading industrial states. Manufacturing, the state's most important economic activity, employs more than 875,000 workers in about 14,000 plants. These plants are mainly in the Elizabeth-Jersey City-Newark area in the northeast, and in the Trenton-Camden area in the west. New Jersey is sometimes called the *Workshop of the Nation* because of the great number of manufactured products its factories turn out.

The beach-lined Atlantic seaboard is the center of New Jersey's flourishing tourist trade. Tourism ranks as the state's second most important economic activity. The millions of tourists who visit the state each year contribute more than $2½ billion to the economy.

New Jersey's location between New York City and Philadelphia helps the state's economy. Thousands of New Jerseyans work in these two cities.

Natural Resources of New Jersey include fertile soils, large forests, and small deposits of minerals. Unlike many other states, New Jersey does not rely on its own resources for the raw materials of its industries.

Soil. Three types of soil are most common in New Jersey. In the north, the soil has a high limestone and glacial mineral content. Farmers in this region raise field crops and operate dairy farms. A rich subsoil of greensand marl lies under rich loam in central New Jersey. This mixture yields good vegetable crops. When mixed with fertilizer, the sandy soil of the south supports fruit orchards and vegetable farms.

Minerals. Stone (especially basalt, diabase, granite, limestone, and serpentine) is New Jersey's most abundant mineral. The counties in northern New Jersey produce all the stone. Sand and gravel deposits are found throughout New Jersey. Bergen, Passaic, and other northern counties produce sand and gravel for construction. Cumberland, Camden, and other southern counties produce industrial sand for glassmaking and foundry work. Other minerals include clay, greensand marl, peat, and zinc.

Forests cover almost half of New Jersey. Beech, birch, black tupelo, maple, oak, sweet gums, and other hardwoods are the most valuable trees in the north. Important trees of southern New Jersey include cedar, pitch pine, and shortleaf pine.

Plant Life. The violet, New Jersey's state flower, grows in wooded areas throughout the state. Honeysuckle, goldenrod, and Queen Anne's lace grow in many areas. Other flowers include azaleas, buttercups, mountain laurels, rhododendrons, and Virginia cowslips.

Animal Life. New Jersey animals include deer, foxes, minks, muskrats, opossums, otters, rabbits, raccoons, and skunks. Hunters shoot wild ducks and geese along the marshy shores of the Atlantic Ocean. Game birds of the meadows and woodlands include partridges, pheasants, quail, ruffed grouse, and wild turkeys.

Clams, crabs, lobsters, menhaden, and oysters live in New Jersey's coastal waters. The state's bays and streams abound with bass, bluefish, crappies, pickerel, pike, salmon, shad, sturgeon, trout, and weakfish.

Manufacturing accounts for about 97 per cent of the value of goods produced in New Jersey. Goods manufactured there have a *value added by manufacture* of about

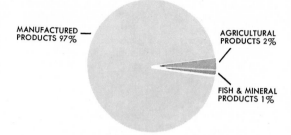

NEW JERSEY'S PRODUCTION IN 1967

Total value of goods produced—$13,162,163,000

MANUFACTURED PRODUCTS 97%

AGRICULTURAL PRODUCTS 2%

FISH & MINERAL PRODUCTS 1%

Note: Manufacturing percentage based on value added by manufacture. Other percentages based on value of production.

Sources: U.S. Government statistics

NEW JERSEY'S EMPLOYMENT IN 1967

Total number of persons employed—2,471,200

		Number of Employees
Manufacturing	𝄃𝄃𝄃𝄃𝄃𝄃𝄃	876,000
Wholesale & Retail Trade	𝄃𝄃𝄃𝄃	481,100
Services	𝄃𝄃𝄃	358,300
Government	𝄃𝄃𝄃	324,100
Transportation & Public Utilities	𝄃𝄃	166,700
Construction	𝄃	120,700
Finance, Insurance & Real Estate	𝄃	107,700
Agriculture & Mining	𝄃	36,600

Source: U.S. Department of Labor

$12,800,000,000 a year. This figure represents the value created in products by New Jersey's industries, not counting such costs as materials, supplies, and fuels. New Jersey is a leader among the states in manufacturing and processing. New Jersey's chief manufacturing industries are, in order of importance, (1) the chemical industry, (2) electrical machinery manufacturing, and (3) food processing.

The Chemical Industry has a yearly value added of about $2,825,000,000. New Jersey leads the states in chemical production. Important products include basic chemicals, drugs and vitamins, cleaning solutions, explosives, paints and varnishes, plastics, and soaps. New Jersey has about 1,000 chemical plants. Most of them are near the Hudson River across from New York City, and in an area stretching from Newark to Camden.

Electrical Machinery Manufacturing in New Jersey has a value added of about $1,738,000,000 a year. More New Jerseyans work in this industry than in any other activity. New Jersey factories make lamps, phonographs, radios, stoves, television sets, washing machines, driers, and other electrical products for home use. They also turn out generators, motors, transformers, and other machines for industrial use. Homes and factories throughout the United States use telephones made by New Jersey manufacturers. The electrical machinery industry in New Jersey is centered in three small northeastern counties. They are Essex, Hudson, and Union.

Food Processing accounts for about $1,249,000,000 of New Jersey's value added by manufacture. Factories in northeastern New Jersey process a wide variety of foods, including meats, vegetables, and fruits. Plants in the southwest can and process fruits and vegetables from nearby truck gardens and orchards.

Other Industries, in order of importance, make nonelectrical machinery, fabricated metal products, transportation equipment (including automobiles), clothing, and primary metal products. Ranking next in importance are printing and publishing; the manufacture of stone, clay, and glass products; and the making of paper and allied products.

Industrial Research plants in New Jersey number more than 725. These plants spend about $200 million a year to develop and improve products. This figure is about a tenth of all the money spent on industrial research in the United States. New Jersey researchers developed the transistor, and the electronic "brain" used for missiles. They also improved fuels, color television, and other products.

Agriculture accounts for about 2 per cent of the value of goods produced in New Jersey. New Jersey farmers earn about $281,200,000 a year. The state's 10,640 farms average about 109 acres in size. They have an average annual income of about $275 an acre, which is among the highest gross incomes per acre in the country.

Seabrook Farms, New Jersey's largest farm, covers nearly 15,000 acres in Cumberland County. The Seabrook company also leases land or buys crops from 30,000 to 40,000 other farm acres. Seabrook Farm scientists carry on extensive studies of soil, weather, and growing methods to improve farm techniques.

Vegetables earn about one-third of New Jersey's farm income. New Jersey is an important vegetable-growing state. It ranks high in the production of tomatoes, its chief vegetable crop. New Jersey farmers also raise asparagus, lettuce, peppers, potatoes, and sweet corn. Vegetable farms thrive throughout New Jersey, but the largest ones are in the southwest.

Poultry and Poultry Products account for about 15 per cent of New Jersey's farm income. New Jersey chickens lay over 1 billion eggs annually. Most of the eggs are sold as food, but about 3 million of them hatch into commercially valuable baby chicks. New Jersey farmers sell thousands of chickens and turkeys each year. Poultry farms are especially numerous in the southeastern part of the state.

Dairy Products account for about a fifth of New Jersey's farm income. Milk, milkfat, and ice cream are the state's leading dairy products. Dairy farms flourish in the northwest, especially in Hunterdon and Warren counties.

Fruits. Farmers in southern New Jersey grow large peach crops. Several varieties, including the Jerseyland and Sunhigh, were developed in the state. Many apple orchards dot central and southern New Jersey. The state ranks high in blueberry production. Other fruits include cranberries and strawberries.

Field Crops grown in the state are used chiefly to feed livestock. They include barley, corn, hay, and wheat.

WORLD BOOK photo by Three Lions

A Research Chemist conducts an experiment on pigments and dyes in a laboratory in Toms River. New Jersey has about 1,000 chemical plants, and leads the states in chemical production.

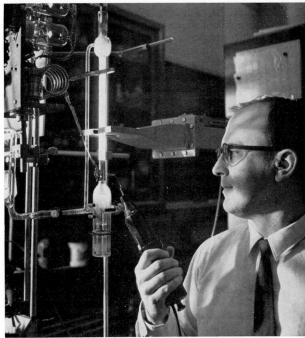

Bell Telephone Laboratories

An Electronics Researcher demonstrates a new electronic technique at the Bell Telephone Laboratories in New Providence. Electrical machinery manufacturing is a leading New Jersey industry.

Urwiller, Three Lions

FARM, MINERAL, AND FOREST PRODUCTS

This map shows where the state's leading farm, mineral, and forest products are produced. The major urban areas (shown on the map in red) are the state's important manufacturing centers.

0   10   20   30   40 Miles

0 10 20 30 40 50 60 Kilometers

WORLD BOOK map

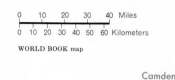

George Washington Bridge crosses the Hudson River, and links Fort Lee with New York City, background. The bridge is used daily by thousands of commuters who live in New Jersey and work in New York City.

Greenhouse and Nursery Products are raised chiefly in northeastern New Jersey for sale in the New York City area. These products have an annual value of more than $32 million. Nearly 13 million roses are grown in the state yearly. About 2 million orchids a year come from Middlesex. New Jersey greenhouses also raise African violets, azaleas, chrysanthemums, geraniums, hydrangeas, lilies, and poinsettias. Leading nursery products in New Jersey include arborvitae, holly, junipers, yews, and a wide variety of other shrubs.

Mining adds about $73 million a year to New Jersey's economy. Sand and gravel are the state's most important minerals. Basalt and diabase, kinds of stone used to build roads, are also leading minerals in New Jersey. Miners take basalt and diabase from quarries in Essex, Hudson, Hunterdon, Mercer, Passaic, Somerset, and Union counties. Zinc also comes from Sussex County. Clay from Camden, Cumberland, Middlesex, and Somerset counties is used in the state's brick and tile industries. Hunterdon, Morris, and Sussex counties produce granite. Sussex and Warren counties are leading producers of crushed limestone. Warren County also yields serpentine. Most of the nation's greensand marl comes from Gloucester County. It is used chiefly as a water-softening agent. Peat from Sussex and Warren counties is used to enrich soil.

Fishing Industry. New Jersey's fish catch has an annual value of about $10,716,000. New Jersey fishermen take in about two-thirds of the clams caught in the United States. Huge clam beds extend from Barnegat

Bay to Cape May. Oysters come from the Maurice River Cove in Delaware Bay. New Jersey fishermen also catch butterfish, flounders, lobsters, menhaden, porgy, scallops, sea bass, tuna, and whiting.

Electric Power. Almost all New Jersey's electric power comes from privately owned steam-generating plants. These plants burn coal, oil, or natural gas. A few hydroelectric plants operate on the Passaic River and swift northern streams. One of the world's largest privately owned nuclear research reactors was built at Plainsboro in 1959. For New Jersey's kilowatt-hour production, see ELECTRIC POWER (table).

Transportation. New Jersey lies in the path between New York City and the western and southern states. This location makes New Jersey highways and railroads important links in the U.S. transportation system.

About 15 airlines serve New Jersey. The state has over 150 airports. Newark Airport is one of the nation's chief air terminals. The first regular airplane passenger service in the United States began operating in 1919 between Atlantic City and New York City.

Railroads operate on about 2,000 miles of track in New Jersey. Most large eastern railroads have terminals in Jersey City and Hoboken. Swift commuter trains serve thousands of New Jerseyans who work in New York City and Philadelphia.

In 1891, New Jersey became the first state to help local communities build roads. New Jersey now has about 32,000 miles of roads and highways, most of which are surfaced. The 131-mile New Jersey Turnpike

A Flower Grower waters plants in one of northeastern New Jersey's many greenhouses. Large numbers of roses, orchids, and geraniums are raised for sale in the New York City area. Many New Jersey nurseries grow ornamental landscaping shrubs.

runs from Deepwater in the southwest to Ridgefield Park in the northeast. The turnpike was opened in 1952 and was extended in 1956. The 173-mile Garden State Parkway crosses New Jersey from the New York state line near Montvale to Cape May, at New Jersey's southern tip. The Garden State Parkway was completed in 1957. The Pulaski Skyway is a four-lane elevated road between Jersey City and Newark.

Bridges and tunnels link New Jersey and neighboring states. The George Washington Bridge, one of the world's longest suspension bridges, spans the Hudson River between Fort Lee and New York City. The Bayonne Bridge, the longest steel arch bridge in the world, crosses Kill Van Kull, a channel between Bayonne and Staten Island. Bridges across the Delaware River include the Benjamin Franklin Bridge between Camden and Philadelphia and the Delaware Memorial Bridge Twin Span between Deepwater and the New Castle, Del., area. The Holland and Lincoln tunnels and the Hudson tubes under the Hudson River link New Jersey and New York City.

New Jersey has important ports along the Hudson and Delaware rivers, in Newark and Raritan Bay, and along Kill Van Kull and Arthur Kill. New Jersey's part of the Atlantic Intracoastal Waterway extends for 117 miles from Manasquan Inlet to Cape May. The waterway is protected from the ocean by barrier beaches, and offers safe passage for small boats.

Communication. About 315 daily and weekly newspapers are published in New Jersey. The leading ones include the *Courier-Post* of Camden, the *Evening News* of Newark, the *Herald-News* of Passaic, the *Newark Star-Ledger*, and *The Record* of Hackensack. New York City and Philadelphia newspapers have wide circulation in New Jersey. The *New Jersey Gazette*, the state's first weekly newspaper, began in Burlington in 1777. New Jersey's first daily newspaper, the *Newark Daily Advertiser*, was founded in 1832.

New Jersey has over 50 radio stations and 3 television stations. Many pioneer efforts in radio broadcasting took place in New Jersey. Joseph Henry transmitted the first radio impulse at Princeton in 1840. WJZ, the second licensed commercial broadcasting station in the United States, was established in Newark in 1921. This station now operates in New York City. The oldest radio station still broadcasting in New Jersey is WAAT, which was established in 1923. The first New Jersey television station, WATV, began operating in Newark in 1948. It is now WNDT of New York City. Today, only *UHF* (ultra high frequency) commercial stations broadcast in New Jersey. But stations broadcasting from New York and Pennsylvania also serve New Jersey.

New Jersey boasts many other "firsts" in communication. The first interstate long-distance telephone call was made from New Brunswick, N.J., to New York City in 1877. The first coast-to-coast direct dialing system was established in Englewood in 1951. *Telstar I*, the first communications satellite to transmit live television across the Atlantic, was designed at the Bell Laboratories in New Jersey. It was launched in 1962.

208g

Inventions Developed in New Jersey include Samuel F. B. Morse's electric telegraph (1838), Thomas A. Edison's electric light bulb (1879), and John P. Holland's submarine (1898).

Alexander Hamilton was killed in 1804 in a duel with Aaron Burr at Weehawken.

Caldwell ●

Weehawken ●

● Hoboken

The First Game of Organized Baseball took place at Hoboken in 1846. The New York Nine defeated the New York Knickerbockers, 23 to 1.

Princeton ●

Freehold (formerly Monmouth)
●

TRENTON
★

Princeton was the capital of the United States from June 30 to Nov. 4, 1783. Nassau Hall, built in 1756 as part of Princeton University, served for a time as the meeting place of Congress.

Washington Crossed the Delaware at the head of the American army on Christmas night, 1776. The next day, his forces defeated a Hessian army at Trenton.

● Indian Mills

Indian Mills in 1758 became the site of the first Indian reservation in what is now the United States.

Princeton University, founded in 1746, is the fourth oldest in the United States. Part of the Battle of Princeton was fought inside Nassau Hall in 1777.

Molly Pitcher took the place of her fallen husband on a cannon crew during the Battle of Monmouth in 1778.

The First Steam Locomotive in the United States was built by John Stevens in 1825 at Hoboken.

Grover Cleveland
born in Caldwell

HISTORIC
NEW JERSEY

Indian Days. About 8,000 Indians probably lived in what is now New Jersey before the white man came. The Indians belonged to the Delaware tribe of the Algonkian Indian family. They called themselves *Lenni-Lenape*, which means *original people*. The Indians spent most of their time hunting, but they also raised *maize* (corn), beans, squash, and other crops.

Exploration. Giovanni da Verrazano, an Italian navigator in the service of France, was probably the first white man to explore the New Jersey coast. He reached the coast in 1524. Henry Hudson, an English sea captain employed by The Netherlands, explored the Sandy Hook Bay area in 1609. He also sailed up the river that now bears his name. The Dutch explorer Cornelius Mey sailed the Delaware River in 1614. Cape May was later named for him. Many Dutch trading ships visited the New Jersey area during the 1600's.

Settlement. The Dutch and the Swedes were the first white settlers in New Jersey. The Dutch founded an outpost in Pavonia (now part of Jersey City) about 1630. Indian uprisings prevented permanent settlement until 1660. That year, the Dutch built the fortified town of Bergen (now part of Jersey City). Bergen was New Jersey's first permanent white settlement.

Traders and settlers from Sweden arrived in southern New Jersey in 1638. The Dutch settlers feared Swedish competition in the fur trade. The Dutch forced the Swedes out of the New Jersey area in 1655.

English Control. English armies won control of New Jersey and other Dutch North American possessions in 1664. King Charles II of England gave the New Jersey area to his brother, James, Duke of York. James, in turn, gave it to two of his friends, Lord John Berkeley and Sir George Carteret. Berkeley and Carteret offered to sell the land to colonists at low prices. They also allowed settlers to have political and religious freedom in their colony. These policies attracted many settlers to New Jersey.

In 1674, a group of Quakers headed by Edward Byllynge bought Berkeley's share of New Jersey. Two years later, the colony was divided into two sections—West Jersey and East Jersey. Byllynge and his associates made West Jersey the first Quaker colony in America. Carteret owned East Jersey until his death in 1680. Another group of Quakers, called the *Twenty-Four Proprietors*, bought East Jersey in 1682.

During the late 1600's, the owners of East and West Jersey became unpopular with the colonists. Land grants made many years earlier caused disputes over property rights. The colonists also objected to paying rent to the owners. Many colonists rioted during the 1690's. The owners gave up East and West Jersey in 1702. England then united the two colonies as a single royal colony.

Colonial Days. New Jersey had twin capitals from 1703 to 1775. They were Perth Amboy, the former capital of East Jersey, and Burlington, the former capital of West Jersey. At first, the governor of New York also ruled New Jersey. But strong protests from the colonists forced England to give New Jersey its own governor in 1738. Lewis Morris, the first colonial governor, served from 1738 to 1746.

Colonial New Jersey was a rural society. Most of the people kept busy growing their own food and building homes. By the 1760's, the colony had about 100,000 persons. The English king appointed the colonial governor and a 12-member council. The people elected a colonial assembly. But only freeholders who owned property valued at £50 (50 pounds) or more were allowed to vote. This sum equals about $140 today.

The Revolutionary War. During the 1760's, Great Britain passed a series of laws that caused unrest in New Jersey and the other American colonies. Most of these laws either set up severe taxes or restricted colonial trade. Some New Jerseyans urged the colonists to remain loyal to Britain in spite of the laws. But most of the colonists favored independence.

In 1774, a group of New Jerseyans dressed as Indians burned a supply of British tea stored in a ship at Greenwich, near Salem. This event, called the *Greenwich Tea Burning*, was similar to the more famous Boston Tea Party of 1773. Like the Boston Tea Party, the action symbolized colonial opposition to British taxation policies. See BOSTON TEA PARTY.

The Revolutionary War began in Massachusetts in 1775. Hundreds of New Jersey men joined the patriots in their fight for independence. New Jersey's location between New York City and Philadelphia made it a major battleground during the war. The Americans and British fought nearly a hundred engagements in New Jersey. The most important ones included the battles of Trenton in 1776, Princeton in 1777, and Monmouth in 1778. Before the Battle of Trenton, George Washington made his famous surprise crossing of the Delaware River on Christmas night. During the war, Washington's army camped two winters at Morristown and a third at Bound Brook. See REVOLUTIONARY WAR IN AMERICA (The Middle Years).

During the Revolutionary period, two New Jersey cities served as the temporary national capital. They were Princeton, from June 30 to Nov. 4, 1783, and Trenton, from Nov. 1 to Dec. 24, 1784.

New Jersey declared its independence from Great Britain and adopted its first constitution on July 2, 1776. On Nov. 26, 1778, New Jersey ratified the Articles of Confederation (the forerunner of the United States Constitution). New Jersey became a state on Dec. 18, 1787, when it ratified the U.S. Constitution. It was the third state to do so. William Livingston became New Jersey's first state governor.

The New Jersey delegates to the Constitutional Convention of 1787 proposed a plan to protect the interests of small states. This *New Jersey Plan* suggested that all states have equal representation in Congress. But the convention adopted the *Connecticut Compromise* instead. The compromise created the present two-house Congress. The states have equal representation in the Senate. Their representation in the House of Representatives is based on population.

The 1800's. During the early 1800's, New Jersey made many major improvements in its transportation system. These improvements included new turnpikes, canals, and railroads. Improved transportation in the state helped lead to industrial growth that has continued to the present day.

One of the most famous duels of all time was fought

New Jersey Dept. of Conservation and Economic Development
Urban-Renewal Project in Trenton calls for tearing down slums and building state office buildings and a cultural center.

at Weehawken in 1804. Aaron Burr, the Vice-President of the United States, shot and killed his political rival, Alexander Hamilton.

Public demand for a more democratic state government led to the adoption of a new state constitution in 1844. The new constitution provided for separation of powers among the legislative, judicial, and executive branches of the state government. It also provided for a bill of rights and for the election of the governor by the people. In 1845, Charles C. Stratton became the first New Jersey governor elected by the people.

About 88,000 New Jersey men served in the Union army during the Civil War (1861-1865). But there was much pro-Southern sympathy in the state during the Civil War period. In 1864, for example, New Jersey was one of only three states that voted against the re-election of President Abraham Lincoln.

During the late 1800's, New Jersey became the home of many of the nation's *trusts* (industrial monopolies). Trusts were illegal in many other states, but New Jersey law allowed them. New Jersey also attracted many *holding companies* during this period. A holding company is a company that controls the stock and policies of one or more other companies. By 1900, hundreds of large corporations obtained charters under New Jersey laws and set up headquarters in the state.

Industrial Development increased greatly after the Civil War. New Jersey factories turned out elevators, sewing machines, steam locomotives, and other new products. The great population growth of neighboring New York City helped New Jersey's food-processing industry expand by providing a larger market. The iron and steel industry and other businesses also expanded rapidly in the state.

As industry grew, thousands of Europeans came to New Jersey cities to work in factories. By 1910, more than half the state's people had been born outside the United States or had parents who were born in other countries. With the growth of industry, city populations increased and farm populations decreased. By 1900, more New Jerseyans were living in cities and towns than in rural areas.

The Early 1900's saw the rise of progressive government in New Jersey. In 1910, the people elected Woodrow Wilson governor. Under Wilson, the state passed laws providing for direct primary elections, workmen's compensation, and a public utilities commission. The legislature also passed laws restricting business monopolies. Wilson's achievements as governor helped lead to his election as President of the United States in 1912. He was re-elected in 1916.

Thomas A. Edison helped develop the motion picture while working in New Jersey. Fort Lee became the motion picture capital of the world in the early 1900's. There, "Fatty" Arbuckle, Mary Pickford, Pearl White, and other stars made movies that introduced a new era in entertainment.

After the United States entered World War I in 1917, Hoboken became a major port for shipping troops overseas. Thousands of American soldiers sailed for France from this Hudson River port. During the war, Camp Dix and Camp Merrit served as military training centers. New Jersey factories contributed chemicals, munitions, and ships to the war effort.

Between 1900 and 1930, New Jersey's population

more than doubled. During the same period, the state's annual value of manufacturing rose from about $500 million to almost $4 billion. New Jersey, like other states, suffered widespread unemployment during the Great Depression of the 1930's.

The Mid-1900's. New Jersey's electronics and chemical industries began large-scale operations about 1940. These industries grew during World War II (1939-1945), when the state produced communications equipment, ships, and weapons and ammunition.

In 1947, New Jersey voters approved a new state constitution. The constitution extended the governor's term from three to four years and increased his powers. It also reorganized the state's court system.

During the mid-1900's, the state's population expanded steadily into many rural areas. The expansion included construction of homes and of commercial and industrial plants. Commercial and industrial growth occurred most rapidly among chemical, electronics, food-processing, pharmaceutical, and research firms.

The New Jersey Turnpike opened in 1952 and soon became one of the nation's busiest highways. The turnpike links the Philadelphia and New York City metropolitan areas. The Garden State Parkway, completed in 1955, runs along the New Jersey coast. This highway played an important role in the residential and industrial growth of the state's coastal region.

Although passenger railroad travel declined nationally during the mid-1900's, New Jersey kept its position as a major rail center. The freight yards in Hudson County remained among the largest in the world. In 1958, construction began on a $232-million project to develop port facilities on Newark Bay. Newark Airport started a major construction program in 1963 to expand passenger and cargo service.

During the 1960's, older New Jersey cities faced the problem of spreading slums, especially in Negro neighborhoods. In July, 1967, riots broke out in black neighborhoods of several cities. The worst riot occurred in Newark, where 26 persons were killed and more than 1,000 were injured. Property damage totaled between $10 million and $15 million.

New Jersey Today, like many other states, has trouble providing enough money to run the state government. In the late 1960's, the state adopted a sales tax and several bond issues that will help pay for major programs. One of these bond issues will supply money during the 1970's for new state colleges, highways, institutions, and commuter train facilities. Another will pay for water conservation projects and for a program to fight water pollution. In 1969, the voters approved a state lottery to raise money for the state government and for the schools.

Large urban renewal projects are underway in several New Jersey cities. The program in Trenton includes construction of a $35-million group of state government office buildings and a cultural center. In Newark, the state is building or expanding several college and uni-

---

THE GOVERNORS OF NEW JERSEY

	Name	Party	Term		Name	Party	Term
1.	William Livingston	Federalist	1776-1790	35.	George B. McClellan	Democratic	1878-1881
2.	Elisha Lawrence	Federalist	1790	36.	George C. Ludlow	Democratic	1881-1884
3.	William Paterson	Federalist	1790-1793	37.	Leon Abbett	Democratic	1884-1887
4.	Elisha Lawrence	Federalist	1793	38.	Robert S. Green	Democratic	1887-1890
5.	Richard Howell	Federalist	1793-1801	39.	Leon Abbett	Democratic	1890-1893
6.	Joseph Bloomfield	*Dem.-Rep.	1801-1802	40.	George T. Werts	Democratic	1893-1896
7.	John Lambert	Dem.-Rep.	1802-1803	41.	John W. Griggs	Republican	1896-1898
8.	Joseph Bloomfield	Dem.-Rep.	1803-1812	42.	Foster M. Voorhees	Republican	1898
9.	Charles Clark	Dem.-Rep.	1812	43.	David O. Watkins	Republican	1898-1899
10.	Aaron Ogden	Federalist	1812-1813	44.	Foster M. Voorhees	Republican	1899-1902
11.	William S. Pennington	Dem.-Rep.	1813-1815	45.	Franklin Murphy	Republican	1902-1905
12.	William Kennedy	Dem.-Rep.	1815	46.	Edward C. Stokes	Republican	1905-1908
13.	Mahlon Dickerson	Dem.-Rep.	1815-1817	47.	John Franklin Fort	Republican	1908-1911
14.	Jesse Upson	Dem.-Rep.	1817	48.	Woodrow Wilson	Democratic	1911-1913
15.	Isaac H. Williamson	Dem.-Rep.	1817-1829	49.	James E. Fielder	Democratic	1913
16.	Garret D. Wall	Democratic	1829 (declined)	50.	Leon R. Taylor	Democratic	1913-1914
				51.	James E. Fielder	Democratic	1914-1917
17.	Peter D. Vroom	Democratic	1829-1832	52.	Walter E. Edge	Republican	1917-1919
18.	Samuel L. Southard	Whig	1832-1833	53.	William N. Runyon	Republican	1919-1920
19.	Elias P. Seeley	Whig	1833	54.	Edward I. Edwards	Democratic	1920-1923
20.	Peter D. Vroom	Democratic	1833-1836	55.	George S. Silzer	Democratic	1923-1926
21.	Philemon Dickerson	Democratic	1836-1837	56.	A. Harry Moore	Democratic	1926-1929
22.	William Pennington	Whig	1837-1843	57.	Morgan F. Larson	Republican	1929-1932
23.	Daniel Haines	Democratic	1843-1845	58.	A. Harry Moore	Democratic	1932-1935
24.	Charles C. Stratton	Whig	1845-1848	59.	Clifford R. Powell	Republican	1935
25.	Daniel Haines	Democratic	1848-1851	60.	Horace G. Prall	Republican	1935
26.	George F. Fort	Democratic	1851-1854	61.	Harold G. Hoffman	Republican	1935-1938
27.	Rodman M. Price	Democratic	1854-1857	62.	A. Harry Moore	Democratic	1938-1941
28.	William A. Newell	Republican	1857-1860	63.	Charles Edison	Democratic	1941-1944
29.	Charles S. Olden	Republican	1860-1863	64.	Walter E. Edge	Republican	1944-1947
30.	Joel Parker	Democratic	1863-1866	65.	Alfred E. Driscoll	Republican	1947-1954
31.	Marcus L. Ward	Republican	1866-1869	66.	Robert B. Meyner	Democratic	1954-1962
32.	Theodore F. Randolph	Democratic	1869-1872	67.	Richard J. Hughes	Democratic	1962-1970
33.	Joel Parker	Democratic	1872-1875	68.	William T. Cahill	Republican	1970-
34.	Joseph D. Bedle	Democratic	1875-1878				

*Democratic-Republican

versity facilities, including a new campus for Rutgers University.

Another renewal plan involves the Meadowlands area of northeastern New Jersey. Some real estate experts believe that the Meadowlands—about 18,000 acres of marshes—could be the most valuable undeveloped land in the world. For many years, nearby communities op-

posed the development of the marshland. But in 1969, the Hackensack Meadowlands Development Commission was established to plan industrial, commercial, residential, and recreational uses for the area.

In 1970, William T. Cahill became New Jersey's first Republican governor in 16 years. Cahill promised to fight organized crime and government corruption in the state. Several state and local government officials had been accused of having connections with organized crime.   ARTHUR GETIS, RICHARD P. McCORMICK, and MORT PYE

NEW JERSEY/Study Aids

Related Articles in WORLD BOOK include:

BIOGRAPHIES

Brearley, David
Burr, Aaron
Case, Clifford P.
Clark, Abraham
Cleveland, Grover
Dayton, Jonathan
Dayton, William L.
Edison, Thomas Alva
Einstein, Albert
Hague, Frank
Halsey, William F., Jr.
Hart, John
Hobart, Garret A.

Hudson, Henry
Lawrence, James
Livingston, William
McClellan, George B.
Paterson, William (1745-1806)
Pitcher, Molly
Roth, Philip
Schirra, Walter M.
Stockton, Richard
Van Fleet, James A.
Verrazano, Giovanni da
Wilson, Woodrow
Witherspoon, John

CITIES

Asbury Park
Atlantic City
Bayonne
Bloomfield
Camden
Clifton
East Orange
Elizabeth
Hoboken
Irvington
Jersey City
Kearny
Lakehurst

Montclair
Morristown
New Brunswick
Newark
North Bergen
Passaic
Paterson
Perth Amboy
Plainfield
Princeton
Trenton
Union City

MILITARY INSTALLATIONS

Cape May Receiving
    Center
Fort Dix
Fort Monmouth

Lakehurst Naval Air
    Station
McGuire Air Force Base

PHYSICAL FEATURES

Delaware Bay
Delaware River
Delaware Water Gap
Hudson River

Palisades
Piedmont Region
Raritan River
Sandy Hook

PRODUCTS AND INDUSTRIES

For New Jersey's rank among the states in production, see the following articles:

Automobile
Chemical
    Industry

Clothing
Publishing
Strawberry

Tomato
Wine

OTHER RELATED ARTICLES

Atlantic Intracoastal Waterway
Celluloid
George Washington Bridge
Hudson River Tunnels
Middle Atlantic States

New Netherland
Port of New York Authority
Pulaski Skyway

Outline

I. **Government**
  A. Constitution
  B. Executive
  C. Legislature
  D. Courts
  E. Local Government
  F. Taxation
  G. Politics
II. **People**
III. **Education**
  A. Schools
  B. Libraries
  C. Museums
IV. **A Visitor's Guide**
  A. Places to Visit
  B. Annual Events
V. **The Land**
  A. Land Regions
  B. Coastline
  C. Mountains
  D. Rivers and Lakes
VI. **Climate**
VII. **Economy**
  A. Natural Resources
  B. Manufacturing
  C. Agriculture
  D. Mining
  E. Fishing Industry
  F. Electric Power
  G. Transportation
  H. Communication
VIII. **History**

Questions

What unique name do New Jersey county governments have?

How did Lord John Berkeley and Sir George Carteret attract settlers to New Jersey?

What parts of New Jersey are included in a Standard Consolidated Metropolitan Area?

What is New Jersey's best-known annual event?

What New Jersey governor became President of the United States?

What is New Jersey's chief economic activity?

What percentage of New Jerseyans live in cities and towns?

What are New Jersey's six largest cities?

When and where was New Jersey's first library established?

What New Jersey cities served as the national capital?

Books for Young Readers

BAILEY, BERNADINE F. *Picture Book of New Jersey.* Rev. ed. Whitman, 1965.

DE ANGELI, MARGUERITE L. *Jared's Island*. Doubleday, 1947. Jared finds an Indian friend and treasure on the New Jersey coast in the 1670's.

MEADER, STEPHEN W. *Fish Hawk's Nest*. Harcourt, 1952. An exciting story of farmers and smugglers on the Jersey coast about 1820. This book gives a picture of life near Cape May and in Philadelphia at the time. *Guns for the Saratoga*. 1955. How Gid Jones helped forge the ship's guns at his father's ironworks in south Jersey, and fought on the ship during the Revolutionary War.

SAYRE, ARLENE R. *Jersey Voices from the Past*. Phillips-Campbell, 1964. Twelve dramatizations from New Jersey's colorful history.

STOCKTON, FRANK R. *Stories of New Jersey*. Rutgers Univ. Press, 1961.

Books for Older Readers

BAKELESS, KATHERINE and JOHN. *Spies of the Revolution*. Lippincott, 1962.

BECK, HENRY C. *Roads of Home: Lanes and Legends of New Jersey*. Rutgers Univ. Press, 1956. *Tales and Towns of Northern New Jersey*. 1964.

CAWLEY, JAMES S. and MARGARET. *Exploring the Little Rivers of New Jersey*. Rev. ed. Rutgers Univ. Press, 1961.

CUNNINGHAM, JOHN T. *This Is New Jersey: From High Point to Cape May*. Rutgers Univ. Press, 1953. *Made in New Jersey: The Industrial Story of a State*. 1954. *Garden State: The Story of Agriculture in New Jersey*. 1955. *The New Jersey Shore*. 1958. Surveys of various aspects of the state which describe its people, geography, agriculture, and industry. *New Jersey: America's Main Road*. Doubleday, 1966.

MCCORMICK, RICHARD P. *New Jersey from Colony to State, 1609-1789*. Van Nostrand, 1964. The first volume of the *New Jersey Historical Series*, edited by Richard M. Huber and Wheaton J. Lane. *New Jersey: A Students' Guide to Localized History*. Teachers College Press, 1965.

New Jersey: A Guide to Its Present and Past. Rev. ed. Hastings, 1959.

WILDES, HARRY E. *The Delaware*. Rinehart, 1940 (Rivers of America series). A description of life along the banks of the river. *Twin Rivers: The Raritan and the Passaic*. 1943.

NEW JERSEY PLAN. See UNITED STATES CONSTITUTION (The Compromises).

NEW JERSEY TURNPIKE. See NEW JERSEY (Transportation).

NEW LEFT is a radical political and social movement in the United States. It began in the early 1960's and includes many college students and other young people. The New Left is "new" in relation to the "old left" of the 1930's, which generally was guided by Marxist ideas and supported Soviet policies.

Members of the New Left demand sweeping and fundamental changes in American society. They attack most major institutions for claiming to support democratic principles but failing to end such injustices as poverty, racial discrimination, and class distinctions. Many New Leftists oppose capitalism and believe the desire for profits leads to *imperialism*, a national policy that favors extending influence over another country.

People who identify themselves with the New Left are not all members of a single organization, and they frequently disagree among themselves. Members of the New Left range from pacifists to violent revolutionaries. Many New Leftists favor such tactics as nonviolent civil disobedience. But their actions have often led to bloody clashes with the police and other law-

enforcement officials. The most important elements of the New Left include the militant wings of the peace movement, the movement for racial equality, and the students' rights movement.

The peace and civil rights movements have appealed especially to young people. Their experiences in civil rights and peace demonstrations have convinced many of them that war and discrimination can be ended only by a general reformation of American society. Several radical student organizations appeared in the early 1960's, including the Students for a Democratic Society (SDS) and the Free Speech Movement. Radical students began to consider the university as an accomplice of war and racism. They used disruptive tactics in an effort to reform their universities or to use them as a base for revolutionary activities.

Most members of the New Left have shown little interest in conventional politics and have done little to get sympathetic candidates elected to public office. However, many people believe that the antiwar movement helped persuade President Lyndon B. Johnson not to run for re-election in 1968.

After 1968, the New Left split into several factions. For example, the revolutionaries split over tactics for defeating imperialism. Some urged an alliance with American workers, but others favored organizing the world's poor and nonwhite peoples.   CHRISTOPHER LASCH

See also RADICALISM; BLACK PANTHER PARTY; STUDENTS FOR A DEMOCRATIC SOCIETY; RIOT (The 1960's).

NEW LONDON, Conn. (pop. 31,630; alt. 35 ft.), is the home of the United States Coast Guard Academy. It is also the trading, banking, and distribution center for southeastern Connecticut. The city's position at the mouth of the Thames River, near the eastern entrance of Long Island Sound, makes it an important seaport (see CONNECTICUT [political map]). New London, Groton, and Norwich form a metropolitan area with 208,412 persons. Military bases in the area include the U.S. Submarine Base and the U.S. Underwater Sound Laboratory. Factories make antibiotics, paper boxes, clothing, tooth paste, and burial vaults. The city is the home of Connecticut College. New London was founded in 1646 and incorporated in 1784. It has a council-manager form of government.   ALBERT E. VAN DUSEN

NEW LONDON NAVAL SUBMARINE BASE, Conn., is the chief training center of the United States Navy's submarine force. It also houses the Submarine School and headquarters of the Atlantic Fleet Submarine Force. The base covers 497 acres on the Thames River, a mile northeast of New London. Connecticut gave the land to the federal government in 1868 for naval purposes. The navy established a coaling station there in 1872. The navy first used submarines at the New London base in 1900.

The New London Naval Submarine Base added a medical research laboratory after World War II. The laboratory conducts research on problems related to shipboard, submarine, and diving medicine. The New London base also houses a nuclear power school. The world's first atomic submarines were built in nearby Groton.   JOHN H. THOMPSON

NEW MATHEMATICS. See NUMERATION SYSTEMS; SET THEORY.

The Big Pasture by Peter Hurd for the Field Enterprises Educational Corporation Collection

Pastureland near the Sacramento Mountains

Capital: Santa Fe.

Government: *Congress*—U.S. senators, 2; U.S. representatives, 2. *Electoral Votes*—4. *State Legislature*—senators, 42; representatives, 70. *Counties*—32. *Voting Age*—21 yrs. (state and local elections); 18 yrs. (national elections).

Area: 121,666 square mi. (including 221 square mi. of inland water), 5th in size among the states. *Greatest Distances*—(north-south) 391 mi.; (east-west) 352 mi.

Elevation: *Highest*—Wheeler Peak in Taos County, 13,160 feet above sea level; *Lowest*—2,817 feet above sea level at Red Bluff Reservoir in Eddy County.

Population: *1970 Census*—1,016,000; 37th among the states; density, 8 persons to the square mile; distribution, 69 per cent urban, 31 per cent rural. *1960 Census*—951,023.

Chief Products: *Agriculture*—beef cattle, cotton, dairy products, grain sorghum, hay, lettuce, sheep, wheat. *Manufacturing*—chemicals; food and food products; lumber and wood products; machinery; metal products; printed materials; stone, clay, and glass products. *Mining*—coal, copper, natural gas, natural gas liquids, petroleum, potash, sand and gravel, uranium.

Statehood: Jan. 6, 1912, the 47th state.

State Motto: *Crescit eundo* (We grow as we go).

State Song: "O, Fair New Mexico." Words and music by Elizabeth Garrett.

NEW MEXICO
THE LAND OF ENCHANTMENT

NEW MEXICO is called the *Land of Enchantment* because of its scenic beauty and rich history. Every year, thousands of tourists go to this southwestern state for hunting, fishing, skiing, or sightseeing. New Mexico is the fifth largest state in area. Only Alaska, Texas, California, and Montana cover more square miles. But New Mexico is thinly populated. The state averages only about eight persons to each square mile. Much of New Mexico consists of mountain ranges, rugged canyons, and rocky deserts.

A vacationer might see New Mexico as a land of beautiful scenery, Spanish fiestas, and Indian ceremonies. But a scientist would think of it as a center of research into rockets and atomic energy. An oil company executive might regard the state as a rich source of gasoline for automobiles, or of natural gas for cooking and heating. A retired couple might choose to live in New Mexico because its location and high altitude provide warm, sunny days and cool nights. A farmer might be disappointed in the state because of the lack of rain. But a rancher might be impressed by the millions of acres of grazing land.

The earth and its riches provide the basis of New Mexico's economy. About nine-tenths of the value of New Mexico's production comes from two industries that use the land, mining and agriculture. In addition to oil and gas, the mineral riches include two products important for the future— uranium and potash. Uranium is the raw material for atomic power. Potash is used to make fertilizer that helps increase food production. Millions of cattle and sheep graze on the plains and in mountain valleys.

Much of New Mexico's growing industry springs from the science of the atomic age. The first atomic bomb was built and exploded in New Mexico in 1945. Today, scientists in New Mexico search for a way to make space rockets travel on atomic power. Others work on methods for using atomic power to generate electricity, or to improve atomic weapons for defense.

New Mexico's colorful past gives the state important tourist attractions. Still standing are the ruins of an 800-room apartment house built by the Indians hundreds of years before Columbus discovered America. Spain ruled the land for more than 250 years. The Spanish influence may be seen today in the names of places, in the churches of early missionaries, in foods, and in customs and holidays. Colorful men such as Kit Carson, Geronimo, and Billy the Kid played major parts in the history of the area in territorial days.

New Mexico has the oldest road in the United States, *El Camino Real* (the Royal Road). It also has the oldest seat of government, Santa Fe. Santa Fe was the capital of a Spanish province in 1610, and is the capital of New Mexico today. The state's largest city is Albuquerque, founded by the Spaniards in 1706.

For the relationship of New Mexico to other states in its region, see the article on the SOUTHWESTERN STATES.

The contributors of this article are James B. Colegrove, Editor of Enchantment *magazine; B. LeRoy Gordon, Professor of Geography at San Francisco State College, and former Chairman of the Geography Department of the University of New Mexico; and Lynn I. Perrigo, Head of the Department of History and Social Science at New Mexico Highlands University.*

New Mexico (blue) ranks fifth in size among all the states, and second in size among the Southwestern States (gray).

Constitution. New Mexico is governed under its original state constitution. The constitution was adopted in 1911, a year before New Mexico became a state. It has been amended more than 60 times. Amendments may be proposed by either house of the state legislature. They must be approved by a majority of the voters in a regular or special election. Some sections of the constitution require special majority votes to be amended. These sections guarantee the voting rights and education of Spanish-speaking persons. Amendments to these sections must be approved by three-fourths of the voters in the state and by two-thirds of the voters in each county. A constitutional convention may be called by a two-thirds vote of the legislature, if a majority of the voters approve. The voters must approve any amendments proposed by a constitutional convention.

Executive. The governor of New Mexico holds office for a two-year term. He is paid $20,000 a year. The governor may be re-elected once, but he cannot hold any state office within two years after the second term. This same limitation applies for the lieutenant governor, secretary of state, auditor, treasurer, attorney general, and commissioner of public lands. The 10 members of the state board of education are also elected by the people, for six-year terms.

Much of the governor's authority lies in his broad power of appointment. For example, he appoints three of the seven members of the powerful state board of finance, and is a member of the board himself. He also appoints most of the directors or board members who run state agencies and institutions. The governor may veto legislation passed by the state legislature. For a list of all the governors of New Mexico, see the *History* section of this article.

Legislature of New Mexico consists of a 42-member senate and a 70-member house of representatives. There are 42 senatorial districts and 70 representative districts. Voters in each senatorial district elect one senator. Voters in each representative district elect one repre-

sentative. Senators serve four-year terms. Members of the house of representatives serve two-year terms.

The legislature meets every year on the third Tuesday in January. The sessions are limited to 60 days in odd-numbered years, and to 30 days in even-numbered years. The governor may call the legislature into special session. The legislature may call itself into extraordinary session. The constitution provides for a referendum, but not for initiative (see INITIATIVE AND REFERENDUM).

Courts. The state supreme court, New Mexico's highest court, has five justices. They are elected to eight-year terms. Terms are staggered so an entirely new court is not elected in any one election. The justice with the shortest time to serve on the state supreme court acts as chief justice.

The court of appeals has four judges, who are elected to eight-year staggered terms. Panels made up of three judges hear appellate cases. Most cases which this court hears may be taken to the supreme court.

District courts are the state's principal trial courts. New Mexico has 21 district judges elected from 11 judicial districts. They hold district court sessions in each of the state's 32 counties. District judges are elected for terms of six years. They also serve as juvenile judges if the defendant is under 18 years old. Other courts include probate courts and magistrate courts.

Local Government. New Mexico has 32 counties, each administered by a board of three commissioners. The commissioners are elected to two-year terms. The state has about 90 *municipalities* (towns, villages, or cities).

State law gives municipalities a wide choice of form of government. Most common are the mayor-council, commission, and city manager-commission forms. Cities can adopt and amend their own charters. Albuquerque, Gallup, and Silver City have charters of their own. Towns and villages may elect trustees, one of whom serves as mayor. Municipal elections are held every two years in New Mexico.

New Mexico Dept. of Development

The Governor's Mansion stands on spacious landscaped grounds at the northeastern edge of Santa Fe. The simple lines of the building mark it as a fine example of the territorial style of architecture characteristic of New Mexico.

The State Seal

The State Flag

Symbols of New Mexico. On the state seal, adopted in 1913, the two eagles represent the annexation of New Mexico by the United States. The scroll beneath the birds bears the state's motto, *Crescit Eundo* (We grow as we go). On the flag, adopted in 1925, the ancient sun symbol of the Zia pueblo of Indians appears in red on a yellow field. The colors represent the Spanish flag, recalling the fact that New Mexico was once Spanish territory.

Flag and flower illustrations, courtesy of Eli Lilly Company

Taxation. A sales tax is the largest single source of tax income for the state. New Mexico also has a state income tax on both individuals and corporations. In addition, the state collects taxes on cigarettes, alcoholic beverages, gasoline, and property. Almost all the rest of the state government's income, about 28 per cent, comes from federal grants and other U.S. government programs.

The State Bird
Road Runner

Politics. New Mexico has voted for the winner in every presidential election since it became a state in 1912. In voter registration, Democrats usually outnumber Republicans by about 2 to 1. Democrats have won a majority of the state offices since the 1930's. But some Republicans have won election by large margins.

The eastern part of New Mexico was settled largely by southerners, who generally vote for Democrats. In the north-central counties, the Spanish-American population has been largely Democratic since the early 1930's. Centers of Republican strength lie in the northeast, northwest, and central portions of the state. For New Mexico's electoral votes and voting record in presidential elections, see ELECTORAL COLLEGE (table).

The State Flower
Yucca Flower

The State Capitol in Santa Fe was completed in 1967. Santa Fe has been the state's capital since the city was established in 1610. San Gabriel served as the capital from 1599 to 1610.

New Mexico Department of Development

The State Tree
Piñon, or Nut Pine

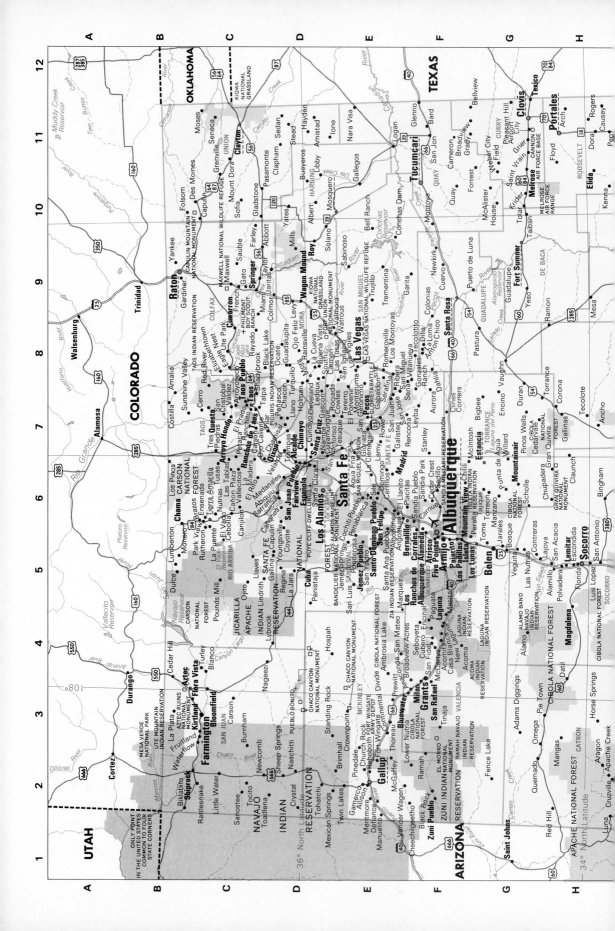

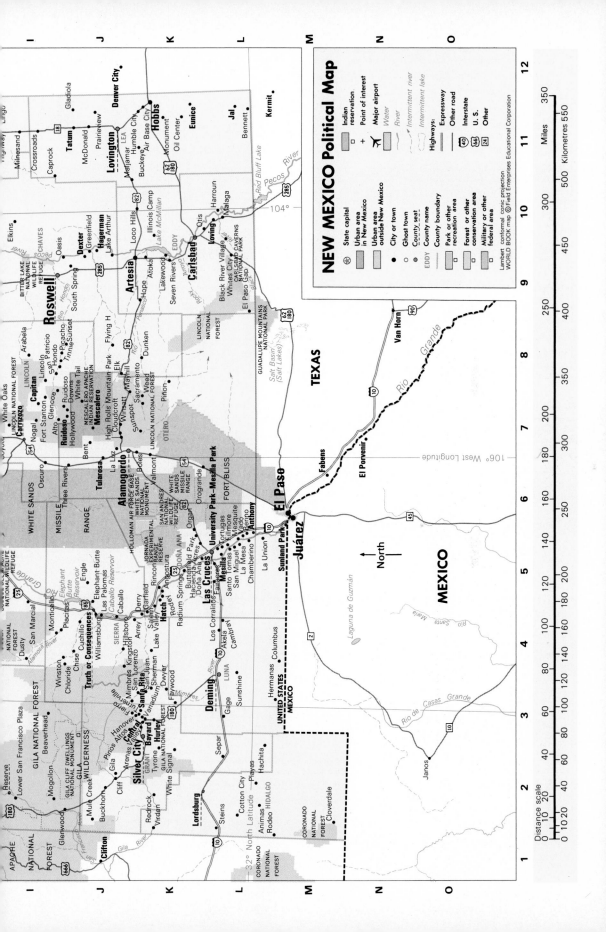

The 1970 United States census reported that New Mexico had 1,016,000 persons. The population had increased 7 per cent over the 1960 figure of 951,023. New Mexico averages only about eight persons to the square mile. Almost a third of the people in New Mexico live in the Albuquerque metropolitan area, the state's only Standard Metropolitan Statistical Area (see METROPOLITAN AREA).

Most New Mexicans are descended from one of the three major groups that settled the area—Indians, Spaniards, and English-speaking Americans. The modern Indian's way of life may be much like that of his ancestors. He might live in a *pueblo* (village) or on a large reservation.

Spanish Americans in New Mexico take part in most state activities, including politics. A Spanish American, Dennis Chavez, represented New Mexico in Congress for 31 years. The Spanish influence shows strongly in place names, foods, and holiday customs. Many New Mexicans speak both Spanish and English. About 98 out of 100 New Mexicans were born in the United States.

Albuquerque is the state's chief industrial, transportation, and trading center. Santa Fe, the capital and second largest city of New Mexico, has many quaint, narrow streets, with buildings made of *adobe* (sun-dried

An Indian Family buys food in a Gallup supermarket. The city is a shopping center for Indians of nearby reservations.

C. W. Herbert, Western Ways

bricks). See the separate articles on the cities of New Mexico listed in the *Related Articles* at the end of this article.

The majority of the people of New Mexico are Protestants, but Roman Catholics make up the largest single religious group. The largest Protestant groups are the Baptists, Episcopalians, Methodists, and Presbyterians.

POPULATION

This map shows the *population density* of New Mexico, and how it varies in different parts of the state. Population density means the average number of persons who live on each square mile.

PERSONS PER SQUARE MILE

| 0 to 3 | 3 to 10 | 10 to 90 | 90 to 250 |

Albuquerque

| 0 | 50 | 100 | 150 Miles |
| 0 | 50 | 100 | 150 | 200 Kilometers |

WORLD BOOK map

Schools. Education in New Mexico began in the early 1600's, when Spanish priests started teaching the Indians. The state's first permanent school was established by the Roman Catholic Church at Santa Fe in 1853. The present system of free public education started in 1891.

The state board of education, an elected body, establishes school policies. The policies are carried out by a superintendent of public instruction hired by the board. The state constitution requires children between the ages of 6 and 17 to attend school. For the number of students and teachers in New Mexico, see EDUCATION (table).

Libraries and Museums. The New Mexico Territorial Library, sometimes called the Supreme Court Library, was established in Santa Fe in 1851. The first public library in New Mexico was founded in Cimarron in 1881. New Mexico has about 40 public libraries.

The Museum of New Mexico in Santa Fe includes the Laboratory of Anthropology and the Museum of International Folk Art. The Los Alamos Scientific Laboratory Science Hall traces the development of the atomic bomb.

UNIVERSITIES AND COLLEGES

New Mexico has eight state universities and colleges accredited by the North Central Association of Colleges and Secondary Schools. For enrollments and further information, see UNIVERSITIES AND COLLEGES (table).

Name	Location	Founded
Albuquerque, University of	Albuquerque	1940
Eastern New Mexico University	Portales	1934
New Mexico, University of	Albuquerque	1889
New Mexico Highlands University	Las Vegas	1893
New Mexico Institute of Mining and Technology	Socorro	1889
New Mexico State University	Las Cruces	1888
Santa Fe, College of	Santa Fe	1859
Western New Mexico University	Silver City	1893

NEW MEXICO / A Visitor's Guide

New Mexico's scenery and outdoor activities attract visitors throughout the year. The state offers skiing in winter, fishing in spring and summer, and hunting in the fall. Scenic beauty ranges from rose-colored deserts to snow-capped mountains. Lovers of history can visit Indian ruins, frontier forts, and Spanish missions.

Shostal

Fiesta in Santa Fe

Zimmerman, New Mexico State Tourist Bureau

Gila Wilderness near Silver City

FPG

Old Mission at the Isleta Pueblo

--- PLACES TO VISIT ---

Following are brief descriptions of some of New Mexico's most interesting places to visit.

Carlsbad Caverns National Park. This series of huge caves in southeastern New Mexico is one of the world's great natural wonders. Lighted trails offer an excellent opportunity for visitors to see fantastic rock formations. Tens of thousands of bats fly out at dusk and return at dawn. See CARLSBAD CAVERNS NATIONAL PARK.

Gila Wilderness, near Silver City, was the first area in the country to be set aside as a national wilderness. It is kept in its natural condition.

Glorieta Battle Site, west of Pecos, is the place where Union and Confederate troops fought for control of New Mexico during the Civil War.

Los Alamos Museum shows the history of the atomic bomb near the site of its development.

Philmont Boy Scout Ranch is a 170,000-acre Boy Scout recreational area and a working ranch. It has a museum at ranch headquarters near Cimarron.

Puye Cliff Dwellings are ancient Indian "apartment houses" west of Española.

San Miguel Mission, in Santa Fe, was built by the Spaniards in 1636 and was restored in 1710.

National Forests, Monuments, and Wilderness Areas. New Mexico has seven national forests, each with recreational areas. Gila Forest, west of Silver City, is the largest. The others are Apache, near Datil; Carson, near Taos; Cibola, which consists of several separate forests; Coronado, near Rodeo; Lincoln, near Lincoln; and Santa Fe, near Santa Fe. For the areas and chief features of these forests, see NATIONAL FOREST (table).

In September, 1964, Congress designated five areas of the forests as national wilderness areas. These areas will be preserved in their natural form.

There are ten national monuments in New Mexico. They include some of the outstanding remains of ancient Indian civilization. These monuments are Aztec Ruins, an ancient pueblo; Bandelier, the ruins of four pueblos; Capulin Mountain, the cone of an extinct volcano; Chaco Canyon, the site of 18 pueblo ruins; El Morro, the site of Inscription Rock; Fort Union, an old military post; the Gila Cliff Dwellings, a onetime Indian settlement; Gran Quivira and Pecos, both with ruins of a pueblo and a Spanish mission; and White Sands, a large deposit of gypsum sand. Each monument is described in its own article in WORLD BOOK.

State Parks and Monuments cover thousands of acres in New Mexico. There are 22 state parks and 9 state monuments. For detailed information, write Superintendent, State Park and Recreation Commission, P.O. Box 1147, Santa Fe, N.M. 87501.

220b

Ceremonial Indian Dance at San Ildefonso Pueblo near Santa Fe

Herbert Lanks, Black Star

Rock Formations in Carlsbad Caverns near Carlsbad

FPG

ANNUAL EVENTS

Indian ceremonies and local rodeos are among the most interesting events for visitors. The dates of events may vary from year to year, and among the different tribes and pueblos. Numerous Indian ceremonies are held throughout the year. Other annual events in New Mexico include the following.

January-March: King's Day Dances in most of the Indian pueblos (Epiphany, Jan. 6); Winter Carnival in Santa Fe (late February); Penitente Services and Processions at various villages (Good Friday); Dances at most Indian pueblos (Easter).

April-June: State Science Fair in Socorro (mid-April); Raft Races, Rio Grande River (mid-May); New Mexico High School Championship Rodeo in Santa Rosa (early June); Eugene Rhodes Tour in Alamogordo (early June); Annual All Breeds Horse Show in Silver City (mid-June).

July-September: Apache Indian Ceremonial in Mescalero (July 4th weekend); Rodeo de Santa Fe (mid-July); Puye Cliff Ceremonial at Santa Clara Pueblo (last Saturday and Sunday in July); New Mexico Arts and Crafts Fair in Albuquerque (late July or early August); "Billy the Kid" Pageant in Lincoln (late July or early August); World Championship Steer Roping Contest in Clovis (August); Inter-Tribal Indian Ceremonial in Gallup (mid-August); Annual Connie Mack World Series in Farmington (late August); Fiesta de Santa Fe (Labor Day weekend); New Mexico State Fair in Albuquerque (mid-September); Feast Day in Taos Pueblo (Sept. 30).

October-December: Eastern New Mexico State Fair in Roswell (early October); Pinata Festival in Tucumcari (early October); Navaho Fair in Shiprock (early October); Pecan Festival in Carlsbad (Thanksgiving weekend); Christmas Eve Dances in Mission Churches at many Indian pueblos (Dec. 24); Christmas Eve Luminaria Tours in Albuquerque (Dec. 24).

220C

NEW MEXICO / The Land

Land Regions. New Mexico has four main land regions: (1) the Great Plains, (2) the Rocky Mountains, (3) the Basin and Range region, and (4) the Colorado Plateau.

The Great Plains of New Mexico are part of the vast Interior Plain that sweeps across North America from Canada to Mexico. In New Mexico, the Great Plains cover roughly the eastern third of the state. They extend from a high plateau in the north to the Pecos River Valley in the south. Streams have cut deep canyons in the plateau as it slopes away from the Rocky Mountains. Cattle and sheep graze there. To the south are dry farming and irrigation. The eastern edge of the state, south of the Canadian River, is called the *High Plains* or *Llano Estacado* (Staked Plain). The Llano Estacado also covers much of northwestern Texas (see Texas [Land Regions]).

The Rocky Mountains extend into north-central New Mexico from Colorado south to a point near Santa Fe. In winter, deep snow piles up on the mountains. In spring, the snow melts and provides moisture for irrigated crops in the fertile Rio Grande Valley. The Rio Grande, which rises in Colorado, cuts between ranges of mountains. To the east is the lofty Sangre de Cristo (Blood of Christ) Range. Wheeler Peak, which rises 13,160 feet, is the highest point in the state. The Nacimiento and Jemez ranges are west of the river.

The Basin and Range Region covers about a third of the state. It extends south and west from the Rockies to the borders with Arizona and Mexico. This region includes scattered ranges of rugged mountains—the Guadalupe, Mogollon, Organ, Sacramento, and San Andres ranges. Broad desert *basins* (low places where the streams have no outlet) lie between the mountains. The largest basins are the Jornada del Muerto (Journey of the Dead) and the Tularosa. The Rio Grande cuts through the Basin and Range region.

The Colorado Plateau, in the northwest, is a broken country of wide valleys and plains, deep canyons, sharp cliffs, and rugged, lonely, flat-topped hills called *mesas*. The best known mesa is Acoma, on top of which the Indians built a city. Shiprock Butte, in San Juan County, has been a famous landmark for hundreds of years. A *butte* is a steep hill that stands alone. Shiprock, which resembles a ship under full sail, rises 1,678 feet

Dick Kent

Rugged Rock Formations are found in the Bottomless Lakes State Park near Roswell in the Great Plains region. Dry, treeless land makes up much of New Mexico's Great Plains. The soil of the region produces excellent crops when irrigated or dry farmed.

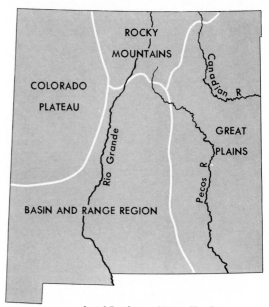

Land Regions of New Mexico

Map Index

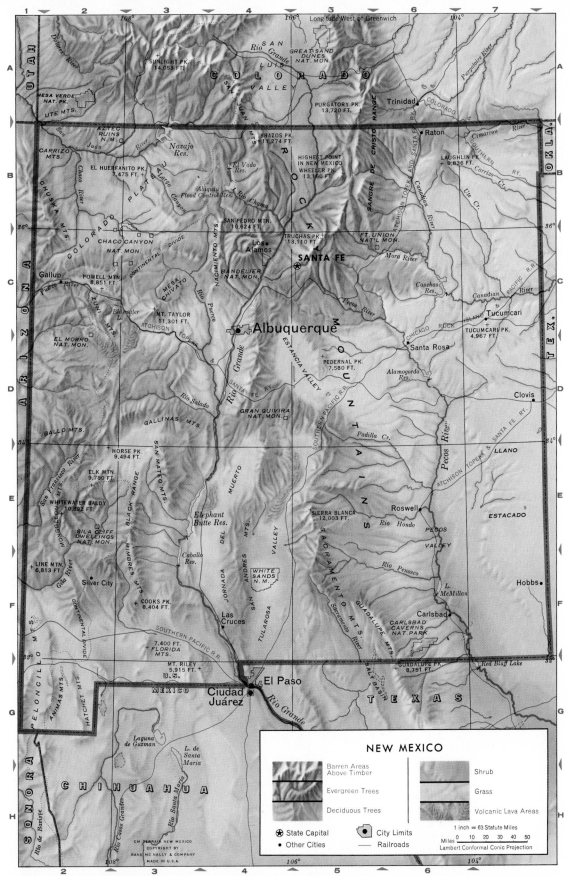

NEW MEXICO

Barren Areas Above Timber
Evergreen Trees
Deciduous Trees
Shrub
Grass
Volcanic Lava Areas

✪ State Capital
● Other Cities
City Limits
— Railroads

1 inch = 63 Statute Miles

Miles 0 10 20 30 40 50
Lambert Conformal Conic Projection

CM TERRAIN NEW MEXICO
COPYRIGHT BY
RAND MCNALLY & COMPANY
MADE IN U.S.A.

Especially created for **World Book Encyclopedia** by Rand McNally and World Book editors

Huge Shifting Dunes of White Sands National Monument near Alamogordo form a magnificent scene of white gypsum sand.

This arid wilderness of southern New Mexico lies among the rugged mountain ranges and desert basins of the Basin and Range Region.

above the flat land surrounding it. The San Juan Basin lies in the northwest section of the Colorado Plateau. To the south is a 40-mile strip of *malpais*, a badland of extinct volcanoes and lava plains. The *Continental Divide* winds through the Colorado Plateau. Streams west of it run into the Pacific Ocean. Water east of the divide runs to the Gulf of Mexico.

Rivers and Lakes. The Rio Grande runs like a backbone down the length of New Mexico. At the state's southern boundary it turns east and forms the border between Texas and Mexico. A series of dams stores water for irrigation. Elephant Butte Dam, near Truth or Consequences, backs up the Rio Grande and forms Elephant Butte Reservoir, New Mexico's largest lake. Its water irrigates land in New Mexico, Texas, and Mexico. Another important river is the Pecos. It rises in the Sangre de Cristo mountains, and then flows south. The Pecos provides irrigation water for the land around Carlsbad and Roswell. The San Juan River drains the northwest corner of the state. The Canadian River rises in the northeast part. Its waters are stored at the Conchas Dam, near Tucumcari, for irrigation. The Gila River, in the southwest, flows west into Arizona.

New Mexico has few natural lakes. Most famous are the deep Bottomless Lakes, a group of pools near Roswell. In addition to Elephant Butte, other man-made lakes are Abiquiu, Alamogordo, Avalon, Bluewater, Conchas, Eagle Nest, El Vado, McMillan, and Navajo.

Mesas and Desert Valleys form a landscape of rugged isolation. This stream and group of steep cliffs north of Gallup are part of the Colorado Plateau region of northwestern New Mexico.

Grazing Land in the Rocky Mountains region of northern New Mexico provides rich grass for cattle and sheep. These animals

find feed on much land that is too steep or too rocky to grow crops. Ranching is the chief agricultural activity in New Mexico.

NEW MEXICO / Climate

New Mexico has a dry, warm climate. It is not too unusual to see a housewife hanging out clothes in the rain. She knows the rain will stop soon, and the air will dry the clothes quickly. The state averages less than 20 inches of *precipitation* (rain, melted snow, and other forms of moisture) a year. It varies from less than 10 inches in the south and central areas to more than 20 inches in the northern mountain regions. Snow falls throughout the state. It averages only about 2 inches a year in the south. The high mountains may get as much as 300 inches of snow a year.

The average July temperature is about 74° F. January temperatures vary from an average of 55° F. in the south to about 35° F. in the north. Day and night temperatures vary widely on the same day. The thin, dry air does not stay warm after sundown because of the high altitude. The state's lowest recorded temperature was −50° F. at Gavilan on Feb. 1, 1951. The highest temperature was 116° F. at Artesia on June 29, 1918, and at Orogrande on July 14, 1934.

New Mexico Dept. of Development

New Mexico's Warm Climate helps produce rich crops if farmers irrigate the fertile land. This field is near Las Cruces. Not enough rain falls there to produce good crops without irrigation.

SEASONAL TEMPERATURES

JANUARY

AVERAGE OF DAILY LOW TEMPERATURES

Degrees Centigrade	Degrees Fahrenheit
-4 to 0	24 to 32
-9 to -4	16 to 24
-13 to -9	8 to 16
-18 to -13	0 to 8

AVERAGE OF DAILY HIGH TEMPERATURES

Degrees Fahrenheit	Degrees Centigrade
56 to 64	13 to 18
48 to 56	9 to 13
40 to 48	4 to 9
32 to 40	0 to 4

JULY

AVERAGE OF DAILY LOW TEMPERATURES

Degrees Centigrade	Degrees Fahrenheit
18 to 22	64 to 72
13 to 18	56 to 64
9 to 13	48 to 56
4 to 9	40 to 48

AVERAGE OF DAILY HIGH TEMPERATURES

Degrees Fahrenheit	Degrees Centigrade
96 to 104	36 to 40
88 to 96	31 to 36
80 to 88	27 to 31
72 to 80	22 to 27

AVERAGE YEARLY PRECIPITATION
(Rain, Melted Snow, and Other Moisture)

Inches	Centimeters
12 to 24	30 to 61
0 to 12	0 to 30

0   100   200   300 Miles
0   100 200 300 400 Kilometers

WORLD BOOK maps

MONTHLY WEATHER IN ALBUQUERQUE AND ROSWELL

	JAN	FEB	MAR	APR	MAY	JUNE	JULY	AUG	SEPT	OCT	NOV	DEC	Average of:
ALBUQUERQUE	46	52	60	69	79	89	92	89	82	71	57	47	High Temperatures
	22	27	32	42	52	61	66	65	58	45	31	25	Low Temperatures
	4	4	4	4	4	4	9	10	5	5	3	4	Days of Rain or Snow
	3	4	2	3	4	4	9	7	4	4	2	2	Days of Rain or Snow
ROSWELL	54	60	66	75	83	91	92	91	85	75	64	55	High Temperatures
	25	30	35	45	54	62	66	65	58	47	33	27	Low Temperatures

Temperatures are given in degrees Fahrenheit.

Source: U.S. Weather Bureau

New Mexico's land is rich in many kinds of minerals, and at least part of the soil is fertile. But water is scarce. This lack of water has limited New Mexico's growth. The people are learning to make better use of the water resources they have. New industries that use little water are growing. But water remains a problem.

The federal government owns about half the land in New Mexico. Much of it is rangeland. The rest includes Indian reservations, national forests, and military reservations. Many government agencies, among them the Atomic Energy Commission, spend large sums of money in New Mexico. This makes the federal government vital to New Mexico's economy.

Natural Resources of New Mexico include large mineral deposits and rich, renewable resources based on the soil—forests, grasses, plants, and animals.

Minerals. New Mexico is rich in minerals that supply energy. The state has large reserves of coal, natural gas, petroleum, and uranium. Uranium is the main source of atomic energy. New Mexico has more than 30 million tons of ore—nearly one-half of the nation's known uranium reserves. The largest U.S. reserves of potash, a vital fertilizer material, are also in New Mexico. The state ranks as a leader in copper reserves. It also has important deposits of helium gas, natural gas liquids, perlite, salt, sand and gravel, stone, and zinc. Other minerals include clays, gemstones, gold, gypsum, iron, lead, manganese, mica, pumice, and silver.

Soil of New Mexico varies widely. More than half the soil is stony and shallow, and not good for farming. Some desert land contains chemicals that prevent trees from growing. But this land supports shrubs, flowers, and grasses. The eastern section has brown and reddish-brown sandy soil.

Water is precious in New Mexico, and water resources are extremely important. New Mexico and other western states have joined with Mexico to share the use of water in various streams. Each area gets a share. For example, Colorado users must allow a certain amount of Rio Grande water to flow into New Mexico. New Mexico's resources include underground water. Some comes from *artesian wells* (see ARTESIAN WELL).

New Mexico has seven major storage projects that help make good use of water. These projects regulate the flow of the Canadian, Pecos, Rio Grande, and San Juan rivers, and some of their tributaries.

Forests cover about 21 million acres, or more than a fourth of the state. There are commercially valuable timberlands in eight mountain areas. The most common trees include the aspen, cottonwood, Douglas fir, juniper, piñon (nut pine), ponderosa pine, scrub oak, spruce, and white fir.

Plant Life. The yucca, New Mexico's state flower, grows in most areas. Its dried stems provided the Indians with fire-making materials in the early days. Cattlemen must guard their livestock from the poisonous locoweed. Desert plants include cactus, creosote bush, grama grass, mesquite, white and purple sage, and soapweed. Wild mountain plants include forget-me-nots, saxifrages, sedges, alpine larkspur, and other flowers.

Animal Life is plentiful in New Mexico. Among the larger animals are black bears, coyotes, mountain lions, pronghorn antelope, and whitetail and mule deer. Others include badgers, beavers, bobcats, chipmunks, foxes, jack rabbits, minks, otters, and prairie dogs.

Among the game birds are ducks, grouse, pheasants, quail, and wild turkeys. Common fish include black bass, catfish, crappies, perch, suckers, and trout.

Two kinds of poisonous snakes, the rattlesnake and the coral snake, live in New Mexico. The southwestern desert is the home of such spiders as the tarantula and the poisonous black widow.

Mining is by far the biggest income-producing activity in New Mexico. Mineral products valued at $874 million a year account for almost two-thirds of the value of all goods produced in the state and make New Mexico a leader in mining.

Petroleum makes up almost half the value of New Mexico's mineral production, with a yearly output of about 126 million barrels. Natural gas is the second most valuable product, and the state is a leader in production of both oil and gas. The biggest producing fields are in San Juan County in the northwest, and in Lea and Eddy counties in the southeast.

New Mexico leads the states in uranium production, with about half the U.S. output. Paddy Martinez, a Navaho Indian, accidentally found the uranium deposits in 1950 in northwestern New Mexico.

NEW MEXICO'S PRODUCTION IN 1967

Total value of goods produced—$1,408,115,000

MINERAL PRODUCTS 62% —
— AGRICULTURAL PRODUCTS 25%
— MANUFACTURED PRODUCTS 13%

Note: Manufacturing percentage based on value added by manufacture. Other percentages based on value of production.

Sources: U.S. Government statistics

NEW MEXICO'S EMPLOYMENT IN 1967

Total number of persons employed—302,200

		Number of Employees
Government	🚶🚶🚶🚶🚶🚶	81,100
Wholesale & Retail Trade	🚶🚶🚶🚶🚶	59,000
Services	🚶🚶🚶🚶🚶	53,800
Agriculture	🚶🚶	23,400
Transportation & Public Utilities	🚶🚶	20,100
Construction	🚶🚶	18,600
Manufacturing	🚶🚶	18,400
Mining	🚶🚶	16,500
Finance, Insurance & Real Estate	🚶	11,300

Source: U.S. Department of Labor

Harvey Caplin, Western Ways

Santa Rita Copper Mine is near Silver City. It has been a rich source of ore since the 1800's, when the Spaniards began to work the mine.

FARM, MINERAL, AND FOREST PRODUCTS

This map shows where the leading farm, mineral, and forest products are produced. The major urban area (shown in red) is the state's important manufacturing center.

```
0    25   50   75   100 Miles
0  25  50  75  100 Kilometers
```

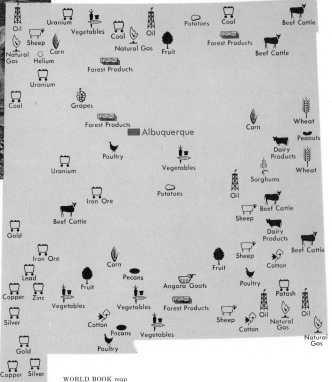

WORLD BOOK map

New Mexico is the leading potash-mining state. Potash is mined in the Carlsbad area. New Mexico is also a leader in copper production. Soft-coal miners dig about $3\frac{1}{2}$ million tons a year in Colfax, McKinley, San Juan, and Sandoval counties. Other important minerals are gypsum, helium gas, natural gas liquids, perlite, pumice, salt, sand and gravel, stone, and zinc.

Agriculture has a value of about $349 million a year, or about a fourth of the value of goods produced in the state. New Mexico has about 14,200 farms and ranches, covering about 47,647,000 acres. Farms in New Mexico cover an average of about 3,350 acres.

The most important agricultural activity is ranching. The state has more than twice as many cattle and sheep together as it has people. There are about 2,220,000 cattle and sheep. Cattle and sheep graze in areas where low rainfall or rough land prevents crop farming. About 44,805,000 acres are used for grazing.

Dry farming is used on about two-thirds of the state's cropland. This method is most successful in the eastern part of the state. But New Mexico's farmers are changing from dry farming to irrigation. New dams are providing more water, and some fields are being irrigated with water from deep wells. About a third of the cropland is irrigated. The most important field crops are cotton, hay, and grain sorghum. Other important crops include lettuce, onions, and wheat. Chili peppers are grown in several southern counties.

Huge Herds of Cattle, such as this one in the Animas Valley near Lordsburg, are rounded up by cowboys for shipment to market. Cattle are one of New Mexico's most important products. The animals graze over vast areas of land unsuitable for crop farming.

Cletis Reaves, Alpha

Fruits and vegetables grow well in the irrigated river valleys, particularly along the Rio Grande. Dona Ana county, near El Paso, Tex., has one of the nation's largest pecan groves. The nearly 200,000 trees in this grove bear about $7\frac{1}{2}$ million pounds of pecans a year.

Manufacturing has expanded since World War II, but it still provides only about one-eighth of the value of all goods produced in New Mexico. Goods manufactured in the state have a *value added by manufacture* of $185 million a year. This figure represents the value created in products by New Mexico's industries, not counting such costs as materials, supplies, and fuel. The state has a large atomic industry, both public and private. The government finances the Los Alamos Scientific Laboratory, where the first atomic bomb was built. Sandia Laboratories, a private corporation in Albuquerque, does research and engineering on both peaceful and military uses of nuclear energy.

Food processing is New Mexico's most important manufacturing activity. Other manufactured products include, in order of value, printed materials; stone, clay, and glass products; lumber and wood products; and machinery.

New Mexico produces about 250 million board feet of lumber a year. The Navaho Indian tribe is one of the major producers. The most important forest product is softwood lumber from ponderosa pine trees.

Electric Power is generated mostly by power plants that burn coal or natural gas. The only hydroelectric plant is a small one at Elephant Butte Dam. Privately owned power plants serve most of the state's urban areas. Municipally owned plants serve many medium-sized towns while electrical cooperatives serve most rural areas. For New Mexico's kilowatt-hour production, see ELECTRIC POWER (table).

Transportation. New Mexico has more than 66,000 miles of roads and highways, including about 20,000 miles of hard-surface roads. The oldest road in the United States—*El Camino Real* (the Royal Road)—runs from Santa Fe to Chihuahua, Mexico. Spaniards first traveled the road in 1581. Another famous road, the Santa Fe Trail, was opened in 1821 between Missouri and New Mexico. Today, U.S. Highway 85 east of Santa Fe follows this old trail. See SANTA FE TRAIL.

Most commercial air traffic is centered around Albuquerque. Four major airlines serve the city. The state has over 120 airports. New Mexico lies on the main lines of several railroads, and has about 2,300 miles of track. The Atchison, Topeka, & Santa Fe was the state's first railroad. It entered New Mexico in 1878.

Communication. The first Spanish-language newspaper in New Mexico, *El Crepúsculo de la Libertad* (The Dawn of Liberty), began publication in 1834 at Santa Fe. The *Santa Fe Republican*, the first English-language paper, was founded in 1847. Today, publishers in New Mexico issue about 55 newspapers, including 19 dailies. The largest papers are the *Albuquerque Journal* and the *Albuquerque Tribune*. The state's first radio station, KOB, began broadcasting from Albuquerque in 1922. The first television station, KOB-TV, started regular programming from Albuquerque in 1948. New Mexico has about 70 radio stations and 7 television stations.

Indian Days. Indians probably have lived in what is now New Mexico for about 20,000 years. Stone spearheads found at Folsom and other places indicate that Indians hunted in northeastern New Mexico at least 10,000 years ago. The spearheads are known as *Folsom points*, and the people who made them are called *Folsom man*. See FOLSOM POINT.

From about 500 B.C. to A.D. 1200, the Mogollon Indians lived in the valleys in the area of the New Mexico-Arizona border. At first they lived in houses dug partly into the ground. Later, they built villages above the ground. See MOGOLLON.

Another group of ancient Indians lived in the region where the borders of New Mexico, Arizona, Utah, and Colorado meet. They were the Anasazi, some of the most civilized North American Indians. The Anasazi raised corn and cotton, and tamed wild turkeys. The big birds provided food and clothing. In winter, the Indians wore robes made of turkey feathers. Some Anasazi were cliff dwellers and built many-storied apartment houses of closely fitted stones. One such building, the *Pueblo Bonito* (pretty village), probably had about 800 rooms. Sometimes the Anasazi built towns on top of steep mesas. The Pueblo Indians are the descendants of these people. See CLIFF DWELLERS.

--- **IMPORTANT DATES IN NEW MEXICO** ---

1540-1542 Francisco Vásquez de Coronado explored New Mexico.

1598 Juan de Oñate founded the first permanent Spanish colony, at San Juan.

1610 Governor Pedro de Peralta established Santa Fe.

1680 The Pueblo Indians revolted and drove the Spaniards out of northern New Mexico.

1692 Diego de Vargas reconquered New Mexico for Spain.

1706 Francisco Cuervo y Valdes founded Albuquerque.

1821 New Mexico became a province of Mexico. William Becknell established the Santa Fe Trail.

1846 General Stephen W. Kearny took possession of New Mexico during the Mexican War.

1848 Mexico ceded New Mexico to the United States in the Treaty of Guadalupe Hidalgo.

1850 Congress created the Territory of New Mexico.

1853 New Mexico acquired part of the Gila Valley through the Gadsden Purchase.

1864 Colonel Kit Carson defeated the Mescalero Apache and Navaho Indians.

1876 Cattlemen began a 5-year series of fights called the Lincoln County War.

1886 The surrender of Geronimo ended the Apache Wars.

1912 New Mexico became the 47th state on January 6.

1916 Mexican bandits raided Columbus. Elephant Butte Dam was completed.

1922 Geologists discovered oil in the southeastern and northwestern regions of New Mexico.

1930 Carlsbad Caverns became a national park.

1945 The first atomic bomb was exploded at Trinity Site near Alamogordo.

1950 Paddy Martinez, a Navaho Indian, found uranium in the northwest region.

1964 Work started on the $86 million San Juan-Chama project to bring water through the Rocky Mountains to the Albuquerque area.

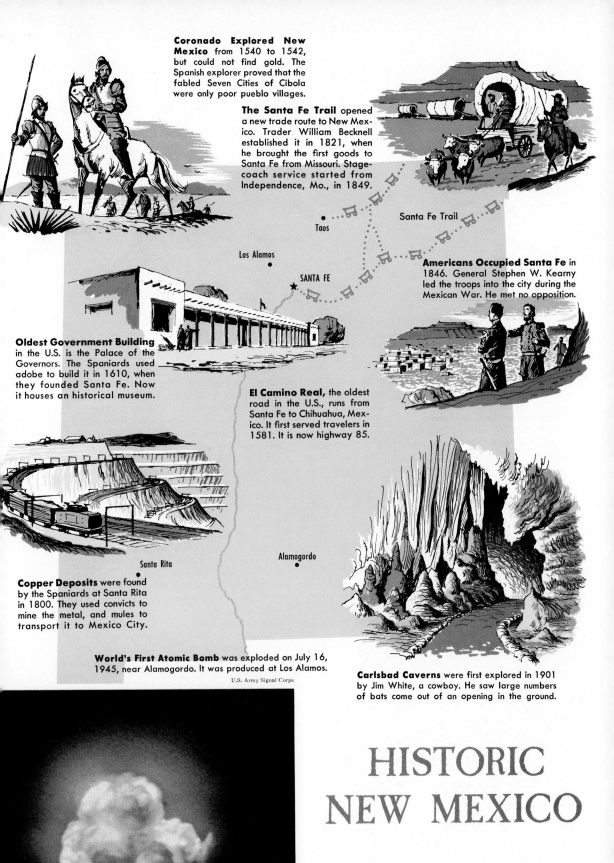

Coronado Explored New Mexico from 1540 to 1542, but could not find gold. The Spanish explorer proved that the fabled Seven Cities of Cibola were only poor pueblo villages.

The Santa Fe Trail opened a new trade route to New Mexico. Trader William Becknell established it in 1821, when he brought the first goods to Santa Fe from Missouri. Stagecoach service started from Independence, Mo., in 1849.

Santa Fe Trail

Taos

Los Alamos

SANTA FE

Americans Occupied Santa Fe in 1846. General Stephen W. Kearny led the troops into the city during the Mexican War. He met no opposition.

Oldest Government Building in the U.S. is the Palace of the Governors. The Spaniards used adobe to build it in 1610, when they founded Santa Fe. Now it houses an historical museum.

El Camino Real, the oldest road in the U.S., runs from Santa Fe to Chihuahua, Mexico. It first served travelers in 1581. It is now highway 85.

Santa Rita

Alamogordo

Copper Deposits were found by the Spaniards at Santa Rita in 1800. They used convicts to mine the metal, and mules to transport it to Mexico City.

World's First Atomic Bomb was exploded on July 16, 1945, near Alamogordo. It was produced at Los Alamos.

U.S. Army Signal Corps.

Carlsbad Caverns were first explored in 1901 by Jim White, a cowboy. He saw large numbers of bats come out of an opening in the ground.

HISTORIC
NEW MEXICO

Pueblo Ruins in Coronado State Monument near Bernalillo symbolize the Indian and Spanish heritage of New Mexico. Indians lived in the pueblo before Columbus discovered America. The Spanish explorer Coronado camped nearby in the 1540's.

The Navaho and Apache tribes came from the north about A.D. 1500. Utes and Comanches came into the region a few years later. See INDIAN, AMERICAN (table, Indian Tribes).

Exploration and Settlement. The first Spanish explorers reached the area almost by accident. Álvar Núñez Cabeza de Vaca was a member of a group seeking gold in Florida in 1528. The expedition was shipwrecked near the Texas coast. Most of the men were drowned. But Cabeza de Vaca and three companions —two white men and a Negro—landed on the Texas coast. In 1536, after wandering for eight years, they reached a settlement near the Pacific Coast of New Spain (now Mexico). They told stories of seven cities of great wealth, called the *Seven Cities of Cibola*, to the north. See CIBOLA, SEVEN CITIES OF.

The Spaniards were determined to find the seven rich cities. Guided by Cabeza de Vaca's Negro companion, Estéban, a priest named Marcos de Niza made a search in 1539. He claimed the area as a province of Spain. Marcos de Niza also reported that he had seen the cities from a distance.

Francisco Vásquez de Coronado, also in search of the seven cities, explored present-day New Mexico and Arizona from 1540 to 1542. But he found only the pueblos of the Indians. Fray Augustín Rodríguez and Captain Francisco Sánchez Chamuscado traveled up the Rio Grande from New Spain in 1581. The report of a later explorer, Antonio de Espejo, led to colonization.

The first Spanish colony in New Mexico was established in 1598 at the Pueblo of San Juan de Los Caballeros, near the Chama River. The colony was financed and established by Juan de Oñate. He became governor of the province of New Mexico. Oñate was succeeded as governor by Pedro de Peralta, who moved the capital to Santa Fe in 1610. Santa Fe is the oldest seat of government in the United States.

The colony had little wealth and grew very slowly. It was kept alive mainly by the efforts of missionaries. Roman Catholic priests from Spain established schools to teach Christianity to the Indians. But repeated quarrels occurred between the church and civil authorities, and between the Spaniards and the Indians.

The Spaniards set up a system of forced labor for the Indians that was almost like slavery. The Spaniards also kept the Indians from worshiping their ancient gods. Popé, an Indian from the San Juan Pueblo, led a revolt in 1680. The Indians killed more than 400 Spaniards, and drove the rest to El Paso del Norte (now El Paso, Tex.). The Indians destroyed almost every trace of the Roman Catholic Church. But they could not set up a permanent government.

In 1692, the Spanish governor Diego de Vargas took back the province with little trouble. Four years of scattered fighting broke the power of the Pueblo Indians. The colonists and priests returned to build homes and missions in and near Santa Fe. For the next 125 years, the Spaniards and Pueblo Indians lived fairly peacefully. The area remained a lonely outpost of the Spanish Empire.

Mexican Rule. Trappers and traders came to New Mexico from the United States during the early 1800's. Spanish officials feared the newcomers, and expelled them or put them in prison. But the Spanish officials were replaced in 1821, after Mexico won its freedom from Spain. New Mexico became a province of Mexico. That same year, William Becknell, an American trader, opened the Santa Fe Trail to bring goods to New Mexico from Missouri.

Mexico ruled the area for the next 25 years, a period filled with unrest. In 1837, Mexicans and Indians in New Mexico rebelled against the Mexican government. They executed the governor and seized the Palace of Governors in Santa Fe. A Taos Indian, José Gonzales, was installed as their chief executive. But a month later, Mexico's General Manuel Armijo crushed the rebellion and became governor.

In 1841, an expedition from Texas (then an independent country) invaded New Mexico. The Texans claimed the land east of the Rio Grande. However,

Taos Chamber of Commerce

The Taos Rio Grande Gorge Bridge is a link in a highway that runs across northern New Mexico. The concrete and steel bridge crosses a 650-foot-deep gorge near Taos. It replaced a road that zigzagged down the sides of the gorge.

Mexican troops defeated the invaders and sent them as captives to Mexico City. They were later freed.

The Mexican War. As colonists from the United States pushed west, trouble developed between the United States and Mexico. In 1846, war broke out, and U.S. forces under General Stephen W. Kearny took control of New Mexico with little resistance. The Treaty of Guadalupe Hidalgo ended the war in 1848, and the U.S. took possession of the region. See MEXICAN WAR.

Territorial Days. In 1850, Congress organized New Mexico as a territory. James C. Calhoun was the first territorial governor. The territory also included what is now Arizona and parts of present-day Colorado, Nevada, and Utah. In 1853, the Gadsden Purchase enlarged the territory (see GADSDEN PURCHASE). Mexico sold the United States land south of the Gila River, between the Rio Grande and the Colorado River. New Mexico got its present boundaries in 1863, after Congress organized the territories of Colorado and Arizona.

Early in the Civil War (1861-1865), Confederate forces from Texas captured much of the region, including Albuquerque and Santa Fe. Union forces recaptured the territory in March, 1862, after two battles southeast of Santa Fe. The first clash was fought in Apache Canyon, and the second in Glorieta Pass. Between 1862 and 1864, Colonel Kit Carson, a famous frontier scout, led the New Mexicans in forcing both the Mescalero Apache and the Navaho Indian tribes to live on reservations.

During the late 1870's, cattlemen and other groups fought for political control of Lincoln County. The bitterness burst into open violence with the murder of rancher John G. Tunstall. Billy the Kid and other outlaws took a leading part in the fighting, which became known as the Lincoln County War. General Lew Wallace was appointed territorial governor in 1878. He declared martial law and used troops to end the bloodshed.

In the late 1800's, after the railroads linked the territory to the rest of the nation, New Mexico experienced a cattle and mining boom. Geronimo, one of the last hostile Apache chiefs, spread terror through the area until he surrendered on Sept. 4, 1886.

Early Statehood. New Mexico became the 47th state on Jan. 6, 1912. It had a population of about 330,000. The people elected William C. McDonald as the first state governor, for a term of five years. Thereafter, all governors were elected to two-year terms.

Mexican bandits, probably led by Pancho Villa, raided the town of Columbus in 1916, killing 16 Americans. The U.S. Army sent an expedition into Mexico to catch Villa, but it failed. During World War I, New Mexico sent more than 17,000 men into the armed forces.

In the early 1920's, a long drought made life difficult for farmers and ranchers. Livestock prices dropped,

	THE GOVERNORS OF NEW MEXICO				
		Party	Term		Party	Term

	Party	Term		Party	Term
1. William C. McDonald	Democratic	1912-1917	12. John E. Miles	Democratic	1939-1943
2. Ezequiel C. de Baca	Democratic	1917	13. John J. Dempsey	Democratic	1943-1947
3. Washington E. Lindsey	Republican	1917-1919	14. Thomas J. Mabry	Democratic	1947-1951
4. Octaviano A. Larrazolo	Republican	1919-1921	15. Edwin L. Mechem	Republican	1951-1955
5. Merritt C. Mechem	Republican	1921-1923	16. John F. Simms	Democratic	1955-1957
6. James F. Hinkle	Democratic	1923-1925	17. Edwin L. Mechem	Republican	1957-1959
7. Arthur T. Hannett	Democratic	1925-1927	18. John Burroughs	Democratic	1959-1961
8. Richard C. Dillon	Republican	1927-1931	19. Edwin L. Mechem	Republican	1961-1963
9. Arthur Seligman	Democratic	1931-1933	20. Jack M. Campbell	Democratic	1963-1967
10. A. W. Hockenhull	Republican	1933-1935	21. David F. Cargo	Republican	1967-1971
11. Clyde Tingley	Democratic	1935-1939	22. Bruce King	Democratic	1971-

and the stockmen's financial troubles spread. Banks closed and many persons lost their savings. But new businesses developed. Oil was discovered in the 1920's, and huge potash deposits at Carlsbad were opened. In 1930, the famous caverns near Carlsbad became a national park, and the tourist industry grew.

World War II. When the United States entered World War II in 1941, the 200th Coast Artillery, composed of New Mexico soldiers, was in the Philippine Islands. The Japanese overwhelmed the regiment, along with the rest of the U.S. forces on Bataan Peninsula. Many of the men were killed, and others spent more than three years in Japanese prison camps. The war ended after U.S. planes dropped two atom bombs on Japan in August, 1945. The bombs had been produced at Los Alamos, a town and laboratory built secretly in the New Mexico mountains. The world's first atomic bomb was exploded at Trinity Site, near Alamogordo, on July 16, 1945.

The Mid-1900's. After World War II ended in 1945, the government continued to spend large amounts of money in New Mexico for research. The state's economy and population both grew rapidly as the government provided funds for work on atomic power development and experiments with rockets. The economy also was aided by the discovery of uranium in northwestern New Mexico in 1950.

During the 1960's, Albuquerque and Roswell went through a slowdown in their rate of growth. The government reduced the number of people it employed in Albuquerque and closed several military bases near Roswell. By the late 1960's, both cities had recovered from their losses by attracting nongovernment industries.

The state's coal industry grew in the mid-1960's. A large coal mine was opened near Raton, and coal-burning electric generating plants were built near Farmington. A molybdenum mine went into operation near Questa, a village in Taos County. But production of potash decreased in the Carlsbad area because of competition from Canadian potash mines.

New Mexico Today is maintaining its rank as a leading center of space and atomic research. The largest private employer in the state is the Sandia Laboratories of Albuquerque, which conducts research and does engineering work on the uses of nuclear energy. At Los Alamos, government scientists are working on many projects involving both military and nonmilitary uses of atomic energy. Near Las Cruces, technicians are developing a nuclear-powered engine that may carry men beyond the moon.

The New Mexico tourist industry continues to grow. Income from tourists almost doubled from the mid-1960's to 1970. One reason for the increase was the construction and improvement of winter sports resorts.

Lack of water has always created problems in New Mexico. Many of these problems were expected to be solved with completion of the San Juan-Chama project in the early 1970's. This project, which was started in 1964, will bring water to the state through three tunnels from rivers in the Rocky Mountain area. The project will also create large reservoirs near Chama and Santa Fe. The reservoir on the Rio Grande near Santa Fe will provide recreational facilities, flood control, and water for irrigation.

JAMES B. COLEGROVE, B. LEROY GORDON, and LYNN I. PERRIGO

NEW MEXICO/Study Aids

Related Articles in WORLD BOOK include:

BIOGRAPHIES

Anderson, Clinton P.
Billy the Kid
Carson, Kit
Chavez, Dennis
Condon, Edward U.
Coronado, Francisco
    Vásquez de

Garrett, Patrick F.
Geronimo
Hilton, Conrad N.
Oñate, Juan de
Ross, Edmund G.
Villa, Pancho
Wallace, Lew

CITIES

Albuquerque
Gallup

Las Cruces
Los Alamos

Roswell
Santa Fe

Taos

HISTORY

Apache Indians
Cibola, Seven Cities of
Cliff Dwellers
Gadsden Purchase
Guadalupe Hidalgo,
    Treaty of
Hopi Indians
Indian, American
Indian Wars

Jefferson Territory
Mexican War
Mogollon
Navaho Indians
Pueblo Indians
Santa Fe Trail
Western Frontier Life
Zuñi Indians

PHYSICAL FEATURES

Canadian River
Carlsbad Caverns
    National Park
Dust Bowl
Elephant Butte
    Dam

Gila River
Mesa
Pecos River
Rio Grande
Rocky Mountains
Sangre de Cristo Mountains

PRODUCTS

For New Mexico's rank among the states in production, see the following articles:

Copper
Gas (fuel)
Helium

Lettuce
Manganese
Mining

Petroleum
Uranium

OTHER RELATED ARTICLES

Holloman Air Force Base
Kirtland Air Force Base
Rocky Mountain States

Sandia Base
Southwestern States
White Sands Missile Range

Outline

I. Government
    A. Constitution
    B. Executive
    C. Legislature
    D. Courts

    E. Local Government
    F. Taxation
    G. Politics

II. People

III. Education
    A. Schools

    B. Libraries and Museums

IV. A Visitor's Guide
    A. Places to Visit

    B. Annual Events

V. The Land
    A. Land Regions

    B. Rivers and Lakes

VI. Climate

VII. Economy
    A. Natural Resources
    B. Mining
    C. Agriculture
    D. Manufacturing

    E. Electric Power
    F. Transportation
    G. Communication

VIII. History

What contribution did missionaries make to the development of New Mexico?

When and why did the Pueblo Indians revolt in New Mexico?

How is the Spanish influence evident in New Mexico today?

Where is the oldest road in the United States? What is its name?

Why is New Mexico sometimes called the *Land of Enchantment?*

What states were formed from the New Mexico Territory?

Where is the oldest seat of government in the United States?

What historic weapons were built in New Mexico during World War II?

New Mexico leads the states in the production of what important minerals?

What is the principal agricultural activity of New Mexico?

Books for Young Readers

ALLEN, T. D. *Tall as Great Standing Rock.* Westminster, 1963. This book is the story of a Navaho boy who learns to combine the best of two different cultures for the good of his people.

BAKER, BETTY. *Killer-of-Death.* Harper, 1963. Haunting story of a young Apache who grows up in the last days of his tribe's greatness.

BLEEKER, SONIA. *The Apache Indians: Raiders of the Southwest.* Morrow, 1951. *The Pueblo Indians: Farmers of the Rio Grande.* 1955. *The Navajo: Herders, Weavers, and Silversmiths.* 1958.

CLARK, ANN N. *In My Mother's House.* Viking, 1941. Pueblo Indian life today. *Medicine Man's Daughter.* Farrar, 1963. A sensitive, poetic story of present-day Navahos.

DAVIS, JULIA. *Ride with the Eagle; the Expedition of the First Missouri in the War with Mexico, 1846.* Harcourt, 1962.

GARST, DORIS S. *Kit Carson.* Messner, 1942. *Dick Wootton.* 1956. *William Bent and His Adobe Empire.* 1957. Biographies of three men who were prominent in the history of New Mexico.

KRUMGOLD, JOSEPH. . . . *And Now Miguel.* Crowell, 1953. This Newbery medal winner describes 12-year-old Miguel Chavez, whose family has raised sheep near Taos for generations.

LAVENDER, DAVID S. *The Trail to Santa Fe.* Houghton, 1958.

Books for Older Readers

BARKER, ELLIOTT S. *Beatty's Cabin: Adventures in the Pecos High Country.* Univ. of New Mexico Press, 1953.

BECK, WARREN A. *New Mexico: A History of Four Centuries.* Univ. of Oklahoma Press, 1962.

CATHER, WILLA. *Death Comes for the Archbishop.* Knopf, 1927. This book by one of America's best-known novelists portrays the character of the people and the region in the 1800's.

FERGUSSON, ERNA. *New Mexico: A Pageant of Three Peoples.* Knopf, 1951.

HORGAN, PAUL. *Great River; the Rio Grande in North American History.* 2 vols. in 1. Holt, Rinehart & Winston, 1960. This two-volume work won the 1955 Pulitzer prize for history.

HUNT, FRAZIER. *The Tragic Days of Billy the Kid.* Hastings, 1956.

MARRIOTT, ALICE. *Maria: The Potter of San Ildefonso.* Rev. ed. Univ. of Oklahoma Press, 1958. This biography tells the story of a Pueblo Indian potter who became world famous.

New Mexico: A Guide to the Colorful State. Rev. ed. Hastings, 1962.

NEW MEXICO, UNIVERSITY OF, is a state-controlled coeducational school at Albuquerque, N.Mex. It has colleges of arts and sciences, business administration, education, engineering, fine arts, nursing, and pharmacy. The university also has a graduate school, law school, government research division, bureau of engineering research, bureau of business research, extension division, summer session, adult education program, and community college for non-degree work.

The university's Institute of Meteoritics was the first of its kind in the world. The University of New Mexico also has anthropology, biology, and geology museums; art galleries; and an audio-visual center. The Peace Corps has a training center on the campus for volunteers going to Latin America. The University of New Mexico was founded in 1889. For enrollment, see UNIVERSITIES AND COLLEGES (table).   TOM L. POPEJOY

NEW MEXICO HIGHLANDS UNIVERSITY. See UNIVERSITIES AND COLLEGES (table).

NEW MEXICO INSTITUTE OF MINING AND TECHNOLOGY. See UNIVERSITIES AND COLLEGES (table).

NEW MEXICO STATE UNIVERSITY is a coeducational institution on the outskirts of Las Cruces, N.Mex. It has colleges of agriculture and home economics, arts and science, engineering, and education. The graduate school grants M.A., M.S., and Ph.D. degrees. Cooperative programs in engineering, mathematics, physics, and accounting provide for six months' study at the university and six months' employment at White Sands Missile Range and other government agencies. The university carries on scientific study and agricultural research. The university was founded in 1888 as Las Cruces College, and in 1889 became New Mexico College of Agriculture and Mechanic Arts. It received its present name in 1960. For enrollment, see UNIVERSITIES AND COLLEGES (table).   ROGER BAILEY CORBETT

NEW NETHERLAND was a region in America claimed by the Dutch in the early 1600's. It included parts of what are now Connecticut, Delaware, New Jersey, and New York. In 1621, merchants in The Netherlands formed the Dutch West India Company to compete with the Spanish Empire, colonize New Netherland, and develop the region's fur trade. Thirty families of Dutch settlers, sponsored by the company, established a Dutch colony at the mouth of the Hudson River in 1624. The company bought Manhattan Island from the Indians in 1626, and founded New Amsterdam (now New York City) there. Dutch traders founded trading posts at the present sites of Albany, N.Y., Hartford, Conn., and Trenton, N.J.

The governors of New Netherland were harsh rulers. They allowed no religious freedom and quarreled with their own people and with neighboring colonies. They mistreated the Indians, and so the colony was often in danger of Indian attack. Many colonists became discontented. By the 1650's, a fierce trading rivalry had built up between the Dutch and the English. In 1664, the English sent a fleet of warships to capture New Netherland for the Duke of York. Many Dutch colonists refused to fight, and Governor Peter Stuyvesant was forced to surrender to the English. New Netherland became the English colony of New York.   MARSHALL SMELSER

See also NEW YORK (History); STUYVESANT, PETER.

NEW ORLEANS

NEW ORLEANS, *AWR lee unz,* is the largest city in Louisiana and one of the great ports of the world. It lies on the Mississippi River, near the Gulf of Mexico. For more than 200 years, the city has served as an important commercial link between the Mississippi and the Atlantic Ocean. Much of America's trade with Latin America flows through New Orleans. The city is also a center of industry, finance, and education.

New Orleans is often called *America's Most Interesting City.* Four flags—those of France, Spain, the Confederate States, and the United States—have flown over it. The city still has many reminders of Old Europe and the Old South. The historic French Quarter and the exciting Mardi Gras festival are two links with the past.

The city also has earned another nickname, the *City Care Forgot.* The people of New Orleans have always been ready to lay aside their business and have a good time. Many of the city's restaurants are world famous for their cooking. New Orleans is also famous as the birthplace of jazz. The city is remembered in such jazz classics as "Basin Street Blues" and "Way Down Yonder in New Orleans."

Location and Description

The Mississippi River sweeps past New Orleans in an easterly direction, forming a giant curve. The curve gave New Orleans the nickname of the *Crescent City.* The main part of the city is wedged between the river on the south and Lake Pontchartrain on the north. Lake Pontchartrain connects to Lake Borgne. Lake Borgne, which is actually an arm of the Gulf of Mexico, can be navigated only by small boats. To reach the Port of New Orleans, ocean-going ships must sail about a hundred miles up the Mississippi River. The city limits of New Orleans also include an area south of the river and a thinly populated, swampy section to the east of the main part of the city.

Part of the land on which the city was built lies below sea level. The land is so low that New Orleans has little natural drainage. A heavy rainstorm could flood the city. To prevent such a disaster, New Orleans has a large pumping system to keep it dry. The system's pumps can draw off 19 billion gallons of water a day.

Part of New Orleans is below the normal levels of Lake Pontchartrain and the Mississippi. The river and the lake are both walled in by levees to prevent floods (see LEVEE). When the Mississippi is high, a person standing at the base of a levee sees an unusual sight—

The French Quarter is the heart of old New Orleans. Parts of it look as they did more than 150 years ago. The lacy grillwork that decorates many French Quarter buildings is a New Orleans trademark. Famed St. Louis Cathedral, *below,* built in 1794, faces Jackson Square.

State of Louisiana

--------- **FACTS IN BRIEF** ---------

Population: 593,471; metropolitan area, 1,045,809.

Area: land, 199.4 sq. mi.; water, 164.1 sq. mi.; total, 363.5 sq. mi.; metropolitan area, 1,118 sq. mi.

Altitude: 5 feet above sea level.

Climate: For the monthly weather in New Orleans, see LOUISIANA (Climate).

Government: Mayor-council (four-year terms).

Founded: 1718. Incorporated as a city, 1805.

Seal: An Indian brave and maiden stand on each side of a shield. A figure lying on the shield salutes the sun as it rises above mountains and sea. Twenty-five stars grouped in a circle are above the shield. Below it is an alligator.

Flag: The white field has a red stripe at the top and a blue stripe at the bottom. The stripes symbolize democracy. Three fleurs-de-lis are on the white field. See FLAG (color picture: Flags of Cities of the U.S.).

ships steaming on the river above his head.

Canal Street. The business district of New Orleans centers on 171-foot-wide Canal Street, the city's main street. This broad thoroughfare runs northward from the river. A visitor walking north along Canal Street from the Mississippi passes the city's largest department stores and goes within a few steps of several of its finest hotels. To his right is the French Quarter. To his left are the buildings of the business and financial district.

Farther north, Canal Street changes to a tree-shaded residential street that ends in an area called the *cemeteries*. Some of the city's oldest and most historic graveyards are in this area. One of them, Metairie Cemetery, was once a race track. Here, as in most other New Orleans cemeteries, the tombs rest above the ground. This is because water lies just a few feet below the surface. For the same reason, few homes have basements.

The French Quarter is the oldest and most famous section of New Orleans. It is also known as the *Vieux Carré* (pronounced *vyuh car RAY*), or Old Square. The area looks much as it did in the 1700's and 1800's. Buildings crowd the edges of the narrow sidewalks, which New Orleanians call *banquettes*. A person strolling through the French Quarter passes under graceful balconies built of iron grillwork. From the street, visitors can look through shady passageways into colorful patios. These patios are a feature of many French Quarter houses. Their fountains, flowers, and leafy banana trees provide cool relief from the hot New Orleans sun.

The Garden District was settled by Americans who came to New Orleans after the Louisiana Purchase in 1803. Some of the city's finest homes stand in this tree- and flower-filled area, which borders on St. Charles Avenue. Many of the homes have fragrant gardens shaded by magnolias, live oaks, and other graceful trees. Homes in the garden district are known for their wide porches and spacious rooms. They are built in a combination of Greek and other classic styles.

Uptown New Orleans is a pleasant residential area. It centers around Audubon Park and the campuses of Tulane and Loyola universities. The park covers about 315 acres between the Mississippi River and St. Charles Avenue. It includes a zoo, a golf course, and an outdoor swimming pool. The park also has a man-made hill that was built to show the children of this flat city what a hill looks like. Tulane and Loyola face the St. Charles Avenue entrance to the park.

City Park and the Lakefront, two of the city's chief playgrounds, lie in the northern section of New Orleans. City Park covers 1,500 acres. It includes three golf courses, a swimming pool, the Isaac Delgado Museum of Art, and the 27,000-seat Municipal Stadium.

The lakefront area is just north of City Park. Scenic Lakeshore Drive follows the shoreline of Lake Pontchartrain. Motorists on the drive see the cool lake on one side and a luxurious residential area on the other. Pontchartrain Amusement Park is at the eastern end of Lakeshore Drive. The New Orleans campus of Louisiana State University lies just south of the park.

Other Sections. The area of New Orleans on the south side of the river is called *Algiers*, or New Orleans West. But no one knows where the name Algiers came from. The Greater New Orleans Bridge connects Algiers to the rest of the city. The chief suburbs of New

Orleans lie in neighboring Jefferson Parish (county). Main suburbs include the towns of Kenner, Metairie, Westwego, Marrero, Harvey, and Gretna.

The People

The *Creoles* (descendants of the early Spanish and French settlers) probably contribute the most toward making New Orleans unusual among American cities. Most Creoles speak French at least as well as they speak English. Today, the Creoles make up only a small part of the population. They take part in the general life of the city, but follow many customs of their ancestors. Other New Orleanians have also adopted these customs. For example, All Saints' Day (November 1) is a city-wide holiday that honors the dead. The people follow the Creole custom of going to the cemeteries in family groups. The cemeteries take on a holiday air as families stroll around the flower-laden tombs.

Negroes make up about 45 per cent of the population. Jazz still plays an important part in the life of New Orleans' Negroes, just as it has since the 1890's. Negro jazz bands still play for Negro funeral processions to and from the cemeteries. See JAZZ.

Work of the People

Foreign Trade. Almost two billion dollars worth of imports and exports flows through the Port of New Orleans every year. Ships from all parts of the world dock at the wharves along both banks of the Mississippi and the Innerharbor Navigation Canal. This canal connects the river with Lake Pontchartrain. New Orleans' imports include bananas, coffee, sugar, and petroleum. Exports include cotton, salt, sulfur, and tobacco.

The city has two important organizations devoted to international trade. The International Trade Mart gives businessmen from many lands a place to buy and sell their goods. International House serves as a clearinghouse for information on world trade. It is also a club-like meeting place for persons interested in improving trade relations.

Industry and Business. Nearby sources of petroleum, natural gas, sulfur, salt, lime, and wood provide raw materials for the factories of New Orleans. The city also has two of the most important needs of modern industry —cheap electricity and a large supply of fresh water. Some of the largest industries in the area produce aluminum, chemicals, building materials, rocket boosters, and ships and boats. The city and its suburbs have more than 900 manufacturing and processing plants that employ about 45,000 persons.

Transportation and Communication

The Union Passenger Terminal in downtown New Orleans serves seven railroads. Moisant International Airport, west of the city, is the largest of the region's three airports. New Orleans Airport on Lake Pontchartrain serves private and business planes.

In addition to the Greater New Orleans Bridge, two other bridges serve motorists entering or leaving the city. The Huey P. Long Bridge crosses the river nine miles west of New Orleans. The 24-mile-long Lake Pontchartrain Causeway, the world's longest bridge,

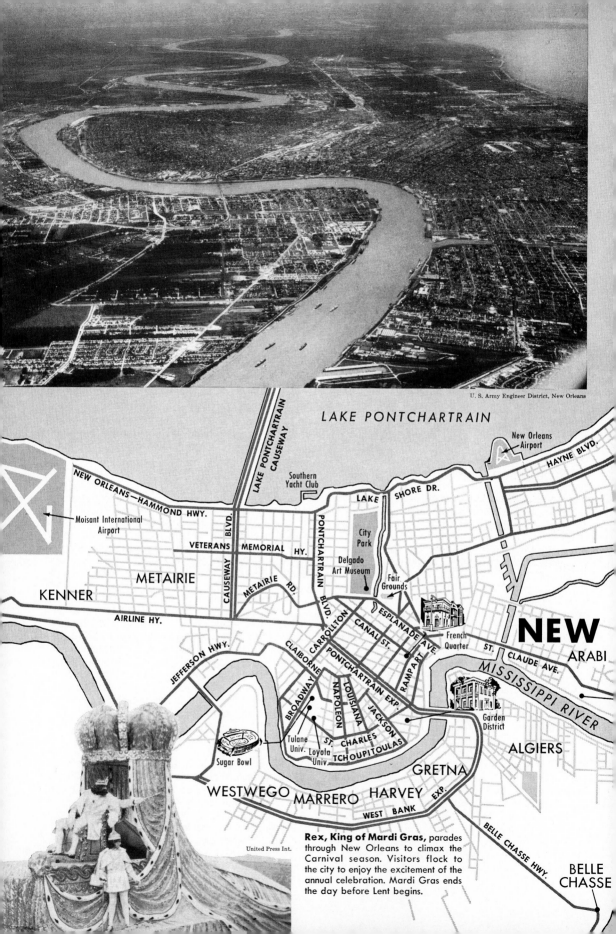

LAKE PONTCHARTRAIN

New Orleans
Airport

HAYNE BLVD.

NEW ORLEANS—HAMMOND HWY.

LAKE PONTCHARTRAIN CAUSEWAY

Southern
Yacht Club

LAKE SHORE DR.

Moisant International
Airport

VETERANS MEMORIAL HY.

CAUSEWAY BLVD.

PONTCHARTRAIN BLVD.

City
Park

Delgado
Art Museum

Fair
Grounds

METAIRIE

METAIRIE RD.

ESPLANADE AVE.

French
Quarter

NEW

ST. CLAUDE AVE.

ARABI

KENNER

AIRLINE HY.

CARROLLTON

CANAL ST.

RAMPART

MISSISSIPPI RIVER

JEFFERSON HWY.

CLAIBORNE

PONTCHARTRAIN EXP.

NAPOLEON

LOUISIANA

JACKSON

Garden
District

BROADWAY

ST. CHARLES

TCHOUPITOULAS

ALGIERS

Sugar Bowl

Tulane
Univ.

Loyola
Univ.

GRETNA

WESTWEGO

MARRERO

HARVEY

HARVEY EXP.

WEST BANK

BELLE CHASSE HWY.

BELLE
CHASSE

Rex, King of Mardi Gras, parades
through New Orleans to climax the
Carnival season. Visitors flock to
the city to enjoy the excitement of the
annual celebration. Mardi Gras ends
the day before Lent begins.

New Orleans, the Crescent City, originally lay within a broad, crescent-shaped curve of the Mississippi River. Today, the city occupies land on both banks of the river and has spread northward to the shore of Lake Pontchartrain, *upper right.*

N

W   E

S

1 inch = 0.37 Statute Miles

0   1   2   3   4

MILES

FORT PIKE

LAKE ST. CATHERINE

INTERSTATE EXPRESSWAY 10

U.S. 11

LITTLE WOODS

BLIND LAGOON

FORT MACOMB

(U.S. 90)

CHEF MENTEUR HY.

MICHOUD

CHEF MENTEUR HY.

INTRACOASTAL WATERWAY

LAKE BORGNE

GULF

BIENVENUE

BAYOU

TIDEWATER

CHANNEL

ORLEANS

CHALMETTE

Chalmette National Historic Park

ST. BERNARD HWY.

H. Armstrong Roberts

A Modern Civic Center covers 14 acres near the downtown business district of New Orleans. Built during the late 1950's, the center includes City Hall, *above,* and other government buildings.

The Port of New Orleans is one of the world's busiest. A ship docks at one of the city's wharves on the average of every 90 minutes. Longshoremen load or unload cotton, coffee, bananas, and other cargo.

Bureau of New Orleans News

Metropolitan New Orleans is shown in light gray. The city is in black. The dotted line encloses the area on the large map.

ST. TAMMANY PARISH

LAKE PONTCHARTRAIN

ORLEANS PARISH

JEFFERSON PARISH

ST. BERNARD PARISH

provides a shortcut across the lake.

New Orleans has two daily newspapers, both under the same ownership. The morning *Times-Picayune* was founded in 1837. The newspaper originally sold for a picayune, a small coin. The city's afternoon paper is the *States-Item*. Three commercial television stations and an educational TV station broadcast from New Orleans. The city has fourteen radio stations.

Cultural Life

The New Orleans Opera House Association produces six operas every year at the Municipal Auditorium. This group brings some of the world's leading singers to New Orleans. The New Orleans Symphony Orchestra also performs in the auditorium. Top jazz musicians play in French Quarter night clubs and in concerts presented by the New Orleans Jazz Club. The club also sponsors a jazz museum in the French Quarter.

New Orleans is the home of Tulane University, Loyola University, Dillard University, Xavier University, St. Mary's Dominican College, Notre Dame Seminary, New Orleans Baptist Theological Seminary, and a branch of Louisiana State University.

New Orleans has more than 225 public, private, and parochial elementary and high schools. About 93,000 students attend the public schools, and about 53,000 go to the private and parochial schools.

The Louisiana State Museum exhibits items related to Louisiana history. Its collection is housed in the Cabildo and other French Quarter buildings. The Tulane University Institute of Middle American Research owns a world-famous collection of relics of the ancient Maya Indians.

Visiting New Orleans

Annual Events make New Orleans interesting to visit almost any time of the year.

Mardi Gras is a gay holiday that reaches a climax on Shrove Tuesday, the day before Lent begins. Street parades begin 10 days earlier. Masquerade balls are an exciting feature of the New Orleans Carnival season. See MARDI GRAS.

Spring Fiesta, usually held shortly after Easter, celebrates the city's historic past. The fiesta includes guided tours of famous old homes.

Sugar Bowl Football Game is held on New Year's Day. The Sugar Bowl festivities also include a week of tennis, basketball, and other sports.

Other Events in and around New Orleans are listed in the LOUISIANA article, under Annual Events.

Things to See and Do. Tourists who visit New Orleans usually spend most of their time sight-seeing in the French Quarter. Jackson Square, the heart of the old French Quarter, is one of the chief attractions. The tall, gray spires of the St. Louis Cathedral rise on one side of the square. This church was built in 1794. Flanking the cathedral are the Cabildo, the old Spanish courthouse; and the Presbytere, another old Spanish building. The beautiful, block-long Pontalba Buildings stand along two sides of the square. Completed in 1850, they are believed to be the oldest apartment buildings in the United States. Other French Quarter sights include the antique shops along Royal Street and the old French

Market near the river. Professional football fans can watch the games of the New Orleans Saints of the National Football League.

New Orleans is an ideal place for those who enjoy fine dining. The city has won fame throughout the world for its Creole cooking, a blend of French and Spanish cuisines. Seafood is a specialty, and almost every restaurant serves fresh oysters, shrimps, crabs, pompano, and other salt-water delicacies.

History

French and Spanish Rule. New Orleans was founded in 1718 by Jean Baptiste le Moyne, Sieur de Bienville, the governor of the French colony of Louisiana. He chose the site on a curve in the Mississippi River because it was protected from hurricanes and tidal waves. Bienville sent some men to the site to build huts and storage houses. In 1721, Adrien de Pauger, a French engineer, arrived. He laid out the plans for what is now the French Quarter. In 1722, Bienville made the town the capital of the colony. He named it *La Nouvelle Orléans* (New Orleans) after the regent of France, Philippe, Duc d'Orléans.

New Orleans came under Spanish rule in 1762 when France ceded Louisiana to Spain. The people of the city did not learn about the transfer until 1764 because of slow communications. The Spaniards did not bother to take over the colony until 1766, when the first Spanish official arrived. The French settlers hated the Spaniards. In 1768, they ousted the Spanish governor. The colony remained free of Spanish rule until 1769, when Spanish soldiers arrived to put down the revolution. A Spanish governor again ruled New Orleans.

A fire swept the city in 1788, destroying more than 800 buildings. Most of them were replaced by Spanish-style structures. This is why most buildings in the French Quarter look more Spanish than French.

Under Three Flags. Spain returned Louisiana to France in 1800. A French official arrived in New Orleans in March, 1803, to govern the city. The next month, the United States purchased Louisiana from France. The French official wondered whether to take over the city for the short period before the Americans arrived. Finally, on November 30, the Spanish flag was hauled down and the French flag was raised. On December 20, American troops hoisted the United States flag over the city. Thus, New Orleans was under three flags in less than a month. See JEFFERSON, THOMAS (color picture: The Louisiana Purchase).

New Orleans was incorporated as a city on Feb. 17, 1805. When Louisiana joined the Union in 1812, New Orleans became the first capital of the state.

During the War of 1812, British troops tried to capture the city. General Andrew Jackson stopped the British in the Battle of New Orleans at nearby Chalmette on Jan. 8, 1815. See WAR OF 1812 (The Needless Battle); NATIONAL PARK (Chalmette).

Before the Civil War. In the early 1800's, New Orleans became one of the leading cities in the United States. Its population rose from about 10,000 persons in 1805 to 46,000 in 1830. By 1850, New Orleans was the fifth largest city in the country, with a population of more than 116,000.

Trade was the city's lifeblood. Colorful paddle-wheel steamboats and clumsy barges brought the products of mid-America down the Mississippi to New Orleans. There, sailing ships took on cargoes and carried them across the oceans. New Orleans' reputation for gaiety and culture won the exciting city the nickname of the *Paris of America*.

New Orleans also had a reputation for disease. Malaria, cholera, and yellow fever frequently swept the great port. The worst yellow fever epidemic occurred in the summer of 1853, when about 7,200 persons died of the disease.

Union Occupation. Union troops captured New Orleans a little more than a year after the Civil War began. Union ships commanded by Admiral David G. Farragut forced New Orleans to surrender on April 28, 1862. General Benjamin F. Butler commanded the troops that occupied the city. Butler's stern military rule of New Orleans earned him the nickname *Beast*. See BUTLER, BENJAMIN F.

After the Civil War, New Orleans faced many of the problems that affected other Southern cities during the Reconstruction period. Federal troops occupied New Orleans until 1877. See LOUISIANA (The Civil War and Reconstruction).

The city began to boom again after 1877. In 1879, James B. Eads completed construction of a series of jetties designed to prevent sand and silt from blocking the mouth of the Mississippi (see JETTY). The jetties made it possible for large ocean-going steamships to dock at New Orleans. In 1884 and 1885, New Orleans played host to the Cotton Centennial Exposition, a world's fair that was held on the site of present-day Audubon Park.

The 1900's. The Huey P. Long Bridge opened in 1935. It was the first span to cross the river in the New Orleans area. That same year, the completion of the Bonnet Carré Spillway almost eliminated the danger of floods from the Mississippi. This channel connects the river to Lake Pontchartrain west of the city. When floods threaten, water from the river is diverted to the lake through the spillway.

In 1946, New Orleans entered a period of spectacular growth and change. Led by Mayor deLesseps S. Morrison, New Orleanians began to change the face of their city and make it an important industrial center. The first major step was a $55 million project to eliminate 144 railroad crossings and consolidate five railroad stations into one. This project was completed with the opening of the Union Passenger Terminal in 1954. Other projects included the Civic Center, begun in 1955; the Greater New Orleans Bridge, completed in 1958; and the Pontchartrain Expressway, which began serving motorists in 1960. From 1946 to 1960, more than a billion dollars was spent to build or expand industrial plants in the New Orleans area.

In the 1960's, New Orleans started several large development projects. For example, in 1960, pumps began to draw water from New Orleans East, 50 square miles of swampy land northeast of the city. Many buildings have been built there.   ROBERT O. ZELENY

Critically reviewed by THOMAS KURTZ GRIFFIN

Related Articles in WORLD BOOK include:

Outline

Questions

Why is New Orleans called the *Crescent City?*
Why is water a problem in New Orleans?
Why was a hill built in Audubon Park?
What two organizations in New Orleans help promote world trade?
When does Mardi Gras take place?
Who led the Americans in the Battle of New Orleans?
What kind of music is New Orleans famous for?
How do New Orleanians celebrate All Saints' Day?
What is *Creole cooking?* a *picayune?* a *banquette?*

NEW ORLEANS, BATTLE OF. See JACKSON, ANDREW (Glory at New Orleans); LAFFITE, JEAN; WAR OF 1812.

NEW ORLEANS BAPTIST THEOLOGICAL SEMINARY. See UNIVERSITIES AND COLLEGES (table).

NEW PROVIDENCE. See BAHAMAS.

NEW RIVER. See KANAWHA RIVER.

NEW ROCHELLE, N.Y. (pop. 75,385; alt. 70 ft.), a residential suburb of New York City, is one of the richest cities, in wealth per person, in the United States. It was named for La Rochelle, France, the home of the early Huguenot settlers. New Rochelle lies on Long Island Sound, 15 miles northeast of the heart of Manhattan (see NEW YORK [political map]). It is noted for its bathing beaches, golf clubs, parks, and homes. New Rochelle has excellent transportation connections with New York City. It has the College of New Rochelle for women, and Iona College for men. New Rochelle was founded in 1688, became a village in 1857, and a city in 1899. The city has a council-manager government.   WILLIAM E. YOUNG

NEW ROCHELLE, COLLEGE OF. See UNIVERSITIES AND COLLEGES (table).

NEW SALEM. See ILLINOIS (Places to Visit); LINCOLN, ABRAHAM (New Salem Years).

NEW SCHOOL FOR SOCIAL RESEARCH. See UNIVERSITIES AND COLLEGES (table).

NEW SOUTH WALES is the oldest and most heavily populated state in Australia. It lies in the east, facing the Pacific Ocean. New South Wales has high mountains and wide, rolling plains. Sydney is the capital and largest city (see AUSTRALIA [political map]).

The Land. New South Wales covers 309,433 square miles. Its coastline is 700 miles long. The New South

NEW SOUTH WALES

Wales coast rises sharply from the Pacific Ocean in rugged, broken cliffs. These form rocky headlands that shelter several good harbors. Beyond the coast, a narrow strip of fertile land borders the mountains of the Great Dividing Range. The highest point in the range is 7,316-foot Mount Kosciusko. West of the mountains, the land broadens into a rolling plateau that slopes to grass-covered plains.

The state has a mild climate. Temperatures average about 50° F. in July and 75° F. in January. Average annual rainfall ranges from 100 inches in the eastern highlands to less than 10 inches on the western plains.

The People. Most of the 4,382,404 people of New South Wales are of British descent, and more than half of them live in or near Sydney. The population includes about 14,000 aborigines.

Economy. Most of the land suitable for agriculture lies along the coast and in the tablelands west of the mountains. Irrigation canals supply water for many areas. The chief industry in New South Wales centers around its grazing lands. About half of Australia's sheep graze on pastures there. Stock raising, dairy farming, and crop farming account for about a fourth of the state's total annual production of goods. Farmers grow wheat on over half of the farmland in New South Wales. Other products include bananas, citrus fruits, corn, hay, oats, potatoes, sugar, and tobacco.

More than half of Australia's mineral output comes from New South Wales. Coal production averages about 17 million tons a year. The first gold discovery in Australia was made in New South Wales in 1851. Other minerals include copper, iron, lead, magnesite, opals, silver, tin, and zinc.

Most manufacturing is closely connected with stock raising and mining. The state has over 23,000 factories, including iron and steel foundries and woolen mills.

New South Wales has more than 6,000 miles of railroads, all state owned. It has about 130,000 miles of roads. Chief exports include butter, coal, drugs, flour, fruits, hides and skins, iron and steel, lead, machinery, meats, textiles, wheat, and wool. The chief imports are manufactured goods.

Education and Religion. Children under 15 are required to attend school. About 590,000 students attend state public schools and 192,000 attend nongovernmental schools. The University of Sydney has over 16,000 students. The state also has the University of New South Wales, the University of New England, the University of Newcastle, and Macquarie University.

The Church of England has the largest number of members. There is no official state church.

Government. The chief executive of New South Wales is a governor appointed by the British monarch. The actual head is the premier, assisted by a Cabinet made up of the heads of the government departments. The state's Parliament consists of a 60-member Legislative Council, and a 94-member Legislative Assembly.

History. Captain James Cook discovered and named the area in 1770 (see COOK, JAMES). Captain Arthur Phillip landed with convict settlers at Port Jackson in New South Wales in 1788 to found the first settlement in Australia. At that time, New South Wales covered the eastern part of Australia and included land that now makes up the states of Queensland and Victoria and part of the state of South Australia. Free settlers began to arrive in the early 1800's, and convict immigration ended in 1852. The colonists drew up a constitution in 1853. The colony became self-governing in 1856.

In 1901, New South Wales became one of the six states of the Commonwealth of Australia. The state transferred 911 square miles of territory to the federal government in 1911. This area became the Australian Capital Territory, surrounding Canberra. C. M. H. CLARK

See also CANBERRA; LORD HOWE ISLAND; MURRAY RIVER; MURRUMBIDGEE RIVER; SYDNEY.

NEW SWEDEN was the only Swedish colony in America. It extended along the Delaware River from the mouth of Delaware Bay to about what is now Trenton, N.J. Swedish settlers founded the colony in 1638, and built Fort Christina at what is now Wilmington, Del. The population of New Sweden never reached 200. The Dutch in New Netherland to the north tolerated Swedish competition in the fur trade as long as Sweden and The Netherlands were allies. In 1655, the Dutch took over New Sweden by a threat of force. See also DELAWARE (History). MARSHALL SMELSER

New South Wales lies in southeastern Australia. State agricultural societies stage annual shows where livestock are judged. The grand parade at Sydney's Royal Easter Show, *right,* displays some of the country's finest livestock.

NEW TESTAMENT is part of the Christian Bible. It is a record of the new *testament*, or promises made by God to man, as shown in the teachings and experiences of Christ and His followers.

Contents of the New Testament

Books. The New Testament consists of 27 books, and is about a third as long as the Old Testament. The first four books are the Gospels according to Matthew, Mark, Luke, and John. They represent a collection of the acts and words of Jesus. The authors wrote them for teaching purposes. The Acts of the Apostles, a continuation of the Gospel of Luke, is a volume of history. Twenty-one documents called *epistles*, or letters, follow. St. Paul is supposed to have written 13 of these; 7 books are the Epistles of Peter, James, John, and Jude; and the Epistle to the Hebrews is anonymous. The New Testament ends with the Book of Revelation, or Apocalypse.

The 27 books make up the *canon* of the New Testament, or all the books that Christians consider to be authoritative Scripture. During early Christian times, there were many books of religious writings, some of doubtful value and authority. These included fanciful gospels and acts designed to fill in details of the life of Jesus and His Apostles. By about the A.D. 300's, church scholars regarded the present books of the New Testament as authoritative Scripture. They considered other writings as *apocryphal*, or of doubtful authorship (see APOCRYPHA). Later, church councils ratified the decisions regarding the canon.

Writing the New Testament. The original language of the New Testament is the common vernacular Greek that was widely used at the time of Jesus. The Greek in the New Testament includes some Hebrew phrases and idioms, because all the New Testament writers except Luke were Jews. The authors of the original books of the New Testament wrote them on papyrus scrolls, none of which now exist. Scholars have used early Latin, Syriac, and Coptic translations of the Greek New Testament to help reconstruct the original text. They have also studied quotations of the New Testament. Several appear in the writings of the church fathers as early as about A.D. 150.

Dating the New Testament

It is impossible to give definite dates for all the events of the New Testament, just as it is impossible to give definite dates for many other incidents in ancient history. But scholars have been able to set approximate dates by connecting Bible narratives with facts known from history.

The Birth of Jesus. The Christian Era is represented by the Latin words *anno Domini*, which mean *in the year of our Lord*. The abbreviation A.D. is written before the year, as A.D. 1000. A mistake occurred when our calendar was set up. Early Christians dated the Christian Era about six years after the actual birth of Jesus.

Scholars have determined this in the following way: In Matthew 2 we learn that Jesus was born during the rule of Herod the Great. Herod died in 4 B.C. Some scholars believe that the birth of Jesus probably occurred two or three years before, or about 6 B.C.

Another attempt to find evidence for the date of Jesus' birth concerns the star of Bethlehem. Johannes Kepler, a great German astronomer, said that two planets seemed to come together in the skies over Bethlehem in 7 B.C. They must have looked like one bright star.

More evidence comes from Luke's mention of a decree of the Emperor Augustus (Luke 2: 1-3). The emperor, according to Luke, ordered that "all the world should be enrolled." Scholars have found documents that seem to show that a *census* (count of the people) took place in 8 B.C. Some persons believe it may have been shortly after this time that Joseph and Mary went to Bethlehem.

Nothing in the Bible tells us the day or month when Jesus was born. But the 25th of December comes at about the time of year called the winter *solstice* (see SOLSTICE). At this time, the days stop growing shorter as winter turns toward spring. The date serves as a symbol of the new life that came to the world when Jesus was born.

The Public Ministry of Jesus. The Gospel of Luke tells us that Jesus was about 30 years old when He began to preach (Luke 3: 23). The length of His public ministry is determined by the number of *Passovers* (annual Jewish Festivals) that He celebrated. The *Synoptic Gospels* (Matthew, Mark, and Luke) refer to only one Passover during Jesus' adult life, the one at the time of His Crucifixion. The Gospel of John mentions at least three Passovers, and the feast mentioned in John 5: 1 may have been a fourth Passover. The mention of these Passovers has led many scholars to believe Jesus' public ministry lasted for about two and a half or three and a half years.

The Crucifixion. All the Gospels imply that Jesus was crucified on a Friday. All except John tell us that this Friday was the day after Passover. In John, the Crucifixion occurs on the day of the Passover. Many scholars believe that the Crucifixion took place on either April

A Scene from the New Testament, *The Raising of Lazarus* by Peter Paul Rubens, shows Jesus calling Lazarus from his grave.

7, A.D. 30, or April 3, A.D. 33. The Jewish year differs in length from the calendar year now in general use. This difference makes it necessary to go through a complicated process of figuring to determine when Jesus died according to the calendar of the Christian Era.

The Conversion of Paul followed several incidents described in the opening chapters of Acts. These were the holiday of Pentecost, the organization of the church, and the martyrdom of Stephen. Paul was probably converted between A.D. 34 and 37.

Paul's Missionary Journeys. Paul and Barnabas brought food to the Christians at Jerusalem because of an expected famine, according to Acts 11: 27-30. Non-Biblical records show that a famine did occur in Judea about A.D. 46, during the rule of Claudius (41-54). Therefore, the visit of Paul and Barnabas must have taken place about A.D. 45 or 46. Paul made his first missionary journey soon afterward, and thus it must have occurred in A.D. 47 or 48. Two other missionary journeys followed. Then Paul was arrested in Jerusalem and put into prison by Felix, the Roman governor of Judea. Festus became governor two years later, and he allowed Paul to plead his cause before Herod Agrippa II. These references to names recorded in history make it possible for scholars to fix fairly precise dates for several events in Paul's life. An interesting inscription found at Delphi dates the governorship of Gallio (Acts 18: 12) in A.D. 50 or 51. Paul was probably in prison at Caesarea for two years, beginning about A.D. 58. From there, he was taken to Rome, where he remained in custody for two more years. Many scholars believe he wrote the Epistles to the Philippians, the Colossians, Philemon, and the Ephesians during this time.

Some scholars think that Paul may have made a missionary journey to Spain in about A.D. 64, and that he was again put in prison in Rome about the year 66. Tradition says that he died a martyr during the rule of Nero (54-68). We know that this emperor put a number of Christians to death after the burning of Rome in order to turn people's suspicions away from himself.

Critical Studies of the New Testament

The original manuscripts of the books of the New Testament, as they were written by the Apostles, have all been lost. Only copies remain, and none of them dates from the time when the Apostles were still living. Thousands of later copies exist. Many variations of wording occur in the old copies, although the variations in the Greek manuscripts rarely affect the meaning of the passage. But these differences have made it difficult to determine the original wording of some passages.

Efforts to determine original wordings through careful study and comparison of old manuscripts have sometimes met with opposition. But most churchmen now accept such studies as necessary to determine the purpose and the original meaning of the Biblical writings. A study of this kind is called *criticism*. Biblical criticism is divided into two classes, lower criticism and higher criticism.

Lower, or Textual, Criticism is concerned with the recovery of the author's own wording, before copies were made. The process of making copies gave rise to errors, most of which were accidental. Lower criticism

requires a great deal of research and comparison, and scholars have spent years of work on it. They have put together all the variations of wording for the passages of the New Testament, and for the wording of the Old Testament as well.

Higher Criticism covers a broader field than textual criticism. The higher critic learns what he can of the Bible by comparing one passage with another. He also compares statements in the Bible with literary and historical works of the period. He studies the literary form of the Biblical writings. By such means he can draw conclusions concerning the nature and authenticity of the sacred record. Higher critics have not always agreed in their findings. The more extreme higher critics have made such prejudiced interpretations that the general movement has at times met with hostile charges. Sometimes these charges are well-founded and sometimes not. Most persons believe that many good results have come from a wise and unprejudiced study of the Bible. The advanced schools of religious studies teach the New Testament in the light of all that modern learning and scholarship have achieved.   BRUCE M. METZGER

Related Articles. See BIBLE with its list of Related Articles. See also the following articles on Books of the New Testament:

Acts of the Apostles	Jude
Colossians, Epistle to the	Peter, Epistles of
Corinthians, Epistles to the	Philemon, Epistle to
Ephesians, Epistle to the	Philippians, Epistle to the
Galatians, Epistle to the	Revelation
Gospels (Matthew, Mark, Luke, John)	Romans, Epistle to the
	Thessalonians, Epistles to the
Hebrews, Epistle to the	
James, Saint (Epistles of)	Timothy
John, Epistles of	Titus

NEW THOUGHT is a philosophical idea that the mind is superior to all material conditions and circumstances. The idea was advanced in the 1800's by Ralph Waldo Emerson, American author and lecturer. It was somewhat revived in the early 1900's.

NEW WESTMINSTER, British Columbia (pop. 38,013; alt. 34 ft.), was the first Canadian city on the Pacific Coast. It became the first incorporated city in British Columbia in 1860. The second largest industrial center in the province, the city lies 12 miles southeast of Vancouver on the Fraser River. For location, see BRITISH COLUMBIA (political map).

New Westminster's lumber industry produces about a billion board feet of lumber a year. The city serves as headquarters of the International Salmon Fishing Commission and the Fraser River salmon fishing fleet. New Westminster is a distributing and canning center for Fraser Valley farm produce. Its port serves oceangoing ships.

Simon Fraser, a British fur trader and explorer, discovered the site in 1808. The city served as the capital of the colony of British Columbia from 1859 to 1868. British Royal Engineers named the city Queensborough in 1858. Queen Victoria changed the name to New Westminster in 1859, after the town of Westminster, England. Fire destroyed the main business district in 1898, but it was rebuilt. New Westminster has a mayor-council government.   RODERICK HAIG-BROWN

NEW WORLD is another name for the Western Hemisphere, which includes the continents of North America and South America. See OLD WORLD; HEMISPHERE.

Buon Capo d'Anno (Italy)
Bonne Année (France)
С новым годом (Russia)
Gott Nytt År (Sweden)
Hauoli Makahiki Hou (Hawaii)
शुभ नव वर्ष (India)
Godt Nytt År (Norway)
Gelukkig Nieuwjaar (Netherlands)
(Saudi Arabia)
Εὐτυχὲς τό Νέον Ἔτος (Greece)
(Japan)
Happy New Year
Szczęśliwego Nowego Roku (Poland)
Maligayang Bagong Taon (Philippines)
Feliz Año Nuevo (Spain)
Shana Tova (Israel)
Gutes Neues Jahr (Germany)
Aith-bhliain fé mhaise dhuit (Ireland)

On New Year's Eve, thousands of people jam Times Square in New York City to welcome the new year, *right*. Around the world, new year greetings are sounded in almost every language, *above*.

United Press Int.

NEW YEAR'S DAY is the first day of the calendar year. It is celebrated as a holiday in almost every country. Generally, church services are held, with parties before or after them. New Year's Day is a time of gaiety in the Orient. Homes are decorated, and friends give one another gifts. In Europe, the day is celebrated by family parties, the giving of gifts, and visiting.

In the United States, people attend church, go to the theater, or to various places of entertainment. Parties are held on New Year's Eve to "watch the old year out." At one time, formal calls were made on New Year's Day, but this is no longer a general custom. Many persons hold "open house" on the afternoon or evening of New Year's Day. Their friends come to call, and refreshments are sometimes served.

Early Customs. Even the earliest of the ancient nations had customs that celebrated New Year's Day. The Chinese, Egyptian, Jewish, Roman, and Mohammedan years all began at different times. But the first day of each year was marked with elaborate ceremonies. Thousands of years ago, the Egyptians celebrated the new year about the middle of June. This was the time when the Nile River usually overflowed its banks.

In ancient Rome, the first day of the year was given over to honoring Janus, the god of gates and doors and of beginnings and endings. The month of January was named after this god. Janus had two faces, and looked both ahead and backward. On the first day of the year the Roman people looked back to what had happened during the past year and thought of what the coming year might bring. Romans gave one another presents on New Year's Day. Many persons brought gifts to the Roman emperor and wished him good fortune. At first, the gifts were simply branches of bay and palm trees, but later more expensive presents were given. Roman senators received flowers and fruits and sometimes beautiful materials from persons who wanted favors. Roman merchants carried this custom of giving gifts as far east as Persia (now Iran). There the ancient Iranians, or Persians, followed the custom of giving eggs to their friends. Since an egg hatches into life, this custom meant much the same thing as "turning over a new leaf."

When the Romans invaded England, they found that the Druid priests celebrated New Year's Day on March 10. The priests cut off branches of mistletoe, which grew on their sacred oak trees, and gave them to the people

for charms. The early English took over many of the Roman New Year's Day customs. Later, English people followed the custom of cleaning the chimneys on New Year's Day. This was supposed to bring good luck to the household during the coming year. Today we say "cleaning the slate," instead of "cleaning the chimney." This means making resolutions to correct faults and bad habits, and resolving to make the new year better.

The Roman custom of giving gifts to the emperor was revived by the English in the 1200's. Jewelry, gloves, and other presents were brought to the English king or queen. Queen Elizabeth I (1533-1603) built up a collection of hundreds of pairs of richly embroidered and bejeweled gloves through this custom. By another English custom, English husbands gave their wives money on New Year's Day to buy enough pins for the whole year. This custom disappeared in the 1800's, when machines were developed to manufacture pins. But the term "pin money" still refers to small amounts of spending money.

The Date of New Year's. New Year's Day became a holy day in the Christian church in A.D. 487, when it was declared the Feast of the Circumcision. At first, parties were not allowed on this day because the pagans had followed that custom. This was gradually changed and celebrations could again be held. The opening of the new year has been celebrated on many different days in different countries. These days of celebration have included Christmas Day, Easter Day, March 1, and March 25, which is the time of the Feast of Annunciation.

January 1 became generally recognized as New Year's Day in the 1500's, when the Gregorian calendar was introduced. The Julian calendar places the first day of the year 13 days later, on January 14. The Jewish New Year's Day, a feast day, is celebrated about the time of the autumnal equinox, in late September. The Chinese used the lunar calendar for about 4,000 years. This is based on the waxing and waning of the moon. Today the Chinese New Year's Day falls between January 21 and February 19 each year.

The new year begins on March 21 in Iran. The date of the Hindu's new year depends upon his religion. The Hindus belong to many different religious groups, and each group considers a different date as the beginning of the year.   ELIZABETH HOUGH SECHRIST

See also JANUARY.

237

NEW YORK

The Empire State

NEW YORK has richly earned its nickname—the *Empire State*. It is the greatest manufacturing state in the United States. It also far outranks all other states in foreign trade, and in wholesale and retail trade. It is the national center of transportation and communication, and of banking and finance. New York ranked first in population for more than a hundred years, until California gained first place during the early 1960's.

Much of the state's greatness lies in huge, exciting New York City. New York City is the largest city in the United States and the second largest in the world. It is the nation's leading center of business and industry. Its many theaters, museums, and musical organizations make it the cultural center of the Western Hemisphere. New York City is the world's biggest and busiest seaport. In its harbor stands the Statue of Liberty, long a symbol of freedom to people in all parts of the world. As the headquarters of the United Nations, New York City can be called the "capital of the world."

New York's factories turn out an incredible variety of products. The state makes about a third of all the clothes worn by Americans. New York City does almost a fourth of the nation's printing, and publishes about three-fourths of its books. New York makes more electrical machinery than any other state. Only California processes more food than New York. Only New Jersey and Texas manufacture more chemical products.

In addition to New York City, the state has five other cities with populations over 100,000. One of them is Albany, the state capital. These cities also are important manufacturing and trading centers.

But New York is not just a state of business and industry. It is also a land of fertile river valleys, forested hills, tall mountains, and sparkling lakes. New York's many scenic attractions draw countless vacationers. Niagara Falls, the state's most magnificent natural wonder, attracts millions of visitors every year.

New York was one of the original 13 states. Henry Hudson, an English explorer sailing under the Dutch flag, claimed the New York region for The Netherlands in 1609. The Dutch named the region *New Netherland*. On Manhattan Island, the Dutch established New Amsterdam, which later became New York City. The English took control of New Netherland in 1664. They renamed it New York in honor of the Duke of York (later King James II).

About a third of all the battles of the Revolutionary War were fought in New York. New York City became the first capital of the United States under the Constitution. George Washington took the oath of office there as the nation's first President. In the early 1800's, New York began its great era of canal and railroad building. By 1820, it had become the most populated state. By 1850, it was the leading manufacturing state.

Some historians believe New York's nickname—the *Empire State*—came from a remark made by George Washington. When Washington visited New York in 1783, he predicted that it might become the seat of a new empire. New York is also called the *Excelsior State*. *Excelsior*, a Latin word meaning *ever upward*, is the state motto. For the relationship of New York to other states in its region, see MIDDLE ATLANTIC STATES.

The contributors of this article are James A. Frost, Vice-Chancellor for University Colleges at the State University of New York; John J. Leary, Executive Editor of the Albany Times-Union; and John H. Thompson, Professor of Geography at Syracuse University.

The Lights of Manhattan

Three Lions

New York (blue) ranks 30th in size among all the states. It is the largest of the Middle Atlantic States (gray).

Delaware River Valley Between Delhi and Stamford

FACTS IN BRIEF

Capital: Albany.

Government: *Congress*—U.S. senators, 2; U.S. representatives, 39. *Electoral Votes*—41. *State Legislature*—senators, 57; assemblymen, 150. *Counties*—62. *Voting Age*—21 years (state and local elections); 18 years (national elections).

Area: 49,576 square miles (including 1,707 square miles of inland water), 30th in size among the states. *Greatest Distances*—(east-west) 314 miles; (north-south) 307 miles. *Coastline* (along the Atlantic Ocean)—127 miles. *Shoreline*—775 miles (along Lakes Ontario and Erie, 371 miles; St. Lawrence and Niagara rivers, 192 miles; islands, 212 miles).

Elevation: *Highest*—Mount Marcy in the Adirondack Mountains, 5,344 feet above sea level. *Lowest*—sea level along the Atlantic Ocean.

Population: *1970 Census*—18,190,740; 2nd among the states; density, 367 persons to the square mile; distribution, 86 per cent urban, 14 per cent rural. *1960 Census*—16,782,304.

Chief Products: *Agriculture*—apples, beef cattle, dairy products, eggs, greenhouse and nursery products, potatoes. *Fishing Industry*—clams, flounders, lobsters, porgy, scallops. *Manufacturing and Processing*—chemicals; clothing; electrical machinery; fabricated metal products; food and related products; nonelectrical machinery; primary metals; printed materials; scientific instruments and photographic equipment; transportation equipment. *Mining*—iron ore, salt, sand and gravel, stone, zinc.

Statehood: July 26, 1788, the 11th state.

State Motto: *Excelsior* (Ever Upward).

State Song: None official.

Constitution. New York adopted its first constitution in 1777. The present constitution was adopted in 1894, and has been *amended* (changed) more than 250 times. An amendment may be proposed in the state legislature. The proposal must be approved by a majority in both houses of two successive, separately elected legislatures. It must then be approved by a majority of the persons who vote on the proposal in an election. The constitution may also be amended by a constitutional convention. A proposal to call a convention must be approved by a majority of the legislature and by a majority of the voters. Amendments suggested by the convention become law after they have been approved by a majority of the citizens voting on them.

Executive. The governor of New York is elected to a four-year term. He may serve an unlimited number of terms. The governor receives a yearly salary of $50,-000—the highest salary paid any governor in the United States. For a list of all the governors of New York, see the *History* section of this article.

The lieutenant governor, attorney general, and comptroller are also elected to four-year terms. The secretary of state is appointed by the governor with the approval of the state senate. The governor heads the executive department, one of the 20 departments that administer the state government. The governor, with senate approval, appoints most other department heads.

Legislature of New York consists of a senate of 57 members and an assembly of 150 members. Voters in senatorial and assembly districts elect the members of both houses to two-year terms. The legislature meets every year on the first Wednesday after the first Monday in January. There is no time limit on regular sessions. The governor may call special sessions of the legislature, which also have no time limit.

Courts. New York is divided into 11 judicial districts. The voters in each district elect a varying number of supreme court judges to 14-year terms. Altogether, New York has about 250 supreme court justices. They make up the state supreme court. New York is also divided into four judicial departments. Each department has an appellate division of the supreme court.

The appellate divisions hear appeals from the supreme court. The governor selects the supreme court justices of the appellate divisions. Two appellate divisions have seven justices each, and the other two have five each.

The highest court in New York is the court of appeals. It has a chief judge and six associate judges, all elected to 14-year terms. The court of appeals hears cases only from the appellate divisions of the supreme court.

Each New York county, except those that make up New York City, has a county court. County courts hear civil and criminal cases. A surrogate court in each county deals with wills and estates. Some counties have family courts that handle domestic matters. New York City has a civil court and a criminal court. There are also many justices of the peace, city courts, and village police courts in the state.

Local Government. New York has 62 counties, including the 5 that make up New York City. A board of supervisors governs each county except the New York City counties. The supervisors are elected either from the towns and cities of the county, or from county legislative districts. The supervisors' duties include adopting local laws, creating county departments, and levying taxes. Other county officials include the county clerk, district attorney, sheriff, and treasurer.

Within New York's counties are villages, towns, and cities. An elected mayor and board of trustees governs each village. Each town is governed by an elected supervisor and town board. Most New York cities have the mayor-council form of government. Some cities, including Niagara Falls, Rochester, and Yonkers, have the city manager form. A few small cities operate under the commission plan. The state legislature has the power to draw up city charters. Cities, in turn, may adopt and amend local laws and revise their charters, thus determining their own form of government. New York City, because of its large population and area, has a different government from that of the other cities (see NEW YORK CITY [Government]).

Taxation. Taxes bring in nearly four-fifths of the state government's income. Almost all the rest comes from federal grants and other U.S. government programs. A tax on personal income provides about a third of the state's income. It is the largest single source of income. New York has a sales tax, and taxes on alcoholic beverages, cigarettes, and motor fuels. It also taxes estates, race tracks, corporations and other businesses, stock transfers, and truck mileage.

Since 1967, the state has operated a lottery to raise educational funds from nontax sources.

Politics. Enrolled Democratic voters in New York City usually outnumber Republicans about 3 to 1. But there are about twice as many enrolled Republicans as Democrats in the rest of the state. Albany County is often the only upstate county to vote Democratic. Thus, the two parties are fairly evenly matched, because New York City has almost half the state's total population. Republicans, however, have generally controlled the legislature. From 1964 to 1966, the Democrats controlled the legislature for the first time in 30 years. In 1964 and 1965, Republicans and Democrats battled over *reapportionment* (redivision) of the

Governor's Mansion in Albany stands south of the Capitol. The building, begun in the mid-1850's, was originally a private home. The state bought it in 1877 for the governor's residence.
New York State Dept. of Commerce

The State Seal

Symbols of New York. On the seal, the figure on the left represents Liberty. The crown at her feet signifies that Liberty has rejected kings and monarchies. The figure on the right symbolizes Justice. A typical New York river scene is in the center of the seal, and an American eagle perches on the globe at the top. The seal was adopted in 1778. The state flag, adopted in 1909, has a reproduction of the seal.

legislative districts. But they did not agree on a reapportionment plan. In 1966, the court of appeals appointed a *bipartisan* (representing both parties) commission to draw up a plan. The court approved the commission's plan.

New York has 41 electoral votes—more than any other state except California. For this reason, New York plays a key role in presidential elections. Its governors have always been considered possible presidential candidates because of the importance of the state's electoral votes. They often have introduced national issues into state politics. Four men served as governor of New York before becoming President—Martin Van Buren, Grover Cleveland, Theodore Roosevelt, and Franklin D. Roosevelt. Five other governors—Horatio Seymour, Samuel J. Tilden, Charles Evans Hughes, Alfred E. Smith, and Thomas E. Dewey—were unsuccessful candidates for the presidency.

Since 1880, New Yorkers have voted for the winning presidential candidate in every election except those in 1916, 1948, and 1968. For New York's electoral votes and voting record in presidential elections, see ELECTORAL COLLEGE (table).

State Capitol in Albany was first occupied in 1879. Albany has been the capital since 1797. Kingston, Poughkeepsie, and New York City served as temporary capitals between 1777 and 1797.

New York State Dept. of Commerce

The State Flag

The State Bird
Bluebird

The State Flower
Rose

The State Tree
Sugar Maple

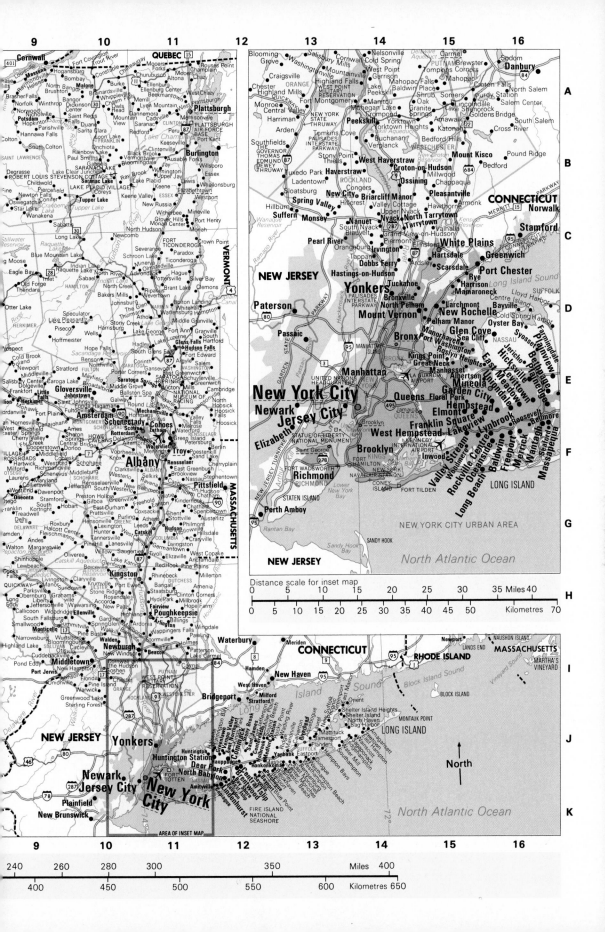

Lloyd Harbor ......3,371..D 16
Lockport ...25,399.°E 3
Locust Grove* ...11,626..J 11
Long Beach 33,127..F 16
Lorenz Park* 1,995..G 11
Loudonville* 9,299..F 11
Lowville ....3,671.°C 8
Lynbrook ..23,776..F 16
Lyndonville ..888..E 3
Lyons ......4,496.°E 5
Lyons Falls ..852..D 8
Macedon ....1,168..E 5
Mahopac ...5,265..A 15
Malone .....8,048.°A 10
Malverne* .10,036..K 11
Mamaroneck .....18,909..D 15
Manchester .1,305..E 5
Manhasset ..8,541..E 15
Manhattan 1,524,541..E 14
Manlius ....4,295..E 7
Manorhaven .5,710..E 15
Marathon ...1,053..G 7
Marcellus* ..1,456..E 7
Margaretville .816..G 9
Marlboro ...1,580..I 11
Massapequa 26,951..F 16
Massapequa Park* ...22,112..K 11
Massena ...14,042..A 9
Mastic Beach 4,870..J 13
Matinecock* ..841..J 11
Mattituck ...1,995..J 13
Mattydale* .8,292..E 7
Maybrook* ..1,536..I 10
Mayfield ......981..E 10
Mayville ....1,567.°G 1
McGraw ....1,319..F 7
Mechanicville ......6,247..F 11
Medina .....6,415..E 3
Melrose Park .....2,189..F 6
Melville* ....5,999..J 12
Menands ....3,449..F 11
Merrick ....25,904..F 16
Merriewold Lake* ....2,564..I 10
Mexico .....1,555..D 7
Middleburg .1,410..F 10
Middlehope* 2,327..I 10
Middleport ..2,132..E 3
Middletown 22,607..I 10
Middleville ...725..E 9
Milford ......527..F 9
Mill Neck* ...982..J 11
Millbrook ...1,735..H 11
Millerton ...1,042..H 11
Millport ......480..G 6
Milton* .....1,861..E 11
Mineola ...21,845.°E 16
Mineville [-Witherbee] ......1,967..C 11
Minoa ......2,245..E 7
Mohawk .....3,301..E 9
Monroe .....4,439..A 13
Monsey .....8,797..C 13
Montgomery* 1,533..I 10
Monticello ..5,991.°H 9
Montour Falls .....1,534..G 6
Mooers ......536..A 11
Moravia ....1,642..F 6
Morris ....675..F 8
Morrisonville 1,276..A 11
Morristown ....532..B 8
Morrisville ..2,296..F 8
Mount Kisco 8,172..B 15
Mount Morris ....3,417..F 4
Mount Vernon ..72,778..D 15
Munsey Park* ....2,980..J 11
Munsons Corners* ..2,076..F 7
Muttontown* 1,919..J 11
Myers Corner* ...2,826..I 11
Nanuet ....10,447..C 14
Naples ......1,324..F 4
Nassau .....1,466..F 11
Nelliston* ....716..F 9
Nelsonville ...583..A 14
Nesconset* .10,048..J 12
New Berlin ..1,369..F 8
New Cassel* 8,554..J 11
New City ..27,344.°B 14
New Hackensack* .....1,111..I 11
New Hamburg* .1,064..H 11
New Hartford* .....2,433..E 8
New Hyde Park* ...10,116..K 11
New Paltz ..6,058..H 10
New Rochelle ...75,385..D 15
New Square* 1,156..J 10
New Windsor ..8,803..I 11
New York City ..7,867,760.°K 11
New York Mills* ....3,805..E 8
Newark ....11,644..E 5
Newark Valley ....1,286..G 7
Newburgh ..26,219..I 11
Newfane ....2,588..E 2
Newport ......908..E 9
Niagara Falls ....85,615..E 2
Nichols ......638..H 6
Nimmonsburg [-Chenango Bridge] ...5,059..G 7
Niskayuna* .6,186..F 11
Nissequogue* 1,120..J 12
Norfolk .....1,379..A 9
North Amityville* ....11,905..K 12
North Babylon .39,556..K 12
North Ballston Spa* ......1,296..E 11
North Bellmore* 22,893..K 11
North Bellport* .5,903..J 13
North Boston* ..1,635..F 2
North Chili 3,163..E 4
North Collins ...1,675..F 2
North Great River* ...12,080..K 12
North Haven ..694..J 14
North Hornell 919..G 4
North Lindenhurst* ...11,205..K 12
North Massapequa* .23,101..K 11
North Merrick* .13,650..K 11
North New Hyde Park* ....17,945..J 11
North Patchogue* 6,383..J 13
North Pelham ...5,184..D 15
North Syracuse ..8,687..E 7
North Tarrytown ......8,334..C 14
North Tonawanda ...36,012..E 2
North Valley Stream* .14,881..F 15
North Wantagh* 15,053..K 11
Northport* ..7,440..J 12
Northville ...1,192..E 10
Norwich ....8,843.°F 8
Norwood ....2,098..A 9
Nunda ......1,254..F 4
Nyack ......6,659..C 14
Oakdale* ...7,334..K 12
Oakfield ....1,964..E 3
Oceanside ..35,028..F 16
Odessa ....606..G 6
Ogdensburg 14,554..A 8
Olcott ......1,592..D 2
Old Bethpage* .....7,084..K 11
Old Brookville* .....2,502..J 11
Old Field* ....812..J 12
Old Westbury* .....2,667..J 11
Olean ......19,169..G 3
Oneida .....11,658..E 8
Oneida Castle* .....788..E 8
Oneonta ...16,030..G 9
Oniad Lake* 1,587..I 11
Orange Lake* 4,348..I 10
Orchard Park ......3,732..F 2
Oriskany* ...1,627..E 8
Oriskany Falls* ......927..E 8
Ossining ...21,659..B 14
Oswego ....23,844.°D 6
Otego ....956..G 8
Otisville ......933..I 10
Ovid ....779..F 6
Owego ......5,152.°G 7
Oxford ......1,944..G 8
Oyster Bay Cove* .....1,320..J 11
Painted Post 2,496..G 5
Palatine Bridge* .....601..F 10
Palmyra ....3,776..E 5
Parish ....634..D 7
Patchogue .11,582..J 12
Pawling .....1,914..I 11
Pearl River 17,146..C 14
Peekskill ...18,881..A 14
Pelham* ....2,076..J 11
Pelham Manor ....6,673..D 15
Penn Yan ...5,168.°F 5
Perry ....4,538..F 4
Peru ....1,261..B 11
Phelps ......1,989..E 5
Philadelphia .858..C 8
Philmont ...1,674..G 11
Phoenix ....2,617..E 7
Piermont ...2,386..C 14
Pine Bush ..1,183..I 10
Pine Neck-West Tiana* ....1,326..J 13
Pittsford ....1,755..E 5
Plainedge ..10,759..E 16
Plainview ..32,195..E 16
Plandome* ..1,593..J 11
Plandome Heights* ..1,032..J 11
Plandome Manor* .....835..J 11
Plattsburgh 18,715.°A 11
Plattsburgh Base ......7,078..A 11
Pleasant Valley* ...1,372..H 11
Pleasantville 7,110..B 15
Poland ....629..E 9
Pomona* ....1,792..J 11
Ponquogue* .1,474..J 13
Port Byron .1,330..E 6
Port Chester ..25,803..C 15
Port Dickinson ....2,132..G 7
Port Ewen ..2,882..H 11
Port Henry .1,532..C 11
Port Jefferson ....5,515..J 12
Port Jefferson Station* ..7,403..J 12
Port Jervis ..8,852..I 9
Port Leyden ..862..D 8
Port Washington ......15,923..E 15
Port Washington North* ....2,578..J 11
Portville ....1,304..H 3
Potsdam ....9,985..A 9
Poughkeepsie ...32,029.°H 11
Prattsburg ....765..F 5
Prospect ....392..E 8
Pulaski ......2,480..D 7
Putnam Lake* .....1,425..I 11
Queens .1,973,708..F 14
Quogue ....865..J 13
Randolph ...1,498..G 2
Ransomville .1,034..E 2
Ravena .....2,797..G 11
Red Creek ...626..E 6
Red Hook ..1,680..H 11
Red Oaks Mill* .....3,919..H 11
Remsen ....602..E 8
Rensselaer .10,136..F 11
Rhineback ..2,336..H 11
Richfield Springs ...1,540..F 9
Richmond .295,443..F 13
Richmondville 826..F 10
Ripley ......1,173..G 1
Riverhead ..7,585.°J 13
Riverside .....911..G 5
Rochdale* ...1,849..H 11
Rochester .296,233.°E 4
Rockville Centre ...27,444..F 16
Roessleville* 5,476..F 11
Rolling Acres* ....1,152..E 4
Rome ......50,148..E 8
Ronkonkoma 7,284..J 12
Roosevelt ..15,008..F 16
Rosendale ..1,220..H 10
Roslyn* ....2,546..J 11
Roslyn Estates* ..1,420..J 11
Roslyn Harbor* ....939..J 11
Roslyn Heights ...7,140..E 16
Rotterdam .25,153..F 11
Round Lake ..886..E 11
Rouses Point 2,250..A 11
Rushville .....568..F 5
Russell Gardens* .1,174..J 11
Rye ....15,869..D 15
Sackets Harbor ....1,202..C 7
Saddle Rock* .895..J 11
Sag Harbor .2,363..J 14
St. George ....°F 13
St. James ..10,818..J 12
St. Johnsville ......2,089..E 9
Salamanca ..7,877..G 2
Salem ......1,025..E 12
San Remo* .8,302..J 12
Sand Ridge* 1,109..E 7
Sandy Beach* ...1,691..E 2
Sands Point* 2,916..J 11
Sandy Creek ..731..D 7
Saranac Lake ....6,086..B 10
Saratoga Springs ..18,845..E 11
Saugerties ..4,190..G 11
Saugerties South* ....3,159..G 11
Savannah ....636..E 6
Savona ....933..G 5
Sayville ....11,680..K 12
Scarsdale ..19,229..C 15
Schaghticoke ..860..F 11
Schenectady 77,859.°F 11
Schenevus ....540..F 9
Schoharie ...1,125.°F 10
Schuylerville 1,402..E 11
Scotchtown* 2,119..I 10
Scotia ......8,224..F 11
Scottsville ..1,967..E 4
Sea Cliff ...5,890..D 16
Seaford ....17,379..F 16
Selden* ....11,613..J 12
Seneca Falls 7,794..F 6
Setauket [-South Setauket]* 6,857..J 12
Sherburne ..1,613..F 8
Sherman .....769..G 1
Sherrill .....2,986..E 8
Shirley .....6,280..J 13
Shoreham* ....524..J 13
Shortsville ..1,516..E 5
Sidney .....4,789..G 8
Silver Creek 3,182..F 2
Silver Springs 823..F 4
Sinclairville ..772..G 1
Skaneateles .3,055..E 6
Slabtown* ..2,753..G 5
Sloan ....5,216..F 2
Sloatsburg ..3,134..B 13
Sodus ......1,813..E 5
Sodus Point 1,172..E 5
Solvay ......8,280..E 7
South Corning ..1,414..G 5
South Dayton .688..G 2
South Fallsburg .....1,590..H 9
South Farmingdale* .20,464..J 11
South Floral Park* ....1,032..J 11
South Glens Falls .....4,013..E 11
South Holbrook* ....6,700..K 12
South Hudson Falls* ....2,097..E 11
South Huntington* ......8,946..J 12
South Lockport* .1,341..E 3
South Nyack 3,435..C 14
South Setauket, see Setauket [-South Setauket]
South Stony Brook* ..15,329..J 12
South Valley Stream* ..6,595..K 11
South Westbury* ....10,978..J 11
Southampton 4,904..J 13
Southold* ...2,030..J 13
Spackenhill* 2,725..H 11
Spencer ......854..G 6
Spencerport .2,929..E 4
Spring Valley ...18,112..C 13
Springville ..4,350..F 3
Sproutville* .1,871..I 11
Stamford ....1,286..G 9
Stewart .....1,230..I 10
Stewart Manor* ...2,183..J 11
Stillwater ...1,428..E 11
Stony Brook 6,391..J 12
Stony Point .....8,270..B 14
Stottville ...1,106..G 11
Suffern .....8,273..C 13
Syosset ....9,970..E 16
Syracuse ..197,208.°E 7
Tannersville ..650..G 10
Tappan .....7,424..C 14
Tarrytown ..11,115..C 14
Theresa ......985..B 7
Thomaston* .2,486..J 11
Thornwood* .6,874..J 11
Ticonderoga .3,268..C 11
Tillson* ....1,256..H 10
Tivoli ....739..G 11
Tonawanda 21,898..E 2
Town Line* .2,434..E 3
Tribes Hill* .1,184..F 10
Troy ......62,918.°F 11
Trumansburg .....1,618..F 6
Tuckahoe ...6,236..D 15
Tully ....899..F 7
Tupper Lake 4,854..B 10
Tuxedo Park .861..B 13
Twin Orchards, see Vestal [-Twin Orchards]
Unadilla ....1,489..G 8
Union Springs ...1,183..F 6
Uniondale .22,077..E 16
Unionville ....576..I 10
Upper Brookville* .....1,182..J 11
Upper Nyack ....2,096..C 14
Utica ......91,611.°E 8
Valatie .....1,288..G 11
Valley Cottage ...6,007..C 14
Valley Falls ..681..F 11
Valley Stream ..40,413..F 15
Van Etten ....522..G 6
Van Keurens* ..3,292..H 11
Vernon .....1,108..E 8
Vernon Valley ....7,925..J 12
Vestal [-Twin Orchards] .8,303..G 7
Victor .....2,187..E 5
Victory Mills .718..E 11
Village of the Branch* ..1,675..J 12
Viola* ......5,136..I 10
Voorheesville ......2,826..F 11
Waddington ..955..A 8
Walden .....5,277..I 10
Wallkill ....1,849..I 10
Walton .....3,744..G 9
Wampsville ...586.°E 8
Wantagh ...21,873..F 16
Wappingers Falls .....5,607..I 11
Wappingers Falls East* .....2,017..I 11
Wappingers Lake* ....1,958..H 11
Warrensburg 2,743..D 11
Warsaw ....3,619.°F 3
Warwick ....3,604..I 10
Washington Heights* ..1,204..I 10
Washingtonville ....1,887..A 13
Waterford ..2,879..F 11
Waterloo ...5,418.°F 6
Watertown .30,787.°C 7
Waterville ..1,808..E 8
Watervliet .12,404..F 11
Watkins Glen .....2,716.°G 6
Waverly ....5,261..H 6
Wayland ....2,022..F 4
Webster .....5,037..E 5
Weedsport ..1,900..E 6
Wellsburg ....779..H 6
Wellsville ...5,815..G 4
West Amityville* .....6,393..K 11
West Babylon* 12,788..K 12
West Carthage .2,047..C 8
West Elmira ....5,901..G 6
West End ...1,692..G 9
West Glens Falls* ...3,363..D 11
West Haverstraw .....8,558..B 14
West Hempstead .....20,375..E 16
West Islip .16,711..K 12
West Nyack* 5,510..I 11
West Point ....A 14
West Sand Lake* .....1,875..F 11
West Sayville* .....7,386..K 12
West Tiana, see Pine Neck-West Tiana
West Winfield ..1,018..F 8
Westbury* .15,362..J 11
Westfield ...3,651..G 1
Westhampton 1,156..J 13
Westhampton Beach ....1,926..J 13
Westmere* ..6,364..F 11
Westport .....673..C 11
Westvale* ...7,253..E 7
White Plains ...50,220.°C 15
Whitehall ...3,764..D 11
Whitesboro ..4,805..E 8
Whitney Point .....1,058..G 7
Williamson .1,991..E 5
Williamsville ......6,835..E 2
Williston Park* .....9,154..J 11
Wilson .....1,284..E 2
Windsor ....1,098..G 8
Witherbee, see Mineville [-Witherbee]
Wolcott ....1,617..E 6
Woodbourne* 1,155..I 9
Woodmere ..19,831..F 15
Woodridge ..1,071..H 10
Woodsburgh* .817..K 11
Woodstock* .1,073..G 10
Wurtsboro ....732..I 10
Wyandanch* 14,906..K 12
Yaphank ....5,460..J 13
Yonkers ..204,370..J 11
Yorktown Heights ...6,805..B 15
Yorktown [-Jefferson Valley] ...9,008..A 15
Yorkville ...3,425..E 8
Youngstown .2,169..E 2

*Does not appear on the map; key shows general location.
°County seat

Source: Latest census figures (1970). Places without population figures are unincorporated areas and are not listed in census reports.

NEW YORK/People

The 1970 United States census reported that New York had 18,190,740 persons. The population had increased 8 per cent over the 1960 figure of 16,782,304. The 1960 census had reported that New York ranked as the top state in population. But during the 1960's, California overtook New York, and became the leader in population by about 1,700,000 persons.

About 85 of every 100 of New York's people live in urban areas. That is, they live in or near cities and towns of 2,500 or more persons. The state has seven Standard Metropolitan Statistical Areas (see METROPOLITAN AREA). For the populations of these areas, see the *Index* to the political map of New York.

New York City, with 7,867,760 persons, is the largest city in the United States. It ranks second in the world, after Tokyo. The New York City metropolitan area, which includes nine counties in New York, is the largest metropolitan area in the world. The state has five other cities with more than 100,000 persons. They are, in order of size, Buffalo, Rochester, Yonkers, Syracuse, and Albany. See the separate articles on the cities of New York listed in the *Related Articles* at the end of this article.

New York, especially New York City, has long been known as a *melting pot*. Here, peoples of various races and many countries have settled and adopted a common culture. About one of every seven persons in New York was born in another country. In addition, one or both parents of a fourth of the American-born New Yorkers were born in other countries. The largest groups born in other lands include, in order of size, Italians, Germans, Russians, Poles, Irish, Canadians, Austrians, and English. Many Puerto Ricans have come to New York since the end of World War II. More than 600,000 Puerto Ricans live in New York City. There are also more Negroes living in New York than in any other state—over 2 million.

Roman Catholics make up the largest single religious group in New York. Other large religious groups in the state include Baptists, Episcopalians, Jews, Lutherans, Methodists, Presbyterians, and members of the Reformed Church of America and the United Church of Christ. New York has more Roman Catholics and more Jews than any other state.

Ruth Sondak, FPG

Parade Watchers line the sidewalks in downtown Manhattan. New York City is the largest city in the United States. About 85 of every 100 persons in the state live in urban areas.

WORLD BOOK photo by Three Lions

Mohawk Indian works on a construction project in New York City. Indians come to the city from other parts of the state to find jobs. Many of them live in Brooklyn.

POPULATION

This map shows the *population density* of New York, and how it varies in different parts of the state. Population density means the average number of persons who live on each square mile.

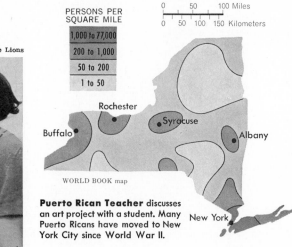

PERSONS PER SQUARE MILE
1,000 to 77,000
200 to 1,000
50 to 200
1 to 50

0   50   100 Miles
0   50 100 150 Kilometers

Rochester
Buffalo
Syracuse
Albany
New York

WORLD BOOK map

WORLD BOOK photo by Three Lions

Puerto Rican Teacher discusses an art project with a student. Many Puerto Ricans have moved to New York City since World War II.

Schools. In 1784, the New York Legislature established an agency called the University of the State of New York. This agency controls and supervises the educational system in New York. The University of the State of New York is not a university in the usual sense of the word. A 15-member board of regents governs the University of the State of New York. The Legislature elects the regents, one each year, to 15-year terms. The regents receive no pay, but serve for the honor. The board of regents has sweeping powers over all education in the state—elementary, secondary, and higher education—both private and public. Its powers include setting educational standards, distributing public funds, awarding scholarships, and incorporating colleges and universities.

The powers and duties of the regents are administered by the state education department. The state commissioner of education heads the department. He is appointed by the regents for an indefinite term. In 1948, the Legislature established the State University of New York. This statewide university system has one of the largest enrollments of any university in the United States. Headquarters of the State University of New York are in Albany.

The state education department, responsible to the board of regents, supervises more than 800 local school districts. Each district has its own school board and superintendent. Children between 6 and 16 must attend school. For the number of students and teachers in New York, see EDUCATION (table).

Libraries. The first libraries in New York were church libraries and private libraries established by Dutch colonists. The first libraries in the English colony of New York were set up about 1698 in New York City and Albany through the efforts of Thomas Bray, an Anglican missionary. The first public library in the New York region was founded in New York City about 1730. Today, the state has more than 700 public libraries. They own over 45 million books, magazines, and other reading materials. New York City has three independent library systems including more than 200 branches. One system, the New York Public Library, has the largest free circulating library in the nation.

Columbia University's libraries in New York City have about 4 million books. Other large college and university libraries include those at the City College of New York, Cornell University in Ithaca, the State University of New York in Buffalo, the University of Rochester in Rochester, and Syracuse University. The Sibley Musical Library of the University of Rochester has the only library building in the nation devoted entirely to music.

New York's many special libraries include the Grosvenor Collection in the Buffalo and Erie County Public Library, an outstanding reference library; the Pierpont Morgan Library in New York City, which has a fine collection of rare manuscripts and early books; and the Frick Art Reference Library in New York City.

The New York State Library was founded in Albany in 1818. It is directed by the regents of the University

State University of New York in Buffalo is part of the state's university system which includes 4 four-year state universities, 2 medical centers, 17 four-year state colleges, 6 two-year state colleges, and over 30 two-year community colleges.
Three Lions

Pickow, Three Lions

Baseball Hall of Fame and Museum in Cooperstown includes displays of equipment, trophies, and documents. The standing figure, above, represents the hero of the famous poem "Casey at the Bat."

of the State of New York. The library has a general reference collection of about 4 million books, pamphlets, manuscripts, and prints. It has an almost complete collection of state and local histories on New York. The library's treasures include the autographs of all the signers of the Declaration of Independence, and the original copy of the first draft of Abraham Lincoln's Emancipation Proclamation.

Museums. New York has about 370 museums. About 130 of them deal with history, 90 with the fine arts, 20 with natural history and applied science, 5 with children's exhibits, and about 125 are historic houses. The New York State Museum, founded in Albany in 1836, is the nation's oldest state museum. The regents of the University of the State of New York supervise this museum. Its collections deal with natural history, science, and the art and history of the state. The Metropolitan Museum of Art in New York City is the largest art museum in the United States. Other outstanding museums include the Museum of Modern Art, the American Museum of Natural History, and the Guggenheim Museum, all in New York City; and the National Baseball Hall of Fame and Museum, in Cooperstown.

--- **UNIVERSITIES AND COLLEGES** ---

New York has 86 universities and colleges accredited by the Middle States Association of Colleges and Secondary Schools. For enrollments and further information, see UNIVERSITIES AND COLLEGES (table).

Name	Location	Founded	Name	Location	Founded
Adelphi University	Garden City	1896	Molloy Catholic College		
Alfred University	Alfred	1857	for Women	Rockville Centre	1955
Bank Street College of			Mount Saint Mary College	Newburgh	1954
Education	New York City	1916	Mount Saint Vincent,		
Bard College	Annandale-on-		College of	New York City	1847
	Hudson	1860	Nazareth College of Rochester	Rochester	1924
Brentwood College	Brentwood	1955	New Rochelle, College of	New Rochelle	1904
Briarcliff College	Briarcliff Manor	1965	New School for Social Research	New York City	1919
Brooklyn, Polytechnic			New York, City University of	*	1847
Institute of	New York City	1854	New York, State University of	*	1844
Canisius College	Buffalo	1870	New York University	New York City	1831
Clarkson College of Technology	Potsdam	1896	Niagara University	Niagara	
Colgate University	Hamilton	1819		University	1856
Columbia University	*	1754	Notre Dame College of		
Cooper Union	New York City	1859	Staten Island	New York City	1931
Cornell University	Ithaca	1865	Nyack Missionary College	Nyack	1882
D'Youville College	Buffalo	1908	Pace College	New York City	1906
Elmira College	Elmira	1855	Pratt Institute	New York City	1887
Finch College	New York City	1900	Rensselaer Polytechnic Institute	Troy	1824
Fordham University	New York City	1841	Roberts Wesleyan College	North Chili	1866
Good Counsel College	White Plains	1923	Rochester, University of	Rochester	1850
Hamilton College	Clinton	1793	Rochester Institute of		
Hartwick College	Oneonta	1928	Technology	Rochester	1829
Hobart and William Smith			Rosary Hill College	Buffalo	1947
Colleges	Geneva	1822	Russell Sage College	Troy	1916
Hofstra University	Hempstead	1935	St. Bonaventure University	St. Bonaventure	1856
Houghton College	Houghton	1883	St. Francis College	New York City	1858
Insurance, College of	New York City	1962	St. John Fisher College	Rochester	1951
Iona College	New Rochelle	1940	St. John's University	New York City	1870
Ithaca College	Ithaca	1892	St. Joseph's College for Women	New York City	1916
Jewish Theological Seminary			St. Joseph's Seminary and		
of America	New York City	1887	College	Yonkers	1833
Julliard School	New York City	1887	St. Lawrence University	Canton	1856
Keuka College	Keuka Park	1892	St. Rose, College of	Albany	1920
King's College	Briarcliff Manor	1938	Sarah Lawrence College	Bronxville	1928
Ladycliff College	Highland Falls	1933	Siena College	Loudonville	1937
Le Moyne College	Syracuse	1946	Skidmore College	Saratoga Springs	1911
Long Island University	*	1926	Syracuse University	*	1870
Manhattan College	New York City	1853	Union College and University	*	1795
Manhattan School of Music	New York City	1920	Union Theological Seminary	New York City	1836
Manhattanville College	Purchase	1841	United States Merchant		
Marist College	Poughkeepsie	1946	Marine Academy	Kings Point	1938
Mary Rogers College	Maryknoll	1931	United States Military Academy	West Point	1802
Maryknoll Seminary	Maryknoll	1911	Vassar College	Poughkeepsie	1861
Marymount College	Tarrytown	1907	Wagner College	New York City	1883
Marymount Manhattan			Webb Institute of Naval		
College	New York City	1936	Architecture	Glen Cove	1889
Medaille College	Buffalo	1937	Wells College	Aurora	1868
Mercy College	Dobbs Ferry	1961	Woodstock College	New York City	1869
Mills College of Education	New York City	1909	Yeshiva University	New York City	1886

*For the campuses of City University of New York, Columbia University, Long Island University, State University of New York, Syracuse University, and Union College and University, see UNIVERSITIES AND COLLEGES (table).

United States Military Academy in West Point, *right*, trains young men to be military officers. Another federal academy, the U.S. Merchant Marine Academy, is in Kings Point.

Guggenheim Museum in New York City, *below*, displays works of art in an unusual building designed by Frank Lloyd Wright.

New York State Museum in Albany, *below*, has displays of natural science and state art and history.

Cornell University, *right,* is in Ithaca. Cornell also has schools of medicine and nursing in New York City.

NEW YORK / *A Visitor's Guide*

New York is one of the most popular vacationlands in the United States. Its forested mountains, shimmering lakes, sandy beaches, and vast areas of unspoiled wilderness attract millions of summer vacationers yearly. Winter sports fans enjoy New York's excellent facilities for skiing, tobogganing, iceboating, and ice skating. Visitors also come to see New York's many historic forts and houses, and such magnificent wonders of nature as Niagara Falls. New York City's cultural and recreational attractions draw over 16 million visitors a year. See NEW YORK CITY.

Osborne, Three Lions
Niagara Falls at Night

--- PLACES TO VISIT ---

Following are brief descriptions of some of New York's many interesting places to visit.

Corning Glass Center, in Corning, includes the world's largest library devoted to glass, and a museum with exhibits of 3,500 years of glassmaking.

Doubleday Field and National Baseball Hall of Fame and Museum, in Cooperstown, commemorate the birthplace of baseball.

Farmers' Museum, near Cooperstown, has early agricultural tools and appliances. Nearby stands the **Village Crossroads.** It includes a country school, law office, village store, blacksmith shop, print shop, doctor's office, church, tavern, and farmhouse and barn. All were built in the late 1700's or early 1800's.

Fort Niagara, near Youngstown, was the scene of fighting during the French and Indian Wars and the American Revolution.

Fort Ticonderoga, on Lake Champlain, is a reconstruction of the colonial fort where Ethan Allen and his Green Mountain Boys defied the British and forced them to surrender in 1775.

Franklin D. Roosevelt National Historic Site, in Hyde Park, includes the President's home, grave, and library. The library has many of his books, ship models, and other personal belongings.

Howe Caverns, near Cobleskill, are colorfully lighted caves. Some of them are 200 feet underground.

Lake Placid, a village in the Adirondack Mountains, is a world-famous resort. It is noted for its glacial lake and its excellent facilities for winter and summer sports. John Brown, the abolitionist, is buried there.

Literary Shrines may be seen throughout New York. They include John Burroughs' birthplace in Roxbury, Thomas Paine's home in New Rochelle, and Walt Whitman's birthplace near Huntington. Mark Twain's home and grave are in Elmira. The cottage in which Robert Louis Stevenson wrote several of his books is in Saranac Lake. The cottage in which Edgar Allan Poe wrote many poems is in New York City.

Niagara Falls, in the city of Niagara Falls, is the most famous waterfall in the world. About 500,000 tons of water plunge into a steep-walled gorge every minute.

Saranac Lake, in the Adirondacks, is a famous summer and winter sports center.

Saratoga Springs is noted for its health resort, owned and operated by the state, and for its race track. The National Museum of Racing has many exhibits of famous thoroughbred horses.

Vanderbilt Mansion, near Hyde Park, was the luxurious 50-room home of Frederick W. Vanderbilt. The

Watkins Glen State Park
Dean, Three Lions

Corning Glass Center in Corning
WORLD BOOK photo by Three Lions

WORLD BOOK photo
Fort Niagara near Youngstown

WORLD BOOK photo by Three Lions
Howe Caverns near Cobleskill

mansion was made a national historic site in 1940.

West Point, on the Hudson River north of New York City, is the home of the U.S. Military Academy.

National Parks and Monuments. Saratoga National Historical Park, near Stillwater, includes the battlefield on which the Americans defeated the British in the Battle of Saratoga in 1777. The park was established in 1948. Fire Island National Seashore Park was established in 1964 on Fire Island, a reef off Long Island. The Statue of Liberty National Monument, established in 1924, stands in New York Harbor. Castle Clinton National Monument, in New York City, was once a landing depot for immigrants. Here, 7,500,000 persons entered the United States from 1855 to 1890. The monument was established in 1950.

State Parks and Forests. New York has more than 100 state parks and about 400 forest areas. One of its most popular parks is Watkins Glen State Park, near Watkins Glen. This park is one of the scenic wonders of North America. It has eight waterfalls, many caverns, Hollow Lake, and a deep glen in which the water drops about 700 feet within two miles. For information on the state parks of New York, write to the Director, Division of Parks, Department of Conservation, State Campus Site, Albany, N.Y. 12226.

Franklin D. Roosevelt Home in Hyde Park
WORLD BOOK photo by Three Lions

ANNUAL EVENTS

Many cultural festivals, historical celebrations, and sports competitions are held throughout New York every year. One of the most popular annual events is the New York State Fair, held in Syracuse in late August and early September. The opening of each theatrical and opera season in New York City is a glittering, exciting event. New York City also holds many gay and colorful holiday parades every year.

Other annual events in New York include the following.

January-March: Kennedy Games in Lake Placid (January-March); Winter Carnival in Saranac Lake (February); St. Patrick's Day Parade in New York City (March 17); International Flower Show in New York City (March).

April-June: North American Indoor Speed Skating Championships in Lake Placid (April); Hudson River White Water Derby in North Creek (May); Tulip Festival in Albany (May); Festival of Lilacs in Rochester (May); June Week Ceremonies at the United States Military Academy at West Point (June); Jaycee Canoe Race on the Ausable River in Lake Placid (June); National Lake Trout Derby on Seneca Lake near Geneva (May-June); Intercollegiate Rowing Association Championship in Syracuse (June); Old Whaler's Festival in Sag Harbor, L.I. (June); National (Glider) Soaring Contest in Elmira (May-June).

July-September: Annual Summer Ski Jump in Lake Placid (July); Grand Prix Sports Car Races in Watkins Glen (July); Hall of Fame Baseball Exhibition Game in Cooperstown (July); Mormon Religious Pageant at Hill Cumorah near Palmyra (July or August); Rodeo at Madison Square Garden in New York City (August); U.S. Lawn Tennis Association Championships in Forest Hills, L.I. (August or September); Bridgehampton Grand Prix Sports Car Race in Bridgehampton, L.I. (September); Song Festival in Utica (September).

October-December: Columbus Day Parade in New York City (October 12); National Horse Show at Madison Square Garden in New York City (November); Thanksgiving Day Parade in New York City (November); Rockefeller Center Tree Lighting Ceremony in New York City (December).

246e

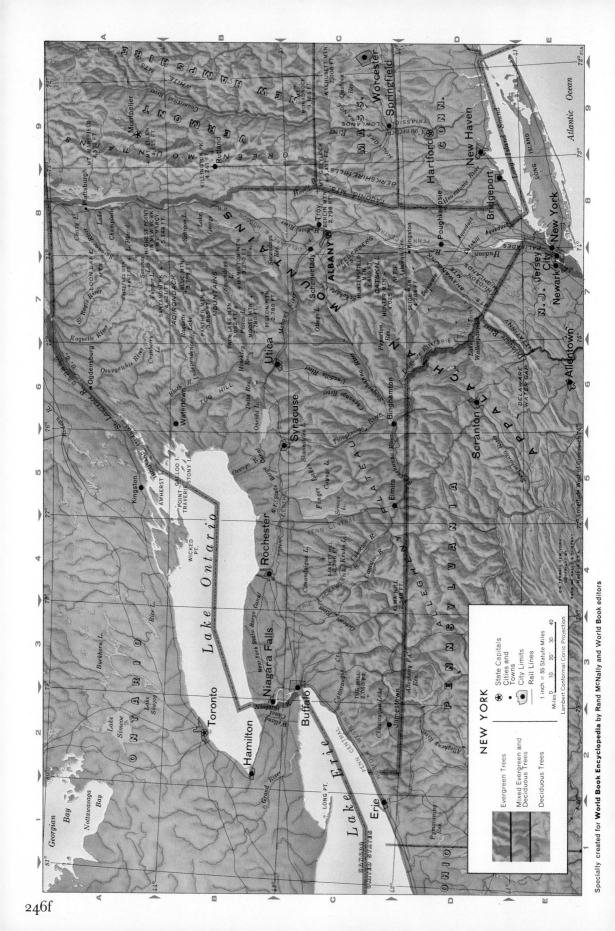

246f

Land Regions. During the Ice Age, which ended about 10,000 years ago, glaciers spread across almost all the area now covered by New York. They formed many of New York's most striking natural features, and deposited stones, pebbles, and other materials. Most of New York's soils have been formed from materials deposited by the glaciers.

New York has seven major land regions: (1) the Atlantic Coastal Plain, (2) the New England Upland, (3) the Hudson-Mohawk Lowland, (4) the Adirondack Upland, (5) the St. Lawrence Lowland, (6) the Erie-Ontario Lowland, and (7) the Appalachian Plateau.

The Atlantic Coastal Plain covers Long Island and Staten Island. It forms part of the low, almost level coastal plain that stretches along the Atlantic Ocean from Massachusetts to the southern tip of Florida. Staten Island and the western end of Long Island lie within New York City. Both islands are important residential districts. Broad sandy beaches along the southern end of Long Island make it a popular summer resort area. Fishing is an important source of income on the Atlantic Coastal Plain. Farmers raise vegetables, fruits, flowers, and poultry.

The New England Upland, a region of hills and low mountains, extends along about half of New York's eastern border. The region includes the Taconic Mountains and the southern part of the Hudson River Valley. Manhattan Island, the heart of New York City, lies in the New England Upland. Lovely, forested Westchester County is also part of this region.

The Hudson-Mohawk Lowland covers most of the Hudson River Valley and the Mohawk River Valley. The Hudson Valley is part of the Appalachian Ridge and Valley Region of New Jersey and Pennsylvania. The Hudson-Mohawk Lowland is about 10 to 30 miles wide. It cuts through highlands a thousand or more feet high. The region is the only great break in the Appalachian Mountains. Since pioneer days, it has served as a major highway into the interior. It is the only natural trade route within the United States between the Atlantic Ocean and the Great Lakes.

The fertile plains bordering the Hudson and Mohawk rivers are used for general farming, fruit growing, and dairying. Falls along the rivers provide abundant water power for generating electricity. Many of New York's great industrial and population centers are in the Hudson-Mohawk Lowland.

The Adirondack Upland is a roughly circular hill and mountain region in the northeastern part of New York. The region's mountains are formed of hard, ancient rocks, perhaps the oldest in North America. Many mountain peaks rise above 4,000 feet. Mount Marcy rises 5,344 feet in the northeastern part of the region, and is the highest point in New York. The Adirondack Upland is famous for its wild and beautiful scenery, sparkling lakes, rushing streams, splashing waterfalls, and purple-tinted peaks. It ranks as one of the most popular recreation areas in the eastern United States. The Adirondack soils are poor for farming. But there

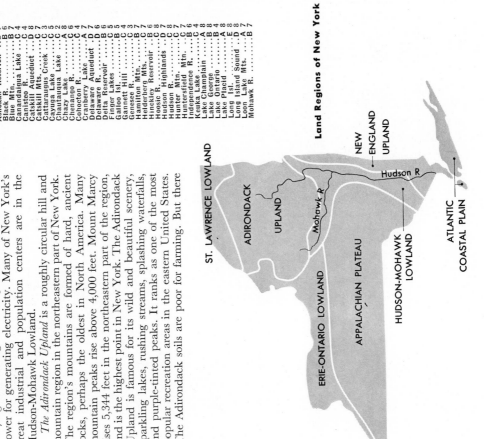

Land Regions of New York

ST. LAWRENCE LOWLAND

ERIE-ONTARIO LOWLAND

ADIRONDACK UPLAND

APPALACHIAN PLATEAU

HUDSON-MOHAWK LOWLAND

NEW ENGLAND UPLAND

ATLANTIC COASTAL PLAIN

Mohawk R.

Hudson R.

Broad Sandy Beaches on the Atlantic Ocean, *left*, border Long Island's southern shores. The area is in the Atlantic Coastal Plain.

Mohawk River, *right*, serves as a major water link between the Atlantic Ocean and the Great Lakes. It is in the Hudson-Mohawk Lowland.

Southern Hudson River Valley, *below*, at Bear Mountain Bridge is in the New England Upland. This region extends along about half of New York's eastern border.

NEW YORK

is some lumbering in the region, as well as iron, lead, titanium, and zinc mining.

The Tug Hill Plateau lies in the western part of the Adirondack Upland region. This high, flat, rocky area has fewer lakes and smaller mountains than the rest of the region.

The St. Lawrence Lowland lies along the south bank of the St. Lawrence River. It borders the Adirondack Upland on the north. The region is less than 20 miles wide. The land is level to rolling, but seldom rises more than a few hundred feet above sea level. Some of the milk from the region's dairy farms is shipped all the way to New York City. Fruit growing is common near Lake Champlain on the New York-Vermont boundary.

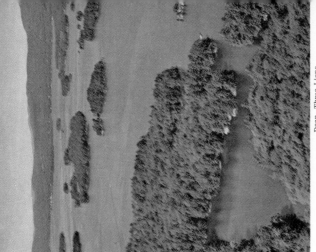

Summer homes line the banks of the St. Lawrence River. Many resorts have been built on the river's beautiful Thousand Islands.

The Erie-Ontario Lowland is a low-lying region south of Lake Erie and Lake Ontario. Part of the region was once the flat bottom of ancient glacial lakes. Elsewhere, glacial deposits called *moranes* have produced a low, rolling surface. The glaciers also formed many *drumlins* in the area southeast of Rochester. Drumlins are oval-shaped hills about 50 to 300 feet high. The Erie-Ontario Lowland has unusually fertile soils. Fruit growing is a specialty. The region also has prosperous truck gardens, greenhouses, plant nurseries, and dairy farms. Excellent transportation and abundant water power have spurred

Eisenhower Lock, *right,* is part of the St. Lawrence Seaway. The lock is in the St. Lawrence Lowland region of northern New York.

Wooded Islands dot Paradise Bay, *right,* near Thousand Islands in the St. Lawrence River. The area is in the Erie-Ontario Lowland.

Vineyards thrive near Seneca Lake, *below,* in the Finger Lakes area of the Appalachian Plateau. Fertile farmland lies in this area, which is also a famous resort center.

Tiny Village, *below,* nestles in the Keene Valley in the Adirondack Upland. The mountains in this region may be the oldest in North America. The region is famous for its beautiful scenery.

the growth of such industrial and commercial cities as Buffalo and Rochester.

The Appalachian Plateau, the state's largest land region, covers most of southern New York. It lies south and west of the Hudson-Mohawk Lowland, and south of the Erie-Ontario Lowland. The plateau stretches westward almost to Lake Erie. Glaciers and rivers have produced a wide variety of surface features. These features range from rolling hills near the northern end of Finger Lakes to the mountainous country of the beautiful Catskills in the east. The Catskill Mountains, with peaks rising from 2,000 to more than 4,000 feet above sea level, are a favorite tourist area. Large reservoirs created in the Catskill Mountains help supply New York City with water (see WATER [map: How New York City Gets Its Water]).

Most farms of the Appalachian Plateau specialize in dairying. The region's best farming area lies in the Finger Lakes section in the north. Vineyards, nurseries, and truck gardens thrive here. The Finger Lakes received their name because they look like the outstretched fingers of a hand. The sparkling beauty of the lakes and the wooded, rolling country surrounding them provide an outstanding scenic attraction for vacationers. Many summer homes line their shores.

Coastline and Shoreline. New York's general coastline stretches 127 miles along the Atlantic Ocean. New York City has one of the world's best natural harbors. The harbor is almost completely protected by land. The state also has 371 miles of shoreline along Lakes Erie and Ontario, 174 miles along Lake Champlain, and 192 miles along the St. Lawrence and Niagara rivers. Buffalo is New York's chief lake port. Oceangoing ships reach it through the St. Lawrence Seaway.

Mountains. The Adirondacks, in northeastern New York, are the state's largest mountain range. In addition to 5,344-foot Mount Marcy, two other peaks in the Adirondacks rise more than 5,000 feet. They are Mount McIntyre and Algonquin Peak, both 5,112 feet high. The tallest peak in the Catskill Mountains is 4,204-foot Slide Mountain, west of the lower Hudson River. The Catskill's second highest peak, Hunter

Mountain, rises 4,025 feet. The low, narrow Shawangunk Mountains are south of the Catskills, and also form part of the Appalachian Plateau. The Shawangunks extend southward into New Jersey. The Taconic Mountains rise east of the Hudson River along the Massachusetts border. They are a western extension of Massachusett's Berkshire Hills. The Helderberg Mountains rise northeast of the Catskills.

Rivers. New York's most important rivers are the Hudson and the Mohawk. They make up one of the greatest trade waterways in the United States. The Hudson River rises in the wildest part of the Adirondacks, in a little lake called Tear-of-the-Clouds. The river flows almost straight south to New York Bay, where it becomes an arm of the Atlantic Ocean. The Hudson is 306 miles long—the largest river lying entirely within the state. Along its upper course, the Hudson is a narrow stream breaking into many falls and rapids, which are used to produce electric power. The Hudson widens and deepens as it flows to the sea. Some sections of the river are quite beautiful with their huge rock cliffs called the *Palisades*. Oceangoing ships can sail up the Hudson as far as Albany, about 150 miles from the river's mouth.

The Mohawk River is the chief branch of the Hudson. It connects the Hudson with the Great Lakes lowland. The Mohawk drains central New York, and has been important in the development of the interior. The river rises in Oneida County and flows southeastward for about 145 miles. It enters the Hudson River at Cohoes.

The Genesee River starts in Pennsylvania, flows northward through western New York, and empties into Lake Ontario north of Rochester. The Oswego River and its branch, the Seneca, also empty into Lake Ontario. The Delaware, Susquehanna, and Allegheny rivers drain the southern part of the state. The Delaware forms part of the boundary between New York and Pennsylvania. The Susquehanna rises in Otsego Lake in central New York and flows southward into Pennsylvania. The Allegheny begins in Pennsylvania, curves across the southwestern corner of New York, and swings

back into Pennsylvania. The East River, which is actually a strait, separates Manhattan from Long Island. It is only about 16 miles long, but is an important New York City waterway. The St. Lawrence River, between New York and Canada, is one of the great water routes of North America.

Waterfalls. Many of New York's larger rivers flow through wide, fertile valleys for most of their courses. At certain points, some of the rivers pass through deep, rock-walled gorges and become plunging waterfalls. The smaller mountain streams have many small falls and swirling rapids. Many of these falls provide water power for industries. Thundering Niagara Falls is the grandest and most famous of all waterfalls in the state. Taughannock Falls, near Cayuga Lake in the Finger Lakes region, is one of the highest falls east of the Rocky Mountains. Its waters drop 215 feet. Near Portageville, the Genesee River breaks into three falls, the largest of which has a drop of 110 feet. Other falls in the Genesee at Rochester are used to generate power for the city's industries.

Lakes. New York has more than 8,000 lakes. Most of them were created by glaciers of the Ice Age. Lake Oneida, northeast of Syracuse, is the largest lake lying entirely within the state. It covers about 80 square miles, and empties into Lake Ontario. Lake George is a popular summer vacation area. It empties into Lake Champlain, which lies on the New York-Vermont border and extends into the Canadian province of Quebec. Lake Champlain covers a total area of about 500 square miles.

The glacial Finger Lakes consist of six bodies of water covering more than 10 square miles each, and several smaller lakes. All are long and narrow, and lie nearly parallel in a north-south direction. The Adirondack Mountains have about 2,000 small lakes. Two of the most beautiful ones—Lake Placid and Saranac Lake—are popular summer and winter resorts. Chautauqua Lake, in southwestern New York, is a favorite summer vacation spot. It is also the birthplace of the Chautauqua Institution, famous for its summer adult education program.

NEW YORK / Climate

New York's climate varies greatly throughout the state because of differences in land forms and exposure to large bodies of water. The Adirondacks have the coldest winters, the heaviest snowfalls, and the coolest summers. The Atlantic Coastal Plain has the mildest winters, the lightest snowfalls, and the hottest summers.

The average January temperature in the Adirondacks is 17° F., and on the coastal plain, 32° F. The average July temperature in the Adirondacks is 66° F., and on the coastal plain, 74° F. About 122 inches of snow falls yearly in the Adirondacks. The coastal plain receives about 26 inches yearly. The climate in New York's other land regions varies between the extremes of these two regions. New York's record high temperature, 108° F., was set at Troy on July 22, 1926. The record low, −52° F., was set at Stillwater Reservoir on Feb. 9, 1934.

New York's annual *precipitation* (rain, melted snow, and other forms of moisture) ranges between 32 and 54 inches. The southwestern slopes of the Adirondacks, Catskills, and other mountains, and the coastal plain receive the most precipitation.

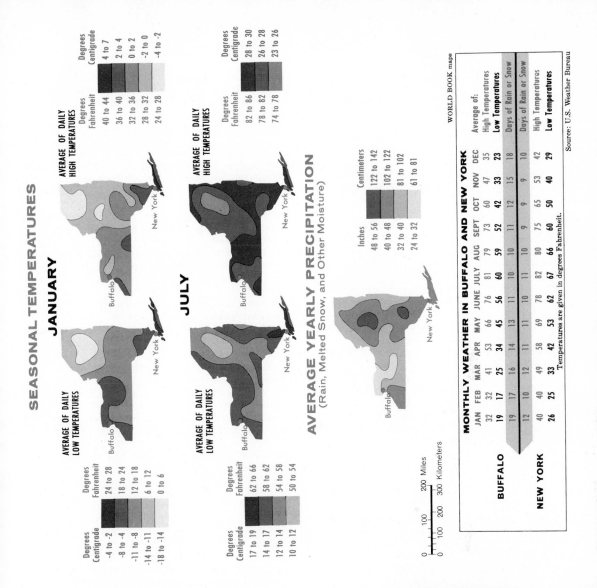

SEASONAL TEMPERATURES

JANUARY

AVERAGE OF DAILY LOW TEMPERATURES

Degrees Centigrade	Degrees Fahrenheit
-4 to -2	24 to 28
-8 to -4	18 to 24
-11 to -8	12 to 18
-14 to -11	6 to 12
-18 to -14	0 to 6

AVERAGE OF DAILY HIGH TEMPERATURES

Degrees Fahrenheit	Degrees Centigrade
40 to 44	4 to 7
36 to 40	2 to 4
32 to 36	0 to 2
28 to 32	-2 to 0
24 to 28	-4 to -2

JULY

AVERAGE OF DAILY LOW TEMPERATURES

Degrees Centigrade	Degrees Fahrenheit
17 to 19	62 to 66
14 to 17	58 to 62
12 to 14	54 to 58
10 to 12	50 to 54

AVERAGE OF DAILY HIGH TEMPERATURES

Degrees Fahrenheit	Degrees Centigrade
82 to 86	28 to 30
78 to 82	26 to 28
74 to 78	23 to 26

AVERAGE YEARLY PRECIPITATION
(Rain, Melted Snow, and Other Moisture)

Inches	Centimeters
48 to 56	122 to 142
40 to 48	102 to 122
32 to 40	81 to 102
24 to 32	61 to 81

0   100   200 Miles
0   100   200   300 Kilometers

WORLD BOOK maps

MONTHLY WEATHER IN BUFFALO AND NEW YORK													
	JAN	FEB	MAR	APR	MAY	JUNE	JULY	AUG	SEPT	OCT	NOV	DEC	Average of:
BUFFALO	32	32	41	53	66	76	81	79	73	60	47	35	High Temperatures
	19	17	25	34	45	56	60	59	52	42	33	23	Low Temperatures
	19	17	16	14	13	11	10	10	11	12	15	18	Days of Rain or Snow
	12	10	12	11	11	10	11	10	9	9	9	10	Days of Rain or Snow
NEW YORK	40	40	49	58	69	78	82	80	75	65	53	42	High Temperatures
	26	25	33	42	53	62	67	66	60	50	40	29	Low Temperatures

Temperatures are given in degrees Fahrenheit.

Source: U.S. Weather Bureau

Winter Snow covers Whiteface Mountain. This area in the Adirondack Mountains attracts skiers from New York and other states.
Dean, Three Lions

New York is the greatest manufacturing and trading state in the nation. Its excellent location, huge population, and outstanding transportation facilities have helped make it the leader in business and industry. New York is also an important agricultural state. The state's farmers produce an enormous amount of food—especially dairy products and fresh vegetables—for the big cities of New York and other East Coast states.

Natural Resources of New York include fertile soils, mineral deposits, and abundant water supplies. The state has thick forests and other plant life, and a plentiful supply of fish and game.

Soil. In general, the soils of the Appalachian Plateau tend to be poor. Most of them are gray-brown, silty loam soils developed from glacial *drift*. Drift is material ranging in size from great boulders to fine rock dust laid down by melting glaciers. Soils of the New England Upland vary between stony and gravelly loams. Most of these soils also developed from glacial drift. The Adirondack Upland has rough, stony soils. The St. Lawrence Lowland, the Hudson-Mohawk Lowland, and the Erie-Ontario Lowland have fertile, loamy, well-drained soils. The Atlantic Coastal Plain has rich sandy and alluvial soils.

Minerals. New York's chief metallic mineral is iron ore. Deposits lie throughout the Adirondacks. Valuable clay deposits are found in the middle Hudson Valley, in Erie County south of Buffalo, and in Onondaga County near Syracuse. Many sections of the state have sand and gravel deposits. Reserves of petroleum and natural gas lie in the southwest. Fibrous talc, used in ceramics, paints, and roofing, and lead and zinc come from St. Lawrence County. The Adirondacks supply a large part of the country's industrial garnets, used for watch jewels and in the manufacture of abrasives.

New York has large salt and gypsum deposits. The largest salt beds are in the Genesee Valley. Gypsum is also found in this area. The state has valuable deposits of granite, limestone, marble, and sandstone. Mines in Westchester County produce emery, used in grinding metals, gems, and lenses. This is the only emery-producing area in the United States. Slate deposits are found in Washington County.

Water is one of New York's most valuable resources, and the state has plentiful supplies. The water is used in homes and factories, for transportation, for recreation, and for powering electric generators.

Forests once covered all New York. In the 1800's and early 1900's, lumberjacks logged the forests heavily. Forested areas suitable for farms and cities also were cleared. Today, forests cover about half the state. Great tracts of trees grow throughout the Adirondacks. Smaller forests thrive throughout the Appalachian region. Trees of commercial importance include the ash, birch, cherry, maple, spruce, walnut, and white pine.

Other Plant Life. Many wild flowers bloom in river valleys throughout the state. They include black-eyed Susans, devil's-paintbrush, Queen Anne's lace, and white daisies. Buttercups, clover, goldenrod, strawberries, violets, and wild roses grow along the borders of wood lots. White and yellow water lilies thrive in many Adirondack lakes. Other common wild flowers include bunchberries, enchanter's nightshade, goldthreads, Indian pipes, starflowers, and trilliums.

Animal Life. Animals trapped for their furs in New York include foxes, gray squirrels, minks, muskrats, pine martens, raccoons, and skunks. Deer roam the forests, and rabbits range throughout the state.

More than 400 kinds of fresh- and salt-water fish live in New York waters. The most common include black crappies; brook, brown, and lake trout; northern and walleyed pike; pickerel; sunfish; white bass and smallmouth black bass; and yellow perch. New York's chief game birds include grouse, partridges, pheasants, quail, wild ducks, wild geese, and woodcocks.

Manufacturing accounts for about 95 per cent of the value of all goods produced in New York. Goods manufactured in the state have a *value added by manufacture* of about $25,331,000,000 yearly. This figure represents the value created in products by New York's industries, not counting such manufacturing costs as materials, supplies, and fuel.

New York far outranks all other states in manufacturing. The value of its manufactured products accounts for about one-tenth of the total U.S. output. New York has over 40,000 industrial plants. They employ about 1,900,000 workers. New York's factories turn out an amazing variety of products—from huge machines to hairpins. New York is the industrial giant of the United States for many reasons. These include the state's favorable location, excellent air, rail, and water transportation facilities, and the markets provided by the large population of the East Coast. New York's chief manufacturing activities, in order of importance, are (1) printing and publishing, (2) the manufacture of clothing, (3) the manufacture of electrical machinery, and (4) the manufacture of nonelectrical machinery.

Printing and Publishing have a value added of about $3½ billion yearly. New York is by far the leading state in this activity. New York City is the center of the publishing industry. It has more printing plants than any other U.S. city. New York City does almost a fourth of the nation's printing and a third of its photoengraving. It publishes about three-fourths of all the books published in the United States.

Clothing manufactured in New York has a value added of about $2,882,000,000 yearly. New York leads all the states in the production of clothing and related products. The state makes over 40 per cent of all the dresses, coats, and blouses worn by American women. About 95 per cent of the nation's furs, and about 25 per cent of all other clothing, come from New York. New York City is the nation's chief center for the manufacture of women's garments. New York City and Rochester are the leading men's clothing centers. New York City, Syracuse, and the Triple Cities (Binghamton, Johnson City, and Endicott) produce shoes. New York makes one of every nine pair of shoes manufactured in the United States. Factories in Gloversville and Johnstown specialize in leather gloves and mittens. New York turns out almost half the nation's gloves. Shirtmaking centers include New York City and Troy.

Electrical Machinery produced in New York factories has a value added of about $2,679,600,000 yearly. New

York ranks first in the manufacture of electrical machinery. Most of the factories are in Schenectady and Syracuse, and in cities on Long Island. Electrical machinery produced includes household appliances, lighting and wiring devices, and radio and television equipment.

Nonelectrical Machinery has a value added of about $2,302,700,000 annually. New York is a leading state in the production of nonelectrical machinery. The manufacture of computers is the leading activity in the industry. Chief production centers for these machines are Binghamton, Poughkeepsie, and White Plains.

Other nonelectrical machinery made in the state includes construction equipment; general and special industrial, metalworking, and service-industry machinery; and office machines. Chief production centers are Buffalo, New York City, Rochester, and Syracuse.

Other Leading Industries produce chemicals and related products, food and related products, metal products, photographic equipment and scientific instruments, and transportation equipment. The Hudson Valley is an important producer of cement. This region also makes bricks, porcelain for electrical appliances, tiles, and many similar products. Rome is a major center for the manufacture of copper products. Industries in Albany County manufacture products that include abrasives, paper goods, and steel. Buffalo is a major steel producer. Rochester is a center for the production of instruments.

Agriculture. New York's farm income totals about $1,126,000,000 yearly. But this enormous sum amounts to only about 4 per cent of the value of all goods produced in the state. New York has about 66,500 farms. They average 185 acres in size. The state's farms cover a total of about 12,275,000 acres.

Dairy Products are New York's most valuable source of farm income. They bring in about $533 million yearly. New York's cool, moist climate and excellent pastureland have contributed to the development of the state's great dairy industry. But more important has been the huge demand for dairy products from New York City and other large cities on the East Coast. Dairying is carried on in almost every part of the state. Only Wisconsin and Minnesota have more milk cows than New York. New York is one of the leading milk-producing states. It also ranks high among the states in the production of butter and cheese.

Vegetables are the second most important farm products. They account for about $114 million annually. The demand for fresh vegetables from the big cities has encouraged the growth of New York's great truck farms (see TRUCK FARMING). New York ranks high among the states in the value of its vegetable crops. It is a leader in growing celery, lettuce, onions, potatoes, snap beans, and tomatoes.

Poultry and Eggs bring New York's farmers about $81 million annually. Long Island is the state's main poultry-raising area. It supplies the nation with more than half of all the ducks marketed each year. People throughout the country enjoy Long Island ducklings. Over 2¼ billion eggs and 22 million chickens are produced on New York farms each year. Farmers also raise large numbers of geese, turkeys, and guinea fowl.

Beef Cattle and Calves are also leading farm products in New York. They provide about $73 million annually. Cattle and calves are raised throughout most of the state.

Other Farm Products. New York's most important fruit crops include apples, cherries, grapes, peaches, pears, and strawberries. Only California grows more grapes than New York. Most of New York's grapes come from vineyards along the Lake Erie shore in the far southwestern part of the state. Wine grapes are important in the Finger Lakes district. Only Washington raises more apples than New York. New York also ranks high among the states in growing pears and strawberries. Other fruits include blackberries, currants, gooseberries, plums, and raspberries. There are many plant nurseries throughout the state, especially along the shores of Lakes Erie and Ontario, and on Long Island. These nurseries produce large quantities of flowers.

Other important New York farm products include hay, grown for dairy and beef cattle, and maple syrup. New York ranks among the leading hay-producing states. New York and Vermont are leaders in the production of maple syrup.

Mining. New York's most important mineral products include iron ore, petroleum, salt, sand and gravel, stone, and zinc. New York ranks high among the states in iron-ore production. Petroleum is produced in Clin-

NEW YORK'S PRODUCTION IN 1967

Total value of goods produced—$26,768,929,000

MANUFACTURED PRODUCTS 95%

AGRICULTURAL PRODUCTS 4%

FISH & MINERAL PRODUCTS 1%

Note: Manufacturing percentage based on value added by manufacture. Other percentages based on value of production.

Sources: U.S. Government statistics

NEW YORK'S EMPLOYMENT IN 1967

Total number of persons employed—7,009,000

		Number of Employees
Manufacturing	🚶🚶🚶🚶🚶🚶	1,866,300
Wholesale & Retail Trade	🚶🚶🚶🚶🚶	1,383,300
Services	🚶🚶🚶🚶🚶	1,256,300
Government	🚶🚶🚶🚶	1,076,200
Finance, Insurance & Real Estate	🚶🚶	534,800
Transportation & Public Utilities	🚶🚶	491,700
Construction	🚶	285,800
Agriculture & Mining	🚶	114,500

Source: U.S. Department of Labor

NEW YORK

ton, Essex, and St. Lawrence counties. New York is also a leading salt-producing state. Most of the salt comes from the west-central counties. The nation's largest underground salt mine is in the Genesee Valley in Livingston County. Sand and gravel come from various parts of the state. The most valuable stones include basalt, limestone, marble, and sandstone. The state is the leading producer of emery and industrial garnets. New York mines also make the state a top producer of ilmenite and zinc. Other minerals in the state include clay, gypsum, natural gas, and talc.

Fishing Industry. New York has an annual fish catch valued at about $13 million. Fishermen take large quantities of fish from New York's rivers and inland lakes. But most of the commercial fishing takes place in Long Island waters and in Lakes Erie and Ontario. Bluefish, butterfish, clams, flounders, lobsters, oysters, porgy, scallops, striped bass, and whiting are taken from Long Island Sound. Fishermen catch bullheads, eels, perch, and pike in Lakes Erie and Ontario. In the mid-1960's, the state began a water pollution crackdown to clear rivers and streams.

Electric Power. New York ranks third, behind California and Texas, in electric power production. Fuel-burning steam plants provide about 70 per cent of New York's electric power. Most of the rest comes from water power. New York's two greatest hydroelectric power projects are the St. Lawrence Power Project and the Niagara Power Project. They were developed jointly by the Power Authority of the State of New York and Canada. In July, 1955, the General Electric Company plant in West Milton, near Schenectady, produced electricity through nuclear fission for commercial use. It was the first time this had been done anywhere. For New York's kilowatt-hour production, see ELECTRIC POWER (table).

Transportation. New York lies in the heart of the most thickly populated part of the United States. It is the chief gateway to the United States from other countries. New York is the nation's greatest industrial state. It has one of the finest natural harbors in the world,

WORLD BOOK photo by Three Lions

Printer Checks Proofs in a New York City printing plant. New York City has more printing houses than any other U.S. city. It produces about three of every four books published in the country.

and an excellent system of inland waterways. All these factors have helped New York become one of the nation's leaders in transportation.

Railroads. About 35 railroad companies serve New York. They operate on about 6,200 miles of track in the state. New York's first railroad, the Mohawk and Hudson, began running between Albany and Schenectady in 1831. New York City's subway system, the world's busiest, covers about 237 miles. More than $4\frac{1}{2}$ million passengers jam these trains every working day.

Aviation. New York has about 350 airports, 25 seaplane bases, and 40 heliports. All the principal cities have commercial airline service. About 40 domestic and international airlines serve New York. The John F. Kennedy International Airport in New York City handles more international flights than any other U.S. airport—about 240 every day. New York City is also served by La Guardia Airport and by two airports in New Jersey, Newark Airport and Teterboro Airport.

WORLD BOOK photo by Three Lions

Racks of New Clothes are pushed through New York City's bustling garment district. New York leads all states in the production of clothing.

FARM, MINERAL, AND FOREST PRODUCTS

This map shows the areas where the state's leading farm, mineral, and forest products are produced. The major urban areas (shown in red) are the state's important manufacturing centers.

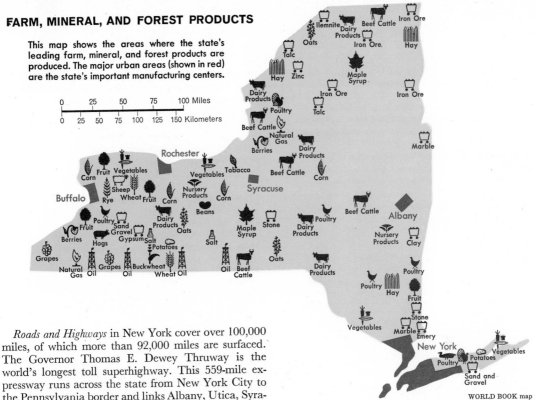

WORLD BOOK map

Roads and Highways in New York cover over 100,000 miles, of which more than 92,000 miles are surfaced. The Governor Thomas E. Dewey Thruway is the world's longest toll superhighway. This 559-mile expressway runs across the state from New York City to the Pennsylvania border and links Albany, Utica, Syracuse, Rochester, and Buffalo. The Northway superhighway links Albany with the Canadian border. New York has many great bridges. The George Washington, Bear Mountain, Mid-Hudson, Newburgh-Beacon, and Rip Van Winkle bridges span the Hudson River. The Brooklyn and Triborough bridges cross the East River. The Peace Bridge links Buffalo with Fort Erie in Canada. The Verrazano-Narrows Bridge across the Narrows channel connects Brooklyn and Staten Island. Its 4,260-foot center span is the world's longest.

Waterways. New York has one of the nation's largest internal waterway systems—the New York State Barge Canal System. The system was completed in 1918, and includes parts of the old Erie Canal and several other waterways. The Erie Canal, which was opened in 1825, connected the Hudson River with Lake Erie. It played an important part in the economic growth of New York and the entire United States. The New York State Barge Canal System and its connecting waterways cover about 800 miles. They extend from Lake Champlain and the Hudson River to Lake Erie and Lake Ontario. The St. Lawrence Seaway, which was opened in 1959, turned New York's Great Lakes ports into seaports.

Shipping. The Port of New York is the world's largest and busiest seaport. It handles more tonnage than any other U.S. port. It also handles more tonnage of foreign trade than any other American port. Huge ocean liners and freighters from all parts of the world dock at hundreds of piers in this great port. The port handles about 175 million tons of cargo each year. This cargo includes imports, exports, goods coming from other East Coast ports, and goods going to other coastal points.

Other major New York ports include Albany, Buffalo, Ogdensburg, and Rochester. Buffalo, on Lake Erie, generally outranks all other Great Lakes ports in value of tonnage handled. Ogdensburg, on the St. Lawrence River, is an important shipping center for newsprint, petroleum products, pulpwood, and other products. Albany is a major shipping center although it lies almost 150 miles from the Atlantic Ocean. The Hudson River has been deepened so that ocean ships can reach Albany.

Communication. New York leads the nation in producing books, magazines, and newspapers. William Bradford established New York's first newspaper, the *New York Gazette*, in New York City in 1725. Today, New York has about 100 daily newspapers and over 550 weeklies. One of the world's most influential newspapers, the *New York Times*, is published in New York City. Other well-known New York City newspapers are the *Daily News*, which has the largest circulation of any newspaper in the country, and the *New York Post* which is one of the nation's oldest papers. The Associated Press and United Press International have headquarters in New York City.

The General Electric Company set up New York's first radio station, WGY, in its Schenectady laboratories in 1922. The National Broadcasting Company established the first coast-to-coast radio network in 1926 in New York City. On Jan. 1, 1927, NBC made a 4,000-mile hookup with Pasadena, Calif., and carried the first broadcast of a Rose Bowl football game. The nation's first commercial television station, WNBT, began operating in New York City in 1941. New York has over 230 radio stations and 26 TV stations.

IMPORTANT DATES IN NEW YORK

1609 Henry Hudson explored the Hudson River. Samuel de Champlain visited the northern part of the New York region.

1624 The Dutch established Fort Orange (Albany), the first permanent white settlement in the New York region.

1625 Dutch settlers began building New Amsterdam (New York City).

1664 The Dutch surrendered New Amsterdam to England.

1735 Editor John Peter Zenger was found innocent of libel, an important victory for freedom of the press.

1776 New York approved the Declaration of Independence.

1779 Military expeditions under Generals James Clinton and John Sullivan broke the power of the Iroquois Indians and opened Iroquois land to white settlement.

1788 New York became the 11th state on July 26.

1789 George Washington was inaugurated in New York City as the first President of the United States.

1825 The Erie Canal was opened, linking the Hudson River and the Great Lakes.

1831 New York's first railroad, the Mohawk and Hudson, began running between Albany and Schenectady.

1863 Mobs rioted in New York City in opposition to drafting men into the Union Army.

1901 President William McKinley was assassinated at the Pan American Exposition in Buffalo.

1918 The New York State Barge Canal System was opened.

1939-1940 New York held a World's Fair.

1952 United Nations Headquarters was completed in New York City.

1959 The St. Lawrence Seaway opening made "ocean" ports of New York's ports on Lake Erie and Lake Ontario.

1960 The New York State Thruway (now the Governor Thomas E. Dewey Thruway) was completed.

1964 The Verrazano-Narrows Bridge, with the world's longest center span, was opened.

1964-1965 New York held another World's Fair.

1967 The state legislature established a lottery to help pay for education.

Martin Van Buren
born at Kinderhook

Millard Fillmore
born at Locke

Theodore Roosevelt
born in New York City

Franklin Delano Roosevelt
born at Hyde Park

HISTORIC NEW YORK

First Woman Suffrage Convention in the United States was organized in Seneca Falls in 1848 by Lucretia Mott and Elizabeth Cady Stanton.

The Erie Canal, completed in 1825, helped to open the Midwest to settlers. It linked the Hudson River with the Great Lakes by way of the Mohawk Valley.

Indian Days. Two of the largest and most powerful Indian groups in North America lived in the New York region before the white man came. One group consisted of the Delaware, Mohican, Montauk, Munsee, and Wappinger tribes of the Algonkian family of Indians. The other was the fierce and greatly feared Iroquois, or Five Nations. The Cayuga, Mohawk, Oneida, Onondaga, and Seneca tribes made up the Five Nations (see IROQUOIS INDIANS). Both Indian groups

farmed, hunted, and fished. The Iroquois were especially advanced in political and social organization. See INDIAN, AMERICAN (Table of Tribes).

Exploration and Early Settlement. Giovanni da Verrazano, an Italian navigator and pirate, was probably the first white man to visit the New York region. Verrazano supposedly was hired by King Francis I of France to explore the northern part of America. Historians believe Verrazano may have sailed into New

George Washington took the oath of office as the nation's first President in New York City on April 30, 1789. New York City served as the capital of the United States from 1785 to 1790.

Turning Point of the Revolutionary War was General John Burgoyne's surrender to General Horatio Gates on Oct. 17, 1777, after the Second Battle of Saratoga.

Freedom of the Press won its first victory in the American colonies when John Peter Zenger, Editor of the *New York Weekly Journal*, was acquitted of criminal libel in 1735. He had criticized the British governor.

The National Baseball Hall of Fame and Museum at Cooperstown, the "birthplace" of baseball, honors outstanding players of the game.

Saratoga

Cooperstown

ALBANY ★

Locke

Henry Hudson, an English explorer, sailed up the Hudson River in 1609. He explored the New York region as far as the area near the present site of Albany.

Kinderhook

The First Successful Steamboat, the *Clermont,* built by Robert Fulton, completed a trip from New York City to Albany in 32 hours on Aug. 19, 1807.

Hyde Park

West Point

West Point, home of the United States Military Academy, lies on bluffs rising above the Hudson River. Congress established the school on Mar. 16, 1802, after George Washington had twice recommended a national military academy be founded.

Manhattan Island Was Bought for $24. In 1626, Peter Minuit, director-general of New Netherland, paid the Manhattan Indians $24 in trinkets for Manhattan Island.

New York City

NEW YORK

York Bay and discovered the Hudson River in 1524.

In 1609, Henry Hudson, an Englishman employed by the Dutch, sailed up the river that now bears his name. He was looking for a Northwest Passage to the Orient. Hudson's voyage gave The Netherlands a claim to the territory covering much of present-day New York, New Jersey, Delaware, and part of Connecticut. The territory was named *New Netherland*.

Also in 1609, the French explorer Samuel de Champlain entered the northern part of New York from Quebec. His visit gave France a claim to the land.

The Dutch established several trading posts and prosperous settlements in the Hudson Valley soon after Hudson's visit. They built up a profitable fur trade with the Indians. In 1621, a group of Dutch merchants formed the Dutch West India Company. The government of The Netherlands gave the company all rights to trade in New Netherland for the next 24 years. In 1624, the company sent about 30 families to the region. Some of these families founded Fort Orange (now Albany), the first permanent white settlement in the colony. The rest established settlements in other parts of New Netherland. In 1625, a group of Dutch colonists began building a fort and laying out a town on Manhattan Island. They named their settlement *New Amsterdam*. In 1626, Peter Minuit, the Dutch governor (or director-general), bought Manhattan from the Indians for goods worth 60 Dutch guilders, or about $24. During the next few years, Wiltwyck (now Kingston), Rensselaerswyck (now Rensselaer), Breuckelen (now Brooklyn), Schenectady, and other settlements were established by Dutch colonists.

In 1629, the Dutch West India Company set up the *patroon* (landowner) system to speed the settlement of New Netherland. Members of the company were given huge tracts of land, which they could keep if they colonized the land with settlers. Only one patroonship was successful, that of Kiliaen Van Rensselaer, an Amsterdam diamond merchant. His land covered much of present-day Albany, Columbia, and Rensselaer counties. Van Rensselaer began the practice of leasing his land. He established the tenant system in New

York, which lasted until the tenant farmers rebelled in the early 1800's. See PATROON SYSTEM.

Under English Rule. Many English colonists from Connecticut and Massachusetts settled on Long Island. For a long time, they cooperated with the Dutch. But gradually the English began to oppose the Dutch. In addition, King Charles II of England decided to take over New Netherland. He gave his brother James, the Duke of York, a charter for the territory. In 1664, the English sent a fleet to seize New Netherland. The warships dropped anchor in the harbor of New Amsterdam. Peter Stuyvesant, the Dutch governor, surrendered the settlement without a fight.

Under the Treaty of Breda, signed in 1667, the Dutch formally gave up all New Netherland to England. The English renamed the territory *New York*, after the Duke of York, a famed naval hero who later became King James II.

At first, the colony prospered under English rule. Later, dishonest governors kept New York from developing rapidly. The farm tenant system further discouraged progress. Most of the land lay in large estates. Poor persons who wanted land of their own had to settle outside the colony.

Soon after the English won control of southern New York, the French began to take great interest in the northern part. In 1669, the French explorer Robert Cavelier, Sieur de la Salle, entered the Niagara region. In 1731, the French built a fortress at Crown Point on Lake Champlain. They prepared to take permanent possession of northern New York. Meanwhile, in 1689, war had broken out in Europe between England and France. New York soon became a battleground in the struggle between the two countries.

From 1689 until 1763, the region suffered severely through four wars, known in America as the French and Indian Wars. Battles were fought at Crown Point, Fort Niagara, Fort Ticonderoga, and many other places. The French received aid from the Algonkian Indians in the wars, but the Iroquois helped the English. The French and Indian Wars delayed settlement of the frontier regions and slowed the growth of sections that had already been settled. England and France signed a peace treaty—the Treaty of Paris—in 1763. But the wars cost France almost all its possessions in

Erie Canal opened in 1825 with a huge celebration. The canal provided an all-water route between the Hudson River and Buffalo. It greatly lowered the cost of transporting goods.

Immigrants of the 1880's wait for permission to enter the United States. The immigration station was on Ellis Island in New York Harbor. More than 16,000,000 persons passed through the station before it closed in 1954.

Three Lions

Pan American Exposition, held in Buffalo in 1901, sought to promote unity and understanding among the nations of North and South America. President William McKinley was shot on September 6 during a public reception at the exposition's Temple of Music.

Buffalo and Erie County Historical Society

North America. See FRENCH AND INDIAN WARS.

In 1735, John Peter Zenger, publisher of the *New York Weekly Journal*, won a great victory for freedom of the press. Zenger had criticized the English governor, and was charged with libel. In a historic trial, the jury found Zenger innocent.

The Revolutionary War. British policies angered many people of New York. They did not like the presence of British troops, the authority of royal judges, or the taxes passed by the British Parliament. Other New Yorkers, called Loyalists or Tories, did not oppose the British. Nobody knows how many persons were Loyalists. But after the Revolutionary War, more than 30,000 persons left the state. During the war, New York was the scene of many battles, on both land and water. The Loyalists helped the British and persuaded the Iroquois Indians to fight the patriots. American patriots won two of the most important battles of the war in New York. These were the Battle of Oriskany in August, 1777, and the Battle of Saratoga in October, 1777. See REVOLUTIONARY WAR IN AMERICA.

Statehood. On July 9, 1776, the provincial congress of New York met in White Plains. It approved the Declaration of Independence which the Continental Congress had adopted on July 4. The congress also organized an independent government. The next year, New York adopted its first constitution. George Clinton, who later became Vice-President of the United States, was elected as the first governor of New York. On Feb. 6, 1778, New York approved the Articles of Confederation. On July 9, it ratified the Articles in the Continental Congress. New York did not want a strong federal government. But it finally ratified the United States Constitution on July 26, 1788. New York was the 11th state to enter the Union. New York City served as the capital of the United States from 1785 to 1790. In 1789, George Washington was inaugurated as the nation's first President. The inauguration took place in Federal Hall in New York City.

Settlement of the interior progressed rapidly. In 1779, General Washington sent an expedition to crush the mighty Iroquois. Troops commanded by General James Clinton raided Indian villages up through the Mohawk Valley. The soldiers then moved down the Susquehanna River to Tioga, Pa. There, they joined troops commanded by General John Sullivan. The combined force of about 3,500 men marched through the Finger Lakes region to the Genesee Valley. The soldiers wiped out Indian villages, killed the Indians' livestock, and burned their fields. The heart of the Iroquois territory was left in ruin. The military power of the Iroquois lay broken forever, leaving the area open to white settlement. After the Revolutionary War, soldiers who had fought in the area told of its level, fertile land. Many veterans settled on grants of land they received there.

War broke out between the United States and Great Britain in 1812 (see WAR OF 1812). Much of the fight-

255

ing took place in frontier regions near the New York-Canada border. After the war, pioneers began to settle in the northern and western sections of the state. Many came from other parts of New York, but many also came from New England, Canada, New Jersey, Delaware, and Pennsylvania. By 1820, about 500,000 persons lived in frontier settlements. New York had a population of over 1,370,000, more than any other state.

Growing Prosperity. As the frontier was opened, the people of New York realized that better transportation would be needed between the coast and the interior. Governor De Witt Clinton had long urged the construction of a canal to link the Atlantic Ocean and the Great Lakes. In 1825, the famous Erie Canal was completed. It crossed New York from Buffalo on Lake Erie to Troy and Albany on the Hudson River. The canal provided an important link in an all-water route between New York City and Buffalo. It greatly lowered the cost of transporting goods. Farmers in the West shipped their produce to the East by way of the Great Lakes and the Erie Canal. Products from New York's growing factories were, in turn, shipped on the canal to western markets (see ERIE CANAL).

The development of railroads across the state soon followed the opening of the Erie Canal. The canal and railroads greatly encouraged the state's growing prosperity. They also provided jobs for many of the thousands of European immigrants who were pouring into the state. By 1850, New York was firmly established as the *Empire State*. It led the nation in population, in manufacturing, and in commerce.

Wealthy merchants and great landowners had controlled New York since colonial days. During the early 1800's, the state adopted more and more democratic practices. In the 1820's, white men no longer had to own property to be able to vote. A new constitution adopted in 1846 required that all major state officials be elected by the voters. In 1839, the *antirent movement* began when tenant farmers refused to pay rent to wealthy landowners. The antirenters, disguised as Indians, ranged the countryside and terrorized the landlords. The antirent movement grew rapidly and became a powerful political force. During the 1840's, the great landlords began breaking up their estates into small independent farms. See ANTIRENTER.

Long before the Civil War began in 1861, many of New York's people strongly opposed slavery. But some did not. In July, 1863, mobs rioted for four days in New York City. They objected to drafting men into the Union Army. The mobs burned, robbed, and murdered recklessly. They killed or wounded about a thousand persons and destroyed more than $1½ million worth of property. Troops called from the battlefield finally ended the riots. Despite the draft riots, New York provided more soldiers, supplies, and money to the Union war effort than any other state.

After the Civil War ended in 1865, new manufacturing centers grew up in various parts of New York. More and more products of the Middle West flowed through Buffalo, the state's western gateway. Increased commerce between the United States and other countries passed through New York City, the state's eastern gate-

way. New York City, already the nation's industrial and financial capital, also became a leading cultural center. As manufacturing continued to increase, new waves of immigrants poured in, drawn by employment opportunities. They came from Italy, Poland, Russia, and other southern and eastern European countries. By 1900, the state had more than 7 million persons.

The Early 1900's. In 1901, a Pan American Exposition was held in Buffalo. The exhibition sought to promote unity and understanding between North and South America.

Theodore Roosevelt, a Republican, served as governor of New York in 1899 and 1900. He supported a number of reform bills, especially in the field of labor. In 1901, Roosevelt became Vice-President of the United States under President William McKinley. On Sept. 6, 1901, six months after the inauguration, an assassin shot McKinley at the opening ceremonies of the Pan American Exposition. McKinley died eight days later, and Roosevelt became President.

The United States entered World War I in 1917. New York City served as the great port from which thousands of American soldiers sailed for and returned from the battlefields of Europe.

The Great Depression of the late 1920's and the 1930's hit New York hard. Unemployment was severe. Men and women sold apples on street corners. Hungry persons lined up at soup kitchens, or stood in bread lines that stretched for blocks.

Alfred E. Smith, a Democrat, served as governor of New York from 1919 to 1921 and from 1923 to 1929. He lost to Republican Herbert Hoover in the 1928 presidential election. Franklin D. Roosevelt was governor from 1929 to 1932. He served as President from 1933 until his death in 1945. Herbert H. Lehman succeeded Roosevelt as governor and served until 1942. Much of the social legislation supported by Governors Roosevelt and Lehman attacked the depression. This legislation later served as a model for federal laws urged by President Roosevelt.

The Mid-1900's. New York became a center of the country's defense industry in the mid-1900's. Factories produced large amounts of war materials during World War II (1939-1945), the Korean War (1950-1953), and the Vietnam War. These materials came from the state's industrial centers—Buffalo, New York City, Rochester, Schenectady, and Syracuse—and hundreds of smaller communities. Growth occurred in several fields, including agriculture, banking, insurance, and manufacturing.

In 1946, the United Nations selected New York City as the site of its permanent home. Construction of UN headquarters was completed in 1952. Two world's fairs were held in New York City during the mid-1900's—in 1939 and 1940 and in 1964 and 1965.

In 1948, New York established its first state university—the State University of New York. The university has grown into a system of more than 60 campuses.

During the 1950's, New York and the Canadian province of Ontario developed a large hydroelectric project on the St. Lawrence River. In 1961, the first generator of a giant hydroelectric power plant began to produce electric power at Niagara Falls.

New York also greatly improved its transportation system. The St. Lawrence Seaway opened in 1959, allowing ocean-going ships to sail to ports on the Great

Lakes. In 1960, New York completed the world's longest toll superhighway, the New York State Thruway. This 559-mile expressway was renamed the Governor Thomas E. Dewey Thruway in 1964. Also in the 1960's, the state opened the 180-mile North-South Expressway and the 176-mile Adirondack Northway. The expressway runs through the middle of the state, connecting Pennsylvania with the province of Ontario. The scenic northway extends from Albany to Quebec. In 1964, the Verrazano-Narrows Bridge opened in New York City. This bridge includes the world's longest center span.

During the 1960's, the Lincoln Center for the Performing Arts was built in New York City. The center serves as a home for some of the country's leading cultural institutions. These institutions include the Juilliard School of Music, the Metropolitan Opera, and the New York Philharmonic Orchestra.

New York Today needs more and better health facilities, schools, transportation, and welfare services. The state has pioneered in much social legislation—and its people continue to expect broad social programs. Welfare costs rank second only to education expenses in New York. Both state and local governments have raised taxes and borrowed more and more money to pay for their social programs. The people of New York pay more taxes per person than the residents of any other state.

The cost of education accounts for more than 40 per cent of New York's budget. The state uses profits from a lottery established in 1967 to help pay for education.

Racial segregation is an urgent problem in New

THE GOVERNORS OF NEW YORK

		Party	Term			Party	Term
1.	George Clinton	None	1777-1795	28.	Samuel Jones Tilden	Democratic	1875-1876
2.	John Jay	Federalist	1795-1801	29.	Lucius Robinson	Democratic	1877-1879
3.	George Clinton	*Dem.-Rep.	1801-1804	30.	Alonzo B. Cornell	Republican	1880-1882
4.	Morgan Lewis	*Dem.-Rep.	1804-1807	31.	Grover Cleveland	Democratic	1883-1885
5.	Daniel D. Tompkins	*Dem.-Rep.	1807-1817	32.	David Bennett Hill	Democratic	1885-1891
6.	John Taylor	*Dem.-Rep.	1817	33.	Roswell Pettibone Flower	Democratic	1892-1894
7.	De Witt Clinton	*Dem.-Rep.	1817-1822	34.	Levi Parsons Morton	Republican	1895-1896
8.	Joseph C. Yates	*Dem.-Rep.	1823-1824	35.	Frank Sweet Black	Republican	1897-1898
9.	De Witt Clinton	*Dem.-Rep.	1825-1828	36.	Theodore Roosevelt	Republican	1899-1900
10.	Nathaniel Pitcher	Independent	1828	37.	Benjamin B. Odell, Jr.	Republican	1901-1904
11.	Martin Van Buren	*Dem.-Rep.	1829	38.	Frank Wayland Higgins	Republican	1905-1906
12.	Enos T. Throop	Democratic	1829-1832	39.	Charles Evans Hughes	Republican	1907-1910
13.	William L. Marcy	Democratic	1833-1838	40.	Horace White	Republican	1910
14.	William H. Seward	Whig	1839-1842	41.	John Alden Dix	Democratic	1911-1912
15.	William C. Bouck	Democratic	1843-1844	42.	William Sulzer	Democratic	1913
16.	Silas Wright	Democratic	1845-1846	43.	Martin Henry Glynn	Democratic	1913-1914
17.	John Young	Whig	1847-1848	44.	Charles S. Whitman	Republican	1915-1918
18.	Hamilton Fish	Whig	1849-1850	45.	Alfred E. Smith	Democratic	1919-1920
19.	Washington Hunt	Whig	1851-1852	46.	Nathan L. Miller	Republican	1921-1922
20.	Horatio Seymour	Democratic	1853-1854	47.	Alfred E. Smith	Democratic	1923-1928
21.	Myron Holley Clark	Whig	1855-1856	48.	Franklin D. Roosevelt	Democratic	1929-1932
22.	John Alsop King	Republican	1857-1858	49.	Herbert H. Lehman	Democratic	1933-1942
23.	Edwin Denison Morgan	Republican	1859-1862	50.	Charles Poletti	Democratic	1942
24.	Horatio Seymour	Democratic	1863-1864	51.	Thomas E. Dewey	Republican	1943-1954
25.	Reuben Eaton Fenton	Republican	1865-1868	52.	W. Averell Harriman	Democratic	1955-1958
26.	John Thompson Hoffman	Democratic	1869-1872	53.	Nelson A. Rockefeller	Republican	1959-
27.	John Adams Dix	Republican	1873-1874		*Democratic-Republican		

Richard A. Peer

Robert Moses Power Dam is part of a large hydroelectric project on the St. Lawrence River. The project was developed jointly by the state of New York and the province of Ontario in the 1950's.

York's elementary and high schools, especially those in New York City. The population of certain areas of the city consists largely of Negroes and Puerto Ricans. As a result, school enrollment in those areas is almost entirely Negro and Puerto Rican. Demands to end this *de facto* segregation have created intense disagreement and sometimes violence. The state has attempted to eliminate de facto segregation by changing the boundaries of school districts and by busing children to schools outside their own districts.

New York is attacking the problem of water pollution

with a $1-billion program. This program was designed to eliminate pollution from all state waterways by 1975. New York is also spending $2½ billion to expand its highway system, to add to or improve major state airports, to rebuild rapid transit systems, and to assist local railway and bus operations.

New York City and upstate New York have long tended to distrust each other. The city has claimed for years that it does not receive a fair share of state aid. The state legislature was *reapportioned* (redivided) in 1966 to give New York City more representation. But conflict between the city and upstate New York remains a major problem.

JAMES A. FROST, JOHN J. LEARY, and JOHN H. THOMPSON

NEW YORK/Study Aids

Related Articles. See NEW YORK CITY with its list of Related Articles. See also the following articles:

BIOGRAPHIES

Arthur, Chester A.	Johnson, Sir William
Astor (family)	La Guardia, Fiorello H.
Bausch (family)	Leisler, Jacob
Bohlen, Charles Eustis	Lewis, Francis
Bryant, William Cullen	Lindsay, John Vliet
Burr, Aaron	Livingston, Philip
Cabrini, Saint Frances	Livingston, Robert R.
Champlain, Samuel de	Miller, William E.
Clark, Mark W.	Minuit, Peter
Cleveland, Grover	Morris, Gouverneur
Clinton, De Witt	Morris, Lewis
Clinton, George	Ochs, Adolph S.
Cooper, James Fenimore	Paine, Thomas
Cooper, Peter	Powell, Adam Clayton, Jr.
Cornell, Ezra	Pulitzer, Joseph
Curtiss, Glenn H.	Rockefeller (family)
Dewey, Thomas E.	Rogers, William P.
Eastman, George	Roosevelt, Eleanor
Fargo, William G.	Roosevelt, Franklin D.
Farley, James A.	Roosevelt, Theodore
Fillmore, Millard	Roosevelt, Theodore, Jr.
Fish (family)	Root, Elihu
Flemming, Arthur S.	Runyon, Damon
Floyd, William	Schuyler, Philip J.
Forrestal, James V.	Seymour, Horatio
Fulton, Robert	Smith, Alfred E.
Gates, Horatio	Spellman, Francis Cardinal
Goodrich, Benjamin F.	Stuyvesant, Peter
Gould (family)	Sulzberger, Arthur H.
Greeley, Horace	Tilden, Samuel J.
Hale, Nathan	Tompkins, Daniel D.
Hamilton, Alexander	Van Buren, Martin
Harriman (family)	Vanderbilt (family)
Hayes, Patrick Cardinal	Van Rensselaer (family)
Hearst (family)	Wagner, Robert F.
Hudson, Henry	Walker, James J.
Hughes, Charles Evans	Wharton, Edith N. J.
Irving, Washington	Wheeler, William A.
Javits, Jacob K.	Whitman, Walt
Jay, John	Zenger, John Peter

CITIES AND OTHER COMMUNITIES

Albany	Levittown	Rome
Binghamton	Mount Vernon	Saratoga Springs
Buffalo	New Rochelle	Schenectady
Cooperstown	Niagara Falls	Syracuse
Corning	Oswego	Troy
Elmira	Plattsburgh	Utica
Ithaca	Poughkeepsie	White Plains
Jamestown	Rochester	Yonkers
Kingston		

HISTORY

Albany Congress	French and Indian Wars
Antirenter	Hunker
Barnburner	Iroquois Indians
Bucktail	Loco-Foco
Colonial Life in America	New Netherland
Crown Point	Patroon System
Dutch West India Company	Revolutionary War
Federal Hall	in America
Fort Niagara	Tammany, Society of
Fort Ticonderoga	War of 1812
Free Soil Party	

PHYSICAL FEATURES

Adirondack Mountains	Lake Placid
Allegheny River	Long Island
Catskill Mountains	Mohawk River
Delaware River	Montauk Peninsula
Finger Lakes	Niagara Falls and Niagara
Genesee River	River
Hudson River	Palisades
Lake Champlain	Saint Lawrence River
Lake Erie	Saranac Lakes
Lake George	Susquehanna River
Lake Oneida	Thousand Islands
Lake Ontario	

PRODUCTS AND INDUSTRY

For New York's rank among the states in production, see the following articles:

Aluminum	Cherry	Maple Sugar	Salt
Apple	Clothing	Milk	Textile
Bean	Grape	Onion	Timothy
Cattle	Iron and Steel	Potato	Vegetable
Cheese	Leather	Publishing	Wine
Chemical	Manufacturing		
Industry			

OTHER RELATED ARTICLES

Castle Clinton	New York State Barge
National Monument	Canal System
Chautauqua	Oneida Community
Erie Canal	Peace Bridge
Fort Stanwix	Sing Sing
George Junior Republic	United Nations
Middle Atlantic States	

Outline

I. Government

A. Constitution	E. Local Government
B. Executive	F. Taxation
C. Legislature	G. Politics
D. Courts	

II. People

Questions

Why have New York's governors always been considered possible presidential candidates?

Why has New York earned its nickname the *Empire State?*

How many visitors does New York City usually have every year?

Why was the Erie Canal so important in New York's history?

Where did George Washington take the oath of office as the first President of the United States?

What are some of the reasons that New York is the greatest industrial state?

How does New York City rank in size with other cities in the United States? In the world?

Why has the Hudson-Mohawk Lowland been so important in the development of New York?

How was the power of the Iroquois Indians broken in New York in 1779?

Why is New York known as a *melting pot?*

Books for Young Readers

COOPER, JAMES FENIMORE. *The Spy.* Many editions are available.

DELEEUW, CATEAU. *Determined to be Free.* Nelson, 1963.

EARLE, ALICE. *Colonial Days in Old New York.* Friedman, 1962.

EDMONDS, WALTER D. *They Had a Horse.* Dodd, 1962. A story of tough pioneer life in the 1700's in the Scoharie Valley.

EDMONDS, WALTER D. *Two Logs Crossing.* Dodd, 1943. A 16-year-old boy does a man's job and finds himself during the hard pioneer days of the early 1800's.

EDMONDS, WALTER D. *Wilderness Clearing.* Dodd, 1944. A 16-year-old boy becomes a man during the tense Revolutionary War days in the Mohawk Valley.

FAXON, LAVINIA. *A Young Explorer's New York.* New York Graphic Society, 1962. Maps of Manhattan.

VROOMAN, JOHN J. *Council Fire and Cannon.* Follett, 1962.

Books for Older Readers

DANGERFIELD, GEORGE. *Chancellor Robert R. Livingston of New York, 1746-1813.* Harcourt, 1960.

ELDRIDGE, PAUL. *Crown of Empire: A Story of the State of New York.* Barnes, 1962.

ELLIS, DAVID M. *New York: The Empire State.* 2nd ed. Prentice-Hall, 1964. With J. A. Frost, and others: *A Short History of New York State.* Cornell, 1957.

HISLOP, CODMAN. *The Mohawk.* Rinehart, 1948. The river and its history.

IRVING, WASHINGTON. *Knickerbocker's History of New York.* Ed. by Anne Carroll Moore. Ungar, 1959.

LYMAN, SUSAN E. *The Story of New York: An Informal History of the City.* Crown, 1964.

MANLEY, SEON. *Long Island Discovery: An Adventure into the History, Manners, and Mores of America's Front Porch.* Doubleday, 1966.

NEW YORK, CITY UNIVERSITY OF, consists of nine senior colleges, six junior colleges, and a Graduate Center in New York City. The Mount Sinai School of Medicine is also affiliated with the university. The nine senior colleges are Bernard M. Baruch College, City College, Hunter College, and John Jay College of Criminal Justice, all in Manhattan; Herbert H. Lehman College in the Bronx; Brooklyn College in Brooklyn; Queens College and York College in Queens; and Richmond College on Staten Island. These colleges offer liberal arts and science programs leading to bachelor's degrees. Master's degrees are offered in liberal arts, education, engineering, social work, nursing, business, and public administration. Doctor's degrees are offered in 25 fields.

The six junior colleges are Bronx, Kingsborough, New York City, Queensborough, Staten Island, and Borough of Manhattan community colleges. They offer associate degrees in arts and applied science.

The university is supported by the city, state, and federal governments, and by fees and gifts. Tuition is free to qualified city residents studying for bachelor's degrees, to state residents preparing to teach, and to disadvantaged students enrolled in special programs. Master's degree programs for teachers are tuition-free to state residents. All other students pay tuition.

The City University of New York gained university status in 1961. It is one of the largest systems of higher education in the United States. For enrollment, see UNIVERSITIES (table).　　HENRY D. PALEY

NEW YORK, STATE UNIVERSITY OF, is the statewide public system of higher education in the state of New York. It includes 4 university centers, 10 colleges of arts and science, 2 medical centers, 8 specialized colleges, 6 agricultural and technical colleges, and 30 community colleges.

The four university centers are in Albany, Binghamton, Buffalo, and Stony Brook. The 10 state colleges are in Brockport, Buffalo, Cortland, Fredonia, Geneseo, New Paltz, Oneonta, Oswego, Plattsburgh, and Potsdam. The Downstate Medical Center is in Brooklyn, a borough of New York City; and the Upstate Medical Center is in Syracuse. Other professional colleges include the College of Forestry at Syracuse University; the Maritime College in the Bronx, a borough of New York City; and the College of Ceramics at Alfred University. State university colleges of agriculture, home economics, and veterinary medicine, and a school of industrial and labor relations are at Cornell University. The graduate school of public affairs is in Albany.

The master's degree is offered at 24 of the campuses. The doctor of philosophy degree is granted at the four university centers and nine other campuses of the State University of New York.

Two-year courses are offered at the agricultural and technical colleges at Alfred, Canton, Cobleskill, Delhi, Farmingdale, and Morrisville. The community colleges are also two-year institutions. The community colleges and the technical colleges offer associate degrees.

State University of New York was established in 1948. Headquarters are at Albany. For enrollment, see UNIVERSITIES AND COLLEGES (table).　　SAMUEL B. GOULD

New York City is the world's largest and busiest seaport. Ocean liners and freighters from all parts of the world dock at piers on the Hudson and East rivers. Ships come and go past the towering buildings of the financial district at the tip of Manhattan Island.

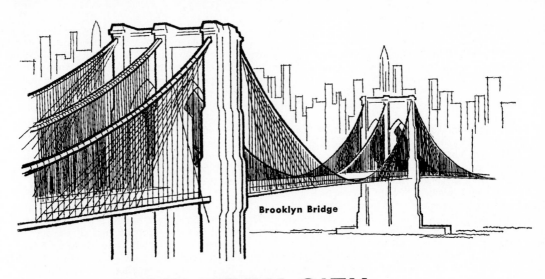
Brooklyn Bridge

NEW YORK CITY

NEW YORK CITY (pop. 7,867,760; met. area 11,528,-649; alt. 55 ft.) is one of the greatest cities in the world. It ranks as the world's second largest city, after Tokyo. New York City is a center of many large industries, and of business and finance. It also is a center of shipping, of educational and cultural facilities, and of theatrical and other amusements. The United Nations has its headquarters in New York City.

New York City is sometimes called *Gotham*, after a legendary English village whose inhabitants were noted for their foolishness. This name was humorously given to the city by Washington Irving because so many "wiseacres" (persons pretending to have great knowledge) lived there in his time. But today this city is the cultural center of the nation.

New York City is one of the most important financial centers in the world. Along Wall Street are the banks, stock exchanges, and other financial institutions that provide working capital for most of the largest corporations in the United States. These organizations have great power in the world's money markets. Lower Broadway, Park Avenue, and Madison Avenue are lined with skyscrapers that house the home offices of many national and international business concerns.

As a cultural center, New York City has no equal in the United States. Here are most of the publishing houses that select and produce the nation's books. Plays or musical shows usually succeed or fail depending on reactions of New York critics and audiences. This city also is the center of other fine arts—painting, sculpture, opera, and dancing.

New York City is the fashion center of the United States. Copies of dresses and hats designed on Seventh Avenue are shipped to countless small-town stores.

This metropolis has a great influence on the entire nation. Interest in New York City is keen everywhere. Many newspapers from Maine to California contain a column devoted to news and gossip about people in New York City.

Manhattan, which is the heart of New York City, is an island on which most of the large buildings are located.

Peter Minuit, the governor of the Dutch West India Company, bought this island of 14,272 acres from the Indians in 1626. He paid the Indians with beads, cloth, and trinkets worth about $24. Today, the land and buildings together are valued at about $29 billion.

Location, Size, and Description

New York City is made up of five boroughs: Manhattan, the Bronx, Queens, Brooklyn, and Richmond. They lie at the mouth of the Hudson River in the southeastern corner of the state of New York. Together they cover an area of about 365 square miles, including 65 square miles of inland water. For location, see NEW YORK (political map). Manhattan, the smallest borough, covers about 31 square miles. It lies between the East and Hudson rivers. The section of the Hudson River from about 51st Street to the Battery is often called the North River. The East River is actually a strait separating Manhattan from Long Island. Manhattan is 13.4 miles long and 2.3 miles wide at its widest point. Originally, all of New York City lay in Manhattan. But in 1874 and 1895, parts of Westchester County were annexed to form what is now the Bronx. The Bronx lies north and east of Manhattan. It covers about 54 square miles, and is mainly residential.

In 1898, Brooklyn, Richmond, and Queens counties were united with Manhattan and the Bronx to form Greater New York. Queens, the largest borough, covers about 127 square miles. It forms part of the western end of Long Island. Brooklyn, also part of Long Island, has the second largest area, about 89 square miles. More people live in Brooklyn than any other borough. Richmond, better known as Staten Island, lies in the bay. Richmond (about 64 square miles) has the smallest population. Its small farms and truck gardens make it appear quite countrified.

The little island of Manhattan, where over $1\frac{1}{2}$ million people live, is the most important of the boroughs of New York City. Here one finds the tallest skyscrapers, the chief shipping port, some of America's largest schools and colleges, and the most famous theatrical district in the world. Also, much of the early history of the city centers on this tiny island.

Manhattan is surrounded by rivers and small islands. From the lower end, at Battery Park, one can see the whole length of Upper New York Bay to the Narrows, a distance of seven miles. The Narrows is a passage leading from the Lower Bay, part of the Atlantic Ocean, into the Upper Bay, New York City's harbor. The East and North (Hudson) rivers meet in the harbor and form the east and west boundaries of Manhattan. The Harlem River divides Manhattan and the Bronx. A channel, Spuyten Duyvil Creek, connects the North and Harlem rivers. Washington Irving told the legend of Antony van Corlear to explain this Dutch name. Corlear drowned while trying to swim the channel one stormy night "in spite of the devil."

The rivers surrounding Manhattan and Upper New York Bay are filled with smaller islands. One of them, just off the lower end of Manhattan, is almost as famous as Manhattan itself. This is Liberty Island, on which the Statue of Liberty stands. France gave the statue to the United States in 1884 as a symbol of "Liberty Enlightening the World." Nearby is Ellis Island, which, until 1954, was used as a detention and deportation center by the U.S. Immigration Service. Ellis and Liberty islands now form the Statue of Liberty National Monument. Coney Island is no longer an island. Land has been filled in connecting it with the south side of Brooklyn. Governors Island, at the entrance to the East River, is the site of one of the city's oldest military fortifications. Welfare, Ward's, Randall's, and Riker's islands lie in the East River. Welfare institutions are located on them.

The most noted of the famous streets of New York is usually agreed to be Fifth Avenue, which begins at the Washington Memorial Arch and runs for seven miles through the heart of the city. It is lined with fine stores, hotels, churches, clubs, museums, and fashionable apartment houses. World-famous Broadway cuts diagonally across the city from the Battery to the north end of Manhattan. North of the intersection of Broadway, Seventh Avenue, and 42d Street is Times Square, named for the old New York Times Building. In the mid-1960's, the Allied Chemical Corporation bought the building and remodeled its exterior. Times Square, or the *Great White Way*, is a patch of light and color.

North of Washington Square, Manhattan is laid out in a regular pattern of cross streets. The avenues run north and south and the numbered streets run east and west. South of the square is a jumble of small, crooked streets. In this section is the Bowery, the "East Side," Chinatown, and all the vast mixture of old and new New York City. Wall Street, home of the nation's financial institutions, and the great commercial districts of the city are farther south, near Battery Park.

Suburbs. All the millions of persons who work in New York City cannot live there. Millions live in suburbs in New York, New Jersey, and Connecticut. They commute by automobiles, subways, trains, ferries, and buses.

The People

It is the people of a city who tell the real story of its growth and importance. Manhattan was first settled by

the Dutch in the 1620's. During the Dutch and English wars, England took the city and changed its name from New Amsterdam to New York. All during the 1600's the city grew rapidly, and became one of the busiest shipping centers of the Western Hemisphere. Its importance as a port attracted new colonists, and by 1700 there were over 7,000 inhabitants, who spoke 18 different languages.

Today, New York City has more people from other lands than any city in the world. There are people from 60 nations living within its boundaries. About 2,650,000 of these persons were born abroad, and another 2,700,000 are the children of immigrants.

It is said that there are more Jews in New York City than in Israel; almost as many persons of Italian descent as in Rome, Italy; almost as many of German descent as in Bremen, Germany; and almost as many of Irish descent as in Dublin, Ireland. More Negroes live in New York City than in any other U.S. city. The Puerto Rican population more than doubled between 1950 and 1955. Over 600,000 Puerto Ricans live in the city. Because all these people are so much a part of New York City, and have contributed so much to making it what it is, it is almost impossible to classify them in special industrial groups. They work together at the thousands of jobs that make the city a business and cultural center.

Religion. Greater New York has about 4,000 churches of various faiths. The Roman Catholics make up the leading religious group, with the Jews next in number of members. Other leading faiths include the Lutherans, Methodists, Presbyterians, Congregationalists, Episcopalians, Baptists, and Friends (Quakers).

Culture Groups. Only a few of the many culture groups that make up the population of New York City have established colonies with definite boundaries. For the most part, these descendants of many races may be found in all the neighborhoods throughout the city. The Lower East Side contains thousands of Jews, Italians, Poles, Greeks, Russians, Spaniards, Puerto Ricans, and Lithuanians, as well as some Turks, Persians, and Chinese. Districts of New York City which represent races or nationalities include the following:

Chinatown lies west of Chatham Square and the Bowery, between Canal Street on the north and Worth Street on the south. The Oriental atmosphere of the

Towering Skyscrapers cast brilliant reflections on the East River at night. The 1,250-foot-high Empire State Building, *far right*, in Manhattan, is one of the world's tallest buildings.

Chinese section attracts many New York City visitors. Approximately 5,000 of the city's 30,000 Chinese live here.

Harlem is between the Harlem and Hudson rivers from Morningside Heights to Washington Heights. Most of Harlem's residents are Negroes and Latin Americans.

Cultural Life

Education. New York City has the largest school system in the world. There are more than 800 public schools with nearly one million pupils. There are also hundreds of parochial schools.

The colleges, seminaries, and universities of New York City are known throughout the country. Columbia University is one of the oldest universities in the United States. It was chartered as King's College in 1754. Barnard College, the College of Pharmaceutical Sciences, and Teachers College are affiliated with Columbia. The City University of New York has the largest enrollment. It includes Bernard M. Baruch, Brooklyn, City, Herbert H. Lehman, Queens, Richmond, and York colleges; the John Jay College of Criminal Justice; and six community colleges. The Mount Sinai School of Medicine is affiliated with it.

New York University, another school with a large enrollment, has several professional schools. Fordham University in Manhattan and the Bronx is a Roman Catholic college founded in 1841. Other schools include Polytechnic Institute of Brooklyn, Pratt Institute, the New School for Social Research, Manhattan and Pace colleges, and Long Island and St. John's universities. Peter Cooper founded Cooper Union in 1859 to furnish free education to the citizens of New York City.

Architecture. If there is one thing more than any other for which New York City is famous throughout the world, it is its towering skyscrapers. The giant spires and towers of the lofty buildings on the Manhattan skyline amaze visitors who see them for the first time. This small island has the tallest buildings in the world.

The oldest skyscraper in New York City is the Flatiron Building on 23d Street where Broadway crosses Fifth Avenue. Completed in 1902, it is built in the shape of a triangle, which makes it look somewhat like an old-fashioned flatiron. Today the 21 stories of this structure seem unimpressive beside newer buildings.

One of New York's most famous skyscrapers is the Empire State Building, erected in 1931 on Fifth Avenue

between 33rd and 34th streets. Its 102 stories are a landmark to every New Yorker. The building is 1,250 feet high. The world's tallest building, the 110-story World Trade Center, stands on the east bank of the Hudson River in lower Manhattan. It is 1,350 feet high.

There are other great skyscrapers in the midtown and Times Square sections. The New York Central Building on Park Avenue and the Daily News and Chanin buildings on East 42d Street are all fine examples of this typically American style of architecture. Other skyscrapers include the Chrysler Building at 42d Street and Lexington Avenue, the RCA Building at Sixth Avenue and 50th Street, Sixty Wall Tower (Cities Service Building) at 70 Pine Street, and the Chase Manhattan Bank at 1 Chase Manhattan Plaza. See SKYSCRAPER (table).

Port of New York Authority; Ewing Galloway

NEW YORK CITY

Manhattan Island, the heart of New York City, is about 13 miles long and 2 miles wide. This small area contains the financial capital of the world, the cultural and theatrical center of the Western Hemisphere, and the headquarters of the United Nations.

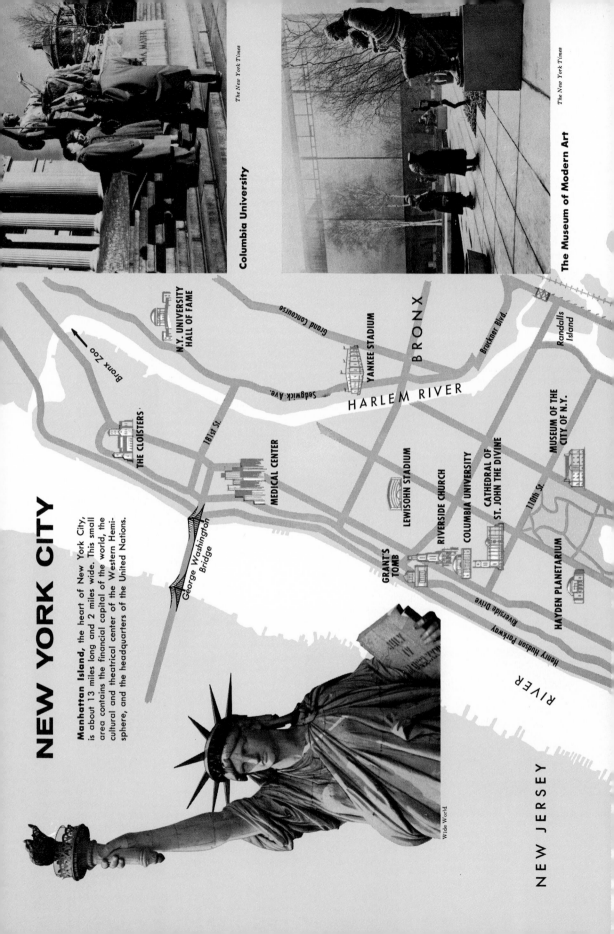

Columbia University

The New York Times

The Museum of Modern Art

The New York Times

Wide World

N.Y. UNIVERSITY HALL OF FAME

Bronx Zoo

THE CLOISTERS

181st St.

George Washington Bridge

MEDICAL CENTER

Grand Concourse

YANKEE STADIUM

Sedgwick Ave.

B R O N X

Bruckner Blvd.

Randall's Island

HARLEM RIVER

LEWISOHN STADIUM

RIVERSIDE CHURCH

GRANT'S TOMB

COLUMBIA UNIVERSITY

CATHEDRAL OF ST. JOHN THE DIVINE

110th St.

MUSEUM OF THE CITY OF N.Y.

HAYDEN PLANETARIUM

Riverside Drive

Henry Hudson Parkway

R I V E R

NEW JERSEY

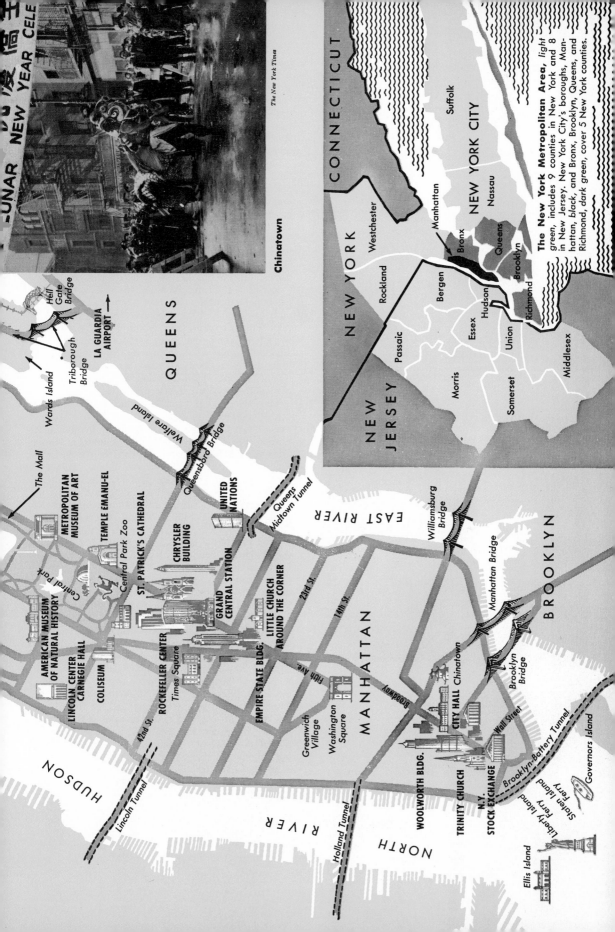

LUNAR NEW YEAR CELE

The New York Times

Chinatown

The New York Metropolitan Area, *light green, includes 9 counties in New York and 8 in New Jersey. New York City's boroughs, Manhattan, black, and Bronx, Brooklyn, Queens, and Richmond, dark green, cover 5 New York counties.*

CONNECTICUT

NEW YORK CITY

Suffolk

Manhattan

Nassau

Bronx

Queens

Westchester

Brooklyn

Rockland

Bergen

Richmond

NEW YORK

Hudson

Passaic

Essex

Union

Middlesex

NEW JERSEY

Morris

Somerset

QUEENS

Hell Gate Bridge

LA GUARDIA AIRPORT →

Triborough Bridge

Wards Island

Welfare Island

Queensboro Bridge

The Mall

METROPOLITAN MUSEUM OF ART

TEMPLE EMANU-EL

Central Park Zoo

ST. PATRICK'S CATHEDRAL

CHRYSLER BUILDING

UNITED NATIONS

Central Park

GRAND CENTRAL STATION

Queens Midtown Tunnel

EAST RIVER

AMERICAN MUSEUM OF NATURAL HISTORY

LINCOLN CENTER CARNEGIE HALL

COLISEUM

ROCKEFELLER CENTER

Times Square

LITTLE CHURCH AROUND THE CORNER

23rd St.

Williamsburg Bridge

42nd St.

EMPIRE STATE BLDG.

14th St.

Manhattan Bridge

BROOKLYN

HUDSON

Fifth Ave.

Greenwich Village

Washington Square

MANHATTAN

Broadway

Chinatown

Brooklyn Bridge

Lincoln Tunnel

CITY HALL

WOOLWORTH BLDG.

TRINITY CHURCH

N.Y. STOCK EXCHANGE

Wall Street

Brooklyn-Battery Tunnel

NORTH

Holland Tunnel

Liberty Island

Staten Island Ferry

Governors Island

RIVER

Ellis Island

Riverside Church. People of all religious denominations attend services in this lovely Gothic church.

Ewing Galloway

St. Patrick's Cathedral. Roman Catholic services are held in this block-square cathedral on Fifth Avenue.

Temple Emanu-El. Rich carvings set off the plain front of this impressive synagogue on Fifth Avenue.

Many outstanding buildings have been built in the midtown area since World War II. These include the United Nations Secretariat Building (see UNITED NATIONS [picture]), Lever House, the Colgate-Palmolive, Seagram, and Arabian-American Oil buildings, as well as the Manufacturer's Trust Company Building, Canada House, and the Socony-Mobil Building. These structures are notable for their use of steel or copper and glass.

On lower Broadway, on the southern end of the island, are some of the great buildings of the commercial and banking houses. The Cunard Steamship Company and the American Telephone and Telegraph Company are two of the well-known concerns that own large buildings in this bustling financial and business district. The Woolworth Building, which is headquarters for the famous five-and-ten-cent stores, stands as one of the tallest of the huge structures in the area. It has 54 stories and contains 40 acres of floor space.

Rockefeller Center includes 16 massive buildings extending from 48th to 52d streets between Fifth Avenue and the Avenue of the Americas (formerly Sixth Avenue). This is really a "city within a city." One could live a long time in the Center without leaving it. About 160,000 people work in or visit Rockefeller Center every day. This number is larger than the total population of Tacoma, Wash. The buildings are fine examples of modern American architecture.

The RCA Building, in the center of the group, is the tallest of all. It is 70 stories high. The consulates of many different nations occupy buildings in Rockefeller Center. The British Empire Building and La Maison Française face Fifth Avenue. Between them is the lovely Promenade, lined with flowers and shrubs, which leads down to the sunken Plaza. The Plaza is an outdoor dining area in summer and a skating rink during the cold months. In 1935 the International Building was finished. It stands between 50th and 51st streets on Fifth Avenue. The Palazzo d'Italia is part of this building. On the roofs of the foreign buildings are the Gardens of the Nations, a beautiful array of botanical specimens from various parts of the world.

Outstanding contemporary sculpture and painting can be seen in Rockefeller Center. The huge statue of Prometheus in the Plaza, the figure of Atlas before the International Building, and other sculptural pieces in various buildings are well worth seeing. Mural paintings by famous artists are on exhibit in many of the buildings.

Several buildings of Rockefeller Center make up what is known as *Radio City*. These include the Music Hall, the largest theater in the world; the RKO Building; the RCA Building, which houses the studios of the National Broadcasting Company; and the RCA Building West. The Center Theatre, also one of the original Radio City group, was torn down in 1954. It was replaced by a 19-story addition to the United States Rubber Building. In 1956, New York City erected the Coliseum, the largest building in the world devoted to fairs, trade gatherings, and displays. It stands at Columbus Circle. The exhibition area covers 300,000 square feet.

Churches. The Episcopal Cathedral of St. John the Divine, between 110th and 113th streets, was designed as the largest Gothic cathedral in the world (see SAINT JOHN THE DIVINE, CATHEDRAL OF). Trinity Church, on Wall Street, is the most famous of the old

Episcopal churches. The brownstone church was built in English Gothic style. The churchyard has headstones marking the graves of Alexander Hamilton, Robert Fulton, and other famous Americans. The Church of the Transfiguration, on East 29th Street, is known as "The Little Church Around the Corner." It is a popular Episcopal church, especially among people of the theatrical world.

The best known of Roman Catholic churches in New York City is the great Cathedral of St. Patrick on Fifth Avenue. This is a beautiful building, and it has played an important part in the religious life of the city since it was opened in 1879. St. Ignatius Loyola and Notre Dame de Lourdes are among the best known of the many other Roman Catholic churches.

Riverside Church, on Riverside Drive, is one of the loveliest of New York City churches. Its structure follows the Gothic tradition. People of all faiths come to this interdenominational church to worship.

Among the churches of historical interest in New York City are St. Paul's Chapel, the city's oldest church building (1766), where George Washington once worshiped; Plymouth Church of the Pilgrims, where Henry Ward Beecher preached; and St. Mark's-in-the-Bouwerie, in the churchyard of which Peter Stuyvesant is buried. Temple Emanu-El and the Free Synagogue are distinctive among Jewish places of worship.

Private Houses. The public buildings of New York City are so numerous and impressive that people sometimes do not notice the old private houses that once belonged to New York City's first families. Unfortunately, many of these are fast disappearing. They are being torn down to make way for office buildings, or the apartment houses in which most New Yorkers live. A few of these old residences have been turned into small art galleries to show the collections made by their wealthy owners. The Morgan home, on East 36th Street, houses the Pierpont Morgan Library. The Frick Gallery, on East 70th Street, has paintings by old masters, as well as early, rare furniture. Many old private houses are built of brownstone, a building material typical of Old New York. Many side streets are lined with tall,

narrow brownstone houses that once belonged to single families, but are now divided into small apartments. These old homes are very much a part of the architectural scene in New York City.

Historic Houses. New York's three hundred years have given the city a rich history. There is little now to remind one of the early days except certain old houses that still remain to show us something of the past. Among these is City Hall, a beautiful example of post-colonial architecture, which today houses the offices of the mayor and his staff. There are chairs and desks here that were used by George Washington and his Cabinet when New York City was the nation's capital. On the second floor is a collection of paintings of some of the early governors and mayors of New York, painted by the well-known American artist John Trumbull (1756-1843).

North of Manhattan, in the Bronx, is the stately Van Cortlandt Mansion, once owned by a family that lived here when New York City was still New Amsterdam. This building is now a museum.

The Jumel Mansion on 160th-162nd streets has perhaps more historical interest than any other house in New York City. It was built in 1765, and Washington used it as his headquarters in 1776. From here he sent Nathan Hale on his ill-fated spy mission. Aaron Burr lived here, and Benjamin Franklin and Lafayette visited the house. Now it is a museum, furnished with pieces chiefly from the mid-1700's and early 1800's.

Fraunces Tavern in downtown Manhattan, originally built in 1719, is one of the city's oldest houses. The Revolutionary leaders often met here and Washington

FAMOUS CHURCHES
OF NEW YORK CITY

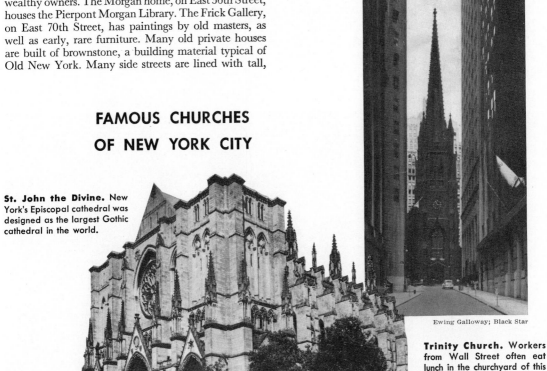

St. John the Divine. New York's Episcopal cathedral was designed as the largest Gothic cathedral in the world.

Ewing Galloway; Black Star

Trinity Church. Workers from Wall Street often eat lunch in the churchyard of this Episcopal church.

Greenwich Village artists often work on their paintings near the memorial arch in Washington Square.

said goodby to his men here in 1783. The first floor is still a restaurant. On the third floor there is a museum for documents and mementos of Revolutionary times.

There are other noted old houses in New York City, all of them of historical interest. Some of the most interesting of these are the Poe Cottage, in the Bronx, where Edgar Allan Poe wrote some of his best-known poems; the Dyckman House, in uptown Manhattan, which is still preserved as an old farmhouse; the Gracie Mansion, on East River Drive, which is now the Mayor's house; and India House, on Hanover Square, where relics of the days of the Yankee clipper ships have been preserved.

Libraries. New York City has three independent library systems—the New York Public Library, the Brooklyn Public Library, and the Queens Borough Public Library. Together, the three systems have more than 200 branches.

The New York Public Library, the largest public library in the country, has 80 branches and over 7,000,000 volumes. Every year, more than 3,000,000 persons enter the famous Central Building on Fifth Avenue at 42d Street. This building houses the central circulation branch of the library. Its reference collections of about 4,100,000 books are known as the Astor, Lenox, and Tilden Foundations. All the cards in its vast card index have been put on microfilm. During the summer, vast crowds stop to hear the noon-hour concerts of classical music on records played over loudspeakers just behind the Central Building, in Bryant Park.

Horse-Drawn Carriages in Central Park give visitors a leisurely, scenic drive. Central Park covers 840 acres in the center of Manhattan Island.

In addition to the many special divisions and collections in the Central Building, the library maintains special libraries housed elsewhere in the city. These include the Music Library, the Municipal Reference Library, the Newspaper Division, the Library for the Blind, and the Schomburg Collection of Negro Literature and History. The Donnell Library Center on West 53rd Street houses the union catalogue (central catalogue) of branch library collections. Many branches of the New York Public Library have special foreign-language collections for the various foreign-born groups.

Scattered throughout the city are about 1,000 special libraries in museums, colleges, clubs, and corporations. One of the oldest of these, the New York Society Library, was founded in 1754.

Museums. The museums of the city have also been important in its artistic development. The largest is the famed Metropolitan Museum of Art at 82nd Street and Fifth Avenue. This enormous building holds priceless collections of paintings, sculpture, prints, furniture, textiles, armors, and art objects from every age and country. The Egyptian, Greek, and Roman collections are comprehensive, and they present a vivid picture of these ancient cultures. The Cloisters, a granite tile-roofed building at Fort Tryon Park, is a reproduction of a medieval monastery. It is part of the Metropolitan Museum. Old tapestries, paintings, and sculpture are arranged here exactly as they would have been in the Middle Ages. A visit to the Cloisters is like taking a trip into

Three Lions, Inc.

Times Square lies in the heart of the theater and entertainment district. Broadway, 42nd Street, and Seventh Avenue cross each other at the square.

Rockefeller Center sparkles at night with lights from many windows. Skaters glide on the ice near a huge Christmas tree at Christmas time.
Robert Bagby, F.P.G.

monastic life as it was during medieval times.

Another famous New York City museum is the American Museum of Natural History at 77th Street and Central Park West. This museum contains a marvelous collection of stuffed birds and animals arranged in backgrounds that are exact reproductions of their natural surroundings. Connected with this museum are the Akeley Memorial Hall of African Mammals, the Hall of the Birds of the World, the Hall of Ocean Life, and the Hayden Planetarium. Here the story of the stars of all seasons and ages is projected by rays of light on a 75-foot domed ceiling. Another scientific museum is the Museum of the American Indian. The New York Historical Society, the Museum of the City of New York, the Jewish Museum, and the Hispanic Society have interesting historical relics. The Museum of Modern Art on West 53rd Street, the Whitney Museum of American Art on Madison Avenue and 75th Street, the Guggenheim Museum on Fifth Avenue, and the Huntington Hartford Gallery of Modern Art on Columbus Circle show contemporary art.

The Arts. New York has many cultural establishments, such as art galleries, orchestral societies, and musical and literary groups. Dozens of small art galleries display works of noted artists. The New York Philharmonic (formerly the New York Philharmonic-Symphony Orchestra) played many years at Carnegie Hall on West 57th Street. On Nov. 6, 1964, this building was proclaimed a national historic landmark. The 1960's brought the gradual completion of the Lincoln Center for the Performing Arts. The center's Philharmonic Hall became the home of the New York Philharmonic in 1962. The Vivian Beaumont Theater and the library museum opened in 1965. The Metropolitan Opera Association moved to the center in 1966. Lincoln Center is located at West 62nd Street and Columbus Avenue (see LINCOLN CENTER FOR THE PERFORMING ARTS). The New York City Center of Music and Drama on West 55th Street also offers varied fine arts programs.

Almost every large book-publishing house in America has offices in New York. The city is considered the literary center of the country. Many literary groups and societies have grown up here. Poets, artists, and writers have made New York their headquarters. The cultural activity among the literary, musical, and artistic people who live here has made New York the goal for those who hope to be a part of this creative world.

The theater is also very much a part of New York life. The theatrical district is on or near Broadway between 41st and 62nd streets. Nearly every important play is shown in one of the theaters here. The reception a play receives in New York usually determines its success or failure. There are more than 500 theaters in the city, including motion-picture houses. Among the movie theaters are large ones, such as the Paramount and Radio City Music Hall. Because of its many theaters, New York is sometimes called the *Entertainment Capital of the World.*

Newspapers and Magazines. New York City has some of the largest and most famous newspapers in the world. The city is headquarters for the editorial offices of a majority of the well-known national magazines that are read by millions of persons every week.

Newspapers began in New York City with the first appearance of William Bradford's *New York Gazette* in 1725. Freedom of the press was established in the early days of New York journalism with the trial and acquittal of Peter Zenger, editor of the *Weekly Journal*, in 1735. The modern American newspaper grew out of the efforts of a number of famous New York City publishers, including Horace Greeley, Joseph Pulitzer, James Gordon Bennett, Frank A. Munsey, and Adolph Ochs.

Today New York City daily newspapers include the *Times*, the *Daily News*, and the *Post*. There are also hundreds of foreign-language newspapers, daily and weekly, and many special trade and union newspapers. While the editorial and business offices of important magazines also are located in New York City, the printing is often done in other cities.

A 114-day strike stopped newspaper publishing in New York City from December, 1962, to April, 1963.

Radio and Television. The four largest national broadcasting networks have their headquarters in New York City. The city is also the home of regional broadcasting systems which serve the New York area.

Social Welfare

The city's Department of Welfare has charge of home relief, child welfare, old-age and blind assistance, rehabilitation of the disabled, and shelter for the homeless. In addition, about 2,000 social agencies, both public and private, give special aid to needy inhabitants of New York City. The city is the home of many national welfare organizations, whose work is coordinated by the Community Council of Greater New York.

Many of New York City's hospitals rank among the best in the country. Among the outstanding medical centers in the city are the New York Hospital, which is associated with Cornell University Medical College; and the Presbyterian Hospital, associated with Columbia University. Bellevue Hospital started as a charity institution with six beds in 1736. Today, it can accommodate hundreds of patients. There are also about 150 smaller hospitals in New York City. Many of these care for special diseases. Municipal hospitals, such as Coler Memorial Hospital and Goldwater Memorial Hospital, are on Welfare Island. Other large hospitals include Kings County, Metropolitan, Mount Sinai, Montefiore, Post-Graduate, Neurological, Polyclinic, Saint Luke's, Roosevelt, Beth Israel, and Columbus.

Recreation

The parks, playgrounds, and other places of recreation in New York City have resources for swimming, tennis, golf, baseball, skating, boating, and horseback riding. New York City has two major-league baseball teams. The Yankees play in the American League, and the Mets in the National League. The city's oldest park is Bowling Green, on Manhattan's lower end. Early Dutch settlers used this park as a playground, a parade ground, and an annual fair ground.

Central Park, stretching from 59th to 110th Street, contains 840 acres and is the best known of all the more than one hundred big and little parks in Greater New York. Each day, during the warm months, huge crowds visit Central Park's zoo, the Shakespeare Garden, the Mall, the conservatory, the outdoor concert stadium, the children's zoo, and the many playgrounds. Monuments and statues decorate the park's wooded grounds and formal gardens. Cleopatra's Needle, a slender stone obelisk more than 3,500 years old, was presented to the United States by the *khedive* (governor) of Egypt in 1881. This famed landmark is near the Metropolitan Museum. The statue of General Sherman near 59th Street, the memorial to those who lost their lives on the battleship *Maine*, near Columbus Circle, and a large variety of smaller statues and monuments make Central Park continually interesting to visitors.

Other large parks in the city include Van Cortlandt Park in the Bronx, Prospect Park in Brooklyn, and Riverside Park in Manhattan. Grant's Tomb and the Soldiers' and Sailors' Monument are in Riverside Park.

The Bronx Zoo is a vast parkland where live animals from every country in the world can be seen in reproductions of their natural surroundings. There are more than a thousand species of animals, birds, and reptiles. This is one of the outstanding United States zoos.

Small parks and squares that are especially well-known include Gramercy Park and Madison Square, where an "Eternal Light" atop a 125-foot monument burns continuously to the memory of the soldiers who died during World War I. Washington Square, at the foot of Fifth Avenue near Greenwich Village, is noted for the Washington Memorial Arch that forms its entrance. Union Square, between 14th and 17th streets and Broadway and Fourth Avenue, was laid out as a park in 1830. During the early 1900's, it became noted as a gathering place for radical political speakers.

Interesting Places to Visit include:

Battery Park, at the tip of Manhattan. This park commands a view of the harbor and the canyon of lower Broadway. Situated in the park is Castle Clinton, which was once a harbor fort. See CASTLE CLINTON NATIONAL MONUMENT.

Brooklyn Children's Museum, on Brooklyn Avenue, the first of its kind in the world, founded in 1899 by the Brooklyn Institute of Arts and Sciences. It offers exhibits, lectures, films, and story hours in science and history.

Coney Island, a famous seaside amusement center, is part of Brooklyn. It has a bathing beach, dance halls, side shows, and is the site of the New York Aquarium.

Greenwich Village near Washington Square is the "home of artists." Painters, singers, musicians, and poets come to live in the colorful Village. The Village lies between West Street and Broadway.

Madison Square Garden, in Pennsylvania Plaza on Eighth Avenue, is a seven-story entertainment center. It includes an arena, art gallery, bowling alleys, convention hall, exposition hall, and theater. It was opened in 1968. See MADISON SQUARE GARDEN.

Staten Island is reached by the Verrazano-Narrows Bridge. It features Richmondtown, a village that is being restored and rebuilt to appear as it did in colonial times. The project is scheduled for completion in the 1970's. See RICHMONDTOWN; STATEN ISLAND.

United Nations Headquarters cover 18 acres between 42nd and 48th streets along the East River. There are lectures and films, and guided tours through the Secretariat, General Assembly, and Conference buildings. See UNITED NATIONS.

Industry and Trade

The Port of New York includes more than 1,600 piers, wharves, and bulkheads on its 650-mile-long waterfront. The great oceangoing ships that use these vast shipping facilities touch at nine out of ten of the world's ports. New York City is the largest export center in the world. The New York Customs Office handles almost half the overseas commerce of the United States.

New York City is the heart of the country's banking and business activity. The Wall Street financial district, where the New York Stock Exchange and so many of the great commercial houses and banks are located, is an international symbol of financial affairs.

The largest industry in New York City is the garment trade, which employs more than 300,000 workers. New York City does almost one-fourth of the nation's printing and one-third of its photoengraving, and publishes about three-fourths of all its books. The city also conducts the largest wholesale dry-goods business and the largest wholesale grocery business in the United States. Fulton Fish Market, on the Lower East Side, is the largest wholesale fish market on the Atlantic Coast. Some important manufactures in the city include food products, furniture, paper products, furs, and millinery.

Transportation

The transportation system of New York City is a vast and complicated one. It requires many terminals, airports, bridges, and tunnels for the millions of passengers and millions of tons of freight that are handled every day by trains, buses, trucks, ships, ferries, and planes.

Railroads. The Grand Central station at 42nd Street and the Penn Central Railroad terminal on Seventh Avenue handle a total of more than 500,000 passengers each day. As many as 550 trains of the Penn Central

New York City's Harlem is a district near the Harlem River. In Central Harlem, nearly 250,000 persons, most of them Negroes and Latin Americans, are crowded into a 1½-square-mile area.

and New York, New Haven, and Hartford railroads arrive at or leave the Grand Central Terminal daily. Every day, hundreds of trains of the Penn Central, Long Island, and Lehigh Valley railroads use "Penn Station." In the mid-1960's, the upper structure of Penn Station was torn down, but trains continue to operate beneath street level. Other railroad lines, such as the Lackawanna, the Erie, and the Reading, have terminals in New Jersey. Trains and buses carry the passengers into the city. Freight trains are ferried across the Hudson and East rivers on barges.

Bridges. "Walls are built to keep people out, bridges to bring them closer together." This quotation applies well to New York City, for the city has dozens of railroad and vehicular bridges connecting the different boroughs. The Brooklyn Bridge crosses the East River in downtown Manhattan, at Park Row. It was opened in 1883 and is still one of the city's great sights. In 1964, the bridge was designated as a national historic landmark by the National Park Service. Since 1883 eight other bridges have been built across the East River. They are the Manhattan, Williamsburg, Queensboro, Welfare Island, Triborough, Hell Gate, Bronx-Whitestone, and Throgs Neck bridges. The Y-shaped Triborough Bridge links Manhattan, the Bronx, and Queens.

The Harlem River is spanned by High Bridge, Harlem Bridge, Henry Hudson Bridge, Alexander Hamilton Bridge, and several other smaller bridges. High Bridge, opened in 1848, is the oldest bridge in the city.

The city has one bridge spanning the Hudson River. It is the George Washington Bridge. The Bayonne Bridge is the longest arch span in the world. It stretches 1,675 feet over Kill Van Kull channel, between Staten Island and New Jersey. Goethals Bridge and Outerbridge Crossing, both crossing the Arthur Kill channel, also connect Staten Island and New Jersey.

The Verrazano-Narrows Bridge, linking Staten Island and Brooklyn, was opened to traffic in November, 1964. It has a suspension span that is 4,260 feet long.

Highways and Tunnels. New York City has developed an impressive arterial highway system to speed travel in and out of the city. It includes Deegan Parkway in the Bronx, the Shore and Gowanus parkways in Brooklyn, the Cross Island and Grand Central parkways in Queens, the East and West Side highways in Manhattan, and many others. The Queens-Midtown Tunnel under the East River connects Manhattan with Queens, and the Brooklyn-Battery Tunnel connects it with Brooklyn. The Brooklyn-Battery Tunnel is the longest underwater tunnel in the United States. The Lincoln and Holland tunnels run under the North River (part of the Hudson River) into New Jersey.

Airports. The metropolitan district has many commercial and military airports. Staten Island has Miller Field, and Governors Island Army Airfield is on Governors Island. The United States Naval Air Station at Floyd Bennett Field, opened in 1931, was the first municipal airport. It covers 387 acres on Jamaica Bay.

La Guardia Airport, once one of the busiest in the world, covers 575 acres on Flushing Bay. Opened in 1939, it was long the main eastern terminal for major airlines, as well as a base for Atlantic Clippers. In 1947,

N.Y. Central

Grand Central Station faces 42nd Street at the south end of Park Avenue. Hundreds of trains come and go each day.

this airport was leased to the Port of New York Authority. In 1948, its overseas operations were transferred to New York International Airport at Idlewild, which opened that year. New York International Airport was renamed the John F. Kennedy International Airport in 1963. Kennedy International is one of the largest and most modern airports in the world. It covers about 5,000 acres in Queens. Kennedy Airport has 10 giant hangars, about 13 miles of concrete runways for land planes, and three huge landing areas in the bay for seaplanes. The Port Authority also maintains Battery Park Heliport and Newark and Teterboro airports in New Jersey. Other commercial airports include Curtiss Field and Rockaway Airfield on Long Island; Bendix Airport and Hadley Field in New Jersey, and Westchester County Airport.

Local Transportation. About 237 miles of subway stretch beneath the city like the web of a giant spider. The first subway, the Interborough, was opened in 1904. It operates throughout Manhattan, and through a large part of the Bronx. It has branch lines in Brooklyn and Queens. A large subway system called the Independent Subway serves all the boroughs except Richmond. The Brooklyn-Manhattan Transit Company has lines in Brooklyn, Manhattan, and Queens. The New York City Transit Authority controls all three subways. Subways have replaced almost all elevated railways. Bus lines provide most of the surface transportation.

Public Services

Gas and Electric Power. The Consolidated Edison Company, established in 1882, supplies Greater New York with gas and electricity for light, heat, and power.

Water Supply. The water system is owned by the city. Vast reservoirs supply the city's needs. About half the water used in New York City comes from the Schoharie and Ashokan reservoirs in the Catskill Mountains. The Kensico Dam, the Catskill Aqueduct, and the bombproof Delaware Aqueduct also are part of New York

TRANSPORTATION IN NEW YORK CITY

Ken Regan, Pictorial Parade

Verrazano-Narrows Bridge connects Brooklyn with Staten Island, *foreground.* Opened in 1964, it is one of the world's longest suspension bridges.

Passenger Liners dock on the Hudson River. Freighters unload along the East River, or on the New Jersey shore of the Hudson.

Air Traffic from all parts of the world flows through the John F. Kennedy International Airport at Idlewild.

UNDERGROUND NEW YORK

A complex maze of tunnels and tubes under the city is filled with vital public utilities and transportation systems.

Public Utilities, such as gas and water mains, and power and telephone lines, run under streets.

Subway Tunnels burrow beneath the public-utility lines.

Railroad Tunnels carry passengers to busy rail terminals.

Sewers lie deepest so they will not leak onto power lines.

City's water system. There are four reservoirs within the city limits. See WATER (map: How New York City Gets Its Water).

Government

New York City is governed by a charter that was adopted in 1961 and became effective in 1963. The mayor, elected for four-year terms, is the chief executive. Each of the five boroughs has an independently elected president who also serves four years. The mayor is responsible for city administration, except for the financial work done by the comptroller's office and the duties assigned to each borough president. He may appoint two or more deputy mayors. One deputy mayor acts as the mayor's representative at ceremonial functions, council meetings, and board and committee meetings. He advises the mayor on policy, and supervises the mayor's staff. A second deputy mayor supervises most other city offices and departments. Councilmen, elected for four-year terms, pass the city's laws.

The borough presidents, the comptroller, the mayor, and the president of the council make up the board of estimate. With the council, the board of estimate controls the city's financial affairs. The mayor submits the city budget to the council and board of estimate for approval and possible amendment. Most department and bureau heads, such as those in charge of welfare or police, are appointed by the mayor.

In addition to state courts, New York City has several courts with jurisdiction within the city. One court deals with civil cases. Another handles criminal cases. New York City also has a family court.

History

The slim viking ships of Leif Ericson are believed to have sailed the North American coast from Maine to Virginia in the 1000's. Very probably one of them entered the mouth of the Hudson, but these ancient mariners sailed past the little rocky island in the bay without a second glance. In 1524, Giovanni da Verrazano, a Florentine explorer in the service of the king of France, visited New York Harbor on a westward voyage in search of a new route to the Indies. But not until Henry Hudson, an English navigator working for the Dutch, sailed up the river that bears his name, did anyone notice the island the Indians called *Man-a-hat-ta* (Heavenly Land). Hudson entered the name in his logbook and brought to Holland stories of the new land.

Settlement. In 1613, the Dutch explorer Adriaen Block and his men spent the winter on Manhattan Island. They put up a few huts where 41-45 Broadway is today. In 1624 and 1625, the Dutch West India Company sent settlers to the New York area. Some went to Manhattan. By 1626, they had laid out a town and built Fort Amsterdam. Peter Minuit, the Dutch governor, bought Manhattan from the Indians in that year. He paid them in goods worth about $24.

Soon after Fort Amsterdam was built, the entire settlement was named New Amsterdam. Peter Stuyvesant was sent as governor in 1647, and the town grew rapidly under his administration. About 1,000 persons lived there in the 1650's. In 1653, Stuyvesant built a *palisade* (wall) on the northern boundary of the village. This wall ran the same way as Wall Street does now, and gave the street its name.

Since most of the colony's business had to do with trading and shipping, the life of the community was centered below Wall Street. When New Amsterdam was incorporated as a city in 1653, it was like a small country village with narrow dirt roads and a few scattered houses. During the Dutch-English wars of the period, England took the city and named it New York. The Dutch regained it for a short time, but the English recovered the settlement and controlled it until after the Revolutionary War. The English made many improvements, such as a postal service and street lights, and in 1686 granted the city a charter.

The City Grows. By this time, Harlem was part of New York. The two towns were joined by a dirt road that cut through the island to Grand Street, then the northern end of the city. By 1700, there were 7,000 people in New York. Eighteen languages were spoken. The first newspaper was published in 1725. Kings College, now Columbia University, was founded in 1754.

New York played a leading part in the American fight for freedom. The Stamp Act Congress met there in 1765. In 1770, New Yorkers fought British soldiers in a battle on Golden Hill, now John Street. But the British were able to keep New York until after the surrender of Cornwallis at Yorktown. The national Congress met in City Hall (later called Federal Hall) on Wall Street from 1785 to 1790. Washington was inaugurated there as the first President in 1789.

After the Revolutionary War, New York continued to expand. By 1800, it had a population of 60,000. The number of immigrants increased, and New York became the melting pot of nations that it remains today.

The Erie Canal, now a part of the New York State Barge Canal System, was opened in 1825. Greater New York, containing the five boroughs, was established in 1898. In 1913, the Catskill Aqueduct was completed.

The New York World's Fair, with its hundreds of exhibits dramatizing "The World of Tomorrow," was held in the city in 1939 and 1940. During World War II, the offices and factories in the New York City area turned to war work.

In 1946, an 18-acre riverfront site in east Manhattan was bought by John D. Rockefeller, Jr., and accepted by the United Nations for its permanent site.

A New Era. New York City's Golden Anniversary Exposition was opened on August 21, 1948. The dedication of the new airport at Idlewild in the same month made New York City the greatest air terminal in the world. New York City erected the Coliseum at Columbus Circle in 1956. It is designed especially for expositions and fairs. The 12-acre Lincoln Center, north of the Coliseum from West 60th to West 70th streets, was completed in 1969. The city held another world's fair in 1964 and 1965.

A 12-day strike by transit workers closed the city's subway and bus lines in January, 1966. With the transportation system shut down, many persons could not get to work or to stores. Estimates of losses in wages, business, and taxes ran as high as $800 million.

New York City Today faces problems that reflect the pressures of living in a highly populated major city during a time of rapid social and technological change. These problems include racial conflict, physical decay, overcrowded highways and airports, outdated public and mass transportation, riots, and crime in the streets. New York City also has faced crippling strikes, air and water pollution, student unrest, growing welfare rolls, and inadequate housing, parks, and medical services.

During the 1960's, thousands of people moved out of the city because they believed it could not solve these problems. Many people went to residential areas at the outer edges of the city, but most moved to the suburbs. At the same time, the slum areas of the city became more crowded as many blacks, Puerto Ricans, and members of other minority groups migrated to the city. Families who could afford to move out of the slums did so. Most of them moved to nearby neighborhoods where the majority of people were whites of European ancestry. Many whites in those areas moved farther away to avoid mixed neighborhoods, and the inner city became mostly nonwhite.

Some families who remained in New York City could afford to live in areas away from the changing neighborhoods. Others, who could not afford to leave the slums, stayed there. The two groups had little to do with each other, and the results were a breakdown of community relations and a lack of common goals.

One result of the lack of closeness among New Yorkers was a *decentralization* (splitting up) of the school system. In April, 1969, the state legislature approved a plan to divide the city into districts and give some control to local school boards. In 1968, an experiment in local control had led to a five-week strike by public school teachers. A nonwhite section of Brooklyn had been given control of its schools. The local board tried to transfer a group of white and mostly Jewish teachers out of the district, saying the teachers were trying to ruin the experiment. A federal judge ruled the board had no transfer power, and the teachers were reinstated. The city school board then developed a workable decentralization plan.

Conflicts still existed in New York City during the late 1960's. But improved social agencies and successful experiments in cooperative, biracial social and economic organizations gave hope of solutions to some of the city's social problems.　　　　　B. A. BOTKIN

Related Articles in WORLD BOOK include:

BUSINESS LEADERS

Astor (William Backhouse)	Rockefeller (family)
Baruch, Bernard M.	Sarnoff, David
Birdseye, Clarence	Tiffany (family)
Douglas, Donald W.	Vanderbilt
Morgan (John P.; John P., Jr.)	(Cornelius III)

POLITICAL LEADERS

Arthur, Chester A.	Roosevelt, Theodore
Fish (Hamilton [1808-1893])	Smith, Alfred E.
La Guardia, Fiorello	Stimson, Henry L.
Lindsay, John V.	Tilden, Samuel J.
Luce (Clare B.)	Tompkins, Daniel D.
Mitchel, John Purroy	Walker, James J.
Morgenthau, Henry, Jr.	Welles, Sumner
Roosevelt, Franklin D.	

PUBLISHERS AND WRITERS

Bennett (family)	Day, Benjamin H.
Bourke-White, Margaret	Greeley, Horace
Brisbane, Arthur	Irving, Washington
Broun, Heywood C.	Lippmann, Walter
Dana, Charles A.	Luce (Henry R.)

Questions

How does New York City compare in size with other cities of the world?

What was the original price Peter Minuit paid for Manhattan?

What famous islands lie in Upper New York Bay?

Where is New York's "Great White Way"?

What is Rockefeller Center? Why can it be called "a city within a city"?

Why is New York City often called the "Entertainment Capital of the World"?

Where is Central Park? How large is it?

How much of the country's foreign commerce is handled in New York City?

What is New York City's oldest bridge? What other bridges in the city are well known?

Where does the city get its water supply?

NEW YORK FOUNDATION is a fund for charitable purposes. The foundation was established in 1909 by Louis A. Heinsheimer, an American banker, by a grant under his will. This grant gave $1 million to be used for the Jewish charities in New York City. In 1926, the foundation received $2,200,000 from the estate of Lionel J. Salomon and, in 1929, $6 million from the estate of Alfred M. Heinsheimer.

The New York Foundation is nonsectarian and supports many organizations in the fields of public health, social welfare, and education, chiefly in New York City. The foundation's headquarters are located at 4 West 58th Street, New York, N.Y. 10019. For assets, see FOUNDATIONS (table).   Critically reviewed by NEW YORK FOUNDATION

NEW YORK LIFE INSURANCE COMPANY. See INSURANCE (table).

NEW YORK PORT AUTHORITY. See PORT OF NEW YORK AUTHORITY.

NEW YORK PUBLIC LIBRARY is the largest city public library in the United States in terms of its number of volumes and number of branch libraries. The library operates a central reference library from its endowment funds. Public funds from the city support the system of branches that operate in the boroughs of Manhattan, the Bronx, and Richmond. Two additional library systems that serve New York City are the Brooklyn Public Library and the Queens Borough Public Library.

The Reference Department of the New York Public Library occupies a white marble structure at Fifth Avenue and 42nd Street. The main building contains over 4 million books. Its 81 branch libraries have about 3 million additional books. The library also has about 9 million manuscripts, $3\frac{1}{2}$ million pictures, 260,000 maps, 34,000 reels of film and microfilm, and 67,000 books for the blind. The library also offers lectures, concerts, film showings, book discussions, and story hours for children. The New York Public Library was founded in 1895.   Critically reviewed by NEW YORK PUBLIC LIBRARY

NEW YORK STATE. See NEW YORK.

NEW YORK STATE AGRICULTURAL AND TECHNICAL INSTITUTE. See ALFRED UNIVERSITY.

NEW YORK STATE BARGE CANAL SYSTEM connects the state's principal natural waterways. The toll-free canal system and its connecting waterways extend 800 miles from Lake Champlain and the Hudson River to Lakes Erie and Ontario. Nearly half of the state of New York and 90 per cent of its population lie within 20 miles of some point on this huge waterways system. The canal system proper is 524 miles long.

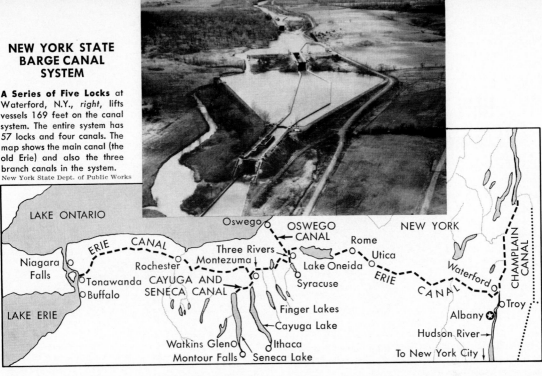

NEW YORK STATE BARGE CANAL SYSTEM

A Series of Five Locks at Waterford, N.Y., *right*, lifts vessels 169 feet on the canal system. The entire system has 57 locks and four canals. The map shows the main canal (the old Erie) and also the three branch canals in the system.
New York State Dept. of Public Works

LAKE ONTARIO

ERIE CANAL

NEW YORK

Oswego

OSWEGO CANAL

Rome

Utica

Niagara Falls

Rochester

Three Rivers

Montezuma

Lake Oneida

ERIE

Waterford

CHAMPLAIN CANAL

Tonawanda

CAYUGA AND SENECA CANAL

Syracuse

CANAL

Buffalo

Troy

LAKE ERIE

Finger Lakes

Albany

Cayuga Lake

Hudson River

Watkins Glen

Ithaca

To New York City

Montour Falls

Seneca Lake

The system consists of a main canal, the old Erie, and three branches—the Champlain, the Oswego, and the Cayuga and Seneca. The 338-mile Erie Canal connects Tonawanda on the Niagara River with Troy and Albany on the Hudson River. The Champlain Canal, between Whitehall on Lake Champlain and Waterford near Troy, is 60 miles long. The 24-mile Oswego Canal links Oswego on Lake Ontario and Three Rivers. The Cayuga and Seneca Canal extends 92 miles from Montezuma, on the Seneca River and the Erie Canal, to Ithaca and Watkins Glen. This waterway includes passages through Cayuga and Seneca lakes and to Montour Falls.

The New York state legislature authorized construction of the New York State Barge Canal System in 1903. The $155 million system was opened in 1918. It has 57 locks, each 310 feet long and 45 feet wide. The locks have a water depth of 12 feet, but are being deepened to 13 feet.

The locks can handle a tug and a 3,000-ton barge that has the capacity of 85 railroad tank cars. A vessel can pass through a lock in 20 minutes. About three million tons of goods and thousands of pleasure boats move through the system each year. WILLIAM E. YOUNG

See also ERIE CANAL.

NEW YORK UNIVERSITY, in New York City, is a privately endowed nonsectarian coeducational institution. It is the largest privately supported university in the United States. The university offers more than 2,600 courses of study in many subject fields. It has more than 4,500 faculty members.

Eight major divisions of the university are located around Washington Square: three graduate schools (Arts and Science, Public Administration, and Social Work), the Division of General Education and Extension Services, Washington Square College of Arts and Science, and three professional schools (Law, Education, and Commerce).

The University College of Arts and Science and the School of Engineering and Science are in the Bronx. The New York University Medical Center has a program of medical education, research, and patient care. The College of Dentistry offers instruction and conducts extensive clinics and research units. The Graduate School of Business Administration carries on an extensive educational program for business students and industrial executives. The Institute of Fine Arts specializes in scholarly studies of the history of art and in archaeological investigations. The Courant Institute of Mathematical Sciences is among the world's largest mathematics research and teaching centers. The university was founded in 1831. For enrollment, see UNIVERSITIES AND COLLEGES (table). JAMES M. HESTER

See also HALL OF FAME.

NEW YORK WORLD'S FAIR has been held twice in New York City. The first fair opened in 1939. Its theme was *The World of Tomorrow*, and its symbols were a *trylon* (a 700-foot-high triangular obelisk) and a *perisphere* (a 200-foot-wide ball-like structure). The fair was held in Flushing Meadow Park in Queens. It promoted inventions of that period, including television, nylon, and air conditioning. Scheduled to end in 1939, the fair was reopened in 1940 because of its popularity. It attracted almost 45 million persons.

The second New York World's Fair, held in 1964 and 1965, used the theme *Peace Through Understanding*. Its symbol was a *unisphere* (a 140-foot-high stainless steel globe). It was held on the same site as the first fair. The inventions displayed at the second fair included color television, picture telephones, computers, and communications satellites. Several art treasures were also displayed. Vatican City sent Michelangelo's famous sculpture *Pieta* to the fair. The fair attracted about 51 million persons.

See also FAIRS AND EXPOSITIONS (picture, The Unisphere); TIME CAPSULE.

NEW
ZEALAND

NEW ZEALAND is a country made up of several islands in the South Pacific Ocean. This self-governing country is a member of the Commonwealth of Nations. Snow-covered mountains, green plains and forests, and sparkling white beaches make it one of the most beautiful lands in the world. New Zealand is also famous for bold experiments in social welfare. Wellington is the capital. Auckland's metropolitan area has the largest population.

The islands of New Zealand have a total area a little smaller than Colorado, but the country has about a million more people than Colorado. About 93 of every 100 New Zealanders are descendants of settlers who came to the country from Great Britain and other European countries. They came to New Zealand in search of a chance to make a good living in a new country. The rest of the people are brown-skinned Maoris who lived in New Zealand before the settlers arrived. The Maoris have adopted most of the ways of the white man.

Two-thirds of the people live in busy, modern cities. Most of the others live on the sheep and dairy farms that dot the foothills and rolling plains. New Zealanders have kept many British customs. For example, they drive on the left side of the street and enjoy such sports as cricket and *Rugby* (a football game).

In 1893, New Zealand became the first country to give women the right to vote. It was also one of the first countries to provide old-age pensions and social security for all citizens and to require workers and employers to settle their differences by arbitration (see ARBITRATION). New Zealand has an excellent public-health program, and the country's infant death rate is one of the lowest in the world.

The Land and Its Resources

Location and Size. New Zealand lies in the South Pacific Ocean about 1,200 miles southeast of Australia. The part of the Pacific Ocean between New Zealand and Australia is called the Tasman Sea.

The *Color Map* shows that New Zealand has three main islands: North, South, and Stewart. These main

John Bell Condliffe, the contributor of this article, is a consultant at the Stanford Research Institute and the author of New Zealand in the Making.

islands stretch about 1,000 miles from north to south. New Zealand has several smaller islands, but most of them lie hundreds of miles from the main islands.

North Island has more than half of the country's population, and covers an area of 44,281 square miles. The northern part of North Island is a narrow peninsula with rolling hills and low mountains. The southern half of the island rises from fertile plains along the coast to volcanic mountain peaks in the center.

South Island has about 30 per cent of the population and an area of 58,093 square miles. It is separated from

---
FACTS IN BRIEF

Capital: Wellington.

Official Language: English.

Form of Government: Constitutional monarchy.

Area: 103,736 square miles. *Greatest Distances*—(north-south) about 1,000 miles; (east-west) about 280 miles. *Coastline*—3,000 miles.

Population: *1966 Census*—2,676,919; distribution, 62 per cent urban, 38 per cent rural. *Estimated 1971 Population*—2,894,000; density, 28 persons to the square mile. *Estimated 1976 Population*—3,148,000.

Chief Products: *Agriculture*—barley, beef, grass and clover seeds, hay, hides and skins, lamb, milk, mutton, oats, wheat, wool. *Manufacturing and Processing*—books, butter, cheese, clothing, furniture, machinery, motor vehicles. *Forest Products*—cardboard, newsprint, lumber. *Fishing*—crayfish, flounder, grouper, snapper, sole, tarakihi, trout. *Mining*—coal, gold.

Flag: The British Union Flag appears at the upper left on a blue field, with the Southern Cross constellation on the right. The flag has been used since 1869. See FLAG (color picture: Flags of Asia and the Pacific).

National Anthem: "God Save the Queen (or King)." *National Song*—"God Defend New Zealand."

Money: *Basic Unit*—dollar. For its value, see MONEY (table: Values).

278

Coronet Peak, one of New Zealand's many mountains, is used by skiers in August. New Zealand seasons are the reverse of those in the United States.

Sheep thrive on New Zealand's fertile plains. The country ranks as one of the world's leading sheep producers. New Zealanders raise livestock on nine-tenths of their farmland. ▶

Wide World

North Island by the 16-mile-wide Cook Strait. South Island is narrow, and stretches 480 miles from northeast to southwest. The great Southern Alps mountain range and its branches extend the entire length of the island. The mountains slope down to fertile coastal plains. New Zealand's highest peak, 12,349-foot Mount Cook, looms over the west-central part of South Island.

Stewart Island has several hundred residents, and covers an area of 670 square miles. The 20-mile-wide Foveaux Strait separates Stewart and South islands. Rugged, forest-covered peaks rise more than 3,000 feet.

Other Islands. The Chatham Islands consist of one large island and three small islands 422 miles southeast of North Island. The islands have a total area of 372 square miles. Several hundred people raise sheep on the two inhabited Chatham Islands. For descriptions of other New Zealand islands, see COOK ISLANDS; KERMADEC ISLANDS; TOKELAU ISLANDS.

Coastline. The 3,000-mile-long New Zealand coast has many stretches of smooth white sand beaches. However, rugged rocks and cliffs stand along most sections of the coast. Beautiful *fiords* (long, narrow inlets of the sea) cut deeply into the southwestern coast of South Island. The chief bays include the Bay of Plenty, South Taranaki Bight, and Hawke Bay on North Island; and Pegasus Bay on South Island.

Rivers, Waterfalls, and Lakes. Swift rivers rise in the mountains and flow to the sea. Few of the rivers can be navigated because of their strong currents. The chief rivers include the Waikato, Wanganui, Rangitikei, and Wairoa on North Island; and the Clutha, Waitaki, Taieri, Mataura, Waimakariri, and Waiau on South Island.

Sutherland Falls plunges 1,904 feet down a mountainside near Milford Sound on the west coast of South Island. It is the fifth highest waterfall in the world.

Location Map

New Zealand's largest lake, 238-square-mile Lake Taupo, lies on North Island. North Island has few other lakes. Its *thermal region* has geysers, boiling mud, and hot pools and springs. This region, near Rotorua, is like Yellowstone National Park in Wyoming. Many large lakes dot the mountains of South Island.

Natural Resources. New Zealand's soil is the country's chief natural resource. Much of it has been enriched by treatment with chemical fertilizers. About two-thirds of the country has soil suitable for forestry, stock raising, or farming.

Forests. Beech, fir, pine, and other trees grow in thick forests that cover about one-fifth of the land. The government has set aside national forests. A forest products industry is based on tree plantations established in New Zealand.

Minerals. The mountains contain deposits of gold, coal, and other minerals. These include small deposits of limestone, silver, and tungsten.

Animal Life. New Zealand is the home of the strange *kiwi* bird. The kiwi has no tail and cannot fly because its wings are too small. Other distinctive New Zealand birds include the olive-green *kea* parrot and the rare, noisy *kaka* parrot. See KEA; KIWI.

Climate. New Zealand has a mild, pleasant climate similar to that of the state of Washington. Sea breezes cool the islands in the summer and keep them fairly

New Zealand Has an Area Almost the Size of Colorado.

1 INCH = 1,200 MILES

279

warm in winter. Because New Zealand lies below the equator, its summer comes when the United States is experiencing winter. Average temperatures in Wellington range from 68°F. in January to 42°F. in July.

Between 20 and 200 inches of rain falls on various parts of the islands every year. About 49 inches of rain falls in the Wellington area annually.

New Zealanders experience about 100 earthquakes each year. Most of the quakes occur in southern North Island and northern South Island. The country's worst earthquake occurred at Napier in 1931, killing 255.

Life of the People

The People. About two-thirds of the people live in city areas and one-third in farming regions.

Over 90 of every 100 New Zealanders are descendants of people who came to the country from England, Scotland, Wales, and Ireland after 1840. About 7 of every 100 persons are Maoris. The rest of the New Zealanders come chiefly from European countries outside of the British Isles. New Zealanders sometimes use the term *European* to refer to anyone who is not a Maori. The Maori word for a European is *pakeha*.

The Maoris are a Polynesian people related to the Hawaiians, Samoans, Tahitians, and other Pacific island people. The Maoris also have some Melanesian blood. Some Maoris have intermarried with Europeans. Many Maoris have gained prominence in the government and the professions. See MAORI.

About 835,000 New Zealanders belong to the Church of England. There are about 539,000 Presbyterians, 364,000 Roman Catholics, and 174,000 Methodists.

Language. New Zealanders speak English. The Maoris also speak their own language, Maori. It is a part of the Malayo-Polynesian group of languages, written in a modified form of the English alphabet. See LANGUAGE (Other Language Families).

Family Life. New Zealand has one of the highest standards of living in the world. New Zealanders earn almost as much as do people in the United States. They pay less for food, clothing, and shelter than Americans, but mechanical products such as automobiles cost more than in the United States.

Shelter. Most of the people live in one-story houses made of wood, but sometimes built of stone or brick. Many homes have porches that extend along one or two sides. Most New Zealanders plant flower gardens, and many also raise vegetables.

NEW ZEALAND MAP INDEX

Main Islands

Map Key	Island	Population	Area (Sq. Mi.)
B 4	North Island	1,893,326	44,281
F 3	South Island	783,261	58,093
G 2	Stewart Island	332	670

Cities and Towns

Alexandra ...2,979..F 2
Ashburton ..12,672...E 3
Auckland ..149,989
  *548,293...B 5
Balclutha ...4,419...G 2
Birkenhead .11,388..H 8
Blenheim ..13,242...D 4
Bluff ......3,279...G 2
Bulls* .....1,803...D 5
Cambridge ..5,962...B 5
Carterton ...3,536..D 5
Christ-
  church ...161,566
  *247,248...E 4
Dannevirke ..5,728..D 6
Dargaville ..3,902...A 4
Devonport ..11,092..B 5
Dunedin ...77,149
  *108,734..F 3
East Coast
  Bays* ...12,357..H 9
Eastbourne ..4,545..J 11
Ellerslie ....4,284...H 9
Eltham .....2,319...C 5
Featherston* 1,857...D 5
Feilding ....9,031..D 5
Foxton .....2,819..D 5

Geraldine ...1,876...F 3
Gisborne ..24,939
  *27,804...C 7
Glen Eden ..6,045..H 8
Glenfield ..13,335..H 8
Gore ......8,104...G 2
Green Bay* .2,022..B 5
Green
  Island ...5,849..F 3
Greymouth ..8,781..E 3
Hamilton ..63,000
  *63,303...B 5
Hastings ..26,867
  *37,466...C 6
Havelock
  North .....5,472...C 6
Hawera ....8,142...C 5
Henderson ..5,604..H 8
Heretaunga-
  Pinehaven* 4,539..D 5
Hokitika ....3,258...E 3
Hornby .....6,484..E 4
Howick .....9,189..B 5
Huntly .....5,401..B 5
Inglewood ..2,003..C 5
Invercargill 43,572
  *46,016...G 2

Kaiapoi ...3,528...E 4
Kaikohe ...3,134...A 4
Kaitaia ...3,056...A 4
Kawerau ...5,826...C 6
Kelston
  West* ....4,937...H 8
Levin .....11,402...D 5
Lower Hutt .57,403
  *114,628...J 11
Lyttelton* ..3,493...E 4
Manukau* .73,218..H 9
Marton ....4,731...D 5
Masterton ..17,596..D 5
Matamata ...3,810..B 5
Mataura ...2,629...G 2
Milton .....1,861...G 2
Morrinsville .4,497...B 5
Mosgiel ....7,488...F 3
Motueka ...3,748...D 4
Mount
  Albert ...25,721..H 8
Mount Eden 18,392..H 9
Mount
  Maunganui 6,815..B 5
Mount
  Roskill ..33,472..H 9
Mount Wel-
  lington ..18,857..H 9
Murupara ..2,670...C 6
Napier 28,645
  *38,309...C 6
Nelson 26,218
  *27,615...D 4
New Lynn ..9,957..H 8
New
  Plymouth 31,843
  *35,280...C 5
Ngaruawahia 3,769..B 5

Ngongotaha* 1,994...C 6
Northcote ..8,144...H 9
Oamaru ...13,186...F 3
One Tree
  Hill ....12,905...H 9
Onehunga ..16,238..H 9
Opotiki ....2,588...C 6
Otahuhu ....9,821..H 9
Otaki .....3,573...D 5
Otorohanga ..1,951...C 5
Paekakariki* 1,934..D 5
Paeroa ....3,129...B 5
Pahiatua ...2,597...D 5
Palmerston
  North 46,832
  *49,140...D 5
Papakura* .11,278..B 5
Papatoetoe .20,576..H 9
Patea .....2,013...C 5
Petone ...10,143...J 11
Picton ....2,560...D 5
Plimmerton-
  Paremata* 3,774...D 5
Porirua ...22,190..D 5
Port
  Chalmers .3,071...F 3
Pukekohe ..6,547...B 5
Putaruru* ..4,435...C 5
Rangiora ...4,117...E 4
Riccarton ...7,253..E 4
Richmond ..4,574...D 4
Rotorua ...25,978
  *33,229...C 6
St. Kilda ..6,726...F 3
Sockburn ...5,529...E 4
Stratford ...5,441...C 5
Taihape ...2,861...C 5
Takapuna ..23,098..H 9

Taradale ...6,253...C 6
Taumarunui 5,864...C 5
Taupo .....7,311...C 6
Tauranga ..23,390
  *31,606..B 6
Tawa ......9,852...J 11
Te Aroha* ..3,212...B 5
Te Awamutu 6,719...C 5
Te Kuiti ...4,825...C 5
Te Puke ...2,601...B 6
Temuka ...2,703...F 3
Thames ....5,599...B 5
Timaru 27,314
  *27,946...F 3
Titirangi ..5,568...H 8
Tokoroa ..11,229...C 5
Upper Hutt 19,084
  *114,628...D 5
Waihi* ....3,169...B 5
Waimate ...3,300...F 3
Wainui-
  omata ...13,948...J 11
Waipawa ...1,848...C 6
Waipukurau 3,569...D 6
Wairoa ....5,100...C 6
Waitara ....4,790...C 5
Waiuku ...1,759...B 5
Wanganui ..35,629
  *38,174..C 5
Wellington 131,655
  *167,859...D 5
Westport ...5,271...D 3
Whakatane ..8,637...B 6
Whangarei .27,560
  *29,503...A 5
Winton ....1,740...G 2

Physical Features

Awarua Bay ....F 2
Banks Peninsula ....E 4
Baring Head (Cape) .J 11
Bay of Islands ....A 5
Bay of Plenty .....B 6
Browns (Motukorea)
  Isl. ....H 9
Buller R. ....D 4
Canterbury Bight ..F 3
Cape Brett ....A 5
Cape Campbell .....D 5
Cape Egmont ......C 4
Cape Farewell .....D 4
Cape Foulwind .....D 3
Cape Karikari .....A 4
Cape Kidnappers ...C 6
Cape Maria
  Van Diemen ....A 4
Cape Palliser .....D 5
Cape Turnagain ...D 6
Cascade Pt. ....E 2
Clarence R. ....E 4
Cloudy Bay ....D 5
Clutha R. ....F 2
Cook, Mt. ....E 3
Cook Strait ....D 5
Devil River Peak ..D 4

Doubtful Sound ....F 1
D'Urville (Isl.) ....D 4
Dusky Sound ......F 1
East Cape ....B 7
Firth of Thames ...B 5
Fitzroy Bay ....J 11
Flat Mtn. ....D 3
Foveaux Strait ....G 1
Golden Bay ....D 4
Gollans R. ....J 11
Great Barrier Isl. ..B 5
Great Mercury (Isl.) B 5
Grey R. ....E 3
Hauraki Gulf ......B 5
Hawke Bay ....C 6
Herbert Peak .....E 4
Hikurangi (Mtn.) ..B 7
Kaikoura Peninsula .E 4
Kaipara Harbour ...B 5
Karamea Bight ....D 3
Karori R. ....J 10
Kawhia Harbour ...C 5
Lake Brunner .....E 3
Lake Hawea ......F 2
Lake Pupuke ......H 9
Lake Taupo ....C 5
Lake Te Anau .....F 1

Lake Tekapo ......E 3
Lake Wakatipu ....F 2
Lake Wanaka .....F 2
Lyall Bay ....J 11
Mahia Peninsula ...C 6
Main Entrance ....J 11
Manukau Entrance .I 8
Manukau Harbour .B 5
Mercury Bay ......B 6
Milford Sound ....F 1
Mitre (Mtn.) ......D 5
Mt. Allen ....G 1
Mt. Anglem ......G 1
Mt. Aspiring .....F 2
Mt. Cook ....E 3
Mt. Egmont ......C 5
Mt. Lyall ....F 1
Mt. Ngauruhoe ...C 5
Mt. Owen ....D 4
Mt. Ross ....D 5
Mt. Ruapehu .....C 5
Mt. Stokes ......D 5
Mt. Tapuaenuku ..D 5
Mt. Taylor ......E 3
Mt. Tongariro ....C 5
Mt. Travers .....E 4
Mt. Whitcombe ...E 3

North Cape ......A 4
North Isl. ....B 4
North Taranaki
  Bight ....C 5
Ohau Bay ....J 10
Ohau Pt. ....J 10
Oreti R. ....G 2
Orongorongo R. ...J 11
Otago Harbour ....F 3
Otago Peninsula ..F 3
Otari Mt. ....J 11
Outlook Hill (Mtn.) J 10
Owhariu Bay .....J 10
Pegasus Bay .....E 4
Poor Knights Is. ..A 5
Port Nicholson
  (Harbor) ......J 11
Poverty Bay .....C 7
Pukeamaru (Mtn.) .B 7
Puketutu (Weeks)
  Isl. ....H 8
Rakaia R. ....E 3
Rangaunu Bay ....A 4
Rangitata R. .....E 3
Rangitikei R. .....D 5
Rangitoto Channel .H 9
Rangitoto Isl. .....H 9

Sinclair Head
  (Cape) ....J 10
Solander (Isl.) .....G 1
Somes Isl. ....J 11
South Isl. ....F 3
South Taranaki
  Bight ....C 5
Southern Alps (Mts.) E 3
Southwest Cape ...G 1
Stewart (Isl.) .....G 1
Summit (Mtn.) ....D 6
Tamaki R. ....H 9
Tasman Bay ......D 4
Tasman Sea ......C 3
Tauroa Pt. ....A 4
Te Waewae Bay ...G 1
Teana-Katuku
  (Mtn.) ....H 8
Three Kings Is. ...A 4
Waiau R. ....E 4
Waikato R. ....B 5
Wainuiomata R. ..J 11
Waitaki R. ....F 3
Waitemata Harbour .H 8
Wanganui R. .....C 5
Ward Isl. ....J 11
Whangarei Harbour .A 5

*Population of metropolitan area, including suburbs.

*Not on map; key shows general location.

Source: Latest census (1966).

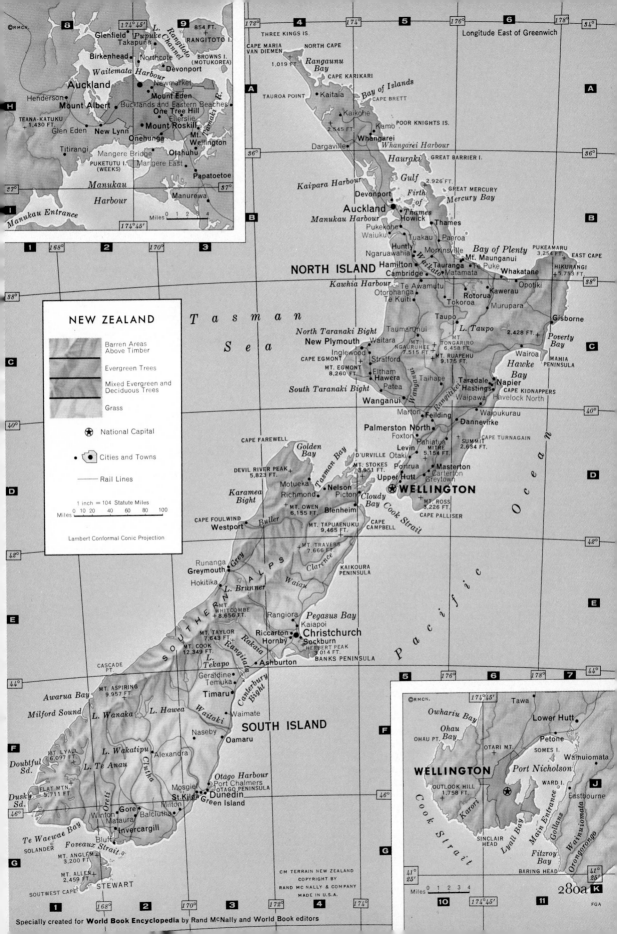

Electric Cable Cars in Wellington carry passengers up the steep hills that border the city's harbor. Wellington ranks among New Zealand's chief seaports. Its huge harbor provides ample space for the merchant ships that make port there.

Food. The people eat about the same food as people enjoy in the United States and Canada. However, New Zealanders eat more butter and meat than do people in those countries.

Tea is the national drink in New Zealand. The people like their tea brewed stronger than do people in the United States. New Zealanders, following British custom, call their late afternoon meal *tea*. They have tea about 6 o'clock. This meal usually includes meat, vegetables, and dessert as well as tea.

Clothing. New Zealanders wear much the same types of clothing as are worn in North America and England. The Maoris sometimes dress in their national costume to welcome distinguished visitors. The costume is woven from flax. The men wear only knee-length skirts. Women dress in skirts and tight, bare-shouldered blouses decorated with bright patterns. The Maoris also wear ornaments made of stone, shark teeth, and feathers.

Recreation. New Zealanders like the outdoors, and enjoy many sports and games. Their favorite game is rugby, which they play in winter. Cricket is the main team sport in the summer. Other sports include horse racing, golf, tennis, boxing, skiing, and baseball.

Waitangi Day, Feb. 6, is a national holiday commemorating the 1840 Treaty of Waitangi which established friendly relations between the Maoris and the Europeans. Anzac Day, April 25, is another national holiday. Anzac stands for the *Australian and New Zealand Army Corps* that fought in World War I. Anzac Day marks the landing of the Anzacs on the Gallipoli Peninsula in Turkey (see GALLIPOLI PENINSULA). Memorial services are held and armed forces veterans parade on Anzac Day. Other important holidays include the monarch's birthday in June, and Labor Day in October.

City Life. Auckland, Christchurch, Dunedin, and Wellington are the largest cities in New Zealand. For

Rugged George Sound flows into the Tasman Sea. Like Norway, New Zealand has many rocky, picturesque fiords.

the populations of these and other New Zealand cities, see the *Map Index* with this article. Many of New Zealand's cities lie along the coasts and overlook fine harbors. They look like many of the smaller cities in the United States and Canada. See AUCKLAND; CHRISTCHURCH; WELLINGTON.

Country Life. Almost all the farms have electricity to provide light and run modern machinery such as milking machines, cream separators, and refrigerators. New Zealand farmers call their fields *paddocks*. Their sheep and cattle can graze on the grass-covered paddocks throughout the year because of the mild climate. Trained sheep dogs help herd the sheep.

Work of the People

About one-fourth of the New Zealanders make their living in manufacturing, and about one-sixth are employed in farming and livestock-raising. About one-fifth are employed by the national and local governments. Farming and livestock-raising rank as the chief industry, however, because the value of their products is larger than that of any other industry.

Agriculture. About half of New Zealand is used for agriculture. The average farmer owns between 100 and 200 acres of land. New Zealand farmers use up-to-date methods of breeding, fertilization, and cultivation.

Stock Raising. Farmers raise cattle and sheep on about nine-tenths of the farmland. Dairy farming and sheep raising are the chief sources of farm income. Most of the dairy cows graze on small farms on the plains of North Island. Farmers also raise beef cattle to provide meat for local use and for export.

New Zealand ranks among the leading sheep-producing countries of the world. South Island and the east coast of North Island have great sheep *runs*, or grazing farms. See SHEEP (Long-Wooled Sheep).

Crops. Farmers grow wheat, barley, and oats for local use. Most of the grains grow in the west-central region of South Island. New Zealand also produces high-quality grass and clover seeds. Other crops include fruits, potatoes, and various garden vegetables.

Manufacturing and Processing. Wellington, Auckland, and Christchurch are the principal manufacturing centers. The chief manufactured products include aluminum, flour, clothing, beer, iron and brass products, machinery, motor vehicles, furniture, shoes, and textiles. Co-operative plants process butter, cheese, and meat.

Forest Products. The forests provide about 600 million board feet of lumber every year. Types of wood in-

New Zealand Traffic Keeps to the Left just as it does in Great Britain. Many New Zealanders ride bicycles to work and to school in the city of Christchurch, *below.*

McGovern, Black Star

New Zealand Consulate General

Lamb Carcasses Ready for Export are inspected before being packed for shipment at a North Island packing company.

clude beech, fir, and pine. Large paper mills located on North Island manufacture newsprint, pulp, and cardboard.

Fishing Industry. Commercial fishermen catch flounder, grouper, snapper, sole, and tarakihi in the shallow water along the coasts. Oysters and crayfish are other important products of the coastal waters.

Electric Power. The many rushing mountain rivers supply power for hydroelectric projects throughout the country. These projects generate most of the 9 billion kilowatt hours of electricity used every year. About 93 of every 100 homes have electricity.

Trade. Wool, butter, cheese, and frozen meats (mainly mutton and lamb) account for more than four-fifths of the country's exports. Over 95 per cent of the exports come from the land. Almost three-fourths of the exports go to the members of the Commonwealth of Nations. More New Zealand exports go to Great Britain than any other country. About half the butter used in Great Britain comes from New Zealand.

Chief imports include textiles, petroleum, machinery, motor vehicles, and paper. The Commonwealth nations supply more than four-fifths of New Zealand's imports. Great Britain is New Zealand's chief source of imports.

Transportation. A government-owned airline and a few small privately-owned airlines fly within the country. Several international airlines fly to New Zealand. The 3,420 miles of railroads, all government-owned, link the chief cities. Trucks, buses, and automobiles travel on 56,275 miles of paved public roads. New Zealand has several merchant ships. Many international shipping lines also serve the country. Small steamboats carry passengers and goods between the three main islands. Wellington and Auckland are the country's chief ports.

Communication. More than 380 companies print or publish books, newspapers, and other printed matter. Most of these companies are in Wellington and Auckland. More than 40 daily newspapers are published throughout New Zealand. Government-owned telephone and telegraph lines connect all parts of the country. The government also owns all but two of the nearly 30 radio stations in New Zealand.

Education

The law requires all children between the ages of 7 and 15 to attend school. The primary schools and high schools are free. The government operates special schools for Maori children in thickly-settled Maori districts. The country also has several private schools, most of them operated by various churches. The percentage of people who can read and write is higher in New Zealand than in almost any other country.

New Zealand has six government-supported universities. They are at Auckland, Christchurch, Dunedin, Hamilton, Palmerston North, and Wellington.

The Arts

Several New Zealanders have won fame in the arts. The sensitive short stories of Katherine Mansfield (1888-1923) are famous throughout the world. The detective story writer Dame Ngaio Marsh (1899-   ), the political cartoonist David Low (1891-1963), and the painter Frances Hodgkins (1869-1947) are also famous in many countries.

The Maoris have won fame for their great skill in wood carving and weaving. Some of the most beautiful Maori carvings appear on their canoes, churches, meeting houses, and homes. The Maoris weave cloth from flax, and decorate the cloth with elaborate designs.

What To See and Do in New Zealand

New Zealand's scenic beauty and excellent sporting facilities attract thousands of visitors from other countries every year. The country's beautiful mountains, glaciers, lakes, rivers, and fiords are easily reached. Many sportsmen think that New Zealand has the best fishing in the world. Anglers catch salmon, trout, and other fish in the streams and lakes. Deep-sea fishermen catch shark, tarpon, and swordfish in the ocean. The miles of white sand beaches provide fine swimming. Skiers speed down the snow-covered mountain slopes. Hunters stalk deer and other wild game in the thick forests. The thermal regions on North Island are popular as health resorts and vacation centers. The picnic grounds and beautiful scenery of Stewart Island also attract many visitors. A series of caves at Waitomo, near Auckland, contains millions of tiny glowworms. The light from these insects shining on rock formations in the caves creates a fascinating fairyland effect.

Government

New Zealand, like Canada, is a self-governing member of the Commonwealth of Nations. The government of New Zealand is modeled after that of Great Britain. The British monarch is also the monarch of New Zealand. The governor-general represents the British Crown in New Zealand. However, the actual political leader of New Zealand is the prime minister, who heads the cabinet (see CABINET). The New Zealand legislature has one house (the House of Representatives). The Court of Appeal is the highest court in New Zealand.

Governor-General. The British Crown appoints the governor-general for an indefinite term. The governor-general has little real power and serves chiefly as a symbol of New Zealand's membership in the British Commonwealth of Nations.

Prime Minister. The leader of the majority party in the House of Representatives automatically becomes prime minister. He appoints the other members of the cabinet. The cabinet must have the support of a majority of the representatives to remain in office.

House of Representatives. The people elect the 80 members of the House of Representatives for three-year terms. The members are elected from districts. If the legislative program of the prime minister loses the support of the House of Representatives, elections are held before the end of the three-year term.

Courts. New Zealand law comes from English common law, certain statutes passed by the British Parliament, and statutes passed by the House of Representatives (see COMMON LAW; LAW [Sources of Law]). The Supreme Court ranks second to the Court of Appeal. The lowest courts are called Magistrates' Courts. The governor-general appoints all judges for life terms.

Local Government. New Zealand has three major subdivisions for local government. These subdivisions include about 120 counties, 140 boroughs, and 25 town districts. The people elect councils to administer each of these subdivisions. The council members serve three-year terms. The voters also elect many special boards to handle such community problems as water supply, land drainage, roads, and public health.

Taxation. Income taxes provide about 36 per cent of the government income. Social security taxes provide about 26 per cent, import taxes about 13 per cent, and sales taxes about 8 per cent.

Politics. All citizens who are 20 years old or older may vote. The country has three political parties—the National, the Labour, and the Social Credit.

Armed Forces. New Zealand's army, navy, and air force have a total of about 10,000 men in peacetime. Many of these men are volunteers.

History

Early Days. The Maoris probably arrived in New Zealand sometime between A.D. 950 and 1350. The warlike Maoris conquered the small Moriori tribes that lived on the islands. The Moriois were a primitive group related to the Maoris and other Polynesians. The Maoris settled mainly in the coast lands of North Island.

In 1642, Abel Janszoon Tasman, a sea captain working for the Dutch East India Company, became the first European to sight New Zealand. The Dutch company kept Tasman's discovery a secret in order to prevent its rival, the British East India Company, from taking over the islands. The Dutch named the islands *Nieuw Zeeland*, or New Zealand, after the Zeeland province in The Netherlands. See DUTCH EAST INDIA COMPANY; EAST INDIA COMPANY.

British Colonization. No other Europeans came to New Zealand until 1769, when Captain James Cook, a British navigator, rediscovered and charted the islands. Escaped convicts from Australia, deserters from whale- and seal-hunting vessels, and other adventurers established lawless settlements along the coasts during the early 1800's. Edward Gibbon Wakefield (1796-1862), a British statesman, was interested in the development of British colonies. He formed the New Zealand Company to colonize the islands. In late 1839, the com-

pany sent the first group of settlers to New Zealand. This forced the British government to claim the islands, in order to set up a government to protect the settlers. The British made New Zealand a part of the colony of New South Wales in Australia, and sent a lieutenant governor, William Hobson (1793-1842), to the islands. He signed the treaty of Waitangi with the Maori chiefs. The Maoris recognized the British queen, Victoria, as ruler of the islands. The British promised to protect the Maoris and to recognize Maori property rights. The British made New Zealand a separate colony in 1841.

RED-LETTER DATES IN NEW ZEALAND

A.D. 1300's The Maoris came to New Zealand.
1642 Abel Janszoon Tasman discovered New Zealand.
1769 Captain James Cook explored the islands.
1839 The New Zealand Company sent settlers to the islands.
1840 The Maoris signed the Treaty of Waitangi, ceding New Zealand to Great Britain.
1845-1870 The Maoris fought several wars against the Europeans.
1852 The British granted New Zealand a constitution.
1861 The New Zealand gold rush began.
1890 The government began a program of social legislation.
1907 The British made New Zealand a dominion.
1914-1918 New Zealand fought with the Allies against Germany in World War I.
1939-1945 New Zealand fought against the Axis in World War II.
1950-1953 New Zealand fought with other United Nations forces in the Korean War.
1954 New Zealand joined the Southeast Asia Treaty Organization (SEATO).
1955 New Zealand sent troops to help the British fight communist rebels in Malaya.
1965 New Zealand sent troops to support the South Vietnamese government in the Vietnam War.

A Maori Child plays near wooden sculptures, for which Maoris are famous. About 7 of every 100 New Zealanders are Maoris.
Waagenaar, Pix

NEW ZEALAND

The Maori Wars. Fighting between the Maoris and settlers broke out in 1845. The Maoris felt that the settlers were buying Maori land illegally. The British sent George Grey (1812-1898) to New Zealand as governor. Grey settled the disputes, and fighting ended by 1848.

In 1852, the British gave New Zealand a constitution that granted self-government. The constitution provided for a parliament that included an elected house of representatives and an appointed legislative council.

The Maoris revolted again in 1860 because of land disputes similar to those of the 1840's. Small-scale fighting flared until 1870.

The Gold Rush. New Zealand's population grew slowly until gold was discovered in 1861. The gold strike brought a rush of new immigrants to the islands from Great Britain. The miners soon dug most of the surface gold. But many miners liked New Zealand so well that they remained there after the gold was gone, and turned to other ways of making a living.

New Zealand first shipped frozen meat to England in 1882. This marked the beginning of the growth of the country's great meat and dairy-products industry.

Social Progress. During the 1890's and early 1900's, the government introduced many reforms. These included old-age pensions, an income tax, regulation of employment conditions, breaking up large estates for sale to farmers, and compulsory arbitration of labor disputes. In 1893, New Zealand became the first country to grant women the right to vote.

Dominion Status. In 1907, Great Britain granted New Zealand's request to be a dominion within the British Empire. The country prospered during the early 1900's as a result of rising prices for exports and an increase in production. New Zealand troops served with the Allied forces during World War I.

Depression. The great world depression that began in 1929 hit New Zealand hard. Export prices fell and many persons lost their jobs. The Labour party, under the leadership of Michael Joseph Savage (1872-1940), won the election of 1935. The government began a new period of experimental legislation. In 1938, the government established a complete social security program that included full dental, medical, and hospital care, and benefits for widows, orphans, and the aged. It also acted to control imports, guarantee export prices, and develop local industry. Peter Fraser (1884-1950) succeeded Savage as prime minister and Labour party leader in 1940.

World War II. During World War II, New Zealand fought with the Allies against Germany, Italy, and Japan. New Zealand became a charter member of the United Nations in 1945.

The conservative National party defeated the Labour party in 1949, and the National party leader, Sidney G. Holland (1893-1961), became prime minister. The National party continued most of the social welfare program started by the Labour party. Until 1951, New Zealand had a two-house parliament. In that year, the government abolished the legislative council which had been the upper house of the parliament. New Zealand army and navy units fought alongside other United Nations forces in the Korean War (1950-1953).

Recent Developments. The nation prospered during the 1950's and had almost no unemployment. In 1951,

New Zealand, Australia, and the United States signed a mutual-defense pact known as the Anzus treaty. The three countries agreed to come to each other's aid in case of attack. In 1954, New Zealand signed the Southeast Asia Collective Defense Treaty with the United States, the Philippines, Great Britain, France, Pakistan, Australia, and Thailand (see SOUTHEAST ASIA TREATY ORGANIZATION). In 1955, New Zealand dispatched army, navy, and air force units to Malaya to bolster the British defense against communist rebels. Holland resigned as prime minister in September, 1957. He was replaced by Keith J. Holyoake (1904-   ). Holyoake and the National party held office until December, 1957, when the Labour party won the national election. Walter Nash (1882-   ) then became prime minister. In 1960, Holyoake's National party regained control, and Holyoake again became prime minister. Holyoake's party was re-elected in 1963, in 1966, and in 1969. In the mid-1960's, New Zealand sent troops to South Vietnam to help the South Vietnamese in the Vietnam War (see VIETNAM WAR).   JOHN BELL CONDLIFFE

Related Articles in WORLD BOOK include:

BIOGRAPHIES

Hillary, Sir Edmund P.	Rutherford, Ernest
Mansfield, Katherine	Walpole, Sir Hugh Seymour

CITIES

Auckland	Christchurch	Wellington

ISLANDS

Auckland Islands	Kermadec Islands	Ross Dependency
Cook Islands	Niue Island	Tokelau Islands

OTHER RELATED ARTICLES

Anzus	Moa	Sutherland Falls
Colombo Plan	Mount Cook	Tasman Sea
Maori	Pacific Islands	

Outline

I. **The Land and Its Resources**
   A. Location and Size   D. Natural Resources
   B. Coastline   E. Climate
   C. Rivers, Waterfalls, and Lakes
II. **Life of the People**
   A. The People   C. Family Life   E. Country Life
   B. Language   D. City Life
III. **Work of the People**
   A. Agriculture   E. Electric Power
   B. Manufacturing and Processing F. Trade
   C. Forest Products   G. Transportation
   D. Fishing Industry   H. Communication
IV. **Education**
V. **The Arts**
VI. **What To See and Do in New Zealand**
VII. **Government**
VIII. **History**

Questions

How did gold help New Zealand's development?

Who are the Maoris?

What part has New Zealand taken in the development of social welfare?

Why are rivers important to New Zealand?

How does the government of New Zealand differ from that of the United States or Canada? How is it the same?

When did New Zealand women receive the right to vote? Compare this with the United States.

What is New Zealand's chief industry? What industry employs the most people?

What may cause members of the House of Representatives to serve less than three-year terms?

What country imports most of New Zealand's products? What kinds of products does New Zealand import?

NEWAR. See NEPAL (The People).

NEWARK, Del. (pop. 20,757; alt. 135 ft.), is one of the major fiber-making centers of the United States. It also manufactures fine book papers, and has an automobile-assembly plant. Newark lies in northern Delaware, about halfway between New York City and Washington, D.C. For location, see DELAWARE (political map). The University of Delaware and the Biochemical Research Foundation of the Franklin Institute are there. Newark was chartered in 1758. It has a council-manager government.   JOHN A. MUNROE

NEWARK, N.J. (pop. 382,417; met. area 1,856,556; alt. 55 ft.), is the largest city in New Jersey. It is an industrial center and an important port. The city is the seat of Essex County.

Location, Size, and General Description. Newark lies on the shore of Newark Bay, at the mouth of the Passaic River. Railways, subways, and bus lines connect Newark with New York City. The city covers an area of about 24 square miles. The surface of the city is fairly flat for a mile inland. Then it rises in terraces. To the west are the Watchung Mountains. For location, see NEW JERSEY (political map). For information on the monthly weather there, see NEW JERSEY (Climate).

A ring of suburban cities and towns lies around Newark. These suburbs include Montclair, Glen Ridge, Bloomfield, Maplewood, Belleville, Nutley, Irvington, Caldwell, Orange, and East, West, and South Orange. The industrial neighbors of Newark are Elizabeth, Bayonne, Passaic, Hoboken, East Newark, and Pater-son. Jersey City is about 4 miles east of Newark. On the west coast of the bay is the Port of Newark, a shipping terminal that handles worldwide trade.

Cultural Life. Newark was a pioneer in the educational field. In 1794, Moses Combs, a shoe manufacturer, started a school for his workers. Newark was one of the first U.S. cities to establish a summer school (1885); the second to establish all-year schools (1912); and the third to erect a high school (1838).

Newark's schools include the Newark College of Engineering, the New Jersey College of Medicine and Dentistry, and the Newark Colleges of Rutgers University. The Museum of Art was founded in 1909.

The People. The first settlers on the site of Newark were Connecticut Puritans who came from the former colony of New Haven. As the community grew industrially, large groups of immigrants from many countries in Europe came to work in the factories. By 1970, Negroes made up more than half of Newark's population.

Industries. Newark factories make many products. Several of the nation's leading electrical goods plants are located there. With 19 insurance companies there, Newark ranks second in the volume of life insurance business. Among the other important products are paint and varnish, leather goods, steel bearings, malt liquors, machinery, jewelry, hats, electrical apparatus, clothing, furs, enamelware, trunks, bags, tobacco, and coal tar.

Fairchild Aerial Surveys, Inc.

Newark, N.J., lies on the west bank of the Passaic River where it joins Newark Bay. The city forms the hub of a large industrial area in the northeastern part of New Jersey.

Transportation. Port Newark, built at a cost of $90 million, has a deepwater harbor. It covers 2,200 acres, with 12,000 feet of docks and space for 20 freight steamers. It is an important lumber and building materials center. The city airport was constructed in 1928 at a cost of more than $10 million. The Port of New York Authority operates the seaport and airport.

History. An entire Connecticut community moved to the site of Newark in 1666. They first named it Milford. They changed the name to Newark, perhaps in honor of the first minister, Abraham Pierson, who had been ordained at Newark-on-Trent in England. Newark was incorporated as a city in 1836. From 1748 until 1756, the College of New Jersey was in Newark. Then the school was moved to Princeton, N.J. This school later became known as Princeton University.

Newark's first tannery was established in 1698. In 1819, Seth Boyden of Newark developed the process for making patent leather. He later discovered a process for making cast iron that was not brittle. A monument to Boyden stands in Washington Park.

In 1967, riots broke out in a largely Negro section of Newark. During the five-day riots, 23 persons were killed and over 1,000 were injured. Property damage was estimated at between $10 million and $15 million.

A major scandal shocked the city in 1969, when Mayor Hugh Addonizio and other Newark officials were charged with sharing illegal refunds on city contracts. Addonizio ran for re-election in 1970 and was defeated by Kenneth A. Gibson, who became Newark's first Negro mayor. Later that year, a jury convicted Addonizio and four other defendants.

In 1971, a dispute over working conditions developed between white Newark teachers and the city's board of education, which had a black and Puerto Rican majority. The dispute led to an 11-week strike by the teachers, the longest in the history of a major American city. This strike greatly increased racial tension in Newark.   RICHARD P. McCORMICK

NEWARK, Ohio (pop. 41,836; alt. 820 ft.), is an important industrial and agricultural center surrounded by fertile farms rich in grains, fruit, livestock, and dairy products. Newark lies at the meeting point of the north and south branches of the Licking River, about 35 miles east of Columbus (see OHIO [political map]). The city is famous for its glass and stove works. Other industries make fiber glass, truck axles, power lawnmowers, aluminum cable, and parts for electrical appliances. General W. C. Schenck founded Newark in 1802 and named it for Newark, N.J. Tourists enjoy visiting the city's prehistoric mounds. Newark has a mayor-council government.   JAMES H. RODABAUGH

NEWARK COLLEGE OF ENGINEERING. See UNIVERSITIES AND COLLEGES (table).

NEWARK STATE COLLEGE. See UNIVERSITIES AND COLLEGES (table).

NEWBERRY, WALTER LOOMIS (1804-1868), was an American businessman and philanthropist. He left about half of his fortune to found the Newberry Library in Chicago (see NEWBERRY LIBRARY).

Newberry was born in East (now South) Windsor, Conn. His family moved to Sangerfield, N.Y., when he was a year old. He had little schooling, and went to work in his brother's store when he was 16. The two moved to Detroit, Mich., in 1826, where they built up a prosperous dry-goods business. Later, Newberry became interested in Chicago, which was then only a tiny trading community. He moved to Chicago in 1833, and made a fortune in real estate.   ROBERT H. BREMNER

NEWBERRY COLLEGE. See UNIVERSITIES AND COLLEGES (table).

NEWBERRY LIBRARY is a privately supported research library in Chicago. It specializes in books and manuscripts on literature, languages, history, genealogy, and music. The institution has about 850,000 volumes. Outstanding collections include the Edward E. Ayer collection on American Indians, the John M. Wing collection on printing, and the Louis H. Silver collection on European history and literature. The library, founded by Walter L. Newberry, opened in 1887. It is at 60 W. Walton Place, Chicago, Ill., 60610.

NEWBERY, JOHN (1713-1767), was an English publisher and bookseller. He is famous in the history of children's literature as the first person to print and sell books for children. He published *Mother Goose's Melodies* and *Goody-Two-Shoes* (1765) and many other little volumes bound in "flowery gilt," a gay paper imported from The Netherlands. Many of Newbery's books were reprinted in America between 1749 and 1831.

Reprinted from *Records of the House of Newbery*, Bemrose & Sons, Ltd., London.

John Newbery

Newbery's bookshop, The Bible and Sun, was in St. Paul's Churchyard, London. He was the friend and patron of Oliver Goldsmith, Samuel Johnson, and many other literary men of his day. Goldsmith portrayed him in his novel, *The Vicar of Wakefield* (1766). It is believed that Goldsmith wrote some of the quaint penny books published by Newbery. These little books are now highly prized. Thomas Babington Macaulay, a famous English essayist of the 1800's, called Newbery the "friend of children."

Newbery was born in Berkshire. The Newbery medal, which has been awarded each year since 1922 for the finest children's book written by an American, was named for him (see NEWBERY MEDAL).   JEAN THOMSON

See also LITERATURE FOR CHILDREN (The 1700's).

NEWBERY MEDAL is an annual award given to the author of the most distinguished contribution to American children's literature published in the preceding year. The award was established and endowed in 1921 by Frederic G. Melcher, chairman of the board of R. R. Bowker Co., publishers of the *Library Journal* and *Publishers' Weekly*. He named it for John Newbery, an English publisher. Melcher also founded the Caldecott medal, awarded annually to the illustrator of the outstanding children's picture book of the preceding year.

René Chambellan designed the medal. It is awarded by the Children's Services Division of the American Library Association.   ANNE J. RICHTER

See also NEWBERY, JOHN; MELCHER, FREDERIC GERSHOM; CALDECOTT MEDAL.

The Newbery Medal is presented annually to the author of the year's most distinguished book for children.

NEWBERY MEDAL WINNERS

Year	Author	Winning Book
1922	Hendrik Van Loon	The Story of Mankind
1923	Hugh Lofting	The Voyages of Dr. Dolittle
1924	Charles Hawes	The Dark Frigate
1925	Charles Finger	Tales from Silver Lands
1926	Arthur Chrisman	Shen of the Sea
1927	Will James	Smoky
1928	Dhan Mukerji	Gay-Neck
1929	Eric P. Kelly	The Trumpeter of Krakow
1930	Rachel Field	Hitty, Her First Hundred Years
1931	Elizabeth Coatsworth	The Cat Who Went to Heaven
1932	Laura Armer	Waterless Mountain
1933	Elizabeth Lewis	Young Fu of the Upper Yangtze
1934	Cornelia Meigs	Invincible Louisa
1935	Monica Shannon	Dobry
1936	Carol Ryrie Brink	Caddie Woodlawn
1937	Ruth Sawyer	Roller Skates
1938	Kate Seredy	The White Stag
1939	Elizabeth Enright	Thimble Summer
1940	James Daugherty	Daniel Boone
1941	Armstrong Sperry	Call It Courage
1942	Walter D. Edmonds	The Matchlock Gun
1943	Elizabeth Janet Gray	Adam of the Road
1944	Esther Forbes	Johnny Tremain
1945	Robert Lawson	Rabbit Hill
1946	Lois Lenski	Strawberry Girl
1947	Carolyn S. Bailey	Miss Hickory
1948	William Pène du Bois	The Twenty-One Balloons
1949	Marguerite Henry	King of the Wind
1950	Marguerite De Angeli	The Door in the Wall
1951	Elizabeth Yates	Amos Fortune, Free Man
1952	Eleanor Estes	Ginger Pye
1953	Ann Nolan Clark	Secret of the Andes
1954	Joseph Krumgold	. . . And Now Miguel
1955	Meindert DeJong	The Wheel on the School
1956	Jean Lee Latham	Carry on, Mr. Bowditch
1957	Virginia Sorensen	Miracles on Maple Hill
1958	Harold V. Keith	Rifles for Watie
1959	Elizabeth G. Speare	The Witch of Blackbird Pond
1960	Joseph Krumgold	Onion John
1961	Scott O'Dell	Island of the Blue Dolphins
1962	Elizabeth G. Speare	The Bronze Bow
1963	Madeleine L'Engle	A Wrinkle in Time
1964	Emily C. Neville	It's Like This, Cat
1965	Maia Wojciechowska	Shadow of a Bull
1966	Elizabeth Borton de Treviño	I, Juan de Pareja
1967	Irene Hunt	Up a Road Slowly
1968	Elaine Konigsburg	From the Mixed-Up Files of Mrs. Basil E. Frankweiler
1969	Lloyd Alexander	The High King
1970	William H. Armstrong	Sounder
1971	Betsy Byars	Summer of the Swans

Each author has a separate biography in WORLD BOOK.

NEWCASTLE (pop. 233,967; alt. 25 ft.) is at the mouth of the Hunter River in New South Wales, Australia (see AUSTRALIA [political map]). It is the second largest city and the chief coal-mining town of the state of New South Wales. Newcastle exports chiefly coal, iron and steel, wool, timber, copper, and agricultural products.

NEWCASTLE UPON TYNE (pop. 244,880; metropolitan area 842,630; alt. 175 ft.) is one of the chief coal centers of England. It has given to the English language the expression "carrying coals to Newcastle," which means taking something to a place that already has more of it than is needed. Newcastle is near the northern border of England, about 7 miles from the North Sea. For location, see GREAT BRITAIN (political map).

The city received its name from a castle built by the son of William the Conqueror about 1080. Shipbuilding and the manufacture of locomotives are among the chief industries. FRANCIS H. HERRICK

NEWCOMB, *NOO kum,* **SIMON** (1835-1909), was an American astronomer. He became famous for his studies of the motions of the moon and other heavenly bodies.

In 1861, Newcomb was named professor of mathematics by the United States Navy, and assigned to the Naval Observatory in Washington, D.C. There, he supervised the construction of a 26-inch equatorial telescope. With George W. Hill (1838-1914), he used this instrument to determine the orbits of the moon, Venus, Mars, Uranus, Neptune, and Saturn. In 1877, he became director of the Observatory's *Nautical Almanac.*

From 1880 to 1882, Newcomb conducted experiments on the velocity of light. He used fixed and revolving mirrors on opposite banks of the Potomac River to gain his result of 186,328 miles per second.

Newcomb was born in Wallace, Nova Scotia, and came to the United States in 1853. He studied at Harvard University. From 1884 to 1894 and from 1898 to 1900, he served as a professor of mathematics at Johns Hopkins University. HELEN WRIGHT

NEWCOMEN, THOMAS (1663-1729), an English inventor, built one of the first practical steam engines in 1712. His atmospheric-pressure steam engine was used to pump water from British mines for almost 75 years. It was gradually replaced by James Watt's separate condenser engine (see WATT, JAMES).

Newcomen's was the first known engine to use a piston successfully. A water jet inside the piston cylinder condensed the steam, creating a vacuum. Air pressure then pushed the piston head into the vacuum. This engine was safer and more efficient than a similar machine designed by Thomas Savery and used at the time, because it avoided high steam pressures and wasted less fuel. Newcomen later worked with Savery in producing and building the new engine.

Newcomen was born in Dartmouth, England. He worked as a blacksmith until the problem of draining water from English tin mines caught his interest. According to tradition, Robert Hooke, the famous English scientist, directed Newcomen's attention to developing a steam engine that could drain the mines. Many Newcomen engines were used in Great Britain and on the continent of Europe. ROBERT E. SCHOFIELD

See also STEAM ENGINE.

Open Pit Mines Contain Labrador's Rich Iron Ore Deposits.

NEWFOUNDLAND

NEWFOUNDLAND, *new fun LAND,* is Canada's newest province. It includes the island of Newfoundland and the coast of Labrador, a part of the Canadian mainland. Newfoundland became a province of Canada in 1949. St. John's is the capital and largest city of Newfoundland. This bustling city ranks among the oldest communities in North America.

Fewer persons live in Newfoundland than in any other province except Prince Edward Island. Most of Newfoundland's land is rugged, especially along the rocky coast. Thick forests grow along tumbling rivers and around sparkling blue lakes. Barren, rocky ridges rise above the green valleys. The ridges surround many brown *peat bogs* (swamps of decayed plants). Arctic winds and ocean currents chill the land and keep the climate generally cool. Storms occur frequently, and fog often covers the coast.

Almost all Newfoundlanders live within a few miles of the sea. Hundreds of villages and fishing settlements nestle in small, sheltered bays along the jagged coast. Some places, too small to appear on maps, have such unusual names as Blow-Me-Down, Little Heart's Ease, and Dragon Bay. One of the world's largest factories that produces paper for newspapers is in Corner Brook.

Most Newfoundlanders belong to families that originally came from the British Isles. The people of many lonely fishing settlements have kept much of the language and customs of their forefathers. Newfoundland fishermen are famed as a people made hardy by their struggle to earn a living from the sea.

Cod, salmon, and other fishes thrive along Newfoundland's shores. The fishing fleets of some nations sail halfway around the world to fish in an area called the Grand Banks, southeast of Newfoundland. Sportsmen come to the province to catch salmon in the streams or

bluefin tuna in the offshore waters. Caribou and moose roam the wilderness areas. In winter, seals sun themselves on ice packs that drift down from the north.

Manufacturing is Newfoundland's leading industry. Manufacturers use the province's extensive timber resources to produce its most valuable products—wood pulp and paper. Food processors prepare salted and frozen fish, and pack live lobsters for shipment to other countries. Miners dig iron ore and other minerals from deposits that rank among the world's largest.

Newfoundland has a longer history than any other region of North America where the people speak English. Viking adventurers may have established settlements in Newfoundland as early as A.D. 1000. Sailors from the English port of Bristol probably reached the island of Newfoundland in 1481. In 1497, John Cabot, an Italian explorer in the service of England, sailed through the rich fishing grounds near Newfoundland. He brought news of the fishing grounds back to Europe. The fisheries attracted many fishermen, and some of them settled on the island. Newfoundland is sometimes called "Britain's oldest colony." But Great Britain considered Newfoundland only a fishing ground for English ships. It did not recognize Newfoundland as a colony until 1824.

For the relationship of Newfoundland to the other provinces, see CANADA; CANADA, GOVERNMENT OF; CANADA, HISTORY OF. See also LABRADOR.

The contributors of this article are Gordon Oliver Rothney, Professor of History at Lakehead University, Ontario; Arch Sullivan, writer for the Newfoundland Herald, CJON *radio and* CJON-TV; *and William F. Summers, Professor and Head of the Department of Geography at the Memorial University of Newfoundland.*

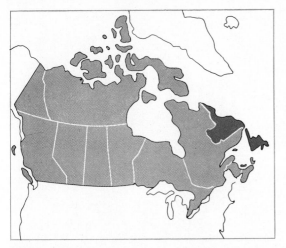

Newfoundland (blue) ranks seventh in size among the Canadian provinces, and is the largest of the Atlantic, or Maritime, Provinces.

———————————— FACTS IN BRIEF ————————————

Capital: St. John's.

Government: *Parliament*—senators, 6; members of the House of Commons, 7. *Provincial*—members of the House of Assembly, 42. *Voting Age*—19 years (provincial elections); 18 years (national elections).

Area: 156,185 square miles (the island of Newfoundland, 43,359 square miles; Labrador, 112,826 square miles), 7th in size among the provinces. *Greatest Distances*—(north-south) the island of Newfoundland, 326 miles; Labrador, 650 miles; (east-west) the island of Newfoundland, 320 miles; Labrador, 450 miles. *Coastline*—the island of Newfoundland, 6,000 miles; Labrador, 4,560 miles.

Elevation: *Highest*—Cirque Mountain in northern Labrador, 5,160 feet above sea level. *Lowest*—sea level.

Population: *1966 Census*—493,396, 9th among the provinces; density, 3 persons to the square mile; distribution, 54 per cent urban, 46 per cent rural. *Estimated 1971 Population*—532,000.

Chief Products: *Manufacturing*—clay products, food products, lumber products, paper, stone products, wood pulp. *Mining*—asbestos, copper, fluorite, iron ore, zinc. *Fishing Industry*—cod, herring, lobsters, salmon, seals, trout, turbot. *Agriculture*—dairy products, vegetables.

Entered the Dominion: March 31, 1949, the 10th province.

Provincial Motto: *Quaerite Prime Regnum Dei* (Seek Ye First the Kingdom of God).

Provincial Song: "The Ode to Newfoundland." Words by Sir Cavendish Boyle; music by Sir Hubert Parry.

Bonavista, a Fishing Village on Bonavista Bay

The Legislative Assembly Meets in the Confederation Building

NEWFOUNDLAND/*Government*

Lieutenant Governor of Newfoundland must approve all laws and executive orders. His position is largely honorary, like that of the governor general of Canada. The lieutenant governor always acts on the advice of the premier. He is appointed by the governor-general-in-council and serves as the representative of Queen Elizabeth in the province.

Premier of Newfoundland is the actual head of the provincial government. He is a member of the Legislative Assembly, and is usually the leader of a political party. He must have the support of a majority of the Assembly. The premier receives $12,000 a year. He also receives allowances as a member of the Assembly.

The premier presides over the Executive Council, or Cabinet. The council includes ministers chosen by the premier, usually from among his party's members in the Legislative Assembly. Most ministers direct one or more branches of the provincial government. The Executive Council, like the premier, must have the support of the majority of the Assembly. Otherwise, it must resign, or else its supporters must win a majority of seats in the Assembly in a new general election.

Legislative Assembly makes the provincial laws. This one-house legislature has 42 members—two from the Harbour Main district and one from each of the 40 other electoral districts. A new Assembly must be elected at least once every five years. Usually, the lieutenant governor calls for the election after a shorter time, on the advice of the premier.

Courts of Newfoundland include the Supreme Court, district courts, and magistrate's courts. The Supreme Court consists of a chief justice and three other judges. Members of the Supreme Court and judges of the four district courts are appointed by the Canadian governor-general-in-council. The lieutenant governor of Newfoundland appoints magistrates.

Local Government. St. John's and Corner Brook, Newfoundland's only cities, operate under special city charters. Each of the province's towns and rural districts is governed by an elected council. Town councils have from 5 to 10 members who serve four-year terms. In some areas, the whole community meets once a year to elect a governing body called a community council.

Taxation. Federal grants, corporation taxes, and personal income taxes account for most of Newfoundland's income. The rest comes from service fees and from sales taxes on gasoline, tobacco products, alcoholic beverages, and other products. The province also collects license fees and royalties on the use of natural resources.

Politics. The people of Newfoundland have strongly supported the Liberal Party since 1949. That year, Newfoundland became a province of Canada. The voters elected Liberals led by Premier Joseph R. Smallwood to a majority of seats in the Assembly. In the next five elections, Smallwood and other Liberals won re-election and kept control of the Assembly. The Progressive Conservative Party forms the opposition in the Assembly.

The Provincial Coat of Arms

The Provincial Flag

Symbols of Newfoundland. On the coat of arms, *above*, the white cross of St. George divides the shield into four parts. The lions and unicorns represent Newfoundland's ties to Great Britain. The coat of arms was granted by King Charles I of England in 1638. The British Union Jack, *above right*, was adopted as the provincial flag in 1952.

The Floral Emblem
Pitcher Plant

Confederation Building is in St. John's, Newfoundland's capital since 1729. The building serves as government headquarters, and the legislature meets there.

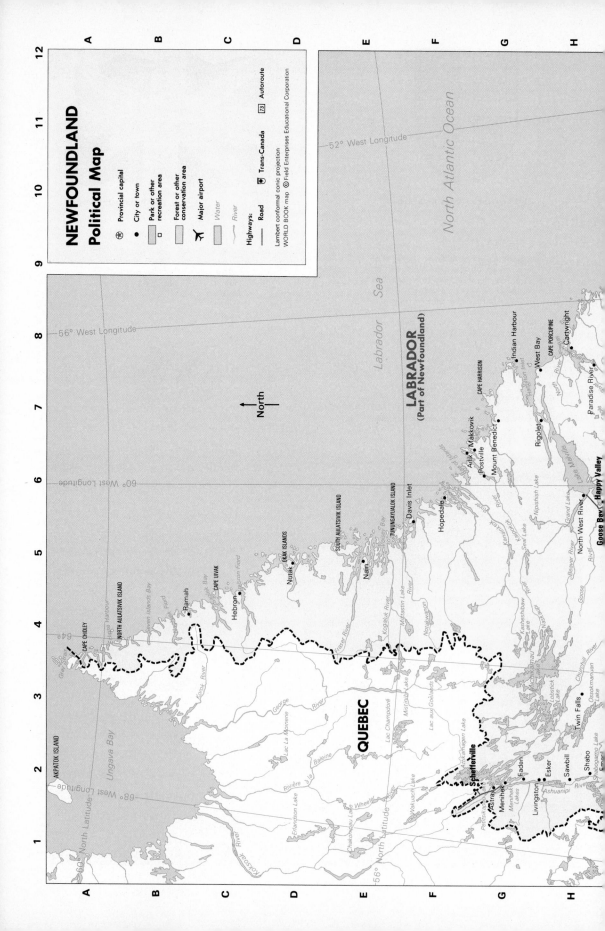

NEWFOUNDLAND
Political Map

⊛ Provincial capital

• City or town

□ Park or other recreation area

Forest or other conservation area

✈ Major airport

Water

River

Highways:

Road

[73] Trans-Canada

Autoroute

Lambert conformal conic projection
WORLD BOOK map © Field Enterprises Educational Corporation

LABRADOR
(Part of Newfoundland)

QUEBEC

North Atlantic Ocean

Labrador Sea

Ungava Bay

North

52° West Longitude

56° West Longitude

60° West Longitude

68° West Longitude

64° North Latitude

60° North Latitude

56° North Latitude

AKPATOK ISLAND

CAPE CHIDLEY

NORTH AULATSIVIK ISLAND

Ramah

CAPE UIVAK

Hebron

OKAK ISLANDS

Nutak

SOUTH AULATSIVIK ISLAND

TUNUNGAYUALOK ISLAND

Nain

Davis Inlet

Hopedale

Aillik

Makkovik

Postville

Mount Benedict

CAPE HARRISON

Indian Harbour

West Bay

CAPE PORCUPINE

Cartwright

Rigolet

Paradise River

North West River

Goose Bay

Happy Valley

Twin Falls

Shabo

Sawbill

Esker

Livingston

Faden

Menihek

Strait

Schefferville

Kogaluk River

Fraser River

Korok River

George River

Lac Champdoré

Lac aux Goélands

Mistastin Lake

Michikamau Lake

Kaniapiskau River

Ashuanipi River

Churchill River

Grand Lake

Lake Melville

North River

Kenamu River

Goose River

Eagle River

Ungava Bay

Grey Strait

Nachvak Fiord

Saglek Bay

Seven Islands Bay

Voisey Bay

Ossokmanuan Lake

Lobstick Lake

Menihek Lakes

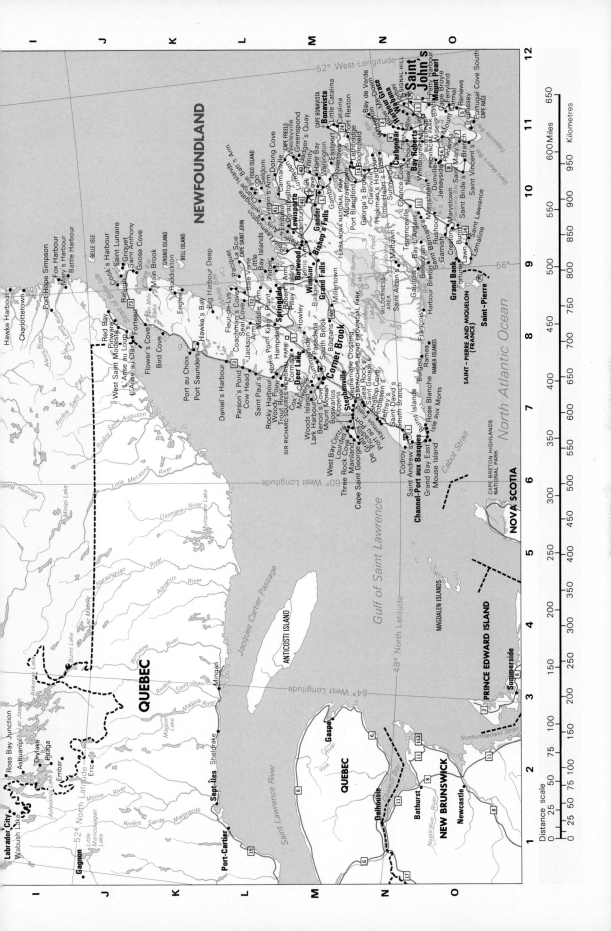

NEWFOUNDLAND/People

The 1966 Canadian census reported that Newfoundland had 493,396 persons. The population of the province had increased 8 per cent over the 1961 figure, 457,853. By 1971, Newfoundland had an estimated population of 532,000. Most persons in Newfoundland are of English, Irish, Scottish, or French descent.

St. John's, on the Avalon Peninsula, is Newfoundland's capital and largest city. It is the center of the province's only Census Metropolitan Area as defined by the Dominion Bureau of Statistics. For the population of this metropolitan area, see the *Index* to the political map of Newfoundland. About 40 of every 100 persons live on the Avalon Peninsula.

Corner Brook is Newfoundland's only other city. Over half of Newfoundland's people live in communities with populations of more than 1,000 persons. Almost all these settlements lie near the coast. Only about 3 of every 100 Newfoundlanders live in communities on the coast of Labrador. See the articles on Newfoundland cities and towns listed in the *Related Articles* at the end of this article.

Less than 2 per cent of Newfoundland's population was born outside Canada. Most of these persons came to the province from England, Scotland, and the United States. The churches with the largest memberships in Newfoundland are, in order of size, the Roman Catholic Church, the Anglican Church of Canada, and the United Church of Canada. Many persons in Newfoundland also belong to the Salvation Army and to Pentecostal assemblies.

POPULATION

This map shows the *population density* of Newfoundland, and how it varies in different parts of the province. Population density is the average number of persons who live on each square mile.

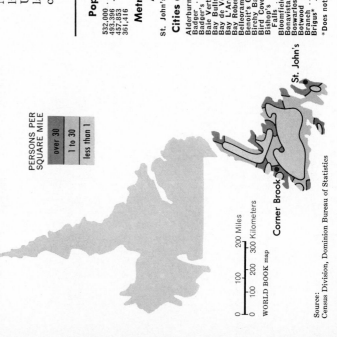

PERSONS PER SQUARE MILE

- over 30
- 1 to 30
- less than 1

WORLD BOOK map

0   100   200 Miles
0   100   200   300 Kilometers

Corner Brook   St. John's

Source: Census Division, Dominion Bureau of Statistics

NEWFOUNDLAND MAP INDEX

*Does not appear on map; key shows general location.

Source: Census Division, Dominion Bureau of Statistics

NEWFOUNDLAND / *Education*

National Film Board of Canada

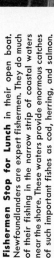

Memorial University of Newfoundland

Schools in Newfoundland are organized mainly on the basis of its five largest religious denominations: Anglican, Pentecostal, Roman Catholic, the Salvation Army, and the United Church of Canada. These denominations have their own school districts, which overlap one another. Each district has a school board and a superintendent of education appointed by the lieutenant governor. The district superintendents represent the religious denominations in the provincial department of education. The minister of education, a member of the Cabinet, directs the department of education. Newfoundland established this department in 1920.

Provincial law requires children to attend school from age 7 through 15. The provincial government pays almost all educational costs. Local taxes and assessments collected by some school districts pay for the rest. The province has one university, the Memorial Uni-

versity of Newfoundland, in St. John's. The provincial legislature made it a degree-granting university in 1949. For the university's enrollment, see CANADA (table: Universities and Colleges).

Libraries and Museums. About 60 libraries serve the province. Organized library service began in 1926 with bookmobiles sent out by the department of education. In 1936, Newfoundland established its first public library, the Gosling Memorial Library in St. John's. The provincial government operates the Newfoundland Museum and the Military and Naval Museum, both in St. John's. The Newfoundland Museum features historical exhibits including relics of the Beothuk Indians. The Military and Naval Museum features weapons from early battles fought in the Newfoundland area. An aviation museum at Gander Airport has displays dealing with pioneer transatlantic flights.

Houses of St. John's line the streets in areas familiar to such famous early explorers as Jacques Cartier and Sir Humphrey Gilbert. St. John's, settled in the 1500's, is one of the oldest continuously occupied North American cities. It serves as Newfoundland's capital, and is the industrial center of the province.

Fishermen Stop for Lunch in their open boat. Newfoundlanders are expert fishermen. They do much of their fishing in the narrow strip of coastal waters near the shore. These waters provide enormous catches of such important fishes as cod, herring, and salmon.

Memorial University of Newfoundland stands on a spacious new campus near the outskirts of St. John's. The first four buildings were completed in 1961. The university was founded as Memorial University College in 1925. The Newfoundland legislature made it a degree-granting university in 1949.

Miller Services

George Hunter, Publix

St. John's on the Atlantic Coast

NEWFOUNDLAND/*A Visitor's Guide*

Newfoundland's many bays and inlets offer camera fans a variety of colorful scenes. The blue waters of the bays may be rimmed by a sprawling city, wooded hills, or barren rocks. The resorts are all near the sea. Guides lead sportsmen inland to hunt bears, caribou, and moose, or to fish for salmon and trout.

PLACES TO VISIT

Following are brief descriptions of some of Newfoundland's most interesting places to visit.

Bell Island, in Conception Bay, has rich iron-ore deposits with mine tunnels extending nearly three miles beneath the floor of the bay.

Gander Airport, one of the finest air terminals in Canada, is North America's chief refueling point for non-jet transatlantic flights.

Placentia, on the west coast of the Avalon Peninsula, was established by the French in 1662. Prime Minister Winston Churchill and President Franklin D. Roosevelt drew up the Atlantic Charter on a warship near Placentia in 1941.

Saint Pierre and Miquelon Islands, two small islands that belong to France, lie about 10 miles off Newfoundland's south coast. The language and customs of the islands resemble those of northwest France. See SAINT PIERRE AND MIQUELON.

Witless Bay, a small fishing village 20 miles south of St. John's, offers boat trips to nearby islands and to villages along the coast.

Parks and Historic Sites. Terra Nova National Park is Newfoundland's only national park. For the area and features of this park, see CANADA (National Parks). Signal Hill, a national historic site, overlooks the harbor at St. John's. It marks the scene of a battle in which the English defeated the French in 1762. In 1901, Guglielmo Marconi received the first transatlantic radio message on Signal Hill. See MARCONI, GUGLIELMO.

Newfoundland has three regional provincial parks. The largest is Butter Pot Park, on the Avalon Peninsula. Barachois Pond Park lies near St. George's, amid the towering Long Range Mountains. Sir Richard Squires Memorial Park, on the Humber River, includes the famous Big Falls. Every spring, Atlantic salmon make spectacular jumps up the falls to reach their *spawning* (egg-laying) grounds upstream.

The province also maintains 16 camping and picnic parks along the Trans-Canada Highway. For information on the provincial parks of Newfoundland, write to Chief Parks Officer, Department of Mines, Agriculture, and Resources, St. John's, Nfld.

Boats in a Harbor
on Conception Bay

Malak, Miller Services

Placentia Bay West of
the Avalon Peninsula
Horwood, Miller Services

Signal Hill Overlooking
the Harbor of St. John's

Jackson, Miller Services

ANNUAL EVENTS

Newfoundlanders observe Commemoration Day on the Sunday nearest July 1. This day honors the Newfoundland regiment that was almost wiped out by German troops in the 1916 Battle of Beaumont-Hamel in France. Other annual events in Newfoundland include the following.

January-March: Robert Burns's birthday, province-wide (Jan. 25); Sports Day in St. Anthony, featuring a dog-team race across 10 miles of ice in St. Anthony Harbour (March); St. Patrick's Day celebrations (March 17).

April-June: Kiwanis Music Festival in St. John's (Easter Week); St. George's Day celebrations, province-wide (April 23); Drama Festival in St. John's (May).

July-September: Regattas at Harbour Grace and Placentia (July); Orangemen's Day celebrations, province-wide (July 12); Regatta Day boat races at Quidi Vidi Lake (August).

October-December: Agricultural and Homecrafts Exhibition in St. John's (October).

NEWFOUNDLAND

Evergreen Trees

Mixed Evergreen and
Deciduous Trees

Tundra

⊛ Provincial Capitals
• Cities and Towns — Rail Lines
1 inch = 115 Statute Miles
Miles 0 20 40 60 80 100
Lambert Conformal Conic Projection

Specially created for **World Book Encyclopedia** by Rand McNally and World Book editors

NEWFOUNDLAND / The Land

Land Regions. Newfoundland includes parts of two land regions: (1) the Canadian Shield, and (2) the Appalachian Region.

The Canadian Shield covers about half of Canada, including all Labrador. It is a rough plateau made up of ancient rocks. In Labrador, the edge of this plateau is cut by valleys and by swift rivers that drain into the Atlantic Ocean. Forests cover more than half of Labrador. Southwestern Labrador has many lakes. It also has rich deposits of iron ore. See CANADIAN SHIELD.

The Appalachian Region extends through the eastern part of North America from the island of Newfoundland to Alabama. Lowlands form the eastern edge of the island of Newfoundland. Toward the west, the land gradually rises to a plateau with several areas higher than 2,000 feet above sea level. In the central part of the island, barren rocky ridges rise from forested valleys. Many lakes, ponds, and bogs dot the area. Three peninsulas—the Great Northern, the Avalon, and the Burin—stick out from the island. The Great Northern Peninsula points northeastward toward Labrador. Forests cover most of this mountainous strip of land. The Avalon Peninsula, on the island's southeast corner, is the most heavily populated part of Newfoundland. About 40 per cent of the people live there. The hilly Burin Peninsula lies west of the Avalon Peninsula, across Placentia Bay.

Coastline of Newfoundland is broken by scenic *fiords* (long, narrow inlets) and by many bays. Several of these bays rank among the largest in Canada. The island of Newfoundland has 6,000 miles of coastline. Labrador's coastline is 4,560 miles long. Thousands of small islands dot the coastal waters.

Mountains. Cirque Mountain, one of the towering Torngat Mountains in northern Labrador, is the highest point in Newfoundland. It rises 5,160 feet above sea level. The Mealy Mountains, in southern Labrador, are over 4,000 feet high. On the island of Newfoundland, the chief mountains are the Long Range Mountains, which rise along the Great Northern Peninsula. The Lewis Hills, southwest of Corner Brook, have the island's highest elevation—2,672 feet above sea level.

Rivers and Lakes. The Churchill River in Labrador is Newfoundland's longest river. It rises near the Quebec border and flows 600 miles to the Atlantic Ocean. On the island of Newfoundland, the Exploits River flows 153 miles northeast from Red Indian Lake into Notre Dame Bay.

Labrador's largest lake is Lake Melville, which covers 1,133 square miles. The next largest Labrador lakes are Michikamau, Lobstick, and Dyke lakes, and Lac Joseph. On the island of Newfoundland, Grand Lake is the largest, followed by Red Indian and Gander lakes. Grand Lake covers 205 square miles.

CANADIAN SHIELD

Churchill R

Naskaupi R

APPALACHIAN REGION

Exploits R.

Land Regions of Newfoundland

Rocky Ridges rise near the village of Trinity on the shore of Trinity Bay. Trinity is in the Appalachian Region, which covers the entire island of Newfoundland. Many lakes, ponds, and bogs dot the area.

Miller Services

The cold Labrador Current and arctic winds keep Newfoundland generally cool (see LABRADOR CURRENT). But the climate varies greatly between Labrador and the island of Newfoundland. On the island, average January temperatures range from 24° F. in St. John's to 11° F. at the tip of the Great Northern Peninsula. Along the Labrador coast, average January temperatures range from 4° F. to −2° F. In July, St. John's has an average temperature of about 60° F., and coastal Labrador has one of about 50° F. The temperature may rise above 80° F. during the summer in any part of the province. The highest and lowest temperatures in the province both were recorded in central Labrador. Goose Bay had the highest temperature, 100° F., on July 4, 1944. The lowest temperature, −55° F., was recorded at Sandgirt Lake on Jan. 17, 1946, and at Ashuanipi on Feb. 7, 1950.

Frequent storms bring Newfoundland strong winds and regular *precipitation* (rain, melted snow, and other forms of moisture) throughout the year. Annual precipitation in the province ranges from between 50 and 60 inches around St. John's to less than 20 inches in the northernmost part of Labrador.

Much of Newfoundland's precipitation falls as snow in the north. Snowfall is greatest in southern Labrador and in the central part of the island. These regions may receive up to 200 inches of snow annually. In the southern part of the island, the average yearly snowfall is 80 inches. Some years, this region's snowfall amounts to 5 inches or less.

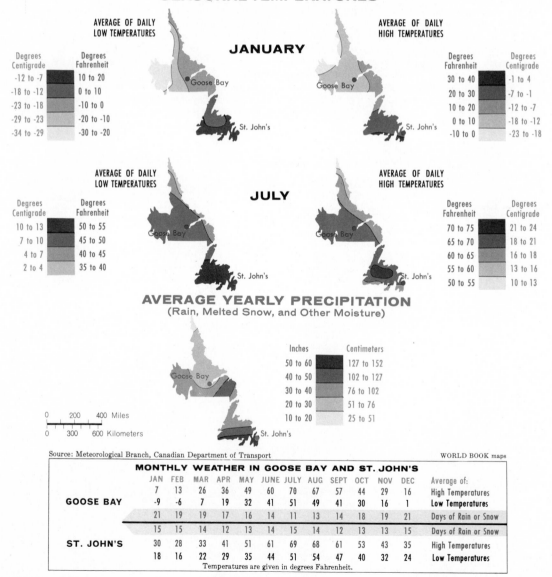

SEASONAL TEMPERATURES

JANUARY

AVERAGE OF DAILY LOW TEMPERATURES

Degrees Centigrade	Degrees Fahrenheit
-12 to -7	10 to 20
-18 to -12	0 to 10
-23 to -18	-10 to 0
-29 to -23	-20 to -10
-34 to -29	-30 to -20

AVERAGE OF DAILY HIGH TEMPERATURES

Degrees Fahrenheit	Degrees Centigrade
30 to 40	-1 to 4
20 to 30	-7 to -1
10 to 20	-12 to -7
0 to 10	-18 to -12
-10 to 0	-23 to -18

JULY

AVERAGE OF DAILY LOW TEMPERATURES

Degrees Centigrade	Degrees Fahrenheit
10 to 13	50 to 55
7 to 10	45 to 50
4 to 7	40 to 45
2 to 4	35 to 40

AVERAGE OF DAILY HIGH TEMPERATURES

Degrees Fahrenheit	Degrees Centigrade
70 to 75	21 to 24
65 to 70	18 to 21
60 to 65	16 to 18
55 to 60	13 to 16
50 to 55	10 to 13

AVERAGE YEARLY PRECIPITATION
(Rain, Melted Snow, and Other Moisture)

Inches	Centimeters
50 to 60	127 to 152
40 to 50	102 to 127
30 to 40	76 to 102
20 to 30	51 to 76
10 to 20	25 to 51

0   200   400 Miles
0   300   600 Kilometers

Source: Meteorological Branch, Canadian Department of Transport

WORLD BOOK maps

MONTHLY WEATHER IN GOOSE BAY AND ST. JOHN'S													
	JAN	FEB	MAR	APR	MAY	JUNE	JULY	AUG	SEPT	OCT	NOV	DEC	Average of:
GOOSE BAY	7	13	26	36	49	60	70	67	57	44	29	16	High Temperatures
	-9	-6	7	19	32	41	51	49	41	30	16	1	Low Temperatures
	21	19	19	17	16	14	11	13	14	18	19	21	Days of Rain or Snow
	15	15	14	12	13	14	15	14	12	13	13	15	Days of Rain or Snow
ST. JOHN'S	30	28	33	41	51	61	69	68	61	53	43	35	High Temperatures
	18	16	22	29	35	44	51	54	47	40	32	24	Low Temperatures

Temperatures are given in degrees Fahrenheit.

The leading industry of Newfoundland is manufacturing, followed by mining and forestry. All production values given in this section are in Canadian dollars. For the value of the Canadian dollar in U.S. money, see MONEY (table).

Natural Resources. Newfoundland's most valuable resources are its large forests, extensive mineral deposits, and rich fishing grounds.

Soil of Newfoundland is coarse and rocky in most places. It contains granite, limestone, quartz rocks, sandstones, shales, slate, and other deposits left by ancient glaciers. The province's richest soil is in the valleys of the Codroy and Humber rivers.

Minerals in Newfoundland include some of the world's largest known iron-ore deposits. The iron field beneath Conception Bay has about 10 billion tons of low grade ore that is no longer mined. Some of the world's most important gypsum deposits are on the west coast of the island. Other important minerals include asbestos, ceramic shales, copper, fluorite, gold, lead, limestone, pyrophyllite, silver, uranium, and zinc.

Plant Life. Forests cover about 88,000 square miles of the province. Balsam firs and black spruces, the most common trees, supply wood for Newfoundland's pulp and paper industry. Other trees include the aspen, birch, larch, pine, and poplar. In areas over 1,200 feet above sea level, the climate is too cold for trees to grow. Only small shrubs, lichens, and mosses grow at these elevations.

Animal Life. Newfoundland's fishing grounds became famous within a few years after their discovery by John Cabot in 1497. Fisheries surround the island of Newfoundland and extend along the Labrador coast. Even fishermen from Europe and Japan fish on Newfoundland's Grand Banks, an underwater plateau. The Grand Banks extend hundreds of miles southeastward from the island. Fishermen catch cod, haddock, redfish, salmon, turbot, and lobsters.

About 30 kinds of animals live in the province. They include arctic hares, bears, beavers, caribou, foxes, lynxes, moose, otters, rabbits, seals, and weasels. Two famous breeds of dogs, the Labrador retriever and the Newfoundland, were developed in Newfoundland (see LABRADOR RETRIEVER; NEWFOUNDLAND DOG).

Few birds live in Newfoundland all year, but many kinds visit the province. Ptarmigans and ruffed grouse live on the island and in Labrador. Ducks, geese, and snipes visit the province every summer. Gulls, loons, murres, puffins, terns, and other sea birds feed in Newfoundland's coastal waters.

Manufacturing. Newfoundland's industrial products have a *value added by manufacture* of about $70,010,000 a year. This figure represents the value created in products by Newfoundland's industries, not counting such costs as materials, supplies, and fuels. The province's pulp and paper industry earns more than all other manufacturing activities together. Corner Brook has one of the world's largest pulp and paper mills. Every day it produces more than 180 tons of pulp and over 1,000 tons of newsprint.

Fish processing ranks second to the pulp and paper industry. The chief fish products are dry salted cod

PRODUCTION IN NEWFOUNDLAND

Total yearly value of goods produced—$158,996,000

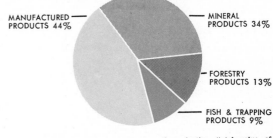

MANUFACTURED PRODUCTS 44%

MINERAL PRODUCTS 34%

FORESTRY PRODUCTS 13%

FISH & TRAPPING PRODUCTS 9%

Note: Percentages based on net value of production (total value of shipments less such costs as materials, fuel, electricity, and supplies). Trapping Products are less than 1 per cent.

Source: Dominion Bureau of Statistics

EMPLOYMENT IN NEWFOUNDLAND

Average yearly number of persons employed—96,100

	Number of Employees
Services	15,923
Wholesale & Retail Trade	14,552
Transportation, Communications & Utilities	14,352
Government & Defense	12,579
Manufacturing	11,549
Construction	8,894
Forestry	6,569
Mining	4,288
Fishing	2,195
Finance, Insurance & Real Estate	1,354
Agriculture	596
Other	3,249

Source: 1961 Census of Canada

and frozen *fillets* (boneless strips of fish). Every year, Newfoundland ships more than 50 million pounds of frozen fillets to the United States and England.

Factories in Newfoundland produce plywood, plasterboard and lath, wallboard, and cement. A large plant near St. John's makes plywood, doors, furniture, and flooring from birch and imported mahogany logs. Another plant manufactures wallboard from fir and spruce timber. Industrial plants also make clothing, leather goods, margarine, phosphorus, steel, textiles, and clay, petroleum, and stone products.

Mining in Newfoundland has an annual income of about $53,753,000. Iron-ore mining accounts for more than two-thirds of all mining income. All of the iron ore comes from mines in Labrador. One of the world's largest iron-ore mines is in a border town known in Labrador as Knob Lake and in Quebec as Schefferville. Labrador City and Wabush, two thriving mining communities, grew up among valuable iron-ore fields in southwestern Labrador.

Mines at Buchans, near Red Indian Lake, produce most of Newfoundland's gold, lead, silver, and zinc. Buchans, Baie Verte, Gull Pond, Little Bay, Tilt Cove,

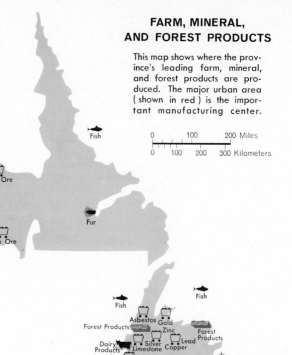

FARM, MINERAL, AND FOREST PRODUCTS

This map shows where the province's leading farm, mineral, and forest products are produced. The major urban area (shown in red) is the important manufacturing center.

WORLD BOOK map

Lyn; APF

Workers Prepare Codfish for Export in a port on Conception Bay. They spread the fish on wire racks to dry in the sun. Drying keeps the fish from spoiling. Newfoundland also exports large amounts of frozen fish.

and Whalesback have copper mines, and Corner Brook has two limestone quarries. Other mining products include asbestos from Baie Verte, fluorite from St. Lawrence, and gypsum from Flat Bay.

Forestry in Newfoundland has an annual income of about $20,265,000. Every year, lumbermen cut more than 1,200,000,000 board feet of timber, mainly pulpwood for Newfoundland's paper mills. The province has about 1,500 sawmills.

Fishing Industry. Newfoundland ranks among the top fishing industry provinces and states, with an annual fish catch valued at $14,922,000. Every year, the province's fisheries produce more than 525,000,000 pounds of fish, including cod, herring, salmon, trout, turbot, and lobsters. Newfoundland fishermen also catch seals that are processed for fur, leather, and oils.

Agriculture. Newfoundland has more than 1,700 farms. They average about 29 acres in size. Most of the farms supply food for their owners. Less than 500 farms grow products for sale. About half the farms are on the Avalon Peninsula. Farms in the fertile areas of the west coast produce about a third of the farm income. The chief farm products include hay, oats, and potatoes. In addition to potatoes, other vegetables include beets, cabbages, carrots, parsnips, and turnips. Dairy and poultry farms operate on the Avalon Peninsula.

Electric Power in Newfoundland comes almost entirely from hydroelectric plants. Steam or diesel-driven generators supply the rest of the electricity. One of the largest hydroelectric projects, Bay d' Espoir, is located on the south coast. Other large hydroelectric plants on the Humber and Exploits rivers supply power for the

paper and pulp mills at Corner Brook and Grand Falls. A Twin Falls power plant serves the Labrador City mining area. For Newfoundland's kilowatt-hour production, see ELECTRIC POWER (table).

Transportation. Newfoundland lies nearer Europe than any other part of North America except Greenland. This location makes the province an important stopping point for transatlantic airplanes and ships.

Two airlines serve Newfoundland. Some propeller-driven airplanes refuel at Gander Airport during transatlantic flights to and from Canada and the United States. Other important airports are at Torbay near St. John's, and at Goose Bay in Labrador. A 547-mile railway connects St. John's and Channel-Port aux Basques with Corner Brook and towns near the northern coast. In Labrador, trains carry iron ore 357 miles from Knob Lake to Sept-Îles, Que.

Newfoundland has about 7,300 miles of roads. Most of the roads are not paved. Part of the Trans-Canada Highway runs from St. John's to Channel-Port aux Basques (see TRANS-CANADA HIGHWAY). Freighters sail to St. John's and Corner Brook from Toronto, Montreal, and Halifax, and from Boston, New York City, and Liverpool, England.

Communication. Newfoundland has three daily newspapers and three weekly papers. The *Evening Telegram*, the oldest and largest daily, was established in St. John's in 1879. The province's first radio station, VOWR, began broadcasting from St. John's in 1924. In 1955, Newfoundland's first television station, CJON-TV, began operating in St. John's. Eleven television stations and 19 radio stations now serve the province.

294f

Discovery. Viking explorers probably were the first white men to live in Newfoundland. In 1961, archaeologists discovered the ruins of a viking settlement on the northern tip of the island. This settlement may have been built as early as A.D. 1000. English fishermen from Bristol probably reached Newfoundland in 1481. John Cabot, an Italian explorer in the service of England, may have landed on Newfoundland or Nova Scotia in 1497. Cabot thought he had reached Asia. He brought to Europe news of Newfoundland's rich fishing grounds.

Indian Days. After Cabot discovered the fishing grounds, hundreds of French, Portuguese, and Spanish fishermen visited Newfoundland. At that time, Beothuk Indians lived on the island. Early explorers named the Beothuks the Red Indians because they painted their bodies with a red mineral substance. For many years, the white settlers and fishermen on the island killed the Beothuks. During the late 1700's, Micmac Indians invaded Newfoundland from what is now Nova Scotia. The Micmacs, like the white settlers, fought the Beothuks. This fighting, together with disease and starvation, wiped out the Beothuks by 1829.

The Micmacs settled around St. Georges Bay and along Newfoundland's southern coast. Naskapi and Montagnais Indians have lived in Labrador for as long as white men have known about the region.

Colonization. By the late 1500's, fishermen of several countries had established small settlements on Newfoundland. English fishermen worked and settled mainly along the southern part of the east coast. French fishing fleets controlled the north and south coasts. But English, French, Spanish, and Portuguese ships often anchored in the same harbor. Each harbor was ruled by a "fishing admiral." He was the master of the first ship to arrive at the beginning of the fishing season. He ruled until the end of the fishing season in early autumn. In 1634, King Charles I officially gave authority to the fishing admirals.

In 1583, the English explorer Sir Humphrey Gilbert landed at St. John's harbor. He claimed "200 leagues" (about 600 miles) in every direction for England. John Guy, a merchant, arrived in 1610 with settlers sent by an English company. Guy formed a colony at Cupids, on Conception Bay. But English fishermen and pirates from the Mediterranean Sea attacked the colony, and it failed. In 1621, Sir George Calvert sent agents to set up a colony at Ferryland, in an area he named Avalon. French raiders and the harsh climate forced Calvert to abandon the project in 1629. In 1637, Charles I granted Newfoundland to Sir David Kirke and other nobles. Kirke set up headquarters at Ferryland, but he had no authority over the English fishermen who came to the island each summer. In 1651, the English government called Kirke back to England.

War with France. French settlers founded Placentia in 1662. Placentia quickly grew into a fortified colony that threatened the English in Newfoundland. But the English government considered Newfoundland only a fishery. English settlers were not allowed to own land within six miles of the sea. England and France did not quarrel openly until William III became king of England in 1689. William declared war on France, and Newfoundland became a battleground. The English and French attacked each other's ships and settlements until 1713, when they signed the Treaty of Utrecht. The treaty gave Britain the entire island. France kept only the privilege of using part of the northern and western shore for drying fish. That area became known as the *French Shore*.

In 1729, the British government began to appoint naval officers as royal governors to rule Newfoundland. Captain Henry Osborne became the first such "naval governor." He appointed justices of the peace and constables to enforce law among the settlers. But Britain continued to favor the interests of the fishermen and to discourage the development of communities. Newfoundland's early governors did not even remain on the island all year. They lived there during the fishing season, and returned to England for the winter.

During the Seven Years' War (1756-1763), English fishermen drove the French fishermen from the French Shore. In 1762, a French fleet seized St. John's and controlled the east coast for a few months. Britain finally obtained all of Canada by the Treaty of Paris in 1763. France received Saint Pierre and Miquelon islands from Britain, and also regained its right to use Newfoundland's French Shore. France gave up this right in 1904.

After the Treaty of Paris, the British government placed the Labrador coast under the authority of Newfoundland's royal governor. Newfoundland lost Labrador to Quebec in 1774, regained it in 1809, and then divided it with Quebec in 1825.

Representation and Independence. By the early 1800's, about 20,000 persons were living in Newfoundland. In 1817, Sir Francis Pickmore became the first governor to remain on the island after the close of the fishing season. Many Newfoundlanders wanted a strong local government. Led by William

The First Successful Atlantic Cable was completed in 1866 at the village of Hearts Content. Four previous attempts had failed. Cyrus W. Field, *second from right,* financed the project. He rented the British steamship *Great Eastern* to lay the cable, which stretched from Valencia, Ireland, to Hearts Content.

Newfoundland's Annual Seal Hunt takes place in spring. In the 1800's, schooners sailed out to the icefields.

The Labrador Boundary Decision of 1927 rejected Quebec claims, *dark area, left,* and defined Newfoundland's boundaries clearly, *right.*

Transatlantic Air Service made Goose Bay and Gander airports famous throughout the world.

Sir Humphrey Gilbert landed on Newfoundland in 1583 and claimed it in the name of Elizabeth I of England.

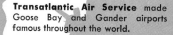

The First Transatlantic Flight, flown nonstop, left Lester's Field near St. John's on June 14, 1919.

Goose Bay •

HISTORIC NEWFOUNDLAND

John Cabot discovered the Newfoundland fisheries in 1497, and may have landed on the island of Newfoundland.

The First House of Assembly in Newfoundland was elected in the fall of 1832 and met on Jan. 1, 1833.

Corner Brook •

Gander •

1st Transatlantic Wireless Signal was received by Marconi in 1901 at Cabot Tower on Signal Hill, St. John's.

Torbay •

ST. JOHN'S ★

The Corner Brook Mill, one of the world's largest pulp and paper mills, turns out over 1,000 tons of paper daily.

Carson, a Scottish surgeon, the people repeatedly asked Parliament for authority to make their own laws. Finally, in 1832, the British government established a legislature for Newfoundland. It consisted of a governor, his council, and a general assembly elected by the people.

Newfoundland's new government was a "representative government" because the legislature could make laws. But the British Parliament had to approve the laws, and a British governor enforced them. Soon, the assembly began to ask the British government for a "responsible government"—one in which the cabinet was controlled by the elected assembly and not by the governor. The British colonies in Canada had been granted this form of government in the 1840's. In 1855, Newfoundland was also allowed to set up a responsible government.

Economic Growth. In 1857, prospectors discovered copper at Tilt Cove. By 1888, copper mining had become an important industry. During the 1880's and 1890's, Sir William Whiteway served several terms as prime minister of Newfoundland. Whiteway encouraged the building of a Newfoundland Railway that later became part of Canadian National Railways. The Wabana iron mine at Bell Island opened in 1895, and Newfoundland's first paper mill began operating in Grand Falls in 1909. The colony's fishing industry boomed during World War I (1914-1918) because of top prices paid for wartime food supplies.

In 1927, the Judicial Committee of the British Privy Council in London established the present boundary between the coast of Labrador and Quebec. This decision gave Newfoundland the vast mineral resources of the Knob Lake and Wabush Lake regions. See LABRADOR (History).

Ruin and Recovery. After World War I, Newfoundland's prosperity began to fade because there was no longer a demand for the province's products. During the 1920's, Newfoundland desperately tried to revive its lagging industries and to develop new ones. But by 1930, the Great Depression had struck most of the world. Newfoundland's fish, iron ore, and newsprint markets collapsed. Its government sank deeply into debt.

Under Prime Minister Frederick C. Alderdice, Newfoundland appealed to Great Britain for financial assistance under a new form of government. In 1934, Britain suspended Newfoundland's government and established a *Commission of Government*. This government consisted of a British governor and six other men, three of them Newfoundlanders. Newfoundland became a *dependency*, and Great Britain took over its debts.

Economic recovery came slowly. The Commission of Government reorganized the civil service, improved education and health facilities, and sponsored research to improve agriculture. Newfoundland's fishing and logging industries received much-needed financial aid.

World War II (1939-1945) gave new life to Newfoundland's economy. The fisheries, factories, and mines once again increased production to fill wartime demands. Canada and the United States built military bases in Newfoundland. Servicemen stationed at these bases, and persons employed there, created new demands for local products.

Confederation with Canada. In 1948, Newfoundland voters chose to unite with Canada rather than keep the Commission of Government or return to independ-

ent self-government. On March 31, 1949, Newfoundland became Canada's 10th province. Joseph R. Smallwood, a Liberal, took office as the province's first premier.

Newfoundland was in sound financial condition at the time of confederation. But a wide gap existed between the standard of living in Newfoundland and many of the other nine provinces. Through confederation, the people of Newfoundland began to share in federal social security benefits. The province participated in a number of federal programs, including development of trade schools and the construction of more than 500 miles of the Trans-Canada Highway.

A major federal-provincial project, begun in the 1950's, involved resettlement of a number of fishing outposts and villages. This program brought higher standards of living and greater educational opportunities to many fishermen and their families.

During the 1960's, Newfoundland expanded its industrial and educational facilities and its production and distribution of electricity. Following a boom in mineral production, mining began to rival manufacturing as the province's chief industry. New mines were opened, most of them in Labrador. Many new schools and trade schools were established to meet the demand

--- **IMPORTANT DATES IN NEWFOUNDLAND** ---

1497 John Cabot raised the banner of King Henry VII on a "new found land" which may have been the island of Newfoundland or Nova Scotia.

1583 Sir Humphrey Gilbert landed in Newfoundland and claimed the region for England.

1610 John Guy established a colony on Conception Bay that lasted for about 10 years.

1637 Charles I granted Newfoundland to Sir David Kirke and his partners.

1662 The French established a garrison at Placentia.

1713 The Treaty of Utrecht gave Newfoundland to Britain.

1729 Captain Henry Osborne became Newfoundland's first royal governor.

1763 In the Treaty of Paris, France gave Labrador to Britain.

1832 Great Britain granted Newfoundland the right to elect a general assembly.

1855 Newfoundland gained a "responsible government" that was controlled by an elected assembly.

1866 The steamship *Great Eastern* completed laying the first successful Atlantic cable at Hearts Content.

1904 France gave up its right to use Newfoundland's northern shore.

1909 Newfoundland's first paper mill began production in Grand Falls.

1927 The Judicial Committee of the Privy Council in London determined the Labrador-Quebec boundary.

1934 Great Britain suspended Newfoundland's government, established a Commission of Government, and assumed Newfoundland's debts.

1949 Newfoundland became Canada's 10th province on March 31.

1958 Newfoundland introduced free hospitalization and programs for educational improvements.

1967 Construction began on a $950-million hydroelectric plant in Churchill Falls in Labrador.

for skilled workers. In 1964, the College of Fisheries, Navigation, Marine Engineering, and Electronics opened in St. John's. In the mid-1960's, the province abolished tuition fees for needy students at Memorial University and began paying allowances to them.

By the mid-1960's, Newfoundland's rural electrification program had brought electricity to more than 100 isolated communities. The principal project in the program was a $950-million hydroelectric plant in Churchill Falls in Labrador. Construction started in 1967, and the plant—the largest hydroelectric facility in the Western Hemisphere—was scheduled to begin operating in 1972.

Newfoundland Today has a major problem finding jobs to keep up with its rapidly increasing population. The province has one of the highest birth rates and one of the lowest death rates in Canada.

Two major projects are expected to provide more jobs during the 1970's and help boost Newfoundland's economy even further. Construction of a $149-million linerboard mill in Stephenville, begun in 1969, was scheduled for completion in 1972. A $130-million oil refinery was to be completed in the 1970's in Come by Chance, near Sunnyside.

Another big problem of Newfoundland is to find income to maintain the standards of public service reached since confederation. The cost of government programs has soared during that period.

GORDON OLIVER ROTHNEY, ARCH SULLIVAN, and WILLIAM F. SUMMERS

NEWFOUNDLAND / Study Aids

Related Articles in WORLD BOOK include:

BIOGRAPHIES

Bartlett, Robert A.	Grenfell, Sir Wilfred T.
Gilbert, Sir Humphrey	Prendergast, Maurice B.

CITIES AND TOWNS

Bonavista	Corner Brook	Saint John's
Carbonear	Placentia	

PHYSICAL FEATURES

Belle Isle, Strait of	Gulf of Saint Lawrence
Churchill River	Gulf Stream
Grand Banks	Labrador Current

OTHER RELATED ARTICLES

Atlantic Provinces	Goose Bay	Lead
Cod	Iron and Steel	Memorial University
Gander Airport	Labrador	of Newfoundland

Outline

I. Government
   A. Lieutenant-Governor
   B. Premier
   C. Legislative Assembly
   D. Courts
   E. Local Government
   F. Taxation
   G. Politics
II. People
III. Education
   A. Schools
   B. Libraries and Museums
IV. A Visitor's Guide
   A. Places to Visit
   B. Annual Events
V. The Land
   A. Land Regions
   B. Coastline
   C. Mountains
   D. Rivers and Lakes
VI. Climate
VII. Economy
   A. Natural Resources
   B. Manufacturing
   C. Mining
   D. Forestry
   E. Fishing Industry
   F. Agriculture
   G. Electric Power
   H. Transportation
   I. Communication
VIII. History

Questions

What part of Newfoundland is most heavily populated?
What are Newfoundland's chief manufactured products? What are the two most important fish products?
How are Newfoundland's schools organized?
What part of Newfoundland produces most of the province's iron ore?

What are Newfoundland's only two cities?
When did Great Britain gain control of Labrador?
Why did Britain give Newfoundland a Commission of Government in 1934?
Why has Newfoundland lost some importance as a base for military operations?

Books for Young Readers

BICE, CLARE. *The Great Island: A Story of Mystery in Newfoundland*. Macmillan (Toronto), 1954.
COCHRANE, JAMES A. *The Story of Newfoundland*. Revised by A. W. Parsons. Ginn (Toronto), 1949.
PUMPHREY, GEORGE H. *Grenfell of Labrador*. Clarke, Irwin (Toronto), 1958.
SUMMERS, WILLIAM F. *The Geography of Newfoundland*. Copp (Toronto), 1965.

Books for Older Readers

HARRINGTON, MICHAEL F. *Sea Stories from Newfoundland*. Ryerson (Toronto), 1958.
KERR, LENNOX J. *Wilfred Grenfell, His Life and Work*. Clarke, Irwin (Toronto), 1959.
PERLIN, ALBERT B. *The Story of Newfoundland*. Dicks (St. John's), 1959.
ROTHNEY, G. O. *Newfoundland: A History*. Canadian Historical Association (Ottawa), 1964.

NEWFOUNDLAND DOG, *NEW fund LAND*, is a breed developed by the earliest settlers of Newfoundland. It is famous for its work in saving people from drowning. One of the few truly American breeds, it is believed to have been the *forerunner* (ancestor) of the Labrador retriever.

The Newfoundland dog is a powerful, intelligent animal, which looks somewhat like the Saint Bernard or great pyrenees. It has a noble appearance, with a great head and somewhat shortened muzzle. The color of the Newfoundland dog may vary, but the best-known type is black with a bronze tinge.

The Newfoundland has a dense oily coat which keeps water away from its body. The dog retrieves ducks, and can swim in the coldest water for hours. The males weigh between 140 and 150 pounds. The Newfoundland is an excellent companion and guardian for children. It is fearless and has an even temper.

Few of the dogs live in Newfoundland today. Most of them have been taken to other countries. OLGA DAKAN

See also DOG (color picture: Working Dogs).

NEWGATE PRISON, a London jail, was England's main criminal prison for more than 700 years. It was torn down in 1902, after many years of protest about its shameful condition.

The prison originally was part of London's West Gate, an entranceway to the city. West Gate was rebuilt and renamed Newgate in the 1100's. Prisoners were held in a room above the entranceway. Newgate was rebuilt again about 1423. But the Great Fire of London damaged it in 1666, and its condition grew steadily worse. Many prisoners died because of overcrowded rooms, poor food, and such contagious diseases as *jail fever* (typhus). Women, children, and debtors lived with hardened criminals. Few reforms were adopted until the 1800's. After 1815, debtors were held elsewhere. After 1847, only persons awaiting trial were kept at Newgate Prison. VERNON F. SNOW

NEWMAN, JOHN HENRY CARDINAL (1801-1890), became a convert to the Roman Catholic Church in 1845, and was made a cardinal in 1879. Before his conversion, he had distinguished himself as a scholar and a preacher of the Church of England at Oxford University. In 1833, he joined the movement within that church to rid it of political domination and to ground it more firmly in traditional beliefs (see OXFORD MOVEMENT). The movement helped strengthen the established church, but Newman shocked his fellow reformers when he joined the Roman Catholic Church. In 1846, he became a Catholic priest.

Newman was born in London. For most of his life as a Catholic, he lived in Birmingham as rector of an *oratory*, a group of men devoted to prayer and studies. He was considered one of the great thinkers of the 1800's.

Cardinal Newman's autobiography, the *Apologia pro Vita Sua* (1864), was an answer to an attack upon him by Charles Kingsley, an Anglican minister and author. Among his many lectures is "The Idea of a University" (1852). *The Grammar of Assent* (1870) was his answer to religious skepticism. He also wrote the famous hymn "Lead, Kindly Light" (see HYMN [Some World-Famous Hymns]). JOHN T. FARRELL and FULTON J. SHEEN

NEWMAN APOSTOLATE is a Roman Catholic organization in the United States. It serves students on campuses of universities and colleges not affiliated with the Roman Catholic Church. It has centers on about 1,250 campuses, serving more than 1½ million students.

Newman centers sponsor lectures, seminars, conferences, and study groups. They also conduct educational, leadership, religious, and social programs. A chaplain serves each center. The national office provides information, program aids, and publications for members. It sponsors chaplains' training schools, educational conferences, and a national student congress.

The first Newman group began in 1893. Headquarters are at 1312 Massachusetts Avenue NW, Washington, D.C. 20005.

Critically reviewed by the NATIONAL NEWMAN APOSTOLATE

NEWPORT, R.I. (pop. 34,562; alt. 10 ft.), is best known as a summer colony and resort. The city lies on Narragansett Bay. For location, see RHODE ISLAND (political map). In 1954, Newport began a series of jazz festivals. Many fans attend this summer event.

Newport was founded in 1639 by nine families from the Massachusetts Bay Colony who sought religious freedom in Rhode Island. There are more than 300 colonial buildings in Newport, including the Old Colony House, which became a National Historic Landmark in 1962. Before the Revolutionary War, Newport rivaled Boston and New York City as a shipping center. It has a council-manager government. CLARKSON A. COLLINS III

See also JEWS (picture: The Oldest Synagogue).

NEWPORT, CHRISTOPHER. See NEWPORT NEWS.

NEWPORT NAVAL BASE, R.I., is a training center for the United States Navy and a supporting base for units of the U.S. Atlantic Fleet. The base includes many schools, such as the Naval Justice School and the Naval Officer Candidate School. The base covers 6,370 acres and was established in 1946. During the Civil War, the government moved the U.S. Naval Academy from Annapolis, Md., to Newport for a time. JOHN A. OUDINE

See also RHODE ISLAND (color picture).

NEWPORT NEWS, Va. (pop. 138,177; alt. 20 ft.), is one of the largest Southern shipbuilding and coal-exporting centers. It stands on the northern shore of the harbor called Hampton Roads. See HAMPTON ROADS; VIRGINIA (political map). Newport News is a seafood center. It also produces automotive parts; electrical machinery; paints; ships and boats; and fish, foundry, paper, tobacco, and wood products.

The Mariners Museum in Newport News has more than 45,000 articles from ships of many countries. The city's War Memorial Museum of Virginia houses a large collection of relics from World Wars I and II.

The city is named after Captain Christopher Newport, who unloaded supplies there for the Jamestown colonists. He also brought news that more settlers were on the way. Permanent settlement began in 1621. Newport News grew rapidly during the 1800's. It merged with Warwick and took over Warwick County in 1958. The metropolitan area population of 292,159 persons includes Hampton. Newport News has a council-manager government. FRANCIS B. SIMKINS

NEWS COMMENTATOR. See JOURNALISM (Journalism in Radio and Television).

NEWS SERVICE is an organization for the collection and distribution of news. News services make it possible for newspapers to give their readers news from all parts of the world. They furnish telegraphic news to radio and television stations and news magazines, as well as to newspapers. They also furnish photographs by messenger, mail, telegraph, or radio.

The five principal news services in the world are the *Associated Press* and *United Press International* in the United States; *Agence France-Presse* in France; *Reuters* in Great Britain; and *Tass* in Russia. All except Tass are free from direct government control. Some 75 national news services distribute news daily.

During the Middle Ages, hand-written newsletters kept groups of nobles and business firms informed of recent events. Later, coffeehouses became the centers of news distribution. The *Father of all News Services* was the General News Association of the City of New York, started in 1849. EARL F. ENGLISH

Related Articles in WORLD BOOK include:

Agence France-Presse	North American
Associated Press	Newspaper Alliance
International News	Reuters
Service	Tass
Kyodo	United Press International

NEWSPAPER

The Newsroom of a daily newspaper is staffed with experienced rewritemen and editors. They quickly translate each day's important events into headlines, news stories, feature stories, editorials, and pictures which inform and entertain a nation.

NEWSPAPER. In the United States, where about 97 out of 100 persons who are old enough have learned to read, almost everyone reads newspapers. Every day people in the United States buy about $60\frac{1}{2}$ million daily newspapers. They also purchase over $48\frac{1}{2}$ million Sunday newspapers and about 24 million weekly newspapers. These daily, Sunday, and weekly newspapers have become a part of the home life of most American families. They are so familiar to us all that we do not think of them as anything wonderful. But the newspaper is a daily miracle—a marvel of machinery, business organization, news coverage, and fast and clear writing.

In the United States there are about 1,750 daily and 8,200 weekly and semiweekly papers. These represent many differences in policy and great range in ethical standards and excellence. In discussing newspapers, therefore, we should keep in mind the fact that their great differences make many generalizations unsafe.

A large daily newspaper contains a variety of information. Up-to-the-minute news stories tell of foreign, national, state, and local affairs. Articles and columnists report developments in sports, society, finance, science, religion, education, and agriculture. Comment on the

Robert U. Brown, the contributor of this article, is editor and publisher of Editor & Publisher *magazine.*

news appears in editorials and signed columns. Feature articles bring readers information on fashions, health, housekeeping, and child care. Comic strips and crossword puzzles appear regularly. Big Sunday and weekend editions may contain magazine sections, book review sections, and guides to the week's television viewing. Pictures and other illustrations appear throughout all the sections.

Advertising usually fills about 50 to 70 per cent of a newspaper's space. The classified advertising section is filled with many small advertisements.

A large newspaper would make a sizable volume if printed in book form. And, like a book, it has a contents guide that tells where each feature may be found. Many families divide the newspaper. Father may look first at the main news or financial section while Mother reads the women's pages and the children grab for the "funnies," sports, or other sections.

A newspaper that comes into any home with such a wide scope of reading matter can exert a great deal of influence. The modern newspaper, with its large circulation, usually tries to present both sides of a problem, instead of presenting only one viewpoint as newspapers usually did until the early 1900's. Nevertheless, it continually suggests ideas, beliefs, and ways of judging persons and events that help form our attitudes toward the important things of life.

What Is a Newspaper?

A newspaper is a publication devoted basically to presenting current news and commenting upon the news and related matters. The newspaper is usually

raphers, rewrite men, and copyreaders. Certain departmental editors, as those for sports and finance, have similar staffs. There is now a strong trend toward the "universal copydesk." Copy for all news departments passes over this desk for the inspection of the copyreaders, who edit the stories and write headlines.

The Business Department is headed by the business manager. The publisher also often gives this department a large part of his attention. The business manager has under him the circulation manager, with a large staff to handle distribution by carriers, street sales, mail, and trucks; the advertising manager, with assistants in charge of national, classified, department store, automotive, and other advertising fields; the promotion manager, with a staff whose job it is to advertise the newspaper itself in many ways; and the auditor, with his accounting staff.

The Mechanical Department is headed by a production manager or chief. It includes the composing room, where the type is set and made up into pages; the engraving room, where the photographers' prints are made into "cuts" for insertion into the pages for printing; the stereotyping room, where these pages go for casting before they are locked on the presses; the pressroom, where the papers are printed and folded; and the mailing room, where the papers are assembled, and turned over to the circulation department. Each of these divisions is headed by a foreman.

Each of the workers in these departments must do his

printed on cheap paper known as *newsprint*. Neither the page size of a newspaper nor the number of pages has ever been standardized. But throughout the 1800's the folio page (about 16 by 23 inches) was commonly considered the true newspaper form. Today, the folio (about 15 by 23 inches) and the tabloid of about two-thirds that size are the common page sizes.

The *news magazine* is also devoted to news and comment, but it is issued with a cover and better paper. It is published weekly, but, unlike most weekly newspapers, it covers national and international news (see MAGAZINE). House organs, camp and army papers, and school papers are often newspapers in purpose and form.

Organization of a Newspaper

The number of men and women necessary to produce a newspaper varies greatly. There are some small one-man weekly papers, though the larger weeklies may have ten to thirty workers on their payrolls. The largest city papers have about 2,000 employees, organized into large and complex staffs.

Such a staff, headed by the publisher, is divided into three departments: editorial, business, and mechanical.

The Editorial Department is headed by the editor in chief, who is nearly always called just the editor, or (by irreverent reporters) "the old man." Under the editor is the news staff, and a board of editorial writers who produce the editorial page. News is the paper's lifeblood, and the news staff is its heart. It is headed by the managing editor or by a news editor whom he appoints. Under the managing editor (or news editor) are the city editor, in charge of local news; the foreign (or cable) editor; the telegraph (or wire) editor; the state editor; and special editors for sports, society, the Sunday paper, the financial page, features, the book section, the woman's page, pictures, and similar special departments. The city editor has a staff of reporters, photog-

---

NEWSPAPER TERMS

Banner. The top headline on page 1.

Beat. A story obtained by a newspaper before rival papers publish it. A beat may not be exclusive, as a scoop. Also, a beat is any news source to which a reporter is regularly assigned, such as the city hall.

By-Line. The name of the writer of a news or feature story, or special column, usually carried between the headline and the item.

Copy. The manuscript of any kind of news matter prepared for the typesetter.

Date Line. The location and origin and date of a news story, such as, "New York, Sep. 4., (AP)—"

Deadline. The time limit for stages in preparing copy to get out a certain edition of a newspaper.

Edition. Any issue of the newspaper. Large newspapers issue several editions during the day or night.

Extra. An edition of a newspaper published at a time other than a scheduled regular edition.

Gazette. An ancient name for newspaper, often used today as part of newspaper titles. The term originated from a Venetian coin, *gazzetta*, which was the price of an early newspaper of Venice.

Lead. The opening paragraph of a news story. A *buried lead* consists of important facts which an inexpert writer has placed in the body of the story.

Line. See *Banner* (above).

Masthead. The title of the newspaper and statement of its ownership and policy, usually carried on the editorial page.

Morgue. The research library of a newspaper.

Obit. An obituary.

Scoop. A story obtained exclusively by a newspaper without the knowledge of its competitors.

Squib. A brief story, unimportant from a news standpoint and used primarily to fill space.

Subhead. Short headings used to break up the paragraphs of a long news story.

Reporters rush to the scene of an important event. They get the facts quickly and report them to the newsroom.

Photographers receive radio dispatches from the newsroom to get pictures while the news is "hot." When they have the photos, they speed them to the newspaper.

Chicago *Sun-Times*

job with the deadlines of each edition of the paper in mind. His own job must be finished at a certain time in order to fit in with the job that follows. For the newspaper must do its chief work not on a schedule of weeks or days or even hours, but minutes. It has to get its news on the street and in the home in the shortest possible time after an event occurs.

From News-Break to Fireside

Let us see how a typical news event is handled. A fire breaks out in an apartment house in the west end of a large city. A "beat" reporter from the *News*, who is at his daily job of visiting police and fire department news sources, telephones the city editor that this is a serious three-alarm fire.

Reporting the Story. The city editor calls to Stubbs, a general assignment man, "Get out to 18th and Oregon, Stubbs—three-alarm fire!" Stubbs crams some copy-paper into his pocket, seizes his hat, hurries to the street, and signals a taxi. There are only fifty minutes before the home edition deadline, he notes by a glance at his wrist watch. When Stubbs arrives at the scene of the fire, he wastes no time observing picturesque effects. He may write a "color" story later, but now he wants facts.

Stubbs finds out from the fire chief the probable cause of the fire, when it broke out, and any such features as rescues of residents or trouble with the water supply. He finds out who owns the property and locates him, getting his estimate of the damage and the amount of insurance. Most important of all, if there have been injuries or deaths, he must get the names and addresses of the injured and the dead, and the extent of their injuries or the causes of their deaths. Watching the time, Stubbs goes to a telephone 25 minutes before his deadline, calls his city editor. "Child dead from burns; fireman injured; $80,000 loss," he sum-

marizes. "Give Wells half a column," says the city editor and switches Stubbs to a rewrite man. There will be a longer story, with pictures, in later editions, but now there is no time or space for more.

Writing the Story. Stubbs gives Wells the details—the location of the fire, the size of the building, the name of the owner, the probable loss, the insurance, and details of the traffic tie-up caused by the blaze. He gives the name, age, and parents of the dead child, and tells how it met its death. He gives the name and address of the fireman, tells the extent of his injuries and how they were received, and gives the name of the hospital to which he has been taken. He is very careful to spell names and to repeat figures. The form of the story takes shape in Wells' practiced mind as he takes down the facts at the telephone. As soon as Stubbs has finished, Wells writes his "lead," giving the chief facts, and then elaborates in succeeding paragraphs.

Editing the Story. The city editor notifies the copy-desk that the story is coming. The news editor orders a headline. A copyreader takes the story in pages from a copy boy. He edits the story, checking accuracy and making it more readable. He writes the headline.

Setting the Story in Type. The news editor sends the copy down a pneumatic chute to the composing room just before the deadline. There it is divided into parts called "takes" so that several linotypers can set it in type. The lines of type, called slugs, are put together and proofs are printed, read, and corrected rapidly. The slugs, complete with head, are delivered to the editorial make-up man, who has left space for them in his front-page form. He shows a printer where to insert them, and gives the form to the stereotypers. During the 1960's, some newspapers began using computers to set type (see PRINTING [Setting the Type]).

Printing and Distributing the Paper. In the stereo-

300

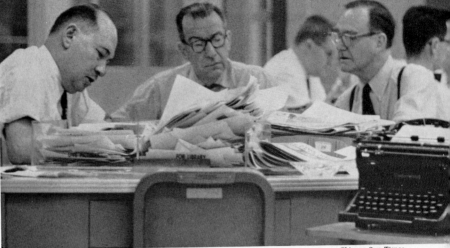

Teletype Machines bring stories from around the world to the newspaper office. News services such as Associated Press and United Press International supply this news.

News Desk Editors determine the banner headline for the front page. They also make a final check on the stories that go into the paper, and then mark them for position on the pages in each edition.

type room, a papier-mâché form, called a "mat," is made of the page. The mat is used as a mold for the plate. The printing plate is then cast from hot metal in the form of a half cylinder. This goes by roller conveyer to the press and is locked on a cylinder in printing position. The signal to start the presses is given, and the great press goes into action. The roll of paper is drawn through the length of the press, receiving the print of all the plates. At the farther end of the machine it is folded, trimmed, and counted.

The piles of paper are hurried to the mailing room, made into counted bundles, delivered methodically to a fleet of trucks, and rushed to newsstands, carriers, and post office. Two hours from the time Stubbs was assigned to cover the fire, the paper containing the fire story is delivered to your door. This kind of speed is common for a newspaper. A news bulletin often appears in an edition 15 minutes after it reaches a newspaper office in a large city.

News-Gathering Services

The chief U.S. services in covering world news are the Associated Press, which is owned by its member newspapers, and United Press International, owned by the Scripps-Howard chain of newspapers and serving many others as well. Each of these services has hundreds of correspondents at home and in most other countries. Each has regional bureaus and staffs of editors. Their dispatches and news photographs come into the newspaper offices over electrical Teletype and facsimile machines. They also serve radio and television stations.

In addition to these services, some large newspapers have their own staffs of foreign correspondents. These papers often *syndicate* (sell) their reports to other papers. Organizations with photographers and writers throughout the world syndicate pictures and features. Popular

syndicated features include comic strips, public affairs columns, puzzles, and serialized books.

All this material comes into the newspaper office in various ways. Feature stories, often called "time copy," usually come by mail. Most of these syndicated features can be prepared well in advance of their publication date. But most of the news from outside the local area comes in by Teletype. The stories are typed out on a Teletype recorder which receives electrical impulses over wires from a transmitter in a distant news bureau. Foreign dispatches come by cable or radio to New York or San Francisco and are then transmitted by Teletype. Radio was first used for reporting in 1899, and has been used increasingly since. Transmission of pictures by wire was begun by the Associated Press in 1935. A few years later, pictures were being sent by radio.

The Newspaper as a Business

Newspapers in the United States represent a $4\frac{1}{4}$-billion-a-year business. Newspapers receive about 70 per cent of their revenue from advertising and 30 per cent from newspaper sales. Newspapers get about one-third of all money spent for advertising in the U.S. In the mid-1960's, newspapers received over $3 billion a year from advertisers. Circulation (the sale of papers) brought about $1\frac{1}{4}$ billion.

Newspapers have billions of dollars invested in plants and equipment. Between 1954 and 1964, newspapers spent more than $100 million a year on plant modernization and expansion alone.

Daily newspapers employ about 250,000 persons. The weekly papers employ about 55,000. In addition, several hundred thousand carrier boys deliver daily, Sunday, and weekly newspapers to homes.

Newsprint is the largest expense item in operating

Production begins with Linotype operators, *above*, who set articles in columns of metal type. Compositors set advertisements by hand, *below*. Impressions of each page are made on paper *mats* used to mold metal printing plates.

Printing Plates travel to the presses on an automatic conveyer. Machines cast the plates by pouring hot metal on the mats. Then the plates are trimmed and sent to the presses.

all but the smallest newspapers. Each year, U.S. newspapers use over 6,500,000 tons of newsprint costing about $900 million. Newsprint costs rise with increases in circulation, and increases in the volume of advertising and news. Newsprint accounts for about one-third of the total expense in operating a large metropolitan newspaper. Among the smallest papers, it amounts to 15 per cent or less of total expenses.

Mechanical department costs range from 25 per cent for the smallest papers to about 15 per cent on the largest dailies. Editorial expenses account for about 14 per cent of total costs.

Newspapers in Other Countries

The circulation of newspapers for the entire world is about 350 million copies daily, or about one daily paper for every 10 persons. Sweden leads the world with about 500 copies sold daily for every 1,000 persons.

British newspapers greatly resemble American papers. This has been true ever since Lord Northcliffe (1865-1922), the most famous of modern British newspaper publishers, adapted many American techniques on his *London Daily Mail*. It is not true of the more conservative *London Times*, which greatly influences English opinion. The *Times* carried classified advertising on its front page until early in 1966.

Many of the leading papers of France were founded during or after World War II. *France-Soir*, founded in Paris in 1941, has a circulation of over a million. Other papers include *Le Parisien Libéré*, *Le Figaro*, and *L'Aurore*, all published in Paris.

Leading independent papers published in West Ger-

many are the *Telegraf Am Sonntag*, and *Morgenpost*. The largest paper in East Berlin is the communist-controlled *Taegliche Rundschau*. In Italy, outstanding papers are the independents, *Il Messaggero* and *Il Tempo*, and the communist *L'Unità*, all in Rome; the Roman Catholic *L'Osservatore Romano*, in Vatican City; and *Corriere della Sera*, in Milan. Japanese papers include Tokyo's *Mainichi Shimbun* and *Yomiuri Shimbun*.

In Russia, the Moscow *Izvestia* and *Pravda* are under strict communist control. They are only four-page papers, but claim to have daily circulations of several million. Among other Russian papers are the army *Red Star* and the navy *Red Fleet*. Russia claims a daily newspaper circulation of more than thirty-three million.

In China, mother of printing, papermaking, and the printed newspaper, newspapers have suffered from national disorders and wars. The Chinese tendency has been to develop many small dailies instead of a few papers with mass circulation. Once there were over a hundred dailies published at the same time in Peking.

In India, there are English-language papers in large cities, and many papers printed in other languages.

Australia and Canada have many prosperous and growing newspapers. The *Melbourne Sun News-Pictorial*, with more than 500,000 circulation, is the largest Australian daily paper. The *Toronto Star*, with 350,000, is the largest Canadian newspaper.

The Latin-American republics have many powerful and active newspapers. In a few of them the press is controlled in various degrees by the governments. *La Prensa* of Argentina, long outstanding for its full coverage of news, was taken over by Juan Perón's dictatorial

In the Pressroom, giant rolls of paper unwind through rows of presses that can print, cut, fold, and count as many as 1,000 newspapers a minute.

government in 1951. After a revolution overthrew Perón, *La Prensa* was returned to its owners early in 1956. *La Nación, La Critica,* and *El Mundo* are other influential Argentine papers. *El Comercio* is the oldest paper of Peru. *El Mercurio* and *La Nación* of Chile have circulations of 100,000 or more. Mexico has about 100 dailies. The largest have circulations of over 100,000.

History

Beginnings. Probably the first newspaper was *Tsing Pao,* a court journal published in Peking. It is said to have started as early as the 500's, and was continued until 1935. At first it was produced from carved blocks instead of from type. This method of printing was hundreds of years old in China by the time the paper began.

In Europe, the forerunners of printed newspapers were written newsletters. These were sent out regularly by Roman scribes to businessmen and politicians in distant cities to keep them informed of happenings in Rome. Newsletter service from European capitals continued to be used in the 1700's, even after printed papers had become common. Another Roman news publication was the posted bulletin. The leading bulletin was the *Acta Diurna* (Daily Events). This began to be posted in the Forum in 60 B.C., and was often copied by the scribes and dispatched abroad in newsletters.

After Gutenberg's invention of printing from movable type, there were occasional news pamphlets (news-

Ready to "Hit the Street," the papers go by conveyer from the presses to the circulation department. There, they are bundled and rushed to newsstands by trucks.

Chicago *Sun-Times*

303

books) issued in Europe, especially in Germany. But these pamphlets were not published frequently, since rulers generally frowned on news or comment on public affairs. In addition, only a few people were able to read. Apparently the first regularly published papers were issued in Germany in the early 1600's. The oldest on record is the *Strasbourg Relation* of 1609.

Early English Newspapers. The first paper to be published continuously in England was the *Courant*, or *Weekly Newes*, of 1621. This paper and those which followed were very small in page size. The first English newspaper of full size was the Oxford *Gazette*, which soon moved from Oxford to London. This was a court journal begun in 1665 and devoted to official notices of the royal court. It still continues with much the same function. The first daily paper in England was the *London Daily Courant*, begun in 1702 by a woman, Elizabeth Mallett. The *London Times* was founded in 1785 under the name of the *Daily Universal Register*.

First American Newspapers. The first newspaper published in the American colonies was *Publick Occurrences Both Forreign and Domestick*. It was issued in Boston in 1690 by Benjamin Harris, who had already been in trouble for bold publishing in England. His Boston paper was suppressed after the first issue. After that no paper was attempted until John Campbell began his *Boston News-Letter* in 1704. After that, other papers were attempted in Boston. One was the *New England Courant*, begun in 1721 by James Franklin, who employed his brother Benjamin in his shop.

The first paper outside Boston was Andrew Bradford's *American Weekly Mercury*, founded in Philadelphia in 1719. Andrew's father, William Bradford, started the first New York paper, the *Gazette*, in 1725. Benjamin Franklin published the *Pennsylvania Gazette* from 1729 to 1766. The first daily newspaper in America, the *Pennsylvania Evening Post and Daily Advertiser*, began in 1783 in Philadelphia. At the outbreak of the Revolutionary War, there were 35 newspapers being published in the colonies. The first published west of the Appalachian Mountains was the *Pittsburgh Gazette* in 1786. The *Alexandria* (Va.) *Gazette*, published daily since 1797, is the oldest continuously-published U.S. daily.

The Penny Papers. In the early 1800's, the newspapers were chiefly political in both news and editorials.

They were often very large in page-size (blanket-sheets) and commonly sold for six cents. This put them out of reach of the poorer classes of people. When the penny papers were started in the 1830's, America had its first genuinely popular journalism. The first successful penny paper was the *New York Sun*, founded in 1833 by Benjamin H. Day. It was lively, gave more attention to news than politics, and was small in size. After the Civil War, the *Sun* came under the control of Charles A. Dana, a believer in independent journalism.

In 1835, James Gordon Bennett founded the *New York Herald*, which came to be considered by many people as the great representative American paper. In spite of his sensationalism, Bennett originated many new journalistic techniques, and is regarded as one of the greatest of American editors.

Another paper which started at one cent was the *New York Tribune*, founded in 1841 by Horace Greeley. Greeley was an outstanding humanitarian. He developed the modern editorial page and exerted a wide national influence. The Bennett and Greeley papers were merged in 1924 into the *Herald Tribune*. The *New York Times*, too, was a penny paper when it was started in 1851 by Henry J. Raymond and two associates. Adolph S. Ochs brought the *Times* to its present position in the top rank of journalism. Another penny paper was the *Baltimore Sun*, founded by A. S. Abell and two friends.

Other Great American Papers. Joseph Pulitzer, an immigrant boy, made both fortune and reputation in St. Louis, where he founded the *Post-Dispatch*. Later he bought the *New York World* (1883) and greatly influenced American journalism by his highly successful enterprise. The *World* was bought by the Scripps-Howard chain in 1931, and merged with the *New York Evening Telegram*. In 1950, the *World-Telegram* bought the *New York Sun* and became the *World-Telegram and The Sun*. The first Chicago paper was the *Chicago Democrat*, begun in 1833. The *Chicago Tribune* was founded in 1847. Joseph Medill and C. H. Ray made it an important paper in the 1850's.

A second penny-press movement developed in the 1870's and early 1880's. The *Chicago Daily News* was founded by Victor Lawson and Melville Stone in 1876. The *Kansas City Star* was founded by William Nelson in 1880. Certain Southern papers are historically important. These include the *New Orleans Picayune* (now *Times-Picayune*), founded in 1837 by George Kendall and his friend Francis Lumsden; and the *Atlanta Constitution*, edited in the 1880's by Henry Grady. Similarly important are two Western papers—the *San Francisco Chronicle*, started in 1865 by two teen-aged brothers named De Young, and the *Portland Oregonian*, edited from 1877 to 1910 by Harvey Scott.

Tabloids. During the 1920's, many tabloids adopted a policy of sensationalism coupled with large-scale use of illustrations. Most important of these newspapers was Joseph Patterson's *New York News*, founded in 1919. Many tabloids later gave up sensationalism and became respectable newspapers. Today there are a number of excellent tabloids published. Marshall Field III established the *Chicago Sun* in 1941. In 1948, he merged this paper with the *Chicago Times* to form a tabloid, the *Chicago Sun and Times*, now called the *Chicago Sun-Times*. See FIELD (family).

Consolidation and Expansion. In the 1900's the number of newspapers in the United States was cut by consolidations, or combining of two or more papers. Advertisers found it cheaper to buy space in one paper with general circulation, even at increased rates, than in two with overlapping coverage. Combination papers often made special efforts to represent all points of view fairly, and they were able to avoid ruinous competition. Frank A. Munsey, millionaire magazine publisher, led a great movement of merging newspapers.

Newspapers expanded through modern chain ownership. E. W. Scripps established the first chain with his penny papers in 1878. William Randolph Hearst's chain began with the *San Francisco Examiner* in 1885. In 1895, he bought the *New York Journal* and made it the model of sensational papers. This sensationalism was called "yellow journalism," after the "Yellow Kid," a comic strip character (see OUTCAULT, RICHARD FELTON). In 1964, the Hearst chain had 10 daily papers and 8 Sunday papers. The Samuel Newhouse chain had 16 dailies and 10 Sunday papers, and a financial interest in 3 other dailies and 2 Sunday papers. The Scripps-Howard chain had 18 dailies and 8 Sunday papers.

In 1962, the *New York Times* began a West Coast edition in Los Angeles. This marked the first time a daily newspaper of general readership was published in two U.S. cities at the same time. But the western edition was suspended in 1964 after financial losses. For several years, the *Wall Street Journal* has been printed simultaneously in seven plants across the country.

Newspapers Today. Population shifts from large cities to suburban areas since the mid-1940's have changed the newspaper business. Large metropolitan papers must now compete with smaller suburban papers. These suburban papers give their readers more news of their local communities than the larger papers do. Metropolitan papers must appeal to readers over a wide area. They sometimes publish *zone* sections that feature local news and advertising for particular areas.

New York City, Detroit, Houston, Los Angeles, and San Francisco lost newspapers in the early 1960's through mergers or closings. Because of costly strikes, New York City and Cleveland were without local newspapers during the winter of 1962-63. The *New York Mirror* went out of business as an indirect result of the New York City strike.

By 1964, only New York City, Boston, and Washington, D.C., had more than two separately owned newspapers with large circulations. The number of U.S. dailies remained about the same from 1945 to the mid-1960's. But total circulation increased about 12 million during that period.

In 1966, three New York City newspapers—the *Herald Tribune*, the *Journal-American*, and the *World-Telegram and the Sun*—merged to form the *World-Journal-Tribune*, an afternoon and Sunday paper. But the merger only consolidated the financial problems of the past. In 1967, the paper suspended publication.   ROBERT U. BROWN

Related Articles. See the Communication section of the various state, province, and country articles. See also JOURNALISM with its list of Related Articles. Other related articles in WORLD BOOK include:

Outline

I. **What Is a Newspaper?**
II. **Organization of a Newspaper**
   A. The Editorial Department
   B. The Business Department
   C. The Mechanical Department
III. **From News-Break to Fireside**
   A. Reporting the Story
   B. Writing the Story
   C. Editing the Story
   D. Setting the Story in Type
   E. Printing and Distributing the Paper
IV. **News-Gathering Services**
V. **The Newspaper as a Business**
VI. **Newspapers in Other Countries**
VII. **History**

Questions

About how many newspapers are distributed daily in the United States?

What is the greatest single expense in operating a large newspaper? What department costs the most to operate on a small newspaper?

What was probably the first known newspaper?

What different kinds of material or information are usually found in a daily paper?

How did the term "yellow journalism" get started?

What country leads the world in the number of newspapers sold daily per 1,000 persons?

Into what three departments is a newspaper staff usually divided?

What is the work of the city editor?

What facts would a reporter covering a fire try to get?

What is (a) a beat reporter, (b) writing a lead, (c) a "mat," (d) a syndicated feature?

NEWSPAPER GUILD, AMERICAN (ANG), is a labor union whose members work in the news and commercial departments of newspapers, news magazines, news services, and related enterprises. The Guild has local organizations in 100 cities in Canada, Puerto Rico, and the United States. For membership, see LABOR (table).

The American Newspaper Guild has advocated shorter hours, higher wages, severance pay, and greater job security for its members. It has contracts with newspapers whose combined circulation totals about one-half of the daily newspaper circulation in the United States.

The American Newspaper Guild is affiliated with the AFL-CIO and the Canadian Labour Congress. It was founded in 1933. Its headquarters are at 1126 16th St. NW, Washington, D.C. 20036.

Critically reviewed by the AMERICAN NEWSPAPER GUILD

NEWSPAPER SYNDICATE. For a few cents a person can buy a newspaper that contains outstanding photographs and comics, and columns and features by famous writers, cartoonists, medical authorities, and other specialists. Newspaper syndicates make it possible for even small newspapers to carry features by highly paid contributors, because the syndicates sell the same material to many papers. They differ from *news services* because they do not deal in "spot news."

The amount of money a newspaper pays for a syndicated feature depends on the size of the newspaper's circulation. A paper with a circulation of 200,000 might pay $50 a week for a feature that would cost a smaller paper only $3.50 a week. Many syndicates are owned or controlled by newspapers which develop features for their own use and to sell to other newspapers.

There are several important newspaper syndicates in the United States. The best-known syndicates include Bell, King Features, Publishers-Hall Syndicate (formerly called Publishers Newspaper Syndicate), and United Features. EARL F. ENGLISH

See also NORTH AMERICAN NEWSPAPER ALLIANCE; NEWS SERVICE; PUBLISHERS-HALL SYNDICATE.

NEWSPRINT. See NEWSPAPER (What Is a Newspaper?); PAPER (Special Kinds of Paper).

A Red-Spotted Newt is shown in the *eft* phase, during which it lives on land in wooded places.

Hugh Spencer

NEWT, *noot,* is a small animal with a slender body, thin skin, and four weak legs. It is a type of salamander, and is classified as an amphibian, along with frogs and caecilians (see AMPHIBIAN).

Newts and other salamanders are *tailed amphibians.* The tail of the adult newt is flatter than that of most other salamanders. Newts hatch from eggs which are laid singly in the spring on the leaves of plants under water. The young hatch after three to five weeks. They live in the water and breathe by means of gills. In time, they develop lungs and may take to the land. People then call them *efts.* The efts stay on land up to three years before they return to water to breed. They often shed their skins. If an eft loses a leg, it can grow it back. The United States has several kinds of newts. The best known is the *red-spotted* newt, which is about 4 inches long. Newts eat insects, worms, and mollusks.

Scientific Classification. Newts are in the class *Amphibia.* They belong to the salamander family, *Salamandridae.* The American red-spotted newt is genus *Diemictylus,* species *D. viridescens.* W. FRANK BLAIR

NEWTON, Mass. (pop. 91,066; alt. 35 ft.), is a suburban community 7 miles west of Boston. Often called the *Garden City,* Newton lies on the Charles River in a region of great natural beauty (see MASSACHUSETTS [political map]). Newton produces electrical equipment, knit goods, paper products, and plastics. Boston College is in the Chestnut Hill section of Newton. Other schools in the city are the Andover-Newton Theological School and Newton College of the Sacred Heart.

Settlers first came to Newton in 1639. The settlement was then part of Cambridge. It consisted of 14 villages which still retain their separate identities within the city. John Eliot, called "The Apostle of the Indians," arrived in 1646, and later became pastor of Newton's first church. Other noted residents have included educator Horace Mann, and the authors Nathaniel Hawthorne and Ralph Waldo Emerson. Newton was known as New Cambridge until 1692, and received its city charter in 1873. It has a mayor-council type of government. WILLIAM J. REID

NEWTON, SIR ISAAC (1642-1727), an English scientist, astronomer, and mathematician, invented a new kind of mathematics, discovered the secrets of light and color, and showed how the universe is held together. He is sometimes described as "one of the greatest names in the history of human thought," because of his great contributions to mathematics, physics, and astronomy.

Newton discovered how the universe is held together through his theory of gravity. He discovered the secrets of light and color. He invented a branch of mathematics, *calculus* (see CALCULUS). He made these three discoveries within 18 months from 1665 to 1667.

The Theories of Motion and Gravitation. Newton said the concept of a universal force came to him while he was drinking tea in the garden and saw an apple fall. He suddenly realized that one and the same force pulls the apple to earth and keeps the moon in its orbit. He found that the force of universal gravitation makes every pair of bodies in the universe attract each other. The force depends on (1) the amount of matter in the bodies being attracted and (2) the distance between the bodies. The force by which the earth attracts or pulls a large rock is greater than the pull on a small pebble, because the rock contains more matter. The earth's pull is called *the weight* of the body. With this theory, Newton explained why a rock weighs more than a pebble.

He also proved that many types of motion are due to one kind of force. He showed that the gravitational force of the sun keeps the planets in their orbits, just as the gravitational force of the earth attracts the moon and an apple. The falling of an apple seems different from the motion of the moon, because the apple falls straight down to the earth, while the moon moves approximately in a circle around the earth. Newton showed that the moon falls just like the apple. If the moon did not fall constantly toward the earth, it would move in a straight line and fly off at a tangent to its orbit. Newton calculated how much the moon falls in each second and found the distance is $\frac{1}{3600}$ of the distance an apple falls in a second. The moon is 60 times as far from the earth's center as a falling apple. Consequently, the force of the earth on an object 60 times as far away as another object is $\frac{1}{3600}$.

The Principia. Newton concluded his first investigations on gravity and motion in 1665 and 1666. Nothing was heard of them for nearly 20 years. His original theory had been based on an inaccurate measurement of the earth's radius, and Newton realized differences between the theory and the facts. Although he later learned the true value of the earth's size, he was not led to complete his investigation or to produce a book for publication.

One day in 1684, Edmund Halley, an English astronomer, Robert Hooke, an English scientist, and Christopher Wren, the architect, were discussing what law of force produced the visible motion of the planets around the sun. They could not solve this problem. Halley went to Cambridge to ask Newton about it. He found Newton in possession of complete proof of the law of gravity. Halley persuaded Newton to publish his findings. Halley paid all the expenses, corrected the proofs, and laid aside his own work to publish Newton's discoveries. Newton's discoveries on the laws of motion and theories of gravitation were published in 1687 in *Philosophiae Naturalis Principia Mathematica* (Mathematical Principles of Natural Philosophy). The book generally is considered one of the greatest single contributions in the history of science. The book includes Newton's fundamental laws of motion and theory of gravitation. It was the first book to contain a unified system of scientific principles explaining what happens on the earth and in the heavens.

Light and Color. Newton's discoveries in optics were equally spectacular. He published the results of his experiments and studies in *Opticks* (1704).

Newton's discoveries explained why bodies appear to be colored. They laid the foundation for the science of spectrum analysis. This science allows us to determine the chemical composition, temperature, and even the speed of such hot, glowing bodies as a distant star or an object heated in a laboratory.

Newton discovered that sunlight is a mixture of light of all colors. He passed a beam of sunlight through a glass prism and studied the colors that were produced. A green sweater illuminated by sunlight looks green, because it largely reflects the green light in the sun and absorbs most of the other colors. If the green sweater were lighted by a red light or any color light not containing green, it would not appear green.

Bausch & Lomb

By Passing a Beam of Sunlight through a prism, Newton showed that white light is made up of the rainbow's colors.

He Constructed a reflecting telescope to use in his studies.

He Made Great Discoveries in the field of mathematics. He is credited with inventing integral and differential calculus.

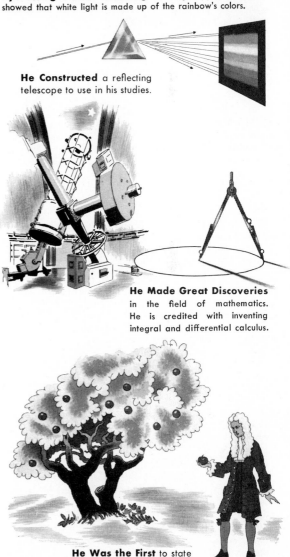

He Was the First to state the laws of gravitation.

NEWTON, SIR ISAAC

The study of light led Newton to consider constructing a new type of telescope in which a reflecting mirror was used instead of a combination of lenses. Newton's first reflecting telescope was 6 inches long, and, through it, Newton saw Jupiter's satellites.

Early Life. Newton was born at Woolsthorpe, Lincolnshire, on Dec. 25, 1642. He attended Grantham grammar school. As a boy, he was more interested in making mechanical devices than in studying. He was considered a poor student. His youthful inventions included a small windmill that could grind wheat and corn, a water clock run by the force of dropping water, and a sundial. He left school when he was 14 to help his widowed mother manage her farm. But he spent so much time reading, he was sent back to school.

He entered Trinity College, Cambridge University, in 1661. He showed no exceptional ability during his college career, and was graduated in 1665 without any particular distinction. He returned to Cambridge as a fellow of Trinity College in 1667.

Newton became professor of mathematics at Cambridge in 1669. He lectured once a week on geometry, astronomy, optics, arithmetic, or other mathematical subjects. He was elected a fellow of the Royal Society in 1672.

Public Life. Newton became active in public life after the publication of *Principia*. He became the Cambridge University member of Parliament in 1689 and held his seat until Parliament dissolved the following year. He became warden of the mint in 1696. He was appointed master of the mint in 1699, a position he held until his death.

In 1699, he also became a member of the Royal Society council and an associate of the French Academy. He was elected to Parliament again from the university in 1701. He left Cambridge and settled permanently in London in 1701. He became president of the Royal Society in 1703 and was re-elected annually until his death. Queen Anne knighted Newton in 1705. He died on March 20, 1727, and was buried in Westminster Abbey.

Personal Characteristics. Newton did not enjoy the scientific arguments that arose from his discoveries. Many new scientific theories are opposed violently when they are first announced, and Newton's did not escape criticism. He was so sensitive to such criticism that his friends had to plead with him to publish his most valuable discoveries.

Newton was a bachelor who spent little of his time studying mathematics, physics, and astronomy. He was a student of alchemy, and made many alchemical experiments. He also spent a great deal of his time on questions of theology and Biblical chronology.

As a professor, he was very absent-minded. He showed great generosity to his nephews and nieces and to publishers and scientists who helped him in his work.

He was modest in his character. He said of himself shortly before his death, "I do not know what I may appear to the world, but to myself I seem to have been only like a boy playing on the seashore, and diverting myself in now and then finding a smoother pebble or a prettier shell than ordinary, whilst the great ocean of truth lay all undiscovered before me."

Albert Einstein, the German-American physicist, rejected Newton's explanation of universal gravitation but not the fact of its operation. He said that his own work would have been impossible without Newton's discoveries. He also said that the concepts Newton developed "are even today still guiding our thinking in physics." I. BERNARD COHEN

Related Articles in WORLD BOOK include:

Color (History)	Force	Jet Propulsion	Motion
	Gravitation	Light	Tide

NEWTON COLLEGE OF THE SACRED HEART. See UNIVERSITIES AND COLLEGES (table).

NEWTON'S LAWS OF MOTION. See MOTION.

NEWTON'S RINGS are a series of alternately bright and dark circles that can be seen when a slightly convex piece of glass is placed against a flat piece of glass. If the viewing light is a single color, the rings will have this color. If the light is white, the rings will have the colors of the spectrum from violet through red. Newton's rings are caused by interference between the light waves reflected from the top of the flat surface and those reflected from the bottom of the curved surface. The point of contact is dark. The rings were named for Sir Isaac Newton, who first observed them. ROBERT LINDSAY

NEXT OF KIN is a legal phrase for the closest blood relatives of a person who has died without making a will. These next of kin are entitled to share in whatever personal property the dead person owned. Laws of descent and distribution are complicated, and differ in the various states. The laws of each state determine how and to what extent the next of kin will share in the personal property left by a resident of that state who did not leave a will. In some instances such laws provide for the distribution of both real and personal property to the same people and to the same extent, thus treating next of kin the same as heirs. See HEIR.

People sometimes use the term *next of kin* to mean a person's nearest relative, without regard for the legal meaning of the phrase. WILLIAM TUCKER DEAN

NEY, *nay,* **MICHEL** (1769-1815), was one of Napoleon Bonaparte's great soldiers. He served with great distinction in the campaign of 1792, when the French Army of the North defeated the Prussians and Austrians. His cool courage and military skill soon marked him as a most notable soldier. Napoleon made him a marshal of France in 1804. He received the title duke of Elchingen for defeating the Austrians at Elchingen in 1805. He fought at Jena and Eylau and commanded an army at Friedland, where the French defeated the Russians in the summer of 1807. His conduct at Friedland won him Napoleon's praise. He took charge of Napoleon's army for the march into Russia in 1812, and became Prince of Moscow. Napoleon and Joachim Murat left the army after its defeat and hastened back to France (see MURAT, JOACHIM). But Ney remained with the Grand Army during the terrible retreat.

When Napoleon was forced from power in 1814, Ney abandoned him, and became a supporter of King Louis XVIII, who succeeded Napoleon. But Napoleon escaped from Elba in 1815, and landed on the coast of France. Ney declared himself loyal to King Louis. He told the king that he would "bring Napoleon back in an iron cage," and started out with an army. He met Napoleon, who was marching toward Paris with a new army. But emotion swayed Ney. He embraced Napoleon, and joined him in the march on Paris. The king fled, and Ney and Napoleon entered the capital together.

The period of Napoleon's return to power, called the *Hundred Days*, ended in defeat. Ney led the last French charge at Waterloo in 1815. But the soldier who had fought so well for France was seized and tried for treason and rebellion. A court of his fellow officers refused to try him. But the House of Peers tried him, and condemned him to death. He was shot on Dec. 7, 1815. Ney was born in Saarelouis, in the Saar Basin. VERNON J. PURYEAR

See also NAPOLEON I.

NEZ PERCÉ INDIANS, *NAY pehr SAY*, or *nez PURSE*, of Idaho were known for their bravery, independence, and almost constant friendship for the white men. The French gave them their name, which means *pierced nose*. But this group of Indians probably did not pierce their noses for shell jewelry.

In the early days, the Nez Percé lived on salmon, which they trapped in mountain streams, and such wild bulbs as bitterroot and camas. When white men brought horses, the Nez Percé moved to the plains and became hunters. They made their clothing of deerskin, and covered their gabled shelters with brush mats.

The Nez Percé met white trappers and explorers in the early 1800's. Later, they asked for missionaries, and most of the tribe became Christian.

In 1855, they agreed to go on a reservation. But one group refused to move, and the Nez Percé War resulted (see INDIAN WARS [The Nez Percé War]). JOHN C. EWERS

See also JOSEPH, CHIEF; NATIONAL PARK SYSTEM (table: National Historical Parks).

NFO. See FARMERS ORGANIZATION, NATIONAL.

NGO DINH DIEM, *noh din ZEE em* (1901-1963), was the first president of South Vietnam. He served from 1955 until a group of army officers seized control of the government and killed him in 1963.

Diem was born in central Vietnam, the son of a government official. During the 1940's, he worked for Vietnam's independence from France and opposed Communist control of Vietnam. Vietnam was divided into two independent countries after Communist-led rebels defeated the French in 1954. Bao Dai, emperor of South Vietnam, appointed Diem as his prime minister. Diem was elected president when South Vietnam became a republic in 1955.

At first, Diem restored some order to his war-torn country. But he soon began ruling like a dictator, and he became increasingly unpopular. Special police units brutally crushed his opponents. Also, Diem was unable to stop *Viet Cong* (Communist-led guerrilla) attacks on villages in South Vietnam. Many of his harsh actions were attributed to advice from his brother Ngo Dinh Nhu, and his sister-in-law, Madame Nhu. Nhu and Diem were killed together. BERNARD B. FALL

See also VIETNAM (History); VIETNAM WAR.

NGUYEN VAN THIEU, *nwin vahn tyoo* (1923-   ), was elected president of South Vietnam in September, 1967. He became head of the country's first constitutional government since the overthrow of President Ngo Dinh Diem in 1963. Thieu was South Vietnam's deputy prime minister and defense minister in 1965. From 1965 to 1967, he served as chief of state and chairman of the Directory, a 10-member executive committee in the military government that ruled South Vietnam.

Thieu was born in Phan Rang, and graduated from the Vietnamese National Military Academy. As a division commander, Thieu led a major attack during the military revolt that overthrew Diem. Born a Buddhist, he became a Roman Catholic in 1958. WESLEY R. FISHEL

See also VIETNAM (History); VIETNAM WAR.

NIACIN. See VITAMIN (Vitamin B Complex).

NIAGARA FALLS, N.Y. (pop. 85,615; alt. 570 ft.), is an industrial center on the Niagara River at Niagara Falls (see NEW YORK [political map]). The falls provide the greatest single natural source of water power in North America. The water power generated supplies homes and industries throughout New York and Pennsylvania, as well as the province of Ontario. The scenic beauty of the falls attracts thousands of tourists.

The city of Niagara Falls is a center for electrochemical and electrometallurgical industries. Factories in the city make paper and paper products, carbons, graphite, abrasives, storage batteries, printed business forms, and aerospace equipment. The municipal airport serves several charter lines. Several railroads and bus lines serve the city.

Father Louis Hennepin visited Niagara Falls in 1678 and sketched the falls. Sieur de la Salle later built Fort Conti, the first fort on the Niagara River, at this point. In 1759, this fort, later known as Fort Niagara, was captured by English forces. In 1819, Canada and the United States made the center line of the Niagara River their international boundary.

Niagara Falls was incorporated as a village in 1848, and as a city in 1892. In 1914, the city adopted a charter which provided for a city-manager form of government.

A footbridge over the Niagara River was completed in 1848. In 1855, John A. Roebling built the first railroad bridge. The twelfth bridge, a steel arch span known as the Rainbow Bridge, was completed in 1941. The development of Niagara power began in 1852. At that time, construction started on a hydraulic canal to lead the water from the upper river around the falls. The first electric power was delivered to the village of Niagara Falls in 1881. By 1895, electric power was available in quantity. In the early 1960's, the New York State Power Authority completed the $720 million Niagara Power Project, one of the largest hydroelectric facilities in the world. WILLIAM E. YOUNG

See also NIAGARA FALLS AND NIAGARA RIVER.

NIAGARA FALLS, Ont. (pop. 56,891; alt. 570 ft.), is a gateway used by visitors to Canada from the United States. Niagara Falls lies on the Niagara River overlooking the Canadian side of the famous Niagara Falls (see ONTARIO [political map]). Driveways, parks, and gardens stretch along the river.

Niagara Falls has become an industrial center of Ontario because of its location near the Queenston hydroelectric power development. The city's chief products include abrasives, chemicals, cereals, canned goods, industrial machinery, leather goods, iron and steel products, nitrogen fertilizers, paper, and silverware.

The city was incorporated in 1904. It has a mayor-council government. It became a gateway between Canada and the U.S. when a railroad bridge connected Canadian and U.S. railroads. Several bridges now cross the river at Niagara Falls. D. M. L. FARR

NIAGARA FALLS (ONT.)   Oneida Tower

Skylon Tower

Seagram Tower

Niagara Falls carries about 500,000 tons of water a minute from one level of the Niagara River to the other. Horseshoe Falls, on the Canadian side of the river, is larger than American Falls. Four observation towers, from 282 to 500 feet high, give visitors a view of the falls. Rainbow Bridge links Niagara Falls, N.Y., *upper right,* and Niagara Falls, Ont.

NIAGARA FALLS AND NIAGARA RIVER. This waterway and its famous Falls make up one of the most beautiful natural regions in the world. The Falls have become a favorite tourist center and are known throughout America as a *honeymooners' paradise.*

The River. The Niagara River connects Lake Erie and Lake Ontario. It forms part of the boundary line between New York and the Canadian province of Ontario. All the Great Lakes except Lake Ontario empty into this stream, which is only about 35 miles long.

The river flows quietly northward after leaving Lake Erie. Here, the stream is 326 feet higher than the surface of Lake Ontario, toward which it winds. Farther along in its course, the river divides and passes on either side of Grand Island, which is about 6 miles wide. Beyond the island, the river again forms a shallow stream. Goat Island then separates the river just before the Falls and a series of rapids occur. Then, the waters again flow quietly along the Ontario plain for the last 7 miles. Ships can sail the length of the river except the 9 miles of waterfalls and rapids. The Welland Canal, which was built by the Canadian government, provides a shipping route around the Falls and rapids.

The Falls. The famous Falls are about midway in the river. At this point, the river plunges 500,000 tons of water a minute into a steep-walled gorge. The water drops in two streams. The larger one falls over a rocky ledge of Niagara limestone on the Canadian side and forms the famous Horseshoe Falls. The smaller stream drops over the eastern shore and forms the American Falls. Horseshoe Falls are 186 feet high and 2,100 feet wide at their widest point (see ONTARIO [color picture]). This waterfall carries nearly the entire volume of the Niagara River. The American Falls are 193 feet high and about 1,100 feet wide. At night, wide beams of white and colored lights illuminate the Falls and present a beautiful picture of colored water. *The Maid of the Mist,* a steamer, takes visitors around the river at the base of the Falls.

The Whirlpool. The Whirlpool Rapids, near the northern end of the river, are almost as famous as the Falls. The current is so violent that it has carved a round basin out of the rock. Here, the rapids circle and twist about as fast as any other whirlpool in the world.

A cableway has been built in Ontario, high above the whirlpool. This cableway carries tourists from Colt's Point to Thompson's Point, on the opposite bank. A passenger car provides seating space for 24 people, and standing room for 21 others. The car is hung from six cables, which are 1,800 feet long.

The Gorge. The steep-walled canyon through which the river flows downstream from Niagara Falls is 7 miles long. It stretches from the edge of Horseshoe Falls to Lewiston, N.Y. The gorge is made up of layers of dif-

NIAGARA FALLS (N.Y.)

American Observation Tower

AMERICAN FALLS

HORSESHOE FALLS

James Studio, Niagara Falls

ferent kinds of stone. The top layer of hard limestone is about 80 feet thick. Beneath this layer are softer layers of limestone, shale, and sandstone. The ledge rests on a bed of soft shale. The top layer stretches out farther than the lower layers. The Cave of the Winds is under an extended shelf of hard rock. It is possible to see the falls from the inside by going down to the cave. Spray and water are wearing away at the base of the gorge. The gorge walls are steep but smooth at the southern and northern ends. But the rocks have been carved into strange shapes at the whirlpools and falls section.

The gorge is becoming longer, because the water pounds against it, wearing it down. The Falls were once at Lewiston, but they gradually moved back upstream toward Lake Erie. The ledge of Horseshoe Falls is being worn away at the rate of about three feet a year. The cutting away at the American Falls is much slower, since the action of the water is not so strong at this point. The rock bed of the American Falls moves back about 4 to 7 inches a year. In addition, slides have changed the appearance of the gorge. About 80,000 tons of rock fell from the face of the American Falls in 1931. Several years later, 30,000 tons of rock cracked off the upper edge of Horseshoe Falls. In 1934, 200 tons of rock broke off from under Table Rock. On July 28, 1954, an estimated 185,000 tons of rock tumbled from the American Falls and nearby Prospect Point into

the Niagara River. It was the biggest slide ever to occur at Niagara Falls. Engineers took steps to halt further erosion at the Falls. But on June 7, 1956, a series of giant rockfalls about a half mile below the Falls sent two-thirds of a huge power plant tumbling into the Niagara River gorge. A power-company employee was swept to his death, and damage to the power station totaled several million dollars. Seepage of water into rock crevices between the lip of the gorge and the hydraulic canal feeding into the power station from above the Falls caused the collapse.

In 1969, U.S. Army engineers built a dam to temporarily stop the flow of water over the American Falls. They did this so they could study the rock ledge to find a way to prevent further erosion.

Origin of the Niagara Region. Niagara Falls was formed after the last great ice sheet withdrew from this region. The ice changed the surface of the land so much that waterways and streams were forced to seek new channels. The waters of Lake Erie overflowed and formed the Niagara River. This river had to pass a high cliff, known as the Niagara Escarpment, on its way northward. It is very difficult to tell when this occurred, because the water does not flow at an even rate, and it cuts away at both hard and soft rock. In some places, hard layers of rock cover softer layers, and the river cuts away the soft layers underneath to form caves. The Cave

311

HOW NIAGARA FALLS IS CHANGING

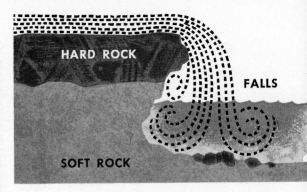

HARD ROCK

FALLS

SOFT ROCK

Swirling Currents, gaining force from plunging over the falls, eat away the soft under rock. The hard top rock then breaks off.

Erosion since Niagara Falls was first sketched in 1678 is shown by dotted lines, *below.* Horseshoe Falls, over which 95 per cent of the Niagara River flows, has eroded about a quarter of a mile. The American Falls has receded only about 90 feet since 1842. In 1969, engineers temporarily stopped the flow over the American Falls, *left,* to study possible ways to prevent further erosion.

U.S. Army

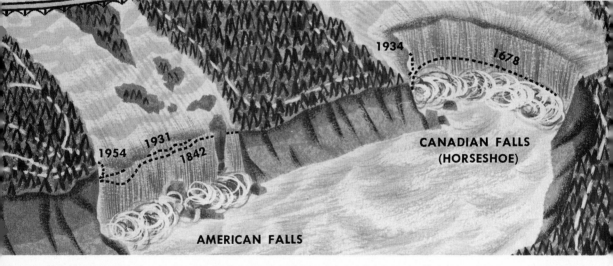

1934

1678

1954

1931

1842

CANADIAN FALLS
(HORSESHOE)

AMERICAN FALLS

of the Winds was made in this way. Scientists believe tnat the Falls cannot be more than 20,000 years old.

Parks. In 1885, the New York state government took control of the land surrounding the falls on the American side and established Niagara Falls Park. The reservation covered about 430 acres. There are now about 1,700 acres of parks on the United States side. In 1886, Canada set aside 196 acres on its shore and established Queen Victoria Park. The entire Canadian side near the falls is now reserved as a park.

A drive follows the edge of the gorge in Canada. The drive is connected with Niagara Falls, N.Y., by the Niagara Rapids Boulevard and the Queenston-Lewiston Bridge. Niagara Rapids Boulevard links Devil's Hole State Park and Whirlpool State Park.

Bridges. The Cantilever Bridge, built in 1883 into solid rock, spanned the gorge above the whirlpool. It was the first bridge of its kind in America. A steel arch bridge replaced it in 1920. The famous Rainbow Bridge

was completed in 1941 between Niagara Falls, N.Y., and Niagara Falls, Ont. It replaced a bridge that collapsed under the weight of ice in 1938.

Water Power at the Falls was used as early as 1757 to run a sawmill built by a Frenchman, Chabert Joncaire, Jr. In 1881, the first hydroelectric power was generated at the Falls. But the first generators for the large-scale production of electric power were not installed on both sides of the Falls until the mid-1890's. Today, large power plants line both sides of the river. They have attracted to the Falls region electrochemical processing plants and other firms that require large amounts of electricity.

In 1950, the United States and Canada signed a treaty raising the amount of water that can be used to generate power. The authorized flow was increased from a total of 56,000 cubic feet a second to 100,000 to 150,000 cubic feet a second. The province of Ontario completed a power plant in 1958. This gave the Sir

Adam Beck generating plants on the Canadian side of the Falls a total capacity of 1,811,000 kilowatts. That year, the United States began building a $720 million power plant with a capacity of 2,190,000 kilowatts. The plant, the largest hydroelectric project outside Russia, was completed in 1962.   GEORGE MACINKO

NIAGARA MOVEMENT was an organization founded by Negroes to fight racial discrimination in the United States. It existed from 1905 to 1910. At its height, the Niagara Movement had 30 branches in various U.S. cities. The movement failed to win the support of most Negroes, but many of its ideas and programs were adopted in 1909 by a new interracial organization—the National Association for the Advancement of Colored People (NAACP).

The Niagara Movement was founded in Niagara Falls, Ont. W. E. B. Du Bois, a black professor at Atlanta University, led the organization (see DU BOIS, W. E. B.). The movement placed the responsibility for racial problems in the United States on whites. The movement thus opposed the view of the great Negro educator Booker T. Washington, who urged blacks to stop demanding equal rights (see WASHINGTON, BOOKER T.). Various branches of the movement demanded voting rights for Negroes, opposed school segregation, and worked to elect candidates who promised to fight race prejudice.   ELLIOTT RUDWICK

See also NEGRO (After Reconstruction).

NIAGARA UNIVERSITY is located in the town of Niagara University, just outside the city of Niagara Falls, N.Y. It is conducted by the Roman Catholic Church, and has the following divisions: Seminary of Our Lady of Angels, College of Arts and Sciences, College of Business Administration, School of Education, College of Nursing, and the Graduate School. The majority of the university's students are men. Courses are offered leading to degrees of B.B.A., B.A., B.S., M.A., and M.S. Niagara University was founded in 1856. For the university's enrollment, see UNIVERSITIES AND COLLEGES (table).   ROBERT J. RIVARD

NIAMEY, *nyah MAY* (pop. 78,991; alt. 886 ft.), is the capital of the Republic of Niger in western Africa. An inland port on the Niger River, Niamey exports agricultural products of the region. For location, see NIGER (map).

NIBELUNG, *NEE buh loong,* was any one of a group of dwarfs in German mythology. They also were called *the children of the mist.* The Nibelungs owned a golden treasure that cursed all who seized it. The name Nibelung was later applied to anyone possessing the treasure. In the *Nibelungenlied,* a German epic of about A.D. 1200, the Burgundian kings are called Nibelungs.

See also OPERA (Some of the Famous Operas).

NIBELUNGENLIED, *NEE buh LOONG un LEET,* is a German epic poem written about A.D. 1200. The title means *Song of the Nibelungs.* The author is unknown, but he undoubtedly came from the Danube area of southeastern Germany or Austria.

The poem tells of Siegfried, king of the Nibelungs. Siegfried owns the fabulous Nibelung treasure and a cloak of invisibility. He has also killed a dragon and bathed in its blood. The blood hardened Siegfried's flesh, protecting it from wounds. But a linden leaf had fallen between his shoulders while he bathed, leaving an unprotected spot on his back.

Siegfried wants to marry Kriemhild, the sister of King Gunther of Burgundy. To gain Kriemhild, Siegfried helps Gunther win the maiden Brunhild, Queen of Iceland. Brunhild will marry only the man who can overcome her in combat. So Siegfried disguises himself as Gunther, and beats Brunhild, winning her for Gunther. Years later, Kriemhild tells Brunhild that Siegfried, not Gunther, had beaten her. In revenge, Brunhild orders Hagen, one of Gunther's *vassals* (servants), to murder Siegfried. Hagen kills Siegfried by shooting an arrow into the unprotected spot on his back.

Several years later, Kriemhild marries Etzel, mighty king of the Huns. But she never forgets Siegfried. She invites the Burgundians to visit her, and has them slaughtered. Only Hagen survives. Kriemhild asks him to reveal where he has hidden the Nibelung treasure. When he refuses, she kills him. Hildebrand, a warrior at the court of Etzel, horrified by Kriemhild's treachery, kills her.

The Background. Two actual events form the basis for parts of the *Nibelungenlied.* In A.D. 437, the Huns destroyed the Burgundians, an east Germanic tribe. The Burgundian king and members of his royal household died in the battle. The king of the Huns, Attila (called Etzel in the poem), was not connected with this event. Attila died suddenly on his wedding night in 453. Some historians said that he was murdered by his Germanic bride.

The Nibelungen-poet clearly was not the first to deal with this story material. The Icelandic *Edda,* composed before the *Nibelungenlied,* contains *lays* (short poems) on the same themes. The early Germanic peoples also composed lays to celebrate the great heroes and events of their past. The lays were revised, and in the course of centuries the original historical events were greatly altered. Unknown poets combined the events of 437 and 453 into a single historic lay. In this lay, a Burgundian bride kills Attila to gain revenge for the death of her relatives, who were killed by Attila's Huns.

Many of the themes and much of the plot of the older Germanic lays can still be found in the *Nibelungenlied,* but the poet changed the material. Scholars have not been able to trace the *Nibelungenlied* story of Siegfried's death to particular historical personalities and events. In fact, Siegfried's supernatural powers give his story the quality of a fairy tale.

The Style. The *Nibelungenlied* is written in stanzas. Each stanza consists of four long lines of two pairs of rhymed couplets. The author shows a keen understanding of human psychology as he develops the motives that cause the proud figures in his poem to act as they do. The great climaxes lie in the tense dialogues in which the rivals confront each other.

Scholars cannot say precisely what the Nibelungen-poet retained and what he added. The courtly aspects were probably added around 1200, however, when courtly culture flourished in Germany. The tender love between Siegfried and Kriemhild, the festivals of knights and ladies, and the many heroes of the epic reflect courtly virtues. These aspects provide the softer accents that contrast with and heighten the effect of the tragic ending.   JAMES F. POAG

NICAEA, COUNCILS OF. See NICENE COUNCILS.

313

Managua, the Capital and Largest City of Nicaragua, Lies on Lake Managua.

NICARAGUA

NICARAGUA, NICK *ah* RAH *gwah*, is the largest country of Central America. It is a little larger than North Carolina, but has only about a third as many people as that state. Nicaragua extends from the Pacific Ocean to the Caribbean Sea. Most of the people live in a fertile region on the Pacific side. In this region is Managua, the capital and largest city of Nicaragua. About 15 per cent of Nicaragua's people live in Managua.

Most Nicaraguans have both Indian and Spanish ancestors. During the early 1500's, the Spaniards began arriving in what is now Nicaragua. They named the land for an Indian chief and his tribe—both called Nicarao—who lived there. The Nicarao way of life, like that of most other Indians of Nicaragua, has blended with Spanish customs and traditions. Today, Nicaragua has only a few Indian groups that still follow their old way of life.

Cotton is Nicaragua's leading source of income. It is grown on large farms in the Pacific Region. Few people live in the thickly forested Caribbean Region, on the other side of the country. In between, the people of the rugged Central Highlands raise beans, coffee, corn, and sugar cane on small farms.

Government

The Nicaraguan government has been controlled by the Somoza family since 1937. That year, General Anastasio Somoza became president of Nicaragua. Partly by using terrorist methods, he achieved great political power and wealth. Each of Somoza's two

Richard N. Adams, the contributor of this article, is Professor of Anthropology at the University of Texas. He is the author of The Second Sowing: Power and Secondary Development in Latin America *and the coauthor of* Contemporary Cultures and Societies in Latin America.

sons later became president and tightened the family's control of the nation. Today, members of the Somoza family own all or part of almost every major economic operation in Nicaragua.

National elections are controlled to discourage voting against the Nationalist Liberal Party, which is run by the Somozas. There are no local elections. Politicians opposed to the Somozas have never been a serious threat to their power. Opposition to the Somozas has been continuous, but it has been ineffective against their economic strength and government troops.

People

The great majority of Nicaraguans are *mestizos* (persons with white and Indian ancestors). Their general way of life is somewhat similar to that of Spanish-

--- FACTS IN BRIEF ---

Capital: Managua.

Official Language: Spanish.

Area: 50,193 square miles. *Greatest Distances*—(north-south) 293 miles; (east-west) 297 miles. *Coastlines*—(Pacific) 215 miles; (Caribbean) 297 miles.

Elevation: *Highest*—8,000 feet above sea level in the Cordillera Isabella. *Lowest*—sea level along the coasts.

Population: *1963 Census*—1,535,588; distribution, 59 per cent rural, 41 per cent urban. *Estimated 1970 Population*—1,988,000; density, 40 persons to the square mile. *Estimated 1975 Population*—2,384,000.

Chief Products: *Agriculture*—bananas, beans, beef cattle, coffee, corn, cotton, rice, sesame, sugar cane. *Manufacturing*—clothing and textiles, processed foods and beverages.

National Holiday: Independence Day, September 15.

National Anthem: "Himno Nacional de Nicaragua."

Money: *Basic Unit*—cordoba. One hundred centavos equal one cordoba. For the value of the cordoba in dollars, see MONEY (table: Values). See also CORDOBA.

GOVERNMENT IN BRIEF

Form of Government: Republic.

Head of State and Government: President (elected to a 5-year term). He cannot serve two terms in a row.

Congress: *Senate*—16 members (elected to 5-year terms), plus the second-place presidential candidate (5-year term) and ex-presidents (life terms); *Chamber of Deputies*—42 members (elected to 5-year terms).

Courts: The Supreme Court of Justice (7 judges elected by Congress until the age of 75) appoints judges of most lower courts to varying terms.

Political Divisions: 16 departments divided into about 120 *municipios* (cities or townships), all headed by administrators appointed by the president.

Voting Age: 21; 18 for persons who can read and write or are married; under 18 for those with a high school degree.

Armed Forces: The National Guard of about 5,500 men is both an army and a police force. There are a small coast guard and air force. Military service may be required by law at any time.

Americans in other Central American countries. Most of the people of Nicaragua belong to the Roman Catholic Church and speak Spanish. The only Indian groups that still generally speak their own languages and follow their other old ways of life live in the thinly populated Caribbean Region. This region also has some Negro and mixed Indian-Negro communities that largely follow Indian customs and traditions.

Most of Nicaragua's people are poor farmers. Many of those in the Pacific Region are peasants who work on large estates owned by wealthy Nicaraguans. They live on or near the estates in shacks with palm-leaf roofs and walls of poles and branches. In the Central Highlands, many of the farmers have their own small farms. In the colder areas of that region, the farmers live in adobe homes with tile roofs. The Indians and Negroes of the Caribbean Region live chiefly by farming small plots, or by fishing, lumbering, or mining.

Education. Nicaraguan law requires children to go to school from the age of 6 through 12. But only about half the children do so, and most of these live in cities or towns. Nicaragua does not have enough schools for all its youngsters, and many farm areas have no schools at all. There is also a shortage of teachers. About half the people cannot read and write.

Nicaragua has two universities. The National University of Nicaragua, in León and Managua, is the older and larger one. It was founded in 1812, and has more than 3,000 students. The Central American University is a Roman Catholic institution in Managua.

Population of Nicaragua increases about 3 per cent a year. To ease the pressure of this increase, the government encourages people of the Pacific Region, with loans and other help, to move to other regions. The Pacific Region still has more than two-thirds of Nicaragua's population, although many people have moved to northern areas of the Central Highlands.

In 1970, Nicaragua had an estimated population of 1,988,000. The following table shows census figures of Nicaragua through the years:

1963 1,535,588	1920 638,119
1950 1,057,023	1906 505,377
1940 835,686	

Nicaragua has five cities with populations over 20,000. In order of size, they are Managua, León, Granada, Masaya, and Chinandega. See the separate articles on MANAGUA; LEÓN; and GRANADA.

The Land and Climate

Nicaragua has three main land regions: (1) the Pacific Region, (2) the Central Highlands, and (3) the Caribbean Region. The climate is chiefly tropical, with some differences among these regions.

The Pacific Region is largely a low area extending from Honduras to Costa Rica. Several volcanoes, some of them active, are in this low area. Lake Managua and Lake Nicaragua lie in the central and southern sections. West of these lakes, mountains up to 3,000 feet high rise along the Pacific coast. Nicaragua's largest cities and many large farms are in the Pacific Region.

The region receives about 60 inches of rain a year. The rainy season lasts from May to November. Temperatures average about 80° F. throughout the year.

The Central Highlands make up Nicaragua's highest

Nicaragua's Flag was adopted in 1908 from that of the United Provinces of Central America. This union of the early 1800's consisted of Nicaragua and four other nations.

The Coat of Arms appears on the flag. The volcanoes stand for the Central American union, the triangle for equality, the rainbow for peace, and the cap for liberty.

Nicaragua, the largest Central American nation, is 1½ per cent as large as the United States, not counting Alaska and Hawaii.

WORLD BOOK map

NICARAGUA

Leon V. Kofad

Cotton, Nicaragua's Chief Product, makes up about 40 per cent of the country's exports. It grows in lowlands along the Pacific Ocean.

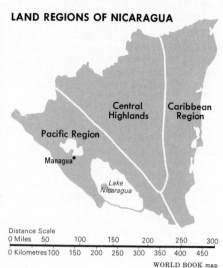

LAND REGIONS OF NICARAGUA

Central Highlands

Caribbean Region

Pacific Region

Managua

Lake Nicaragua

Distance Scale
0 Miles 50   100   150   200   250   300
0 Kilometres 100   150   200   250   300   350   400   450

WORLD BOOK map

and coolest region. They include the country's highest point, an unnamed peak that rises 8,000 feet above sea level in the Cordillera Isabella, a mountain range. Forests cover most of the region's slopes. Deep valleys lie between the mountains.

Some areas receive more than 100 inches of rain a year, and most of the people live on farms in the drier areas. Like the Pacific Region, the Central Highlands have a rainy season from May to November. Temperatures average between 60° F. and 70° F.

The Caribbean Region is mostly a flat plain, with some highlands sloping upward toward the west. Many rivers that rise in the Central Highlands flow through the plain. The region's only good farmland lies along the riverbanks. Rain forests cover most of the region. There are grasslands with palm and pine forests in the north. A number of small islands lie off the coast.

Easterly trade winds drench the Caribbean Region with an annual average of 165 inches of rain, which falls

throughout most of the year. Temperatures in the region average 80° F.

Economy

Nicaragua's major natural resource is the rich soil of the Pacific Region. Ash from volcanoes makes this soil especially fertile. Farming is the country's leading industry, though farmland makes up less than 15 per cent of the land area.

Nicaragua has some deposits of copper, gold, and silver, but mining provides only a small part of the nation's income. United States and Canadian companies own most of the mines. Thick forests cover about half the land, and foreign firms also own much of the Nicaraguan lumber industry. Many mountain streams in the Central Highlands could furnish cheap hydroelectric power, but few of them have been used. The country is developing these power sources.

Agriculture. Exported farm products provide most of

NICARAGUA MAP INDEX

*Does not appear on the map; key shows general location.   Sources: 1965 official estimate for capital; 1963 census for departments and other cities.

NICARAGUA

Nicaragua's income. Cotton, the most valuable crop, is grown in the low Pacific areas. It accounts for about 40 per cent of the country's exports. Coffee and sugar cane are grown in the Central Highlands and the Pacific Region. Other farm exports include bananas, beef, rice, and sesame. Corn and beans are the main food crops raised for use in Nicaragua. They are grown in all regions, but chiefly in the Central Highlands.

Manufacturing. Nicaragua's chief industrial center is Managua, where most of the nation's electric power is generated. As in most other Central American countries, the major manufactured products are processed foods and beverages, clothing, and textiles. Other products include cement, cigarettes, and goods made of leather, petroleum, and wood. Almost all the manufacturing companies are privately owned, about a third of them by foreign firms.

Foreign Trade. In many years, Nicaragua exports more goods than it imports. The country's main trading partner is the United States, and others include West Germany and Japan. Nicaragua belongs to the Central American Common Market, an economic union of five nations. This organization is based on the General Treaty for Central American Economic Integration (see COMMON MARKET). Nicaragua's trade with the other four market countries increased rapidly during the 1960's.

Transportation. Nicaragua has more than 4,000 miles of roads, of which about 650 miles are paved. The Pan American Highway is the major highway (see PAN AMERICAN HIGHWAY). Several roads branch off the highway to various parts of Nicaragua. But many populated areas cannot be reached by automobile, and the people use mules or oxcarts to travel over crude trails. There are about 250 miles of railways, all in the Pacific Region. Managua has an international airport. The major seaport, Corinto, is on the Pacific Ocean.

Communication. Nicaragua has few newspapers. The largest, *La Prensa* of Managua, has a daily circulation of about 40,000 copies. The government-operated postal, telegraph, and telephone systems serve only cities and towns. Most of the many radio stations and the two television channels are privately operated.

History

The Indian Period. Little is known of what is now Nicaragua before the Spaniards arrived in the early 1500's. A series of Indian states occupied the Pacific Region and the Central Highlands. They built fortified towns, and had highly developed markets and a system of social classes that included slaves. Less developed Indian societies lived in the Caribbean Region.

The Colonial Period. In 1502, Christopher Columbus discovered what is now Nicaragua, and claimed the land for Spain. A Spanish expedition from Panama explored the Pacific Region in 1522. The Spaniards baptized many Nicarao Indians of the region into the Roman Catholic Church. Another expedition from Panama came to the Pacific Region in 1524. The leader, Fernández de Córdoba, founded Granada and León near the main sources of Indian labor. The Indians worked on the Spaniards' farms and in their mines.

In 1570, Nicaragua came under the control of the Audiencia of Guatemala, a high court of Spanish judges and administrators that ruled most of Central America. Nicaragua was part of the colony of New Spain, but the court had great power because it was so far from Mexico City, the colonial capital.

The Spaniards explored the Caribbean coast of Nicaragua, but did not settle there. During the 1600's and 1700's, other Europeans—chiefly the English—occupied that region from time to time. English, Dutch, and French pirates had hideouts there, and attacked Spanish shipping in the Caribbean Sea. The pirates also raided Spanish towns to the west. During the 1700's, the English established control over the Miskito, or Mosquito, Indians of the Caribbean coast. Great Britain gave up its hold on the region to Nicaragua in the mid-1800's, under an agreement with the United States.

Independence. On Sept. 15, 1821, Nicaragua and other Central American states also declared their independence. They later became part of the Mexican empire, but broke away in 1823 and formed the United Provinces of Central America. This union generally followed liberal economic and political policies. For ex-

NICARAGUA'S GROSS NATIONAL PRODUCT IN 1967

Total gross national product—$638,000,000

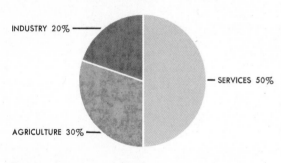

INDUSTRY 20%

SERVICES 50%

AGRICULTURE 30%

The gross national product (GNP) is the total value of goods and services produced by a country in a year. The GNP measures a nation's total annual economic performance. It can also be used to compare the economic output and growth of countries.

PRODUCTION AND WORKERS BY ECONOMIC ACTIVITIES

Economic Activities	Per Cent of GDP* Produced	Labor Force Number of Persons	Labor Force Per Cent of Total
Agriculture, Forestry, & Fishing	30	314,842	57
Commerce	20	46,007	8
Manufacturing	14	65,407	12
Government	9	†	†
Other Services	7	85,917	15
Housing	7	—	—
Transportation & Communication	5	14,412	3
Construction	3	21,618	4
Banking, Insurance, & Real Estate	2	†	†
Utilities	2	**	**
Mining	1	6,087	1
Total	100	554,290	100

*GDP is gross domestic product (gross national product less net income from abroad).
†Included in Other Services.   **Included in Mining.
Sources: Central Bank of Nicaragua; National Economic Council, Nicaragua.

ample, the member states established various civil rights, and ended the special rights of powerful nobles and the Roman Catholic Church.

The union began to fall apart under various pressures, including efforts by the conservative landowners and churchmen to regain their old privileges. In 1838, Nicaragua left the union. By that time, a great dispute had developed between León, the liberal center, and Granada, the conservative center. The cities struggled for control of Nicaragua, and fighting often broke out.

The liberals of León asked William Walker, an American military adventurer, to help them. In 1855, Walker arrived with a band of followers and captured Granada in a surprise attack. But instead of helping the liberals, he seized control of the government in 1856. The next year, the liberals and conservatives joined forces and drove Walker from the country.

The United States and Nicaragua. For many years, the United States had wanted to build a canal across Nicaragua to link the Atlantic and Pacific oceans. In 1901, President José Santos Zelaya of Nicaragua set certain limits on U.S. rights in the proposed canal zone. The United States did not accept these limits, and shifted its attention to Panama as the site of the canal. Zelaya then threatened to sell rights to the canal to some rival country of the United States. He also canceled contracts with a number of U.S. firms.

In 1909, a revolt broke out against Zelaya, a harsh ruler. He was driven from office after the United States sided with the rebels. In 1911, U.S. banks began to lend money to Nicaragua under agreements that gave them control over its finances until the debts were paid in 1925. At the request of the banks and President Adolfo Díaz, U.S. marines landed in Nicaragua in 1912 to put down forces that opposed American control. The marines remained there almost continuously until 1933 to protect U.S. interests and supervise elections.

In 1916, the Bryan-Chamorro Treaty between the two nations gave the United States permanent, exclusive canal rights and 99-year leases on naval bases in Nicaraguan waters. Nicaragua received $3 million in return. United States plans for the canal have never been developed.

Rebels led by General Augusto César Sandino made many raids on the U.S. marines from hideouts in the mountains. The Americans trained a new Nicaraguan army, called the National Guard, to help the marines. In 1934, after the marines had left, national guardsmen murdered Sandino under a flag of truce.

The Somoza Period. In 1936, General Anastasio Somoza, the head of the National Guard, forced President Juan Sacasa to resign. Somoza, who was Sacasa's nephew, became president the next year after an election in which he was the only candidate. He ruled as a dictator, and established great political and economic power for himself and his family.

Since 1937, a Somoza has ruled Nicaragua either as president or as the real power behind the presidency. Anastasio Somoza was assassinated in 1956, and his older son, Luis, replaced him as president. Luis held the presidency until 1963. His brother, Anastasio Somoza Debayle, became president in 1967. The Somozas have generally been eager to cooperate with the United States, and have always been supported by the U.S. government.

NICARAGUA

Wide World

The Somoza Family has controlled Nicaragua's government since 1937. Anastasio Somoza, *second from right,* shown with his wife, ruled from 1937 until 1956. His sons, Anastasio Somoza Debayle, *left,* and Luis Somoza, *right,* also became president.

Nicaragua's economy is expanding faster per person than that of any other Central American country. Political stability under the Somozas has attracted public and private American investments. Tax reductions offered by the Somozas have been especially attractive to private investors.

In 1968, the 160-mile Rama Road, built with U.S. aid, helped connect the Pacific and Caribbean coasts of Nicaragua. It greatly improved the movement of people and goods, and became an important part of Nicaragua's expanding economy. RICHARD N. ADAMS

Related Articles in WORLD BOOK include:

Central America	Lake Nicaragua	Mosquito Coast
Cordoba	Larreinaga, Miguel	Nicaragua Canal
Corinto	León	Somoza (family)
Darío, Rubén	Managua	Walker, William
Granada		

Outline

I. Government
II. People
    A. Education   B. Population
III. The Land and Climate
    A. The Pacific Region   C. The Caribbean
    B. The Central Highlands   Region
IV. Economy
    A. Agriculture   D. Transportation
    B. Manufacturing   E. Communication
    C. Foreign Trade
V. History

Questions

How did Nicaragua get its name?

What is the main source of Nicaragua's income?

What family has controlled Nicaragua since 1937?

What is the most heavily populated part of Nicaragua?

What events led to the landing of U.S. marines in Nicaragua in 1912?

What are the main foods of the Nicaraguans?

Which two cities struggled for power in Nicaragua during the 1800's?

What are Nicaragua's chief manufactured products?

Why is the Pacific Region's soil especially fertile?

What country is Nicaragua's major trading partner?

NICARAGUA, LAKE. See LAKE NICARAGUA.

NICARAGUA CANAL is a ship canal which engineers for many years have proposed to extend across the Isthmus of Nicaragua to connect the Atlantic and Pacific oceans. Although the oceans have since been connected by the Panama Canal, the Nicaragua waterway plan has not been entirely abandoned. The Nicaragua Canal would extend from Greytown, on the Atlantic Coast, to Brito, on the Pacific Coast, passing through Lake Nicaragua (see LAKE NICARAGUA).

The Nicaragua Canal was first discussed in 1826 at the Panama Congress. Henry Clay instructed his commissioners to report whether the project was practical. Partial surveys were made in 1826 and 1837-1838. But nothing else was done until 1849, when Cornelius Vanderbilt formed and headed a company which was granted the right to build the canal. It never began construction, and the concession was annulled in 1856.

In 1849, Great Britain seized the land around the mouth of the San Juan River, which was to be the eastern end of the canal. Then the United States entered into the Clayton-Bulwer Treaty of 1850 with Great Britain. The treaty provided that, if the canal were built, Great Britain and the United States would control it (see CLAYTON-BULWER TREATY). The canal project was put off repeatedly, although surveys and plans to start construction were made from time to time. In 1887, a private company called the Nicaragua Canal Association was granted exclusive rights to build and operate the proposed canal. Two years later construction began, but cost of the canal was higher than had been expected, and within four years the company had spent $6,000,000. It then asked Congress for an additional $100,000,000. Congress denied the grant, and work was stopped.

The federal government appointed commissions to survey a route for a canal connecting the Pacific and Atlantic oceans in 1872, 1895, 1897, and 1899. Each time, the commissions favored a route across Nicaragua. But in 1909, Congress finally decided on a route through Panama. In 1914, the Panama Canal was completed. In 1916, the United States made a treaty with Nicaragua in which the Nicaraguan government granted the United States perpetual canal rights and other privileges for $3,000,000. In 1929, 1931, and 1938, Congress again authorized surveys. Further planning has taken place since World War II.   ROLLIN S. ATWOOD

NICE, *nees* (pop. 292,958; alt. 94 ft.), is a leading resort city on the French Riviera. It is also a Mediterranean Sea port. Nice lies at the foot of the Alps near the Italian border (see FRANCE [color map]).

The beautiful city has wide avenues, luxurious hotels, and villas surrounded by gardens. The Paillon River divides it into the Old Town to the east and the modern, western part. The Alps protect Nice from cold northern winds and give it a mild winter climate. Most of the people depend for their living on the tourist trade. Most tourists come during the winter vacation season between January and April, or else from July to September. The Mardi Gras, which marks the height of the Riviera Carnival, is one of the city's many winter festivals (see MARDI GRAS). The industries of Nice produce olive oil, perfumes, processed fruit, soap, cement, and other products. Railroad lines to Marseille and to the Italian cities

of Genoa and Turin pass through Nice. Greek settlers founded Nice about 400 B.C.   ROBERT E. DICKINSON

NICENE COUNCILS, *ny SEEN*, were two councils of the Christian Church held in Nicaea (Nice), in Asia Minor.

The first council was called in 325 by Emperor Constantine to settle the dispute caused by the Arian views of the Trinity. Arius was a priest of Alexandria who believed that Christ is not of the same essence as God, but of similar substance. The Council adopted the so-called *Nicene Creed*. This declared that God and Christ as God are of one substance. The Council also fixed the time for observing Easter. It was questioned whether the Christian Easter should be on the same day as the Jewish observance (Passover), or on a Sunday.

The *Nicene Creed* summarized the chief articles of the Christian faith of that time. It is next oldest to the Apostles' Creed. It was adopted originally in the following form, but has been amplified since:

We believe in one God, the Father Almighty, maker of all things, both visible and invisible; and in one Lord, Jesus Christ, the Son of God, Only begotten of the Father, that is to say, of the substance of the Father, God of God and Light of Light, very God of very God, begotten, not made, being of one substance with the Father, by whom all things were made, both things in heaven and things on earth; who, for us men and for our salvation, came down and was made flesh, was made man, suffered, and rose again on the third day, went up into the heavens, and is to come again to judge both the quick and the dead; and in the Holy Ghost.

The second Council was called in 787 by the Empress Irene and her son Constantine. The Emperor Leo, Irene's deceased husband, had forbidden the use of images for any purpose. The Council was called because of opposition to the decree. The Empress revoked the decree after the Council had laid down principles governing the veneration of images.   FULTON J. SHEEN

See also ARIANISM; EASTER; ICONOCLAST; TRINITY.

NICHOLAS is the name of five popes of the Roman Catholic Church. Their terms were as follows:

Nicholas I, Saint	(858-867)
Nicholas II	(1059-1061)
Nicholas III	(1277-1280)
Nicholas IV	(1288-1292)
Nicholas V	(1447-1455)

Saint Nicholas I was a vigorous administrator. He asserted papal authority by excommunicating the archbishops of Cologne and Trier for approving King Lothair's second, adulterous marriage. He also excommunicated the archbishop of Ravenna for oppressing the poor.

Nicholas II called a council to set rules for electing future popes. He confined the election to a vote of the cardinals. This rule excluded the emperor and Roman nobility from papal elections.

The next two popes of this name were unimportant.

Nicholas V became famous as a scholar of the humanities. He founded the Vatican Library (see VATICAN LIBRARY). He started a vast building program that renovated Rome, and welcomed humanist scholars to Rome.   THOMAS P. NEILL and FULTON J. SHEEN

Nicholas II, the Last Czar of Russia, and His Family posed for this photograph shortly before the Russian Revolution of 1917. The Czar's family included his wife, Empress Alexandra; his son, Grand Duke Alexis; and his four daughters, the Grand Duchesses Maria, Tatiana, Olga, and Anastasia, *left to right.* Nicholas abdicated at the start of the revolution.

NICHOLAS was the name of two Russian czars.

Nicholas I (1796-1855) was noted for his harsh rule. He became emperor when his brother Alexander I died in 1825, and an older brother, Constantine, renounced his claim to the throne. Nicholas first put down a revolution staged by liberal-minded noblemen who desired reforms. This was called the *Decembrist* revolution because it occurred in December. Nicholas had five of the leaders executed, and exiled the rest to Siberia.

Nicholas fought all political reform after that. He created a powerful police, banned political organizations, introduced strict censorship, exiled liberal writers, and refused to abolish outdated institutions such as *serfdom* (see SERF). Corruption continued. He helped suppress revolutions abroad, and put an end to Polish independence when a revolution occurred there.

Despite these harsh measures, Nicholas eased and fixed the economic burdens of the farming class, and promoted the economic growth of the country through protective tariffs and a stable currency. He started railway construction. He introduced a new law code. Literature prospered despite persecution of liberal writers. Vocational schools were founded, but a free spirit in the universities was held in check.

Nicholas engaged in wars of expansion in Central and East Asia. He made war on Turkey in 1828, and almost achieved his aim of dominating the Bosporus and Dardanelles, exit to the Black Sea. Western Powers stemmed the Russian drive in the Crimean War (see CRIMEAN WAR). Nicholas died during the war. He was born at Tsarskoye Selo (now Pushkin).

Nicholas II (1868-1918), the last czar of Russia, ruled the country from 1894 to 1917. He was a charming and well-intentioned person, but he was politically weak and unreliable. Russia made economic progress, and became a major industrial power in oil, coal, iron, and textile production during his reign, with the help of loans from other countries. A trans-Siberian railway was completed. Science, music, and literature prospered. But Nicholas failed to re-establish good relations with his powerful neighbors, Germany and Austria. He allowed himself to become involved in a war with Japan in 1904, in an effort to control the Far East. Russia was defeated in 1905 (see RUSSO-JAPANESE WAR).

The lost war strengthened the disappointed Russian liberals, the discontented farmers and industrial workers, the oppressed Jews, and Polish, Finnish, and Baltic nationalists. Revolution broke out in 1905. Nicholas tried to crush it, but he was forced to compromise. He formed an elected assembly called the *Duma*, introducing a measure of representative government (see DUMA). He abolished flogging and canceled farm debts dating back to the time of emancipation. Farmers won the right to own their land. Although he introduced these reforms, broadened legislation, improved education, and increased industries, the lot of the common people seemed little improved. Nicholas disregarded demands for further reforms. This caused a renewal of revolutionary activities.

Russia entered World War I on the side of France and England. Soon terrible military defeats, coupled with an incapable, corrupt government, led to further suffering and unrest. Yet Nicholas, ill-advised by reactionaries, continued to neglect demands for reform. A new revolution broke out in 1917. Nicholas was forced to abdicate, and the rule of the czars ended. Nicholas and the members of his family were held as prisoners for a year. They were all reported shot on July 16, 1918, after Communists (bolsheviks) seized the government. Nicholas was born at Tsarskoye Selo (now Pushkin), the son of Alexander III.   W. KIRCHNER

See also RUSSIA (History).

NICHOLAS, SAINT (A.D. 300's), one of the most popular saints of the Christian church, is the patron saint of sailors, travelers, bakers, merchants, and especially children. Little is known about his life except that he was Bishop of Myra in Lycia, on the coast of Asia Minor. It is believed that he was born in Patara in Lycia. Some stories say that he made a pilgrimage as a boy to Egypt and Palestine, that he was imprisoned during Diocletian's persecution, and released under Constantine. Some legends say he attended the Council of Nicaea in 325. Many miracles were credited to him.

Much of Europe still observes December 6, the date of Saint Nicholas' death, as a special holiday. In Germany, Switzerland, The Netherlands, and Belgium, men in bishops' robes pose as Saint Nicholas. They visit children, examine them on their prayers, urge them to be good, and give them gifts. This custom probably originated in the legend that Saint Nicholas gave gold to each of three girls who did not have dowries and so could not get married.

The Dutch brought "the visit of Saint Nicholas" to America. The visit of Santa Claus came from this custom. The name Santa Claus comes from *Sinterklaas*, Dutch for Saint Nicholas.   WALTER J. BURGHARDT

See also BARI; CHRISTMAS (St. Nicholas); SANTA CLAUS; SAINT NICHOLAS, FEAST OF.

NICHOLLS STATE UNIVERSITY. See UNIVERSITIES AND COLLEGES (table).

NICHOLS COLLEGE. See UNIVERSITIES AND COLLEGES (table).

NICHOLSON, BEN (1894-   ), is an English artist noted for his abstract paintings, which feature geometric forms and pale colors. He also created *reliefs*, which combine the techniques of painting and sculpture. In these, Nicholson created three-dimensional abstract pictures by cutting flat boards down to various levels and painting them.

Saint Nicholas was a kind-hearted Christian bishop who lived in the A.D. 300's. He became the patron saint of many European countries.

Bettmann Archive

Nicholson was born near Uxbridge, in England. His father was Sir William Nicholson (1872-1949), also an artist. Ben Nicholson's early works were realistic decorative paintings of great charm. He turned to abstract painting in the 1930's. He was especially influenced by the work of painters Piet Mondrian and Joan Miró. In 1956, he won the first $10,000 Guggenheim International Award for his painting, *August 1956—Val D'Orcia*.   ALLEN S. WELLER

NICKEL (chemical symbol, Ni) is a white metallic chemical element often used in alloys. Its atomic number is 28 and its atomic weight is 58.71. Nickel is magnetic, takes a high polish, and does not tarnish easily or rust. It can be hammered into thin sheets or drawn into wires. One pound of pure nickel could be drawn into a wire 80 miles long. Axel Cronstedt, a Swedish scientist, discovered nickel in 1751.

Industrial Uses. Nickel is used in structural work and in electroplating chiefly because of its resistance to corrosion. Publishers often have printing plates electroplated with nickel to make them able to withstand hard use (see ELECTROPLATING). *Nickel peroxide*, a nickel compound, forms the active material of the positive electrode in the Edison storage battery. Nickel is also used in the nickel-cadmium storage battery (see BAT-

A Giant Nickel Ore Crusher, left, handles about 500 tons of ore an hour, reducing it to 8-inch chunks. The 185-ton machine operates in an underground mine in northern Ontario. Seven huge chains, foreground, regulate the flow of ore to the crusher.

The International Nickel Co., Inc.

LEADING NICKEL-PRODUCING COUNTRIES
Tons of nickel produced in 1967

Canada 247,000 tons	🛒🛒🛒🛒🛒🛒🛒🛒🛒🛒
Russia 105,000 tons	🛒🛒🛒🛒🛒
New Caledonia 67,900 tons	🛒🛒🛒🛒
Cuba 26,000 tons	🛒🛒
United States 14,600 tons	🛒

Source: *Minerals Yearbook, 1967,* U.S. Bureau of Mines

TERY [picture: Nickel-Cadmium Storage Battery]).

An important use for nickel is to promote certain chemical reactions by *catalysis* (see CATALYSIS). The nickel itself is not changed in the process and can be used repeatedly. Nickel is used as a catalyst in a process called *hydrogenation*. In this process, the nickel causes some organic compounds to combine with hydrogen to form new compounds. Hydrogenation is used in producing solid vegetable oils for use in cooking. See HYDROGENATION.

Nickel-Iron Alloys. Perhaps the largest use for nickel is as an additive to cast iron and steel. It improves the properties of these substances in many ways. It makes iron more *ductile* (easily formed) and increases its resistance to corrosion. Nickel also makes steel more resistant to impact. For this reason manufacturers frequently use steel alloyed with nickel to make armor plate and machine parts.

Invar, an alloy of nickel, iron, and other metals, is valued for meter scales and pendulum rods. It expands or contracts very little as its temperature changes.

Monel Metal is an alloy of copper and nickel used in sheet-metal work. See MONEL METAL.

Nickel Silver, also called *German silver*, is a nickel alloy used in tableware. See NICKEL SILVER.

Mining Nickel. The chief mineral ore of nickel is *pentlandite*, a mixture of sulfur, iron, and nickel. Other nickel ores include *millerite* and *niccolite*.

Sudbury District, in Ontario, supplies about half of the world's nickel. Ores obtained there contain pentlandite and iron and copper sulfides. Other nickel-producing areas include Russia, New Caledonia, Cuba, and the United States.　　　　　ALBERT J. PHILLIPS

NICKEL is the common name for a U.S. copper-nickel coin. It is worth five cents, and its official name is the *five-cent piece*. The current Jefferson nickel has been minted since 1938. It has a profile of Thomas Jefferson

The U.S. Nickel Shows Thomas Jefferson and Monticello.
Chase Manhattan Bank Money Museum

on the obverse side, and a picture of Monticello, Jefferson's home, on the reverse side. A nickel with an Indian head on the obverse and a buffalo on the reverse was minted from 1913 through 1938. Nickels made from 1883 through 1912 had a head of Liberty on the obverse and a *V* (Roman numeral five) on the reverse. The earliest U.S. five-cent pieces had a shield on the obverse and a *5* on the reverse. They were minted between 1866 and 1883.　　　　　BURTON H. HOBSON

NICKEL SILVER is an alloy of copper, nickel, and zinc. A common composition is 60 parts copper, 25 parts zinc, and 15 parts nickel. The alloy is also called *German silver* because it was first made in the town of Hildburghausen, Germany. It is a yellowish metal that is harder than silver. It tarnishes easily but takes a good polish.

Much of the silverware used today is made of nickel silver plated with real silver. It looks like solid silver when new, but the plate wears off with use.

The amounts of copper, zinc, and nickel are not always 60-25-15. Different proportions make the alloy better for some purposes. When it is used to make casts and candlesticks, a little lead is added. Iron or steel makes the alloy harder, whiter, and more brittle. Vinegar and strong salt solutions may combine with nickel silver to form poisons. Silver-plated tableware should not be used with these liquids, or with fruits, after the silver plate has worn away. See also ALLOY.　　　　WILLIAM W. MULLINS

NICKELODEON. See MOTION PICTURE (History).

NICKLAUS, *NIK lus,* **JACK WILLIAM** (1940-　　), of the United States, is one of the world's leading golfers. He became the first golfer to win all four of the world's major golf titles at least twice. He won the U.S. Open in 1962 and 1967, the British Open in 1966 and 1970, the Professional Golfers' Association (PGA) tournament in 1963 and 1971, and the Masters tournament in 1963, 1965, and 1966. Before becoming a professional late in 1961, Nicklaus won the U.S. Amateur title in 1959 and 1961. He was born in Columbus, Ohio.

NICKNAME. See NAME, PERSONAL (Nicknames).

NICOBAR ISLANDS, *NICK oh bahr,* are a group of 19 islands in the Bay of Bengal. They have an area of 635 square miles, and a population of 12,000. The islands, with the Andaman Islands, form a territory of India. For location, see INDIA (physical map).

People live on only 12 of the 19 islands. The thick forests and hot, wet climate make living conditions unpleasant. Most of the people on the islands trade in coconuts and copra.　　　　　ROBERT I. CRANE

NICODEMUS, *NICK oh DEE mus,* was a Pharisee and a member of the Sanhedrin, the Jewish court in Jerusalem. When Jesus Christ was tried before the Sanhedrin Nicodemus spoke in His behalf. He later helped care for and bury Christ's body. See PHARISEE; SANHEDRIN.

NICOLAITANS, *NICK oh LAY uh tunz,* members of an early religious sect, followed the doctrine of Balaam (see BALAAM). They believed that Christians could eat foods offered to idols, and could indulge in moral extremes. Their leader was Nicolas. Scholars doubt that he was the same Nicolas who was a deacon in Jerusalem.

NICOLAY, JOHN GEORGE (1832-1901), an American newspaperman, served as President Abraham Lincoln's private secretary from 1860 to 1865. With John Hay, he wrote *Abraham Lincoln: A History* (1890), a 10-volume biography. He also served as U.S. Consul in Paris from 1865 to 1869, and as Marshal of the Supreme Court of the United States from 1872 to 1887. He was born in Essingen, Bavaria, and came to the United States in 1838. He became editor of a Pittsfield, Ill., newspaper in 1854.　　　　　MERLE CURTI

NICOLET, *nick oh LAY* or *nee kuh leh,* **JEAN** (1598-1642), was an early French explorer in America. Historians believe he was the first European to enter Lake Michigan and to travel in the territory that is now the state of Wisconsin. Little was known of his explorations until the middle 1800's when an account of his western journey was found in the *Jesuit Relations*.

It is now believed that Nicolet made a voyage up through Lake Huron in a large canoe in 1634. He passed through the Straits of Mackinac and entered Lake Michigan. Nicolet's party crossed the lake to Green Bay on the west side. There they met a tribe of Winnebago Indians, with whom Nicolet made a peace treaty. They honored him as a son of the gods. Nicolet is believed to have gone a short way inland and then to have returned to the French outposts.

Hank Lefebvre

Jean Nicolet

Nicolet was born in Cherbourg, France, and came to America when he was 20 with explorer Samuel de Champlain. He drowned when his boat overturned on the St. Lawrence River in a storm. FRANKLIN L. FORD

NICOMACHEAN ETHICS. See ETHICS (Greek and Roman).

NICOSIA, NICK uh SEE uh (pop. 47,000; met. area 103,000; alt. 734 ft.), is the capital of Cyprus, an island in the Mediterranean Sea. It lies in the north-central part of the island, 150 miles northwest of Beirut, Lebanon. For location, see TURKEY (color map). The city serves as the business and administration center of the island. It is also a trade center in the Messaori Plain. This region produces wheat, wine, olive oil, almonds, and citrus fruit. FREDERICK G. MARCHAM

NICOTIANA. See FLOWERING TOBACCO.

NICOTINE, NICK oh teen or NICK oh tin (chemical formula $C_{10}H_{14}N_2$), is a colorless, oily, transparent vegetable chemical compound of the type called an *alkaloid*. It has a hot and bitter taste. It is found in small quantities in the leaves, roots, and seeds of the tobacco plant. It can also be made synthetically.

The quantity of nicotine in most tobaccos ranges from 2 to 7 per cent. Turkish tobacco has practically no nicotine. Good Havana tobacco contains little of it. Nicotine is most abundant in cheaper and domestic varieties. The amount of nicotine in the tobacco from which cigars, cigarettes, or pipe tobacco may be made is not the same as the amount in the finished product.

Nicotine is exceedingly poisonous. In a pure state, even a small quantity will cause vomiting, great weakness, rapid but weak pulse, and possibly collapse or even death. Tobacco varies in its effect. Nicotine harms some persons less than others. But physicians generally agree that use of tobacco in any form is not wise for young people. Overuse of tobacco may cause nausea, indigestion, and heart disturbances.

Nicotine is valuable as an insecticide. Physicians sometimes use nicotine compounds to treat tetanus and strychnine poisoning. A. K. REYNOLDS

See also TOBACCO (Effects of Using Tobacco).

NICOTINIC ACID. See VITAMIN (Vitamin B Complex).

NICTITATING MEMBRANE is a thin membrane under the eyelid that can be pulled over the eyeball. Birds and many reptiles have the membrane, but man does not have it.

NIDAROS, old name of Trondheim. See TRONDHEIM.

NIEBUHR, NEE boor, is the family name of two American brothers who became leading Protestant theologians.

Reinhold Niebuhr (1892-1971) won fame as a writer and teacher. He became dean of Union Theological Seminary in New York City in 1950 and served until 1960.

Niebuhr was ordained in 1915 and became pastor of an Evangelical church in Detroit, Mich. Detroit was growing into a vast, industrial city. Niebuhr defended labor and criticized such industrialists as Henry Ford. He became an active Socialist and a leader of the "social gospel" liberal Christians.

In 1928, he became an assistant professor of the philosophy of religion at Union Seminary. He was gradually disillusioned by Marxism, fascism, pacifism, and the "social gospel" theology. By 1939, he ranked as a leading anti-social gospel theologian. He worked on a theology that would retain Reformation values, especially those of Martin Luther, and that would apply to present-day social problems. He edited a small journal, *Christianity and Society.*

His writings include *Moral Man and Immoral Society* (1932), the two-volume *Nature and Destiny of Man* (1941 and 1943), *Christianity and Power Politics* (1940), and *Discerning the Signs of the Times* (1946).

Niebuhr was born in Wright City, Mo. He was graduated from Yale Divinity School in 1915.

H. Richard Niebuhr (1894-1962) was an authority on Christian ethics and the history of Christian thought. He was a professor at Yale Divinity School from 1931 until his death. His writings include *The Kingdom of God in America* (1937), *The Purpose of the Church and Its Ministry* (1956), and *Radical Monotheism and Western Culture* (1960). Helmut Richard Niebuhr was born in Wright City, Mo. L. J. TRINTERUD

NIELLO. See ENAMEL (Decorative Enameling).

NIELSEN, NEEL sun, **CARL AUGUST** (1865-1931), was a Danish composer. He is best known for six symphonies and a comic opera, *Maskarade* (1906). He also composed chamber and choral music, and concertos. Nielsen was conductor of the Royal Opera from 1908 to 1914, and became director of the Royal Conservatory in Copenhagen in 1915. He was born on the island of Fyn, near Odense. HOMER ULRICH

NIEMEYER, OSCAR (1907-), is a Brazilian architect. He is best known as the designer of the principal buildings of Brasília, the Brazilian capital (see BRASÍLIA). Niemeyer often uses decorative shapes for entire buildings, and in repetitious architectural elements. He has said that his designs are inspired by Brazilian climatic and social conditions, and the nation's colonial baroque art heritage.

Niemeyer was born in Rio de Janeiro. His early work was influenced by brief contact with the architect Le Corbusier. An example of this work is the Ministry of Education (1937-1943) in Rio de Janeiro. It is shaped like a concrete slab, with windows set deeply into the building to provide sun shades. In the early 1940's, Niemeyer served as chief architect for Pampulha, a new residential suburb near Belo Horizonte. For pictures of his work, see ARCHITECTURE (Today) and LATIN AMERICA (Arts). STANFORD ANDERSON

NIÉPCE, nyeps, **JOSEPH NICÉPHORE** (1765-1833), a French scientist, invented the first photographic technique, *heliography*. Niépce began experimenting in 1816. He succeeded in making a crude photograph of a courtyard in 1826. He sensitized a metal plate with bitumen and exposed it eight hours. This plate, the world's first photograph, is in the Gernsheim Collection in London. Niépce also produced photogravure plates from engravings.

In 1829, Niépce became the partner of L. J. M. Daguerre, who based his researches for his daguerreotype process on Niépce's earlier technique of heliography (see DAGUERRE, LOUIS J. M.). Niépce was born in Chalon-sur-Saône: BEAUMONT NEWHALL

See also PHOTOGRAPHY (History).

NIER, *near,* **ALFRED OTTO CARL** (1911-   ), an American physicist, won distinction for his development of a mass spectrograph and his use of it in nuclear research. He specialized in the study of *isotopes* (atoms of the same element with different atomic weights) and their accurate mass determination.

Nier separated a small amount of the two principal isotopes of uranium, U-235 and U-238, in 1940. This allowed physicist J. R. Dunning and his associates at Columbia University to prove that U-235 *fissions* (splits) when bombarded with slow neutrons. This discovery ranks as a milestone in the development of practical atomic energy. Nier also studied thermal diffusion, electronics, and the application of the mass spectrograph to chemistry, geology, and medicine.

Nier was born in St. Paul, Minn. He was graduated from the University of Minnesota. He became chairman of the physics department there in 1953.   RALPH E. LAPP

NIETZSCHE, *NEE chuh,* **FRIEDRICH** (1844-1900), was a German philosopher, poet, and classical scholar. Many philosophers, writers, and psychologists of the 1900's have been deeply influenced by him.

Nietzsche greatly admired classical Greek civilization. In his first book, *The Birth of Tragedy* (1872), he presented a revolutionary theory about the nature of Greek tragedy and civilization. He said they could best be understood as the results of a conflict between two basic human tendencies. The *Apollonian* tendency was a desire for clarity and order, represented by the Greek sun god, Apollo. The other, *Dionysian,* tendency was a wild, irrational drive toward disorder, represented by the god of wine, Dionysus.

The Palace of Justice was one of many buildings designed by Oscar Niemeyer in the 1950's for Brasília, the capital of Brazil.
Pictorial Parade

Nietzsche criticized religion. In *Thus Spake Zarathustra* (1883-1885), he proclaimed, "God is dead." He meant that religion, in his time, had lost its meaningfulness and power over people. Thus, he argued, religion could no longer serve as the foundation for moral values. He believed that the time had come for man to critically examine his traditional values and their origins.

Nietzsche tried to begin this "re-evaluation of all values" in such works as *Beyond Good and Evil* (1886) and *Genealogy of Morals* (1887). He said that the warriors who originally dominated society had defined their own strength and nobility as "good," and the weakness of the common people as "bad." Later, when the priests and common people came to dominate society, they redefined their own weakness and humility as "good" and the strength and cruelty of the warriors whom they feared as "evil." Nietzsche criticized this second set of values because it was based on fear and resentment, and he associated these values with the Judeo-Christian tradition. He repeatedly criticized Christianity, particularly in *The Antichrist* (1895).

Nietzsche boasted that he was one of the few philosophers who was also a psychologist. Nietzsche's major psychological theory is that all human behavior is basically motivated by the "will to power." He did not mean that men wanted only to overpower each other physically. He thought that men also wanted to gain power and control over their own unruly passions. He thought that the self control exhibited by ascetics and artists was a higher form of power than the physical bullying of the weak by the strong. Nietzsche's ideal, the *overman* or *superman,* is the passionate man who learns to control his passions and use them in a creative manner.

Nietzsche said that one should accept and love one's own life so completely that he would choose to relive it, with its joys and sufferings, an infinite number of times.

Nietzsche was born in Saxony, the son and grandson of Protestant ministers. He studied at the universities of Bonn and Leipzig. When he was only 24, he became professor of classics at the University of Basel in Switzerland. There he became the close friend of the composer Richard Wagner, but the friendship ended in hostility. In 1870, Nietzsche became a Swiss citizen. After teaching at the university for only 10 years, he retired because of poor health. He then devoted all his time and energy to his writing. In 1889, Nietzsche suffered a mental breakdown from which he never recovered.

Nietzsche has unjustly suffered notoriety as a racist, anti-Semite, and forerunner of Nazism. This is largely due to the editing of his writings and misrepresentation of his ideas by Nazi propagandists and by his racist sister Elizabeth.   IVAN SOLL

NIFLHEIM, *NIHV'l haym,* in Norse mythology, was the land of mist and cold. Odin cast Hel, goddess of death, into Niflheim to rule over the "nine unlighted worlds" of the dead. All who died of sickness and old age went to Niflheim. It included the spring, Hvergelmin, from which ice streams flowed; the root of the world-tree that supported the universe; and Uller, god of winter. A bridge called Bifrost stretched from Niflheim to the world of men and gods.   CHARLOTTE E. GOODFELLOW

See also HEL; ODIN.

NIGER

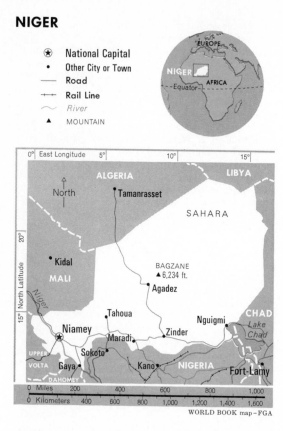

Legend:
- ⊛ National Capital
- • Other City or Town
- — Road
- ┼┼ Rail Line
- 〜 River
- ▲ MOUNTAIN

Globe inset: EUROPE, NIGER, AFRICA, Equator

Map labels: 0° East Longitude, 5°, 10°, 15°, ALGERIA, LIBYA, North, Tamanrasset, SAHARA, 20°, Kidal, BAGZANE ▲6,234 ft., MALI, North Latitude, Agadez, 15°, Tahoua, Nguigmi, CHAD, Niger, Niamey, Zinder, Lake Chad, Maradi, UPPER VOLTA, Sokoto, Gaya, Kano, NIGERIA, Fort-Lamy, DAHOMEY

Scale: 0 Miles 200 400 600 800 1,000 / 0 Kilometers 400 600 800 1,000 1,200 1,400 1,600

WORLD BOOK map–FGA

NIGER, *NYE jur,* is a thinly populated country in western Africa. It sprawls over an area greater than the combined areas of California, Louisiana, and Texas. But Niger has only about as many people as the state of Louisiana.

Much of Niger is desert or semidesert. Most persons in the north are *nomads* (wanderers) who move from place to place in search of water and pasture for their livestock. The areas in the extreme southwest around the Niger River and along the southern border are the only places with enough water for farming. Farmers in the south raise millet, peanuts, and sorghum.

Niger is completely surrounded by other countries and has no outlet to the sea. Algeria and Libya border it on the north. Chad lies to the east and Nigeria and Dahomey to the south. Upper Volta borders Niger on the southwest, and Mali lies to the west.

Niger was once a territory in French West Africa. It became independent as the REPUBLIC OF NIGER in 1960. Its name in French, the official language, is RÉPUBLIQUE DU NIGER. Niamey (pop. 40,172) is the capital and most important town.

Government. Niger is a republic, with a president as head of state. The people elect the president for a five-

---

The contributor of this article, R. J. Harrison Church, is Professor of Geography at the University of London and author of Africa and the Islands *and* West Africa.

---

year term. He is president of the *Council of Ministers* (Cabinet), and selects the ministers from the members of the National Assembly. The people elect the 60 members of the National Assembly for five-year terms.

People of Niger belong to four main groups: (1) the Fulani, (2) the Tuareg, (3) the Djerma, and (4) the Hausa. These peoples live in widely separated areas, have little in common, and speak different languages. French is the official language of Niger, but few persons speak it.

There are about 414,000 Fulani in Niger. They live in the northern and central part of the country. About 250,000 Tuareg also live in the north. The Fulani and Tuareg are Moslems, but the Tuareg women do not wear veils, as most Moslem women do.

The Fulani and Tuareg are herdsmen who travel from place to place with their livestock. The cattle are not raised as a source of income, but as the chief source of food. The Fulani and Tuareg live almost entirely on animal products. Their diet includes blood (which they draw regularly from healthy animals), meat, milk, and milk products. Men who own many animals have a high standing among their neighbors. Fulani and Tuareg sell animals only when they need money for paying taxes or for special occasions such as a birth, death, or marriage.

About 545,000 Djerma, a branch of the Songhai peoples of western Africa, live in the southwestern part of Niger. Most Djerma raise such crops as rice, cotton, millet, and peanuts on small farms near the Niger River.

About 1,125,000 Hausa tribesmen live in Niger. Most of them are farmers in the south. Their main food crops include beans, manioc, millet, peanuts, peas, and sorghum. Many other Hausa tribesmen live in Nigeria.

About 8 of every 10 persons in Niger are Moslems. Most of the other people practice *fetish* religions, in which they worship objects such as stones or images (see FETISH). Many of the older people of Niger cannot read or write. The country suffers from a shortage of schools and teachers, partly because Christian mission schools were not encouraged in this Moslem country. Only about 6 of every 10 school-age children go to school.

─────────── **FACTS IN BRIEF** ───────────

Capital: Niamey.
Official Language: French.
Official Name: Republic of Niger.
Form of Government: Republic.
Head of State: President.
Area: 489,191 square miles. *Greatest Distances*—(east-west) 1,100 miles; (north-south) 825 miles.
Population: No census figures available. *Estimated 1971 Population*—3,946,000; density, 8 persons to the square mile. *Estimated 1976 Population*—4,508,000.
Chief Products: *Agriculture*—beans, chillies, cotton, henna, hides and skins, livestock (cattle, goats, sheep), manioc, millet, okra, onions, peanuts, peas, rice, sorghum. *Mining*—natron, salt, tin.
Flag: The flag has horizontal stripes of orange (for the Sahara), white (for purity), and green (for agriculture). An orange circle (for the sun) is in the center. See FLAG (color picture: Flags of Africa).
National Holidays: Independence Day, August 3, and Republic Day, December 18.
Money: *Basic Unit*—franc. See MONEY (table: Values).

Land. Most parts of Niger lie less than 1,500 feet above sea level. The only extensive areas higher than 1,500 feet lie in the north-central part of the country. The Sahara covers northeastern and east-central Niger. The southern part of the country is a grassy plain. The Niger River flows through the southwestern corner of the country, and farmers plant crops there when the river floods. They also practice some irrigation near the river. Part of shallow Lake Chad lies in the southeast corner of Niger (see LAKE CHAD).

Niger has a hot, dry climate. The hottest season around Niamey in the southwest extends from March to late June when temperatures rise to about 110° F. The rainy season, from late June to mid-September, is the coolest season. Temperatures average about 94° F. during the day and about 73° F. at night. They reach about 102° F. in October and November, and range between 94° and 99° F. from December to February.

At Agadez, in central Niger, May is generally the hottest month. Temperatures average up to 112° F. Short rains occur in July and August, and January is the coolest month.

Average annual rainfall in Niger is 7 inches. Only about one-tenth of the country receives more than 21 inches of rainfall a year. About half of the country receives less than 4 inches, causing true desert conditions.

Economy. The economic development of Niger has been more difficult than that of many other African countries. Most of the people are herdsmen or farmers, but less than one-fourth of the country can be used for farming. Pasture for livestock is scarce. Niger's remote inland position makes the transportation of exports difficult and expensive. The country has few manufacturing and mining industries.

Most farmers produce just enough food for their families. Some sell peanuts, cotton, and millet, however, and some animals and hides are exported to Nigeria. Mining companies produce a little tin in the north-central part of the country, and local residents dig salt and the mineral natron near Lake Chad. A rich deposit of uranium lies near Agadez.

Niger has no railroads, but it has 3,500 miles of roads and trails. Niamey has an international airport, and there are smaller airports at Agadez, Maradi, Tahoua,

and Zinder. A government radio station broadcasts from Niamey.

The most direct route for eastern Niger's overseas trade runs from Zinder or Maradi about 900 miles through Nigeria to the Nigerian port of Lagos. A 660-mile route from Niamey to the port of Cotonou in Dahomey is used for most of western Niger's trade. Niger is a member of the Council of the Entente, which promotes regional economic cooperation. Other members are Dahomey, Ivory Coast, Togo, and Upper Volta.

History. Areas of what is now Niger were part of the Kanem, Mali, and Songhai empires. These empires were powerful states that began during the Middle Ages. See KANEM; MALI EMPIRE; SONGHAI EMPIRE.

European explorers arrived in what is now Niger during the 1700's. The French began to occupy the area in 1897 and completed the occupation in 1900. They created the colony of Upper Senegal and Niger in French West Africa in 1904. In 1922, Niger became a separate colony in French West Africa.

Niger's first national assembly met in 1946. Also in 1946, representatives from Niger entered the French parliament in Paris, and the Grand Council of French West Africa in Dakar. Niger became an independent state on Aug. 3, 1960. Hamani Diori was elected president of Niger in November, 1960. Niger retains close links with France.   R. J. HARRISON CHURCH

See also FRENCH WEST AFRICA; NIAMEY; NIGER RIVER.

NIGER RIVER is the third largest river in Africa. The Nile and Congo rivers are larger.

The Niger rises in West Africa, only 150 miles from the Atlantic Ocean. But the river travels a winding course of about 2,600 miles before it reaches the Gulf of Guinea. The Niger River drains an area of 584,000 square miles—almost equal to the area of Alaska. The middle Niger is navigable for about 1,000 miles. But rapids interrupt its course for about 300 miles between the Republic of Mali and Nigeria. The lower Niger is navigable from Jebba to Onitsha, Nigeria. The delta begins at Onitsha, about 150 miles from the Atlantic. It is Africa's largest river delta.   KENNETH ROBINSON

See also AFRICA (physical map); RIVER (chart: Longest Rivers).

Marc Riboud, Magnum

A Young Hausa Girl gathers wood for the family fire near the town of Tahoua in southwestern Niger. The Hausa tribe is one of the most important groups in Niger. Most Hausa tribesmen make their living by farming in southern Niger and the northern parts of Nigeria.

NIGERIA

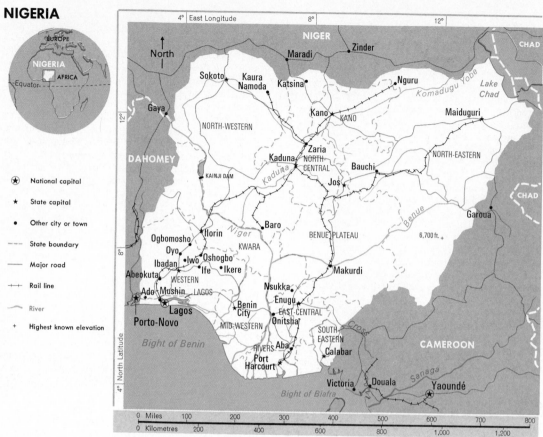

Legend:
- ⊛ National capital
- ★ State capital
- • Other city or town
- --- State boundary
- — Major road
- +++ Rail line
- ∿ River
- + Highest known elevation

WORLD BOOK map

NIGERIA, *ny JIHR ee ah,* has more people—about 68,580,000—than any other African country. It ranks among the world's 10 largest nations in population. Nigeria is also one of the most densely populated countries in Africa. It has an average of 192 persons per square mile.

Nigeria, a land of great contrasts, lies in western Africa. It extends from the rainy, swampy coast on the Gulf of Guinea near the equator to the edges of the hot, dry Sahara in the north. Nigeria has bustling commercial cities, but it also has large areas of tropical forests and *savannas* (grasslands). Nigeria is mainly a farming country and produces cacao, cotton, palm kernels and oil, and peanuts. The nation also has great artistic traditions. Ancient Nigerian art influenced some of the finest artists of the 1900's, including Pablo Picasso.

The official name of the country is the FEDERAL REPUBLIC OF NIGERIA. Nigeria was a British colony and protectorate until it gained independence in 1960. In 1963, it became a republic with a central government

The contributor of this article, J. F. Ade Ajayi, is Professor of History at the University of Ibadan in Nigeria and the author of Milestones in Nigerian History.

and four regional governments. In 1967, the federal government created 12 states to replace the regions. Lagos is the capital and largest city of Nigeria and the nation's main port and business center.

Government

The federal government of Nigeria has sole power in such activities as defense, foreign affairs, and trade. It shares power with the state governments in several fields, including economic development, education, and health. The state governments have sole power in all matters not assigned to the federal government.

Since January, 1966, Nigeria's military leaders have ruled the country. The commander in chief of the armed forces serves as head of state and chairman of the supreme military council. The leaders of the army, navy, air force, and police, plus the military governors of the 12 states, make up this council and establish policies. A federal executive council, consisting of 12 civilian commissioners appointed by the state governors, runs the government. The two councils rule by decree. The military governor of each state has a cabinet of civilian commissioners to assist him.

Before the military government took power, a president served as head of state. A federal legislature, made up of a House of Representatives and a Senate, passed Nigeria's laws. The people elected the members

Capital: Lagos.

Official Language: English.

Form of Government: Republic.

Area: 356,669 sq. mi. *Greatest Distances*—(north-south) 665 miles; (east-west) 825 miles. *Coastline*—475 miles.

Population: *1963 Census*—55,670,046. *Estimated 1972 Population*—68,580,000; density, 192 persons to the square mile. *Estimated 1977 Population*—77,214,000.

Chief Products: *Agriculture*—bananas, cacao, cassava, corn, cotton, livestock (cattle, goats, sheep), millet, palm kernels and oil, peanuts, rice, rubber, yams. *Mining*—columbite, petroleum, tin. *Manufacturing and Processing*—beer, canned fruit and soft drinks, cement, cigarettes, palm oil, peanut oil and cakes, plastics, plywood, shoes, textiles. *Forestry*—tropical woods.

Flag: The flag has three vertical stripes (green, white, and green). See FLAG (picture: Flags of Africa).

Money: *Basic Unit*—pound. See MONEY (table: Values).

Almasy

Lagos, Nigeria's Bustling Capital, lies partly on an island. It is the country's business, industrial, and shipping center.

of the House of Representatives, and regional legislatures chose the senators. The leader of the majority party in the House served as prime minister.

People

Most Nigerians are Negroes. They belong to about 250 *ethnic* (cultural) groups, each of which speaks its own language. English, the official language, is taught in most schools.

The three largest ethnic groups in Nigeria are the Hausa-Fulani, the Ibo, and the Yoruba. The Hausa-Fulani live in the northwestern part of the country. Most Ibo live in the southeast. The Yoruba live in the southwest, often called Yorubaland. Other ethnic groups include the Edo, Efik, Ibibio, Idoma, Ijo, Itsekiri, Kanuri, Tiv, and Uhobo. Only about 27,000 non-Africans live in Nigeria.

About half the Nigerians are Moslems, and a fourth are Christians. The rest of the people practice traditional religions.

Nigeria has eight cities with populations of more than 200,000. In order of size, they are Lagos, Ibadan, Ogbomosho, Kano, Oshogbo, Ilorin, Abeokuta, and Port Harcourt. Most of these cities have modern glass and steel dwellings and office buildings. In the towns and villages, many of the people live in houses with mud walls. At one time, most of these houses had mud floors and thatched roofs. Today, many of them have cement floors and corrugated iron or asbestos roofs.

Many of the older people of Nigeria cannot read or write. But the country has developed its educational system greatly since World War II ended in 1945. More than three-fifths of the children now attend school. Christian churches and missionary societies run many of the schools in southern Nigeria. Northern Nigeria also has schools run by Christian missionaries, but most children in the north attend local government or Moslem schools. Nigeria has five universities.

Land

Nigeria covers 356,669 square miles. The Niger River flows south through the country and enters the Gulf of Guinea through a huge delta. The delta has great swamps and mangrove forests. The Niger's biggest tribu-

On the Way to Market, cattle from northern Nigeria pass through a village in a cacao-farming area near the town of Enugu.

Marc and Evelyn Bernheim, Rapho-Guillumette

tary, the Benue River, enters Nigeria from Cameroon.

The Yorubaland Plateau lies south and west of the Niger. Most of this plateau is between 1,000 and 1,600 feet above sea level, but in some areas it reaches 2,000 feet. The Bauchi Plateau lies north of the Niger and Benue rivers. It slopes gently to the north from about 4,000 feet to 2,000 feet. Hills near the town of Jos rise more than 5,000 feet. In the far north, the country slopes toward Lake Chad and merges with the Sahara (see LAKE CHAD; SAHARA). The lower slopes of the Cameroon mountains along the country's eastern border form the other highland area of Nigeria.

Swamps and mangrove forests form a belt from 10 to 16 miles wide along the coast. A region of tropical forests 40 to 100 miles wide lies behind the coastal strip. The forests merge into woodlands and savannas in central Nigeria. Grasslands cover most of northern Nigeria.

Nigeria has a tropical climate. Northern Nigeria is drier and hotter than the south. On the coast, the annual average temperature is about 80° F. In the north, temperatures may rise above 100° F. The wet season lasts from about May to October. Areas in the extreme north have an average annual rainfall of about 20 inches. The rainfall increases toward the south and averages more than 150 inches a year on the coast.

Economy

Nigeria is rich in natural resources. But many of these resources have been developed only since the early 1960's. In 1962, the government began a six-year national development plan to increase agricultural production and develop industry and education.

Most Nigerians farm the land. Their food crops include bananas, cassava, corn, millet, rice, and yams. They export cacao, cotton, hides and skins, palm kernels and oil, peanuts, and rubber. Nigeria is one of the world's leading producers of cacao, palm kernels, and peanuts. Farmers in the forest areas of the southwest raise cacao. Oil palms grow throughout the forests. Farmers in the far north raise peanuts. They also cultivate cotton and raise cattle, goats, and sheep. Nigeria exports large quantities of lumber and plywood.

Nigeria ranks as the world's leading producer of columbite, a mineral ore, and stands sixth in tin production. Other minerals and metals of Nigeria include coal, gold, iron, lead, limestone, and zinc. Important petroleum reserves were found in the southeast in the 1950's. By 1970, Nigeria had become an important oil producer. In 1969, a new dam at Kainji on the Niger River began producing power for industry.

Nigeria has about 2,000 miles of railroads, more than 40,000 miles of roads, and about 4,000 miles of navigable waterways. Nigerian Airways flights link many of the country's towns. This airline also flies to other countries. Lagos and Kano have international airports. Lagos and Port Harcourt are the leading ports. Enugu, Ibadan, Kaduna, and Lagos have radio and television stations.

History

Early Times. Archaeologists have found stone tools, rock paintings, and other evidence of ancient civili-

zations in Nigeria. The most interesting discoveries include pottery figures and stone and tin ornaments from Nok, a civilization that flourished in central Nigeria from about 500 B.C. to A.D. 200 (see NOK).

During the A.D. 700's, a civilization grew up in Kanem in what is now Chad. The ruler of Kanem moved to Bornu in northeastern Nigeria in the 1300's, and the kingdom continued to exist there until the mid-1800's. During the 1000's, Bornu's rulers converted to Islam, the religion of the Moslems. The kingdom traded widely with countries in Africa, Asia, and Europe. See KANEM.

By the 1300's, the Hausa people had developed a number of states in the area west of Bornu. All of these states shared the same language and similar cultures. Many of the Hausa later converted to Islam. During the 1300's, Fulani herders from the west began to move into the Hausa region in search of grazing land. Some settled down and became teachers, scribes, and judges in Hausa cities. See FULANI.

A great Yoruba civilization grew up around Ife in southwestern Nigeria between the 800's and 1100's (see IFE). Yorubas from Ife established states in different parts of Yorubaland. One of these states, Oyo, built an empire that included Dahomey. A Yoruba became king of Benin. In the 1400's, Benin gained control over much of southern Nigeria. The kingdom reached a high degree of civilization. Its brass, bronze, and ivory sculptures are world famous. See BENIN; SCULPTURE (picture: A Royal Group).

The Coming of the Europeans. In the late 1400's, the Portuguese became the first Europeans to visit Nigeria. The slave trade began soon after the Europeans arrived. British, Dutch, and other European traders bought slaves from African chiefs along the coast. The slave trade continued until the 1800's.

In 1804, Usman dan Fodio, a Fulani and a Moslem teacher, declared war on the Hausa states. By 1811, he had gained control of almost all northern Nigeria except Bornu and made it one Moslem empire called the Sokoto Caliphate. About the same time, Great Britain, which had outlawed the slave trade in 1807, captured large numbers of slaves along the coast and freed them in Sierra Leone. The freed slaves helped British missionaries and traders move into Nigeria.

In 1851, Britain seized Lagos. British influence then spread to Yorubaland, the Niger River delta and valley, the Sokoto Caliphate, and Bornu. The British government assumed direct control of northern Nigeria in 1900 and southern Nigeria in 1906. In 1914, it merged those two territories into the colony and protectorate of Nigeria.

Independence. Under British rule, southern Nigeria advanced more rapidly than northern Nigeria in economic development and education. But political power passed to the north because of its larger population. After World War II ended in 1945, Nigeria moved toward independence. In 1946, Britain set up regional councils in the north, east, and west to advise a central legislative council in Lagos. In 1954, the councils gained more power and Nigeria became a federation. Sir Abubakar Tafawa Balewa, leader of the Northern People's Congress, became prime minister of the federation. Balewa remained as prime minister after the 1959 federal election. He led Nigeria to independence in 1960.

In 1961, the United Nations held a referendum in western Cameroon, a UN trust territory. The people in the north voted to join Nigeria, and those in the south voted to join the Republic of Cameroon (see CAMEROON).

Different ethnic groups and regions competed for power in Nigeria's central government during the early 1960's. The people of southern Nigeria, especially the Ibo, resented the power of the Hausa people of the north. Many southerners protested the results of a census taken in 1962 to determine the distribution of seats in the House of Representatives. Another census, taken in 1963, also caused widespread anger. The federal election of 1964 and a regional election in 1965 led to fighting between the police and citizens who charged that those elections were dishonest.

Civil War. In January, 1966, southern army officers overthrew the government. They murdered Balewa and other leaders. General Johnson Aguiyi-Ironsi, an Ibo and commander of the army, restored order. He suspended the constitution and appointed military officers to run the government.

In May, 1966, Aguiyi-Ironsi abolished the federal republic and made Nigeria a republic with a strong central government. He chose Ibo as his closest advisers. Many Nigerians feared that the Ibo would take over the country. Fighting broke out between the Hausa and the Ibo.

In July, 1966, northern army officers rebelled and killed Aguiyi-Ironsi. Colonel Yakubu Gowon, army chief of staff, became head of state in August. He restored the federal republic, but the Ibo of the Eastern Region refused to accept him as head of state. In May, 1967, Gowon assumed greater powers and divided Nigeria into 12 states. The Eastern Region then declared itself an independent republic named *Biafra*.

Civil war broke out between Biafra and the rest of Nigeria in June, 1967. The fighting lasted until January, 1970, when Biafra surrendered and accepted Gowon as head of state. During the early 1970's, Nigerian leaders worked to repair war damage and to heal the bitterness caused by the fighting.   J. F. ADE AJAYI

See also AFRICA (pictures); CHOCOLATE (graph); IBADAN; LAGOS; VEGETABLE (graph).

NIGHT. See DAY.

NIGHT BLINDNESS. See BLINDNESS (Kinds).

NIGHT-BLOOMING CEREUS. See CACTUS (picture); FLOWER (color picture).

NIGHT HERON is a medium-sized heron which remains quiet during the day, and begins its activities at sundown. There are several species. They live in most parts of the world except the far northern regions. In America, the black-crowned night heron lives in colonies from Manitoba and New Brunswick, Canada, southward through South America. It is about 2 feet long, with a black head and back, grayish tail and wings, and white throat, breast, and forehead. In the spring, three white feathers hang from its crown. It usually nests in colonies and builds its bulky nest in a treetop, in a bush, in reeds, or on the ground. The female lays from four to six pale blue eggs.

Scientific Classification. The night heron is in the heron family, *Ardeidae.* The black-crowned night heron is genus *Nycticorax,* species *N. nycticorax.*   GEORGE J. WALLACE

NIGHT LETTER. See TELEGRAPH (Kinds of Telegrams).

NIGHT SCHOOL provides instruction after regular school hours. Most night schools teach people who work during the day.

Many night school students want to complete the requirements for a high school diploma or a college degree. Others wish to increase their knowledge or skill in a certain field. The first night school in North America opened in Nieuw Amsterdam (New York City) in 1661.   THOMAS J. McLERNON

NIGHTHAWK, also called *bullbat* and *mosquito hawk,* is a bird that looks much like the whippoorwill, to which it is related. It is not a hawk. The nighthawk is about 10 inches long, and has mixed black, white, and buff plumage, and a white throat patch. It has a white bar on each wing. Soon after sunset the nighthawk flies high to look for insects. The nighthawk breeds throughout most of the United States and Canada. In winter, it is found in South America. The female lays two speckled eggs on the bare ground or on gravel roofs of buildings.

Scientific Classification. The nighthawk belongs to the nightjar family, *Caprimulgidae.* The eastern nighthawk is genus *Chordeiles,* species *C. minor.*   HERBERT FRIEDMANN

See also BIRD (color picture: Color Protects Them).

NIGHTINGALE is a small bird of the thrush family. It lives in western and central Europe. The nightingale is famed for its beautiful voice, which has a sad quality.

The nightingale has a plain appearance, and shy habits. It is about 6 inches long, with russet-brown upper parts, changing to reddish on the rump and tail. The breast and underparts are mostly white. The bird is most at home deep in the woods and hedges, especially along streams. It lives mainly on insects. It hops rapidly along the ground for a few moments and then stands motionless as if listening, as the robin does.

Nightingales have only one brood of young in a season. They build their nests near the ground in thickets or hedges. The female lays from four to six olive-brown eggs. The birds migrate to Africa for the winter.

Scientific Classification. The nightingale belongs to the thrush family, *Turdidae.* It is genus *Luscinia,* species *L. megarhynchos.*   GEORGE E. HUDSON

See also BIRD (color picture: Birds of Other Lands).

Fish and Wildlife Service

The Black-Crowned Night Heron is sometimes called the *quabird,* or the *squawk,* because of the croaklike notes it utters.

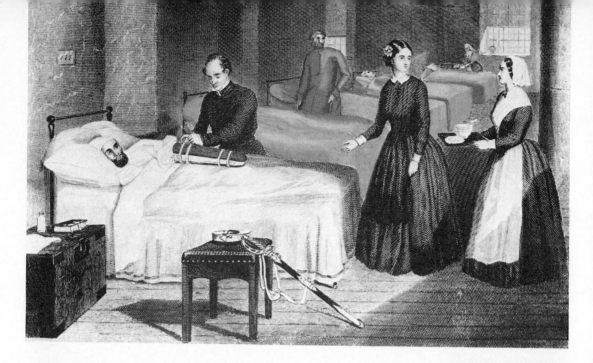

NIGHTINGALE, FLORENCE

NIGHTINGALE, FLORENCE (1820-1910), was the founder of the nursing profession as we know it today, and one of the greatest women of England's Victorian Age. British soldiers, wounded in the Crimean War, called her the *lady with the lamp* when she walked the halls of their hospital at night.

To all the world, the light that Florence Nightingale carried has come to mean care for the sick, concern for the welfare of the ordinary soldier, and freedom for women to choose their own work. She was called a "saintly woman." But her success was also due to her brilliant mind and her ability to organize and administer the details of hospital work.

Early Years. Florence Nightingale was named for Florence, Italy, where she was born on May 12, 1820, while her wealthy British parents were living abroad. Her childhood was spent at the two family estates in England, with her mother, father, and sister Parthenope. Her mother filled their home with guests. Mrs. Nightingale taught her daughters the social graces and how to manage a large household well. William Nightingale was his daughters' only teacher, and a strict one. From him, they learned Greek, Latin, mathematics, and philosophy.

Florence liked books better than parties. She was even more devoted to helping others. An example of her first handwriting is a copy of a medical prescription written in a book measuring only an inch square. She enjoyed caring for visiting babies and looking after the sick farmers on her father's estates. She nursed her dolls in their imagined illnesses, and saved the life of an old shepherd's dog when its broken leg had condemned it to death. As Florence grew older, she took over the management of the large Nightingale households.

When she was 16, Florence Nightingale made a difficult personal decision. She decided that she must devote herself to service for others, but she did not yet know how she could do this. Both Florence and her sister were presented to Queen Victoria when they en-

Florence Nightingale, *right,* introduced sanitary methods of nursing in wartime. She attended to the nursing needs of British soldiers wounded in the Crimean War, *above center.* It marked the first time that soldiers wounded while fighting away from home received good hospital care.

Culver; Brown Bros.

tered British society. Travels in Europe followed.

But Florence had not forgotten her purpose in life. Slowly, she began to realize what her work must be. She turned down suitors, declined many parties, and spent much of her time studying health and reforms for the poor and suffering. This was unheard-of behavior for a wealthy girl. Mrs. Nightingale could not accept her daughter's wish to do hospital work.

Her family's opposition prevented Florence from working in a hospital, for at that time such places were dirty and disreputable. Nurses were often drunken women, unfit to care for the sick. Florence took her first step toward independence when she went to study in a hospital in Paris. She then entered nursing training at the Institute of Protestant Deaconesses in Kaiserswerth, Germany. At 33, she became superintendent of a women's hospital in London.

Service in Crimea. Great Britain and France went to war with Russia in the Crimea in 1854. The British people were angry when they heard that their troops had been sent to battle without enough supplies, to die under terrible conditions. The Secretary of War asked Florence Nightingale to take charge of nursing. She sailed for the Crimea with 38 nurses.

This little band, in ugly gray uniforms, stepped ashore in the mud of Scutari, across from Constantinople (now

Istanbul), in late 1854. They faced a job which seemed impossible. Five hundred wounded troops had just arrived, from the Battle of Balaclava, where the charge of the Light Brigade (made famous later in a poem by Alfred, Lord Tennyson) had taken place. Two-thirds of the British cavalrymen had been killed or wounded there in 25 minutes.

The hospital was an old Turkish barracks, huge, dirty, and unfurnished. The wounded lay on floors, bleeding and uncared-for. How much could 38 nurses do? Medical supplies, food, and bedding were not arriving. There were no cots, mattresses, or bandages. Miss Nightingale found a few men well enough to clean the place, and she put them to work at once. She set up a nursing schedule for care, kitchen work, and diets. At night, her lamp burned as she walked the four miles of corridors and wrote countless letters demanding supplies from British military officials.

At first, doctors and officials resented the "dictatorship of a woman," as they regarded it, for Florence Nightingale stood for no delays or slipshod ways. Then they came over to her side. Many people told her that the British soldiers were no better than animals and that she was "spoiling the brutes." But she believed that every human being's life was valuable. When the hospital was running better, she started classes to teach convalescent soldiers to read and write.

While on a visit to the front lines, Miss Nightingale caught Crimean fever, and nearly died. By that time, she had become famous, and even Queen Victoria kept an anxious watch on her recovery.

After she returned to the Scutari hospital, Miss Nightingale was urged to go to England to get her strength back. She replied firmly, "I can stand out the war with any man." Her success at Scutari became so widely recognized that she was given charge of all the army hospitals in the Crimea. By the end of the war, she had saved countless lives, and brought about worldwide reforms in hospital administration and nursing.

Return to England. England greeted her arrival in 1856 with big celebrations. Instead of attending them, Miss Nightingale went quietly home to her family, and then moved to London. She used a gift of $150,000 from her grateful public to found the Nightingale Home for Nurses at Saint Thomas Hospital in London. She became a world authority on scientific care of the sick. The United States asked her advice for setting up military hospitals during the Civil War.

The strain of overwork and her Crimean illness had injured her health. Miss Nightingale became a semi-invalid and seldom left her rooms. Instead, the world came to her. Ministers, heads of government, authors, reformers, and politicians came to ask her advice. By correspondence and by constant reading, she made studies of conditions in the British Army in India and in hospitals. Health conditions among the people of India especially concerned her. Her 800-page report to the War Department brought about the formation of the Royal Commission on the Health of the British Army in 1858. She received many public honors, and was the first woman to be given the British Order of Merit.   MAY McNEER

NIGHTJAR. See GOATSUCKER.

NIGHTMARE is a frightening dream or dreamlike experience that awakens a sleeper. After awakening from most nightmares, the sleeper can recall the dream that caused his fright. But in another kind of nightmare, sometimes called an *incubus attack*, a deeply sleeping person feels a pressure as if a great weight were on his chest. He wakes up in terror and does not remember much about any dream.

Nightmares may occur in times of severe tension. They have been experienced by many soldiers in combat and by persons withdrawing from alcohol or certain other drugs. All children between the ages of 2 and 6 probably have some nightmares. Some nightmares seem entirely real to a youngster after awakening. Most adults do not have nightmares. Frequent nightmares among older children or adults may indicate a physical or emotional problem.   ERNEST HARTMANN

See also DREAM.

NIGHTSHADE is the common name of a family of plants that have the scientific name *Solanaceae*. The nightshade family includes herbs, shrubs, and tropical trees. The plants grow most abundantly in warm regions.

Among the more than 2,000 members of this family are such useful plants as the potato, tomato, ground cherry, capsicum (red pepper), and eggplant. The family also includes poisonous plants like belladonna (deadly nightshade), Jimson weed (stramonium), and bittersweet (woody nightshade). People in the United States once thought tomatoes were poisonous. The tobacco plant and the petunia also are members of the nightshade family.   GEORGE H. M. LAWRENCE

Related Articles in WORLD BOOK include:

Apple of Sodom	Capsicum	Petunia	Tobacco
Belladonna	Eggplant	Potato	Tomato
Bittersweet	Jimson Weed	Solanum	

SOME MEMBERS OF THE NIGHTSHADE FAMILY

POTATO

JIMSON WEED

NIGHTSHADE

TOMATO

J. Horace McFarland Co.

PETUNIA

NIHILISM, *NI uh liz'm,* was a movement of ideas in Russia during the middle of the 1800's. The name comes from the Latin word *nihil,* which means *nothing.* It first appeared in Ivan Turgenev's novel *Fathers and Sons.* One character in the book says, "A nihilist is a man who does not bow down before any authority; who does not take any principle on faith, whatever reverence that principle may be enshrined in."

The idea of rejecting all authority greatly influenced the revolutionary movement in Russia. People in other countries believed that the nihilists were responsible for acts of terrorism against the Russian government. *Nihilism* and *revolution* came to have the same meaning when applied to Russia.

In Western Europe, nihilism meant a denial of objective truths and values. Friedrich Nietzsche called himself a nihilist because he attacked accepted ideas. Most Western nihilists find that they cannot remain wholly negative. They tend to replace old values with new ones. Pure nihilism seldom exists.   JAMES COLLINS

See also NIETZSCHE, FRIEDRICH; TURGENEV, IVAN S.

NIIHAU. See HAWAII (The Islands).

NIJINSKY, *nih ZHIN ski,* **VASLAV** (1890-1950), was the most famous male dancer of his time. He was short, with thick thighs and sloping shoulders. Yet he acted out his roles so completely that his appearance seemed to change from one role to another.

Nijinsky had such amazing body control that his dancing looked spontaneous and effortless. One legend tells of a dramatic leap he made through an open win-

Vaslav Nijinsky created the choreography and also danced the part of the faun in *The Afternoon of a Faun* in 1912.

Bettmann Archive

dow as his exit in *Le Spectre de la Rose.* He rose slowly, soared high across the window ledge, appeared to stop in midair, and was still at the height of his jump as he disappeared.

Nijinsky was born in Kiev, Russia. He first studied dancing at the St. Petersburg Imperial School of Ballet at the age of 10. He traveled with Sergei Diaghilev's ballet company to Paris in 1909, and enjoyed great international success until 1913. He married a dancer in the company in 1913, and Diaghilev dismissed him. Nijinsky rejoined the company in the United States in 1916, dancing as brilliantly as ever. But in 1917, mental illness ended his career.   P. W. MANCHESTER

NIKE. See GUIDED MISSILE.

NIKE, TEMPLE OF. See ACROPOLIS.

NIKE OF SAMOTHRACE. See WINGED VICTORY.

NIKISCH, *NEE kish,* **ARTHUR** (1855-1922), was a Hungarian conductor, violinist, and pianist. He conducted the Leipzig Opera in Germany from 1879 to 1889, and then led the Boston Symphony Orchestra for four years. He conducted the Royal Hungarian Opera and the Philharmonic concerts in Budapest from 1893 to 1895. Nikisch became conductor of the Leipzig Gewandhaus Orchestra in 1895, and of the Berlin Philharmonic Orchestra in 1897. He held both positions until his death. He toured the United States in 1912.

Nikisch was born in Szent Miklós, Hungary, and performed as a pianist when only 8 years old. He began to study at the Vienna Conservatory at 11.   DAVID EWEN

NIKOLAYEV, ANDRIAN G. See ASTRONAUT (table: Cosmonauts; pictures).

NILE, BATTLE OF THE, took place between English and French fleets off the Egyptian coast on Aug. 1, 1798. Rear Admiral Horatio Nelson's British fleet defeated the French fleet, commanded by Admiral Francois-Paul Brueys. The battle re-established British supremacy in the Mediterranean Sea, and contributed to the failure of Napoleon's campaign in Egypt.

Napoleon's army had landed in Egypt early in July, 1798. It captured Alexandria, routed the Mameluke army near the pyramids outside Cairo, and then took Cairo. Nelson, who had been searching in the eastern Mediterranean for the French fleet, sailed for Egypt after he learned of Napoleon's landing. He found the French fleet anchored by the island of Aboukir in the mouth of the Nile River. Nelson's fleet sank several of the 13 French ships, and damaged and captured most of the others. Brueys and several hundred French sailors were killed. Napoleon's army soon ran out of supplies, and he returned to France. Nelson was made Baron Nelson of the Nile and given a pension.   VERNON F. SNOW

See also MAMELUKE; NAPOLEON I (Egypt Invaded).

NILE RIVER is the longest river in the world. An early civilization was born along the banks of this river in Egypt. As early as 5000 B.C. farmers were planting crops in the rich soil of the Nile Delta, one of the most fertile farming regions in the world. Every year during the summer, the Nile overflows its banks, flooding the lowlands. Alluvial soils that have resulted from this annual flooding rank among the richest in the world.

The Nile flows 4,160 miles. It is the only river in the world that rises near the equator and flows into the middle latitudes. It irrigates about 6,300,000 acres of land in Egypt, about 2,800,000 acres in Sudan, and small areas in Ethiopia and Uganda.

Course of the Nile. Ptolemy, the famous geographer who lived in Egypt around A.D. 150, said that the Nile rose south of the equator, near a range of mountains called *Mountains of the Moon.* Centuries later, he was proved nearly correct. The Mountains of the Moon, now called the Ruwenzori, rise between Lakes Albert and Edward. Water from the lakes flows into the Nile. Lake Victoria is often called the source of the Nile. But the Luvironza River in Burundi is the river's most remote headstream. The Luvironza flows into the Ruvuvu River, one of the headstreams of the Kagera, which drains into Lake Victoria.

The Nile flows generally northward from its headwaters. If the river were placed in the United States, it would reach almost from the West Coast to the East Coast. Many streams join the Nile just northeast of the Congo River. Here it is called the White Nile. When it reaches Khartoum, it is joined by the Blue Nile from Ethiopia. The Nile becomes narrower as it flows north-

The World's Longest River, the Nile, winds 4,160 miles through northeastern Africa. If the Nile flowed across the United States, it would extend from the California-Oregon border near the Pacific Ocean to the West Virginia-Virginia border about 250 miles from the Atlantic Ocean.

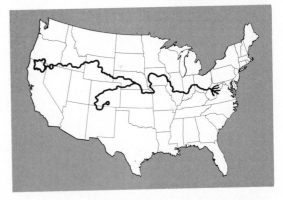

The Mighty Nile spills over Ripon and Owen Falls as it leaves Lake Victoria, *below,* one of its sources. The Nile rises in the lake regions of Burundi, Congo (Kinshasa), Rwanda, Tanzania, and Uganda. It flows northward through the Sudan and Egypt, and empties into the Mediterranean Sea.

Cowling, Ewing Galloway

ward through a desert region. The river is less than 100 yards wide just south of Cairo. The Nile has no branches for its last 1,600 miles. The delta begins at Cairo.

The region most benefited by the yearly Nile flood lies north of Aswan, where two dams have been built. At Aswan the floodwaters usually rise about 26 feet. They rise about 23 feet at Cairo. These floodwaters are caused by heavy rains that fall in the upper valley of the Blue Nile, in Ethiopia's highlands. *Cataracts* (rapids) make navigation difficult for small craft between Khartoum and Aswan.

The Nile Valley. The Nile Delta region is as thickly populated as many large cities. Every bit of the fertile soil is farmed throughout the year. During the long rainless summer, dams and canals provide irrigation. Winter crops include wheat, barley, beans, and vegetables. The chief summer crops include cotton, sugar cane, and corn. Cotton is the most important crop financially.   GEORGE H. T. KIMBLE

See also ASWAN DAM; DELTA; EGYPT (The Land; color picture); LAKE TANA; RIVER (chart).

NILGAI. See ANTELOPE (Kinds of Antelope).

NILOTE. See AFRICA (People).

NILSSON, BIRGIT (1918-   ), is a Swedish dramatic soprano. She became noted for the power and clarity of her voice. Critics generally regard Miss Nilsson as the finest singer of heroic roles in the operas of Richard Wagner. Kirsten Flagstad of Norway formerly held this distinction. Miss Nilsson's performances as the Wagnerian heroines Isolde and Brünnhilde set the standard for her time. She also achieved fame as Aïda, Elektra, Lady Macbeth, Salome, and Tosca. But many critics rate her performance in the title role of Giacomo Puccini's opera *Turandot* as her outstanding achievement.

Birgit Nilsson was born in Västra Karup, near Malmö, Sweden. She began her career with the Stockholm Opera in 1947. She made a successful debut at the Metropolitan Opera in 1959 as Isolde. MAX DE SCHAUENSEE

NIMBA MOUNTAINS. See LIBERIA (The Land; map).

NIMBUS. See CLOUD.

NIMBUS is another name for *halo* in painting. It was developed in Christian art in the 400's. According to Greek myths, a radiant nimbus surrounded the heads of gods and goddesses when they came to earth.

NIMBUS WEATHER SATELLITE. See SPACE TRAVEL (Artificial Satellites).

NÎMES, *neem,* or NISMES (pop. 123,292; met. area 124,854; alt. 203 ft.), is an industrial city of southern France. It is the center of a wine- and brandy-producing district. Its factories produce silks, cotton goods, and carpets. Nîmes was one of the most magnificent cities of the Roman Empire. For location, see FRANCE (political map). See also FRANCE (picture: The Amphitheater).

NIMITZ, CHESTER WILLIAM (1885-1966), served as commander in chief of the United States Pacific Fleet during World War II. He took command on Dec. 31, 1941, about three weeks after the fleet had been almost completely disabled in the Japanese attack on Pearl Harbor.

Admiral Nimitz painstakingly rebuilt U.S. strength in the Pacific. As commander of the Pacific Fleet and the Pacific Ocean Areas, Admiral Nimitz directed the Navy and the Marine Corps forces. The admiral's calm assurance of final victory did much to restore the U.S. Navy's faith in its own power and ability.

In the early months of the war, Admiral Nimitz refused to attack before U.S. forces were fully ready, in spite of angry questions from congressmen and newspapers. He waited until he had enough ships, supplies, and men to assure victory. Nimitz developed much of the strategy of *island hopping* (seizing only key islands from which attacks on other key islands could be launched). This strategy saved lives and time. Nimitz led the fleet through many victories until it drove the Japanese back to Japan. He was promoted to fleet admiral in 1944. Nimitz signed for the United States at the Japanese surrender ceremonies in Tokyo Bay.

After the war, Nimitz became chief of naval operations. He left active duty in 1947, and then became special assistant to the secretary of the Navy. Nimitz headed the United Nations commission that mediated the dispute over Kashmir in 1949. Nimitz was born in Fredericksburg, Tex., and graduated from the U.S. Naval Academy in 1905.   DONALD W. MITCHELL

See also WORLD WAR II (The War in Asia).

NIMROD is a Bible character mentioned in Genesis 10: 8-10 as a descendant of Noah. He lived some centuries after the Flood, when people were wandering over the earth. He is said to have been a grandson of Ham. He was a mighty ruler and builder of cities. His kingdom included Babylon, Erech, and Accad in Mesopotamia. He is supposed to have founded Nineveh in Assyria. He became famous as a hunter, and today we speak of a skillful hunter as a *Nimrod.*   JOHN BRIGHT

NIÑA. See CARAVEL; COLUMBUS, CHRISTOPHER (First Voyage to America; picture: The Niña).

NINE-POWER TREATY. At the Washington Conference in 1921 and 1922, Belgium, China, France, Great Britain, Italy, Japan, The Netherlands, Portugal, and the United States signed a treaty to respect the independence and territorial integrity of China, and to maintain the Open Door there. But these powers failed to provide guarantees to keep the pledges. DWIGHT E. LEE

NINEPINS. See BOWLING (Other Kinds; History).

NINETEENTH AMENDMENT. See UNITED STATES CONSTITUTION (Amendment 19); WOMAN SUFFRAGE.

NINETY-FIVE THESES. See LUTHER, MARTIN.

NINEVEH was the last capital of the ancient Assyrian Empire. It stood on the east bank of the Tigris River, about 230 miles north of present-day Baghdad. The site of Nineveh was settled as early as 5000 B.C. In 612 B.C., a combined army of Babylonians and Medes captured and destroyed the city. In the 1800's, archaeologists unearthed the site and discovered the great royal library of King Ashurbanipal. This library included business documents, letters, and many examples of Babylonian and Sumerian literature. See also ASSYRIA; NIMROD.   JACOB J. FINKELSTEIN

NINGPO (pop. 237,500), also called YIN-HSIEN, is an industrial center and port in the Chinese province of Chekiang. For location, see CHINA (political map). In 1842, Ningpo became one of five Chinese "treaty ports" in which Great Britain won special trading rights (see CHINA [The "Unequal Treaties"]). Today, the city produces heavy industrial equipment. Nearby iron mines help supply the raw materials for its factories.   RICHARD H. SOLOMON

NIO. See IOS.

NIOBE, *NYE oh be,* was the daughter of King Tantalus in Greek mythology (see TANTALUS). She married Amphion, the king of Thebes, and had seven strong, talented sons and seven beautiful daughters. But her pride brought disaster. She boasted that she deserved more worship than the goddess Leto (Latona), mother of Apollo and Artemis (Diana), because she had so many children (see APOLLO; DIANA). This angered Leto. She sent Apollo and Artemis to slay the children of Niobe with their arrows. Niobe's grief was so great that she could not stop weeping. The gods changed her into a stone cliff with a waterfall.   PHILIP W. HARSH

NIOBIUM, or COLUMBIUM, one of the chemical elements, is a shiny-white, soft metal. It is used to toughen and harden steel. Niobium allows atomic particles called *neutrons* to pass through it without interference. For this reason, it may someday be used in atomic reactors. Niobium occurs as niobium pentoxide (Nb_2O_5) in a mineral called columbite. It is always found with a similar element called tantalum.

Niobium (symbol Nb) has the atomic number 41 and the atomic weight 92.906. It melts at 2468° C. ($\pm10°$ C.) and boils at 4927° C. It was discovered in 1801 by Charles Hatchett of England.   ALAN DAVISON

See also ELEMENT, CHEMICAL (tables).

NIOBRARA RIVER. See NEBRASKA (Rivers and Lakes).

NIPKOW, PAUL G. See TELEVISION (Beginnings).

NIPPON. See JAPAN.

NIRENBERG, MARSHALL W. See NOBEL PRIZES (table [1968]).

NIRVANA. See BUDDHISM; TRANSMIGRATION OF THE SOUL.

NISEI, *nee say,* is the Japanese name for the children of Japanese families who have migrated to other countries. The people who migrate are called *Issei.* Their children born in the new country are *Nisei.* The children of Nisei are called *Sansei.* The largest Japanese-American groups live in Hawaii and California. The Nisei and their Sansei children have rapidly adopted American ways of life.   FELIX M. KEESING

See also HAWAII (World War II); WORLD WAR II (Internment of Aliens).

NIT. See LOUSE.

NITER. See SALTPETER.

NITERÓI, *NEE tuh ROY* (pop. 287,000; alt. 80 ft.), is the capital of the state of Rio de Janeiro in Brazil. It lies on Guanabara Bay, facing the city of Rio de Janeiro (see BRAZIL [political map]). Many people who work in Rio de Janeiro live in Niterói.

NITRATE is any one of a number of chemical compounds. They always contain the nitrate radical (NO^-_3) and some other element, such as sodium or calcium. Some nitrates are salts of nitric acid. Others are formed by microorganisms that act on organic nitrogen compounds. They have many important uses in industry, medicine, and agriculture. Some heart remedies come from nitrates. Nitrates are also used in photographic films, fireworks, and explosives. The nitrates of sodium and calcium add nitrogen directly to the soil, and make valuable fertilizers. The large natural deposits of sodium nitrate found in Chile were long the chief source of nitrogen fertilizer. Synthetic nitrates are now being produced.   K. L. KAUFMAN

See also CHILE (Mining); FERTILIZER (Sources).

NITRATE OF SILVER. See SILVER NITRATE.

NITRIC ACID is a strong inorganic acid that has many industrial uses. Its principal use is for the production of fertilizers, drugs, and explosives. Large quantities of nitric acid are produced during thunderstorms. It is also a by-product of nuclear explosions set off in the atmosphere. Nitric acid was one of the first acids known to man. Many alchemists of the Middle Ages used it in their experiments.

Nitric acid is such a powerful oxidizing agent that it dissolves many metals. But it does not attack two precious metals, gold and platinum. A drop of nitric acid on a piece of jewelry tells whether it is made of genuine gold or platinum. These two metals can be dissolved by *aqua regia,* a mixture of nitric acid and hydrochloric acid (see AQUA REGIA).

Nitric acid is used to manufacture ammonium nitrate, NH_4NO_3, an ingredient of many fertilizers, and to make explosives. The chemical industry uses nitric acid to prepare such organic compounds as dyes, drugs, and nitrate salts. Nitric acid reacts with toluene in the presence of sulfuric acid to form trinitrotoluene, better known as TNT. Cellulose is treated with nitric acid to make cellulose nitrate, which is used for guncotton and other explosives.

Commercially, most nitric acid is produced by oxidizing ammonia using a platinum catalyst. Ammonia and air are passed through heated platinum gauze. The gases react to form nitrogen oxide and water. Upon cooling, this gaseous mixture reacts further to form nitric acid. This method is called the *Ostwald process,* after Wilhelm Ostwald, the German chemist who developed it. Nitric acid is also produced by heating saltpeter with sulfuric acid. In this process, nitric acid is recovered by distillation.

Nitric acid is a colorless liquid with a suffocating odor. It develops a yellow color if kept in bottles that are not tightly stoppered. This is due to nitrogen dioxide gas, NO_2, that results from decomposition of the acid. Nitric acid is highly caustic and corrosive and can cause painful burns on the skin. Its chemical formula is HNO_3. The metal salts of nitric acid, called *nitrates,* are soluble in water.   S. YOUNG TYREE, JR.

See also ACID; OSTWALD, WILHELM; NITRATE.

NITRIFYING BACTERIA are bacteria that provide the necessary nitrates for green plants. The bacteria enrich soil by converting nitrogen from the air into usable nitrogen compounds that plants must have. Some nitrifying bacteria live in soil, and others live in plants. For example, nitrifying bacteria live in the nodes found on the roots of such legumes as clover and alfalfa.

See also NITROGEN CYCLE (picture: Nitrogen Cycle).

NITRITES are compounds of the nitrite radical (NO^-_2) and some other element. Inorganic nitrites are stable and soluble. Organic nitrites are made from alcohol and aromatic substances, such as toluene. They are unstable when in the presence of acid, but they are preserved satisfactorily in neutral or mildly alkaline solutions. Nitrites are used in medicine for heart ailments. Sodium nitrite is important in making dyes. Nitrites are also used for explosives and to produce other chemicals.   K. L. KAUFMAN

NITROCELLULOSE, also called cellulose nitrate. See CELLULOID; GUNCOTTON.

NITROGEN

NITROGEN, *NI troh jen* (chemical symbol, N), is the chief gas in the air. It forms about 75 per cent of the air by weight, and about 79 per cent by volume. Almost all the rest of the air is oxygen. Daniel Rutherford, a Scottish physician, discovered nitrogen in 1772.

Nitrogen is a chemical element, one of the nonmetals. Its atomic number is 7. Its atomic weight is 14.0067. The gas is colorless, tasteless, and odorless. Pure nitrogen is a little lighter than air, and fourteen times as heavy as hydrogen, the lightest known element. Nitrogen is not very soluble in water and does not combine easily with oxygen or any other element. The nitrogen in the air serves to dilute the oxygen, so combustion in air is slower than in pure oxygen.

Nitrogen is one of the substances necessary for life in plants and animals. The element is found in protoplasm, the living material in plant and animal tissues. It is also part of all protein foods.

Man and animals must get their nitrogen by eating plant or animal food that contains compounds of the element. But any nitrogen in the animal food really comes from plants. When animals breathe, they draw nitrogen and oxygen into their lungs. Only the oxygen unites with the blood. Some nitrogen dissolves in the blood, but most of it is breathed out again.

Most plants get nitrogen from soluble nitrogen compounds in the soil. Nitrogen in the soil may come from the atmosphere, with the help of lightning and rain. The action of electricity in the air causes oxygen and nitrogen to form oxides of nitrogen. Then the rain carries these oxides into the soil. Mineral compounds of nitrogen are also often present in soil, and certain bacteria form nitrogen compounds from nitrogen of the air.

As it takes different forms in air, soil, plants, and animals, nitrogen goes through a circle of changes called the *nitrogen cycle.* See NITROGEN CYCLE.

Nitrogen in Agriculture. If the soil is in use, the rain does not supply enough nitrogen to keep it rich. Thus, farmers have to renew the nitrogen in their fields by rotating their crops, or by using nitrogenous fertilizers.

In crop rotation, plants which consume nitrogen are followed by plants which restore it. Wheat and corn take nitrogen from the soil, while clover and other legumes return nitrogen. The legumes include plants such as peas, beans, or alfalfa. Their roots bear small growths, or nodules, which contain bacteria that take nitrogen from the air and change the nitrogen into compounds suitable for plant food. Legumes are also planted to furnish green manure. The crop is plowed under, and it decays and adds nitrogen to the soil.

Other nitrogenous fertilizers include both natural and manufactured kinds. Guano is the body waste material of sea birds used for fertilizer. Garbage, sewage, fish scraps, packing-house refuse, and ordinary barnyard manure are all sources of nitrogen compounds. More important than these fertilizers are sodium and calcium nitrates, which are salts of nitric acid. Sodium nitrate is commonly called Chile saltpeter. Large natural beds of this material in Chile were once the world's chief source of nitrogenous fertilizer. There are now synthetic methods for manufacturing this and other nitrogen compounds from the free nitrogen of the air. The various synthetic processes for changing nitrogen of the air into

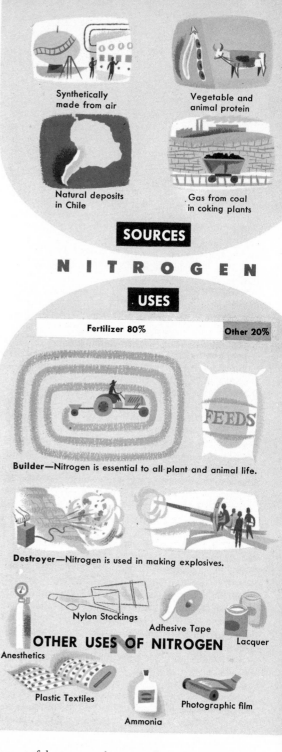

Synthetically made from air

Vegetable and animal protein

Natural deposits in Chile

Gas from coal in coking plants

SOURCES

NITROGEN

USES

| Fertilizer 80% | Other 20% |

Builder—Nitrogen is essential to all plant and animal life.

Destroyer—Nitrogen is used in making explosives.

OTHER USES OF NITROGEN

Nylon Stockings

Adhesive Tape

Lacquer

Anesthetics

Plastic Textiles

Ammonia

Photographic film

more useful compounds are called the *fixation* of nitrogen.

Other Important Compounds. Borazon, an artificially produced crystal with the hardness of a diamond, is a compound of nitrogen and boron. Ammonia is a compound of nitrogen and hydrogen. Ammonia is used to make nitric acid, an ingredient of TNT and other high-powered explosives. This important acid is a compound of the elements nitrogen, hydrogen, and oxygen.

There are five oxides of nitrogen. Nitrous oxide is the "laughing gas" which is used as an anesthetic. Nitric oxide is used to carry oxygen in the manufacture of sulfuric acid. Nitrogen trioxide, nitrogen peroxide, and nitrogen pentoxide are oxidizing agents.

Liquid nitrogen is used as a cooling agent. It is also used as a pulverizing agent.

Related Articles in WORLD BOOK include:

Air (Gases)	Gas	Nitroglycerin
Ammonia	Liquid Air	Nitrous Oxide
Borazon	Nitrate	Protein
Fertilizer	Nitric Acid	Saltpeter

NITROGEN CYCLE. Nitrogen, like other elements used by plants and animals, passes through a cycle of chemical changes, and eventually returns to its original form.

Although nitrogen makes up almost eight-tenths of the air, ordinary green plants cannot use it. They absorb nitrogen from the soil as nitrates (NO_3 compounds). The nitrates are used in making proteins and other substances. If an animal eats the plant, some of the proteins and other nitrogenous compounds are changed into animal proteins and similar compounds. The animal then excretes nitrogenous wastes. Decay bacteria act upon these wastes and upon the dead bodies of plants and animals. They produce ammonia (NH_3) as

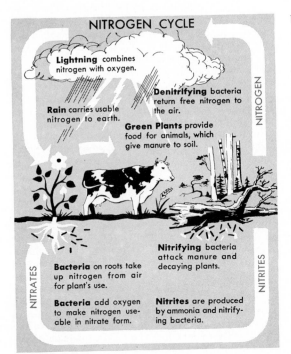

NITROGEN CYCLE

NITROGEN

Lightning combines nitrogen with oxygen.

Rain carries usable nitrogen to earth.

Denitrifying bacteria return free nitrogen to the air.

Green Plants provide food for animals, which give manure to soil.

Nitrifying bacteria attack manure and decaying plants.

NITRATES

Bacteria on roots take up nitrogen from air for plant's use.

Bacteria add oxygen to make nitrogen useable in nitrate form.

NITRITES

Nitrites are produced by ammonia and nitrifying bacteria.

a waste product. Ammonium (NH_4) compounds are used by nitrifying bacteria, which release nitrites (NO_2 compounds) as waste products. Another group of bacteria change the nitrites to nitrates, which again can be used by green plants.   ARTHUR CRONQUIST

See also LEGUME; NITROGEN.

NITROGLYCERIN, *NY troh GLISS ur in*, is a powerful explosive. Its chemical formula is $C_3H_5(ONO_2)_3$. It is

the principal explosive ingredient of dynamite. Pure nitroglycerin is a heavy, oily liquid that is as clear as water. But the commercial product is usually straw-colored. When nitroglycerin explodes, it expands to form gases that take up more than 3,000 times as much space as the liquid. The explosion of nitroglycerin is about three times as powerful as that of an equal amount of gunpowder, and the explosion speed is 25 times as fast as that of gunpowder.

Chemists make nitroglycerin by slowly adding glycerin to concentrated nitric and sulfuric acids. The nitroglycerin forms a layer on top of the acids. This layer is drawn off and washed, first with water, and then with a sodium carbonate solution.

Ascanio Sobrero, an Italian chemist, discovered nitroglycerin in 1846. For many years, it was not used widely because it could not be depended on. In 1864, Alfred Nobel, a Swedish chemist, obtained a patent on a detonating cap made of mercury fulminate, which proved ideal for exploding nitroglycerin. In 1867, he invented dynamite, which provided a safe and convenient means for the transportation and use of nitroglycerin. Nitroglycerin quickly became the most widely used explosive.

Nitroglycerin is an ingredient of many smokeless powders, such as cordite and ballistite. It is seldom used alone as an explosive, except for blasting in oil wells.

Doctors use nitroglycerin to treat certain heart and blood-circulation diseases.   JULIUS ROTH

See also DYNAMITE; EXPLOSIVE; GLYCERIN (Uses).

NITROUS OXIDE, *NY trus AHK side*, is a gas used as an *anesthetic* because it deadens pain. Nitrous oxide is commonly called "laughing gas," although people do not laugh when under its influence. When a person inhales nitrous oxide it causes loss of the sensation of pain. If a person inhales enough, he may lose consciousness. But the effect does not last long. Nitrous oxide is used widely in dental and minor surgical procedures, because it acts quickly and because the patient recovers quickly.

Nitrous oxide is a relatively weak anesthetic, and must be used in high concentrations to be effective. The gas is usually mixed with pure oxygen. A mixture of air and nitrous oxide may not provide enough oxygen, because air is only 20 per cent oxygen. The body cannot use the oxygen found in the nitrous oxide compound itself.

Nitrous oxide is a colorless gas that has a sweetish odor and taste. Its chemical formula is N_2O. It does not burn, but wood will burn in an atmosphere of pure nitrous oxide. The gas was first prepared in the 1770's by English chemist Joseph Priestley.   SOLOMON GARB

See also ANESTHESIA.

NIUE ISLAND, *nee OOH ay*, or SAVAGE ISLAND, is a coral island in the South Pacific. It belongs to New Zealand. The island covers about 100 square miles and has a population of about 5,000. Niue exports copra and bananas. Alofi is the island's chief town.

NIX was the name of a water sprite in German folklore. The nixes were little people with golden hair and green teeth, and they lived in lakes and rivers. Nixes were fond of music and dancing, and sometimes invited humans to their feasts. They were said to appear before anyone died of drowning. See also FAIRY; NEREID.

RICHARD M. NIXON

KENNEDY
35th President
1961—1963

JOHNSON
36th President
1963—1969

NIXON, RICHARD MILHOUS (1913-), climaxed one of the most extraordinary political comebacks in U.S. history when he was elected President. Only a few years before, Nixon's political career appeared to have ended when he lost two major elections in a row.

In 1960, while serving as Vice-President under President Dwight D. Eisenhower, Nixon ran for the presidency and lost to John F. Kennedy. In 1962, Nixon was beaten when he ran for governor of California, his home state at that time. Following this defeat, most political experts agreed that Nixon had lost his voter appeal. One television network even presented a program called "The Political Obituary of Richard Nixon."

But in 1968, Nixon showed that he was politically very much alive. He won several primary elections, and again became the Republican candidate for President. This time, Nixon defeated Vice-President Hubert H. Humphrey, his Democratic opponent, and former Governor George C. Wallace of Alabama, the candidate of the American Independent Party.

Nixon was the 12th former Vice-President who became President. He was the first of this group who did not succeed the President under whom he had served. Nixon became Vice-President at the age of 40, and was the second youngest man to hold that office. John C. Breckinridge was 36 when he became Vice-President under James Buchanan in 1857. Before Nixon was elected Vice-President, he was elected twice to the U.S. House of Representatives and once to the U.S. Senate.

When Nixon took office as President, the United States faced two main problems—Vietnam and racial unrest in U.S. cities. Americans were bitterly divided over the nation's role in Vietnam. At home, millions of Negroes were demanding long-promised equality in education, jobs, and housing. Many whites felt that Negroes were pushing too hard for social and economic gains.

In politics, Nixon won fame as a tough, forceful campaigner. But friends knew him as a painfully sensitive man. Nixon felt especially hurt by what he considered unfair criticism. He believed his personal success story fulfilled the American dream.

Early Life

Boyhood. Richard Milhous Nixon was born on Jan. 9, 1913, in Yorba Linda, Calif., a village 30 miles southeast of Los Angeles. He was the second of the five sons of Francis Anthony Nixon and Hannah Milhous Nixon. As a young man, Nixon's father had moved from Ohio to southern California. There he met and married Hannah Milhous, who had come from Indiana with her parents and a group of other Quakers. After his marriage, Francis Nixon gave up his Methodist faith and became a Quaker. At one time or another he worked as a streetcar conductor, a motorman, a carpenter, a day laborer, and a farmer.

When Richard was 9 years old, the family moved to nearby Whittier. There the elder Nixon opened a combination grocery store and gasoline station. One of the President's four brothers, Harold (1909-1932), died of tuberculosis and another, Arthur (1918-1925), of meningitis. His other brothers are Donald (1914-) and Edward (1930-).

At the age of about 10, Richard began working part time as a bean picker. As he grew older, he helped in his father's store. During his teens, he held many other jobs, working as handyman in a packing house, janitor at a swimming pool, and barker at an amusement park. While in college, Nixon served as bookkeeper and as manager of the vegetable department of the store.

Nixon spent much of his early life at the East Whittier Friends Meeting House. He attended Quaker services four times on Sunday and several times during the week. While in high school, Richard played the organ at the meeting house and taught Sunday school.

Education. Nixon attended elementary schools in Yorba Linda, Whittier, and nearby Fullerton. At Whittier High School, history and civics were his favorite subjects. He played football and starred in debating. At the age of 17, Nixon entered Whittier College, a Quaker institution. He won several debating awards, and became president of the student body.

Nixon graduated from Whittier in 1934 and won a scholarship from the Duke University School of Law in Durham, N.C. Walter F. Dexter, then president of Whittier College, wrote in a letter of recommendation for Nixon: "I believe he will become one of America's important, if not great, leaders." At Duke, Nixon was elected president of the student law association. He also won election to the Order of the Coif, the national law fraternity for honor students. Nixon ranked third in the 1937 graduating class of 44 students.

Lawyer. The Great Depression still gripped the United States when Nixon left Duke. There were few jobs. Nixon tried unsuccessfully to join the Federal

Earl Mazo, the contributor of this article, is a White House correspondent for Reader's Digest *and the author of* Richard Nixon: A Political and Personal Portrait.

The White House

Bureau of Investigation and then a law firm in New York City. He finally returned home and joined a Whittier law firm, in which he became a partner. Nixon and several investors later formed a company to make and market frozen orange juice, but the company went bankrupt in 18 months.

At the age of 26, Nixon became the youngest member of the Whittier College Board of Trustees. There he served with Mrs. Herbert Hoover, wife of the former President. He also taught a law course at Whittier.

Nixon's Family. Shortly after returning to Whittier from the East, Nixon met Thelma Patricia (Pat) Ryan

─────── **IMPORTANT DATES IN NIXON'S LIFE** ───────

1913 (January 9) Born in Yorba Linda, Calif.
1934 Graduated from Whittier College.
1940 (June 21) Married Thelma Patricia (Pat) Ryan.
1942-1946 Served in the U.S. Navy during World War II.
1946 Elected to the U.S. House of Representatives.
1948 Re-elected to the House.
1950 Elected to the U.S. Senate.
1952 Elected Vice-President of the United States.
1956 Re-elected Vice-President.
1960 Defeated for President by John F. Kennedy.
1962 Defeated for governor of California by Governor Edmund G. (Pat) Brown.
1968 Elected President of the United States.

(March 16, 1913-   ). She had been born in a mining camp at Ely, Nev. When Pat was a baby, her parents moved to a farm in California. They died before Pat finished high school, but she put herself through the University of Southern California. Pat won high scholastic honors though working part time in a department store.

When Nixon met Pat, she was teaching commercial subjects at Whittier High School. Friends introduced them during tryouts for a community theater play. They were married on June 21, 1940. The Nixons have two daughters. Patricia (Tricia) was born on Feb. 21, 1946, and Julie on July 5, 1948. Julie was married to David Eisenhower, grandson of former President Dwight D. Eisenhower, on December 22, 1968, in New York City. Tricia was married to Edward Ridley Finch Cox in the White House Rose Garden on June 12, 1971. Tricia became the eighth daughter of a President to be married at the White House.

Naval Officer. A movement among the Whittier faculty and alumni to choose Nixon as president of the school was halted by World War II. In January, 1942, while awaiting assignment by the Navy, he took a job in the tire rationing section of the Office of Price Administration in Washington, D.C. Eight months later, Nixon was called to active duty as a lieutenant junior grade. He served in a naval air transport unit in the

Wide World

Wide World

Nixon's Birthplace was this small frame house in Yorba Linda, Calif. In the family picture, Nixon and two of his four brothers, Harold, *left*, and Donald, *center*, are shown with their parents. Richard went to work part time as a bean picker when he was about 10 years old.

Pacific, and was promoted to lieutenant commander before the war ended in 1945.

Career in Congress

Nixon entered politics by invitation. Since 1936, the voters of his home congressional district had elected a Democrat, Jerry Voorhis, to the U.S. House of Representatives. Republican leaders searched for a "new face" to oppose Voorhis in the 1946 election. They turned to Walter F. Dexter, state superintendent of education and former president of Whittier College. Dexter declined, but suggested Nixon. Nixon, then awaiting discharge from the Navy, agreed to run.

Professional politicians gave Nixon little chance of defeating Voorhis, a veteran campaigner. At first, Voorhis ignored his relatively unknown opponent. Then he agreed to a series of public debates, and the campaign became a tough, hard-hitting race. Nixon's skill in debating helped him win the election.

U.S. Representative. In the House of Representatives, Nixon was proudest of his work on a committee that laid the groundwork for the Marshall Plan and other foreign aid programs (see FOREIGN AID). Nixon helped write the Taft-Hartley Act, which set up controls over labor unions. He also became a member of the House Committee on Un-American Activities (now Committee on Internal Security).

In 1948, Nixon was re-elected to the House as the nominee of both the Republican and Democratic parties. At that time, California had a unique "cross-filing" system that allowed candidates to enter each party's primary election. Nixon won both primaries.

The Alger Hiss case, which began in 1948, brought Nixon into national prominence. Hiss, a former State Department official, was accused of having passed government information to a Russian spy ring during the 1930's. The matter rested with Hiss's word against that of his accusers. Many members of the Un-American Activities Committee wanted to drop the case, but Nixon insisted that the charges against Hiss be either proved or disproved. The question of Communists in government was a fierce political issue at the time. In 1950, a Federal District Court jury convicted Hiss of perjury in denying that he had ever given secret documents to Russian agents. See HISS, ALGER.

U.S. Senator. At the peak of his prominence in the Hiss case, Nixon ran for the U.S. Senate in 1950. He opposed Representative Helen Gahagan Douglas, a New Deal Democrat. Conservative Democrats regarded Mrs. Douglas as an extreme liberal. During the campaign, Nixon emphasized charges, made originally by Mrs. Douglas' foes in the Democratic primary election, that she did not realize the threat of Communism. In one of California's most savage political contests, Nixon defeated Mrs. Douglas by nearly 700,000 votes.

Nixon worked hard in the Senate, serving on the Labor and Public Welfare Committee. He also became a popular speaker at Republican Party affairs and at civic meetings in all parts of the United States.

The 1952 Campaign. In 1952, the Republican National Convention nominated Nixon for Vice-President to run with General Dwight D. Eisenhower. A highlight of the campaign was a dispute over an $18,000 fund set up by Nixon's supporters in California. They had organized the fund in 1950 to enable Nixon to campaign for Republican programs and candidates in both election and nonelection years. Nixon and his friends showed that they had used the money only for political expenses, but his Democratic opponents called it a "secret slush fund." Some Republicans, fearing that Nixon might hurt Eisenhower's chances of victory, demanded that Nixon withdraw from the campaign.

Nixon's cause seemed hopeless. Then, on Sept. 23, 1952, Nixon stated his case in an emotional address over television and radio. He discussed his personal finances in detail, showing that he had not profited personally from the fund. He said that "Pat doesn't have a mink coat. But she does have a respectable Republican cloth coat." And he vowed to keep Checkers, a cocker spaniel that had been a gift to his daughters. After the program, Republicans hailed Nixon as a hero. Eisenhower put his arm around Nixon when they next met and declared: "You're my boy." Eisenhower and Nixon went on to defeat their Democratic opponents, Governor Adlai E. Stevenson of Illinois and Senator John J. Sparkman of Alabama.

Vice-President (1953-1961)

Eisenhower succeeded Democratic President Harry S. Truman in 1953. He gave Nixon the job of working with members of Congress to smooth out possible quarrels with the new administration. Eisenhower also assigned Nixon to preside over Cabinet meetings and the National Security Council in the President's absence. Nixon took a greater role in the executive branch of the government than any previous Vice-President.

Eisenhower's Illnesses. Nixon's biggest test as Vice-President began Sept. 24, 1955, when Eisenhower suffered a heart attack. Nixon calmly went about his normal duties, presided at Cabinet meetings, and kept the wheels of government moving smoothly. He also stepped in when the President suffered another illness in June, 1956, and a stroke in November, 1957.

The 1956 Election. Many persons wondered whether Eisenhower would ask Nixon to run with him again in 1956. Angered by rumors that he planned to drop Nixon, the President declared: "Anyone who attempts to drive a wedge of any kind between Dick Nixon and me has just as much chance as if he tried to drive it between my brother and me." Eisenhower and Nixon defeated the Democratic nominees, Stevenson and Senator Estes Kefauver of Tennessee.

Overseas Missions. Nixon often acted as spokesman for the government on trips to other nations. As Vice-President, he toured nearly 60 countries, visiting every continent except Antarctica. During a tour of Latin America in the spring of 1958, Nixon faced violence and danger. In Peru, Communist agents led groups that booed and stoned him. In Venezuela, mobs smashed the windows of Nixon's car, but he was not hurt.

Nixon traveled to Russia in July, 1959, to open an American exhibit in Moscow. As he and Premier Nikita S. Khrushchev walked through a model home, they argued about Russian and U.S. plans for world peace. At one point in the "kitchen debate," Nixon startled the Russians by pointing his finger at Khrushchev and saying bluntly: "You don't know everything."

Defeat by Kennedy. Few persons doubted that Nixon would be the Republican presidential candidate in 1960. For a time, some party leaders thought that Governor Nelson Rockefeller of New York might make an

United Press Int.

Representative Nixon won national fame during the Alger Hiss case. Nixon worked with Whittaker Chambers, *left*, who accused Hiss of spying, and investigator Robert Stripling, *right*.

United Press Int.

Nomination in 1952 brought this joyful gesture from Nixon and Dwight D. Eisenhower. Their wives shared the excitement.

The "Kitchen Debate" between Nixon and Russian Premier Khrushchev occurred during a tour of a U.S. exhibit in Moscow.
Wide World

United Press Int.

John F. Kennedy and Nixon discussed the issues of the 1960 presidential campaign during four televised "great debates."

all-out fight for the nomination. But Rockefeller withdrew, and the Republican National Convention nominated Nixon on the first ballot. The delegates chose Henry Cabot Lodge, Jr., American ambassador to the United Nations, as Nixon's vice-presidential running mate. The Democrats nominated Senator John F. Kennedy of Massachusetts for President and Senator Lyndon B. Johnson of Texas for Vice-President.

The campaign was close and hard-fought from start to finish. Kennedy argued that Republican methods had slowed U.S. economic growth, contributing to what he called a loss of American prestige on the international scene. Nixon cited figures to show that the economy was growing at a satisfactory rate. Nixon and Kennedy took part in a unique series of four televised debates. The television and radio audiences included most of the nation's voters. These "great debates" marked the first time in American history that presidential candidates argued campaign issues face-to-face.

Nixon lost to Kennedy in the closest presidential election since Grover Cleveland defeated James G. Blaine by 23,005 popular votes in 1884. Kennedy won by 119,-450 popular votes out of nearly 69 million. Nixon carried 26 states to 22 for Kennedy, but Kennedy received 303 electoral votes compared to Nixon's 219. Senator Harry F. Byrd of Virginia received 15 electoral votes.

Political Comeback

Defeat in California. In 1961, Nixon began to practice law in Los Angeles. In 1962, friends encouraged him to run for governor of California. Nixon won the Republican nomination for governor by defeating Joseph C. Shell in the state primary election. But the victory was costly. Conservative Republicans had supported Shell, and Nixon's triumph split the party. Democratic Governor Edmund G. (Pat) Brown beat Nixon by about 300,000 votes.

New York City Lawyer. Nixon moved to New York City in 1963 and began a new law practice. He became

a partner in a Wall Street law firm, and his associates placed his name first in the list of partners.

Some of Nixon's supporters wanted him to run for President in 1964, but Nixon felt that most Republicans favored Senator Barry M. Goldwater of Arizona. Goldwater won the Republican presidential nomination, and Nixon campaigned for him and other party candidates. President Lyndon B. Johnson, seeking his first full term, defeated Goldwater by a huge margin.

Goldwater's overwhelming defeat put Nixon back into the political limelight. Liberal and conservative Republicans were quarreling bitterly, and he was the only nationally prominent man whom both groups could accept. In 1966, Nixon campaigned vigorously for Republican candidates in congressional elections. He helped build party organizations, raise funds, and promote candidates in 35 states and 61 congressional districts. Republicans won 47 House seats, 3 Senate seats, and 8 governorships that had been held by Democrats. Nixon received much credit for the Republican victories.

In 1967, Nixon traveled around the world. His trip included visits to the Soviet Union and South Vietnam.

The 1968 Election. In February, 1968, Nixon announced that he would be a candidate for the Republican presidential nomination. Many Republicans wondered whether he could regain his voter appeal. They feared that his defeats by Kennedy and Brown had given him the image of a loser. But Nixon won primary elections by large margins in New Hampshire, Wisconsin, Indiana, Nebraska, Oregon, and South Dakota.

Nixon's chief opponents for the presidential nomination were Governors Nelson Rockefeller of New York and Ronald Reagan of California. But Nixon easily won nomination on the first ballot at the Republican National Convention in Miami Beach. The convention nominated Nixon's choice as running mate, Governor Spiro T. Agnew of Maryland.

The Democrats chose Vice-President Hubert H. Humphrey and Senator Edmund S. Muskie of Maine to oppose Nixon and Agnew. Former Governor George C. Wallace of Alabama and retired General Curtis E. LeMay ran as the candidates of the American Independent Party.

Both Nixon and Humphrey promised to make peace in Vietnam their main goal as President. Nixon called for a program of what he termed "new internationalism." Under this program, other nations would take over from the United States more of the responsibility for preserving world peace and helping underde-

---

NIXON'S ELECTION

Place of Nominating Convention....Miami Beach, Fla.
Ballot on Which Nominated........1st
Democratic Opponent............Hubert H. Humphrey
American Independent Opponent....George C. Wallace
Electoral Vote...................301 (Nixon) to 191
                                    (Humphrey) and 46
                                    (Wallace)
Popular Vote....................31,710,470 (Nixon)
                                    to 30,898,055 (Humphrey) and 9,446,167
                                    (Wallace)
Age at Inauguration.............56

veloped countries. Nixon also pledged to strengthen law enforcement in the United States.

In the election, Nixon defeated Humphrey by only about 812,000 popular votes, 31,710,470 to 30,898,055. Wallace received 9,446,167 popular votes. But Nixon won a clear majority of electoral votes, with 301. Humphrey received 191 electoral votes, and Wallace got 46. For the electoral vote by states, see ELECTORAL COLLEGE (table).

Nixon's Administration (1969-   )

As President, Nixon chose to act slowly at first in dealing with the nation's problems. He spent much time studying alternatives and made few proposals to Congress during his first months in office.

Foreign Policy. Nixon's major goal was settlement of the Vietnam War. In his inaugural address, Nixon said: "The greatest honor history can bestow is the title of peacemaker. This honor now beckons America."

The Vietnam War. The Vietnam peace talks, begun in 1968, continued in Paris. But the negotiators made little progress. In March, 1969, Nixon ordered a stepped-up training program for South Vietnamese forces so that they could gradually take over the major burden of fighting the war. In July, he began a gradual withdrawal of U.S. combat troops from Vietnam. This policy became known as *Vietnamization.* Many Americans favored the gradual withdrawal, but many others wanted the U.S. involvement to end immediately.

In April, 1970, Nixon sent U.S. troops into Cambodia to destroy Communist bases there. He said the operation would save American lives in South Vietnam and shorten the war. Nixon promised to withdraw all U.S. troops from Cambodia by the end of June. College students on campuses across the country protested what they felt was a widening of the war. All U.S. troops were withdrawn from Cambodia by the end of June. Nixon called the mission the "most successful operation of this long and very difficult war."

In February, 1971, South Vietnamese forces launched a campaign to disrupt Communist supply routes in neighboring Laos. The operation lasted 45 days and ended under heavy Communist fire. American troop

withdrawals from South Vietnam continued during 1971.

The Nixon Doctrine. In 1969, during a visit to Southeast Asia, Nixon proposed a new Asian policy for the United States. He declared that, in the future, Asian nations would have to bear the main responsibility for their defense. He pledged the aid of U.S. troops only if a non-Communist Asian nation were threatened by a major foreign power. This policy became known as the *Nixon Doctrine.*

Relations with China. In 1969, Nixon approved the removal of some restrictions on travel by Americans to Communist China. He also encouraged the reopening of trade between China and the United States. The two nations had stopped trading with each other during the Korean War (1950-1953). In April, 1971, the Chinese invited a U.S. table tennis team playing in Japan to visit China and compete against their players. A few days later, the team began a weeklong visit to China. Nixon then announced that the U.S. government would allow the export of certain goods to China.

The National Scene. In August, 1969, Nixon proposed a series of major domestic reforms, which he termed the *New Federalism.* One of the reforms called for a minimum federal payment to every needy family with children. Nixon also suggested that the federal government share its tax revenues with state and local governments. But action on the reforms was stalled as key Democrats in Congress asked for major changes.

The Democrats, who had kept control of both houses of Congress in the 1968 elections, also slowed the passage of many of Nixon's other proposals. In 1970, Nixon campaigned for Republican congressional candidates in more than 20 states. In elections that year, the Democrats retained control of the House and the Senate.

Major Legislation. In spite of the legislative slowdown, Congress did enact several far-reaching laws. In 1969, it passed Nixon's proposal to establish a lottery system for the military draft. Also in 1969, Congress

President Nixon, in his inaugural address on Jan. 20, 1969, pledged that the United States would seek "the title of peacemaker." Vice-President Spiro T. Agnew sat to Nixon's left.

Wide World

approved the most extensive reforms in federal tax laws in U.S. history. These reforms included increases in personal income tax deductions and cuts in tax benefits for foundations and oil companies. In 1970, Congress established independent agencies to replace the Post Office Department and to operate the passenger trains that linked the nation's major cities. Also in 1970, Congress lowered the minimum voting age in federal elections to 18. The 26th Amendment to the U.S. Constitution, ratified in 1971, set the voting age at 18 for all elections.

Inflation was one of Nixon's chief domestic concerns. In 1969, prices rose faster than at any time since 1951, during the Korean War. Many Americans found that although they were earning more money than ever before, rising prices sharply cut their gains. Nixon tried to keep government spending at a minimum and acted to reduce the amount of money available for loans by banks. He also proposed a one-year extension of a 10 per cent federal surtax on incomes that Congress had adopted in June, 1968. In August, Congress extended the tax to the end of 1969. In December, as part of the tax reform bill, Congress dropped the tax to 5 per cent and extended it through June 30, 1970.

Business fell sharply in 1970, and more than 6 per cent of the nation's workers were unemployed. In spite of the slump, prices continued to climb. Nixon ordered federal agencies to reduce their budgets. He also vetoed some bills that called for large increases in government spending. The economy began to improve in 1971, though unemployment remained high. The cost of living also continued to rise.

The ABM System. In March, 1969, Nixon proposed a plan to build an antiballistic missile (ABM) system called *Safeguard.* Nixon said the new missiles were needed to protect U.S. underground missiles and bomber bases from enemy missile attack. The plan became one of the most heavily debated issues of Nixon's Administration. Critics charged that the system would step up the arms race between the United States and Russia. They also claimed that the new missiles would not only cost too much money, but would also fail to destroy enemy missiles.

In August, the Senate narrowly approved construction of the two ABM bases. The ABM debate was the first time a national defense program had been seriously challenged in Congress since 1941. That year, the House of Representatives approved extension of the first peacetime draft in U.S. history by only one vote. In 1970, Nixon proposed building four more ABM bases. But Congress approved the construction of only two more.

School Desegregation. In 1969, the U.S. Department of Justice began to file an increasing number of suits against segregated school districts in both the North and the South. But Nixon felt that some Southern districts needed more time to prepare for integration.

In August, 1969, the Administration asked a U.S. circuit court to delay plans calling for the desegregation of 33 Mississippi school districts by September 1. Critics charged that the request was part of Nixon's "Southern strategy" to attract white Southerners to the Republican Party. The circuit court approved the Administration's request, but civil rights leaders appealed

the decision. In October, the Supreme Court of the United States overturned the lower court decision. It ruled that all public school districts must end segregation "at once." This ruling replaced a 1955 decision of the Supreme Court calling for an end to segregation "with all deliberate speed." In 1971, the Supreme Court ruled that children could be bused to integrate public schools in areas where state laws had required segregation.

Supreme Court Nominations. In 1969 and again in 1970, Nixon suffered a stinging defeat when he tried to appoint a conservative Southerner to the Supreme Court. In May, 1969, Associate Justice Abe Fortas resigned from the court under charges of personal misconduct (see FORTAS, ABE). Nixon nominated Judge Clement F. Haynsworth, Jr., of South Carolina to succeed Fortas. Some critics claimed that Haynsworth was anti-Negro. Others charged he was unethical for ruling in a case in which he had a financial interest. In November, the Senate rejected the nomination by a 55 to 45 vote.

In January, 1970, Nixon nominated Judge G. Harrold Carswell of Florida for the seat. Opposition to Carswell grew quickly after several judges and law school deans rated him unqualified for the Supreme Court. In April, the Senate defeated the nomination by a 51 to 45 vote. It was the first time that two Supreme Court nominees of a President had been rejected since 1894, when Grover Cleveland was chief executive.

After Carswell's defeat, Nixon accused the Senate of "regional discrimination." He charged that the Senate would not confirm a Southerner to the court. In May, the Senate unanimously approved Nixon's third choice, Judge Harry A. Blackmun of Minnesota.

The U.S. Space Program opened a new era of exploration and discovery in 1969. On July 20, Apollo 11 astronauts Neil A. Armstrong and Edwin E. Aldrin, Jr., became the first men to set foot on the moon. Nixon spoke to the men through a special telephone connection while they were on the moon. "Because of what you have done," he told them, "the heavens have become part of man's world." See SPACE TRAVEL.

Environmental Problems attracted more and more attention during Nixon's Administration. Many Americans began to realize that pollution of the air, land, and water endangered not only the quality of life but also life itself. In July, 1970, Nixon announced a plan to merge into one agency a number of federal operations dealing with environmental pollution. This agency, the Environmental Protection Agency, was established in October. In December, Congress passed a bill requiring automobile manufacturers to develop an engine that by 1976 would eliminate nearly all pollution caused by cars.

The SST Debate. Continued federal aid for a supersonic transport (SST) airplane program became a major issue in 1971. The government had established the program in 1963 to develop a commercial jetliner that would fly faster than the speed of sound and reduce overseas travel time. Opposition to the SST increased rapidly in 1971 after conservationist groups warned that the plane would harm the environment. Other critics claimed that the nation had higher priorities than the SST program. Nixon argued that the United States needed the SST to preserve its leadership in commercial aviation. He pointed out that France, Great Britain,

The Nixon Family. From left to right are daughter Julie Nixon Eisenhower, the President, Mrs. Nixon, and daughter Patricia Nixon Cox.

and Russia were working to develop an SST. In March, 1971, Congress voted to end federal support of the program.

The Calley Trial. In 1971, Nixon became involved in the Army court-martial of First Lieutenant William L. Calley, Jr. In March, Lieutenant Calley was sentenced to life imprisonment for the 1968 murder of at least 22 South Vietnamese civilians in the village of My Lai. The sentence created a nationwide debate. Many Americans supported the sentence, but others called it too harsh. Still others argued that Lieutenant Calley's sentence was unfair because the Army had dropped charges against most of the officers accused in the case. In April, Nixon ordered the lieutenant released from the stockade at Fort Benning, Ga. The President directed that Lieutenant Calley be restricted to his quarters at the Army base until his appeals had been ruled on. Nixon said he would review the case before any sentence went into effect.

Life in the White House. The Nixons brought a calm and reserved way of life to the White House. The Johnsons and their two daughters had liked informal dress and some jazz and rock music at their receptions. The Nixons preferred formal dress, including white ties and coats with tails for men and long gowns for women. They also favored fox trots and waltzes for dancing. The Nixons' taste in art also was conservative. They replaced many of the op art paintings on office walls with traditional landscapes and portraits.

Nixon was the first President to play the piano since Harry Truman. He occasionally played the White House piano for guests. The President followed sports closely, especially professional football. He impressed many White House visitors with his knowledge of baseball and football.

Pat Nixon worked hard to encourage Americans to volunteer for social work. She occasionally traveled across the country to support volunteer groups. "I want to make volunteerism the 'in' thing to do," she said.

Shortly after Nixon took office, he bought a large estate in San Clemente, Calif., a beach resort between San Diego and Los Angeles. The residence became known as the Western White House because Nixon spent working vacations there.   EARL MAZO

Related Articles in WORLD BOOK include:

Agnew, Spiro T.
Eisenhower, Dwight D.
Hiss, Alger
Humphrey, Hubert H.
Kennedy, John F.
Kissinger, Henry A.
Lodge (family)
Moynihan, Daniel P.
President of the United States
Republican Party
Urban Affairs, Council for
Vice-President of the United States
Vietnam War

Outline

I. **Early Life**
  A. Boyhood
  B. Education
  C. Lawyer
  D. Nixon's Family
  E. Naval Officer

II. **Career in Congress**
  A. U.S. Representative
  B. U.S. Senator
  C. The 1952 Campaign

III. **Vice-President (1953-1961)**
  A. Eisenhower's Illnesses
  B. The 1956 Election
  C. Overseas Missions
  D. Defeat by Kennedy

IV. **Political Comeback**
  A. Defeat in California
  B. New York City Lawyer
  C. The 1968 Election

V. **Nixon's Administration (1969-   )**
  A. Foreign Policy
  B. The National Scene
  C. Life in the White House

Questions

How did Nixon happen to enter politics?

What was the "kitchen debate"?

Why was Nixon's election as President one of the greatest political comebacks in U.S. history?

How did Nixon first win national prominence?

Where did Nixon meet his future wife?

How was Nixon's career almost ruined in 1952?

What was unique about the 1960 presidential campaign?

How did Nixon's role as Vice-President differ from that of previous Vice-Presidents?

What were some of the jobs Nixon held as a boy?

What kind of way of life did the Nixons bring to the White House?

337

Noah and His Family, happy to see land again, watch as the birds, beasts, and reptiles stream from the Ark, two by two, on Mount Ararat. Noah offered a sacrifice to God in thanksgiving for being delivered from the Flood.

Culver

NIZA, MARCOS DE. See ARIZONA (Exploration); NEW MEXICO (Exploration and Settlement).

NIZHNI NOVGOROD. See GORKI.

NKRUMAH, *en KROO mah,* **KWAME,** *KWAH meh* (1909-   ), was president of Ghana from 1960 to 1966. Army leaders ousted him in 1966, and Nkrumah went into exile in nearby Guinea. Guinea's President Sékou Touré made Nkrumah honorary president of that country.

As president of Ghana, Nkrumah worked to develop the country's economy and improve the living conditions of its people. He promoted industrialization, introduced health and welfare programs, and expanded the educational system. But Nkrumah made enemies with the methods he used to achieve these goals. Nkrumah imprisoned his opponents. Taxes rose, the price of cacao (Ghana's chief export) fell, corruption became widespread, and government debt mounted. Army leaders took over the government while Nkrumah was visiting Communist China.

Nkrumah was born in Nkroful, a village in Ghana. He led his country's drive for independence from Great Britain in the 1950's. He was prime minister of the Gold Coast, and kept that office when the colony became Ghana, an independent country, in 1957. His goal was to form a union of African nations. IMMANUEL WALLERSTEIN

See also GHANA.

Kwame Nkrumah
Wide World

NKVD. See MVD.

NLRB. See NATIONAL LABOR RELATIONS BOARD.

NO PLAY. See JAPANESE LITERATURE (Drama); DANCING (The Far East).

NOAH was the only righteous, God-fearing man of his time. Genesis 6-9 tells that he was chosen by God to keep some people and animals alive during the Deluge, or great Flood. Noah warned his countrymen for 120 years that the Flood was coming. He built his huge 450-foot-long ship, called the Ark, during that time. He took into the Ark his family, and enough birds and animals to repopulate the earth. The rain poured for 40 days and 40 nights (Gen. 7:12, 24). Even when the water rose above the highest mountaintops, all who were in the Ark floated safely on the water.

The waters dropped enough 150 days after the Flood started that the Ark was able to rest on top of Mount Ararat (see ARARAT). Noah let loose a raven which did not return. Then he sent out a dove, and it returned because it could find no place to perch. Later, he sent out the same dove two more times. On the second flight, it returned with an olive branch in its mouth. Noah and all the animals came out of the Ark later to begin a new life. Noah offered sacrifice to God for deliverance, and God promised him that He would never send another flood to destroy the earth. He made the rainbow a sign of that promise. He commanded Noah and his descendants to respect human life and to punish murder with the death penalty.

Noah's sons were Shem, Ham, and Japheth. Shem became father of the *Semitic* peoples, including the Hebrews and the Arabs. Ham was father of the Hamitic peoples, and Japheth was father of peoples of Asia Minor and Europe. GLEASON L. ARCHER, JR.

NOBEL, *noh BEHL,* **AL-FRED BERNHARD** (1833-1896), a Swedish chemist, invented dynamite and founded the Nobel prizes (see NOBEL PRIZES). As a young man, Nobel experimented with nitroglycerin in his father's factory. He hoped to make this dangerous substance into a safe and useful explosive. He prepared a nitroglycerin explosive, but so many accidents occurred when it was put on the market that for a number of years many persons considered Nobel almost a public enemy.

Amer. Swedish News Exch., Inc.
Alfred Nobel

Finally, in 1867, Nobel combined nitroglycerin with an absorbent substance. This explosive could be handled and shipped safely. Nobel named it *dynamite* (see DYNAMITE). Within a few years, he became one of the world's richest men. He set up factories throughout the world, and bought the large Bofors armament plant in Sweden. He worked on synthetic rubber, artificial silk, and many other patented products. He was also fond of literature and wrote several novels and plays, but with little success.

Nobel was never in good health. In later years, he became increasingly ill and nervous. He suffered from a feeling of guilt at having created a substance that caused so much death and injury. He hated the thought that dynamite could be used in war when he had invented it for peace. Nobel set up a fund of about $9 million. The interest from the fund was to be used to award annual prizes, one of which was for the most effective work in promoting international peace.

Nobel was born on Oct. 21, 1833, in Stockholm, the son of an inventor. He was educated in St. Petersburg (now Leningrad), Russia, and later studied engineering in the United States. K. L. KAUFMAN

NOBEL PRIZES are awarded each year in six different fields to persons, regardless of nationality, who have made valuable contributions to the "good of humanity." The awards are given for the most important discovery or invention in the fields of physics; chemistry; physiology and medicine; the most distinguished literary work of an idealistic nature; the most effective work in the interest of international peace; and the outstanding work in the field of economic science. Prizes in the first five fields were first presented in 1901. The economics award was offered for the first time in 1969. The original five prizes consist of equal shares from the income of the $9 million estate of the Swedish inventor Alfred Nobel. In his will, Nobel directed that his fortune be used in this way. The Swedish Central Bank established and provided money for the economics prize. In 1970, the value of each of the prizes was $78,400.

The Royal Academy of Science in Stockholm chooses the physics, chemistry, and economics winners. The Caroline Institute, the faculty of medicine in Stockholm, awards the prize for medicine. The Swedish Academy of Literature in Stockholm awards the prize for literature. A committee of five elected by the Norwegian *Storting* (parliament) awards the prize for peace.

A candidate may not apply directly for a prize. A qualified person must submit each name in writing. For the literary prize, the Swedish Academy considers only works that have appeared in print and have been "proved by the test of experience or by the examination of experts." The academy usually selects an author on the basis of his complete work, rather than an individual book.

The organizations that award the prizes appoint 15 deputies who elect a board of directors. The board holds office for two years and administers the fund. Winners receive their awards on December 10, the anniversary of the death of Alfred Nobel. The peace prize is awarded in Oslo, Norway. The other prizes are awarded in Stockholm, Sweden. Two or more persons may share a prize. Occasionally, prizes are not awarded or are awarded in a later year.

Through 1970, 107 persons who won a Nobel prize came from the United States, 61 from Great Britain, 58 from Germany, 42 from France, 19 from Sweden, 11 from Switzerland, 11 from The Netherlands, and 10 from Italy. Eleven organizations have won prizes.

More Americans have won prizes in the fields of physics, physiology and medicine, and peace than persons of any other country. The Germans lead in chemistry prizes and the French in literature.

There is a biography in WORLD BOOK of each prizewinner whose name is marked with an asterisk in the table on the following pages.

Nobel Prizes are presented in Stockholm and Oslo in December of each year. Willis E. Lamb, *left,* one of the winners of the 1955 prize for physics, received his award from King Gustaf VI of Sweden.
Text & Bilder, Stockholm

Nobel Foundation; Bettmann Archive

The Nobel Prize for Physics was awarded to Marie Curie and others in 1903. Mme. Curie won the chemistry prize in 1911. Both medals are the same. The obverse, with the bust of Alfred Nobel, is also used on the medals shown below.

	PHYSICS	CHEMISTRY	PHYSIOLOGY AND MEDICINE	LITERATURE	PEACE
1901	*Wilhelm K. Roentgen (German) for discovering X rays.	*Jacobus Henricus Van't Hoff (Dutch) for discovering laws of chemical dynamics and osmotic pressure.	*Emil von Behring (German) for discovering the diphtheria antitoxin.	*René Sully-Prudhomme (French) for his poems.	*Jean Henri Dunant (Swiss) for founding the Red Cross and originating the Geneva Convention, and Frédéric Passy (French) for founding a French peace society.
1902	*Hendrik Antoon Lorentz and *Pieter Zeeman (Dutch) for discovering the Zeeman effect of magnetism on light.	*Emil Fischer (German) for synthesizing sugars, purine derivatives, and peptides.	*Sir Ronald Ross (British) for working on malaria and discovering the malarial parasite and mosquito.	*Theodor Mommsen (German) for his historical narratives, particularly his history of Rome.	Élie Ducommun (Swiss) for his work as honorary secretary of the International Peace Bureau, and Charles Albert Gobat (Swiss) for his work as administrative head of the Interparliamentary Union.
1903	*Antoine Henri Becquerel and *Pierre and Marie Curie (French) for discovering radioactivity and studying uranium.	*Svante August Arrhenius (Swedish) for his dissociation theory of ionization in electrolytes.	*Niels Ryberg Finsen (Danish) for treating diseases, especially *lupus vulgaris*, with concentrated light rays.	*Björnstjerne Björnson (Norwegian) for his novels, poems, and dramas.	Sir William R. Cremer (British) for his activities as founder and secretary of the International Arbitration League.
1904	*Baron Rayleigh (British) for studying the density of gases and discovering argon.	*Sir William Ramsay (British) for discovering helium, neon, xenon, and krypton, and determining their place in the periodic system.	*Ivan Petrovich Pavlov (Russian) for his work on the physiology of digestion.	*Frédéric Mistral (French) for his poems, and *José Echegaray y Eizaguirre (Spanish) for his dramas.	The Institute of International Law for its studies on the laws of neutrality and other phases of international law.
1905	Philipp Lenard (German) for studying the properties of cathode rays.	*Adolph von Baeyer (German) for his work on dyes and organic compounds, and for synthesizing indigo and arsenicals.	*Robert Koch (German) for working on tuberculosis and discovering the tubercule bacillus and tuberculin.	*Henryk Sienkiewicz (Polish) for his novels.	Baroness Bertha von Suttner (Austrian) for promoting pacifism and founding an Austrian peace society.
1906	*Sir Joseph John Thomson (British) for studying electrical discharge through gases.	Henri Moissan (French) for preparing pure fluorine and developing the electric furnace.	*Camillo Golgi (Italian) and Santiago Ramon y Cajal (Spanish) for their studies of nerve tissue.	*Giosuè Carducci (Italian) for his poems.	*Theodore Roosevelt (American) for negotiating peace in the Russo-Japanese War.

1907	*Albert A. Michelson (American) for inventing optical instruments and measuring the speed of light.	Eduard Buchner (German) for his biochemical researches and for discovering cell-less fermentation.	*Charles Louis Alphonse Laveran (French) for studying diseases caused by protozoa.	*Rudyard Kipling (British) for his stories, novels, and poems.	Ernesto T. Moneta (Italian) for his work as president of the Lombard League for Peace, and Louis Renault (French) for organizing international conferences and representing France at two peace conferences.
1908	Gabriel Lippmann (French) for his method of color photography.	*Ernest Rutherford (British) for discovering that alpha rays break down atoms and studying radioactive substances.	*Paul Ehrlich (German) and *Élie Metchnikoff (Russian) for their work on immunity.	*Rudolf Eucken (German) for his philosophic writings.	Klas Pontus Arnoldson (Swedish) for founding the Swedish Society for Arbitration and Peace, and Fredrik Bajer (Danish) for his work on the International Peace Bureau.
1909	*Guglielmo Marconi (Italian) and Karl Ferdinand Braun (German) for developing the wireless telegraph.	Wilhelm Ostwald (German) for his work on catalysis, chemical equilibrium, and the rate of chemical reactions.	Emil Theodor Kocher (Swiss) for his work on the physiology, pathology, and surgery of the thyroid gland.	*Selma Lagerlöf (Swedish) for her novels and poems.	Auguste M. F. Beernaert (Belgian) for his work as a member of the Permanent Court of Arbitration, and *Paul d'Estournelles (French) for founding and directing the French Parliamentary Arbitration Committee and League of International Conciliation.
1910	Johannes D. van der Waals (Dutch) for studying the relationships of liquids and gases.	*Otto Wallach (German) for his work in the field of alicyclic substances.	Albrecht Kossel (German) for studying cell chemistry, proteins, and nucleic substances.	Paul von Heyse (German) for his poems, novels, and dramas.	The International Peace Bureau for promoting international arbitration and organizing many peace conferences.
1911	Wilhelm Wien (German) for his discoveries on the heat radiated by black objects.	*Marie Curie (French) for discovering radium and polonium, and for isolating radium and studying its compounds.	*Allvar Gullstrand (Swedish) for his work on dioptrics, the refraction of light through the eye.	*Maurice Maeterlinck (Belgian) for his dramas.	Tobias M. C. Asser (Dutch) for organizing conferences on international law, and Alfred H. Fried (Austrian) for his writings on peace as editor of *Die Friedenswarte*.

Nobel Foundation; Bettmann Archive

The Literature Prize was awarded to Rudyard Kipling in 1907. Most of Kipling's writings tell about life in India.

The Physiology Prize was won by Ivan Petrovich Pavlov in 1904. Pavlov and his staff studied the process of digestion by experimenting on dogs.

Bettmann Archive; Nobel Foundation

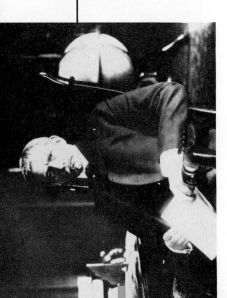

The Nobel Peace Prize was presented to the great American statesmen Elihu Root, *left*, in 1912, and Woodrow Wilson, *right*, in 1919. A committee elected by the Norwegian Parliament awards this prize.

Bettmann Archive; Nobel Foundation

	PHYSICS	CHEMISTRY	PHYSIOLOGY AND MEDICINE	LITERATURE	PEACE
1912	Nils Dalén (Swedish) for inventing automatic gas regulators for lighthouses.	*François Auguste Victor Grignard (French) for discovering the Grignard reagent to synthesize organic compounds, and Paul Sabatier (French) for his method of adding hydrogen to organic compounds, using metals as catalysts.	*Alexis Carrel (French) for suturing blood vessels and grafting vessels and organs.	*Gerhart Hauptmann (German) for his dramas.	*Elihu Root (American) for peacefully settling the problem of Japanese immigration to California and organizing the Central American Peace Conference.
1913	Heike Kamerlingh Onnes (Dutch) for experimenting with low temperatures and liquefying helium.	*Alfred Werner (Swiss) for his coordination theory on the arrangement of atoms.	Charles Robert Richet (French) for studying allergies caused by foreign substances, as in hay fever.	*Sir Rabindranath Tagore (Indian) for his poems.	Henri Lafontaine (Belgian) for his work as president of the International Peace Bureau.
1914	*Max T. F. von Laue (German) for using crystals to measure X rays.	Theodore W. Richards (American) for determining the atomic weights of many elements.	Robert Bárány (Austrian) for work on function and diseases of organs of equilibrium in the inner ear.	No Award	No Award
1915	*Sir William Henry Bragg and Sir William L. Bragg (British) for using X rays to study crystal structure.	*Richard Willstätter (German) for his research on chlorophyll and other coloring matter in plants.	No Award	*Romain Rolland (French) for his novels.	No Award
1916	No Award	No Award	No Award	Verner von Hiedenstam (Swedish) for his poems.	No Award
1917	Charles Barkla (British) for studying the diffusion of light and the radiation of X rays from elements.	No Award	No Award	Karl Gjellerup (Danish) for his poems and novels, and *Henrik Pontoppidan (Danish) for his novels and short stories.	The International Red Cross for doing relief work during World War I.
1918	*Max Planck (German) for stating the quantum theory of light.	*Fritz Haber (German) for the Haber process of synthesizing ammonia from nitrogen and hydrogen.	No Award	No Award	No Award

Year	Peace	Literature	Physiology or Medicine	Chemistry	Physics
1919	*Woodrow Wilson (American) for attempting a just settlement of World War I and advocating the League of Nations.	*Carl Spitteler (Swiss) for his epics, short stories, and essays.	Jules Bordet (Belgian) for his discoveries on immunity.	No Award	*Johannes Stark (German) for discovering the Stark effect of spectra in electric fields.
1920	Léon Bourgeois (French) for his contribution as president of the Council of the League of Nations.	*Knut Hamsun (Norwegian) for his novels.	August Krogh (Danish) for discovering the system of action of blood capillaries.	*Walther Nernst (German) for his discoveries concerning heat changes in chemical reactions.	Charles E. Guillaume (French) for discovering nickel-steel alloys with slight expansion, and the alloy invar.
1921	Karl Hjalmar Branting (Swedish) for promoting social reforms in Sweden and serving as Sweden's delegate to the League of Nations, and Christian Louis Lange (Norwegian) for his work as secretary-general of the Inter-Parliamentary Union.	*Anatole France (French) for his novels, short stories, and essays.	No Award	*Frederick Soddy (British) for studying radioactive substances and isotopes.	*Albert Einstein (German) for contributing to mathematical physics and stating the law of the photoelectric effect.
1922	*Fridtjof Nansen (Norwegian) for doing relief work among Russian prisoners of war and in famine areas in Russia.	*Jacinto Benavente y Martínez (Spanish) for his dramas.	Archibald V. Hill (British) for his discovery on heat production in the muscles, and Otto Meyerhoff (German) for his theory on the production of lactic acid in the muscles.	*Francis W. Aston (British) for discovering many isotopes by means of the mass spectrograph and discovering the whole number rule on the weight of atoms.	*Niels Bohr (Danish) for studying the structure of atoms and their radiations.
1923	No Award	*William Butler Yeats (Irish) for his poems.	*Sir Frederick Grant Banting (Canadian) and *John J. R. Macleod (Scottish) for discovering insulin.	Fritz Pregl (Austrian) for inventing a method of microanalyzing organic substances.	*Robert A. Millikan (American) for measuring the charge on electrons and working on the photoelectric effect.
1924	No Award	Ladislaw S. Reymont (Polish) for his novels, particularly The Peasants.	*Willem Einthoven (Dutch) for inventing the electrocardiograph.	No Award	*Karl M. G. Siegbahn (Swedish) for working with the X-ray spectroscope.
1925	*Sir Austen Chamberlain (British) for helping to work out the Locarno Peace Pact, and *Charles G. Dawes (American) for originating a plan for payment of German reparations.	*George Bernard Shaw (British) for his plays and satires.	No Award	*Richard Zsigmondy (German) for his method of studying colloids.	*James Franck and *Gustav Hertz (German) for stating laws on the collision of an electron with an atom.
1926	*Aristide Briand (French) for his part in forming the Locarno Peace Pact, and *Gustav Stresemann (German) for persuading Germany to accept plans for reparations.	Grazia Deledda (Italian) for her novels.	*Johannes Fibiger (Danish) for discovering a parasite that causes cancer.	*Theodor Svedberg (Swedish) for his work on dispersions and on colloid chemistry.	Jean Baptiste Perrin (French) for studying the discontinuous structure of matter and measuring the sizes of atoms.

	PHYSICS	CHEMISTRY	PHYSIOLOGY AND MEDICINE	LITERATURE	PEACE
1927	*Arthur H. Compton (American) for discovering the Compton effect on X rays reflected from atoms, and *Charles T. R. Wilson (British) for discovering a method for tracing the paths of ions.	*Heinrich O. Wieland (German) for studying gall acids and related substances.	Julius Wagner von Jauregg (Austrian) for discovering the fever treatment for paralysis.	*Henri Bergson (French) for his philosophic writings.	Ferdinand Buisson (French) for his work as president of the League of Human Rights, and Ludwig Quidde (German) for writing on peace and taking part in many international peace congresses.
1928	Owen W. Richardson (British) for studying thermionic effect and electrons sent off by hot metals.	Adolf Windaus (German) for studying sterols and their connection with vitamins.	Charles Nicolle (French) for his work on typhus.	*Sigrid Undset (Norwegian) for her novels.	No Award
1929	*Louis Victor de Broglie (French) for discovering the wave character of electrons.	Sir Arthur Harden (British) and Hans August Simon von Euler-Chelpin (German) for their research on sugar fermentation and enzymes.	Christiaan Eijkman (Dutch) for discovering vitamins that prevent beriberi, and Sir Frederick G. Hopkins (British) for discovering vitamins that help growth.	*Thomas Mann (German) principally for his novel, *Buddenbrooks*.	*Frank Billings Kellogg (American) for negotiating the Kellogg-Briand Pact.
1930	*Sir Chandrasekhara Venkata Raman (Indian) for discovering a new effect in radiation from elements.	*Hans Fischer (German) for studying the coloring matter of blood and leaves and synthesizing hemin.	*Karl Landsteiner (American) for discovering the four main human blood types.	*Sinclair Lewis (American) for his novels.	*Nathan Söderblom (Swedish) for writing on and working for peace.
1931	No Award	*Carl Bosch and *Friedrich Bergius (German) for inventing high-pressure methods of manufacturing ammonia and liquefying coal.	Otto H. Warburg (German) for discovering that enzymes aid in respiration by tissues.	*Eric A. Karlfeldt (Swedish) for his lyric poetry.	*Jane Addams (American) for her work with the Women's International League for Peace and Freedom, and *Nicholas M. Butler (American) for his work with the Carnegie Endowment for International Peace.
1932	*Werner Heisenberg (German) for founding quantum mechanics, which led to discoveries in hydrogen.	*Irving Langmuir (American) for his discoveries about molecular films absorbed on surfaces.	Edgar D. Adrian and *Sir Charles S. Sherrington (British) for their discoveries on the function of neurons.	*John Galsworthy (British) for his novels, plays, and short stories.	No Award
1933	*Paul Dirac (British) and *Erwin Schrödinger (Austrian) for discovering new forms of atomic theory.	No Award	*Thomas H. Morgan (American) for studying the function of chromosomes in heredity.	*Ivan Alexeyevich Bunin (Russian) for his novels, short stories, and poems.	*Sir Norman Angell (British) for his work with the Royal Institute of International Affairs, the League of Nations, and the National Peace Council.
1934	No Award	*Harold Clayton Urey (American) for discovering deuterium (heavy hydrogen).	*George Minot, William P. Murphy, and George H. Whipple (American) for their discoveries on liver treatment for anemia.	*Luigi Pirandello (Italian) for his dramas.	*Arthur Henderson (British) for his contribution as president of the World Disarmament Conference.
1935	*Sir James Chadwick (British) for discovering the neutron.	*Frédéric and Irène Joliot-Curie (French) for synthesizing new radioactive elements.	*Hans Spemann (German) for discovering the organizer-effect in the growth of an embryo.	No Award	*Carl von Ossietzky (German) for writing to promote world disarmament. (Award delayed until 1936.)

Year	Physics	Chemistry	Medicine	Literature	Peace
1936	*Carl David Anderson (American) for discovering the positron, and Victor F. Hess (Austrian) for discovering cosmic rays.	*Peter J. W. Debye (Dutch) for his studies on molecules, dipole moments, the diffraction of electrons, and X rays in gases.	Sir Henry H. Dale (British) and Otto Loewi (Austrian) for their discoveries on the chemical transmission of nerve impulses.	*Eugene O'Neill (American) for his dramas.	*Carlos Saavedra Lamas (Argentinian) for negotiating a peace settlement between Bolivia and Paraguay in the Chaco War.
1937	Clinton Davisson (American) and George Thomson (British) for discovering the diffraction of electrons by crystals.	*Sir Walter N. Haworth (British) for his research on carbohydrates and vitamin C, and Paul Karrer (Swiss) for studying carotenoids, flavins, and vitamins A and B$_2$.	*Albert Szent-Györgyi (Hungarian) for his discoveries in connection with oxidation in tissues, Vitamin C, and fumaric acid.	Roger Martin du Gard (French) for his novels.	Robert A.T.G. Cecil (British) for promoting international arbitration as Assistant Secretary of State for Foreign Affairs.
1938	*Enrico Fermi (Italian) for discovering new radioactive elements beyond uranium.	*Richard Kuhn (German) for his work on carotenoids and vitamins (declined).	Corneille Heymans (Belgian) for his discoveries concerning the regulation of respiration.	*Pearl S. Buck (American) for her novels.	The International Office for Refugees for directing relief work among refugees.
1939	*Ernest O. Lawrence (American) for inventing the cyclotron and working on artificial radioactivity.	Adolph Butenandt (German) for studying the chemistry of sex hormones (declined), and *Leopold Ružička (Swiss) for his work on polymethylenes.	*Gerhard Domagk (German) for discovering prontosil, the first sulfa drug (declined).	Frans Eemil Sillanpää (Finnish) for his novels.	No Award
1940-42	No Award	No Award	No Award	No Award	No Award

Niels Bohr, a Danish scientist, was awarded the prize for physics in 1922.
Black Star

Sinclair Lewis' satirical novels won him the literature prize in 1930.
United Press Int.

Harold C. Urey won the chemistry prize in 1934 for his work with hydrogen.
Town and Country

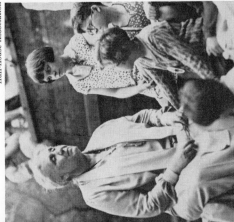

Jane Addams, an American social worker, won the Nobel peace prize in 1931.
Hull-House Association

	PHYSICS	CHEMISTRY	PHYSIOLOGY AND MEDICINE	LITERATURE	PEACE
1943	*Otto Stern (American) for discovering the molecular beam method of studying the atom.	*Georg von Hevesy (Hungarian) for using isotopes as indicators in chemistry.	Henrik Dam (Danish) for discovering vitamin K, and *Edward A. Doisy (U.S.) for synthesizing vitamin K.	No Award	No Award
1944	*Isidor Isaac Rabi (American) for recording the magnetic properties of atomic nuclei.	Otto Hahn (German) for his discoveries in atomic fission.	Joseph Erlanger and Herbert Gasser (American) for their work on single nerve fibers.	*Johannes V. Jensen (Danish) for his poems and novels.	The International Red Cross for doing relief work during World War II.
1945	*Wolfgang Pauli (Austrian) for discovering the exclusion principle (Pauli principle) of electrons.	*Artturi Virtanen (Finnish) for inventing new methods in agricultural biochemistry.	*Sir Alexander Fleming, *Sir Howard W. Florey, and *Ernst B. Chain (British) for discovering penicillin.	*Gabriela Mistral (Chilean) for her poems.	*Cordell Hull (American) for his peace efforts as Secretary of State.
1946	*Percy Williams Bridgman (American) for his work in the field of very high pressures.	*James B. Sumner (American) for discovering that enzymes can be crystallized, and *Wendell M. Stanley and *John H. Northrop (American) for preparing enzymes and virus proteins in pure form.	*Hermann Joseph Muller (American) for discovering that X rays can produce mutations.	*Hermann Hesse (German) for his novels, poems, and essays.	*John R. Mott (American) for his YMCA work, and for aiding displaced persons, and *Emily G. Balch (American) for her work as president of the Women's International League for Peace and Freedom.
1947	*Sir Edward V. Appleton (British) for exploring the ionosphere.	*Sir Robert Robinson (British) for his research on biologically significant plant substances.	*Carl F. and Gerty Cori (American) for their work on insulin, and *Bernardo Houssay (Argentinian) for studying the pancreas and the pituitary gland.	*André Gide (French) for his novels.	The Friends Service Council (British) and the American Friends Service Committee (American) for their humanitarian work.
1948	*Patrick M. S. Blackett (British) for his discoveries in cosmic radiation.	*Arne Tiselius (Swedish) for his discoveries on the nature of the serum proteins.	*Paul Mueller (Swiss) for discovering the insect-killing properties of DDT.	*T. S. Eliot (British) for his poems, essays, and plays.	No Award
1949	*Hideki Yukawa (Japanese) for discovering the meson.	*William Francis Giauque (American) for studying reactions to extreme cold.	Walter F. Hess (Swiss) for discovering how certain parts of the brain control organs of the body, and *António E. Moniz (Portuguese) for originating prefrontal lobotomy.	*William Faulkner (American) for his novels. (Award delayed until 1950.)	*John Boyd Orr (British) for directing the United Nations Food and Agriculture Organization.
1950	*Cecil Frank Powell (British) for his photographic method of studying atomic nuclei and his discoveries concerning mesons.	*Otto Diels and *Kurt Alder (German) for developing a method of synthesizing organic compounds of the diene group.	*Philip S. Hench, *Edward C. Kendall (American), and *Tadeus Reichstein (Swiss) for their discoveries on Cortisone and ACTH.	*Bertrand Russell (British) for his philosophic writings.	*Ralph J. Bunche (American) for his work as United Nations mediator in Palestine in 1948 and 1949.
1951	*Sir John D. Cockcroft (British) and *Ernest T. S. Walton (Irish) for working on the transmutation of atomic nuclei by artificially accelerated atomic particles.	*Edwin M. McMillan and *Glenn T. Seaborg (American) for discovering plutonium and other elements.	*Max Theiler (American) for developing the yellow fever vaccine known as 17-D.	*Pär Fabian Lagerkvist (Swedish) for his novels, particularly Barabbas.	*Léon Jouhaux (French) for helping to organize national and international labor unions.

1952

*Felix Bloch and *Edward Mills Purcell (American) for developing magnetic measurement methods for atomic nuclei.

*Archer J. P. Martin and *Richard Synge (British) for developing the partition chromatography process, a method of separating compounds.

*Selman A. Waksman (American) for his work in the discovery of streptomycin.

*François Mauriac (French) for his novels, essays, and poems.

*Albert Schweitzer (German) for his humanitarian work in Africa. (Award delayed until 1953.)

1953

*Frits Zernike (Dutch) for inventing the phase contrast microscope for cancer research.

*Hermann Staudinger (German) for discovering a way to synthesize fiber.

*Fritz Albert Lipmann (American) and *Hans Adolf Krebs (British) for their discoveries in biosynthesis and metabolism.

*Sir Winston Churchill (British) for his essays, speeches, and historical writings.

*George C. Marshall (American) for promoting peace through the European Recovery Program.

1954

*Max Born (German) for his basic research in quantum mechanics, and *Walther Bothe (German) for discoveries he made with his coincidence method.

*Linus Pauling (American) for his work on the forces that hold matter together.

*John F. Enders, *Thomas H. Weller, and *Frederick C. Robbins (American) for discovering a simple method of growing polio virus in test tubes.

*Ernest Hemingway (American) for his novels and short stories.

The United Nations High Commission for Refugees for providing international protection for millions of refugees and seeking permanent solutions to their problems. (Award delayed until 1955.)

1955

*Willis E. Lamb, Jr. (American) for discoveries on the structure of the hydrogen spectrum, and *Polykarp Kusch (American) for determining the magnetic moment of the electron.

Vincent Du Vigneaud (American) for discovering a process for making synthetic hormones.

*Hugo Theorell (Swedish) for his discoveries on the nature and action of oxidation enzymes.

*Halldór K. Laxness (Icelandic) for his novels.

No Award

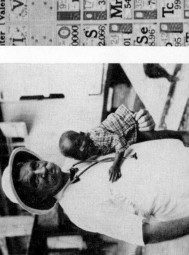

Glenn T. Seaborg, *far right*, shared the Nobel chemistry prize with Edwin M. McMillan in 1951.

Albert Schweitzer, winner of the peace prize for 1952, devoted his life to helping others.

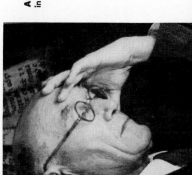

André Gide, *left*, won the Nobel literature prize in 1947. His novel *The Counterfeiters* is famous.

	PHYSICS	CHEMISTRY	PHYSIOLOGY AND MEDICINE	LITERATURE	PEACE	ECONOMICS
1956	*John Bardeen, *Walter H. Brattain, and *William Shockley (American) for inventing the transistor.	*Sir Cyril Hinshelwood (British) and *Nikolai N. Semenov (Russian) for their work on chemical chain reactions.	*André F. Cournand, *Dickinson W. Richards, Jr. (American), and *Werner Forssmann (German) for using a catheter to chart the interior of the heart.	*Juan Ramón Jiménez (Spanish) for his poems.	No Award	The prize in economics was established in 1969.
1957	*Tsung Dao Lee and *Chen Ning Yang (American) for disproving the law of conservation of parity.	*Lord Todd (British) for his work on the protein composition of cells.	*Daniel Bovet (Italian) for discovering antihistamines.	*Albert Camus (French) for his novels.	*Lester B. Pearson (Canadian) for organizing a United Nations force in Egypt.	
1958	*Pavel A. Cherenkov, *Ilya M. Frank, and *Igor Y. Tamm (Russian) for discovering and interpreting the Cherenkov effect in studying high-energy particles.	*Frederick Sanger (British) for discovering the structure of the insulin molecule.	*George Wells Beadle and *Edward Lawrie Tatum (American) for their work in biochemical genetics, and *Joshua Lederberg (American) for his studies of genetics in bacteria.	*Boris Pasternak (Russian) for his novels, especially Dr. Zhivago (declined).	*Dominique Georges Pire (Belgian) for his work in resettling displaced persons.	
1959	*Emilio Segrè and *Owen Chamberlain (American) for demonstrating the existence of the antiproton.	*Jaroslav Heyrovský (Czech) for developing polarographic method of analysis.	*Severo Ochoa and *Arthur Kornberg (American) for producing nucleic acid by artificial means.	*Salvatore Quasimodo (Italian) for his lyric poems.	*Philip Noel-Baker (British) for his work in promoting peace and disarmament.	
1960	*Donald A. Glaser (American) for inventing the bubble chamber to study subatomic particles.	*Willard F. Libby (American) for developing a method of radiocarbon dating.	*Sir Macfarlane Burnet (Australian) and *Peter B. Medawar (British) for research in transplanting human organs.	*Saint-John Perse (French) for his poems.	*Albert John Luthuli (African) for his peaceful campaign against racial restrictions in South Africa.	
1961	*Robert Hofstadter (American) for his studies of nucleons, and *Rudolf L. Mössbauer (German) for his research on gamma rays.	*Melvin Calvin (American) for his research on photosynthesis.	*Georg von Békésy (American) for demonstrating how the ear distinguishes between various sounds.	*Ivo Andrić (Yugoslavian) for his novels, especially The Bridge on the Drina.	*Dag Hammarskjöld (Swedish) for his efforts to bring peace to the Congo (awarded posthumously).	
1962	*Lev Davidovich Landau (Russian) for his research on liquid helium gas.	*John Cowdery Kendrew and *Max Ferdinand Perutz (British) for studies on globular proteins.	*James D. Watson (American) and *Francis H. Crick and *Maurice H. F. Wilkins (British) for their work on nucleic acid.	*John Steinbeck (American) for his novels, especially The Winter of Our Discontent.	*Linus Pauling (American) for trying to effect a ban on nuclear weapons.	
1963	*Eugene Paul Wigner (American) for his contributions to the understanding of atomic nuclei and elementary particles, and *Maria Goeppert-Mayer (American) and *J. Hans Jensen (German) for their work on the structure of atomic nuclei.	*Giulio Natta (Italian) for his contributions to the understanding of polymers, and *Karl Ziegler (German) for his production of organometallic compounds. The work of both men led to the production of improved plastics products.	*Sir John Carew Eccles (Australian) for his research on the transmission of nerve impulses, and *Alan Lloyd Hodgkin (British) and *Andrew Fielding Huxley (British) for their description of the behavior of nerve impulses.	*George Seferis (Greek) for his lyric poetry.	The International Committee of the Red Cross and The League of Red Cross Societies for humanitarian work.	

Year	Physics	Chemistry	Physiology or Medicine	Literature	Peace	Economics
1964	*Charles H. Townes (American) and *Nikolai G. Basov and *Alexander M. Prokhorov (Russians) for developing *masers* and *lasers*.	*Dorothy C. Hodgkin (British) for X-ray studies of compounds such as vitamin B₁₂ and penicillin.	*Konrad E. Bloch (American) and *Feodor Lynen (German) for their work on cholesterol and fatty acid metabolism.	*Jean-Paul Sartre (French) for his philosophical works (declined).	*Martin Luther King, Jr. (American), for leading the Negro struggle for equality in the U.S. through nonviolent means.	
1965	*Sin-itiro Tomonaga (Japanese) and *Julian S. Schwinger and *Richard P. Feynman (Americans) for their fundamental work in quantum electrodynamics.	Robert Burns Woodward (American) for his contributions to organic synthesis.	*François Jacob, *André Lwoff, and *Jacques Monod (French) for their discoveries concerning genetic control of enzyme and virus synthesis.	*Mikhail Sholokhov (Russian) for his novels.	United Nations Children's Fund (UNICEF) for its aid to children.	
1966	Alfred Kastler (French) for his work on the energy levels of atoms.	Robert S. Mulliken (American) for developing the *molecular-orbital* theory of chemical structure.	Francis Peyton Rous (American) for discovering a cancer-producing virus, and Charles B. Huggins (American) for discovering uses of hormones in treating cancer.	*Shmuel Yosef Agnon (Israeli) for his stories of Eastern European Jewish life, and *Nelly Sachs (Jewish) for her poetry about the Jewish people.	No Award.	
1967	Hans Albrecht Bethe (American) for his contributions to the theory of nuclear reactions, especially his discoveries on the energy production in stars.	Manfred Eigen (German) and Ronald G. W. Norrish and George Porter (British) for their work in high speed chemical reactions.	Ragnar Granit (Swedish) and H. Keffer Hartline and George Wald (Americans) for their work on the chemical and physiological visual processes in the eye.	*Miguel Angel Asturias (Guatemalan) for his writings rooted in national individuality and Indian traditions.	No Award.	
1968	Luis W. Alvarez (American) for his contributions to the knowledge of subatomic particles, including a technique for detecting these particles.	Lars Onsager (American) for developing the theory of reciprocal relations of thermodynamic activity.	Robert W. Holley, H. Gobind Khorana, and Marshall W. Nirenberg (Americans) for explaining how genes determine the function of cells.	Yasunari Kawabata (Japanese) for his novels about the Japanese people.	René Cassin (French) for furthering the cause of human rights.	
1969	Murray Gell-Mann (American) for his discoveries concerning the classification of nuclear particles and their interactions.	Derek H. R. Barton (British) and Odd Hassel (Norwegian) for their studies relating chemical reactions with the three-dimensional shape of molecules.	Max Delbrück, Alfred Hershey, and Salvador Luria (American) for their work with *bacteriophages*.	*Samuel B. Beckett (Irishborn) for his novels and plays.	*International Labor Organization (ILO) for its efforts to improve working conditions.	*Ragnar Frisch (Norwegian) and *Jan Tinbergen (Dutch) for work in *econometrics*, the developing of mathematical models to analyze economic activity.
1970	Hannes Olof Gösta Alfven (Swedish) for his work in *magnetohydrodynamics*, the study of electrical and magnetic effects in fluids that conduct electricity; and Louis Eugène Félix Néel (French) for his discoveries of magnetic properties that applied to computer memories.	Luis Federico Leloir (Argentinian) for his discovery of chemical compounds that affect the storage of chemical energy in living things.	Julius Axelrod (American), Bernard Katz (British), and Ulf Svante von Euler (Swedish) for their discoveries of the role played by certain chemicals in the transmission of nerve impulses.	*Alexander Solzhenitsyn (Russian) for his novels.	Norman E. Borlaug (American) for his central role in developing high-yield disease-resistant grains that increased food production in underdeveloped countries.	*Paul A. Samuelson (American) for his efforts to raise the level of scientific analysis in economic activity.

NOBELIUM

NOBELIUM (chemical symbol, No) is a man-made element with the atomic number 102. Its most stable isotope has a mass number of 255. The element was prepared by bombarding curium with carbon-13 ions in a cyclotron. It is unstable, and has a half-life of about 10 minutes (see RADIOACTIVITY [Half-Life]). This short half-life is characteristic of all man-made elements. Scientists from the United States, Sweden, and Great Britain isolated nobelium in 1957 at the Nobel Institute for Physics in Stockholm, Sweden.   PAUL R. FREY

NOBILE, UMBERTO. See AMUNDSEN, ROALD; EXPLORATION AND DISCOVERY (table: Famous Explorers).

NOBILITY, *no BIL uh tih*, of a country makes up a class of persons who have titles and certain privileges. Republics do not have titles of nobility. The Constitution of the United States forbids the government from giving these titles. European countries, especially Great Britain, have continued the custom of having nobility. The British nobility is called the *peerage*, and members of the peerage are called *peers*, meaning *equals*.

The British peerage began after the Norman Conquest of 1066, when William the Conqueror declared his followers *barons*. More powerful barons gradually came to be called *earls*. In 1337, the title of *duke* was added. The peerage now includes the following titles in descending order of rank: duke, marquis, earl, viscount, and baron.   MARION F. LANSING

Related Articles in WORLD BOOK include:

Baron	Earl	Marquis	Prince
Burke's Peerage	Lady	Middle Ages	Viscount
Duke	Lord	Parliament	

NOBLE GAS. See ELEMENT, CHEMICAL (How to Use the Periodic Table).

NODULE. See LEGUME.

NOËL. See CHRISTMAS.

NOEL-BAKER, PHILIP JOHN (1889-   ), British statesman and author, won the 1959 Nobel peace prize for his work in promoting international disarmament. He served at the Paris peace conference in 1919 and the Geneva disarmament conference in 1932. He also helped draft the United Nations Charter in 1945. Noel-Baker was born Philip John Baker in London. He studied at Haverford College in Pennsylvania, and at Cambridge University in Great Britain.

NOGUCHI, ISAMU (1904-   ), is an American sculptor whose work represents a wide variety of styles. Noguchi has said that he is "suspicious of the whole business of style— again it is a form of inhibition."

Noguchi works directly in nearly every sculptural material, avoiding such processes as casting, welding, or painting. Almost all his work has no recognizable subject matter. Noguchi seeks to preserve the nature of the sculptural material. He is intrigued

Isamu Noguchi became famous for his abstract sculpture. He created these three works in the mid-1940's. Their smooth, highly polished surfaces show the influence of the sculptor Constantin Brancusi.

Kaz Inouye

by problems of weight, mass, and tension, and these elements are his constant themes.

Noguchi was born in Los Angeles of an American mother and a well-known Japanese poet and scholar. He lived in Japan from the age of 2 until he was 13. Noguchi gave up medical studies at Columbia University to return to sculpture, his earlier ambition. In the late 1920's, he studied in Paris with Constantin Brancusi, who had a strong influence on his work. Noguchi has designed furniture and settings for ballets. He also has collaborated with architects in planning gardens, playgrounds, and bridges.   DOUGLAS GEORGE

NOISE may be random sound or unwanted sound. It may also be unwanted signals, such as static that interferes with radio transmission. The sound we hear is caused by vibrations in air, water, steel, or other substances. A tuning fork produces an almost *pure tone*, with only one *frequency*, or rate of vibration (see TONE). Musical instruments produce *harmonic sound*. Such sound contains many frequencies, called *overtones*, that are harmonically related (see HARMONICS). *Random sound* has many overtones that are not harmonically related. Mechanical devices produce such sound.

Unwanted sound can be caused by any kind of sound— tones, harmonic sound, or random sound. Sound is unwanted if it interferes with talking or listening to speech or music, if it is annoying or distracting, or if it damages the hearing mechanism. Persons exposed to a loud noise for a long time may suffer temporary or permanent loss of hearing. Workers continually exposed to loud noises may protect their hearing by wearing earplugs, earmuffs, or specially designed helmets. Noise can also be controlled by using heavy walls and tight doors to block its passage, or by using sound-absorptive materials to reduce its intensity. See ACOUSTICS; INSULATION (picture: Sound Insulation).

Unwanted signals can mean anything that interferes

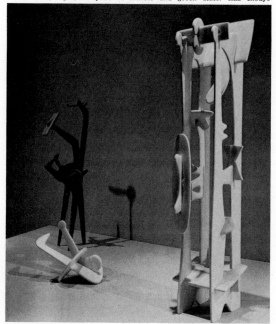

View Through Kouros, left rear; The Seed, left front; and Strange Bird, right; in polished marble and green slate. Kaz Inouye

with any kind of communication. Flickers of light that may be confused with blips on a radar screen are unwanted signals, or a form of noise. RICHARD H. BOLT

See also SOUND; DECIBEL; MUFFLER.

NOK was a West African civilization that flourished from about 500 B.C. until at least A.D. 200. The civilization was centered in the valley where the Niger and Benue rivers meet. Today, Nok is the name of a village in Nigeria, about 100 miles northeast of the city of Baro.

The people of ancient Nok produced the oldest sculptures found so far in black Africa. These sculptures of animal and human figures were identified by the British archaeologist Bernard Fagg, who named them after the village of Nok. Similar sculptures have been discovered at many other sites in the river valley.

The Nok sculptures are made of terra cotta, a kind of earthenware. They vary in size from an inch high to life size. All the human heads have pierced ears, and the eyes are hollowed out. Scholars do not know what function these sculptures had in the Nok society. However, some believe that the sculpture of other West African peoples shows Nok influence.

The people of Nok probably farmed the land, but they also hunted and gathered food. They made tools and weapons of stone and at least started to learn to smelt and use iron. Scholars know from the decorations on Nok sculpture that the people probably wore beaded jewelry, including anklets, bracelets, and heavy collars. The Nok people apparently lived in clay huts in the lowlands and hills. The people, like some Nigerians today, worshiped their ancestors and had many gods. Historians know little about the end of the Nok culture. LEO SPITZER

NOLAN, PHILIP. See HALE, EDWARD EVERETT.

NOM DE PLUME. See NAME, PERSONAL (Pseudonym).

NOMAD, *NO mad*, is a person who wanders about and has no settled home. The word *nomad* is from a Greek word that means *one who wanders for pasture*. Most nomadic peoples wander through a general area in a cycle according to the seasons. The African Pygmies, the Negritos of Malaya, and the Australian Aborigines hunt animals and gather wild vegetables and fruits. Many of the American Indians lived as nomadic hunters and gatherers. There are few true nomads today.

Pastoral nomads live in the deserts of Arabia, Central Asia, and North Africa. These regions cannot be farmed, but have enough grass to feed grazing animals. Pastoral nomads raise camels, horses, sheep, and goats, and move seasonally to find new pastures. They generally live in portable tents, and have a simpler life than settled peoples. The Hebrews and other wandering tribes of Biblical times were pastoral nomads. This way of life still exists in the Middle East. FRED EGGAN

See also ARAB (Nomadic Life); BEDOUIN; GYPSY; MIGRATION (History); MONGOLIA (People; picture).

NOME, Alaska (pop. 2,488; alt. 20 ft.), an ocean port and gold-mining center, lies on the northern shore of Norton Sound of the Bering Sea. It is about 2,400 miles by sea northwest of Seattle, Wash. For location, see ALASKA (political map).

Placer gold mining forms the backbone of Nome's economy. Three large dredges operate near the city. Ivory carving is the principal industry of the Eskimos in the area. Military construction and governmental

offices also contribute to the income. The port of Nome is open from June to October. Two airlines serve the region. It also has a radio station.

Nome began as a boom town in 1899 when gold was discovered nearby. Within a short time, 40,000 miners, merchants, and adventurers had set up a tent city. Many of Nome's structures today are built on skids because permanent foundations are difficult to sink in the frozen subsoil. Nome was incorporated in 1901. It has a mayor-council government. LYMAN E. ALLEN

NOMINATING CONVENTION. See POLITICAL CONVENTION.

NOMINATING ELECTION. See PRIMARY ELECTION.

NOMINATIVE CASE. See CASE.

NONAGGRESSION PACT is a treaty by which two or more nations agree to settle mutual disputes by peaceful means and not to attack each other. Between World War I and World War II, many nations signed nonaggression pacts because there was no international force strong enough to prevent aggression. See LEAGUE OF NATIONS.

Nonaggression pacts sometimes were not effective because they lacked enforcement procedures, and also because participating nations violated their agreements. For example, during the 1920's and 1930's, Russia signed pacts with many of its neighbors. But Russia violated its agreements with Estonia, Finland, Latvia, and Lithuania when it occupied them in 1939 and 1940.

Since the end of World War II, there have been fewer attempts to establish nonaggression pacts. Many nations feel that the United Nations charter contains adequate pledges against aggression. See UNITED NATIONS.

One of the major problems with nonaggression pacts is to determine an acceptable definition of *aggression*. The UN has debated this question, but has not been able to reach any agreement. Some nations believe that aggression includes only direct military attacks. Others feel that when one country aids revolution in another country through propaganda, subversion, or by taking over government posts, it constitutes indirect aggression. ELTON ATWATER

NONCOMMISSIONED OFFICER. See RANK IN ARMED SERVICES.

NONCONDUCTOR. See ELECTRICITY (Current Electricity).

NONCONFORMIST, *NAHN kun FAWR mist*, is one who refuses to conform, especially to the regulations of an established religion. More specifically, the term refers to one of the Protestant dissenters who refused to conform to the Church of England and various Acts of Uniformity passed by Parliament. These acts were based on the belief of the Middle Ages that it was the duty of the government to enforce a common form of worship on all the people.

During the English Civil War and the Commonwealth (1642-1660), about 8,000 nonconformist ministers and teachers replaced the Anglican clergy. But in 1662, Parliament passed an Act of Uniformity which provided that every minister and teacher who did not agree to use the Book of Common Prayer be expelled from the churches and schools. Other curbs followed, but relief came with the Toleration Act of 1689. WALTER H. STOWE

NONELECTROLYTE. See ELECTROLYTE.

NONES. See MONTH.

NONESUCH. See SHAMROCK.

NON-EUCLIDEAN GEOMETRY. See GEOMETRY.

NONILLION, *noh NILL yun.* In the United States and France, nonillion is a thousand octillions, or a unit with 30 zeros. In England, it is a unit with 54 zeros.

NON-IMPORTATION ACT. See WAR OF 1812 (American Reaction).

NON-INTERCOURSE ACT. Congress passed the Non-Intercourse Act in 1809. The act prohibited American shippers from trading with Great Britain and France, which were then at war with each other. Both warring nations had interfered with American commerce by taking American ships. The British offense was aggravated by the policy of *impressing* (seizing) British, and sometimes American, sailors. President Jefferson felt that the Non-Intercourse Act would compel Britain and France to recognize American commercial rights.

In 1810, Congress passed the so-called Macon's Bill No. 2, which restored trade with both Great Britain and France. But Great Britain continued to interfere with American shipping until 1812, when open warfare broke out.   RAY ALLEN BILLINGTON

NONMETAL. See METAL.

NONPARTISAN LEAGUE, a political organization of farmers, was founded in North Dakota in 1915. Its aims were to restore government control to the farmers and to establish state-owned institutions for their benefit. From 1916 to 1921, the league controlled the government of North Dakota, and its influence spread to neighboring states. In Minnesota, it helped to create the powerful Farmer-Labor party.

After 1921, the power of the Nonpartisan League declined, except in North Dakota. For many years, most of the league candidates ran as Republicans, though they had little in common with Republicans elsewhere. In 1956, the league officially aligned itself with the Democratic party in North Dakota.   HAROLD W. BRADLEY

See also FARMER-LABOR PARTY.

NONSCHEDULED AIRLINE. See AIRLINE (Kinds).

NONVIOLENT RESISTANCE. See KING, MARTIN LUTHER, JR.; NEGRO (The Civil Rights Movement); GANDHI, MOHANDAS K.; CHAVEZ, CESAR E.

NOODLE. See MACARONI.

NOON. See DAY; TIME.

NOOTKA INDIANS, *NOOT kuh,* were noted for the beauty and seaworthiness of their cedar canoes. No other hunting and fishing people in the world made such fine canoes. Some people say that this Nootka craft influenced the New England designers of the superb American clipper ships of the early 1800's.

Nootka villages dotted northwestern Washington state and the west side of Vancouver Island. Nootka craftsmen made remarkable wooden mechanical devices, such as puppets and masks with movable parts. The Nootka used Dentalium shells as a kind of money, and this custom spread to many other Indian groups in the Northwest region. In other respects, the Nootka way of life resembled that of other fishing groups in the Pacific Northwest (see INDIAN, AMERICAN [Indians of the Northwest Coast]). Little remains of the Nootka way of life. But many still speak the language and remember some of the old beliefs and customs.   MELVILLE JACOBS

NOPAL. See PRICKLY PEAR.

NORAD. See AIR FORCE, UNITED STATES (Defense); NATIONAL DEFENSE (Air Defense).

NORDENSKJÖLD, *NOOR dun SHOOLD,* **NILS ADOLF ERIK** (1832-1901), BARON NORDENSKJÖLD, was a Swedish polar explorer, mineralogist, and map authority. In 1878 and 1879, he became the first man to sail through the Northeast Passage between the Atlantic and Pacific oceans. He accomplished this feat by sailing along the northern coast of Europe and Asia. Nordenskjöld tells of this journey in his book, *Voyage of the Vega* (1881).

Nordenskjöld was born in Helsinki, Finland. He moved to Sweden in 1857, and became a Swedish citizen. He led two expeditions in an attempt to reach the North Pole. On the first one in 1868, he pushed to within about 400 nautical miles of the Pole. This was farther north (81°42') than anyone had gone before.

Nordenskjöld studied the geology of Greenland in 1870. He returned in 1883, and penetrated the ice barrier off the east coast. He traveled far enough over the inland ice to determine that it covered the interior of the island.   JOHN EDWARDS CASWELL

NORDHOFF, CHARLES BERNARD, and **HALL, JAMES NORMAN,** were a team of American novelists. Together they wrote a number of adventure stories of the South Seas. The best-known are *Mutiny on the Bounty* (1932), *Men Against the Sea* (1933), *Pitcairn's Island* (1934), and *The Hurricane* (1935). *Mutiny on the Bounty* and *The Hurricane* were made into movies.

Charles Bernard Nordhoff (1887-1947) wrote *The Fledgling* (1919), *The Pearl Lagoon* (1924), and *The Derelict* (1928). His first work with Hall was *Lafayette Flying Corps* (1920), a history of the famous World War I air group in which both served.

Nordhoff was born in London of American parents. During World War I, he served as a pilot, first in the French volunteer squadron the Lafayette Escadrille, and then in the United States Army Air Service. After the war, he and Hall lived in Tahiti.

James Norman Hall (1887-1951) wrote *Kitchener's Mob* (1916), *Dr. Dogbody's Leg* (1940), and his autobiography *My Island Home* (1952). He was born in Colfax, Iowa. He spent four years as a social worker. In 1916, he joined the French Air Force, where he met Nordhoff.   JOHN O. EIDSON

NORFOLK. See ENGLAND (political map).

NORFOLK, Va. (pop. 307,951; alt. 10 ft.), is an important shipping and shipbuilding center on one of the world's great harbors, Hampton Roads. Norfolk lies at the mouth of the Elizabeth River, about 150 miles south of Washington, D.C. (see VIRGINIA [political map]). The 20-mile Chesapeake Bay Bridge-Tunnel across the Chesapeake Bay links Norfolk with the Delmarva Peninsula. Norfolk and nearby Portsmouth form a metropolitan area with a population of 680,600. For the monthly weather in Norfolk, see VIRGINIA (Climate).

Norfolk ranks as one of the world's leading coal-shipping ports. It is the site of the nation's largest naval installation, the Norfolk Naval Base. Here the United States Navy maintains its largest supply depot, an aircraft landing field, and the headquarters of the Atlantic Fleet and Fifth Naval District. See NORFOLK NAVAL BASE.

Recreation and Cultural Life. Norfolk has two municipal golf courses and a city auditorium. Other recreational centers include Foreman Field and more than 100 playgrounds. Ocean View, a popular bathing and fishing area, lies within the city limits. The Back Bay section and nearby Dismal Swamp offer abundant wildlife for hunting. Virginia Beach, an ocean resort, lies about 20 miles east of Norfolk.

The city is the home of Norfolk State College and Old Dominion University. Other cultural and educational centers include the Museum of Arts and Sciences and the Norfolk Public Library. Each spring, many persons visit Norfolk's 100-acre Municipal Gardens, which has over 120,000 azalea plants.

Industry. Norfolk's major industries include automobile assembly, fertilizer production, and repair and building of ships. The chief exports from Norfolk include chemicals, clothing, coal, tobacco, food products, cotton goods, machinery, and lumber. Many of the city's people work in the seafood industry.

History. Norfolk was founded in 1682 and incorporated as a town in 1705. It served as a colonial tobacco and naval supply port. In 1736, it became a borough, a political unit separate from a county. American forces burned Norfolk in 1776, in an attack on British troops and sympathizers. Incorporated as a city in 1845, Norfolk has a council-manager government.   FRANCIS B. SIMKINS

NORFOLK ISLAND is an isolated island in the South Pacific Ocean. It lies 930 miles northeast of Sydney, Australia, and 630 miles northwest of New Zealand. For location, see PACIFIC ISLANDS (color map). Many of the inhabitants are descendants of the crew of the sailing ship, *Bounty*. The sailors of the *Bounty* mutinied against their captain's treatment and settled on Pitcairn Island in 1790.

In 1774, Captain James Cook discovered Norfolk Island. For many years, the island was a part of the Australian state of New South Wales, which used it as a penal colony until 1856. In that year, settlers were moved to the island from Pitcairn Island, more than 3,000 miles across the Pacific. In 1914, Norfolk Island was separated from New South Wales and became a federal territory of the Australian Commonwealth. The island's administrator has his office in Kingston.

Norfolk Island has a population of about 1,000, and covers an area of 13 square miles. It has fertile soil. The people who live on the island grow citrus fruits, bananas, and vegetables.   EDWIN H. BRYAN, JR.

See also PITCAIRN ISLAND.

NORFOLK NAVAL BASE, Va., is the largest naval base in the United States. It includes the headquarters of the Atlantic Fleet, the Fifth Naval District, and the North Atlantic Treaty Organization (NATO) Allied Command Atlantic. Commissioned in 1917, the base houses the Armed Forces Staff College and the navy's oldest supply center. Nearby are the Naval Amphibious Base at Little Creek, a weapons station at Yorktown, and a shipyard at Portsmouth.   JOHN A. OUDINE

NORFOLK STATE COLLEGE. See UNIVERSITIES AND COLLEGES (table).

NORGAY, TENZING. See MOUNT EVEREST (with picture).

NORGE. See AIRSHIP (Italian Airships).

NORMAL SCHOOL is another name for a teacher-training institution. See TEACHING (Preparation).

NORMAN. The Normans were a group of Vikings, or *Norsemen* (Scandinavians), who first settled in France, then spread into England, southern Italy, and Sicily. In the 800's, Norman warriors began their conquests by raiding French coasts and river valleys. By the early 900's, they had colonized the French territory near the mouth of the Seine River that is now known as Normandy. In 911, the Norman chief Hrolf, or Rollo (860?-931?), became a duke in the service of the Frankish king, Charles the Simple. The Normans became Christians and adopted French customs. Many of the Normans became famous as administrators, church leaders, and crusaders.

In 1066, Norman warriors under the leadership of William, Duke of Normandy, conquered England, and Norman influence spread throughout the British Isles. During the same period, Norman groups won great victories in other lands. Robert Guiscard (1015?-1085), son of Tancred of Hauteville, conquered southern Italy. Roger, another of Tancred's sons, took the island of Sicily from the Moslems. These two territories were later united in the famous Kingdom of the Two Sicilies by Roger's son, Roger II.   WILLIAM C. BARK

See also NORMAN CONQUEST; NORMANDY; VIKING.

NORMAN, Okla. (pop. 52,117; alt. 1,170 ft.), an educational center in the heart of a fertile farming region, is the home of the University of Oklahoma. Norman is the seat of Cleveland County. The city lies about 20 miles south of Oklahoma City. For location, see OKLAHOMA (political map). Oklahoma pioneers founded Norman in 1889. The city has a mayor-council type of government.   JOHN W. MORRIS

NORMAN ARCHITECTURE is a style of building which had its origin in Normandy, in northwestern France. It reached a high development in England after the Norman Conquest of 1066 and during the 1100's. Norman architecture is bold and massive, with short, heavy columns supporting semicircular arches. Geometric patterns of zigzags and similar forms are highly developed. Parts of some English Gothic cathedrals were done in the Norman style.   BERNARD LEMANN

NORMAN CONQUEST is the name given to the conquest of England in 1066 by William, Duke of Normandy. The duke, known as William the Conqueror, led a Norman army across the Channel into England.

William was a proud and ruthless ruler, and a vassal of the King of France. He hoped to follow his cousin, King Edward the Confessor, as King of England. William claimed that Edward had named him as his successor. The chief contender for the English throne was Harold, Earl of Wessex. But William also claimed that Harold, who had been shipwrecked on the Norman coast in 1064, had sworn a solemn oath to support William's claim to the throne. In 1066, King Edward died. The Anglo-Saxon Witan (Great Council) elected Harold king (see HAROLD [II]).

William at once declared his right to the throne. He secured the support of the pope and gathered an army of about 5,000 men. William landed in England without opposition at Pevensey, near Hastings, on the coast of Sussex.

The Normans were aided in their successful landing by a chance happening. While Harold was waiting for

Culver

The Norman Conquest of England Began in 1066 When William the Conqueror Sailed His Army Across the Channel.

the Normans to arrive, he received news that a Norwegian force had landed in the north of England. He hastened north and defeated the Norwegians. Meanwhile, William landed his force on the unprotected coast. Harold then marched back across England and attacked the Norman army near Hastings on October 14, 1066. This was the historic Battle of Hastings, which established the Norman rule of England. King Harold was defeated and slain. William marched on to London, where he was crowned King of England on Christmas Day, 1066. The Conqueror spent several years subduing the Saxons. At first he tried to win over the Saxon nobles, but they opposed him stubbornly.

William established the Norman rule in England on a strong foundation. He hesitated at no act which he thought would increase the power of the crown. He took the land of most of the English nobility, who had opposed him. However, William was generous in some cases and did not deprive the rebel of his lands or titles. The confiscated land was then divided among William's Norman followers. William forced all these landholders to swear direct loyalty to himself. In this way, he put all the lords of England under his direct control. In order to know conditions in England, the Conqueror directed the preparation of the famous Domesday Book. This was a survey of all the regions in his kingdom. Many English families trace their names to entries in the Domesday Book (see DOMESDAY BOOK).

The descendants of the Normans became the ruling class in England. For a time, they kept themselves aloof from the Anglo-Saxons and treated them as a conquered people. But as the years went by the Normans and the Anglo-Saxons intermarried. The two races, which even in the beginning were similar, blended into one.

The Normans were a race of conquerors, with a genius for law and government, and they ruled England with great ability. In addition, English language, literature, and architecture owe much to the Normans. At first the Normans spoke French. Later, the Norman French blended with the Germanic tongue of the Anglo-Saxons and became English.   BASIL D. HENNING

See also ENGLAND (The Norman Conquest); HASTINGS, BATTLE OF; IRELAND (History); WILLIAM (I).

NORMANDY is a region in northwestern France. It was named after the Norsemen who conquered the area in the 800's. It lies along the English Channel coast between the regions of Picardy and Brittany. The famous towns of Normandy include Rouen, the capital of the old province; Le Havre, Harfleur, Caen, Bayeux, and Cherbourg. The inhabitants are well known as sailors and farmers. The farmers specialize in dairying and raising fruits, especially apples for cider and brandy. Iron ore is mined near Caen.

In A.D. 911, the Carolingian king, Charles the Simple, made Normandy a duchy under the Norman chieftain Hrolf, or Rollo. One of Rollo's most famous descendants was William the Conqueror, who won the English crown after the Battle of Hastings in 1066. Normandy was united with England during the reign of the English king, Henry I (1100-1135). England and France struggled for control of Normandy during the Hundred Years' War. The English recovered the region twice, but finally lost it in 1449 to Charles VII, king of France. Joan of Arc became famous as the leader of French troops in the fight for Normandy.

Normandy attracted world-wide attention on June 6, 1944, when Allied troops landed on its beaches. From Normandy, the Allies drove the Germans out of France. Visitors to the beaches may still see the wreckage of ships that took part in the historic invasion. Many Norman towns were damaged in the fighting, but have been repaired.   ROBERT E. DICKINSON

See also CLOTHING (color picture, Europe); FURNITURE (Norman); NORMAN; WORLD WAR II (D-Day).

NORMANDY, DUKE OF. See WILLIAM (I, the Conqueror).

NORNS were the three Fates of Scandinavian mythology. They were three sisters: Urd (Past), Verdandi (Present), and Skuld (Future). Urd was old and looked toward the past. Verdandi faced straight ahead into the present. Skuld represented the future, and looked in a direction opposite from that of Urd. The fate of men and gods was decided by the Norns.

The Norse people believed that there were many lesser Norns, and one for each person.   PADRAIC COLUM

See also FATES.

NORODOM SIHANOUK, *NOR ah dum SEE hah nook* (1922-   ), ruled Cambodia as chief of state from 1960 to 1970. He became king in 1941. But in 1955, he gave up the throne, made his father king, and served as premier. After his father died in 1960, Sihanouk became chief of state. In March, 1970, pro-Western military leaders overthrew Sihanouk's government. Sihanouk then went to Peking and set up a government-in-exile there.

During the Vietnam War, Prince Sihanouk followed a zigzag course in foreign relations. At times he co-operated with the United States and South Vietnam. At other times he cooperated with North Vietnam. The prince claimed that his goal was to maintain Cambodia's independence and territorial integrity.

Sihanouk was born in Cambodia when it was part of French Indochina. His grandfather and great-grandfather had been Cambodian kings. He attended French schools in Saigon and Paris, and was elected king by the royal council with French approval in 1941. At first, Prince Sihanouk accepted French rule of his country. But in 1953, he demanded complete independence for Cambodia. Within a few months, the French agreed.

NORRIS, FRANK (1870-1902), was an American novelist and journalist and a leader of the naturalism movement in literature. Norris believed that a novel should serve a moral purpose. The novelist, he said, must "sacrifice money, fashion and popularity for the greater reward of realizing that he has told the truth." See NATURALISM.

Benjamin Franklin Norris was born in Chicago. He moved to San Francisco with his family in 1884 and attended the University of California from 1890 to 1894. At the university he came under the influence of the writings of the French naturalist writer Émile Zola and began to write *McTeague*, one of his finest novels. Norris then spent a year at Harvard University, where he wrote part of an unfinished novel, *Vandover and the Brute*. In 1895 and 1896, during the Boer War, Norris was a reporter in South Africa for *Collier's* magazine and the *San Francisco Chronicle*. In 1896, he returned to San Francisco where he became assistant editor of a magazine called *The Wave*. In 1899, he took a job as manuscript reader for a publisher in New York City. That same year Norris published *McTeague*, which tells how circumstances and a greedy wife force a man to become a murderer.

Norris planned a three-novel series called *Epic of the Wheat* to tell about the production, distribution, and consumption of wheat in the United States. *The Octopus* (1901) dramatizes how a railroad controlled a group of California wheat farmers by such means as charging excessive freight rates for hauling wheat. It ranks with *McTeague* as Norris' finest work. Both novels show the author's weakness for melodrama but illustrate his genius for revealing character and writing exciting action scenes. The second volume of the series, *The Pit*, was published in 1903, after Norris died following an operation for appendicitis. The final volume, *The Wolf*, was never written. DOMINICK CONSOLO

NORRIS, GEORGE WILLIAM (1861-1944), was one of the great independent statesmen of American public life. During 40 years in Congress, he ignored party politics to fight for whatever he believed to be right.

Norris was elected to the United States House of Representatives as a Republican from Nebraska in 1902. He served for 10 years. In 1910, he led the fight to free the House from the dictatorial power of Speaker Joseph Cannon.

Norris was elected a United States senator from Nebraska in 1912. He opposed American entry into World War I and into the League of Nations. But his main interest lay in the development of public ownership of public utilities. He wanted the U.S. government to develop the electric power of the Tennessee River Valley, despite the policies of his own Republican Party. In 1933, Congress finally passed his bill to create the Tennessee Valley Authority (TVA). A dam on the Tennessee was named in his honor.

Norris also helped pass the 20th (Lame Duck) Amendment to the United States Constitution. This shortened the time gap between congressional elections and the first meeting of the new Congress. The amendment reduced the influence of defeated congressmen.

Norris realized the danger to America resulting from the rise of Naziism and Fascism in Europe. He supported aid to Great Britain in the early years of World War II. Norris was defeated for re-election in 1942. He was born in Sandusky County, Ohio, and studied law at Valparaiso University. He moved to Beaver City, Nebr., in 1885. JOHN A. GARRATY

NORRIS DAM. See TENNESSEE (color picture: Norris Dam); TENNESSEE VALLEY AUTHORITY (The Dams; picture: Norris Dam).

NORRIS-LAGUARDIA ACT OF 1932. See YELLOW-DOG CONTRACTS.

NORRISH, RONALD G. W. See NOBEL PRIZES (table [1967]).

NORSE MYTHOLOGY. See MYTHOLOGY.

NORSEMAN. See VIKING.

NORTH, LORD (1732-1792), FREDERICK, EARL OF GUILFORD, was a British prime minister whose short-sighted treatment of the American Colonies helped bring on the Revolutionary War.

North was closely associated with King George III, and managed the House of Commons in the king's interests (see GEORGE [III] of England). Even when he disagreed with his master's policy, he did not oppose it. He often asked to resign, but the king would not allow it. North supported the tea tax that became one of the causes of the Revolutionary War (see BOSTON TEA PARTY). As the Revolutionary War progressed, North's administration became increasingly disorganized and demoralized. He finally persuaded the king to accept his resignation in 1782. He became joint secretary of state with Charles Fox in 1783, but resigned after only nine months in office.

He was born in London on April 13, 1732. He attended Eton College and Oxford University. His father had him elected to Parliament in 1754 from a "pocket borough" owned by the family. North later served in the Treasury and as a member of the Privy Council. He became chancellor of the exchequer and leader of the House of Commons in 1767. In 1770, North became prime minister. W. B. WILLCOX

NORTH ADAMS STATE COLLEGE. See UNIVERSITIES AND COLLEGES (table).

Yukon Territory, Canada

Alaskan Eskimo Girl

NORTH AMERICA

Clarence W. Olmstead, the contributor of this article, is Professor of Geography at the University of Wisconsin at Madison.

Niagara Falls

Guard at the Citadel, Quebec

New York City Harbor

Roundup in Wyoming

Panama Girl in Costume

Street in Mexico

--------- FACTS IN BRIEF ---------

Area: 9,416,000 square miles. *Greatest Distances* (mainland)—(north-south) 4,500 miles; (east-west) 4,000 miles. *Coastline*—96,459 miles.

Population: 329,000,000; density, 35 persons to the square mile.

Physical Features: *Chief Mountain Ranges*—Alaska, Appalachian, Cascade, Coast, Rocky, Sierra Madre, Sierra Nevada. *Highest Peaks*—McKinley (alt. 20,320 feet), Logan (19,850 feet), Orizaba (18,-701 feet), Saint Elias (18,008 feet). *Lowest Point*—Death Valley (282 feet below sea level). *Chief Rivers*—Arkansas, Colorado, Columbia, Fraser, Mackenzie, Mississippi, Missouri, Nelson, Ohio, Rio Grande, St. Lawrence, Yukon. *Chief Lakes*—Athabasca, Erie, Great Bear, Great Salt, Great Slave, Huron, Michigan, Nicaragua, Ontario, Superior, Winnipeg. *Chief Deserts*—Chihuahuan, Colorado, Great Basin, Mojave, Painted, Sonoran, Vizcaíno, Yuma. *Chief Waterfalls*—Niagara, Ribbon, Silver Strand, Takakkaw, Upper Yosemite. *Chief Islands*—Cuba, Greenland, Hispaniola, Jamaica, Newfoundland, Puerto Rico, Vancouver.

Chief Products: *Manufacturing and Processing*—airplanes, automobiles, cement, chemicals, clothing, electrical products, food products, furniture, leather products, locomotives, machinery, metals, paper, rubber products, textiles, tobacco products, wood products. *Agriculture*—beef cattle, coffee, corn, cotton, dairy products, fruits and vegetables, hay, hogs, oats, poultry and eggs, soybeans, sugar, tobacco, wheat. *Mining*—asbestos, bauxite, building stone, coal, copper, gold, gypsum, iron ore, lead, molybdenum, natural gas, nickel, petroleum, phosphate, potash, salt, silver, sulfur, uranium ore, zinc.

Credits: Bob and Ira Spring, Publix; WORLD BOOK Photo; WORLD BOOK Photo; WORLD BOOK Photo; Martin Helfer, Shostal; Hal Rumel, Publix; Max Tatch, Shostal; WORLD BOOK Photo.

NORTH AMERICA, the third largest of the seven continents, extends from the cold Arctic Ocean in the north to the warm tropics in the south. Only Asia and Africa have greater areas. Canada and the United States occupy the northern four-fifths of North America. Mexico and Central America make up the southern part. North America also includes many widely separated islands, such as Greenland and the West Indies.

With about a tenth of the earth's people and about a sixth of its land area, North America produces about half the world's manufactured goods and a large share of its mineral, forest, and farm products. Most of North America's vast wealth, however, is centered in the United States and Canada. These countries, with great industries and vast natural resources, have the highest standards of living in the world. The Central American and Caribbean countries have fewer industries and resources, and much lower living standards.

Nature gave North America many varieties of beautiful landscapes. The seacoasts of the Atlantic and Pacific oceans have thousands of miles of sandy beaches and rocky cliffs. In the interior, snow-capped mountains tower above gently rolling plains. The largest freshwater lakes in the world, the Great Lakes, are in North America. The continent also includes the world's most spectacular canyon, the Grand Canyon of the Colorado River. Fertile, green fields cover much of North America, but there also are immense, dry deserts.

When European explorers and colonists reached North America nearly 500 years ago, they found it largely a wilderness inhabited by primitive Indians. Only the Aztec and Maya Indians of Mexico and Central America had developed advanced civilizations that included written languages and large cities. The northern part of the continent was settled mostly by English-speaking (Anglo-Saxon) people. This region is sometimes called *Anglo-America.* The southern part of the continent was settled mostly by Spanish-speaking people. It is sometimes called *Middle America,* because it lies between Anglo-America and South America.

INDEPENDENT COUNTRIES OF NORTH AMERICA

Map Key	Name	Area (sq. mi.)	Population	Capital	Government	Date of Independence	Official Language
M12	Barbados	166	263,000	Bridgetown	Monarchy	1966	English
G7	Canada	3,851,809	21,979,000	Ottawa	Monarchy	1931	English, French
N9	Costa Rica	19,575	1,808,000	San José	Republic	1821	Spanish
L9	Cuba	44,218	8,693,000	Havana	Communist Dictatorship	1898	Spanish
L10	Dominican Republic	18,816	4,480,000	Santo Domingo	Republic	1821	Spanish
N8	El Salvador	8,260	3,642,000	San Salvador	Republic	1821	Spanish
M8	Guatemala	42,042	5,331,000	Guatemala City	Republic	1821	Spanish
M10	Haiti	10,714	4,960,000	Port-au-Prince	Republic	1804	French
M8	Honduras	43,277	2,811,000	Tegucigalpa	Republic	1821	Spanish
M9	Jamaica	4,232	2,054,000	Kingston	Monarchy	1962	English
L6	Mexico	761,602	52,406,000	Mexico City	Republic	1821	Spanish
N8	Nicaragua	50,193	2,048,000	Managua	Republic	1821	Spanish
N9	Panama	29,209	1,512,000	Panamá	Republic	1903	Spanish
M12	Trinidad and Tobago	1,980	1,099,000	Port-of-Spain	Monarchy	1962	English
J7	United States	3,675,545	212,161,000	Washington, D.C.	Republic	1776	English

OTHER POLITICAL UNITS IN NORTH AMERICA

Map Key	Name	Area (sq. mi.)	Population	Capital	Status
L12	Antigua	171	64,000	Saint John's	State associated with Great Britain
L9	Bahamas*	4,403	161,000	Nassau	British colony with some self-government
L9	Bermuda*	21	53,000	Hamilton	British colony with some self-government
M8	British Honduras*	8,867	127,000	Belize City	British colony with some self-government
M9	Cayman Islands*	100	9,000	Georgetown	British colony
M12	Dominica	290	78,000	Roseau	State associated with Great Britain
D9	Greenland*	840,000	52,000	Godthåb	Province of Denmark
M12	Grenada	133	110,000	Saint George's	State associated with Great Britain
L12	Guadeloupe*	687	343,000	Basse-Terre	Overseas department of France
M12	Martinique*	425	357,000	Fort-de-France	Overseas department of France
L11	Montserrat*	38	16,000	Plymouth	British colony
M11	Netherlands Antilles*	371	222,000	Willemstad	Self-governing part of The Netherlands
N9	Panama Canal Zone*	553	50,000	Balboa Heights	United States leasehold from Panama
L11	Puerto Rico*	3,435	2,856,000	San Juan	United States commonwealth
L11	Saint Christopher (St. Kitts)-Nevis-Anguilla	138	57,000	Basseterre	State associated with Great Britain
M12	Saint Lucia	238	117,000	Castries	State associated with Great Britain
H11	Saint Pierre and Miquelon*	93	5,000	Saint Pierre	French territory with some self-government
M12	Saint Vincent	150	99,000	Kingstown	State associated with Great Britain
L10	Turks and Caicos Islands*	166	6,000	Grand Turk	British colony
L11	Virgin Islands, British*	59	10,000	Road Town	British colony with some self-government
L11	Virgin Islands, U.S.*	133	80,000	Charlotte Amalie	United States territory

Populations are 1971 estimates based on the latest official figures.
Each independent country has a separate article in WORLD BOOK.

*Has a separate article in WORLD BOOK.

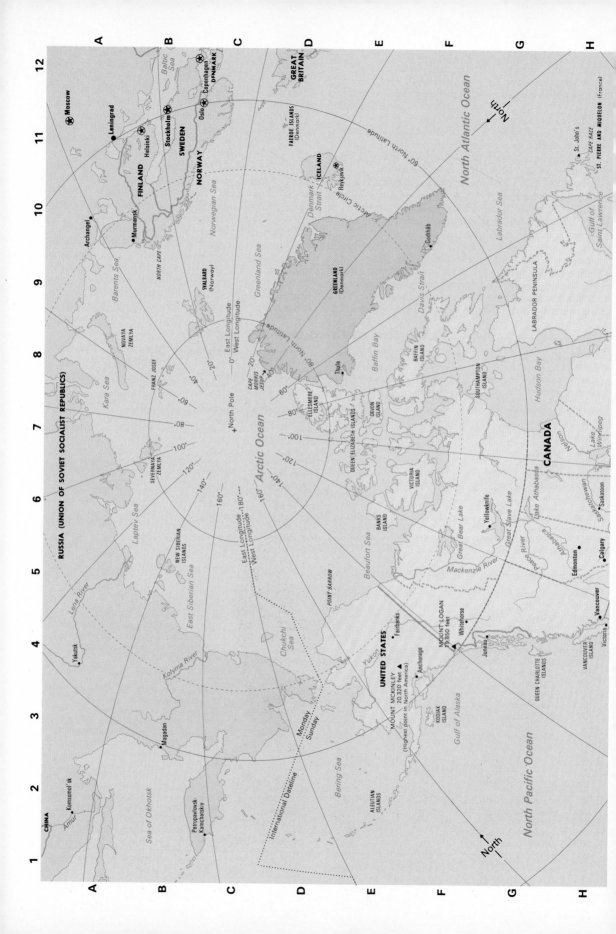

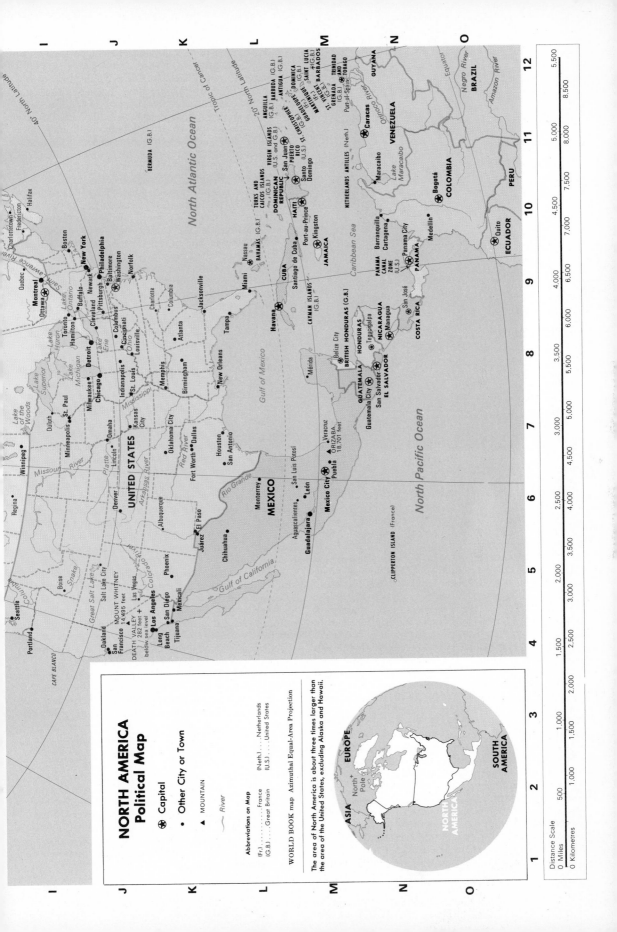

NORTH AMERICA
Political Map

✪ Capital

• Other City or Town

▲ MOUNTAIN

〰 River

Abbreviations on Map

(Fr.) . . . . France   (Neth.) . . . . . Netherlands
(G.B.) . . . . Great Britain   (U.S.) . . . . . United States

WORLD BOOK map   Azimuthal Equal-Area Projection

The area of North America is about three times larger than the area of the United States, excluding Alaska and Hawaii.

Distance Scale
0 Miles   500   1,000   1,500   2,000   2,500   3,000   3,500   4,000   4,500   5,000   5,500
0 Kilometres   1,000   1,500   2,500   3,500   4,000   5,000   5,500   6,000   6,500   7,000   7,500   8,000   8,500

North Pacific Ocean

North Atlantic Ocean

Gulf of Mexico

Caribbean Sea

UNITED STATES

MEXICO

Mexico City

Guatemala City

Havana

CUBA

BAHAMAS (G.B.)

Caracas

VENEZUELA

COLOMBIA

Bogotá

ECUADOR

Quito

PERU

BRAZIL

Amazon River

Negro River

Equator

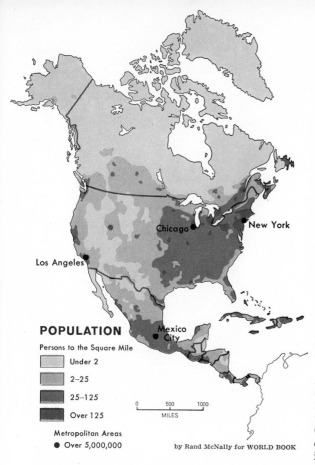

POPULATION

Persons to the Square Mile

- Under 2
- 2–25
- 25–125
- Over 125

Metropolitan Areas
● Over 5,000,000

0   500   1000
MILES

by Rand McNally for WORLD BOOK

NORTH AMERICA / *The People*

The people of North America represent four vastly different backgrounds—European, African Negro, American Indian, and Eskimo.

The largest number of people of North America have European ancestors. About half of all Canadians trace their origin to Great Britain and Ireland, and about a third are the descendants of early French settlers. The United States became a melting pot of immigrants from many European countries. South of the United States, most of the European settlers came from Spain.

Negroes were originally brought to North America from Africa as slaves. In the United States, nearly 11 of every 100 persons is a Negro or has mixed Negro and white ancestry. The islands of the Caribbean also have large Negro populations. Nearly all the people of Haiti are Negroes or of mixed Negro and white descent.

Indians were the first North Americans. They have occupied the continent at least 20,000 years. Their ancestors probably came from Asia by way of a narrow crossing to Alaska. When Europeans first settled North America, the largest number of Indians lived in present-day Mexico and Central America. Today, many people in these regions have pure Indian ancestry, and even larger numbers are *mestizos* of mixed Indian and European descent. See INDIAN, AMERICAN; MESTIZO.

The Eskimos arrived after the Indians. They came from Asia by boat about 6,000 years ago and settled in Alaska, northern Canada, and Greenland. Today,

the descendants of these Arctic pioneers number about 60,000. See ESKIMO.

Language and Education. Most North Americans speak English, Spanish, or French. Generally, the early European colonists gave the language of their native countries to the regions that they settled. English is spoken throughout the United States and most of Canada. English and French both are spoken in Quebec and some other parts of Canada. Mexicans and most of the people of Central America and the Caribbean islands speak Spanish, although French, English, or Dutch is the language of some areas. Many Indians and Eskimos still use their native languages.

Most of the people of North America can read and write. Canada and the United States have extensive systems of public and private schools that provide the education needed to support a modern industrial democracy. The Latin-American countries south of the United States have been slower in providing mass education for all their young people.

The oldest university in North America is the University of Santo Domingo in the Dominican Republic. It was founded in 1538. For more about education in North America, see the *Education* section of the various country, state, and province articles.

Religion. Christianity is the major religion of North America. In the United States, the largest number of church members are Protestants. Roman Catholics account for about two-fifths of the church members of the United States, about half the church members of Canada, and nearly all of those in the Latin-American countries. Other chief religious groups in North America include Jews and Eastern Orthodox Christians.

Transportation and Communication. The most extensive transportation and communication systems in the world spread a network over a large part of the North American continent. On the Pan American Highway, automobiles can travel from Mexico in the north to Panama in the south and continue far into South America. In Canada and the United States, coast-to-coast highway systems connect most towns and cities. Airlines serve the cities of North America and provide jet travel across the continent in about five hours. They carry about 70 million passengers a year. The St. Lawrence Seaway, the Great Lakes, and the Mississippi River and its tributaries form the greatest inland waterway system in the world. In addition, intracoastal waterways run along the Atlantic and Gulf coasts of the United States and along the Pacific coast from Seattle to Alaska. The Panama Canal near the southern tip of the continent connects the Atlantic and Pacific oceans.

North Americans read more than 2,000 daily newspapers. Canada and the United States have an average of one telephone for about every three persons. More television sets are in North America than in all the rest of the world. In the United States alone, the Postal Service carries about 85 billion pieces of mail a year.

The continent's Latin-American and far-northern regions have fewer transportation and communication facilities than the United States and Canada. For example, Mexico has an average of only one telephone for about every 60 persons. Some areas of Central America cannot be reached by highway. In northern Canada and Alaska, airplanes provide much of the transportation in sparsely settled areas.

TRANSPORTATION

North America's vast system of transportation by air, land, and water is concentrated most heavily in the thickly populated industrial areas of the United States and Canada.

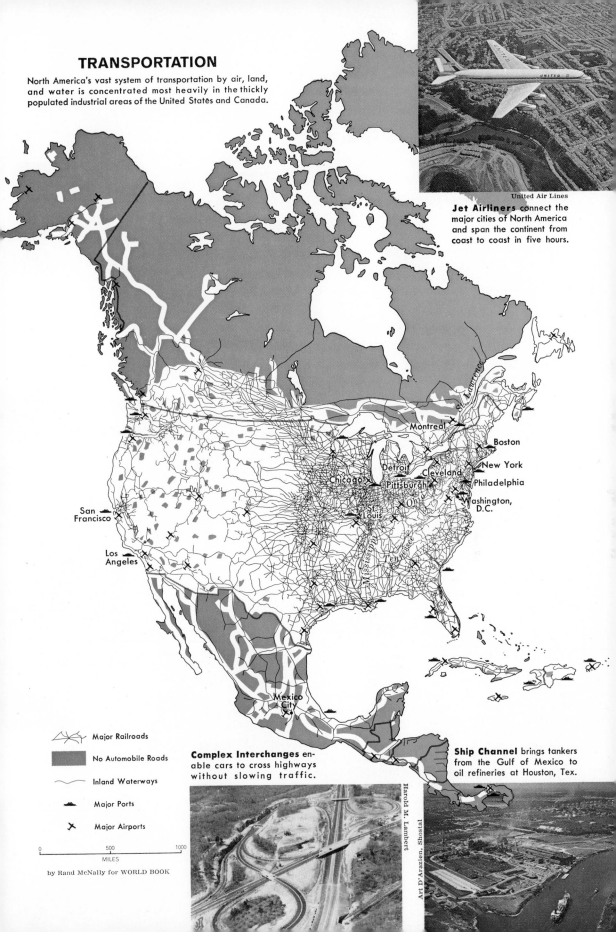

United Air Lines

Jet Airliners connect the major cities of North America and span the continent from coast to coast in five hours.

Montreal

Boston

Detroit
Chicago
Pittsburgh
Cleveland
New York
Philadelphia

St. Louis
Washington, D.C.

San Francisco

Tennessee

Los Angeles

Mississippi

Mexico City

Legend

- Major Railroads
- No Automobile Roads
- Inland Waterways
- Major Ports
- ✕ Major Airports

0   500   1000
MILES

by Rand McNally for WORLD BOOK

Complex Interchanges enable cars to cross highways without slowing traffic.

Harold M. Lambert

Ship Channel brings tankers from the Gulf of Mexico to oil refineries at Houston, Tex.

Art D'Arazien, Shostal

NORTH AMERICA / Land Regions

North America is shaped roughly like a vast triangle. One point of the triangle connects with South America. The Atlantic, Pacific, and Arctic coasts form the three sides. Great mountain systems separated by wide plains run parallel to the Atlantic and Pacific coasts.

North America has seven major land regions: (1) the *Pacific Coastland*, (2) the *Intermountain Region*, (3) the *Rocky Mountains*, (4) the *Interior Plain*, (5) the *Canadian Shield*, (6) the *Appalachian Mountains*, and (7) the *Coastal Plain*.

The Pacific Coastland extends from Alaska into Mexico. It consists of two roughly parallel mountain chains separated by valleys such as the Central Valley of California. The outer chain rises steeply from the Pacific Ocean. It includes the Olympic Mountains in Washington and the coastal mountains of Oregon and California. The inner chain includes the Alaska Range, the Coast Mountains of Canada, the Cascade Range in Washington and Oregon, and the Sierra Nevada in California. The Sierra Madre Occidental and the mountains of Lower California may be thought of as extensions of the Pacific Coastland mountains. Mount McKinley, North America's highest peak, rises 20,320 feet in the Alaska Range.

The Intermountain Region divides the Pacific Coastland from the Rocky Mountains. Its basins and high plateaus include the Yukon River Basin in Alaska and Canada, the Interior Plateau of British Columbia, the Colorado Plateau, the Great Basin centered in Nevada, and the Mexican Plateau. This region includes such spectacular land features as the Grand Canyon. California's Death Valley, the lowest point in North America, lies 282 feet below sea level in the Great Basin.

The Rocky Mountains form the high inland spine of North America. They run from northern Alaska into New Mexico, and can be traced southward into Mexico as the Sierra Madre Oriental. In the Colorado Rockies, 55 peaks rise to heights of 14,000 feet or more.

The Interior Plain is a vast lowland area in the central part of the continent. It includes the Midwestern States of the United States and part of central Canada. The Rocky Mountains rise to the west, and the Appalachian Mountains are to the east. The Interior Plain has some hilly areas, such as the Ozark Mountains. The drier, higher western part of this region is called the *Great Plains*.

The Canadian Shield stretches across half of Canada north and east of the Interior Plain. It also extends into northern Minnesota, Wisconsin, Michigan, and New York. The region is called a *shield* because of the old, hard rock that lies under the poor soil. Large forests cover much of the southern part of this region.

The Appalachian Mountains run parallel to the Atlantic coast. These low mountains extend about 1,500 miles from the Gulf of St. Lawrence into northern Alabama. The highest peak, Mount Mitchell in North Carolina, has an altitude of only 6,684 feet. A belt of hilly land called the *Piedmont Region* lies along the eastern edge of the central and southern Appalachians.

The Coastal Plain is a lowland area along the Atlantic Ocean and the Gulf of Mexico. It extends from Cape Cod in Massachusetts, through the Yucatán Peninsula in Mexico, and into Central America.

362

The Pacific Coastland—Ray Atkeson, Publix

The Intermountain Region—Hal Rumel, Publix

The Rocky Mountains—John D. Freeman, Publix

The Interior Plain—Richard W. Hufnagle, Publix

The Canadian Shield—George Hunter, Shostal

The Appalachian Mountains—Martin W. Swithinbank, P.I.P. Photos

The Coastal Plain—Joe E. Steinmetz, Publix

NORTH AMERICA

Barren Areas
Above Timber

Evergreen Trees

Deciduous Trees

Shrub

Grass

Tundra

Snow and Ice

Ice Pack

● Cities and Towns

- - - Boundary of
North America

1 inch = 670 Statute miles

Miles 0 100 200 300 400 500 600

Lambert Azimuthal Equal Area Projection

CM TERRAIN NORTH AMERICA
COPYRIGHT BY
RAND McNALLY & COMPANY
MADE IN U.S.A.

363

NORTH AMERICA / *Natural Features*

Coastline. North America has a longer total coastline than any other continent. Including the many islands of North America, the total coastline is more than 96,000 miles long. The coastline of mainland North America measures about 39,000 miles. The Atlantic coastline is steep and rocky in the north, but south of Cape Cod it slopes gently to the sea. Along stretches of the Pacific coast, high mountains rise abruptly from the sea. Great gulfs and bays jut into North America's mainland. The largest are the Gulf of Mexico in the south and Hudson Bay in the north.

Offshore Islands lie along North America's coasts. Greenland, the largest island in the world, is considered part of North America although it is a province of Denmark. Cuba, Hispaniola, and the other islands of the West Indies are part of North America. The Pacific coast islands, of which Vancouver is the largest, lie off southern Alaska and British Columbia. Other important North American islands include the Aleutians, Bermuda, Long Island, and Newfoundland.

Rivers. The crest of the Rocky Mountains divides North America into two great watersheds. West of this crest, called the *Great Divide*, water flows toward the Pacific Ocean. East of it, water flows toward the Arctic Ocean, the Atlantic Ocean, or the Gulf of Mexico. Together, the Mississippi and Missouri rivers form a river system of 3,710 miles—the longest on the continent. This system drains much of the Interior Plain before emptying into the Gulf of Mexico. The Rio Grande is the boundary between Texas and Mexico.

The Mackenzie River, which forms part of the longest river system in Canada, flows from Great Slave Lake into the Arctic Ocean. The St. Lawrence River carries water from the Great Lakes to the Atlantic Ocean.

Great rushing streams that drain the western slopes of the Rocky Mountains include the Yukon, Fraser, and Columbia rivers. One of the western rivers, the Colorado, cuts through the Grand Canyon before it reaches the Gulf of California. Shorter, slower streams, such as the Hudson and Potomac rivers, drain the eastern slopes of the Appalachians.

Lakes. The Great Lakes are the most important group of lakes in the world. They make up part of North America's great inland waterway system. One of them, Lake Superior, is the world's largest body of fresh water. Four of the Great Lakes—Ontario, Erie, Huron, and Superior—lie between Canada and the United States. The fifth, Lake Michigan, lies entirely within the United States. Utah's Great Salt Lake, one of the natural wonders of North America, is from four to seven times saltier than the ocean. Great Bear Lake is the largest lake in Canada.

Waterfalls. North America's most famous waterfall is 167-foot-high Niagara Falls. It is partly in Canada and partly in the United States. More water passes over Niagara Falls than over any other falls in North America. Yosemite Falls in California, the highest waterfall in North America, has a drop of 2,425 feet.

Deserts. North America's major deserts are in the southwestern United States and northern Mexico. Like other west coast areas of similar latitude, this region receives scanty and irregular rainfall. The Chihuahuan, Sonoran, and Colorado deserts extend from Mexico into the United States. The largest North American desert region includes the area along the lower Colorado River, and the Mojave Desert and Death Valley of southeastern California. The land near the Arctic Ocean is a treeless area called the *tundra*.

NORTH AMERICA / *Climate*

The climate of North America is cold most of the year in the far north. In the far south, it is always hot except in the highlands. The greater part of the continent, however, has a mixed climate, with warm summers and cold winters. In Chicago, for example, the average temperature in January is 26° F., and the average temperature in July is 74° F. The highest temperature ever recorded in North America was 134° F. at

Death Valley in 1913. The lowest temperature was −81° F. at Snag in the Yukon Territory in 1947.

The amount of rain and snow varies from one region to another. On the western slopes of the Olympic Mountains in Washington, rainfall totals about 140 inches a year. The region between the Pacific coast ranges and the Rockies is one of the driest areas. In Death Valley, only about 1½ inches of rain falls each year.

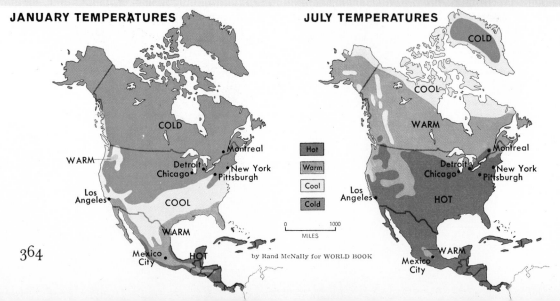

JANUARY TEMPERATURES

COLD

WARM

COLD

Montreal
Detroit
Chicago
New York
Pittsburgh

Los
Angeles

COOL

WARM

Mexico
City   HOT

Hot
Warm
Cool
Cold

0   1000
MILES

JULY TEMPERATURES

COLD

COOL

WARM

Montreal
Detroit
Chicago
New York
Pittsburgh

Los
Angeles

HOT

WARM

Mexico
City

by Rand McNally for WORLD BOOK

Eskimos build shelters of snow in the arctic wasteland.
Douglas Sinclair, Shostal

MAJOR CLIMATE REGIONS

POLAR

COLD MOIST

WARM RAINY
with Dry Summer

San Francisco

SEMIARID

Los Angeles

DESERT

WARM RAINY

St. Louis

Montreal

Boston

Detroit
Cleveland
New York
Chicago
Pittsburgh
Philadelphia
Washington, D.C.

Mexico City

TROPICAL WET AND DRY

500   1000
MILES
by Rand McNally for WORLD BOOK

Swimmers and Sunbathers enjoy warm sunshine on the beach at Acapulco, Mexico.
Otto Done, Shostal

RAINFALL

LIGHT

HEAVY

Detroit   Montreal
Chicago   New York
Pittsburgh

Los Angeles

MODERATE

	Inches
Heavy	Over 60
Moderate	20-60
Light	0-20

0   1000
MILES

Mexico City

HEAVY

NORTH AMERICA /*Animals*

North America's wildlife varies from the polar north to the tropical south. Arctic foxes, caribou, fur seals, musk oxen, polar bears, and walruses live in the far north. Alligators, anteaters, armadillos, jaguars, monkeys, and colorful birds such as parrots are found in Central America. Eagles, elk, grizzly bears, and moose inhabit the forested western mountains. The wooded areas of the central and eastern regions have beavers, black bears, deer, muskrats, and porcupines. Smaller animals, such as pigeons, rabbits, and squirrels, live in and around populated regions and farm areas.

As more and more people settled the continent, many kinds of animals decreased in number or became extinct. Millions of buffalo once roamed the plains. Today, only a few scattered herds of buffalo live in game preserves. The passenger pigeon, native to North America, has disappeared entirely. Game laws and refuge areas protect wildlife today.

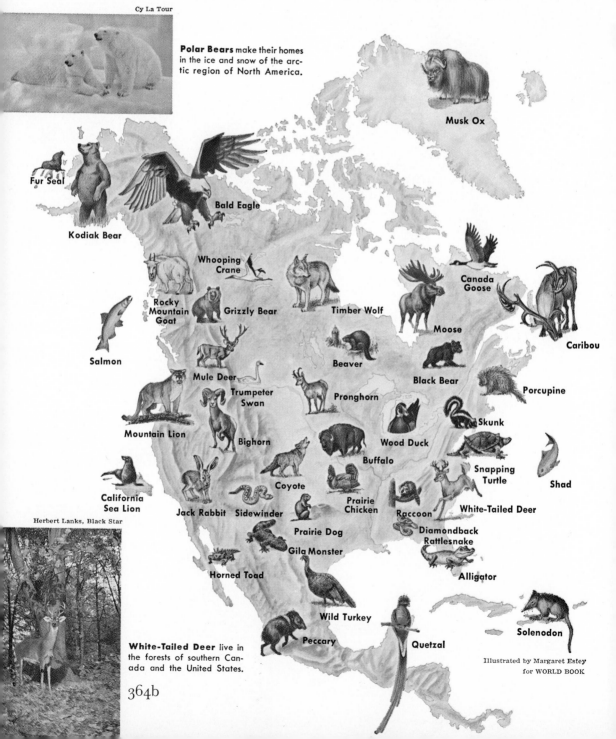

Cy La Tour

Polar Bears make their homes in the ice and snow of the arctic region of North America.

Musk Ox

Fur Seal

Kodiak Bear

Bald Eagle

Whooping Crane

Rocky Mountain Goat

Grizzly Bear

Timber Wolf

Canada Goose

Moose

Caribou

Salmon

Mule Deer

Trumpeter Swan

Pronghorn

Beaver

Black Bear

Porcupine

Mountain Lion

Bighorn

Wood Duck

Skunk

Buffalo

Snapping Turtle

Shad

California Sea Lion

Coyote

Jack Rabbit   Sidewinder

Prairie Chicken

Raccoon

White-Tailed Deer

Prairie Dog

Diamondback Rattlesnake

Gila Monster

Horned Toad

Alligator

Wild Turkey

Quetzal

Solenodon

Herbert Lanks, Black Star

White-Tailed Deer live in the forests of southern Canada and the United States.

Peccary

Illustrated by Margaret Estey
for WORLD BOOK

364b

NORTH AMERICA / *Plant Life*

The plant life of North America ranges from desert cactus to the largest trees in the world, the redwoods and sequoias of California. On the tundra, only moss, lichens, and some flowering plants can grow.

Trees and grass once covered most of North America. But as people settled the continent, they turned large areas of prairie and forest into farmland. Nevertheless, forests and grasslands are still two important natural resources. The grasslands of the Great Plains provide pasture for large herds of sheep and cattle. Evergreen forests of fir, spruce, and pine trees cover much of Canada and the western mountains of the United States. Large areas of hardwood and softwood trees grow in the forests that extend from Maine to Minnesota. The wooded regions of the eastern coastal plain produce several kinds of oak and pine. Forests near the Gulf of Mexico and the Caribbean Sea have palm, mahogany, cypress, mangrove, and other tropical trees.

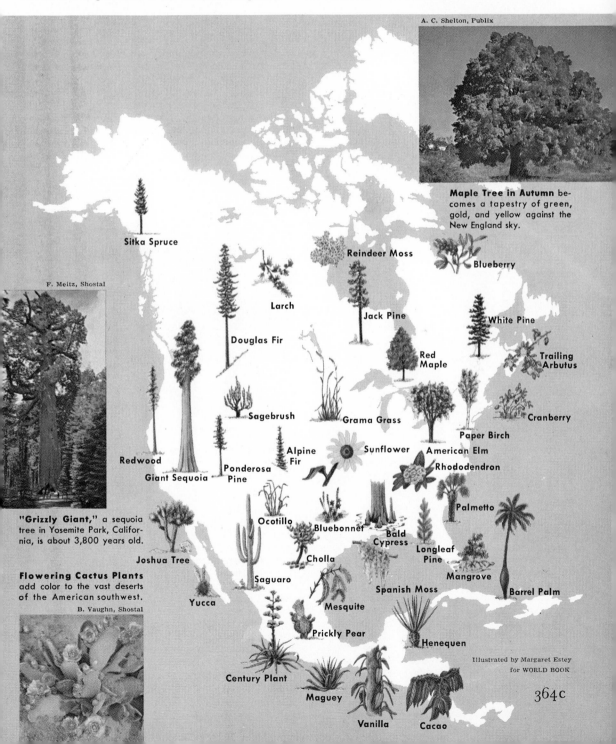

A. C. Shelton, Publix

Maple Tree in Autumn becomes a tapestry of green, gold, and yellow against the New England sky.

F. Meitz, Shostal

"Grizzly Giant," a sequoia tree in Yosemite Park, California, is about 3,800 years old.

Flowering Cactus Plants add color to the vast deserts of the American southwest.

B. Vaughn, Shostal

Sitka Spruce
Reindeer Moss
Blueberry
Larch
Jack Pine
White Pine
Douglas Fir
Red Maple
Trailing Arbutus
Sagebrush
Grama Grass
Cranberry
Redwood
Paper Birch
Giant Sequoia
Ponderosa Pine
Alpine Fir
Sunflower
American Elm
Rhododendron
Joshua Tree
Ocotillo
Bluebonnet
Bald Cypress
Palmetto
Cholla
Longleaf Pine
Saguaro
Mangrove
Yucca
Spanish Moss
Barrel Palm
Mesquite
Prickly Pear
Henequen
Century Plant
Maguey
Vanilla
Cacao

Illustrated by Margaret Estey
for WORLD BOOK

364c

NORTH AMERICA / *Manufacturing and Mining*

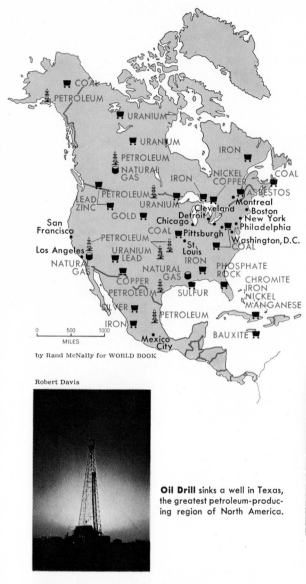

by Rand McNally for WORLD BOOK

North America has large supplies of important minerals. The hills and plains contain some of the world's richest deposits of coal, gold, iron ore, nickel, petroleum, and other minerals. The United States produces about one-fourth of the world's petroleum and nearly a fifth of its coal. Canada is the leading producer of asbestos and nickel, and one of the leading producers of gold. Canada and the United States together mine about a third of the copper and about a fifth of the iron ore produced in the world. Mexico leads in the production of silver, and is a major source of lead and zinc. Jamaica is the world's largest producer of bauxite, the ore from which aluminum is made.

Many of the large cities of the United States and Canada are important industrial centers. As a result, both these countries rank among the leading manufacturing nations of the world. Their industrial greatness is based on their rich natural resources, their skilled workers, and their use of highly developed machinery, automation, and mass production.

The Latin-American countries of North America must import many of their manufactured goods. Most manufacturing is still done by hand, and cannot supply even all local needs. Modern factories are being established in some cities, especially in Mexico.

Robert Davis

Oil Drill sinks a well in Texas, the greatest petroleum-producing region of North America.

Devaney from Publix

Yankee Atomic Power Plant, opened in 1960 at Rowe, Mass., produces 150,000 kilowatts of electricity for 10 privately owned power companies serving the New England area of the United States.

NORTH AMERICA / *Agriculture*

The United States and Canada have some of the largest and most fertile agricultural areas in the world. Their farms not only produce enough food for all their people, but also supply large quantities for export. Canada, for example, sends more than half its wheat to other parts of the world. Through the use of machinery and scientific methods of farming, the United States and Canada constantly increase the output of their land. In the United States, an acre of corn produced about 26 bushels in 1940. The yield per acre had more than doubled by the 1960's, and continues to increase.

The Latin-American countries of North America produce barely enough food for their own people. Large areas are either too dry or too wet for farming. Where farming is possible, primitive agricultural methods, such as the use of hand tools for tilling the soil, often prevent a large output. In some of these countries, one or two crops dominate the economy. Cuba, for example, depends largely on sugar for its foreign trade. Most Central American countries specialize in growing bananas in the lowlands and coffee in the highlands. In such regions, a poor growing season or low prices result in widespread hardship for the people.

Forests cover about a third of North America. This vast natural resource supplies more than a fourth of the world's lumber and half its pulpwood, from which paper is made. CLARENCE W. OLMSTEAD

364d

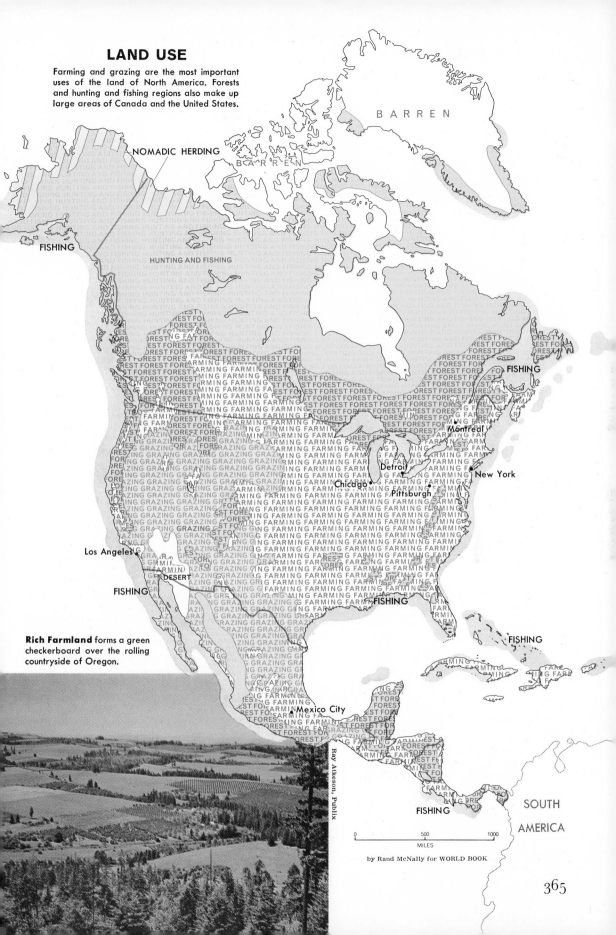

LAND USE

Farming and grazing are the most important uses of the land of North America. Forests and hunting and fishing regions also make up large areas of Canada and the United States.

BARREN

NOMADIC HERDING

BARREN

FISHING

HUNTING AND FISHING

HUNTING AND FISHING

FISHING

FOREST FOREST

FARMING FARMING

Montreal

GRAZING

Detroit

New York

Chicago

Pittsburgh

GRAZING

Los Angeles

FISHING

DESERT

FISHING

Rich Farmland forms a green checkerboard over the rolling countryside of Oregon.

GRAZING

FARMING

FISHING

Mexico City

FISHING

SOUTH

AMERICA

FISHING

Ray Atkeson, Publix

0   500   1000

MILES

by Rand McNally for WORLD BOOK

365

NORTH AMERICA /Study Aids

Related Articles in WORLD BOOK include:

COUNTRIES, COLONIES, AND TERRITORIES

Bahamas	Martinique
Bermuda	Mexico
British Honduras	Netherlands Antilles
Canada	Nicaragua
Costa Rica	Panama
Cuba	Panama Canal Zone
Dominican Republic	Puerto Rico
El Salvador	Saint Pierre and Miquelon
Greenland	Trinidad and Tobago
Guadeloupe	United States
Guatemala	Virgin Islands
Haiti	Virgin Islands, British
Honduras	West Indies (British)
Jamaica	

CITIES

See the following articles on the 15 largest cities of North America:

Baltimore	Houston	New York City
Chicago	Los Angeles	Philadelphia
Cleveland	Mexico City	Saint Louis
Detroit	Milwaukee	San Francisco
Havana	Montreal	Washington, D.C.

NATURAL FEATURES

See the list of Related Articles with the articles on DESERT; INLAND WATERWAY; ISLAND; LAKE; MOUNTAIN; RIVER; WATERFALL; WATERWAY. See also the following articles on some of the most important physical features of North America:

Appalachian Mountains	Mississippi River
Arkansas River	Missouri River
Bridalveil Fall	Multnomah Falls
Canadian Shield	Nelson River
Coast Range	Newfoundland
Colorado River	Niagara Falls and
Columbia River	Niagara River
Death Valley	Orizaba
Fairy Falls	Parícutin
Grand Canyon National Park	Piedmont Region
Great Basin	Popocatepetl
Great Bear Lake	Ribbon Falls
Great Divide	Rio Grande
Great Lakes	Rocky Mountains
Great Plains	Saint Lawrence River
Great Salt Lake	Sierra Madre
Great Slave Lake	Sierra Nevada
Greenland	Takakkaw Falls
Ixtacihuatl	West Indies
Lake Nicaragua	Yosemite Falls
Lake Winnipeg	Yosemite National Park
Mackenzie River	Yukon River

COASTAL WATERS

Arctic Ocean	Gulf of California
Atlantic Ocean	Gulf of Mexico
Baffin Bay	Gulf of Saint Lawrence
Bay of Fundy	Hudson Bay
Belle Isle, Strait of	James Bay
Bering Sea	Juan de Fuca, Strait of
Caribbean Sea	Long Island Sound
Chesapeake Bay	Pacific Ocean
Delaware Bay	Puget Sound
Florida, Straits of	

PEOPLE

City	Negro
Clothing	Population
Eskimo	Shelter (Shelter
Food	Around the World)
Indian, American	World
Metropolitan Area	

HISTORY

See the History section of the articles on the countries, states, and provinces of North America. See also the following articles:

Canada, History of	Latin America (History)
Central America (History)	United States, History of
Exploration and Discovery	

Outline

I. People
  A. Language and Education
  B. Religion
  C. Transportation and Communication
II. Land Regions
  A. The Pacific Coastland
  B. The Intermountain Region
  C. The Rocky Mountains
  D. The Interior Plain
  E. The Canadian Shield
  F. The Appalachian Mountains
  G. The Coastal Plain
III. Natural Features
  A. Coastline
  B. Offshore Islands
  C. Rivers
  D. Lakes
  E. Waterfalls
  F. Deserts
IV. Climate
V. Animals
VI. Plant Life
VII. Manufacturing and Mining
VIII. Agriculture

Questions

What mountain ranges rise to the east and west of the Interior Plain?

What is the largest island in the world?

What is North America's highest mountain?

What country is the world's leading producer of bauxite?

What is the largest body of fresh water in the world?

Which land region includes both the Grand Canyon and Death Valley?

What is the Great Divide?

What is North America's highest waterfall?

Which of the Great Lakes lies entirely within the United States?

Which countries form Anglo-America?

NORTH AMERICAN AIR DEFENSE COMMAND. See NATIONAL DEFENSE (Air Defense); AIR FORCE, UNITED STATES (Why We Have an Air Force).

NORTH AMERICAN NEWSPAPER ALLIANCE (NANA) is a world-wide independent news agency. It specializes in exclusive news coverage and in articles by famous persons. NANA provides its subscribing newspapers with important feature stories. The agency is noted for its memoirs of well-known statesmen. NANA was founded as a cooperative news alliance in 1922. Headquarters are at 229 West 43d St., New York City.

NORTH AMERICAN ROCKWELL CORPORATION. See AIRPLANE (Leading Airplane Companies).

NORTH ATLANTIC CURRENT is the continuation of the Gulf Stream that is carried northeastward by winds. It sweeps along the northwest coast of Europe, past the British Isles and Norway, and into the Arctic Ocean. See also GULF STREAM (map); OCEAN (How the Ocean Moves).

NORTH ATLANTIC TREATY ORGANIZATION (NATO) provides unified military leadership for the common defense of 15 Western nations. NATO was established in 1950 by the nations allied by the North

The North Atlantic Council, *above,* is the highest authority in NATO. It plans for the collective defense of North America and Western Europe. It consists of the representatives of the member countries. The NATO secretary general serves as council chairman. The presidency of the council rotates annually.

Atlantic Treaty, which provided for their collective defense against a possible attack by Russia or any other aggressor. Article 5 of the treaty provides that an armed attack against one or more member nations in Europe or North America shall be considered an attack against all members.

Twelve nations signed the North Atlantic Treaty on April 4, 1949, in Washington, D.C. They were Belgium, Canada, Denmark, France, Great Britain, Iceland, Italy, Luxembourg, The Netherlands, Norway, Portugal, and the United States. Greece and Turkey signed the treaty in October, 1951, and West Germany signed it in October, 1954.

Organization. NATO's military forces are organized into three main commands: the Atlantic Command, Channel Command, and Allied Command Europe. Most of NATO's forces are in Allied Command Europe, which is directed by the Supreme Allied Commander in Europe (SACEUR). The Military Committee of NATO, consisting of the chiefs of staff of the member nations, establishes military policy to be carried out by SACEUR. The committee is responsible to the North Atlantic Council, which consists of the heads of the member nations or their representatives. All decisions of the council must be unanimous.

NATO members have never been willing to maintain an army large enough to stand off the Russian Army. As a result, in order to prevent a Soviet attack, the United States has said it will use the nuclear weapons of its Strategic Air Command (SAC) against Russia if Russia starts a war in Europe. NATO's dependence on American nuclear weapons has made the United States the dominant member, and the supreme allied commander in Europe has always been an American general.

History. In 1949, the nations of Western Europe were weak and could not easily defend themselves against attack. The Communist seizure of power in Czechoslovakia in February, 1948, and the Russian blockade of Berlin in June, 1948, raised fears that Russia might use armed force to gain control of Western Europe.

By signing the treaty, the United States for the first time in its history joined a peacetime alliance that committed it to fight in Europe. United States leaders felt that the U.S. would have to fight against Russian seizure of Western Europe because this would add greatly to the power of Russia to attack the U.S. The United States hoped that Russia would not attack Western Europe if it knew it would have to fight the United States, too. At the same time, the United States also acted to help the nations of Western Europe to defend themselves by providing them with military weapons and economic aid as part of the Marshall Plan. The Communist attack on South Korea in June, 1950, increased fears of a Russian attack on Western Europe, and in September, 1950, the members of the alliance formed NATO.

Most alliances owe their unity to the fear of a common enemy. When this fear decreases, differences among the members can develop. In the 1960's, NATO members became less worried about the possibility of a Russian attack. At the same time, the European members began to wonder if the United States would really start a nuclear war in defense of Western Europe, in view of Russia's growing nuclear power. European members of NATO resented the fact that NATO had no control over SAC, the main instrument of European defense. They also disliked the fact that NATO could not influence U.S. foreign policy in other parts of the world, even though these policies might lead to a war in Europe. For their part, Americans resented the fact that Europeans did not furnish more ground forces, and Britain and France instead spent their money developing nuclear weapons.

These differences reached a climax in March, 1966, when France decided to withdraw its troops from NATO. No French forces are now under NATO command, and no NATO forces are permitted in France. In 1967, the Supreme Headquarters Allied Powers Europe (SHAPE) moved from Paris to Brussels, Belgium.

Both the United States and the West European nations are still interested in common defense. France is still a member of the North Atlantic alliance, but may eventually withdraw. The treaty permits a member to withdraw after 20 years. France opposes U.S. domination, not U.S. protection. As long as American forces remain in West Germany as part of NATO, France will continue to enjoy that protection.   WARNER R. SCHILLING

See also FLAG (color picture: Flags of World Organizations); WARSAW PACT.

NORTH BERGEN, N.J. (pop. 47,751; alt. 220 ft.), is one of the largest townships in the state. It lies in Hudson County, on the northern boundary of Jersey City. See NEW JERSEY (political map).

North Bergen factories make batteries, clothing, ink, machinery, paper boxes, and electric, electronic, and metal products. The township was founded in 1660, and was incorporated in 1843. North Bergen has a commission form of government.   RICHARD P. McCORMICK

NORTH BORNEO. See BORNEO; MALAYSIA.

NORTH CAPE is a rocky point of land on the small island of Magerøy, which lies at the very northernmost tip of Norway on the shore of the Arctic Ocean. The cape has many cliffs and rocks which rise to 1,000 feet above the sea. Many tourists visit North Cape during the summer to see the *midnight sun.*

Cape Hatteras—Graveyard of the Atlantic

NORTH CAROLINA

THE TAR HEEL STATE

NORTH CAROLINA is the leading tobacco state of the United States. It leads the nation in tobacco farming and in the manufacture of tobacco products. North Carolinians grow tobacco, cure it, transport it, market it, and manufacture it. North Carolina also leads the nation in two other important areas. It manufactures more cloth and makes more wooden furniture than any other state. Most homes in the United States have wooden furniture that was made in North Carolina.

North Carolina is a southern state with a long coastline on the Atlantic Ocean. Islands, reefs, and sand bars make its shores some of the most treacherous in the world. Many ships have been wrecked at Cape Hatteras by the rough seas and difficult currents. Cape Hatteras is called the *Graveyard of the Atlantic*.

The state stretches westward from the coast across swamps and fertile farms. The land rises through lovely sand hills into industrial cities and towns. Tobacco farms, with neat rows of tobacco plants, are scattered throughout the state. The tobacco fields extend from the lowlands near the eastern coast high into the mountains that cross the western edge of the state. Mount Mitchell, more than a mile and a quarter above sea level, is the highest peak in the eastern United States.

Manufacturing earns more money and provides more jobs than any other industry in North Carolina. But North Carolina's manufacturing depends on other industries and on the state's natural resources. Cotton and tobacco farms, on rich soils, provide the textile and tobacco industries with necessary raw materials. North Carolina's thick forests and its huge forest industry furnish wood for the furniture plants.

In 1585 and 1587, the first groups of English settlers in America built colonies on Roanoke Island off the

Thurston Hatcher, Shostal

North Carolina Burley Tobacco Field

Hallinan, FPG

The Blue Ridge Mountains near Waynesville

FACTS IN BRIEF

Capital: Raleigh.

Government: *Congress*—U.S. senators, 2; U.S. representatives, 11. *Electoral Votes*—13. *State Legislature*—senators, 50; representatives, 120. *Counties*—100. *Voting Age*—21 years (state and local elections); 18 years (national elections).

Area: 52,586 square miles (including 3,706 square miles of inland water), 28th in size among the states. *Greatest Distances*—(east-west) 503 miles; (north-south) 187 miles. *Coastline*—301 miles.

Elevation: *Highest*—Mount Mitchell, 6,684 feet above sea level, in Yancey County. *Lowest*—sea level, along the coast.

Population: *1970 Census*—5,082,059; 12th among the states; density, 97 persons to the square mile; distribution, 55 per cent rural, 45 per cent urban. *1960 Census*—4,556,155.

Chief Products: *Agriculture*—beef cattle, broilers, corn, dairy products, eggs, hogs, peanuts, soybeans, tobacco. *Fishing Industry*—crabs, flounders, menhaden, shrimps. *Manufacturing*—chemicals; clothing; electrical machinery; food products; furniture and fixtures; nonelectrical machinery; paper and paper products; textiles and related products; tobacco products. *Mining*—clays, feldspar, lithium, mica, phosphate, sand and gravel, stone.

Statehood: Nov. 21, 1789, the 12th state.

State Motto: *Esse quam videri* (To be, rather than to seem).

State Song: "The Old North State." Words by William Gaston; musical arrangement by Mrs. E. E. Randolph.

North Carolina coast. The first group returned to England. The later group vanished from the island, leaving behind only a mystery that has puzzled the ages. This group has been named the *Lost Colony*. Virginia Dare, the first child born to English parents in America, was a member of the Lost Colony. During colonial days, groups in North Carolina such as the *Sons of Liberty* defied English taxes and English rule. After the Revolutionary War began, North Carolina was the first colony to instruct its delegates at the Continental Congress to vote for independence.

Before the outbreak of the Civil War, North Carolina tried to preserve the Union. But after North Carolina left the Union, it did its best to help the Confederate cause. More than 10 battles were fought on North Carolina soil. During one fierce battle, some Confederate troops retreated, leaving North Carolina forces to fight alone. The North Carolinians supposedly threatened to put tar on the heels of the other troops so they would "stick better in the next fight." Since then, North Carolina has been called the *Tar Heel State*.

Raleigh is North Carolina's capital, and Charlotte is its largest city. For North Carolina's relationship to other states in its region, see SOUTHERN STATES.

North Carolina (blue) ranks 28th in size among all the states, and 4th in size among the Southern States (gray).

The contributors of this article are Robert Eli Cramer, Chairman and Professor in the Department of Geography at East Carolina University; Blackwell Pierce Robinson, Associate Professor of History and Political Science at the University of North Carolina at Greensboro; and Sam Ragan, Editor and Publisher of The Pilot *in Southern Pines.*

Constitution. North Carolina has had the same constitution since 1868. It had one earlier constitution, adopted in 1776. North Carolina adopted this earlier constitution several months after the American colonies declared independence from Great Britain.

The North Carolina constitution has had more than 80 amendments. An amendment must first be approved by three-fifths of both houses of the state legislature. Then it must be approved by a majority of the voters in a general election. Constitutional amendments can be proposed by the legislators, or by delegates to a constitutional convention. A constitutional convention must be approved by two-thirds of both houses, and by the voters, before it can meet to propose amendments.

Executive. North Carolina's governor and lieutenant governor serve four-year terms. They cannot serve two terms in a row. The governor receives a yearly salary of $35,000. For a list of North Carolina's governors, see the *History* section of this article.

The governor has limited powers to appoint state officials. The voters elect all top administrative officers —the secretary of state, attorney general, auditor, treasurer, superintendent of public instruction, and commissioners of agriculture, insurance, and labor. All these officers except the attorney general make up the council of state, an advisory board to the governor. Each serves a four-year term and can be re-elected. North Carolina is the only state in which the governor cannot veto a bill passed by the legislature.

Legislature, called the *general assembly*, consists of a 50-member senate and a 120-member house of representatives. Senators are elected from 33 senatorial districts. Representatives are elected from 49 representative districts. Members of both houses serve two-year terms from the day they are elected. The lieutenant governor is president of the senate. The house of representatives elects a speaker to preside over it. Both houses meet in odd-numbered years, beginning on the Wednesday after the second Monday in January.

In 1965, a federal court ordered North Carolina to redraw its legislative districts to provide equal representation. The general assembly set up its present districts in 1966, and the court approved them.

Courts. North Carolina's court system consists of an appellate division, a superior court division, and a district court division.

The appellate division consists of the supreme court, the state's highest court; and the court of appeals, an intermediate appellate court. The appellate courts hear cases appealed from lower courts. The supreme court has a chief justice and six associate justices, and the court of appeals has nine judges.

The superior and district court divisions consist of 30 judicial districts. Each of these 30 districts is served by one or more superior court judges who hear civil and criminal trials. Each district also has two or more district court judges who handle minor civil and criminal cases.

Supreme court justices and superior court judges are elected to eight-year terms. Judges on the court of appeals are elected to six-year terms and district court judges to four-year terms. If any justice or judge leaves office, the governor appoints a successor.

Local Government. North Carolina has 100 counties. Each county is governed by a board of county commissioners. The boards consist of three to seven members, elected to two- or four-year terms, depending on the county. They meet monthly to supervise county affairs, and to perform such duties as appropriating funds and levying taxes. County officials include the sheriff, register of deeds, superior court clerk, treasurer, coroner, accountant, attorney, and tax officials.

State laws permit cities and towns to have *home rule* (self-government) to the extent that they can amend existing charters or adopt new ones. But control must remain in the hands of the general assembly. North Carolina has about 465 incorporated cities and towns. An area may incorporate by petitioning the general

The Legislative Building, *below,* is often called the *State House.* It was first used in 1963. The state senate and house of representatives meet there. It was the first building constructed by a state for the exclusive use of the legislature.

The Governor's Mansion, *right,* stands several blocks east of the Capitol. The red brick and sandstone building, completed in 1889, has many gables and porches. It is considered a classic example of the Victorian style of architecture.

North Carolina Dept. of Conservation and Development

North Carolina Dept. of Conservation and Development

The State Seal

Symbols of North Carolina. On the seal, the standing figure represents *Liberty* and holds a scroll inscribed "Constitution." The seated figure symbolizes *Plenty*. The date "May 20, 1775" is that of the supposed Mecklenburg Declaration of Independence. The seal was adopted in 1893. The state flag, adopted in 1885, bears the dates of the two North Carolina declarations of independence that were made before the national Declaration.

Flag, flower, and bird illustrations, courtesy Eli Lilly and Company

assembly. Most of the larger cities have the council-manager form of government. Other forms of municipal government are mayor-council and commission.

Taxation. Corporate and individual income taxes provide about 35 per cent of the state government's income. Sales and gross receipts taxes bring in about 25 per cent. Other sources of revenue include license fees and vehicle registrations. More than 20 per cent of the state government's income comes from federal grants and other U.S. government programs.

Politics. The Democratic Party dominates the state's politics. But the Republican Party is gaining strength. Since the Reconstruction period (1865-1877), only two Republican presidential candidates have won the state's electoral votes—Herbert Hoover in 1928 and Richard Nixon in 1968. For North Carolina's voting record in presidential elections, see ELECTORAL COLLEGE (table). Only one Republican has been elected governor since Reconstruction—D. L. Russell in 1896. North Carolina's voters elect 11 members to the U.S. House of Representatives. In 1966, when the general assembly redrew its districts, it also redrew the state's congressional districts. Federal courts approved the new congressional districts for the 1966 elections, but required the legislature to redraw the districts again in 1967.

The Capitol Building is in Raleigh. The city became the capital in 1791, but was not used until 1794. New Bern was the capital from 1771 to 1776. There was no fixed capital, 1776 to 1794.

North Carolina Dept. of Conservation and Development

The State Flag

The State Flower
Flowering Dogwood

The State Bird
Cardinal

The State Tree
Pine

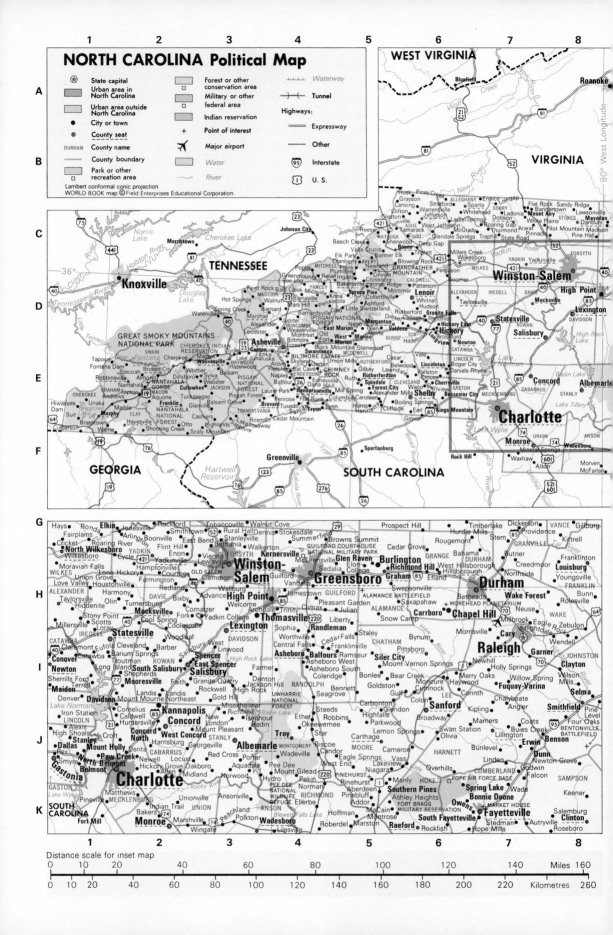

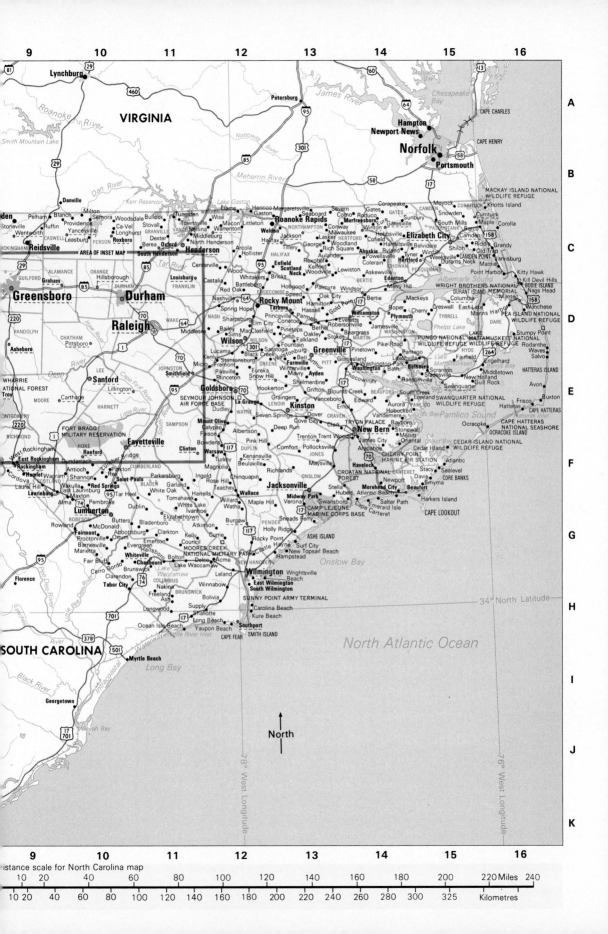

Huntersville 1,538..J 1
Hurdle Mills .....G 6
Husk ....B 6
Icard ....D 6
Indian Trail ..405..K 2
Ingalls ....D 5
Ingold ....F 11
Iron Station ......J 1
Ivanhoe ....G 12
Jackson ......762.°C 13
Jackson Hill ....I 3
Jacksonville 16,021.°F 13
James City ..2,577..F 14
Jamestown ..1,297..H 4
Jamesville ....533..D 14
Jarvisburg ....C 16
Jefferson .....943.°C 6
Jonas Ridge ....D 5
Jonesville ...1,659..G 1
Julian ....H 5
Jupiter ....208..D 4
Kannapolis 36,293..J 2
Kelford ......295..C 13
Kelly ....G 11
Kenansville ...762.°F 12
Kenly ......1,370..E 12
Kernersville ......4,815..G 3
Kill Devil Hills ....357..C 16
King* ......1,033..C 8
Kings Mountain ......8,465..E 6
Kinston ...22,309.°E 13
Kipling ....J 7
Kittrell ......427..G 8
Kitty Hawk ....C 16
Knightdale ...815..I 8
Knotts Island .....B 16
Kona ....D 4
Kure Beach ...394..H 12
La Grange ..2,558..E 12
Lake Junaluska ....E 3
Lake Lure* ...456..E 5
Lake Toxaway .....F 3
Lake Waccamaw .924..G 11
Lakeview ....J 5
Landis .....2,297..I 2
Landis Northeast ......1,353..I 2
Lansing ......283..C 6
Lasker ....114..C 13
Lattimore* ...257..E 5
Laurel Hill .1,215..F 9
Laurel Park ..581..E 4
Laurinburg ......8,859.°F 9
Laurinburg West* ....1,156..F 9
Lawndale ....544..E 6
Lawsonville ....C 8
Leasburg ....C 10
Leechville ....E 15
Leicester ....D 4
Leland ....G 12
Lemon Springs .....J 6
Lenoir .....14,705.°D 6
Lewiston .....327..C 13
Lewisville ....H 2
Lexington ..17,205.°D 8
Liberty .....2,167..H 5
Lilesville .....641..K 4
Lillington ...1,155.°E 10
Lincolnton ..5,293.°E 6
Linden ....205..J 7
Linville ....D 5
Linwood ....I 3
Little Switzerland ......D 5
Littleton .....903..C 12
Locust ....J 2
Lone Hickory ......H 2
Long Beach ...493..H 12
Longhurst ..1,485..C 10
Longview ...3,360..D 6
Longwood ....H 11
Longwood Park* ....1,284..F 9
Loray ....H 1
Louisburg ..2,941.°C 11
Love Valley ...40..H 1
Lowell* ....3,307..E 6
Lowgap ....C 7
Lowland ....E 14
Lucama ......610..D 12
Lumber Bridge 117..F 10
Lumberton .16,961.°G 10
Lynn ....E 4
Macclesfield ..536..D 13
Mackeys ....D 14
Macon ....179..C 12
Madison ....2,018..C 8
Maggie ....E 3
Magnolia .....614..F 12
Maiden ......2,416..I 1
Mamers ....J 6
Mamie ....C 16
Manly ....K 5
Manns Harbor .....D 16
Manteo ......547.°D 16
Maple ....C 15
Maple Hill ....G 13

Marble ....E 1
Margaretsville ..95..B 13
Marietta ......70..G 10
Marion .....3,335.°D 5
Mars Hill ...1,623..D 4
Marshall .....982.°D 4
Marshville ..1,405..K 3
Marston ....K 5
Matthews ....783..K 2
Maury ....421..E 13
Maxton .....1,885..F 10
Mayodan ...2,875..C 8
Maysville .....912..F 13
McAdenville* .950..E 6
McCain ....K 5
McDonald .....80..G 10
McFarlan .....140..F 8
McGrady ....C 6
McLeansville ....H 5
Mebane* ....2,433..C 10
Merritt ....F 14
Merry Hill ....D 14
Merry Oaks ....I 6
Micaville ....D 4
Micro ....300..E 12
Middleburg ...149..C 11
Middlesex ....729..D 12
Midland ....J 2
Midway Park .....F 13
Mill Spring ....E 4
Millbrook ....H 7
Millers Creek ......C 6
Millersville ....H 1
Milton ....235..C 10
Milwaukee ....376..C 13
Mineral Springs ...F 7
Misenheimer ....J 3
Mocksville ..2,529.°D 7
Moncure ....I 6
Monroe ....11,282.°F 7
Montreat ....D 4
Mooresville ..8,808..I 1
Moravian Falls ....H 1
Morehead City ......5,233..F 14
Morganton .13,625.°D 5
Morgantown* 3,547..C 9
Morrisville .....192..H 7
Mortimer ....27..D 5
Morven ....562..F 8
Mount Airy .7,325..C 7
Mount Gilead ....1,286..J 4
Mount Holly 5,107..J 1
Mount Mourne ......I 1
Mount Olive 4,914..E 12
Mount Pleasant ..1,174..J 2
Mount Vernon Springs ....I 5
Moyock ....B 15
Murfreesboro 3,508..C 13
Murphy .....2,082.°F 1
Nags Head ...414..D 16
Nakina ....H 11
Naples ....E 4
Nashville ...1,670.°D 12
Nebo ....D 5
Neuse ....H 7
New Bern .14,660.°F 14
New Holland ....E 15
New London ..285..J 3
New River-Gieger* ....8,699..G 13
New Topsail Beach ....41..G 13
Newell ....J 2
Newhill ....I 6
Newland .....524.°C 5
Newport .....1,735..F 14
Newton .....7,857.°D 6
Newton Grove .546..J 4
Niagara ....J 5
Norlina ......969..C 12
Norman ....K 4
North Belmont .10,759..J 1
North Henderson 1,997..C 11
North Wilkesboro 3,357..G 1
Northside ....H 7
Norwood ....1,896..J 3
Oak City .....559..D 13
Oakboro ......568..J 3
Ocean Isle Beach ....78..H 11
Ocracoke ....E 16
Okeewemee ....J 4
Old Fort .....676..D 4
Old Trap ....C 15
Olin ....H 1
Olivia ....J 6
Oriental ......445..F 14
Orrum ....162..G 10
Otto ....F 2
Owens ....K 6
Oxford ....7,178.°C 11
Paint Rock ....D 3
Palmyra ....27..C 13
Pantego ......218..D 14
Parkersburg ....56..F 11
Parkton ......550..F 10

Parkwood ...2,267..J 5
Parmele ......373..D 13
Patterson .....344..D 6
Paw Creek ....J 1
Peachland ....556..K 3
Pee Dee ....J 4
Pekin ....K 4
Pelham ....C 9
Pembroke ...1,982..G 10
Pensacola ....D 4
Phillipsville* 1,239..E 3
Pike Road ....D 14
Pikeville ......580..E 12
Pilot Mountain .1,309..C 8
Pine Hall ....C 8
Pine Level ....983..J 8
Pinebluff .....570..K 5
Pinehurst ...1,056..K 5
Pinetops ....1,379..D 13
Pinetown .....278..D 14
Pineville ....1,948..K 1
Pink Hill .....522..F 12
Pinnacle ....C 8
Pisgah Forest ....E 3
Pittsboro ....1,447.°D 10
Pleasant Garden ...H 4
Plumtree ....D 5
Plymouth ...4,774.°D 14
Point Harbor ......C 16
Polkton ......845..K 3
Pollocksville ..456..F 13
Poplar ....C 4
Porter ....J 3
Powellsville ...247..C 14
Princeton ...1,044..E 12
Princeville ....654..D 13
Proctorville ...157..G 10
Prospect Hill ......G 6
Providence ....C 9
Providence ....G 7
Raeford .....3,180.°F 10
Raleigh ..121,577.°D 11
Ramseur ....1,328..I 5
Randleman ..2,312..I 4
Ranlo* .....2,092..E 6
Ransomville ....E 14
Red Cross ....J 3
Red Oak ......359..D 12
Red Springs .3,383..F 10
Redland ....H 2
Reidsville ..13,636..C 9
Relief ....D 4
Rex ....F 10
Rex ....J 1
Rhodhiss ......784..D 6
Rich Square 1,254..C 13
Richfield .....306..J 3
Richlands ....935..F 13
Richmond Hill .....H 5
Riddle ....C 15
Roanoke Rapids ...13,508..C 12
Roaring Gap ....C 7
Roaring River .....G 1
Robbins .....1,059..J 5
Robbinsville ...777.°E 1
Roberdel ....K 4
Robersonville 1,910..D 13
Rockford ....G 2
Rockingham .5,852.°F 9
Rockwell ......999..I 3
Rocky Mount ...34,284..D 12
Rocky Point ....G 12
Rodanthe ....D 16
Roduco ....C 14
Rolesville .....529..H 8
Ronda ....465..G 1
Roper ....649..D 14
Rose Hill ...1,448..F 12
Roseboro ....1,235..K 8
Rosman ......407..E 3
Rougemont ....G 6
Rowan Mill* 1,184..D 7
Rowland ....1,358..G 10
Roxboro .....5,370.°C 10
Roxobel ....347..C 13
Royal Pines* 2,041..E 4
Ruffin ....C 9
Rural Hall ..2,338..G 3
Ruth ....360..E 5
Rutherford College ....D 6
Rutherfordton ....3,245.°E 5
Rhyne, see Daniels-Rhyne
Ryland ....C 14
St. Pauls ...2,011..F 10
Salemburg ....669..K 8
Salisbury ..22,515.°D 8
Salter Path ....F 14
Saluda ....546..E 4
Salvo ....D 16
Sandy Ridge ....C 8
Sanford ....11,716.°E 10
Sapphire ....F 3
Saratoga .....391..D 12
Saxapahaw ....H 5
Scaly Mountain ....F 2
Scotland Neck .....2,869..C 13

Scotts ....H 1
Scranton ....E 15
Seaboard .....611..C 13
Seagrove .....354..I 4
Sealevel ....F 15
Sedalia ....H 5
Selma ......4,356..I 8
Semora ....C 10
Seven Springs .188..E 12
Severn ....356..B 13
Seymour Johnson ...8,172..E 12
Shallotte .....597..H 11
Shannon ....F 10
Sharpsburg ...789..D 12
Shelby .....16,328.°E 6
Shelmerdine ....E 13
Sherrills Ford ......I 1
Sherwood ....C 5
Shiloh ....C 15
Shooting Creek .....F 2
Siler City ...4,689..I 5
Sims ....205..D 12
Skyland .....2,177..E 4
Sladesville ....E 15
Smithfield ..6,677.°E 11
Smithtown ....196..G 2
Smyre ....J 1
Smyrna ....F 15
Sneads Ferry ......G 13
Snow Hill ..1,359.°E 13
Snowden ....C 15
Sophia ....H 4
South Belmont* .2,278..F 6
South Creek ...73..E 14
South Fayetteville ..K 7
South Gastonia* .3,718..F 6
South Goldsboro* 2,094..E 12
South Henderson 1,843..C 11
South Mills ....C 15
South Rosemary, see Belmont-South Rosemary
South Salisbury .2,199..I 2
South Wadesboro* .109..F 8
South Weldon* ..1,630..C 13
South Wilmington ..H 12
Southern Pines .....5,937..K 5
Southport ..2,220.°H 12
Sparta ......1,304.°C 6
Speed ....142..D 13
Spencer .....3,075..I 2
Spencer Mountain* ..300..E 6
Spindale ....3,848..E 5
Spring Hope 1,334..D 12
Spring Lake 3,968..K 6
Spruce Pine 2,333..D 5
Stacy ....F 15
Staley ....239..I 5
Stanfield* .....458..E 8
Stanley .....2,336..J 1
Stanleyville .2,362..G 3
Stantonsburg ..869..E 12
Star ....892..J 4
State Road ....C 7
Statesville .19,996.°D 7
Stecoah ....E 2
Stedman ......505..K 7
Stella ....F 13
Stem ....242..G 7
Stokes ....D 13
Stokesdale ....G 4
Stoneville ...1,030..C 9
Stonewall .....335..F 14
Stony Point .1,001..H 1
Stovall ....405..C 11
Stumpy Point ......D 16
Suit ....F 1
Summerfield ....G 4
Sunbury ....C 14
Sunset Beach* 108..H 12
Supply ....H 12
Surf City .....166..G 13
Swan Station .196..J 6
Swannanoa .1,966..E 4
Swanquarter ......°E 15
Swansboro ..1,207..F 14
Swepsonville ....H 5
Sylva ....1,561.°E 3
Tabor City ..2,400..H 10
Tapoco ....E 1
Tar Heel ......87..F 11
Tarboro ......9,425.°D 13
Taylorsville ..1,231.°D 6
Teachey ......219..F 12
Terrell ....I 1
Thomasville 15,230..H 3
Thurmond ....C 7
Tillery ....C 13
Timberlake ....G 6
Toast* ....2,635..C 7
Tobaccoville ....G 3
Todd ....98..C 6
Topton ....E 2

Townsville ....C 11
Traphill ....C 7
Trent Woods ..719..F 14
Trenton ....539.°F 13
Trinity ....H 4
Triplett ....C 6
Troutman .....797..I 1
Troy ....2,429.°E 9
Tryon ......1,951..E 4
Tungsten ....C 11
Turkey ....329..F 12
Turnersburg ....H 1
Tuxedo ....E 4
Tyner ....C 14
Unaka ....E 1
Union Grove ....H 1
Union Mills ....E 5
Unionville ....K 2
Valdese .....3,182..D 6
Valle Crucis ....C 5
Vanceboro ....758..E 13
Vandalia ....H 4
Vandemere ....379..E 14
Vass ....885..J 6
Verona ....G 13
Vienna ....G 3
Waco ....245..E 6
Wade ....315..K 7
Wadesboro ..3,977.°F 8
Wadeville ....J 4
Wagram ....718..F 9
Wake Forest 3,148..H 8
Wakulla ....F 10
Walkerton ...1,652..G 3
Wallace ....2,905..F 12
Wallburg ....H 3
Walnut ....D 3
Walnut Cove 1,213..G 3
Walstonburg ..176..E 12
Wanchese ....D 16
Warrensville ..224..C 6
Warrenton ..1,035.°C 12
Warsaw .....2,701..F 12
Washington .8,961.°E 14
Washington Park ....517..E 14
Waterville ....D 3
Watha ....181..G 12
Waves ....D 16
Waxhaw .....1,248..F 7
Waynesville .6,488.°E 3
Weaverville .1,280..D 4
Webster ....181..E 3
Weeksville ....C 15
Welcome ....H 3
Weldon .....2,304..C 13
Wendell .....1,929..I 8
Wentworth ....°C 9
West Burlington* ......1,471..C 9
West Concord ...5,347..J 2
West End ....J 5
West Hillsborough ...1,696..H 6
West Jefferson ...889..C 6
West Marion 3,034..D 5
West Rockingham ..F 9
West Statesville* .....3,079..D 7
Whispering Pines* ......362..F 10
Whitakers .....926..C 12
White Lake ....232..G 11
White Oak ....F 11
White Plains ....C 7
Whitehead ....C 6
Whiteville ...4,195.°G 11
Whitnel ....D 6
Whittier ....E 2
Wilkesboro ..1,974.°C 6
Willard ....G 12
Williamston .6,570.°D 14
Willow Spring ......I 7
Wilmington 46,169.°H 12
Wilson .....29,347.°D 12
Wilson Mills ..283..I 8
Windsor .....2,199.°D 14
Winfall ....581..C 15
Wingate ....2,569..K 2
Winnabow ....H 12
Winston-Salem ...132,913.°C 8
Winterville ...1,437..E 13
Winton ....917.°C 14
Wise ....C 12
Wood ....C 12
Woodland .....744..C 13
Woodleaf ....I 2
Woodsdale ....C 10
Woodville .....253..C 13
Worthville ....I 4
Wrightsville Beach .....1,701..H 12
Yadkin College ....H 3
Yadkinville ..2,232.°C 7
Yanceyville ..1,274.°C 10
Yaupon Beach 334..H 12
Youngsville ....555..H 8
Zebulon .....1,839..H 8
Zionville ....C 5

*Does not appear on the map; key shows general location.
°County seat

Source: Latest census figures (1970). Places without population figures are unincorporated areas and are not listed in census reports.

NORTH CAROLINA/*People*

The 1970 United States census reported that North Carolina had a population of 5,082,059 persons. The population had increased about 12 per cent over the 1960 figure of 4,556,155.

About 45 per cent of North Carolina's people live in urban areas. That is, they live in or near cities and towns of 2,500 or more persons. About 55 per cent live in rural areas. But increasing numbers of people are moving from rural to urban parts of the state. About two-fifths of the people live in one of the state's seven Standard Metropolitan Statistical Areas (see METRO-POLITAN AREA). These areas are Asheville, Charlotte, Durham, Fayetteville, Greensboro-Winston-Salem-High Point, Raleigh, and Wilmington. For their populations, see the *Index* to the political map of North Carolina.

Charlotte is the state's largest city. Other large cities, in order of population, are Greensboro, Winston-Salem, and Raleigh, the state capital. See the list of separate articles on the cities of North Carolina in the *Related Articles* at the end of this article.

More than 99 of every 100 North Carolinians were born in the United States. Most of those from other countries came from England, France, or other Euro-

North Carolina Dept. of Conservation and Development

Tobacco Auctioneers and Buyers work rapidly. In these warehouses in Wilson, the world's largest bright-leaf tobacco market, more than 400 lots of tobacco can be sold in an hour.

pean nations. About 22 of every 100 North Carolinians are Negroes. Large numbers of Negroes have left North Carolina and moved to the industrialized areas of the North.

Baptists make up North Carolina's largest religious group. Methodists are the second largest, and Presbyterians rank third in number.

POPULATION

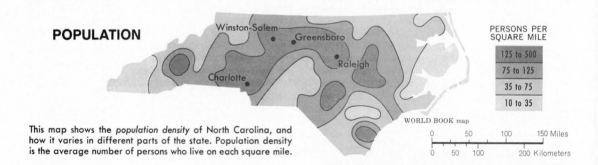

PERSONS PER SQUARE MILE

125 to 500
75 to 125
35 to 75
10 to 35

WORLD BOOK map

0   50   100   150 Miles
0 50 100   200 Kilometers

This map shows the *population density* of North Carolina, and how it varies in different parts of the state. Population density is the average number of persons who live on each square mile.

WORLD BOOK photo

Handicraft Skills are part of the heritage of many persons who live in the mountain areas of western North Carolina. This potter makes graceful bowls and vases, using techniques that have been handed down through many generations.

Skills of the Past still form part of the daily life of Indians on the Qualla Reservation. This aged Cherokee woman pounds cornmeal with a mortar and pestle. Her full, pleated skirt and bandana are traditional garments for women.

North Carolina Dept. of Conservation and Development

Schools. Churches and religious leaders controlled most of the early education in North Carolina. In 1705, Charles Griffin, a schoolteacher and member of the Anglican Church, established what was probably North Carolina's first school. It was at Symons Creek near Elizabeth City. Early attempts at public education were opposed by church members, who believed that education belonged in the hands of the church. The constitution of 1776 provided for the establishment of a public school system and for chartering the University of North Carolina. In 1795, this university became the first state university in the United States to hold classes. But the state did not build its first public school until 1840. In 1901, Governor Charles B. Aycock began to improve North Carolina's system of public education.

The lieutenant governor serves as chairman of the state board of education, and the superintendent of public instruction is its secretary. The state treasurer also serves on the board, as do 10 other members appointed by the governor. Children between 6 and 16 must attend school. For the number of students and teachers in North Carolina, see EDUCATION (table).

Libraries. The state's first public library was founded about 1700 by Thomas Bray, an English missionary. At this time, early groups of settlers were beginning to make their way into North Carolina. About five years later, Bray's library became part of Bath, the first town in North Carolina. In 1897, the state passed its first public-library law. That same year, the first tax-supported library in North Carolina opened in Durham.

The Duke University library owns the largest collection of books in the state. The University of North Carolina at Chapel Hill also has an enormous collection of over a million volumes. Both universities have outstanding collections of documents relating to southern history and to the social sciences. The state library and the state department of archives and history, both in Raleigh, keep records of the history of North Carolina.

Museums. One of the outstanding art museums in the South, the North Carolina Museum of Art, opened in Raleigh in 1956. Among its exhibits are nearly 3,000 artistic treasures. The University of North Carolina's art museums include the William Hayes Ackland Memorial Art Center in Chapel Hill and the Weatherspoon Art Gallery in Greensboro. Other art galleries include the Mint Museum of Art in Charlotte and the Hickory Museum of Art in Hickory. The Greensboro Historical Museum and the North Carolina Museum of History at Raleigh portray the history of the state.

UNIVERSITIES AND COLLEGES

North Carolina has 36 universities and colleges accredited by the Southern Association of Colleges and Schools. For enrollments and further information, see UNIVERSITIES AND COLLEGES (table).

Name	Location	Founded	Name	Location	Founded
Appalachian State University	Boone	1903	Mars Hill College	Mars Hill	1964
Atlantic Christian College	Wilson	1902	Meredith College	Raleigh	1891
Barber-Scotia College	Concord	1867	Methodist College	Fayetteville	1964
Belmont Abbey College	Belmont	1876	North Carolina, University of	*	1789
Bennett College	Greensboro	1873	North Carolina Agricultural and		
Campbell College	Buies Creek	1963	Technical State University	Greensboro	1891
Catawba College	Salisbury	1851	North Carolina Central University	Durham	1910
Davidson College	Davidson	1836	North Carolina Wesleyan		
Duke University	Durham	1838	College	Rocky Mount	1964
East Carolina University	Greenville	1907	Pembroke State University	Pembroke	1887
Elizabeth City University	Elizabeth City	1891	Pfeiffer College	Misenheimer	1885
Elon College	Elon College	1889	Queens College	Charlotte	1857
Fayetteville State University	Fayetteville	1877	Saint Andrews Presbyterian		
Greensboro College	Greensboro	1838	College	Laurinburg	1858
Guilford College	Greensboro	1834	Saint Augustine's College	Raleigh	1867
High Point College	High Point	1920	Salem College	Winston-Salem	1772
Johnson C. Smith			Shaw University	Raleigh	1865
University	Charlotte	1867	Wake Forest University	Winston-Salem	1834
Lenoir Rhyne College	Hickory	1891	Western Carolina University	Cullowhee	1889
Livingstone College	Salisbury	1879	Winston-Salem State University	Winston-Salem	1892

*For location of the campuses of the University of North Carolina, see UNIVERSITIES AND COLLEGES (table).

North Carolina Dept. of Conservation and Development

North Carolina Museum of Art, in Raleigh, has a collection valued at more than $12 million. The museum has had strong state support. In 1947, the state gave $1 million to buy 200 paintings to start the first collection. In 1953, a state-owned building was remodeled to house the museum. The museum opened in 1956.

NORTH CAROLINA / *A Visitor's Guide*

Many Northerners come to North Carolina's sandhills area for relief from the cold winter weather. Blossoming mountain laurels, azaleas, and rhododendrons in spring and summer, and the beautiful colors of autumn, lure visitors to the mountains. Hunters track quail, deer, and black bears through the mountains. Fishermen, swimmers, and sunbathers enjoy North Carolina's lakes, rivers, and coastlines. Historic sites, battlefields, old mansions, and beautiful gardens throughout the state attract sightseers and students of American history.

All photos from North Carolina Dept. of Conservation and Development unless otherwise indicated.

Old Salem Restoration in Winston-Salem

Kabel, Publix

Wright Brothers National Memorial near Kitty Hawk

Annual *Lost Colony* Drama in Manteo

Chimney Rock in the Blue Ridge Mountains

——— PLACES TO VISIT ———

Following are brief descriptions of some of North Carolina's many interesting places to visit.

Alamance Battlefield, near Burlington, was the scene of a historic battle shortly before the Revolutionary War. About 2,000 frontiersmen, called the Regulators, rebelled against the eastern planters and suffered heroic defeat on May 16, 1771.

Bentonville Battlefield, near Smithfield, was the scene of one of the last important Civil War battles. There, on March 25, 1865, General William T. Sherman's Union forces defeated the Confederate troops of General Joseph E. Johnston.

Biltmore Estate covers about 12,000 acres of forests and farmlands near Asheville. The majestic Biltmore House, a masterpiece of early French Renaissance architecture, is the chief feature of the estate.

Chimney Rock towers high above the mountains in Rutherford County, offering an excellent view of the Blue Ridge Mountains. Some persons believe that spirits, called the *Little People,* can be seen there.

Grandfather Mountain, near Linville, looks like the huge sleeping face of an old man. Brave tourists may walk across a mile-high swinging bridge.

Azaleas at Greenfield Park in Wilmington **Tryon Palace in New Bern**

Market House, in Fayetteville, was once a slave market and now houses the local chamber of commerce. It stands on the site of the convention hall, where North Carolina ratified the U.S. Constitution in 1789.

Morehead Planetarium, at the University of North Carolina in Chapel Hill, is one of the nation's better-known planetariums. Spectators can watch the movements of stars and planets across a 68-foot dome.

Nantahala Gorge, in Swain County, plunges hundreds of feet down into the mountains. Indians believed the deep, beautiful canyon was haunted.

Ocracoke Island, a hideout of Blackbeard, the pirate, and the site of many shipwrecks, lies about 20 miles beyond the coastline, southeast of Pamlico Sound.

Old Salem is a restored colonial village in Winston-Salem. Moravians founded the village of Salem in 1766.

Pinehurst, a popular and charming winter resort village in the sandhills region, is famous for its peaceful atmosphere and its golf tournaments.

Tryon Palace, in New Bern, is the restored governor's mansion originally built by William Tryon, a royal governor. American patriots defied British authority by meeting in the palace in 1774.

National Parks, Forests, and Memorials. Carolina has four national forests: Croatan, Nantahala, Pisgah, and Uwharri. It shares another, the Cherokee National Forest, with Tennessee. For the area of each forest, see NATIONAL FOREST (table). In September, 1964, Congress set aside two areas of the national forests as national wilderness. These areas are to be preserved in their natural condition. North Carolina shares the Blue Ridge Parkway with Virginia, and the Great Smoky Mountains National Park with Tennessee (see GREAT SMOKY MOUNTAINS NATIONAL PARK). The Wright Brothers National Memorial at Kill Devil Hills near Kitty Hawk honors the first powered airplane flight. North Carolina has two military parks—Guilford Courthouse National Military Park near Greensboro and Moores Creek National Military Park near Wilmington (see NATIONAL PARK [National Military Parks]). Other areas include Fort Raleigh National Historic Site in Manteo, Cape Hatteras National Seashore on Cape Hatteras, and Cape Lookout National Seashore, which lies south of Cape Hatteras.

State Parks. North Carolina has 12 state parks. For information about them, write to Director, Division of State Parks, Department of Conservation and Development, Box 2719, Raleigh, N.C. 27602.

--------- **ANNUAL EVENTS** ---------

One of North Carolina's most popular annual events is the story of the *Lost Colony.* This historical drama is staged at Fort Raleigh in Manteo each night in July and August. It portrays some of the hardships faced by the early English colonists who disappeared mysteriously from Roanoke Island.

Other annual events in North Carolina include the following.

January-March: Field Trials in Pinehurst (January); Old Christmas Celebration in Rodanthe (January); Snow Carnival in Boone (January); Camellia Show in Wilmington (February); Fox Hunt in Nags Head (March); Bird Dog Field Trials in Tryon (March); Moravian Easter Service in Old Salem (March or April).

April-June: Mountain Youth Jamboree in Asheville (April); Azalea Festival in Wilmington (April); North and South Invitation Golf Championships in Pinehurst (April); Stoneybrook Steeplechase in Southern Pines (April); Sports Car Hill Climb at Chimney Rock (April); Old Time Fiddlers Convention in Union Grove (April); Sedgefield Horse Show in Greensboro (May); Blueberry Festival in White Lake (May); Strawberry Festival in Chadbourn (May); Summer Festival of Music in Brevard (June-August); Singing on the Mountain at Grandfather Mountain (June); Rhododendron Festival in Roan Mountain (June).

July-September: Craftsman's Fair in Asheville (July); Highland Games and Gathering of Scottish Clans at Grandfather Mountain (July); Mountain Dance and Folk Festival in Asheville (August); Mineral and Gem Festival in Spruce Pine (August); International Cup Regatta in Elizabeth City (September); State Championship Horse Show in Raleigh (September); Mule Days Celebration in Benson (September).

October-December: State Fair in Raleigh (October); National 500 Auto Race in Charlotte (October); Surf Fishing Tournament in Nags Head (October); Carolinas Carousel in Charlotte (November); Formal Fox Hunt Meets, statewide (November); Anniversary of First Powered Airplane Flight in Kitty Hawk (December 17).

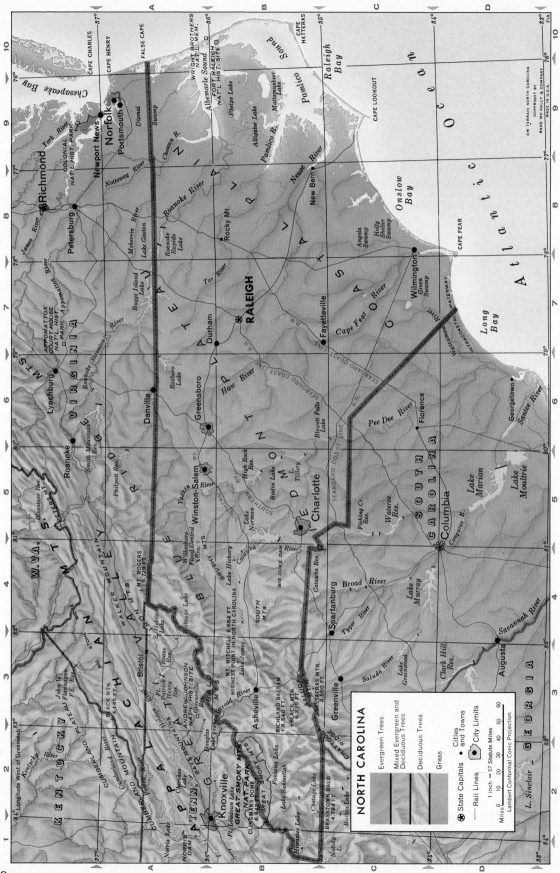

NORTH CAROLINA

Evergreen Trees

Mixed Evergreen and
Deciduous Trees

Deciduous Trees

Grass

⊛ State Capitals   ● Cities
                        and Towns
— Rail Lines   ⊙ City Limits

1 inch = 57 Statute Miles
Miles 0 10 20 30 40 50 60
Lambert Conformal Conic Projection

Specially created for **World Book Encyclopedia** by Rand McNally and World Book editors

NORTH CAROLINA / The Land

Land Regions. North Carolina has three main land regions. These are, from east to west: (1) the Atlantic Coastal Plain, (2) the Piedmont, and (3) the Blue Ridge.

The Atlantic Coastal Plain extends from New Jersey to southern Florida. In North Carolina it looks somewhat like a giant foot, whose heel consists of a chain of slender land ridges several miles out to sea. The coastal plain has swamps, prairies, and rich farmland. It rises from sea level at the ocean to about 300 feet at the *Fall Line* of the rivers. The Fall Line is the zone in which the soft, low country ends and the rockier, hilly area begins.

The sand dunes, reefs, sand bars, and islands beyond North Carolina's shoreline are called the *outer banks*. Some of their individual names are far more colorful—Cape Fear, Cape Hatteras, Cape Lookout, and Nags Head. Like monsters of the deep, the outer banks have sent many ships to the bottom. Cape Hatteras has earned its nickname, the *Graveyard of the Atlantic*.

From the shore, the coastal plain extends inland through an area of low, level marshland, covered by trees and water. Many swamps, shallow lakes, and rivers reflect moss-hung cypress trees. The Dismal Swamp in the northeast is one of the country's largest swamps. Treeless, grassy prairies called *savannas* cover the eastern coastal plain. The western coastal plain has rich farmland. Sand hills rise along the southern part of the Fall Line. Popular winter resort areas such as Pine-

hurst and Southern Pines are in the sandhills region.

The Piedmont extends from Delaware to Alabama. In North Carolina, its shape resembles the face of an elderly man, whose brow, nose, and jaw point westward. The region rises to about 1,500 feet at the mountains. Most of the state's manufacturing industries are in this region. The Piedmont has more people than either the coastal or mountain regions.

The Blue Ridge, or *Mountain*, region stretches from southern Pennsylvania to northern Georgia. It is named for the Blue Ridge Mountains, North Carolina's chief range. But in North Carolina the region also includes a number of other ranges. They include the Bald, Black, Brushy, Great Smoky, Iron, South, Stone, and Unaka ranges. All these mountains form part of the Appalachian Mountains. The Blue Ridge region rises from the Piedmont to heights of more than a mile above sea level. Mount Mitchell rises 6,684 feet and is the highest peak east of the Mississippi River. Forests cover much of the mountains, and the valley bottoms have good farmland. Great Smoky Mountains National Park and the Blue Ridge Parkway are in this region.

Rivers, Waterfalls, and Lakes. Most of North Carolina's rivers start in the Blue Ridge Mountains or in the Piedmont. They flow southeastward down the slopes of the mountains and hills until they reach the rich farmland. There, they plunge down-

ward in waterfalls and rapids to the Fall Line. The rivers race along narrow channels above the Fall Line. Then they become wider and flow slowly below the Fall Line, and end in wide *estuaries* (river mouths). Boats can sail inland from the coast as far west as the Fall Line. Some of the waterfalls and rapids at the Fall Line generate much of North Carolina's electric power.

One of the state's largest rivers, the Roanoke, flows into northeastern North Carolina, and empties into Albemarle Sound. The Neuse and Tar rivers drain the central part of North Carolina and flow into Pamlico Sound. The Cape Fear River crosses the southeastern portion of the Atlantic Coastal Plain. Several swift streams west of the Blue Ridge Mountains drain into Tennessee. North Carolina's largest dams are in this western area on the Hiwassee, Little Tennessee, and Nantahala rivers. A large dam also spans the Catawba River, east of the Blue Ridge Mountains near Marion.

Many lovely waterfalls add to the beauty of southwestern North Carolina. Some of the prettiest include Linville Falls and Bridal Veil Falls. Whitewater Falls, near Brevard, plunges 411 feet and is one of the highest falls in the eastern United States.

North Carolina's only natural lakes are on the Atlantic Coastal Plain. Lake Mattamuskeet, the largest, is about 15 miles long and 6 miles wide.

Land Regions of North Carolina

NORTH CAROLINA/Climate

Temperatures in southeastern Brunswick County average 80° F. in July and 48° F. in January. The western mountains average between 60° F. and 70° F. in July, and as low as 28° F. in January. The highest recorded temperature in the state was 109° F., at Albemarle on July 28, 1940, and at Weldon on Sept. 7, 1954. The state's all-time low temperature, −29° F., was recorded on Mount Mitchell on Jan. 30, 1966.

Most of the state's *precipitation* (rain, melted snow, and other forms of moisture) comes in the form of rain. The Atlantic Coastal Plain averages about 50 inches a year, the Piedmont about 47, and the Blue Ridge region about 60 inches. Snowfall ranges from 40 inches a year in some mountain areas to only a trace in some coastal areas. Since 1900, North Carolina has averaged nearly one hurricane a year. One of the worst to hit the state struck in 1954. It killed 19 persons, injured 200 others, and caused more than $100,000,000 in damage.

Frank J. Miller

Mount Mitchell, the highest peak east of the Mississippi River, overlooks the scenic Blue Ridge Parkway. Rhododendrons and many other kinds of plants thrive in this region. The usually mild climate and heavy rainfall are ideal for plants.

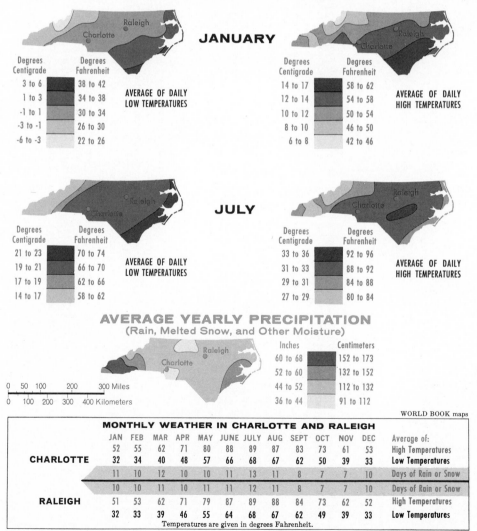

SEASONAL TEMPERATURES

JANUARY

Degrees Centigrade	Degrees Fahrenheit	AVERAGE OF DAILY LOW TEMPERATURES
3 to 6	38 to 42	
1 to 3	34 to 38	
-1 to 1	30 to 34	
-3 to -1	26 to 30	
-6 to -3	22 to 26	

Degrees Centigrade	Degrees Fahrenheit	AVERAGE OF DAILY HIGH TEMPERATURES
14 to 17	58 to 62	
12 to 14	54 to 58	
10 to 12	50 to 54	
8 to 10	46 to 50	
6 to 8	42 to 46	

JULY

Degrees Centigrade	Degrees Fahrenheit	AVERAGE OF DAILY LOW TEMPERATURES
21 to 23	70 to 74	
19 to 21	66 to 70	
17 to 19	62 to 66	
14 to 17	58 to 62	

Degrees Centigrade	Degrees Fahrenheit	AVERAGE OF DAILY HIGH TEMPERATURES
33 to 36	92 to 96	
31 to 33	88 to 92	
29 to 31	84 to 88	
27 to 29	80 to 84	

AVERAGE YEARLY PRECIPITATION
(Rain, Melted Snow, and Other Moisture)

Inches	Centimeters
60 to 68	152 to 173
52 to 60	132 to 152
44 to 52	112 to 132
36 to 44	91 to 112

0   50 100   200   300 Miles
0   100 200   300   400 Kilometers

WORLD BOOK maps

	JAN	FEB	MAR	APR	MAY	JUNE	JULY	AUG	SEPT	OCT	NOV	DEC	Average of:
MONTHLY WEATHER IN CHARLOTTE AND RALEIGH													
CHARLOTTE	52	55	62	71	80	88	89	87	83	73	61	53	High Temperatures
	32	34	40	48	57	66	68	67	62	50	39	33	Low Temperatures
	11	10	12	10	10	11	13	11	8	7	7	10	Days of Rain or Snow
	10	10	11	10	11	11	12	11	8	7	7	10	Days of Rain or Snow
RALEIGH	51	53	62	71	79	87	89	88	84	73	62	52	High Temperatures
	32	33	39	46	55	64	68	67	62	49	39	33	Low Temperatures

Temperatures are given in degrees Fahrenheit.

Source: U.S. Weather Bureau

The line that separates the Atlantic Coastal Plain from the Piedmont also separates North Carolina's two major industrial areas. The state's richest farmland is in the Atlantic Coastal Plain. Most of the manufacturing takes place in the Piedmont. Mining industries operate in many parts of the state.

Natural Resources of North Carolina include rich soils and mineral deposits, thick forests, and plentiful plant and animal life.

Soil. Red and yellow soils cover most of North Carolina, except along the coast and in the mountains. Light and level sandy loam soils make the central and western coastal plain the richest farmland in the state. A strip of coastal land from 30 to 60 miles wide has marshy soils formed by dark peat or muck. These soils have poor drainage, but if drained properly, they provide good farmland. Deep sandy soils cover the sand hills along the Fall Line. The Piedmont has sandy, clay, and silt loams, mostly red in color. Strips of dark *alluvial* (water-deposited) soils lie along most of the streams. Grayish-brown loams cover most of the mountain section.

Minerals. Deposits of more than 300 kinds of minerals and rocks have been found in North Carolina. The mountains contain rich stores of feldspar and kaolin. The Blue Ridge and Piedmont regions have large deposits of gneiss. Sand and gravel are found in the coastal plain and in the Piedmont. The Piedmont region is also rich in clays, granite, kyanite, and shale. Beaufort County, on the coastal plain, has one of the largest phosphate deposits in the world. Each of North Carolina's three main land regions has deposits of limestone.

Forests cover about 20 million acres, or about two-thirds of the state. Pines are North Carolina's most common trees. Hardwoods, including hickories, maples, oaks, and tulip trees, grow in the Blue Ridge and Piedmont regions. Black tupelo and sweet gum forests line the eastern coastal plain rivers. Loblolly pine, the state's most common softwood tree, grows in the swamplands along with bald cypress, pond pine, and water ash.

Plant Life. Every January, camellias bloom along North Carolina's coastline. By April, redbud and dogwood blossoms have spread across the state. Each May and June, azaleas and rhododendrons color the mountainsides. Orchids, and insect eaters such as pitcher plants, sundews, and Venus's-flytraps flourish in the savannas.

Animal Life. Black bear and deer live in the western mountains and in the lowlands near the coast. North Carolina's fields, forests, and streams are filled with beavers, foxes, gray squirrels, opossums, otters, rabbits, raccoons, and skunks. Common songbirds include Carolina wrens and mockingbirds. Ducks, geese, and swans spend the winter near the coast. Mourning doves, partridge, and woodcocks inhabit much of the state. Dolphins, marlin, menhaden, sailfish, and sturgeon are found in the coastal waters. Fresh-water lakes and streams have bass, bluegills, crappies, sunfish, and trout.

Manufacturing accounts for about four-fifths of the value of goods produced in North Carolina. Manufactured goods have a *value added by manufacture* of about $6,600,000,000 a year. This figure represents the value created in products by North Carolina's industries, not counting such costs as materials, supplies, and fuels. The state's chief manufacturing industries, in order of importance, are (1) textiles and related products, (2) tobacco products, and (3) furniture.

Textiles and Related Products. North Carolina leads the United States and most nations of the world in textile production. The state's textile and apparel industries have a value added of about $2 billion a year. This amount is about a third of North Carolina's total manufacturing income. The state has more than a thousand textile plants. Most of them are in the Piedmont region. Gaston County has more cotton mills than any other county in the United States. North Carolina produces nearly half the nation's hosiery. Greensboro has the world's largest mill for weaving denim, and the world's largest overall factory. Kannapolis has the world's largest producer of household textiles, such as sheets and towels. Elkin has the world's largest manufacturer of woolen blankets. Other leading textile products include Dacron, nylon, and rayon.

Tobacco Products. North Carolina leads all the states in the production of tobacco products. This industry has a value added of about $976 million a year. Cigarette factories at Durham, Greensboro, Reidsville, and Winston-Salem account for more than half the nation's cigarette production. North Carolina ranks among the leading states in the amount of taxes paid to the federal government. This is because a tax must be paid with the purchase of cigarettes or processed tobacco.

NORTH CAROLINA'S PRODUCTION IN 1967

Total value of goods produced—$8,180,322,000

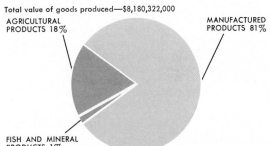

AGRICULTURAL PRODUCTS 18%

MANUFACTURED PRODUCTS 81%

FISH AND MINERAL PRODUCTS 1%

Note: Manufacturing percentage based on value added by manufacture. Other percentages based on value of production.

Sources: U.S. Government statistics

NORTH CAROLINA'S EMPLOYMENT IN 1967

Total number of persons employed—1,754,000

	Number of Employees
Manufacturing	647,700
Wholesale & Retail Trade	280,900
Government	202,000
Agriculture	197,100
Services	183,500
Construction	96,600
Transportation & Public Utilities	81,800
Finance, Mining & Other	64,400

Source: U.S. Department of Labor

FARM, MINERAL, AND FOREST PRODUCTS

This map shows where the state's leading farm, mineral, and forest products are produced. The major urban areas (shown on the map in red) are the state's important manufacturing centers.

WORLD BOOK map

Furniture has a value added of about $519 million yearly. North Carolina leads the states in the production of household furniture. High Point, the chief furniture manufacturer, attracts buyers from all parts of the United States. Factories at Lenoir, Lexington, Mount Airy, Statesville, Thomasville, and other towns produce a variety of wooden furniture.

Other Important Industries. Electrical machinery ranks fourth in North Carolina, with a value added of about $450 million yearly. Food products rank next in importance. Bread, butter, and flour are the chief food products. Other leading industries include the manufacture of chemicals; clothing; nonelectrical machinery; and paper and paper products.

North Carolina stands among the leading lumber-producing states. About a hundred pulp, paper, and paper-products mills use the wood from sweet gums, pines, soft maples, and tulip trees. Canton, Plymouth, and Roanoke Rapids have large pulp and paper mills. Most of the pulpwood comes from the coastal plain. Lumber for the construction-lumber industry comes chiefly from bald cypress, pines, and tulip trees. Other important wood products include cabinets, paneling, poles and piling, and veneer. Processed pine wood is used to make rayon fiber and a variety of chemicals.

Agriculture provides a yearly gross income of about $1½ billion, or almost a fifth of the value of all goods produced. Farmland covers over 14 million acres, or nearly half the state.

Tobacco. North Carolina is the leading tobacco state, raising about 40 per cent of the nation's crop. Tobacco provides a yearly income of about $535 million—nearly two-fifths of the state's total farm income.

The heart of the coastal plain is known as *Tobaccoland.* But farmers in most parts of the state raise tobacco. Most of the tobacco is the bright-leaf variety. But mountain farmers east of Jackson County raise golden-leaf Burley tobacco. Wilson sells more bright-leaf tobacco than any other city in the Western Hemisphere. North Carolina has about 50 tobacco markets.

Soybeans rank second among crops grown in North Carolina. They provide a yearly income of about $69 million. Soybeans grow chiefly in the eastern half of the state.

Corn is the third-ranking cash crop. Farmers throughout the state raise corn, which they use both as livestock feed and as a cash crop.

Other Field Crops. Peanuts rank fourth in North Carolina. Much of the peanut crop comes from the northern coastal plain. Sweet potatoes are raised in the warm, humid regions of the southern coastal plain. North Carolina ranks second only to Louisiana in sweet potato production. Coastal areas and the northern part of the mountain region supply Irish potatoes. Other crops raised in North Carolina include cotton, greenhouse and nursery products, hay, oats, and wheat.

Fruits and Truck Crops are raised mainly on the coastal plain and in the mountains. Some fruits, especially peaches, thrive in the sandhills region. Leading fruit crops include apples, grapes, melons, peaches, and strawberries. Burgaw is noted for its blueberries. Washington and other nearby coastal plain towns ship scuppernongs, a kind of grape. Cucumbers, snap beans, and tomatoes are among the most valuable *truck crops* (vegetables grown for market). Truck farmers also grow cabbages, peppers, and sweet corn.

Livestock Products provide a yearly income of about $462 million. North Carolina ranks among the leading raisers of *broilers* (chickens from 9 to 12 weeks old). Stanley, Surry, Wilkes, and Yadkin counties raise the most chickens. Eggs are the third most valuable farm product. Duplin, Robeson, Scotland, Union, and Wayne counties raise the most turkeys. Most dairy farming takes place in the Piedmont and Blue Ridge regions. Hogs and beef cattle provide an important source of income for farmers.

Mining in North Carolina earns about $77 million a year. Stone provides the greatest income. Sand and gravel rank next in value, followed by phosphate, feldspar, and lithium. North Carolina is the leading producer of feldspar, lithium, and mica. It also leads the nation in crushed granite production. A huge quarry at Mount Airy supplies beautiful white granite. Other granite quarries operate in over 40 counties. Avery County supplies all the state's kaolin, a type of clay used in making pottery, porcelain, and book paper. Other pottery clays are mined in about 20 counties in North Carolina.

Pottery made in Jugtown, in northern Moore County, has won national fame. Most counties supply sand and gravel. Other important minerals include asbestos, barite, gemstones, olivine, and talc. One of the largest supplies of phosphate in the United States and in the world was discovered in Beaufort County in eastern North Carolina in the early 1960's.

Fishing Industry. North Carolina has an annual fish catch valued at more than $8 million. Shellfish and menhaden provide much of the income. Shellfish include crabs, oysters, scallops, and shrimps. The state's leading fish products include alewives, flounders, and sea bass.

Electric Power. Fuel-burning steam plants produce over 90 per cent of the state's electric power. Rural electric cooperatives and private companies furnish electricity to nearly all of the state's farms. North Carolina leads the nation in the percentage of farms with electrification. Fontana Dam, the largest in the state, spans the Little Tennessee River near the western tip of North Carolina. It belongs to the Tennessee Valley Authority, from which North Carolina buys some of its power. The state imports its coal, oil, and natural gas from other states. For North Carolina's kilowatt-hour production, see ELECTRIC POWER (table).

Transportation. Rivers served as the first highways in North Carolina. Roads began to appear in the 1700's. But most of the roads remained poor until well into the 1900's. The first two major railroads—the Wilmington and Raleigh, and the Raleigh and Gaston—began service in 1840. At that time, the 161-mile Wilmington line was the longest in the world.

Today, about 77,000 of the state's 85,000 miles of roads are surfaced. The Blue Ridge Parkway connects Great Smoky Mountains National Park with Shenandoah National Park in Virginia. Many bridges span rivers and inlets along the coast. The state has about 4,300 miles of railroad track. Five commercial airlines serve the state. Harbors at Morehead City, Southport, and Wilmington are part of the Atlantic Intracoastal Waterway (see ATLANTIC INTRACOASTAL WATERWAY).

Communication. James Davis, a printer and editor, established North Carolina's first newspaper, the *North Carolina Gazette*, at New Bern in 1751. The weekly *Raleigh Register* was founded in 1799. The state's largest daily newspapers today are the *Charlotte Observer* and the *Raleigh News and Observer*. North Carolina publishers print about 200 newspapers, of which about 50 are dailies. Over 100 periodicals are produced in the state.

North Carolina's oldest radio station, WBT of Charlotte, began broadcasting in 1922. Television in the state started in 1949, with stations WBTV in Charlotte and WFMY in Greensboro. Today, North Carolina has more than 250 radio stations, 17 commercial television stations, and an educational television network.

NORTH CAROLINA/*History*

Indian Days. About 35,000 Indians, belonging to about 30 tribes, lived in the North Carolina region when white men first arrived. The most important tribes were the Cherokee in the western mountains; the Hatteras along the coast; and the Catawba, Chowanoc, and Tuscarora of the coastal plain and the Piedmont.

Exploration and Settlement. Giovanni da Verrazano, sailing in the service of France, was the first known white man to explore the North Carolina coast. He visited the Cape Fear area in 1524. Verrazano sent glowing reports of what he saw to King Francis I of France. But the king was not interested in colonizing the region. About two years later, Lucas Vásquez de Ayllón of Spain established a colony near Cape Fear. But disease and starvation killed so many of his followers that the survivors soon fled the area. In 1540, Hernando de Soto, also of Spain, led an expedition over the mountains at the southwestern tip of the North Carolina region. De Soto hoped to find gold. Instead, he later discovered the Mississippi River in 1541. Other Spaniards also came to the region, but neither they nor the French established any permanent settlements. In 1585, Sir Walter Raleigh of England sent an expedition to settle on Roanoke Island. This group became the first English colony in America. But misfortunes forced the settlers to return to England in 1586. Raleigh sent a later expedition to Roanoke Island in 1587, with John White as governor. White established a colony, and sailed back to England for supplies that same year. When Queen Elizabeth allowed White to return to Roanoke Island in 1590, his colony had disappeared. No one knows what happened to the more than a hundred men, women, and children of what has come to be called the *Lost Colony* (see LOST COLONY).

In 1629, King Charles I of England granted his attorney general, Sir Robert Heath, the southern part of the English claim in America. This included a strip of land containing what is now both North Carolina and South Carolina, and extending westward to the Pacific Ocean. The land was named the Province of *Carolana* (land of Charles). Heath made no attempts at settlement.

The first permanent white settlers in Carolina came from Virginia. They settled in the Albemarle Sound region around 1650. In 1663, Charles II of England regranted Carolina to eight of his favorite nobles. He made them *lords proprietors* (ruling landlords) of the colony. The proprietors divided Carolina into three counties: (1) Albemarle, in the northern part; (2) Clarendon, in the Cape Fear region; and (3) Craven, in what is now South Carolina. In 1664, William Drummond was appointed governor of Albemarle County, and government began in Carolina. Clarendon County lasted only until 1667. From then until 1689, Albemarle County had the only government in the North Carolina region.

Colonial Days. The colonists of Albemarle County believed that the proprietors and governors were more interested in making money than in governing wisely. In 1678, some Albemarle colonists revolted against their governor. They controlled the county for a year, with John Culpeper as governor. The revolt became known as *Culpeper's Rebellion*. Between 1664 and 1689, the colonists drove five of the Albemarle governors out of office.

After 1691, governors were appointed to govern the entire Carolina colony, with a deputy governor for the North Carolina region. The deputy governors ruled wisely and the colonists accepted them. The North Carolina region became a separate colony in 1712.

During the late 1600's and early 1700's, increasing numbers of settlers came to North Carolina. In 1705,

——— IMPORTANT DATES IN NORTH CAROLINA ———

1524 Giovanni da Verrazano, a Florentine explorer sailing in the service of France, visited the North Carolina coast.

1585 The English established at Roanoke Island their first colony in what is now the United States.

1629 King Charles I of England granted *Carolana* to Sir Robert Heath.

1650? The first permanent settlers came to the Albemarle region from Virginia.

1663 King Charles II granted the Carolina colony to eight lords proprietors.

1664 North Carolina's first government was established in Albemarle County.

1711 The Tuscarora Indians attacked settlements between the Neuse and Pamlico rivers. The colonists defeated the Indians in 1713.

1729 North Carolina came under direct royal rule.

1765 Colonists in North Carolina began to resist enforcement of the British Stamp Act and other tax laws.

1774 North Carolina sent delegates to the First Continental Congress in Philadelphia.

1776 The Whigs defeated the Tories at Moore's Creek Bridge. North Carolina adopted its first constitution.

1781 British forces withdrew from North Carolina and surrendered in Virginia.

1789 North Carolina became the 12th state on Nov. 21.

1835 Constitutional changes gave equal representation to most North Carolina taxpayers.

1861 North Carolina seceded from the Union.

1865 General Joseph E. Johnston surrendered to General William T. Sherman near Durham.

1868 North Carolina was readmitted to the Union.

1903 The Wright brothers made the first successful powered airplane flight at Kitty Hawk.

1915 The legislature established a highway commission.

1933 The state took over the support of public schools.

1945 Fontana Dam, the largest in the state, was completed.

1949 The people approved a large bond issue for road and public-school construction.

1950 Great industrial expansion began.

1958 Three North Carolina universities joined in the Research Triangle program for industry.

1962 The state's courts were reorganized under a general court of justice.

1963 The University of North Carolina adopted a single university plan, beginning with branch campuses at Chapel Hill, Greensboro, and Raleigh.

1964 A North Carolina antipoverty plan became the pilot for the national campaign to wipe out poverty.

1969 The state legislature established a public school kindergarten program. It also adopted a state tax on cigarettes.

North Carolina's first town, Bath, was incorporated near the mouth of the Pamlico River. By 1710, settlements had spread down the coast and along the riverbanks as far south as the Neuse River. In 1710, Swiss and Germans founded New Bern, a community several miles inland on the Neuse, in Tuscarora Indian territory. New Bern was one of the most peaceful and prosperous settlements in North Carolina. Then, at dawn on Sept. 22, 1711, disaster struck. Enraged Tuscarora tribesmen, whose land had been seized by white settlers, attacked New Bern and other settlements. Within two hours, most of the settlements between the Neuse and Pamlico rivers lay in ruins. The Indians had massacred hundreds of settlers, burned their homes, stolen their valuables, and destroyed their crops. The massacre marked the beginning of the Tuscarora War, the worst Indian war in North Carolina's history. The colonists finally defeated the Indians on March 25, 1713.

While settlers battled the wilderness and the Indians during the late 1600's and early 1700's, pirates ter-

President Andrew Johnson
born in Raleigh

President James K. Polk
born near Pineville

Lifeline of the Confederacy. North Carolina, "First at Bethel, farthest at Gettysburg, and last at Appomattox," furnished more than one sixth of the Confederate soldiers in the Civil War.

State of Franklin. In 1784, settlers in the western part of North Carolina (now east Tennessee) set up a state when cession of the territory to the United States left them without state or federal protection.

rorized North Carolina's coastline. Most piracy along the Atlantic Coast ended with the death of the famous pirate Blackbeard in a battle near Ocracoke Island in 1718.

In 1729, the lords proprietors sold their land back to England. North Carolina became a royal colony, ruled by royal governors appointed by the king. These royal governors ruled wisely and well, and helped the colony grow. In 1729, only about 36,000 persons lived in North Carolina, mostly along the coast. By 1775, the population had grown to nearly 350,000, and settlement had spread westward across the Piedmont and into the mountains.

Colonial Wars. North Carolina contributed money and troops to help England fight several colonial wars. The War of Jenkins' Ear (1739-1744) was fought against the Spaniards in what is now Georgia. The war was named for Robert Jenkins, an Englishman whose ear was believed to have been cut off by Spaniards. Other colonial wars included Queen Anne's War (1702-1713), King George's War (1744-1748), and the French and Indian War (1754-1763). In 1760, Hugh Waddell of Wilmington led North Carolina troops to an important victory over the Cherokee Indians. This battle took place at Fort Dobbs, near present-day Statesville. In 1761, the Cherokee signed a peace treaty that opened a vast area of western Virginia and the Carolinas to settlement. See FRENCH AND INDIAN WARS.

Revolution and Independence. England had gone into debt as a result of the colonial wars. In an attempt to solve some of its financial problems, England imposed a series of taxes on the American colonies. But the colonists objected to these taxes. A group of North Carolinians called the *Sons of Liberty* led demonstrations and even armed rebellion against the taxes. Some western North Carolina farmers called the *Regulators* rebelled against taxes and against unjust treatment from eastern officials. William Tryon, the royal governor, needed more than a thousand troops to defeat the Regulators

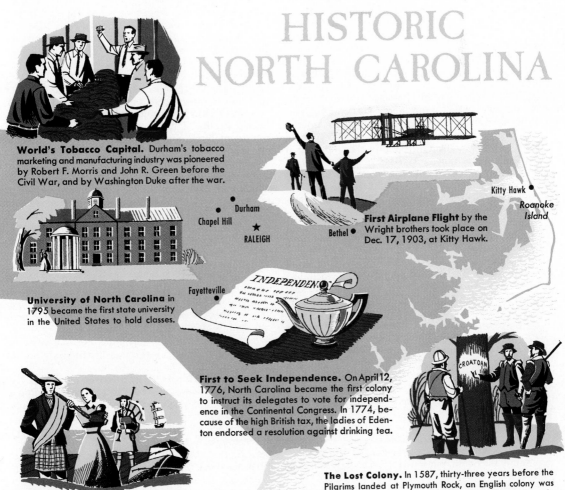

HISTORIC NORTH CAROLINA

World's Tobacco Capital. Durham's tobacco marketing and manufacturing industry was pioneered by Robert F. Morris and John R. Green before the Civil War, and by Washington Duke after the war.

First Airplane Flight by the Wright brothers took place on Dec. 17, 1903, at Kitty Hawk.

University of North Carolina in 1795 became the first state university in the United States to hold classes.

First to Seek Independence. On April 12, 1776, North Carolina became the first colony to instruct its delegates to vote for independence in the Continental Congress. In 1774, because of the high British tax, the ladies of Edenton endorsed a resolution against drinking tea.

Scottish Highlanders settled around Fayetteville after Bonnie Prince Charlie was defeated in Scotland in 1746.

The Lost Colony. In 1587, thirty-three years before the Pilgrims landed at Plymouth Rock, an English colony was founded on Roanoke Island. Three years later, a supply ship found no trace of the colony except for the word "Croatoan" carved on a tree. Virginia Dare, first child born of English parents in America, was among the missing.

Kitty Hawk

Roanoke Island

Durham

Chapel Hill

★ RALEIGH

Bethel

Fayetteville

382e

in the Battle of Alamance, fought on May 16, 1771.

North Carolina sent delegates to Philadelphia to attend the First Continental Congress in 1774. After the Revolutionary War began in April, 1775, North Carolinians quickly took sides. Those who opposed the British were called *Whigs*. Those who remained loyal to the king were called *Tories*. On Feb. 27, 1776, Whig forces, under Colonels Richard Caswell and Alexander Lillington, crushed the Tories in the Battle of Moore's Creek Bridge. This was the first battle of the Revolutionary War in North Carolina. The Whig victory prevented a planned British invasion of North Carolina. On April 12, 1776, North Carolina became the first colony to instruct its delegates to the Continental Congress to vote for independence. Later that year, North Carolina adopted its first constitution and chose Richard Caswell as governor. On July 21, 1778, North Carolina *ratified* (approved) the Articles of Confederation.

Much of the Revolutionary War was fought outside North Carolina's borders. But North Carolinians joined the fight against the British in Virginia, Georgia, and South Carolina. In 1780, British forces led by Lord Charles Cornwallis marched toward North Carolina from the south. Part of Cornwallis's army was slaughtered in the Battle of Kings Mountain, just south of North Carolina. But after a retreat, Cornwallis moved northward again, this time into North Carolina. On March 15, 1781, General Nathanael Greene's forces outlasted Cornwallis' troops in the Battle of Guilford Courthouse. The British abandoned North Carolina.

Statehood. North Carolinians delayed approving the United States Constitution because they opposed a strong federal government. At the Hillsboro Convention of 1788, they rejected the Constitution and suggested many amendments to it. The Bill of Rights to the Constitution, proposed by Congress in 1789, included some of these suggestions. North Carolina finally ratified the Constitution on Nov. 21, 1789.

North Carolina was called the *Rip Van Winkle State* from about 1800 to 1835. The state was so backward that it seemed to be asleep. It had little commerce or industry. It lacked seaports and transportation facilities. Most of its people worked on farms, using poor tools and wasteful methods. Many persons left North Carolina, including three men who later became President—Andrew Jackson, James K. Polk, and Andrew Johnson.

An age of progress began in 1835, when North Carolina revised its constitution, giving most taxpayers the right to vote. By granting equal representation, the constitution gave more power to the people of the western region and encouraged the development of that area. Public schools, railroads, and roads were built. Agriculture increased, and manufacturing started to grow. North Carolina led the nation in gold production until the California Gold Rush of 1849.

The Civil War and Reconstruction. North Carolina was part of the South, but it was also one of the original 13 states of the Union. It tried to preserve the Union even after most southern states had *seceded* (withdrawn). The Civil War began on April 12, 1861. When President Abraham Lincoln asked North Carolina for troops to fight the Confederate States, North Carolina refused.

The state seceded from the Union on May 20, 1861.

Union forces captured much of eastern North Carolina early in the war. But the port at Wilmington remained open to Confederate supply ships until January, 1865. More than 10 battles took place in North Carolina. The bloodiest of these was fought at Bentonville, on March 19-21, 1865. There, Union forces under General William T. Sherman defeated the Confederate troops of General Joseph E. Johnston. Johnston surrendered to Sherman near Durham on April 26. During the war, North Carolina supplied 125,000 men to the Confederate cause. About a fourth of all the Confederate soldiers killed came from North Carolina.

During the Reconstruction period, North Carolinians lived under federal military authority from 1867 until 1877. The Republican party, consisting mostly of Negroes, Union sympathizers, and Northerners called *carpetbaggers* gained control of the state government after the Civil War (see CARPETBAGGER). The Republicans drew up a new state constitution in 1868 which abolished slavery and gave Negroes the right to vote. The state rejoined the Union on June 25, 1868.

During the Reconstruction years, bitter struggles took place between Republicans and Democrats, and between Negroes and whites. The Ku-Klux Klan and other secret groups supported white supremacy and tried to keep Negroes from voting. Democrats gained control of the state legislature in 1870. They impeached Republican Governor William W. Holden in 1871, and removed him from office. Democratic influence spread to other state government departments. In 1875, the Democratic legislature added 30 amendments to the constitution. This action ensured white, Democratic control of North Carolina. See CIVIL WAR; RECONSTRUCTION.

Economic Progress. The Civil War had brought death, despair, and destruction to North Carolina. The abolition of slavery caused the loss of inexpensive farm labor. As a result, large plantations were divided into small farms. The number of farms in the state grew from about 75,000 in 1860 to about 150,000 in 1880.

The people of North Carolina rebuilt their state quickly. By the late 1800's, farm production equaled what it had been before the war. Tobacco and cotton crops led the growth. Industry also grew rapidly. Washington Duke opened a smoking-tobacco business at Durham in 1865. His son, James Buchanan Duke, founded the American Tobacco Company (now American Brands, Inc.), in 1890. Tobacco factories in the state numbered nearly 130 by 1880. Furniture making and cotton processing also became large-scale industries by 1900.

The Early 1900's. In 1901, Governor Charles B. Aycock started a vast, long-reaching program to improve North Carolina's public education system. Since then, the state's schools have continued to improve. In 1915, the legislature created the State Highway Commission. The commission began the largest road-building program in the state's history. This program earned for North Carolina the nickname of the *Good Roads State* during the 1920's.

The state's industries developed at a tremendous rate during the early 1900's. By the late 1920's, North Carolina led the nation in the production of cotton textiles, tobacco products, and wooden furniture.

The depression of the 1930's brought sudden drops in prices and wages. Businesses failed and banks closed. Workers lost their jobs and farmers lost their farms.

The federal and state governments tried to fight the effects of the depression. The North Carolina government reduced local taxes and took control of all highways and public schools. Federal control of agricultural production raised farm prices and income. The state passed welfare measures, raised teachers' salaries, and reduced working hours to help North Carolina out of the depression by the late 1930's.

The Mid-1900's. During World War II (1939-1945), North Carolina mills supplied the armed forces with more textile goods than any other state. North Carolina also mined more than half the mica used in United States war production.

In the late 1940's, North Carolina built new hospitals and mental health facilities. The state also paved more than 13,000 miles of rural roads with funds from a $200-million bond issue. Two dams increased the state's power output. Fontana Dam, at the edge of the Great Smoky Mountains, started operating in 1945, and Kerr Dam, near Henderson, went into operation in 1954.

In 1954, the Supreme Court of the United States ruled that compulsory school segregation was unconstitutional. North Carolina had separate schools for Negroes and whites. By 1970, almost all the state's school districts had been integrated.

During the 1950's, North Carolina continued to shift from a rural, agricultural economy to an urban, industrial economy. The state worked to attract new industries by providing businesses with technical and engineering assistance and by reducing taxes on corporations. In 1958, three universities—Duke University at Durham, North Carolina State University at Raleigh, and the University of North Carolina at Chapel Hill—combined their research resources. They formed the North Carolina Research Triangle, which provides research facilities for industry. The locations of the three universities form a triangle on the state map.

In 1962, the voters approved an amendment to the North Carolina Constitution that brought sweeping changes to the state's court system. All the courts became unified under a general court of justice.

Also in 1962, the state established the North Carolina Fund. The fund, financed by private foundations, grants money to local communities for projects that help needy persons. Congress used the fund as a guide in planning the national fight against poverty that began in 1964. In 1965, North Carolina voters passed a $300-million bond issue to expand and improve major highways.

In 1963, the University of North Carolina adopted a single university plan, with three branches of equal standing. By 1969, it had six branch campuses—at Asheville, Chapel Hill, Charlotte, Greensboro, Raleigh, and Wilmington. Also in 1963, the state set up a system of community colleges and technical institutes. The nation's first state-supported school for the arts, the North Carolina School of the Arts, opened in Winston-Salem in 1965. In 1969, all other state-supported schools of higher education became regional schools. That same year, the legislature voted $1 million to set up a public school kindergarten program.

North Carolina Today faces growing demands for government services. These demands resulted largely

——— THE GOVERNORS OF NORTH CAROLINA ———

		Party	Term
Under Articles of Confederation			
1.	Abner Nash	None	1780-1781
2.	Thomas Burke	None	1781-1782
3.	Alexander Martin	None	1782-1784
4.	Richard Caswell	None	1784-1787
5.	Samuel Johnston	Federalist	1787-1789
Under United States Constitution			
1.	Alexander Martin	Unknown	1789-1792
2.	R. D. Spaight, Sr.	*Dem.-Rep.	1792-1795
3.	Samuel Ashe	*Dem.-Rep.	1795-1798
4.	W. R. Davie	Federalist	1798-1799
5.	Benjamin Williams	*Dem.-Rep.	1799-1802
6.	James Turner	*Dem.-Rep.	1802-1805
7.	Nathaniel Alexander	*Dem.-Rep.	1805-1807
8.	Benjamin Williams	*Dem.-Rep.	1807-1808
9.	David Stone	*Dem.-Rep.	1808-1810
10.	Benjamin Smith	*Dem.-Rep.	1810-1811
11.	William Hawkins	*Dem.-Rep.	1811-1814
12.	William Miller	*Dem.-Rep.	1814-1817
13.	John Branch	*Dem.-Rep.	1817-1820
14.	Jesse Franklin	*Dem.-Rep.	1820-1821
15.	Gabriel Holmes	Unknown	1821-1824
16.	H. G. Burton	Federalist	1824-1827
17.	James Iredell, Jr.	*Dem.-Rep.	1827-1828
18.	John Owen	Unknown	1828-1830
19.	Montfort Stokes	Democratic	1830-1832
20.	D. L. Swain	Whig	1832-1835
21.	R. D. Spaight, Jr.	Democratic	1835-1836
22.	E. B. Dudley	Whig	1836-1841
23.	J. M. Morehead	Whig	1841-1845
24.	W. A. Graham	Whig	1845-1849
25.	Charles Manly	Whig	1849-1851
26.	D. S. Reid	Democratic	1851-1854
27.	Warren Winslow	Democratic	1854-1855
28.	Thomas Bragg	Democratic	1855-1859
29.	John W. Ellis	Democratic	1859-1861
30.	Henry T. Clark	Democratic	1861-1862
31.	Z. B. Vance	Democratic	1862-1865
32.	†W. W. Holden	Republican	1865
33.	Jonathan Worth	Democratic	1865-1868
34.	W. W. Holden	Republican	1868-1871
35.	T. R. Caldwell	Republican	1871-1874
36.	C. H. Brogden	Republican	1874-1877
37.	Z. B. Vance	Democratic	1877-1879
38.	T. J. Jarvis	Democratic	1879-1885
39.	A. M. Scales	Democratic	1885-1889
40.	D. G. Fowle	Democratic	1889-1891
41.	Thomas M. Holt	Democratic	1891-1893
42.	Elias Carr	Democratic	1893-1897
43.	D. L. Russell	Republican	1897-1901
44.	C. B. Aycock	Democratic	1901-1905
45.	R. B. Glenn	Democratic	1905-1909
46.	W. W. Kitchin	Democratic	1909-1913
47.	Locke Craig	Democratic	1913-1917
48.	Thomas W. Bickett	Democratic	1917-1921
49.	Cameron Morrison	Democratic	1921-1925
50.	Angus Wilton McLean	Democratic	1925-1929
51.	O. Max Gardner	Democratic	1929-1933
52.	J. C. B. Ehringhaus	Democratic	1933-1937
53.	Clyde R. Hoey	Democratic	1937-1941
54.	J. Melville Broughton	Democratic	1941-1945
55.	R. Gregg Cherry	Democratic	1945-1949
56.	W. Kerr Scott	Democratic	1949-1953
57.	William B. Umstead	Democratic	1953-1954
58.	Luther H. Hodges	Democratic	1954-1961
59.	Terry Sanford	Democratic	1961-1965
60.	Daniel K. Moore	Democratic	1965-1969
61.	Robert W. Scott	Democratic	1969-

*Democratic-Republican   †Provisional Governor

from population movements. More than half the state's people now live in cities and towns rather than in rural areas.

North Carolina also faces increased spending for community colleges, health programs and hospitals, highways, and prison improvement. In 1969, the state legislature increased some taxes and passed North Carolina's first cigarette tax. The state is the nation's leading tobacco producer.

Other problems of North Carolina in the 1970's include conservation and pollution. In 1969, the legislature passed laws to protect coastal waters where fish and some game animals breed. The legislature also increased the powers of the state board of water and air resources. Cities and counties received permission to adopt air pollution laws.

The Republican Party is expected to continue to increase its strength in the state during the 1970's. In 1968, the Republican candidate for governor, though defeated, received more than 47 per cent of the vote.

ROBERT ELI CRAMER, BLACKWELL PIERCE ROBINSON, and SAM RAGAN

NORTH CAROLINA/*Study Aids*

Related Articles in WORLD BOOK include:

BIOGRAPHIES

Aycock, Charles B.	Hooper, William
Blackbeard	Iredell, James
Blount, William	Johnson, Andrew
Bragg, Braxton	King, William R. D.
Daniels (family)	Penn, John
Dare, Virginia	Polk, James Knox
Duke, James B.	Spaight, Richard D.
Gaston, William	Vance, Zebulon B.
Hewes, Joseph	Williamson, Hugh
Hodges, Luther H.	

CITIES

Asheville	Greensboro	Wilmington
Charlotte	High Point	Wilson
Durham	New Bern	Winston-Salem
Fayetteville	Raleigh	

HISTORY

Civil War	Mecklenburg Declaration
Colonial Life in	of Independence
America	Reconstruction
Franklin, State of	Revolutionary War in
Lost Colony	America

PHYSICAL FEATURES

Black Mountains	Kill Devil Hill
Blue Ridge Mountains	Mount Mitchell
Cape Fear	Ocracoke Island
Cape Hatteras	Pee Dee River
Dismal Swamp	Piedmont Region
Fall Line	Roanoke River
Great Smoky Mountains	

PRODUCTS

For North Carolina's rank among the states, see:

Building	Clothing	Peanut	Textile
Stone	Lumber	Sweet	Tobacco
Chicken	Nut	Potato	Turkey

OTHER RELATED ARTICLES

Camp Lejeune	Fort Bragg	Tennessee Valley
Cherry Point Marine	Southern States	Authority
Corps Air Station		

Outline

I. **Government**
 A. Constitution   D. Courts   F. Taxation
 B. Executive   E. Local   G. Politics
 C. Legislature   Government
II. **People**
III. **Education**
 A. Schools   B. Libraries   C. Museums
IV. **A Visitor's Guide**
 A. Places to Visit   B. Annual Events
V. **The Land**
 A. Land Regions   B. Rivers, Waterfalls, and Lakes

VI. **Climate**
VII. **Economy**
 A. Natural Resources   E. Fishing Industry
 B. Manufacturing   F. Electric Power
 C. Agriculture   G. Transportation
 D. Mining   H. Communication
VIII. **History**

Questions

What was the *Lost Colony?*

Why is North Carolina one of the largest payers of federal taxes in the nation?

What North Carolina town attracts furniture buyers?

For what textile products does North Carolina have the world's largest factories?

How did North Carolina attract industries in the 1950's?

What is the *Graveyard of the Atlantic?*

Why did North Carolina delay in approving the United States Constitution?

Who were the *Sons of Liberty?*

What is unique about the relationship between the governor of North Carolina and the state legislature?

Books for Young Readers

CARROLL, RUTH and LATROBE. *Tough Enough's Trip.* Walck, 1956.

CHASE, RICHARD, ed. *Grandfather Tales.* Houghton, 1948.

CREDLE, ELLIS. *Down, Down the Mountain.* Nelson, 1934.

GRAY, ELIZABETH J. *Jane Hope.* Viking, 1933. *Meggy MacIntosh.* 1930. The Scots on the eve of the Revolution.

LENSKI, LOIS. *Blue Ridge Billy.* Lippincott, 1946.

MEADER, STEPHEN W. *Wild Pony Island.* Harcourt, 1959.

STREET, JULIA M. *Fiddler's Fancy.* Follett, 1955. *Drover's Gold.* Dodd, 1961.

WORTH, KATHRYN. *The Middle Button.* Doubleday, 1941. *They Loved to Laugh.* 1959.

Books for Older Readers

DYKEMAN, WILMA. *The French Broad.* Univ. of Tennessee Press, 1965.

FRIES, ADELAIDE L. *The Road to Salem.* Univ. of North Carolina Press, 1944.

HARDEN, JOHN W. *The Devil's Tramping Ground.* Univ. of North Carolina Press, 1949. *Tar Heel Ghosts.* 1954.

HOBBS, SAMUEL H., JR. *North Carolina: An Economic and Social Profile.* Univ. of North Carolina Press, 1958.

HOYLE, BERNADETTE. *Tar Heel Writers I Know.* Blair, 1956.

LEFLER, HUGH T., ed. *North Carolina History Told by Contemporaries.* 3d ed. Univ. of North Carolina Press, 1956. With NEWSOME, ALBERT R. *North Carolina: The History of a Southern State.* Rev. ed. 1963.

POWELL, WILLIAM S. *North Carolina: A Students' Guide to Localized History.* Teachers College Press, 1965.

RAGAN, SAM. *The New Day.* Davis Press, 1964.

ROBINSON, BLACKWELL P., ed. *The North Carolina Guide.* Univ. of North Carolina Press, 1955.

STICK, DAVID. *The Outer Banks of North Carolina, 1584-1958.* Univ. of North Carolina Press, 1958.

North Carolina State University at Raleigh is part of the University of North Carolina. Harrelson Hall, *above*, a circular classroom building, can seat more than 3,500 students.

University of North Carolina campus at Chapel Hill includes the Louis Round Wilson Library, *right*. The library contains more than 1,200,000 volumes.

University of North Carolina

NORTH CAROLINA, UNIVERSITY OF, consists of

four state coeducational institutions. They are at Chapel Hill, Charlotte, Greensboro, and Raleigh. Each institution has its own chancellor, who is responsible to the university president. The administrative office of the university is at Chapel Hill.

The University of North Carolina at Chapel Hill grants degrees in arts and science, business administration, dentistry, education, journalism, law, library science, medicine, nursing, public health, pharmacy, and social work. It has a full graduate and research program. The Wilson Library contains over 1,200,000 volumes. The university at Chapel Hill also has an art museum, botanical gardens, and a large planetarium. It was chartered in 1789 and opened in 1795.

North Carolina State University at Raleigh grants degrees in agriculture; architecture, landscape architecture, and product design; education; engineering; forestry; liberal arts; physical sciences and applied mathematics; and textiles. It has a full graduate and research program. The university operates agricultural extension and research services, continuing education programs, a forestry laboratory, and a nuclear reactor. North Carolina State University at Raleigh was founded as a land-grant college in 1887 and became part of the University of North Carolina in 1931 (see LAND-GRANT COLLEGE OR UNIVERSITY).

The University of North Carolina at Greensboro grants degrees in arts and science, education, home economics, and music. It has graduate courses. The University of North Carolina at Greensboro was founded in 1891 as a college for women. It became part of the University of North Carolina in 1931, and became a coeducational university in 1964.

The University of North Carolina at Charlotte grants bachelor's degrees in liberal arts and science. It was founded in 1949 as a two-year community college. It became a four-year college in 1963, and became part of the University of North Carolina in 1965.

For enrollment of the four institutions, see UNIVERSITIES AND COLLEGES (table).   WILLIAM C. FRIDAY

NORTH CAROLINA AGRICULTURAL AND TECHNICAL STATE UNIVERSITY. See UNIVERSITIES AND COLLEGES (table).

NORTH CAROLINA CENTRAL UNIVERSITY. See UNIVERSITIES AND COLLEGES (table).

NORTH CAROLINA WESLEYAN COLLEGE. See UNIVERSITIES AND COLLEGES (table).

NORTH CASCADES NATIONAL PARK is in northwestern Washington. The park's magnificent scenery includes mountain ridges, forested valleys, alpine lakes and meadows, waterfalls, and glaciers. Among the animals that live in the park are bears, cougars, deer, moose, mountain goats, and wolverines. The park also has valuable cedar and fir forests and mineral deposits. The 505,000-acre park was established in 1968, along with the adjacent 62,000-acre Lake Chelan National Recreation Area and 107,000-acre Ross Lake National Recreation Area. For location, see WASHINGTON (political map).   GEORGE B. HARTZOG, JR.

NORTH CENTRAL COLLEGE. See UNIVERSITIES AND COLLEGES (table).

NORTH CENTRAL STATES are the 12 states in the north-central part of the United States. They include Illinois, Indiana, Iowa, Kansas, Michigan, Minnesota, Missouri, Nebraska, North Dakota, Ohio, South Dakota, and Wisconsin. The western North Central States, sometimes called the Great Plains States, contain some of the richest farming land in the world. Corn and wheat fields cover the plains. The states on the eastern edge of the region are sometimes called the Lake States. They have great industrial centers, as well as farms. See also MIDWESTERN STATES.

385

NORTH DAKOTA

The Flickertail State

NORTH DAKOTA is a Midwestern state in the center of the North American continent. The geographic center of North America is near the town of Rugby. North Dakota is the nation's most agricultural state. Its economy is based more heavily on farming than that of any other state. North Dakota has a larger percentage of workers in agriculture than any other state. About 65 of every 100 North Dakotans live on farms or in farming areas.

Farms and ranches cover nearly all North Dakota. They stretch from the flat Red River Valley in the east, across rolling plains, to the rugged Badlands in the west. North Dakota's chief crop is wheat, which is grown in every county. Only Kansas raises more wheat. North Dakota harvests more than half the country's flaxseed. It is also the top producer of barley and a leader in rye production.

Soil is North Dakota's most precious resource. It is the base of the state's great agricultural wealth. But North Dakota also has enormous mineral resources. The nation's largest coal reserves—about 350 billion tons of lignite coal—are in North Dakota. The state's oil reserves are among the nation's largest. Petroleum was not discovered in North Dakota until 1951. But it quickly became the state's most valuable mineral.

Few settlers came to the North Dakota region before the 1870's. Transportation was poor, and newcomers feared attacks by Indians. During the 1870's, the Northern Pacific Railroad began to push across the Dakota Territory. Large-scale farming also began during the 1870's. Eastern corporations and some families established huge wheat farms covering thousands of acres in the Red River Valley. The farms made such enormous profits that they were called *bonanza* farms. Settlers flocked to North Dakota, attracted by the success of the bonanza farms. In 1870, North Dakota had 2,405 persons. By 1890, only 20 years later, its population had grown to 190,983. Farming became firmly established as North Dakota's major industry.

North Dakota was named for the Sioux Indians who once roamed the territory. The Sioux called themselves *Dakota* or *Lakota*, meaning *allies* or *friends*. One of North Dakota's nicknames is the *Sioux State*. But it is more often called the *Flickertail State*, because of the many flickertail ground squirrels that live in central North Dakota.

Bismarck is the capital of North Dakota, and Fargo is the largest city. For the relationship of North Dakota to other states in its region, see the article on MIDWESTERN STATES.

Cattle Ranch near Amidon

Harley Hettick, Alpha

Oil Well near Tioga

Harley Hettick, Alpha

Wendler, FPG
Rolling Hills in the Sheyenne River Valley

--- FACTS IN BRIEF ---

Capital: Bismarck.

Government: *Congress*—U.S. senators, 2; U.S. representatives, 1. *Electoral Votes*—3. *State Legislature*—
senators, 49; representatives, 98. *Counties*—53. *Voting
Age*—21 years (state and local elections); 18 years
(national elections).

Area: 70,665 square miles (including 1,385 square miles
of inland water), 17th in size among the states.
Greatest Distances—(east-west) 360 miles; (north-south)
210 miles.

Elevation: *Highest*—White Butte, 3,506 feet above sea level
in Slope County. *Lowest*—750 feet above sea level
along the Red River in Pembina County.

Population: *1970 Census*—617,761; 45th among the states;
density, 9 persons to the square mile; distribution,
56 per cent rural, 44 per cent urban. *1960 Census*—
632,446.

Chief Products: *Agriculture*—barley, beef cattle, dairy
products, flaxseed, hogs, oats, potatoes, wheat. *Manufacturing*—metal products; nonelectrical machinery;
printed materials; processed foods; stone, clay, and
glass products. *Mining*—coal, natural gas, natural gas
liquids, petroleum, sand and gravel, stone.

Statehood: Nov. 2, 1889, the 39th state.

State Motto: *Liberty and Union, Now and Forever, One
and Inseparable.*

State Song: "North Dakota Hymn." Words by James W.
Foley; music by C. S. Putnam.

North Dakota (blue) ranks 17th in size among all the states,
and 5th in size among the Midwestern States (gray).

*The contributors of this article are Jack U. Hagerty, Man-
aging Editor of the* Grand Forks Herald; *Russell S. Reid,
Former Historian of the State Historical Society of North
Dakota; and Bernt Lloyd Wills, Professor of the Department
of Geography at the University of North Dakota.*

387

Constitution. North Dakota is governed under its original constitution, adopted in 1889. An *amendment* (change) to the constitution may be proposed in the state legislature. The proposed amendment must be approved by a majority of each house of the legislature. Then a majority of citizens voting on the proposal must approve it. The people may also sign a *petition* (formal request) proposing an amendment. After 20,000 voters have signed the petition, the proposal is put on a state-wide ballot. The proposal becomes law if a majority of voters approve it.

North Dakota's constitution is one of four in the country that do not provide for a constitutional convention. The other states that do not have this provision are Indiana, New Jersey, and Vermont.

Executive. The governor of North Dakota is elected to a four-year term. He may serve an unlimited number of terms. The governor receives a yearly salary of $18,-000. For a list of all the governors of North Dakota, see the *History* section of this article.

The lieutenant governor, attorney general, secretary of state, treasurer, auditor, and superintendent of public instruction are also elected to four-year terms. All except the treasurer may serve an unlimited number of terms. The treasurer may serve only two terms in a row. The people also elect three public-service com-

missioners, and one commissioner each of agriculture, of labor, of insurance, and of taxation.

The governor, attorney general, and commissioner of agriculture make up the state industrial commission. This commission regulates the North Dakota oil industry. It also oversees the operation of the Bank of North Dakota in Bismarck and of the North Dakota Mill and Elevator in Grand Forks. Both these firms are state-owned and compete with private companies.

Legislature of North Dakota is called the *legislative assembly*. It consists of a 49-member senate and a 98-member house of representatives. Voters in each of the state's 39 legislative districts elect from one to four senators to four-year terms. They elect from two to eight representatives, depending on population, to two-year terms. The legislature begins its regular session on the first Tuesday after the first Monday in January in odd-numbered years. Regular sessions are limited to 60 legislative days. The governor may also call special sessions, which have no time limit.

Courts of North Dakota are headed by the state supreme court. The supreme court has five judges, all elected to 10-year terms. The judge with the shortest remaining term serves as the chief justice. The people of the state's six judicial districts elect a total of 16 district court judges to six-year terms. Each county has a county court with one judge elected to a four-year term. All North Dakota judges are elected on a "no party" ballot—the ballot has no political party labels.

Local Government. North Dakota has 53 counties. Each is governed by a board of commissioners of three to five members elected to four-year terms. Other elected county officials include the auditor, sheriff, superintendent of schools, and treasurer. North Dakota has 357 cities. The 1967 legislature classed all cities and towns as cities. The cities have limited *home rule* (self-government). They are organized under either mayor-council or commission forms of government, with or without city managers.

Taxation. Taxes and license fees bring in nearly three-fourths of the state government's income. Almost all the rest comes from federal grants and other U.S. government programs. Retail sales taxes and motor vehicle license fees account for more than half the state's revenue collections. North Dakota also collects taxes on alcoholic beverages, cigarettes, corporation and personal incomes, property, and other items.

Memorial to Pioneer Families in North Dakota adds beauty to the Capitol grounds. The bronze statue was completed in 1947.

Eva Luoma Photos

North Dakota Travel Dept.

Governor's Mansion stands southwest of the state Capitol in Bismarck. The building was completed in 1960.

The State Seal

Symbols of North Dakota. On the seal, the elm tree and the setting sun represent the state's landscape. The plow, sheaves of wheat, and anvil symbolize agriculture. The bow and arrows and the Indian hunting a buffalo represent North Dakota's history. The seal was adopted in 1889. The regimental flag of the First North Dakota Infantry was adopted as the state flag in 1911. The design is a modified version of the coat of arms of the United States.

Bird and flower illustrations, courtesy of Eli Lilly and Company

Politics. Throughout most of its history, North Dakota has strongly favored the Republican party. In 1889, the people elected a Republican as the first governor of their state. Since then, the state has had only five Democratic governors. North Dakotans have voted for Republican candidates in about three of every four presidential elections. For North Dakota's electoral votes and voting record in presidential elections, see ELECTORAL COLLEGE (table).

There are signs that North Dakota is becoming a two-party state. In 1915, the Nonpartisan League, a political organization of farmers, was founded in North Dakota. During its early years, the league often controlled the Republican party. In 1956, the league joined with the state Democratic party. In 1958, this new, strong political force elected the state's first Democrat to the U.S. House of Representatives. He was Quentin N. Burdick. Two years later, Burdick was elected to the U.S. Senate and William L. Guy, a Democrat, was elected governor. In 1964, Guy was re-elected to a third term and Burdick to a second term. Also in 1964, Democrats won control of the state house of representatives for the first time in the state's history. But in 1966, the Republicans swept the election and regained control of the legislature. In 1968, Guy again won re-election as governor.

State Capitol in Bismarck is 18 stories tall. Bismarck has been the capital since 1889, when North Dakota became a state.

North Dakota Travel Dept.

The State Flag

The State Bird
Western Meadow Lark

The State Flower
Wild Prairie Rose

The State Tree
American Elm

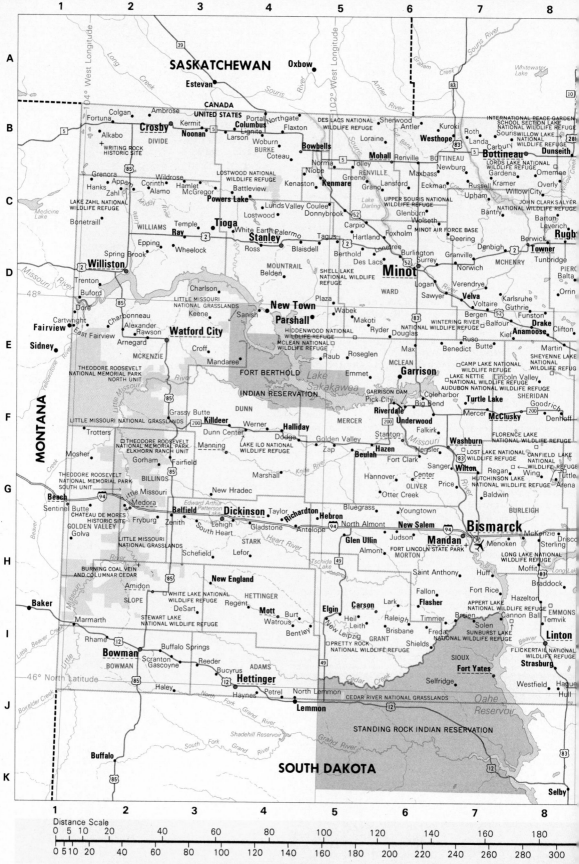

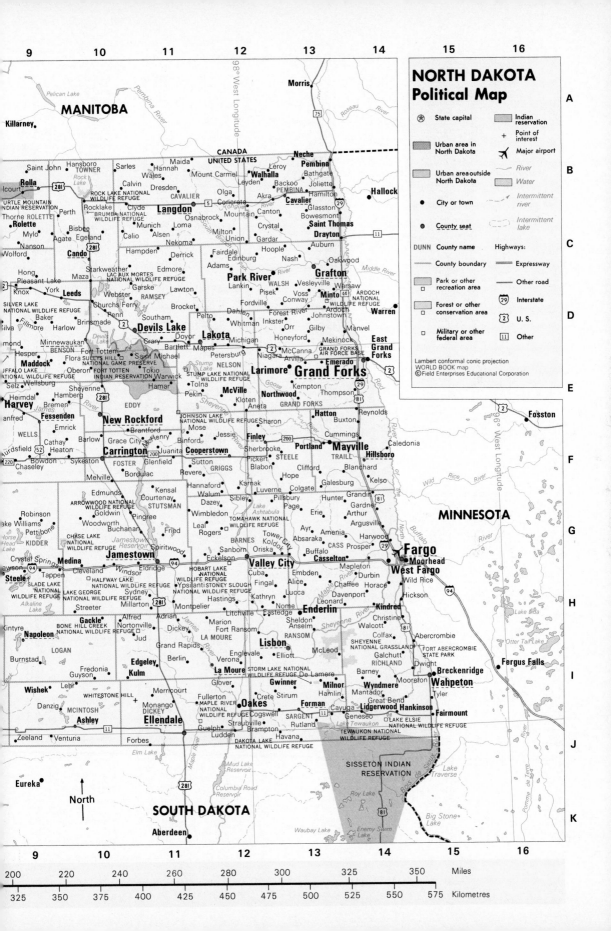

Population

617,761 ...Census...1970
632,446 ......"....1960
619,636 ......"....1950
641,935 ......"....1940
680,845 ......"....1930
646,872 ......"....1920
577,056 ......"....1910
319,146 ......"....1900
190,983 ......"....1890
36,909 ......"....1880
2,405 ......"....1870

Metropolitan Area

Fargo-Moorhead (Minn.) ......120,238 (73,653 in N. Dak.; 46,585 in Minn.)

Counties

Adams ......3,832..J 4
Barnes .....14,669..G 12
Benson .....8,245..D 9
Billings .....1,198..G 2
Bottineau ...9,496..B 6
Bowman ....3,901..J 2
Burke ......4,739..B 4
Burleigh ...40,714..G 8
Cass ....73,653..G 13
Cavalier ....8,213..B 11
Dickey ......6,976..J 11
Divide ......4,564..B 2
Dunn ....4,895..F 4
Eddy ....4,103..E 10
Emmons ....7,200..I 8
Foster ......4,832..F 10
Golden Valley ....2,611..H 1
Grand Forks ....61,102..E 13
Grant ....5,009..I 6
Griggs ......4,184..F 12
Hettinger ...5,075..I 4
Kidder ......4,362..G 9
La Moure ...7,117..I 12
Logan ....4,245..I 9
McHenry ....8,977..D 7
McIntosh ....5,545..I 10
McKenzie ...6,127..E 2
McLean ....11,251..E 6
Mercer ......6,175..F 5
Morton ....20,310..H 6
Mountrail ...8,437..D 4
Nelson ......5,776..D 12
Oliver ......2,322..G 6
Pembina ...10,728..B 13
Pierce ......6,323..D 8
Ramsey ....12,915..D 11
Ransom .....7,102..H 13
Renville ....3,828..C 5
Richland ..18,089..I 14
Rolette ....11,549..C 9
Sargent .....5,937..J 13
Sheridan ....3,232..F 8
Sioux ....3,632..I 7
Slope ....1,484..I 2
Stark ......19,613..H 4
Steele ......3,749..F 13
Stutsman ..23,550..G 11
Towner .....4,645..B 10
Traill ......9,571..F 13
Walsh ......16,251..D 13
Ward ......58,560..D 6
Wells ....7,847..F 9
Williams ...19,301..C 2

Cities

Abercrombie ..262..I 15
Adams ....284..C 12
Adrian ....H 11
Alamo ....124..C 2
Alexander ....208..E 2
Alfred ....H 10
Alice ....83..H 13
Alkabo ....B 2
Almont ....109..H 6
Alsen ....201..C 11
Ambrose ......109..B 2
Amenia ....80..G 14
Amidon ....54.°H 2
Anamoose ....401..E 8
Aneta ....376..E 12
Antler ....135..B 6
Ardoch ....70..D 13
Argusville ....118..G 14
Arnegard .....141..E 2
Arthur ....412..G 14
Arvilla ....E 13
Ashley ......1,236.°J 10
Ayr ....48..G 13
Baker ....D 9
Baldwin ....G 7
Balfour ....93..E 8
Balta ....133..D 8
Bantry ....40..C 7
Barlow ....F 10
Barney ....81..I 14
Bartlett ....19..D 11
Barton ....34..C 8
Bathgate ......133..B 13
Battleview ....C 4
Beach ......1,408.°G 1
Belcourt ....B 9
Belfield .....1,130..G 3
Benedict ....72..E 7
Bentley ....I 5
Bergen ....24..D 7
Berlin ....76..I 11
Berthold ......398..D 5
Berwick ....33..D 8
Beulah .....1,344..F 5
Big Bend ....F 6
Binford ....242..F 11
Bisbee ....305..C 10
Bismarck ..34,703.°H 7
Blaisdell ....D 5
Blanchard ....F 14
Bordulac ....F 10
Bottineau ...2,760.°B 8
Bowbells .....584.°B 4
Bowdon ....229..F 9
Bowesmont ....C 14
Bowman ....1,762.°I 2
Braddock ......106..H 8
Brampton ....J 13
Brantford ....F 10
Bremen ....E 10
Brinsmade .....36..D 10
Brocket ....95..D 11
Buchanan ....G 11
Bucyrus ....42..J 3
Buffalo ....241..G 13
Burlington ....247..D 6
Burnstad ....I 9
Burt ....I 4
Butte ....193..E 7
Buxton ....235..E 14
Caledonia ....F 14
Calio ....75..C 10
Calvin ....78..B 10
Cando ....1,512.°C 10
Cannon Ball ....I 7
Canton ....81..C 13
Carpio ....215..C 5
Carrington ..2,491.°F 10
Carson ....466.°I 6
Cartwright ....E 1
Casselton ....1,485..G 14
Cathay ....110..F 10
Cavalier .....1,381.°B 13
Cayuga ....116..J 13
Center ....619.°G 6
Chaffee ....H 13
Chaseley ....F 9
Christine ....H 14
Churchs Ferry 139..D 10
Cleveland .....128..G 10
Clifford ....84..F 13
Clyde ....B 10
Cogswell ....203..J 13
Coleharbor .....78..F 6
Colfax ....70..I 14
Colgate ....F 13
Columbus .....465..B 4
Conway ....57..D 13
Cooperstown .1,485.°F 12
Coteau ....B 4
Coulee ....C 5
Courtenay .....125..G 11
Crary ....150..D 11
Crosby ......1,545.°B 3
Crystal ....272..C 13
Cummings ....F 14
Dahlen ....D 12
Davenport ....147..H 14
Dawson ....131..H 9
Dazey ....128..G 12
Deering ....75..C 7
De Lamere ....I 13
Denhoff ....F 8
Des Lacs ......197..D 6
Devils Lake .7,078.°D 11
Dickey ....118..H 11
Dickinson ..12,405.°G 3
Dodge ....121..F 4
Donnybrook ...163..C 5
Douglas ....144..E 6
Doyon ....D 11
Drake ....636..E 8
Drayton .....1,095..C 14
Driscoll ....H 8
Dunn Center ..107..F 4
Dunseith ......811..B 8
Dwight ....93..I 15
East Fairview ....E 1
Eckleson ....G 12
Eckman ....9..C 7
Edgeley ....888..I 11
Edinburg ....315..C 12
Edmore ....398..C 11
Egeland ....96..C 10
Eldridge ....G 11
Elgin ....839..I 5
Ellendale ....1,517.°J 11
Elliott ....50..I 13
Emerado ....515..E 13
Enderlin .....1,343..H 13
Englevale ....I 12
Epping ....140..D 2
Erie ....G 13
Esmond ....416..D 9
Fairdale ....102..C 12
Fairmount .....412..J 15
Fargo .....53,365.°G 14
Fessenden .....815.°E 9
Fillmore ....D 9
Fingal ....166..H 13
Finley ....809.°F 12
Flasher ....467..I 6
Flaxton ....286..B 4
Forbes ....88..J 11
Fordville ....361..D 12
Forest River ..169..D 13
Forman ....596.°J 13
Fort Ransom ....H 12
Fort Totten ....E 10
Fort Yates ..1,153.°J 7
Fortuna ....216..B 2
Foxholm ....C 6
Fredonia ....100..I 10
Fullerton ....110..I 11
Gackle ....470..H 10
Galchutt ....I 14
Galesburg ....134..F 13
Gardar ....C 12
Gardena ....84..C 8
Gardner ....96..G 14
Garrison ....1,614..E 6
Gascoyne ....34..I 3
Geneseo ....J 14
Gilby ....268..D 13
Gladstone ....222..G 4
Glasston ....C 13
Glen Ullin ..1,070..H 5
Glenburn ....381..C 6
Glenfield ....127..F 11
Golden Valley ......235..F 5
Golva ....104..H 1
Goodrich ....300..F 8
Grace City ....F 11
Grafton .....5,946.°C 13
Grand Forks ....39,008.°E 14
Grand Forks Base* ....10,474..E 13
Grandin ....187..F 14
Grano ....4..C 6
Granville ....282..D 7
Grassy Butte ....F 3
Great Bend ....86..I 14
Grenora ....401..C 1
Guelph ....J 12
Gwinner ....623..I 13
Hague ....146..J 8
Halliday ....413..F 4
Hamar ....E 11
Hamberg ....51..E 9
Hamilton ....110..B 13
Hampden ....114..C 11
Hankinson ..1,125..J 14
Hanks ....13..C 2
Hannaford ......244..F 12
Hannah ....145..B 11
Hansboro ....49..B 10
Harlow ....D 9
Harvey ....2,361..E 9
Harwood ....G 14
Hastings ....H 12
Hatton ....808..E 13
Havana ....156..J 13
Haynes ....53..J 4
Hazelton ....374..I 8
Hazen ....1,240..F 6
Heaton ....F 9
Hebron ....1,103..G 5
Heil ....I 5
Heimdal ....E 9
Hettinger ...1,655.°J 4
Hickson ....H 14
Hillsboro ...1,309.°F 14
Hoople ....330..C 13
Hope ....364..F 13
Horace ....276..H 14
Huff ....H 7
Hunter ....362..G 14
Hurdsfield ......139..F 9
Inkster ....198..D 13
Jamestown .15,385.°G 11
Jessie ....F 12
Johnstown ....D 13
Jud ....110..H 11
Judson ....H 6
Karlsruhe ....172..D 7
Kathryn ....109..H 12
Keene ....E 3
Kempton ....E 13
Kenmare ....1,515..C 5
Kensal ....263..F 11
Kief ....46..E 8
Killdeer ....615..F 3
Kindred ....495..H 14
Kloten ....E 12
Knox ....104..D 9
Kramer ....125..C 7
Kulm ....625..I 10
Lakota ....964.°D 11
La Moure ......951.°I 12
Landa ....61..B 7
Langdon ....2,182.°B 11
Lankin ....221..D 12
Lansford ....296..C 6
Larimore ....1,469..E 13
Larson ....35..B 3
Lawton ....123..D 11
Leal ....41..G 12
Leeds ....626..D 9
Lefor ....H 4
Lehr ....287..I 10
Leith ....92..I 5
Leonard ....221..H 14
Leroy ....B 12
Lidgerwood ..1,000..J 14
Lignite ....354..B 4
Linton ....1,695.°I 8
Lisbon ......2,090.°I 13
Litchville ....294..H 12
Loma ....6..C 11
Loraine ....33..B 6
Ludden ....44..J 12
Luverne ....84..F 12
Maddock ....708..E 9
Makoti ....159..E 5
Mandan ...11,093.°H 7
Mandaree ....E 4
Manfred ....E 9
Manning ....°G 3
Mantador ....95..I 14
Manvel ....265..D 14
Mapes ....D 12
Mapleton ....219..G 14
Marion ....215..H 12
Marmarth ....247..I 1
Martin ....120..E 8
Max ....301..E 6
Maxbass ....174..C 6
Mayville ....2,554..F 13
Maza ....20..C 10
McCanna ....D 13
McClusky ....664.°F 8
McGregor ....C 3
McHenry ....152..F 11
McKenzie ....H 8
McLeod ....I 13
McVille ....583..E 12
Medina ....488..G 10
Medora ....129.°G 2
Mekinock ....D 13
Menoken ....H 7
Mercer ....132..F 7
Merricourt ....22..I 11
Michigan ....447..D 12
Milnor ....645..I 13
Milton ....198..C 12
Minnewaukan .496.°D 10
Minot ......32,290.°D 6
Minot Base* ...12,077..C 6
Minto ....636..D 13
Moffit ....H 8
Mohall ....950.°B 6
Monango ....112..I 11
Montpelier ....116..H 11
Mooreton ....158..I 14
Mott ....1,368.°I 4
Mountain ....146..C 12
Munich ....249..C 11
Mylo ....51..C 9
Napoleon ...1,036.°I 9
Nash ....G 13
Neche ....451..B 13
Nekoma ....84..C 11
New England ...906..H 3
New Hradec ....G 3
New Leipzig ..354..I 5
New Rockford 1,969.°E 10
New Salem ......943..H 6
New Town ..1,428..E 4
Newburg ....125..C 7
Niagara ....115..D 12
Niobe ....C 5
Nome ....103..H 12
Noonan ....403..B 3
Norma ....C 5
North Lemmon ....J 4
Northgate ....B 4
Northwood ..1,189..E 13
Nortonville ....H 11
Norwich ....D 7
Oakes ....1,742..I 12
Oakwood ....C 13
Oberon ....151..E 10
Olga ....B 12
Omemee ....5..C 8
Oriska ....128..G 13
Orr ....D 13
Orrin ....D 8
Osnabrock ......255..C 12
Overly ....28..C 8
Page ....367..G 13
Palermo ....146..D 4
Park River ..1,680..C 13
Parshall ....1,246..E 5
Pekin ....120..E 12
Pembina ....741..B 13
Penn ....D 10
Perth ....44..B 9
Petersburg ......266..D 12
Pettibone ....173..G 9
Pick City ....119..F 6
Pillsbury ....50..G 12
Pingree ....76..G 10
Pisek ....154..D 13
Plaza ....291..D 5
Portal ....251..B 4
Portland ....534..F 13
Powers Lake .523..C 4
Raleigh ....I 6
Rawson ....10..E 2
Ray ....776..C 3
Reeder ....306..I 3
Regan ....74..G 8
Regent ....344..I 4
Reynolds ....236..E 14
Rhame ....206..I 2
Richardton ...799..G 4
Riverdale ....F 6
Robinson ....125..G 9
Rocklake ....270..B 10
Rogers ....96..G 12
Rolette ....579..C 9
Rolla ....1,458.°B 9
Ross ....125..D 4
Rugby ....2,889.°D 8
Ruso ....15..E 7
Russell ....14..C 7
Rutland ....225..J 13
Ryder ....211..E 5
St. Anthony ....H 7
St. John ....367..B 9
St. Thomas ...508..C 13
Sanborn ....255..G 12
Sanish ....25..E 4
Sarles ....148..B 10
Sawyer ....373..D 7
Scranton ....360..I 3
Selfridge ....346..J 7
Selz ....E 9
Sentinel Butte 125..G 1
Sharon ....201..F 12
Sheldon ....192..H 13
Sherwood ....369..B 6
Sheyenne ....362..E 10
Shields ....I 6
Sibley ....20..G 12
Solen ....180..I 7
Souris ....151..B 7
South Heart ..132..G 3
Spiritwood ....G 11
Spring Brook ..27..D 2
Stanley ....1,581.°D 4
Stanton ....517.°F 6
Starkweather .193..C 10
Steele ....696.°H 9
Sterling ....H 8
Stirum ....I 13
Strasburg ....642..J 8
Streeter ....324..H 10
Surrey ....361..D 6
Sutton ....F 11
Sykeston ....232..F 10
Tagus ....14..D 5
Tappen ....294..H 9
Taylor ....162..G 4
Temvik ....I 8
Thompson ....291..E 14
Tioga ....1,667..C 3
Tokio ....E 11
Tolley ....163..C 5
Tolna ....247..E 11
Tower City .....289..G 13
Towner ....870.°D 8
Trenton ....D 2
Turtle Lake ..712..F 7
Tuttle ....216..G 8
Underwood ......781..F 6
Upham ....272..C 7
Valley City .7,843.°G 12
Velva ....1,241..D 7
Venturia ....77..J 9
Verona ....140..I 12
Veselevville ....D 13
Voltaire ....54..D 7
Wabek ....E 5
Wahpeton ...7,076.°I 15
Walcott ....H 14
Wales ....116..B 11
Walhalla .....1,471..B 12
Walum ....F 12
Warsaw ....D 13
Warwick ....168..E 11
Washburn ....804.°F 7
Watford City 1,768.°E 3
Webster ....D 10
Wellsburg ....E 9
Werner ....21..F 4
West Fargo .5,161..G 14
West Fargo Industrial Park* ......104..G 14
Westfield ....J 8
Westhope ....705..B 7
Wheelock ....21..D 3
White Earth ..128..C 4
Whitman ....D 12
Wild Rice ....H 14
Wildrose ....235..C 3
Williston ....11,280.°D 2
Willow City ....403..C 8
Wilton ....695..G 7
Wimbledon ......337..G 11
Wing ....223..G 8
Wishek ....1,275..I 9
Wolford ....81..C 9
Woodworth ....139..G 10
Wyndmere ....516..I 14
York ....102..D 9
Ypsilanti ....H 11
Zahl ....C 2
Zap ....271..F 5
Zeeland ....313..J 9

*Does not appear on map; key shows general location.
°County seat

Source: Latest census figures (1970). Places without population figures are unincorporated areas and are not listed in census reports.

The 1970 United States census reported that North Dakota had 617,761 persons. The state's population had decreased 2 per cent from the 1960 census figure, 632,446.

About 45 per cent of the people of North Dakota live in urban areas. Among the states, North Dakota has one of the lowest percentages of city dwellers. North Dakota has only one Standard Metropolitan Statistical Area (see METROPOLITAN AREA). This is the Fargo-Moorhead (Minn.) metropolitan area. For the population of the Fargo-Moorhead area, see the *Index* to the political map of North Dakota.

North Dakota has no large manufacturing industries to encourage the growth of big cities. Only 16 cities in the state have more than 2,500 persons. Only four have more than 25,000 persons. They are, in order of size, Fargo, Grand Forks, Bismarck, the state capital, and Minot. North Dakota's larger cities still serve their original function as centers of shipping, supply, and trade for the surrounding agricultural region. Most of the factories in North Dakota's cities are small. They

manufacture, pack, and process food and food products. See the separate articles on the cities of North Dakota listed in the *Related Articles* at the end of this article.

Settlers began to pour into North Dakota by the thousands in the late 1800's. They were attracted by reports of the large profits that had been made in wheat farming. Most of the settlers came from states to the east and south. The largest number from other nations came from Norway. They settled throughout the region. Germans and Russians settled in the south-central area, and Canadians moved into the Red River Valley. Today, about 95 of every 100 North Dakotans were born in the United States. Most of the others came to North Dakota from Canada, Germany, Norway, and Russia.

The majority of immigrants who arrived in the late 1800's belonged to the Lutheran and Roman Catholic churches. Today, more than half the church members in North Dakota belong to these two churches. Other large religious groups in the state include Methodists and Presbyterians.

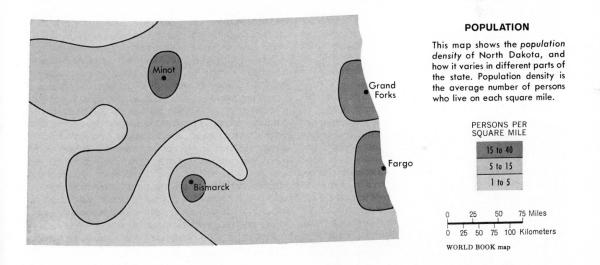

POPULATION

This map shows the *population density* of North Dakota, and how it varies in different parts of the state. Population density is the average number of persons who live on each square mile.

PERSONS PER
SQUARE MILE

| 15 to 40 |
| 5 to 15 |
| 1 to 5 |

0   25   50   75 Miles
0   25 50 75 100 Kilometers

WORLD BOOK map

Indian Chief greets a young paleface. Indians in North Dakota wear feathered headdresses at many ceremonies.
Alpha Photo Assoc.

Cowboys perform in exciting rodeos in Mandan and Dickinson every summer. These rodeos help preserve North Dakota's "wild west" heritage.
Greater North Dakota Assn.

Schools. In 1818, Roman Catholic missionaries established the first school in the North Dakota region, at Pembina in the extreme northeast. They taught the children of Scottish and Irish settlers who came from Canada. The school was discontinued in 1823, when the settlement was abandoned. In 1848, Father George Belcourt reopened the Pembina school as an Indian mission.

In the early days, teachers traveled from village to village, teaching groups of children in the settlers' homes. As the settlements grew, the colonists built new schools and hired teachers. Railroad companies, anxious to attract settlers to the region, helped by supplying building materials.

In 1862, the first legislature of the Dakota Territory passed "An Act for the Regulation and Support of Common (public) Schools." Between 1862 and statehood in 1889, the territory reorganized its educational system several times. The first state legislature created a fund for the support of all schools teaching the English language. State and local taxes now support the public schools.

The superintendent of public instruction administers the North Dakota public school system. The people elect him to a four-year term. The superintendent and his staff make up the state department of public instruction. Children must attend school between the ages of 7 and 16. For the number of students and teachers in North Dakota, see EDUCATION (table).

Libraries and Museums. Women's clubs did much to organize and improve North Dakota's early libraries. In 1897, a women's club opened the first public library in the state, at Grafton. Today, North Dakota has

North Dakota's crisp autumn days attract thousands of hunters to streams and lakes where migrating waterfowl pause on their way south. Sportsmen also shoot grouse, Hungarian partridges, pheasants, and other game birds. Fishermen catch catfish, perch, pike, trout, and other fishes. Favorite summer-resort areas include the Badlands region; Devils Lake; and the Killdeer, Pembina, and Turtle mountains.

Rodeo in White Earth

Harley Hettick, Alpha

Relics of Fort Abercrombie in Abercrombie

Bernie Donahue, Publix

———————— PLACES TO VISIT ————————

Following are brief descriptions of some of North Dakota's many interesting places to visit.

Burning Lignite Beds, near Amidon, can be seen for miles at night. The lignite beds were probably set afire by lightning or by prairie or camp fires. The fire has advanced only a few hundred feet since 1900, although it has burned continuously.

De Mores Chateau, near Medora, was the home of a Frenchman, the Marquis de Mores, who founded Medora in 1883.

Fort Abercrombie, at Abercrombie, was the first U.S. military post in present-day North Dakota. The fort was established in 1857.

Lake Sakakawea, the reservoir for Garrison Dam, is about 60 miles north of Bismarck. The site is popular for swimming, boating, fishing, camping, and picnicking.

Whitestone Hill, near Merricourt, is the site of a battle in 1863 in which U.S. soldiers defeated the Sioux. The site has a monument of a cavalry bugler, and the graves of soldiers who died in the battle.

Writing Rock, near Grenora, is a large glacial boulder covered with Indian picture writing.

National Memorial Park. Theodore Roosevelt National Memorial Park lies in the scenic Badlands. It was established in 1947 in memory of President Roosevelt, who operated two ranches in the area in the 1880's. The park is a wildlife sanctuary, and has petrified forests, prairie dog towns, and many other features.

State Parks. North Dakota has 14 state and recreational parks and many state historic and military sites. Its most famous park is the beautiful International Peace Garden, which it shares with the Canadian province of Manitoba. The park lies in the Turtle Mountains. It symbolizes the long friendship between the United States and Canada. Fort Abraham Lincoln State Park, near Mandan, is one of the state's most important historic sites. In 1876, General George A. Custer and the 7th Cavalry set out from Fort Abraham Lincoln on the expedition that ended in the disastrous Battle of the Little Bighorn. For information on the state parks, write to Director, Division of State Parks, Liberty Memorial Building, Bismarck, N.Dak. 58501.

about 30 public libraries. In 1898, the state department of public instruction set up a system of traveling libraries to serve the schools. In 1907, the legislature established the state library commission, which provides library services for rural areas.

The University of North Dakota at Grand Forks has the largest library in the state. It owns about 350,000 books. The library's collection includes Scandinavian literature, manuscripts on North Dakota's history, and a complete set of the papers of the original Nuremberg trial (see NUREMBERG TRIALS).

The state historical society was organized as a state corporation in Bismarck in 1895. It operates a library with a large collection of books, manuscripts, maps, and papers relating to the state's history. The society also has a museum in Bismarck. The museum's collection includes exhibits dealing with the life of early North Dakota Indians, pioneer days, and natural history. The society has smaller collections in museums at Fort Lincoln and Fort Abercrombie state parks, and at Camp Hancock, Fort Buford, Pembina, and Whitestone Hill historic sites.

UNIVERSITIES AND COLLEGES

North Dakota has eight universities and colleges accredited by the North Central Association of Colleges and Secondary Schools. For enrollments and further information, see UNIVERSITIES AND COLLEGES (table).

Name	Location	Founded
Dickinson State College	Dickinson	1917
Jamestown College	Jamestown	1884
Mary College	Bismarck	1955
Mayville State College	Mayville	1889
Minot State College	Minot	1913
North Dakota, University of	Grand Forks	1883
North Dakota State University	Fargo	1889
Valley City State College	Valley City	1889

ANNUAL EVENTS

During the summer, musical comedies are offered at old Fort Totten, on an Indian reservation south of Devils Lake. Fort Totten has the nation's only restored "cavalry square." Variety shows are offered in the Burning Hills Amphitheater near Medora and in the Theodore Roosevelt National Memorial Park. Medora, a picturesque old cow town that has been restored, is a popular tourist attraction. Summer visitors to North Dakota also enjoy colorful Indian ceremonies conducted on reservations and exciting rodeos held in many communities. Other annual events are:

January-March: Ice Carnival in Fargo (January 1); Farmers' and Homemakers' Week in Fargo (January); Ski Tournament in Valley City (January); North Dakota Winter Show in Valley City (March).

April-June: Norwegian Independence Day, statewide (May 17); Chippewa Indian Sun Dance at Turtle Mountain Indian Reservation (June); International Peace Garden Music Camp (June and July); Miss North Dakota Pageant in Bismarck (June).

July-September: Rodeos in Mandan and Dickinson (July 4); Greater Grand Forks Fair in Grand Forks (July); North Dakota State Fair in Minot (July or August); State Dairy Show and Stutsman County Fair in Jamestown (July); Lake Metigoshe Water Carnival in Bottineau (July); Champions Ride Rodeo in Sentinel Butte (August); Red River Valley Fair in Fargo (August); Cowboys' Reunion in Beulah (September); Indian Pow-Wow and Rodeo in Fort Totten (September).

October-December: Minot Indoor Rodeo (October); U.S. Durum Show in Langdon (October); State Art Exhibit in Bismarck (November).

Theodore Roosevelt National Memorial Park
Harley Hettick, Alpha

Indian Ceremonies near Mandan
Harley Hettick, Alpha

395

Land Regions. North Dakota has three major land regions: (1) the Red River Valley, (2) the Young Drift Plains, and (3) the Great Plains. These regions rise in three broad steps from east to west.

The Red River Valley lies along the Minnesota border. This region is extremely flat. The valley is part of the bed of an ancient glacial lake, Lake Agassiz (see LAKE AGASSIZ). The *silt* (soil particles) of the former lake bottom makes this valley one of the most fertile farming areas in the world. Dairy farms and fields of wheat and other crops cover most of the region. The valley is the most heavily populated part of North Dakota.

The Young Drift Plains rise on the western border of the Red River Valley. An *escarpment* (steep slope) separates the two regions. The escarpment is steepest in the north in the Pembina Mountains. The mountains tower several hundred feet above the Red River Valley. Generally, the Drift Plains rise gradually toward the west

and southwest. Near the region's western border, the land is from 300 to 2,000 feet above the Red River Valley. The glaciers that crossed the Drift Plains during the Ice Age left rich deposits of earth materials called *drift.* Most of the region has rolling hills, and is cut by stream valleys. In the north, the Turtle Mountains rise about 550 feet above the surrounding plains.

The Great Plains cover the southwestern half of North Dakota. This region is part of the immense highland that extends from northern Canada to southern Texas (see GREAT PLAINS). North Dakotans call the region the *Missouri Plateau.* The region begins at the Missouri Escarpment. The escarpment rises 300 to 400 feet above the Drift Plains just east of the Missouri River. It crosses the state from northwest to southeast. The area is hilly, and is used for grazing cattle. It is also rich in mineral deposits. The area has many small lakes where thousands of wild ducks nest every year.

A narrow band of lowlands called the *Missouri Breaks* follows the sweep of the Missouri River. The area south and west of the river is called the *Slope.* There, rough valleys and *buttes* (steep hills that stand alone) break up the flatness of the plains. Many small streams wind around the hills as they flow toward the larger rivers.

The Badlands of the Little Missouri River lie in the southwest. This strip of rough and strangely beautiful land is from 6 to 20 miles wide and about 190 miles long. The Badlands are a sandstone, shale, and clay valley in which wind and water have carved weird formations. Buttes, domes, pyramids, and cones—colored with bands of browns, reds, grays, and yellows—rise from the valley floor. One of the buttes, White Butte, is 3,506 feet above sea level, the highest point in North Dakota. In some places of the Badlands, the rocks contain lignite coal. Some coal beds have been burning for hundreds of years, turning the clay above them bright red and pink. This burned material, called *scoria,* is used for surfacing roads.

Rivers and Lakes. The Missouri and Red river systems drain most of North Dakota. The great Missouri winds through the western part of the state. Its branches include the Cannonball, Heart, Knife, and Little Missouri rivers. The James River begins in central North Dakota and flows southward into South Dakota. Gar-

Map Index

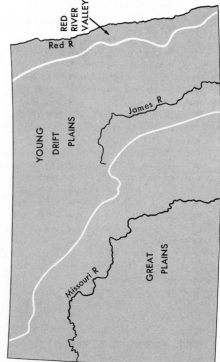

Land Regions of North Dakota

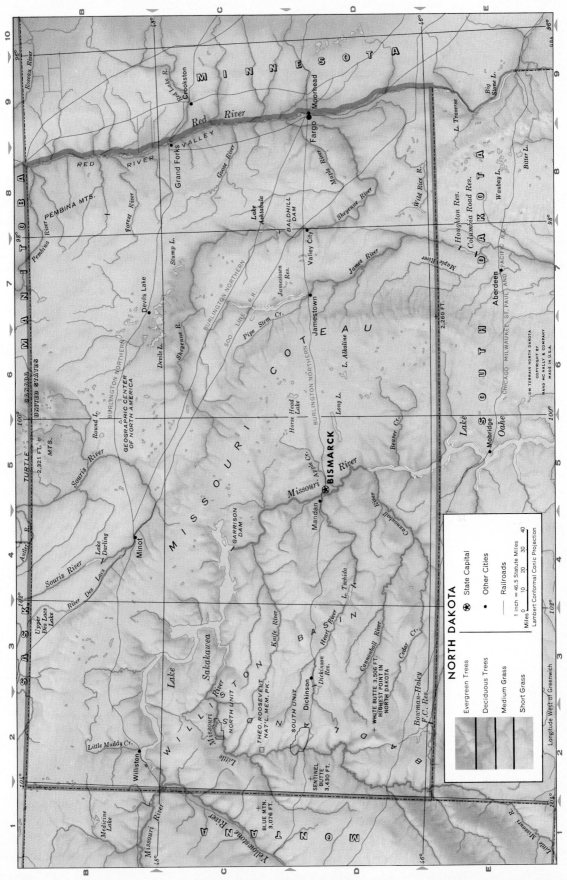

NORTH DAKOTA

✹	State Capital
●	Other Cities
—	Railroads

1 inch = 46.5 Statute Miles

Miles | 0 10 20 30 40

Lambert Conformal Conic Projection

Evergreen Trees

Deciduous Trees

Medium Grass

Short Grass

Specially created for **World Book Encyclopedia** by Rand McNally and World Book editors

GEOGRAPHIC CENTER
OF NORTH AMERICA

BISMARCK

Bismarck
Mandan
Fargo
Moorhead
Grand Forks
Crookston
Minot
Williston
Dickinson
Jamestown
Valley City
Devils Lake
Aberdeen
Mobridge

MINNESOTA
SOUTH DAKOTA
MANITOBA
CANADA
UNITED STATES
SASKATCHEWAN
MONTANA

Red River
Red River Valley
Missouri River
James River
Sheyenne River
Souris River
Yellowstone River
Little Missouri River
Cannonball River
Heart River
Knife River
Cedar Cr.
Beaver Cr.
Maple River
Wild Rice R.
Pembina River
Forest River
Goose River
Roseau River
Apple Cr.
Pipe Stem Cr.
Little Muddy Cr.
Antler R.
River Des Lacs

Lake Sakakawea
Lake Darling
Devils Lake
Lake Ashtabula
Round L.
Stump L.
Long L.
Horse Head Lake
L. Alkaline
Medicine Lake
Upper Des Lacs Lake
L. Tschida
L. Traverse
Big Stone L.
Bitter L.
Waubay L.
Oahe

GARRISON DAM
BALDHILL DAM

PEMBINA MTS.
TURTLE MTS.
COTEAU
MISSOURI PLATEAU
MISSOURI COTEAU
WILLISTON BASIN
DRIFT PRAIRIE

2,321 FT.
2,260 FT.

THEO. ROOSEVELT NAT'L. MEM. PK.
NORTH UNIT
SOUTH UNIT

WHITE BUTTE 3,506 FT.,
HIGHEST POINT IN
NORTH DAKOTA

SENTINEL BUTTE 3,430 FT.
BLUE MTN. 3,076 FT.

BURLINGTON NORTHERN
SOO LINE R.R.
CHICAGO MILWAUKEE, ST. PAUL AND PACIFIC R.R.

Bowman-Haley F.C. Res.
Jamestown Res.
Dickinson Res.
Houghton Res.
Columbia Road Res.

CM TERRAIN NORTH DAKOTA
COPYRIGHT BY
RAND McNALLY & COMPANY
MADE IN U.S.A.
GBA

102° 100° 98° 96°

48° 46°

Longitude West of Greenwich

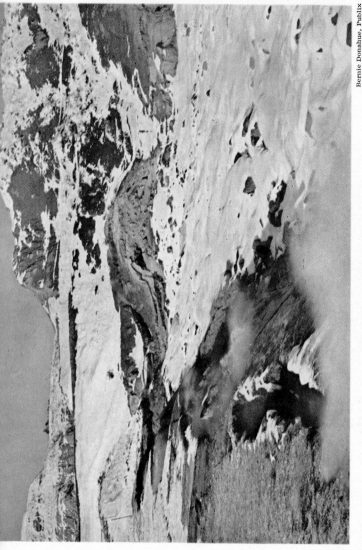

Bernie Donahue, Publix

Beds of Lignite smolder near Amidon in the Badlands of North Dakota. Some of these coal beds in the Great Plains have been burning for hundreds of years.

NORTH DAKOTA

rison Dam, 11,300 feet long, spans the Missouri near Riverdale. The waters above the dam form a reservoir 178 miles long and an average 3½ miles wide. The dam helps control floods, and provides water for irrigation and hydroelectric power.

The Red River and its branches flow northward through eastern North Dakota and empty into Hudson Bay in Canada. The largest branches include the Goose, Park, Pembina, and Sheyenne rivers. The Souris River drains a flat, fertile area in the north-central section. It flows southward from Saskatchewan, and then circles back north into Manitoba.

Numerous small lakes dot the Young Drift Plains. Many lie in beds scooped out by the glaciers. Devils Lake, in the north-central part of the region, is the largest natural lake in the state. It has no outlet, and its water is salty. The lake has been shrinking, and the state plans to raise the water level.

Fields of Soybeans ripen near Fargo in the Red River Valley. This region has some of the nation's most fertile farmland. Dairy farms and fields of crops cover most of the region.

Wendler, FPG

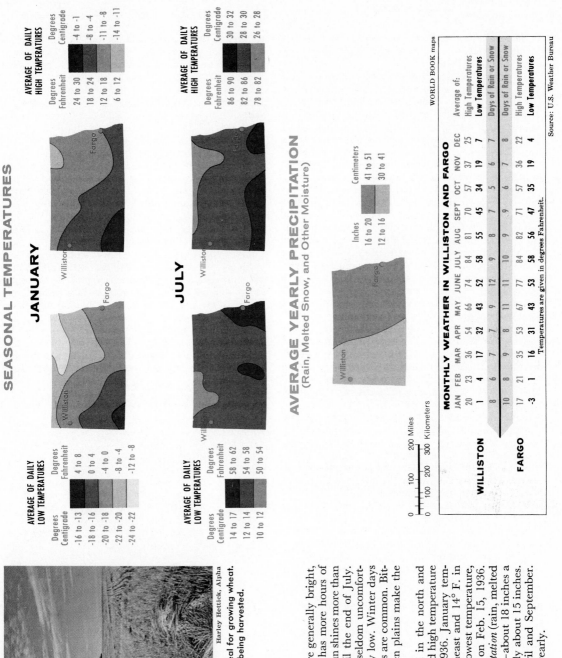

SEASONAL TEMPERATURES

JANUARY

AVERAGE OF DAILY HIGH TEMPERATURES

Degrees Fahrenheit	Degrees Centigrade
24 to 30	-4 to -1
18 to 24	-8 to -4
12 to 18	-11 to -8
6 to 12	-14 to -11

AVERAGE OF DAILY LOW TEMPERATURES

Degrees Centigrade	Degrees Fahrenheit
-16 to -13	4 to 8
-18 to -16	0 to 4
-20 to -18	-4 to 0
-22 to -20	-8 to -4
-24 to -22	-12 to -8

JULY

AVERAGE OF DAILY HIGH TEMPERATURES

Degrees Fahrenheit	Degrees Centigrade
86 to 90	30 to 32
82 to 86	28 to 30
78 to 82	26 to 28

AVERAGE OF DAILY LOW TEMPERATURES

Degrees Centigrade	Degrees Fahrenheit
14 to 17	58 to 62
12 to 14	54 to 58
10 to 12	50 to 54

AVERAGE YEARLY PRECIPITATION
(Rain, Melted Snow, and Other Moisture)

Inches	Centimeters
16 to 20	41 to 51
12 to 16	30 to 41

0 100 200 Miles
0 100 200 300 Kilometers

MONTHLY WEATHER IN WILLISTON AND FARGO	JAN	FEB	MAR	APR	MAY	JUNE	JULY	AUG	SEPT	OCT	NOV	DEC
WILLISTON Average of: High Temperatures	20	23	36	54	66	74	84	81	70	57	37	25
Low Temperatures	1	4	17	32	43	52	58	55	45	34	19	7
Days of Rain or Snow	8	6	9	8	9	12	9	9	8	7	5	6
FARGO High Temperatures	10	21	35	53	67	77	84	82	71	57	36	22
Low Temperatures	-3	1	16	31	43	53	58	56	47	35	19	4

Temperatures are given in degrees Fahrenheit.

Source: U.S. Weather Bureau

Harley Hettick, Alpha

North Dakota's Sunny Weather is ideal for growing wheat. This wheat crop in the Red River Valley is being harvested.

NORTH DAKOTA / Climate

Summer days in North Dakota are generally bright, clear, and pleasant. North Dakota has more hours of sunshine than any other state. The sun shines more than 15 hours a day from mid-May until the end of July. Even the hottest summer days are seldom uncomfortable because the humidity is usually low. Winter days can be severe, and zero temperatures are common. Biting winds that sweep across the open plains make the cold even more bitter.

July temperatures average 69° F. in the north and 72° F. in the south. The state's record high temperature was 121° F., at Steele on July 6, 1936. January temperatures average 3° F. in the northeast and 14° F. in the extreme southwest. The state's lowest temperature, −60° F., was recorded at Parshall on Feb. 15, 1936.

The southeast has the most *precipitation* (rain, melted snow, and other forms of moisture)—about 18 inches a year. Some western areas receive only about 15 inches. Most of the rain falls between April and September. Snowfall averages about 32 inches yearly.

Natural Resources. North Dakota's greatest natural resources are its outstandingly fertile soil and its enormous mineral deposits.

Soil is North Dakota's most valuable resource. It is the basis of the state's major industry—agriculture. North Dakota's richest soil lies in the Red River Valley. This fertile black soil is free of stones and contains much *organic matter* (decayed plant and animal remains). Loamy and sandy soils lie on the Drift Plains west of the Red River Valley. Shale and limestone make up most of the soil of the Great Plains region. The thin, brown soil in parts of the region produces well if irrigated.

Minerals. North Dakota has large deposits of petroleum in the west. These deposits lie in the great Williston Basin, which extends from North Dakota into northern South Dakota, eastern Montana, and southern Canada. In North Dakota, this enormous oil field has been developed in about 15 counties. McKenzie and Williams counties are the leading producers. North Dakota's proved oil reserves are among the largest in the United States. Bowman County in southwestern North Dakota and other oil-producing counties in the northwest have natural-gas wells.

North Dakota has unbelievably huge lignite coal deposits—more than 350 billion tons. No other state has such enormous reserves of coal. North Dakota's lignite deposits lie in the west. Sand and gravel are found throughout the state. The southwestern area has millions of tons of clay, ranging in quality from common brick to the finest pottery clay.

Plant Life. North Dakota has poor forest resources. Forests cover only about 725 square miles of North Dakota, or about 1 per cent of the state's total area. Trees that grow in the east include the ash, aspen, basswood, box elder, elm, oak, and poplar. The largest stands of timber are in the Turtle and Pembina mountains and in the hills surrounding Devils Lake. Ash, cottonwood, elm, and willow trees grow along the Missouri and its branches.

In spring and summer, brilliantly colored flowers bloom throughout the countryside. They include beard-tongues, black-eyed Susans, gaillardias, pasqueflowers, prairie mallows, red lilies, and wild prairie roses. The wild prairie rose is the state flower. Chokecherries, high-bush cranberries, and wild plums grow in many parts of the state. Bluegrass thrives in the northeast, and buffalo and gama grasses in the southwest.

Animal Life. White-tailed deer graze throughout North Dakota. Mule deer and pronghorns range the western plains. In the Badlands, prairie dogs live in scattered colonies called *dog towns.* Fur-bearing animals include badgers, beavers, bobcats, coyotes, foxes, lynxes, minks, muskrats, rabbits, raccoons, skunks, and weasels. Flickertail ground squirrels are commonly seen.

Every summer, ducks migrate to North Dakota to breed in the lakes, marshes, and grainfields. More waterfowl hatch in North Dakota than in any other state. Hunters shoot grouse, Hungarian partridges, pheasants, and other game birds. Fishermen catch bass, carp, catfish, perch, pike, trout, and other fishes.

Agriculture is by far the leading industry in North Dakota. The state's farm income totals about $882 million yearly. This is more than four-fifths of the value of all goods produced in North Dakota. Crops are the largest source of farm income. They bring in about $437,325,000 yearly.

North Dakota has about 49,000 farms and ranches. They average about 875 acres in size. North Dakota farms cover a total of about 42,700,000 acres. Of this total, over 50,000 acres are irrigated.

Wheat is the most important crop in both value and production. It accounts for about $249 million of the state's annual farm income. Over 175 million bushels of wheat are harvested each year on about 8 million acres of land. Most of it is *spring wheat* (wheat planted in the spring). More than 50 million bushels of *durum wheat* (a variety of hard spring wheat used for making spaghetti and macaroni) are grown in North Dakota each year. Durum wheat is harvested on more than 2 million acres. North Dakota usually ranks second only to Kansas in total wheat production. But it leads the nation in durum wheat production. Wheat is grown throughout North Dakota, but the heaviest output is in the northern areas. The north-central areas lead in durum wheat production.

Other Field Crops. Farmers raise flaxseed on about 1,700,000 acres, chiefly in the eastern and central sections. They raise about 9 million bushels of flaxseed annually, about half the nation's harvest. North Dakota

NORTH DAKOTA'S PRODUCTION IN 1967

Total value of goods produced—$1,092,282,000

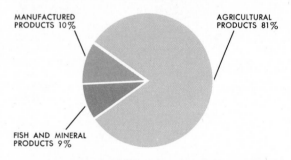

MANUFACTURED PRODUCTS 10%

AGRICULTURAL PRODUCTS 81%

FISH AND MINERAL PRODUCTS 9%

Note: Manufacturing percentage based on value added by manufacture. Other percentages based on value of production. Fish Products are less than 1 per cent.

Sources: U.S. Government statistics

NORTH DAKOTA'S EMPLOYMENT IN 1967

Total number of persons employed—218,000

		Number of Employees
Agriculture	𝝠 𝝠 𝝠 𝝠 𝝠 𝝠	65,200
Wholesale & Retail Trade	𝝠 𝝠 𝝠 𝝠 ∤	42,500
Government	𝝠 𝝠 𝝠 𝝠 ∤	41,700
Services	𝝠 𝝠 𝝠	27,000
Transportation & Public Utilities	𝝠 ∤	12,700
Construction	𝝠 ∤	11,200
Manufacturing	𝝠	9,000
Finance, Insurance & Real Estate	𝝠	6,700
Mining	∤	2,000

Source: U.S. Department of Labor

Greater North Dakota Assn.

Open-Pit Lignite Mine near Bismarck yields large amounts of soft coal. Much lignite is burned to produce electric power for North Dakota and nearby states.

Skyline of Towers rises from an oil refinery near Mandan. Petroleum is the most valuable mineral produced in North Dakota.

Greater North Dakota Assn.

also leads all states in barley production, with about 85,800,000 bushels yearly. Farmers in the eastern counties raise most of the barley. North Dakota also ranks first in rye production. It harvests about 8,300,000 bushels annually. Most of the rye comes from the southeastern and north-central areas. Other important North Dakota crops include oats, potatoes, soybeans, and sugar beets. Farmers also raise corn, dry beans, dry peas, hay, safflower, and sunflowers.

Meat Animals account for about $230 million in annual farm income. The central and western plains provide good pasturage and winter feed. Pastures cover about 14 million acres, or about a third of the state's farmland. Farmers throughout the state raise beef cattle and sell them to eastern dealers who fatten them for market. Sheep are raised mainly in the southeastern counties. Farmers raise hogs in the southeast and south central areas, where corn is plentiful. Dairy cattle also graze in the southeastern part of the state, and in several central counties.

Manufacturing accounts for 10 per cent of the value of all goods produced in North Dakota. Goods manufactured in the state have a *value added by manufacture* of about $113 million yearly. This figure represents the value created in products by North Dakota's industries, not counting such costs as materials, supplies, and fuel. North Dakota ranks last among the states in manufacturing. It has about 450 manufacturing plants. Most of them employ fewer than 50 persons.

Food processing is the chief manufacturing activity. Foods and related products processed in North Dakota have a value added of about $40 million yearly. North Dakota ranks among the leading states in the produc-

tion of butter and cheddar cheese. Creameries ship most of the butter, ice cream, and other dairy products to markets in other states. More than 100 plants in the state process and pack meat. Flour production totals over 3 million barrels yearly. The state-owned flour mill in Grand Forks, established in 1922, is the largest west of Minnesota. Mills in Fargo and Grand Forks produce wheat flour and cereals. A number of North Dakota mills prepare cattle feed. A large sugar refinery in Drayton processes sugar beets grown in North Dakota and Minnesota.

North Dakota's second-ranking manufacturing activity is the production of nonelectrical machinery. The manufacture of machinery is the fastest-growing industry in the state. Nonelectrical machinery has an annual value added by manufacture of about $12 million. Other leading industries in North Dakota produce metal products; printed materials; and stone, clay, and glass products.

Oil refineries are located in Mandan and Williston. Plants in McGregor, Lignite, and Tioga recover gasoline, propane, butane, natural gas, and sulfur from the petroleum deposits of the Williston Basin.

Mining accounts for about $98 million, or about 8 per cent of the value of all goods produced in the state. Petroleum is the most valuable mineral. Over 25 million barrels of oil are pumped annually from the more than 2,000 wells in western North Dakota. Pipelines carry most of the crude oil to North Dakota refineries. Trucks help transport the oil out of the state. North Dakota also produces more than 40 billion cubic feet of natural gas annually.

More than 4 million tons of lignite are mined yearly.

396e

NORTH DAKOTA

More than half of this coal comes from Mercer County. Most of the lignite is taken from *strip* (open) mines. The thin topsoil is removed, leaving the coal at the surface ready for mining by machinery. Coal production began to decline during the 1950's, when many coal users turned to natural gas and oil for fuel, and to the water power of Garrison Dam for electricity. However, construction of huge lignite-burning electric power plants near Stanton and Center has increased coal production. Almost all North Dakota counties produce sand and gravel. Other minerals produced in the state include clay, natural gas liquids, salt, and stone.

Electric Power. Steam plants that burn lignite coal generate about 60 per cent of North Dakota's electric power. The rest of the state's electric power comes from the hydroelectric project at Garrison Dam. Major coal-burning plants are located at Mandan and in the Stanton area. Almost half of the power generated in North Dakota is exported by high voltage transmission lines to other midwestern states. For North Dakota's kilowatt-hour production, see ELECTRIC POWER (table).

Transportation. North Dakota is a large state with a relatively small population. It also lies far from the nation's large population centers. These factors have hindered the growth of transportation in the state. The first railroad in North Dakota, the Northern Pacific, reached Fargo in 1872 and Bismarck in 1873. By 1881, the line ran to the Montana border. Until a bridge was built, trains crossed the Missouri River at Bismarck on a ferry in summer and on tracks over the ice in winter. By 1881, the Great Northern Railway established a

Harley Hettick, Alpha

FARM AND MINERAL PRODUCTS

This map shows where the state's leading farm and mineral products are produced. The major urban areas (shown on the map in red) are the state's important manufacturing centers.

```
0      25     50     75 Miles
0  25  50  75  100 Kilometers
```

WORLD BOOK map

Cowboys Round Up Cattle on a ranch near Sentinel Butte. Farmers throughout North Dakota raise beef cattle. They sell the cattle to eastern dealers, who fatten them for market.

route between Fargo and Grand Forks. It built a line westward through Minot and Williston to the Montana border by 1887. Today, five railroads operate on more than 5,000 miles of track in the state.

North Dakota has about 107,000 miles of roads and highways, of which about two-thirds are surfaced. Three scheduled airlines serve North Dakota, and the state has nearly 200 airports.

Communication. North Dakota's first newspaper, the *Frontier Scout*, was published in Fort Union in 1864. In 1873, Colonel Clement A. Lounsberry founded the *Bismarck Tribune*, the oldest newspaper still published in North Dakota. In 1876, Lounsberry wrote the first story of the Battle of the Little Bighorn. In this famous battle, Indians massacred General George A. Custer and all the troops under his immediate command. In order to write the story, Lounsberry used notes found

in the buckskin pouch of Mark Kellogg, a reporter for the *Tribune* and the *New York Herald*. Kellogg was killed in the battle.

North Dakota dailies with the largest circulations include the *Bismarck Tribune*, the *Fargo Forum*, the *Grand Forks Herald*, and the *Minot Daily News*. The state has about 110 newspapers, of which about 100 are weeklies. North Dakota publishers also issue about 20 magazines.

The first radio station in North Dakota, WDAY, started broadcasting in Fargo in 1922. The state's first television station, KCJB (now KXMC-TV), began operating in 1953 in Minot. North Dakota has 30 radio stations and 11 television stations.

NORTH DAKOTA / History

Indian Days. Several Indian tribes lived in the North Dakota region before white explorers first arrived. The Arikara, Cheyenne, Hidatsa, and Mandan peacefully farmed the land. Most of these Indians lived in the Missouri Valley. They lived in villages fortified against attacks by warring tribes. Hunter and warrior tribes included the Assiniboin, Chippewa, and Sioux. They mainly roamed the northeast. See INDIAN, AMERICAN (table: Indian Tribes).

Exploration and Early Settlement. In 1682, Robert Cavelier, Sieur de la Salle, claimed for France all the land drained by the Mississippi River system. This territory included the southwestern half of present-day North Dakota, because the Missouri River flows into the Mississippi. France also claimed the vast area south of Hudson Bay, which included the northeastern half of North Dakota. In 1713, France gave all this Hudson Bay territory to Great Britain.

North Dakota was first explored by a French Canadian, Pierre Gaultier de Varennes, Sieur de la Vérendrye. He set out from Canada in 1738, and reached the Mandan Indian villages near present-day Bismarck.

In 1762, France gave its land west of the Mississippi to Spain. Spain returned it to France in 1800. In 1803, the United States bought this region, called Louisiana, from France (see LOUISIANA PURCHASE).

In 1804, President Thomas Jefferson sent Meriwether Lewis and William Clark to explore the Louisiana Territory and to blaze a trail to the Pacific Ocean. Lewis and Clark reached central North Dakota in October, 1804. They built Fort Mandan on the east bank of the Missouri River, across from present-day Stanton. The explorers stayed at Fort Mandan until April, 1805. They passed through North Dakota again in 1806 on their return from the Pacific.

In 1812, Scottish and Irish families from Canada made the first attempt at a permanent settlement in North Dakota, in Pembina. In 1818, the United States obtained northeastern North Dakota by a treaty with Great Britain. All of present-day North Dakota then became U.S. territory. The 1818 treaty also set the United States-Canadian border at the 49th parallel. Some of the Pembina settlers moved north, to be sure they were on British territory. The rest left in 1823, when a survey

of the border confirmed that Pembina was actually located in the United States.

Territorial Days. Congress created the Dakota Territory in 1861. President Abraham Lincoln appointed William Jayne as governor. The territory included the present states of North and South Dakota and much of Montana and Wyoming. The first legislature met in Yankton (now in South Dakota) in 1862.

In 1863, the territory was opened for homesteading. Settlers were given free land if they lived on it and improved it. But the territory developed slowly. Transportation was poor, and the settlers feared Indian attacks. In 1862, Sioux Indians killed hundreds of settlers in an uprising in Minnesota. Some of the Indians then fled to the Dakota Territory. During the 1860's and 1870's, the U.S. government sent troops into the territory to punish the Indians who had taken part in the Minnesota massacre. Many battles were fought as the soldiers pursued the Indians across the territory.

The federal government signed several treaties with the Indians in the Dakota Territory, giving them land on reservations. But the whites often broke the treaties, causing more Indian uprisings. Peace came in 1881, when the great Sioux chief Sitting Bull voluntarily surrendered to U.S. troops. See INDIAN WARS (The Sioux Wars); SITTING BULL.

Large-scale farming began about 1875, when eastern corporations and some families established huge wheat farms. Most of the farms were in the Red River Valley, and ranged from 3,000 to 65,000 acres. The farms earned such tremendous profits they became known as *bonanza* farms. The farmers used machinery and orderly methods of planting, harvesting, and marketing. This was possible because only one crop—wheat—was raised. It was easy to cultivate the large, level fields with machinery, and the owners could afford equipment. In time, other crops were introduced on the bonanza farms. But difficulties arose as stockholders quarreled over how to operate the farms. Finally, most of the farms were divided into smaller lots and sold to newcomers.

Statehood. During the 1870's, the people began to ask Congress to divide the Dakota Territory into two parts. The population centers had developed in far cor-

Tioga

The Petroleum Industry in North Dakota began in 1951, when oil was discovered near Tioga. Oil quickly became the state's most valuable mineral.

Ranching Began in North Dakota in the late 1800's, when its western range lands became a fattening-up place for Texas cattle. Famous ranches included one owned by Theodore Roosevelt.

ners of the territory—in the northeast and the southeast. North-south travel between these two centers was difficult because the railroads had laid their tracks in an east-west direction. The two groups of settlers also had little in common, and wanted to develop their own governments.

In February, 1889, Congress established the present boundary between North Dakota and South Dakota. It also passed an enabling act, allowing the two regions to set up the machinery to become states (see ENABLING ACT). On Nov. 2, 1889, North Dakota became the 39th state, and South Dakota the 40th state. John Miller, a Republican, became North Dakota's first governor.

The Early 1900's. North Dakota's population increased rapidly following statehood. The state had 190,983 persons in 1890. In 1910, it had 577,056 persons. Farming also grew rapidly. But the farmers disliked having to deal with banks, grain companies, and railroad interests in Minnesota. They also disliked the power these out-of-state businesses held in North Dakota politics.

In 1915, the Nonpartisan League was founded in North Dakota. This organization supported the farmers. It called for state ownership of grain elevators, flour mills, packing houses, and cold-storage plants. It also wanted banks in farming areas that would grant loans at cost. Thousands of farmers joined the league.

In 1916, a league-supported candidate, Republican

Lynn J. Frazier, was elected governor of North Dakota. During Frazier's administrations, from 1917 to 1921, the state legislature passed a number of progressive laws. Rural schools received more funds. Taxes on farm improvements were lowered. An industrial commission was set up to manage businesses begun by the state. In 1919, the Bank of North Dakota was established in Bismarck. In 1922, the North Dakota Mill and Elevator in Grand Forks began operating.

The Great Depression. North Dakota suffered a severe drought during the 1930's. In addition, the entire nation was hit by the Great Depression. North Dakota's farm production plunged sharply, and its population also began to decline. The population had reached a peak of 680,845 in 1930.

During the 1930's, the state and federal governments took many steps to help North Dakota farmers. In 1937, the state water conservation commission was created. Since that time, state, federal, and private agencies have set up projects to provide irrigation and prevent soil erosion. These agencies also encourage *dry farming*

HISTORIC NORTH DAKOTA

The First Explorer of the North Dakota region reached an Indian village at Mandan in 1738. He was Pierre de la Vérendrye, who was looking for a route west to the Pacific Ocean.

Pembina

Scottish and Irish Families made the first attempts to settle at Pembina in 1812. Before that, only Indians and white fur traders lived in North Dakota.

The Huge Garrison Dam north of Bismarck is one of the largest dams in the world. It forms a reservoir 178 miles long. Work began in 1946. The embankment took seven years to build.

Fargo

The Northern Pacific Railroad built a line to Fargo by 1872, and reached westward to Bismarck in 1873. Railroad building brought a rush of settlers, and farming soon prospered in eastern North Dakota. The state now harvests over half the total U.S. flaxseed crop.

Mandan
BISMARCK ★

Lewis and Clark followed the Missouri into North Dakota in 1804. They wintered among Mandan Indians. On leaving, they took along the young Shoshoni, Sacagawea, who guided the expedition.

Wheat Raising on a Vast Scale boosted agriculture in the 1870's. The crop grew on rich "bonanza farms" that covered up to 65,000 acres. North Dakota now leads all states in durum wheat.

Dome-Shaped Lodges of the Mandan Indians have been restored. This community, near Mandan, is called Slant Village because the land it occupies slopes toward the Heart River.

Bernie Donahue, Publix

Garrison Dam Hydroelectric Project began operating in 1956. The project supplies much of North Dakota's electric power.

(farming methods that make the most of limited rain).

The Mid-1900's. North Dakota's economy recovered during World War II (1939-1945). Farmers broke all their production records in supplying much food for the armed forces. But in the late 1940's, farm prices sagged as a result of farm surpluses throughout the country. The increased use of machines on farms left large numbers of farmworkers unemployed. Many of these workers found jobs in towns and cities, and North Dakota's urban population increased. But thousands of farmworkers could not find other jobs in the state and left in search of opportunities elsewhere.

Construction of the great Garrison Dam near Riverdale began in 1946. This dam provides flood control, hydroelectric power, and water for irrigation. In 1956, the first generator at the dam went into operation. The dam was completed in 1960. Two lignite-burning power plants near Stanton have also helped North Dakota's economy.

Oil was discovered near Tioga in 1951 and became the state's most valuable mineral. By 1970, oil wells were operating in 14 counties of western North Dakota.

In 1957, North Dakota established an economic development commission that works to attract industry to the state. More than 80 North Dakota communities now have their own development commissions. Largely as a result of these commissions, the state's rate of industrial growth ranked among the highest in the country from 1958 to 1969.

The U.S. Air Force gave a boost to the state's economy during the 1960's. It built Strategic Air Command

THE GOVERNORS OF NORTH DAKOTA

		Party	Term
1.	John Miller	Republican	1889-1890
2.	Andrew H. Burke	Republican	1891-1892
3.	Eli C. D. Shortridge	Democratic	1893-1894
4.	Roger Allen	Republican	1895-1896
5.	Frank A. Briggs	Republican	1897-1898
6.	Joseph M. Devine	Republican	1898
7.	Frederick B. Fancher	Republican	1899-1900
8.	Frank White	Republican	1901-1904
9.	E. Y. Sarles	Republican	1905-1906
10.	John Burke	Democratic	1907-1912
11.	L. B. Hanna	Republican	1913-1916
12.	Lynn J. Frazier	Republican	1917-1921
13.	R. A. Nestos	Republican	1921-1924
14.	A. G. Sorlie	Republican	1925-1928
15.	Walter Maddock	Republican	1928
16.	George F. Schafer	Republican	1929-1932
17.	William Langer	Republican	1933-1934
18.	Ole H. Olson	Republican	1934-1935
19.	Thomas H. Moodie	Democratic	1935
20.	Walter Welford	Republican	1935-1936
21.	William Langer	Republican	1937-1938
22.	John Moses	Democratic	1939-1944
23.	Fred Aandahl	Republican	1945-1950
24.	Norman Brunsdale	Republican	1951-1956
25.	John E. Davis	Republican	1957-1960
26.	William L. Guy	Democratic	1961-

(SAC) bomber bases near Grand Forks and Minot. About 17,000 workers and their families live on each of the two bases and in nearby communities.

North Dakota Today is working to broaden its economy, which still depends heavily upon agriculture. State leaders, fearing a possible crop failure or a disastrous drop in farm prices, continue to seek new industry. But the task of attracting new industry is difficult because North Dakota lies so far from the nation's largest population centers.

The state's need for more industry is reflected in three related problems. These problems are (1) lack of job opportunities, (2) low *per capita* (per person) income, and (3) people moving out of the state. The number of nonagricultural jobs has been increasing, but not enough to keep up with the decline in farm jobs. North Dakota also hopes to expand the use of its mineral resources as a step toward broadening its economy.

The Garrison Diversion Project, started in 1968, was scheduled to begin operating in 1975. It includes a 2,000-mile canal system to bring water for irrigation from the Missouri River to 250,000 acres of farmland. It will also supply water to 14 cities and towns.

JACK U. HAGERTY, RUSSELL S. REID, and BERNT LLOYD WILLS

NORTH DAKOTA/Study Aids

Related Articles in WORLD BOOK include:

BIOGRAPHIES

Burke, John   Sacagawea   Sitting Bull
Nye, Gerald Prentice

CITIES

Bismarck   Fargo   Minot
Devils Lake   Grand Forks

HISTORY

Indian Wars (The Sioux Wars)   Louisiana Purchase
Lake Agassiz   Nonpartisan League
Lewis and Clark Expedition   Western Frontier Life

PHYSICAL FEATURES

Badlands   Missouri River
Great Plains   Red River of the North

PRODUCTS

For North Dakota's rank among the states in production, see the following articles:

Barley   Rye   Wheat
Flax

OTHER RELATED ARTICLES

Dry Farming   Geographic Center of North America
Garrison Dam   Midwestern States

Questions

What political organization was founded in North Dakota?

Why did few settlers come to the Dakota Territory in the early days even though they were given free land?

What mineral was discovered in North Dakota in 1951?

Why is soil North Dakota's most precious resource?

How did trains cross the Missouri River at Bismarck before a bridge was built over the river?

North Dakota is the nation's leading producer of what crops?

What were the bonanza farms?

Why did the settlers of the Dakota Territory want the territory divided into two parts?

Where in North Dakota have coal beds been burning for hundreds of years? What use is made of the burned material?

What is the world's tallest man-made structure?

Books for Young Readers

ANDERSON, ANITA M. *Grant Marsh, Steamboat Captain.* Wheeler, 1959. Adventure on the Missouri River.
SAUNDERS, WINNIE C. *Daughters of Dakota.* Caxton, 1960. Incidents of a childhood in Dakota.

Books for Older Readers

BANER, SKULDA V. *First Parting.* McKay, 1960. An account of teaching in a one-room school in the Badlands of North Dakota in early days.
CUSTER, ELIZABETH. *Boots and Saddles: or, Life in Dakota with General Custer.* Univ. of Oklahoma Press, 1961. In this book, originally published in 1885, General Custer's widow gives a dramatic account of life in a frontier garrison in the midst of Indian perils.
DIETRICH, I. T., ed. *Conservation of Natural Resources in North Dakota.* North Dakota Institute for Regional Studies, North Dakota State University, 1962.
HUDSON, L. P. *Bones of Plenty.* Little, Brown, 1962. A novel about a proud family of wheat farmers and their struggles during the depression years.
MILLER, WILFORD L., and LARSON, DELORES. *Animals of the Prairie.* Walsh County Record, Grafton, North Dakota, 1964.
PIPER, MARION J. *Dakota Portraits: A Sentimental Journal of Pictorial History.* The author, Mohall, North Dakota, 1964.
ROBINSON, ELWYN B. *History of North Dakota.* Univ. of Nebraska Press, 1966.
ROLFSRUD, ERLING N. *The Story of North Dakota.* Lantern, 1963.
WILLS, BERNT L. *North Dakota: The Northern Prairie State.* The author, 1963.

NORTH DAKOTA, UNIVERSITY OF, is a state-controlled coeducational school at Grand Forks, N.Dak. It has colleges of science, literature, and arts; education; engineering; nursing; and business and public administration. The University of North Dakota also has a two-year medical school, a law school, and a graduate school. It confers bachelor's, master's, and doctor's degrees. Its students also may take courses in religion at Wesley College, with which the University of North Dakota is affiliated. There are Army and Air Force ROTC units on the campus. The university was founded in 1883. For enrollment, see UNIVERSITIES AND COLLEGES (table). GEORGE W. STARCHER

NORTH DAKOTA STATE UNIVERSITY is a state-controlled coeducational school at Fargo, N.Dak. The university has undergraduate schools of agriculture, home economics, pharmacy, arts and sciences, engineering, and chemical technology. It also has a graduate school. Courses lead to bachelor's, master's, and doctor's degrees.

The university includes the North Dakota Agricultural Extension Service, which is supported by both state and federal funds, and the Cooperative Agricultural Extension, which is maintained by the federal, state, and county governments. The university was founded in 1889. For enrollment, see UNIVERSITIES AND COLLEGES (table). H. R. ALBRECHT

NORTH EQUATORIAL CURRENT. See OCEAN (How the Ocean Moves).

NORTH GEORGIA COLLEGE is a coeducational liberal arts school at Dahlonega, Ga. It is a state-supported senior unit of the University System of Georgia. Courses lead to B.A. and B.S. degrees. The college was founded in 1873. For enrollment, see UNIVERSITIES AND COLLEGES (table).

NORTH GERMAN CONFEDERATION. See GERMANY (The Unification of Germany).

NORTH ISLAND. See NEW ZEALAND (Location and Size).

NORTH KOREA. See KOREA.

NORTH LITTLE ROCK, Ark. (pop. 60,040; alt. 255 ft.), an industrial and transportation center, lies in the center of the state on the north bank of the Arkansas River. For location, see ARKANSAS (political map). North Little Rock has large railroad repair shops. The city manufactures cottonseed products, fertilizer, furniture, concrete, iron products, railroad ties, barrels, and food products.

The city was laid out in 1839 as the town of De Cantillon and was incorporated under its present name in 1904. North Little Rock and Little Rock form a metropolitan area with a population of 323,296. North Little Rock has the mayor-council form of government. WALTER L. BROWN

NORTH MAGNETIC POLE

NORTH MAGNETIC POLE. See NORTH POLE.

NORTH PARK COLLEGE AND THEOLOGICAL SEMINARY. See UNIVERSITIES AND COLLEGES (table).

NORTH PLATTE, Nebr. (pop. 19,447; alt. 2,800 ft.), is the center of an important farming and cattle-raising region in western Nebraska. The people of this railroad and shipping city deal in livestock, grains, dairy products, meat packing, and pet food. Lake McConaughy, the reservoir of nearby Kingsley Dam, provides water for power and irrigation. The city lies at the fork of the North Platte and South Platte rivers. For location, see NEBRASKA (political map).

North Platte was first settled in 1866, as a construction camp for workers of the Union Pacific Railroad. William F. Cody, better known as "Buffalo Bill," operated a large cattle ranch nearby. The city has a mayor-council government. JAMES C. OLSON

NORTH PLATTE RIVER. See PLATTE RIVER.

NORTH POLE is a term used for several invisible surface points located in the Arctic region. The best-known is the *North Geographic Pole*. But other important north poles include the *Instantaneous North Pole*, the *North Pole of Balance*, the *North Magnetic Pole*, and the *Geomagnetic North Pole*.

The North Geographic Pole lies near the center of the Arctic Ocean at the point where all the earth's lines of longitude meet. Explorer Robert E. Peary of the United States was the first man to reach the North Geographic Pole. He made the trip by dog team in 1909. In 1926, Admiral Richard E. Byrd and Floyd Bennett of the United States reached the pole by airplane. In 1958, the U.S.S. *Nautilus* became the first submarine to pass under the arctic ice to the North Geographic Pole.

The Instantaneous North Pole lies at the point where the earth's *axis* (an imaginary line through the earth) meets the surface. The earth wobbles slowly as it turns around its axis, causing the Instantaneous North Pole to move. This pole takes about 14 months to move clockwise around an irregular path called the *Chandler Circle*. The diameter of the Chandler Circle varies from a few inches to about 70 feet.

The North Pole of Balance lies at the center of the Chandler Circle. Its position locates the North Geographic Pole. Each year since 1900, the North Pole of Balance has moved about 6 inches toward North America. This motion has caused tiny changes in the latitude and longitude of points around the earth.

The North Magnetic Pole is the point toward which north-seeking compass needles point. This pole can move many miles in a few years. In 1970, it was located near Bathurst Island in northern Canada.

The Geomagnetic North Pole lies near Thule, Greenland. In the upper atmosphere, the earth's magnetic field points down toward this point. PAUL A. SIPLE

Related Articles in WORLD BOOK include:

Arctic (Arctic Exploration)	Exploration and Discovery
Arctic Ocean (maps)	(Polar Exploration)
Byrd, Richard E.	Henson, Matthew A.
Earth (The Earth's Magnetism)	Peary, Robert E.

NORTH RIVER. See NEW YORK CITY (Location).

NORTH SEA is a wide arm of the Atlantic Ocean that lies between Great Britain and the continent of Europe.

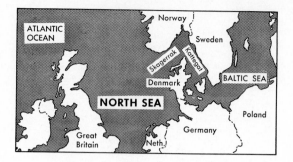

Location Map of the North Sea

In peacetime, heavily burdened ships, carrying food, manufactured products, and passengers, make the North Sea a busy trade highway. In wartime, the North Sea is closely guarded by the countries on its shores.

The harbors of many of the greatest seafaring nations are on the shores of the North Sea. The most important ports of England, Germany, Norway, The Netherlands, and Denmark border the sea. The entire eastern seaboard of England and Scotland is devoted to fishing. Water pollution and excessive fishing have been blamed for reduced catches since the mid-1900's.

The bottom of the North Sea has large deposits of petroleum and natural gas. The sea was expected to become an important European source of oil and gas during the 1970's.

The North Sea is nearly 600 miles long and about 360 miles wide. It has a shore line of about 4,000 miles. The area of the North Sea is 221,000 square miles, or a little smaller than Texas. About 2,500 square miles of this area is taken up by islands.

The average depth of the North Sea varies from 100 feet in the south to 400 feet in the north. The sea is about 250 feet deep in the center. The deepest section of the North Sea is off the Norwegian coast. Here the water is more than 2,400 feet deep. The North Sea contains less salt than the open ocean, because so many rivers empty into it. Among these are the Humber and Thames of Great Britain, and the Rhine, Elbe, Weser, Ems, and Schelde of the European continent.

Skagerrak, an arm of the North Sea, connects it with the Strait of Kattegat and the Baltic Sea. The Kiel Canal also connects the North and the Baltic seas. The English Channel and the Strait of Dover connect the North Sea with the Atlantic Ocean on the south.

Its location as a sea among seas causes strange tides in the North Sea. One tide wave comes through the English Channel and the Strait of Dover and sweeps northward. The other tide wave moves southward along Norway to the Danish coast. The two tides cancel near the southern tip of Norway, and they reinforce each other on the coast of Germany, where the range of the highest tide is about 10 feet. There is little rise and fall in the middle of the North Sea.

The position of the North Sea made it important during both world wars. During World War I, Great Britain controlled these waters and cut off the enemy from this route to the Atlantic. During World War II, both the German and British navies patrolled and mined the North Sea. JOHN D. ISAACS

See also DOGGER BANK.

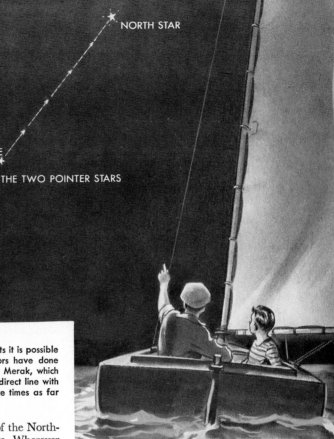

NORTH STAR

BIG DIPPER

DUBHE

THE TWO POINTER STARS

MERAK

How to Locate the North Star. On clear nights it is possible to tell directions by the North Star, just as sailors have done for hundreds of years. The two stars Dubhe and Merak, which form the front of the Big Dipper, are almost in a direct line with the North Star. This star appears to be about five times as far from Dubhe as Dubhe is from Merak.

NORTH STAR, or POLESTAR. This star of the Northern Hemisphere has long guided mariners. Wherever one may be in northern latitudes, the direction north may be found by reference to it (see LATITUDE [picture]). The North Star is also called POLARIS. It is easily located, for two stars in Ursa Major (the Big Dipper), or Great Bear, called the *pointers* always point to it.

The star is about one degree from the *north celestial pole* (see EQUINOX [The North Celestial Pole]). It is the brightest star in the constellation Ursa Minor, or Little Bear. It is of the second magnitude in brightness. The Greeks called the polestar *Cynosura*, meaning *dog's tail*. In English, *cynosure* now means *center of attraction*.

The distance of the polestar from the north celestial pole is gradually becoming less, because of the motion of the pole of the heavens around the pole of the *ecliptic* (see ASTRONOMY [table: Astronomy Terms]). Within the next 100 years the distance will decrease to one-half degree, then begin to increase again. About 2,000 years from now, the star Alpha Cephei will be the polestar for people on earth. CHARLES A. FEDERER, JR.

See also ASTRONOMY (diagram: The North Star); BIG AND LITTLE DIPPERS.

NORTH TEXAS STATE UNIVERSITY is a coeducational school at Denton, Tex. Courses offered include art, business administration, education, English, government, journalism, music, sciences, speech, and drama. The school grants bachelor's, master's, and doctor's degrees. There is a special training program for teachers of audio-visual education.

North Texas State University was established as Texas

Normal College in 1890. It became a state college in 1901, and received its present name in 1961. The graduate division was founded in 1935. The College of Arts and Sciences, and the schools of business administration, education, home economics, and music, were founded in 1946. For enrollment, see UNIVERSITIES AND COLLEGES (table). JAMES CARL MATTHEWS

NORTH VIETNAM. See VIETNAM.

NORTH WEST COMPANY was a famous fur-trading company organized in Canada in 1783. It was set up to compete with the powerful Hudson's Bay Company. The North West Company sent its rugged traders across Canada to the Pacific Ocean and did much to open up the little-known regions of the Canadian Far West.

In the early 1800's, the North West Company began to build trading posts down the Pacific Coast toward the Columbia River. John Jacob Astor's Pacific Fur Company was also establishing posts in the Columbia region. Astor reached the entrance of the Columbia River first and, in 1811, founded Astoria. Later the North West Company bought out the Astor interests in this region. In 1821, the Hudson's Bay Company absorbed the North West Company. JOHN R. ALDEN

See also ASTOR (John Jacob Astor); HUDSON'S BAY COMPANY; FRASER, SIMON.

NORTH WEST MOUNTED POLICE. See ROYAL CANADIAN MOUNTED POLICE.

Smith College

Smith College in Northampton, Mass., was founded in 1871. The housing units, *above,* enclose a terraced quadrangle.

NORTHAMPTON, Mass. (pop. 29,664; alt. 133 ft.), is best known as the home of Smith College, one of the leading colleges for women in the United States.

Northampton lies on the Connecticut River in west-central Massachusetts, 17 miles north of Springfield. For location, see MASSACHUSETTS (political map). The city is noted for its wide, tree-lined streets and fine homes. Brushes, silverware, optical instruments, cutlery, and paper napkins are manufactured here.

Northampton was settled in 1654 and became a city in 1883. The seat of Hampshire County, it has a mayor-council government. Calvin Coolidge, 30th President of the United States, lived there.   WILLIAM J. REID

NORTHAMPTONSHIRE. See ENGLAND (political map).

NORTHCLIFFE, VISCOUNT (1865-1922), ALFRED CHARLES WILLIAM HARMSWORTH, a famous English journalist and publisher, pioneered in the use of comics, special features, religious news, and tabloid newspapers. He had great political influence, and played an important part in the formation in 1916 of the Coalition Cabinet led by David Lloyd George. Northcliffe owned the Amalgamated Press, a large magazine publishing house, and the London *Evening News,* the *Daily Mail,* the *Daily Mirror,* and the *Times.* He was born in County Dublin, Ireland.   JOHN ELDRIDGE DREWRY

NORTHEAST LOUISIANA UNIVERSITY. See UNIVERSITIES AND COLLEGES (table).

NORTHEAST MISSOURI STATE COLLEGE. See UNIVERSITIES AND COLLEGES (table).

NORTHEAST PASSAGE. See ARCTIC OCEAN.

NORTHEASTERN ILLINOIS STATE COLLEGE. See UNIVERSITIES AND COLLEGES (table).

NORTHEASTERN STATE COLLEGE. See UNIVERSITIES AND COLLEGES (table).

NORTHEASTERN UNIVERSITY is a private, coeducational school in Boston, Mass. It offers bachelor's and master's degrees in business administration, education, engineering, pharmacy, and liberal arts. There are doctoral programs in chemistry, electrical engineering, and physics.

Under Northeastern University's Cooperative Plan of Education, it takes five years to earn a bachelor's degree. This is because students alternate 10-week and 16-week periods of study with equal periods of work in business and industry. The plan begins in the second year, except in pharmacy, where it begins in the third year. Graduate level co-op programs lead to the master's degree in two years. Northeastern was established in 1898. For enrollment, see UNIVERSITIES AND COLLEGES (table).   ASA S. KNOWLES

NORTHER is a cold winter wind that sweeps over the southern United States and the Gulf of Mexico, destroying crops and wrecking ships. The northers occur most frequently between September and March. Northers often cause the temperature to drop rapidly as much as 20 to 30 degrees.

The wind usually blows over Texas and other regions that border the western part of the Gulf of Mexico. Sometimes the wind reaches as far south as Panama. Occasionally a norther starts as far north as Canada and extends over the entire Mississippi Valley. Scientists can predict the coming of a norther about 24 hours in advance. A similar cold wind, called *Friagem,* occurs in South America.   GEORGE F. TAYLOR

NORTHERN ARIZONA UNIVERSITY. See UNIVERSITIES AND COLLEGES (table).

NORTHERN BAPTIST THEOLOGICAL SEMINARY. See UNIVERSITIES AND COLLEGES (table).

NORTHERN BLACK RACER. See BLACKSNAKE.

NORTHERN COLORADO, UNIVERSITY OF. See UNIVERSITIES AND COLLEGES (table).

NORTHERN HEMISPHERE. See HEMISPHERE.

NORTHERN ILLINOIS UNIVERSITY is a state-supported coeducational school in De Kalb, Ill. Courses lead to bachelor's and master's degrees in education, fine arts, liberal arts, and science. The graduate school was established in 1951. Northern Illinois was founded in 1895 as a teachers college and became a university in 1957. For the enrollment of Northern Illinois University, see UNIVERSITIES AND COLLEGES (table).

NORTHERN IOWA, UNIVERSITY OF, is a state-supported coeducational liberal arts and teacher education school in Cedar Falls, Iowa. It is controlled by the Iowa State Board of Regents. It offers courses that prepare students for preschool, elementary school, and high school teaching, supervisory, and administrative positions. It has a grade school and high school as a teaching laboratory. Founded in 1876, it grants B.A., M.A., and Ed.S. degrees. For enrollment, see UNIVERSITIES AND COLLEGES (table).   J. W. MAUCKER

Orange Day is a Protestant celebration in Northern Ireland honoring William of Orange's defeat of Roman Catholics in 1690.

Green Valleys and Low Mountains lie along the coast of Northern Ireland. Rolling farmland covers most of the country.

NORTHERN IRELAND

NORTHERN IRELAND is the smallest of the four countries that make up the UNITED KINGDOM OF GREAT BRITAIN AND NORTHERN IRELAND. The other countries are England, Scotland, and Wales. Northern Ireland is slightly larger than the state of Connecticut, but it has only about half as many people as that state. Belfast is the capital and largest city.

Northern Ireland occupies the northeastern corner of the island of Ireland. It takes up about a sixth of the island. The independent Republic of Ireland occupies the rest of the island. Fertile farmland covers most of Northern Ireland, and low mountain ranges rise near the coast.

Most of the people of Northern Ireland are of English or Scottish descent, and they observe many English traditions and customs. Almost half the people live in rural areas. The farmers of Northern Ireland produce large quantities of agricultural products for the rest of Great Britain. About a fourth of the people live in Belfast, the country's manufacturing and trading center.

Northern Ireland is often called *Ulster*. Ulster was the name of a large province of Ireland until 1920, when Northern Ireland was separated from the rest of Ireland. The province covered what are now Northern Ireland and three counties of the Republic of Ireland.

This article tells about the people, geography, econ-

The contributors of this article are John Magee, Senior Lecturer in History at St. Joseph's College of Education, Belfast, Northern Ireland; Norman Runnion, Editor of the Brattleboro (Vt.) Daily Reformer and former London Correspondent for United Press International; and J. Wreford Watson, Professor of Geography at Edinburgh University, Edinburgh, Scotland.

omy, and history of Northern Ireland. For a discussion of Great Britain as a whole and of Northern Ireland's relation to the other British countries, see the WORLD BOOK article on GREAT BRITAIN.

Government

Northern Ireland is part of Great Britain, a constitutional monarchy. Queen Elizabeth II is the head of state, but a Cabinet of government officials called *ministers* actually rules Britain. The *prime minister*

--------- FACTS IN BRIEF ---------

Capital: Belfast.

Official Language: English.

Form of Government: Constitutional monarchy; part of the United Kingdom of Great Britain and Northern Ireland (see GREAT BRITAIN [Government]).

Area: 5,462 square miles. *Greatest Distances*—(north-south) 85 miles; (east-west) 111 miles. *Coastline*—330 miles.

Elevation: *Highest*—Slieve Donard, 2,783 feet above sea level. *Lowest*—The Marsh, near Downpatrick, 1.3 feet below sea level.

Population: *1966 Census*—1,484,775; distribution, 53 per cent urban, 47 per cent rural. *Estimated 1971 Population*—1,539,000; density, 282 persons to the square mile. *Estimated 1976 Population*—1,601,000.

Chief Products: *Agriculture*—cattle, eggs, hogs, milk, potatoes. *Manufacturing*—aircraft, alcoholic beverages, animal feeds, canned foods, Irish linen and other textiles, ships, tobacco products.

Money: *Basic Unit*—pound. Effective Feb. 15, 1971, 100 new pence equal one pound. For the value of the pound in dollars, see MONEY (table: Values [Great Britain]). See also POUND STERLING.

is the chief ruling official. *Parliament* makes the laws of Great Britain. Parliament is made up of the *House of Commons* and the *House of Lords*. Northern Ireland elects 12 of the 630 members of the House of Commons. Most members of the House of Lords are noblemen who inherit their seats. For more information on the British government, see GREAT BRITAIN (Government).

Northern Ireland is the only British country that has its own governor, parliament, prime minister, and cabinet. Its relationship with the British government is somewhat similar to that of a state with the federal government in the United States.

The Governor of Northern Ireland is the country's official head of state. He represents the British monarch and is appointed by the monarch to a six-year term. The governor's duties include approving or rejecting bills passed by the Parliament of Northern Ireland. But he is more of a symbol than a ruler and almost never rejects a bill. As in the British government,

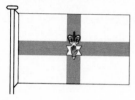

Northern Ireland's Flag has the country's coat of arms over the St. George's cross of the English flag.

The Coat of Arms of Northern Ireland has a six-pointed star and the ancient Ulster symbol of a red hand.

Northern Ireland occupies about a sixth of the island of Ireland. The country is slightly larger than Connecticut.

WORLD BOOK map

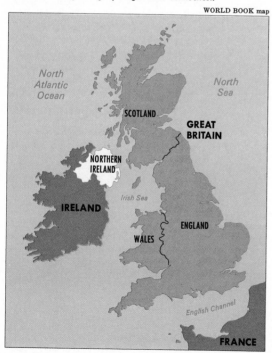

Northern Ireland's prime minister and Cabinet actually hold most of the power.

Parliament of Northern Ireland has two houses—the *House of Commons* and the *Senate*. The House of Commons has 52 members. They are elected but have no fixed terms. Elections must be held at least every five years. But they may be called sooner, and many Parliaments do not last five years. The Senate has 26 members. The lord mayor of Belfast and the lord mayor of Londonderry are honorary members. The members of the House of Commons elect the remaining 24 senators to eight-year terms.

The Parliament of Northern Ireland deals with local matters, such as maintaining law and order, administering the educational system, and regulating commerce and agriculture. Certain other powers, such as maintaining armed forces, levying income taxes, and dealing with other nations, are reserved for the Parliament of Great Britain.

The Prime Minister and Cabinet. The prime minister is the leader of the political party that has a majority in the House of Commons. He selects other members of Parliament to serve as ministers in the Cabinet and to head the various government departments.

The Unionist Party has controlled the government throughout the history of Northern Ireland. Other parties include the Nationalist Party and the Northern Ireland Labour Party.

The Courts. The Supreme Court of Judicature is Northern Ireland's highest court. It consists of a chief justice and six associate justices. The British monarch appoints the justices on the advice of the British government. Other courts include the Court of Criminal Appeal and county and civil courts.

Local Government in Northern Ireland is divided into various units. The main units are two *county boroughs* and six *counties*. The country's two largest cities—Belfast and Londonderry—make up the county boroughs, which are independent of the counties. The counties are subdivided into 27 *rural districts*, 24 *urban districts*, and 9 *boroughs*. Rural districts cover farm areas. Urban districts and boroughs cover small cities and villages. Each unit has its own elected council. The councils are responsible for such services as public health, public welfare, and sanitation.

Plans are being made to reorganize Northern Ireland's system of local government. The plans call for a sharp reduction in the number of local councils.

People

The way of life in Northern Ireland is closer to that in the rest of Great Britain than to that in the Republic of Ireland. This is because about two-thirds of the people of Northern Ireland are descended from English and Scottish Protestants. Most of the remaining third are of Irish Catholic descent.

Many Protestants of Northern Ireland belong to an organization called the *Orange Order* and are known as *Orangemen*. These terms date back to the late 1600's, when William of Orange, a Protestant, defeated James II, a Roman Catholic, in a struggle for the English throne. William became a hero to the Protestants of Ulster. On Orange Day, July 12, Orangemen still

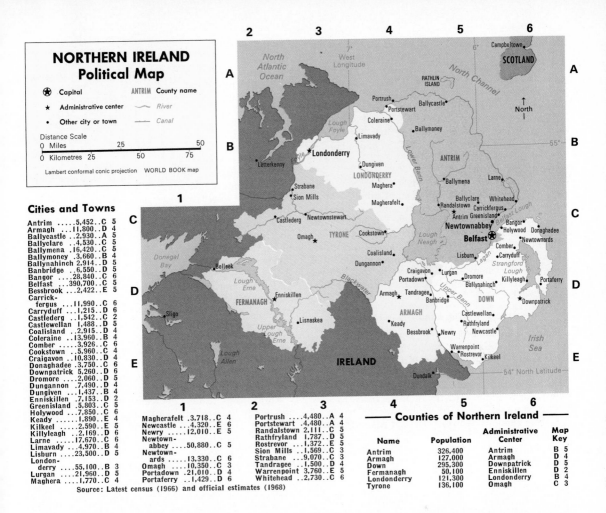

Cities and Towns

Antrim .....5,452..C 5
Armagh ...11,800..D 4
Ballycastle ..2,930..A 5
Ballyclare ..4,530..C 5
Ballymena .16,420..C 5
Ballymoney .3,660..B 4
Ballynahinch 2,914..D 5
Banbridge .6,550..D 5
Bangor ...28,840..C 6
Belfast 390,700..C 5
Bessbrook ..2,422..E 5
Carrick-
  fergus ..11,990..C 6
Carryduff ..1,215..D 6
Castlederg ..1,542..C 2
Castlewellan 1,488..D 5
Coalisland ..2,915..D 4
Coleraine .13,960..B 4
Comber ....3,926..C 6
Cookstown ..5,960..C 4
Craigavon .10,830..D 4
Donaghadee .3,750..C 6
Downpatrick 5,260..D 6
Dromore ...2,060..D 5
Dungannon .7,490..D 4
Dungiven ...1,437..B 4
Enniskillen .7,153..D 2
Greenisland .5,803..C 5
Holywood ..7,850..C 6
Keady .....1,890..E 4
Kilkeel ....2,590..E 5
Killyleagh ..2,169..D 6
Larne ....17,670..C 6
Limavady ..4,970..B 4
Lisburn ...23,500..D 5
London-
  derry ...55,100..B 3
Lurgan ...21,960..D 5
Maghera ...1,770..C 4

Magherafelt .3,718..C 4
Newcastle ..4,320..E 6
Newry ....12,010..E 5
Newtown-
  abbey ...50,880..C 5
Newtown-
  ards ....13,330..C 6
Omagh ...10,350..C 3
Portadown .21,010..D 4
Portaferry ..1,429..D 6

Portrush ...4,480..A 4
Portstewart .4,480..A 4
Randalstown 2,111..C 5
Rathfryland 1,787..D 5
Rostrevor ..1,372..E 5
Sion Mills ..1,569..C 3
Strabane ...9,070..C 3
Tandragee ..1,500..D 4
Warrenpoint 3,760..E 5
Whitehead ..2,730..C 6

Source: Latest census (1966) and official estimates (1968)

Counties of Northern Ireland

Name	Population	Administrative Center	Map Key
Antrim	326,400	Antrim	B 5
Armagh	127,000	Armagh	D 4
Down	295,300	Downpatrick	D 5
Fermanagh	50,100	Enniskillen	D 2
Londonderry	121,300	Londonderry	B 4
Tyrone	136,100	Omagh	C 3

celebrate his victory in the Battle of the Boyne (see BOYNE, BATTLE OF THE).

Population. Northern Ireland has a population of about 1,539,000. More than half the people live in cities, towns, or villages. The country has three cities with over 50,000 persons. Belfast, the capital, has a population of 390,700. Londonderry has 55,100 persons, and Newtownabbey has 50,880.

Language. English is the official language throughout Great Britain, and nearly all the people of Northern Ireland speak it. A few persons in rural areas speak Gaelic, which was once used throughout Ireland (see GAELIC LANGUAGE).

Food and Drink. The people of Northern Ireland enjoy simple meals of meat, potatoes, vegetables, and bread. They also eat large amounts of poultry, eggs, dairy products, and fish.

Tea is the most popular drink in Northern Ireland. A favorite alcoholic beverage is beer. Many people enjoy drinking it in their local *pub* (public house). Pubs play an important role in social life throughout Great Britain.

Recreation. Northern Ireland's most popular organized sport is *football*, or soccer. The Irish Football Association regulates the country's nearly 600 amateur football teams. Professional and semiprofessional teams belong to the Irish League. Both amateur and profes-

sional teams compete in British and international football matches. See SOCCER.

Other popular sports include cricket, which is played with a bat and ball; Gaelic football, which resembles soccer; handball; hurling and camogie, which are somewhat similar to field hockey; and Rugby, a form of football. Many people enjoy boating, fishing, golf, hunting, and swimming. See CRICKET; FIELD HOCKEY; HANDBALL; RUGBY FOOTBALL.

Education in Northern Ireland is supervised by the Ministry of Education and local education authorities. These local groups are committees of county and county borough councils.

All children in Northern Ireland between the ages of 5 and 15 are required to attend school. Nearly all of them go to schools that are supported by public funds.

Northern Ireland has three types of high schools—grammar schools, secondary schools, and technical schools. *Grammar schools* prepare students for college. *Secondary schools* provide general and vocational education. *Technical schools* offer specialized courses, with emphasis on mathematics and science. Education in secondary and technical schools is free. Grammar school students must pay fees, but about 90 per cent of them receive scholarships.

There are two universities in Northern Ireland—the Queen's University of Belfast and the New University of Ulster in Coleraine. The Queen's University has more than 6,000 students, and the New University has about 400.

Religion. About two-thirds of the people of Northern Ireland are Protestants. The Church of Ireland, also called the Anglican Church, and the Presbyterian Church are the country's largest Protestant churches. Most of the remaining third of the people are Roman Catholics.

One of Northern Ireland's major problems is the serious split between Protestants and Catholics. Many Protestants fear that Catholics in both Northern Ireland and the Republic of Ireland want to unite the two countries and put Northern Ireland under Catholic control. On the other hand, Roman Catholics in Northern Ireland claim that the Protestants have violated their civil rights. For more information on the split between the Protestants and Catholics, see the *History* section of this article.

The Land

Northern Ireland occupies the northeastern corner of the island of Ireland. It covers 5,462 square miles. The country is bordered on the south and west by the Republic of Ireland, which occupies the rest of the island. The North Channel separates Northern Ireland from Scotland to the northeast, and the Irish Sea separates it from England to the southeast.

Surface Features. Northern Ireland is a land of rolling plains and low mountains. The plains, which cover the central part of the country, include fertile fields and pasturelands. The mountains, which are near the coast, have many deep, scenic valleys. In some areas, the plains reach to the coast.

The highest peak in Northern Ireland, 2,783-foot Slieve Donard, rises in the Mourne Mountains near the southeast coast. Other mountain ranges include the Sperrin Mountains in the northwest and the Mountains of Antrim in the northeast.

Lakes, Rivers, and Bays. Smooth, clear lakes, which are called *loughs* (pronounced *lahks*), lie throughout Northern Ireland. Lough Neagh, near the center of the country, covers 147 square miles and is the largest lake in the British Isles (see LOUGH NEAGH).

The largest river in Northern Ireland is the River Bann. The Bann actually is two rivers. The Upper Bann, which is 47½ miles long, begins in the Mourne Mountains and flows northwestward into the southern end of Lough Neagh. The Lower Bann begins at the northern end of the lake and flows north 38 miles into the Atlantic Ocean. Many small, winding rivers empty into the Bann.

Several large bays, which are also called loughs, cut into Northern Ireland's coast. Lough Foyle and Belfast Lough provide excellent harbors for Londonderry and Belfast.

Economy

The economy of Northern Ireland depends mainly on manufacturing and agriculture. Manufacturing has been important since the Industrial Revolution began in Great Britain in the 1700's. Agriculture is important because more than 80 per cent of the land in Northern

Ireland is fertile enough for crop farming or grazing.

Natural Resources. Fertile fields and pasturelands are Northern Ireland's chief natural resources. The country also has large deposits of peat. The peat, which is cut from *bogs* (swamplands), is burned for heating and cooking (see PEAT). Other natural resources include chalk, granite, and sandstone. Excellent fishing grounds lie off the coast.

Manufacturing. Northern Ireland's chief manufactured product is Irish linen, which is world famous for its excellent quality. Most linen mills are near Belfast and Londonderry.

Other mills in Northern Ireland produce cord, twine, and rope; woolen and cotton textiles; and man-made fibers. The production of man-made fibers has grown rapidly with the construction of new factories near Belfast and Carrickfergus.

Heavy manufacturing in Northern Ireland is centered in the Belfast area. Shipyards there have built many warships and ocean liners, including the famous *Titanic*. Aircraft plants in the area make airliners and military planes. Aluminum produced in nearby Larne is used by the aircraft industry. Other products manufactured in Northern Ireland include alcoholic beverages, animal feeds, beet sugar, canned foods, chemicals, tobacco products, and vegetable oils.

Agriculture. Cattle, eggs, hogs, milk, and potatoes are Northern Ireland's most important agricultural products. Much barley, hay, and oats are grown for animal feed. Other farm products include butter,

PHYSICAL MAP OF NORTHERN IRELAND

A large plateau about 500 feet above sea level covers most of Northern Ireland. The surface is lowest near the center around Lough Neagh, the largest lake in the British Isles. The land rises gently in the mountains surrounding the plateau.

Distance Scale
0 Miles 20 40 60
0 Kilometres 40 60 80

WORLD BOOK map

poultry, sheep, and turnips. Orchards in the south produce apples, pears, and plums.

Transportation and Trade. More than 14,000 miles of roads and highways and about 200 miles of railroad track crisscross Northern Ireland. Ships from many countries dock at Belfast, the country's main seaport. Ferry services run between various ports in Northern Ireland and cities on the west coasts of England and Scotland. More than 150 miles of rivers and canals provide inland water routes. Aldergrove Airport, near Belfast, has flights to several countries.

Northern Ireland trades mainly with the Republic of Ireland and with the other countries of Great Britain. Its chief exports include clothing; finished cotton, linen, and rayon fabrics; and machines for weaving textiles. Northern Ireland also ships large quantities of eggs, livestock, meat, and poultry to the other British countries. Chief imports include cotton, flax, and rayon yarn; machinery; and unfinished cotton and woolen goods. Most of the flax fiber used in making Irish linen is imported from Belgium and France.

History

Protestant Settlement. Ireland came under English rule in 1541, when Henry VIII of England declared himself king of Ireland. Henry tried to introduce Protestantism into Ireland. But the Irish people, most of whom were Roman Catholics, objected and began a series of revolts against English rule. In 1603, Elizabeth I of England put down an uprising led by Catholics in Ulster, a large province in northeastern Ireland. James I, who followed Elizabeth as ruler of England, tried to prevent further revolts by seizing the Catholics' land in Ulster and giving it to English and Scottish Protestants. This action was partly responsible for the Prot-

estant majority that still exists in Northern Ireland.

Economic and Political Differences began to develop during the 1700's between Catholics in southern Ireland and Protestants in Ulster. In the south, an increasing population, unequal distribution of the land, and declines in industry led to low standards of living. In the north, textile manufacturing and shipbuilding flourished, and standards of living rose. The Protestants controlled Ireland's Parliament and, together with the British, restricted the rights of Catholics.

In 1800, the British and Irish parliaments each passed the Act of Union, which ended Ireland's Parliament and made the country part of Great Britain. But many Catholics still demanded freedom from Britain.

In 1886, the British Liberal Party supported a plan called *home rule*. Under this plan, all Ireland would have remained part of Great Britain, but the country would have had its own parliament for domestic affairs. Ulster Protestants, who feared a Catholic parliament, formed the Unionist Party to oppose the plan. The British Parliament passed a home rule bill over Ulster opposition in 1914. But the outbreak of World War I (1914-1918) prevented home rule from going into effect.

The Division of Ireland. In 1919, 73 Irish members of the British Parliament met in Dublin and declared all Ireland an independent republic. Violent fighting then broke out between the Irish rebels and British forces. In 1920, the British Parliament passed the Government of Ireland Act. This act divided Ireland into two separate countries and gave each some powers of self-government. Ulster Protestants accepted the act, and the state of Northern Ireland was formed from 6 counties in Ulster. But southern Catholics rejected the act and demanded complete independence. In 1921, southern leaders and Great Britain signed a treaty that

Textile Manufacturing is an important industry in Northern Ireland. These wool yarns will be woven into tweed, one of the many types of cloth made in Belfast and Londonderry mills.

NORTHERN IRELAND

Pictorial Parade

British Troops built barricades in 1969 to separate the Protestant and Roman Catholic areas of Belfast. The troops were sent in following bloody fighting between the two religious groups.

created the Irish Free State from 23 southern counties and 3 counties of Ulster. In 1949, the Irish Free State cut all ties with Britain and became the independent Republic of Ireland.

Problems of Division. Many Roman Catholics in Northern Ireland refused to accept the 1920 division of Ireland, and the new government made little effort to win their loyalty. In some parts of the country where Catholics formed a majority, election districts were set up to make sure that Unionist minorities won control of local councils. The councils tried to establish separate living areas for Catholics and Protestants. As a result, the two groups, in time, became almost completely separated.

The division of Ireland was also opposed by the Irish Free State and, later, by the Republic of Ireland. Beginning in 1921, armed groups crossed into Northern Ireland and attacked British government installations. Between 1956 and 1962, frequent attacks were carried out by a group called the Irish Republican Army (I.R.A.). The raiders hoped to force the British to give up control of the country. Because of these attacks, Northern Ireland's police force, the Royal Ulster Constabulary, was given heavy arms. In addition, an all-Protestant volunteer force called the Ulster Special Constabulary was formed to assist the police.

The Civil Rights Movement. Catholics in Northern Ireland have long claimed that Protestants have violated their civil rights and discriminated against them in jobs, housing, and other areas. In 1967, the Northern Ireland Civil Rights Association was established to work for equal rights for all citizens.

On Oct. 5, 1968, the association planned a march in Londonderry to demonstrate its strength and to demand reforms. The government tried to stop the march, and bloody riots broke out. Following the riots, the British government persuaded Northern Ireland's prime minister, Terence M. O'Neill, to establish a number of reforms. But conservative Unionists objected, and O'Neill resigned in 1969. James D. Chichester-Clark then became prime minister.

Serious riots occurred again in July and August, 1969, in Belfast and Londonderry. British troops were sent to Northern Ireland to maintain order, and the British government persuaded Chichester-Clark to accept far-reaching reforms, including an unarmed, nonpolitical police force and agencies to guard against discrimination. A new Cabinet post, that of minister for community relations, was also created. British troops remained in Northern Ireland, but they were unable to prevent bloody rioting from occurring again during the early 1970's. The continuing conflict led Chichester-Clark to resign in 1971. He was succeeded as prime minister by Brian Faulkner, a former Cabinet member.

Before 1920, the history of Northern Ireland was part of the history of Ireland. Since 1920, it has been part of the history of Great Britain. For the story of Ireland and Britain, see IRELAND (History) and GREAT BRITAIN (History).

JOHN MAGEE, NORMAN RUNNION, and J. WREFORD WATSON

Related Articles in WORLD BOOK include:

Belfast	Linen	Lough Neagh
Giant's Causeway	Londonderry	Ulster

Outline

I. Government
 A. The Governor
 B. Parliament
 C. The Prime Minister and Cabinet
 D. The Courts
 E. Local Government

II. People
 A. Population
 B. Language
 C. Food and Drink
 D. Recreation
 E. Education
 F. Religion

III. The Land
 A. Surface Features
 B. Lakes, Rivers, and Bays

IV. Economy
 A. Natural Resources
 B. Manufacturing
 C. Agriculture
 D. Transportation and Trade

V. History

Questions

What are Northern Ireland's most important natural resources?

How does the government in Northern Ireland differ from that in the other British countries?

What political party has controlled the government of Northern Ireland throughout the country's history? Why was this party formed?

What is Northern Ireland's chief manufactured product?

Why is there a split between Protestants and Roman Catholics in Northern Ireland?

What countries are Northern Ireland's chief trading partners?

Why was the Ulster Special Constabulary formed?

What is Northern Ireland's most popular organized sport?

What was the Government of Ireland Act?

Why is agriculture important in Northern Ireland?

NORTHERN LIGHTS. See Aurora Borealis.

NORTHERN MICHIGAN UNIVERSITY is a coeducational liberal arts school at Marquette. Its graduate-school courses are conducted in cooperation with the University of Michigan. It grants A.B., B.S., and B.Mus. degrees. The library contains the Moses Coit Tyler Collection of Americana. The university was opened in 1899. For enrollment, see Universities and Colleges (table).

NORTHERN MONTANA COLLEGE. See Universities and Colleges (table).

NORTHERN RHODESIA. See Zambia.

NORTHERN STATE COLLEGE is a coeducational school at Aberdeen, S.Dak. The college offers bachelor's degrees in education and liberal arts, and master's degrees in education. Courses include fine arts, humanities, science, and mathematics. It was founded in 1901. For enrollment, see Universities and Colleges (table).

NORTHERN TERRITORY is a tropical area in north-central Australia. It has large regions of only partly explored land. It covers 520,280 square miles. Its population of 62,524 includes about 21,120 aborigines whose ancestors lived in Australia before white people arrived (see Australia [The Aborigines]). Tribal conditions still exist among some of the territory's aborigines. Darwin is the territory's administrative center and largest city. For location, see Australia (political map).

The territory's flat coastline of 1,040 miles has many bays. The interior is mostly flat. The northern area has excellent grazing regions. The south is sandy. Rivers include the Victoria, Daly, and Roper. Average January temperatures range between 80° and 90° F., and July temperatures average about 70° F. The annual rainfall varies greatly. Darwin, on the northern coast, has an average of 58 inches. In the dry interior, rainfall seldom exceeds 11 inches a year.

Cattle breeding is the chief industry in the Northern Territory. Large cattle *stations* (ranches) cover thousands of miles in the territory. About 1,067,000 cattle, 36,000 horses, and 9,000 sheep graze in the Northern Territory. Other important industries include pearling and mining. Bauxite, copper, gold, mica, tantalite, tin, tungsten, and uranium are the chief minerals. Mining has developed slowly, because mineral deposits are located far from supply sources. The lack of good transportation and the distance from markets have delayed the full development of the Northern Territory.

Some of the people ride on horseback to hunt smooth-haired water buffaloes. These animals were imported from India about a hundred years ago, and now roam the Northern Territory plains in great numbers.

The federal government provides medical services for the Northern Territory. A "Flying Doctor" operation uses radio and aircraft service to help the sick and injured at isolated mines and cattle stations.

The government of South Australia operates the educational system in the Northern Territory for the federal government.

The Northern Territory

The Northern Territory was part of New South Wales until 1863 when it was annexed to the province of South Australia. The Australian Commonwealth government took over the administration in 1911. A commonwealth administrator now handles the territory's affairs. The territory has an 18-member council. The commonwealth appoints 10 of them. The people elect the other 8. The Legislative Council can adopt non-financial measures. The Northern Territory elects one member to the federal House of Representatives. He can vote only on matters solely relating to the territory.

The explorer John McDouall Stuart entered the Northern Territory in 1860. His explorations opened up much of the Northern Territory. An overland telegraph line, completed in the 1870's, followed Stuart's trail from Adelaide to Darwin.　　　　C. M. H. Clark

See also Darwin.

NORTHFIELD, Minn. (pop. 10,235; alt. 915 ft.), in the center of Minnesota's dairy country, is known for its Holstein-Friesian cattle and its large creameries. It lies about 40 miles south of St. Paul in southeastern Minnesota (see Minnesota [political map]). Industries of Northfield include the manufacture of cereal, wood-working machines, sheet-metal products, and plastics goods. The city is named after John W. North, who founded it in 1856. It is the home of St. Olaf and Carleton colleges. Northfield has a mayor-council form of government.　　　　Harold L. Hagg

NORTHLAND COLLEGE. See Universities and Colleges (table).

NORTHMAN. See Viking.

NORTHROP, JOHN HOWARD (1891-　　), an American biochemist, shared the 1946 Nobel prize in chemistry with James B. Sumner and W. M. Stanley. They prepared in crystalline form several pure enzymes and one of the viruses which destroy bacteria (see Enzyme). Northrop's writings on enzymes include *Crystalline Enzymes* (1939). He was born in Yonkers, N.Y. He received his doctoral degree from Columbia University in 1915 and became a member of the Rockefeller Institute (now Rockefeller University) in New York City in 1924.

NORTHROP INSTITUTE OF TECHNOLOGY is a privately controlled school of engineering for men in Inglewood, Calif. It offers B.S. degrees in various fields of engineering. The school operates throughout the year, and students may complete the regular four-year program in three years. Northrop Institute was founded in 1942. For enrollment, see Universities and Colleges (table).

NORTHUMBERLAND. See England (political map).

NORTHWEST CHRISTIAN COLLEGE. See Universities and Colleges (table).

NORTHWEST MISSOURI STATE COLLEGE is a state-controlled, coeducational teachers college at Maryville, Mo. It offers A.B. and B.S. degrees, and master's degrees in education. The college was founded in 1905, as the Fifth District Normal School. The school received its present name in 1949. For the enrollment of Northwest Missouri State College, see Universities and Colleges (table).

NORTHWEST NAZARENE COLLEGE. See Universities and Colleges (table).

MINN

Lake Superior

MICHIGAN

WISCONSIN

Lake Michigan

MICHIGAN

Lake Huron

ILLINOIS

INDIANA

Lake Erie

OHIO

The Northwest Territory, governed by the Ordinance of 1787, was formed into five complete states and a part of Minnesota.

Freedom of Religious Worship was guaranteed to all settlers in the Northwest Territory by the Ordinance of 1787.

The Ordinance Laid the Basis for education in the Northwest Territory by its declaration for the encouragement of schools.

NORTHWEST ORDINANCE

Before State Governments were set up in the Northwest Territory, the laws of the thirteen original states were enforced there.

Just Dealing with Indians in the Northwest Territory was provided for in the Ordinance.

The Prohibition of Slavery strengthened the ranks of the antislavery states in the Union.

NORTHWEST ORDINANCE, passed by the United States Congress on July 13, 1787, was one of the most important laws ever adopted. The ordinance provided for the government of the region north of the Ohio River and west of Pennsylvania, then called the Northwest Territory. It became a model for all territories that later entered the Union as states. The ordinance was largely the work of General Nathan Dane, Rufus King, and Manasseh Cutler (see KING [Rufus]).

Under the terms of the ordinance, the territories could achieve equality with the older states by passing through three steps leading to full self-government. (1) Congress, which governed the territory, appointed a governor, a secretary, and three judges. (2) When the territory, or any division of it, attained an adult male population of 5,000, it could choose a legislature and send to Congress a delegate who could speak but not vote. (3) When the total population reached 60,000, the territory could apply for admission into the Union on terms of full equality with the older states. The ordi-

nance removed the danger of colonial rebellion, because it assured the territories of participation in the national government.

The Northwest Ordinance contained more than a plan of government. It laid the groundwork for social and political democracy in the West. It forbade slavery. All persons were guaranteed trial by jury and freedom of religious worship. The ordinance guaranteed fair treatment for the Indians, and declared that "means of education shall forever be encouraged."

The terms of the ordinance were so attractive that pioneers poured into the new territory. In 1788, one of the first groups of settlers founded the town of Marietta, Ohio. Thousands of families followed the first settlers in the westward movement. The territory eventually became five states—Ohio, Indiana, Illinois, Michigan, and Wisconsin. It included what is now the part of Minnesota east of the Mississippi River. RAY ALLEN BILLINGTON

See also NORTHWEST TERRITORY; OHIO COMPANY.

NORTHWEST ORIENT AIRLINES. See AIRLINE.

NORTHWEST PASSAGE. The explorers who followed Columbus soon found that North America was not a part of Asia, as they had believed at first. At this time, British, French, and Dutch adventurers were more interested in finding an easy route to Asia than they were in exploring and settling North America. So they began to look for a "Northwest Passage," or waterway, that would take them around or through the continent.

The story of the search for the Northwest Passage is an exciting tale of adventure and heroism. In 1524, Giovanni Verrazano, sailing under the French flag, tried to find the Northwest Passage. He probably explored as far north as Maine.

Jacques Cartier, while exploring for France in 1535, found the St. Lawrence River. He was seeking a route to China. Henry Hudson was sent out many years later by the Dutch East India Company to find a shorter route to the South Seas. He thought he had found that route in 1609 when he sailed into New York Bay and some distance up the Hudson River.

No country tried harder than England to find the passage. Sir Martin Frobisher began a series of English expeditions in 1576. Other Englishmen continued these explorations for 300 years. These men sailed far to the north in their search. Frobisher made many important discoveries, including Frobisher Bay, an indentation in Baffin Island (later called Baffin Land). John Davis followed Frobisher, and sailed into the strait that now bears his name. In 1616, William Baffin and Robert Bylot sailed up Davis Strait and around the great channel ever since known as Baffin Bay. Russia, Holland, and Denmark took an interest in the search.

By the close of the 1700's, the territory that had been explored included Hudson Strait, Hudson Bay, Davis Strait, Baffin Bay, and the icy seas from Greenland to Spitsbergen (now Svalbard) and from Spitsbergen to Novaya Zemlya. For details of this important period of exploration, see EXPLORATION AND DISCOVERY.

Commander John Ross (1777-1856), a Scottish explorer, began the final series of expeditions in 1818. The most noted of the explorers to follow him was Sir John Franklin, a British explorer. Franklin died trying to find

a passage to Asia. Many people honor Franklin as the first discoverer of the passage, although he never completed the voyage through it. His ships reached a point within a few miles of waters that lead directly to the Asiatic shore. In 1850 Sir Robert McClure (1807-1873) forced a passage northward to the northern shore of the island Banks Land. He anchored his ship in a bay which he named God's Mercy, and tried to continue his trip by foot. But his attempt did not succeed.

In 1906, Roald Amundsen's ship, the *Gjoa*, completed the first trip through the Northwest Passage. Amundsen traveled from east to west. The first west-to-east voyage was completed in 1942 by the Royal Canadian Mounted Police schooner, *St. Roch*. McClure Strait was conquered in 1954 by U.S. Navy and Coast Guard icebreakers. Three U.S. Coast Guard cutters, the *Spar*, the *Bramble*, and the *Storis*, aided by the Canadian Navy icebreaker, the *Labrador*, made the west-to-east trip in 1957. They traveled through a narrow channel called *Bellot Strait*. This passage is big enough for freighters. It permits cargo ships to unload supplies for the Distant Early Warning radar line in Northern Canada. The *Spar* was the first ship ever to sail completely around North America. It started from Bristol, R.I., and went south to the Panama Canal, then up the Pacific Coast, through the Northwest Passage, and back to Bristol.

In 1958, the U.S. atomic submarine *Seadragon* made the first Atlantic to Pacific crossing of the Northwest Passage. It traveled 850 miles from Lancaster Sound, through the Canadian Arctic islands, and into McClure Strait. In 1969, the U.S. icebreaker-tanker *Manhattan* became the first commercial ship to complete the passage. It sailed to Alaska by way of the Prince of Wales Strait.   RAY ALLEN BILLINGTON

Map of the Northwest Passage Shows the Different Routes Traveled by Explorers.

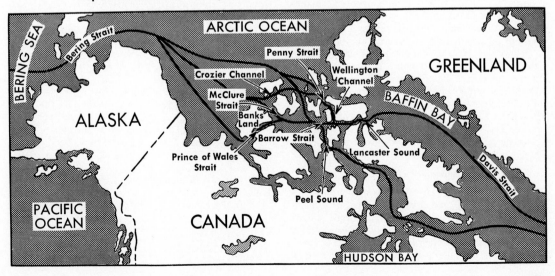

NORTHWEST TERRITORIES

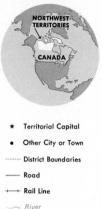

★   Territorial Capital

●   Other City or Town

-----   District Boundaries

——   Road

+—+—+   Rail Line

～～   River

All islands in Hudson Bay, James Bay, and Ungava Bay are part of the Northwest Territories.

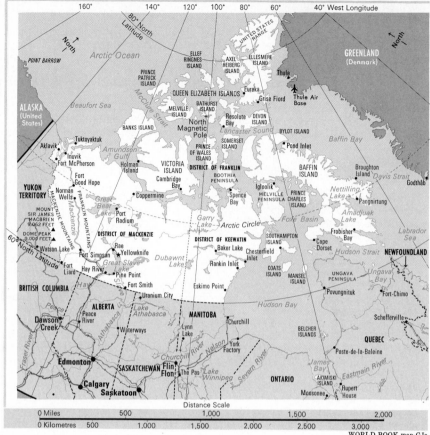

WORLD BOOK map-GJa

NORTHWEST TERRITORIES is a vast region that covers almost a third of Canada. It stretches from the northern boundaries of the Canadian provinces to within 500 miles of the North Pole. The region includes the Arctic homeland of some 8,000 Canadian Eskimos and about 6,000 northern Indians.

Until the 1950's, the Northwest Territories remained one of the world's last undeveloped frontiers. The region has one railroad and only one major highway. Pioneers are developing its great mineral wealth.

Yellowknife serves as the capital of the Northwest Territories. A commissioner and a 12-man council govern the Territories. The Canadian Department of Indian Affairs and Northern Development once handled the administration of the Northwest Territories. A territorial public service now handles most of the administrative duties.

For the relationship of the Northwest Territories to the rest of Canada, see CANADA.

The Land and Its Resources

Location and Size. The Northwest Territories lies west of Greenland, and north and west of Quebec. The provinces of Manitoba, Saskatchewan, Alberta, and British Columbia border the Territories on the south. The Yukon Territory lies to the west. The Northwest Territories includes a group of Arctic islands north of the Canadian mainland, and all the islands in Hudson, James, and Ungava bays. The Territories covers 1,304,903 square miles. The *Map* shows that about half the Northwest Territories is located north of the Arctic Circle.

Districts. The Northwest Territories is divided into three geographic districts: Mackenzie, Keewatin, and Franklin.

The District of Mackenzie (527,490 sq. mi.) lies east of the Yukon Territory. The rugged Mackenzie Mountains rise along the Yukon boundary. High peaks include Mount Sir James MacBrien (9,062 feet) and Dome Peak (9,000 feet).

East of the Mackenzie Mountains is the Mackenzie River Valley, a northward continuation of the Great Central Plain of North America (see PLAIN). The Mackenzie River is the longest waterway in Canada. From its most distant source to the point at which it empties into the Arctic Ocean, the river is 2,635 miles long. The Franklin Mountains rise to elevations of about 5,000 feet, and lie along the east bank of the Mackenzie River.

More than half of Mackenzie District is east of the

S. M. Hodgson, the contributor of this article, is Commissioner of the Northwest Territories.

plains region in the rocky Canadian Shield area (see CANADIAN SHIELD). Lakes, swamps, and sand plains cover much of this area. Two of the largest lakes in Canada, Great Bear Lake and Great Slave Lake, lie east of the plain of the Mackenzie River.

The first main settlements of the Territories grew along the banks of the Mackenzie River during the late 1700's. In the 1930's, the center of population began to shift to mining areas around Great Slave Lake and Great Bear Lake, which supply most of the minerals mined in the Territories. Minerals include gold, petroleum, lead, zinc, and natural gas. The Mackenzie District is also the main source of forestry and fishery products.

The District of Keewatin (228,160 sq. mi.) lies east of Mackenzie District, within the Canadian Shield region. Keewatin extends eastward to Quebec and includes all the islands in Hudson, James, and Ungava bays. *Keewatin* means *north wind* in the language of the Cree Indians, who once hunted in the region. Most of Keewatin is a rocky plateau called the *Barrens*. It has little vegetation.

The District of Franklin (549,253 sq. mi.) includes the Canadian Arctic islands and the Melville and Boothia peninsulas in the northeast. Large islands near the mainland include Baffin, one of the largest islands in

Heavy Polar Ice dots the northern waters of the Northwest Territories the year around, often making navigation difficult.

────────── **FACTS IN BRIEF** ──────────

Capital: Yellowknife.

Government: *National*—member of the House of Commons from the Northwest Territories, 1. *Territorial*—members of the territorial legislative council, 12.

Area: 1,304,903 square miles (including 51,465 square miles of inland water). *Greatest Distances*—(east-west) 1,800 miles; (north-south) 1,660 miles.

Elevation: *Highest*—Mount Sir James MacBrien in the Mackenzie Mountains, 9,062 feet above sea level; *Lowest*—sea level along the coast.

Population: 28,738 (1966). *Density*—2.2 persons to every 100 square miles.

Chief Products: *Mining*—gold, petroleum, lead, zinc. *Fishing Industry*—lake trout, whitefish. *Fur Industry*—muskrat, white fox, mink, beaver, seal.

Territorial Coat of Arms: Two golden whales at the top guard the compass rose. The wavy line crossing the white chief (top of the shield) is blue. The field below has red and green sections. The bars of gold stand for mineral resources, and the fox for the fur industry.

Territorial Flag: The flag has three vertical panels. The panels on the left and right are blue for the skies and waters, and the wider center panel is white for the snows of the Territories. The shield from the territorial coat of arms appears in the center of the white panel. The flag was adopted in 1969.

Territorial Motto: Canada's Northland.

Territorial Flower: Mountain Avens.

National Film Board

The Territorial Coat of Arms

Small White Whales come into the coastal waters in July. Eskimos of the Mackenzie River Delta harpoon the animals from small boats and bring them to shore stations to be cut up.

A Gleaming White Mace rests on the table at meetings of the Northwest Territories council. It symbolizes royal and legislative authority.

the world; Banks; and Victoria. The Arctic islands, north of McClure Strait and Lancaster Sound, are known as the Queen Elizabeth Islands. Ellesmere Island, the largest in the group, has a high mountain range, the United States Range. Its highest peak is about 8,200 feet above sea level. Baffin and Ellesmere islands have spectacular, rugged mountain formations and deeply cut fiords.

Not one tree grows in the whole District of Franklin, because the average July temperature is below 50° F. But colorful flowers bloom abundantly in some places during the summer.

The northern part of the District of Franklin is almost completely uninhabited. There are some employees of government weather and radio stations, and of an airfield at Resolute Bay on Cornwallis Island. Some Eskimos live at Resolute Bay and at Grise Fiord. The Royal Canadian Mounted Police are also stationed in these two places.

Climate. Most of the District of Mackenzie has fairly warm summers and cold winters. The towns of Aklavik

and Inuvik have average temperatures of 56° F. in July, and −18° F. in January. Temperatures in Fort Smith, near the Alberta border, average 61° F. in July, and −13° F. in January.

The District of Keewatin has an Arctic climate, with long, cold winters and short, cool summers. The average July temperature is about 42° F., and January temperatures range around −25° F.

Temperatures on the Arctic islands vary little from those in the District of Keewatin, except in the Queen Elizabeth group. Weather stations in the far north report averages of 25° F. in July, and −40° F. in January.

Most of the Northwest Territories receives little moisture. Average annual precipitation ranges from 15 inches in the southern part of Mackenzie District to about 2½ inches on Ellesmere Island. Most of it falls as snow. About 40 inches of snow falls every year on the mainland, and about 60 inches on some of the islands.

The highest temperature recorded in the Territories was 103° F. at Fort Smith on July 18, 1941. The lowest, −69° F., occurred at Fort Simpson on Feb. 1, 1947; at Fort Good Hope on Feb. 4, 1947; and at Lake Hazen on Jan. 4, 1958.

Life of the People

The People. According to the Dominion Bureau of Statistics, the Northwest Territories had a population of 28,738 in 1966. This was an increase of about 25 per cent over the 1961 population. The Territories has an average of about 2.2 persons per 100 square miles. The towns of Yellowknife, Fort Smith, Hay River, and Inuvik have a combined population of about 9,900. Most of the rest of the people live in small mining and fur-trading settlements. The population includes whites, Indians, Eskimos, and *métis* (persons of mixed French and Indian descent).

Most of the Eskimos live in the interior of Keewatin, around the shores of Hudson Bay, and on Baffin and some southern Arctic islands. Most of the whites live in Mackenzie District.

The Village of Tuktoyaktuk lies on Beaufort Sea in the northwestern part of the Mackenzie District. The village serves as a cargo transfer point from Mackenzie River steamers to sea-going vessels.

National Film Board

Eskimo Children in the Northwest Territories attend schools that are run by the government. Children from remote areas live in student dormitories during the school year.

All of the Indians live in the District of Mackenzie, and make their living mainly by trapping and hunting. They also work for government agencies, in industry and commerce, and as guides for tourists.

The income of the Eskimos in Keewatin and on the eastern Arctic islands comes from trapping, hunting, and handicrafts. Eskimos also work on government defense projects and in the public service. Many Eskimos in the west have gradually adopted the way of life of the white settlers. Most Eskimos now live in small, prefabricated houses. Igloos have almost disappeared.

The Roman Catholic, Anglican, and Pentecostal churches are the largest churches in the Northwest Territories. Most of the Indians are Catholics. Most of the Eskimos belong to the Anglican Church. Most of the whites belong to one of those three churches or to the United Church of Canada.

Towns. Yellowknife, Hay River, and Fort Smith are the only incorporated towns in the Northwest Territories. Inuvik is the only incorporated village. Yellowknife, the capital, is in the center of a gold-mining area, and is by far the largest town. Aklavik, on the Mackenzie River Delta, long ranked second in size. But frequent flooding of the area discouraged further growth. For this reason, the federal government began building Inuvik, about 30 miles away, in 1955. Inuvik has replaced Aklavik as the administrative, educational, and medical care center in the area. Most communities in the Northwest Territories were once fur-trading posts.

Work of the People

Mining is the most important activity in the Northwest Territories. Geologists believe that almost every known mineral can be found in the region, except bauxite and some others produced in tropical climates. However, mining companies have developed only a small portion of the resources. Gold and other base metals account for most of the mineral output. Gold mining centers in and around Yellowknife. Mines in this area yield over 400,000 ounces of gold a year. Petroleum, also produced in important quantities, comes from the Norman Wells area. A small refinery in the town proc-

esses more than 400,000 barrels of crude oil annually. Pine Point, on the shore of Great Slave Lake, is the site of a lead and zinc mine which was completed in 1966. A railroad leading to the mine was built at the same time. The Northwest Territories is a leading North American producer of lead and zinc. One of the richest iron ore deposits in the world was found on northern Baffin Island near Milne Inlet in the early 1960's. But developers had difficulty transporting the ore out of the island's wilderness. Exploration for minerals continued in the late 1960's.

Fishing Industry ranks second in product value. Almost all commercial fishing is on Great Slave Lake, which supplies whitefish and lake trout. The summer catch brings in nearly 6 million pounds, and winter fishing more than 3 million pounds. *Char* (trout) fishing in the Arctic has attracted both sport and commercial interests. Commercial projects process about $1 million worth of fish a year.

Fur Trapping, which first attracted white men to the Territories in the late 1700's, remained the main source of income for more than a hundred years. It lost some of its importance as mining began to develop after 1920.

413

NORTHWEST TERRITORIES

It also suffered a great setback during the 1940's and 1950's, as fur prices fell and game became scarcer. The principal furs include white fox, muskrat, mink, beaver, and seal. Muskrat and white fox make up a large part of the income from trapping.

Forest Industry and Agriculture have little importance in the Northwest Territories. The only forests are in the District of Mackenzie. The most common trees include spruce, pine, poplar, and birch. Sawmills are located on the Slave and upper Mackenzie rivers.

All the land that could be used for agriculture lies in the District of Mackenzie. The area has nearly 2,000,000 acres of possible farming land, including some grassland now used only for the grazing of buffaloes. Agriculture has not developed beyond the testing stages. The government has operated an experimental farm in Fort Simpson since 1947. The crops produced on this farm include wheat and such coarse grains as oats and barley; root vegetables, such as turnips and radishes; and potatoes, tomatoes, berries, and tree fruits. Most of the food for the people in the territories must be imported from the Canadian provinces.

Transportation. The great distances and the small number of passengers make transportation very expensive. The cheapest and oldest form of transportation is by water. But the Mackenzie River, the main water route, remains frozen for 8 to 9 months each year. A tug and barge service operates from the northern Canadian railroads in Hay River and Waterways, Alta. Waterways is the starting point of a historic route down the Athabasca and Slave rivers. The route then continues across Great Slave Lake to Yellowknife, or down the Mackenzie River to the Arctic Ocean.

Scheduled air services operate in each of the districts. Seaplanes that can land on lakes take supplies to mining and prospecting communities during the summer. After the lakes freeze, airplanes use skis for landing. In 1969, jet aircraft began serving Fort Smith, Frobisher Bay, Hay River, and Yellowknife. Motor vehicles use the highways south of Great Slave Lake. The Great Slave Lake Railroad provides freight service to Hay River and Pine Point. It runs parallel to Mackenzie Highway.

Communication. The Territories has four weekly newspapers, *News of the North*, published in Yellowknife; *Tapwe* and *Hay River News*, published in Hay River; and *Norther*, circulated in Fort Smith; and one biweekly newspaper, *Drum*, published in Inuvik. The Canadian Broadcasting Corporation has radio stations in Frobisher Bay, Inuvik, and Yellowknife. It also provides taped television programs to several areas.

Education

Schools. The Northwest Territories has more than 50 elementary and high schools. These include schools built and operated by the federal government, and school districts financed by local taxation and grants from both the territorial and federal governments. The federal government pays for the education of Indians and Eskimos. Students from isolated areas live in dormitories during the school term. The Territories has no universities or colleges. But the Territories government provides grants and interest-free loans for students who wish to attend universities and colleges elsewhere.

Government

The people elect one representative to the Canadian House of Commons. A commissioner and a legislative

Laying of the Oil Pipeline which supplies the joint United States and Canadian radio and weather station in Eureka was hindered by chunks of ice in Eureka Sound. The station was established on the northwestern shore of Ellesmere Island.

National Film Board

council of 12 members govern the Territories. The federal government appoints the commissioner and five of the council members. The voters elect the other seven every three years from seven electoral districts—Central Arctic, Eastern Arctic, Western Arctic, Mackenzie Delta, Mackenzie North, Mackenzie River, and Mackenzie South. The council meets at least twice a year. It has legislative powers similar to those of provincial legislatures.

The territorial government maintains a departmentalized public service similar to those of provincial governments. The public service handles most of the administration in the Territories. But the federal government controls and administers the Territories' land and resources because their development requires substantial government investment in surveys, exploration, communications, and transportation.

The Northwest Territories Court has one judge appointed by the governor general of Canada. The judge holds court in Yellowknife and in other areas.

History

Exploration. The Vikings were probably the first Europeans to visit the Northwest Territories. They may have sighted the Arctic shores about A.D. 1000. The search for a Northwest Passage to the riches of China encouraged many explorers to look for a route around or through the North American continent to the West. Until 1770, all expeditions traveled by ship. Martin Frobisher, an English seaman, was the first known discoverer of any part of the Northwest Territories. He reached Baffin Island in 1576. See NORTHWEST PASSAGE.

The first man to cross the Territories by land was Samuel Hearne, of the Hudson's Bay Company. He set out in 1770 from Churchill in present-day Manitoba. Traveling overland, Hearne reached the mouth of the Coppermine River in 1771, and explored the Great Slave Lake region on the return journey. In 1789, Sir Alexander Mackenzie discovered the Mackenzie River.

Northwest Territories. The eastern part of the Northwest Territories had belonged to the Hudson's Bay Company since 1670. In that year, King Charles II of England granted the company a vast area called Rupert's Land (see RUPERT'S LAND). In 1870, the Dominion of Canada acquired Rupert's Land, which the British government had bought from the Hudson's Bay Company. At the same time, it obtained from Great Britain a region called the North West Territory which lay north, west, and south of Rupert's Land. The Canadian government organized these two new possessions into the North West Territories, which later became known as the Northwest Territories. See SASKATCHEWAN (North West Territories).

The Territories lost part of the Manitoba area in 1870, when Manitoba became a province. The Yukon Territory was cut off in 1898, and the provinces of Alberta and Saskatchewan in 1905. In 1912, Manitoba, Ontario, and Quebec acquired certain areas.

1930's and 1940's. The discovery of radium ore on the shore of Great Bear Lake in the early 1930's brought the Northwest Territories into world prominence. During World War II, the importance of the radium mine increased because of the demand for uranium, which is found in the same ore as radium. Also, the requirements of the Allied armies brought

about an intensified program for the building of airfields and weather stations in the Territories.

The Canadian government did little to develop the Territories until after World War II. But then, it increased the number of the Royal Canadian Mounted Police detachments, and began to establish weather stations, post offices, schools, and medical services.

Recent Developments. The government expanded its programs for education and medical and social welfare during the 1950's. Interest in mineral and oil exploration also increased. Scheduled airplane flights to Mackenzie District and Baffin Island began in the 1950's. In the 1960's, the government carried on a major road building program. A railway was built from Peace River, Alta., to Great Slave Lake in the mid-1960's to serve mining operations in Pine Point. In 1967, Yellowknife became capital of the Territories. Ottawa had been the previous seat of government. In 1968, the federal government transferred most of its responsibilities in the Northwest Territories to the territorial government in Yellowknife.   S. M. HODGSON

Related Articles in WORLD BOOK include:

HISTORY

Canada, History of	Northwest Passage
Hudson's Bay Company	Rupert's Land
Mackenzie, Sir Alexander	

PHYSICAL FEATURES

Arctic Ocean	Great Slave Lake
Baffin Bay	Mackenzie River
Boothia Peninsula	Melville Island
Canadian Shield	Melville Peninsula
Ellesmere Island	Southampton Island
Great Bear Lake	Slave River

OTHER RELATED ARTICLES

Aklavik	Gold (table)	Lead (table)
Athabaska	Igloo	Mackenzie
Eskimo	Inuvik	Yellowknife
Franklin, District of	Keewatin	Zinc (table)

Outline

I. **The Land and Its Resources**
   A. Location and Size   B. Districts   C. Climate

II. **Life of the People**
   A. The People   B. Towns

III. **Work of the People**
   A. Mining   D. Forest Industry and
   B. Fishing   Agriculture
      Industry   E. Transportation
   C. Fur Trapping   F. Communication

IV. **Education**

V. **Government**

VI. **History**

Questions

What is the longest waterway in Canada?

What three groups of people make up the majority of the population of the Northwest Territories?

Why are there no trees in the District of Franklin?

What two large lakes are in Mackenzie District?

What firm once owned the land of the territories?

Why was the construction of a new town named Inuvik begun in the territories in 1955?

How do the people obtain most of their food?

What minerals account for much of the mining activity in the Northwest Territories?

What attracted explorers to the area of the Northwest Territories in the 1500's and 1600's?

How is public education provided in the territories?

NORTHWEST TERRITORY

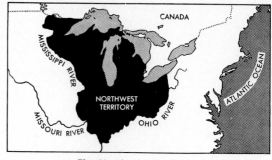

The Northwest Territory

NORTHWEST TERRITORY was a vast tract of land lying north of the Ohio River, west of Pennsylvania, and east of the Mississippi River. It extended to the northern limits of the United States. The states of Ohio, Indiana, Illinois, Michigan, Wisconsin, and part of Minnesota east of the Mississippi were carved out of the Northwest Territory.

Early History. The French, who first occupied the region, had established posts by the early 1700's. Competition between French traders operating from these posts and English trappers from Pennsylvania helped start the French and Indian War (1754-1763). The war ended with the cession of the area to victorious England. See FRENCH AND INDIAN WARS.

During the Revolutionary War (1775-1783), violent fighting took place in the Northwest between the settlers and the British and their Indian allies. The campaign of George Rogers Clark against British-held posts helped win the territory for the United States. The region was ceded after the war. Before the government could open the region to settlement, it had to deal with the claims of Massachusetts, Connecticut, Virginia, and New York. These states insisted that their colonial charters extended their boundaries into this area. The states ceded their claims to Congress between 1781 and 1785, because Maryland refused to approve the Articles of Confederation until it received assurance that the other states would yield their claims.

The land then became a territory of the United States. Congress, eager for revenue from the sale of lands there, adopted the Ordinance of 1785. This law provided for orderly rectangular surveys into mile-square units called *sections*. These were sold at auction at a minimum price of $1 an acre. Congress also struggled with the problem of a government for the territory. Thomas Jefferson in 1784 had drafted a plan that would have divided the territory into several units. These could become states when the population of any one unit equaled the population of the smallest state in the Union. The Eastern States rejected this pro-

posal, because they feared that the many Western States would dominate Congress. Instead, Congress adopted the Northwest Ordinance, or Ordinance of 1787. This provided for the division of the region into from three to five states, and the establishment of a governmental system that would allow them eventual membership in the Union. See NORTHWEST ORDINANCE.

Settlement began at once. The first arrivals were sent out by a New England speculating group called the Ohio Company (see OHIO COMPANY). They founded the town of Marietta at the mouth of the Muskingum River in Ohio. Other interests soon established rival settlements at such villages as Gallipolis and Cincinnati. To the north, colonists clustered about Cleveland in the "Western Reserve" area retained by Connecticut when it ceded its lands to Congress (see WESTERN RESERVE). Arthur St. Clair became the first governor of the Northwest Territory in 1787. He inaugurated the first territorial government on July 15, 1788.

The population grew slowly at first because of the continual Indian attacks. President George Washington sent three expeditions to fight the Indians, but the first two met with disaster. The territory became more peaceful after General Anthony Wayne defeated the Indians in the Battle of Fallen Timbers in 1794. In 1795, Wayne forced the Treaty of Greenville on the defeated Indians. In this treaty, they ceded most of the lands of southern

The Garrison That Later Became the Site of Marietta, Ohio, Was Founded Soon After the Ordinance of 1787.

Deering Library, a Handsome Gothic Structure, Stands on the Evanston Campus of Northwestern University.

Ohio and part of eastern Indiana to the United States. Other land cessions followed during the early 1800's. See INDIAN WARS (Along the Frontier).

As more settlers moved into the region, the Northwest Territory was divided. In 1800, the western part of the region became the Territory of Indiana, with William Henry Harrison as governor. The Michigan Territory was created in 1805, and the Illinois Territory in 1809. Ohio became a state in 1803, Indiana in 1816, Illinois in 1818, Michigan in 1837, and Wisconsin in 1848.   RAY ALLEN BILLINGTON

See also WESTWARD MOVEMENT (pictures); CLARK, GEORGE ROGERS; HARRISON, WILLIAM HENRY; SAINT CLAIR, ARTHUR.

NORTHWESTERN COLLEGE. See UNIVERSITIES AND COLLEGES (table).

NORTHWESTERN STATE UNIVERSITY OF LOUISIANA. See UNIVERSITIES AND COLLEGES (table).

NORTHWESTERN UNIVERSITY is a privately controlled coeducational institution with separate campuses in Evanston and Chicago, Ill. Located on the Evanston campus are the college of liberal arts, the graduate school, and schools of music, speech, education, journalism, and business. A technological institute and a summer session are also located there. The Chicago campus serves as a center for professional studies. It includes the medical, dental, and law schools, the graduate school of business administration, and the evening divisions of the university.

Four Chicago hospitals and Evanston Hospital are affiliates of the medical school. Chicago affiliates include Passavant Memorial, Chicago Wesley Memorial, Veterans Administration Research Hospital, and Children's Memorial. The Morton Medical Research building on the Chicago campus provides facilities for clinical research in all branches of medicine and surgery.

Northwestern offers bachelor's, master's, and doctor's degrees. A United States Navy R.O.T.C. unit is on campus. The university takes part in research programs in many fields. The university's libraries contain more than 1,375,000 volumes. Northwestern has cooperative relations with Garrett Biblical Institute of the United Methodist Church and Seabury-Western Seminary of the Episcopal Church, both in Evanston.

Northwestern University was founded in 1851. In 1926, various professional schools previously affiliated with it were brought together on the new Chicago campus. Northwestern was the first university in the United States to establish a school of speech and sponsor a children's theater. Its law school was first to organize a scientific crime detection laboratory, and its dental school was the first to introduce an independent course in care of children's teeth and organize a children's dental clinic. The university also established the first program in African studies. For enrollment, see UNIVERSITIES AND COLLEGES (table).   J. ROSCOE MILLER

See also LAW (picture: Northwestern University's cloister and garden).

NORWALK, Calif. (pop. 91,827; alt. 97 ft.), is a residential city 14 miles southeast of Los Angeles (see CALIFORNIA [political map]). The city's most important industry is oil refining. Norwalk was settled in 1868 and incorporated as a city in 1957. The city's greatest growth took place between 1940 and 1960, when its population grew from less than 4,000 to almost 90,000. It has a council-manager government.   GEORGE SHAFTEL

NORWALK, Conn. (pop. 79,113; met. area 120,099; alt. 40 ft.), is an industrial city which takes its name from the Norwalk Indians who once lived in the area. It lies at the mouth of the Norwalk River, about 40 miles northeast of New York City. For location, see CONNECTICUT (political map). Norwalk's manufactured products include automobile accessories, clothing, compressors, computers, electrical and electronic equipment, laboratory apparatus, optical systems, and pumps.

Hartford colonists settled Norwalk in 1649. It was incorporated as a town in 1651. British Redcoats burned much of the town in 1779, during the Revolutionary War. Norwalk received a city charter in 1893. It has a mayor-council form of government.   ALBERT E. VAN DUSEN

417

WORLD BOOK photo   George Holton, Photo Researchers

Norway's Rugged Coast is indented by many long inlets of the sea called fiords, *left.* Another famous symbol of Norway is the midnight sun. Every year, the sun shines day and night for 10 weeks at North Cape, *right.*

NORWAY

NORWAY is a long, narrow kingdom on the northwestern edge of the European continent. The northern third of Norway lies above the Arctic Circle and is called the *Land of the Midnight Sun.* Because this region is so far north, it has long periods every summer when the sun shines 24 hours a day. Oslo, Norway's capital and largest city, is in the southern part of the country.

Most of the Norwegian people live near or along the sea. Winds warmed by the sea give the coast much warmer winters than other regions so far north, and snow melts quickly there. Even north of the Arctic Circle, nearly all of Norway's harbors are free of ice the year around. Inland areas are colder, and snow covers the ground much of the year. For thousands of years, the people have used skis for travel over the snow. Today, skiing is Norway's national sport. Most Norwegians learn to ski before they even start school.

Norway, along with Denmark and Sweden, is one of the Scandinavian countries. Vikings lived in all three countries about a thousand years ago. Norwegian Vikings sailed west and established colonies in Iceland and Greenland. About A.D. 1000, Leif Ericson sailed from Greenland and made what historians believe was the first voyage to the North American continent.

Since the time of the Vikings, the Norwegians have been a seafaring people. Norway's coast is famous for its many long, narrow inlets of the sea called *fiords,* which provide fine harbors. Rich fisheries lie off the west coast, and dried fish were an important export as early as the 1200's. Norway began developing its great shipping fleet during the 1600's. Today, the Norwegian fishing and shipping industries rank among the largest in the world.

Norway is mostly a high, mountainous plateau covered chiefly by bare rock, and it has little farmland. But the rivers that rush down from the mountains provide much cheap electricity. Norway generates more hydroelectric power per person than any other country. Norwegian manufacturing industries are based on this cheap power. Important products of Norway include chemicals, metals, processed foods, and wood pulp and paper.

The contributors of this article are H. Peter Krosby, Associate Professor of History and Scandinavian Studies at the University of Wisconsin; Mark W. Leiserson, Associate Professor of Economics at Yale University; and William C. Wonders, Professor of Geography at the University of Alberta.

FACTS IN BRIEF

Capital: Oslo.

Official Languages: Bokmål and Nynorsk.

Official Name: *Kongeriget Norge* (Kingdom of Norway).

Form of Government: Constitutional monarchy. *Head of State*—King. *Head of Government*—Prime Minister. *Legislature*—Storting (150 members, 4-year terms).

Area: 125,182 square miles. *Greatest Distances*—(northeast-southwest) 1,100 miles; (northwest-southeast) 280 miles. *Coastline*—1,650 miles.

Elevation: *Highest*—Galdhøpiggen, 8,097 feet above sea level. *Lowest*—sea level along the coast.

Population: *1960 Census*—3,591,234; distribution, 57 per cent urban, 43 per cent rural. *Estimated 1971*

Population—3,911,000; density, 31 persons to the square mile. *Estimated 1976 Population*—4,070,000.

Chief Products: *Agriculture*—barley, dairy products, hay, livestock, oats, potatoes. *Fishing*—cod, herring, mackerel, salmon. *Forestry*—timber. *Manufacturing*—aluminum, chemicals, processed foods, ships, wood pulp and paper. *Mining*—ilmenite, iron ore, lead, molybdenite, pyrites, zinc.

National Anthem: "Ja vi elsker" ("Yes, We Love with Fond Devotion").

National Holiday: Constitution Day, May 17.

Money: *Basic Unit*—krone. For the value of the krone in dollars, see MONEY (table: Values). See also KRONE.

418

Norway is a constitutional monarchy with a king, a prime minister and cabinet, and a parliament. The government is based on the Norwegian constitution of 1814. This constitution, like that of the United States, divides the government into three branches—executive, legislative, and judicial. The prime minister is the actual head of the government. The king has little real power, and no queen can be the head of state.

The king usually appoints the leader of the strongest party in the parliament to be prime minister. Other high government officials, including judges and county governors, are appointed by the king on the advice of the cabinet. Most of them may serve until the age of 70, but the king can dismiss them earlier on the cabinet's advice. Like the other Scandinavian countries, Norway has a government official called an *ombudsman*. He investigates complaints by citizens against government actions or decisions. See OMBUDSMAN.

Cabinet of the Norwegian prime minister is also called the Council of State. It is formed by the prime minister to run the various government departments. There are 15 members, including the prime minister. The cabinet must resign if it receives a vote of no confidence from the parliament. Norway's cabinet system differs sharply from that of Canada and Great Britain. In those countries, cabinet members are generally also members of parliament. In Norway, a cabinet member cannot also be a member of the parliament.

Parliament of Norway is called the *Storting*. It has 150 members elected to four-year terms. Each of Norway's 20 counties elects from 4 to 13 members, depending upon its population. The Storting consists of one house, but its members form two sections to discuss and vote on proposed laws. They elect 38 of their number to the *Lagting*, and the other 112 make up the *Odelsting*.

To become law, most bills must first be approved by the Odelsting, and then by the Lagting. If the two sections do not agree on a bill, it can be approved by two-thirds of the parliament as a whole. Certain matters are voted on only by the entire parliament.

Courts. Norway's highest court is the Supreme Court of Justice. Five Courts of Appeal hear appeals of decisions made by the county and town courts. Each county and town also has a Conciliation Council, which tries to settle disputes before they go to court. This body consists of three persons elected to four-year terms.

Local Government. Norway has 20 counties, 2 of which are the cities of Oslo and Bergen. Each county, except Oslo and Bergen, has a governor. Cities, towns, and village districts elect councils of varying size to four-year terms. These councils select a chairman, or mayor, to serve two years.

Politics. Norway has seven political parties. The Labor party has been the largest since the 1920's. The others are the Center, Christian People's, Communist, Conservative, Liberal, and Socialist People's parties. Norwegians who are at least 20 years old can vote if they have lived in Norway five years or more.

Armed Forces. Norway's army, navy, and air force have a total of about 32,000 men. Norwegian men between the ages of 20 and 44 are required to serve from 12 to 15 months in the armed forces.

Sven Samelius from Carl Östman

Parliament Building in Oslo is the home of the *Storting*, Norway's one-house legislature. The Storting has 150 members.

Barto, Photo Researchers

King Olav V, *left,* came to Norway's throne in 1957. He heads the armed forces and the nation's Evangelical Lutheran Church.

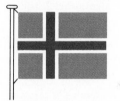

H. E. Harris & Co.

The Norwegian Flag was first approved for use by merchant ships in 1821. It became the national flag in 1898.

Norway's Coat of Arms dates from the 1280's, when the ax and crown of Saint Olav were added to the lion.

Norway is 4 per cent as large as the United States, not counting Alaska and Hawaii. The country lies just west of Sweden.

WORLD BOOK map

The Norwegians are a Scandinavian people, closely related to the Danes and the Swedes. The people of Norway have strong ties with Americans. During the late 1800's and early 1900's, more than 600,000 Norwegians migrated to the United States in search of better job opportunities. No other country except Ireland has provided the United States with so many immigrants in proportion to population.

About 20,000 Lapps live in far northern Norway (see LAPLAND). That region also has about 10,000 persons of Finnish ancestry.

Population. In 1971, Norway had a population of about 3,911,000. The following table shows some official census figures for Norway through the years:

1960	3,591,234	1910	2,391,782
1950	3,278,546	1900	2,240,032
1946	3,156,950	1855	1,490,047
1930	2,814,194	1801	883,487
1920	2,649,775	1769	723,618

More than 40 per cent of the people live in villages of fewer than 200 persons. Only five cities have populations over 50,000. They are Bergen, Kristiansand, Oslo, Stavanger, and Trondheim. See the separate articles on Norwegian cities listed in the *Related Articles* at the end of this article.

Food. Norwegians usually eat four meals a day, but many farm families have five. Breakfast generally includes cereal and open-faced sandwiches with cheese, jam, or marmalade. Goat cheese is a favorite sandwich spread. Sandwiches are also eaten at lunch and at a late-evening supper. Dinner is usually the only hot meal of the day. It includes soup, meat or fish, potatoes, vegetables, and dessert. People in the cities and towns eat dinner in the evening, and those in farm areas have it at midday.

Language. Norway has two official languages—Bokmål and Nynorsk. They are gradually being combined into a language called Samnorsk. Bokmål and Nynorsk are similar enough for someone who speaks either language to understand a person who speaks the other. Both belong to the Scandinavian group of Germanic languages. Local school boards may select either as the chief language in a school, but all students learn to read both languages. The Lapps also use their own language, which is much like Finnish.

Bokmål, also called Riksmål, is the major language of the cities and towns, and in most Norwegian schools. Bokmål is a Norwegian form of Danish. It has almost the same vocabulary and spelling as Danish, but is pronounced much differently. Bokmål developed during Norway's political union with Denmark, which lasted from 1380 to 1814. During that period, it replaced Old Norse, the early Norwegian language.

Nynorsk, originally called Landsmål, was created during the mid-1800's as a reaction against the Danish influence. Nynorsk was based on the many *dialects* (local forms of speech) that developed in the villages during Norway's union with Denmark.

Religion. The Norwegian Constitution establishes the Evangelical Lutheran Church as the nation's official church. About 96 per cent of the people are Evangelical Lutherans. Other religious groups have complete freedom of worship. They include members of the Baptist, Free Lutheran, Methodist, Pentecostal, and Roman Catholic churches.

The government largely controls the Evangelical Lutheran Church. It appoints the pastors and church officials, and pays their salaries. In 1956, the parliament passed a law permitting women to become pastors. The first woman pastor was named in 1961.

Education. Almost all the people of Norway can read and write. Norwegian law requires children from the age of 7 to either 14 or 16 to go to school. Until 1959, the elementary school program lasted seven years, until the age of 14. That year, the government provided for nine-year elementary schools. Each city, town, and village decided whether to adopt the new system, which required children to attend school until the age of 16. Today, about half the youngsters of Norway attend nine-year schools.

Norway's high schools offer three- or five-year programs. Norway also has many technical and specialized schools at the high school or college level. There are two universities, one in Oslo and the other in Bergen.

The University of Oslo Library, which owns about 1,400,000 volumes, is the largest library in Norway. Oslo also has the country's largest city library, with about 720,000 volumes. All Norwegian cities and towns are required by law to have free public libraries. These libraries are partly supported by government grants.

Arts. Norwegians have contributed much to the development of the arts. Henrik Ibsen's realistic plays of the late 1800's brought him worldwide fame as the father of modern drama. Three Norwegian writers—Bjørnstjerne Bjørnson, Knut Hamsun, and Sigrid Undset—have won the Nobel prize for literature.

The painter Edvard Munch was a strong influence on the expressionist art style of the early 1900's. Statues by Gustav Vigeland, perhaps Norway's greatest sculptor, stand in Oslo's Frogner Park. Edvard Grieg, Norway's best-known composer, used many melodies from Norwegian folk songs and dances in his orchestral works. For more information on Norwegians in the various arts, see the biographies listed in the *Related Articles* at the end of this article.

Social Welfare. The government of Norway provides the people with many welfare services. All families with more than one child receive a yearly allowance for each youngster under the age of 16, beginning with the second one. These families also may receive financial aid in paying their rent. The government guarantees all employed persons an annual four-week vacation with full pay. Large families with medium or low incomes pay little or no national taxes, and their local taxes are reduced.

The National Insurance Act, which went into effect in 1967, combined many existing welfare programs. All Norwegians are required to take part in this combined plan. It includes old-age pensions, job retraining, and aid for mothers, orphans, widows, widowers, and handicapped persons. Another insurance plan provides free medical and hospital care, plus cash payments to employees during illness. The costs of these plans are shared by the insured persons, their employers, and the national and local governments.

Sports.

Outdoor sports are an important part of Norwegian life. Recreation areas lie within short distances of all homes. Skiing, Norway's national sport, may have started there thousands of years ago as a means of crossing the snow-covered land. Many Norwegians take cross-country ski trips to the country's mountains or wooded hills. Almost every town has a ski jump. The second most popular winter sport is ice skating. Norwegians also have long enjoyed *bandy*, a form of hockey played by 11-man teams on large rinks.

Soccer is the favorite summer sport. Sailing is popular along the coast. The lakes and rivers attract many fishermen, and a number of towns have rowing clubs. The people also enjoy hiking, hunting, and swimming.

John LaDue

Frogner Park, in Oslo has about 150 works by Gustav Vigeland, one of Norway's greatest sculptors. The 75-acre park, laid out by Vigeland, attracts visitors from many parts of the world.

Nordisk Pressefoto from Keystone Press

Lapp Children attend modern schools in the larger towns of far northern Norway. About 20,000 Lapps live here. They make their living largely by fishing or raising reindeer.

Oslo, the capital and largest city of Norway, has many colorful outdoor cafes. It is one of the most popular tourist centers of northern Europe, as well as a major industrial city.

Bob Serating, Birnback

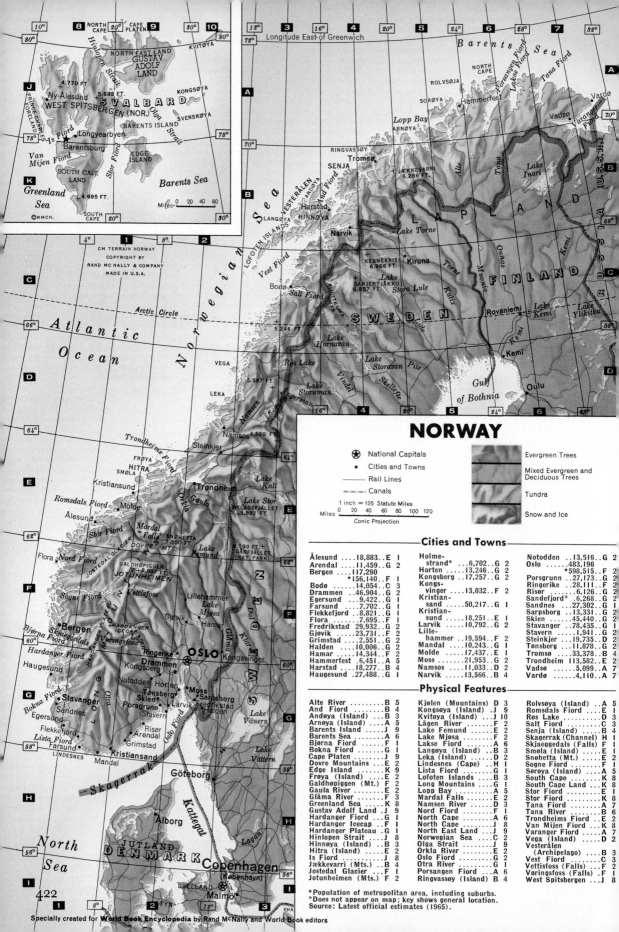

NORWAY

⊛ National Capitals
• Cities and Towns
═══ Rail Lines
═══ Canals

1 inch = 125 Statute Miles

Miles 0 20 40 60 80 100 120
Conic Projection

Evergreen Trees
Mixed Evergreen and Deciduous Trees
Tundra
Snow and Ice

Cities and Towns

Ålesund . . . . .18,883. .E 1	Holme-	Notodden . .13,516. .G 2
Arendal . . . .11,459. .G 2	strand* . . . .6,702. .G 2	Oslo 483,196
Bergen · · · ·117,290	Horten . . . .13,246. .G 2	*598,515. .F 2
*156,140. .F 1	Kongsberg .17,257. .G 2	Porsgrunn . .27,173. .G 2
Bodø . . . . .14,054. .C 3	Kongs-	Ringerike . .28,111. .F 2
Drammen . .46,904. .G 2	vinger . . . .13,032. .F 2	Risør . . . . . .6,126. .G 2
Egersund . . .9,422. .G 1	Kristian-	Sandefjord* . .6,268. .G 2
Farsund . . . .7,702. .G 1	sand . . . . .50,217. .E 1	Sandnes . . .27,302. .G 1
Flekkefjord . .8,821. .G 1	Kristian-	Sarpsborg . .13,331. .G 2
Flora . . . . . .7,695. .F 1	sund . . . . .18,251. .E 1	Skien . . . . .45,440. .G 2
Fredrikstad 29,932. .G 2	Larvik . . . .10,792. .G 2	Stavanger . .78,435. .G 1
Gjøvik . . . .23,731. .F 2	Lille-	Stavern . . . . .1,941. .G 2
Grimstad . . .2,551. .G 2	hammer . .19,594. .F 2	Steinkjer . . .19,735. .D 2
Halden . . . .10,006. .G 2	Mandal . . .10,243. .G 1	Tønsberg . . .11,878. .G 2
Hamar . . . .14,344. .F 2	Molde . . . .17,437. .E 1	Tromsø . . . .33,378. .B 4
Hammerfest . .6,451. .A 5	Moss . . . . .21,953. .G 2	Trondheim 113,582. .E 2
Harstad . . .18,277. .B 4	Namsos . . .11,033. .D 2	Vadsø . . . . . .5,099. .A 7
Haugesund .27,488. .G 1	Narvik . . . .13,566. .B 4	Vardø . . . . . .4,110. .A 7

Physical Features

Alte River . . . . .B 5	Kjølen (Mountains) D 3	Rolvsøya (Island) . .A 5
And Fiord . . . . .B 4	Kongsøya (Island) . .J 9	Romsdals Fiord . . . .E 1
Andøya (Island) . . . .B 4	Kvitøya (Island) . . . .J 10	Røs Lake . . . . .D 3
Arnøya (Island) . . . .A 5	Lågen River . . . . . . .F 2	Salt Fiord . . . . .C 3
Barents Island . . . . .J 9	Lake Femund . . . . . .E 2	Senja (Island) . . . . .B 4
Barents Sea . . . . . . .A 6	Lake Mjøsa . . . . . . .F 2	Skagerrak (Channel) .H 1
Bjørna Fiord . . . . . . .G 1	Lakse Fiord . . . . . . .A 6	Skjaeggedals (Falls) .F 1
Bokna Fiord . . . . . . .G 1	Langøya (Island) . . .B 3	Smøla (Island) . . . . .E 1
Cape Platen . . . . . . .J 9	Leka (Island) . . . . . .D 2	Snøhetta (Mt.) . . . . .E 2
Dovre Mountains . . . .E 2	Lindesnes (Cape) . . .H 1	Sogne Fiord . . . . . . .F 1
Edge Island . . . . . . .K 9	Lista Fiord . . . . .G 1	Sørøya (Island) . . . .A 5
Frøya (Island) . . . . . .E 2	Lofoten Islands . . . .B 3	South Cape . . . . . . .K 8
Galdhøpiggen (Mt.) . .F 2	Long Mountains . . . .G 1	South Cape Land . . .K 8
Gaula River . . . . . . .E 2	Lopp Bay . . . . .A 5	Stor Fiord . . . . .K 8
Glåma River . . . . . . .F 3	Mardal Falls . . . . . . .E 2	Stor Fiord . . . . .E 1
Greenland Sea . . . . .K 8	Namsen River . . . . . .D 2	Tana Fiord . . . . .A 7
Gustav Adolf Land . .J 9	Nord Fiord . . . . .F 1	Tana River . . . . .B 6
Hardanger Fiord . . . .G 1	North Cape . . . . . . .A 6	Trondheims Fiord . . .E 2
Hardanger Icecap . . .F 1	North Cape . . . . . . .J 8	Van Mijen Fiord . . . .K 8
Hardanger Plateau . .F 1	North East Land . . . .J 9	Varanger Fiord . . . . .A 7
Hinlopen Strait . . . . .J 8	Norwegian Sea . . . . .C 2	Vega (Island) . . . . . .D 2
Hinnøya (Island) . . . .B 3	Olga Strait . . . . .J 8	Vesterålen
Hitra (Island) . . . . . .E 2	Orkla River . . . . .E 2	(Archipelago) . . . .B 3
Is Fiord . . . . .J 8	Oslo Fiord . . . . .G 2	Vest Fiord . . . . .C 3
Jækkevarri (Mts.) . . .B 4	Otra River . . . . .G 1	Vettisfoss (Falls) . . .F 2
Jostedal Glacier . . . .F 1	Porsangen Fiord . . . .A 6	Vøringsfoss (Falls) . .F 1
Jotunheimen (Mts.) . .F 2	Ringvassøy (Island) .B 4	West Spitsbergen . . .J 8

*Population of metropolitan area, including suburbs.
*Does not appear on map; key shows general location.
Source: Latest official estimates (1965).

422

Specially created for World Book Encyclopedia by Rand McNally and World Book editors

Land Regions. Most of Norway is a high, mountainous plateau. The average height of the country is more than 1,500 feet above sea level. Only about a fifth of Norway, including two major lowlands, lies under 500 feet. Norway has three main land regions: (1) the Mountainous Plateau, (2) the Southeastern Lowlands, and (3) the Trondheim Lowlands.

The Mountainous Plateau is covered largely by bare rock that was smoothed and rounded by ancient glaciers. The glaciers also formed numerous lakes and deep valleys. Many of these lakes and valleys are in the 4,500-square-mile Hardanger Plateau, the largest highland plain in Europe. In Norway's uplands above 6,500 feet, permanent snow and ice cover a total of about 1,200 square miles. The 300-square-mile Jostedal Glacier is the largest ice field in Europe outside Iceland.

In the narrow northern half of Norway, the Kjølen mountain range extends along the border with Sweden. The jagged peaks form a ridge that looks like the keel on the bottom of an overturned boat. Norway's highest mountains rise in the wider southern half of the country. The Dovre Mountains extend in an east-west direction, and the Long Mountains rise to the south. The Jotunheimen range of the Long Mountains includes the highest point in Norway. It is 8,097-foot Galdhøpiggen, the tallest mountain in northern Europe.

The Southeastern Lowlands consist mostly of the middle and lower valleys of the 380-mile-long Glåma River and several other rivers. The rivers are used to float timber to pulp mills and sawmills, and their many waterfalls provide hydroelectric energy. The region also has long, narrow lakes, including 140-square-mile Lake Mjøsa. Slopes are gentler than in most of the country, and the region is more suitable for farming and forestry. These lowlands are the most thickly settled part of Norway. They include Oslo, the capital and chief commercial, industrial, and shipping center.

The Trondheim Lowlands include the lower ends of several wide, flat valleys. In addition to providing good farmland, the valleys also serve as important railroad routes to other parts of Norway and to Sweden.

The lowlands have long been a major region of settlement. Trondheim, founded in A.D. 998, was once Norway's capital and leading city. Today, it is a leading center of industry and trade.

Coast and Islands. Many long, narrow inlets of the sea indent the rocky coast of Norway. These inlets, called *fiords*, make the coastline one of the most jagged in the world. The longest, Sogne Fiord, extends inland for more than 100 miles. Norway has a coastline of about 1,650 miles. Including all the fiords and peninsulas, the full length of the coast is about 12,500 miles —approximately half the distance around the world.

About 150,000 islands lie off the Norwegian coast, except in some parts of the southwest and far north. Some are only rocky reefs called *skerries*, which shield the coastal waters from stormy seas. The mountainous Lofoten Islands are the largest offshore island group. The waters around these islands have rich cod fisheries. The famous Maelstrom current sweeps between the two outermost Lofotens, and sometimes forms huge, dangerous whirlpools.

Ernst A. Weber, Photo Researchers

The Trondheim Lowlands are among Norway's few farm regions. Crops include barley and potatoes. The region also has much dairy farming.

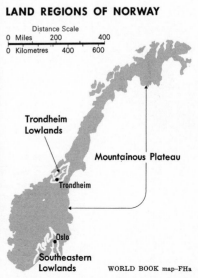

LAND REGIONS OF NORWAY

Distance Scale

0 Miles 200 400

0 Kilometres 400 600

Trondheim Lowlands

Mountainous Plateau

Trondheim

Oslo

Southeastern Lowlands

WORLD BOOK map—FHa

423

The climate of Norway is much milder than that of most other regions as far north, especially along the country's west coast. Near the Lofoten Islands, for example, January temperatures average 45° F. higher than the world average for that latitude. Most of the coast has warmer winters than Chicago, which lies much farther south. Snow that falls along the coast melts almost immediately. The warm North Atlantic Current of the Gulf Stream keeps nearly all the seaports ice-free, even in the Arctic (see GULF STREAM).

Norway's inland regions are colder because mountains block the warm west winds that come from the sea. Snow covers the ground at least three months a year. Deep snow may block mountain roads for as long as six months. In summer, when the sea is cooler than the land, the west winds cool the coast more than the inland areas. Norway's warmest summers occur in the inland valleys of the southeast. Less rain also falls inland than along the coast.

The far north, known as the *Land of the Midnight Sun*, has continuous daylight from mid-May through July. The period of midnight sun decreases southward, and there is no 24-hour sunshine south of the Arctic Circle. In winter, northern Norway has similar periods of continuous darkness. See MIDNIGHT SUN.

Ingmar Holmasen from Carl Östman

Permanent Ice and Snow cover about 1,200 square miles of Norway's uplands. The 190-square-mile Svartisen Glacier, near the Arctic Circle, is one of the largest glaciers in Norway.

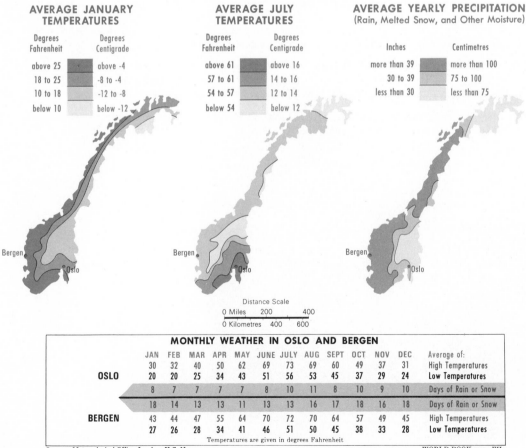

AVERAGE JANUARY TEMPERATURES

Degrees Fahrenheit	Degrees Centigrade
above 25	above -4
18 to 25	-8 to -4
10 to 18	-12 to -8
below 10	below -12

Bergen
Oslo

AVERAGE JULY TEMPERATURES

Degrees Fahrenheit	Degrees Centigrade
above 61	above 16
57 to 61	14 to 16
54 to 57	12 to 14
below 54	below 12

Bergen
Oslo

AVERAGE YEARLY PRECIPITATION
(Rain, Melted Snow, and Other Moisture)

Inches	Centimetres
more than 39	more than 100
30 to 39	75 to 100
less than 30	less than 75

Bergen
Oslo

Distance Scale
0 Miles   200   400
0 Kilometres   400   600

MONTHLY WEATHER IN OSLO AND BERGEN

	JAN	FEB	MAR	APR	MAY	JUNE	JULY	AUG	SEPT	OCT	NOV	DEC	Average of:
	30	32	40	50	62	69	73	69	60	49	37	31	High Temperatures
OSLO	20	20	25	34	43	51	56	53	45	37	29	24	Low Temperatures
	8	7	7	7	7	8	10	11	8	10	9	10	Days of Rain or Snow
	18	14	13	13	11	13	13	16	17	18	16	18	Days of Rain or Snow
BERGEN	43	44	47	55	64	70	72	70	64	57	49	45	High Temperatures
	27	26	28	34	41	46	51	50	45	38	33	28	Low Temperatures

Temperatures are given in degrees Fahrenheit

Sources: Meteorological Office, London; U.S. Navy

WORLD BOOK maps-FHa

Norway has a thriving economy and nearly full employment. Since the late 1940's, the nation's total income from the production of goods and services has more than doubled. Unemployment has been kept below an average of 2 per cent of the labor force. During the 1920's and 1930's, a fourth to a third of the workers were usually jobless. The rapid economic expansion of the mid-1900's has resulted largely from (1) government programs to promote investment in industries, and (2) greater demand by other countries for Norwegian goods and services.

Natural Resources. Norway is not rich in natural resources. About three-fourths of the country consists of mountains and plateaus that are covered mostly by bare rock. Only 3 per cent of Norway is farmland. Forests, chiefly of pines and spruces, cover more than 20 per cent of the country. There are also many ash, beech, birch, and oak trees.

Norway's waters are its greatest natural resource. The many swift mountain rivers are used to produce hydroelectric power. The seas off the northern and western coasts are rich in cod and herring. The seas have also helped Norway carry on an extensive foreign trade and develop a great shipping industry.

The country does not have rich mineral deposits, and its mining industry is small. Iron ore and pyrites, from which copper and sulfur are taken, are mined in Norway. Other minerals include ilmenite, lead, molybdenite, and zinc. Coal is mined only in Svalbard, an island territory far to the north of Norway.

Manufacturing developed much later in Norway than in the major industrial countries. Those countries had their own coal to provide power with which to run machines. During the 1800's, Norway had to import coal for its factories, which made manufacturing expensive and held back its growth. By 1900, Norway had started to develop its great sources of cheap hydroelectric power. The factories turned to hydroelectricity and expanded rapidly.

Today, manufacturing is Norway's most valuable industry. About half the factories are in the Oslo area. The most important products include chemicals and chemical products, such metals as aluminum and magnesium, processed foods, and wood pulp and paper. Norway is one of the world's leading producers of aluminum. This metal is processed from imported bauxite, which Norway lacks. The nation also produces clothing, electrical machinery, furniture, and small ships.

Agriculture. Norway's farms lie on narrow strips of land in inland valleys and along the coast. About 90 per cent of the farms cover 25 acres or less, compared with an average of about 300 acres in the United States. Many farmers have a second occupation so they can earn enough to support their families. Farmers own about two-thirds of Norway's commercial forests, and many of them are also loggers. A number of farmers also work as commercial fishermen.

Dairy farming and livestock production account for more than two-thirds of Norway's farm income. Most of the cropland is used for growing livestock feed. The major crops are barley, fruits and vegetables, hay, oats, and potatoes.

Forestry has been an important industry in Norway for hundreds of years. Lumber became a major export during the 1500's. Today, much timber is also used to produce pulp and paper. The chief commercial trees include birch, pine, and spruce. More than 12,000 miles of forest roads have been built to transport the logs. Much timber is also moved by way of rivers.

Norwegian loggers cut over 335 million cubic feet of timber a year. The forest growth rate is about 415 million cubic feet a year. Timber production could not be increased much without using up the forests, all of which are protected by government regulations.

Fishing. Norway has long been a great fishing country. Its total catch, chiefly cod and herring, is about 1½

NORWAY'S GROSS NATIONAL PRODUCT IN 1965

Total gross national product—$7,780,000,000

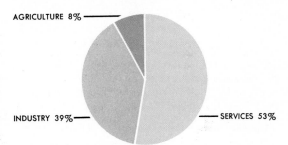

AGRICULTURE 8%

INDUSTRY 39%

SERVICES 53%

The Gross National Product (GNP) is the total value of goods and services produced by a country in a year. The GNP measures a nation's total annual economic performance. It can also be used to compare the economic output and growth of countries.

Production and Workers by Economic Activities

Economic Activities	Per Cent of GDP* Produced	Employed Workers	
		Number of Persons	Per Cent of Total
Manufacturing	27	353,000	32
Trade	12	153,000	14
Water Transportation	11	65,000	6
Construction	8	102,000	9
Health & Educational Services	7	104,000	9
Other Transportation & Communication	7	72,000	7
Government	5	68,000	6
Other Services	5	103,000	9
Agriculture	4	14,000	1
Utilities	3	14,000	1
Housing	3	—	—
Banking, Insurance, & Real Estate	3	29,000	3
Fishing & Whaling	2	6,000	1
Forestry & Hunting	2	15,000	1
Mining	1	7,000	1
Total	100	1,105,000	100

*GDP is gross domestic product (gross national product less net income sent abroad).
Sources: Organization for Economic Cooperation and Development; Central Bureau of Statistics of Norway.

million tons a year. Norwegian fishermen also bring in large numbers of flounder, mackerel, and salmon. Much of the catch is processed for export. Norway's once-great whaling industry declined sharply during the 1960's. Large catches by Norway and other major whaling nations made many kinds of whales increasingly scarce.

Electric Power. Norway produces more electric power in relation to its population than any other country. Industry uses most of it, but almost all Norwegian homes have electricity. Hydroelectric stations produce more than 99 per cent of the power. Since the late 1940's, hydroelectric production has increased 500 per cent. But Norway's still undeveloped sources of power could provide more than is now produced.

Foreign Trade. Norway depends heavily on foreign trade to help keep its standard of living high. The nation's trade is one of the largest in the world in relation to its population. Norway, with limited natural resources, imports a wide variety of foods and minerals as well as machinery and other manufactured goods. The imports have a value equal to about 40 per cent of all goods and services produced in Norway.

Norway's major exports include chemicals, fish, metals, and wood pulp and paper. The exported goods pay for only about half the imports. Income from Norway's merchant fleet, the fourth largest in the world, pays for more than a third of the imports. The fleet provides shipping services for countries in all parts of the world.

Transportation. During World War II (1939-1945),

about half of Norway's merchant fleet was sunk while carrying cargo for the Allies. Since the war, the fleet has expanded 600 per cent to a total of more than 18 million tons. About 450 vessels link Norway's coastal cities and towns. Inland, ferries cross many fiords.

Norway has more than 40,000 miles of roads and highways. Only the major routes are paved, but most of the others have well-kept gravel surfaces. About 10 per cent of the people own automobiles.

The government owns and operates nearly all the railroads. There are about 2,700 miles of track. The government also owns part of the Scandinavian Airlines System, which flies throughout the world. Several airlines provide regular service to all parts of Norway.

Communication. Norway has about 85 daily newspapers with a total circulation of nearly 1½ million. The largest dailies include the *Aftenposten*, *Arbeiderbladet*, and *Dagbladet* of Oslo; the *Bergens Tidende* of Bergen; and the *Adresseavisen* of Trondheim.

The government-owned Norwegian Broadcasting Corporation operates the country's radio and television systems. No advertising is allowed on the programs. The corporation's income is provided by annual taxes on all radio and television sets. Most radio and television programs are cultural or educational, and less than a third of the broadcasting time is used for entertainment.

The government owns and operates the telegraph system and most telephone services. Telegraph and telephone lines connect all sections of Norway.

FARM, MINERAL, AND FOREST PRODUCTS

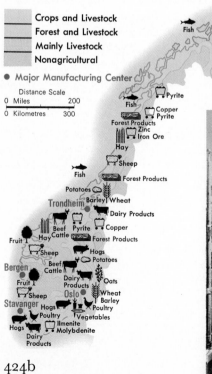

- Crops and Livestock
- Forest and Livestock
- Mainly Livestock
- Nonagricultural
- ● Major Manufacturing Center

This map shows where the most important farm, mineral, and forest products of Norway are produced. Most Norwegian agriculture is in the Southeastern Lowlands. The map also shows the nation's major industrial centers.

Norway's Fishing Fleet brings in one of the world's largest catches every year. From January to April, thousands of tons of cod are caught in waters off the Lofoten Islands.

Herbert Fristedt from Carl Östman

Early Days. Almost 11,000 years ago, people lived along the northern and western coasts of what is now Norway. Most of the region was covered by thick ice sheets, which took thousands of years to melt. By 2,000 B.C., a series of Germanic tribes had started to settle there permanently. They gradually spread throughout the region, and continued to arrive for hundreds of years after the time of Christ. The various tribes formed local and regional communities ruled by chiefs and kings.

The Viking Period. Viking sea raiders from the Norwegian communities spread terror through much of western Europe for about 300 years. Beginning with the British Isles about A.D. 800, they attacked coastal towns and sailed away with slaves and treasure. The Vikings also sailed to the west and established colonies in the Faeroe Islands and other North Atlantic islands. About 870, they explored farther west and colonized Iceland. Eric the Red brought the first group of settlers to Greenland about 985. About 1000, his son, Leif Ericson, made what is believed to have been the first voyage to the North American continent. See ERIC THE RED; ERICSON, LEIF; VIKING (The Norwegian Vikings).

About 900, much of present-day Norway was united under Norway's first king, Harold I (called Fairhair), or Harald I. He defeated many local chieftains and kings, and others recognized his leadership. King Olav I introduced Christianity in Norway during the 990's. During the early 1000's, Olav II achieved full Norwegian unity and firmly established Christianity. He became Norway's patron saint in 1031.

The Viking period ended during the late 1000's. The church grew in power, foreign trade expanded, and religious and trading centers became important cities. Political confusion and bitter struggles for royal power also developed. Beginning in 1130, many regional leaders claimed the throne. They were defeated in a series of civil wars that lasted until 1240. Peace was restored under Haakon IV. By 1300, Norway's economy was largely controlled by north German merchants. Norway had become dependent on them for grain imports. The country was weakened further in 1349 and 1350, when about half the Norwegian people died in an epidemic of bubonic plague.

Union with Denmark. Margaret, the wife of King Haakon VI of Norway, was also the daughter of the king of Denmark. After her father died in 1375, she became the Danish ruler. Haakon died in 1380, and Margaret became ruler of Norway as well. In 1388, during political confusion in Sweden, Swedish noblemen elected her to rule that country, too. In 1397, in the Union of Kalmar, Margaret united Norway, Denmark, and Sweden, with power centered in Denmark. Sweden revolted against the Danish rule several times, and broke away from the union in 1523.

Under the Danish-controlled union, Norway grew weaker and Denmark became stronger. In 1536, Denmark declared Norway a Danish province and made Lutheranism the official Norwegian religion.

During the 1500's, Norway exported increasing amounts of lumber to the countries of western Europe. As a result, Norway began to develop a great shipping

National Museum, Copenhagen

King Olav II became Norway's patron saint in 1031. This wooden statue of Olav was carved by an unknown artist of the 1200's.

--- **IMPORTANT DATES IN NORWAY** ---

c. 870 Norwegian Vikings colonized Iceland.

c. 900 Harold I united Norway.

c. 985 Eric the Red colonized Greenland.

c. 1000 Leif Ericson sailed to North America.

1349-1350 An epidemic of bubonic plague killed about half the people of Norway.

1380 Norway was united with Denmark.

1536 Norway became a Danish province. Lutheranism was made Norway's official religion.

1814 Denmark gave up Norway to Sweden, but kept Norway's island colonies.

1884 The cabinet of Norway became responsible to the parliament instead of the king.

1905 Norway became independent.

1940-1945 German troops occupied Norway in World War II.

1945 Norway joined the United Nations.

1949 Norway became a member of the North Atlantic Treaty Organization.

1957 King Haakon VII died and was succeeded by Olav V.

1959 Norway and six other nations formed the European Free Trade Association.

1967 Norway began its greatest welfare program, which combined many established social security plans under the National Insurance Act.

industry during the late 1600's. The industry expanded rapidly throughout the 1700's.

Union with Sweden. In 1807, during the Napoleonic Wars, Denmark sided with France against Great Britain. Britain had been Norway's chief trading partner, but now the British ended the trade. British warships blockaded Norway's trade with other countries, and many Norwegians starved. Norway was cut off from Denmark by the British blockade, and began to manage its own affairs. The Norwegians secretly began to trade with the British again.

Denmark was defeated in 1813 by Sweden, an ally of Britain against France. In 1814, in the Treaty of Kiel, Denmark gave Norway to Sweden. Denmark kept Norway's island colonies—Greenland, Iceland, and the Faeroe Islands.

The Norwegians did not recognize the Treaty of Kiel. Later in 1814, they elected an assembly to draw up a constitution for an independent Norway. The constitution was adopted on May 17, but Sweden refused to grant Norway independence. Swedish forces attacked Norwegian troops and quickly defeated them. In November, 1814, the Norwegian parliament accepted King Charles XIII of Sweden as Norway's ruler as well. Charles promised to respect the Norwegian constitution.

In 1884, after a long political struggle, the parliament won the right to force the cabinet to resign. Until then, the cabinet had been responsible only to the king.

Independence. During the 1890's, Norway's merchant fleet was one of the largest in the world. But the Swedish foreign service handled Norway's shipping affairs in overseas trading centers. Norway demanded its own foreign service, but Sweden refused. In May, 1905, the Norwegian parliament passed a law creating a foreign service, but the Swedish king vetoed it. On June 7, the parliament ended the union with Sweden.

Sweden nearly went to war against Norway. However, Sweden recognized Norway's independence in September, 1905, after all but 184 Norwegians voted for independence. In November, the people approved a Danish prince as their king. He became Haakon VII.

By the time of independence, Norway had started to develop its many mountain streams to produce hydroelectric power. Its industries expanded rapidly with this cheap power source. Norway's economy increased further during World War I (1914-1918). Norway remained neutral, but its merchant fleet carried much cargo for the Allies. About half its ships were sunk by German submarines and mines.

The Constitution of Norway was adopted in 1814 by an elected assembly at Eidsvoll, near Oslo. It has remained in effect since then with only minor changes. This painting of the assembly, presented to the parliament in 1885, hangs in the Storting's main chamber.

The National Assembly, Eidsvoll 1814 by Oscar Wergeland. Storting, Oslo (O. Vaering)

An economic depression hit Norway after the war. The nation's economy, dependent on trade and shipping, suffered further during the worldwide depression of the 1930's. Between a fourth and a third of Norway's workers were usually unemployed during this period.

World War II began in 1939, and Norway tried to remain neutral. But on April 9, 1940, Germany invaded Norway by attacking all its main seaports at once. The Norwegians fought bravely for two months, aided by some British, French, and Polish troops. On June 10, 1940, Norway surrendered. King Haakon VII and the cabinet fled to London and formed a government-in-exile. The Germans made Vidkun Quisling, a Norwegian who supported them, premier of Norway. His last name became an international word for *traitor*.

A secret Norwegian resistance army conducted sabotage against the German occupation force. These Norwegians were trained chiefly to join a hoped-for Allied invasion of Norway. Other Norwegians fled their country and trained in Sweden or Great Britain for the invasion. Some took part in British commando raids in Norway. After each raid, the Germans shot, tortured, or imprisoned many Norwegians.

Norwegian fighter pilots were trained in Canada, and operated from bases in Britain and Iceland. Norway's merchant fleet carried war supplies for the Allies. The Norwegian navy helped protect Allied shipping, and took part in the invasion of France in 1944.

On May 8, 1945, after Germany fell, the 350,000 German troops in Norway surrendered. Haakon VII returned in triumph on June 7, the 40th anniversary of Norwegian independence. Norway suffered light war losses, compared with those of some other occupied countries. About 10,000 Norwegians died, and about half the merchant fleet was sunk. The far northern counties of Finnmark and Troms lay largely in ruins. For the complete story of the war, see WORLD WAR II.

Postwar Developments. After the war, loans from the United States helped Norway rebuild its merchant fleet and its war-torn industries. By the 1950's, the Norwegian economy was thriving again.

Norway became a charter member of the United Nations in 1945. The next year, Trygve Lie of Norway became the first secretary-general of the UN. Norway later took part in UN military actions in the Congo, Cyprus, Egypt, and South Korea. In 1949, Norway became a charter member of the North Atlantic Treaty Organization (NATO). But Norway refused to permit NATO bases or nuclear weapons on its territory for fear of angering Russia, its neighbor on the northeast. In 1959, Norway and six other countries formed the European Free Trade Association (EFTA), an economic union (see EUROPEAN FREE TRADE ASSOCIATION).

Norway Today. Under Olav V, who became king in 1957, Norway is more prosperous than ever. Less than 1 per cent of the labor force is unemployed. But the cost of living is rising. The government is promoting more foreign trade to help meet this problem.

In 1966, the parliament passed the National Insurance Act, probably the most important social reform in Norway's history. This program began on Jan. 1, 1967. It combines many social security plans, including old-age pensions, job retraining, and aid for mothers, orphans, widows, widowers, and handicapped persons.

H. PETER KROSBY, MARK W. LEISERSON, and WILLIAM C. WONDERS

NORWAY / *Study Aids*

Outline

I. **Government**
II. **People**
    A. Population
    B. Food
    C. Language
    D. Religion
    E. Education
    F. Arts
    G. Social Welfare
    H. Sports
III. **The Land**
    A. Land Regions
    B. Coast and Islands
IV. **Climate**
V. **Economy**
    A. Natural Resources
    B. Manufacturing
    C. Agriculture
    D. Forestry
    E. Fishing
    F. Electric Power
    G. Foreign Trade
    H. Transportation
    I. Communication
VI. **History**

Questions

What families are covered by Norway's family allowance program?

Who is believed to have made the first voyage to the North American mainland?

How does Norway's cabinet system of government differ from that of Canada and Great Britain?

What is the northern third of Norway called? Why?

How did Norway, Denmark, and Sweden become united during the late 1300's?

How did Norway's two official languages develop?

Why is Norway's large merchant fleet essential to the country's economy?

Why does Norway's government regulate all logging?

What natural resource led to the rapid expansion of Norwegian manufacturing?

What led to Norway's independence from Sweden?

NORWAY HOUSE. See MANITOBA (Places to Visit).

NORWEGIAN ELKHOUND is a hunting dog that originated in Norway, probably between 5000 and 4000 B.C. Hunters claim the elkhound can scent an elk three miles away. The elkhound stalks its prey quietly and holds it at bay until the hunter arrives. It is also used in hunting bear and game birds. The elkhound's coat is thick and gray with black tips. The dog stands about 20 inches high at the shoulder and weighs about 50 pounds. See also DOG (color picture: Hounds). OLGA DAKAN

NORWICH TERRIER is an English dog, good at hunting rats and rabbits. It is named for Norwich, England. It has bright eyes and a head like a fox. Some Norwich terriers hold their ears straight up. Others let their ears droop. The Norwich has short legs and a wiry red coat. It weighs from 10 to 15 pounds. The breed was developed in the 1880's by mating a small-sized Irish terrier with an English terrier. JOSEPHINE Z. RINE

The Norwich Terrier Originated in England.
WORLD BOOK photo by Walter Chandoha

NORWICH UNIVERSITY is a privately endowed military college for men at Northfield, Vt. It was founded in 1819. The university offers courses in engineering, aviation administration, sciences, liberal arts, and business administration. Norwich was the first U.S. civilian institution to offer military training. Its program was a forerunner in the ROTC movement. For enrollment, see UNIVERSITIES AND COLLEGES (table).

NOSE is the organ used for breathing and smelling. It forms part of the face, just above the mouth. Outwardly, it appears to be simple, but it is complicated inside.

When we breathe, air enters the nose through two openings called *nostrils*. The nostrils are separated by the *septum*, a thin wall of *cartilage* (tough tissue) and bones. Air passes from the nostrils into two tunnels called the *nasal passages*. The nasal passages lead back to the upper part of the throat. From the nasal passages, air passes through the pharynx and windpipe into the lungs.

Both nasal passages have a lining of soft, moist mucous membrane covered with microscopic, hairlike projections called *cilia*. The cilia wave back and forth constantly, moving dust, bacteria, and fluids from the nose to the throat for swallowing.

Each nasal passage also has three large, shelflike bones that are called *turbinates*. The turbinates warm the air before it enters the lungs. These turbinates also stir up the air so that dust in the air sticks to the mucous membrane of the turbinates and thus does not pass into the lungs.

The sense of smell is located in the highest part of the nasal cavity. The end fibers of the *olfactory nerve* lie in a small piece of mucous membrane about as big as a dime. These fibers carry sensations of smell along the olfactory nerve to the *olfactory lobe* of the brain, the part of the brain that is responsible for smell. The olfactory lobe is located on the lower surface of the brain's frontal lobe.

The sense of smell is closely related to the sense of taste. Some experts believe that much of our taste sensations are really sensations of odor that we have associated with certain tastes. For example, we really smell coffee, tobacco, wine, apples, and potatoes more

THE NOSE

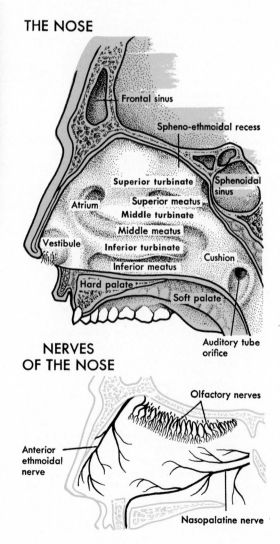

Frontal sinus

Spheno-ethmoidal recess

Superior turbinate

Sphenoidal sinus

Atrium

Superior meatus

Middle turbinate

Middle meatus

Vestibule

Inferior turbinate

Inferior meatus

Cushion

Hard palate

Soft palate

Auditory tube orifice

NERVES OF THE NOSE

Olfactory nerves

Anterior ethmoidal nerve

Nasopalatine nerve

than we taste them. If a person is blindfolded and his nose stopped up so he cannot smell, he has great difficulty telling apples from potatoes by taste. Red wine and plain coffee taste almost alike to such a person when they are at the same temperature and consistency.

We cannot smell when we have a cold, because the infection inflames the mucous membrane of the nasal passages and blocks the passage of air to the center of smell. It is important to keep nasal passages clean and to treat any inflammation of the mucous membrane at once. When neglected, colds can lead to more serious ailments, such as bronchitis and pneumonia. Sinuses, which empty into the nose, may also become infected.

A. C. GUYTON

Related Articles in WORLD BOOK include:

HOW TO STOP NOSEBLEED

The Bleeding may often be stopped by pinching the nostrils together for four or five minutes, so that clots have time to form.

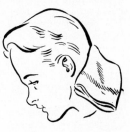

A Cold Compress made of a towel or other cloth wrung out of cold water can be placed at the back of the neck to stop bleeding.

A Small Pad or Roll of paper or cloth may be slid inside the upper lip above the teeth, and pressed from the outside with the finger.

If Bleeding Continues, the person should be seated with his head over a chair back. Cold compresses should then be placed over his nose.

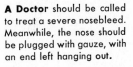

A Doctor should be called to treat a severe nosebleed. Meanwhile, the nose should be plugged with gauze, with an end left hanging out.

HOW WE BREATHE

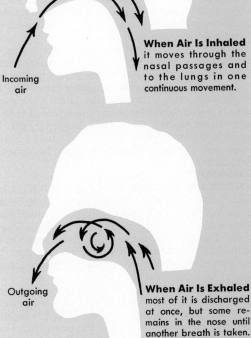

Incoming air

When Air Is Inhaled it moves through the nasal passages and to the lungs in one continuous movement.

Outgoing air

When Air Is Exhaled most of it is discharged at once, but some remains in the nose until another breath is taken.

NOSEBLEED. The medical term for nosebleed, or hemorrhage from the nose, is *epistaxis*. Many different conditions can bring on nosebleed. There are numerous small blood vessels that supply the nasal tissues. These tissues are thin and easily broken. The hemorrhage is not a disease in itself, but may be a symptom of a disease. Nosebleed is frequent in hemorrhagic diseases such as *purpura*, but it may be purely local. Frequent flows of blood from the nose may even cause anemia. Severe bleeding may occur in cases of hardening of the arteries. The high blood pressure breaks small blood vessels, thus resulting in bleeding.

Sometimes a slight excitement can raise a person's blood pressure enough to start a nosebleed. Any hard knock which breaks a blood vessel may also cause it.

Most nosebleeds stop by themselves in about 10 minutes. It is helpful for the person to lie on his back, and to

427

keep cool. The position helps lower the blood pressure. A cold pack against the nose may also be helpful. If the bleeding keeps up, it may be necessary to pack the nose with gauze. A physician may have to pinch off the blood vessel, or give drugs that cause it to close and help to clot the blood.

Nosebleeds that occur often or last a long time require medical care. In any case, a person with a nosebleed should not blow his nose once it has stopped bleeding. If he does, he may disturb the blood clots and start another nosebleed. WILLIAM DAMESHEK

See also FIRST AID (picture: Nosebleed).

NOSTRADAMUS, *NAHS truh DAY mus* (1503-1566) was the Latin name of MICHEL DE NOTREDAME, a French astrologer and physician. His fame rests on his book *Centuries* (1555), a series of prophecies in verse. Nostradamus won lasting fame in 1559 when King Henry II of France died in a manner predicted in the *Centuries*. Nostradamus' prophecies are vague and open to many interpretations. Some persons credit him with predicting various events in French and world history, including the rise of Adolf Hitler in the 1930's.

Nostradamus was born in Saint-Remi, in southern France. In 1525, while a medical student, he showed great courage and skill in caring for victims of a plague. He earned a doctor's degree in 1532, and became a professor at the University of Montpellier. The success of *Centuries* gained him an appointment as court physician to King Charles IX of France. ABRAHAM C. KELLER

NOTARY PUBLIC is an officer who is authorized by state law to certify certain documents, and to take oaths. Many documents must be notarized before they become legally effective. The purpose of notarizing a document is to protect those who use it from forgeries. The notary, when he signs the document, certifies that the person who signed it appeared before him and was personally known to him. The signer of the document swears to the notary that the signature on the document is his own. The notary records that fact, then stamps his seal on the document.

The Notary Public Seal is pressed into paper with a small hand stamp.

In many states, any responsible person can get a commission as a notary public, on payment of a fee. A notary is usually allowed to charge for his services. In Great Britain and Canada, the Court of Faculties appoints notaries. ERWIN N. GRISWOLD

NOTATION, *noh TAY shun,* is any system of symbols and abbreviations that helps people work with a particular subject. Mathematics uses notation to simplify and consolidate ideas and problems. The Arabic numeral system is a notational device for writing numbers and making arithmetic operations easier. Chemistry, music, physics, and other subjects have also developed extensive notation systems. HOWARD W. EVES

See also ARABIC NUMERALS; NUMERATION SYSTEMS; MUSIC (The Language of Music); SYMBOL.

NOTE is an unconditional written promise to pay a specified sum of money on demand or at a given date to a designated person. The one who signs the note is called the *maker*. The one to whom it is made payable is called the *payee*. This written promise is called a *promissory note*. *Note of hand* is a name sometimes used for a promissory note.

Let us suppose that Arnold Shaw is a retail merchant who has a good business and a good financial standing. He needs $500 worth of merchandise, but does not have the cash on hand to pay for it. He knows that he has accounts coming due within 60 days. He will be able to pay the $500 when he is paid by those who owe him. He goes to Henry Brown, a wholesale merchant, who sells him the goods he needs and takes his note. The note is as follows:

$500   San Francisco, Calif.
                     March 1, 1967
Sixty days after date I promise to pay to the order of Henry Brown $500, with interest at 6 per cent. Value received.

         Arnold Shaw

Brown can endorse the note and cash it at the bank, if he needs the money before 60 days. Shaw will then pay the bank when his note becomes due.

Liability of the Maker. A note is *negotiable* when it is made payable to "bearer" or includes the word "order," like the one given above. When a note has been transferred by endorsement, the person in possession of the note is known as the *holder*. He can transfer it to another by adding his endorsement, and so on indefinitely, just as he can transfer a bank check. When the note falls due, the holder looks to the maker for payment. The law protects the holder under almost all conditions, including some kinds of fraud or cheating by the payee.

An endorser is liable in case the maker fails to pay the note when it falls due. The endorser is served with a notice called a *protest*. It is signed by a notary public (see NOTARY PUBLIC), and one copy is sent to each endorser if there is more than one.

Caution. No one should sign a document unless he understands fully what he is signing. The maker should have a lawyer examine any document that he does not understand. The law holds the maker responsible for his signature, except when any part, or all, of the document is proved fraudulent in court, or is proved to have been altered, without the maker's knowledge, after he signed it in good faith. JAMES B. LUDTKE

See also DISCOUNT (Bank Discount); NEGOTIABLE INSTRUMENT.

NOTOCHORD. See AMPHIOXUS.

NOTRE DAME, CATHEDRAL OF, *NO t'r DAHM,* is a famous cathedral in the heart of Paris. It stands on the Île de la Cité, a small island in the Seine River. *Notre Dame* is the French expression for *Our Lady,* the Virgin Mary. The cathedral is one of the finest examples of early Gothic architecture. Its walls are supported by the first well-designed *flying buttresses* (stone beams built against the outside walls).

The cathedral was begun in 1163 and was completed about 150 years later. During the French Revolution in the late 1700's, a mob attacked the cathedral because they regarded it as a symbol of the monarchy. They smashed most of its statues and windows, and damaged the walls. Repairs were begun in 1845. The French ar-

Notre Dame Cathedral in Paris has many gracefully carved stone ornaments, figures, and gargoyles. But many of them are placed so high above the ground that it is said only an angel can admire their details.

Gendreau

chitect and writer Eugène Emmanuel Viollet-le-Duc (1814-1879) directed the restoration, and is largely responsible for the way Notre Dame looks today.

Many historic events have taken place in Notre Dame. Henry VI of England was crowned king of France there in 1431. Mary, Queen of Scots, married Francis II, the *dauphin* (crown prince) of France, there in 1558. Napoleon I was crowned ruler of France there in 1804.

Notre Dame is also the name of other famous cathedrals in France. One is located at Reims (see REIMS [picture]). Another is located at Amiens (see GOTHIC ART [picture]). ALAN GOWANS

See also CATHEDRAL.

NOTRE DAME, COLLEGE OF. See UNIVERSITIES AND COLLEGES (table).

NOTRE DAME, UNIVERSITY OF, is a famous Roman Catholic school for men at Notre Dame, Ind. It is governed by a board of trustees consisting of 30 laymen, and 7 priests of the Congregation of Holy Cross—the Roman Catholic order that founded the university. Notre Dame admits students of all faiths.

The Campus. Notre Dame has a 1,000-acre campus, with twin lakes and wooded areas that provide a beautiful setting for more than 70 buildings. Landmarks include the Log Chapel, which is a replica of the first building erected at Notre Dame; and the Grotto of Our Lady of Lourdes, which is a replica of a shrine at Lourdes, France.

The 13-story Memorial Library, completed in 1963, has a capacity of about 2 million volumes. Nearly half of the university's undergraduates can study there at one time. The library's important collections include the Dante Library of books from the early 1500's; the Hiberniana collection of Irish history and literature; the Kirsch-Wenninger-Niewland Biology Library; and the Zahm South American Library.

Bordering the campus is Notre Dame Stadium where the "Fighting Irish" football team plays. Great football figures such as coach Knute Rockne, George Gipp, and the Four Horsemen of Notre Dame brought the university much fame (see ROCKNE, KNUTE).

Educational Program. Notre Dame's undergraduate school has colleges of arts and letters, business administration, engineering, and science. Courses in these colleges lead to bachelor's degrees. Notre Dame's law school, the first law school at a Roman Catholic university in the United States, offers the Bachelor of Laws degree. The graduate school at the University of Notre

429

The Library at Notre Dame is the tallest building on campus and one of the largest university libraries in the world. The 13-story building, built at a cost of $8 million, seats 2,900. The exterior features a 132-foot-high mural, depicting Christ, the Apostles, and various scholars. The mural is made of 7,000 granite pieces.

The University of Notre Dame

Dame offers advanced degrees in 25 departments.

The university has awarded the Laetare Medal each year since 1883. The award honors a leading U.S. Roman Catholic layman for his contributions to society.

Research Program. Notre Dame places a strong emphasis on research. It receives more than $7 million in grants annually for research. Researchers at the Lobund Institute for Germ-Free Life Studies use germ-free animals to study cancer and other diseases. *Lobund* stands for Laboratories of Bacteriology, University of Notre Dame.

The Medieval Institute conducts research and offers advanced courses in the culture, life, and thought of the Middle Ages. The Jacques Maritain Center conducts philosophical research. A $2,200,000 radiation laboratory, built by the U.S. Atomic Energy Commission, conducts research in radiation chemistry. Notre Dame was founded in 1842. For enrollment, see UNIVERSITIES AND COLLEGES (table).   THEODORE M. HESBURGH

See also HESBURGH, THEODORE MARTIN.

NOTRE DAME COLLEGE. See UNIVERSITIES AND COLLEGES (table).

NOTRE DAME COLLEGE OF STATEN ISLAND. See UNIVERSITIES AND COLLEGES (table).

NOTRE DAME OF MARYLAND, COLLEGE OF. See UNIVERSITIES AND COLLEGES (table).

NOTRE DAME SEMINARY. See UNIVERSITIES AND COLLEGES (table).

NOTRE DAME UNIVERSITY is a private, coeducational university in Nelson, B.C. It offers bachelor's degrees in arts and sciences. The university also trains elementary schoolteachers. It has a special program for student atheletes who represent Canada in international competition, and it is the home of Canada's National Ski Team. Founded in 1950, Notre Dame received its charter in 1963. For enrollment, see CANADA (table: Universities and Colleges).   AQUINAS THOMAS

NOTTINGHAM, *NAHT ing um,* England (pop. 305,-050; alt. 90 ft.) is a manufacturing city on the River Trent, 125 miles northwest of London. For location, see GREAT BRITAIN (political map). The city's industries include textiles and tobacco goods. Many of Robin Hood's legendary adventures took place in Nottingham

and nearby Sherwood Forest. The city was founded in the 800's. In 1769, Richard Arkwright set up the first spinning frame for stockings in Nottingham. Another inventor, John Heathcoat (1783-1861), later produced a machine for making a kind of lace called *bobbinet.*   JOHN W. WEBB

NOTTINGHAMSHIRE. See ENGLAND (political map).

NOUAKCHOTT, *nwahk SHAWT* (pop. 14,500; alt. 7 ft.), is the capital of Mauritania, a West African republic. Nouakchott serves as a market center. The city is developing port facilities. For the location of Nouakchott, see MAURITANIA (map).   CLEMENT H. MOORE

NOUN is a word that refers to one or more persons, places, objects, or ideas. Words such as *car, chalkboard, actor, boy, Sam, town, team, courage,* and *probability* are nouns.

Concrete and Abstract Nouns. Nouns may be divided into classes. Those which occur with the articles *the* and *a* and which have distinct plural forms are called *concrete nouns. Car, chalkboard, boy, team,* and *probability* are some concrete nouns.

Usually, nouns which occur with *the* but not *a* are *abstract nouns.* Examples are *courage, patience, indolence, lightness,* and *warmth.* Similar in usage to abstract nouns are nouns referring to materials or masses, such as *gravel, blood, mahogany,* and *mush.*

The differences between abstract and concrete classes of nouns are easy to see. For instance, we can say *a chair, a boy,* and *a probability,* but not usually, *a courage, a patience, a gravel,* or *a mush.* We can say *chairs, boys,* and *probabilities,* but not usually *courages, patiences, gravels,* or *mushes.* Some nouns, such as *paper, stone,* and *glass,* belong to both concrete and abstract classes. Note the difference between "I bought *a* paper" and "I bought paper." The word *the* occurs with nouns in both classes, and the sentence "I bought *the* paper" has two possible meanings.

Proper and Common Nouns. Some nouns do not ordinarily occur with either *a* or *the. Sam, Sally, Germany,* and *New York* are some of them. These nouns, which refer to particular persons or places, are called *proper nouns. The United States* and *the Red River* are also proper nouns. Such proper nouns are always accompanied by *the* or a similar modifier, such as *our*, *your*, or *his*, but they are not accompanied by modifiers such as *a*, *each*, or *every*.

All nouns which are not proper nouns are *common nouns*. In English writing, proper nouns are regularly capitalized, and common nouns are regularly not capitalized.

Collective Nouns are nouns that refer to groups of persons or animals, such as *team*, *flock*, *crowd*, *class*, *family*, *audience*, and *government*. In British English, collective nouns are usually followed by plural verbs, as "The team were exhausted" or "The government were defeated." In American English, the general practice is to treat collective nouns like other concrete nouns: "The team was exhausted" or "The government was defeated."

Number and Case. English nouns may have endings which show *number* and *case*.

Number is the form which indicates that the noun refers to one (singular) or to more than one (plural). Singular nouns indicate one, such as *pear*, *apple*, *man*, *mouse*, and *memorandum*. Plural forms for these nouns are *pears*, *apples*, *men*, *mice*, and *memorandums*. Abstract nouns, nouns of mass and material, and proper nouns do not ordinarily have distinct plural forms. In special cases, these nouns may be used as concrete nouns, as in the sentence "There were three *Sams* in the room."

Case is the form that helps show the relation of a noun to other words in a sentence. In some languages, words have many different endings to show relationships. In English, word order, rather than endings, shows relationships. Modern English nouns have only two cases: *common case* and *possessive case*. *Boy*, *man*, and *Sam* are common-case forms. *Boy's*, *man's*, and *Sam's* are possessive-case forms.

In English speech, the common case and the possessive case of regular nouns are identical in sound in the plural. In English writing, the possessive case is distinguished from the common case by the addition of an apostrophe after the *s* in the plural. "The boys were going" and "The boys' fathers were going" are examples. The common case and the possessive case of nouns with irregular plurals are usually different in sound as well as in writing, as in such plurals as *men* and *men's*.

As the name suggests, the possessive case frequently expresses ownership or possession, as in "The boy's coat," "Sam's car," and "My father's house." However, the possessive case often expresses various other meanings, as "a day's work."

Gender. In English, nouns are sometimes said to have gender, but this feature is not regularly shown by endings. It is never shown by *inflection*, which marks the difference between a singular and a plural or a possessive. *Lion* and *lioness* are two different words, not two forms of the same word.

An English noun has gender only in the sense that it is referred to by one of three pronouns: *he* or *him*, *she* or *her*, and *it*. "I found Jim and brought him home," "I found Sally and brought her home," or "I found a book and brought it home."

Nouns for which the corresponding pronoun is *he* or *him* are *masculine* nouns. Nouns for which the corresponding pronoun is *she* or *her* are *feminine* nouns. Nouns for which the corresponding pronoun is *it* are *neuter* nouns.

By and large, masculine nouns name males, feminine nouns name females, and neuter nouns name inanimate or sexless things. However, there are some exceptions. We usually think of a *ship* as feminine, and refer to it as *she*. We may use such expressions as "There she goes!" in connection with almost any object. Such nouns as baby, mosquito, and mouse do not name sexless things, but we usually use neuter pronouns in connection with them. In many languages, the connection between sex and gender in grammar is not so close as it is in the English language.   Paul Roberts

See also CASE; DECLENSION; INFLECTION; NUMBER; PERSON.

NOVA is a star that suddenly explodes and blasts part of its matter into space. An exploding nova quickly becomes much brighter than before. It remains bright for a time and then fades slowly. All novae observed so far have been distant stars too faint to be seen without a telescope before they exploded. Most became 10,000 to 100,000 times brighter when they flared up. One nova became several million times brighter. Astronomers do not know what causes novae. The word *nova* comes from the Latin word for *new*. People once believed that novae were newly created stars.

In a typical nova explosion, the star loses only about a hundred-thousandth part of its matter. The matter it throws off is a shell of glowing gases that expands outward into space at a tremendous speed.

Some novae develop so rapidly that they reach their greatest brightness in a few hours or a day. They start to fade gradually almost at once and return to their original brightness in several months or a year. Slower novae may take a month to reach maximum brightness. Their fading process may last many years.

Several novae, called *recurrent novae*, have flared up more than once since they were first observed. Astronomers believe that all novae may be recurrent, but that most flare up so rarely that recurrence has not been noticed.

Astronomers observe about 2 novae a year in the Milky Way galaxy, but between 25 and 40 probably occur. Most novae go unnoticed because they are so far from the earth. Novae in one of the Milky Way's neighboring galaxies occur at about the same rate as novae in the Milky Way.

A *supernova* is a star that explodes much more violently and shines much more brightly than a nova. A supernova throws off as much as 10 per cent of its matter when it explodes. Supernovae and novae differ so much in the percentage of matter thrown off that scientists believe the two probably develop differently. A supernova may increase in brightness as much as a billion times in a few days. Astronomers believe that about 14 supernova explosions have taken place in the Milky Way during the past 2,000 years. The Crab Nebula, a huge cloud of dust and gas in the Milky Way, is the remains of a supernova seen in A.D. 1054. Supernovae are also rare in other galaxies.   Eric D. Carlson

NOVA LISBOA, *NAW vuh leezh BOH uh* (pop. 38,745), is a railroad center in Angola about 200 miles from the Atlantic coast. It was formerly called Huambo. The city lies on a plateau about 5,600 feet above sea level. For location, see ANGOLA (map).

NOVA SCOTIA

NOVA SCOTIA, *SKO shuh*, is one of the four Atlantic Provinces of Canada. It includes a peninsula of the Canadian mainland and also Cape Breton Island. The province sticks out into the Atlantic Ocean from the Canadian mainland. Resorts along Nova Scotia's coast have earned the province the nickname *Canada's Ocean Playground*.

No part of Nova Scotia is more than 50 miles from the sea. The Atlantic Ocean, the Gulf of St. Lawrence, and the Bay of Fundy almost surround the province. Only a narrow strip of land—the Isthmus of Chignecto—joins the peninsula to the Canadian mainland. Ocean tides may rise higher in Nova Scotia than anywhere else in the world. Sometimes the tide rises more than 50 feet at the head of the Bay of Fundy. Sable Island, formed entirely of sand, lies about 100 miles off Nova Scotia's southern coast. Sailors call it the *Graveyard of the Atlantic* because it has caused many shipwrecks.

The sea keeps the climate of Nova Scotia from becoming either extremely hot or extremely cold. Thick forests cover much of the province. In the north, ranges of low hills stretch across parts of Nova Scotia. Seawater reaches far inland in many rivers that irrigate the rich soil of lowland farms. The Annapolis-Cornwallis Valley, famous for its apple orchards, glows with pink and white apple blossoms in spring.

White-tailed deer roam the wilderness areas. Many kinds of sea birds nest along the shore and on offshore islands. Cod, lobsters, and other seafood caught off Nova Scotia help make the province a leader in the Canadian fishing industry.

Manufacturing is Nova Scotia's chief industry. The province's leading products include boats and ships, dairy products, iron and steel, paper, processed seafoods, and wood pulp. Nova Scotia leads all the provinces in mining barite, coal, and gypsum.

Nova Scotia is one of the four original Canadian provinces. In 1867, it joined with New Brunswick, Ontario, and Quebec to form the Dominion of Canada. The first British settlers in Nova Scotia had arrived from Scotland in 1629. The Latin words *Nova Scotia* mean *New Scotland*.

The American poet Henry Wadsworth Longfellow made Nova Scotia famous in his poem *Evangeline*. This partly fictional poem tells how French colonists, called *Acadians*, were driven from their homes in Nova Scotia by British colonial troops from New England. The Acadians had remained loyal to France after Great Britain won control of Nova Scotia in the mid-1700's. The poem gave part of the province the nickname *Land of Evangeline*.

After the Revolutionary War in America, many

Angus L. Macdonald Bridge Across Halifax Harbor

November Sunset by Gerald Roach for the Field Enterprises Educational Corporation Collection

Countryside near Halifax

persons who remained loyal to Britain fled to Nova Scotia from the United States. These United Empire Loyalists, as they were called, nicknamed the Nova Scotians *bluenoses*. This nickname may have come from the "bluenose" potato, which the Nova Scotians grew and shipped to New England. Today, the people still call themselves bluenoses.

For the relationship of Nova Scotia to other provinces, see ATLANTIC PROVINCES; CANADA; CANADA, GOVERNMENT OF; CANADA, HISTORY OF.

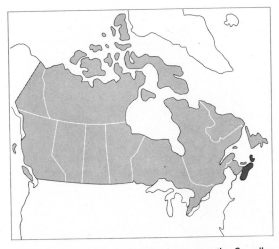

Nova Scotia (blue) ranks ninth in size among the Canadian provinces, and third among the Atlantic, or Maritime, Provinces.

FACTS IN BRIEF

Capital: Halifax.

Government: *Parliament*—members of the Senate, 10; members of the House of Commons, 12. *Provincial*—members of the House of Assembly, 46. *Voting Age*—19 years (provincial elections); 18 years (national elections).

Area: 21,425 square miles (including 1,023 square miles of inland water), ninth in size among the provinces. *Greatest Distances*—(southeast-northwest) 374 miles; (north-south) 100 miles. *Coastline*—about 1,000 miles.

Elevation: *Highest*—Ingonish Mountain, 1,747 feet above sea level. *Lowest*—sea level.

Population: *1966 Census*—756,039, seventh among the provinces; density, 35 persons to the square mile; distribution, 58 per cent urban, 42 per cent rural. *Estimated 1971 Population*—775,000.

Chief Products: *Manufacturing*—boats and ships, electrical and electronics equipment, iron and steel, lumber, paper, processed fish, transportation equipment, wood pulp. *Mining*—barite, coal, gypsum, salt, sand and gravel. *Fishing Industry*—cod, haddock, halibut, herring, lobster, scallops, swordfish. *Agriculture*—apples, barley, beets, dairy products, oats, potatoes, poultry and eggs, turnips.

Entered the Dominion: July 1, 1867; one of the four original provinces.

Provincial Motto: *Munit haec et altera vincit* (One labors, the other defends).

The contributors of this article are Basil W. Deakin, Editorial Page Editor of the Chronicle-Herald *of Halifax; Charles Bruce Fergusson, Provincial Archivist of Nova Scotia and Associate Professor of History at Dalhousie University; and Bernard J. Keating, Professor of Geology at St. Francis Xavier University.*

433

Lieutenant-Governor of Nova Scotia represents Queen Elizabeth in the province. He is appointed by the governor-general-in-council of Canada to a term of not less than five years. The lieutenant-governor's position, like that of the Canadian governor-general, is largely honorary.

Premier of Nova Scotia is the actual head of the provincial government. He is the leader of the majority party in the legislative assembly. The premier receives $26,000 a year, which includes his salary and the allowances he gets as a member of the assembly. For a list of all the premiers of Nova Scotia, see the *History* section of this article.

The premier presides over the executive council, or cabinet. The council is made up of the premier and other ministers. All the ministers are members of the majority party of the assembly. They are chosen by the premier. Each council member usually directs one or more departments of the government. The council resigns if it loses the support of a majority of the assembly.

Legislative Assembly makes the provincial laws. This one-house legislature has 46 members elected by the people. An election must be held at least every five years. But the lieutenant-governor, on the advice of the premier, may call for an election at any time. If the premier loses the support of a majority of the assembly he resigns, or else a new election is held.

Courts. The supreme court has an appeal court division and a trial court division. The governor-general-in-council of Canada appoints all supreme court members. The appeal division has a chief justice and two justices. The trial division has a chief justice and five justices. Justices serve until they are 75. The governor-general-in-council also appoints seven county court judges. Nova Scotia's lieutenant-governor-in-council appoints provincial magistrates, justices of the peace, and judges of probate and juvenile courts.

Local Government. Nova Scotia has 18 counties. They serve as the province's main judicial and administrative districts. The province has three cities, which operate under special charters, and 39 towns. Voters in each city and town elect a mayor and a council. All other communities in Nova Scotia are part of 24 districts called municipalities. Each of 12 counties is a single municipality, and each of the other 6 counties is divided into two municipalities. An elected council governs each rural municipality. Members of the council, called councilors, elect a *warden* (chief councilor) from their group.

Taxation. Nova Scotia's main source of income is a tax-sharing agreement with the Canadian government. Under this arrangement, the Canadian government collects income taxes and returns a special yearly grant to the province. The provincial government collects taxes on gasoline and alcoholic beverages. In 1959, Nova Scotia began collecting a sales tax to support a free-hospitalization plan.

Politics. Nova Scotia's leading political parties are the Liberal Party and the Progressive Conservative Party. An earlier Conservative Party changed its name to the Progressive Conservative Party in 1942. Since 1867, when Nova Scotia became a province, almost twice as many Liberals as Conservatives have been elected premier.

Nova Scotia Information Service

Government House in Halifax is the home of Nova Scotia's lieutenant-governor. The mansion was first occupied in 1805. It is surrounded by parklike grounds.

The Provincial Coat of Arms

The Provincial Flag

Symbols of Nova Scotia. On the coat of arms, the center shield bears the blue cross of St. Andrew and a lion that represents Nova Scotia's ties with Scotland. An Indian, symbolizing the province's first inhabitants, and a unicorn, representing England, flank the shield. Charles I of England granted the coat of arms to Nova Scotia in 1626. The flag, granted by royal charter in 1621, bears the cross of St. Andrew and the lion of the Scottish kings.

The Floral Emblem
Trailing Arbutus

Province House in downtown Halifax is the meeting place of the Nova Scotia legislature. The three-story stone building was completed in 1818, and was first used by the legislature in 1819. Halifax, Nova Scotia's largest city, has been the provincial capital since 1749. Nova Scotia has had only one other capital—Annapolis Royal, from 1710 to 1749.

Nova Scotia Information Service

NOVA SCOTIA / People

The 1966 Canadian census reported that Nova Scotia had 756,039 persons. The population of Nova Scotia had increased almost 3 per cent over the 1961 figure, 737,007. By 1971, Nova Scotia had an estimated population of 775,000.

Most Nova Scotians belong to families that originally came from the British Isles or from France. Some persons in the province still speak the Gaelic language of their Scottish ancestors. During Scottish celebrations held each year in some Nova Scotia communities, many persons wear colorful costumes and sing and dance to bagpipe music. Such gatherings are held in Antigonish and St. Anns.

Persons in the province who had French forefathers hold festivals in Cheticamp, Church Point, and Pubnico. These celebrations feature the dress and customs of old France.

Halifax is the capital of Nova Scotia and the largest of the province's three cities. It is one of Canada's most important ports and the chief railway and air terminal in Nova Scotia. Halifax is the population center of the province's only Census Metropolitan Area as defined by the Dominion Bureau of Statistics. For the population of this metropolitan area, see the *Index* to the political map of Nova Scotia. Dartmouth, the second largest city in the province, lies across the harbor from Halifax. Sydney, the province's only other city, is on Cape Breton Island.

Nova Scotia's towns have populations of less than 25,000. See the list of articles on Nova Scotia cities and towns listed in the *Related Articles* at the end of this article.

The churches with the largest memberships in Nova Scotia are, in order of size, the Roman Catholic Church, the United Church of Canada, and the Anglican Church of Canada. Other churches in Nova Scotia that also have many members include the Baptist Church and the Presbyterian Church.

POPULATION

This map shows the population density of Nova Scotia, and how it varies in different parts of the province. Population density means the average number of persons who live on each square mile.

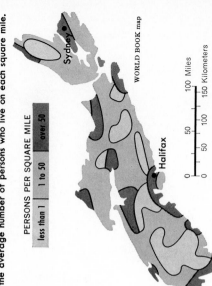

PERSONS PER SQUARE MILE		
less than 1	1 to 50	over 50

Sydney
Halifax

WORLD BOOK map

0   50   100 Miles
0   50   100   150 Kilometers

Source: Census Division, Dominion Bureau of Statistics

NOVA SCOTIA MAP INDEX

Population

775,000	..Estimate	.1971
756,039	..Census	.1966
737,007	"	.1961
642,584	"	.1951
577,962	"	.1941
512,846	"	.1931
523,837	"	.1921
492,338	"	.1911
459,574	"	.1901
450,396	"	.1891
440,572	"	.1881
387,800	"	.1871

Metropolitan Area

Halifax 198,193

Counties

Annapolis ..21,579. .E	5
Antigonish .14,890. .C	9
Cape	
Breton .129,572. .C11
Colchester .35,700. .C 7
Cumberland 35,933. .C 6
Digby 19,827. .D 4
Guysborough 12,830. .D 9
Halifax .244,893. .D 8
Hants 18,152. .B10
Inverness 18,152. .B10
Kings 43,249. .E 4
Lunenburg 36,114. .E 5
Pictou 44,490. .D 8
Queens 11,218. .F 5
Richmond 16,284. .F 5
Shelburne 8,001. .B10
Victoria 23,552. .F 4
Yarmouth	

Cities and Towns

Abercrombie ..387. .C 8	
Advocate	
Harbour .... 261. .D 5
Aldershot ..2,059. .D 6
Amherst ..10,551. .°C 6
Annapolis	
Royal ....805. .°E 5
Antigonish ..4,856. .°C 9
Arichat ....652. .°C10
Athol ....182. .C 6
Baddeck ....778. .°B11
Baddeck Bay .191. .B11
Barrington	
Passage ...370. .G 4
Bass River ...352. .D 7
Bear River ...679. .E 4
Bedford	
Belle Côte ...239. .B10
Belliveau Cove .429. .E 7
Berwick ..1,311. .D 5
Bible Hill ..2,901. .D 7
Bickerton	
West ....366. .D 9
Bramber ....303. .D 6
Bridgetown ..1,060. .E 5
Bridgewater .4,755. .E 6
Brookfield ...654. .C 7
Brooklyn* ..1,245. .F 5
Caledonia ....367. .E 5
Cambridge ...196. .D 6
Central ..1,190. .D10
North River .357. .C 7
Centreville ..278. .E 4
Charles Cove .176. .D10
Chester* ..1,014. .E 6
Cheticamp ..1,118. .A10
Clark's	
Harbour ..1,002. .G 4
Clementsport .424. .E 4

Collingwood	
Corner ....252. .C 7
Concession ..313. .F 4
Country Harbour	
Mines ....272. .D 9
Dalhousie East 163. .E 5
Dalhousie West 158. .C 6
Danesville ...158. .C 6
Dartmouth .58,745. .D 7
Debert ....805. .°E 5
Deep Brook ..469. .E 4
Digby ....2,305. .°E 4
Dingwall ....278. .A11
Dominion ..2,960. .B12
Donkin* ..1,013. .B11
East Bay ....350. .B11
East Uniacke .215. .D 7
East Walton ..190. .D 7
Ecum Secum ..241. .C 9
Eureka ....321. .C 8
Five Islands .195. .D 6
Florence* ..2,059. .B11
Fort Lawrence 273. .C 6
Gabarus ....225. .C11
Glace Bay ..23,516. .B12
Grand-Étang ..253. .A10
Greenfield ...184. .F 5
Guysborough ..502. .°E 7
Hammonds	
Plains ....512. .D 7
Hantsport ..1,438. .E 6
Havre Boucher .290. .D10
Hazel Hill ...271. .D10
Head of	
Amherst ...164. .C 6
Herring	
Cove* ..1,458. .E 7
Hilden ....656. .D 7
Hopewell ....399. .C 8
Ingonish ....364. .A11

Ingonish	
Beach ....642. .A11
Ingonish	
Centre ....169. .A11
Inverness ..2,022. .B10
Joggins ....799. .C 6
Jordan Falls .191. .°F 5
Kentville ..5,176. .°D 5
L'Ardoise ....400. .C10
Kingston* ..1,210. .D 5
L'Ardoise ...400. .C10
Linwood ...385. .C11
La Have	
Islands ....241. .F 6
Lakeside ..1,636. .E 7
Larry's River .218. .D10
Lawrencetown .495. .E 5
Linwood ....201. .C10
Little Dover ..527. .D10
Little Narrows 180. .B10
Liverpool ..3,607. .°F 6
Lockeport ..1,284. .G 5
Lorne ....179. .D 8
Louisbourg ..1,617. .C12
Louisdale ....733. .C10
Lower Argyle .209. .G 4
Lower	
L'Ardoise ...247. .C11
Lower West	
Pubnico ....709. .G 4
Lower Woods	
Harbour ....563. .G 4
Lunenburg ..3,154. .°E 6
Mabou ....290. .B10
Macean ....339. .C 6
Mahone Bay .1,296. .E 6
Main-à-Dieu ..437. .B12
Maitland	
Bridge ....201. .E 5
Margaree	
Centre ....250. .B10
Margaree	
Forks ....296. .B10

Martins Point 374. .E 6	
Medford ....175. .D 6
Melvern	
Square ....396. .D 5
Meteghan ....991. .F 4
Meteghan	
River ....350. .F 4
Middleton ..1,765. .D 5
Milton ....1,210. .F 5
Mira Road* ..1,201. .B11
Moser River ..334. .D 9
Mount	
Pleasant ....345. .E 4
Mulgrave ..1,124. .C10
Musquodoboit	
Harbour ....749. .E 8
Neil Harbour .299. .A11
New	
Glasgow ..10,489. .C 8
New Minas* ..1,007. .D 5
New Road ...1,310. .E 7
New	
Victoria* ..1,415. .B11
New	
Waterford 9,725. .B11
Newellton ....382. .G 4
North	
Brookfield ..194. .E 5
North	
Sydney ..8,752. .B11
Oxford ....1,426. .D 7
Parrsboro ..1,835. .C 6
Petit-de-Grat .945. .C10
Petit-Étang ..435. .A10
Pictou ....4,254. .°C 8
Port Mouton 321. .F 5
Southampton .180. .C 6
Springfield ...283. .E 5
Springhill ..5,380. .C 6
Stellarton ..5,191. .C 8
Stewiacke ....982. .D 7

Port Hawkes-	
bury ....1,366. .C10
Port Hood ..472. .°B10
Port Maitland .487. .F 4
Pugwash ....799. .C 7
Queensport ...158. .D10
Reserve	
Mines* ..2,710. .B11
River Hébert .896. .C 6
River John ..401. .C 8
Rockville ....221. .G 4
Round Hill ..256. .E 5
Sackville* ..2,613. .E 7
St.-Joseph-	
du-Moine ....273. .B10
Salmon	
River* ..1,219. .D 7
Samsonville ..345. .C11
Saulnierville .442. .F 4
Scotchtown ..2,038. .B11
Scotts Bay ...160. .D 6
Shag Harbour .260. .G 4
Sheet	
Harbour ....647. .D 8
Shelburne ..2,654. .°G 5
Sherbrooke ...379. .D 9
Ship Harbour .209. .E 8
Smith's Cove .393. .E 4
South Bar	
of Sydney ..1,061. .B11
South West	
Margaree ...204. .B10
South West	
Port Mouton 321. .F 5
Stony Island .248. .G 4
Sydney ...32,767. .°B11
Sydney	
Mines ....9,171. .B11
Sydney River 2,166. .C11
Tangier ....210. .E 8
Tatamagouche .559. .C 7
Terence Bay 1,079. .E 7
The Hawk ....896. .C 6
Three Mile	
Plains* ..1,247. .D 6
Timberlea ..1,269. .E 7
Tiverton ....334. .E 4
Tracadie ....315. .C 9
Trenton ..3,229. .C 8
Truro ....13,007. .°D 7
Upper Musquo-	
doboit ....315. .D 8
Upper Nappan 300. .C 6
Wallace ....270. .C 7
Walton ....273. .D 6
Waverley ....737. .E 7
Wedgeport ...218. .G 4
West Arichat .477. .C10
Westchester ..225. .C 6
Westfield	
Station ....287. .C 7
Westmount* ..1,823. .B11
Westport ....367. .F 3
Westville ..4,147. .C 8
Weymouth ....573. .E 4
Weymouth	
North ....301. .E 4
Whycocomagh .304. .B10
Windsor ..3,765. .°D 6
Windsor Forks 282. .D 6
Wolfville ..2,533. .D 6
Woodside ....212. .D 7
Yarmouth ..8,319. .°F 4

°County Town
*Does not appear on map; key shows general location

Source: Latest census (1966)

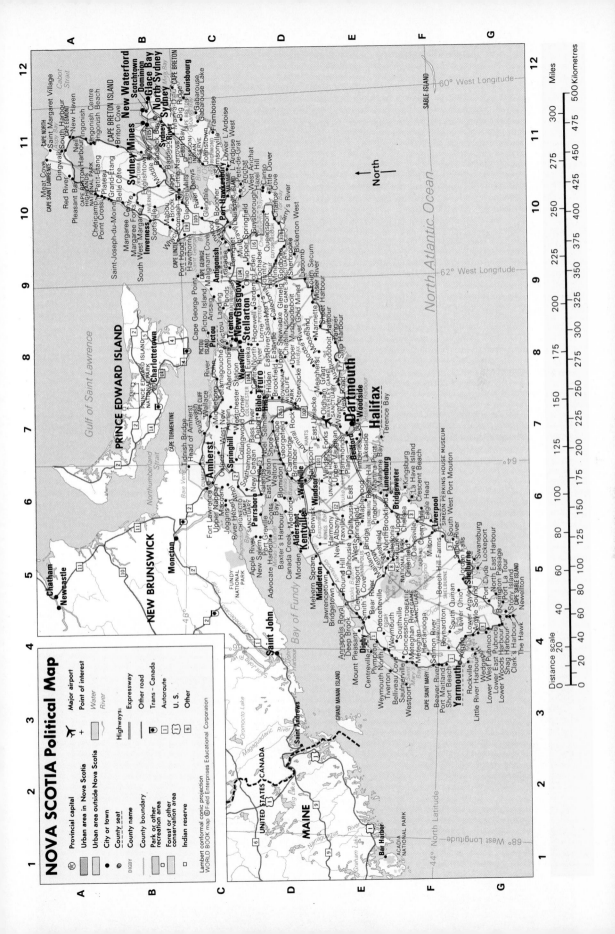

NOVA SCOTIA Political Map

⊛ Provincial capital

Urban area in Nova Scotia

Urban area outside Nova Scotia

✈ Major airport

+ Point of interest

● City or town

◉ County seat

DIGBY County name

County boundary

Park or other recreation area

Forest or other conservation area

Indian reserve

Water

River

Highways:

Expressway

Other road

Trans-Canada

Autoroute

U.S.

Other

Lambert conformal conic projection
WORLD BOOK map ©Field Enterprises Educational Corporation

North

North Atlantic Ocean

Gulf of Saint Lawrence

PRINCE EDWARD ISLAND

NEW BRUNSWICK

MAINE

UNITED STATES
CANADA

Bay of Fundy

Northumberland Strait

60° West Longitude

62° West Longitude

68° West Longitude

44° North Latitude

46° North Latitude

Distance scale

Miles

500 Kilometres

Schools. Public schools in Nova Scotia operate under the provincial Education Act. Nova Scotia's first Education Act was passed in 1766. The provincial department of education supervises the school system. Schools are controlled by local school boards. Municipal councils and the lieutenant-governor-in-council appoint the members of these boards. Local taxes and grants from the provincial government provide the chief sources of income for the schools. Provincial law requires children in urban areas to attend school from age 6 through 16. It requires children in rural areas to attend school from age 7 through 14, though rural school boards may adopt the urban area requirements.

Libraries. Nova Scotia has about 50 libraries. Local taxes and grants from the provincial government support regional libraries that operate in cities, towns, and rural areas. Libraries that are not classified as regional are supported by funds collected in local areas.

Museums. The Citadel, a national historic park in Halifax, includes two military museums and a provincial museum. The Public Archives of Nova Scotia, at Dalhousie University in Halifax, contain public records and historic documents. The archives also have maps, ship models, and art collections. Other museums include the Alexander Graham Bell Museum in Baddeck, Fort Anne Historical Museum in Annapolis Royal, Fortress of Louisbourg Museum in Louisbourg, Nova Scotia Museum of Science in Halifax, and Uniacke House in Mount Uniacke.

UNIVERSITIES AND COLLEGES

Nova Scotia has seven degree-granting universities and colleges. See the separate articles on these institutions. For enrollments, see CANADA (table: Universities and Colleges).

Name	Location	Founded
Acadia University	Wolfville	1838
Dalhousie University	Halifax	1818
Mount Saint Vincent University	Halifax	1873
Nova Scotia College of Art and Design	Halifax	1969
Nova Scotia Technical College	Halifax	1907
Saint Francis Xavier University	Antigonish	1853
Saint Mary's University	Halifax	1841

NOVA SCOTIA/A Visitor's Guide

Nova Scotia's beaches and shoreline resorts have given the province the nickname *Canada's Ocean Playground*. Fishermen can catch swordfish and tuna along the coast, and salmon and trout in the inland streams. In the forests, sportsmen hunt deer, snowshoe rabbits, and grouse.

Tourists who spend three days or more in Nova Scotia may become members of the Order of the Good Time. This social club was founded at Port Royal in 1606 by the French explorer Samuel de Champlain.

Many visitors come to the Gaelic festival in St. Ann's and the Highland Games in Antigonish. They enjoy watching the Scottish sport of tossing the caber. In this contest, men throw the *caber* (a heavy wooden pole) as far as they can. Hunting guides and lumbermen match skills during Guides' Meets held at Beaver Dam near Shelburne and in Stillwater in Guysborough County. These contests include canoe racing and *log birling* (balancing on a spinning, floating log). Winter sports include curling, hockey, skating, and skiing.

Queen and Her Court at Annapolis Valley Apple Blossom Festival
Nova Scotia Information Service

Boat Races at Lunenburg

Bagpipers at Antigonish

Tossing the Caber in a Highland Games Contest

PLACES TO VISIT

Following are brief descriptions of some of Nova Scotia's many interesting places to visit.

Alexander Graham Bell Museum, in Baddeck, displays inventions, models, notes, and photographs of Alexander Graham Bell, inventor of the telephone.

Cabot Trail offers motorists a magnificent view of the sea. This highway winds through the wilderness areas of northern Cape Breton Island.

Cape Blomidon, near Wolfville, overlooks Minas Basin and nearby apple orchards.

Parrsboro Shore, on Minas Basin, has rocks formed into odd shapes by the tides that rise and fall more than 50 feet in the Bay of Fundy.

Sunrise Trail runs along the shore of Northumberland Strait between Amherst and New Glasgow. The highway is more than 100 miles long.

Parks and Historic Sites. Until 1965, Cape Breton Highlands National Park was Nova Scotia's only national park. For the area and features of this park, see CANADA (National Parks). In 1965, Nova Scotia began to develop Kejimkujik National Park in the southwestern part of the province. The Canadian government also operates five historic parks: the Citadel in Halifax, Fort Anne in Annapolis Royal, the Fortress of Louisbourg in Louisbourg, Grand Pré in the Annapolis Valley, and Port Royal near Annapolis Royal.

The Nova Scotian government has set aside four large wooded areas—the Chignecto, Liscomb, Tobeatic, and Waverley game sanctuaries—to protect wildlife in the province. Other tourist attractions include Wildlife Park in Shubenacadie, and three historic homes: Haliburton Memorial Museum in Windsor, Perkins House in Liverpool, and Uniacke House in Mount Uniacke. For information on the provincial parks and historic sites of Nova Scotia, write to Director of Parks, Nova Scotia Department of Lands and Forests, Halifax, N.S.

A Trout Fisherman Tries the Rough Waters near Maitland

ANNUAL EVENTS

One of Nova Scotia's best-known annual events is the Annapolis Valley Apple Blossom Festival in Kentville and nearby towns. The festival is held during late May or early June. Other annual events in Nova Scotia include the following.

April-June: John Cabot Day in Cape North (June 24).

July-September: Gathering of the Clans and Fishermen's Regatta in Pugwash (Dominion Day, July 1); Lobster Fisheries Carnival in Pictou (July); Highland Games in Antigonish (July); Nova Scotia Festival of the Arts in Wolfville (August); Nova Scotia Gaelic Mod in St. Ann's (August); Festival of the Tartans in New Glasgow (August); Nova Scotia Fisheries Exhibition in Lunenburg (September).

October-December: Atlantic Winter Fair in Halifax (late October or early November).

439

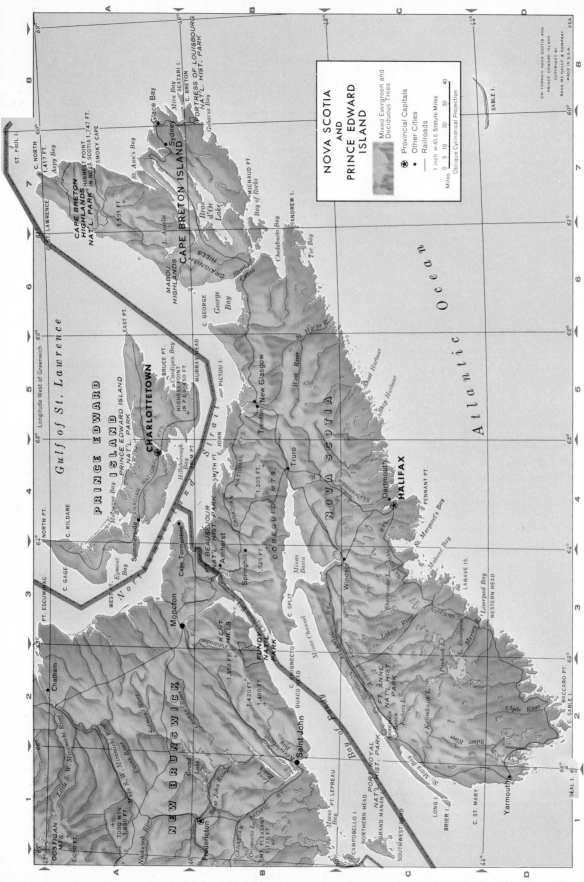

NOVA SCOTIA
AND
PRINCE EDWARD
ISLAND

Mixed Evergreen and
Deciduous Trees

⊛ Provincial Capitals
• Other Cities
Railroads

1 inch = 43.5 Statute Miles

Miles 0 5 10 20 30 40

Oblique Cylindrical Projection

ON TERRAIN NOVA SCOTIA AND
PRINCE EDWARD ISLAND
COPYRIGHT BY
RAND MCNALLY & COMPANY
MADE IN U.S.A.

Especially created for **World Book Encyclopedia** by Rand McNally and World Book editors

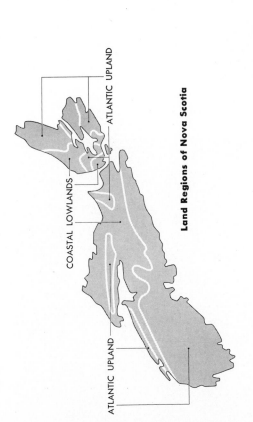

Land Regions of Nova Scotia

NOVA SCOTIA/*The Land*

Land Regions. Nova Scotia has two main land regions: (1) the Atlantic Upland and (2) the Coastal Lowlands.

The Atlantic Upland slopes upward from the Atlantic Ocean to hilly ranges near the northern shores of the province. The northern slopes of these hills drop steeply to the Bay of Fundy and to lowlands along the Gulf of St. Lawrence. North Mountain rises along the Bay of Fundy. The Cobequid Mountains extend along the northern shore of the Minas Basin.

The Atlantic Upland is part of a plain that once lay almost at sea level. Geologists believe this plain stretched northeast from Alabama to perhaps as far as the Arctic Ocean. About 70,000,000 years ago, the plain tilted upward so that it sloped gently to the southeast. In Nova Scotia, this rocky slope is covered with forests. Rivers that flow down the slope are the source of most of the hydroelectric power generated in Nova Scotia.

The Strait of Canso separates the Nova Scotia mainland from Cape Breton Island. At its narrowest point, the strait is only three-fourths of a mile wide. Steep hills rise in the northern part of Cape Breton Island. Thick forests grow close to the shores. Ingonish Mountain is the highest point in Nova Scotia. It rises 1,747 feet above sea level in Cape Breton Highlands National Park.

The Coastal Lowlands extend through central Nova Scotia and Cape Breton Island, and also surround the Cobequid Mountains. These lowlands were carved into the Atlantic Upland when rivers and the weather wore away areas made up of soft rocks. In some places, the hard rocks of the upland region remained and formed flat-topped hills rising from the lowlands.

The lowlands have Nova Scotia's most valuable soils and mineral deposits. The rich farmland of the Annapolis-Cornwallis Valley is south of North Mountain. Fertile marshlands lie along the Bay of Fundy, Chignecto Bay, and the Minas Basin. These marshlands also extend far inland along many rivers. Beneath the lowlands are rich deposits of coal and gypsum. Limestone, rock salt, sandstone, and shale are also found there.

Coastline of Nova Scotia measures about 1,000 miles. The province's rocky southern shore is broken by many inlets. If these inlets are added to the coastline, they increase its length to 4,625 miles. Fishing fleets use the large inlets as harbors. Small islands dot the waters along the southern coast.

Rivers and Lakes. Nova Scotia's rivers are all narrow, and few are more than 50 miles long. The Mersey and the St. Marys rivers, both 72 miles long, are the longest in the province. The Mersey rises on South Mountain and flows through several lakes, including Lake Rossignol. Rich farmland lies along the Annapolis and Shubenacadie rivers, which flow into the Bay of Fundy. Other important rivers include the Lahave and Musquodoboit, which flow into the Atlantic, and the Mira on Cape Breton Island. Ocean ships can sail 30 miles inland on the Mira River. Many of Nova Scotia's rivers rise and fall with the tides, and carry salt water

NOVA SCOTIA

inland. Dikes protect some of the lowlands from rivers that could overflow their banks at high tide.

Nova Scotia has more than 400 lakes. Most of them are small. Bras d'Or Lake, the largest, covers 360 square miles on Cape Breton Island. This salt-water lake nearly divides the island in two. The largest fresh-water lakes are, in order of size, Lake Rossignol in Queens County, Lake Ainslie on Cape Breton Island, Kejimkujik Lake in Queens and Annapolis counties, and Grand Lake near Halifax.

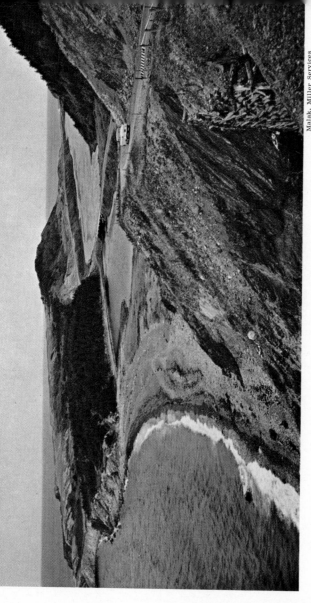

Malak, Miller Services

Russ Kinne, Photo Researchers

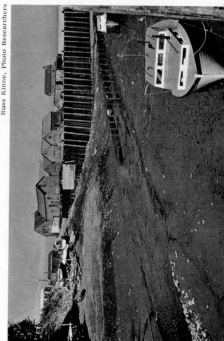

Cabot Trail, *above,* winds along steep bluffs overlooking the sea in northern Cape Breton Island. It is a favorite route for visitors.

Bay of Fundy Coast, *right,* in the Coastal Lowlands region, may have the world's highest tides. Low tide leaves boats on dry land.

Wild Daisies, *below,* brighten the rocky hillsides in the northern section of Cape Breton Island. These steep hills, part of the Atlantic Upland region, are among the highest in Nova Scotia.

Chas. R. Belinky, Photo Researchers

JANUARY

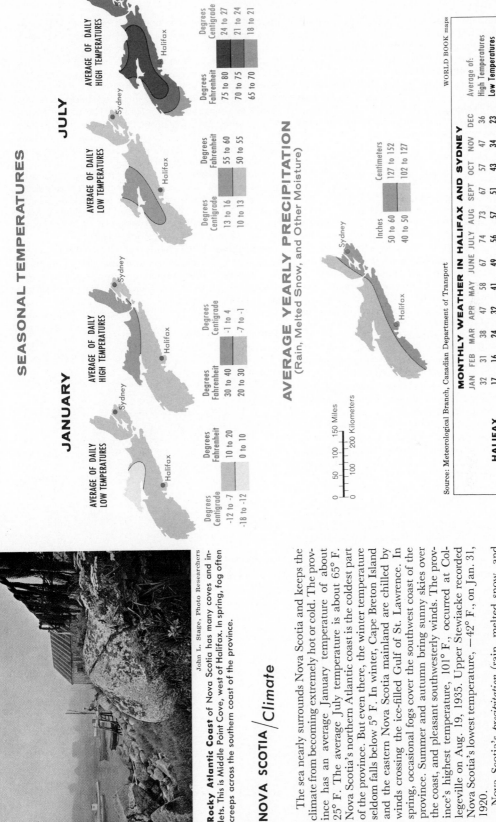

AVERAGE OF DAILY LOW TEMPERATURES

Degrees Fahrenheit	Degrees Centigrade
10 to 20	-12 to -7
0 to 10	-18 to -12

AVERAGE OF DAILY HIGH TEMPERATURES

Degrees Fahrenheit	Degrees Centigrade
30 to 40	-1 to 4
20 to 30	-7 to -1

JULY

AVERAGE OF DAILY LOW TEMPERATURES

Degrees Fahrenheit	Degrees Centigrade
55 to 60	13 to 16
50 to 55	10 to 13

AVERAGE OF DAILY HIGH TEMPERATURES

Degrees Fahrenheit	Degrees Centigrade
75 to 80	24 to 27
70 to 75	21 to 24
65 to 70	18 to 21

AVERAGE YEARLY PRECIPITATION
(Rain, Melted Snow, and Other Moisture)

Inches	Centimeters
50 to 60	127 to 152
40 to 50	102 to 127

0   50   100   150 Miles
0   100   200 Kilometers

WORLD BOOK maps

Source: Meteorological Branch, Canadian Department of Transport

MONTHLY WEATHER IN HALIFAX AND SYDNEY

		JAN	FEB	MAR	APR	MAY	JUNE	JULY	AUG	SEPT	OCT	NOV	DEC	Average of:
HALIFAX		32	31	38	47	58	67	74	73	67	57	47	36	High Temperatures
		17	16	24	32	41	49	56	57	51	43	34	23	Low Temperatures
		15	14	14	13	14	13	12	10	12	12	15	15	Days of Rain or Snow
SYDNEY		16	15	15	14	12	11	11	14	14	16	18		Days of Rain or Snow
		30	28	35	44	56	67	75	74	66	56	45	35	High Temperatures
		15	11	20	29	37	46	55	56	50	41	33	23	Low Temperatures

Temperatures are given in degrees Fahrenheit.

John L. Stage, Photo Researchers

Rocky Atlantic Coast of Nova Scotia has many coves and inlets. This is Middle Point Cove, west of Halifax. In spring, fog often creeps across the southern coast of the province.

NOVA SCOTIA / Climate

The sea nearly surrounds Nova Scotia and keeps the climate from becoming extremely hot or cold. The province has an average January temperature of about 25° F. The average July temperature is about 65° F. Nova Scotia's northern Atlantic coast is the coldest part of the province. But even there, the winter temperature seldom falls below 5° F. In winter, Cape Breton Island and the eastern Nova Scotia mainland are chilled by winds crossing the ice-filled Gulf of St. Lawrence. In spring, occasional fogs cover the southwest coast of the province. Summer and autumn bring sunny skies over the coast, and pleasant southwesterly winds. The province's highest temperature, 101° F., occurred at Collegeville on Aug. 19, 1935. Upper Stewiacke recorded Nova Scotia's lowest temperature, −42° F., on Jan. 31, 1920.

Nova Scotia's *precipitation* (rain, melted snow, and other forms of moisture) averages from 35 to 50 inches a year. Rainfall is heaviest along the Atlantic coast. The annual snowfall totals about 90 inches on the uplands. The lowlands receive from 60 to 80 inches of snow a year.

The leading industry of Nova Scotia is manufacturing. Mining and fishing follow in importance. All production values given in this section are in Canadian dollars. For the value of the Canadian dollar in United States money, see MONEY (table).

Natural Resources. Nova Scotia's most valuable resources are its extensive mineral deposits, fertile lowlands, and rich fishing grounds.

Soil. The Annapolis-Cornwallis Valley has the best farmland. Other good farming areas include the marshlands along the Bay of Fundy and the plains between the Shubenacadie River and the Northumberland Strait. The Atlantic Upland has shallow, rocky soil.

Minerals in Nova Scotia include one of North America's largest deposits of gypsum, near Halifax. Valuable coal deposits lie underground from Chignecto on the Nova Scotia mainland to Glace Bay on Cape Breton Island. Other important minerals include barite, salt, and ores containing copper, lead, and zinc.

Plant Life. Forests cover more than 55 per cent of the province. Firs, hemlocks, maples, pines, and spruces are the most common trees. They supply wood for Nova Scotia's lumber, wood pulp, and paper industries. Other plants found throughout the province include the blueberry, bracken, lambkill, mayflower, raspberry, rhodora, sweet fern, and wintergreen.

Animal Life. The white-tailed deer is Nova Scotia's most common large animal. Some black bears, moose, and wildcats also are found in wilderness areas. Small animals of Nova Scotia include minks, muskrats, otters, porcupines, red foxes, skunks, weasels, and woodchucks. The province has several kinds of geese and ducks, as well as pheasants, ruffed grouse, and woodcocks. Cormorants, gulls, terns, and other sea birds nest along the coast and on the offshore islands. Salmon and trout swim in Nova Scotia's streams. The coastal waters contain cod, flounders, haddock, halibut, herring, lobsters, mackerel, pollacks, swordfish, and tuna.

Manufacturing. Nova Scotia's industrial products have a *value added by manufacture* of about $159,218,000 yearly. This figure represents the value created in products by Nova Scotia's industries, not counting such costs as materials, supplies, and fuels. The leading manufacturing activities of Nova Scotia include the production of iron and steel; the processing of fish and dairy products; the manufacture of transportation equipment; the production of lumber, wood pulp, and paper; and shipbuilding and repair. Most of Nova Scotia's iron and steel mills operate in Sydney and Trenton. Halifax, Lunenburg, Louisbourg, and many other ports have fish processing plants. The chief dairying regions lie around the Minas Basin and along the Bay of Fundy.

Other Nova Scotia products include automobiles, batteries, bricks, cans, carpets, electrical and electronics equipment, plastics, textiles and clothing, and tile. Refineries in Dartmouth produce gasoline and other petroleum products. Tankers bring the raw petroleum from Peru, Venezuela, Iraq, and other countries. Steel mills in Sydney make steel from iron ore mined in the neighboring province of Newfoundland.

Mining in Nova Scotia has an annual income of about $45,489,000. The province's most valuable minerals, in order of importance, are coal, gypsum, and barite. Nova Scotia ranks first among the provinces in the production of these minerals. The chief coal mines are on Cape Breton Island. Some coal is mined in Cumberland and Pictou counties. Much of the coal is used for fuel in the province's steam-driven electric power plants. Gypsum comes from Halifax, Hants, and Inverness counties. Hants County also produces barite. Salt is mined in Cumberland County. Nova Scotia also produces some copper, lead, silver, and zinc from ores recovered in the mining of barite.

Fishing Industry. Nova Scotia ranks among the top fishing industry provinces. Its annual catch is valued at $27,741,000. Nova Scotia leads the provinces in lobster production. Other valuable seafoods include cod, haddock, halibut, scallops, and swordfish. Fish are sold fresh or shipped to food processing plants.

Agriculture. Nova Scotia has about 9,600 farms. They average about 192 acres in size. Dairy farming is the province's most important agricultural activity. Dairy cattle graze on the Truro plain and around the cities and large towns.

Apples are Nova Scotia's leading crop. The annual

PRODUCTION IN NOVA SCOTIA

Total yearly value of goods produced—$270,010,000

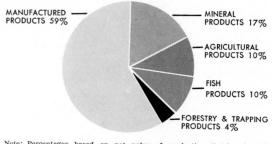

MANUFACTURED PRODUCTS 59%

MINERAL PRODUCTS 17%

AGRICULTURAL PRODUCTS 10%

FISH PRODUCTS 10%

FORESTRY & TRAPPING PRODUCTS 4%

Note: Percentages based on net value of production (total value of shipments less such costs as materials, fuel, electricity, and supplies). Trapping Products are less than 1 per cent.

Source: Dominion Bureau of Statistics

EMPLOYMENT IN NOVA SCOTIA

Average yearly number of persons employed—203,322

		Number of Employees
Services	👤👤👤👤👤👤👤	39,437
Government & Defense	👤👤👤👤👤👤👤	36,816
Manufacturing	👤👤👤👤👤👤	32,660
Wholesale & Retail Trade	👤👤👤👤👤👤	29,910
Transportation, Communications & Utilities	👤👤👤👤👤	23,408
Construction	👤👤👤	13,249
Mining	👤👤	10,069
Finance, Insurance & Real Estate	👤	5,274
Agriculture	👤	3,311
Forestry	👤	3,298
Fishing	👤	2,094
Other	👤	3,796

Source: 1961 Census of Canada

FARM, MINERAL, AND FOREST PRODUCTS

This map shows where the province's leading farm, mineral, and forest products are produced. The major urban area (shown in red) is the province's most important manufacturing center.

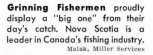

WORLD BOOK map

Grinning Fishermen proudly display a "big one" from their day's catch. Nova Scotia is a leader in Canada's fishing industry.
Malak, Miller Services

apple production totals almost 3,000,000 bushels. Most of the province's apple orchards are in the Annapolis-Cornwallis Valley. Other fruits include apricots, cherries, grapes, pears, plums, raspberries, strawberries, and tomatoes. The province's leading grain is oats. Barley, hay, and wheat are grown on the Bay of Fundy marshlands. Farmers in the western part of the province grow beets, cabbages, potatoes, and turnips.

Forestry. Nova Scotia's forests supply wood for its pulp and paper mills, boatyards, and furniture factories. Hard maples and soft maples are the chief hardwoods of the province. The chief softwoods include balsam firs, red spruces, and white spruces. Nova Scotia exports many Christmas trees to the United States. The province has more than 450 sawmills.

Electric Power. About three-fourths of Nova Scotia's electric power comes from coal-burning power plants. Hydroelectric dams produce the rest. Hydroelectric plants operate on the Avon, Bear, East, Indian, Mersey, Northeast, and Sissiboo rivers. For Nova Scotia's kilowatt-hour production, see ELECTRIC POWER (table).

Transportation. Nova Scotia has about 15,000 miles of roads. About a fifth of them are paved. Automobiles and trains travel about a mile and a half from the Nova Scotia mainland to Cape Breton Island over a *causeway* (a road built on a high, man-made mound). Two airlines serve Nova Scotia. Halifax is a center for air traffic. Nova Scotia has about 1,700 miles of railroad track. Halifax is the province's largest seaport. Steamship lines connect Nova Scotia's coastal towns with Maine, New Brunswick, Newfoundland, and Prince Edward Island.

Communication. Nova Scotia has more than 30 newspapers, including 6 dailies. The *Halifax Gazette*, founded in 1752, was the first newspaper published in Canada. It is still published as the *Royal Gazette* by the provincial government. The province's main daily newspapers include the *Chronicle-Herald* and the *Mail-Star*, both of Halifax, and the *Cape Breton Post*, published in Sydney.

The province has 17 radio stations and 3 television stations. The first radio station, CHNS, began broadcasting from Halifax in 1920. The first television station, CJCB-TV, began operating in Sydney in 1954.

Trainloads of Coal from Cape Breton Island feed the steel mill furnaces of Sydney. Iron ore for Nova Scotia's mills comes from mines in nearby Newfoundland.
Malak, Shostal

Statue of Evangeline honors the French Acadians who were expelled from Grand Pré in 1755. Many of them were sent to what is now Louisiana.

First British Victory in Nova Scotia came when seamen captured and burned the French colony of Port Royal in 1613.

● **Port Royal**

Grand Pré ●

HISTORIC NOVA SCOTIA

Port Royal, one of the oldest cities in North America, was founded about 1605. It is now known as Annapolis Royal.

★ **HALIFAX**

Halifax Was Founded in 1749 by the English governor Edward Cornwallis. He made it the capital of Nova Scotia.

NOVA SCOTIA / History

Indian Days. When white explorers first came to the Nova Scotia region in the early 1500's, they found Micmac Indians living there. These Indians were the earliest known settlers in Nova Scotia. They fished along the coast in summer, and hunted moose and caribou in the forests in winter.

Exploration and Settlement. The English explorer John Cabot may have landed in Nova Scotia or in Newfoundland as early as 1497. Cabot believed he had landed in Asia. Between 1520 and 1524, several other explorers reached Nova Scotia while trying to find a westward sea route to Asia. These explorers included the Italian navigator Giovanni da Verrazano and two Portuguese sailors, João Alvarez Fagundes and Estevan Gomez. Verrazano explored in the service of France. Gomez sailed in the service of Spain. During the summers of the late 1500's, French fishermen used the Nova Scotia shore for drying codfish they had caught in the nearby fishing grounds. These fishermen returned to France every autumn.

In 1603, King Henry IV of France gave land including Nova Scotia to a French explorer, Pierre du Guast, Sieur de Monts. De Monts and another French explorer, Samuel de Champlain, sailed along the Nova Scotia coast in 1604. Champlain made the first accurate chart of the coast. The French called the Nova Scotia region and the land around it *Acadia* (see ACADIA). De Monts and Champlain established a colony in the New Bruns-

wick region near the mouth of the St. Croix River. In 1605, this colony was moved to Nova Scotia and became Port Royal.

The Struggle in Acadia. In 1613, the French colony at Port Royal was captured and burned by English raiders from Virginia. Samuel Argall, a sea captain, led the attack. For more than a hundred years the English and the French battled, off and on, for control of Acadia.

In 1621, King James I of England and Scotland granted Acadia to Sir William Alexander. The grant included what is now Nova Scotia and also New Brunswick, Prince Edward Island, part of Quebec, and part of Maine. Alexander named the region *Nova Scotia*, Latin for *New Scotland*. In 1629, Alexander's son, Sir William the younger, built a new fort at Port Royal. But the colony lasted only until 1632.

The English gave Port Royal to France in 1632, under the Treaty of St. Germain-en-Laye. Colonists sent by a French company took control of Port Royal and also settled at La Have. These settlers became known as Acadians. In 1636, the French built a new fort near Port Royal, on the present site of the town of Annapolis Royal.

English troops under Sir William Phips captured Port Royal in 1690. But England gave Port Royal back to France under the Treaty of Ryswick in 1697. A combined force of troops from England and New England

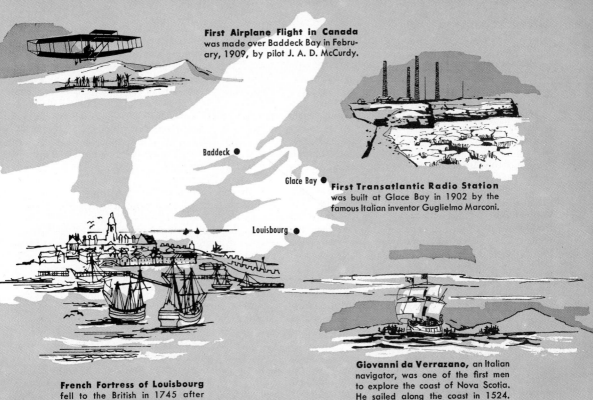

First Airplane Flight in Canada was made over Baddeck Bay in February, 1909, by pilot J. A. D. McCurdy.

First Transatlantic Radio Station was built at Glace Bay in 1902 by the famous Italian inventor Guglielmo Marconi.

Baddeck ●

Glace Bay ●

Louisbourg ●

French Fortress of Louisbourg fell to the British in 1745 after English warships bombarded the fort.

Giovanni da Verrazano, an Italian navigator, was one of the first men to explore the coast of Nova Scotia. He sailed along the coast in 1524.

took Port Royal again in 1710. That year, the British changed the name of the fort from Port Royal to Annapolis Royal.

The French finally gave up Nova Scotia under the Peace of Utrecht in 1713. This treaty made British subjects of the French Acadians who remained in Nova Scotia. It also gave Cape Breton Island and Prince Edward Island (then called *Ile Saint Jean*) to France. The French built a fortress at Louisbourg on Cape Breton Island to guard the entrance to the Gulf of St. Lawrence. British troops from New England captured the fortress in 1745 with the aid of the Royal Navy. France regained Louisbourg in 1748 under the Treaty of Aix-la-Chapelle, which settled a European war. But the French held the fortress for only 10 years. Louisbourg fell to the British during the Seven Years' War (1756-1763).

British settlers established Halifax in 1749, and it became the capital of Nova Scotia the same year. Many French, German, and Swiss Protestants came to Nova Scotia during the early 1750's to escape religious persecution in Europe.

In 1755, British colonial troops from New England began to drive out of Nova Scotia the Acadians who refused to swear allegiance to Britain. Several thousand Acadians fled to Prince Edward Island, Quebec, the French colony of Louisiana, and British colonies in America.

─── **IMPORTANT DATES IN NOVA SCOTIA** ───

1497-1524 European explorers reached Nova Scotia while seeking a sea route to Asia.

1603 King Henry IV of France commissioned Pierre du Guast, Sieur de Monts, to colonize Acadia.

1604 Samuel de Champlain charted the Nova Scotia coast.

1605 Champlain and De Monts founded Port Royal.

1710 The British captured Port Royal and changed its name to Annapolis Royal.

1713 Under the Peace of Utrecht, France gave Britain all Acadia except Cape Breton Island and Prince Edward Island.

1749 The British founded Halifax.

1755 British colonial troops from New England began to drive French Acadians from Nova Scotia.

1758 The British won Cape Breton Island from France. Nova Scotia's first provincial parliament met in Halifax.

1776-1785 United Empire Loyalists came to Nova Scotia from the United States.

1867 Nova Scotia joined with New Brunswick, Ontario, and Quebec in forming the Dominion of Canada.

1917 A French munitions ship exploded in Halifax harbor and killed more than 1,600 persons.

1939-1945 Halifax became a base for warships sailing to and from Europe during World War II.

1955 The Canso Causeway was opened, linking the Nova Scotia mainland with Cape Breton Island.

1967 The Canadian Parliament established the Cape Breton Development Corporation to help attract new industry to the area.

Progress as a Province. In 1758, the British government allowed colonists in Nova Scotia to elect a representative assembly. The first assembly met in Halifax. It gave the people some voice in their government. But a governor and a council appointed by the king really ruled the province.

In 1760, more than 20 ships carrying New Englanders arrived in Nova Scotia. The New Englanders took over the land the Acadians had cleared, and established many new settlements. During and after the Revolutionary War in America (1776-1785), about 35,000 United Empire Loyalists came to Nova Scotia from the United States. The Loyalists were British colonists in America who refused to take up arms against Great Britain in the Revolutionary War. They established Shelburne and also settled in Aylesford, Digby, and other towns.

Settlers from Scotland began arriving in 1773. The greatest number of Scots arrived between 1815 and 1850. They settled in the eastern part of the Nova Scotia peninsula and in Cape Breton. Irish immigrants came to Nova Scotia after the 1845 potato famine in Ireland.

Nova Scotians gained complete control over their local affairs in 1848. That year, the British government granted Nova Scotia a governing council controlled by the elected assembly. Nova Scotia became the first completely self-governing colony within the British Empire. Joseph Howe, a forceful editor and statesman of Nova Scotia, had led the fight to win the new government for the colony.

During the 1800's, Nova Scotia thrived with growing industries and increasing world trade. Shipbuilders used timber from the province's forests to build merchant ships. By 1860, Nova Scotia had one of the largest merchant fleets in the world. For a short time, these ships and the profitable lumber industry made Nova Scotia the most prosperous Canadian province. But during the 1860's, steamships largely replaced sailing vessels. Nova Scotia then lost much of its shipping business. The lumber industry also suffered because of reckless tree cutting.

In 1867, Nova Scotia joined with New Brunswick, Ontario, and Quebec in forming the Canadian confederation (see BRITISH NORTH AMERICA ACT). During the next 30 years, economic difficulties slowed the growth of all the provinces. Nova Scotia began to recover during the late 1890's when farm production increased and the iron and steel industry developed.

The 1900's. During World War I (1914-1918), Halifax served as the headquarters of Allied fleets sailing between North America and Europe. In 1917, a French military supply ship exploded in Halifax Harbor. The blast killed more than 1,600 persons and damaged much of the city.

In 1933, Angus L. Macdonald became premier of the province. Macdonald, a Liberal, served until 1940, when he resigned to take an administrative post in the Canadian government during World War II (1939-1945). He returned as premier in 1945 and served until his death in 1954. During Macdonald's administration, the Legislative Assembly passed new tax laws, a civil service act, and other laws dealing with economic, legislative, and social problems.

School expansion, highway construction, and industrial development marked the 1950's and 1960's in Nova Scotia. Several vocational and technical schools were built in the 1950's to meet the rising demand for skilled workers. The Nova Scotia Institute of Technology opened in Halifax in 1963. The Nova Scotia section of the Trans-Canada Highway—about 300 miles long—was built across the province. In 1955, the Canso Causeway was completed. It provided a highway and railway link between the mainland and Cape Breton Island. The causeway contributed to the province's economic growth and to expansion of the tourist industry. A suspension bridge across the northern part of Halifax harbor was also completed in 1955.

In 1957, the provincial government established Industrial Estates Limited, a corporation designed to attract new industry to Nova Scotia. This nonprofit corporation leases or sells manufacturing space and facilities to companies that wish to expand or to move into Nova Scotia. In 1967, the Canadian government set up the Cape Breton Development Corporation. This corporation was designed both to attract new industry and to close unprofitable coal mines. For almost 20 years, Nova Scotia's coal industry had suffered from rising production costs and a loss of markets.

Nova Scotia Today is developing industrially and its people have a higher standard of living than in past years. But a wide gap still exists in job opportunities, living standards, and wage levels between Nova Scotia and the heavily populated areas of Canada.

At the beginning of the 1970's, industrial expansion centered on Cape Breton Island. A new coal mine and new industries valued at about $35 million were under construction in the Sydney area. A $300-million industrial park was being built on the shores of Canso Strait. The park will include a deepwater port, a $60-million oil refinery, and a $65-million plant for making *heavy water*, used in atomic reactors for producing electric power. The projects at Sydney and on the strait were scheduled to be completed by the mid-1970's.

BASIL W. DEAKIN,
CHARLES BRUCE FERGUSSON, and BERNARD J. KEATING

THE PREMIERS OF NOVA SCOTIA		
	Party	Term
1. Hiram Blanchard	Conservative	1867
2. William Annand	Liberal	1867-1875
3. Philip C. Hill	Liberal	1875-1878
4. Simon H. Holmes	Conservative	1878-1882
5. John S. D. Thompson	Conservative	1882
6. William T. Pipes	Liberal	1882-1884
7. William S. Fielding	Liberal	1884-1896
8. George H. Murray	Liberal	1896-1923
9. Ernest H. Armstrong	Liberal	1923-1925
10. Edgar N. Rhodes	Conservative	1925-1930
11. Gordon S. Harrington	Conservative	1930-1933
12. Angus L. Macdonald	Liberal	1933-1940
13. A. Stirling MacMillan	Liberal	1940-1945
14. Angus L. Macdonald	Liberal	1945-1954
15. Harold Connolly	Liberal	1954
16. Henry D. Hicks	Liberal	1954-1956
17. Robert L. Stanfield	*Progressive Cons.	1956-1967
18. George I. Smith	*Progressive Cons.	1967-1970
19. Gerald Regan	Liberal	1970-

*Progressive Conservative

Outline

I. Government
  A. Lieutenant-Governor   E. Local Government
  B. Premier   F. Taxation
  C. Legislative Assembly   G. Politics
  D. Courts
II. People
III. Education
  A. Schools   B. Libraries   C. Museums
IV. A Visitor's Guide
  A. Places to Visit   B. Annual Events
V. The Land
  A. Land Regions   C. Rivers and Lakes
  B. Coastline
VI. Climate

VII. Economy
  A. Natural Resources   F. Forestry
  B. Manufacturing   G. Electric Power
  C. Mining   H. Transportation
  D. Fishing Industry   I. Communication
  E. Agriculture
VIII. History

Questions

Where is Nova Scotia's best farmland?
How does Nova Scotia's provincial corporation attract new industries to the province?
What are Nova Scotia's three cities?
Who heads the provincial government?
What are Nova Scotia's chief manufactured products?
What bodies of water nearly surround Nova Scotia?
What are the leading mining products of Nova Scotia?
What is Nova Scotia's most valuable land region?
What was the first newspaper published in Canada?
Who were the United Empire Loyalists?

Books for Young Readers

BANNON, LAURA M. *The Tide Won't Wait: A Nova Scotia Story.* McLeod (Toronto), 1957.
BLAKELEY, PHYLLIS R. *Nova Scotia: A Brief History.* Dent (Toronto), 1955.
HILL, KAY. *Glooscap and His Magic: Legends of the Wabanaki Indians.* McClelland (Toronto), 1963.

Books for Older Readers

BECK, JAMES M. *The Government of Nova Scotia.* Univ. of Toronto Press (Toronto), 1957.
BIRD, MICHAEL J. *The Town That Died.* Ryerson (Toronto), 1963.
CAMPBELL, GEORGE G. *The History of Nova Scotia.* Ryerson (Toronto), 1949.
HALIBURTON, THOMAS C. *Sam Slick.* McClelland (Toronto), 1941.
RADDALL, THOMAS H. *Halifax: Warden of the North.* McClelland (Toronto), 1950.

NOVA SCOTIA COLLEGE OF ART AND DESIGN is the only specialized school in Canada that offers degrees in fine arts and design. It is located in Halifax, N.S., and receives most of its financial support from the provincial government. The college offers four-year programs of study, some of which include preparation for careers in teaching, environmental design, and communication design. The college was founded in 1887. For enrollment, see CANADA (table: Universities and Colleges).   JAMES DAVIES

NOVA SCOTIA TECHNICAL COLLEGE is a coeducational college in Halifax, N.S. It is privately controlled, but receives grants from the provincial and federal governments. The college grants bachelor's, master's, and doctor's degrees. The undergraduate division offers the final two years of a five-year engineering course, and the final four years of a course in architecture. The earlier years are offered by universities associated with the college. Nova Scotia Technical College was founded in 1907. For enrollment, see CANADA (table: Universities and Colleges).   C. J. FEAR

NOVACULITE. See WHETSTONE.

NOVALIS (1772-1801) was the pen name of FRIEDRICH VON HARDENBERG, a German romantic poet. Five poems by Novalis, called *Hymns to the Night* (1800), express his religious, mystical nature, and a longing for death. In the essay *Christianity or Europe* (1799), Novalis tried to show that people lived more meaningful lives in the spiritual unity of the Catholic Middle Ages than in his own troubled time. This attitude became a major theme of German romanticism. Novalis died before finishing *Heinrich von Ofterdingen*, a novel about a legendary medieval poet.

Novalis was born in Saxony. The death of his 15-year-old fiancée in 1797 deepened his melancholy and his religious temperament. Novalis' work as a mining engineer brought him close to the land and intensified his love of nature and its mysteries.   JEFFREY L. SAMMONS

NOVAYA ZEMLYA, *NAW vuh yuh zyim LYAH,* is the Russian name for two islands in the Arctic Ocean that belong to Russia. The name means *new land.* The northern island is about 20,000 square miles in area, and the southern island is about 15,000 square miles. The islands have a combined coastline of 1,700 miles. Novaya Zemlya has an arctic climate. The islands have large deposits of coal, and smaller quantities of gold and copper. Russia has used the islands to test nuclear bombs.

Russians first discovered Novaya Zemlya, probably in the A.D. 1000's, but the islands remained uninhabited until 1877. The Russian government has built villages for hunters, and a small colony of Russians and Samoyeds live on the southern island. Islanders raise reindeer, trap animals, and collect *eider down* (the feathers of eider ducks).   THEODORE SHABAD

441

NOVEL

NOVEL. A novel is a long prose story that is largely imaginary. Its chief purpose is usually to entertain, but its underlying aim is to help readers to understand life. Charles Dickens' *The Pickwick Papers* is mainly a funny story. Leo Tolstoy's great novel *War and Peace* not only gives pleasure but also offers much wisdom. While the reader is laughing at Mark Twain's humor in *Huckleberry Finn*, he learns about human nature and the history of part of the United States.

The novel is perhaps the broadest and least confined of all literary forms. It may be comparatively short. For example, Edith Wharton's *Ethan Frome* can be read in less than two hours. It may be long. Herman Melville's *Moby Dick* probably takes about twenty hours to read.

The novel is usually about people, but it is sometimes about animals or fabulous beings, such as those in *Gulliver's Travels* by Jonathan Swift. In George Stewart's *Storm*, the chief character is a wind. If the characters are people, they may be of high or low rank. They may be emperors or page boys. They may be saints or thieves.

Real people and imaginary people may appear in the same novel. In James Fenimore Cooper's *The Spy*, George Washington appears among "made-up" characters. Sir Walter Scott included King Richard I of England with many nonhistorical characters.

There is also much flexibility of action in the novel. The story can take place anywhere, and at any time. The action may occur in unexplored regions near the South Pole, as in Edgar Allan Poe's *The Narrative of A. Gordon Pym*. It can go under the sea. Its action can go through distant space, as in Jules Verne's *Hector Servadac*, the story of life on a comet.

The time of a novel may be in the past, the present, or the future. Sigrid Undset's *Kristin Lavransdatter* is a *trilogy* (series of three) of novels set in Norway in the 1300's. *Looking Backward* by Edward Bellamy is actually a forecast with events occurring in A.D. 2000.

Perhaps the great quality of the novel is the great variety of its subject matter. It may tell of practically unknown adventures. For example, few persons have had experiences like those of Robinson Crusoe. It may deal interestingly with familiar, everyday occurrences. For example, Sinclair Lewis' *Main Street* throws a new light on life in a small midwestern town. Reader interest is held by both types: *romantic* novels, which explore the new, and *realistic* novels, which recognize, analyze, and "check" the familiar.

The Power of the Novel

People read novels for fun, yet often they get much more than fun from them. The novel mirrors the history of mankind. W. M. Thackeray's *Henry Esmond* teaches us facts in English history; John Steinbeck's *The Grapes of Wrath* tells of the plight of United States dust-bowl farmers during the depression; George Santayana's *The Last Puritan* shows how a New England heritage shaped the character of a young man.

The novel may do more than mirror history: it may even influence it. Harriet Beecher Stowe's *Uncle Tom's Cabin* gave great impetus to the movement to free the slaves. Charles Dickens' *Nicholas Nickleby* told such a pathetic story of the treatment of children in an English school that it led to a movement to reform education.

The novel not only can teach people and help to shape society, but also it can make the reader a more understanding person, more tolerant and more sympathetic toward suffering. Reading a great novel like Fyodor Dostoevsky's *The Brothers Karamazov* or Victor Hugo's *Les Misérables* is an emotional experience that can serve to broaden the humanity of the reader. Like a great play such as William Shakespeare's *King Lear*, a great novel enriches the human spirit.

How the Novel Developed

The novel as it is now known in Western Europe and the Americas got its real start in the 1700's. Yet its beginnings are ancient. Many of the earliest narratives told for entertainment were about historical persons, but prose tales about imaginary persons are to be found even in ancient Greek writings.

Early Beginnings. The Italian stories called *novelle* are closely related to the novel of today in form. They are shorter than most novels of today. Giovanni Boccaccio's *Decameron* (1348-1353) is the most noted collection of novelle. The stories in the *Decameron* are supposedly told by a group of persons who left the city of Florence to escape the plague.

In Spain, two works of fiction became models for later writers. Garci Rodríguez de Montalvo published a romantic narrative, *Amadis of Gaul*, in 1508. This work was the most influential of the *romances of chivalry*. The first *picaresque novel*, *Lazarillo de Tormes*, appeared anonymously in 1554. It told of the adventures of a *pícaro*. A *pícaro* is a clever, witty, unscrupulous youngster who travels about in the service of various masters. He engages in cheating, practical jokes, and petty thievery. This type of story became very popular.

The most famous of all Spanish stories, *Don Quixote* by Miguel de Cervantes, was published early in the 1600's. Cervantes poked fun at the popular romances of chivalry through the idealistic knight Don Quixote. With his realistic squire Sancho Panza, Don Quixote, in a real world, tries to have the same kind of adventures that the knights did in the unreal, dreamy world of the old romances of chivalry. The effect is comic, but the tale is also sad. Don Quixote suffers much in body and in spirit.

In England, prose fiction began significantly during the Elizabethan period. The first notable work was John Lyly's *Euphues* (1578), remembered today for its

finished style, which set *euphuism* (artificial, elegant, alliterative style) as a standard for writers. There is very little incident, and the book is chiefly a running discussion of love, honor, and manners among fine ladies and gentlemen. Imitations of this popular piece included Thomas Lodge's *Rosalind* (1590). In the same year came Sir Philip Sidney's *Arcadia*, a long story using some materials of the romances of chivalry, but quieter in tone. It is partly pastoral; that is, it emphasizes the quiet charm of country living.

The Elizabethans wrote much picaresque material, especially after *Lazarillo de Tormes* was translated into English in 1576. Most notable was *The Unfortunate Traveller, or The Life of Jack Wilton* (1594) by Thomas Nash.

In the 1600's came many long, tedious romances, but no narratives of importance in the development of the novel until 1678. In that year, the first part of John Bunyan's *The Pilgrim's Progress* appeared. This is an allegory; that is, the characters and actions are represented by personifications, or symbols. It is the story of Christian, who left the City of Destruction as a pilgrim to the Celestial City. And yet it gives some realistic glimpses of English village life in the settings for its allegory. Bunyan's beautifully simple style reflects his familiarity with the Bible.

Mrs. Aphra Behn's short *Oroonoko* (1688) was notable as one of the first stories to try to create sympathy for a slave.

The 1700's in England saw the novel well started. Defoe's *Robinson Crusoe* (1719) is the first novel of incident in which the author seems to try deliberately to create belief in the reality of his invented material. It has been said that Defoe "lied like truth." All his writings seem sincerely realistic. With Defoe, fiction seems more real than reality. The best known of his many other novels is *Moll Flanders* (1722).

Defoe's stories are not fully-developed novels. Each is mainly a simple succession of adventures without a continued plot. Plot is a planned groundwork of action leading to a climax, which is the logical result. It creates suspense by the pattern of arrangement. This kind of planned action first appeared in *Pamela* (1740) by Samuel Richardson, the story of a servant girl's efforts to defend her honor. This was a long tale in the form of letters, but it had plot. Richardson's *Clarissa Harlowe* (1747-1748) was a long novel in which the young woman was defeated instead of victorious like Pamela.

Henry Fielding also wrote novels in the modern sense of the word. His works were mainly humorous, as opposed to Richardson's seriousness. His novel, *Joseph Andrews* (1742), made fun of *Pamela* by showing, in highly exaggerated incidents, a young man trying to defend his honor against an older woman.

Some critics have said that Fielding's *Tom Jones* (1749) has the most perfect plot in all English fiction. It tells of the adventures of a lively young man who gets into many situations, both serious and humorous, before the mystery of his parentage is cleared up. Fielding used the picaresque method in much of his writing. Tobias Smollett, who wrote *Roderick Random* (1748), also used a picaresque framework for comic stories.

A very different kind of novel was produced by Laurence Sterne, who was interested in character more than incident. His *Tristram Shandy* (1760-1767) has been called a forerunner of the modern psychological novel. Oliver Goldsmith introduced the story of sentiment in his *The Vicar of Wakefield* (1766), one of the most loved English novels. In it, the gentle, humorous Dr. Primrose meets many family troubles with strength and courage before his story reaches a happy ending.

The Gothic novel appeared in the late 1700's. A Gothic novel belongs to what has been called the *goose-flesh* type of fiction. In it, the heroine in a lonely castle is exposed to such things as ghosts, strange lights, pictures that seem alive, mysterious voices, trapdoors, and statues that seem to drip blood. The first such English novel was Horace Walpole's short *The Castle of Otranto* (1764). The most famous was, perhaps, Ann Radcliffe's *The Mysteries of Udolpho* (1794). Many lesser and often more horrifying such novels were written.

The 1800's in England. The first novelist of importance was Jane Austen, who relied less on excitement than on careful use of detail. Her *Pride and Prejudice* (1813) is the story of a small-town family with several daughters to marry off. The chief interest lies in Mr. Darcy's courtship of Elizabeth Bennett, who is at first prejudiced against him because of his proud attitude toward village girls.

Sir Walter Scott had great success in colorful historical romance. His materials were often lovely ladies and gallant knights who were involved in tournaments, sieges, crusades, piracy, or border warfare. Scott did not forget the common people, however, and he was skilled in both tragic and comic action. His first novel, *Waverley*, appeared in 1814. Among his most famous were *The Bride of Lammermoor* (1819), *Ivanhoe* (1820), and *Kenilworth* (1821). Many persons think his best novel was *Old Mortality* (1816), about a religious problem among the Covenanters of Scotland at the end of the 1600's.

Charles Dickens' novels were compounded chiefly of humor, pathos, and interest in the welfare of the common people. His career began with the humorous *Pickwick Papers* in 1836-1837. In *Oliver Twist* (1837), Dickens' talent for portraying pathos and tragedy was revealed, as well as his sympathy for the poor. His novels are especially informative on English schools, elections, poorhouses, prisons, and legal matters. Dickens also created memorable characters, such as Micawber in *David Copperfield* (1849). *A Tale of Two Cities* (1859) is a vivid story of adventures, escapes, and heroism during the French Revolution.

443

NOVEL

William Makepeace Thackeray in *Vanity Fair*, published as a serial in 1847 and 1848, pictured the folly, insincerity, and emptiness of the London society of his time. His *Henry Esmond* (1852) is a historical novel of England in the early 1700's. Charlotte Brontë in 1847 brought out *Jane Eyre*, a story of the problems of a struggling young governess. Her sister, Emily Brontë, told in *Wuthering Heights* a tale of character conflict and violent incident in England's North Country.

The best of George Meredith's finely written, rather hard-to-read, psychological novels is probably *The Ordeal of Richard Feverel* (1859). About the same time, George Eliot (the pen name of Mary Ann Evans) was producing her stories of the English Midlands, notably *The Mill on the Floss* (1860) and *Silas Marner* (1861). Like Emily Brontë, George Eliot was deeply interested in the effects of environment on character.

Robert Louis Stevenson's novels *Treasure Island* (1883) and *Kidnapped* (1886) are exciting romantic stories of adventure, often involving young people.

On the Continent. François Rabelais's *Gargantua and Pantagruel* appeared in France in the 1500's. He specialized in exaggerated tales of gross humor. The psychological romance *La Princesse de Clèves* (*The Princess of Cleves*, 1678) by Madame de La Fayette was the only influential novel of the 1600's. As in England, the novel did not get under way until the 1700's.

In 1715 came the first part of Alain René Le Sage's picaresque novel *Gil Blas*. L'Abbé Prévost produced a tragic love novel, *Manon Lescaut*, in 1731. Pierre Carlet de Marivaux published his *Marianne* in parts from 1731 through 1741. Perhaps the most famous early French novel was Jean Jacques Rousseau's *La Nouvelle Héloïse* (*The New Heloise*, 1761), a sentimental and tragic narrative about love problems.

The 1800's were rich in French novels. Stendhal's *The Red and the Black* (1831) showed an ambitious young man in complicated French society. Honoré de Balzac wrote many realistic novels. He intended an entire collection of novels (*La Comédie Humaine*) to give a picture of all life in France. The most famous single novel of the group is *Le Père Goriot* (1834).

Dumas produced many spectacular romances, *The Three Musketeers* (1844) being the most famous. Victor Hugo's *Les Misérables* (1862) is a complicated story springing from a poor man's theft of a loaf of bread. One of the most famous French novels of this time was *Madame Bovary* (1857), Gustave Flaubert's carefully finished study of a dissatisfied wife.

In the 1870's, Émile Zola's novels started the theory of naturalism. Naturalism treated character scientifically as the product of heredity and environment. Naturalism did not shrink from showing the most unpleasant or degrading aspects of life.

The novel as such developed late in Germany. Goethe's sentimental, tragic love story *The Sorrows of Young Werther* (1774) was read throughout Europe. His *The Apprenticeship of Wilhelm Meister* (1795-1796) is a study of character development.

In Russia, Pushkin pioneered in 1836 with *The Captain's Daughter*. This novel treats of an unsuccessful Cossack revolt, led by peasants. Gogol's *Dead Souls* (1842) comically pictures a shrewd, scheming man, planning to gain money and land, but also gives realistic pictures of many aspects of Russian society.

Perhaps the most famous of all Russian novels is Tolstoy's *War and Peace* (1865-1869), a tremendous work portraying many aspects of society during the Napoleonic wars. His *Anna Karenina* (1875-1877) is a study of a tragic marriage.

Ivan Turgenev, also a powerful writer who used a finished style, brought out his most notable novel, *Fathers and Sons*, in 1862. During his life in Paris, he influenced and was influenced by French novelists.

Fyodor Dostoevsky, one of the most vivid Russian writers, wrote *Crime and Punishment* (1866). His novel *The Brothers Karamazov* (1880) has tremendous scope, including almost every range of human emotion from highest religious devotion to the most diabolical hatred. Dostoevsky was one of the most powerful shapers of the novel of today.

In the United States, sustained prose fiction became important with Charles Brockden Brown's *Wieland* (1798), a story of ventriloquism and religious mania. His *Edgar Huntly* (1799) has been called the first American detective novel.

James Fenimore Cooper, the "American Scott," wrote many historical novels, some of the best of which feature Indians. His *The Spy* (1821) was the first important novel to emphasize the American scene. Probably the most famous of his novels are the *Leatherstocking Tales*, with Natty Bumppo, master woodsman and brave fighter, as hero. *The Deerslayer* (1841) is perhaps his best. His pictures of frontier America and Indian life were excellently done. The heroines in his novels were usually weak and lovely.

Nathaniel Hawthorne wrote novels in which the "action" was often the destructive psychological effect of concealing sin, as in *The Scarlet Letter* (1850), picturing Puritan times, and in *The House of the Seven Gables* (1851), which mingles New England witchcraft and the inevitable punishment.

The greatest novel of the 1800's is probably Herman Melville's *Moby Dick* (1851). It is the story of a captain's pursuit of a huge white whale which symbolizes evil. Melville gave his readers both exciting incident and profound interpretation of man's problems.

William Dean Howells tried to make the novel realistic in *The Rise of Silas Lapham* (1885). Henry James used a rather difficult style for his *The American* (1877), in which the fine American characters face social and ethical problems in Europe.

Mark Twain's humorous stories of American boyhood, *Tom Sawyer* (1876) and *Huckleberry Finn* (1884), created patterns of natural speech and action that greatly influenced the novelists who came after him.

Stephen Crane treated war truthfully rather than romantically in *The Red Badge of Courage* (1895).

In the 1900's, most serious authors have been far more concerned with probing deep and even desperate problems than with entertainment. They show man as individual (in the psychological novel), and man's place in society (in the social novel). Joseph Conrad's *Lord Jim* (1900) shows what goes on in the mind of a chief mate after he deserts a sinking ship. Thomas Mann's *Buddenbrooks* (1901) is a study of the development and decay of a German merchant family. Mann's *The Magic Mountain* (1924) interprets the confusing world before World War I through the eyes of a sensitive young man in an Alpine tuberculosis sanitarium.

Sigmund Freud's studies of the unconscious mind strongly influenced the writing of novels concerned with the fears, frustrations, and anxieties of modern man. Such a novel is James Joyce's *Ulysses* (1922), which gives a full account of one man's inner life during a period of 18¾ hours. D. H. Lawrence's *Sons and Lovers* (1913) studies the personality problems of a young Englishman torn between love of his mother and love of young women.

Thomas Wolfe's *Look Homeward, Angel* (1929) tells vividly of a young man who felt he did not "belong" to any social group in America. Marcel Proust's long and brilliant *À la Recherche du Temps Perdu* (*The Remembrance of Things Past*), published in several volumes from 1913 to 1927, deals in detail with the psychological states of several sensitive Frenchmen and women.

André Gide's *Les Faux-Monnayeurs* (1926; English title, *The Counterfeiters*) analyzes the lives and personalities of a group of characters, and the problems involved in writing a novel. In Ernest Hemingway's *The Sun Also Rises* (1926) and Aldous Huxley's *Point Counter Point* (1928), the chief characters suffer from lack of faith. Virginia Woolf made penetrating character studies in *Mrs. Dalloway* (1925) and *To the Lighthouse* (1927).

Problems of being a Negro are presented in William Faulkner's *Light in August* (1932). The horrors of modern war is the theme of Hemingway's *A Farewell to Arms* (1929), Erich Maria Remarque's *All Quiet on the Western Front* (1929), and Faulkner's *A Fable* (1955).

Three novels of World War II are outstanding. Norman Mailer's *The Naked and the Dead* is long, but honestly and brilliantly written. It is noted for its stark realism. Irwin Shaw's *The Young Lions* is the dramatic, eloquent story of three young men in World War II, only one of whom survives. Herman Wouk's *The Caine Mutiny* traces the career of a Princeton graduate from midshipman to captain of the old minesweeper *Caine*.

Fear of mechanized control of human life is shown in Huxley's *Brave New World* (1932). Jakob Wassermann in *The World's Illusion* (1918) wrote of the need of faith, and kindness to fellowmen.

Some novelists of the 1900's have dealt largely with economic problems. Erskine Caldwell's *Tobacco Road* (1932) pictures severe poverty in the South. In *My Ántonia* (1918), Willa Cather reported difficult pioneering conditions on the Nebraska prairie, as Ole Rölvaag did for Minnesota in *Giants in the Earth* (1927).

Sometimes the novelist blames society when his characters violate moral codes, as Theodore Dreiser did in *Sister Carrie* (1900) and *An American Tragedy* (1925).

Other twentieth-century novelists deal with characters as groups. John Steinbeck did this in his realistic story of migrant workers, *The Grapes of Wrath* (1939). John Dos Passos in *Manhattan Transfer* (1925) presents the confused struggle for success, and the involved psychological and economic problems that are a part of city life today. In *The Emigrants* (1951), Vilhelm Moberg vividly recounts the extreme hardships of Swedish families voyaging to America.

Technique of the Novel

As the novel developed, its form changed almost as much as its content. At first, authors emphasized action, and it was generally easy to follow, as in the simple narrative *Tom Jones* (Fielding), or in the form of letters (Richardson's *Pamela*). Sometimes they used an autobiographical form, as Dickens did in *David Copperfield*.

The action was usually crystallized in a plot. Plot is organized action concerning a definite problem with foreshadowing (clues), climax, and dénouement (unfolding or untying). But even these rules were not always followed. Many novels have no recognizable plot.

The novel may be merely a description of a kind of life, as Dos Passos' *U. S. A.* (1937). It may have no central character wholly admirable. Often the novelist seems to be just an observer of what he describes. He is impartial, remote, as anonymous as a newswriter. He offers no sympathy and no religious consolation. This is especially true of naturalistic writers.

Authors sometimes use special techniques to present setting and establish tone. Dos Passos uses the "camera-eye" and "newsreel" technique. Psychological novelists follow the "stream of consciousness" technique—giving the character's thoughts and feelings without any apparent selection, and without comment. Many modern novelists use symbolism, whereby an object represents an abstract quality, such as goodness or evil. In Franz Kafka's *The Castle* (1930), the castle symbolizes faith. Albert Camus' *The Plague* (1947) outwardly describes an epidemic of bubonic plague, but symbolically relates man to the problem of evil in general.

The modern novelist probably does not offer as much clear explanation as the earlier novelist did. Sometimes the reader is lost in the complex presentation, which reflects the complexity of modern life.

The novel is not entirely different from all other forms of literature. It is most closely related to the short story, but it is longer and usually has more characters and more complicated events than the short story. It differs from drama because a play is more narrowly focused than a novel and the playwright seldom offers any explanation of the action.

The novel is not only the least confined and most experimental form of literature, but is also the longest lasting. If one form of the novel falls in popular favor, the novel can regain its vitality and its position in some new form. People write novels for self-expression, and read them to fill instinctive needs. Novels help people to endure and to enjoy life.   ALEXANDER COWIE

Related Articles. See LITERATURE and the articles on the various national literatures, such as AMERICAN LITERATURE and FRENCH LITERATURE. See also the following articles:

NOVELS

Anna Karenina	Les Misérables
Brothers Karamazov	Pilgrim's Progress
Candide	Red and the Black, The
David Copperfield	Robinson Crusoe
Gulliver's Travels	Three Musketeers, The
Huckleberry Finn,	Uncle Tom's Cabin
Adventures of	Vanity Fair
Iron Mask, Man in the	War and Peace
Last of the Mohicans	

OTHER RELATED ARTICLES

Fiction	Romance
Legend	Short Story
Mystery Story	

NOVEMBER

NOVEMBER is the eleventh month of the year. *Novem* is the Latin word for *nine*. In the Roman calendar, November was the ninth month. Because July was named for Julius Caesar and August for Augustus Caesar, the Roman Senate offered to name the eleventh month for Tiberius Caesar. He refused modestly, saying, "What will you do if you have thirteen emperors?" Originally there were thirty days in November, then twenty-nine, then thirty-one. From the time of Augustus, it has had thirty days.

Nature in November. November comes between autumn and winter. In the North Temperate regions during November, the trees are bare, and the dead leaves on the earth have lost the brilliant color they had in October. Soft snow seldom hides the bareness of the fields, but the grays and browns of the landscapes are sometimes relieved by delightful days of hazy sunshine. The Anglo-Saxons referred to November as "the wind month" and sometimes "the blood month," probably because during this period they killed animals for their winter meat.

Many outdoor activities in the North come to a halt in November. Nature seems to be resting after the harvest. The crops have been stored away or have been shipped to processing plants and mills, and the farmer knows whether or not he has had a successful year. Near the end of November, the people of the United States celebrate Thanksgiving Day. The Pilgrims originated this Thanksgiving festival to express their gratitude for their first harvests in the hard new land. In Canada, where the colder climate forces farmers to harvest their crops earlier, Thanksgiving is celebrated in October.

IMPORTANT NOVEMBER EVENTS

1 Benvenuto Cellini, Italian goldsmith, born 1500.
—Dr. Crawford W. Long, first to use ether as an anesthetic in surgery, born 1815.
—Sholem Asch, American novelist, born 1880.
—France gave up its Indian settlements to India, 1954.
2 Daniel Boone, American frontiersman, born 1734.
—Marie Antoinette, French queen, born 1755.
—Gaspar de Portolá discovered San Francisco Bay, 1769.
—James K. Polk, 11th President of the United States, born near Pineville, N.C., 1795.

Warren G. Harding   **James K. Polk**

—Warren G. Harding, 29th President of the United States, born near Blooming Grove, Ohio, 1865.
—North Dakota became the 39th state, 1889.
—South Dakota became the 40th state, 1889.
—Arthur Balfour, British Foreign Secretary, proposed settlement of Jewish people in Palestine, 1917.
—First regular radio broadcasts began, over station KDKA in Pittsburgh, 1920.
3 Stephen Austin, colonizer of Texas, born 1793.
—William Cullen Bryant, American poet, born 1794.
—Canadian explorer Vilhjálmur Stefánsson born 1879.
4 Erie Canal formally opened at New York, 1825.
—Auguste Rodin, French sculptor, born 1840.
—Will Rogers, American humorist, born 1879.
5 Gunpowder Plot to blow up Parliament failed, 1605. This day is celebrated as Guy Fawkes Day.
—Eugene V. Debs, American socialist and labor leader, born 1855.
—Will Durant, American historian, philosopher, and educator, born 1885.
—England and France declared war on Turkey, 1914.
—Reconstructed Vienna Opera House opened, 1955.
6 John Philip Sousa, American bandmaster, born 1854.
—Ignace Jan Paderewski, Polish pianist, composer, and statesman, born 1860.
—First intercollegiate football game in United States,

Rutgers *vs.* Princeton, at Rutgers, 1869.

7 Gen. William Henry Harrison defeated Indians in Battle of Tippecanoe, 1811.
—Nobel physicist Marie Curie born 1867.
—Last spike driven in Canadian Pacific Railway, 1885.
—Bolsheviks ousted provisional Russian government, 1917.
—United States troops landed in North Africa, 1942.
8 Edmund Halley, British astronomer, born 1656.
—Mt. Holyoke Seminary for women opened, 1837.
—Montana became the 41st state, 1889.
9 Ivan Turgenev, Russian novelist, born 1818.
—Edward VII of England born 1841.
—Kaiser Wilhelm II abdicated German throne, 1918.
—The CIO established, 1935.
10 Martin Luther, German religious leader, born 1483.
—William Hogarth, English painter, born 1697.
—German poet Friedrich von Schiller born 1759.
—Arctic explorer Donald MacMillan born 1874.
11 Russian novelist Fyodor M. Dostoevsky born 1821.
—Thomas Bailey Aldrich, American writer, born 1836.
—Maude Adams, American actress, born 1872.
—Washington became the 42nd state, 1889.
—Armistice signed ending World War I, 1918.

—Veterans Day first celebrated in United States, 1954 (now observed on fourth Monday in October).
12 Joseph Hopkinson, American jurist and author of "Hail Columbia," born 1770.
—Reformer Elizabeth Cady Stanton born 1815.
13 Joseph Hooker, Union general, born 1814.
—James C. Maxwell, Scottish physicist, born 1831.
—Novelist Robert Louis Stevenson born 1850.
—John Drew, American actor, born 1853.
—Louis D. Brandeis, American jurist, born 1856.
—Holland Tunnel opened in New York City, 1927.
14 Robert Fulton, American inventor, born 1765.
—Claude Monet, French painter, born 1840.
—Leo H. Baekeland, American inventor, born 1863.
—Indian leader Jawaharlal Nehru born 1889.

446

Football is the outstanding sport in November. The weather is usually ideal for the exciting games, and thousands of spectators do not seem to mind sitting several hours in the frosty air to watch their favorite football teams play.

Special Days. Election Day in the United States falls on the first Tuesday after the first Monday in November. Thanksgiving Day is celebrated on the fourth Thursday of the month. Children's Book Week is also observed in November.

November Symbols. The topaz is the November birthstone, and the special flower of the month is the chrysanthemum. GRACE HUMPHREY

Quotations

November's sky is chill and drear,
November's leaf is red and sear.
Sir Walter Scott

Autumn wins you best by this, its mute
Appeal to sympathy for its decay.
Robert Browning

The wild November comes at last
Beneath a veil of rain;
The night wind blows its folds aside,
Her face is full of pain.
Richard Henry Stoddard

November woods are bare and still;
November days are clear and bright;
Each noon burns up the morning's chill,
The morning's snow is gone by night.
Helen Hunt Jackson

See also CALENDAR; CHRYSANTHEMUM; THANKSGIVING DAY; TOPAZ.

IMPORTANT NOVEMBER EVENTS

14 Canadian physician Frederick Grant Banting, famous for discovering insulin, born 1891.
—John Steuart Curry, American painter, born 1897.
—Aaron Copland, American composer, born 1900.
15 William Pitt, British statesman, born 1708.
—William Herschel, English astronomer, born 1738.
—Draft of Articles of Confederation approved by Congress, 1777.
—Zebulon Pike first sighted Pikes Peak, 1806.
—American jurist Felix Frankfurter born 1882.
—First meeting of League of Nations Assembly, Geneva, 1920.
—Manuel Quezon inaugurated as first president of the Philippines, 1935.
16 John Bright, English statesman, born 1811.
—Canadian poet Louis H. Fréchette born 1839.
—Composer Paul Hindemith born 1895.
—Oklahoma became the 46th state, 1907.
—The United States recognized the Communist government of Russia, 1933.
17 Congress first met in Washington, D.C., 1800.
—Suez Canal opened, 1869.
—British General Bernard L. Montgomery, commander of the British 8th Army in World War II, born 1887.
18 Louis Jacques Daguerre, French painter and inventor of the daguerreotype, born 1787.
—Asa Gray, American botanist, born 1810.
—Standard time began in the United States, 1883.
—Sir William S. Gilbert, English dramatist who worked with composer Sir Arthur Sullivan, born 1836.
—Eugene Ormandy, American conductor, born 1899.
—United States and Panama signed treaty providing for Panama Canal, 1903.
—Haakon VII elected king of Norway, 1905.
19 Frontiersman George Rogers Clark born 1752.
—Sculptor Bertel Thorvaldsen born 1770.
—Ferdinand de Lesseps, French promoter of Suez Canal, born 1805.
—James A. Garfield, 20th President of the United States, born in Orange, Ohio, 1831.
—Abraham Lincoln delivered Gettysburg Address, 1863.

James A. Garfield

19 Allen Tate, American poet and critic, born 1899.
20 Sir Wilfrid Laurier, Canadian statesman, born 1841.
—Selma Lagerlöf, Swedish novelist, born 1858.
—Kenesaw Mountain Landis, first commissioner of professional baseball, born 1866.
—United States forces landed on Tarawa, 1943.
21 Voltaire, French author and philosopher, born 1694.
—North Carolina ratified the Constitution, 1789.
22 French explorer La Salle born 1643.
—George Eliot, English novelist, born 1819.
—Charles de Gaulle, French statesman, born 1890.
—Benjamin Britten, British composer, born 1913.
—First transpacific air-mail flight began, 1935.
—U.S. President John F. Kennedy assassinated, 1963.
23 Franklin Pierce, 14th President of the United States, born in Hillsboro, N.H., 1804.
—Canadian novelist Sir Gilbert Parker born 1862.

Franklin Pierce

Zachary Taylor

24 Baruch Spinoza, Dutch philosopher, born 1632.
—Missionary Father Junípero Serra born 1713.
—Laurence Sterne, British novelist, born 1713.
—Zachary Taylor, 12th President of the United States, born near Barboursville, Va., 1784.
—French painter Henri de Toulouse-Lautrec born 1864.
25 Lope de Vega, Spanish playwright, born 1562.
—Andrew Carnegie, American industrialist, born 1835.
—Joe DiMaggio, American baseball star, born 1914.
26 First national Thanksgiving Day in United States proclaimed by President George Washington, 1789.
27 Charles A. Beard, American historian, born 1874.
28 William Blake, English poet and artist, born 1757.
—Stefan Zweig, Austrian biographer, born 1881.
29 Louisa M. Alcott, American author, born 1832.
—Commander Richard E. Byrd and crew of three were first to fly over South Pole, 1929.
30 Jonathan Swift, who wrote *Gulliver's Travels*, born 1667.
—Theodor Mommsen, German historian, born 1817.
—Mark Twain, American author, born 1835.
—British statesman Sir Winston Churchill born 1874.

NOVENA is a period of private or public devotion and prayer lasting nine days. It is used in the Roman Catholic Church as a period in which to obtain special graces. It is patterned after the action of the apostles. They gathered together for prayer during the nine days between Ascension Thursday and Pentecost. The Novena of the Sacred Heart and the Novena to the Holy Ghost are important novenas. FULTON J. SHEEN

NOVERRE, JEAN GEORGES. See BALLET (History).

NOVI SAD, *NAW vee SAHD* (pop. 126,000; alt. 276 ft.), is a railroad center in Yugoslavia. It lies at the junction of the Danube River and the Mali Bački Canal (see YUGOSLAVIA [color map]). It serves as a market for the agricultural products of the region. GEORGE KISH

NOVOBIOCIN. See ANTIBIOTIC (Kinds).

NOVOCAIN is a trade name for PROCAINE, a drug used as a local anesthetic. When injected, novocain paralyzes nearby nerves for a short time. The paralysis usually leaves no permanent or damaging effect. Novocain is not habit-forming and is rarely poisonous. Dentists often inject novocain into the gums before pulling or filling teeth. An American physician, Albert Einhorn, discovered the drug in 1905. It is the most widely used local anesthetic. SOLOMON GARB

NOVOSIBIRSK, *NAW vuh see BEERSK* (pop. 1,064,-000; alt. 400 ft.), the largest city in Siberia, lies 1,700 miles east of Moscow (see RUSSIA [political map]). It is western Siberia's industrial and transportation center.

NOX. See SOMNUS.

NOYES, *noiz,* **ALFRED** (1880-1958), an English poet and critic, was noted for his stirring ballads. His most famous is "The Highwayman." He also wrote epic poems, short stories, and novels. His works include *Collected Poems* (1947); *Two Worlds from Memory* (1953), an autobiography; and *A Letter to Lucian and Other Poems* (1957). He was born in Staffordshire and studied at Oxford University. He was converted to the Roman Catholic religion in 1925, and his religious views influenced his later writings. WILLIAM VAN O'CONNOR

British Information Services
Alfred Noyes

NOYES, JOHN HUMPHREY. See ONEIDA COMMUNITY.

NSA. See NATIONAL SECURITY AGENCY.

NSC. See NATIONAL SECURITY COUNCIL.

NU, U (1907-   ), is a Burmese politician and statesman. In the 1930's, he was a leader of a student strike that helped obtain independence for Burma. In 1948, he became the first prime minister of independent Burma. He left his post for eight months during 1956 and 1957 to reorganize the Anti-Fascist People's Freedom League, the country's most important political party. After a split in the ruling party, he resigned in 1958. He was named prime minister again in 1960, but was forced out of office in 1962 and placed under detention. He was released in 1966. U Nu was born in Wakema, in the Myaungmya District of Burma. *U* is an honorary title similar to *mister*. In March, 1960, U Nu be-

came a Buddhist priest and took the name U DHAMMA DASA. See also BURMA (History). GEORGE E. TAYLOR

NUBIA, *NYOO bee uh,* was a region in what is now the Sudan. It extended along the Nile River from ancient Egypt almost to what is now Khartoum, Sudan. Nubia was an important source of gold. Egypt ruled parts of it until about 750 B.C. Then, Nubian kings conquered Egypt, and ruled for a short time. BARBARA MERTZ

NUCLEAR ENERGY. See ATOMIC ENERGY.

NUCLEAR ENGINEERING. See ENGINEERING (table).

NUCLEAR FISSION. See FISSION.

NUCLEAR NON-PROLIFERATION TREATY. See UNITED NATIONS (Arms Control).

NUCLEAR PHYSICS is the science that deals with the nature of the nucleus, the tiny dense core deep within the atom. Nuclear physicists seek to understand the structure of the nucleus and how the particles within it act upon one another. The supreme achievement of nuclear physicists has been the development of practical atomic energy. See ATOMIC REACTOR.

The fundamental problem confronting nuclear physicists is the study of nuclear forces. We know that in the nucleus the two nuclear building blocks are the *neutron* and the *proton*. These two particles make up 99.9 per cent of all matter. When they are close together, the neutron and the proton are strongly attracted and resist efforts to pull them apart. This cohesion of neutrons and protons is called *binding energy*, and explains why nuclei do not fly apart.

Nuclear scientists study the nucleus by bombarding it with high-speed particles. Some of these nuclear projectiles merely glance off the nucleus or are scattered. This scattering allows physicists to gain knowledge about nuclear forces, particularly about the size of the nucleus. Other particles do not bounce off the nucleus, but penetrate into it. These may produce nuclear disintegrations or transformations. In a few cases, as in the bombardment of an isotope of the element uranium (U-235), the atom *fissions* (splits in two). This process releases a large amount of nuclear energy.

Bombardment of the nucleus with very high-energy particles has resulted in the artificial production of subnuclear particles known as *mesons*. These are of special interest to nuclear physicists, because they may explain the nature of the nuclear forces. RALPH E. LAPP

Related Articles in WORLD BOOK include:

Atom	Plasma (in	Transmutation
Atom Smasher	physics)	of Elements
Atomic Energy	Radiation	Uranium
Meson	Radioactivity	

NUCLEAR REACTOR. See ATOMIC REACTOR.

NUCLEAR ROCKET. See ROCKET (Nuclear Rockets).

NUCLEAR WEAPON. See ATOMIC BOMB; HYDROGEN BOMB.

NUCLEIC ACID is a complex compound found in all living cells. Two types of nucleic acids are *deoxyribonucleic acid* (DNA) and *ribonucleic acid* (RNA). DNA is usually found only in the nucleus of a cell. But RNA may be found throughout the cell. Certain viruses, such as the plant viruses and poliomyelitis virus, contain only RNA. Other viruses contain only DNA.

DNA plays a vital part in heredity. It is the chief material in *chromosomes*, the cell bodies that control the heredity of an animal or a plant. When a cell divides, the chromosomes in its nucleus must be duplicated exactly in the daughter cells. The DNA in the chromosomes furnishes the daughter cells with a complete set of "instructions" for the cells' own development and the development of their descendants for generations.

DNA contains *phosphate*, a sugar called *deoxyribose*, and compounds called *bases*. These are arranged in units of phosphate-sugar-base—phosphate-sugar-base, repeated thousands of times to form long, coiled chains. This fundamental chemical structure is common to all DNA. However, there are four different bases in DNA— *adenine*, *guanine*, *thymine*, and *cytosine*. The exact proportions of each of the bases, and the precise order in which they are arranged, are unique for each *species* (kind) of living thing. It is this exact order and composition that must be faithfully copied each time a cell divides. Each DNA molecule contains about 20,000 such phosphate-sugar-base units. A chromosome contains many thousands of DNA molecules. Scientists can *synthesize* (chemically reconstruct) some kinds of DNA molecules that are able to reproduce themselves.

RNA also consists of long chains of repeating phosphate-sugar-base units. However, the sugar in RNA is *ribose*. Its bases are *adenine*, *guanine*, *cytosine*, and *uracil* (rather than thymine as in DNA). Scientists believe that some RNA carries the materials used in making proteins. Other RNA carries the "instructions" for making different proteins.   ARTHUR and SYLVY KORNBERG

For a more complete discussion and diagrams, see CELL. See also HEREDITY; WATSON, JAMES D.

NUCLEON. See ATOM (Inside the Atom).

NUCLEONICS is the study of nucleons, the central particles of atoms. See ATOM (Inside the Atom).

NUCLEUS. See AMEBA; ATOM; CELL; COMET.

NUEVA ISABELA. See SANTO DOMINGO.

NUEVO LEÓN, *NWAY voh lay AWN,* is a state in northeastern Mexico (see MEXICO [political map]). It has an area of 24,925 square miles and a population of 1,653,808. A dry, rolling plain covers northern Nuevo León. The Sierra Madre Oriental mountains rise across the southern part. Nuevo León grows grapes, cotton, wheat, corn, barley, and citrus fruits. It also produces cattle and lumber. Monterrey is the state capital (see MONTERREY).   CHARLES C. CUMBERLAND

NUISANCE. When someone annoys you while you are working, you may call him a nuisance. In law, the term *nuisance* has much the same meaning.

A nuisance that annoys a large part of the community, such as an odorous slaughterhouse, is called a *public nuisance*. A slaughterhouse in open country that affects few people is a *private nuisance*. Most states have laws forbidding public nuisances.   FRED E. INBAU

NUKUALOFA, *NOO koo ah LOH fah* (pop. 15,545; alt. 10 ft.), is the capital of Tonga. The town lies on the northern coast of Tongatapu, one of the many islands of the South Pacific kingdom (see TONGA [map]).

Nukualofa is Tonga's chief port and commercial center. Small shops and business offices line its wide streets. Most of the buildings are made of wood, and many of the streets are unpaved. Important landmarks in Nukualofa include the Legislative Assembly building and the royal palace and chapel.

In 1643, Abel Tasman, a Dutch sea captain, became the first European to land at Nukualofa. Nukualofa was named Tonga's capital during the reign of King George Tupou I, who ruled from 1845 to 1893.   STUART INDER

NULL SET. See SET THEORY (Empty Sets).

NULLIFICATION is the action of setting aside a law by declaring it *null and void*. The United States Constitution does not provide any way for a law of Congress to be declared unconstitutional after it has been signed by the President. Some delegates to the Constitutional Convention believed that the courts would naturally assume this authority. But only in 1803, with the case of *Marbury vs. Madison*, did the Supreme Court flatly assert the right of the courts to pass on the constitutionality of an act of Congress.

The theory that the states, rather than any branch of the federal government, should have the right to *nullify* (declare unconstitutional) a law of Congress, developed slowly. The Kentucky and Virginia Resolutions of 1798 protested the Alien and Sedition Acts passed by Congress. Many persons believed that these acts violated Amendment I. They wanted the states to join together to declare the acts unconstitutional. But no other state would join in the action. In 1799, the Kentucky legislature stated its belief in the legality of nullification, but merely entered a protest against the Alien and Sedition Acts.

Nullification was next seriously proposed in 1828, when John C. Calhoun prepared a document known as the "South Carolina Exposition." Rising industrial interests of the Northeast had persuaded Congress to include in the tariff law of 1828 (the "tariff of abominations") protective duties that the cotton-growing South disliked. Sentiment against the tariff was strongest in South Carolina. There was even talk of secession.

Calhoun's motive in recommending nullification was to provide an alternative to secession. He argued that the federal government had no right to judge the constitutionality of its own acts. He also insisted that the states had given certain powers to Congress, and were alone competent to say whether or not Congress had exceeded its powers. Calhoun's reasoning was set forth by Senator Robert Y. Hayne in his famous debate with Webster in 1830. Webster said nullification would break up the Union, and closed with the words: "Liberty *and* Union, now and forever, one and inseparable!"

In 1832, Congress again passed a protective tariff act. South Carolina passed an ordinance which declared the tariff laws of 1828 and 1832 null and void in that state. It threatened to leave the Union if the federal government attempted to enforce the tariff laws anywhere in South Carolina. President Andrew Jackson met this challenge by a proclamation warning the people that the laws would be enforced. He also took measures to make sure that the tariff would be collected at the important port of Charleston. After Congress passed a Force Bill to uphold Jackson's position, it became clear that resistance was unwise. Besides, the Compromise Tariff of 1833, engineered through Congress by Henry Clay, greatly reduced the tariff duties.

Nullification was only one manifestation of the doctrine of states' rights which, insofar as it meant the supremacy of the states over the nation, was ended by the Civil War.   JOHN DONALD HICKS

See also CALHOUN, JOHN C.; FORCE BILL; HAYNE, ROBERT Y.; STATES' RIGHTS; WEBSTER, DANIEL.

NUMA POMPILIUS, the second of the seven legendary kings of Rome, reigned from 715 to 673 B.C. Many of his deeds are legendary. Supposedly, he became king a year after Romulus died and had a reign of unbroken peace. His chief contributions to the state were in religion. He established the priesthoods, and created a calendar form which was used until the time of Julius Caesar. He also built a *shrine* (sacred place) to the god Janus (see JANUS). Numa, a Sabine, consulted the nymph Egeria who is said to have given Numa advice on religious matters (see EGERIA).   HERBERT M. HOWE

NUMBER, in grammar, is a feature of language that indicates how many persons or objects are referred to. In English, the form of a noun shows whether the reference is to one person, place, object, or idea, or to more than one. The form that indicates only one is called the *singular.* The form that indicates more than one is called the *plural.* Some languages have a singular form, indicating one, a *dual* form, indicating two, and a plural form, indicating more than two.

The plurals of English nouns may be divided into *regular* and *irregular* plurals. In speech, the regular plurals are formed by adding an *s, z,* or *ez* sound to the singular. For example, add an *s* sound to *cap, bet,* and *back,* to form *caps, bets,* and *backs.* Add a *z* sound (in writing, spelled *s*) to *cab, bed,* and *bag,* to form *cabs, beds,* and *bags.* Add an *ez* sound (spelled *es*) to *witch, smash, pass,* and *judge,* to form *witches, smashes, passes,* and *judges.*

Irregular Plurals must be learned as we learn the language. The English language has seven nouns, plus their compounds, which form the plural by changing the vowel sound. For example, the plural for *man* is *men.* Other examples include tooth, *teeth;* goose, *geese;* foot, *feet;* mouse, *mice;* and louse, *lice.* In woman, *women,* the sound changes in the first syllable also, although the spelling shows a change in the second syllable only.

One noun, *ox,* forms the plural by adding *en* to make *oxen.* A few nouns have the *en* plural and other changes as well, as in child, *children,* and brother, *brethren.*

About a dozen nouns ending in *f* change the *f* sound to a *v* sound, and then add a *z* sound, spelling it *ves.* Examples are half, *halves,* wife, *wives,* and leaf, *leaves.*

Some nouns remain unchanged in the plural, as in *sheep, deer, quail, partridge, moose,* and *bison.* Certain dialects use this plural form for words of measurement. Britishers, in some areas, say *two pound of butter.*

Some English nouns have no plural at all. These are abstract nouns, such as *cowardice* and *geniality,* and nouns of mass, such as *gravel* and *mush.* They are not like *sheep* or *deer.* We say *two sheep* but not *two cowardices.*

Foreign Plurals. Words coming into English from foreign languages sometimes keep their foreign plurals. Such foreign plurals are mostly from Greek and Latin words. Some of these are phenomenon, *phenomena;* criterion, *criteria;* alumnus, *alumni;* alumna, *alumnae;* fungus, *fungi;* and thesis, *theses.* There is a strong tendency for such words to go into the regular English plural group. For example, at an earlier period the plural of *stadium* was the foreign form *stadia.* Now, however, *stadiums* is the plural form commonly used. Sometimes such nouns become regular when used figuratively. We might use the Hebrew plural *cherubim* when referring to the angels, but we would call children *cherubs.*

The spelling of plurals in English has many irregularities that reflect nothing in speech. Singular nouns that end in *y,* following a consonant, change their endings to *ies* in plural, as in lady, *ladies;* flurry, *flurries;* candy, *candies.* Many nouns ending in *o* add a *z* sound in the plural, spelling it *oes,* as in hero, *heroes,* potato, *potatoes,* and mosquito, *mosquitoes.*

English Pronouns also have plurals, but the relationship is not so consistent as in nouns. *We* can be called the plural of *I,* and *they* the plural of *he, she,* and *it. These* is the plural of *this,* and *those* the plural of *that.*

English Verbs do not have plurals in the sense that they can mean "do a thing once" or "do it several times." Verbs do have forms that vary according to the number of the subject involved. For example, the verb *play* occurs with a plural subject in "The boys *play* golf," and *plays* occurs with a singular subject in "The boy *plays* golf."   PAUL ROBERTS

See also DECLENSION; INFLECTION; NOUN (Number and Case); PRONOUN; VERB.

NUMBER AND NUMERAL. Numbers are ideas. We think of a number when we consider how many objects are in a certain group. Numerals are names for number ideas. For example, we can use the word *five* or the symbol *5* to stand for the number of fingers on one hand. Both *five* and *5* are numerals.

Counting means arranging numerals in a certain order. In counting, each number is one more than the number that comes before it. Systems of counting or of naming numbers are called *numeration systems.* Today, most peoples use the *Hindu-Arabic* numeration system, also called the *decimal number system.* This system includes the familiar symbols 1, 2, 3, 4, 5, and so on.

Numbers used in counting are also called *natural numbers, positive numbers,* and *cardinal numbers. Ordinal numbers* such as "first," "second," "third," and so on, indicate an object's position in a series.

See also NUMERATION SYSTEMS; DECIMAL NUMERAL SYSTEM; ARABIC NUMERALS.

NUMBER LINE. See ADDITION (Regrouping).

NUMBERING MACHINE is a device for printing numbers on such papers as checks, invoices, and orders. It may print one number after another—1, 2, 3—or it may repeat the same number as many times as desired. The machines are either automatic or hand-operated.

A numbering machine consists of a set of little wheels, all mounted on the same shaft. Each of these wheels has numbers from 0 to 9 on its rim. The first wheel prints 0, 1, 2, 3, 4, 5, 6, 7, 8, 9. As it returns to 0, a tooth engages the second wheel and turns the wheel from 0 to 1, printing 10. After the number 99 has been printed, a tooth turns the third wheel from 0 to 1, printing 100. There are some numbering machines that can count as high as 99,999,999.   WILLIAM H. FISH

NUMBERS is the fourth book of the Bible. Its name comes from the *census,* or counting, of the Israelites in the desert after their escape from Egypt. The book includes experiences of the Hebrew tribes interwoven with important laws and poetic material. It contains the famous priestly blessing "The Lord bless thee, and keep thee" (6: 24), and the law of the Nazarites, who dedicated themselves to the service of God. It also tells the story of the prophet Balaam, who was hired to curse Israel. The book describes the grandeur and tragedy of Moses' career as leader of his people.   ROBERT GORDIS

See also BALAAM; NAZARITE; PENTATEUCH.

NUMERAL. See NUMBER AND NUMERAL.

NUMERATION SYSTEMS, or NUMERAL SYSTEMS, are ways of counting and of naming numbers. We cannot see or touch numbers, because they are ideas. But we can use symbols to stand for numbers. These symbols are called *numerals.* Here are four numerals that represent the number in a half dozen: 6, six, VI, and ⅢⅢ I. Each of these numerals is a name for the number in a half dozen.

Our numeration system has only 10 basic numerals, called *digits:* 0, 1, 2, 3, 4, 5, 6, 7, 8, 9. With these 10 symbols we can represent any number, regardless of size. This system is called a *decimal* system because it is based on 10. The word decimal comes from the Latin word *decem,* which means *ten.* Ten is the *base* or the *scale* of the decimal system.

Kinds of Numeration Systems

It is possible to use any number as a base in building a numeration system. The number of digits used in the system is always equal to the base. For example, (1) the *decimal,* or *base 10,* system uses 10 digits; (2) the *quinary,* or *base 5,* system uses 5 digits; (3) the *binary,* or *base 2,* system uses 2 digits; and (4) the *duodecimal,* or *base 12,* system uses 12 digits.

The Decimal System represents numbers in terms of groups of ten. Suppose you wanted to count the pennies you have saved. Instead of counting them one by one, you could count them in groups of 10. You would put them in stacks of 10. Then you would arrange the stacks in groups, putting 10 in each group, as shown.

2 Groups of 10 Stacks of 10 Pennies   **4 Stacks of 10 Pennies**   **8 Pennies**

How many pennies are there? You could count them like this: 2 groups of 10 stacks of 10 = 2 × (10 × 10) = 200; 4 stacks of 10 = 4 × 10 = 40; plus 8 single pennies. In all, you have 200 + 40 + 8 = 248 pennies.

If you had counted the pennies one by one, you would have counted the same total. In decimal counting, you use one-digit numerals to count from 1 to 9. Then you use two-digit numerals to count from 10 to 99. In two-digit numerals, the digit on the left stands for the number of groups of ten. The digit on the right shows the number of ones. For example, the numeral 14 stands for 1 group of ten plus 4 ones. After 99, you use three-digit numerals. The first digit on the left of these numerals stands for the number of *hundreds* (groups of ten tens). Thus, the numeral 248 stands for 2 hundreds + 4 tens + 8, as shown in the illustration.

The value of each digit in a decimal numeral depends on its *place* (position) in the numeral. For example, the numeral 482 contains the same digits as the numeral 248. But 482 represents a different number because the digits are in different positions.

Charlotte W. Junge, the contributor of this article, is Professor of Education at Wayne State University, and Assistant Editor of The Arithmetic Teacher.

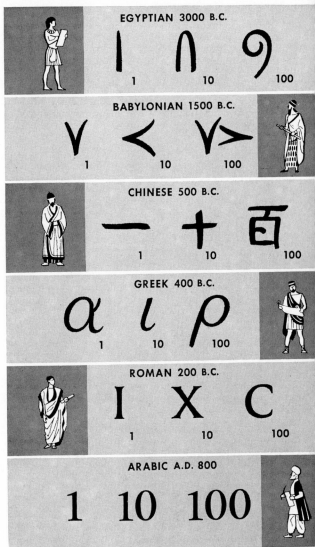

Numerals from Five Early Civilizations

Each position has a name that tells its value in terms of 10. In the numeral 248, the 8 is in the *ones* place; the 4 is in the *tens* place; and the 2 is in the *hundreds* place. In numerals with more than three digits, the additional positions are called the *thousands* place, the *ten thousands* place, and so on. Each position has a value 10 times greater than the position to its right.

Another way of expressing place value is to use *powers of 10* (10 multiplied by itself a certain number of times). The following table shows the meaning of several powers of 10.

Place Name	Power of 10	Meaning	Symbol
Ones		1	10^0
Tens	1st	1 × 10	10^1
Hundreds	2nd	10 × 10	10^2
Thousands	3rd	10 × 10 × 10	10^3
Ten Thousands	4th	10 × 10 × 10 × 10	10^4

The 2 in 10^2, the 3 in 10^3, and the 4 in 10^4 are called *exponents.* The 10 is called the *base.* The exponent tells the number of times the base is to be used as a *factor*. For example, 10^2 means 10 is used as a factor twice, or 10×10; and 10^4 means $10 \times 10 \times 10 \times 10$. We can write the numeral 248 as $200 + 40 + 8$, or we can write it as $(2 \times 10^2) + (4 \times 10^1) + 8$.

The value of any numeral is the sum of the values of the digits. The numeral 4,206 means "4 thousands plus 2 hundreds plus no tens plus 6 ones," or $(4 \times 10^3) + (2 \times 10^2) + (0 \times 10^1) + (6 \times 1)$. We could also write 4,206 as $(4 \times 10^3) + (2 \times 10^2) + (0 \times 10^1) + (6 \times 10^0)$. The exponent zero means ten is not used as a factor. 6×10^0 is another expression for 6×1.

The Quinary System groups numbers by fives and by powers of five. The word *quinary* comes from the Latin word *quinque*, meaning *five*. This system uses five digits: 0, 1, 2, 3, and 4. In the quinary system, the numeral 10 (one, zero) stands for *five*, the base of the system. It means "1 five plus no ones." To avoid confusion between quinary numerals and decimal numerals, you can write the word "five" next to a quinary numeral: 10_{five}. This numeral is read "one, zero, base 5."

Grouping by Fives. The groups of stars below show the meaning of several quinary numerals:

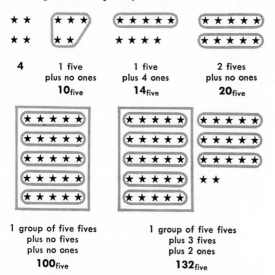

| 4 | 1 five plus no ones **10**$_{\text{five}}$ | 1 five plus 4 ones **14**$_{\text{five}}$ | 2 fives plus no ones **20**$_{\text{five}}$ |

1 group of five fives plus no fives plus no ones **100**$_{\text{five}}$

1 group of five fives plus 3 fives plus 2 ones **132**$_{\text{five}}$

In quinary counting, the digits 1, 2, 3, and 4 are used to express numbers from 1 to 4. To show 5 in this system, we use the first two basic symbols. The number five is written 10_{five}. Two-digit numerals are used from 10_{five} to 44_{five} (4 fives plus 4 ones). The digit on the left represents the number of fives, and the righthand digit represents the number of ones. In the numeral 32_{five}, the 3 means 3 groups of 5, and the 2 means 2 ones. To show the counting numbers past 44_{five}, three basic symbols are used. The numeral 100_{five} means 1 twenty-five (5 fives) plus no tens and no ones. After 444_{five}, four-digit numerals are used, and so on.

Finding Place Value in Base 5. In a quinary numeral, the last digit on the right is in the ones place. Every other position has a value 5 times the value of the position to its right. In the quinary numeral 1402_{five}, the 2 means 2×1; the 0 means 0×5; the 4 means $4 \times 5 \times 5$; and the 1 means $1 \times 5 \times 5 \times 5$.

You can express the place value of each position in terms of powers of 5. The following table shows the meaning of several powers of 5 and their values in decimal numerals.

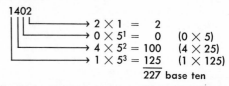

Base 5 Numeral		Meaning		Decimal Numerals		
1$_{\text{five}}$	=	1	=	1	=	5^0
10$_{\text{five}}$	=	5×1	=	5	=	5^1
100$_{\text{five}}$	=	5×5	=	25	=	5^2
1,000$_{\text{five}}$	=	$5 \times 5 \times 5$	=	125	=	5^3
10,000$_{\text{five}}$	=	$5 \times 5 \times 5 \times 5$	=	625	=	5^4

In the numeral 1402_{five}, 2 is in the ones place; 0 is in the 5^1 place; 4 is in the 5^2 place; and 1 is in the 5^3 place.

Quinary numerals may be changed to decimal numerals by adding the values of the digits in terms of decimal numerals. The following calculation shows how to change the quinary numeral 1402_{five} to the decimal numeral 227:

$$
\begin{aligned}
1402 \\
2 \times 1 &= 2 \\
0 \times 5^1 &= 0 \quad (0 \times 5) \\
4 \times 5^2 &= 100 \quad (4 \times 25) \\
1 \times 5^3 &= 125 \quad (1 \times 125) \\
\hline
227 \text{ base ten}
\end{aligned}
$$

The Binary System groups numbers by twos and by powers of two. The word *binary* comes from the Latin word *bini*, meaning *two at a time*. This system uses only two digits: 0 and 1. The numeral 10_{two} (one, zero, base two) stands for *two*, the base of the system. It means "1 two plus no ones."

Grouping by Twos. The groups of squares below show the meaning of several binary numerals:

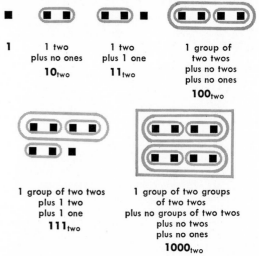

| 1 | 1 two plus no ones **10**$_{\text{two}}$ | 1 two plus 1 one **11**$_{\text{two}}$ | 1 group of two twos plus no twos plus no ones **100**$_{\text{two}}$ |

1 group of two twos plus 1 two plus 1 one **111**$_{\text{two}}$

1 group of two groups of two twos plus no groups of two twos plus no twos plus no ones **1000**$_{\text{two}}$

In binary counting, single digits are used for *none* and *one*. Two-digit numerals are used for 10_{two} and 11_{two} (2 and 3 in decimal numerals). For the next counting number, 100_{two} (4 in decimal numerals), three digits are necessary. After 111_{two} (7 in decimal numerals), four-digit numerals are used until 1111_{two} (15 in decimal numerals) is reached, and so on.

Finding Place Value in Base 2. In a binary numeral, every position has a value 2 times the value of the position to its right. For example, in the numeral 1010_{two}, the 0 on the right means 0×1; the 1 at the left of this 0 means 1×2; the next 0 means $0 \times 2 \times 2$; and the 1 at the far left of the numeral means $1 \times 2 \times 2 \times 2$.

The place value of each position can be expressed in terms of powers of 2. The following table shows the meaning of several powers of 2.

Base 2 Numeral		Meaning		Decimal Numerals		
1_{two}	=	1	=	1	=	2^0
10_{two}	=	2×1	=	2	=	2^1
100_{two}	=	2×2	=	4	=	2^2
$1,000_{two}$	=	$2 \times 2 \times 2$	=	8	=	2^3
$10,000_{two}$	=	$2 \times 2 \times 2 \times 2$	=	16	=	2^4

In the numeral 1010_{two}, the 0 at the right is in the ones place; the 1 next to it is in the 2^1 place; the next 0 to the left is in the 2^2 place; and the 1 at the far left is in the 2^3 place.

Binary numerals may be changed to decimal numerals by adding up the place values of the digits in terms of decimal numerals. The following calculation shows how to change the binary numeral 1010_{two} to the decimal numeral 10:

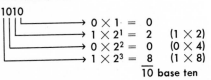

$$
\begin{aligned}
0 \times 1 &= 0 \\
1 \times 2^1 &= 2 \quad (1 \times 2) \\
0 \times 2^2 &= 0 \quad (0 \times 4) \\
1 \times 2^3 &= 8 \quad (1 \times 8) \\
\hline
&\ 10 \text{ base ten}
\end{aligned}
$$

The Duodecimal System groups numbers by twelves and powers of twelve. The word *duodecimal* comes from the Latin word *duodecimus*, meaning *twelfth*. It is a combination of the Latin words *duo*, meaning *two*, and *decem*, meaning *ten*. Because the duodecimal system is based on 12, it uses 12 digits: 0, 1, 2, 3, 4, 5, 6, 7, 8, 9, T, and E. The symbols T and E stand for the number of objects called *ten* and *eleven* in the decimal system. The numeral 10_{twelve} (one, zero, base twelve) means "1 twelve plus no ones." The numeral 12_{twelve} (one, two, base twelve) stands for "1 twelve plus 2 ones." It represents the numeral 14 in the decimal system.

Grouping by Twelves. The groups of dots below show the meaning of various duodecimal numerals.

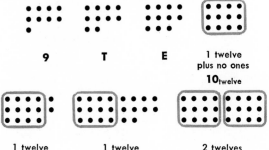

| 9 | T | E | 1 twelve plus no ones 10_{twelve} |

| 1 twelve plus 2 ones 12_{twelve} | 1 twelve plus T ones $1T_{twelve}$ | 2 twelves plus no ones 20_{twelve} |

In duodecimal counting, you use single digits to count from 1 to E. Then you use two-digit numerals to count from 10_{twelve} to EE_{twelve}. The digit on the left stands for the number of twelves, and the digit on the right shows the number of ones. For example, in the numeral 45_{twelve}, the 4 stands for 4 twelves and the 5 for 5 ones. After EE_{twelve}, you use three-digit numerals. The first digit on the left then stands for the number of twelve twelves. For example, the number in one *gross* is twelve twelves (144 in decimal numerals). In the duodecimal system, one gross is written 100_{twelve}. This

numeral means "1 group of twelve twelves plus no twelves plus no ones." After EEE_{twelve}, you use four-digit numerals, and so on.

Finding Place Value in Base 12. In a duodecimal numeral, the last digit on the right is in the ones place. Every other position has a value 12 times the value of the position to its right. For example, in the numeral $E0T5_{twelve}$, 5 means 5×1; T means $T \times 12$; 0 means $0 \times 12 \times 12$; and E means $E \times 12 \times 12 \times 12$.

You can express the place value of each position in terms of powers of 12. The following table shows the meaning of several powers of 12 and their values in decimal numerals.

Base 12 Numeral		Meaning		Decimal Numerals		
1_{twelve}	=	1	=	1	=	12^0
10_{twelve}	=	12×1	=	12	=	12^1
100_{twelve}	=	12×12	=	144	=	12^2
$1,000_{twelve}$	=	$12 \times 12 \times 12$	=	1,728	=	12^3
$10,000_{twelve}$	=	$12 \times 12 \times 12 \times 12$	=	20,736	=	12^4

In the numeral $E0T5_{twelve}$, 5 is in the ones place; T is in the 12^1 place; 0 is in the 12^2 place; and E is in the 12^3 place.

Duodecimal numerals can be changed to decimal numerals by adding up the place values of the digits in terms of decimal numerals. The following calculation shows how to change the duodecimal numeral $E0T5_{twelve}$ to the decimal numeral 19,133:

E0T5

$$
\begin{aligned}
5 \times 1 &= 5 \\
10 \times 12^1 &= 120 \quad (10 \times 12) \\
0 \times 12^2 &= 0 \quad (0 \times 144) \\
11 \times 12^3 &= 19,008 \quad (11 \times 1,728) \\
\hline
&\ 19,133 \text{ (base ten)}
\end{aligned}
$$

Working with Numeration Systems

Suppose you are asked to solve an addition problem: $4 + 4 + 4 = ?$. If you use the base 10 system, you know the answer is 12, as shown by these groups of dots:

| 4 ones | 4 ones | 4 ones | 12 1 group of ten plus 2 ones |

But if you use the base 5 system, the sum of 4 plus 4 plus 4 is 22_{five}, as shown below:

| 4 ones | 4 ones | 4 ones | 22_{five} 2 groups of five plus 2 ones |

On the other hand, if you use the base 12 system, $4 + 4 + 4 = 10_{twelve}$:

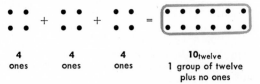

| 4 ones | 4 ones | 4 ones | 10_{twelve} 1 group of twelve plus no ones |

NUMERATION SYSTEMS

The numerals differ in each answer, but the number of dots is the same. The numerals are formed according to the principles of grouping and place value. Subtraction, multiplication, and division also follow these principles. You can study these principles by working problems in various numeration systems. In this way, you will get a better understanding of the use of numerals in arithmetic.

Decimal Arithmetic. Statements such as $4 + 5 = 9$, $9 - 4 = 5$, $9 \times 5 = 45$, and $45 \div 9 = 5$ are called *arithmetic facts*. We use many such facts in addition, subtraction, multiplication, and division.

Decimal Addition is a way of combining two or more groups into only one group. The principle of place value is used in adding ones to ones, tens to tens, and so on, as in the following example:

$$
\begin{array}{r}
24 \\
+12 \\
\hline
36
\end{array}
\quad
\begin{array}{l}
\text{2 tens} + \text{4 ones} \\
\text{1 ten} + \text{2 ones} \\
\hline
\text{3 tens} + \text{6 ones}
\end{array}
$$

In this example, you use the addition fact $4 + 2 = 6$ and the fact $2 + 1 = 3$ (meaning 2 tens + 1 ten = 3 tens, or 30). Therefore, the sum is 3 tens plus 6, or 36. In some problems, the sum in one or more places is 10 or more. Then you must *regroup* the sum. Regrouping in addition is sometimes called *carrying*. The next problem shows how to regroup in decimal addition.

$$
\begin{array}{r}
1 \\
48 \\
+25 \\
\hline
73
\end{array}
\quad
\begin{array}{l}
\text{4 tens} + \text{8 ones} \\
\text{2 tens} + \text{5 ones} \\
\hline
\text{6 tens} + \text{13 ones} \\
\text{or, after regrouping,} \\
\text{7 tens} + \text{3 ones}
\end{array}
$$

In this problem, the ones add up to 13, which can be regrouped into 1 ten plus 3 ones. So you write 3 in the ones place and a small 1 in the tens place above the 4. Then you add the tens: $1 + 4 + 2 = 7$ tens, or 70. Therefore, the sum is $70 + 3$, or 73.

Decimal Subtraction is a way of "undoing" addition. It follows the same principles as decimal addition:

$$
\begin{array}{r}
65 \\
-23 \\
\hline
42
\end{array}
\quad
\begin{array}{l}
\text{6 tens} + \text{5 ones} \\
\text{2 tens} + \text{3 ones} \\
\hline
\text{4 tens} + \text{2 ones}
\end{array}
$$

In this example, you use the subtraction fact $5 - 3 = 2$, and the fact $6 - 2 = 4$ (meaning 6 tens − 2 tens = 4 tens). To subtract a large number from a smaller number in any place, you have to regroup. Regrouping in subtraction is sometimes called *borrowing*. The next example shows how to regroup in decimal subtraction.

$$
\begin{array}{r}
6\,1 \\
\cancel{7}3 \\
-25 \\
\hline
48
\end{array}
\quad
\begin{array}{l}
\text{6 tens} + \text{13 ones} \\
\text{2 tens} + \text{5 ones} \\
\hline
\text{4 tens} + \text{8 ones}
\end{array}
$$

In the ones place, you must subtract 5 from 3, which is smaller. So you regroup 7 tens plus 3 ones to make 6 tens plus 13 ones. Show this by writing a small 1 in front of the 3, and by crossing out the 7 and writing a small 6 above it. Then use the subtraction fact $13 - 5 = 8$ to subtract the ones, and the fact $6 - 2 = 4$ to subtract the tens.

Decimal Multiplication is a way of putting together equal groups. The multiplication fact $4 \times 6 = 24$ means that 4 groups of 6 objects contain 24 objects. Here is the way you use place value to multiply 23 by 3:

$$
\begin{array}{r}
23 \\
\times 3 \\
\hline
69
\end{array}
\quad
\begin{array}{l}
\text{2 tens} + \text{3 ones} \\
\text{3 ones} \\
\hline
\text{6 tens} + \text{9 ones}
\end{array}
$$

First, think: "3×3 ones = 9 ones, and 3×2 tens = 6 tens, or 60." Then add $60 + 9 = 69$.

In multiplication, you regroup when the product in any place is 10 or more:

$$
\begin{array}{r}
1 \\
49 \\
\times 2 \\
\hline
98
\end{array}
\quad
\begin{array}{l}
\text{4 tens} + \text{9 ones} \\
\text{2 ones} \\
\hline
\text{8 tens} + \text{18 ones} \\
\text{or, after regrouping,} \\
\text{9 tens} + \text{8 ones}
\end{array}
$$

In this problem, the product of 2×9 is 18, which can be regrouped into 1 ten plus 8 ones. So you write 8 in the ones place and a little 1 in the tens place above the 4. Next, multiply $2 \times 4 = 8$ in the tens place, and add the 1 to make 9.

When the multiplier has more than one digit, you repeat the operation for each digit and add the products:

$$
\begin{array}{r}
24 \\
\times 12 \\
\hline
48 \\
24 \\
\hline
288
\end{array}
\quad
\begin{array}{l}
\text{2 tens} + \text{4 ones} \\
\text{1 ten} + \text{2 ones} \\
\hline
\text{4 tens} + \text{8 ones} \\
\text{2 hundreds} + \text{4 tens} \\
\hline
\text{2 hundreds} + \text{8 tens} + \text{8 ones}
\end{array}
$$

First, multiply 24 by 2, writing 8 in the ones place, and 4 in the tens place. Then multiply 24 by 1 ten, writing 4 in the tens place and 2 in the hundreds place. Then add the products to get 288.

Decimal Division is a way of "undoing" multiplication. It is a grouping apart of one group into several groups of equal size. Here is the way you divide 69 by 3:

$$
\begin{array}{r}
23 \\
3\overline{)69} \\
6 \\
\hline
9 \\
9
\end{array}
\quad
\begin{array}{l}
\text{2 tens} + \text{3 ones} \\
\text{3 ones } \overline{)\text{6 tens} + \text{9 ones}} \\
\quad\text{6 tens} \\
\hline
\qquad\qquad\text{9 ones} \\
\qquad\qquad\text{9 ones}
\end{array}
$$

First, think: "6 tens $\div$ 3 = 2 tens." Write 2 in the tens place above the 6. Then think: "9 ones $\div$ 3 = 3 ones." Write 3 in the ones place above the 9. Therefore, $69 \div 3 = 2$ tens + 3 ones, or 23.

The principle of place value also makes it easy to divide larger numbers:

$$
\begin{array}{r}
82 \\
2\overline{)164} \\
16 \\
\hline
4 \\
4
\end{array}
$$

First, think: "16 tens $\div$ 2 = 8 tens." Write 8 in the tens place above the 6. Then think: "4 ones $\div$ 2 = 2 ones." Write 2 in the ones place above the 4. Therefore, $164 \div 2 = 8$ tens + 2 ones, or 82.

Quinary Arithmetic has fewer arithmetic facts than decimal arithmetic because it uses only 5 digits instead of 10. These digits are: 0, 1, 2, 3, 4.

Quinary Addition. You can use the following table to find the basic facts of quinary addition.

+	0	1	2	3	4
0	0	1	2	3	4
1	1	2	3	4	10
2	2	3	4	10	11
3	3	4	10	11	12
4	4	10	11	12	13

The numerals in the table run from left to right in *rows*, and from top to bottom in *columns*. Each row and each column begins with a digit from 0 through 4. You can use these digits to locate various sums in the chart. To find the sum of 3 + 3, for example, first find the row that begins with 3. Then run your finger to the right along this row until you come to the column that has 3 at the top. Your finger will be on 11 (1 five plus 1), the sum of 3 plus 3. You can use the table to solve the following problem:

Quinary Addition	Meaning	Decimal Addition
21	2 fives + 1 one	11
+13	1 five + 3 ones	+8
34	3 fives + 4 ones	19

When the sum in any place is greater than 4, you have to regroup, as shown in the next example.

Quinary Addition	Meaning	Decimal Addition
¹24	2 fives + 4 ones	14
+14	1 five + 4 ones	+9
43	3 fives + 13 ones	23
	or, after regrouping,	
	4 fives + 3 ones	

First, use the fact 4 + 4 = 13 to add the ones. Regroup 13 ones into 1 five plus 3 ones. Write 3 in the ones place and a small 1 in the fives place above the 2. Next, add the fives: 1 + 2 + 1 = 4.

Quinary Subtraction. You can use the quinary addition facts table to find subtraction facts, too. For example, to subtract 3 from 11, first find the column that begins with 3. Next, run your finger down this column until you come to 11. Then run your finger to the left along this row to the beginning digit to find the answer, 3.

Use the table to solve the next problem:

Quinary Subtraction	Meaning	Decimal Subtraction
33	3 fives + 3 ones	18
−12	1 five + 2 ones	−7
21	2 fives + 1 one	11

The following problem shows how you regroup in quinary subtraction.

Quinary Subtraction	Meaning (after regrouping)	Decimal Subtraction
²1 3̶1	2 fives + 11 ones	16
−14	1 five + 4 ones	−9
12	1 five + 2 ones	7

To subtract in the ones place, you must regroup 3 fives plus 1 one into 2 fives plus 11 ones. Then use the subtraction fact 11 − 4 = 2. Next, use the fact 2 − 1 = 1 to subtract the fives.

Quinary Multiplication also uses fewer facts than decimal multiplication. You can use the following table to find the basic quinary multiplication facts.

×	1	2	3	4
1	1	2	3	4
2	2	4	11	13
3	3	11	14	22
4	4	13	22	31

For example, to find the product of 3 × 4, first find the row that begins with 3. Then run your finger to the right until you come to the column that has 4 at the top. Your finger will be on the answer, 22 (2 fives plus 2 ones).

Here is a simple problem to solve with the table:

Quinary Multiplication	Meaning	Decimal Multiplication
21	2 fives + 1 one	11
×2	2 ones	×2
42	4 fives + 2 ones	22

When the product in any place is greater than 4, you have to regroup, as shown in the next example.

Quinary Multiplication	Meaning	Decimal Multiplication
¹14	1 five + 4 ones	9
×2	2 ones	×2
33	2 fives + 13 ones	18
	or, after regrouping,	
	3 fives + 3 ones	

First, you use the fact 2 × 4 = 13 to multiply in the ones place. Regroup 13 ones into 1 five plus 3 ones. Write 3 in the ones place and a small 1 in the fives place above the 1. Then use the fact 2 × 1 = 2 (meaning 2 × 1 five = 2 fives). Add the 1 five you got by regrouping in the ones place to make 3 fives, or 30 (three, zero) in quinary numerals. The sum is therefore 30 + 3, or 33 (three, three).

When the multiplier has more than one digit, repeat the operation for each digit and add the products:

Quinary Multiplication	Meaning	Decimal Multiplication
21	2 fives + 1 one	11
×12	1 five + 2 ones	×7
42	4 fives + 2 ones	77
21	2 twenty-fives + 1 five	
302	2 twenty-fives + 10 fives + 2 ones	
	or, after regrouping,	
	3 twenty-fives + 0 fives + 2 ones	

Quinary Division. You can also use the quinary multiplication table to find division facts. For example, to find the quotient 22 ÷ 4, first find the column that begins with 4. Next run your finger down this column until you come to 22. Then run your finger to the left

450e

along this row until you come to the beginning digit, 3. Use the table to work the following problem:

Quinary Division	Meaning	Decimal Division
12	1 five + 2 ones	7
2/24	2 ones/2 fives + 4 ones	2/14
2	2 fives	14
4	4 ones	
4	4 ones	

The next example shows how to divide with larger numerals.

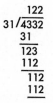

In this problem, think "3 will go into 4 once, so 31 will go into 43 once." Write 1 above the 3. Then finish the problem as you would a decimal division problem. But remember to use quinary arithmetic facts.

Binary Arithmetic has only a few facts because it uses only two digits—0 and 1.

Binary Addition is based on only these facts:

$$0 + 0 = 0 \quad 0 + 1 = 1 \quad 1 + 0 = 1 \quad 1 + 1 = 10$$

Here is the way you use these facts to add 11 + 11:

Binary Addition	Meaning	Decimal Addition
1		
11	1 two + 1 one	3
+11	1 two + 1 one	+3
110	10 twos + 10 ones	6
	or, after regrouping,	
	1 four + 1 two + 0 ones	

First, you use the addition fact $1 + 1 = 10$ (meaning one 2) to add the ones. Regroup 10_{two} into 1 two plus no ones. Write 0 in the ones place, and a small 1 above the twos column. Then add the twos: $1 + 1 = 10$; $10 + 1 = 11$. Write 1 in the twos place, and 1 in the fours place. Thus, $11_{two} + 11_{two} = 110_{two}$.

Binary Subtraction is based on four facts:

$$0 - 0 = 0 \quad 1 - 0 = 1 \quad 1 - 1 = 0 \quad 10 - 1 = 1$$

Use these facts to subtract 11 from 110:

Binary Subtraction	Meaning (after regrouping twice)	Decimal Subtraction
110	0 fours + 10 twos + 10 ones	6
−11	1 two + 1 one	−3
11	1 two + 1 one	3

In the ones place, you have to subtract 1 from 0. So you regroup 1 four plus 1 two plus no ones into 1 four plus no twos plus 10 ones. Then use the fact $10 - 1 = 1$ to subtract the ones. To subtract the twos, you again have to take 1 from 0 because your first regrouping has left a 0 in the twos place. You regroup 1 four plus no twos

into no fours plus 10 twos, and use the fact $10 - 1 = 1$.

Binary Multiplication uses the following facts:

$$0 \times 0 = 0 \quad 0 \times 1 = 0 \quad 1 \times 0 = 0 \quad 1 \times 1 = 1$$

The product of two single digits is always either 0 or 1. However, you may have to regroup when adding products to complete a multiplication problem. For example, here is the way you multiply 11×11:

Binary Multiplication	Meaning	Decimal Multiplication
11	1 two + 1 one	3
×11	1 two + 1 one	×3
11	1 two + 1 one	9
11	1 four + 1 two	
1001	1 four + 10 twos + 1 one	
	or, after regrouping,	
	1 eight + 0 fours + 0 twos + 1 one	

Multiply and write the products as you do in the decimal system. When you add the partial products, use binary addition facts. Bring down the 1 in the ones place. Add the twos: $1 + 1 = 10$. Regroup 10 twos to 1 four plus no twos. Write 0 in the twos place and add 1 to the 1 in the fours place: $1 + 1 = 10$. Write 0 in the fours place and 1 in the eights place to get 1001.

Binary Division "undoes" binary multiplication. The following example shows how to divide with a two-digit binary numeral:

$$\begin{array}{r} 11 \\ 11\overline{)1001} \\ \underline{11} \\ 11 \\ \underline{11} \end{array}$$

To divide 11 into 1001, think, "11 is larger than 10, but smaller than 100. So it must go into 100 once." Write 1 over the second zero. Then complete the problem by multiplying and subtracting as in a decimal numeral problem. But remember to use binary subtraction facts.

Duodecimal Arithmetic has more facts than decimal arithmetic because it uses more digits—0 through 9, plus T and E.

Duodecimal Addition. You can use the following table to find the basic facts of duodecimal addition.

+	0	1	2	3	4	5	6	7	8	9	T	E
0	0	1	2	3	4	5	6	7	8	9	T	E
1	1	2	3	4	5	6	7	8	9	T	E	10
2	2	3	4	5	6	7	8	9	T	E	10	11
3	3	4	5	6	7	8	9	T	E	10	11	12
4	4	5	6	7	8	9	T	E	10	11	12	13
5	5	6	7	8	9	T	E	10	11	12	13	14
6	6	7	8	9	T	E	10	11	12	13	14	15
7	7	8	9	T	E	10	11	12	13	14	15	16
8	8	9	T	E	10	11	12	13	14	15	16	17
9	9	T	E	10	11	12	13	14	15	16	17	18
T	T	E	10	11	12	13	14	15	16	17	18	19
E	E	10	11	12	13	14	15	16	17	18	19	1T

To find the sum of 6 + T, for example, first find the row that begins with 6. Then run your finger to the right along this row until you come to the column that has T at the top. Your finger will be on 14 (meaning 1 twelve plus 4), the sum of 6 plus T.

Use the table to solve the following problem:

Duodecimal Addition	Meaning	Decimal Addition
2T	2 twelves + T ones	34
+81	8 twelves + 1 one	+97
TE	T twelves + E ones	131

First, use the fact T + 1 = E to add the ones. Then use the fact 2 + 8 = T (meaning 2 twelves + 8 twelves = T twelves).

When the sum in any place is greater than E, you have to regroup in terms of the base, 12, as shown in the next example.

Duodecimal Addition	Meaning	Decimal Addition
^{1} 6E	6 twelves + E ones	83
+34	3 twelves + 4 ones	+40
T3	9 twelves + 13 ones *or, after regrouping,* T twelves + 3 ones	123

In the ones place, E + 4 = 13, as shown in the table. Regroup 13 ones into 1 twelve plus 3 ones. Write 3 in the ones place and a small 1 in the twelves place over the 6. Then add the twelves: 6 + 3 = 9 twelves; 9 plus the 1 twelve you got by regrouping equals T twelves.

Duodecimal Subtraction. You can use the duodecimal addition facts table to find subtraction facts, too. For example, to subtract T from 14, first find the column that begins with T. Next, run your finger down this column until you come to 14. Then run your finger to the left along this row to the beginning digit to find the answer, 6.

Use the table to solve the next problem.

Duodecimal Subtraction	Meaning	Decimal Subtraction
E6	E twelves + 6 ones	138
−T4	T twelves + 4 ones	−124
12	1 twelve + 2 ones	14

First, use the fact 6 − 4 = 2 to subtract the ones. In the twelves place, use the fact E − T = 1 (meaning E twelves − T twelves = 1 twelve).

The next example shows how to regroup when the number you are subtracting in any place is larger than the one you are subtracting it from.

Duodecimal Subtraction	Meaning *(after regrouping)*	Decimal Subtraction
^{6}~~7~~^{1}T	6 twelves + 1T ones	94
−3E	3 twelves + E ones	−47
3E	3 twelves + E ones	47

In the ones place, E is larger than T. So you regroup 7 twelves plus T ones into 6 twelves plus 1T ones. Cross out the 7 and write a small 6 above it, and write a small 1 in front of the T. Then use the subtraction fact 1T − E = E to subtract the ones. Use the fact 6 − 3 = 3 to subtract the twelves.

Duodecimal Multiplication also uses more facts than decimal multiplication. You can use the following table to find the basic duodecimal multiplication facts.

×	1	2	3	4	5	6	7	8	9	T	E
1	1	2	3	4	5	6	7	8	9	T	E
2	2	4	6	8	T	10	12	14	16	18	1T
3	3	6	9	10	13	16	19	20	23	26	29
4	4	8	10	14	18	20	24	28	30	34	38
5	5	T	13	18	21	26	2E	34	39	42	47
6	6	10	16	20	26	30	36	40	46	50	56
7	7	12	19	24	2E	36	41	48	53	5T	65
8	8	14	20	28	34	40	48	54	60	68	74
9	9	16	23	30	39	46	53	60	69	76	83
T	T	18	26	34	42	50	5T	68	76	84	92
E	E	1T	29	38	47	56	65	74	83	92	T1

For example, to find the product of 4 × 6, first find the row that begins with 4. Then run your finger to the right until you come to the column that has 6 at the top. Your finger will be on the answer, 20 (2 twelves plus no ones). Use the table to work the following problem:

Duodecimal Multiplication	Meaning	Decimal Multiplication
15	1 twelve + 5 ones	17
×2	2 ones	×2
2T	2 twelves + T ones	34

If the product in any place is greater than E, you have to regroup:

Duodecimal Multiplication	Meaning	Decimal Multiplication
^{2}3T	3 twelves + T ones	46
×3	3 ones	×3
E6	9 twelves + 26 ones *or, after regrouping,* E twelves + 6 ones	138

In the ones place, use the fact 3 × T = 26. Regroup 26 ones into 2 twelves plus 6 ones. Write 6 in the ones place and a small 2 in the twelves place above the 3. Then multiply 3 × 3 to get 9 and add the 2 to get E.

When the multiplier has more than one digit, repeat the operation for each digit and add the products. Can you find a mistake in the next duodecimal problem?

```
 ¹24
 ×13
  70
 24
 310
```

First multiply 24 × 3. In the ones place, use the fact 3 × 4 = 10. Regroup 10 ones into 1 twelve plus 0 ones. Write 0 in the ones place and a small 1 in the twelves place above the 2. Then use the fact 3 × 2 = 6 in the twelves place, and add the 1 to get 7. Next, multiply 24×1 twelve: $1 \times 4 = 4$ in the twelves place, and $1 \times 2 = 2$ in the one hundred forty-fours place. Finally, add the products. Bring down the 0. Add $7 + 4 = E$ (not $7 + 4 = 11$). Bring down the 2. The correct answer is 2E0 (not 310).

Duodecimal Division. You can also use the duodecimal multiplication table to find division facts. For example, to find the quotient $42 \div T$, first find the column that begins with T. Next, run your finger down this column until you come to 42. Then run your finger to the left along this row until you come to the beginning digit, 5.

Use the table to work the following problem:

Duodecimal Division	Meaning	Decimal Division
17	1 twelve + 7 ones	19
5)7E	5 ones)7 twelves + E ones	5)95
5	5 twelves	5
2E	2 twelves + E ones	45
2E	2 twelves + E ones	45

Think, "7 twelves divided by 5 is 1 twelve." Write 1 above the 7. Multiply 1×5 and write the product 5 below the 7. Complete the problem as you would in decimal division, but use duodecimal arithmetic facts.

History

How Numeration Systems Began. Primitive man had several ways of recording the few numbers he needed. A shepherd could collect pebbles to represent the number of sheep in his flock. Each pebble meant one sheep. A bag of pebbles stood for the whole flock. By matching the pebbles against his flock, he could see if he had all his sheep. Mathematicians call this kind of matching *one-to-one correspondence*.

Later, man developed other ways to record the number of his possessions. He tied knots in a leather thong, or he scratched tally marks (**JH**) on the side of a rock. He matched the knots or marks against each item.

Then man began to use words to represent numbers. These words told him "how many." They helped him to match items mentally. For example, he used the word for "wings" to mean two objects. To refer to four things, he used the name of a fruit that grew in clusters of four. For five items, he used the word that meant "hand." Such number-names appeared in various primitive languages. They showed that man had begun to form ideas of numbers. Whether he had three fish, three pebbles, or three tally marks, he recognized a "threeness" about each of these groups.

Finally, man began to *count* by arranging his number-names in a certain order. To count, he spoke or wrote the word that meant "one," next the word for "two," then the word for "three," and so on. In time, people in many parts of the world developed various kinds of counting systems. Some were based on five, others on ten, and still others on twelve or sixty. We still use such measures as 12 inches in a foot and 60 minutes in an hour, taken from these ancient systems.

In most early systems, people formed numerals simply by repeating basic symbols and adding their values to get the number they wanted. The Egyptians, Greeks, and Romans used numeral systems of this kind.

The Hindus used a system superior to all others. It followed the principle of place value and used a symbol that meant *not any*. This system became the decimal numeral system, which is now used in most parts of the world.

The Egyptian Numeral System. About 3000 B.C., the ancient Egyptians used *hieroglyphics* (picture writing) to write numerals, as shown below.

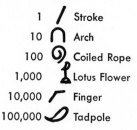

1	/	Stroke
10	∩	Arch
100	9	Coiled Rope
1,000	🪷	Lotus Flower
10,000	/	Finger
100,000	𝄢	Tadpole

This system was based on 10. But it did not include a zero symbol, nor did it use the principle of place value. The Egyptians formed numerals by putting basic symbols together. For example, they wrote the numeral 1,326 like this:

With this system, Egyptians could put symbols in any order, because the value of a symbol did not depend on its position.

The Greek Numeral System. About 500 B.C., the Greeks developed a system based on ten. In this system, the first nine letters of the Greek alphabet stood for numbers, from 1 through 9. The next nine letters stood for tens, from 10 through 90. The last nine letters were symbols for hundreds, from 100 through 900. The Greeks, like the Egyptians, formed numerals by combining these symbols and adding their values.

The Roman Numeral System uses letters as symbols for numbers. But the early Roman system of about 500 B.C. differed from the system we use today. For example, the ancient Romans wrote 4 as IIII and 9 as VIIII. They used the symbol ↓ for 50 and CIↃ for 1,000. Today, we use IV for 4, IX for 9, L for 50, and M for 1,000. The numerals VI, XV, and LX illustrate the *additive* principle. When the first of two symbols stands for a larger number than the second, you *add* the value of the first to the second to get the value of the combination. Thus, the Roman numeral VI represents 6, or $5 + 1$; XV represents 15 as $10 + 5$; and LX represents $50 + 10 = 60$.

The numerals IV and IX illustrate the *subtractive* principle. When the first of two symbols stands for a smaller number than the second, you subtract the value of the first from that of the second to get the value of the combination. Thus, in the Roman numeral IV, you subtract 1 from 5 to get 4.

The Babylonian Numeral System used *cuneiform* (wedge-shaped) symbols. An early system of about 3000 B.C. was based on 60. In this system, a numeral contained groups of symbols. One group stood for the number of ones, the next group stood for 60's, the next for (60×60)'s, and so on.

By 1500 B.C., the Babylonians had also developed

a system based on 10. In this system, the numeral for "one thousand" was a combination of the symbols for "ten" and "one hundred."

The Hindu-Arabic Numeral System. Hindu mathematicians of the 300's and 200's B.C. used a system based on 10. The Hindus had symbols for each number from one to nine. They had a name for each power of 10, and used these names when writing numerals. For example, a Hindu wrote "1 sata, 3 dasan, 5" to represent the number we write as 135. He wrote "1 sata, 5" for the number we write as 105.

Probably about A.D. 600, the Hindus found a way of eliminating place names. They invented the symbol *sunya* (meaning *empty*), which we call *zero*. With this symbol, they could write "105" instead of "1 sata, 5."

During the 700's, the Arabs learned Hindu arithmetic from scientific writings of the Hindus and the Greeks. Then, in the 800's, a Persian mathematician wrote a book that was translated into Latin about 300 years later. This translation brought the Hindu-Arabic numerals into Europe.

Several hundred years passed before the Hindu-Arabic system became widely used. Many persons liked Hindu-Arabic numerals because they could easily use them to write out calculations. Others preferred Roman numerals because they were accustomed to solving problems on a device called an *abacus* without writing out the calculations. After the development of printing from movable type in the 1400's, many mathematics textbooks were published. Most of them showed calculations using the Hindu-Arabic system. These books brought the system into widespread use.

Mathematicians regard the Hindu-Arabic system as one of the world's greatest inventions. Its greatness lies in the principle of place value and in the use of zero. These two ideas make it easy to represent numbers and to perform mathematical operations that would be difficult with any other kind of system.

Rediscovering Numeration Systems. During the late 1600's, the German mathematician and philosopher Gottfried Wilhelm Leibniz (1646-1716) developed the binary numeration system. However, mathematicians found no practical use for the system until the 1940's, when computers were developed. Today, many electronic computers use the binary system. Binary numerals are easy to represent with electrical circuits. The 0 can be an open switch, or a light that is "off." The 1 can be a closed switch, or a light that is "on."

During the 1950's and 1960's, many educators recognized the value of teaching numeration systems. Students began studying various systems as a part of what was called the "new mathematics." By doing arithmetic with unfamiliar systems, students gained a better understanding of the familiar decimal system and of arithmetic in general. CHARLOTTE W. JUNGE

NUMERATION SYSTEMS PROBLEMS

1. The dots in the pattern below have been grouped by 10. Copy the dot pattern on a piece of paper. Then draw lines around the dots to group them by 5. Write the base 5 numeral for the number of dots.

2. How many stars are shown below? Give your answer in base 12 and in base 2.

★ ★ ★ ★ ★ ★ ★ ★
★ ★ ★ ★ ★ ★ ★ ★

3. What is the base of the system that uses the following numerals in counting?

1, 2, 3, 4, 5, 6, 7, 10, 11, 12, . . .

4. Fill in the digits for evaluating the binary numeral 101101. Write the decimal value of this numeral.

$1 \times 2^5 + \underline{\quad} \times 2^4 + \underline{\quad} \times 2^3 + 1 \times 2^2 + \underline{\quad} \times 2^1 + 1$

5. Make groups of dots showing the numbers represented by the numeral 11 in (a) the duodecimal system, (b) the quinary system, (c) the binary system.

6. Write the decimal numeral for the number represented by the quinary numeral 243.

7. What base has been used to solve this addition problem: 12 + 43 = 110?

8. What is the product of 4 × 4 (a) in base 5, and (b) in base 12?

9. Write the quinary numeral for the duodecimal numeral 1T.

10. What Arabic digits would you use in a numeration system based on the number 3?

ANSWERS

1. 23$_{\text{five}}$

2. 16$_{\text{twelve}}$; 10010$_{\text{two}}$

3. Base 8

4. 0×2^4; 1×2^3; 0×2^1; decimal value = 45

5.
Base 12   Base 5   Base 2

6. 73

7. Base 5

8. 31$_{\text{five}}$; 14$_{\text{twelve}}$

9. 1T$_{\text{twelve}}$ = (1 × 12) + 10 = 22$_{\text{ten}}$ = (2 × 10) + 2 = (4 × 5) + 2 = 42$_{\text{five}}$

10. 0, 1, 2, 10, 11, 12, 20, 21, . . .

NUMERATOR. See ARITHMETIC (Common Fractions); FRACTION.

NUMEROLOGY, *NOO mer AHL oh jih,* is the practice of using a person's name and birth date in an attempt to tell his character and abilities, and see into his past and future. It is a *pseudo* (false) science. It has no scientific standing, and is not based on facts. Historians believe the ancient Chinese and Hebrews used it. The supposed basis for numerology is that all numbers vibrate. Each letter of the alphabet is supposed to have a numerical value. A person's name and birth date are said to give information about his vibrations.   JOHN MULHOLLAND

NUMIDIA was an area in northern Africa during ancient times. It occupied part of what is now Algeria. Numidia was allied with nearby Carthage when the Second Punic War between Carthage and Rome began in 218 B.C. But Massinissa, a Numidian chieftain, sided with the Roman general Scipio. In return, Scipio made Massinissa king of all Numidia in 203 B.C. The next year, Numidians helped Scipio defeat the Carthaginians, led by Hannibal, at Zama in North Africa.

Several times after the war, Massinissa seized land from Carthage. Finally, Carthage fought back, helping bring about the Third Punic War (149-146 B.C.). Rome destroyed Carthage in the war, but also halted Numidian expansion. By 112 B.C., Jugurtha, adopted grandson of Massinissa, had seized all of Numidia in defiance of Rome. He was defeated by the Roman general Marius in 106 B.C. In 46 B.C., Numidian King Juba fought Julius Caesar and was defeated. The Roman emperor Augustus made Numidia part of the Roman province of Africa in 25 B.C.   HENRY C. BOREN

NUMISMATIST. See COIN COLLECTING.

NUMITOR. See ROMULUS AND REMUS.

NUMMULITE, *NUHM yoo lite*, is the name for a large number of marine one-celled fossil animals. They can be recognized by their shells, which are shaped like flat disks. On the inside, each shell is coiled and divided into many little chambers. Some nummulites are smaller than a dime, others larger than a half dollar. The large-shelled nummulites are really giants among one-celled animals. During the Eocene and Oligocene periods of geologic time, nummulites lived in great numbers in the sea. Their shells made up thick layers of rock, especially in southern Asia and in the Mediterranean. The pyramids of ancient Egypt were built with blocks of such *nummulitic* limestone taken from large quarries.

Scientific Classification. Nummulites belong to the phylum *Protozoa* and the order *Foraminifera*. They are in the camerind family, *Camerinidae*.   SAMUEL PAUL WELLES

NUN is a woman who gives up worldly things and enters a religious community. The word *nun* is supposed to have come from a *Coptic* (Christian Egyptian) word meaning *pure*. A nun spends her life in religious service, and usually lives in a convent. There are many societies of nuns. Some care for sick or old people. Others are teachers. But all make similar vows, or promises, when they enter the religious life. The first convent for women was founded about A.D. 320 by the sister of Saint Pachomius, in the Egyptian desert. The first one in England was started by Eadbald, king of Kent, in 620 at Folkestone. See also CONVENT.   FULTON J. SHEEN

NUNCIO, *NUN shih oh*, or APOSTOLIC NUNCIO, is a Roman Catholic official somewhat like an ambassador. Nuncios represent the pope and are sent by the church to many countries that are largely Catholic. Nuncios are accredited, as are temporal ambassadors. They are concerned with the welfare of the church in countries to which they are accredited. *Internuncios* are officials with the same power as nuncios, but of a lesser rank. See also LEGATE.   FULTON J. SHEEN

NUREMBERG, *NYOOR um berg* (pop. 471,997; alt. 1,110 ft.), is one of the oldest cities in Germany. Its German name is NÜRNBERG. The city is in West Germany and lies on the Pegnitz River, 92 miles northwest of Munich (see GERMANY [political map]). Nuremberg is noted for its historical landmarks and its toy industry. The city manufactures pencils, chemicals, and electrical supplies.

In the Middle Ages, the city was one of the most important cultural centers in Germany. The first German *gymnasium* (higher school) was established in Nuremberg. The first German paper mill stood in this city. About 1500, Peter Henlein invented in Nuremberg what may have been the first watch (see WATCH [History]).

The heart of Nuremberg was once its walled inner quarter. Many famous buildings, which were hundreds of years old, stood there. The Burg (royal palace), built between 1024 and 1158, stood on a hill overlooking the city. Allied bombs almost destroyed this section during World War II.

Nuremberg was known as a city as early as the 1000's. It became a Protestant center during the Reformation. Nuremberg was a free city at the time it became part of the kingdom of Bavaria in the early 1800's.

Nuremberg became an important political center after the National Socialists (Nazis) came to power in Germany in 1933. The Nazis held their nationwide

Nuns, or Sisters, in the Roman Catholic and Episcopal churches spend their time in prayer and in charitable, medical, or educational work. The robed nuns, *below, left to right,* represent these orders: Roman Catholic Sisters of the Sacred Hearts of Jesus and Mary, Sisters of St. Francis of Assisi, Congregation de Notre Dame Sisters, and the Episcopalian Order of St. Anne.

German Tourist Information Office

An Old Wine-Storage House in Nuremberg, now a college dormitory, is one of Germany's finest medieval structures.

assemblies and congresses in Nuremberg. In 1935, the Nazi-controlled national assembly (*Reichstag*) met at Nuremberg and approved the "Nuremberg Laws." These laws forbade Germans to marry Jews, deprived Jews of citizenship, and made the swastika Germany's flag.

American forces occupied Nuremberg in the last months of the war and continued to hold the city as part of the American zone. In 1945, various former officials of the German government, army, and navy were placed on trial in Nuremberg. JAMES K. POLLOCK

See also NUREMBERG TRIALS.

NUREMBERG TRIALS were a series of 13 trials held in Nuremberg, Germany, from 1945 to 1949. In these trials, leaders of Nazi Germany were accused of crimes against international law. Some of the defendants were charged with causing World War II deliberately, and with waging aggressive wars of conquest. Nearly all were charged with murder, enslavement, looting, and other atrocities against soldiers and civilians of occupied countries. Some were also charged with responsibility for the persecution of Jews and other racial and national groups.

The Nuremberg trials were a new development in international law. Trials of war criminals have been carried on in one form or another for hundreds of years. But at Nuremberg, for the first time, the leaders of a government were brought to trial on the charge of starting an aggressive war.

The First Trial was held before the International Military Tribunal. This tribunal was set up under an agreement signed by representatives of the United States, Great Britain, France, and Russia at London in August, 1945. Judges and prosecutors from all four countries took part in the first trial. In it, 22 officials of Nazi Germany were the defendants. Among these leaders were Hermann Goering, Rudolf Hess, Joachim von Ribbentrop, and Hjalmar Schacht. Martin Bormann was tried *in absentia* (while absent). On Oct. 1, 1946, the court convicted 19 defendants, and acquitted Schacht and two others. Seven, including Hess, were sentenced to prison. Bormann, Goering, von Ribbentrop, and nine others were condemned to death. Goering killed himself on October 15, and Bormann could not be found. The other condemned men were hanged at Nuremberg on October 16.

Further Trials. The four nations occupying Germany decided that additional war crimes trials should be held in each of the occupation zones. In the American zone, 12 trials were held in Nuremberg from 1946 to 1949. There were three trials of military leaders, three trials of principal officers in the SS (Hitler's private army), three trials of industrialists, one trial of government officials and diplomats, one trial of Nazi judges, and one trial of doctors who had conducted cruel and deadly medical experiments in concentration camps. About 200 leaders were brought to trial. Many were sentenced to prison, a few were sentenced to death and hanged, and some were acquitted.

Importance of the Trials. The nations responsible for conducting trials at Nuremberg hoped they would mark a great forward step in the development of international law, and in the preservation of peace and civilization. But some persons criticized the trials as acts of vengeance by the victorious nations. Others argued that there was no basis in international law for trying the German leaders on the charge of starting a war. TELFORD TAYLOR

See also INTERNATIONAL LAW; WAR CRIME.

NUREYEV, *NUH reh yef*, **RUDOLF** (1938-   ), is a Russian dancer who *defected* (deserted) to the West in 1961. He joined England's Royal Ballet in 1962 as partner to Dame Margot Fonteyn, the company's prima ballerina. Nureyev and Dame Margot won praise for their performances in the classics of the 1900's and in *Marguerite and Armand*, created for the pair by Sir Frederick Ashton in 1963. See FONTEYN, DAME MARGOT (picture).

Critics have praised Nureyev for the apparently natural ease of his dancing. In addition to performing, he re-created several Russian works for the Royal Ballet. In 1966, he restaged Marius Petipa's four-act ballet *Don Quixote* for the Vienna State Opera. The next year, he composed a new version of *The Nutcracker*, which is based on Peter Tchaikovsky's music, for the Royal Swedish Ballet. SELMA JEANNE COHEN

NURMI, *NOOR mih,* **PAAVO** (1897-   ), a Finnish runner, excelled in distance races. He performed at his best from 1918 through 1932, and held world records for distances from 1 mile to 14 miles. He won seven championships in Olympic Games competition. His record for the mile run was 4 minutes 10.4 seconds, and it stood as the world record from 1923 until 1931. Nurmi planned every race precisely, and carried a stop watch as he ran to insure perfection. As a boy, he practiced by running behind trolley cars. He was born in Turku, Finland. PAT HARMON

NURSE. See NURSING; HOSPITAL; AIRLINE STEWARDESS.

NURSERY raises trees, shrubs, and vines until they are ready for permanent planting elsewhere. Nurseries also scientifically develop such plants. People use these plants to beautify public and private property, to reforest vacant land, to control soil erosion, and in many other ways. The United States has more than 100,000 acres devoted to nurseries. The federal and state governments operate many nurseries, but most are commercial enterprises. William Prince founded the first American nursery in New York about 1770.

From *Mother Goose*, illustrated by Pelagie Doane, and published by Random House. © 1940, by Random House, Inc. By permission of Artists and Writers Guild, Incorporated

"Pease Porridge Hot, Pease Porridge Cold."

NURSERY RHYME. Ever since the world was young, children have danced and played games. They have made up songs and rhymed words to go with their game-playing. This is as natural for children as their love of fairy tales and music. We do not know how most of these old rhymes began. The children probably made up many and passed them along to other children. Adults may have made up other rhymes.

The rhymes of childhood cover every subject and game a child is interested in. Some of these things are chasing games, counting games, guessing games, and games that are contests. Other rhymes are about familiar birds and beasts, the villages and cities that children know, the bridges they have crossed, and the activities and trades that go on around them. Almost everything has been made into rhyme. Children hear the rhymes and change them to fit their country and times.

Little girls have skipped rope in almost every country in the world, and counted the number of skips in rhymes such as this:

> Apple, peach, pumpkin pie,
> How many years before I die?
> One, two, three, - - - - - - - .

The following poem is usually recited to the clapping of hands.

> Pease porridge hot,
> Pease porridge cold,
> Pease porridge in the pot,
> Nine days old;
> Some like it hot,
> Some like it cold,
> Some like it in the pot,
> Nine days old.

Children of all time have been delighted with hunting games. They have used buttons, thimbles, handkerchiefs, and other small objects. A flower or nut was probably used the first time the game was played. All the players but the one who is *it* form a circle. The handkerchief, or other object, is hidden while the players sing:

> Drop the handkerchief Saturday night,
> Where do you think I found it?
> Up in the sky, ever so high,
> A thousand stars around it.
>   Itiskit, Itaskit,
>   Green and yellow basket,
>   I sent a letter to my love
>   And on the way I lost it.
>   I lost it once; I lost it twice;
>   I lost it three times over.

Riddles have always been among the best-loved rhymes. One that has a *river* for an answer is:

> Runs all day and never walks,
> Often murmurs, never talks;
> It has a bed and never sleeps;
> It has a mouth and never eats.

There have always been games to play with the baby's toes, or for children to play with their fingers. It is said that Oliver Goldsmith (1730?-1774), famous English writer, had one he taught to all the children he knew. He put two small pieces of black paper on the nails of his index, or pointing, fingers, palms down, and then sang:

> Two bonnie blackbirds sitting on a hill;
> One named Jack and one named Jill.
> Fly away Jack; fly away Jill.
> Come back Jack; come back Jill.

Goldsmith would bend his fingers at the proper time in the rhyme and conceal the paper in his hand.

Children have had fun with tongue-twisters in rhyme in all languages. A famous tongue-twister in English is *Peter Piper*. Most of the fun from these rhymes comes in reciting them as fast as possible.

> Peter Piper picked a peck of pickled peppers;
> A peck of pickled peppers Peter Piper picked;
> If Peter Piper picked a peck of pickled peppers,
> Where's the peck of pickled peppers Peter Piper picked?

A counting rhyme that has delighted young and old for many generations is:

> One-ery, you-ery, e-kery, heaven,
> Hollow-bone, willow-bone, ten or eleven.
> Spin, spun—must be done—
> Hollow-bone, willow-bone, twenty-one.

Some rhymes are made up for their complete nonsense. One of these is:

> If all the world were paper,
> And all the sea were ink,
> And all the trees were bread and cheese,
> What would we have to drink?

The rhyme of *Little Jack Horner* has an interesting history. It is a tale of dishonest dealings in the days of King Henry VIII of England.

> Little Jack Horner,
> Sat in the corner,
> Eating his Christmas pie;
> He stuck in his thumb,
> And pulled out a plum,
> And cried, "What a bright boy am I."

But there is more to the story than appears in the nursery rhyme. It seems that a man by the name of John Horner, a steward of Glastonbury, England, was sent to London with a pie for the King. Title deeds for several estates in Somersetshire were baked in the pie. The greedy John Horner *stuck in his thumb* in the pie before he got to London. In other words, he stole the King's *plum*, which was the land deed for the Abbey of Mells. The estate formerly belonged to the Church of England. Another story is that Queen Jane's brother, Edward Seymour, received a pie in the 1500's from which some valuable papers had been stolen. Some scholars prefer this story to the first.

This legend seems more believable when we know that papers were often baked in pies at this time. It was a favorite trick in the 1500's to hide surprises of all kinds in pies. A rare old book of recipes tells a similar tale. It instructs a chef to make pies with live birds in them so that they may fly out when the pie is cut. This is probably the origin of the famous nursery rhyme:

> Sing a song of sixpence,
> Pocket full of rye,
> Four and twenty blackbirds,
> Baked in a pie;
> When the pie was opened,
> The birds began to sing,
> Was not that a dainty dish,
> To set before a king?

Several jingles were made up when the kings from the House of Hanover took over the English throne in 1714. A political party called *Jacobites* supported James III for the crown. They considered that George of Hanover, as a German, had no right to be King of England. They recited this rhyme when he became George I.

> Hark, hark, the dogs do bark,
> The beggars are coming to town;
> Some are in rags, and some are in tags,
> And some are in velvet gowns.

The Jacobites also used this rhyme:

> Jim and George were two great lords,
> They fought all in a churn;
> And when that Jim got George by the nose,
> Then George began to girn (whine).

This rhyme may shed some light on the same George's friendships with the women of the court.

> Georgey Porgey, pudding and pie,
> Kissed the girls and made them cry;
> When the boys came out to play,
> Georgey Porgey ran away.

A more recent rhyme tells of the adventures of Mary and her lamb. Here are the first three verses.

> Mary had a little lamb,
> Its fleece was white as snow,
> And everywhere that Mary went,
> The lamb was sure to go.

> He followed her to school one day;
> Which was against the rule;
> It made the children laugh and play,
> To see a lamb at school.

> And so the teacher turned him out;
> But still he lingered near,
> And waited patiently about,
> Till Mary did appear.

The *Mary* of the poem is generally said to be Mary Elizabeth Sawyer. Her lamb followed her to the Old Redstone Schoolhouse, near Sterling, Mass. Polly Kimball was the teacher who sent the lamb out. Sarah Josepha Hale wrote the verses, although they have been claimed by several others, including John Roulstone. The incident is a common one, and many have claimed to be the Mary of the poem.

The following rhyme is usually sung as a group of children dance in a circle. The first two verses are:

> Here we go round the mulberry bush,
> The mulberry bush, the mulberry bush,
> Here we go round the mulberry bush,
> So early in the morning.
> This is the way we wash our clothes,
> Wash our clothes, wash our clothes,
> This is the way we wash our clothes,
> On a cold and frosty morning.

Many of these nursery rhymes were written to tell a story with a lesson in it. This one suggests that little details are as important as big ones:

> For want of a nail, the shoe was lost;
> For want of the shoe, the horse was lost;
> For want of the horse, the rider was lost;
> For want of the rider, the battle was lost;
> For want of the battle, the kingdom was lost;
> And all for the want of a horseshoe nail!

For hundreds of years mothers have lulled their babies to sleep to the tune of *Bye, Baby Bunting*.

> Bye, baby bunting,
> Daddy's gone a-hunting,
> To get a little rabbit skin,
> To wrap the baby bunting in.

The Lord Mayor is another famous rhyme. Each line of the song represents a part of the face, which is touched as the line is recited:

> Here sits the Lord Mayor, (forehead)
> Here sit his two men, (eyes)
> Here sits the cock, (right cheek)
> Here sits the hen, (left cheek)
> Here sit the little chickens, (tip of nose)
> Here they all run in; (mouth)
> Chinchopper, chinchopper,
> Chinchopper chin! (chuck the chin)

There are many short verses that are probably as well known as many of the great classics of poetry. Some of them are:

> Star light, star bright,
> First star I see to-night;
> I wish I may, I wish I might,
> Have the wish I wish to-night.

> A diller, a dollar,
> A ten o'clock scholar,
> What makes you come so soon?
> You used to come at ten o'clock,
> And now you come at noon.

> Pussy-cat, pussy-cat, where have you been?
> I've been to London to see the Queen.
> Pussy-cat, pussy-cat, what did you there?
> I frightened a little mouse under the chair.

> Peter, Peter, pumpkin-eater,
> Had a wife and couldn't keep her;
> He put her in a pumpkin-shell,
> And there he kept her very well.

The MOTHER GOOSE article in THE WORLD BOOK EN-CYCLOPEDIA contains the nursery rhymes *Old King Cole*, *Little Jack Horner*, and *Hey Diddle Diddle*. The most popular nursery rhymes can be found illustrated in color in Volume I of CHILDCRAFT. This is published by Field Enterprises Educational Corp., publishers of THE WORLD BOOK ENCYCLOPEDIA. For other books of nursery rhymes, see the Books to Read section (Books for Young Children) following the article entitled LITERATURE FOR CHILDREN.   DOROTHY ELIZABETH SMITH

See also GAME (Games for Young Children).

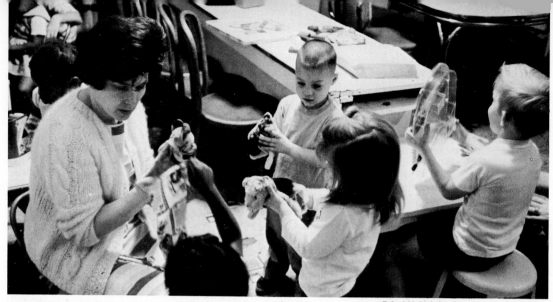

Children in Nursery Schools learn how to work and play together. They also learn how to work out individual tasks by themselves. Good nursery-school teachers help youngsters realize that learning—as well as playing—can be fun and rewarding.

NURSERY SCHOOL is a school for children from 3 to 4 years old. A child this age forms important basic attitudes toward himself, the people around him, and the world in which he lives. These early attitudes strongly influence his behavior throughout later life. The nursery school aims at helping a child's physical, emotional, intellectual, and social growth during this critical period.

Nursery Schools in the United States

The United States has about 4,000 nursery schools. Most of these are private. *Cooperative nursery schools*, owned and operated by parents, form the next largest group. Some churches have weekday nursery schools, and many colleges and universities operate them for educational research and practice-teaching.

A small but growing number of nursery schools care for handicapped children. For example, special nursery schools help crippled children and youngsters who suffer from defects in hearing, speech, and sight. Public-school systems seldom include nursery schools. But they often give funds to the special schools for handicapped children. *Day nurseries* or *child-care centers* are nursery schools that care for the children of working mothers.

Most private and cooperative nursery schools in the United States are half-day schools. Some schools, especially college-laboratory nursery schools, have full-day programs. They give the children luncheon at school and see that the children rest after the meal. Day nurseries and child-care centers are usually full-day schools, open from 6 A.M. to 6 P.M. Mothers who work can bring their children to the school at any time during the day.

Instruction in the Nursery School

Learning Through Play. Most nursery schools follow the principle that children from 3 to 4 can learn best through play. The youngsters spend a large part of their time playing with toys. A nursery school usually has many kinds of toys and equipment, including wagons, trucks, and boats; blocks, puzzles, and beads; clay, paints, and crayons; dolls, stuffed animals, and toys for make-believe housekeeping; sandboxes and sand toys; books; and a framework made of metal pipes on

which the children can climb. There are also boards, planks, sawhorses, boxes, shovels, wheelbarrows, water, and pots and pans. In addition, nursery schools have some equipment, usually found in schools for older children.

Selection of Play Materials. Nursery-school teachers select toys and other equipment with great care. The toys must promote a youngster's growth. They must also stimulate his development as a creative, self-reliant, and imaginative citizen in a democratic society. Nursery schools usually have few or no mechanical toys. A child only winds most mechanical toys and watches them work. Instead of these, nursery-school teachers choose toys and materials that can be used in many ways. These stimulate a child's imagination, and call for action on his part.

As children develop, they become more interested in other persons. Young children need practice in getting along with people, because a democratic society needs citizens who enjoy working with others. For this reason, nursery-school teachers prefer equipment that can best be used by children playing together.

At the same time, a child is eager to explore the world in which he lives. Nursery-school teachers also use play materials that help introduce a child to this world. For example, nursery-school children often play with finger paints, water, mud, sand, clay, and wood. Each of these acquaints the child with a different feel and texture.

Nursery schools are concerned with the total development of the child. For example, some kinds of equipment, such as a framework to climb on, promote a child's physical growth. Others, such as beads, teach a child to use his eyes and hands together. Still other kinds of play help social, intellectual, and emotional development.

Health forms an important part of most nursery-school programs. Nursery schools usually require a child to have a complete physical examination before entrance. Most nursery schools also require various immunizations and vaccinations. A doctor or nurse pays regular visits to the school, and a nursery-school teacher usually checks the children's health every day.

Most nursery-school programs recognize a child's need for adequate food and rest. They usually have a midmorning rest time and midmorning fruit or vegetable juice. Most full-day nursery schools give milk and crackers to the youngsters who stay through the afternoon. If the nursery school serves lunch, it either has an expert on child nutrition on its staff or follows the advice of an expert.

Other Training includes learning a number of important skills that the children can use in everyday life. The nursery-school teacher plans activities such as dressing and eating, so a child *learns independence.* Nursery schools have specially designed tables, chairs, plates, cups, and tableware that a child can learn to use easily. Almost all nursery-school furnishings, including those in the washrooms and coat closets, are of special design. For example, the designers place the hooks in a coat closet so that a child can reach them.

The Teacher

A child who goes to nursery school leaves his parents for the first time. This departure forms a critical step in his emotional and social development. Nursery-school teachers influence a child's development in almost every way they act toward him. A nursery-school teacher must have a warm personality and the ability to be a friend to each child.

The Teacher's Role in a nursery school often seems different from that in a school for older children. For example, the teacher does not usually stand in the front of the room. Nor does she divide the day into periods for studying particular subjects. A nursery-school teacher's biggest job is to plan indoor and outdoor activities so that the children learn chiefly from what they do, rather than from what they are told. Only rarely—during storytelling time or music time or when the group takes a short trip—does the teacher take the center of the stage. She must spend much time talking with individual children. Youngsters have many questions, and usually need help in solving their problems.

Training. Some nursery-school teachers take their professional training in home economics, because the nursery school in many ways serves as a supplement to the home. Others study in colleges of education or in child-study departments of liberal-arts colleges. They major in such fields as child development, child welfare, or *early childhood education.* Early childhood education is a field that includes educational programs for children from 3 to 8.

Associations. There are two national professional organizations that include nursery-school teachers: the Association for Childhood Education International, with headquarters in Washington, D.C., and the National Association for Nursery Education, with headquarters in Chicago. The National Education Association also has a department that includes nursery-school instruction. Many nursery-school teachers have state and local associations. See CHILDHOOD EDUCATION INTERNATIONAL, ASSOCIATION FOR; NATIONAL EDUCATION ASSOCIATION OF THE UNITED STATES.

History

British factory owners began the first school groups for young children in the late 1700's. Hundreds of factories appeared in Great Britain at this time, and large numbers of women went to work in them. Many working mothers could not leave their younger children at home or keep the children with them at their jobs. The factory owners often provided special rooms for these youngsters, and hired untrained supervisors or older boys and girls to watch the children.

Robert Owen (1771-1858), a social reformer and mill owner, became the first to see the need for improving these schools. Owen set up the first regular teaching program for the children in his own factory in Great Britain. He hired persons with some teaching qualifications to supervise and teach the children. But schools such as Owen's remained rare until after World War I ended in 1918.

British law established the first public nursery schools in 1918. Other European countries, including France and Germany, followed Great Britain's example. In the United States, nursery schools developed on a private or cooperative basis. But the number of nursery schools grew rapidly. In 1918, the United States had only three nursery schools. In 1927-1928, it had 76. By 1930-1931, the number had risen to about 500. During the depression, the federal government maintained nursery schools as part of the Works Progress Administration (see NEW DEAL). The United States had 2,398 such nursery schools by 1933.

The federal government again supported nursery schools during World War II. It helped establish many nursery schools called *child-care centers.* At the peak of this program, these centers cared for 129,476 children. Nursery-school attendance dropped sharply when these centers closed after World War II, but the number of nursery schools, both public and private, continued to grow. JAMES L. HYMES, JR.

Related Articles in WORLD BOOK include:

NURSE'S AIDE is a person who helps nurses in hospitals perform their work. A nurse's aide also may be called a *ward helper,* a *hospital attendant,* or a *nursing aide.* A man who performs this kind of work is usually called an *orderly.*

The nurse's aide does as much of a nurse's work as she can. By doing the jobs that require little or no training, the nurse's aide allows a regular nurse to concentrate on jobs that require her special skills. Nurse's aides answer patients' calls; help feed, wash, and care for them; and keep their rooms in order. If a patient has to go to some other part of the hospital, a nurse's aide may go with him. She may help support a patient during treatment, or help move him onto or off of beds and stretchers. In larger hospitals, nurse's aides may act as diet assistants or as clerks.

There are two kinds of nurse's aides. The Red Cross trains volunteer workers who help out in community hospitals. Most of these are older women. But many nurse's aides are paid workers who have no nursing training. Many young girls work as nurse's aides in a hospital for a while in order to find out whether or not they want to become nurses.

See also NURSING.

NURSING

Ed Wergeles, *Newsweek*

Johns Hopkins Hospital

Queen's Hospital, Honolulu

A Nurse's Cap symbolizes her profession. The style of the cap tells from what school the nurse graduated. A nurse wears the school cap throughout her career. Florence Nightingale's Lamp, *above*, is a common emblem of nursing. The famed English nurse carried a lamp on nightly visits to her patients.

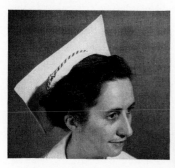

University of California

Presbyterian-St. Luke's Hospital, Chicago

Presbyterian-St. Luke's
Hospital, Chicago

Philadelphia General Hospital

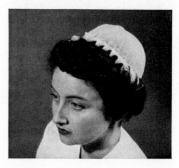

Navy Nurse Corps

Bellevue Hospital, New York City

NURSING. Most nurses work in hospitals taking care of sick persons and helping them get well. Their crisp white uniforms and caps are a familiar sight as they tend to the needs of patients. But nurses work in other places. Visiting nurses go to the homes of the sick. Some nurses assist in the offices of doctors and dentists. Others work in medical clinics, in schools, in stores and factories, in the armed forces, and on ships, trains, and airplanes. Nurses may be found wherever their skills are needed—in big cities, small towns, and farm areas in all parts of the world.

In addition to caring for the sick, nurses help people stay well. They teach children and adults to protect themselves from disease. Nurses with special training may also teach in schools of nursing, where they help others to become professional nurses.

The two main groups of nurses are professional nurses and practical nurses. *Professional nurses*, generally called *registered nurses*, are graduates of two-year junior college programs, three-year hospital programs, or four-year college programs. *Practical nurses* complete a training program that usually lasts 12 months. They perform many duties that relieve professional nurses for duties requiring more preparation.

Most professional nurses are women, but about 1 of every 100 are men. Practical nursing offers many opportunities for men, especially in caring for persons with chronic or mental illnesses.

Professional Nurses

Hospital Nurses. Most professional nurses serve as *general-duty* nurses in hospitals. They work with doctors and other members of the hospital staff to speed a patient's recovery. A general-duty nurse may work in an operating room, where she plays an important role as a member of the surgical team. Elsewhere in the hospital, nurses administer prescribed medicines and treatments to patients. In the nursery, nurses gently care for newborn babies. In other parts of the hospital, nurses may be assisting with blood transfusions, or giving injections of drugs.

The nurse also takes charge of the patient's routine care. She sees that he has his daily bath and that he eats proper foods. She also makes sure he does the exercises or treatments that the doctor has asked him to do on his own. She keeps a watchful eye on the patient and reports to the doctor any change in his physical condition, mental attitude, or reaction to drugs or other treatment.

The well-being of her patient is of first importance to the nurse. She takes time to reassure a worried patient and tries to boost his morale. She is trained to recognize and understand her patient's needs and to provide emotional support as well as physical care. If the nurse has time, she may play with a lonely child, read to a person who cannot see, or write letters for a patient with a broken arm.

A *head nurse* has charge of a group of nurses and patients in a ward or in some other unit of the hospital. With additional education, an experienced nurse may become a supervisor and direct several wards or she may specialize in one kind of nursing. For example, a nurse who specializes in the care of newborn babies might become head of the hospital nursery. Specialization requires a master's degree, which prepares a nurse for teaching, supervision, or administration.

In other institutions, such as sanatoriums or mental hospitals, nurses perform many of the same duties as do hospital nurses. Specialized knowledge or training usually is required because of the special needs of the patients. Many male nurses work in mental hospitals.

Private-Duty Nurses make up the second largest group of professional nurses. They work in hospitals or in private homes. Unlike general-duty nurses, they are employed by the patient rather than by the hospital. Private-duty nurses may devote all their time to only one patient who needs constant care. Sometimes they may attend a small group of patients. Most hospitals keep a *registry*, or file, of nurses who are available for private duty.

Public Health Nurses. Public health offers increasing opportunities for professional nurses. Those who wish to enter this field must take special college courses

approved for public health work. Public health nurses usually help tend large groups of persons outside hospitals. Most of these nurses work for government or private agencies. They often take part in community health programs.

Visiting nurses are public health nurses. So are the nurses employed by city, county, or state health departments. The public health nurse may go into homes to care for patients who have just returned from hospitals. She often teaches patients with chronic illnesses how to care for themselves. She also teaches patients and their families about proper diet, personal cleanliness, and other ways of preventing illness. She may take part in many community projects, such as polio-vaccination and chest X-ray campaigns. Some public health nurses work in schools and summer camps.

Occupational, or Industrial, Health Nurses work in factories, stores, banks, and many business offices. They give first aid to the injured. They treat employees for colds, bruises, and other minor ailments. They also promote safety programs to prevent accidents on the job.

Other Nursing Careers. Many professional nurses combine the professions of teaching and nursing. To teach in a school of nursing, a professional nurse should have advanced college preparation. A master's degree in nursing education is usually required for teaching.

Professional nurses may work in clinics, in doctors' and dentists' offices, or in research laboratories. Some hold positions in nursing organizations. Others write books and articles about nursing. Companies that manufacture drugs and medical equipment often employ nurses as consultants on their products. Nurses serve in the army, navy, and air force. Other branches of the government, such as the Veterans Administration and Department of State, have nurses on their staffs.

Practical Nurses

Practical nurses are specially educated men and women who help professional nurses. They may work in hospitals, private homes, nursing homes, public health agencies, and doctors' offices. Practical nurses often attend mothers and babies, the aged, and chronically ill persons. Frequently they are responsible for such tasks as making beds, giving baths, feeding the helpless, and performing other selected nursing tasks.

Nursing as a Career

Nursing offers daily satisfaction to those who have a genuine desire to help others. It also provides such a wide range of job opportunities that a capable nurse can always be sure of a job.

Among the rewards of nursing are the challenges it offers. A badly injured person may need immediate and expert care. Medicines and equipment must be rushed to his bedside. His family must be comforted, and the doctor must be given a detailed report on his condition. A nurse's greatest reward often is the knowledge that her skill has helped to relieve suffering or to save a life.

Persons planning a career in nursing should also consider a number of other factors. Advances are being made steadily in nurses' salaries. But beginning salaries

Michael Reese Hospital

Classroom Study is part of a nurse's education. Most student nurses in the United States and Canada attend hospital schools.

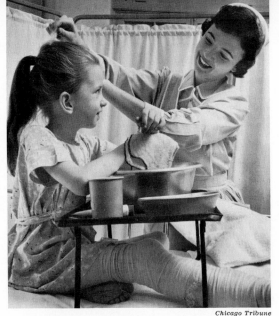

Chicago Tribune

In the Hospital, the student nurse gets varied experiences, such as caring for child patients in the orthopedics department.

may be below those for other professions that require comparable preparation. A person should also consider that some nurses must be active and on their feet a great deal, and may have to do some strenuous work, such as lifting patients. Special *body mechanics* courses taught in nursing schools help the nurse prepare for such tasks.

A nurse must like people and want to help them. She must also have self-reliance and good judgment. Patience, tact, honesty, responsibility, and ability to work easily with others are valuable traits. Good health is another "must."

Most professional nursing schools accept only candidates who rank in the upper half or upper third of their high-school graduating classes. Entrance requirements for practical nursing are less exacting. High-school graduates are preferred, but many practical nursing schools accept candidates with two years of high-school work or less.

Most professional schools admit nursing students between the ages of 17 or 18 and 35. But the upper age limit often is flexible, especially in colleges and universities. Schools of practical nursing admit candidates up to the ages of 45 or 50, but usually also have a flexible upper age limit.

Professional Nursing. Most nurses in the United States and Canada receive their education in hospital schools. During this three-year course, which leads to a diploma, they study nursing in classrooms and laboratories, and work with patients in hospitals and other health agencies. They live in dormitories provided by the hospitals.

Although most nurses take diploma courses, some take regular college courses, with a major in nursing. This requires four to five years and includes work with patients in hospitals and health agencies, in addition to courses in nursing and in the humanities. The student graduates with a bachelor of science degree in nursing. Some junior and community colleges also offer two-year courses of study that lead to an associate degree in nursing.

Classroom Work. Student nurses study such subjects as anatomy, physiology, nutrition, pharmacology, and the fundamentals of nursing care. They often learn to care for the sick by practicing on each other. For example, one girl may take another's temperature, blood pressure, and pulse rate. The students may give their first hypodermic injections to an orange. Then they practice giving "injections," usually small amounts of sterile water, to fellow students.

Clinical Experience. In all schools of nursing, classroom work or theory is interwoven with practice. Clinical experience, or practice, means the time the student spends in learning to care for different types of patients. As part of her clinical experience, she also learns something about hospital routine and the functions of various departments, and gets the "feel" of hospital life.

Student nurses have experience with all types of patients. A teacher who is an expert nurse supervises all their early activities. As the student gains experience and knowledge, she works more independently.

One of the most exciting and important days of a nurse's career is the day she receives her cap. Many nursing schools hold special "capping" ceremonies.

Costs of a nursing education program vary widely. Some hospital schools require an entrance fee. Others do not. Some may require tuition fees. In most college schools of nursing, the student pays tuition and also pays for all or part of her maintenance. Persons who want to enter nursing should inquire about costs at the schools being considered.

Licensing. After graduation from an approved school of nursing, professional nurses in the United States and Canada must pass examinations given by state or provincial boards of examiners. The nurse then receives a license to practice her profession. She is now an R.N., or Registered Nurse.

Nurses may advance their careers by additional study and experience. A master's degree is often the step to specialization, teaching, or administration. A nurse

Visiting Nurses care for sick persons in their homes. During her visit, the nurse may teach the patient to care for himself.

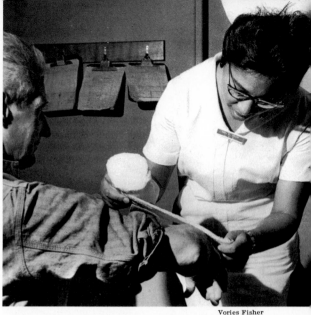

Industrial Nurses, or company nurses, give first aid to injured employees and often set up safety programs for the company.

who wishes to advance her career even further may earn a doctoral degree.

Practical Nursing courses usually last one year. Like professional nursing education, the course combines classroom study with actual experience.

There are two types of schools of practical nursing, public and private. Some public schools teach practical nursing as part of their vocational-training or adult-education programs. Private schools are operated by hospitals, health agencies, and by some junior colleges and universities. Credits from practical nursing schools cannot be transferred to professional nursing schools. If a practical nurse wants to become a professional nurse, she must begin all over again.

In almost all the states, and some Canadian provinces, a practical nurse, like a professional nurse, must obtain a license to practice. She then becomes a Licensed Practical Nurse (L.P.N.), sometimes called a Licensed Vocational Nurse (L.V.N.).

The dress of the graduate practical nurse usually consists of a white cap, uniform, shoes, and stockings. On her sleeve she wears the letters L.P.N. or L.V.N. to show that she is a practical nurse. But dress varies widely according to the school from which the nurse graduates, or the institution for which she works.

Career Information. A high-school student who wants to learn about a nursing career should talk with a vocational guidance counselor, family doctor, school nurse, or other nurses. Many high schools have Future Nurses clubs whose members visit hospitals and schools of nursing and do volunteer work. Serving as a nurse's aide or as an orderly in a hospital is another way to learn more about nursing (see NURSE'S AIDE). Information on professional and practical nursing may be obtained from the Committee on Careers, National League for Nursing, 10 Columbus Circle, New York, N.Y. 10019.

The History of Nursing

Some form of nursing care has probably been practiced for thousands of years. For example, the early Hebrews and Egyptians hired women, later called *midwives*, who assisted at births.

Nurses first organized in groups during early Christian times. Noblewomen, including the wives of the emperors, helped care for the ill in ancient Rome. During the Crusades, military nursing orders of monks and knights tended the sick and wounded.

Many monasteries closed during the Reformation, and there were only a few places where religious orders could nurse the sick. The years from 1600 to 1850 were the darkest period in the history of nursing. Hospitals often were built as charity hospitals, and were usually staffed by untrained, sometimes disreputable, women. Wealthy persons never went to hospitals for treatment. The importance of sanitation and hygiene were unknown. People did not know how diseases spread. Often nurses who took care of patients with contagious diseases contracted these diseases themselves.

Nursing as we know it began in the 1850's with the work of the English nurse, Florence Nightingale, the founder of modern professional nursing. Miss Nightingale established the first school of nursing, the Nightingale Home for Nurses, in London in 1860. Graduates of this school traveled to all parts of the world, including the United States, to teach nursing. The first nursing schools in the United States were established in 1873 at Massachusetts General Hospital in Boston, Bellevue Hospital in New York City, and the New Haven (Conn.) Hospital. The American Nurses Association, Inc., an organization of professional registered nurses, was organized in 1896.

Many nurses have won world fame, including Clara Barton, Edith Cavell, Elizabeth Kenny, and Lillian D. Wald. ELEANOR C. LAMBERTSEN

Related Articles in WORLD BOOK include:

Barton, Clara
Cavell, Edith L.
Hospital
Kenny, Elizabeth
Nightingale, Florence
Nurse's Aide

Pakistan (picture)
Physical Therapy
Red Cross
Safety
Wald, Lillian D.

Ewing Galloway

Nuts Are Nutritious Food and an important source of vegetable oil. This group includes walnuts, almonds, hazelnuts, butternuts, Brazil nuts, and pecans, all widely used.

NUT is the popular name for a type of plant seed or fruit which grows in a shell of woody fiber. The term *nut* may mean the shell as well as the meat inside, or it may refer only to the seed of the fruit, as with the almond. The nut may be one of a large number of seeds lying inside a cone, like the pine nut or Indian nut. In the markets of the United States, whole nuts are called in-shell, or unshelled, nuts. Those with their shells removed are called shelled nuts, kernels, or nut meats.

The kernels of most edible nuts form highly concentrated foods, rich in protein. Most nuts are rich in fat, except the chestnut and a few others, which are fairly high in starch. Nuts are an important source of protein. In parts of Europe, nuts form a large part of the regular diet. Bread is sometimes baked from a flour made from chestnuts.

The Persian or English walnut, pecan, almond,

cashew, pistachio, hickory, black walnut, Brazil nut, filbert or hazelnut, macadamia, and chestnut are the most popular nuts in the United States and Canada. The Persian walnut is usually called the English walnut, although it probably was grown originally in Asia. Many walnuts and almonds are now grown in California. There are many pecan orchards in the southern and southwestern states. The peanut is actually a relative of peas and beans. In the United States, peanuts are grown in many parts of the South (see PEANUT).

Several types of nuts come from the tropics. The coconut is a commercially important nut that grows in many parts of the tropics. The pili nut is a prized food in the Philippines and nearby islands. It is a hardshelled triangular nut about 2 inches long. The sapucaia nut, which is sometimes called the paradise nut or cream nut, is related to the Brazil nut. It is triangular-shaped and about the same size as the Brazil nut. The sapucaia nut grows in the Amazon Basin. Its shell is much like soft cork, and its kernel has a pleasant taste. The ravensara nut and the breadnut are grown in the tropics. But botanists do not consider them to be true nuts. The ravensara nut supplies a spice called Madagascar clove nutmeg.

Several kinds of hickory trees bear nuts that are good to eat. Hickory nuts have hard shells. A hickory tree that grows in eastern United States and Canada bears a seed called a bitternut that is not good to eat. The outer hull is thin, and inside there is a thin inner shell purplish in color. The macadamia nut, sometimes called the Queensland nut or Australian nut, has a thin hard shell, but the kernel is good to eat. It is the fruit of an evergreen tree that comes from Australia, and it is now grown in Hawaii and parts of the American tropics. Some trees have been planted in California and Florida.

Several types of trees that bear pine nuts grow in western North America. The piñon, also called the pine nut, Indian nut, and pinyon, is the small, brown seed of the piñon pine. Its shell has yellow dots. The tree grows in areas between 5,000 and 9,000 feet above sea level. The stone pine, a close relative of the piñon pine, comes from southern Europe. Its kernels are known as pignolia.

Water chestnut, sometimes called water caltrop or Jesuit nut, is the seed of a water plant that grows in Europe. A closely related plant called the Singhara nut, or horn nut, comes from southern Asia.

Nut trees are pollinated by wind or insects. Varieties of *species* (kinds) of nut trees are often crossed. Parts of one variety are *grafted* (joined) to the rootstock of another variety (see GRAFTING).

Those nut trees which come from Europe grow better in the western part of the United States than in the East. Those transplanted from eastern Asia seem to do better in the eastern states.   REID M. BROOKS

Related Articles in WORLD BOOK include:

Acorn	Coconut Palm	Kola Nut
Almond	Filbert	Litchi
Beech	Fruit (picture:	Macadamia Nut
Betel	Nature Designs	Nutmeg
Bitternut	the Fruits)	Pecan
Brazil Nut	Ginkgo	Piñon
Butternut	Hazel	Pistachio Nut
Cashew	Hickory	Walnut
Chestnut	Horse Chestnut	

LEADING NUT-GROWING STATES

Tons of nuts in the shell grown in 1967

Georgia
515,000 tons ⊛⊛⊛⊛⊛⊛⊛⊛⊛⊛⊛⊛⊛⊛⊛⊛⊛⊛⊛⊛

Texas
184,000 tons ⊛⊛⊛⊛⊛⊛⊛

North Carolina
175,000 tons ⊛⊛⊛⊛⊛⊛⊛

California
151,000 tons ⊛⊛⊛⊛⊛⊛

Alabama
132,000 tons ⊛⊛⊛⊛⊛

Oklahoma
131,000 tons ⊛⊛⊛⊛⊛

Virginia
128,000 tons ⊛⊛⊛⊛⊛

Florida
41,000 tons ⊛⊛

South Carolina
13,000 tons ⊛

Louisiana
11,000 tons ⊛

Source: U.S. Department of Agriculture

NUTCRACKER is a bird of the crow family that lives in the mountainous evergreen forests of North America, Europe, and Asia. It received its name because of its supposed ability to crack nuts with its bill. It is somewhat smaller than a crow and has a strong, direct flight. Its feathers are a mixture of brown, white, and black, and its claws are heavy, curved, and very sharp.

The nutcracker feeds chiefly on the seeds of pine cones, and has the rather interesting habit of holding the cones in its claws while opening them. The American nutcracker is called *Clark's crow* and *Clark's nutcracker*. It is found in the western pine regions, usually at high altitudes, from Alaska to Mexico. This nutcracker hides its nest at the top of a tall pine tree. While there is still a deep blanket of snow on the ground, the female lays from three to five speckled, grayish-green eggs in the nest.

Scientific Classification. Nutcrackers belong to the crow family, *Corvidae*. The European nutcracker is genus *Nucifraga*, species *N. caryocatactes*. Clark's nutcracker is *N. columbiana*.   HERBERT FRIEDMANN

NUTHATCH is the name of a group of climbing birds. They are common throughout the temperate regions of

are speckled with reddish-brown or lavender spots.

Other American nuthatches are the *red-breasted* nuthatch found in the northern states, the *brown-headed* nuthatch found in the southern states, and the *pygmy* nuthatch found in the West. The red-breasted and brown-headed nuthatches are smaller than the white-breasted nuthatch.

Scientific Classification. Nuthatches belong to the nuthatch family, *Sittidae*. The white-breasted is genus *Sitta*, species *S. carolinensis*. The red-breasted is classified as *S. canadensis*, the brown-headed as *S. pusilla*, and the pygmy as *S. pygmaea*.   GEORGE J. WALLACE

See also BIRD (color pictures, Birds' Eggs, Birds That Help Us).

NUTMEG is the kernel of a tropical fruit, which is widely used as a spice. When the fruit is ripe it looks like a golden-yellow pear hanging among shiny, gray-green leaves. The tree grows to be as much as 70 feet high and is an evergreen. The trees originally grew in the Molucca (Spice) Islands, but they have been successfully raised in all of the East Indies, the West Indies,

John Sumner, Nat. Audubon Society
Clark's Nutcracker lives in western North America.

Allan Cruickshank
The Red-Breasted Nuthatch lives only in North America.

J. R. Watkins Co.
Kernels of Nutmeg provide the spice used in cooking. A membrane covering the kernel provides mace, another spice.

the world. Nuthatches get their name from their habit of wedging nuts into cracks in the bark of trees and then *hatching* (opening) them with repeated strokes of the bill.

The best-known American species is the *white-breasted* nuthatch. It lives the year-round in the United States and southern Canada. The bird is about 6 inches long. It is dark gray above. The top of its head and upper neck are black, and its under parts are white. These nuthatches are shy in summer, and live in wooded places. But in winter they can be seen around houses and orchards, where they are likely to find food. They particularly like to eat sunflower seed and suet. They are fond of wild nuts, especially beechnuts, and of waste grain and weed seeds. They also eat many insects and insect larvae. In climbing trees, they zigzag in every direction, searching for insects under the bark. Nuthatches can even creep headfirst down trees. They have a peculiar wavering flight. The nuthatch builds its nest in holes in trees or stumps. The female bird lays from 5 to 10 eggs. The eggs are white or creamy in color and

Brazil, Ceylon, and India. Nutmeg trees have long, pointed leaves with well-marked veins. The pale-yellow flowers droop in clusters, and look like lilies of the valley.

As the fruit ripens, the fleshy part becomes rather hard, somewhat like candied fruit. It finally splits open at the top, showing a bright-scarlet membrane, which partly covers the nut. The spice called *mace* comes from this membrane. The kernels are the familiar household nutmegs.

Nutmeg trees do not begin bearing until they are about nine years old. Each tree produces from 1,500 to 2,000 nuts yearly. The fleshy part of the fruit is often preserved and eaten like candy. A clear oil, called *oil of mace*, is made from the kernel.

Scientific Classification. Nutmeg trees belong to the nutmeg family, *Myristicaceae*. They are genus *Myristica*, species *M. fragrans*.   HAROLD NORMAN MOLDENKE

See also MACE.

NUTMEG STATE. See CONNECTICUT (Colonial Life).

NUTRIA. See COYPU; FUR (Names of Furs).

Doris Pinney, Photo Library

Wide World

Nutrition Plays an Important Part in Childhood Development. The child at the left has had a good diet. The child at the right suffers from malnutrition. Her deformed ribs and swollen abdomen are results of malnutrition, and she may also have rickets, a vitamin deficiency disease.

NUTRITION

NUTRITION is the science that deals with foods and the way the body uses them. Good food is essential for health as well as for survival. The word *nutrition* also refers to the process by which living things take in food and use it. Human beings depend for food on plants and on animals that eat plants.

The science of nutrition overlaps into several other fields of science. For example, nutrition is part of medicine because nutritionists study diseases caused

by malnutrition. Nutritionists study digestion as part of physiology, the science that deals with how the body works. They also study biochemistry, the science of the various chemical reactions that take place in the body.

Many nutritionists work with community food programs. They may supervise the diets of patients in hospitals and the food served to children in schools. Nutritionists also develop and test new foods, such as the foods used in space exploration, foods made from *algae* (simple plants), and foods made from chemicals.

Experts in many professions try to solve problems concerning nutrition. Home economists study the management and preparation of food. Chemists make *synthetic* (artificial) foods from chemicals. Educators teach

Jean Mayer, the contributor of this article, is Professor of Nutrition at Harvard University. He was chairman of the First (1969) White House Conference on Food, Nutrition, and Health. He is a Special Consultant to the President and is the author of Overweight: Causes, Cost, and Control.

correct food habits. Agricultural researchers work to develop high-yield and high-quality crops.

Nutrients

The body uses certain parts of foods for energy and growth and for replacement of structures worn out by work or play. These food parts are called *nutrients*. Foods also provide vitamins, which are necessary to get energy out of food. The body needs energy to maintain all its functions. The energy in food is measured in units called *calories*. A food calorie is the amount of energy required to raise the temperature of 1,000 grams of water one degree centigrade.

The amount of energy needed varies from person to person. Children need more energy than adults because they are growing. Children also need more vitamins and nutrients. Pregnant women and nursing mothers require more nutrients than other women. Larger people need more food than smaller individuals. For some nutrients, such as vitamin A, the need is proportional to body size. For example, if one person is twice as large as another, his need for vitamin A is twice as great. The need for total calories also increases with size, though not proportionately. In cold weather, a person must have additional nutrients because his body uses more energy to stay at the same temperature. If a person does physical work or exercise, he also spends more energy than if he is resting.

Nutritionists classify nutrients into five main groups: (1) carbohydrates, (2) fats, (3) proteins, (4) minerals, and (5) vitamins.

Carbohydrates are the starches and sugars in foods. They serve as the main source of energy. Carbohydrates contribute about 45 per cent of the calories in a well-balanced diet. Starches are found in bread, breakfast cereals, flour, and potatoes. The main sugar in food is *sucrose*, ordinary white or brown sugar. Another important sugar, *lactose*, is found in milk.

Fats, another source of energy, furnish a little more than 40 per cent of the calories in the diet. Nutritionists classify fats as *visible* or *invisible*. Visible fats, such as butter, oil, and shortening, are added to foods. Invisible fats are already present in foods. They include the butterfat in milk and the fats in eggs, fish, meat, and nuts.

Fats are made up of substances called *fatty acids* and *glycerol*. Some fatty acids are *saturated*—that is, they contain as many hydrogen atoms as they can hold. Other fatty acids contain fewer hydrogen atoms than possible and are called *unsaturated*. If a fatty acid lacks four or more hydrogen atoms, it is called *polyunsaturated*. Too many saturated fatty acids in the body can raise the amount of *cholesterol*, a fatty substance in the blood and tissues. Too much cholesterol may cause heart attacks. See CHOLESTEROL.

Proteins are especially necessary for the growth and maintenance of body structures. The bones, muscles, skin, and other solid parts of the body are made up largely of proteins. Proteins also provide energy and make up from 12 to 15 per cent of the diet's calories. *Animal proteins* are found in cheese, eggs, fish, meat, and milk. *Vegetable proteins* are found in beans, grains, nuts, and vegetables.

Minerals are also needed for the growth and maintenance of body structures. Calcium, magnesium, and phosphorus are essential parts of the bones and teeth.

CHARACTERISTICS AFFECTING CALORIE REQUIREMENTS

Daily Calorie Requirements depend on many things. For example, a child needs more calories than an old man because the youngster is still growing. A man's body has a greater percentage of muscle tissue than a woman's, and he needs more calories than she does to keep this tissue healthy.

WORLD BOOK illustration

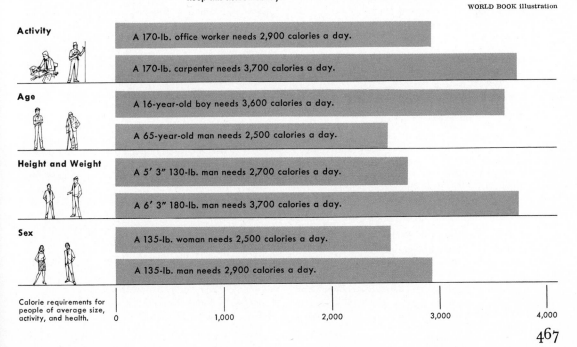

Activity
A 170-lb. office worker needs 2,900 calories a day.
A 170-lb. carpenter needs 3,700 calories a day.

Age
A 16-year-old boy needs 3,600 calories a day.
A 65-year-old man needs 2,500 calories a day.

Height and Weight
A 5' 3" 130-lb. man needs 2,700 calories a day.
A 6' 3" 180-lb. man needs 3,700 calories a day.

Sex
A 135-lb. woman needs 2,500 calories a day.
A 135-lb. man needs 2,900 calories a day.

Calorie requirements for people of average size, activity, and health.

0 — 1,000 — 2,000 — 3,000 — 4,000

467

In addition, calcium is necessary for blood clotting. Iron is an important part of hemoglobin, the red coloring matter in blood. Minerals are also needed to maintain the composition of the digestive juices and the fluids that are found in and around the body cells. Other vital minerals include iodine, potassium, sodium, and sulfur.

Vitamins are essential for good health. The body cannot manufacture vitamins and must depend on food to supply them. Vitamins are named by letters or by their chemical names.

Vitamin A is found in green and yellow plants and in fish liver and fish-liver oils. It is necessary for healthy skin and development of the bones.

Vitamin B1, also called *thiamin*, is found in whole-grain cereals and in meat. It is necessary for the use of starches and sugars by the body.

Vitamin B2, or *riboflavin*, is essential for a number of complicated chemical reactions that take place during the body's use of food. It is found in liver, milk, and vegetables.

Vitamin B12 and *folic acid* are needed for the formation of red blood cells and the proper function of the nerves. Vitamin B12 is found in animal products, especially liver. Folic acid is present in leafy, green, and yellow vegetables.

Vitamin C, also called *ascorbic acid*, is found in fruit—especially oranges and lemons—and in potatoes. It is needed for the maintenance of the ligaments, tendons, and other supportive tissue.

Vitamin D is present in eggs, fish-liver oil, and liver. It is also formed when the skin is exposed to the sun. Vitamin D is necessary for the use of calcium by the body.

Vitamin E is manufactured by bacteria in the intestine. It is necessary for proper clotting of the blood.

Niacin is necessary for respiration of the cells. It is present in liver, yeast, lean meat, and some vegetables.

Pantothenic acid, *pyridoxin*, and *biotin* are other vitamins that play a role in chemical reactions in the body. Small amounts of these vitamins are found in many kinds of foods.

Water plays a vital role in the health of the body, but it is often considered separately from nutrients. Enough water is essential for a good, varied diet. See WATER (Water in Living Things).

Basic Food Groups

The key to good nutrition is a varied diet that includes every kind of nutrient. Nutritionists have grouped foods according to nutrient content to simplify the planning of a varied diet. The *Basic Seven* system of classification divides foods into seven groups.

Another system, called the *Basic Four*, puts foods of different nutritional values into the same groups. This system has (1) a milk group for all milk and milk products, (2) a meat group, (3) a bread and cereal group, and (4) a fruit and vegetable group.

Following are the Basic Seven groups, with the chief foods in each.

Group 1. Meat, Poultry, Fish, Eggs, Dried Beans and Peas, and Nuts. This group is a chief source of proteins and also provides vitamin B1, iron, niacin, phos-

phorus, and some starch. One or two daily servings are recommended.

Group 2. Leafy, Green, and Yellow Vegetables. This group includes greens of all kinds, such as asparagus, broccoli, green peas, and string beans. It also includes carrots, pumpkins, rutabagas, squash, sweet potatoes, and wax beans. All these vegetables supply large amounts of vitamin A, the B vitamins, vitamin C, calcium, and iron. They also provide fiber, which helps regulate the intestines. Nutritionists recommend one or more daily servings from this group.

Group 3. Citrus Fruits, Raw Cabbage, Salad Greens, and Tomatoes. This group includes all citrus fruits—such as grapefruit, lemons, and oranges—and their juices. The foods in this group are good sources of vitamin C, and they also furnish vitamin A, calcium, and iron. One or more daily servings are recommended.

Group 4. Potatoes and Other Vegetables, and Noncitrus Fruits. This group includes all vegetables and fruits not in groups 2 and 3. At least one potato a day is recommended for active people, both children and adults. Potatoes are good sources of vitamin C if baked or boiled. A daily serving of another food from group 4 is also suggested. Group 4 foods supply carbohydrates, minerals, and small amounts of most vitamins.

Group 5. Bread, Breakfast Cereals, and Flour. This group includes biscuits and crackers. All these foods should consist of whole grains or enriched flour. Enriching is important because milling removes much of the grain's outer coat, which is rich in vitamins and minerals. At least four daily servings are recommended.

Group 6. Butter and Fortified Margarine. Margarine must be fortified with vitamin A to equal the amount of this vitamin found in butter. These foods are chiefly energy producers and sources of vitamin A. Butter or margarine should be included in the daily diet, but no specific amount is recommended.

Group 7. Milk and Milk Products. Milk in any form makes up this group. It may be fresh, dried, evaporated, or made into cheese or ice cream. A child needs three to four cups of milk daily, and an adult should have at least two cups. Milk and cheese are valuable sources of vitamin A, vitamin B2, calcium, and proteins.

Selecting and Cooking Foods

Every day's meals should include foods from each group. A wise shopper buys foods that are as fresh as possible because many foods lose vitamins A and C when they become stale. Canned or frozen products add variety to meals because they make most foods available throughout the year. Modern food processing tries to ensure that canned and frozen foods retain their nutritional values. Some high-quality processed foods may be more nutritious than fresh foods. Fresh foods may lose some nutritional value if they are harvested before maturity or if they are kept for long periods before being eaten.

It is important not to add unnecessary calories, saturated fats, or sugar to food. Foods must be kept and cooked carefully to conserve their nutritional value. Many foods should be kept in the refrigerator. They should be cooked quickly and in as little cooking

BASIC FOOD GROUPS

The Basic Food Groups. Nutritionists recommend one daily serving from each of the Basic Seven groups. With the Basic Four system, they suggest four or more servings from both the vegetable-fruit and bread-cereals groups, and two or more servings from the meat group.

The Basic Seven

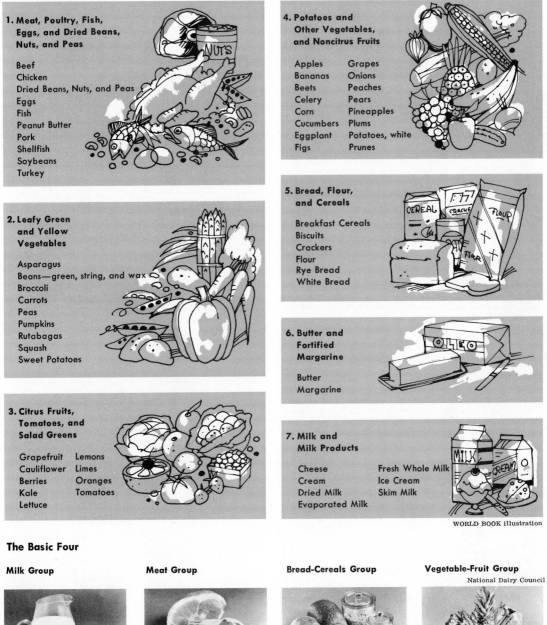

1. Meat, Poultry, Fish, Eggs, and Dried Beans, Nuts, and Peas

Beef
Chicken
Dried Beans, Nuts, and Peas
Eggs
Fish
Peanut Butter
Pork
Shellfish
Soybeans
Turkey

2. Leafy Green and Yellow Vegetables

Asparagus
Beans—green, string, and wax
Broccoli
Carrots
Peas
Pumpkins
Rutabagas
Squash
Sweet Potatoes

3. Citrus Fruits, Tomatoes, and Salad Greens

Grapefruit   Lemons
Cauliflower   Limes
Berries   Oranges
Kale   Tomatoes
Lettuce

4. Potatoes and Other Vegetables, and Noncitrus Fruits

Apples   Grapes
Bananas   Onions
Beets   Peaches
Celery   Pears
Corn   Pineapples
Cucumbers   Plums
Eggplant   Potatoes, white
Figs   Prunes

5. Bread, Flour, and Cereals

Breakfast Cereals
Biscuits
Crackers
Flour
Rye Bread
White Bread

6. Butter and Fortified Margarine

Butter
Margarine

7. Milk and Milk Products

Cheese   Fresh Whole Milk
Cream   Ice Cream
Dried Milk   Skim Milk
Evaporated Milk

WORLD BOOK illustration

The Basic Four

Milk Group

Meat Group

Bread-Cereals Group

Vegetable-Fruit Group

National Dairy Council

468a

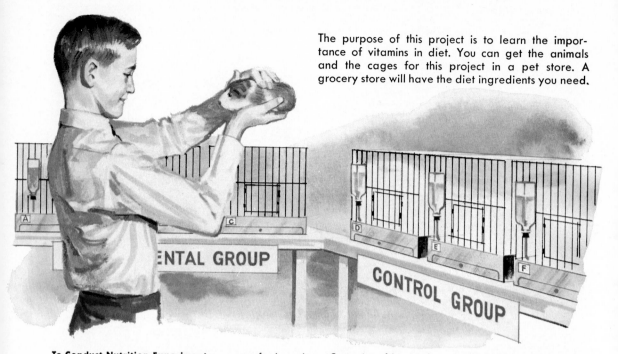

The purpose of this project is to learn the importance of vitamins in diet. You can get the animals and the cages for this project in a pet store. A grocery store will have the diet ingredients you need.

To Conduct Nutrition Experiments, a group of guinea pigs are divided into two groups—a control group and an experimental group. All animals get the same diet, which lacks one vital food element. This element is added to the food for the control group.

Comparison of the control group with the experimental group shows the effect of the deficiency of the food element in which you are interested. This project is concerned with vitamin deficiency. But you can conduct similar experiments with other food elements.

MATERIALS

Materials for this project include six young guinea pigs of about the same size and weight, six cages, a record book, graph paper, and adhesive tape. You will also need a gram scale for weighing the diet ingredients and each of the animals. Most drugstores sell such scales.

Illustrated by Bart Jerner for WORLD BOOK

Scale

Six cages

Six young
guinea pigs

Record book
and growth charts

Adhesive tape labels

NUTRITION EXPERIMENT ON VITAMIN C DEFICIENCY

In this experiment, three guinea pigs make up the experimental group, and three make up the control group. Feed all the animals the same basic diet, which lacks vitamin C. But add foods with vitamin C to the daily ration for the guinea pigs in the control group. The formula for the basic diet and suggestions for foods with a high vitamin C content are given, *below*. Be sure to keep all the animals in comfortable and healthful surroundings. Give them fresh water at least once a day, and clean the cages daily.

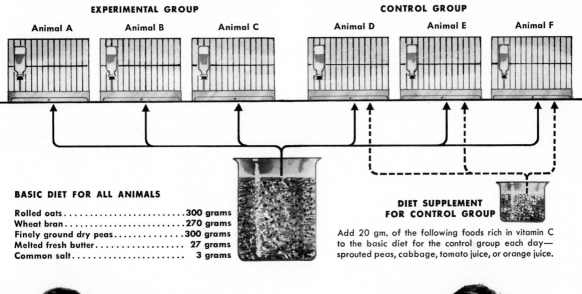

EXPERIMENTAL GROUP

Animal A   Animal B   Animal C

CONTROL GROUP

Animal D   Animal E   Animal F

BASIC DIET FOR ALL ANIMALS

Rolled oats.........................300 grams
Wheat bran........................270 grams
Finely ground dry peas............300 grams
Melted fresh butter.................. 27 grams
Common salt...................... 3 grams

DIET SUPPLEMENT FOR CONTROL GROUP

Add 20 gm. of the following foods rich in vitamin C to the basic diet for the control group each day— sprouted peas, cabbage, tomato juice, or orange juice.

Keeping Records. In the log book, make daily entries for each animal, noting any changes in behavior or appearance. Make separate weight charts for the experimental group and for the control group. Weigh and record the weight of each animal daily. Use a different color lead or a different kind of line for each animal. Compare and analyze all your records at the end of the experiment.

ADDITIONAL EXPERIMENTS ON NUTRITION

You can show the effects of other vitamin deficiencies. For these projects, follow the same routine, but use mice instead of guinea pigs, and feed them a diet lacking the vitamin.

Vitamin A Deficiency. A special diet lacking this vitamin is given, *below*. The recipe makes about 300 grams, which is enough to feed six rats several days. Add 30 grams of fresh butter to this diet for feeding the control group. It may take from 5 to 7 weeks for the test animals to show any signs of vitamin A deficiency. As soon as they do, feed butter to them to restore them to normal health. Keep complete records during this period, too.

BASIC DIET

Wheat.............................114 grams
Dried beef (or lean meat)...................... 30 grams
Starch.............................150 grams
Common salt............................... 3 grams
Slaked lime............................... 3 grams

Vitamin B$_1$ Deficiency. A diet deficient in this vitamin is given, *below*. The recipe makes enough food for several days. To feed the control group, add 5 grams of bakers' yeast, 10 gm. of ground wheat, or 30 gm. of wheat bran to the basic diet. Any of these foods will supply vitamin B$_1$, so you need add only one of them. When the test animals begin to show signs of vitamin deficiency, add the yeast, wheat, or bran to their diet. Keep complete records.

BASIC DIET

White flour.............................150 grams
Butter............................... 30 grams
Dried beef............................... 15 grams
Common salt............................... 3 grams
Slaked lime............................... 3 grams
Starch............................... 99 grams

liquid as possible. Because some vitamins and minerals dissolve in the liquid, it should be eaten with the food. Milk in glass containers should not be exposed to light for long periods because light destroys vitamin B_2.

Results of Malnutrition

Malnutrition is caused by poor intake, absorption, or use of nutrients by the body. If a person does not get enough food, *undernutrition* results. Starvation is extreme undernutrition. If a person does not eat enough food or if his diet lacks certain nutrients, the condition is called *primary malnutrition*. Sometimes, because of disease, the body cannot use nutrients even though they are present in the food eaten. The result is *secondary malnutrition*. A person's diet also may be faulty because it contains too many nutrients. Such a diet may be high in saturated fats or in calories.

Protein-Calorie Malnutrition occurs when the diet is low in both proteins and calories. The condition is called *kwashiorkor* if the diet is especially low in proteins. Symptoms of kwashiorkor include changes in the color and texture of the hair and skin, swelling of the body, and damage to the intestines, liver, and pancreas. The disease generally attacks children and is fatal unless the patient is given protein. If the diet is especially low in calories, the condition is called *marasmus*. Marasmus

DAILY ALLOWANCES OF CHIEF FOOD ELEMENTS

	Age	Weight (lbs.)	Calories	Protein (gm.)	Calcium (gm.)	Iron (mg.)	A (I.U.)	C (mg.)	D (I.U.)	VITAMINS Thiamin (mg.)	Riboflavin (mg.)	Niacin (mg.)
Men	18-35	154	2,900	70	0.8	10	5,000	70		1.2	1.7	19
	35-55	154	2,600	70	0.8	10	5,000	70		1.0	1.6	17
	55-75	154	2,200	70	0.8	10	5,000	70		0.9	1.3	15
Women	18-35	128	2,100	58	0.8	15	5,000	70		0.8	1.3	14
	35-55	128	1,900	58	0.8	15	5,000	70		0.8	1.2	13
	55-75	128	1,600	58	0.8	10	5,000	70		0.8	1.2	13
Children	1-3	29	1,300	32	0.8	8	2,000	40	400	0.5	0.8	9
	3-6	40	1,600	40	0.8	10	2,500	50	400	0.6	1.0	11
	6-9	53	2,100	52	0.8	12	3,500	60	400	0.8	1.3	14
Boys	9-12	72	2,400	60	1.1	15	4,500	70	400	1.0	1.4	16
	12-15	98	3,000	75	1.4	15	5,000	80	400	1.2	1.8	20
	15-18	134	3,400	85	1.4	15	5,000	80	400	1.4	2.0	22
Girls	9-12	72	2,200	55	1.1	15	4,500	80	400	0.9	1.3	15
	12-15	103	2,500	62	1.3	15	5,000	80	400	1.0	1.5	17
	15-18	117	2,300	58	1.3	15	5,000	70	400	0.9	1.3	15

gm. = grams; mg. = milligrams; I.U. = International Units.
Above figures intended for normally active persons in a temperate climate.

Source: National Research Council

NUTRITIONAL VALUES OF COMMON FOODS

Food	Serving	Calories	Protein (gm.)	Calcium (mg.)	Iron (mg.)	A (I.U.)	C (mg.)	D (I.U.)	VITAMINS Thiamin (mcg.)	Riboflavin (mcg.)	Niacin (mg.)
Apple, raw	1 large	117	0.6	12	0.6	180	9	0	80	60	0.4
Banana, raw	1 large	176	2.4	16	1.2	860	20	0	80	100	1.4
Beans, green, cooked	1 cup	27	1.8	45	0.9	830	18	0	90	120	0.6
Beef, round, cooked	3.2 ounces	214	24.7	10	3.1	0	0	0	74	202	5.1
Bread, white, enriched	1 slice	63	2.0	18	0.4	0	0	0	60	40	0.5
Broccoli, cooked	⅔ cup	29	3.3	130	1.3	3,400	74	0	70	150	0.8
Butter	1 tablespoon	100	0.1	33	0.0	460	0	5	tr.	tr.	tr.
Cabbage, cooked	½ cup	20	1.2	39	0.4	75	27	0	40	40	0.3
Carrots, raw	1 cup, shredded	42	1.2	39	0.8	12,000	6	0	60	60	0.5
Cheese, cheddar, American	1 ounce	113	7.1	206	0.3	400	0	0	10	120	tr.
Chicken, fried	½ breast	232	26.8	19	1.3	460	0	0	67	101	10.2
Egg, boiled	1 medium	77	6.1	26	1.3	550	0	27	40	130	tr.
Liver, beef, fried	1 slice	86	8.8	4	2.9	18,658	10	19	90	1,283	5.1
Margarine, fortified	1 tablespoon	101	0.1	3	0.0	460	0	0	0	0	0.0
Milk, whole, cow's	6 ounces	124	6.4	216	0.2	293	2	4	73	311	0.2
Oatmeal, cooked	1 cup	148	5.4	21	1.7	0	0	0	220	50	0.4
Orange, whole	1 medium	68	1.4	50	0.6	285	74	0	120	45	0.3
Pork, shoulder, roasted	2 slices	320	19.2	9	2.0	0	0	0	592	144	3.2
Tomatoes, raw	1 large	40	2.0	22	1.2	2,200	46	0	120	80	1.0
Potatoes, white, baked	1 medium	98	2.4	13	0.8	20	17	0	110	50	1.4
Rice, white, cooked	1 cup	201	4.2	13	0.5	0	0	0	20	10	0.7
Sugar, white, granulated	1 tablespoon	48	0.0	0	0.0	0	0	0	0	0	0.0

gm. = grams; mg. = milligrams; mcg. = micrograms; I.U. = International Units; tr. = trace.

usually attacks infants, causing extreme underweight and weakness.

Vitamin Deficiencies are caused by a diet low in vitamins. Symptoms vary according to which vitamin is missing.

Vitamin A Deficiency causes *night blindness* (lack of vision in dim light) and momentary blinding by sudden exposure to light. It also causes dry, itchy skin. Extreme vitamin A deficiency leads to total blindness and death.

Vitamin B₁ Deficiency, also called *beriberi*, causes swelling, damage to nerves, and a type of heart disease. Beriberi is widespread in many regions of the world. It is a major problem in areas of Asia where polished rice makes up a large part of the people's diet. When rice is polished, the outer shell of the grain is removed by milling. This shell contains most of the grain's vitamin B_1. In the United States, flour is enriched with vitamin B_1, vitamin B_2, iron, and niacin.

Vitamin B₂ Deficiency causes cracking at the corners of the mouth, and itching.

Vitamin B₁₂ Deficiency and lack of folic acid cause blood disorders. Abnormal red cells are formed, and the nervous system is affected.

Vitamin C Deficiency, also called *scurvy*, causes sore and bleeding gums, slow repair of wounds, and painful joints. The walls of the *capillaries*, the smallest blood vessels, become so weak that slight pressure may cause them to break.

Vitamin D Deficiency, also called *rickets*, causes an abnormal development of the bones. Calcium is not properly deposited in the bones. Common results of rickets include such conditions as knock-knees and chicken breast, in which the breastbone sticks out abnormally.

Mineral Deficiencies may also cause severe diseases. Lack of iron can cause *anemia*, an abnormal condition of the blood. *Goiter*, a disease in which the thyroid gland

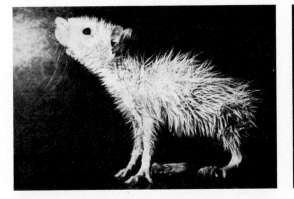

From *Foundations of Nutrition* by Clara Mae Taylor and Orrea F. Pye

Vitamins are essential for important body processes. The two rats above were fed identical diets, except that the rat at the left did not receive vitamin B₂.

Minerals are also important for good health. The chickens below are both five weeks old and were fed identical diets, except that the chicken on the left did not receive zinc.

M. L. Sunde, University of Wisconsin

469

becomes enlarged, is caused by lack of the mineral iodine.

Obesity results from eating more than the body needs for growth, energy, and maintenance. An obese person is simply too fat. More exercise and less food may be necessary to reduce body weight.

Heart and Circulatory Diseases can result from poor nutrition. An increase in the cholesterol in the blood may be caused by a diet with too many saturated fats. Increased cholesterol can increase the chances of heart attacks, strokes, and other diseases of the blood vessels.

History

Nutrition as a Science began in 1780. That year, the French chemist Antoine L. Lavoisier discovered that food and oxygen combine in the body to produce energy. But deficiency diseases had been studied earlier. In 1753, for example, James Lind, a Scottish physician, published a cure for scurvy. He studied the disease in sailors who lived for long periods on salted beef and *hard tack* (dry biscuits). Lind found that adding lemon juice to their diet cured and prevented the disease.

The deficiency diseases were conquered one by one. Christiaan Eijkman, a Dutch scientist, studied beriberi in military prison camps. About 1900, he found that people who depended largely on polished rice for food got beriberi. Those who ate whole rice did not get the disease. Eijkman concluded that something in the hulls was necessary for health.

In the early 1900's, scientists discovered vitamins and *amino acids*, organic acids that make up proteins. The British biochemists Frederick G. Hopkins and Edward Mellanby studied the composition of proteins and the role of vitamins. Mellanby also investigated the cause and cure of rickets. Two American biochemists, Elmer V. McCollum and Lafayette B. Mendel, demonstrated the body's need for amino acids and vitamins. Mendel identified vitamin A in 1913. Vitamin D was identified by McCollum in 1922. Joseph Goldberger, a physician of the U.S. Public Health Service, studied the disease *pellagra*. He found that it is caused by a lack of certain B vitamins.

Increased knowledge about nutrition was accompanied by improved techniques of food production. Intensive use of fertilizers, pesticides, and improved strains of plants greatly increased crop production in the developed countries. This abundance, with increased knowledge of the role of nutrients, led to greater concern for the hungry and undernourished of the world.

International Concern with nutrition began during the 1930's. In 1937, the League of Nations established a committee to study nutrition. During World War II (1939-1945), President Franklin D. Roosevelt of the United States proclaimed "Freedom from Want" as one of the goals of the United States. The United Nations Relief and Rehabilitation Administration (UNRRA) was set up in 1943 to relieve suffering caused by the war. UNRRA distributed food to millions of needy persons, shipped livestock to war-torn areas, and helped revive agriculture.

Other United Nations (UN) agencies also were set up to deal with health and nutrition. The Food and Agriculture Organization (FAO) had its origin at a confer-

ence held in Hot Springs, Va., in 1943. The FAO provides information on the production, consumption, and distribution of food throughout the world. It began working with the UN in 1946. Lord Boyd Orr, a British nutrition and agriculture scientist, headed the FAO from 1945 to 1948. The United Nations Children's Fund (UNICEF), organized in 1946, provides food for needy mothers and children. The World Health Organization (WHO), established in 1948, is the world's principal agency for dealing with worldwide health problems.

Private agencies such as the Ford and Rockefeller foundations contributed to the development of high-yield strains of wheat and rice during the 1960's. In 1963, two American biochemists, Edwin T. Mertz and Oliver E. Nelson, developed corn containing *lysine*, an amino acid that is essential to good health. Seeds for such high-protein corn were marketed for the first time in 1969.

Nutritional research has helped reduce hunger throughout the world. But millions of people still suffer from malnutrition and it remains one of the most important world problems.   JEAN MAYER

Related Articles in WORLD BOOK include:

DIETARY DISEASES

Allergy	Constipation	Rickets
Anemia	Malnutrition	Scurvy
Beriberi	Pellagra	

NUTRIENTS

Albumin	Gluten	Protein
Amino Acid	Iron	Starch
Carbohydrate	Lipid	Sugar
Fat	Pectin	Vitamin

OTHER RELATED ARTICLES

Biochemistry	Food Preservation	Metabolism
Calorie	Food Stamp Program	Starvation
Diet	Health	Trace Elements
Dietician	Homemaking	Vegetarianism
Digestion	Meat	Weight Control
Food		

Outline

I. **Nutrients**
   A. Carbohydrates   D. Minerals
   B. Fats   E. Vitamins
   C. Proteins   F. Water

II. **Basic Food Groups**

III. **Selecting and Cooking Foods**

IV. **Results of Malnutrition**
   A. Protein-Calorie Malnutrition
   B. Vitamin Deficiencies
   C. Mineral Deficiencies
   D. Obesity
   E. Heart and Circulatory Diseases

V. **History**

Questions

What causes malnutrition?

What is a *nutrient*?

Why does the amount of energy needed vary from person to person?

Which group of the Basic Seven contains large amounts of vitamin A?

What is the danger of eating too many saturated fats?

How does careful cooking preserve nutritional values?

What is *kwashiorkor? Marasmus?*

What are the four groups in the Basic Four?

Who identified beriberi?

What was the first international agency to study nutrition?

NUTRITIONIST. See NUTRITION; FOOD (Research).

NUX VOMICA, *nucks VAHM ih kuh,* is the name of a powerful drug containing two alkaloids, brucine and strychnine. It appeared in France during the 1400's or 1500's. Nux vomica is obtained from the dried, ripe seed of the nux vomica tree of India, Ceylon, northern Australia, and South Vietnam. The seed is also called nux vomica. The drug is poisonous to both men and animals except in minute quantities. It is given in small doses as a stimulant in stomach and nervous disorders. In larger quantities, it causes convulsions and even death. Nux vomica is also the principal source of strychnine (see STRYCHNINE). AUSTIN EDWARD SMITH

NYA. See NEW DEAL (Leading New Deal Agencies).

NYACK MISSIONARY COLLEGE. See UNIVERSITIES AND COLLEGES (table).

NYASA, LAKE. See LAKE NYASA.

NYASALAND. See MALAWI.

NYE, BILL (1850-1896), an American humorist, wrote comic histories, such as *Bill Nye's History of the United States* (1894), and *Bill Nye's History of England* (1896). He did not use slang, dialect, or amusing misspellings, as did many other humorists of his time. He edited the *Laramie* (Wyo.) *Boomerang* for three years. He became famous as a staff member of the *New York World.* He made successful lecture tours, both alone and with the poet James Whitcomb Riley. He and Riley wrote *Nye and Riley's Railway Guide* (1888). Nye's other works include *Bill Nye and Boomerang* (1881), *Forty Liars and Other Lies* (1882), and *Baled Hay* (1884). He was admitted to the bar in 1876. Edgar Wilson Nye was born in Shirley, Me. EDWARD WAGENKNECHT

NYE, GERALD PRENTICE (1892-   ), a North Dakota Republican, served in the U.S. Senate from 1925 to 1945. He was a leading isolationist during the 1930's and 1940's. Nye became chairman of the Senate Special Committee Investigating the Munitions Industry in 1934. His committee found that firms making military equipment had made large profits during World War I. Nye believed that the United States had entered the war because of economic ties to the Allies. He sponsored the Neutrality Act of 1935, prohibiting U.S. firms from sending arms to countries during a war and he supported neutrality laws passed in 1936, 1937, and 1939. Nye opposed President Franklin D. Roosevelt's foreign policies before World War II, and supported the America First Committee, which urged U.S. neutrality during the war.

Born in Hortonville, Wis., Nye worked on newspapers in Wisconsin and Iowa before moving to North Dakota in 1919. He was a rural newspaper editor and publisher there when he was appointed to fill a vacant Senate seat in 1925. DAVID A. SHANNON

NYE, JAMES WARREN. See NEVADA (History).

NYERERE, *ny RER ay,* **JULIUS KAMBARAGE** (1922-   ), became president of what is now Tanzania in 1964. He has been head of the Tanganyika African National Union party since 1954. A forceful African nationalist, he led Tanganyika to independence in 1961. In 1964, Nyerere united Tanganyika and Zanzibar to form what is now Tanzania. He introduced government controls to allow for more centralized economic planning. He has tried to set up a democratic society based on equality for all citizens.

Born near what is now Musoma, Tanzania, Nyerere was educated at Makerere University College in Uganda and at the University of Edinburgh in Scotland. He became Tanganyika's first prime minister in 1961, and its first president in 1962. CARL GUSTAF ROSBERG

See also AFRICA (picture).

NYLON is the family name for a group of synthetic products made from coal, water, air, petroleum, agricultural by-products, and natural gas. It is one of the most important of modern chemical discoveries. Nylon is one of the toughest, strongest, and most elastic substances in existence. It can be formed into fibers, bristles, sheets, rods, tubes, and coatings. It can be made in powdered form for use in molding operations.

Nylon fabrics are not weakened by mildew. They are not harmed by most oils, greases, or such chemicals as household cleaning fluids. Nylon absorbs little water.

Uses. Nylon was first made into hosiery in 1938. It was the first synthetic fabric thought to be superior to natural fabrics. Since then, many uses have been found for nylon. Dresses, underwear, bathing suits, lace, tires, carpets, and upholstery are among the many products made of nylon. Industries use nylon to make bearings, gears, wire coatings, and machine parts. During World War II, nylon replaced silk for parachutes made for the United States armed forces. Single threads of coarse-fibered nylon are used for bristles in all types of brushes. Surgeons use nylon thread to sew up wounds.

How Nylon Is Made. Two chemical compounds, called *hexamethylenediamine* and *adipic acid* are used to make nylon. Both of these compounds contain carbon and hydrogen. After these compounds are produced they are combined to form *hexamethylene-diammonium-adipate.* This combination of compounds is known as *nylon salt.*

Most factories make nylon by placing hexamethylenediamine, along with the adipic acid, in a machine called an *autoclave.* Then the mixture is heated under pressure, so that the molecules that make up each of the chemical substances combine into larger molecules. This process of making large molecules out of smaller ones is called *polymerization* (see POLYMERIZATION).

When polymerization is complete, the melted nylon comes out of the machine as a plastic ribbon. This is chilled and hardened on a metal roller. The ribbon is cut into chips and blended for uniformity. Nylon fibers are made by melting the chips over heated grids covered with inert gas to keep the oxygen of the air from getting into the melted nylon. When the nylon becomes liquid, it is pumped through the tiny holes of a device called a *spinneret.* The threads harden as soon as they strike the air, and are wound on spools that handle

Fishing Line   **Furniture Casters**

Du Pont

Nylon Is Used for Many Things. It is tough, strong, and elastic, and it cannot be damaged by oils, greases, and water.

about one-half mile of thread per minute. From one to as many as 2,520 *filaments* (strands) from the spinneret are united into a textile nylon yarn. They are twisted a few turns per inch before they are wound on bobbins.

Nylon is cold-drawn after it is made into yarn. The cold-drawing process makes a great change in the structure of the yarn filaments. Up until this time the thread-like molecules which make up the nylon filament have been widely spaced and lying in a chance arrangement. When the thread is *stretched* (drawn), the molecules fall into parallel lines. This gives the yarn strength and elasticity. The cold-drawing process is carried out by unwinding the filament from one spool and winding it onto another in such a way as to make the winding-up rate 4 or more times as fast as the unwinding rate. The pull between the spools stretches the yarn.

The size of the yarn depends on its original size and the degree of stretching. If the yarn is drawn to 4 times its original length, its diameter is only half its original diameter. The size of nylon yarn is measured in *deniers*. A denier is the weight in grams of 9,846 yards of the yarn. For example, 9,846 yards of nylon yarn that weigh 15 grams is called 15 *denier* (see DENIER). Such yarn is comparable in size to the silk yarn used in one-thread hosiery.

Development of Nylon. Dr. Wallace H. Carothers, a chemist of E. I. du Pont de Nemours & Company at Wilmington, Del., was a leader in the development of nylon. He began work which led to nylon in 1938 by experimenting with polymerization. He used a machine called the "molecular still" which made it possible to make longer molecules than had been made before. Carothers found that many of the fibers made from compounds which he polymerized in the still could be pulled out to several times their original length after they were cooled. This made the fibers much stronger and more elastic. Carothers also found that cold-drawn fibers did not lose strength as do most fibers, such as wool and cotton.

But most of the compounds which Carothers had made so far melted at a temperature too low to make them practical for textiles which must be ironed. Then, in 1935, Carothers polymerized hexamethylenediamine and adipic acid. The product was called by the long chemical name of *pyrehexamethylene adipimide*. But the new substance was soon referred to as "6/6" because both chemicals used in making it contained six carbon atoms. This material had a melting point of 482° F., which is satisfactory for textiles. The new fiber was named nylon and was hailed as a great discovery. But many problems were still to be solved before commercial nylon could be placed on the market in 1938.

The two raw materials of nylon, hexamethylenediamine and adipic acid, had to be produced in large amounts. Up to this time, hexamethylenediamine was considered a laboratory curiosity, and adipic acid was made commercially only in Germany. Then the Du Pont people found a way to make these two raw materials from coal, air, and water. Petroleum, natural gas, and agricultural by-products were developed later as raw materials. Since then, a number of different nylons have been developed.   CHARLES H. RUTLEDGE

NYMPH is a young or immature stage of insect larva of the type which has a gradual metamorphosis (see LARVA; METAMORPHOSIS). The larvae, or nymphs, of these insects are small versions of their parents. They do not pass through four separate stages, taking on four separate appearances, like the insects which have complete metamorphosis. The nymphs look somewhat like the parents, but they have no complete wings, and have much smaller bodies, legs, and mouth parts. They grow gradually into adulthood, and do not pass through different stages. Grasshoppers, crickets, and earwigs have nymph stages.   WILLIAM C. BEAVER

NYMPH was a lovely maiden of mythology who guarded the different realms of nature. *Oreads* watched over the hills and mountains, and *nereids* over the Mediterranean Sea. The *naiads* were the nymphs of the rivers, brooks, and streams. The ocean was protected by the *Oceanids*. The *dryads* and *hamadryads* took care of the trees and forests. Many of the naiads watched over springs that were believed to inspire those who drank their waters. The naiads were thought to have powers to prophesy and to inspire men. The oreads were also known by names that came from the particular mountains where they lived.

Nymphs were friendly and kind to mortals. They were shy and fled from human beings, but sometimes they took revenge on men who hurt the things that were under their protection. Nymphs are represented with fauns and satyrs in the forest, or playing around the keels of ships. Only oreads and naiads were immortal.   PADRAIC COLUM

See also ARETHUSA; DRYAD; NEREID; NIX.

NYNORSK. See NORWAY (Language).

NYSTAGMUS, *nis TAG mus,* is an involuntary, rhythmical movement of the eyes. The eyes may move from side to side, up and down, in a circle, or in a combination of these movements. The motions may be rapid or slow, and jerky or smooth. Nystagmus occurs normally, as when a person watches scenery from a moving train. It may also be produced by diseases of the eye, the ear, or the brain. Some people are born with nystagmus.

A type of nystagmus known as *miner's nystagmus* is caused by darkness, and occurs among miners. *Positional nystagmus* occurs only when the patient's head is placed in an abnormal position or level. *Spontaneous ocular nystagmus* occurs as a result of complete blindness or from defective central vision. *Vertical nystagmus* is an up-and-down movement of the eyes. *Latent nystagmus* occurs when one eye is covered.   JOHN R. McWILLIAMS

See also BIOMEDICAL ENGINEERING (picture).

NYX. See EREBUS.

NZINGA A NKUWA, *en ZING ah ah en KOO wah,* (? -1506), was the divine ruler of the Kongo kingdom in west-central Africa. His subjects believed he was God in human form.

After the first Portuguese trading ships came to Kongo in 1482, Nzinga a Nkuwa tried to increase his country's trade with Europe. At his request, Portugal sent a number of carpenters, farmers, traders, and other specialists to Kongo. But the Europeans became more interested in developing the slave trade than in aiding the Kongolese.

After Christian missionaries came to Mbanza, Kongo's capital, Nzinga a Nkuwa accepted Christianity as one of the country's religions. He was baptized in 1491 and took the name John I, or *João*, the name of the king of Portugal.   LEO SPITZER

See also KONGO.

O o

O o is the 15th letter in our alphabet. It also appeared in the alphabet used by the Semites, who once lived in Syria and Palestine. They called the letter *'ayin*, their word for *eye*. For a symbol, they used a stylized picture of an eye. They probably borrowed it from an Egyptian *hieroglyphic*, or picture letter. The Phoenicians borrowed the letter from the Semites. Later, the Greeks borrowed it from the Phoenicians. They called it *omicron*. See ALPHABET.

Uses. *O* or *o* is about the fourth most frequently used letter in books, newspapers, and other printed material in English. In chemistry, *O* stands for the element *oxygen*. On maps, the letter is the abbreviation for *ocean*, as well as *Ohio*. In modern numbering, it represents the *cipher*, or zero. In medieval Roman numerals, *O* represented the number 11 or, when written $\bar{O}$, stood for 11,000. It may also be used as the abbreviation for *old*, *octavo* (a size of book or method of folding a printed sheet), or *ohm* (a unit used in measuring electrical resistance).

Pronunciation. The letter *o* is a vowel, and has several sounds in English. The main pronunciations are illustrated in the words *November* (long *o*), *not* (short *o*), and *home*, which scholars consider a *diphthong*, or combination of *o* and *u* sounds. Double *o* also has several sounds in English. When pronounced as a single vowel, it may have the sounds represented in the words *food* and *good*. There are some words in English in which each *o* is pronounced separately, as in *cooperate*. See PRONUNCIATION.　　I. J. GELB and J. M. WELLS

The fifteenth letter took its shape from a symbol used in ancient Egypt to represent an eye. Its sound came from the Semitic word *'ayin*, or eye.

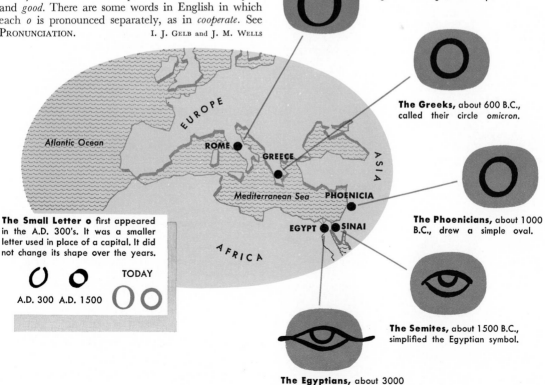

The Romans, about A.D. 114, gave it this graceful shape.

The Greeks, about 600 B.C., called their circle *omicron*.

The Phoenicians, about 1000 B.C., drew a simple oval.

The Semites, about 1500 B.C., simplified the Egyptian symbol.

The Egyptians, about 3000 B.C., drew a symbol for the eye.

The Small Letter o first appeared in the A.D. 300's. It was a smaller letter used in place of a capital. It did not change its shape over the years.

TODAY

A.D. 300　A.D. 1500

473

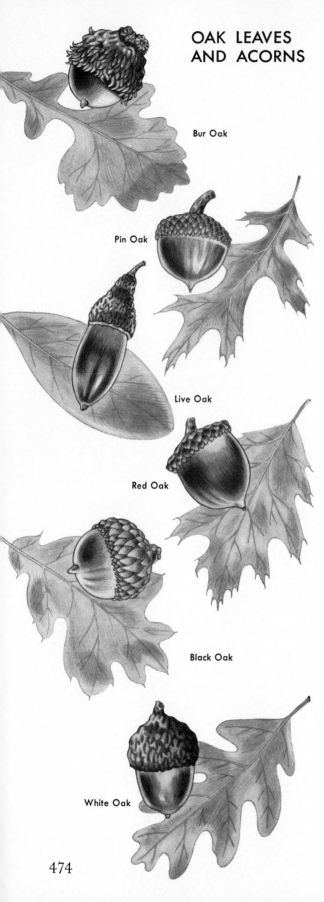

OAK LEAVES
AND ACORNS

Bur Oak

Pin Oak

Live Oak

Red Oak

Black Oak

White Oak

O. HENRY. See HENRY, O.

OAHU. See HAWAII (The Islands).

OAK, *ohk*. For ages the oak tree has symbolized sturdiness and strength. Scientists know of about 275 different *species* (kinds) of oaks. These trees grow in many different lands. Oaks flourish from Malaya and China westward across the Himalaya and the Caucasus. They grow throughout most of Europe, from Sicily northward to the Arctic Circle. In North America, oaks can grow almost any place that other kinds of trees grow. But they do not live in regions of great cold. Oaks grow southward from North America into the Andes.

The acorn is the main feature that sets oaks apart from other trees. The acorn is the fruit of the oak tree. It is a rounded, smooth-shelled nut, pointed at the outer end. A scaly saucer or cup encloses the base of the nut. Most oak trees can also be recognized by their notched or lobed leaves. But a few kinds, including the live oak, have smooth-edged leaves, unlike the others.

Oaks grow slowly, and usually do not bear acorns until they are about 20 years old. But these trees live a long time. Most oak trees live about 200 or 300 years. In England, oak trees were sacred in the days of the Druids, more than 2,000 years ago. Some oak trees still thriving in England may have been seen by the Saxon kings, more than 900 years ago. One oak tree growing in Gloucestershire measures nearly 48 feet around. It has no near rival in size. The oak tree of England closely resembles the white oak of the United States.

The Charter Oak, in Hartford, Conn., is famous in American history. The charter of the colony of Connecticut was hidden from the colony's English governor in this tree. See CHARTER OAK.

Kinds of Oaks. The *white oak* is the noblest of all American oaks. This tree sometimes grows to a height of 150 feet. Its trunk may measure eight feet thick. The bark of the white oak is pale gray. The tree bears leaves with round or finger-shaped lobes. In autumn, these leaves turn a deep red or golden brown. They add charm to autumn landscapes.

The white oak thrives from Canada south to the Gulf of Mexico and west to Texas. In dense forests it has a narrow *crown* (top). But when it grows in the open, it has wide-spreading branches. The wood of the white oak is hard and close-grained. It is valuable for its beauty, strength, and wearing qualities. Furniture makers value the white oak above all other kinds of oaks in the United States. The largest white oak in the United States is the Wye Oak, in Talbot County, Maryland. It is 95 feet high. The trunk is more than 27 feet around.

The *bur oak*, or *mossy-cup oak*, is a rugged tree that is attractive for parks. It has an irregular crown, deeply furrowed bark, and shaggy, spreading branches. It received its name because of its acorns, which are enclosed in a deep, fringed cup. The bur oak has large leaves with *sinuses* (deep notches). The two center sinuses are the deepest. This tree is grown both for shade and for lumber.

The *black oak* grows from Maine to Florida, and west to Minnesota, Kansas, and eastern Texas. Its leaves have broad, bristle-tipped lobes. The upper surface of the leaves is a glossy dark green in summer. In autumn, the leaves may turn a brilliant red. The tree itself does not usually grow more than 90 feet tall. It can be recog-

The Red Oak is one of the most favored American ornamental trees.

The Magnificent Live Oak of the Southern States is famed for the great horizontal spread of its sturdy branches. It has leathery leaves.

The Oregon White Oak closely resembles its better-known relative, the stately white oak of the New England area.

L. W. Brownell; U.S. Forest Service; George J. Baetzhold; Devereux Butcher

The Rugged Bur Oak is sometimes called the mossy-cup oak. It has long, deep-cut leaves and yields valuable lumber.

The Pin Oak, often called the swamp oak, is the fine tree of low, marshy places. It is much used as a shade tree.

nized by its dark gray bark. On old trees, the bark is almost black. It has orange-yellow inner layers rich in tannin.

The *red oak* is a handsome ornamental tree. It is common in the eastern parts of the United States. The red oak has grayish-brown bark. The inner layers of bark are red. The lobes of the leaves of this tree have irregular teeth, bristly points, and a triangular shape. They point forward more than outward. The red oak is the state tree of New Jersey.

The *live oak* ranks as a favorite avenue and park tree in the Southern States. It resembles somewhat an apple tree, because it has a thick, short trunk and long, spreading limbs. The live oak has thick, leathery leaves. They remain on the tree for a year, until new leaves appear. This oak has less showy foliage than some of the northern oaks. But its draperies of Spanish moss give it charm. The live oak has durable wood. See LIVE OAK.

The *holm oak*, sometimes called *holly oak*, or *ilex*, grows mainly in southern Europe. It reaches a height of about 80 feet. Its leaves are dark green above, and light yellow underneath.

Uses. In some kinds of oaks, the acorn is sweet-tasting. But, in others, the acorn is very bitter. People in southern Europe often boil and eat acorns. The American Indians once used meal made from acorns. They first crushed the nuts, and then washed them in water to remove the bitter-tasting material. After the nuts dried, the Indians ground them into a meal. They pressed the meal into cakes which they cooked and ate. Men chiefly eat the acorns of the white oak. Farmers feed all varieties of acorns to their hogs.

Man has made use of timber cut from oak trees for many hundreds of years. The Shrine of Edward the Confessor, in Westminster Abbey, is built of oak. The wood seems as sound today as it was nearly 900 years ago. Oak wood rots very slowly, even if it is often exposed to dampness followed by drying. Oak ranked as the chief kind of lumber used for shipbuilding before the use of steel. The live oak was at one time the favorite kind of oak wood used for ships. Today, oak lumber is valued most of all for its beauty. Oak planks are especially attractive when they are *quartersawed* (cut from logs sawed lengthwise through the center).

Besides their valuable timber, oak trees yield tanbark, which is used in tanning leather. Cork oaks, which grow mainly in Spain and Portugal, produce cork. It comes from the thick, lightweight bark of these trees (see CORK).

An oak fungus that was isolated and identified about 1949 is killing a great many oak trees in the United States. The disease has spread eastward from the central Midwest.

Scientific Classification. Oaks belong to the beech family, *Fagaceae*. They make up the genus *Quercus*. The English oak is genus *Quercus*, species *Q. robur*. The white oak is *Q. alba*. The cork oak is *Q. suber*. The bur oak is *Q. macrocarpa*. The black oak is *Q. velutina*. The red oak is *Q. rubra*. The live oak is *Q. virginiana*. The holm oak is *Q. ilex*.   T. EWALD MAKI

See also ACORN; BIRD (Other Ways Birds Help Man); TREE (Familiar Broadleaf and Needleleaf Trees [picture]); BARK (picture).

OAK LEAF CLUSTER. See DECORATIONS AND MEDALS (Military Awards).

OAK PARK, Ill. (pop. 62,511; alt. 630 ft.), is a residential suburb on the western boundary of Chicago (see ILLINOIS [political map]). It is known for its parks, churches, shops, and fine public school system. Oak Park has a village form of government. Its people elect a president and six trustees who then appoint a village manager.   PAUL M. ANGLE

OAK RIDGE, Tenn. (pop. 28,319; alt. 881 ft.), the *Atomic Bomb City*, sprang up during World War II as a center for developing and producing materials for the atomic bomb. Oak Ridge now ranks as one of the largest cities in Tennessee. It lies about 18 miles northwest of Knoxville. For the location of Oak Ridge, see TENNESSEE (political map).

Federal authorities selected Oak Ridge as the site for atomic laboratories because of the abundance of water and electric power there. Also, its strategic location in hills and valleys helps isolate the various plants. About 1,000 families were removed to clear the area. By 1943, the town had about 50,000 residents. Its existence was not officially known until President Harry S. Truman announced production of the atomic bomb in August, 1945. In 1949, the city was officially opened to the public. The Atomic Energy Communities Act of 1955 authorized self-government for Oak Ridge.

Atomic Energy Commission

The Oak Ridge Gaseous Diffusion Plant was one of the installations that made World War II atomic-bomb materials.

Since 1948, the Oak Ridge National Laboratory has led in developing peaceful uses for atomic energy. The Laboratory began nonatomic work in 1962 with basic research into the problems of changing salt water into fresh water. The Oak Ridge Institute of Nuclear Studies collaborates with the Laboratory. The American Museum of Atomic Energy in Oak Ridge is the world's only museum for the study of the atom.   JEWELL A. PHELPS

See also ATOMIC ENERGY COMMISSION.

OAK RIDGE INSTITUTE OF NUCLEAR STUDIES, Oak Ridge, Tenn., is a nonprofit educational corporation of southern universities. It works with the U.S. Atomic Energy Commission, and offers courses in atomic energy for teachers. The institute also provides lecturers for universities and research opportunities for scientists.

PACIFIC OCEAN

SAUSALITO

SAN FRANCISCO

GOLDEN GATE BRIDGE

San Francisco Bay

SAN FRANCISCO-OAKLAND BAY BRIDGE

Lake Merritt

Oakland, Calif., lies on the eastern shore of San Francisco Bay, six miles across the bay from the city of San Francisco. The Inner Harbor, *left foreground,* which can accommodate ocean freighters separates Oakland, *right,* from the city of Alameda.

OAKLAND, Calif. (pop. 361,561; alt. 25 ft.), is one of several cities that make up the great industrial and residential section known as the San Francisco-Oakland Metropolitan Area, which has a total population of 3,109,519. Today, Oakland is one of the largest cities in the state. It has about 1,500 industrial plants, and the value of tonnage shipped at its harbor ranks next to that of San Francisco and Los Angeles.

Location, Size, and Description. Oakland lies on the eastern shore of San Francisco Bay, six miles across the bay from the city of San Francisco. The great San Francisco-Oakland Bay Bridge connects the two cities. Oakland is near the bay area cities of Albany, Berkeley, Emeryville, Piedmont, Alameda, San Leandro, and Hayward. Oakland is the seat of Alameda County. The city covers about 80 square miles and has a 19-mile waterfront. For location, see CALIFORNIA (political map).

Cultural Life and Recreation. Oakland is the home of Mills College, St. Albert's College, and the California College of Arts and Crafts. Woodminster Memorial Amphitheater and Chabot Observatory are also in Oakland. The city was the home of such famous writers and poets as Jack London, Joaquin Miller, and Edwin Markham. Oakland has three professional sports teams: the Oakland Raiders of the National Football League, the Oakland Athletics baseball team of the American League, and the California Golden Seals of the National Hockey League.

Industry and Commerce. Oakland's manufactured goods include automobiles and trucks, calculating machines, baby foods, pharmaceutical and wood products, beer, wine, and chemicals. Products sent from the harbor include dried and canned fruits, vegetables, grain, salt, lumber, and petroleum. Oakland has a U.S. Naval Supply Center and other military installations.

Transportation. Oakland is one of the western terminals for several transcontinental railways. Airplanes from overseas and from all parts of the United States stop here. Several bus lines also serve the city.

History and Government. Spanish explorers first came to this region in 1770. In 1820, the site of the city was included in a Spanish land grant given to Luis Maria Peralta, a soldier of the Spanish army. The land was divided among his sons in 1842 and worked as large ranches until the 1850's. Then people from the east, some seeking gold near here, settled in this region. Horace W. Carpentier, one of these settlers, succeeded in getting a town charter for Oakland and became its first mayor in 1852. Two years later, the community received a city charter. Its name comes from groves of oaks where the first homes were built.

Cross-country railway lines were extended to the city in 1869. The next year, Oakland had two banks and three newspapers. In 1906, the San Francisco earthquake and fire caused 50,000 persons to flee to Oakland, where many of them stayed. By the end of that year the population reached 125,000. The city adopted city-manager form of government in 1931. The Golden Gate International Exposition, held on Treasure Island in the bay, brought many visitors to Oakland in 1939 and 1940. During World War II and the Korean War, Oakland served as an important port. GEORGE SHAFTEL

OAKLAND UNIVERSITY. See MICHIGAN STATE UNIVERSITY.

Annie Oakley became famous as one of the world's most accurate shots with pistol, rifle, and shotgun.

OAKLEY, ANNIE (1860-1926), an American markswoman, starred in Buffalo Bill's Wild West Show for 17 years. She was popular throughout the United States and Europe. She was an expert shot with a pistol, rifle, or shotgun. Once, with a .22 rifle, she shot 4,772 glass balls out of 5,000 tossed in the air on a single day. At 90 feet, she could hit a playing card with the thin edge toward her, and puncture a card five or six times while it fell to the ground. Since then, free tickets with holes punched in them have been called "Annie Oakleys." She once shot a cigarette from the mouth of the German Crown Prince (later Wilhelm II) at his invitation.

Annie Oakley was born Phoebe Anne Oakley Mozee on Aug. 13, 1860, in a log cabin in Patterson Township, Ohio. She began shooting at the age of 9. After her father died, she supported the family by shooting small game. On a visit to Cincinnati she shot a match with Frank E. Butler, a vaudeville star. She won the match, and later married Butler. She joined his act, and became its star. Only 5 feet tall, she was called "Little Sure Shot." Annie Oakley joined Buffalo Bill's Wild West Show in 1885 (see BUFFALO BILL). The musical play *Annie Get Your Gun* portrayed her life. HOWARD R. LAMAR

OAKUM, *O kum*, is loose fiber obtained by untwisting and picking at old, tarred hemp ropes. The fiber is used mainly to *calk*, or stuff, the seams of wooden ships to make them watertight. Plumbers use oakum for packing joints in waste pipes. *White oakum*, made from clean rope, was formerly used for medical purposes, such as dressings for wounds. JOHN C. LE CLAIR

OAKWOOD COLLEGE is a coeducational liberal arts school at Huntsville, Ala. It is controlled by the Seventh-day Adventist Church. The college was founded in 1896. For enrollment, see UNIVERSITIES AND COLLEGES (table).

OAR. See ROWING.

OARFISH is a large fish that lives in the Atlantic and Pacific oceans. It sometimes reaches a length of 30 feet.

A long fin runs the length of its body. The oarfish swims with a snakelike, undulating motion.

Scientific Classification. The oarfish is in the family *Trachypteridae*. It is genus *Regalecus*, species *glesne*.

OAS. See ORGANIZATION OF AMERICAN STATES.

OASIS, *oh A sis*, is any watered spot in a desert region. In some cases, an oasis is only large enough to sustain the lives of a few persons. In other cases an oasis will be so extensive that 2,000,000 persons may live upon it.

Generally the soil in deserts is fertile but lacks the moisture to encourage plant growths. Oases develop in the places where springs, underground streams, or wells furnish water. The water from hills or mountains commonly percolates through rock debris down to the valleys, where much of it is held. The oases in the North American deserts are mainly formed in this way. Those in the Sahara result from springs, underground streams, or the nearness of mountains which are sufficiently high to cause moisture in the air to condense and rain to fall. Men have reclaimed large tracts of land in these wasteland regions by drilling artesian wells and by irrigating the land from mountain streams. ELDRED D. WILSON

See also DESERT; MERV.

OATCAKE. See BREAD.

OATES, TITUS (1649-1705), was a conspirator who, in 1678, made up the story of a plot by Roman Catholics to assassinate the king of England and destroy Protestantism. He referred to the supposed plan as the *Popish Plot*. This was in 1678, when the English people were suspicious of Roman Catholics in general and of Jesuit priests in particular. Oates claimed knowledge of a Jesuit plot to suppress Protestantism through the assassination of King Charles II. He became a hero at first, and received a reward. But, in 1685, he was charged with perjury, fined, and imprisoned. William III released Oates in 1689, and he received a pension. Oates was born in Oakham, England. F. A. NORWOOD

OATH is a pledge or promise. The *judicial* oath is probably the most common form of pledge. It is used in a court of law. The person taking such an oath swears to the court that all his statements are true. A witness at a trial is given such an oath. Frequently he must lay his hand upon the Bible at the same time that he is taking the oath. This means that he is making his declaration through God. A person swearing to the truth of an affidavit might be given the following oath:

"You do solemnly swear that the contents of this affidavit by you subscribed are true, so help you God."

A person who takes an oath in court and then makes a dishonest statement while under oath is guilty of perjury, which is a crime punishable by a fine or a jail sentence (see PERJURY).

All of us are familiar with oaths in everyday life. A man is said to "take an oath" when he promises either himself or someone else that he will stop smoking cigars or drinking intoxicating liquors. This kind of oath is called *extrajudicial* because it has no force in a court of law. Oaths taken to show good faith in a private transaction are also extrajudicial.

A Man-Made Oasis in the Sahara desert has high sand walls built around it for protection against wind-swept sand.

Irrigation Ditches filled with water from deep wells support the date palms and farm crops raised on El-Goléa, *below,* an oasis in Algeria.

Emil Brunner, Pix

R. Christopher, Pix

Affirmation. Some religious groups, such as the Quakers, do not approve of swearing by an oath. They believe in the Bible's command "Swear not at all." When members of such groups testify in court they take an *affirmation* instead of an oath. The affirmation binds them to the truth just as strongly as an oath would.

Oath of Office. Many important officials take a pledge when they enter a public office. This *oath of office* is a promise to carry on the duties of the office honestly and faithfully. According to the Constitution, the President of the United States must take the following oath at his inauguration:

"I do solemnly swear (or affirm) that I will faithfully execute the office of the President of the United States, and will to the best of my ability preserve, protect, and defend the Constitution of the United States."

All United States officers lower in rank than the President take oaths much like the one above. An officer taking over a state public office promises to protect the state constitution as well as the Constitution of the United States.

In Canada many government officials take a pledge of faithfulness upon entering public office. But members elected to the federal Senate or House of Commons, and members of the legislative bodies of the provinces, must take the following oath of allegiance:

"I do swear that I will be faithful and bear true allegiance to His (or Her) Majesty . . ."

Military Oaths are taken by persons who enter the armed forces. Before a man or woman enters the service, he or she must take the following oath:

"I do solemnly swear (or affirm) that I will bear true faith and allegiance to the United States of America; that I will serve them honestly and faithfully against all their enemies whomsoever; and that I will obey the orders of the President of the United States and the orders of the officers appointed over me, according to the regulations and the Uniform Code of Military Justice."

Members of the armed forces of Canada, Great Britain, and other countries take a similar oath. In Germany, whole regiments were formerly sworn into the service together in a single ceremony. During conscription for World War II, the United States also followed the practice of swearing in large groups of men at the same time. ERWIN N. GRISWOLD

See also CITIZENSHIP (The Oath of Allegiance).

OATS

OATS, *ohts,* is one of the most important of the world's food crops. It belongs to the same family of plants as wheat, rye, barley, corn, and rice. Nearly 100 varieties of oats are raised. They include yellow, white, black, red, and gray oats.

The oat stalk is from 2 to 4 feet long when it is full-grown. It is slender and ends in groups of graceful branches, called *spikelets.* The grain grows at the end of the spikelets. Each seed has a protecting husk around it. The spikelets usually spread out from all sides of the stem. But in one variety, called *horsemane oats,* or *side oats,* the spikelets grow all on one side.

It is thought that oats developed from wild grasses and that the grain first grew in Asia. Oats were not widely known in early Christian times. By the 1200's, oats were grown in England and known there as *pilcorn.*

Oats are best suited to a cool, moist climate. But they are grown throughout the Temperate Zones of the entire world. Some varieties have even been grown near the Arctic Circle.

Oats grow in nearly every state of the United States, but they grow better in the North than in the South.

Oats should not be planted in a low rich soil. It is

OATMEAL is a food product prepared from select cultivated oats. It is eaten chiefly as a cooked breakfast cereal. It is tasty and wholesome, and leads nearly all other grain products in food value. Oatmeal is made by removing the outer husk of the oat kernel. The *grout,* or inner portion of the kernel, is scoured to remove some of the outer skin. Then it is partially cooked by steaming, and rolled. The product is packaged in boxes or sacks for marketing.

The average portion of oatmeal contains about 67 parts carbohydrates, 16 parts protein, 7 parts fat, 2 parts mineral, and 7 parts water. Oatmeal is a good source of Vitamin B$_1$.　　　　W. B. DOHONEY

Oats Growers plant the grain in close rows with a seed drill, *above.* South African farmers, *below,* harvest oats with a binder, which cuts and bundles it. Oats pour into a bin, *right,* after being separated from the straw in a threshing machine.

Carbohydrates, 67.5% →

← Water, 7.3%

Protein, ← 16.1%

← Fat, 7.2%

Ash, 1.9%

The Food Value of Oatmeal makes it one of our best wintertime foods. One pound of oatmeal contains 1,850 Calories.

480

not good to use rich fertilizers, because the grain tends to bend down when it grows too thick. Loam and clay soils are best.

The time for sowing oats is in the spring, except in regions of mild winters, such as the South. There, oats are sown in autumn. If the oats are sown in spring, the ground should be plowed the autumn before. It should also be harrowed soon after the frost is out of the ground. Sowing begins just as soon as the ground is in proper condition. The seed may be sown in close rows (drills), or it may be scattered over the field. Two to three bushels of seed to the acre are usually planted. The crop is usually harvested in July. Reaping times at different latitudes may be a few weeks apart.

The North Central States, Canada, and Russia raise large quantities of oats. The average yield per acre in the United States is about 50 bushels. Scientific methods of cultivation are raising this average almost yearly. In England and Germany, the average yield is about 80 bushels. The world oats crop is about 3 billion bushels a year. The United States raises about one-fourth of this amount. In the United States, a bushel of oats must weigh 32 pounds.

The diseases and insect enemies of the other cereals also attack oats. Smut and rust, both of which are parasitic fungi, destroy millions of bushels each year. Some headway against rust is gained by growing varieties which can resist it. Insect pests that attack and destroy oats include the chinch bug, the "green bug," and the army worm.

Oats are a very nourishing food, rich in starch and proteins. Prepared forms, like oatmeal and rolled oats, are often eaten. The fuel value of both these dishes is about 1,850 calories per pound. Oats are therefore an important food for the winter diet.

The most valuable use of oats, however, is as a food for livestock. Oats are the best of all grains for horses. They are equal to corn as a tissue builder, and are less heating. No other cereal produces straw that makes such good feed and fertilizer.

Scientific Classification. Oats belong to the grass family, *Gramineae*. Most cultivated oats have been developed from genus *Avena*, species *A. sativa*.   WILLIAM R. VAN DERSAL

See also OATMEAL; FURFURAL.

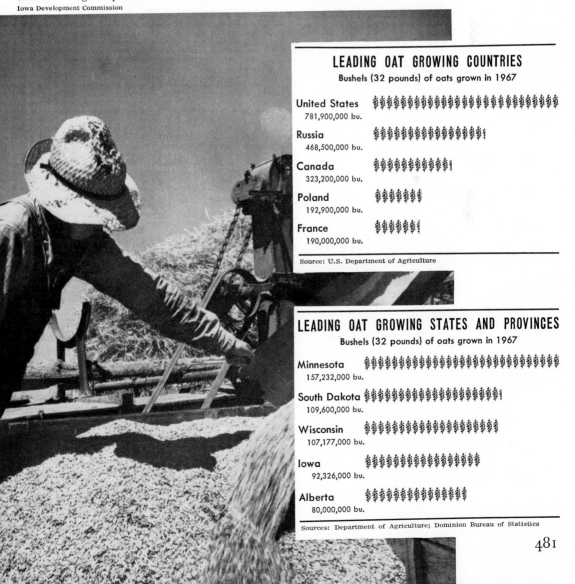

LEADING OAT GROWING COUNTRIES
Bushels (32 pounds) of oats grown in 1967

United States
781,900,000 bu.

Russia
468,500,000 bu.

Canada
323,200,000 bu.

Poland
192,900,000 bu.

France
190,000,000 bu.

Source: U.S. Department of Agriculture

LEADING OAT GROWING STATES AND PROVINCES
Bushels (32 pounds) of oats grown in 1967

Minnesota
157,232,000 bu.

South Dakota
109,600,000 bu.

Wisconsin
107,177,000 bu.

Iowa
92,326,000 bu.

Alberta
80,000,000 bu.

Sources: Department of Agriculture; Dominion Bureau of Statistics

Black Star

The Obelisk of Luxor stands in the Place de la Concorde in Paris. Hieroglyphics telling of the glory of Ramses II cover the 3,000-year-old monument, which was a gift from Egypt.

OAXACA, *wah HAH kah,* officially OAXACA DE JUÁREZ (pop. 72,370; alt. 5,185 ft.), is the capital of Oaxaca, a state in southern Mexico. It stands in a rich mining, farming, and forest region. For location, see MEXICO (political map). Oaxaca has won fame for handicrafts. The ruins of two ancient Indian cities, Mitla and Monte Albán, lie near Oaxaca. Some historians believe the Aztec founded Oaxaca in 1486. But the Zapotec and the Mixtec had lived in the area since the time of the early Christians. Colonial Oaxaca

produced some of the most impressive architecture of the Spanish American empire. JOHN A. CROW

OAXACA, *wah HAH kah,* is a mountainous state on Mexico's South Pacific Coast. It has a population of 2,021,182, and covers 36,820 square miles. For location, see MEXICO (political map). About half of the people are Indians. The chief tribes include the Zapotec and Mixtec. The ruins of their ancient cities show the splendor of these civilizations. Oaxaca's farmers grow wheat, bananas, tobacco, coffee, and other crops. The state also produces lumber, gold, silver, onyx, and marble. Oaxaca was one of the original states of Mexico. The capital is Oaxaca [de Juárez]. See also OAXACA (city); ZAPOTEC INDIANS. CHARLES C. CUMBERLAND

OB RIVER, *ahb,* is one of the chief rivers of Russia in Asia. The Ob rises in the Altai Mountains of western Siberia and flows northwestward for 2,500 miles before it empties into the Arctic Ocean through the Gulf of Ob (Obskaya Guba). It drains 1,125,200 square miles, an area about four times the size of Texas.

The navigable waterways of the Ob and its tributaries total about 19,000 miles. The lower part of the river is 2 to 4 miles wide, while the estuary averages 50 miles in width. It is blocked with ice from October to June. In summer, the Ob River is an important water route for shipping grain, dairy products, livestock, wool, and meat. Most of this moves to the railways for shipment to western Russia, but some is exported by way of the Arctic Ocean. THEODORE SHABAD

See also RIVER (chart: Longest Rivers).

OBADIAH, *OH buh DIE uh,* the fourth book of the minor Hebrew prophets, is the shortest book in the Old Testament. It has only 21 verses. The book contains a prophecy that the kingdom of Edom will be destroyed, and that all nations except Judah will be punished. The name Obadiah (sometimes spelled *Abdias*) means *Servant of the Lord.* Nothing is known of the Obadiah who is supposed to have written this book. He probably lived after 540 B.C. WALTER G. WILLIAMS

OBBLIGATO. See MUSIC (Terms).

OBELISK, *AHB uh lisk,* is a great, upright, four-sided stone pillar. The sides slope slightly so that the top is smaller than the base. The top is shaped like a pyramid and ends in a point. The Washington Monument in Washington, D.C., is an obelisk.

The ancient Egyptians built huge obelisks. Most of them had inscriptions in *hieroglyphics* (picture writing). Two obelisks, now known as Cleopatra's Needles, were originally at Heliopolis, Egypt. In the 1800's, one was taken to New York City, and the other to London (see CLEOPATRA'S NEEDLES). An obelisk from the temple of Luxor, Egypt, now stands in the Place de la Concorde, in Paris.

Obelisks were cut right at the quarry as single blocks of granite. The exact method the ancient Egyptians used is not known. It is believed they first made a horizontal, three-sided form by cutting deep trenches all around the form. Then they split away the fourth side either by inserting copper or wooden wedges, or by pounding through the underside with balls of diorite, a hard rock. Finally they polished the obelisk. Still unexplained is how they raised the huge stone pillar to an upright position at its final site. RICARDO A. CAMINOS

OBERAMMERGAU, *OH ber AHM er gow* (pop. 4,600; alt. 960 ft.), is a Bavarian village 45 miles south-

Picturesque Oberammergau lies in the foothills of the Bavarian Alps in southern Germany. The town's Passion Play is usually presented every 10 years. It was first given in 1634 to fulfill a vow to present it every decade if the Black Plague were ended.

west of Munich in Germany (see GERMANY [political map]). It is famous for its performances of the Passion Play, which normally take place every 10 years. This pageant portrays the suffering and death of Jesus. Residents perform all the parts. See PASSION PLAY.

Colorful Bible scenes cover the outside walls of many of the city's buildings. The largest buildings in the town are the Roman Catholic church and the auditorium. The Passion Play attracts thousands of tourists.

The people earn money from tourist trade and by carving objects from wood and ivory.   JAMES K. POLLOCK

OBERHAUSEN, *OH ber HOW zen* (pop. 259,471; alt. 131 ft.), is a coal-mining and industrial city in West Germany's Ruhr. The city was founded in 1862, and received its charter in 1874. Its industries include zinc refineries, furniture, chemicals, and glass. For location, see GERMANY (political map).   JAMES K. POLLOCK

OBERLIN COLLEGE is a privately controlled, coeducational liberal arts school at Oberlin, Ohio. It was the first coeducational college in the United States. It has a college of arts and sciences, a conservatory of music, and a graduate school of theology. Courses lead to A.B., A.M., M.A.T., Mus.B., B.D., S.T.M., and M.R.E.

degrees. Oberlin was founded in 1833. Oberlin has always had a policy of admitting all students regardless of their race, creed, or color. It was the first school in the United States to award college degrees to women (1841). For enrollment, see UNIVERSITIES AND COLLEGES (table). See also COEDUCATION.   J. ROBERT WILLIAMS

OBERLIN CONSERVATORY OF MUSIC is a coeducational school of music at Oberlin, Ohio. It is a division of Oberlin College. The school grants Mus.B. degrees. It was founded in 1865. Oberlin was the first music school in the United States to become an integral part of a collegiate institution.   J. ROBERT WILLIAMS

OBERON. See FAIRY (Noble Fairies).

OBERTH, HERMANN. See SPACE TRAVEL (Early Developments).

OBESITY. See WEIGHT CONTROL.

OBJECT, in grammar. See CASE; GRAMMAR.

OBJECTIVE CASE. See CASE (Pronouns).

OBJECTIVE LENS. See MICROSCOPE; TELESCOPE.

OBLATE COLLEGE. See UNIVERSITIES AND COLLEGES (table).

OBLATE COLLEGE OF THE SOUTHWEST. See UNIVERSITIES AND COLLEGES (table).

Mouthpiece
(Double Reed)

Keys

Tone Holes

Bell

Bowmar Educational Records

The Oboe has a double-reed mouthpiece. An oboe player blows through the mouthpiece and presses keys and tone holes to produce various tones.

OBOE, *O boh,* is the smallest and highest-pitched of the double-reed wood-wind instruments. The name comes from two French words: *haut,* meaning *high,* and *bois,* meaning *wood.* The oboe is about 21 inches long. It was developed by the French in the late 1700's.

The range of the instrument is almost three octaves, and the tone is made by means of a small double reed. The oboe is hard to play because so little air is needed to blow it. This makes it difficult for the player, because he must breathe more slowly than normally. Early oboes gave off a loud, harsh tone, but today the oboe is known for its smooth and beautiful tone.

The oboe holds an important place in symphony orchestras, concert bands, and small ensembles. Sometimes it is used for solos. Among those who wrote important works for the instrument are Beethoven, Handel, and Mozart. The English horn is an alto oboe, a fifth lower in pitch than the oboe.   CHARLES B. RIGHTER

See also ENGLISH HORN.

OBOLUS. See FUNERAL CUSTOMS; CHARON.

O'BOYLE, PATRICK ALOYSIUS CARDINAL (1896-   ), archbishop of Washington, D.C., was appointed a cardinal of the Roman Catholic Church in 1967 by Pope Paul VI. Archbishop of Washington, D.C., since 1947, he served as chancellor of the Catholic University of America in Washington. Cardinal O'Boyle won recognition for his welfare activities and his work in improving race relations.

From 1933 to 1936, he served as assistant director of the child care department of Catholic Charities of the New York archdiocese. He was executive director of the National Catholic Welfare Conference war relief activities from 1943 to 1947. Cardinal O'Boyle was born in Scranton, Pa. He was ordained a priest in New York City in 1921.   THOMAS P. NEILL

OBREGÓN, *oh bray GAWN,* **ÁLVARO** (1880-1928), a Mexican soldier, statesman, and rancher, was twice president of Mexico. Obregón succeeded Venustiano Carranza as president in 1920 (see CARRANZA, VENUSTIANO). He won the United States' recognition of his government in 1923. He was one of the most capable leaders of the Mexican Revolution. He was re-elected president in 1928, but was assassinated before he could take office.

In 1912, during a revolution against the government of President Francisco Madero, Obregón raised a force of Sonora Indians and went to Madero's aid. In 1913, Victoriano Huerta murdered Madero and seized the presidency. Obregón joined Venustiano Carranza against Huerta.

In 1914 and 1915, Obregón supported Carranza against Pancho Villa (see VILLA, "PANCHO," FRANCISCO). In his battles with Villa, Obregón used barbed-wire entanglements, machine-gun nests, and trench warfare for the first time in Mexico. Obregón was born in the Alamos district of Sonora, where his family had large property holdings.   DONALD J. WORCESTER

See also MEXICO (Economic and Social Changes).

O'BRIEN, LAWRENCE FRANCIS (1917-   ), served as postmaster general of the United States from 1965 to 1968. He had been a special assistant in charge of congressional relations to Presidents John F. Kennedy and Lyndon B. Johnson. He worked to get congressional approval of legislation that Presidents Kennedy and Johnson favored.

O'Brien helped direct John F. Kennedy's campaigns for the United States Senate in 1952 and 1958, and for the presidency in 1960. He helped direct Johnson's presidential campaign in 1964. O'Brien was born in Springfield, Mass. He received a law degree from Northeastern University.   CARL T. ROWAN

OBSERVATORY. An observatory is an institution or a building where astronomers study the sun, planets, stars, and other heavenly bodies.

Men have studied the heavens for thousands of years. More than 2,000 years before the telescope was invented, Egyptian priests watched the rising stars from their temples. The Mayan priests in Yucatán built special towers from which they could observe the stars. Stonehenge, built about 1,800 B.C. in Wiltshire, England, is the oldest existing structure known to have been used as an observatory (see STONEHENGE). In 1576, the Danish astronomer Tycho Brahe founded a large observatory at Uraniborg on the island of Hven. The observatory was built like a castle.

In most observatories, a special building with a domed roof protects the telescope. This roof can revolve, and it has shutters that open to permit the telescope to view the sky. Separate buildings house other instruments. Tall steel towers are used for observing the sun, and a number of platforms and small shelters are used for special instruments. There is usually a central office building with laboratories, photographic dark rooms, and optical and mechanical shops.

During the past 50 years, photography and photoelectric instruments have been used more and more by observatories. These instruments must be located where city lights will not affect the exposure. Several large observatories have been built on high mountains in dry regions where the air is more transparent than at sea

484

Astronomers Sit Here to observe stars reflected up from telescope mirror below.

Astronomers Ascend to observation room at top of telescope by elevator.

Instruments for study and analysis of starlight are contained in this room.

Frame of Telescope is supported at each end by big bearings on which it rotates.

Huge Mirror, ground to one-millionth inch accuracy, is the "lens" of the telescope.

Movement of the 500-ton instrument in following stars is controlled from this desk.

Huge Dome Revolves on wheels and track attached to top of building's base.

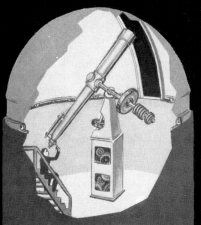

The Refracting Telescope is an older and more common type. Light is not reflected, but comes directly to the eye.

Photographic and other laboratories, shops, and library located in lower part of building.

This Mammoth and Intricate Instrument increases the power of man's eyes more than a million times. This is a reflecting-type telescope in which the light rays are caught by the great lens-mirror at the bottom of the upright framework. These are reflected to the observation chamber above. The telescope is as tall as a six-story building.

level, and where there are few cloudy nights. Most observatories are located in Europe and North America. But several large American and European observatories have stations in South Africa for observing the southern sky. The largest observatory in the Southern Hemisphere is the National Observatory at Canberra, Australia. The center of the Milky Way galaxy can be observed best from the Southern Hemisphere. It lies near the constellation Sagittarius.

The principal instruments of modern observatories are the telescopes. They are not necessarily large. The United States Naval Observatory, for example, uses medium-sized telescopes to measure the positions of relatively bright stars, and to observe the position of the moon from hour to hour. Other observatories use large telescopes to study the spectra and brightness of faint stars and distant galaxies.

Observatories use two kinds of optical telescopes: (1) *refractors*, which focus light rays with a system of lenses; and (2) *reflectors*, which focus light rays with a curved mirror. The Hale telescope, located on Mount Palomar in California, is the world's largest optical telescope. It uses a mirror that measures 200 inches in diameter. Other large optical telescopes include the 100-inch reflector at Mount Wilson Observatory, the 40-inch refractor at Yerkes Observatory, and the 36-inch refractor at Lick Observatory.

The cost of a fully equipped observatory is very high. A telescope of 100-inch diameter may cost several million dollars. Most observatories in Europe in the past were founded by national governments. In America, most of them were founded by private donations to colleges and universities. The 82-inch McDonald Observatory telescope of the University of Texas is used by several other universities on a cooperative plan. The purpose of the plan is to make the equipment available to as many as possible.

An Orbiting Astronomical Observatory offers astronomers a view of the sky without distortions caused by the atmosphere.
NASA

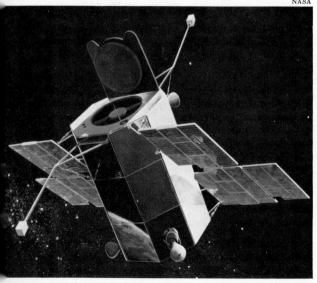

The astronomer begins his work when most persons are preparing for bed. The domes are opened and turned to allow the light of the selected star to reach the lens or mirror of the telescope. The telescope is slowly moved into position by electric motors. The observer stands on an elevated platform which can be raised or lowered until he can reach the eyepiece or the photographic plate-holder. When faint stars are being photographed, the exposure may last for hours. During the exposure, the telescope is slowly turned by a special mechanism so that it automatically follows the star.

Some of the older observatories were built for practical purposes. The Royal Greenwich Observatory in England was founded by Charles II to prepare accurate astronomical tables which British navigators could use in determining the position of a ship at sea. Most modern observatories are research institutes, where scientists try to discover the physical laws of nature. Some may try to learn how different atoms behave when the temperature is extremely hot, as in the atmospheres of the hotter stars. Others study the behavior of atoms when the density is so low that there are only a few atoms per cubic inch, as in the vast spaces between the stars. The scientists may try to discover new facts about the nuclear fusion that takes place in stars and produces their radiant energy.

One of the most famous observatories is the Observatoire de Paris in France, where the finite speed of light was first measured. Another is the national observatory of Russia at Pulkovo, near Leningrad. Here the constant factors which determine the slightly wobbling motion of the earth's rotation were accurately determined from the stars' changes of position. The Potsdam and Neubabelsberg institutes in Germany are also famous.

The Harvard University Observatory is famous for its catalogs of star brightnesses and star spectra. A Dominion Observatory at Victoria, B.C., is devoted to astrophysical work. Another at Ottawa, Ont., does astrometric work. The David Dunlap Observatory of the University of Toronto has a reflecting telescope 74 inches in diameter which is used mostly to determine the velocities of the stars in the line of sight. The Mount Wilson and Palomar observatories specialize in studies of galaxies and of the sun. The Kitt Peak National Observatory, which is located near Tucson, Ariz., conducts solar research.

In addition to optical telescopes, astronomers use radio telescopes. These instruments focus radio waves from space much like optical telescopes focus light. They are usually much larger than optical telescopes. The world's largest radio telescope measures 1,000 feet in diameter (see RADIO TELESCOPE [picture]).

In order to avoid distortion caused by the atmosphere, astronomers have used balloons to send telescopes into the thin upper atmosphere. They have also sent telescopes into space aboard such satellites as *OSO* (Orbiting Solar Observatory).   GERALD S. HAWKINS

Related Articles in WORLD BOOK include:

OBSIDIAN, *ub SID ih un,* is a natural glass formed when hot lava from a volcano or an earth fissure cools quickly. Obsidian contains the same chemicals as granite, but the chemicals are melted together to make glass. Most obsidian is black, or black with red streaks. It is brittle and cannot be quarried in blocks. Indians used obsidian to make arrowheads. Obsidian Cliff, in Yellowstone National Park, is a huge mass of obsidian. See also IGNEOUS ROCK. RICHARD M. PEARL

OBSTETRICS. See MEDICINE (table: Specialty Fields).

OCARINA, *AHK uh RE nuh,* is a small toy wind instrument of the whistle type. It is made of molded clay or plastic, and shaped like a goose egg. Its name is a form of the Italian word for goose. The ocarina has a mouthpiece through which air is blown and 7 to 10 holes that sound a simple scale. Its tone is pleasing and soft. An Italian named Donati developed the ocarina in the 1860's, but forms of the instrument were known in ancient China. CHARLES B. RIGHTER

The Ocarina has a soft sound, almost like a flute. The player makes the notes by covering different holes with his fingers.
Waterbury Companies, Inc.

O'CASEY, SEAN (1880-1964), was perhaps the greatest Irish playwright of his time. Born in the Dublin slums and largely self-educated, he first gained fame when Dublin's Abbey Theatre staged three of his tragicomedies—*The Shadow of a Gunman* (1923), *Juno and the Paycock* (1924), and *The Plough and the Stars* (1926). Each deals with a phase of the violence Ireland experienced from 1916 to 1924, during and after its fight for independence from England. The plays show egotism, slogans, and abstract ideals such as patriotism as the enemies of life and happiness. The plays are full of colorful characters and speech, and are written in a vivid, realistic style.

O'Casey left Ireland for England in 1926, after *The Plough and the Stars* provoked rioting during its opening week. Some of the audience thought the play slandered Ireland's patriots and womanhood. O'Casey broke with the Abbey Theatre in 1928 after it refused to stage his play *The Silver Tassie.* Like his earlier work, this play was antiwar in tone, and shows war as the destroyer of individuality and heroism. The play also developed expressionistic tendencies found in O'Casey's earlier work. Symbolism and expressionism became more important in O'Casey's later plays.

Most of the plays O'Casey wrote during the 1930's and early 1940's have revolutionary heroes and call for a radical transformation of society. These works include the joyously comic *Purple Dust* (1940) and the autobiographical *Red Roses for Me* (1942).

O'Casey returned to Irish themes late in his career. He presented an Ireland that had exchanged British domination for domination by the Roman Catholic Church of Ireland and the new commercial class. Plays of this period include *Cock-a-doodle Dandy* (1949), *The Bishop's Bonfire* (1955), and *The Drums of Father Ned* (1958).

O'Casey's most important nondramatic work is a six-volume autobiography in fictional form. MARTIN MEISEL

OCCIDENTAL COLLEGE. See UNIVERSITIES AND COLLEGES (table).

OCCIPITAL BONE. See HEAD.

OCCLUDED FRONT. See WEATHER (Fronts).

OCCULT, *uh KULT,* or *AHK ult,* is a term which refers to knowledge of a supernatural type, not bounded by the strict laws of modern science. A person may be said to have knowledge of the occult if he claims to understand subjects which cannot be understood by ordinary men, and which are outside the field of recognized science. Occult means secret, or mysterious. A fortuneteller claims to have knowledge of the occult when he tells a fortune, because he says that he can explain things which people in general cannot know.

During ancient times there was wide belief in occult sciences. The best-known of the old occult subjects included astrology, alchemy, necromancy, and magic. Many persons guided their lives by such false sciences. The physical sciences, with their exact answers, had not developed, and people were easily influenced by those who claimed to have unusual knowledge. These leaders were highly respected.

Several branches of the occult sciences are still alive today, and even in civilized countries are believed in by the superstitious. Revivals of occultism occur from time to time in all parts of the world. WILSON D. WALLIS

Related Articles in WORLD BOOK include:

Alchemy	Fortunetelling	Spiritualists
Astrology	Magic	Supernaturalism
Divination	Necromancy	Superstition
Extrasensory	Psychical	Theosophist
Perception	Research	

OCCUPANCY is a legal method by which a person or nation acquires title to a piece of property which does not have an owner. This manner of establishing title to unowned property was first recognized by Roman civil law. It was later taken into the English common law. Occupancy can be described as the act of taking possession of property which belongs to no one, with the intention of keeping that property. Thus, if a man finds property which has been lost, it will become his if the owner makes no effort to reclaim it. If a man captures a wild animal and tames it, the animal becomes his property. British settlers landed in Bermuda in 1609, before there were any other inhabitants, and claimed the island as a British possession. This is an example of an effective occupancy. WILLIAM TUCKER DEAN

OCCUPATION. See VOCATIONAL GUIDANCE.

OCCUPATIONAL DISEASE. See DISEASE (Occupational Diseases).

Crippled Children learn precise finger and muscular control by weaving colored threads through a hand loom.

Occupational Therapists improve the finger movements of crippled children by teaching them to draw with crayons.

An Amputee learns how to handle tools with his artificial arm. Occupational therapy prepares him for a job.

OCCUPATIONAL THERAPY is a kind of treatment prescribed by doctors for persons who are physically or mentally disabled. It includes interesting occupations and pastimes that help patients overcome or reduce their handicaps. A patient with an artificial leg may be taught to dance. In this way he gains confidence in his ability to live a normal life. A blind person who learns to travel, clothe, feed, and care for himself is better prepared to live a useful life. Sometimes patients must relearn such basic skills of everyday living as dressing, writing, or eating. Occupational therapy is often described as "curing by doing," because the patient himself must carry out the activities.

Activities used in occupational therapy are planned and supervised by professional experts called *occupational therapists*. These specialists work in hospitals, rehabilitation centers, and special schools. They also may care for the patient in his own home. Most occupational therapists are women, but an increasing number of men are entering the field.

The therapist determines what kind of therapy, or treatment, will best help a patient. First he must become thoroughly familiar with the patient's illness, interests, and background. Then he can plan a program that will help the patient overcome his disability. The therapist might decide that a woodworking project will provide the best exercise for a boy with an artificial arm. Or he might encourage a mentally ill woman to learn to express her worries through painting.

The rehabilitation of the sick and injured often includes both occupational therapy and *physical* therapy. Therapists use both kinds of treatment to help the physically disabled. See PHYSICAL THERAPY.

The idea behind occupational therapy goes back to

A.D. 172 when Galen, the great Roman physician, said: "Employment is nature's best medicine and essential to human happiness." During the late 1700's, physicians in several countries used occupational therapy in treating mentally ill patients. These doctors included Philippe Pinel in France, Johann Christian Reil in Germany, and Benjamin Rush in the United States. By 1798, the Pennsylvania Hospital for the Insane in Philadelphia was teaching patients carpentry, shoe repairing, needlework, and music. The need to help disabled veterans of World Wars I and II stimulated the growth of occupational therapy.

Modern occupational therapy developed from a nursing course in "Invalid Occupations." This course was first offered to student nurses in 1906 by Susan E. Tracy, a Boston nurse. The term *occupational therapy* was first used in 1914 by George E. Barton, an architect from Clifton Springs, N.Y. He had been treated by this method.

What Occupational Therapy Does

Occupational therapy has two chief goals. These are (1) to help a patient use his body more adequately after an injury or illness and (2) to help a person overcome emotional problems.

Helping the Body is called *physical restoration* or *functional therapy*. Doctors prescribe physical restoration for patients with weak muscles or stiff joints. It is also used when muscles do not work together smoothly, when part of the body is permanently paralyzed, or when a patient must adjust to using an artificial limb.

Physical restoration provides exercise that helps restore muscle strength and usefulness. For example, a

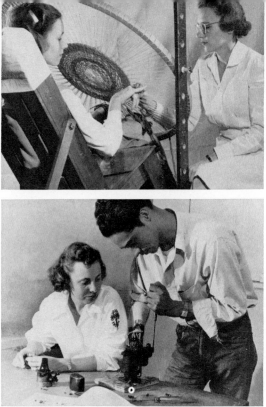

National Society for Crippled Children & Adults

He may be encouraged to read about exploration instead of taking long hikes himself.

Psychological therapy plays a vital part in helping patients with permanent disabilities such as blindness or the loss of a limb. The patient learns that he can do things in spite of his handicap. An amputee might learn to drive a specially equipped car. A blind girl might learn to travel by herself. Each new thing the patient learns to do on his own helps him develop confidence in himself.

Doctors often prescribe psychological therapy for mentally ill patients who have trouble getting along with other people. The therapist plans activities that help the patient develop self-confidence and build satisfying relationships with othes. Folk dancing and dramatics encourage social relationships. Patients may work in hospital kitchens or libraries as the first step toward returning to the responsibilities of home and community.

Careers in Occupational Therapy

A person must like people and enjoy serving them before considering occupational therapy as a career. He must also be physically strong and emotionally stable.

Opportunities. Many positions are available for graduate therapists. They may work in the area of patient treatment, and in professional education, administration, and research. Salaries compare favorably with such professions as nursing and teaching.

Education. A therapist must be graduated from a college or university that offers a program approved by the American Medical Association. Professional subjects of the four-year course include the physical, biological, and social sciences; clinical medicine; rehabilitation; technical skills; and techniques for giving treatments. After their college work, students spend at least nine months in clinical training. They divide this time between general, children's, and tuberculosis hospitals; and in institutions for the mentally ill and those for rehabilitation of the handicapped. Upon completing his studies, the student receives a bachelor's degree in occupational therapy. He may continue his studies for an additional year and earn a master's degree.

After graduation, the therapist takes a national examination administered by the American Occupational Therapy Association. Upon passing the exam, he becomes a Registered Occupational Therapist and uses the letters "O.T.R." after his name. A graduate of a Canadian school may use the letters "O.T.Reg." when he receives his certificate.

To be effective in his work, a therapist must continually add to his knowledge of medicine and psychology, as well as the arts, crafts, recreation, and homemaking skills. This broad range of interests enables him to meet the needs of different patients.

Further information about the various aspects of occupational therapy may be obtained by writing to the American Occupational Therapy Association, 250 W. 57th St., New York 19, N.Y., or to the Canadian Association of Occupational Therapy, 331 Bloor St. W., Toronto, Ont. MARIE LOUISE FRANCISCUS

See also HANDICAPPED; HANDICRAFT; HOBBY.

victim of poliomyelitis may lose the use of some muscles because the nerves that control those muscles have been damaged. The loss may be either partial or complete. The body itself can repair the nerve damage, but the muscles remain too weak to use. The occupational therapist suggests activities designed to strengthen the muscles. He might teach a boy to throw a ball or to do woodwork to build up the arm muscles. A man might operate a potter's wheel, using a kicking motion on the pedal to strengthen the leg muscles.

Sometimes a disease may cripple the body so that stricken muscles remain useless. Then the therapist must teach the patient new ways to perform familiar tasks by substituting one muscle or limb for another. A man might learn to shave and to eat with one hand instead of two. A woman may have to develop strong arm and shoulder muscles to operate the crutches that do the work of her weakened leg muscles.

Physical restoration also helps patients learn how to use artificial limbs. The therapist might teach a man with an artificial hand to assemble an electric circuit. Handling the thin wires gives him skill in using his new hand and provides him with a useful occupation.

Helping the Mind is called *psychological therapy*. Therapists use this technique to help physically or mentally ill patients solve emotional problems.

Patients often worry about the effect their illness will have on their own futures and on that of their families. Some persons are forced to limit their activities because of a disease such as tuberculosis or heart disease. Psychological therapy helps redirect their energies into activities and interests that are within their limitations. For example, a person recovering from a heart attack might substitute chess or checkers for tennis.

OCEAN

OCEAN is the great body of water that covers more than 70 per cent of the earth's surface. The world is really one huge ocean, broken here and there by islands that we call continents. The ocean is so vast that you could sail across it for days without seeing land. It is also deep. In some areas, the bottom of the ocean lies more than six miles below the surface.

Seen from the top of a hill or from an airplane, the ocean seems calm and undisturbed. But the ocean is never still. There are always waves. They lap gently against the shore on calm days and pound heavily against the land on stormy days.

If you take a walk along the ocean shore, you see that the ocean constantly moves and constantly changes. You see what the waves have cast up on the shore—sea shells, starfish, bits of crabs, and stones and pebbles. You may find parts of wrecked ships or huge logs that

have been brought by the current from hundreds of miles away. Every day, changes take place in the shape of the waves and the slope of the beach.

The ocean is filled with life. Plants grow along the shore and on the ocean surface. They are the basis of all animal life in the sea. An amazing variety of animals lives in the ocean. Some of these animals can be seen only with a microscope, and others weigh many tons. Some animals float on the ocean surface, and others live on the ocean floor.

Scientists have only begun to learn many things about the sea, even after more than 90 years of study. There is still much they do not know about life in the sea and about the land beneath the sea. They have much to learn about the movements of the ocean waters. They can only guess how old the sea is and how it began.

Today, man is trying harder than ever to unlock the

Gendreau

INTERESTING FACTS ABOUT THE OCEAN

If the Greenland and Antarctic icecaps should suddenly melt, the world ocean would rise about 200 feet. New York City would be submerged, with only the tops of the tallest buildings sticking out above the water.

The deepest spot in all the oceans, Challenger Deep, is 36,198 feet below the surface of the Pacific. If the highest mountain in the world, 29,028-foot Mount Everest, were put into Challenger Deep, more than a mile of water would cover the mountain.

The Composition of Seawater

All the natural elements can be found in seawater. Among the metallic elements dissolved in the ocean are millions of tons of gold and silver.

CHLORIDE 55.2%

MAGNESIUM 3.7%

OTHERS 3.0%

SULFATE 7.7%

SODIUM 30.4%

secrets of the ocean. Scientists see many new ways to use the sea. The ocean has always been an important source of food. Someday, man may be able to harvest three or four times as much from the sea as he does today. Man also takes minerals from the ocean. As the supply of minerals on land becomes smaller, he will turn more and more to the endless supply in the sea. Man now gets a small amount of fresh water from the sea by removing the salt. In the future, the ocean may be a major source of fresh water. After years of planning, man is harnessing the energy of the ocean's tides for power. The world's first tidal power plant, in France, uses the force of the tides to produce electricity.

Joel W. Hedgpeth, the contributor of this article, is Resident Director and Professor of Oceanography at Yaquina Marine Laboratory, Marine Science Center, at Oregon State University.

Water pressure in the sea increases 14.7 pounds per square inch for every 33 feet of depth. At 30,000 feet, the pressure is more than 6 tons. This could be compared to having the weight of an elephant pressed against every square inch of your body.

DEPTH (In Feet)	PRESSURE (In Pounds per Square Inch)
Ocean Surface	14.7
600	269
1,200	536
3,000	1,338
7,200	3,208
18,000	8,019
30,000	13,363
36,198 (deepest spot)	16,124

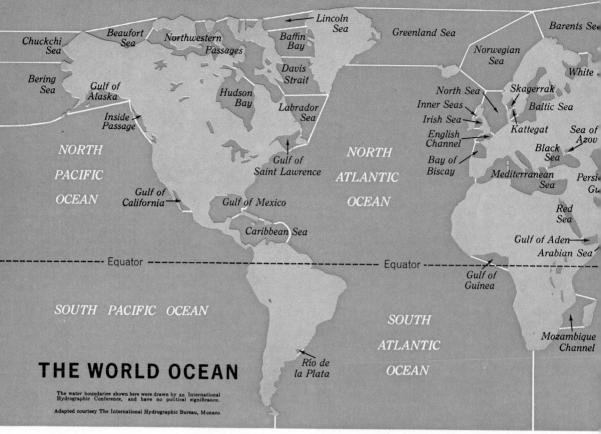

ARCTIC OCEAN

Lincoln Sea · Greenland Sea · Barents Sea

Chuckchi Sea · Beaufort Sea · Northwestern Passages · Baffin Bay · Norwegian Sea · White

Bering Sea · Gulf of Alaska · Hudson Bay · Davis Strait · North Sea · Skagerrak

Inside Passage · Labrador Sea · Inner Seas · Baltic Sea

Irish Sea · Kattegat · Sea of Azov

NORTH PACIFIC OCEAN · English Channel · Black Sea · Persian Gu

Gulf of Saint Lawrence · NORTH ATLANTIC OCEAN · Bay of Biscay · Mediterranean Sea

Gulf of California · Gulf of Mexico · Red Sea

Caribbean Sea · Gulf of Aden · Arabian Sea

Equator — — — — Equator — — —

Gulf of Guinea

SOUTH PACIFIC OCEAN · SOUTH ATLANTIC OCEAN · Mozambique Channel

THE WORLD OCEAN

Río de la Plata

The water boundaries shown here were drawn by an International Hydrographic Conference, and have no political significance.

Adapted courtesy The International Hydrographic Bureau, Monaco

OCEAN / *The World Ocean*

The three great oceans of the world, in order of size, are the Pacific, the Atlantic, and the Indian. Each includes smaller bodies of water called *seas, bays,* and *gulfs,* which are cut off by points of land or by islands. The word *sea* also means the ocean in general.

The three great oceans are really parts of one continuous body of water—the *world ocean.* You can see this if you turn a globe of the world upside down so that the South Pole is on top. The Pacific, Atlantic, and Indian oceans all come together around the continent of Antarctica in the Southern Hemisphere. There they form what is sometimes called the Antarctic Ocean. The Atlantic and Pacific meet again at the top of the globe, in the Arctic Ocean. The continents lie like islands in this vast world ocean.

The waters of the oceans mix together. For example, the waters around Antarctica are so cold that they are heavier than the surface waters of the surrounding oceans. Because they are heavier, they slide under the waters of the other oceans. *Oceanographers* (scientists who study the ocean) have found this cold Antarctic water far north of the equator. Great storm waves on the Indian Ocean may travel all the way across the Pacific to the shores of California. Some oceanographers estimate that one particle of water might find its way through all the oceans in 5,000 years.

The Pacific Ocean is the largest and deepest ocean. It covers about 63,800,000 square miles, more than a third of the earth's surface. The Pacific is so vast that

it could hold all the continents. Near the equator, the Pacific stretches about 11,000 miles, almost halfway around the earth. The average depth of the Pacific is about 14,000 feet. The deepest known spot in the world ocean is Challenger Deep, southwest of the island of Guam. It is 36,198 feet below the ocean's surface.

North America and South America lie to the east of the Pacific, and Asia and Australia are to the west. To the north, Bering Strait links the Pacific with the Arctic Ocean (see STRAIT).

The word *pacific* means *peaceful.* But some of the most disastrous storms on earth blow out of the Pacific. Thousands of volcanoes rise from the ocean floor, and earthquakes occur frequently. See PACIFIC OCEAN.

The Atlantic Ocean is the second largest body of water. Europe and Africa lie to the east, and North America and South America are on the west. The Atlantic meets the Arctic Ocean to the north. The Atlantic covers about 31,530,000 square miles. It has an average depth of about 14,000 feet. The ocean's greatest known depth is Milwaukee Deep, north of Puerto Rico. It is 27,498 feet below the ocean's surface.

Great storms rise in the North Atlantic, but there are also vast regions of quiet waters. The chief industrial countries lie along the coasts of the Atlantic, making it the most important ocean for commerce. See ATLANTIC OCEAN.

The Indian Ocean is somewhat smaller than the Atlantic. Africa borders it on the west, and Australia and the East Indies on the east. Asia lies to the north. The Indian Ocean has an area of about 28,356,000 square miles, and an average depth of 13,000 feet. The

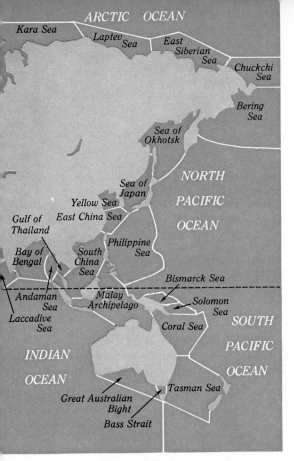

© Rand McNally

deepest known spot, 25,000 feet below the surface, is south of the island of Java.

Gentle winds usually blow across the Indian Ocean, but it is sometimes swept by typhoons. North of the equator, the winds change with the seasons. The ocean currents change with the winds. See INDIAN OCEAN.

The Arctic and Antarctic Oceans are at opposite ends of the earth. The Arctic Ocean lies at the top of the world, north of Asia, Europe, and North America. On the west, Bering Strait links it with the Pacific. On the east, it merges with the Atlantic. Many geographers say it is a sea of the Atlantic, not a separate ocean.

The Arctic Ocean covers about 5,440,000 square miles. Its average depth is 5,010 feet. Its greatest depth is 17,880 feet. Great masses of ice cover much of the ocean during most of the year. In summer, these masses break up into *floes* that drift with the winds and currents. See ARCTIC OCEAN.

The Antarctic Ocean surrounds the continent of Antarctica. Many geographers say these waters are really the southern parts of the Pacific, Atlantic, and Indian oceans, not a separate ocean. See ANTARCTIC OCEAN; ANTARCTICA (The Antarctic Ocean).

The Ocean and Climate. The surface temperature of the ocean ranges from about 28° F. in the polar regions to about 86° F. in the tropics. In the depths, temperatures vary throughout the ocean. But generally, the greater the depth, the lower the temperature. Near the bottom of the deepest parts, it is near freezing.

Water changes temperature more slowly than air and land do. Thus, it takes much longer for the sun to warm up the ocean than the land. The ocean controls the earth's climate because of the great area of the ocean, and the slowness of water to change temperature. The ocean has a steadying influence on land temperatures. It helps keep the air from becoming too hot or too cold.

The ocean also provides rainfall. As water evaporates from the ocean surface because of the sun's heat, it rises and forms clouds. The winds carry the clouds across the land. The clouds provide the rain and snow that form rivers and lakes, and that help make plants grow. Without the ocean, the earth's climate would be like that on Mars—very cold at night and very hot during the day. Man could not live on a planet without an ocean. See CLIMATE (Oceans).

The Composition of Seawater. Swimming in the ocean is easier than in a lake. This is because seawater contains, on the average, about 3.5 per cent salts. These salts help a swimmer float. Seawater is not good to drink. It increases thirst and may make a person ill.

The salty material in the sea is mostly common table salt. Seawater also contains magnesium, sulfur, and calcium. In fact, seawater contains all the elements that make up the minerals in the earth's crust (see ELEMENT, CHEMICAL). The proportions of common salt and other elements in seawater are about the same throughout the world ocean. The mixing action of waves and currents causes this sameness.

Scientists have compared the composition of seawater with the composition of body fluids in man and animals. They have found that the proportions of the elements are much alike in seawater and body fluids. This seems to support the theory that life began in the sea. See LIFE (Later Theories).

493

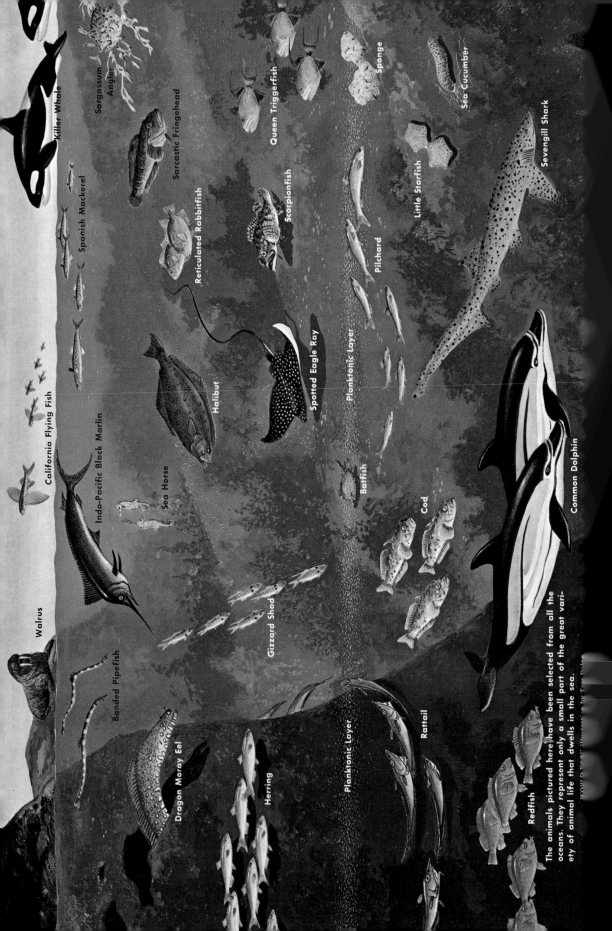

Killer Whale

Sargassum Angler

Spanish Mackerel

Sarcastic Fringehead

Reticulated Rabbitfish

Queen Triggerfish

Sponge

Sea Cucumber

Scorpionfish

Little Starfish

Pilchard

Sevengill Shark

California Flying Fish

Walrus

Indo-Pacific Black Marlin

Sea Horse

Halibut

Spotted Eagle Ray

Planktonic Layer

Batfish

Cod

Common Dolphin

Banded Pipefish

Dragon Moray Eel

Herring

Gizzard Shad

Planktonic Layer

Rattail

Redfish

The animals pictured here have been selected from all the oceans. They represent only a small part of the great variety of animal life that dwells in the sea.

OCEAN / *Life in the Ocean*

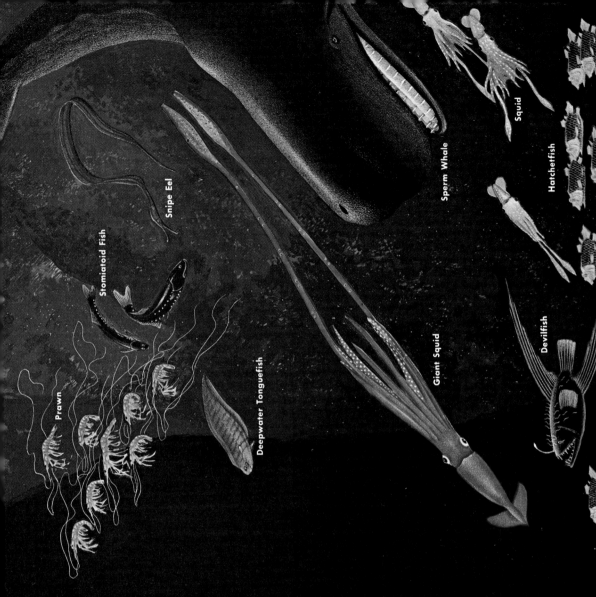

Prawn

Stomiatoid Fish

Snipe Eel

Deepwater Tonguefish

Giant Squid

Sperm Whale

Squid

Hatchetfish

Devilfish

Both plants and animals live in the ocean. Plants can be found wherever there is sunlight—on and near the surface, in shallow waters, and along the shores. They do not live in deep, dark waters. Animals, however, dwell everywhere in the sea—from the surface to the deepest and blackest parts. The ocean is the home of the largest animals that have ever lived, and also some of the smallest ones. Blue whales may grow 95 feet long and weigh 150 tons. They are far larger than any dinosaur that walked the earth millions of years ago. The smallest animals in the sea measure only about 1/25,000 of an inch long.

All life in the ocean can be divided into three groups: (1) the plankton, (2) the nekton, and (3) the benthos. The *plankton* consists of plants and animals that float about, drifting with the currents and tides. The *nekton* is made up of animals that swim freely in the water. The *benthos* consists of animals and plants that live on or in the ocean bottom, from the shore to the greatest depths.

The Plankton. Most of the floating, drifting plants and animals of the sea can be seen only under a microscope. The plants make up the *phytoplankton*, and the animals make up the *zooplankton*.

The Phytoplankton consists of several kinds of plants, including the diatoms, coccolithophores, and dinoflagellates. The most important and the most numerous are the diatoms (see DIATOM). The phytoplankton has been called the "pasture of the sea." It is the basic food supply of the ocean because all the animals feed on it, directly or indirectly.

Sea plants get their energy to grow from the minerals in seawater and from sunlight. But the sun's rays do not go deep into the

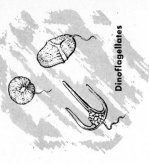

Dinoflagellates

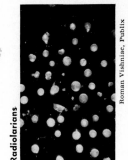

Radiolarians
Roman Vishniac, Publix

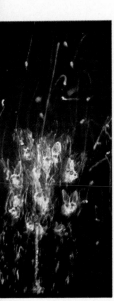

Jerry Greenberg

Copepods

Diatoms

PLANKTON

Paul Popper

Squid

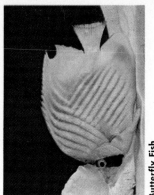

Gene Wolfsheimer, N.A.S.

Butterfly Fish

NEKTON

OCEAN / *Life in the Ocean*

water. In clear tropic seas, away from muddy rivers, light may reach several hundred feet into the ocean. Near shores where rivers bring mud and sand into the ocean, light does not go so deeply. Yet the rivers carry many substances that plants need to grow. For this reason, sea plants may grow thickly near shores.

The *Zooplankton* includes many kinds of animals, such as copepods, radiolarians, jellyfish, and arrowworms. Many of these animals are transparent. Others are brightly colored. Some are light blue, some pink, some lavender. Some of them float because they are mostly water or because their bodies contain bubbles of gas. Other plankton animals have little fins or spines that help them float. See PLANKTON.

The Nekton. The animals of the nekton can swim about freely. The most important ones are the fishes. More than 20,000 kinds of fishes live in the sea. They range in size from sharks 50 feet long to certain gobies less than an inch long. The nekton also includes octopuses, squids, whales, and seals.

Although nektonic animals can swim about freely, they cannot all live anywhere in the world ocean. Some nektonic animals must live in certain parts of the ocean because of the temperature, the food supply, or the saltiness of the water. Most animals of the nekton are found only at certain depths. Sea animals can live under the pressure of the ocean because the pressure inside their bodies equals the water pressure outside. Many fishes have swimming bladders filled with gas that allow them to stay at certain depths. If they swim too high, they can be carried to the surface. This happens because the pressure on the bladder inside no longer equals the water pressure outside. If a fish is carried too high, it dies. A fish that strays too low is also in danger. The increased water pressure compresses the gas in the bladder so that the fish loses its ability to float. It then sinks to the bottom.

Most animals of the nekton, especially the fishes, have streamlined bodies. Their streamlined bodies help them swim easily and quickly through the water in the pursuit of prey or to escape from enemies. Some of these animals can travel at remarkable speeds. The dolphin can swim 25 miles an hour, and the sailfish

Sea Lion

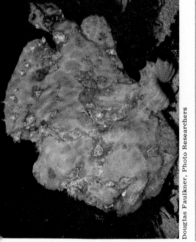

Frog Fish

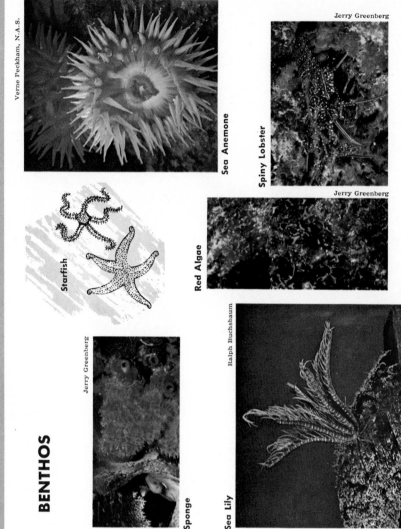

Verne Peckham, N.A.S.

Sea Anemone

Jerry Greenberg

Spiny Lobster

Jerry Greenberg

Red Algae

Starfish

BENTHOS

Jerry Greenberg

Sponge

Ralph Buchsbaum

Sea Lily

and the barracuda can swim 30 miles an hour. Many nektonic animals can also swim great distances. The eel and the salmon, for example, travel thousands of miles to and from their *breeding grounds*, where they lay their eggs.

The Benthos. Animals live everywhere on the sea bottom, from the shore to the deepest parts of the ocean. However, plants of the ocean bottom can be found only as deep as the sun's rays go into the water.

Animals that dwell on the bottom include worms, snails, clams, sponges, sea lilies, and starfish. Some animals with heavy shells, such as crabs and lobsters, can carry this weight because the water buoys them up. Many of them are swimmers or walkers, and move about for food. Some animals are fixed to the bottom in one position throughout their lives. They include oysters, sea anemones, and corals. Ocean currents carry food to these animals, and some food drifts down to them from above.

Seaweeds grow along the shore or in shallow waters. The largest seaweed is the giant kelp. It usually grows about 70 feet long. Many kinds of small, bushy seaweeds grow over rocks that are covered by water at high tide. Man has found many uses for seaweeds. But seaweeds are of little importance to the animals of the open sea. See SEAWEED.

The Food Cycle in the Sea. The phytoplankton is the food base for the animals in the world ocean. Certain animals of the zooplankton eat these plants. These animals, in turn, are eaten by other members of the zooplankton or by fish or other swimming animals. Generally, larger animals eat smaller animals.

After an animal dies, it begins to sink. Before most dead animals sink very far, they are eaten by creatures that dwell at lower depths. When these animals die, they become a source of food for animals that live even deeper. Animals begin to *decompose* (decay) as soon as they die. This decomposition takes place at all depths. In addition, animals give off waste products. These waste products, and dead animals that are not eaten, are broken down into mineral salts by tiny living things called *bacteria* (see BACTERIA). Rising currents carry these minerals to the ocean surface, where plants of the plankton use them as food. Thus, the food cycle in the sea goes on and on.

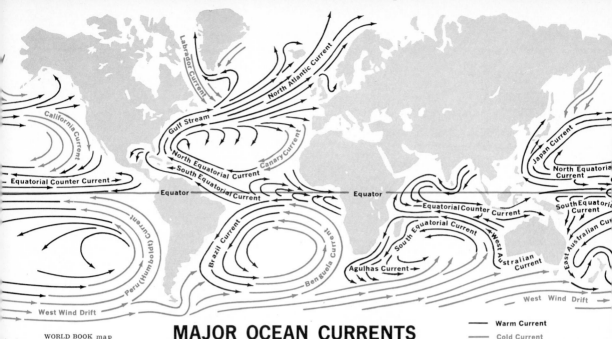

MAJOR OCEAN CURRENTS

WORLD BOOK map

—— Warm Current
—— Cold Current

OCEAN / *How the Ocean Moves*

Ocean Waves. The waters of the ocean never stop moving. The most familiar movements are the waves. Waves are set in motion by winds, earthquakes, and the gravitational pull of the moon and the sun. On shore, we see waves caused by the wind. Their size depends on whether they are driven by winds from storms nearby or from far across the ocean. In an ocean wave, water moves up and down. There is no forward motion of water as the wave goes through the water. This action is like the waves you can make in a rope tied to a tree. When you shake the free end of the rope, waves run along it. But the rope itself does not move forward. When an ocean wave reaches land, however, it starts to drag on the bottom. Then the water also moves.

As waves hit a sandy beach, they carry sand ashore and pile it up. They also move sand along the beach. Sometimes man builds a *breakwater* (a wall to check the force of the waves) and stops the movement of sand along the shore. The sand may then be moved away below the breakwater, and rocks are exposed. This happened at Jones Beach on Long Island, N.Y. Now sand must be brought to this beach so people can use the area.

Storm waves are quite powerful. Out at sea, they may reach heights of 40 feet or higher. Waves can pick up huge boulders and throw them far up on the shore. They have carried large ships against rocks and smashed them. Waves also can cut holes in rocks, forming arches. Waves continually work against the land, breaking the rock into boulders, pebbles, and sand. See WAVES.

Earthquakes and shifts in the sea bottom often set in motion huge waves that move several hundred miles an hour. This type of wave is often called a *tidal wave*, even though it is not caused by the tide. Scientists call these waves *tsunamis*. Most tsunamis start from Japan, Alaska, or Chile. Many earthquakes take place in these regions. Scientists can predict how fast tsunamis are moving, and warn people in their paths.

On the surface of the open ocean, a tsunami is hardly noticeable. But when it reaches a bay or harbor, it may pile up to a tremendous height in the narrow area. It then becomes very dangerous. Waves of this kind have destroyed large towns and drowned hundreds of persons. See TIDAL WAVE.

Ocean Currents. Waters move about in the ocean in streams called *currents*. The mighty Mississippi River is a

HOW OCEAN CURRENTS ARE FORMED

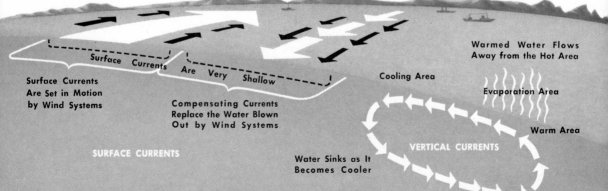

Surface Currents Are Very Shallow

Surface Currents Are Set in Motion by Wind Systems

Compensating Currents Replace the Water Blown Out by Wind Systems

Cooling Area

Warmed Water Flows Away from the Hot Area

Evaporation Area

Warm Area

VERTICAL CURRENTS

SURFACE CURRENTS

Water Sinks as It Becomes Cooler

mere brook compared with the greatest of these streams. The wind systems set the ocean currents in motion (see WIND). Great circular currents move clockwise in the Northern Hemisphere and counterclockwise in the Southern Hemisphere. The earth's rotation makes the currents flow in this way. The strength of the ocean currents changes with the seasons. Often, deeper currents flow below the surface currents. These move in the opposite direction.

The currents move continuously, and they are never quite the same from year to year. The great surface currents of the ocean carry warm water away from the equator. This water gradually cools. When it gets even farther from the equator, it mixes with cold waters from high latitudes. Thus, when the current turns toward the equator again, it is a cold current.

In some years, a current may change its course. Or it may carry less water if the wind is not blowing so hard. Changes in currents may cause changes in the life of the sea. Fishes that depend on a current to bring them food may die if the current changes. A change in a current may change the temperature of the water so that fish eggs will not hatch as well. On the other hand, favorable changes in a current may mean many more fish—and a good year for fishermen.

The Tides. If you stand on the ocean shore, you can see the water slowly rising higher and higher for about six hours. Then it slowly falls back for about six hours. The rise and fall of ocean waters are called *tides*. Tides are caused chiefly by the gravitational pull of the moon. When the moon is directly over any point in the ocean, it pulls the water toward it. The water on the opposite side of the earth also piles up. This action results from the spinning of the earth, which tends to make the water fly off the earth's surface. Tides are not high in mid-ocean, but near shore they may rise 6 to 8 feet. In long, narrow bays, tides may rise 20 to 30 feet. In the Bay of Fundy, between New Brunswick and Nova Scotia, the tide has risen 50 feet.

When the moon is full or new, the earth, sun, and moon are in a straight line. At this time, the sun's gravitational pull, which is about half that of the moon's, combines with the moon's gravitational pull. The incoming tides then are at their highest, and the outgoing tides are at their lowest. These tides are called *spring* tides. At the quarters of the moon, the sun and moon are at right angles to one another. The tides then are neither so high nor so low. These tides are called *neap* tides. See TIDES.

The Changing Shoreline. The movements of the ocean change the shoreline. Waves cut away sloping land and leave steep cliffs. They carve islands from the shore. Waves and currents build up sand bars along the shore. Sometimes waves and currents fill up harbors with sand and mud, making these waters useless for ships.

Shorelines also *emerge* (rise from the water) and *submerge* (sink). When shorelines emerge, all the caves and cliffs made by the waves are found far from the water. The new shore, once part of the ocean bottom, may have many sea shells on it. When shorelines submerge, hilltops become islands, and water flows into the valleys. Shores that have sunk, such as the coast of Maine, are very uneven. Shores that have risen, such as the east coast of Florida, are straighter.

HOW THE OCEAN CHANGES COASTLINES

Cutting Away the Land

As waves pound against the shore, they erode the land and leave a cliff. The earth that is worn away is deposited under water, where it piles up and forms a terrace. Further wave erosion steepens the cliff and cuts a notch in its base. In time, the unsupported earth above the notch falls and more land is carried out to sea.

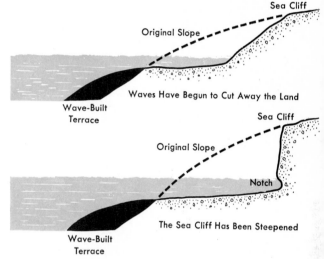

Sea Cliff
Original Slope
Waves Have Begun to Cut Away the Land
Wave-Built Terrace

Sea Cliff
Original Slope
Notch
The Sea Cliff Has Been Steepened
Wave-Built Terrace

Building Up the Land

When large waves break some distance from shore, a sand bar forms as waves scoop up sediment from the ocean floor. Smaller waves build a lower bar near shore. A lagoon is formed after waves build the offshore bar above the water. Waves wash sand into the lagoon, and rivers and winds carry sediment into it. The lagoon becomes a marsh. Finally, the work of the waves, rivers, and winds turns the marsh into an area of sand dunes.

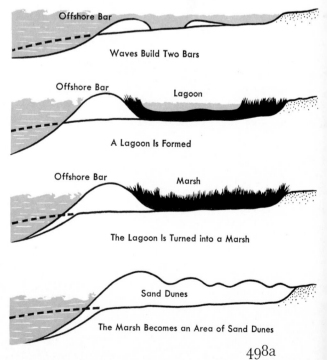

Offshore Bar
Waves Build Two Bars

Offshore Bar — Lagoon
A Lagoon Is Formed

Offshore Bar — Marsh
The Lagoon Is Turned into a Marsh

Sand Dunes
The Marsh Becomes an Area of Sand Dunes

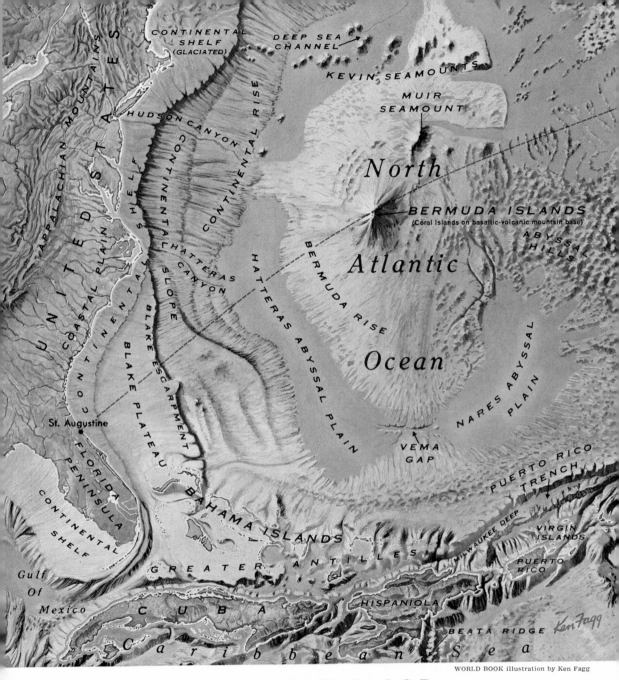

Labels on the map (image):
CONTINENTAL SHELF (GLACIATED) · DEEP SEA CHANNEL · KEVIN SEAMOUNTS · MUIR SEAMOUNT · APPALACHIAN MOUNTAINS · UNITED STATES · HUDSON CANYON · CONTINENTAL SHELF · CONTINENTAL RISE · CONTINENTAL SLOPE · HATTERAS CANYON · HATTERAS ABYSSAL PLAIN · North Atlantic Ocean · BERMUDA ISLANDS (Coral Islands on basaltic-volcanic mountain base) · BERMUDA RISE · ABYSSAL HILLS · COASTAL PLAIN · CONTINENTAL SHELF · BLAKE ESCARPMENT · BLAKE PLATEAU · St. Augustine · FLORIDA PENINSULA · CONTINENTAL SHELF · BAHAMA ISLANDS · GREATER ANTILLES · CUBA · Gulf Of Mexico · NARES ABYSSAL PLAIN · VEMA GAP · PUERTO RICO TRENCH · MILWAUKEE DEEP · VIRGIN ISLANDS · PUERTO RICO · HISPANIOLA · BEATA RIDGE · Ken Fagg · Caribbean Sea

THE ATLANTIC OCEAN FLOOR

The Atlantic Ocean floor off the United States coast consists of broad plains, steep canyons, and towering mountains. The land beneath all the oceans has these varied features. The diagram below shows a profile of the Atlantic floor from St. Augustine, Fla., to Gibraltar. The red line on the physical map corresponds to the part marked off in red on the profile.

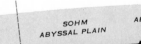

Profile labels: St. Augustine, Fla. · BLAKE PLATEAU · BLAKE ESCARPMENT · HATTERAS ABYSSAL PLAIN · BERMUDA RISE · BERMUDA ISLANDS · MUIR SEAMOUNT · SOHM ABYSSAL PLAIN · ABYSSAL HILLS

People once believed that the floor of the sea was mostly a great level plain. Today, we know that the ocean bottom is just as irregular as the surface of the land. In fact, some of the earth's most spectacular scenery—towering mountains, deep trenches, vast canyons, and broad plains—is beneath the sea.

The Continental Shelf and Slope. In many places around the continents, the land gradually slopes under water to a depth of about 600 feet. This submerged land is called the *continental shelf*. In some areas, the continental shelf extends hundreds of miles. In other areas, it hardly exists, and the coastline drops nearly straight down into deep water. The shelf is covered by material called the *continental deposit*, which has been carried down from the land by rivers. In some ways, the continental shelf is the most important part of the land beneath the sea. The great fisheries of the world are there. The shelf also has rich oil fields.

The continental shelf slopes gently downward to the *continental edge*. There the *continental slope* begins. It is much steeper than the continental shelf. In many parts of the ocean, deep canyons gash the slope. Many of these canyons seem to have been cut by former rivers. Others may have been caused by the movement of sand and mud cutting down into the ocean bottom. The walls of some of the canyons are steeper and higher than the walls of the Grand Canyon. The continental slope plunges to the deep ocean bottom—the *abyss*.

Underwater Mountains and Valleys. Great mountains rise from the bottom of the ocean. Many are volcanoes. In some places, they stick out above the surface of the sea and form islands. The Hawaiian Islands were formed by volcanoes that rose from the sea floor.

Mountain ranges also rise from the bottom. An enormous range, 10,000 miles long, runs down the middle of the Atlantic Ocean. It is called the Mid-Atlantic Ridge. A deep valley cuts down through the middle of it. Some peaks of the Mid-Atlantic Ridge rise above the water's surface and form islands, such as the Azores.

Ridges also rise from the bottom of the Pacific Ocean, but they are smaller than the Mid-Atlantic Ridge. In addition, great cliffs thousands of miles long are found on the Pacific floor. Some of the deepest parts of the world ocean may be found in the western Pacific. They are long, narrow valleys called *trenches*. Challenger Deep, in the Mariana Trench of the Pacific, is 36,198 feet below the surface. It is the deepest known spot in all the oceans.

Layers of muds cover the deep trenches and level parts of the ocean bottom. Some of these muds are full of the shells and skeletons of dead plants and animals from the plankton. Scientists call such muds *oozes*. The oozes have been formed over millions of years. They may be hundreds of feet deep in places. Beneath them lies hard rock called *basalt*. See OOZE.

How the Oceans Began. How did the earth, the oceans, and the continents begin? No one really knows the answers, but scientists have several theories. To understand the theories about how the oceans began, it is helpful to start with theories about how the earth itself began.

Some scientists believe the earth was torn from the sun and spun off into space. As it spun around, it became round and solid. Other scientists think the earth grew slowly, bit by bit. It increased in size by collecting particles floating in space.

Regardless of how the earth began, the rocks in its crust became separated. The heavier rocks sank deeper into the earth's crust, and lighter rocks rose to the surface. Today, the oceans lie in great basins of heavy basalt. Between them, floating on lighter rock called *granite*, are the continents.

According to one theory, the continents began as one great mass. The mass broke up into continents, which slowly drifted apart. This theory explains the similar shapes of the eastern coast of the Americas and the western coast of Africa. You can see this similarity on a globe. The margins of the continents seem to fit together like the pieces of a puzzle. According to another theory, the world is slowly growing larger, carrying North and South America farther away from Europe and Africa.

The great ocean basins became filled with water in two possible ways. Some scientists think the water came from the rocks inside the earth. As these rocks cooled and became solid, they released water. This water filled the depressions in the earth's crust. Other scientists believe that the water came from thick clouds that surrounded the earth. As the earth and clouds cooled, the clouds poured forth rain. The rain fell for hundreds of years, filling the ocean basins.

Many of the salts in the ocean come from the land. Scientists once thought they might learn the ocean's age by figuring out how long it took the ocean to get as salty as it is. But scientists now believe the ocean has been as salty as it is today for as long as there has been life in it. This period of time might be at least 500 million years.

WORLD BOOK illustration by Raymond Perlman

Seawater Becomes Fresh Water at this plant in Israel on the Red Sea. In dry regions near the ocean, man is turning more and more to the sea as a source of fresh water.

The Ocean's Energy is a source of power for man. Incoming and outgoing tides were first used to generate electricity in 1966, at this plant near St.-Malo, France.

State of Israel

OCEAN/*How Man Uses the Ocean*

Since early times, man has used the ocean and its products. He has captured its animals for food, pelts, and oil. He has taken out its valuable minerals. He has used the sea as a source of drinking water and as a highway of commerce. He soon will use its energy to light his homes and to run his factories. Man also uses the ocean as a dumping ground.

Fishing and Whaling. Every year, the world's fishing fleets bring in millions of tons of fish, shellfish, and whales. The best fishing grounds are on the Continental shelves of the North Sea, the Atlantic Ocean near Newfoundland, and the Bering Sea. There the waters teem with haddock, herring, cod, and halibut. Clams, lobsters, oysters, and scallops also are taken in Atlantic waters off New England and Canada. Millions of tons of menhaden live in U.S. waters along the South Atlantic and Gulf coasts. Commercial fishermen of the United States catch more menhaden than any other kind of fish. Menhaden are ground up into meal for livestock, and the oil is pressed from them for use by chemical plants. The world's largest shrimp fisheries are in the same U.S. waters where menhaden are caught.

Other kinds of fishes are caught on the high seas, far from land. The most important is the tuna, which is eaten by the people of many countries. Fishermen catch tuna by hook and line and with nets in the Pacific and Atlantic oceans. See FISHING INDUSTRY.

Whales used to be hunted in the regions where tuna are now caught. Whaling now centers mostly in the waters of Antarctica and the North Pacific. Whales provide meat, oil, and other products. See WHALE.

The Ocean—A Liquid Mine. Seawater contains every mineral found on land. Man knows how to remove many of these minerals. But he must find cheaper ways to do it. For example, seawater holds tons of gold. This gold is so finely dissolved, however, that removing it would cost more than the gold is worth.

Salt was the first mineral that man took from the sea. He let seawater evaporate in shallow basins under sun-light, and used the salt that remained. In many parts of the world, people still gather salt in this way. Other minerals can be taken from the salt left after evaporation. These minerals include iodine, magnesium, and bromine. Evaporation is a cheap but inefficient way to mine the sea, so man uses other methods. Magnesium, for example, is taken by chemical and electrochemical processes (see MAGNESIUM).

On the bottom of the sea lies a fortune in rare minerals. These minerals include manganese, nickel, copper, and cobalt. They occur in lumps called *nodules*. Someday, man may be able to gather up the nodules in a device that works like a giant vacuum cleaner.

Other Products of the Sea include pearls, sponges, seaweeds, and fertilizer.

Pearls have been treasured since ancient times. Valuable pearls are formed between the shell and body of an animal called the pearl oyster. The Japanese make cultured pearls by putting bits of shell in pearl oysters. See PEARL.

Sponges are gathered from the ocean bottom by divers. They also can be gathered by dragging a net along the bottom, but this method removes both young and mature sponges. Natural sponges have a higher quality than man-made ones. See SPONGE.

Seaweeds contain the minerals that are taken from seawater. These weeds are used for food, and as a source of iodine, soda, and potash. Seaweeds also are used in making medicines, ice cream, candy, jellies, salad dressing, and cosmetics. Some types are used as fertilizer. See SEAWEED.

Fertilizer. One of the best fertilizers for plants comes from huge deposits of bird droppings on Pacific islands near Peru. The sea birds of these islands feed on small fishes, which have eaten the rich plant life brought by the Peru Current. The birds fly out from the islands every day to eat the fish, and return at night. The bird droppings are called *guano*. The guano is shipped to many parts of the world. See GUANO.

498d

A Source of Fresh Water. Many parts of the world have a shortage of fresh water. As the population of the world increases, this shortage will become greater. Man now makes a small amount of fresh water from seawater by removing the salt. In the future, he will have to use the sea more and more for water for farms, homes, and factories. He will have to find cheap ways to change seawater into fresh water. Perhaps he will use nuclear energy to do this. See WATER.

Transportation and Communication. The ocean has been a highway for trade ever since man first built sea-going ships. Today, ships are still the most important way to transport heavy machinery and such bulky products as grain and oil.

Telephone and telegraph cables crisscross the ocean bottom. These cables are thousands of miles long. *Oceanographic ships* (ships equipped to explore the ocean) must be careful not to break the cables with instruments dragged along the sea floor. Special cable ships are used to find broken cables and bring them up to the surface for repair. See CABLE.

Harnessing the Sea's Energy. For years, men have tried to figure out ways to use the ocean's tremendous energy to provide electric power. The world's first tidal power plant began operating in June, 1966, on the Rance River, near St.-Malo, France. Twice a day, the incoming tide, up to 44 feet high, surges up the Rance. The tide reaches a volume of as much as 280 million gallons of water a minute. The plant was built to use this energy to produce 544,000,000 kilowatt-hours of electricity a year.

A Vast Dumping Ground. Man dumps all sorts of things into the sea. Barges carry garbage, tons of concrete, unusable parts of wrecked automobiles, and other junk out to sea, where they are thrown overboard. Many great cities dump sewage into the ocean. Radioactive wastes also are emptied into the sea in some places.

The ocean cannot hold all these things without endangering the life in the sea. Man will have to find other ways of getting rid of rubbish. As the world population increases, man will need more products from the sea. If he wants to harvest more fish, he will have to take better care of the ocean in which they live.

Fernand Gigon, Pix from Publix

Seaweeds are used in making foods, drugs, and other products. In Communist China, seaweeds help relieve the food shortage. These Chinese fishermen gather the weeds by age-old methods.

An Endless Supply of Minerals is dissolved in seawater. Magnesium is taken from the water at this plant in England.

WORLD BOOK illustrations by James Dunnington

A Great Highway of Commerce, the ocean has been used for trade ever since man first built ships to carry his goods.

The Port of New York Authority

Morin, Monkmeyer

Animals of the Sea are one of the ocean's greatest resources. Man catches them for food and for their oils and pelts.

OCEAN / *Discovering the Secrets of the Deep*

Early Exploration. Man began to explore the ocean long before he started to record history. First he discovered the seashore. He found that he could use its rocks as weapons and as tools for scraping and breaking things. He soon learned to eat clams, mussels, and seaweed. Then man developed rafts and small boats for fishing away from shore. Later, he built larger boats that could travel long distances for fishing. Now he could also exchange goods with other men in distant places.

Almost as soon as man discovered the sea and the shore, he became curious about them. Since the days of the ancient Greeks and Phoenicians, man has gone on voyages to find out what was beyond his own waters.

More than 2,300 years ago, the Greek explorer Pytheas sailed out of the Mediterranean Sea and far to the north, perhaps beyond the Arctic Circle. About 100 years later, another Greek, Oppian, wrote the first known account of fish and fishing. In those days, man could not bring up fish from deep water. He could not dive far underwater nor take any photographs. Most of the sea was unknown. No one had any idea of what was in the ocean depths or on the bottom of the sea. Men believed that the waters of the sea held many secrets. Today, we still do not know all the secrets of the sea.

Scientific exploration of the ocean did not begin until accurate methods of finding the position of a ship at sea had been developed. The *sextant*, an instrument used for calculating latitude, was invented about 1730. Accurate clocks to help seamen determine longitude became available in the late 1700's. At this time, Captain James Cook, a British explorer, made accurate charts of the South Pacific Ocean. Naturalists accompanied Cook and later explorers who sought to find new lands or to make accurate maps of known regions. The scientists brought back plants and animals of the sea, as well as some knowledge of the behavior of these organisms.

Nature studies by explorers of the early 1800's led to the first expedition to explore the ocean—its depths, waters, and living things. This expedition began in 1872, when the *Challenger*, the first ship equipped for ocean exploration, sailed from England. The *Challenger* expedition, supported by the Royal Society of London and by the British Admiralty, lasted 3½ years. Aboard the ship, British scientists gathered information and specimens. Later, specialists from many parts of the world helped write the 50 volumes of the *Challenger Reports*. The expedition and the information it produced marked the beginning of *oceanography*, the scientific study of the sea.

Why Study the Sea? Today, man studies the sea for many reasons. The oceans cover more than 70 per cent

Ron Church

The *Deepstar*, a submersible, can carry men thousands of feet beneath the surface of the ocean.

Authenticated News   U.S. Navy   Fritz Goro, *Life* © 1962 Time Inc.

A Scuba Diver, *right,* carries his own air supply. He can move more freely than a diver in a diving suit, *left,* but cannot go down so deep.

Portholes in a chamber beneath the bow of *Atlantis II,* a research ship, permit direct undersea observation.

Jenkins Bros. Valves

The *FLIP* (FLoating Instrument Platform), *above,* glides through the water like any other ship. But when tanks in its long hull are filled with water, the stern of the vessel sinks. Its bow rises vertically and becomes a stationary oceanographic research laboratory, *right.*

of the earth, and they affect—directly or indirectly—all life on the earth. Scientists study the ways the ocean surface and the atmosphere act upon each other. They seek knowledge of the various kinds of plant and animal life in the sea. They also investigate the chemical composition of seawater and the structure of the ocean bottom. Scientists also study the behavior of currents, tides, and waves.

The actions of the oceans and the atmosphere on each other control the evaporation of water from the sea. The evaporated water forms *precipitation* (rain, snow, and other forms of moisture) that supplies water to the land. The interactions between the oceans and the atmosphere also affect the earth's climate. Water warms up or cools down much more slowly than do air or land. As a result, the mild temperatures of the air over the vast ocean surface help regulate the temperatures of the air over the land.

Knowledge about sea plants and animals may help man increase his food supply. Today, man gets only a small proportion of his food from the oceans. Yet, this amount is significant for nations that border the sea. Scientists are seeking ways to increase the yield of fish from the sea in order to meet the needs of an expanding world population. This goal involves the wise use of the food cycle in the sea. Scientists are also studying how pollutants dumped into the ocean affect the life cycles of living things of the sea.

Chemists want to know what seawater contains and how it behaves chemically. They seek to identify the materials in seawater that occur in extremely small quantities. Chemists hope to learn how these tiny amounts of material affect the plants and animals of the sea. This knowledge may also help man learn how certain pollutants could harm life in the ocean.

Studies of the sea bottom have revealed deposits of oil and natural gas near many land areas of the world. A number of these offshore sources of oil and natural gas have not yet been tapped by man. Someday they may become vital if man's need for fuel keeps on increasing at its present rate.

Scientists also seek additional knowledge of the currents, tides, and waves of the oceans. The navigation of atomic submarines that can stay underwater for weeks requires detailed understanding of the movements of ocean waters. The study of currents, tides, and waves includes gathering data on the sea's ability to mix and scatter the things that are put into it. Without such knowledge, man might pollute the oceans beyond tolerable limits.

How Man Studies the Depths. The scientists aboard the *Challenger* had only piano wire with which to measure ocean depths. They used heavy rope to tow nets along the ocean bottom to collect plants and animals. The men did have special thermometers to obtain the temperature of the sea at great depths. They also had a special kind of bottle to collect seawater far below the ocean surface. The Norwegian explorer Fridtjof Nansen later perfected this metal bottle. It is known as the *Nansen bottle*, and scientists still use it.

Lockheed Aircraft Corp.

Coring Devices bring up samples of the ocean floor. The corer shown above digs cores 8 feet deep and can cut through almost all sediment on the sea bottom.

Scripps Institution of Oceanography

A Wave-and-Current Channel reproduces the actions of ocean waves for scientific study in a laboratory. The glass-walled channel pictured here is 131 feet long.

498g

UNDERSEA HABITAT A habitat enables divers to remain underwater for several months. The two cylinders are 18 feet high and 12½ feet in diameter. They are divided into four compartments to provide living and working quarters for five divers. A habitat carries equipment for scientific studies of the ocean.

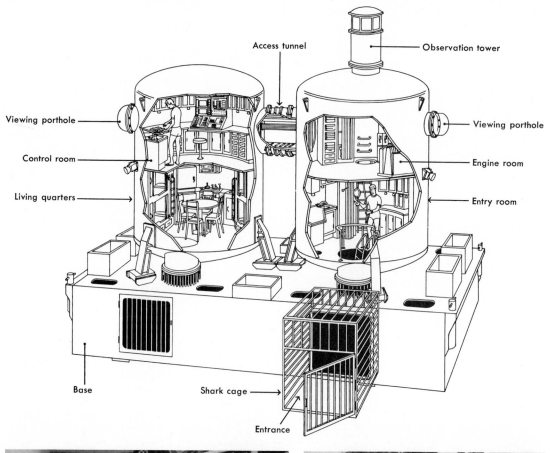

Access tunnel

Observation tower

Viewing porthole

Viewing porthole

Control room

Engine room

Living quarters

Entry room

Base

Shark cage

Entrance

Flip Schulke, Black Star

The Control Room of a Habitat has equipment to monitor activities in the vessel and to communicate with crews on the surface. It also holds instruments used by divers in their experiments.

Flip Schulke, Black Star

Outside a Habitat, a diver examines a marine specimen. The habitat allows divers to stay on the ocean floor far longer than they otherwise could.

498h

Today, oceanographers have many modern instruments—though nets and dredges are still lowered to the bottom to collect specimens. Underwater cameras take photographs of the sea bottom. Devices called *corers* consist of long tubes that can bring up 100-foot-deep samples of bottom mud and sand. Scientists use such samples to study the history of both sea and land. Electronic instruments send back echoes from the bottom that provide information about the depth of the sea. The most powerful of these sounding instruments can send back echoes from layers of the earth deep below the water. Records of the echoes have provided information about the structure of these earth layers.

Other instruments help oceanographers analyze small amounts of various substances in the water. These devices detect the small amounts of the substances needed for life by the plants and animals of the sea. Such instruments also identify the substances that may harm the organisms. Large research vessels carry these delicate instruments and also have computers to help scientists analyze data quickly. The instruments require trained technicians to keep them working properly.

Oceanographic Diving. No oceanographic instrument, no matter how accurate, can take the place of direct inspection of the depths by man. Diving suits equipped with air hoses were developed during the 1800's, but they enabled men to go only about 200 feet down. These suits were so complicated and dangerous that only professional divers used them—and only for ship salvage or treasure hunting.

In the 1840's, the French biologist Henri Milne-Edwards became the first person to use diving gear for scientific studies. But scientists could not actually explore the depths until the invention of the Aqua-Lung in 1943. The Aqua-Lung, a free-diving device, was developed in France by Jacques-Yves Cousteau, an undersea explorer, and Émile Gagnan, an engineer. It gave a diver freedom by enabling him to carry his air supply.

Even with an Aqua-Lung, a diver is limited by the size of his air supply and by the pressure of the water. The pressure underwater increases with the depth of the water. A diver may be seriously injured if he descends or rises faster than his body can adjust to the change in pressure. See DIVING, UNDERWATER.

To eliminate the need for divers to keep adjusting to pressure changes, scientists developed underwater laboratories called *habitats*. Divers can live in a habitat for several months. The air pressure inside is kept equal to that of the surrounding water. The divers can swim away from the habitat, returning only to eat, sleep, or refill their air tanks. Habitats enable underwater explorers to conduct various studies more carefully than was previously possible. These studies include the behavior of living things, the movement of sand along the sea bottom, and the penetration of light into the sea.

Various types of diving spheres and small submarines enable man to descend much deeper than ever before. The first of these was the *bathysphere*, developed in 1930 by William Beebe, an American naturalist. In 1934, Beebe descended half a mile in a bathysphere. The bathysphere was connected to the surface by cables. A later diving craft, the *bathyscaph*, does not need cables.

The bathyscaph was invented in 1948 by Auguste Piccard, a Swiss physicist. It contains large tanks of *ballast* (weights). When the ballast is released into the water, the bathyscaph becomes light enough to rise to the surface. In the bathyscaph, man has descended more than 35,000 feet—or over 6 miles—into the ocean. See BATHYSCAPH; BATHYSPHERE.

A bathyscaph has little ability to move in any direction except down or up. But research submarines called *submersibles* can move about readily. One type has mechanical hands that can pick up objects from the sea bottom. It carries three men and has large windows for underwater study. This submersible goes down about 4,000 feet. Future exploring submarines will probably be able to descend as far as 20,000 feet. Submersibles can stay underwater for a day or two at the most.

Recent Discoveries. Oceanographers constantly discover new and interesting things about the sea. For example, they have found that water in deep pockets at the bottom of the Red Sea is extremely hot and salty. This water has somehow seeped from the underlying rock and does not mix with the water above it.

Oceanographers have collected evidence suggesting that man may be able to obtain four or five times as much food from the sea as he does today. But today's yield of food from the ocean is less than 4 per cent of the world's needs. The expected increase will not be enough to keep up with the increase in population. Much of the additional food might consist of *krill*, a small shrimp found in the Antarctic Ocean. Krill might be made into oil and livestock feed.

Another discovery was based on evidence provided by samples of bottom mud and sand and by *seismic refractions* (echoes from powerful sounding machines). This evidence showed that the sea bottom has large crumpled-up places somewhat like giant cracks. Scientists do not know the causes of these *mid-ocean ridges*. The ridges run down through the middle of the Atlantic Ocean and across the Pacific Ocean. Their existence suggests that the continents may be slowly drifting apart (see CONTINENTAL DRIFT).

Southwest Research Institute

A Naval Experimental Manned Observatory (NEMO) gives scientists a wide view of the undersea environment. The plastic sphere can descend as deep as 600 feet.

498i

Scientific Sailors. The ocean can be studied in many ways, and the science of oceanography has many different specialties. *Physical* oceanographers deal with waves, currents, and tides. *Chemical* oceanographers study the chemicals found in seawater. *Marine biologists* study the animals and plants of the sea. *Marine geologists* are concerned with the rocks beneath the sea, the sand and mud on the ocean floor, and how shores are formed.

An oceanographer, whatever his special interest may be, is really a scientific sailor. He must go to sea for his information. Therefore, he should enjoy life on the ocean. He should not mind being at sea in bad weather because he must understand the ocean on both stormy days and calm days. The oceanographer works on research ships that are equipped with special instruments to study the sea and everything in it.

Some oceanographers work with nets and dredges to capture animals. Others take samples of seawater in special bottles. Still other oceanographers work with echo sounding, or measure temperatures and magnetism in the sea.

Work at sea is often difficult, and research ships cost a great deal of money to operate. The oceanographer must plan trips carefully so he can do as much as possible in the time allowed. After the oceanographer obtains the information he wants, he must study and analyze it. Often he uses instruments that continuously measure and record the information he seeks, such as water temperature. The instruments record such information in the form of marks or numbers on rolls of paper. This data must be carefully analyzed. Animals and plants that have been taken from the sea must be identified. Usually an oceanographer can get enough information in a day at sea to keep him busy for 9 or 10 days on shore.

There are about 500 oceanographers in the United States. Many more will be needed in the future to work on new research vessels. Oceanographers work at institutions devoted to the study of the sea, and on ships maintained by these organizations. Some teach university courses. Oceanographers also work for various agencies of the U.S. government. These agencies include the Oceanographic Office of the Department of the Navy, and the National Marine Fisheries Service of the National Oceanic and Atmospheric Administration.

Education and Training. A number of U.S. universities offer training and degrees in oceanography to students who have a bachelor's degree. A student must meet strict requirements before he can take oceanographic courses. He has little chance to begin actual study of the oceans during his first years at college.

Oceanographers are expected to have had courses in physics, chemistry, biology, and geology. They also should have had enough mathematics—including calculus—to understand the complicated relationships of moving waters in the sea. A thorough knowledge of English is essential so the oceanographer can tell others what he has studied and discovered. An oceanographer must also be able to read about the studies being conducted in such countries as Russia, Germany, and France. His training should include the study of foreign languages, especially Russian and German.

Mechanical ability is valuable in some fields of oceanography. Equipment may break down on research ships and need immediate repair. Sometimes an oceanographer may have to design a special instrument for an unexpected task. Drawing ability is useful for marine biologists because so many of the animals and plants taken from the sea must be illustrated for reports. Most large oceanographic institutions have staffs of mechanics and artists. Electronics technicians are always in demand to care for the many electronic instruments used in oceanography.   JOEL W. HEDGPETH

Chemical Oceanographers study the composition of seawater. This scientist, on a perch on the side of his ship, lowers a *Nansen bottle* into deep water. It will bring up a sample of seawater.

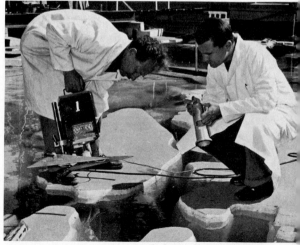

Physical Oceanographers deal with waves, currents, and tides. These men, working with a model built to study the tides, adjust an instrument that measures the rise and fall of the tides.

OCEAN / *Study Aids*

Questions

What would the climate on earth be like if there were no ocean? Why?

Why is it easier to swim in the ocean than in a lake?

What was the importance of the *Challenger* expedition?

What are some ways in which man uses the ocean?

How long might it take for one particle of water to find its way through all the oceans on the earth?

How much of the earth's surface does the ocean cover?

What is meant by the food cycle in the sea?

Which is the largest and deepest ocean?

How do animals attached to the sea-bottom get food?

How can a change in an ocean current affect life in the ocean?

OCEAN CURRENTS. See OCEAN (How the Ocean Moves).

OCEAN ISLAND is a raised reef island near the equator in the west-central Pacific Ocean. It has an area of 2 square miles and a population of about 2,700. It is part of the Gilbert and Ellice Islands Colony. For location, see PACIFIC ISLANDS (color map [Gilbert]).

The British discovered Ocean Island in 1804. They have mined its rich phosphate deposits for use in making fertilizer since 1890. This is the chief activity on the island.　　　　　EDWIN H. BRYAN, JR.

See also GILBERT AND ELLICE ISLANDS.

OCEAN LINER. See SHIP (Ocean Liners).

OCEANARIUM. See AQUARIUM; FISH (picture: Fish Flock for Food).

OCEANIA. See PACIFIC ISLANDS.

OCEANID. See NYMPH (myth).

Marine Biologists study the animals and plants that live in all parts of the ocean. This scientist carefully examines some tiny animals of the plankton group that he has put into a bottle.

The Ocelot prowls about the dense forest underbrush at night to hunt for food. It avoids bright sunlight by sleeping in dark caves or heavy thickets during the day.

OCEANOGRAPHIC OFFICE, UNITED STATES NAVAL, measures and charts the oceans. It distributes nautical and navigational charts, publications, and reports for both military and civilian use. It gathers oceanographic and hydrographic information in cooperation with other U.S. military and government agencies, and with other countries. It has technical direction of a fleet of ships fitted with scientific equipment to gather data about oceans.

The office has headquarters in Suitland, Md., and laboratories in Washington, D.C. The office was established in 1830 as the Depot of Charts and Instruments. Later, it became the U.S. Navy Hydrographic Office. It took its present name in 1962.   JOHN A. OUDINE

OCEANOGRAPHY. See OCEAN (Careers in Oceanography).

OCELLI. See INSECT (Sight).

OCELOT, *O suh laht*, is a medium-sized animal of the cat family. It is known as the *leopard cat* or *tiger cat* of America. It is 3½ to 4 feet long including the tail, which is 15 inches long. The ocelot stands between 16 to 18 inches high at the shoulder. It is one of the most beautiful of the four-footed animals. The ocelot lives in an area ranging from southeastern Arizona and southern Texas to Paraguay in South America. It spends most of its life on the ground, but often hunts in forest trees and is an agile climber. Its principal food is mice, wood rats, rabbits, snakes, lizards, birds, young deer, and monkeys. In the tropics a favorite food is agoutis. If taken young, the ocelot can be tamed and makes an excellent pet.

The ground tint of ocelot fur varies greatly in different animals, from reddish yellow to smoky pearl. Black spots vary in size from dots on the legs and feet to large shell-shaped spots on other parts of the body. The nose is pink, and the eyes are large and translucent.

Scientific Classification. The ocelot belongs to the cat family, *Felidae*. It is classified as genus *Felis*, species *F. pardalis*.   ERNEST S. BOOTH

OCHER, *O ker*, or **OCHRE**, is a mineral which is ground to a fine powder and used as a pigment with linseed oil or some other oil to form paint. Its color varies from pale yellow to brownish red. Some yellow ochers turn red when heated. Ocher consists of iron and lime, often mixed with clay from bogs where ocher forms. Georgia has large yellow ocher deposits.

OCHOA, *oh CHOH uh*, **SEVERO** (1905-   ), a Spanish-American biochemist, shared the 1959 Nobel prize in physiology and medicine. He and Arthur Kornberg won it for discovering ways to *synthesize* (put together) nucleic acids artificially. These acids play a basic role in life and reproduction. Born in Spain, Ochoa moved to the United States in 1940. He became professor of biochemistry at New York University in 1954, and made his discoveries there.   IRWIN H. HERSKOWITZ

OCHS, *ahks*, **ADOLPH SIMON** (1858-1935), rose from a job as a newsboy to become the publisher and guiding influence of *The New York Times*. He separated editorial comment from news in the *Times*, and presented news truthfully and free from prejudice. In 38 years, the daily circulation of the *Times* rose from 9,000 to 460,000. Ochs also founded the magazine *Current History*, and gave $500,000 toward publication of the *Dictionary of American Biography*.

Ochs began his career at 14 as an errand boy at the *Knoxville* (Tenn.) *Chronicle*. Later, he bought a half-interest in the *Chattanooga Times*, and made it one of the region's strongest papers. He became manager of *The New York Times* in 1896, and gained controlling interest in 1900. He was born in Cincinnati, Ohio.   I. W. COLE

OCMULGEE NATIONAL MONUMENT is in central Georgia. It contains the most important prehistoric Indian mounds discovered in the Southeast, including a restored council chamber. Ruins dating back to 8,000 B.C. have been discovered there. The 683.48-acre monument was established in 1936.   C. LANGDON WHITE

O'CONNELL, DANIEL (1775-1847), an Irish statesman, was called the *Liberator*. He formed the Catholic Association in 1823 to help Irish Roman Catholics gain political rights. Pressure from the association and the fact that O'Connell, as a Catholic, could not take his seat in Parliament when he was elected in 1828, brought about the Catholic Emancipation Act of 1829. He was arrested in 1843 for conspiracy in advocating a free Ireland. He was convicted, but the House of Lords released him. He was born in County Kerry. See also DUBLIN (picture).   JAMES L. GODFREY

O'CONNOR, FEARGUS. See CHARTISM.

O'CONNOR, FLANNERY (1925-1964), was an American author whose novels and stories are filled with terror and violence. Many of her characters are physically deformed or emotionally or spiritually disturbed. Some are obsessed with religion and the possibility of their own damnation or salvation. But Miss O'Connor's books also contain humor, irony, and satire.

Mary Flannery O'Connor was born in Savannah,

Ga. Her Southern heritage and her Roman Catholicism strongly influenced her writing. She suffered from poor health most of her life and could complete only a few works. They include two novels, *Wise Blood* (1952) and *The Violent Bear It Away* (1960). Her stories were collected in *A Good Man Is Hard to Find* (1955) and *Everything That Rises Must Converge*, which was published in 1965 after her death. *Mystery and Manners*, a selection of Miss O'Connor's essays and lectures on literature and writing, was published in 1969. JOHN B. VICKERY

OCOTILLO, OH *koh* TEEL *yoh*, is a shrub that grows in the deserts of Mexico and southwestern United States. Other names for it are *candlewood*, *coachwhip*, and *vine cactus*. The plant stands 6 to 25 feet tall, and has many spiny stems growing out like switches from a base. After the wet season, the stems grow leaves and bunches of scarlet flowers. But in the dry season, they stand bare as dry thorny sticks. Ocotillos make good hedges that are hard to pass through.

Scientific Classification. Ocotillos belong to the fouquieria family, *Fouquieriaceae*. They are genus *Fouquieria*, species *F. splendens*. EDMUND C. JAEGER

See also FLOWER (color picture: Flowers of the Desert).

Josef Muench

Ocotillo looks like a bunch of dry sticks thrust into the sand in dry periods. After a wet season, tiny green leaves cover the long spines, and brilliant red blossoms form at the tips.

OCRACOKE ISLAND is an isolated coastal island in Hyde County, North Carolina. It is 16 miles long and about 2 miles wide at its broadest part (see NORTH CAROLINA [political map]). According to tradition, the pirate Blackbeard hid there and was killed in a battle near there in 1718. Ocracoke's chief industry is fishing and shrimping. Before the Civil War, Ocracoke was an important port of entry. HUGH T. LEFLER

OCTAGON, AHK *tuh gahn*, is a plane figure that has eight angles and eight sides. The word comes from the Greek terms for *eight* and *angle*.

OCTAHEDRON is a term used in geometry to mean a solid formed by eight planes. An example would be two solid pyramids with a mutual square base.

OCTANE, AHK *tayn*, is a petroleum hydrocarbon. Octane refers to *n-octane* (normal octane), a colorless, flammable liquid. Its chemical formula is written $CH_3(CH_2)_6CH_3$, and it boils at 125° C. There are 18 octane isomers in the *paraffin* series of hydrocarbons. *Isomers* are compounds that have the same molecular formula, but different chemical or physical properties.

Isooctane, the most important octane isomer, is used as a motor fuel and to determine anti-knock qualities of gasoline. It boils at 99° C. and its chemical formula is written $(CH_3)_2CHCH_2C(CH_3)_3$. LEWIS F. HATCH

See also HYDROCARBON; OCTANE NUMBER.

OCTANE NUMBER is a rating that tells how much a motor fuel "knocks." "Knocking" occurs when the last of the fuel in an engine cylinder burns. It causes some loss in engine power. Two test fuels, normal heptane and isooctane, are blended together for tests to determine octane number. Normal heptane has an octane number of zero, and isooctane a value of 100. Gasolines are then compared with these test fuel blends to find one that produces the same "knock" as the test fuel. If a test blend has 85 per cent isooctane and 15 per cent normal heptane, the gasoline is given an octane number of 85. Most gasolines today have octane numbers of from 90 to 100. CLARENCE KARR, JR.

See also GASOLINE; TETRAETHYLLEAD.

OCTAVE, in music. See MUSIC (Terms).

OCTAVE, in poetry. See SONNET.

OCTAVIA (65?-9 B.C.) was the older sister of the Roman emperor Augustus. She was married to Mark Antony in 40 B.C. to seal a peace agreement that ended a civil war between Augustus and Antony. Octavia and Antony went to Athens and she bore him two daughters, Antonia the Elder and Antonia the Younger. Octavia also raised Antony's children by his former wife, Fulvia.

Antony treated Octavia badly. He had fallen in love with Cleopatra, queen of Egypt, before he married Octavia. About 36 B.C., Antony divorced Octavia and married Cleopatra. Octavia behaved with dignity throughout the civil wars which followed between Antony and Augustus, and won great respect as a virtuous Roman woman. MARY FRANCIS GYLES

See also ANTONY, MARK; AUGUSTUS; CLEOPATRA.

OCTAVIAN, or OCTAVIANUS. See AUGUSTUS.

OCTAVO. See BOOK (Parts of a Book).

OCTILLION, *ahk* TILL *yun*. In France and the United States, an octillion is 1 followed by 27 zeros. In Great Britain, it is 1 with 48 zeros. See also DECIMAL NUMERAL SYSTEM (Larger Numbers).

OCTOBER

OCTOBER is the tenth month of the year. Its name comes from the Latin word for *eight*. October was the eighth month in the Roman calendar. The Roman Senate tried to name the month "Antoninus" after a Roman emperor, "Faustinus" after his wife, and "Tacitus" after a Roman historian. But the people continued to call it October. From the time of Julius Caesar, October has had 31 days.

In the North Temperate Zone, the first frost usually occurs in October. Farmers must finish harvesting most crops, but the cold weather does not come to stay. Days of warm, hazy sunshine come later, with a fresh autumn tang. They inspired poets to sing the praises of October and Indian summer. Leaves change to brilliant crimson, russet, and gold. Wild asters, goldenrod, and fringed gentians bloom at this time. The frost kills many insects, and most birds have left for the South, but sparrows are fond of October. They are seedeaters, and the fields and meadows are rich with seeds. Farmers should welcome sparrows at this time, because the birds eat millions of weed seeds that could otherwise damage the next crop.

Activities. Farmers bring in the fall crops and store them or ship them to market. A few fruits, such as apples and grapes, are still on trees and vines in some areas. Many apples are harvested at the end of October. The excitement of the football season dominates the sports scene, even though the World Series steals some of the spotlight early in the month. Hockey teams also begin their schedules in October.

Special Days. On the second Monday in October, schools and various organizations celebrate Columbus

IMPORTANT OCTOBER EVENTS

1 James Lawrence, the American naval officer who cried "Don't give up the ship!," born 1781.
—William E. Boeing, airplane manufacturer, born 1881.
—First "Model T" Ford put on the market, 1908.
—International Atomic Energy Agency's first general conference opened, Vienna, 1957.
2 Mohandas Gandhi, Indian political leader, born 1869.
—Cordell Hull, American statesman, born 1871.
—First Pan American conference, Washington, 1889.
3 George Bancroft, American historian, born 1800.
—William C. Gorgas, American physician, born 1854.
—Eleonora Duse, Italian actress, born 1859.
4 Rutherford B. Hayes, 19th President of the United States, born at Delaware, Ohio, 1822.

Rutherford B. Hayes

Chester A. Arthur

—Painter Jean François Millet born 1814.
—Michael Pupin, Serbian-American physicist and inventor, born 1858.
—Artist Frederic Remington born 1861.
—Russia launched first artificial satellite, 1957.
5 Gregorian calendar introduced, 1582.
—Denis Diderot, French author, born 1713.
—Chester A. Arthur, 21st President of the United States, born in Fairfield, Vt., 1830.
—Physician Edward L. Trudeau born 1848.
—Joshua Logan, American playwright, born 1908.
—President Harry S. Truman made the first presidential telecast address from the White House, 1947.
6 Jenny Lind, Swedish singer, born 1820.
—George Westinghouse, American inventor, born 1846.
—Le Corbusier, Swiss-born architect, born 1887.
—Austro-German forces invaded Serbia, 1915.
7 First double-decked steamboat, the *Washington*, arrived at New Orleans, 1816.
—James Whitcomb Riley, Hoosier poet, born 1849.
8 John M. Hay, American statesman, born 1838.
—Chicago fire began, and burned for about 30 hours, 1871.
—Edward Rickenbacker, American air ace, born 1890.
9 Camille Saint-Saëns, French composer, born 1835.
—Edward William Bok, noted American journalist, born 1863.

—First telephone conversation using commercial lines between moving automobile and airplane, 1947.
10 Henry Cavendish, English scientist, born 1731.
—Giuseppe Verdi, Italian opera composer, born 1813.
—United States Naval Academy opened at Annapolis, Md., 1845.
—Norwegian explorer and statesman Fridtjof Nansen born 1861.
11 Theodore Thomas, American conductor, born 1835.
—Eleanor Roosevelt born 1884.
—François Mauriac, French novelist, born 1885.
12 Columbus discovered America, 1492.
—Helena Modjeska, Polish actress, born 1840.
—George W. Cable, American author, born 1844.
—Ralph Vaughan Williams, British composer, born 1872.
13 White House cornerstone laid, 1792.
—Rudolf Virchow, German scientist, born 1821.
14 William the Conqueror won the Battle of Hastings, assuring the conquest of England, 1066.
—William Penn, founder of Pennsylvania, born 1644.
—Eamon de Valera, president of the Irish Republic, born 1882.
—Dwight D. Eisenhower, 34th President of the United States, born at Denison, Tex., 1890.
—E. E. Cummings, American poet, born 1894.
—Queen Elizabeth II of England opened Parliament of Canada, 1957.
15 Virgil, Roman poet, born 70 B.C.
—J. F. Pilâtre de Rozier became first person to make an ascent in a captive balloon, 1783.
—Helen Hunt Jackson, American novelist, born 1830.
—Philosopher Friedrich Nietzsche born 1844.
—Clayton Anti-Trust Act became law, 1914.
16 Dictionary editor Noah Webster born 1758.
—Oscar Wilde, Irish dramatist, born 1854.

Dwight D. Eisenhower

Day. This holiday honors the discovery of America by Christopher Columbus on Oct. 12, 1492. In Canada, Thanksgiving Day is celebrated on the second Monday of the month. In the United States, Veterans Day is celebrated on the fourth Monday of October. On the evening of Halloween, the last day of October, children disguise themselves with masks and costumes and go from door to door asking for a treat.

October Symbols. The calendula is the special flower for October. The birthstones for this month are the opal and the tourmaline. GRACE HUMPHREY

Quotations

October turned my maple's leaves to gold;
The most are gone now; here and there one lingers;
Soon these will slip from out the twig's weak hold,
Like coins between a dying miser's fingers.
Thomas Bailey Aldrich

October gave a party;
The leaves by hundreds came;
The ashes, oaks, and maples,
And those of every name.
George Cooper

There is something in October sets
  the gipsy blood astir;
We must rise and follow her,
When from every hill of flame
She calls and calls each vagabond
  by name.
Bliss Carman

Related Articles in WORLD BOOK include:

Autumn	Columbus Day	Indian Summer
Calendar	Cosmos	Opal
Calendula	Halloween	Tourmaline

--- **IMPORTANT OCTOBER EVENTS** ---

16 John Brown and his men seized the United States arsenal at Harpers Ferry, Va., 1859.
—Eugene O'Neill, American playwright and Nobel prizewinner, born 1888.
17 British general John Burgoyne surrendered his army at Saratoga, 1777.
18 Henri Bergson, French philosopher and Nobel prizewinner, born 1859.
—The United States flag was formally raised over Alaska, 1867.

—James Truslow Adams, American historian, born 1878.
19 First general court in New England held, Boston, 1630.
—British troops under Cornwallis surrendered at Yorktown, 1781.
—Thomas Edison began first successful demonstration of his electric light, 1879.
20 Architect Sir Christopher Wren born 1632.
—John Dewey, American philosopher, born 1859.
21 Magellan entered strait that bears his name, 1520.
—Hokusai, Japanese artist, born 1760.
—Samuel Taylor Coleridge, English poet, born 1772.

—U.S.S. *Constitution*, or "Old Ironsides," launched, 1797.
—British Admiral Nelson was killed defeating the French and Spanish at Trafalgar, 1805.
—Alfred Nobel, Swedish philanthropist and founder of the Nobel Prize, born 1833.
22 Franz Liszt, Hungarian composer, born 1811.
—Sam Houston inaugurated as first president of the Republic of Texas, 1836.
23 British began offensive at El Alamein, 1942.
—Battle for Leyte Gulf began, 1944.
24 Anton van Leeuwenhoek, Dutch microscopist and naturalist, born 1632.
—First transcontinental telegram sent, 1861.
—United Nations formally established when necessary number of members ratified charter, 1945.
25 Henry V of England defeated French at Agincourt in Hundred Years' War, 1415.
—Thomas B. Macaulay, English author and historian, born 1800.

25 "Waltz King" Johann Strauss, Jr., born 1825.
—Georges Bizet, French composer, born 1838.
—Painter Pablo Picasso born 1881.
—Richard E. Byrd, American explorer of the North and South poles, born 1888.
26 Helmuth von Moltke, Prussian general, born 1800.
—Erie Canal opened to traffic, 1825.
27 Niccolò Paganini, Italian violinist, born 1782.
—The *Federalist* papers began appearing in New York *Independent Journal*, 1787.
—Theodore Roosevelt, 26th President of the United States, born in New York City, 1858.
—Captain James Cook, English explorer, born 1728.
28 Cuba discovered by Christopher Columbus, 1492.
—Harvard College (now a university) founded, 1636.
—Statue of Liberty dedicated, 1886.
—American composer Howard Hanson born 1896.
—Jonas Salk, American developer of a polio vaccine, born 1914.
29 James Boswell, Scottish biographer of Samuel Johnson, born 1740.
—Cartoonist Bill Mauldin born 1921.
—Blackest day in stock market history, 1929.
30 John Adams, second President of the United States, born in Braintree (now Quincy), Mass., 1735.
—Benito Mussolini, founder of fascism, became premier of Italy, 1922.
31 Martin Luther nailed his 95 theses to the door of a church at Wittenberg, 1517.
—Jan Vermeer, Dutch painter, born 1632.
—King's College (now Columbia University) founded, 1754.
—Nevada became the 36th state, 1864.
—Sir Hubert Wilkins, Australian explorer and aviator, born 1888.

Theodore Roosevelt

John Adams

Douglas P. Wilson

Many Octopuses Find Their Prey on the Ocean Bottom.

OCTOPUS is a sea animal with a soft body and eight arms called *tentacles*. The word *octopus* comes from two Greek words that mean *eight feet*. An octopus's tentacles are called *arms* because the animal uses them to capture its food—crabs, lobsters, and shellfish.

Some people call octopuses *devilfish*, probably because of the animal's frightening appearance. An octopus has large, shiny eyes, and strong, hard jaws that come to a point like a bird's bill. The octopus uses its jaws to tear apart the animals it eats. Some kinds of octopuses inject a poison that paralyzes their prey.

Most scientists believe that octopuses do not attack people. But a person may go into the underwater caves or among the rocks where octopuses live, and be caught by the animal's tentacles. The tentacles do not squeeze the person, but pull him toward the poisoned jaws. Bites from even a small octopus can be dangerous. Some persons have died from octopus bites.

There are about 50 kinds of octopuses, and most are only about as big as a man's fist. The largest ones may measure 28 feet from the tip of one tentacle to the tip of another on the other side of the body.

R. Tucker Abbott, the contributor of this article, holds the du Pont Chair of Malacology at the Delaware Museum of Natural History, and is the author of American Seashells *and* Sea Shells of the World.

Octopuses live chiefly in the China and Mediterranean seas, and along the coasts of Hawaii, North America, and the West Indies. Many people in these regions eat octopus meat.

Octopuses belong to a large group of shellfish called *mollusks*. This group includes clams, oysters, and snails.

BODY OF AN OCTOPUS

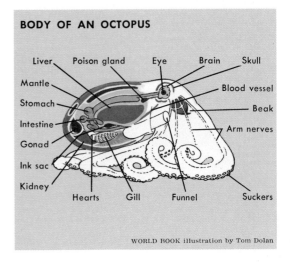

Liver · Poison gland · Eye · Brain · Skull · Mantle · Stomach · Intestine · Gonad · Ink sac · Kidney · Hearts · Gill · Funnel · Suckers · Blood vessel · Beak · Arm nerves

WORLD BOOK illustration by Tom Dolan

504

Like squid and cuttlefish, octopuses are mollusks that have no outside shells. See MOLLUSK.

An octopus has no bones, and no inside shell as squid and cuttlefish do. A tough protective wrapper called a *mantle* covers the body and gives it shape. The tentacles are joined to the body and to one another by a web of tissue at their bases. Rows of round muscles on the underside of each tentacle act much like suction cups. These suckers can fasten tightly to any object, and may hold on even if the tentacle is cut off. If an octopus loses a tentacle, a new one grows in its place.

An octopus has two eyes and sees well. It has three hearts that pump blood through its body. The animal breathes by means of gills, somewhat as fish do. An octopus swims by drawing water into its body. Then the animal squeezes the water out through its *siphon,* a funnel-shaped opening under the head. The force of the expelled water moves the animal forward. The octopus can also squirt a black fluid from the siphon. This fluid forms a dark cloud that hides the animal so it can escape from sharks, whales, men, and other enemies.

A female octopus lays a cluster of as many as 180,000 nearly transparent eggs. The eggs are attached to rocks and hatch in about two months. The female tends the eggs and does not eat during this period. The young begin to find their own food as soon as they hatch.

Scientific Classification. Octopuses are members of the phylum *Mollusca,* and belong to the class *Cephalopoda.* They make up the genus *Octopus.*   R. TUCKER ABBOTT

See also CUTTLEFISH; MOLLUSK; NAUTILUS; SQUID.

OCULAR. See MICROSCOPE; TELESCOPE.

OCULIST is a physician who treats eye disorders and diseases. See OPHTHALMOLOGY.

ODD FELLOWS, INDEPENDENT ORDER OF, is one of the largest fraternal and benevolent orders in the United States. The order was founded in England. The date of its founding is not known, but Odd Fellows' groups probably existed in the early 1700's. The members founded a system of benefits and helped one another in time of misfortune. Branches called *lodges* grew up in the various English cities, but each branch refused to admit the superior rank of any other. Adjustments were finally made, and in 1814 the Manchester Unity of the Independent Order of Odd Fellows was organized. It has branches in various countries but has no present connection with the order in the United States.

The American Order. In 1819, the Washington Lodge of Odd Fellows was organized in Baltimore. The next year, Washington Lodge became a subordinate lodge in the Manchester Unity. Other American lodges were established later and assumed a like position.

But in 1843 the American lodges separated themselves from the parent order in England. The United States grand lodge became the head of the order in America and reserved for itself the right to found new lodges in Europe. The Canadian branch operated under a separate charter until 1852. In that year the society in Canada was merged with the grand lodge of the United States. The Order of Odd Fellows in the United States has a membership of 1,300,000.

Purpose and Organization. The chief purpose of the Order of Odd Fellows is to give aid, assistance, and comfort to its members and their families. It is a secret society and has its own system of rites and passwords. The three links in its symbol represent friendship, love, and truth. The skull and crossbones speak of mortality, and the single eye represents the all-knowingness of God.

A local lodge can confer three degrees of membership upon an Odd Fellow. When a member has reached the highest of these three grades he is ready for membership in an encampment. The encampment also has three degrees of membership, the Patriarchal, the Golden Rule, and the Royal Purple. The Patriarchal is an English degree. Since 1884, there has also been a military or uniformed degree called the Patriarch Militant.

The Rebekah lodges in Odd Fellows are chiefly for women, although some men belong. Rebekah assemblies were organized in 1851 and have more than 1 million members. Headquarters are at 16 W. Chase St., Baltimore, Md. 21201.

ODE, *ohd,* a poem of moderate length, usually expresses exalted praise. Greek dramatists wrote *choral odes* that had three parts. Two parts, a *strophe* and an *antistrophe,* had identical meter. The third part, called an *epode,* had a contrasting meter. Pindar, of ancient Greece, wrote odes in praise of athletic heroes. He used the strophic form, which came to be called *Pindaric* (see PINDAR). Horace, of ancient Rome, wrote odes made up of uniform stanzas, called *stanzaic* form.

English poetry, from the time of Ben Jonson, included a variety of Pindaric odes, stanzaic odes, and *irregular* odes, or those with no particular stanza structure. John Dryden wrote two irregular odes in praise of St. Cecilia. "Ode to Evening," by William Collins, is a notable stanzaic ode. The great irregular and stanzaic odes of the 1800's include William Wordsworth's "Ode: Intimations of Immortality," Percy Bysshe Shelley's "Ode to the West Wind," John Keats' "Ode on a Grecian Urn," and Alfred, Lord Tennyson's "Ode on the Death of the Duke of Wellington." CHARLES W. COOPER

O'DELL, SCOTT (1903-   ), an American author, became known for his historical novels about southern California. He won the Newbery medal in 1961 for *Island of the Blue Dolphins,* his first novel for children. His other novels include *Woman of Spain* (1934) and *Hill of the Hawk* (1947). He was born in Los Angeles.

ODELSTING. See NORWAY (Parliament).

ODENSE, *OH thun suh* (pop. 107,434; alt. 48 ft.), is a seaport on Fyn island in Denmark. It is three miles from Odense fiord. For location, see DENMARK (color map). A canal links the city and the fiord. Odense has important shipyards. Its factories produce machinery, glass, and textiles. Odense was the birthplace of the storyteller Hans Christian Andersen. During World War II, it was a center of Allied resistance against the Germans.   JENS NYHOLM

ODER. See FREYJA.

ODER RIVER is an important waterway of central Europe. It is 550 miles long and drains more than 43,000 square miles, which is about the area of Tennessee.

The Oder rises in the Carpathian Mountains of Czechoslovakia. It then flows northward across western Poland where it joins the Neisse River to form the boundary between Poland and East Germany. It empties into the Baltic Sea by way of the Stettin Lagoon (see POLAND [color map]). Ocean-going vessels can sail into the port of Stettin, on the Polish side of the inlet. Other major cities on the Oder River include Frankfurt in East Germany, and Opole (Oppeln) and Wrocław (Breslau) in Poland.

The Oder's main tributary is the Warta (Warthe). It links the Oder with the Vistula River in Poland by means of the Notéc (Netze) River and a canal.

Because the Oder system provides many nations with an outlet to the sea, the navigable sections were put under international control by the Treaty of Versailles. After World War II, the lower part of the Oder, from about Frankfurt to Stettin, became the boundary between East Germany and Poland. East Germany officially recognized this boundary, called the *Oder-Neisse Line*, in 1950. West Germany opposed the boundary until 1970 and then signed a treaty with Russia confirming the boundary. M. KAMIL DZIEWANOWSKI

ODESSA, Tex. (pop. 78,380; met. area 91,805; alt. 2,890 ft.), is an important petroleum refining center. The city is also the world's largest oil-field service and supply center. It lies in western Texas. The seat of Ector County, Odessa was founded in 1881 and incorporated as a city in 1927. It has a council-manager government. For location, see TEXAS (political map). H. BAILEY CARROLL

ODESSA, oh DES uh (pop. 776,000; alt. 35 ft.), is a seaport in Russia. It lies on the southwestern coast of the Ukraine, near the Romanian border. Odessa is on the Black Sea, 32 miles southwest of the mouth of the Dnepr River (see RUSSIA [political map]).

The harbor at Odessa is divided into five ports. One of these ports is for petroleum trade. Airplane service links Moscow, Kharkov, and Odessa. Odessa is one of the Ukraine's industrial centers. It is also an important transfer point for rail and ocean transportation. Its refineries produce large amounts of petroleum products, and its factories make machinery, automobiles, airplanes, and motion-picture equipment.

The Greeks first settled Odessa around 800 B.C. They named it *Odessos*, or *Ordyssos*. They were followed by the Tartars in the 1200's, the Lithuanians in the 1400's, and the Turks in the 1500's. Russia annexed the city in the 1700's. The Germans captured Odessa in 1941. Russian troops recaptured it later. THEODORE SHABAD

ODETS, CLIFFORD (1906-1963), an American dramatist, is best known for his plays of social conflict written during the 1930's. His most successful works were presented by the famous Group Theatre.

Odets' one-act play *Waiting for Lefty* (1935) is about a taxi drivers' strike. It ranks among the most important of the many plays written in the 1930's that deal with the struggle of the working class. Odets' *Awake and Sing!* (1935) tells the story of a poor Jewish family in the Bronx during the Depression. It is less propagandistic than *Waiting for Lefty*, and its style has been compared to the style in Anton Chekhov's plays. Odets also wrote *Paradise Lost* (1935), *Golden Boy* (1937), *The Big Knife* (1948), and *The Country Girl* (1950).

Odets was born in Philadelphia. He helped form the Group Theatre in 1931. He worked as a film scriptwriter from 1936 until shortly before his death. MARDI VALGEMAE

ODIN, OH din, was the king of the gods in Norse mythology. He held court in Asgard, in the hall named Valhalla, where he gathered all the heroes who had died in battle. He was thought of as an old, one-eyed man, wisest of all the gods. On each shoulder he had a raven which he sent out daily to bring back news.

The worship of Odin came to Scandinavia from Germany, where he was known as *Wotan*. The ancient Anglo-Saxons called him *Woden*. From this name we get *Wednesday* (*Woden's Day*). Thor was the god of the common people. But Odin seems to have been worshiped by viking chieftains. He was above all a god of war, and human sacrifices were made to him. He could be cunning and cruel, but in the final battle of Ragnarok he heroically led the gods against the evil giants that sought to destroy him. EINAR HAUGEN

See also MYTHOLOGY; THOR; VALHALLA.

ODOACER, oh doh AY ser (A.D. 434?-493), was the Germanic leader who overthrew the last emperor of Rome in the West, ending the West Roman Empire.

Odoacer was probably born near the Danube River in what is now Germany. He joined the West Roman army and became a leader of barbarian troops serving the Romans. In 476, when the Roman government refused to give his troops land for settlement, Odoacer led them in a revolt. He deposed the West Roman emperor, Romulus Augustulus, and became the first barbarian king of Italy. Historians consider this event the end of the West Roman Empire. But for years, barbarian generals had been its real rulers. The emperors were symbolic rulers.

Odoacer ruled independently, although he pretended to serve Zeno, the East Roman emperor. Zeno never recognized Odoacer as ruler of Italy. In 489, Zeno sent the Ostrogoth king Theodoric to attack Odoacer. Odoacer retreated to Ravenna, where he surrendered in 493 and was executed (see THEODORIC). WILLIAM G. SINNIGEN

ODOMETER. See SPEEDOMETER.

ODONATA is an order of insects made up of damsel flies and dragonflies. These insects are strong, graceful fliers. The adults spend little time on the ground. They cannot walk, but they use their legs to catch prey in the air. See also DRAGONFLY; INSECT (table).

ODONTOLITE. See TURQUOISE.

ODOR. See SMELL.

ODYSSEUS. See ULYSSES.

Odets' Awake and Sing! is a serious and realistic study of a poor Jewish family in New York City during the Depression.

New York Public Library

ODYSSEY, *AHD ih see,* an epic poem, is perhaps the most influential and most popular work in ancient Greek literature. The *Odyssey* ranks among the greatest adventure stories in literature. It became a model for many later adventure stories.

According to tradition, the *Odyssey* was composed by the Greek poet Homer, probably in the 700's B.C. The central character is Odysseus (Ulysses in Latin), the king of Ithaca. The poem describes Odysseus' adventures as he tries to return home after fighting for Greece against the city of Troy in the Trojan War. The author wrote about this war in the *Iliad,* another great epic poem. For information on the background and authorship of the *Odyssey* and the *Iliad,* see HOMER.

The *Odyssey* consists of 24 *books* (sections). The story takes place during a period of about 10 years in the 1100's B.C. The tale begins after much of the action has already occurred. This device of starting a story in the middle and returning to the start is called *in medias res.* Many later writers used it.

The *Odyssey* Begins on the island of Ogygia, where Odysseus has been the prisoner of the sea nymph Calypso for seven years. At a council of the gods on Mount Olympus, Zeus decides the time has come for Odysseus to return to his wife, Penelope, in Ithaca.

The scene then changes to Odysseus' palace in Ithaca, where a group of unruly young noblemen has settled. The noblemen want Penelope to assume that her husband is dead. They demand that she marry one of them and thus choose a new king of Ithaca. Odysseus' son, Telemachus, resents the noblemen. The goddess Athena suggests that he go on a journey to seek news of his father. Telemachus agrees and leaves Ithaca, and his travels become part of the story.

The tale next returns to Odysseus' adventures. The god Hermes makes Calypso release Odysseus. Odysseus sails away on a raft, but the sea god Poseidon causes a storm and he is shipwrecked on the island of the Phaeacians. Nausicaa, the beautiful daughter of the Phaeacian king, discovers him.

Odysseus Describes His Wanderings since the Trojan War while being entertained by the Phaeacians. He tells of his visit to the land of the lotus-eaters, whose magic food makes people forget their homeland. Some of Odysseus' men who ate the food want to stay with the lotus-eaters, but Odysseus forced them to leave with him. Odysseus and his men then sailed to an island where they were captured by Polyphemus, a one-eyed giant called a *Cyclops.* They escaped, but their ship was blown off course. The ship finally landed on the island of the enchantress Circe. Circe changed Odysseus' men into pigs and made Odysseus her lover. She told Odysseus that to get home, he must visit the underworld to consult the prophet Teiresias. In the underworld, Odysseus saw the ghosts of his mother and of Trojan War heroes. He also witnessed the punishment of sinners.

Teiresias told Odysseus the route home and Circe told him how to sail past the sea monsters Scylla and Charybdis. Circe also warned him about the Sirens, sea nymphs who use their beautiful singing to lure sailors to death on a magic island. Odysseus' ship sailed past these dangers and seemed ready to reach Ithaca without further trouble. But some of Odysseus' men stole and ate the sacred cattle of the sun on the island of Trinacia. As punishment, the ship was de-

Painting (400's B.C.) on a Greek vase by an unknown artist; the British Museum, London

Odysseus Encountered the Sirens during his voyage home. The Sirens, part bird and part woman, lured seamen to their death with beautiful singing. Odysseus filled his sailors' ears with wax but had himself tied to the mast so he could safely enjoy the singing.

stroyed by a thunderbolt and Odysseus' men drowned. Odysseus made his way to Calypso's island—where the story began.

Odysseus Returns Home. After Odysseus finishes his story, the Phaeacians take him to a deserted shore in Ithaca. There, Athena tells him about the noblemen in his palace and advises him to return home in disguise for his own safety.

Odysseus goes to his palace disguised as a beggar. The noblemen are participating in an archery contest, with the winner to marry Penelope. Odysseus wins the contest, kills the noblemen, and is reunited with Penelope.

The *Odyssey* as Literature. The *Odyssey* is a skillfully written adventure story. It combines realistic accounts of life in ancient Greece and elements of historical events with fairy tales about imaginary lands.

The work also contains skillful characterization. Odysseus represents the model of a man of courage and determination. In spite of many setbacks, he never abandons his goal of returning home. But he has other human traits that keep him from being only a symbol. He enjoys life, even while struggling to get home. He is restless, clever, and even tricky and is able to invent lies easily. In fact, some later Greek dramatists made Odysseus a symbol of deceit. Penelope stands for the faithful, loving wife. Telemachus symbolizes the youth who matures by facing a difficult challenge. The travels of Odysseus and Telemachus may represent man's journey through life and his search for self-fulfillment and self-knowledge.　　　　GEORGE KENNEDY

OECD stands for Organization for Economic Cooperation and Development. See EUROPE (Toward European Unity); MARSHALL PLAN.

OEDIPUS, *ED ih pus,* was an unfortunate king of Thebes in Greek mythology. He unknowingly killed his father and married his mother. His father, King Laius of Thebes, received an *oracle* (message) from Apollo which said that a son born to his wife Jocasta would kill him. When Jocasta gave birth to a son, Laius left the baby on a mountainside. But a shepherd found the child and carried him to King Polybus of Corinth. Polybus adopted the boy as his own and named him Oedipus *(swell foot)* because his feet were

From a painting by J. A. D. Ingres, courtesy of Bettmann Archive
Oedipus Solved the Riddle of the Terrible Sphinx.

swollen. Laius had pierced his feet with a spike.

Oedipus grew up in Corinth. One day a companion said that he was not really Polybus' son. Oedipus went to Delphi to find out the truth. Apollo told him not to go back to his own land because he would kill his father and marry his mother. Oedipus thought that Polybus was his father, and that Apollo meant that he should not return to Corinth. So he set out for Thebes.

Oedipus met a man who pushed him off the road. Not knowing that the man was Laius, his father, Oedipus killed him in anger. He found Thebes plagued by the Sphinx, a lioness with a woman's head (see SPHINX). She killed everyone who could not answer her riddle: "What has one voice and yet becomes four-footed and two-footed and three-footed?" Oedipus answered: "Man, who crawls on all fours as a baby, walks on two legs during his lifetime, and needs a cane in old age." The Sphinx killed herself after her riddle was solved.

Oedipus was made king because he had freed Thebes from the Sphinx. He married Jocasta, the widow of King Laius. Oedipus did not find out for many years that he had killed his father and married his mother. A plague came upon Thebes. An oracle said that it would not stop until the murderer of Laius had been driven from Thebes. Oedipus looked for the murderer, and found that he was the man. Horrified, he blinded himself, and Jocasta hanged herself. Oedipus was banished from Thebes. He died at Colonus, near Athens. Sophocles' plays, *Oedipus Tyrannus* and *Oedipus at Colonus*, tell part of the story.   JOSEPH FONTENROSE

OEDIPUS COMPLEX, in psychiatry, is the strong attachment of a child to a parent of the opposite sex. The complex is usually accompanied by dislike for the other parent. The term comes from Oedipus, a hero in Greek mythology, who killed his father and married his mother. Sigmund Freud first used the term. See also OEDIPUS; FREUD, SIGMUND.

OENONE. See PARIS (in legend).

OERSTED is a unit used to measure the intensity, or strength, of a magnetic field in a vacuum. The number of oersteds of a magnetic field equals the number of magnetic lines of force per square centimeter in the field. The unit was named after Hans Christian Oersted, a Danish physicist who pioneered in the study of electromagnetism. The oersted is not as widely used today as another unit called the *weber* (see WEBER).

OERSTED, *UR steth,* **HANS CHRISTIAN** (1777-1851), a Danish physicist and chemist, laid the foundation for the science of electromagnetism (see ELECTROMAGNETISM). In 1819, he noticed that the needle of a compass wavered every time he put it near a wire carrying a current. He had discovered that every conductor carrying an electric current is surrounded by a magnetic field. Oersted is also credited with producing the first aluminum, in 1825 (see ALUMINUM [The First Aluminum]). He wrote *Spirit of Nature* (1850). Oersted was born at the town of Rudkøbing, on the island of Langeland, Denmark.   R. T. ELLICKSON

OFFENBACH, *OHF un bahk,* **JACQUES** (1819-1880), a Franco-German composer, won fame as a manager, director, and composer of 90 French operettas, between 1855 and 1880. Few of the operettas have survived. He is remembered best for his opera, the *Tales of Hoffmann* (see OPERA [Tales of Hoffmann]). He worked on this opera for many years, but died before it was produced. Ernest Guiraud completed it for performance in 1881. His other works include *Orpheus in the Underworld* (1858), *La Belle Hélène* (1865), *La Vie Parisienne* (1866), and *La Grande Duchesse de Gérolstein* (1867).

Chicago Historical Society
Jacques Offenbach

He was born JAKOB OFFENBACH, the son of a synagogue cantor, in Cologne, Germany. He began to study the violoncello at the Paris Conservatory when he was 14, and was shortly playing in the orchestra at the Opéra Comique. He became conductor at the Comédie Française in 1850. He opened his own theater in 1855. Offenbach took his company to London in 1857, and to the United States in 1877.   THEODORE M. FINNEY

OFFICE OF DEFENSE MOBILIZATION (ODM). See NATIONAL DEFENSE (History).

OFFICE OF EDUCATION. See EDUCATION, OFFICE OF.

OFFICE OF PRICE ADMINISTRATION. See PRICE CONTROL.

OFFICE WORK

Skilled Office Workers Are Essential to the Smooth Operation of Modern Industry.

OFFICE WORK. Business firms employ many types of office clerical workers, ranging from office boys to private secretaries. Among other things, office work involves writing and answering letters, keeping records, making out reports, and operating office machines. It does not include selling, buying, or management work. The office workers in large companies may have highly specialized jobs. But small firms often combine several office jobs into one. For example, the work of a ledger clerk may be done by a bookkeeper along with his other duties, and the work of a mail clerk may be done along with her other work by a stenographer.

About 10,000,000 persons in the United States have office clerical jobs. About two-thirds of them are women and about one-third are men. These employees do the detailed work of the many thousands of offices in business and industry. The financial success of a company often may depend on even the most routine job. For example, a slight error in arithmetic made by a bookkeeper might cause a loss of several thousand dollars. A letter misplaced by a file clerk might mean the loss of an important customer.

Many office workers use their jobs as stepping stones to more responsible and better-paying positions in the fields of buying, selling, and management. Persons with years of experience in office work may qualify for such positions as office manager, credit manager, or purchasing agent. Office employees are often called "white-collar workers," because the men usually wear white shirts and ties.

Kinds of Office Workers

The largest group of office workers includes secretaries, stenographers, and typists. Bookkeepers and accountants make up the second largest number. The third largest group includes clerks who perform such jobs as filing, billing, and keeping records. The increasing use of business machines in big offices has opened many jobs for persons trained to use these machines.

Office work varies greatly among different companies. For example, mail-order companies employ more clerks to keep track of orders, shipments, and billing than do manufacturing firms. Insurance companies have more typists and machine operators than do manufacturers.

Typists. Skilled typists who work accurately at high speed are always in demand. Almost all kinds of companies employ typists. These workers may address envelopes, copy letters and manuscripts, or type reports and records. Typists also cut stencils and prepare master copies for duplicating machines. A beginning typist should be able to type at least 50 words a minute accurately. Constant practice and drill should increase this speed to 70 to 100 words a minute. In most offices, typists do not have to know shorthand.

Typists use either standard or electric typewriters. An electric typewriter works no faster than a regular typewriter, because speed depends on the skill of the typist. But the electric typewriter is less tiring, because the typist uses less effort in operating it.

Stenographers form an important link in business communication. They take notes in shorthand, and type letters or reports from these notes (see SHORTHAND). Sometimes an executive dictates letters to a dictating machine. The stenographer then types from the records made on the machine. A stenographer also may use a stenotype machine to take dictation.

A stenographer usually has much more responsibility than a typist. For example, she needs a thorough knowledge of English grammar, punctuation, and spelling in order to type accurately and rapidly the letters dictated to her. She also must be familiar with the special business terms used by her employer so she can take notes and write letters quickly and easily. Stenographers often advance to more responsible secretarial positions.

Stenographers usually work for only one or two persons. Some large companies and government agencies place all of the stenographers in a stenographic *pool* (group), where a supervisor assigns the stenographers various tasks.

Some stenographers work in special fields, such as law or medicine. They need additional training in the methods and terms used in such fields.

Secretaries are usually stenographers who have been promoted to more responsible jobs. They sometimes take dictation in shorthand at a rate of 80 words or more a minute. A stenographer usually performs only the duties that have been directly assigned to her. But a secretary often does work that requires more initiative, responsibility, and executive ability. For example, she may make appointments, answer telephone calls, handle important mail, and answer routine correspondence. Secretaries usually work closely with their employers. They relieve their superiors of much detailed office work, and perform many of their duties when they are away.

Secretaries work for business executives, government officials, and professional persons. Some top secretaries serve as confidential assistants to their employers. An increasing number of young men with secretarial training are being hired for these positions. Secretarial work gives them a chance to learn all the details of a business, and sometimes leads to executive jobs.

Bookkeepers keep detailed records of business transactions (see BOOKKEEPING). They prepare balance sheets and financial reports at regular times of the year. Many bookkeepers who take professional training advance to jobs as accountants (see ACCOUNTING).

Clerks handle most routine office jobs.

Junior Clerks begin with minor duties that require no special training. Their exact duties vary from company to company. A clerk who becomes familiar with a company's methods, and has proved his or her ability, may advance to a position with more responsibility and a higher salary. A clerk can rise to department supervisor or office manager. However, there are few of these positions compared to the number of clerks who have the ability and experience to qualify for them.

File Clerks keep correspondence and records of all kinds in systematic order, so they can be quickly lo-

Many Different Kinds of Office Work play an important part in business operations today. The skill of each worker contributes to the successful operation of the business.

Stenography	Typing	Filing

cated when needed. In many firms, the filing system is alphabetically arranged, and the filing is done by typists and other office workers. Some large firms have complex filing systems that are kept in order by specially trained clerks.

Correspondence Clerks write to customers and to other business firms who want information. They look up needed information and often use standard form letters for their replies. Sometimes they must write special letters. This type of writing requires a clear business-writing style and a knowledge of the company's business details.

Billing Clerks, or *statement clerks*, are widely employed by stores, public utilities, and other companies that send monthly bills to customers. These office workers prepare and verify bills and invoices. They may use typewriters or special billing machines.

Order Clerks often use billing machines to make out purchase orders. They also record and file orders for supplies, merchandise, and equipment.

Mail Clerks handle all the mail that comes in and goes out of an office. They distribute the incoming mail, and stamp outgoing mail and deliver it to the post office.

Payroll Clerks keep salary records and make out payroll checks and envelopes.

Ledger Clerks and *entry clerks* help bookkeepers keep records of a company's business transactions.

Statistical Clerks are usually employed only by large companies. They collect information from various departments, and make charts and graphs for use by salesmen and executives.

Cost Clerks keep production records and use machines to calculate the cost of raw materials, labor and overhead, and office and administrative expenses.

Stock Clerks handle stock and keep records of material that is received, on hand, and sent out. Some large companies have *shipping clerks* and *receiving clerks* in addition to stock clerks.

Business-Machine Operators use many kinds of machines. A machine operator in a large firm may work on only one type of machine. But in most offices these workers must be able to operate several kinds. See BUSINESS MACHINES.

Calculating-Machine Operators figure and check invoices, inventories, payrolls, and costs. They check bookkeeping records and figure profits, losses, discounts, and interest. They also prepare various financial reports. Most large offices employ these workers.

Bookkeeping-Machine Operators work in banks and other companies with large accounts-receivable departments that handle customers' payments. They record amounts directly on depositors' and customers' ledger sheets. They also prepare statements of accounts, and check the work of bank tellers and cashiers.

Tabulating-Machine Operators compile financial and statistical information. The machines work automatically, but skill and careful planning are needed to prepare them properly for each job. Operators use *key-punch* machines to record information on punched cards. A *sorting machine* classifies the cards. The tabulating machine then makes a printed summary of the information. A skilled *wiring technician* prepares the machine so that the information will be properly recorded. Sometimes the wiring is done for one or several specific jobs at the factory that makes the machine.

Other Machine Operators use *adding machines* to add figures on checks, ledger accounts, daily sales records, and other records. *Duplicating-machine operators* make copies of sales letters and a variety of other business forms. *Addressing-machine operators* print addresses on envelopes or long strips of gummed paper for firms that have large mailing lists.

Cashiers handle money and keep records of amounts received and paid in stores, banks, and other firms.

Stock Control

WORLD BOOK photo

Tabulating

WORLD BOOK photo

Order Taking

Eastern Airlines

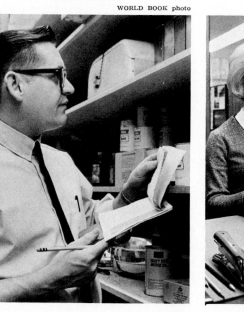

Office Workers Operate Complex Machines such as this proof machine that tabulates and sorts checks in a bank.

They must keep accurate records of their transactions. In some firms, they check cash and merchandise against sales slips, and make reports to the bookkeeper.

Receptionists greet visitors and keep records of their calls. A receptionist with a pleasing personality is an important asset to a company. She may also do some typing or filing tasks. In some offices, the receptionist operates the telephone switchboard.

Messengers, or office boys, run errands, deliver messages, distribute mail, and take care of such details as filling water bottles and changing calendar pads. They may also answer telephones. Messengers who show that they are industrious, dependable, and punctual may advance to more responsible positions.

Timekeepers keep records of the time each employee is at work. This involves solving some arithmetic problems that sometimes require the use of an office machine. Timekeepers have charge of time-recording clocks and time cards. They prepare reports of each employee's hours for the payroll department.

Personal Qualifications

Employers look for intelligent, trained office workers with good characters. Outstanding qualifications for most office positions include: (1) accuracy, (2) systematic habits, (3) a spirit of cooperation, (4) power of concentration, (5) mental alertness, and (6) manual dexterity.

An office worker should be tactful, dependable, and well-groomed. He should be loyal to his employer, have a good attitude toward his work, and have the maturity to behave properly on the job. An employer values these important traits, because they can directly affect the way an employee performs his business duties.

Most office clerical jobs require little executive ability, and an employee can do good work without it. But employers usually give early promotions to workers who show that they can direct other persons.

Many office jobs require workers to have only a fair knowledge of English grammar. However, correspondents, secretaries, and stenographers need superior ability in spelling and grammar. They also must know how to handle letters, records, and other papers that are used in the office. An office worker with such knowledge has a better chance for advancement. All employees should be able to write neatly and clearly.

Skill in arithmetic is an important qualification for much office work. Most office workers often work with figures. Even in large offices, machines have not eliminated the need for this skill.

Office work requires employees to have good eyesight. Good health is also essential. Employers cannot depend upon workers whose health may cause poor attendance. Frequent absences decrease a worker's efficiency.

Educational Requirements

Almost all office jobs require a high-school education. The more education or training a person has, the greater his chances of being hired for a better job. He may also be promoted more rapidly.

Secretarial, Stenographic, and Typing Jobs require at least a high-school education. Employers want persons who have had courses in shorthand, typing, dictating-machine transcription, business English, and office-machine training. Such specialized jobs as medical or legal secretary usually require the applicant to have taken advanced courses.

Employers prefer to hire persons who have taken courses beyond the high-school level. Office workers can get advanced training in junior colleges, vocational and business schools, and colleges and universities. After finishing high school, a person often takes a one- or two-year course in a specialized secretarial school in order to qualify for these positions. Most large cities have such schools. Many of the best jobs in the secretarial field demand several years of working experience.

A person who chooses secretarial work as a career should consider taking a four-year college course to prepare for it. Persons with this advanced training have the maturity and knowledge necessary to do their duties successfully. They usually find outstanding opportunities and earn rapid promotions.

Clerical Jobs generally require a high-school education. The best applicants for these jobs have had such courses as typing, bookkeeping, arithmetic, and business English. A person with one or two years of college has an advantage over other applicants. Some office workers take business courses during their spare time. This helps them in their work and gives them a greater chance for promotion. Some companies offer a tuition plan that pays all or part of an employee's school fees.

Other Office Work. The educational requirements for many other kinds of office jobs also demand high-school graduation as a minimum. Night schools and correspondence courses offer additional educational opportunities that may lead to promotions.

Careers in Office Work

The number of clerical workers has increased greatly. But businesses still report a shortage of well-trained office workers. The Internal Revenue Service and other government agencies require companies to keep an increasing number of tax and other records, and to fill out a large number of forms. This has created a demand for more workers to perform these jobs.

The size of the firm has much to do with opportunities for advancement. Some large firms have established plans for regular salary increases and promotions. These plans specify how large a salary increase each worker can expect, and how often he will receive the increase. The plans sometimes specify how much further education and time on the job is required for promotion. An employer in this kind of company explains these plans to each new worker. An employee also learns what further training he should have in order to advance. Such firms usually have better opportunities than small firms. However, small companies that have no definite promotional plans may have better opportunities for advancement. For example, a small company offers more contact with the employer, who often rewards exceptional work. These companies generally have fewer top jobs than large firms, but there is less competition in reaching them.

An office worker's salary depends on the type of work he does, and on his skill, training, and experience. The size of a company and the amount of business it does also help determine an employee's salary. Federal law sets a minimum wage that companies engaged in interstate commerce must observe (see MINIMUM WAGE).

Office workers who perform routine tasks are generally paid on an hourly basis. They usually earn "time and a half" for overtime. Other workers are paid a set amount for the week. They may be paid each week or every two weeks. Often, a company will offer a yearly bonus based on a percentage of each worker's earnings. Some firms pay according to the amount of work done, instead of paying a definite amount every week. For instance, typists are often paid by the number of lines or the amount of square inches they type. Some companies offer profit-sharing plans that give workers a certain percentage of the firm's net profit (see PROFIT SHARING). Office workers generally earn less than persons who work in factories. But they enjoy better working conditions than do many factory workers. Many office workers believe that the clean, quieter surroundings of an office and the opportunity to wear good clothes makes their work preferable to factory work.

Many office jobs involve doing the same thing over and over again. This sometimes creates a feeling of monotony and a lack of interest. Perhaps the chief disadvantage of some office jobs is the ease with which a worker may find himself in a rut and fail to develop his fullest capacities. However, alert and ambitious workers can avoid this danger by trying to find something interesting in whatever they do.   EARL P. STRONG

Related Articles in WORLD BOOK include:

OFFICE EQUIPMENT

Adding Machine	Calculating Machine	Duplicator
Addressograph	Computer	Typewriter
Business Machines	Dictating Machine	

OTHER RELATED ARTICLES

Accounting	Business Education	Vocations
Bookkeeping	Shorthand	(Business
Business		Organization)

Outline

I. Kinds of Office Workers

A. Typists	F. Business-Machine Operators
B. Stenographers	G. Cashiers
C. Secretaries	H. Receptionists
D. Bookkeepers	I. Messengers
E. Clerks	J. Timekeepers

II. Personal Qualifications

III. Educational Requirements
    A. Secretarial, Stenographic, and Typing Jobs
    B. Clerical Jobs
    C. Other Office Work

IV. Careers in Office Work

Questions

What are several outstanding qualifications that office workers should have?

How do some office workers get additional training for their jobs?

What factors influence an office worker's chances for promotion?

What is the most common type of office work?

What qualifications should a secretary have?

What factors help determine the amount of an office worker's salary?

In what way is the most routine job important to a business?

What is the minimum speed a beginning typist should have?

What duties does a calculating-machine operator have?

About how many women have office clerical jobs?

OFFICER. See RANK IN ARMED SERVICES.

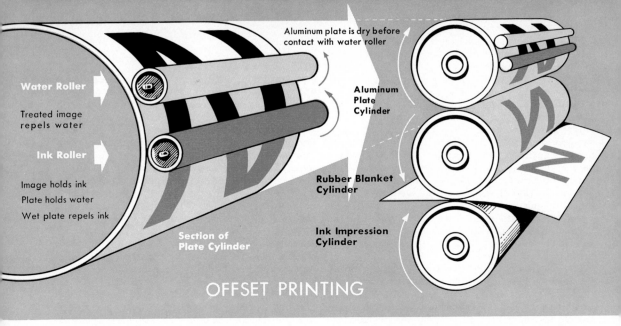

Aluminum plate is dry before contact with water roller

Water Roller

Treated image repels water

Ink Roller

Image holds ink
Plate holds water
Wet plate repels ink

Aluminum Plate Cylinder

Rubber Blanket Cylinder

Section of Plate Cylinder

Ink Impression Cylinder

OFFSET PRINTING

Offset Printing is not done directly from a printing plate or from type. Instead, the ink is transferred from the printing plate to a second roller, which in turn impresses it on the paper or other material to be printed.

OFFSET is a printing process in which the printing is done first on the rubber surface of a rotating cylinder. The impression is then transferred to paper by the pressure of other cylinders. The term *offset* describes the printing, or offsetting, of the ink from the rubber. In recent years, offset has grown more rapidly in popularity than any other printing process.

All ordinary offset printing is done from the metal surfaces of lithographic plates (see LITHOGRAPHY). The material to be printed is transferred onto the plates through a special photographic process. The plates are chemically treated so that only the traced design of the print will take up the ink. But the offset process is used for other methods also. Some printing is done from ordinary type and cuts, some from thin plastic relief or letterpress plates, some from gelatin surfaces, and some from *intaglio* plates, which are metal sheets that carry the ink in sunken lines.

Offset lithography is usually done on a press having three cylinders. A lithographic plate is wrapped around the first cylinder. This plate is a sheet of aluminum or zinc about as thick as heavy paper. The plate prints on a second cylinder which is covered by a rubber blanket. The impression on the rubber is then printed on the paper carried by the third cylinder. The third cylinder is equipped with steel fingers, called *grippers*, to hold the paper in position while it is squeezed against the rubber surface. Three-cylinder presses of this type can turn out 8,000 impressions an hour.

These cylinders are almost hidden while the press is in operation. They are covered by a great number of rollers which supply the lithographic plate with ink and water. The cylinders are also concealed by the mechanism for feeding and removing the sheets of paper.

The offset process has several advantages over other types of printing. The elastic rubber used transfers the impression to a rough surface as easily as to a smooth one. This makes it possible to print on rough paper, as well as on tin, celluloid, and other substances. Another advantage of offset is that the rubber on the cylinder fits itself easily to uneven surfaces. This greatly reduces the time pressmen must spend preparing the presses for printing. Offset is called a *planographic* technique.

Offset was developed in the early 1900's in America as a method of printing tin sheets for making cans and boxes. It has recently been applied to almost every class of printing, from the cheapest to the most expensive. Offset has replaced the older forms of lithography in which the impression was made directly on the paper from stone or metal plates. An offset press can turn out bank notes, stock certificates, letterheads, magazine covers, posters, and mail-order catalogues. The offset press is often used in printing weekly suburban newspapers. Offset is combined with rotogravure to make colored illustrations that are clear and delicate. It is also used for facsimile reproduction of old books.

The process is still being rapidly improved and constantly applied to new purposes. The wearing qualities of the lithographic plates are continually being improved. Offset presses for newspaper work have been designed to print on a *web* (continuous sheet on a spool) of paper. The paper on this *web press* is passed between two rollers covered with rubber blankets, printing on both sides at the same time.   KENNETH G. SCHEID.

See also PRINTING.

OFFUTT AIR FORCE BASE, Nebr., is headquarters of the U.S. Air Force Strategic Air Command. It covers 1,500 acres 9 miles south of Omaha. The base began as Fort Crook, an army post, in the early 1890's. In 1924, the airfield was named for Lt. Jarvis J. Offutt, Omaha's first air casualty in World War I. The Strategic Air Command established headquarters on the base in 1948. See also STRATEGIC AIR COMMAND.   RICHARD M. SKINNER

O'FLAHERTY, LIAM, *LEE uhm* (1897-   ), is an Irish writer of political and psychological novels and short stories. His *The Informer* (1926) and *The Puritan* (1932) made excellent motion pictures. He also wrote the novels *The Black Soul* (1925), *The Assassin* (1928), *Skerrett* (1932), and *Famine* (1937). He was born in the Aran Islands.   JOSEPH E. BAKER

OG, *ahg,* a Bible character, was an Amorite king whom the Israelites fought when they came to the edge of the Promised Land. His kingdom was in Bashan, in what is today southern Syria and northern Jordan. Og was said to have been a giant (Deut. 3). The Israelites defeated and killed him, and took his land.　JOHN BRIGHT

OGASAWARA GUNTO. See BONIN ISLANDS.

OGDEN, Utah (pop. 69,478; met. area 126,278; alt. 4,295 ft.), is the state's second largest city. It lies at the foot of the Wasatch Range, 35 miles north of Salt Lake City. See UTAH (political map). Ogden has the largest stockyards west of Denver. Its factories process agricultural products, and produce canned fruits and vegetables. Missiles are also produced in the area. Ogden is the home of Weber State College, the Utah State Industrial School, and the Utah School for the Deaf and Blind.

Mormons came to the Ogden region in 1847. Ogden was incorporated in 1861, and grew rapidly after the transcontinental railroad came in 1869. The Golden Spike, driven near Ogden in May, 1869, completed the railroad. Ogden was named for Peter Skene Ogden, an early fur trader. Ogden is the seat of Weber County. It has a council-manager government.　A. R. MORTENSEN

OGDEN, CHARLES K. See BASIC ENGLISH.

OGDEN, PETER SKENE. See OGDEN.

OGIER THE DANE, *OH jih er,* was a hero of several French romantic poems of the Middle Ages. The poems tell how he earned his knighthood in Charlemagne's war against the Saracens in Italy. Later, Charlemagne's son killed Ogier's son, and Ogier revolted against Charlemagne. He was imprisoned, but was set free when a Saracen army attacked France. Ogier killed the Saracen leader and saved France.　ARTHUR M. SELVI

OGLETHORPE, JAMES EDWARD (1696-1785), an Englishman, was the founder and first governor of the colony of Georgia.

He was born in London and attended Eton and Oxford. He joined the British Army at 14. He was elected to Parliament in 1722. Here, he became interested in persons who had been imprisoned for not paying their debts. Oglethorpe hoped to help them by establishing an American colony for debtors. In 1732, he and a group of associates received a charter from George II for the colony on territory between the Savannah and Altamaha rivers. Parliament also granted him $50,000.

Oglethorpe and 114 colonists arrived in America in January, 1733. He set up his first settlement where the city of Savannah now stands. He governed wisely for nine years and drove invading Spanish troops back into Florida. He defeated the Spaniards badly in the Battle of Bloody Marsh on St. Simons Island, in 1742.

Oglethorpe was so much in debt from his loans to colonists that he had to return to England in 1743. His enemies called him a coward for not capturing St. Augustine, Fla., when he attacked the Spaniards there in 1743. A court-martial dismissed the charges. He and the other trustees returned the Georgia charter to George II in 1752, and Georgia became a royal province.　JOSEPH CARLYLE SITTERSON

See also GEORGIA (Colonial Period).

OGLETHORPE COLLEGE. See UNIVERSITIES AND COLLEGES (table).

OGOTAI. See MONGOL EMPIRE (Invasions).

OGPU was the Soviet secret police. See MVD.

O'HARA, JOHN (1905-1970), was an American novelist and short-story writer. He is best known for his skillful use of dialogue spoken by middle-class Americans. Many of his novels and stories are set in the fictional town of Gibbsville, Pa.

O'Hara was born in Pottsville, Pa., and worked as a journalist before the success of his first novel, *Appointment in Samarra* (1934). The novel explores the social and psychological difficulties of the upper middle class in America. His short novel *Butterfield 8* (1935) is a study of how sexual freedom affects both society and the individual. Of his later novels, *Ten North Frederick* (1955) has received the greatest praise from both critics and the public.

O'Hara published many collections of stories, including *The Doctor's Son* (1935) and *Sermons and Soda Water* (1960). His story sequence *Pal Joey* (1940) was adapted into a musical by Richard Rodgers and Lorenz Hart. This comic exposé expresses with an authentic American voice the frenzied life of a part of American society.　JOHN CROSSETT

O'HARA, JOHN CARDINAL (1888-1960), was the fifth archbishop of Philadelphia. He was named a cardinal of the Roman Catholic Church in November, 1958, by Pope John XXIII. He was ordained a priest of the Congregation of Holy Cross in 1916. He served as president of the University of Notre Dame from 1934 to 1939, and then became titular bishop of Mylassa. He became bishop of Buffalo in 1945, and archbishop of Philadelphia in 1951. Cardinal O'Hara was born in Ann Arbor, Mich.　JAMES A. CORBETT and FULTON J. SHEEN

O'HARA, MARY (1885-　　), is the pen name of Mary O'Hara Alsop Sture-Vasa, an American author. She wrote of people on the plains and their love for horses in her novels *My Friend Flicka* (1941) and *Thunderhead* (1943). She also wrote *The Son of Adam Wyngate* (1952), a novel of spiritual experiences. She was born in Cape May Point, N.J.

O'HARE INTERNATIONAL AIRPORT. See CHICAGO (Transportation); AIRPORT.

O. HENRY. See HENRY, O.

OHIA, *oh HE uh,* is a mountain apple tree that grows in Hawaii. The wood is used in furniture, flooring, and railroad ties. The ohia belongs to the family *Myrtaceae.*

O'HIGGINS, *oh HIG inz,* is the family name of two South American soldiers and statesmen, father and son.

Ambrosio O'Higgins (1720?-1801) was born in Ireland. He went to Spain, then to Peru to enter business. He became wealthy, and entered Spanish service in Chile. He was captain general of Chile from 1788 to 1796. O'Higgins became Marqués de Osorno in 1792. He served as viceroy of Peru from 1796 until his death.

Bernardo O'Higgins (1778-1842), the son of Ambrosio O'Higgins, was the liberator of Chile. After Spain defeated a Chilean army at Rancagua in 1814, O'Higgins joined the South American liberator José de San Martín, in Argentina. They crossed the Andes Mountains to Chile in 1817 and defeated the Spaniards at Chacabuco. O'Higgins won the final victory over the Spaniards at the Maipo River in 1818. He was ousted from power because of disputes over reform attempts. He was born in Chillán, Chile.　DONALD E. WORCESTER

See also CHILE (Independence; picture).

OHIO is one of the leading industrial states in the United States. It ranks third, behind New York and California, in the total value of manufactured products. Great numbers of people have moved to Ohio so they could work in the state's busy factories. Ohio stands 6th among the states in population, although it is 35th in area. Cleveland, the chief industrial center of Ohio, is the state's largest city. Columbus is the capital.

Ohio took its name from the Iroquois Indian word meaning *something great*. The Iroquois used the word for the Ohio River, which forms the state's southeastern and southern borders. Ohio is called the *Buckeye State*

OHIO *THE BUCKEYE STATE*

because of the buckeye trees that once grew plentifully on its hills and plains. Pioneers cut down many of the buckeyes, or horse chestnut trees, to build log cabins. In 1803, Ohio became the first state to be carved out of the Northwest Territory. Ohio later served as an important link to the West as canals, railways, and roads crossed the state. As a result, Ohio also came to be called the *Gateway State*.

Several natural advantages helped Ohio become a great manufacturing state. Ohio has an abundant supply of water and large deposits of coal, salt, and other important minerals. Its central location, near raw materials and major markets, has helped attract many

Covered Bridge in Southern Ohio Shostal

Sailing on Lake Erie James Busch, Foto/Find

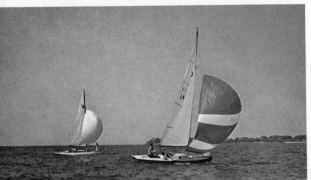

Ohio (blue) ranks 35th in size among all the states, and 11th in size among the Midwestern States (gray).

large industries. Ohio leads the states in the production of such transportation equipment as bus and truck bodies and truck trailers. Ohio's production of iron and steel ranks second only to that of Pennsylvania. No other state manufactures more machine tools or rubber products than Ohio.

But Ohio is not entirely a manufacturing state. Fertile farmlands that make up part of the great midwestern Corn Belt stretch across much of the state. Ohio farmers grow large crops of corn, soybeans, and wheat. Vineyards of colorful grapes dot the shore of Lake Erie to the north. Ohio ranks among the leading hog-raising states.

Ohio claims the title of the *Mother of Presidents*. Seven Presidents of the United States were born in Ohio, more than in any other state except Virginia. In historical order, they were Ulysses S. Grant, Rutherford B. Hayes, James A. Garfield, Benjamin Harrison, William McKinley, William Howard Taft, and Warren G. Harding. In addition, William Henry Harrison was living in Ohio when he became President of the United States.

Astronaut John H. Glenn, Jr., the first American spaceman to orbit the earth, was born in Cambridge and grew up in New Concord. Many famous inventors also came from Ohio. Thomas A. Edison, the wizard of electricity, developed his scientific curiosity as a small boy in Milan. Orville Wright and Wilbur Wright made test flights in their first power-driven airplane from a field near Dayton. Charles F. Kettering of Dayton developed a self-starter for automobiles. The aluminum-refining process was discovered by Charles M. Hall of Oberlin.

For the relationship of Ohio to other states in its geographic region, see the article on the MIDWESTERN STATES.

──────── FACTS IN BRIEF ────────

Capital: Columbus.

Government: *Congress*—U.S. senators, 2; U.S. representatives, 23. *Electoral Votes*—25. *State Legislature*—senators, 33; representatives, 99. *Counties*—88. *Voting Age*—18 years.

Area: 41,222 square miles (including 204 square miles of inland water), 35th in size among the states. *Greatest Distances*—(east-west) 230 miles; (north-south) 210 miles. *Shoreline*—312 miles (on Lake Erie, including 66 miles on islands).

Elevation: *Highest*—Campbell Hill in Logan County, 1,550 feet above sea level. *Lowest*—in Hamilton County, 433 feet above sea level.

Population: *1970 Census*—10,652,017; 6th among the states; density, 258 persons to the square mile; distribution, 75 per cent urban, 25 per cent rural. *1960 Census*—9,706,397.

Chief Products: *Agriculture*—beef cattle, corn, dairy products, eggs, greenhouse and nursery products, hogs, soybeans, tomatoes, wheat. *Fishing Industry*—carp, catfish, sheepshead, white bass, yellow perch, yellow pike. *Manufacturing*—chemicals; electrical machinery; food and related products; metal products; nonelectrical machinery; printed materials; rubber and plastic products; stone, clay, and glass products; transportation equipment. *Mining*—coal, petroleum, salt, sand and gravel, stone.

Statehood: March 1, 1803; the 17th state.

State Motto: *With God, all things are possible.*

State Song: "Beautiful Ohio." Words by Ballard MacDonald; music by Mary Earl.

The contributors of this article are Ralph W. Frank, Professor of Geography at Bowling Green State University; Ben Hayes, Columnist for the Columbus Citizen-Journal; and James H. Rodabaugh, Professor of History at Miami University.

Ohio Oil Refinery

G. Warstler, Foto/Find

Constitution of Ohio, the second in the state's history, was adopted in 1851. Ohioans adopted their first constitution in 1802. An amendment to the constitution may be proposed by (1) the state legislature, (2) a petition signed by 10 per cent of the voters, or (3) a constitutional convention. A convention may be called if it is approved by two-thirds of each house of the legislature and by a majority of the voters. Ohioans also vote every 20 years as to whether they wish to call a convention. Constitutional amendments must be approved by a majority of the persons voting on them in an election.

Executive. The governor of Ohio is elected to a four-year term. He can serve an unlimited number of terms, but not more than two terms in succession. He receives a yearly salary of $40,000. For a list of all the governors of Ohio, see the *History* section of this article.

The governor has the power to appoint the heads of many of the state's administrative departments and agencies. These appointments must be approved by the state senate. The governor also appoints the adjutant general and the trustees of state-supported universities and institutions.

Legislature, called the *General Assembly*, consists of a 33-member Senate and a 99-member House of Representatives. Voters in each of Ohio's 33 senatorial districts elect one senator. Senators serve four-year terms. Voters in each of the state's 99 representative districts elect one representative. Representatives serve two-year terms. The legislature meets on the first Monday of January in odd-numbered years. Sessions have no time limit.

A 1903 amendment to the state constitution required that each county have at least one representative, regardless of its population. In 1964, the Supreme Court of the United States ruled this amendment unconstitutional. In 1965, the governor, the state auditor, and the secretary of state drew up a *reapportionment* (redivision) plan for the Senate and House of Representatives. They set up single-member legislative districts that were as equal in population as possible. A special three-judge federal district court approved the reapportionment plan for temporary use until a permanent plan could be drawn. The Supreme Court of the United States approved the federal district court's decision. In 1967, the state legislature drew up a permanent reapportionment plan.

Courts. The highest appeals court in Ohio is the Supreme Court. It has a chief justice and six judges, elected to six-year terms. Ohio also has 10 courts of appeals. Each court has three judges, except the court in Cuyahoga County, which has six, and the court in Franklin County, which has four.

The highest trial courts are the courts of common pleas. Each of the 88 counties has one. These courts have varying numbers of judges, elected to six-year terms. Other courts in Ohio include county, juvenile, municipal, mayor, and probate courts.

Local Government. Each of Ohio's 88 counties is governed by a three-member board of commissioners, who are elected to four-year terms. By law, counties may have *home rule.* That is, a county may adopt its own charter. But no county in Ohio has done so.

Under Ohio law, cities are communities with at least 5,000 persons. Villages have populations under 5,000. Officially, Ohio has no towns. Ohio law allows cities and villages to adopt home rule, and about a fourth of the cities and villages have done so. The home-rule cities and villages have mayor-council, council-manager, or commission governments. Home rule in Ohio consists mainly of changing the form of local government, not its powers. In 1913, Dayton became the first large U.S. city to adopt council-manager government. About three-fourths of Ohio's cities and villages have the mayor-council government provided by state law.

Taxation. A 4 per cent retail sales tax is the state government's largest single source of tax income. It provides about a fifth of the total income. Other state taxes include those on cigarettes, gasoline, inheritances,

The Governor's Mansion is in Bexley, a suburb east of Columbus. The house, formerly a private residence, was given to the state in 1955 by the owners. The brick and stone structure has 24 rooms. Three acres of parklike grounds surround the mansion.

The State Seal

Symbols of Ohio. On the state seal, a sheaf of wheat represents the richness of Ohio's land. A bundle of arrows symbolizes Ohio's admission to the Union as the 17th state. The sun rising behind the mountains shows that Ohio was the first state west of the Allegheny Mountains. The seal was adopted in 1868 and revised in 1967. On the flag, adopted in 1902, the white circle stands for "O," the state's initial. The red circle represents the buckeye nut. Ohio is the only state with a pennant-shaped flag.

property, and highway use by trucks. Federal grants and other U.S. government programs provide about a fourth of the state's income. The remainder comes from such sources as state-owned liquor stores and various state institutions such as hospitals.

Politics. Since the founding of the Republican party during the 1850's, Republicans have generally controlled Ohio politics. Almost twice as many Republicans as Democrats have been elected governor, and Republicans have usually controlled the state legislature. The rural areas and Cincinnati are centers of Republican strength. They usually combine forces to control the legislature. Cleveland is the major Democratic center.

Ohio is often called a *barometer state* in national politics. That is, Ohioans' political views frequently indicate those of most Americans. For example, the winning presidential candidates have won Ohio's electoral votes in a great majority of presidential elections since 1804. For Ohio's electoral votes and voting record in presidential elections, see ELECTORAL COLLEGE (table).

The State Capitol in Columbus was completed in 1861. The huge limestone building stands in a 10-acre park. Columbus has been Ohio's capital since 1816. Others were Chillicothe (1803-1810), Zanesville (1810-1812), and Chillicothe (1812-1816).
J. H. Hutton, FPG

The State Flag

The State Bird
Cardinal

The State Flower
Scarlet Carnation

The State Tree
Buckeye

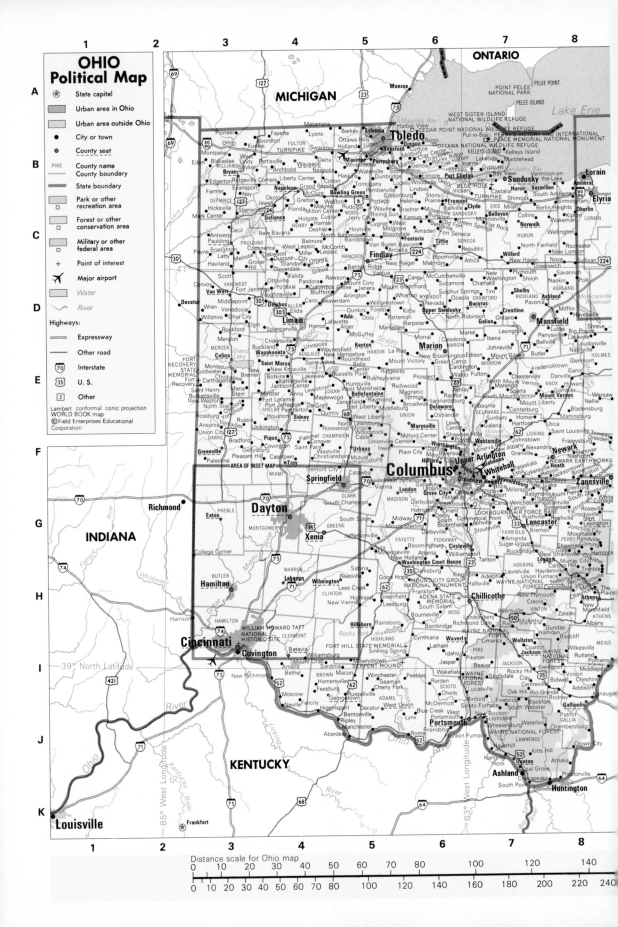

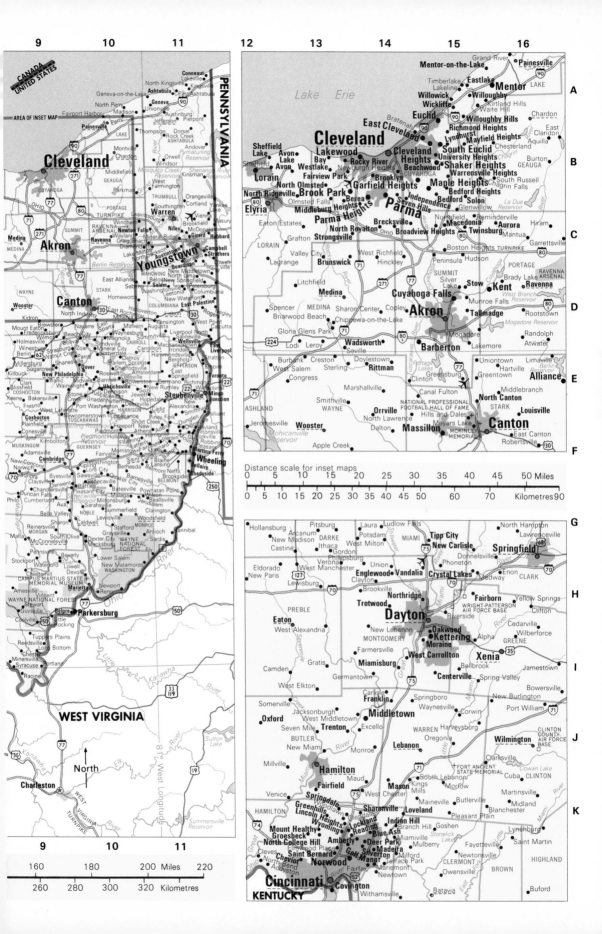

La Rue ......867..E 6
Latty ....269..C 3
Laura ....464..G 14
Laurelville ...624..H 7
Lawrenceville .687..G 16
Lebanon ....7,934.°H 4
Leesburg .....984..H 5
Leetonia ....2,342..D 11
Leipsic .....2,072..C 4
Leroy ....715..D 13
Lewisburg ..1,553..H 13
Lewisville .....294..G 10
Lexington ...2,972..D 7
Liberty Center ....1,007..B 4
Lima ......53,734.°D 4
Limaville .....303..E 16
Lincoln Heights ...6,099..K 13
Lincoln Village* .11,215..F 6
Lindsey ......652..B 6
Lisbon ......3,521.°D 11
Lithopolis ....705..G 7
Lockbourne ...420..G 6
Lockbourne Base .....5,623..G 6
Lockland ...5,288..K 14
Lodi ....2,399..D 13
Logan ......6,269.°H 8
London .....6,481.°G 5
Lorain .....78,185..B 8
Lore City ....401..F 10
Loudonville .2,865..D 8
Louisville ...6,298..E 16
Loveland ...7,144..K 14
Lowell ....852..H 10
Lowellville ..1,836..C 12
Lucas ....771..D 8
Luckey ....996..B 5
Ludlow Falls .292..G 14
Lynchburg ..1,186..K 16
Lyndhurst .19,749..B 15
Lyons ....630..B 4
Macedonia ..6,375..C 15
Macksburg ....266..G 10
Madeira ....6,713..K 14
Madison ....1,678..A 10
Madison North* ...6,882..A 10
Magnetic Springs .....349..E 6
Magnolia ...1,064..D 10
Maineville ....333..K 15
Malinta ......391..C 4
Malta ......1,017..G 9
Malvern ....1,256..D 10
Manchester .2,195..J 5
Mansfield .55,047.°D 7
Mantua ....1,199..C 16
Maple Heights ..34,093..B 15
Marble Cliff ..676..F 6
Marblehead ...726..B 7
Marengo ......330..E 7
Mariemont ..4,540..K 14
Marietta ..16,861.°H 10
Marion ....38,646.°E 6
Marion East* 1,079..E 6
Marshallville .693..E 14
Martins Ferry ....10,757..F 11
Martinsville ..500..K 16
Marysville ..5,744.°F 6
Mason ......5,677..K 14
Massillon ..32,539..F 15
Masury ....2,060..C 12
Maumee ...15,937..B 5
Mayfield* ...3,548..B 10
Mayfield Heights ..22,139..B 15
McArthur ...1,543.°H 7
McClure ......699..B 4
McComb ....1,329..C 5
McConnelsville ......2,107.°G 9
McDonald ..3,177..C 11
McGuffey ....704..D 5
Mechanicsburg ......1,686..F 5
Medina ....10,913.°C 9
Melrose ......302..C 3
Mendon ......672..D 3
Mentor ....36,912..A 16
Mentor-on-the-Lake .....6,517..A 16
Metamora .....594..A 4
Miamisburg 14,797..I 14
Middleburg Heights ..12,367..C 14
Middlefield .1,726..B 10
Middlepoint ..543..D 3
Middleport ..2,784..I 8
Middletown 48,767..J 14
Midland ......388..K 16
Midvale ......636..E 10
Midway ......318..G 5
Milan ....1,405..C 7
Milford .....4,828..K 14
Milford Center 753..F 5
Millbury ......771..B 5
Millersburg .2,979.°E 9
Millersport ...777..G 7
Millville ......697..J 13
Mineral City ..860..E 10
Minerva ....4,359..D 10
Minerva Park ......1,402..F 7
Mingo Junction ......5,278..E 11
Minster .....2,405..E 3
Mogadore ...3,858..D 15
Monroe .....3,492..J 14
Monroeville ......1,455..C 7
Montgomery* ..5,683..H 3
Montpelier ..4,184..B 3
Moraine ....4,898..I 15
Moreland Hills* ....3,000..B 10
Morral ....452..D 6
Morristown ...385..F 10
Morrow .....1,486..K 15
Moscow ......348..I 4
Mount Blanchard ..473..D 5
Mount Cory ..302..D 5
Mount Gilead ....2,971.°E 7
Mount Healthy ...7,446..K 13
Mount Orab .1,306..I 4
Mount Pleasant ...635..F 11
Mount Sterling ...1,536..G 6
Mount Vernon ..13,373.°E 7
Mount Victory 633..E 5
Mowrystown ..465..I 5
Munroe Falls 3,794..D 15
Murray City ..562..H 8
Napoleon ...7,791.°B 4
Navarre .....1,607..D 10
Nelsonville ..4,812..H 8
Nevada ....917..D 6
New Albany ..513..F 7
New Alexandria .425..E 11
New Athens ..450..F 11
New Bloomington ......343..E 6
New Boston .3,325..J 7
New Bremen 2,185..E 3
New Carlisle 6,112..G 15
New Concord 2,318..F 9
New Holland .796..G 6
New Knoxville 852..E 4
New Lebanon 4,248..H 14
New Lexington ....4,921.°G 8
New London 2,336..C 8
New Madison .959..G 12
New Matamoras ....940..H 11
New Miami .3,273..J 13
New Middletown ......1,664..C 12
New Paris ..1,692..H 12
New Philadelphia ..15,184.°E 10
New Richmond .....2,650..I 4
New Riegel ...340..C 6
New Straitsville ....947..G 8
New Vienna ..849..H 5
New Washington ....1,251..D 7
New Waterford 735..D 11
Newark ....41,836.°F 8
Newburgh Heights ...3,396..B 14
Newcomerstown ......4,155..E 9
Newton Falls 5,378..C 11
Newtonsville ..385..K 15
Newtown ....2,047..K 14
Ney ....378..B 3
Niles ......21,581..C 11
North Baltimore 3,143..C 5
North Bend ...638..K 12
North Canton ..15,228..E 15
North College Hill .....12,363..K 13
North Fairfield ...540..C 7
North Hampton ...489..G 16
North Kingsville .2,458..A 11
North Lewisburg ..840..F 5
North Mount Vernon [-Academia] .....1,447..E 7
North Olmsted .34,861..B 13
North Perry ..851..A 10
North Randall* .1,212..B 9
North Ridgeville ......13,152..B 13
North Robinson ...277..D 7
North Royalton .12,807..C 14
North Star ...296..E 3
North Zanesville* .....3,399..F 8
Northfield ..1,089..C 15
Northridge .10,084..H 14
Northwood* .4,222..B 5
Norton* ...12,308..D 9
Norwalk ...13,386.°C 7
Norwood ...30,420..K 13
Oak Harbor .2,807..B 6
Oak Hill ....1,642..I 7
Oakwood* ...3,127..B 10
Oakwood ......804..C 3
Oakwood ....10,095..H 15
Oberlin .....8,761..C 8
Obetz ....2,248..G 6
Ohio City .....816..D 3
Olmsted Falls 2,504..B 13
Ontario .....4,345..D 7
Orange* .....2,112..B 10
Orangeville ...268..B 12
Oregon .....16,563..B 6
Orient ....313..G 6
Orrville .....7,408..E 14
Orwell ....965..B 11
Osgood ....289..E 3
Ostrander ....399..F 6
Ottawa .....3,622.°C 4
Ottawa Hills 4,270..B 5
Ottoville ......914..D 4
Overlook-Page Manor* ..19,596..G 4
Owensville ....707..K 15
Oxford .....15,868..J 12
Page Manor, see Overlook-Page Manor
Painesville .16,536.°A 10
Painesville Southwest* 5,461..A 10
Pandora ......857..D 4
Parma ....100,216..B 14
Parma Heights ..27,192..B 14
Parral ....271..E 10
Pataskala ...1,831..F 7
Paulding ...2,983.°C 3
Payne ......1,351..C 3
Peebles .....1,629..I 6
Pemberville .1,301..B 5
Peninsula .....692..C 15
Pepper Pike* 5,933..B 10
Perry ....917..A 10
Perrysburg ..7,693..B 5
Perrysville ...752..D 8
Phillipsburg ..831..H 14
Philo ....846..G 9
Pickerington ..696..G 7
Piketon .....1,347..I 6
Pioneer ......968..B 3
Piqua .....20,741..F 4
Pitsburg ......462..G 13
Plain City ..2,254..F 6
Pleasant City .494..G 10
Pleasant Hill 1,025..F 3
Pleasantville .754..G 7
Plymouth ...1,993..D 7
Poland .....3,097..C 11
Polk ....435..D 8
Pomeroy ....2,672.°I 8
Port Clinton 7,202.°B 6
Port Jefferson 416..E 4
Port Washington ......550..E 10
Port William .323..J 16
Portage ......494..C 5
Portsmouth 27,633.°J 6
Potsdam ......311..G 14
Powell ....374..F 6
Powhatan Point .....2,167..G 11
Proctorville ..881..K 8
Prospect ...1,031..E 6
Quaker City ..510..F 10
Quincy ....686..E 4
Racine ....583..I 9
Ravenna ...11,780.°C 10
Rawson ....466..D 5
Rayland ....617..F 11
Reading ....14,303..K 14
Reno Beach* 1,049..B 6
Republic .....705..C 6
Reynoldsburg .....13,921..F 7
Richmond .....777..E 11
Richmond Heights ..9,220..A 15
Richwood ...2,072..E 6
Ridgeway .....379..E 5
Rio Grande ...814..I 8
Ripley ......2,745..J 5
Rising Sun ...730..C 5
Rittman .....6,308..E 14
Riverlea ......558..F 6
Riverside .....447..H 15
Rock Creek ...731..B 11
Rockford ....1,207..D 3
Rocky Ridge ..385..B 6
Rocky River ....22,958..B 13
Rogers ....310..D 11
Rosemount* .1,786..J 7
Roseville ....1,767..G 8
Ross* ....1,661..H 3
Rossburg .....275..E 3
Rossford ....5,302..B 5
Roswell ....317..E 10
Rushsylvania .526..E 5
Rushville .....289..G 8
Russells Point .....1,104..E 4
Russellville ...399..I 5
Russia ....420..F 3
Rutland ......663..I 8
Sabina .....2,160..H 5
St. Bernard .6,080..K 13
St. Clairsville ......4,754.°F 11
St. Henry ...1,276..E 3
St. Louisville .385..F 8
St. Marys ...7,699..E 3
St. Paris ...1,646..F 4
Salem .....14,186..D 11
Salineville ..1,686..D 11
Sandusky ..32,674.°B 7
Sandusky South* ...8,501..B 7
Sardinia .....824..I 5
Savannah ....361..D 8
Scio ....1,002..E 10
Scott ....329..C 3
Seaman ....866..I 5
Sebring .....4,954..D 11
Senecaville ...497..F 10
Seven Hills 12,700..B 14
Seven Mile ....699..J 13
Seville ......1,402..E 13
Shadyside ..5,070..F 11
Shaker Heights ..36,306..B 15
Sharon West* ....3,120..B 11
Sharonville 10,985..K 14
Shawnee .....914..G 8
Shawnee Hills 428..F 6
Sheffield ....1,730..B 12
Sheffield Lake .....8,734..B 12
Shelby ....9,847..D 7
Sherrodsville .400..E 10
Sherwood .....784..C 3
Shiloh ....817..D 7
Shiloh* ....11,368..G 4
Shreve .....1,635..D 8
Sidney .....16,332.°E 4
Silver Lake .3,637..D 15
Silverton ...6,588..K 14
Smithfield ..1,245..E 11
Smithville ..1,278..E 13
Solon .....11,519..B 15
Somerset ...1,417..G 8
Somerville ....388..I 13
South Amherst ..2,913..B 8
South Bloomfield .610..G 6
South Charleston 1,500..G 5
South Euclid ...29,579..B 15
South Lebanon ..3,014..K 15
South Mount Vernon ...1,044..E 7
South Point 2,243..K 7
South Russell ...2,673..B 16
South Solon ..415..G 5
South Webster 825..J 7
South Zanesville ......1,436..G 8
Spencer ......758..D 12
Spencerville ......2,241..D 4
Spring Valley 667..I 15
Springboro ..2,799..I 14
Springdale ..8,127..K 13
Springfield 81,926.°F 5
Steubenville 30,771.°E 11
Stockport .....471..G 9
Stony Prairie ...1,913..B 6
Stoutsville ....573..G 7
Stow ......19,847..D 15
Strasburg ...1,874..E 9
Stratton ....386..E 11
Streetsboro* 7,966..C 10
Strongsville 15,182..C 14
Struthers ..15,343..C 11
Stryker .....1,296..B 3
Sugar Grove ..469..G 7
Sugarcreek ..1,771..E 9
Summerfield ..306..G 10
Sunbury .....2,512..F 7
Swanton .....2,927..B 5
Sycamore ...1,096..D 6
Sylvania ...12,031..A 5
Syracuse ......684..I 9
Tallmadge .15,274..D 15
Tarlton ....412..H 7
Terrace Park 2,266..K 14
The Plains .1,568..H 8
Thornville .....679..G 8
Thurston ......428..G 7
Tiffin .....21,596.°C 6
Tiltonsville .2,123..F 11
Timberlake ....964..A 15
Tipp City ....5,090..G 15
Tiro ....310..D 7
Toledo ....383,818.°B 5
Tontogany .....395..B 5
Toronto ......7,705..E 11
Tremont City .426..F 5
Trenton .....5,278..J 13
Trimble ....542..H 8
Trotwood ....6,997..H 14
Troy ......17,186.°F 4
Tuscarawas ...830..E 10
Twinsburg ..6,432..C 15
Uhrichsville 5,731..E 10
Union ......3,654..H 14
Union City .1,808..F 3
Uniopolis ....291..E 4
University Heights .17,055..B 15
Upper Arlington 38,630..F 6
Upper Sandusky .5,645.°D 6
Urbana ....11,237.°F 5
Urbancrest ...754..G 6
Utica ....1,977..F 8
Valley View* 1,422..B 9
Valley View* .909..F 6
Van Buren ...319..C 5
Van Wert .11,320.°D 3
Vandalia ..10,796..H 15
Vanlue ....539..D 5
Vermilion ...9,872..B 8
Verona ....593..H 13
Versailles ...2,441..F 3
Vienna ....545..F 5
Vinton ....352..I 8
Wadsworth 13,142..D 14
Waite Hill ...514..A 15
Wakeman ....822..C 8
Walbridge ..3,208..B 5
Waldo ....428..E 6
Walton Hills* ....2,508..B 9
Wapakoneta 7,324.°E 4
Warren ....63,494.°C 11
Warrensville Heights ..18,925..B 15
Warsaw ......725..E 8
Washington ..346..F 10
Washington Court House ...12,495.°H 5
Washingtonville ....747..D 11
Waterville ..2,940..B 5
Wauseon ...4,932.°B 4
Waverly ....4,858.°I 6
Wayne ....921..C 5
Waynesburg 1,337..D 10
Waynesfield ..704..E 4
Waynesville .1,638..J 15
Wellington ..4,137..C 8
Wellston ....5,410..I 7
Wellsville ...5,891..D 11
West Alexandria 1,553..H 13
West Carrollton 10,748..I 14
West Elkton ..291..I 13
West Farmington 650..B 11
West Jefferson .3,664..F 6
West Lafayette .1,719..E 9
West Leipsic ..378..C 4
West Liberty 1,580..F 5
West Manchester .469..H 13
West Mansfield ..753..E 5
West Milton 3,696..G 14
West Portsmouth ....3,396..J 6
West Richfield .....3,228..C 14
West Salem ..1,058..E 12
West Union .1,951.°J 5
West Unity ..1,589..B 3
West View .2,523..C 13
Westerville 12,530..F 7
Westlake ..15,689..B 13
Weston .....1,269..C 5
Wharton ....422..D 5
Wheelersburg 3,709..J 7
Whitehall ..25,263..F 7
Whitehouse .1,542..B 5
Wickliffe ..21,354..A 15
Willard .....5,510..C 7
Williamsburg 2,054..I 4
Williamsport .857..G 6
Willoughby 18,634..A 15
Willoughby Hills .....5,247..A 15
Willowick ..21,237..A 15
Willshire .....623..D 3
Wilmington 10,051.°H 5
Wilmot ....378..D 9
Winchester ....760..I 5
Windham ...3,360..C 10
Wintersville .4,921..E 11
Woodlawn ..3,251..K 13
Woodmere* ...976..B 10
Woodsfield .3,239.°G 10
Woodstock ....281..F 5
Woodville ..1,834..B 6
Woodworth* 1,054..D 11
Wooster ...18,703.°D 9
Worthington 15,326..F 6
Wren ....282..D 3
Wright-Patterson ...10,151..H 15
Wyoming ....9,089..K 13
Xenia .....25,373.°G 4
Yellow Springs ...4,624..H 16
Yorkville ...1,656..F 11
Youngstown ...139,788.°C 11
Zaleski ....304..H 8
Zanesfield ....272..E 5
Zanesville .33,045.°F 8

°County seat
*Does not appear on the map; key shows general location.

Source: Latest census figures (1970).

523

The 1970 United States census reported that Ohio had 10,652,017 persons, the sixth highest population among the states. Ohio's population had increased 10 per cent over the 1960 figure of 9,706,397.

About three-fourths of Ohio's people live in urban areas, and the rest make their homes in rural communities. About a twentieth of the population live on farms. Almost a third live in the metropolitan areas of Cleveland and Cincinnati. In all, Ohio has 14 Standard Metropolitan Statistical Areas (see METROPOLITAN AREA). For the names and populations of these metropolitan areas, see the *Index* to the political map of Ohio.

Cleveland, with a population of 750,903, is the largest city in Ohio. It lies in the northeast, the most heavily populated section of the state. Ohio has five other cities with populations of more than 200,000. They are, in order of size, Columbus, Cincinnati, Toledo, Akron, and Dayton. See the separate articles on the cities of Ohio listed in the *Related Articles* at the end of this article.

More than 95 of every 100 Ohioans were born in the United States. Most of those born in other countries came from Czechoslovakia, England, Germany, Hungary, Italy, and Poland.

Protestant churches have the largest membership in Ohio. Roman Catholics form the largest single religious group, and total about three-fourths of the number of all Protestants. Large Protestant groups in the state include Disciples of Christ, Lutherans, Methodists, and Presbyterians.

Ohio Dept. of Industrial and Economic Development

The Children's Zoo in Cleveland, Ohio's largest city, is a favorite attraction for children. In this part of the zoo, called "The Red Barn," a child can pet his favorite farm animals.

An Amish Family of Holmes County gathers for a quiet evening at home. These hardworking people lead simple lives and avoid modern ways. The women wear full-skirted dresses and sunbonnets. The men have beards. All the family's clothing is homemade. The Amish have lived in Ohio since the 1800's.

Cornell Capa, Magnum

POPULATION

This map shows the *population density* of Ohio, and how it varies in different parts of the state. Population density means the average number of persons who live on each square mile.

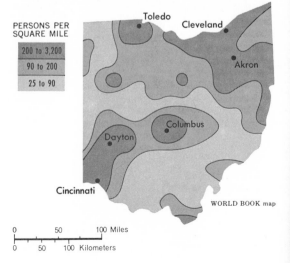

PERSONS PER SQUARE MILE

200 to 3,200
90 to 200
25 to 90

Toledo
Cleveland
Akron
Columbus
Dayton
Cincinnati

WORLD BOOK map

0   50   100 Miles
0   50   100 Kilometers

Schools. The first school in Ohio opened in 1773 at Schoenbrunn, near present-day New Philadelphia. It was set up for Indian children by David Zeisberger, a Moravian missionary. Ohio's public-school system began in 1825, and public high schools were authorized in 1853. During the 1800's, several Ohio educators wrote school textbooks that were used throughout the United States. The most famous of these educators was William H. McGuffey (see McGuffey, William H.).

Many colleges were founded in Ohio during the 1800's, several of them by churches. Oberlin College, established in 1833, became the country's first college for both men and women.

All elementary and high schools in Ohio are under the supervision of the state board of education. This board heads the state department of education. It consists of 24 members elected to six-year terms. These members appoint the state superintendent of public instruction, and can dismiss him at any time. Each of the state colleges and universities of Ohio is supervised by a board of trustees appointed by the governor. Ohio law requires children between the ages of 6 and 18 to attend school. For information on the number of students and teachers in Ohio, see Education (table).

Libraries. A subscription library opened at Belpre in 1796. In 1804, the famous Coonskin Library was founded at Ames (now Amesville). Pioneers bought the library's first 51 books with raccoon skins. Many of these books have been preserved by the Ohio Historical Society in Columbus. In 1817, Governor Thomas Worthington established the Ohio State Library in Columbus as a reference library for state officials. Ohio has 256 tax-supported public libraries and library systems and about 380 branch libraries.

Cleveland is the largest library center in Ohio. The Cleveland Public Library is one of the biggest in the nation. Other large libraries include the Cincinnati Public Library, the University of Cincinnati Library, and the Ohio State University Library in Columbus.

The Rutherford B. Hayes Library in Fremont honors the 19th President of the United States. It opened in 1916 and was the nation's first presidential library. The Historical and Philosophical Society of Ohio in Cincinnati has a collection on early Ohio and the Ohio River. The Martha Kinney Cooper Ohioana Library in Columbus collects the works of Ohio authors and books about Ohio and Ohioans.

Museums. The Cleveland Museum of Art owns the Severance collection of arms and armor, and several items from the famous Guelph Treasure from Germany. The Cincinnati Art Museum is well known for its Greek and Roman statues and other art objects. The Taft Museum in Cincinnati displays excellent collections of paintings and Chinese porcelain. The Toledo Museum of Art has a display of glass from all parts of the world.

Exhibits at the Ohio Historical Society in Columbus show the history of the state. The U.S. Air Force Museum, the only one of its kind, is at Wright-Patterson Air Force Base near Dayton. Its exhibits range from airplanes of World War I to jet aircraft.

UNIVERSITIES AND COLLEGES

Ohio has 56 universities and colleges accredited by the North Central Association of Colleges and Secondary Schools. For enrollments and further information, see UNIVERSITIES AND COLLEGES (table).

Name	Location	Founded	Name	Location	Founded
Air Force Institute of Technology	Wright-Patterson Air Force Base	1946	Malone College	Canton	1957
Akron, University of	Akron	1870	Marietta College	Marietta	1835
Antioch College	Yellow Springs	1852	Mary Manse College	Toledo	1873
Ashland College	Ashland	1878	Miami University	Oxford	1809
Athenaeum of Ohio	Cincinnati	1829	Mount St. Joseph on the Ohio, College of	Mount St. Joseph	1852
Baldwin-Wallace College	Berea	1845	Mount Union College	Alliance	1846
Bluffton College	Bluffton	1900	Muskingum College	New Concord	1837
Borromeo Seminary of Ohio	Wickliffe	1953	Notre Dame College	Cleveland	1922
Bowling Green State University	Bowling Green	1910	Oberlin College	Oberlin	1833
Capital University	Columbus	1830	Ohio Dominican College	Columbus	1911
Case Western Reserve University	Cleveland	1826	Ohio Northern University	Ada	1871
Central State University	Wilberforce	1887	Ohio State University	Columbus	1870
Cincinnati, University of	Cincinnati	1819	Ohio University	Athens	1804
Cleveland Institute of Art	Cleveland	1946	Ohio Wesleyan University	Delaware	1842
Cleveland State University	Cleveland	1923	Otterbein College	Westerville	1847
Dayton, University of	Dayton	1850	Rio Grande College	Rio Grande	1883
Defiance College	Defiance	1850	St. John College of Cleveland	Cleveland	1928
Denison University	Granville	1831	Steubenville, College of	Steubenville	1946
Edgecliff College	Cincinnati	1935	Toledo, University of	Toledo	1872
Findlay College	Findlay	1882	Ursuline College	Cleveland	1871
Hebrew Union College— Jewish Institute of Religion	Cincinnati	1875	Walsh College	Canton	1960
Heidelberg College	Tiffin	1850	Western College	Oxford	1853
Hiram College	Hiram	1850	Wilberforce University	Wilberforce	1856
John Carroll University	Cleveland	1886	Wilmington College	Wilmington	1870
Kent State University	Kent	1910	Wittenberg University	Springfield	1845
Kenyon College	Gambier	1824	Wooster, College of	Wooster	1866
Lake Erie College	Painesville	1856	Wright State University	Dayton	1967
			Xavier University	Cincinnati	1831
			Youngstown State University	Youngstown	1908

Ohio has hundreds of historical, recreational, and scenic attractions. Every year, they draw more than 26 million visitors. Historical points of interest include huge Indian burial mounds and forts that date back to prehistoric times. Ohio's 2,500 lakes and 44,000 miles of rivers and streams offer boating, fishing, and swimming. Hunters shoot deer, ducks, and rabbits in the state's woods and on the rolling plains. Many vacationers enjoy hiking in Ohio's hilly eastern section, which has some of the state's most beautiful scenery.

Great Serpent Mound

PLACES TO VISIT

Following are brief descriptions of some of Ohio's most interesting places to visit.

Adena State Memorial, in Chillicothe, is a restored stone house built in 1807 by Thomas Worthington, who later became governor of Ohio. It is furnished with rare American antiques of the 1700's and early 1800's.

Blue Hole, near Castalia, is a flowing spring that pours forth 10 million gallons of water daily. The water remains at a constant temperature of 48° F.

Campus Martius Museum, in Marietta, has been a state memorial since 1919. It stands on the site of the fortified stockade built by the first permanent white settlers in Ohio. The museum includes the home of Rufus Putnam, the founder of Marietta, and a collection of early Ohio articles. Also on exhibit are models, pictures, and relics of riverboats of the Mississippi, Muskingum, and Ohio rivers.

Fort Recovery, in the village of Fort Recovery, is a reproduction of part of the fort built in 1793 by General Anthony Wayne. He used the fort during the Indian wars in Ohio. Fort Recovery has been a state monument since 1933.

Indian Mounds and Other Earthworks may be seen throughout the state. *Fort Ancient*, near Lebanon, is the largest hilltop earth structure in the United States. Its earthen walls, more than 20 feet high and 3 miles long, enclose an area of more than 100 acres. *Fort Hill*, near Bainbridge, is a 1,200-acre area with a great walled enclosure on a high hill. Nature trails cross the area. *Great Serpent Mound*, near Hillsboro, is one of the best-known prehistoric structures in the world. The mound is shaped like a gigantic snake, with the body forming seven deep curves. It rises several feet and extends for more than a quarter of a mile. *Newark Earthworks*, at Newark, has circular walls 1,200 feet in diameter and from 8 to 14 feet high. They enclose an earthen mound.

Kelleys Island, in Lake Erie near Sandusky, is a summer resort famous for its glacial markings and Inscription Rock. The markings—grooves cut into surface limestone by glaciers—are among the best examples of glacial action in the world. They vary in depth from a few inches to several feet. Inscription Rock is a large limestone boulder with traces of prehistoric Indian carvings.

McKinley Monument, in Canton, is the burial place of President and Mrs. William McKinley. The memorial is a circular structure topped by a dome. It is 75 feet in diameter at the base and 97 feet high.

National Professional Football Hall of Fame, in Canton, honors outstanding professional football players. It includes a museum of equipment worn by famous players and used in famous games.

Schoenbrunn Village, near New Philadelphia, consists of reconstructed portions of the Moravian mission settlement founded there in 1772 for Indians. It includes a replica of the first schoolhouse in what is now Ohio. The village has been a state monument since 1923.

Wright-Patterson Air Force Base, near Dayton, is the largest U.S. Air Force research field in the United States. New and experimental aircraft equipment is tested there. The base includes the field on which the Wright brothers conducted their airplane experiments, and a national aeronautics museum. See WRIGHT-PATTERSON AIR FORCE BASE.

Zoar Village, near New Philadelphia, was founded in 1817 by a group of Germans seeking freedom from religious persecution. The home of their leader, Joseph Bimeler, and the old Zoar Garden can be seen. The village became a state memorial in 1936.

National Forests and Monuments. Wayne National Forest, the only national forest in Ohio, lies in the southeastern part of the state. It was established as a national forest in 1934. For the forest's area and chief features, see NATIONAL FOREST (table). Perry's Victory and International Peace Memorial National Monument stands at Put-in-Bay on South Bass Island in Lake Erie. The monument was completed in 1915. It honors the American victory in the Battle of Lake Erie during the War of 1812, and a hundred years of peace between the United States and Canada. The granite shaft stands 352 feet high, and is one of the tallest monuments in the country. It has an observation deck at the top. Mound City Group National Monument, near Chillicothe, has many prehistoric Indian mounds. It was established in 1923.

State Parks and Forests. Ohio has 55 state parks and 19 state forests. For information on the state parks of Ohio write to Chief, Division of Parks and Recreation, 1500 Dublin Road, Columbus, Ohio 43212.

Steve Bulkley, Foto/Find

Foto/Find

Soap Box Derby

Tom Root, Foto/Find

Schoenbrunn Village **Geauga County Maple Festival**

Perry's Victory Monument

Football Hall of Fame

Shostal   Frank Muth, Foto/Find   G. Warstler, Foto/Find

ANNUAL EVENTS

Ohio has several annual events that attract visitors from all parts of the United States. The most famous event is probably the boys' All-American Soap Box Derby. It also draws young contestants from Canada, Europe, and South America. The Derby is held in Akron on the first Sunday in August (see SOAP BOX DERBY). Other annual events include the following.

January-March: Butler Institute Art Show in Youngstown (January); American-Canadian Sports Show in Cleveland (March); Buzzard Sunday in Hinckley (first Sunday after March 15).

April-June: Geauga County Maple Festival in Chardon (April); Cherry Blossom Festival in Barberton (early in May); May Music Festival in Cincinnati; Annual Show of work by Cleveland artists (throughout May); Bach Festival at Baldwin-Wallace College in

Berea (second week in June); Boy Scout Camporee in Greenville (second week in June).

July-September: Steam Threshers Festival in Urbana (July); Ohio Hills Folk Festival in Quaker City (July); Inter-Lake Yachting Association Regatta in Put-in-Bay (August); Portsmouth Regatta (August); Parade of the Hills in Nelsonville (August); Ohio State Fair in Columbus (late August-early September); Jackson Apple Festival (September); Swiss Festival in Sugarcreek (September); American Indian Festival in Peninsula (September); Ohio State Farm Science Review at Ohio State University in Columbus (late in September).

October-December: Holmes County Antique Festival in Millersburg (early in October); Apple Butter Festival in Burton (October); Pumpkin Show in Circleville (October).

527

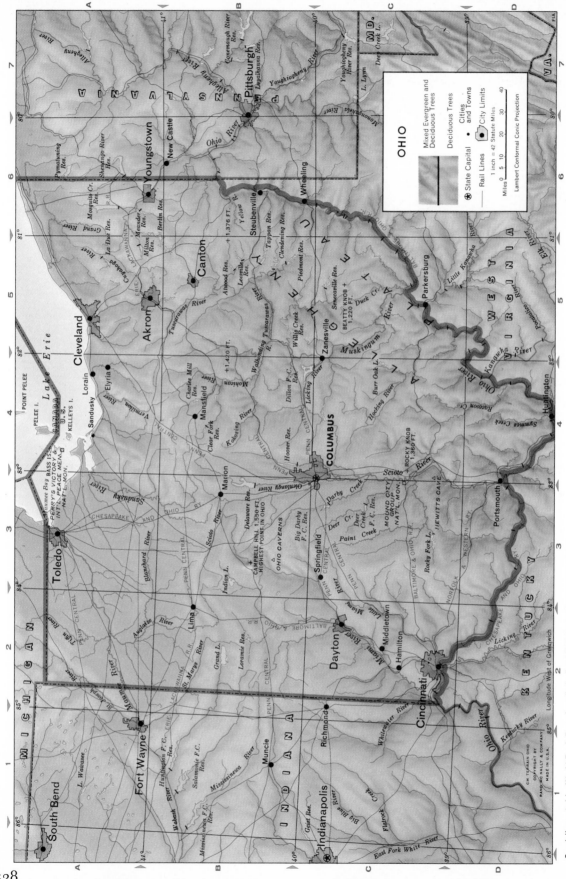

OHIO

Mixed Evergreen and
Deciduous Trees

Deciduous Trees

⊛ State Capital
● Cities and Towns
City Limits

Rail Lines

1 inch = 42 Statute Miles
Miles 0 5 10 20 30 40
Statute Miles

Lambert Conformal Conic Projection

Specially created for **World Book Encyclopedia** by Rand McNally and World Book editors

Meier's Wine Cellars, Inc.

Grape Packers stack wooden boxes of fruit for shipment to a winery in Sandusky. Fruits and vegetables grow well in the fertile soil of northern Ohio. This area is in the Great Lakes Plains region.

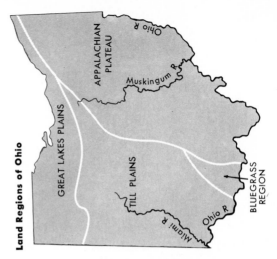

Land Regions of Ohio

Land Regions. Several glaciers moved down from the north thousands of years ago, during the Ice Age. They covered all of what is now Ohio except the southeastern part. These separate glacial movements helped create the state's four main land regions. These four regions are (1) the Great Lakes Plains, (2) the Till Plains, (3) the Appalachian Plateau, and (4) the Bluegrass Region.

The Great Lakes Plains of northern Ohio form part of the fertile lowland that lies along much of the Great Lakes. In Ohio, these plains make up a narrow strip of land that borders Lake Erie. The region is 5 to 10 miles wide in the east, and broadens to more than 50 miles in the Maumee Valley to the west. A few low, sandy ridges along the Lake Erie shore break the flatness of the plains. A wide variety of crops, especially fruits and vegetables, grows in the region's fertile soil. The region is one of the busiest manufacturing, shipping, and trading areas in the United States. It includes many lake ports and large industrial cities. The most heavily populated part of Ohio, the Cleveland metropolitan area, is in this region.

The Till Plains are the easternmost part of the rich midwestern Corn Belt, which stretches westward from Ohio. This region ranks among the most fertile farming areas in the country.

Some hills dot the gently rolling plains, which lie in most of western Ohio. One of them, 1,550-foot-high Campbell Hill in Logan County, is the highest point in Ohio. From there, the land gradually slopes downward to the southwestern corner of the state in Hamilton County. This area, 433 feet above sea level, is Ohio's lowest point. Farmers of the Till Plains produce much grain and livestock. The area has many industrial cities where a wide variety of products is manufactured.

The Appalachian Plateau includes almost all the eastern half of Ohio. This highland extends eastward into Pennsylvania and West Virginia. The southern two-thirds of the region was not covered by glaciers. As a result, this section is the most rugged part of the state, with steep hills and valleys. Most of the soil is thin and

not fertile. Farmers use the land chiefly for grazing cattle or sheep. The northern third of the Appalachian Plateau has rolling hills and valleys, and has less fertile soil than that of the Till Plains. General and dairy farming are the major agricultural activities.

The rugged Appalachian Plateau has some of the most beautiful scenery in Ohio, including the state's largest forests and some waterfalls. It also has Ohio's richest mineral deposits—clay, coal, natural gas, oil, and salt. A few of its cities are important manufacturing centers.

The Bluegrass Region, Ohio's smallest land region, is an extension of the Bluegrass Region of Kentucky. This triangular area in southern Ohio has both hilly and gently rolling land. Many farmers grow tobacco in the flatter sections, which have deep, fertile soil. The hills of the Bluegrass Region have thin, less fertile soil.

Shoreline of Ohio stretches for 312 miles along Lake Erie, from Conneaut in the east to Toledo in the west. It includes 53 miles along Sandusky Bay, and 66 miles

Irvin L. Oakes, Foto/Find

James Busch, Foto/Find

Winter Snow covers a Marion County farm, left. This area of the Till Plains includes some of the country's most fertile farmland.

The Ohio River, right, forms Ohio's southern border. Gallipolis, settled in the 1790's, overlooks West Virginia across the river.

Shostal

Gently Rolling Land of Highland County, below, has deep, fertile soil. The land forms part of the Bluegrass Region, a triangular section in southern Ohio.

along offshore islands. The shoreline is mainly rocky, with a few sandy beaches such as that at Cedar Point. Many fine harbors indent the shoreline. Two of the busy lake ports lie on large bays—Toledo on Maumee Bay, and Sandusky on Sandusky Bay. North and northwest of Sandusky in Lake Erie are some small islands. The largest ones are Kelleys and North, Middle, and South Bass islands. They are used chiefly as recreation areas.

Rivers and Lakes. Ohio has more than 44,000 miles of rivers and streams. They flow either south into the Ohio River or north into Lake Erie. A series of low hills separates the two groups of rivers. This *divide* forms an irregular line from the northeastern corner of Ohio to Mercer County, where it extends into Indiana. Except for the Maumee River, all the longer, wider rivers flow into the Ohio River. They drain about 70 per cent of the state.

The Ohio River, one of the chief rivers of North America, flows more than 450 miles along Ohio's southern and southeastern borders. The northern bank of the river forms the state boundary. Many bluffs between 200 and 500 feet high rise along the river, which winds through a valley less than two miles wide.

The Ohio River's longest tributary in Ohio is the 237-mile-long Scioto River. Other major rivers flowing into the Ohio include the Hocking, Little Miami, Mahoning, Miami, and Muskingum. The largest rivers that flow into Lake Erie include the Cuyahoga, Grand, Huron, Maumee, Portage, Sandusky, and Vermilion. Several underground streams have formed beautiful caverns, such as the Seven Caves near Bainbridge and the Ohio Caverns near West Liberty. Many swift streams in northeastern Ohio have rapids and waterfalls.

Ohio's lake waters include 3,457 square miles of Lake Erie. The International Line between the United States and Canada runs through Lake Erie about 20 miles north of the Ohio shore. The state has more than 2,500 lakes larger than two acres. Only 27 of them are natural lakes with an area of 40 acres or more. These lakes have beds formed by the ancient glaciers. Ohio also has more than 180 man-made lakes that cover at least 40 acres each.

Several man-made lakes were built during the 1800's to feed water into two canals. These canals were the Ohio and Erie Canal, between Cleveland and Portsmouth, and the Miami and Erie Canal, between Toledo and Cincinnati. They were Ohio's chief means of transportation until the coming of the railroads. The largest lake in Ohio is 12,700-acre Grand Lake near Indiana. It was created during the 1840's by damming two nearby creeks to provide water for the Miami and Erie Canal. Other large artificial lakes include three reservoirs—Berlin, Mosquito Creek, and Senecaville—and Indian Lake.

Autumn in Ohio is a season of colorful landscapes. Lake Hope, near Zaleski, is one of many man-made lakes in the state. Its excellent swimming, fishing, and boating attract many tourists.

Shostal

OHIO/*Climate*

Ohio has cold winters and warm, humid summers, with an average annual temperature of 52° F. The average January temperature is 31° F., and the July temperature averages 74° F. Ohio's lowest recorded temperature, −39° F., occurred at Milligan on Feb. 10, 1899. The highest temperature was 113° F. at Thurman on July 4, 1897, and at Gallipolis on July 21, 1934.

Ohio's annual *precipitation* (rain, melted snow, and other forms of moisture) averages 37 inches a year. The wettest area is in the southwest, where Wilmington's yearly precipitation measures 44 inches. The driest part of the state lies along Lake Erie between Sandusky and Toledo. It receives 32 inches of precipitation annually. Snowfall of Ohio averages 29 inches a year. It increases from west to east, and from south to north.

SEASONAL TEMPERATURES

JANUARY

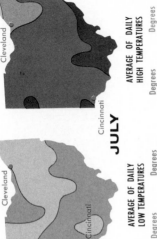

AVERAGE OF DAILY HIGH TEMPERATURES

Degrees Centigrade	Degrees Fahrenheit
8 to 10	46 to 50
6 to 8	42 to 46
3 to 6	38 to 42
1 to 3	34 to 38

AVERAGE OF DAILY LOW TEMPERATURES

Degrees Centigrade	Degrees Fahrenheit
−3 to −1	26 to 30
−6 to −3	22 to 26
−8 to −6	18 to 22

JULY

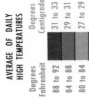

AVERAGE OF DAILY HIGH TEMPERATURES

Degrees Centigrade	Degrees Fahrenheit
31 to 33	88 to 92
29 to 31	84 to 88
27 to 29	80 to 84
24 to 27	76 to 80

AVERAGE OF DAILY LOW TEMPERATURES

Degrees Centigrade	Degrees Fahrenheit
17 to 18	62 to 64
16 to 17	60 to 62

AVERAGE YEARLY PRECIPITATION
(Rain, Melted Snow, and Other Moisture)

Inches	Centimeters
40 to 44	102 to 112
36 to 40	91 to 102
32 to 36	81 to 91

Scale:
0 50 100 150 Miles
0 100 200 Kilometers

WORLD BOOK maps

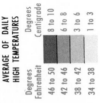
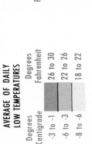

MONTHLY WEATHER IN CLEVELAND AND CINCINNATI

		JAN	FEB	MAR	APR	MAY	JUNE	JULY	AUG	SEPT	OCT	NOV	DEC
CLEVELAND	Average of: High Temperatures	36	36	45	57	70	80	85	83	76	64	49	38
	Low Temperatures	21	21	28	38	48	58	63	61	55	45	34	25
	Days of Rain or Snow	16	15	16	13	12	11	10	9	9	10	15	16
CINCINNATI	Days of Rain or Snow	13	11	13	12	14	11	10	10	9	9	10	11
	High Temperatures	41	43	53	64	74	83	87	85	80	68	53	42
	Low Temperatures	25	27	34	43	53	62	66	64	58	47	36	28

Temperatures are given in degrees Fahrenheit.

Source: U.S. Weather Bureau

The greatest source of income in Ohio is manufacturing. In fact, manufacturing provides all but a small share of the total value of all production in Ohio. Only New York and California rank above Ohio in industrial production. Several important natural advantages have helped develop Ohio's industries. They include large deposits of coal and other minerals, a plentiful water supply, and the state's central location near major markets and supplies of raw materials in other states.

Natural Resources. Fertile soils and valuable minerals are Ohio's most important natural resources. The state also has large forests and varied wildlife.

Soil. Fertile soils deposited by ancient glaciers are found in all parts of Ohio except the southeast. Many layers of these soils are several feet deep. Materials in the various kinds of soils include limestone, sandstone, and shale. Southeastern Ohio, which was not covered by glaciers during the Ice Age, has thin, infertile soil.

Minerals. Coal is Ohio's most important mineral. Deposits in eastern and southeastern Ohio have an estimated 42 billion tons of coal, or about 6 per cent of the country's total supply. Oil and natural gas are found in several parts of Ohio. The state has over 90 million barrels of proven crude oil reserves. Ohio's minerals include huge reserves of rock salt and salt-water brine. The state could supply the United States with all the salt it needs for thousands of years. Most of the salt lies in deep rock-salt beds in the northeastern section of the state. Ohio also has large deposits of clay, limestone, sand and gravel, and sandstone.

Forests cover about a fourth of Ohio. Most of the trees are hardwoods. They include beeches, black walnuts, hickories, maples, sycamores, red and white oaks, tulip trees, white ashes, and white elms. Nearly three-fourths of the state's lumber comes from farm wood lots. This wood consists of second-growth trees, which develop after the first growth of timber has been cut.

Animal Life. Ohio has few large wild animals, except white-tailed deer. Smaller wild animals include minks, muskrats, opossums, rabbits, raccoons, red foxes, squirrels, skunks, and woodchucks. Ohio has about 175 kinds of songbirds. Bald eagles and various shore birds live along Lake Erie. Game birds include ducks, geese, partridges, pheasants, quail, and ruffed grouse. About 170 kinds of fishes live in Ohio's waters. They include bass, bluegills, catfish, muskellunge, perch, and pike.

Manufacturing accounts for over 90 per cent of the value of all goods produced in Ohio. Products manufactured in the state have a *value added by manufacture* of more than $20 billion a year. This figure represents the value created in the products by Ohio's industries, not counting such costs as materials, supplies, and fuel.

The production of nonelectrical machinery is Ohio's chief manufacturing activity. This production has an annual value added by manufacture of about $3,295,-000,000. Ohio has long been a leader in the invention, improvement, and manufacture of farm machinery. Ohio leads the states in the manufacture of machine tools, and Cincinnati leads all U.S. cities. Ohio factories also rank high in the manufacture of blast furnaces and rolling mills, heating and cooling equipment, office machinery, and refrigerating machinery.

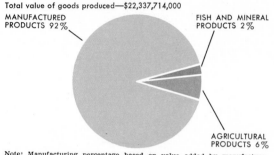

OHIO'S PRODUCTION IN 1967

Total value of goods produced—$22,337,714,000

MANUFACTURED PRODUCTS 92%

FISH AND MINERAL PRODUCTS 2%

AGRICULTURAL PRODUCTS 6%

Note: Manufacturing percentage based on value added by manufacture. Other percentages based on value of production. Fish Products are less than 1 per cent.

Sources: U.S. Government statistics

OHIO'S EMPLOYMENT IN 1967

Total number of persons employed—3,719,200

		Number of Employees
Manufacturing	𝍸𝍸𝍸𝍸𝍸𝍸	1,382,300
Wholesale & Retail Trade	𝍸𝍸𝍸	700,100
Services	𝍸𝍸	489,200
Government	𝍸𝍸	487,500
Transportation & Public Utilities	𝍸	212,900
Construction	𝍸	169,000
Finance, Insurance & Real Estate	𝍸	142,600
Agriculture & Mining	𝍸	135,600

Source: U.S. Department of Labor

Dayton makes more cash registers than any other American city. Toledo has the largest factory in the United States producing weighing scales.

The second-ranking industry is the manufacture of primary metals, especially iron and steel. This industry's products have an annual value added by manufacture of about $2,757,000,000. Among the states, only Pennsylvania's production is greater. Ohio's steel production totals about 23 million tons a year, about a sixth of the nation's total output. The chief steel mills in Ohio include those in the Cleveland-Lorain and Youngstown areas. Convenient transportation routes connect these areas with nearby supplies of coal and iron ore, used in steelmaking.

Ohio's third-ranking manufacturing activity is the production of transportation equipment, with an annual value added by manufacture of about $2,635,-000,000. Ohio leads the states in the production of bus and truck bodies, motorcycles, and truck trailers. Cincinnati, Cleveland, Columbus, Hudson, Lorain, Toledo, and Twinsburg are major manufacturing centers for bodies and parts of automobiles and other motor vehicles. Elyria has the nation's largest factory producing automobile air brakes. Dayton is famous for the manufacture of airplane parts. Ohio factories also produce locomotives and railway cars.

The manufacture of fabricated metal products is Ohio's fourth most important industry. This industry's

Libby-Owens-Ford Glass Co.

Workers Examine Sheets of Plate Glass in a factory in Rossford. They use chalk to mark defects and cutting instructions on ground and polished glass. This eliminates waste when the sheets are cut. Ohio leads the states in the manufacture of glass products.

products have an annual value added by manufacture of about $2,100,000,000. The production of electrical machinery ranks next in importance, with a value added by manufacture of about $2,076,000,000 a year.

Ohio leads the states in the manufacture of rubber products. Its factories produce more than a third of the rubber tires and tubes made in the United States. This industry is centered in Akron, where it was founded in 1870 by Benjamin F. Goodrich. The industry expanded rapidly because of the development of the automobile, and because of the industry's nearness to Michigan automobile factories. The nation's largest factory producing golf balls, a rubber product, is in Elyria.

Ohio also leads the states in the manufacture of clay and glass products. Clay products include bricks and tile, roofing, and tableware. Much pottery is manufactured along the Ohio River, especially in East Liverpool. Toledo and various other cities are centers of the glassmaking industry. Two important natural advantages helped the establishment of this industry in Ohio. These were plentiful deposits of sand and natural gas, both used in glassmaking.

The slaughtering and packing of meat animals is another leading Ohio industry. Important related industries include leather-tanning, shoe-manufacturing, and soapmaking. Ohio leads the states in soap production, and Cincinnati has the largest soap factory in the United States.

Other important Ohio products include aluminum, bicycles, butter and other dairy products, cement, matches, musical instruments, paints and varnishes, and sporting goods. Many Ohio cities manufacture clothing and textiles. Papermaking, developed when the state was still heavily forested, is a profitable industry in Chillicothe, Hamilton, and Middletown. Publishing and printing are centered in Akron, Cincinnati, Cleveland, Columbus, and Dayton. Shipbuilding flourishes in Lorain, and a uranium-diffusion plant operates in Piketon. Several cities have oil refineries. Ohio ranks among the leading states in the production of coke. Important by-products of this steel-making fuel include chemicals, fertilizers, and tar.

Agriculture. Ohio has about 17,600,000 acres of farmland, and a farm population of about 435,000. The state's 120,000 farms average 146 acres in size.

Agriculture in Ohio provides an annual income of about $1½ billion. This amount is only 6 per cent of the state's total value of all production. The most valuable farm activity is the raising of meat animals. Ohio ranks among the leading hog-producing states. Farmers in the Miami River Valley developed the famous Poland China hog during the 1800's. But this breed is no longer produced in Ohio. A monument to the Poland China hog stands near Monroe.

Many Ohio farmers also raise beef cattle or sheep. They raise both mutton and wool breeds of sheep, chiefly in the central part of the state. Ohio produces more wool than any other state east of the Mississippi River.

Dairy farming is Ohio's second-ranking agricultural activity. About 95 per cent of the milk produced on the farms is sold in nearby cities. Cheese is a valuable by-product of the dairy industry. Tuscarawas County is called *America's Little Switzerland* because of its great Swiss cheese production. All Liederkranz cheese is produced in Van Wert.

Ohio cities provide a ready market for the state's large egg production. Poultry farmers also raise chickens and turkeys in hundreds of commercial hatcheries. These hatcheries produce about 30 million chickens a year.

Farmers grow corn and wheat in nearly all parts of the state, especially in the Till Plains region. Ohio is a leading state in the production of these crops, as well as oats, popcorn, and soybeans. The farmers also grow large crops of hay, mushrooms, red clover, and rye. They feed much of the grain crops to their livestock.

Ohio has been an important fruit-producing state since pioneer days, when Johnny Appleseed roamed the countryside planting apple seeds (see APPLESEED, JOHNNY). Ohio farms also produce large crops of grapes and peaches. The plains along Lake Erie and the offshore islands make up one of the leading grape-producing regions of the United States. The warm lake winds protect the grapes from frosts in late spring and early autumn. Ohio's more than 25 wineries produce about a million gallons of wine annually.

Large crops of cabbages, potatoes, sugar beets, sweet corn, tobacco, and tomatoes are grown in Ohio. The rich soils of the Great Lakes Plains and the warmer lowlands along the Ohio River are especially good for

FARM AND MINERAL PRODUCTS

This map shows where the state's leading farm and mineral products are produced. The major urban areas (shown in red) are the state's important manufacturing centers.

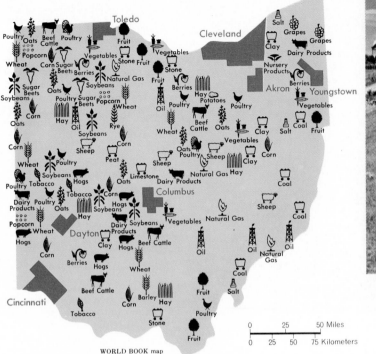

WORLD BOOK map

Shostal

Huge Wheat Harvests provide an important source of farm income in Ohio. Wheat grows particularly well in the Till Plains region.

growing vegetables. These regions also have tree nurseries and flower greenhouses. Ohio leads the states in the production of hothouse vegetables. Ohio has nearly a thousand acres under glass, more than any other state.

Mining in Ohio provides an annual income of about $455 million. Coal is the greatest source of this income. Since coal mining began in Ohio during the early 1800's, about 4 billion tons of coal have been mined. Ohio now produces more than 46 million tons of coal a year, and is a leading coal-producing state. Ohio's great fields of *bituminous* (soft) coal lie mainly in the east and southeast. More than half the coal mined in Ohio comes from Belmont, Harrison, and Jefferson counties. The fields there form part of the great Appalachian coal fields that include parts of Pennsylvania and West Virginia. About two-thirds of the coal is taken from strip mines (see COAL [Mining Methods]). Toledo is an important coal-shipping port.

Petroleum is taken from several parts of Ohio. At one time, most of it came from the Lima-Indiana field, which was opened in 1885. Ohio wells provide about 10 million barrels of oil yearly. The state has over 4,000 natural gas wells. They produce about 41 billion cubic feet of gas annually.

Ohio ranks high among the states in the production of *nonmetallic minerals* (those that are neither metal ores nor fuels). The state leads in the production of building sandstone, supplying over a third of the country's supply. Ohio's best clays come from the eastern part of

the state, in or near the coal fields. These clays are used in the manufacture of such products as bricks and tile, cement, pottery, and stoneware. Sandstone is taken from quarries in many parts of Ohio. The best-known variety of sandstone, Berea or *grit*, comes from Lorain County.

Ohio provides about two-thirds of all the limestone used in the United States to make glass. The state also leads in the production of lime, made from limestone. Other uses of limestone include the manufacture of cement, chemicals, fertilizers, and steel. Limestone is quarried chiefly in north-central Ohio. The nation's deepest limestone quarry—about half a mile deep—is at Barberton.

Ohio's oldest mining industry is the production of salt, and the state is a leading salt producer. The deepest salt mine in the United States is near Fairport Harbor. The mine is about 2,000 feet deep. Sand and gravel are produced throughout the state. Other important minerals include abrasive stones, gypsum, and peat.

Fishing Industry. Ohio has an annual fish catch valued at about $1 million. The state's annual commercial catch amounts to about 10 million pounds. Lake Erie used to be an extremely productive fishing area, but waste from cities and industries has killed off many fish. The cities of Curtice, Port Clinton, Sandusky, and Vermilion are the only remaining fishing ports on Lake Erie today. Many fish caught in Lake Erie are shipped alive to commercial ponds in Kentucky, southern Ohio, and West Virginia. The most important fish caught in

Ohio include carp, channel catfish, sheepshead, white bass, yellow perch, and yellow pike.

Electric Power. Almost all of Ohio's power comes from coal-burning steam plants. About 40 of them operate throughout the state. Ohio also has about 20 other fuel-burning plants and 1 hydroelectric plant. For Ohio's kilowatt-hour production, see ELECTRIC POWER (table).

Transportation. Ohio is a transportation link between the eastern and western United States. Cross-country railways and roads began going westward through the state during the 1800's.

About 10 airlines serve Ohio's cities. The state has more than 400 airports and landing fields, and about 10 seaplane anchorages on Lake Erie and the Ohio River. Seaplane bases for private and training uses have also been established in fishing and hunting areas. Ohio has three federally owned airfields.

Railroads operate on about 9,000 miles of track in Ohio. All the principal railroads connecting the East with Chicago and St. Louis cross the state. Several lines also connect Ohio with the South.

The first east-west roads in Ohio were the natural trails that followed the sandy ridges along Lake Erie. Later roads, paved with logs, followed Indian trails. The historic Zane's Trace, built for the federal government by Ebenezer Zane, opened in 1797. It ran from what is now Wheeling, W.Va., through the present-day Ohio cities of Zanesville, Lancaster, and Chillicothe to Maysville, Ky. Maysville was then the northern end of the road to New Orleans. During the early 1800's, the National (Cumberland) Road became an important link between East and West (see NATIONAL ROAD).

Today, Ohio has about 110,000 miles of roads, almost all of which have hard surfaces. Thirty federal highways and several expressways cross the state. The 241-mile Ohio Turnpike runs from the Pennsylvania border across northern Ohio to Indiana.

The Great Lakes and the St. Lawrence Seaway connect Ohio with the Atlantic Ocean. The lakes also link Ohio with the north-central states and Canada. Another major waterway, the Ohio River, connects the state with the Mississippi River and the Gulf of Mexico. The entire length of this river is navigable throughout the year.

Communication. The first newspaper published north and west of the Ohio River, the *Centinel of the North-Western Territory*, was founded in Cincinnati in 1793. The nation's first antislavery newspaper, the *Philanthropist*, began publication in Mount Pleasant in 1817. Today, Ohio has about 100 daily newspapers and about 300 weeklies. Newspapers with a circulation of over 150,000 are the *Akron Beacon Journal, Cincinnati Enquirer, Cincinnati Post & Times Star, Cleveland Press, Columbus Evening Dispatch, Dayton Daily News, Plain Dealer* of Cleveland, and *Toledo Blade*. More than 300 magazines are published in Ohio. The state is a leader in religious publications, with about 30.

Ohio's oldest radio station, WHK, began broadcasting in Cleveland in 1922. Also that year, Ohio State University in Columbus started WOSU, the first educational radio station in North America. The first Ohio television station, WEWS-TV, opened in Cleveland in 1947. Today, Ohio has over 200 radio stations and 26 television stations.

Indian Days. Thousands of years ago, prehistoric Indians lived in what is now Ohio. These Indians were the ancestors of peoples called *Mound Builders*, some of whom had high forms of civilization. The Mound Builders left more than 6,000 burial mounds, forts, and other earthworks throughout the Ohio region. The Indians included the Adena and Hopewell peoples, who lived there from 1000 B.C. to A.D. 1300. See MOUND BUILDERS.

When the early white settlers arrived, several Indian tribes lived in the Ohio region. These tribes included the Delaware, Miami, Shawnee, and Wyandot, or Huron. See INDIAN, AMERICAN (Table of Tribes).

Exploration and Settlement. The French explorer Robert Cavelier, Sieur de la Salle, was probably the first white man to reach present-day Ohio. He is believed to have visited the region about 1670. The French based their claim to the entire Northwest on La Salle's explorations. But the British claimed all the territory extending inland from their Atlantic colonies. In 1750, the Ohio Company of Virginia sent Christopher Gist to explore the upper Ohio River Valley. This company, organized in 1747, was made up of Englishmen and Virginians who planned to colonize the Ohio region. See GIST, CHRISTOPHER; LA SALLE, SIEUR DE; OHIO COMPANY (The First).

The British-French dispute over territory in North America, including the Ohio region, led to the French and Indian War (1754-1763). In the peace treaty of 1763, France gave Great Britain most of its lands east of the Mississippi River. Pontiac, an Indian chief born in Ohio, started an Indian rebellion against the British in 1763 after the peace treaty was signed. See FRENCH AND INDIAN WARS; PONTIAC.

Fighting during the Revolutionary War forced a Moravian mission settlement named Schoenbrunn, near present-day New Philadelphia, to close down. The settlement, founded in 1772 by David Zeisberger, was abandoned in 1776. In 1780, George Rogers Clark defeated Shawnee Indian allies of the British in the Battle of Piqua, near present-day Springfield. Clark's campaigns in the Northwest helped win the region for the United States during the Revolutionary War.

The region, including Ohio, became the Northwest Territory in 1787. The Northwest Ordinance of 1787 provided for the eventual statehood of Ohio and other divisions of the territory. That year, the Ohio Company of Associates bought land northwest of the Ohio River in the Muskingum River Valley. Members of this company came from New England. On April 7, 1788, the company founded Marietta, the first permanent white settlement in Ohio. Rufus Putnam, a Revolutionary War general, was superintendent of the colony. Marietta became the first capital of the Northwest Territory in July, 1788. Within a short time, several other communities developed along the Ohio River. Many settlers were Revolutionary War veterans who received land in payment for their military service. See NORTHWEST TERRITORY; OHIO COMPANY (The Second); PUTNAM, RUFUS.

For several years, a series of Indian uprisings disturbed the settlers. Several raids were led by Little Tur-

HISTORIC OHIO
The Mother of Presidents

Rutherford B. Hayes
born at Delaware

Ulysses S. Grant
born at Point Pleasant

James A. Garfield
born at Orange

Control of Lake Erie was won for the United States by Commodore Perry's victory over the British near Put-in-Bay in 1813. In reporting the battle, Perry wrote: "We have met the enemy and they are ours."

Lake Erie

• Orange

• Oberlin

Akron •

• Niles

Alliance •

New Ideas in Education. Oberlin College, established in 1833, was the nation's first coeducational college. In 1870, Mount Union College, in Alliance, held one of the first summer schools. The University of Cincinnati began the cooperative plan (classwork combined with part-time employment) in 1906.

Famous Textbooks by Ohio authors were used in American public schools for many years. Best known were *Ray's Arithmetics* (1834), the *McGuffey Readers* (1836), the *Spencerian Writing System* (1848), and *Harvey's Grammar* (1868).

Delaware •
COLUMBUS
★

• Yellow Springs

• Dayton

Rubber Manufacturing Center. B. F. Goodrich began to make fire hose and other products of rubber in 1870 in Akron. After the first pneumatic tire was used in 1895, Akron helped put the world on rubber tires.

Air Pioneers. The Wright brothers built the first wind tunnel in North America at Dayton in 1901 to conduct experiments that led to the first successful airplane flight.

Marietta •

First Permanent White Settlement in Ohio was established in 1788 by General Rufus Putnam, who is sometimes called the Father of Ohio.

• Hillsboro

Home of Many Inventions. James Ritty invented the cash register in 1879 in Dayton. L. E. Custer invented the electric runabout there in 1899. Charles F. Kettering developed an automobile self-starter in Dayton in 1911.

Indian Mounds, near Hillsboro, were built by Indian tribes several thousand years ago. The Great Serpent Mound is about a quarter of a mile long. It looks like a large serpent in the act of uncoiling. The snake has an egg in its jaws.

Benjamin Harrison
born near North Bend

William H. Taft
born at Cincinnati

William McKinley
born at Niles

Warren G. Harding
born near Blooming Grove

──────── **IMPORTANT DATES IN OHIO** ────────

c.1670 The French explorer Robert Cavelier, Sieur de la Salle, probably was the first white man to reach the Ohio region.

1747 The Ohio Company of Virginia was organized to colonize the Ohio River Valley.

1763 France surrendered its claim to the Ohio region to Great Britain.

1787 The Northwest Territory was established.

1788 The first permanent white settlement in Ohio was established in Marietta.

1795 Indian wars in the Ohio region ended with the Treaty of Greenville.

1800 The Division Act divided the Northwest Territory into two parts, and Chillicothe became the capital of the new Northwest Territory.

1803 Ohio became the 17th state on March 1.

1813 Commodore Oliver H. Perry's fleet defeated the British in the Battle of Lake Erie.

1832 The Ohio and Erie Canal was completed.

1836 The Ohio-Michigan boundary dispute was settled.

1845 The Miami and Erie Canal was completed.

1870 Benjamin F. Goodrich began the manufacture of rubber goods in Akron.

1914 Ohio passed the Conservancy Act after tragic floods in 1913.

1922 The Miami River Valley flood-control project was finished.

1938 The flood-control project in the Muskingum River Valley was completed.

1955 The Ohio Turnpike was opened to traffic.

1959 Terms of the governor and other high state officials were increased from two years to four.

1964 The voters approved a $500 million bond issue for highway construction across the state.

1967 Ohio voters approved a plan for reapportionment of the state legislature.

tle, a Miami chief. In 1794, General Anthony Wayne defeated the Indians near present-day Toledo in the Battle of Fallen Timbers. The next year, in the Treaty of Greenville, the Indians ceded the United States about two-thirds of what is now Ohio. The Indians accepted the treaty largely through the influence of Tarhe, or Crane, a Wyandot chief. With peace restored, more and more settlers poured into the region. Many settlements were founded in the valleys of rivers flowing into the Ohio. Some pioneers also settled in northeastern Ohio in the area called the Western Reserve (see WESTERN RESERVE).

In 1800, Congress passed the Division Act. This legislation created the Indiana Territory out of the western part of the Northwest Territory. Chillicothe became the capital of the eastern part, which continued to be called the Northwest Territory.

Statehood. Preparation for Ohio statehood began in November, 1802, when a convention in Chillicothe drew up the state's first constitution. Ohio became the 17th state on March 1, 1803, when the first state legislature met. Edward Tiffin, a Democratic-Republican, was the first governor. The state's population was about 70,000. Chillicothe was Ohio's capital from 1803 to 1810, when Zanesville became the capital. Chillicothe again became the capital of the state in 1812, and Columbus in 1816.

The Louisiana Purchase in 1803 gave Ohio settlers a river outlet for their products. They could ship goods down the Mississippi River and through the port of New Orleans. A thriving river trade with New Orleans soon developed. The first steamboat to travel the Ohio River was the *New Orleans*, a wood-burning sidewheeler. It first went down the river in 1811.

Ohio took an active part in the War of 1812 (1812-1815). Commodore Oliver H. Perry sailed from Put-in-Bay at South Bass Island off the Ohio shore to battle a British fleet on Sept. 10, 1813. Perry won an important naval victory in this Battle of Lake Erie (see PERRY [Oliver H.]). After the war, thousands of persons moved to Ohio from the eastern states. Many came from New England, New York, and Pennsylvania. Immigrants arrived from Germany and Great Britain.

In 1818, the steamboat *Walk-in-the-Water* became the first steamboat on Lake Erie. It demonstrated the practical use of the Great Lakes as a waterway to the West. The Erie Canal across New York from Lake Erie opened in 1825. The Ohio and Erie Canal, joining Cleveland and Portsmouth, was completed in 1832. The Miami and Erie Canal, connecting Toledo and Cincinnati, was completed in 1845. These canals served as busy trade routes for more than 25 years. But the coming of the railroads reduced canal traffic. Ohio canals and railroads brought increased prosperity, and many mills and factories were built between 1830 and 1860.

An old border dispute between Ohio and the Territory of Michigan flared up in 1835 and led to the "Toledo War." Before any actual fighting broke out, President Andrew Jackson sent agents to Toledo to persuade the governors of Ohio and Michigan to accept a truce. In 1836, Congress awarded the disputed area, about 520 square miles along Lake Erie, to Ohio. In 1841, William Henry Harrison of North Bend became the ninth President of the United States.

OHIO

The Civil War. During the years before the Civil War (1861-1865), many Ohioans had strong feelings on the question of slavery. Many *abolitionists* (persons opposed to slavery) lived throughout Ohio. They helped slaves who had escaped across the Ohio River on their flight to Canada (see UNDERGROUND RAILROAD). Most of Ohio's Southern sympathizers lived in the southern and north-central parts of the state. In 1862, Clement L. Vallandigham of Dayton became leader of the Peace Democrats party, which opposed President Abraham Lincoln's administration. Vallandigham and others who sympathized with the South were known as Copperheads.

Many famous Civil War commanders were born in Ohio, including Ulysses S. Grant and William T. Sherman. Ohio supplied about 345,000 men to the Union army. This was more than the total quotas requested by 10 presidential calls for soldiers from the state. In 1863, Confederate cavalrymen known as Morgan's Raiders crossed into Ohio and brought Civil War fighting to its northernmost point. Led by General John Hunt Morgan, they were captured in Columbiana County. Morgan later escaped and returned to the South. See MORGAN, JOHN HUNT.

Ohio's industrial centers grew rapidly after the Civil War. Many workers from other countries settled in the state. The shipping of coal, iron ore, and other bulk goods on Lake Erie increased. Farming continued to be a leading industry, but Ohio also developed into a top manufacturing state. In 1869, the Cincinnati Red Stockings (now Redlegs) became the first all-professional baseball team. Benjamin F. Goodrich began manufacturing rubber products in Akron in 1870.

Five Ohio-born Presidents, all Republicans, were elected during the 1800's. They were Ulysses S. Grant, Rutherford B. Hayes, James A. Garfield, Benjamin Harrison, and William McKinley. President William Henry Harrison of Ohio was born in Virginia.

The Early 1900's. Ohio's government was torn by political scandal and corruption during the late 1800's. Marcus A. "Mark" Hanna, political boss of Cleveland, and George B. Cox, boss of Cincinnati, both Republicans, controlled state politics. Reform movements began about 1900, and promoted honesty in both city and state governments. William Howard Taft of Cincinnati became the 27th President in 1909.

Ohio suffered the worst floods in its history during the spring of 1913. About 500 persons lost their lives after rivers overflowed their banks, and damage totaled about $147 million. Most of the destruction occurred in the Miami River Valley, especially at Dayton. In 1914, the state legislature passed the Conservancy Act, the first legislation of its kind in the United States. The chief purpose of the act was to permit the establishment of flood-control districts based on entire river systems. Many flood-control dams and reservoirs were built under this act, including those completed by 1922 in the Miami River Valley. The federal government also built about 20 flood-control dams in Ohio.

After the United States entered World War I in 1917, the state produced vast supplies of war materials. Newton D. Baker of Cleveland served as Secretary of War in President Woodrow Wilson's wartime Cabinet.

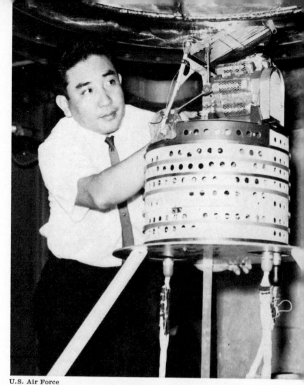

U.S. Air Force

Research in Space Technology contributes to Ohio's industrial expansion today. This scientist is examining the test model of an engine that may propel a spaceship. The engine was tested by the U.S. Air Force Systems Command at Wright-Patterson Air Force Base near Dayton.

Between World Wars. In 1921, Warren G. Harding of Marion became the 29th President. His Democratic opponent was Governor James M. Cox of Dayton. The 1920's were prosperous years in Ohio, because of continued industrial development. Cincinnati, Cleveland, Dayton, Toledo, and other industrial cities expanded rapidly. Many nearby farms disappeared as the cities grew. The Great Depression that began in 1929 hit these cities hardest in Ohio. Thousands of workers lost their jobs as factories closed. Many farmers lost their land when farm prices dropped sharply.

Government funds and federal agencies such as the Works Progress Administration (WPA) helped Ohio recover from the depression during the 1930's. In 1934, work began on the Muskingum River Valley flood-control project. This project came to national attention in the winter of 1937, when most of the dams withstood heavy floodwaters of the Ohio River. The project was completed in 1938. Robert A. Taft of Cincinnati, who became one of the most powerful men in the United States Senate, began his first term as Republican Senator from Ohio in 1939.

The Mid-1900's. During World War II (1939-1945), Ohio produced aircraft, ships, and weapons. It also contributed steel, tires, and materials to the war effort. The armed services established a number of training centers in the state.

During the 1950's, the Atomic Energy Commission (AEC) built several installations in Ohio. They included the Portsmouth Area Project in Pike County, which produces uranium-235 for use in atomic reactors. In 1955, the 241-mile Ohio Turnpike across northern

THE GOVERNORS OF OHIO

	Party	Term		Party	Term
1. Edward Tiffin	*Dem.-Rep.	1803-1807	32. Rutherford B. Hayes	Republican	1876-1877
2. Thomas Kirker	Dem.-Rep.	1807-1808	33. Thomas L. Young	Republican	1877-1878
3. Samuel Huntington	Dem.-Rep.	1808-1810	34. Richard M. Bishop	Democratic	1878-1880
4. Return J. Meigs, Jr.	Dem.-Rep.	1810-1814	35. Charles Foster	Republican	1880-1884
5. Othneil Looker	Dem.-Rep.	1814	36. George Hoadly	Democratic	1884-1886
6. Thomas Worthington	Dem.-Rep.	1814-1818	37. Joseph B. Foraker	Republican	1886-1890
7. Ethan Allen Brown	Dem.-Rep.	1818-1822	38. James E. Campbell	Democratic	1890-1892
8. Allen Trimble	Federalist	1822	39. William McKinley	Republican	1892-1896
9. Jeremiah Morrow	Dem.-Rep.	1822-1826	40. Asa S. Bushnell	Republican	1896-1900
10. Allen Trimble	Federalist	1826-1830	41. George K. Nash	Republican	1900-1904
11. Duncan McArthur	Federalist	1830-1832	42. Myron T. Herrick	Republican	1904-1906
12. Robert Lucas	Democratic	1832-1836	43. John M. Pattison	Democratic	1906
13. Joseph Vance	Whig	1836-1838	44. Andrew L. Harris	Republican	1906-1909
14. Wilson Shannon	Democratic	1838-1840	45. Judson Harmon	Democratic	1909-1913
15. Thomas Corwin	Whig	1840-1842	46. James M. Cox	Democratic	1913-1915
16. Wilson Shannon	Democratic	1842-1844	47. Frank B. Willis	Republican	1915-1917
17. Thomas W. Bartley	Democratic	1844	48. James M. Cox	Democratic	1917-1921
18. Mordecai Bartley	Whig	1844-1846	49. Harry L. Davis	Republican	1921-1923
19. William Bebb	Whig	1846-1849	50. A. Victor Donahey	Democratic	1923-1929
20. Seabury Ford	Whig	1849-1850	51. Myers Y. Cooper	Republican	1929-1931
21. Reuben Wood	Democratic	1850-1853	52. George White	Democratic	1931-1935
22. William Medill	Democratic	1853-1856	53. Martin L. Davey	Democratic	1935-1939
23. Salmon P. Chase	Republican	1856-1860	54. John W. Bricker	Republican	1939-1945
24. William Dennison	Republican	1860-1862	55. Frank J. Lausche	Democratic	1945-1947
25. David Tod	Republican	1862-1864	56. Thomas J. Herbert	Republican	1947-1949
26. John Brough	Republican	1864-1865	57. Frank J. Lausche	Democratic	1949-1957
27. Charles Anderson	Republican	1865-1866	58. John W. Brown	Republican	1957
28. Jacob Dolson Cox	Republican	1866-1868	59. C. William O'Neill	Republican	1957-1959
29. Rutherford B. Hayes	Republican	1868-1872	60. Michael V. DiSalle	Democratic	1959-1963
30. Edward F. Noyes	Republican	1872-1874	61. James A. Rhodes	Republican	1963-1971
31. William Allen	Democratic	1874-1876	62. John J. Gilligan	Democratic	1971-

*Democratic-Republican

Ohio opened to traffic. Since 1958, the National Aeronautics and Space Administration (NASA) has operated the Lewis Research Center in Cleveland. Scientists at the center conduct research on space propulsion systems. In 1959, Ohio voters approved an increase in the terms of the governor and other high state officials from two to four years.

Ohio's industrial growth moved forward rapidly during the 1960's. In 1963, the state launched a giant economic development program to attract more industry. Industrial expansion included new aluminum plants and chemical factories in cities along the Ohio River. Industries came to this area largely because it offered cheap, coal-generated power.

Ohio also entered international trade. Eight Ohio cities on Lake Erie—Ashtabula, Cleveland, Conneaut, Fairport, Huron, Lorain, Sandusky, and Toledo—became ports of the St. Lawrence Seaway, which opened in 1959. By 1970, Ohio ranked fourth among the states in the value of goods exported annually.

In 1963, Ohio voters approved a $250-million bond issue for improvements including expansion of state universities and public schools. In 1964, Ohioans approved a $500-million bond issue to step up expressway construction.

The Supreme Court of the United States ruled in 1964 that Ohio must *reapportion* (redivide) its House of Representatives to provide more equal representation based on population. A special session of the Ohio legislature drew up a reapportionment plan for the House, but the voters rejected it. In 1965, the governor, state auditor, and secretary of state proposed a reapportionment plan for both the House and the Senate. A federal district court approved the plan for temporary use. The state legislature then drew up a permanent plan, which the voters approved in 1967.

Also in 1964, a special legislative session established new congressional districts for Ohio. The legislators drew up 24 districts—one for each of Ohio's 24 representatives. Previously, Ohio had 23 districts, each of which elected one representative. The 24th representative had been elected *at large* (by the entire state). The congressional districts were redrawn in 1968 after a federal court ruled the 1964 action invalid.

Ohio Today faces several problems. One of the state's most serious problems concerns its public school system. Between 1966 and 1970, several Ohio school districts closed their public schools because of lack of funds. Educators predicted more school closings in Ohio in the 1970's unless the voters approve tax increases to pay for higher teachers' salaries and better facilities.

Ohioans are also concerned with providing better police and fire protection for their communities. In 1969, the state established academies to improve the training of policemen and firemen. Another serious problem in Ohio is the pollution of Lake Erie and the state's rivers.

Ohio is promoting tourism in the 1970's. New attractions include lakeside lodges, an Appalachia road through forest preserves in southern Ohio, and an increasing number of summer theaters in the state.

Electric power production has become vital to Ohio's economy. During the 1960's, 11 public utility electric power generators went into operation. Three electric companies are building a nuclear power station at Moscow on the Ohio River. The two-unit station was scheduled for completion in the late 1970's.

RALPH W. FRANK, BEN HAYES, and JAMES H. RODABAUGH

533

Related Articles in WORLD BOOK include:

BIOGRAPHIES

Allen, William	Krol, John Joseph Cardinal
Appleseed, Johnny	Lausche, Frank J.
Brant, Joseph	Logan
Bricker, John W.	Longworth, Nicholas
Bromfield, Louis	McKinley, William
Celebrezze, Anthony J.	Nicklaus, Jack W.
Chase, Salmon P.	Pendleton, George H.
Cox, James M.	Perry (Oliver H.)
Edison, Thomas A.	Pontiac
Firestone, Harvey S.	Putnam, Rufus
Garfield, James A.	Shawnee Prophet
Glenn, John H., Jr.	Sherman (John; William T.)
Goodrich, Benjamin F.	Stokes, Carl B.
Grant, Ulysses S.	Taft, Robert A.
Green, William	Taft, William H.
Hanna, Mark	Tecumseh
Harding, Warren G.	Thurman, Allen G.
Harrison, Benjamin	Vallandigham, Clement L.
Harrison, William Henry	Wayne, Anthony
Hayes, Rutherford B.	Wright Brothers

CITIES

Akron	Euclid	Newark
Canton	Hamilton	Parma
Chillicothe	Kettering	Portsmouth
Cincinnati	Lakewood	Put-In-Bay
Cleveland	Lima	Sandusky
Columbus	Lorain	Springfield
Dayton	Mansfield	Toledo
East Cleveland	Marietta	Warren
East Liverpool	Mount Vernon	Youngstown

HISTORY

French and Indian Wars	Pioneer Life in America
Indian Wars	Underground Railroad
Mound Builders	War of 1812
Northwest Ordinance	Western Reserve
Northwest Territory	Westward Movement
Ohio Company	

PHYSICAL FEATURES

Lake Erie	Perry's Victory and Inter-
Miami River	national Peace Memorial
Mound City Group	National Monument
National Monument	Scioto River
Ohio River	

PRODUCTS AND INDUSTRY

For Ohio's rank among the states in production, see the following articles:

Aluminum	Coal	Salt
Automobile	Corn	Soybean
Building Stone	Iron and Steel	Timothy
Chemical	Manufacturing	Tomato
Industry	Publishing	

OTHER RELATED ARTICLES

Battelle Memorial Institute	National Road
Cleveland Institute of Art	Rookwood Pottery
Erie Canal	Soap Box Derby
Floods and Flood Control	Wright-Patterson Air
Midwestern States	Force Base

Outline

I. Government
  A. Constitution
  B. Executive
  C. Legislature
  D. Courts
  E. Local Government
  F. Taxation
  G. Politics

II. People

III. Education
  A. Schools
  B. Libraries
  C. Museums

IV. A Visitor's Guide
  A. Places to Visit
  B. Annual Events

V. The Land
  A. Land Regions
  B. Shoreline
  C. Rivers and Lakes

VI. Climate

VII. Economy
  A. Natural Resources
  B. Manufacturing
  C. Agriculture
  D. Mining
  E. Fishing Industry
  F. Electric Power
  G. Transportation
  H. Communication

VIII. History

Questions

How many U.S. Presidents came from Ohio? Which one of these men was not born in Ohio?

How did Ohio pioneer in flood-control legislation?

What is Ohio's most valuable farm activity?

Why is Ohio called a *barometer state* in politics?

What was the first U.S. college for both men and women?

What was the "Toledo War"? What was the result of this dispute?

What Ohio educator became famous as an author of reading books for schoolchildren?

What was the first educational radio station in North America? When and where was it established?

What is Ohio's rank among the states in manufacturing?

What city produces all Liederkranz cheese?

Books for Young Readers

BAILEY, BERNADINE. *Picture Book of Ohio*. Whitman, 1963.

CARPENTER, ALLAN. *Ohio: From Its Glorious Past to the Present*. Childrens Press, 1963.

DE LEEUW, CATEAU. *The Proving Years*. Nelson, 1962. General Harrison's 1812 war campaign in Ohio.

DRURY, MAXINE C. *George and the Long Rifle*. Longmans, 1957. The Gray brothers' Ohio venture in 1819.

LINDSEY, DAVID, and Others. *An Outline History of Ohio*. Rev. ed. Howard Allen, 1960.

MASON, F. VAN WYCK. *The Battle of Lake Erie*. Houghton, 1960.

SCHEELE, WILLIAM E. *The Mound Builders*. World Publishing Co., 1960.

STILLE, SAMUEL H. *Ohio Builds a Nation: A Memorial to the Pioneers and the Celebrated Sons of the Buckeye State*. Arlendale Book House, Lower Salem, Ohio, 1962.

Books for Older Readers

BANTA, R. E. *Ohio: A Students' Guide to Localized History*. Teachers College Press, 1965.

COLLINS, WILLIAM R. *Ohio: The Buckeye State*. 2nd ed. Prentice-Hall, 1962.

GOULDER, GRACE. *Ohio Scenes and Citizens*. World Publishing Co., 1964.

HARPER, ROBERT S. *Ohio Handbook of the Civil War*. Ohio State Archaeological and Historical Society, 1961.

IZANT, GRACE G. *Ohio Scenes and Citizens*. World Publishing Co. 1964. Short biographies of famous persons from Ohio. *This Is Ohio*. Rev. ed. 1965. A brief history of each of Ohio's counties.

ROSE, WILLIAM G. *Cleveland: The Making of a City*. World Publishing Co., 1950.

ROSEBOOM, EUGENE H., and WEISENBURGER, F. P. *A History of Ohio*. 5th ed. Ohio State Archaeological and Historical Society, 1961.

SIEDEL, FRANK. *The Ohio Story*. World Publishing Co., 1950.

ZIEGLER, ELSIE R. *The Blowing-Wand*. Winston, 1955. A description of Bohemian glassmaking in Ohio in the mid-1800's.

Pioneers in Ohio settled in the Northwest Territory as a result of the forming of the second Ohio Company in 1786.

OHIO COMPANY. There were two Ohio Companies in American history. The purpose of each was to colonize the Ohio River Valley.

The First Ohio Company was formed in 1747. It is sometimes called the Ohio Company of Virginia. Its members included London merchants and wealthy Virginians. Among them were George Washington's brothers, Lawrence and Augustine Washington. The company in 1749 obtained from King George II a grant of 200,000 acres west of the Allegheny Mountains in Maryland, Pennsylvania, Virginia, and on both sides of the Ohio River. It sent explorers into the Ohio River Valley to survey. The explorers developed trade with the Indians, built storehouses and roads, and established the first fort at the forks of the Ohio. In 1753, the explorers founded a settlement called *Gist's Plantation* near Mount Braddock, Pa. The French destroyed the company's strongholds in 1754. The French and Indian War blocked the company's efforts to settle in the west. The company went out of existence in 1792.

The Second Ohio Company was the more important. Its official name was the Ohio Company of Associates. It was organized at the Bunch of Grapes Tavern in Boston on March 1, 1786. Eleven delegates, elected by persons interested in the venture, set up the company. They planned to raise $1 million in $1,000 shares, which was payable in almost worthless Continental paper money. Within a year the company distributed 250 shares. The company appointed Manasseh Cutler, Rufus Putnam, and Samuel Parsons to petition the Continental Congress to sell it a tract beyond the Ohio River. Congress approved, and later passed the Northwest Ordinance of 1787 (see NORTHWEST ORDINANCE).

At first the Ohio Company contracted to buy 1½ million acres at 66⅔ cents an acre. But because of financial difficulties, these terms were never fully carried out.

Congress finally granted title to 750,000 acres of the land that is now part of southeastern Ohio. The agreement provided that 214,285 acres could be bought with army warrants, and that 100,000 acres were to be offered free to settlers. One section of each township was reserved for schools, one for religion, and three sections for future disposal by Congress. This last term was designed to keep land speculators from monopolizing the territory. Two townships of 46,080 acres were set aside "for the support of an institution of higher learning." This institution was founded at Athens, Ohio, in 1804, and became Ohio University.

The Ohio Company appointed Rufus Putnam as its superintendent. He led an advance party of 47 surveyors, carpenters, boat-builders, blacksmiths, and laborers to lay out a town where the Muskingum and Ohio rivers joined. The group arrived at the mouth of the Muskingum on April 7, 1788. It founded there the first settlement under the Northwest Ordinance, and named it *Marietta* in honor of Queen Marie Antoinette of France. The settlers also built a fort called *Campus Martius* to protect their village. On July 15, Governor Arthur St. Clair established the first capital of the Northwest Territory at Marietta. By April, 1789, three new settlements had been established. The Ohio Company completed its land operations by 1797. It divided its assets among the shareholders, but did not go out of business until about 1832.   JAMES H. RODABAUGH

See also GIST, CHRISTOPHER; NORTHWEST ORDINANCE; NORTHWEST TERRITORY; PUTNAM, RUFUS.

OHIO DOMINICAN COLLEGE. See UNIVERSITIES AND COLLEGES (table).

OHIO NORTHERN UNIVERSITY. See UNIVERSITIES AND COLLEGES (table).

OHIO RIVER is a branch of the Mississippi River. It flows 981 miles through some of the richest farmlands

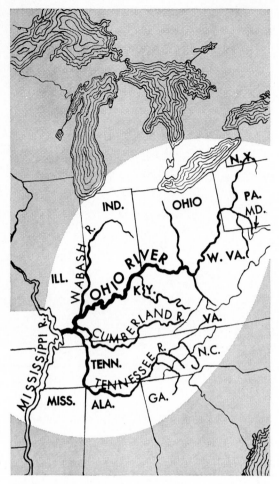

The Ohio and Its Tributaries Drain Parts of 14 States.

and busiest industrial regions in the United States. Its entire length is navigable. Once early pioneers paddled their canoes down the Ohio on their way west. Today large towboats and barges carry more than 85 million tons of commerce on the Ohio every year.

Course and Branches. The Ohio River begins where the Allegheny and Monongahela rivers meet in Pittsburgh. The Ohio flows southwestward, and separates Ohio, Indiana, and Illinois from West Virginia and Kentucky. It empties into the Mississippi at Cairo, Ill. Its chief branches include the Muskingum, Scioto, Kanawha, Miami, Wabash, Big Sandy, Tennessee, Green, and Cumberland rivers. The entire Ohio system drains about 204,000 square miles, or more than twice the size of Wyoming. Among the large cities along the Ohio are Pittsburgh, Pa.; Wheeling, W. Va.; Cincinnati, Ohio; Louisville, Ky.; and Evansville, Ind.

Navigation. By 1929, a series of locks and dams were completed by the federal government to provide a minimum depth of 9 feet in the river. The improvement in navigation resulted in an increase of river traffic from about 10 million tons to over 20 million tons a year. Increased industry in the Ohio River Valley since World War II made a dam replacement and modernization program necessary. During the 1960's, army en-

gineers built 19 modern highlift locks and dams to replace the 46 original structures. The old dams had locks 600 feet long. The new locks are 1,200 feet long.

Floods and Flood Control. The spring floods of the Ohio River often cause great damage. The region gets from 40 to 43 inches of rain each year. As a result of record floods in 1936 and 1937, Congress set up a program of flood control and protection. Dams and reservoirs in upland areas hold back millions of gallons of runoff water until flood crests have passed. In addition, flood walls, levees, and improved channels protect downstream communities.   PAUL B. MASON

Related Articles in WORLD BOOK include:

Allegheny River	Kanawha River	Scioto River
Cumberland River	Miami River	Tennessee River
Floods and Flood Control	Monongahela River	Wabash River

OHIO STATE UNIVERSITY is a state-controlled, coeducational, land-grant institution at Columbus. It also has undergraduate branches at Lima, Mansfield, Marion, and Newark, and a graduate center at Dayton.

The university has 97 departments of instruction. They are in the colleges of administrative science, agriculture and home economics, the arts, biological sciences, dentistry, education, engineering, humanities, law, mathematics and physical sciences, medicine, optometry, pharmacy, social and behavioral sciences, and veterinary medicine. Ohio State also has a graduate school, and special schools in allied medical professions, architecture, art, home economics, journalism, music, natural resources, nursing, physical education, and social work. Courses lead to bachelor's, master's, and doctor's degrees.

The university operates its own radio and television stations. It has a 1,022-acre airport a few miles from the campus. The Franz Theodore Stone Laboratory at Put-in-Bay, Ohio, is the university's center of study and research relating to the biology of the Great Lakes.

Ohio State University was founded in 1870 as the Ohio Agricultural and Mechanical College. First instruction was given in 1873. The name was changed to Ohio State University in 1878. For enrollment, see UNIVERSITIES AND COLLEGES (table).   NOVICE G. FAWCETT

OHIO TURNPIKE. See OHIO (Transportation).

Ohio State University's Stone Laboratory for biological study and research stands on a small island in Lake Erie, *below*. Ivy-covered Orton Hall, *right*, houses the geology department.

Ohio State University

OHIO UNIVERSITY is a state-supported, coeducational school in Athens, Ohio. The university maintains seven branches in southeastern Ohio. The university's six degree-granting colleges offer more than 1,500 courses. Courses lead toward bachelor's, master's, and doctor's degrees. The College of Arts and Sciences offers degrees in the humanities, natural sciences, and social sciences. The College of Business Administration has a School of Journalism as well as business schools. The College of Fine Arts includes schools of architecture, dramatic art, music, and painting and allied arts. The university also has a College of Engineering and Technology, College of Education, and an Honors College.

Founded in 1804, Ohio University was the first institution of higher learning in the vast Midwestern region called the Northwest Territory. For the enrollment of Ohio University, see UNIVERSITIES AND COLLEGES (table). VERNON R. ALDEN

OHIO WESLEYAN UNIVERSITY. See UNIVERSITIES AND COLLEGES (table).

OHM is the unit used to measure resistance to the passage of an electric current. All materials resist the flow of electric current. But some materials offer more resistance than others. Materials that offer little resistance are called *conductors*. Materials that offer great resistance are called *insulators*. Electrical resistance, measured in ohms (*R*), is equal to the electromotive force producing a current, measured in *volts* (*E*), divided by the current, measured in *amperes* (*I*):

$$\text{ohms} = \frac{\text{volts}}{\text{amperes}} \quad \text{or} \quad R = \frac{E}{I}$$

The resistance of a conductor depends on its dimensions and its temperature as well as on the material from which it is made. For example, the resistance of a wire increases as its length increases or as its diameter decreases. Generally, a metal's resistance increases as its temperature rises.

The international standard for the ohm was adopted in 1893. It was defined as the amount of resistance to a uniform electric current offered by a thread of mercury with a cross-sectional area of one square millimeter and a length of 106.3 centimeters, at a temperature of 0° C. Engineers have worked out the resistance of standard-sized wires for the convenience of persons working with electrical circuits. Resistance in an electrical circuit can be measured with an *ohmmeter*. More accurate measurements of resistance can be obtained by using a device called a *Wheatstone bridge* (see WHEATSTONE BRIDGE). BENJAMIN J. DASHER

See also ELECTRIC CURRENT.

OHM, GEORG SIMON (1787-1854), a German physicist, in 1826 discovered the mathematical law of electric currents called Ohm's Law (see OHM'S LAW). The *ohm*, a unit of electrical resistance, was named for him. His discovery was neglected until 1833, when he became a professor of physics at Nuremberg. He was appointed a physics professor at the University of Munich in 1849.

Ohm was born in Erlangen, Germany. He was graduated from the University of Erlangen. SIDNEY ROSEN

OHM'S LAW expresses the relationship between electric current, electromotive force, and the resistance of electrical conductors. The law was discovered by a German physicist, Georg Simon Ohm. Ohm found that a current flowing through a conductor is directly proportional to the electrical force that produces it. In an equation that expresses Ohm's Law, *E* represents electromotive force, measured in *volts; I* represents electric current, measured in *amperes;* and *R* represents electrical resistance, or *ohms*. The relationship is then expressed as:

$$E = IR.$$

For example, an electromotive force of eight volts is required to drive a four-ampere current through a circuit having a resistance of two ohms. The equation also states that if the resistance in a circuit remains constant, doubling the electromotive force doubles the current. BENJAMIN J. DASHER

See also OHM, GEORG SIMON.

OIL. Any greasy substance that does not dissolve in water, but can be dissolved in ether, is classified as an oil. There are many different kinds of oil. Most are lighter than water and are liquid at room temperature. A few, such as lard and butterfat, are solid at room temperature.

Carbon and hydrogen are the chief chemical elements in oil. Some oils also contain oxygen. Oils are classified as animal, mineral, or vegetable, according to their origin. They are further classified as fixed or volatile oils, according to their behavior when heated.

Fixed Oils do not turn to vapor easily when heated. They tend to remain fixed in a liquid state. Scientists sometimes call these oils *glycerides*, or fatty oils, because they are made up chiefly of the glycerides found in animal fat.

Fixed oils may be either animal or vegetable. Most of them can be taken out of the animal or vegetable tissue by pressure alone. But the use of heat and pressure combined is the commonest way to extract them. A larger amount of oil can be obtained by this combined method. The highest-grade oils are obtained by pressure alone and are called *cold-pressed*. When oil is to be taken from vegetable seeds, the seeds are ground before pressing.

Ohio State University

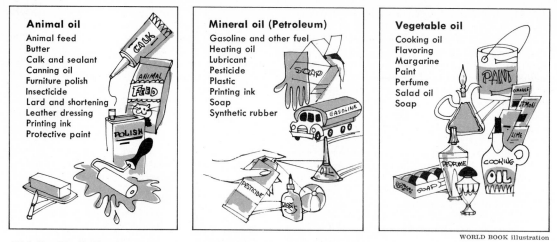

WORLD BOOK illustration

Oil Is Used in Making Many Products. The oil may come from animal, vegetable, or mineral sources. The above lists give examples of products containing oil from these three sources.

The chief animal fixed oils are lard and butterfat. Many oils that come from fish are especially important for their high vitamin content. The chief *marine*, or fish, oils come from the menhaden, salmon, sardine, herring, and sturgeon. The chief vegetable fixed oils include linseed, cottonseed, soybean, castor, corn, and sesame.

Fixed oils have many uses. People use them in food, soap, and paint, and for lighting and lubrication.

Fixed oils can be made by artificial means in the laboratory. Chemists combine one part of glycerin with three parts of the same or different fatty acids. As a rule, each part of glyceride contains more than one kind of fatty acid. The kind of fatty acid in the glyceride determines if the oil is drying, semidrying, or nondrying.

Drying oils absorb oxygen from the air to form a tough film. They are widely used to make paints and varnishes. Important drying oils include linseed, perilla, tung or chinawood, soybean, oiticica, hemp, walnut, poppyseed, and sunflower. Linseed oil comes from flax seeds. It is one of the most important drying oils. It is largely used in making paints and varnishes. Tung oil is a valuable oil. It is used in making waterproof varnishes and quick-drying enamels.

Semidrying oils absorb oxygen from the air to become very thick, but not hard. Cottonseed, corn, and sesame oils are of the semidrying type.

Nondrying oils absorb oxygen from the air with little increase in thickness. But they often develop unpleasant odors and flavors. Olive, peanut, and grape-seed oils, butterfat, and lard are examples of nondrying types.

Volatile Oils, which are sometimes called *essential oils*, turn to gas and evaporate quickly when heated. They usually have a distinctive flavor and odor. Volatile oils may be pressed from plants, or soaked out in water or other liquids. Experts get delicate volatile oils, such as oil of rose, by packing the flowers in a fat, such as lard. The fat absorbs the odor, which is then separated from it by *distillation*. In that process, the fat is heated until the oil turns to gas or vapor. This is piped into a cool container where it turns back to liquid.

Volatile oils are made into *essences* by dissolving them in alcohol. The alcohol causes them to give off more odor. Volatile oils are used in making perfumes (see

PERFUME). For the finest scents, perfumers combine the oils of several plants. Volatile oils also make good flavorings for food and beverages. People use clove, rosemary, lemon, orange, and nutmeg oil in cooking. Peppermint, clove, and wintergreen oils are used in medicines. Manufacturers use grass oils in soaps and insect repellents. Camphor, an oil obtained from the camphor tree, is an important industrial product. It is used in lacquers, moth preventives, and insecticides. Camphorated oil, a camphor product used widely, is a solution of camphor in cottonseed oil. Other products which use the volatile oils include tobacco, paste, and chewing gum.   GEORGE R. GREENBANK

Related Articles in WORLD BOOK include:

Banana Oil	Hydrogenation	Peppermint
Castor Oil	Linseed Oil	Petitgrain Oil
Cod-Liver Oil	Lubricant	Petroleum
Copra	Oil Shale	Sesame
Corn Oil	Olive Oil	Tung Oil
Cottonseed Oil	Palm Oil	Vegetable Oil
Fat	Peanut	Whale
Fusel Oil		

OIL BURNER. See HEATING (Oil Burners).

OIL OF VITRIOL. See SULFURIC ACID.

OIL PAINTING. See PAINTING.

OIL REFINERY. See PETROLEUM.

OIL SHALE. Much of the world's oil is found in rock formed of tightly packed clay, mud, and silt. This rock is called *oil shale*. It contains *kerogen*, a waxy organic substance that gives off liquid oil when it is heated. After oil shale is mined and crushed, it is heated in chambers called *retorts*. When it has been refined, the oil can be made into gasoline and other petroleum products. Shale oil was not used widely by the 1950's, but as the world supply of oil diminishes, it becomes more important. Large deposits lie in Colorado, Utah, and Wyoming, and in Alberta in Canada. RALPH G. OWENS

See also BITUMINOUS SANDS; PETROLEUM (Oil Shale).

OIL WELL. See PETROLEUM.

OILCLOTH is a heavy, waterproof cloth used to cover tables and walls that must often be washed. It is made of coarse cloth coated with heavy paint. The cloth is stretched on a frame and stiffened with glue. The paint is put on in several coats. Each coat is smoothed with pumice stone after it has dried. Patterns are then printed on, from blocks coated with paint. Oilcloth was first used in China between the 600's and 900's, and in England in the 1500's. The first American oilcloth was made in Philadelphia in 1809. The early oilcloths were usually made by hand. EFFA BROWN

OILSTONE is a rock found in Arkansas which can be used as a whetstone. See WHETSTONE.

OISE RIVER. See AISNE RIVER.

OISTRAKH, *OY strahk,* **DAVID** (1908-), Russia's leading violinist, became known for his performances of works by Miaskovsky, Khatchaturian, and Prokofiev. He made his American debut in 1955.

Oistrakh began his concert career at 19. He won a Russian national contest in 1930, the international violinists' contest at Brussels in 1937, and the Stalin prize in 1942. He was born in Odessa. DOROTHY DELAY

OJEDA, ALONSO DE. See COLOMBIA (History).

OJIBWAY INDIANS. See CHIPPEWA INDIANS.

OJOS DEL SALADO, *AW hohz thel sah LAH thoh,* is the second highest mountain in the Western Hemisphere. It rises 22,590 feet. Only Aconcagua is higher. Part of the Andes range, it has four distinct peaks on the border between Argentina and Chile. Snow covers Ojos del Salado the entire year. GEORGE I. BLANKSTEN

O.K. See SLANG (Types of Slang).

OKA RIVER, *uh KAH,* is a tributary of the Volga River in Russia. The Oka rises in central Russia, and flows north and northeast 915 miles to join the Volga at Gorki. Large vessels can sail up the Oka for about 550 miles. But the river freezes over and halts ship traffic for 225 to 240 days each year. See also VOLGA RIVER.

OKAPI, *oh KAH pih,* is a rare and strangely colored animal of the giraffe family. It is about 5 feet high at the shoulders, and has a long neck. Its sloping body makes the forelegs look longer than the hind ones, as

The Rare Okapi Resembles the Giraffe.
Underwood & Underwood

with the giraffe. Its body is reddish-brown, and its legs are marked with creamy-white stripes and bands. Its face is creamy white, but its nose and pointed ears are deep brown or black. The male okapi has a pair of short horns. The okapi has retiring habits and lives in remote jungles. It was discovered in 1900 in the dense forests of the Congo Valley in Africa. See also GIRAFFE.

Scientific Classification. The okapi belongs to the giraffe family, *Giraffidae.* It is genus *Okapia,* species *O. johnstoni.* THEODORE H. EATON, JR.

OKEECHOBEE, LAKE. See LAKE OKEECHOBEE.

O'KEEFFE, GEORGIA (1887-), an American artist, pioneered in modern movements in American painting. Her best-known paintings are those in which she enlarged flowers or the skulls of animals to fill the

Georgia O'Keeffe, *left,* won fame for her stark, simple paintings. She sought beauty by isolating and intensifying such things in nature as the skull and flowers in *Cow's Skull with Calico Roses.*

Candelario, *U.S. Camera Annual*

Courtesy of The Art Institute of Chicago, Gift of Georgia O'Keeffe

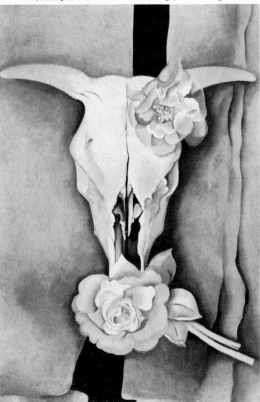

OKEFENOKEE SWAMP

canvas, and transformed them into clear and precise designs. She painted early American buildings and city scenes, but began using subjects near Taos, N.Mex., after moving there in 1929. Her paintings include *A Cross by the Sea*, *Canada*, *Black Iris*, *Farmhouse Window and Door*, and *Lake George*.

Georgia O'Keeffe was born in Sun Prairie, Wis. Her work was first seen in 1916 at "291," the gallery started by Alfred Stieglitz to show work by artists trying new forms. Stieglitz, a famous photographer, encouraged her to seek her personal vision of the abstract design in nature. They were married in 1924 (see STIEGLITZ, ALFRED). Georgia O'Keeffe had exhibitions at the Art Institute of Chicago in 1943, and the Museum of Modern Art in 1946. She had yearly exhibits from 1926 to 1946, and in 1951, at the Intimate Gallery and later at An American Place in New York City. During 1908 and 1909, she worked in advertising art in Chicago. In 1916 and 1917, she was supervisor of public schools at Amarillo, Tex., and in 1918 taught art in Texas. She studied at the Art Institute of Chicago, the Art Students' League in New York City, the University of Virginia, and Columbia University. She was elected to the American Academy of Arts and Letters in 1962.   GEORGE D. CULLER

OKEFENOKEE SWAMP, *O kuh fuh NO kee*, is a marshy, tropical wilderness which lies in southeastern Georgia and northeastern Florida. Most of the swamp was bought by the government in 1937, and 293,826 acres in Georgia were set aside as a wildlife refuge.

The name *Okefenokee* comes from the Indian word *Owaquaphenoga*, which means *trembling earth*. It refers to the trembling of the small bushes and water weeds that float on the lakes of Okefenokee.

The swamp is about 40 miles long and 30 miles wide. It covers an area of 700 square miles. Fine timberlands and fresh-water lakes lie next to the marshy stretches. The region is drained by the St. Marys and the Suwannee rivers. Other bodies of water wind through the swamp. There are about 25 islands. For location, see color maps with FLORIDA; GEORGIA.

The swamp was once a favorite hunting ground of the Creek and Seminole Indians. Today as a government preserve it is the home of many animals, including deer, bears, wildcats, otters, raccoons, opossums, and alligators. The swamp is the winter refuge of many birds that spend the summer in the North. There are about 50 kinds of fish in its waters. Plants that grow there include white and golden lilies, Spanish moss, and cypress trees.   KATHRYN ABBEY HANNA

See also GEORGIA (color picture).

OKHOTSK, *oh KAHTSK*, **SEA OF,** is a large arm of the north Pacific Ocean that forms part of the eastern boundary of Russia. The sea is about 1,000 miles long and 600 miles wide, and covers an area of 589,800 square miles. It is separated from the Bering Sea on the east by the Kamchatka Peninsula. The Kuril Islands on the south separate the sea from the Pacific Ocean. Ice covers the Sea of Okhotsk from November to April, and heavy fogs and storms occur often in this region. But the sea is used as a trade waterway for the ports of Magadan and Okhotsk in Russia. The Amur River and several smaller streams empty into the sea. For location, see RUSSIA (color map).   BOSTWICK H. KETCHUM

OKINAWA

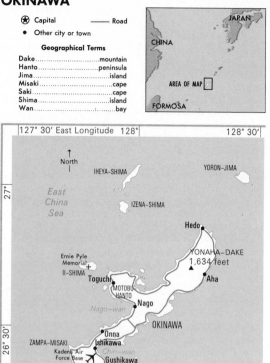

⊛ Capital   ——— Road

● Other city or town

Geographical Terms

Dake	mountain
Hanto	peninsula
Jima	island
Misaki	cape
Saki	cape
Shima	island
Wan	bay

WORLD BOOK map-GA

OKINAWA, OH *kah NAH wuh*, or in Japanese, *AW kee NAH wah*, is the largest and most important island of the Ryukyu Islands, a chain of islands in the western Pacific Ocean. Okinawa covers 454 square miles and has about 759,000 persons. Naha, the capital and largest city of the Ryukyus, is on Okinawa.

Okinawa was a *prefecture* (province) of Japan before World War II (1939-1945). The United States captured the island during the war and has administered it since. The United States also controls the southern Ryukyus. Japan administers the northern Ryukyus. The United States has promised to return Okinawa and the southern islands to Japan in 1972.

Okinawa has had great military importance for the United States because it lies within easy flying distance of China, Formosa, Hong Kong, Japan, the Philippines, and Vietnam. The United States has built air bases and other installations on the island and

Richard Joseph Pearson, contributor of this article, is Associate Professor of Anthropology at the University of Hawaii.

will keep them after giving up control of Okinawa.

Government. A U.S. military officer, who is called the high commissioner, administers Okinawa and the southern Ryukyus. He can overrule all decisions of the local government. The local government consists of a chief executive, a 32-member legislature, and a Supreme Court. The people elect the chief executive and the legislators to three-year terms.

People. The people of Okinawa look much like the Japanese, but Okinawans are shorter and have darker skin. Their language belongs to the Japanese language family, and most Okinawans also speak Japanese.

Many Okinawans live in small villages of red tile-roofed houses. Their main food is rice. Much pork is also eaten. Most village people are farmers or fishermen. Many wear traditional Japanese clothing—kimonos or cotton pants and jackets. Naha and other cities have modern buildings and traffic-choked streets. In the cities, many people wear Western-style clothing.

Okinawa and the southern Ryukyus have about 240 elementary schools, 155 junior high schools, 55 high schools, and 8 colleges. About 95 per cent of the people can read and write.

Land and Climate. Okinawa is 67 miles long and from 2 to 16 miles wide. Mountains and jungle cover the northern part of the island. The southern part has low, rocky hills. Most of the people live in the south.

Okinawa has a subtropical climate. The average daily temperature in Naha is 72° F. the year around. Rainfall averages about 83 inches yearly, most of it falling in the typhoon season, from April to October.

Economy. Before World War II, Okinawa was a poor agricultural island. Today, the Okinawans have the second highest income among the peoples of the Far East. Only the Japanese have a higher income. Okinawa's economy depends largely on U.S. military spending. The principal crops include pineapples, rice, sugar cane, and sweet potatoes. Tourism is growing in importance. Most of the tourists come from Japan.

Okinawan craftsmen make ceramics, lacquerware, and woven and dyed cloth. A pottery kiln in Naha has been operating since the 1600's. Okinawan arts and crafts are prized by art collectors, especially in Japan.

History. Okinawa became a prefecture of Japan in 1879. For the history of the island before that time, see the article on RYUKYU ISLANDS.

One of the bloodiest campaigns of World War II was fought on Okinawa between American and Japanese troops. The Americans landed on the island on April 1, 1945, and conquered it in late June. During the fighting, more than 90 per cent of the island's buildings were destroyed. See WORLD WAR II (Okinawa).

The peace treaty that ended the war gave the United States control of the Ryukyu Islands. In 1950, the United States began to grant some self-rule to the Ryukyuans. It returned the northern Ryukyus to Japan in 1953 but kept Okinawa and the southern islands. The United States built military bases on Okinawa after the Chinese Communists gained control of China in 1949 and the Korean War broke out in 1950.

During the 1950's and 1960's, many Okinawans demanded that the island be returned to Japanese rule. In 1969, the United States agreed to return the island in 1972. Under the agreement, the military bases will remain, but nuclear weapons may not be kept on Okinawa without Japan's consent.   RICHARD JOSEPH PEARSON

A Farmworker in northern Okinawa cuts pineapples from their plants and drops them into a basket strapped to her back. Pineapples rank among the leading exports of Okinawa.

David Moore, Black Star

Naha, Okinawa's Capital and Biggest City, is a busy commercial center. The city was almost completely destroyed during World War II (1939-1945), but it was rebuilt after the war.

Kyodo News Service

An Oil Pump on the Prairie near Oklahoma City

OKLAHOMA

THE SOONER STATE

OKLAHOMA is a major fuel and food producing state in the Southwest. Thousands of oil and natural gas wells dot the Oklahoma landscape. Oil pumps operate even on the front lawn of the state Capitol. Millions of white-faced beef cattle graze on Oklahoma's flat plains and low hills. Fertile fields produce vast crops of wheat.

Oklahoma is also a manufacturing state. Manufacturing and processing rank with mining and farming as major sources of wealth for the people. Busy plants process petroleum and farm products. Factories making glass, construction materials, and metal products produce a wide variety of manufactured goods.

The development of Oklahoma's vast resources began with the Indians. In the 1800's, the U.S. government made most of the region a huge Indian reservation. The Indians established separate nations, with their own governments and schools. The name *Oklahoma* is a combination of two Choctaw Indian words—*okla*, meaning *people*, and *homa*, meaning *red*.

The government first opened Oklahoma to white settlement during the late 1880's. Oklahoma became known as the *Sooner State* because some settlers were there "sooner" than the land was opened. It is also called the *Boomer State*, after the promoters who "boomed" white settlement. The land was settled rapidly, and whites soon far outnumbered the Indians.

During the early 1900's, the farms and ranches of Oklahoma were fertile and productive. In the 1930's, however, a long dry period and low farm prices brought disaster to the farmers. Many farmers and other workers left the state, and Oklahoma's population dropped.

Both these periods of Oklahoma history have become famous. The story of the state's farmers and cattlemen in territorial days is told in the musical play *Oklahoma!* The title song from the play became Oklahoma's state song. John Steinbeck's famous novel *The Grapes of Wrath* included a fictional, but widely accepted, description of the drought of the 1930's.

Today, Oklahoma's industries attract new residents. Hard-working farmers protect their land from drought with modern soil and water conservation methods. The state's oil and gas wells continue to yield their valuable products. Oklahoma City, the state capital and largest city in population, is one of the largest U.S. cities in area. It covers 649 square miles.

For the relationship of Oklahoma to other states in its region, see the article on the SOUTHWESTERN STATES.

Bob Taylor
Combines Harvesting Wheat in Oklahoma

FACTS IN BRIEF

Capital: Oklahoma City.

Government: *Congress*—U.S. senators, 2; U.S. representatives, 6. *Electoral Votes*—8. *State Legislature*—senators, 48; representatives, 99. *Counties*—77. *Voting Age*—21 years (state and local elections); 18 years (national elections).

Area: 69,919 square miles (including 936 square miles of inland water), 18th in size among the states. *Greatest Distances:* (east-west) 464 miles; (north-south) 230 miles.

Elevation: *Highest*—Black Mesa in Cimarron County, 4,978 feet above sea level. *Lowest*—along the Red River in McCurtain County, 300 feet above sea level.

Population: *1970 Census*—2,559,253; 27th among the states; density, 37 persons to the square mile; distribution, 68 per cent urban, 32 per cent rural. *1960 Census*—2,328,284.

Chief Products: *Agriculture*—beef cattle, cotton, dairy products, hogs, peanuts, wheat. *Manufacturing*—food and food products, metal products, nonelectrical machinery, petroleum products, transportation equipment. *Mining*—coal, helium, natural gas, natural gas liquids, petroleum, sand and gravel, stone.

Statehood: Nov. 16, 1907, the 46th state.

State Motto: *Labor Omnia Vincit* (Labor Conquers All Things).

State Song: "Oklahoma!" Words by Oscar Hammerstein II; music by Richard Rodgers.

The contributors of this article are W. Eugene Hollon, former Professor of American History at the University of Oklahoma; John W. Morris, Chairman of the Department of Geography at the University of Oklahoma; and Clarke M. Thomas, Editorial Writer for the Oklahoma City Daily Oklahoman *and the* Oklahoma City Times.

Oklahoma (blue) ranks 18th in size among all of the states, and is the smallest of the Southwestern States (gray).

543

Constitution. The Oklahoma constitution was adopted in 1907, the year Oklahoma became a state. It may be amended by a majority vote of the people. Amendments may be proposed by the legislature or by petitions from the voters. A constitutional convention may be called by the legislature, subject to voter approval. The constitution contains initiative and referendum clauses which allow the voters to propose and pass laws directly (see INITIATIVE AND REFERENDUM).

Executive. The governor is elected to a four-year term. He is paid an annual salary of $35,000. For a list of all the governors of Oklahoma, see the *History* section of this article.

The governor appoints the heads of the chief revenue and budget departments. Some department heads are chosen by a board or by a commission, not by the governor. But the top state officials—the lieutenant governor, secretary of state, attorney general, treasurer, auditor, and superintendent of public instruction— are elected to four-year terms.

Legislature of Oklahoma consists of a senate with 48 members and a house of representatives with 99 members. Each senator and representative is elected from a separate district. Senators are elected to four-year terms and representatives to two-year terms. The legislature meets in annual sessions that begin on the Tuesday after the first Monday in January.

In 1964, a U.S. District Court changed many of the state's legislative districts. This was done to give fair representation to voters in the larger cities. The Oklahoma legislature had been *apportioned* (divided) to give rural areas more than their fair share of representatives. The 1964 reapportionment increased the political power of the cities and decreased the power of rural areas.

Courts. The Oklahoma supreme court has nine justices. They select a chief justice from their group. The governor appoints the justices with the aid of a judicial nominating commission. After serving at least one year,

Kurt Severin, Black Star

The Cowboy, a famous statue by Constance Whitney Warren, stands in front of the state Capitol in Oklahoma City.

a justice must win in the next general election for a six-year term. The court of appeals has six judges elected to four-year terms. The state also has a court of criminal appeals with three judges. These judges are chosen in the same way that supreme court justices are selected. Oklahoma has 25 district court judges elected to four-year terms. Each county also has at least one associate district judge elected to a four-year term.

Oklahoma Industrial Development and Park Department

The Governor's Mansion stands a block east of the Capitol in Oklahoma City. The building, completed in 1928, has a white limestone facing and a red tile roof. Gardens surround the mansion.

The State Seal

Symbols of Oklahoma. On the state seal, the Indian and the white man shake hands before Justice to show the cooperation of all the people of Oklahoma. The large star has symbols of the Five Civilized Tribes, which first settled the region. The seal was adopted in 1907. The state flag, adopted in 1925, has two symbols of peace—a peace pipe and an olive branch. The shield behind these symbols stands for defensive warfare.

Local Government in Oklahoma operates in 77 counties and about 550 cities and towns. The counties have three commissioners, each elected from a separate district. Most cities and towns use the mayor-council or council-manager form of government. The state constitution allows cities of over 2,000 population to adopt and amend their own charters. This gives the cities some control over their own affairs.

Taxation. The state collects a sales tax and individual and corporate income taxes. State taxes, plus revenue from licenses, permits, and fees, provide about two-thirds of the money to run the state government. Almost all the rest of the state's income comes from federal grants and other United States government programs.

Politics. Oklahoma was once almost solidly Democratic. The state began to develop a two-party system in the 1960's. Oklahoma voters elected the state's first Republican governor in 1962, and the second in 1966. Oklahomans favored the Republican presidential candidate in 1952, 1956, 1960, and again in 1968. For Oklahoma's electoral votes and for the state's voting record in presidential elections, see ELECTORAL COLLEGE (table).

The State Capitol was completed in 1917 in an area that later became a major oil field. Oklahoma City has been the capital since 1910. The only other capital was Guthrie (1890-1910).

Bob Taylor

The State Flag

The State Flower
Mistletoe

The State Bird
Scissor-Tailed Flycatcher

The State Tree
Redbud

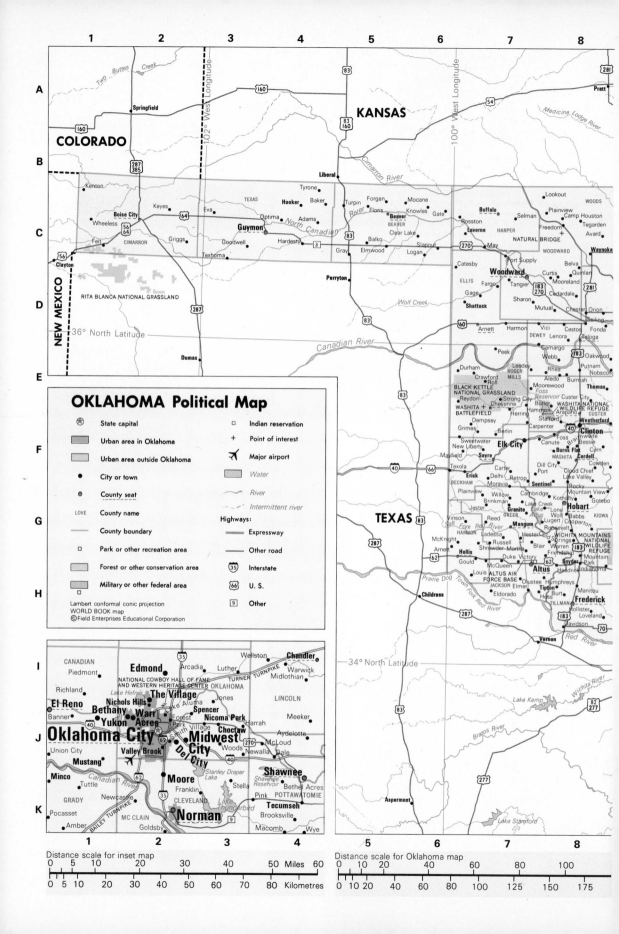

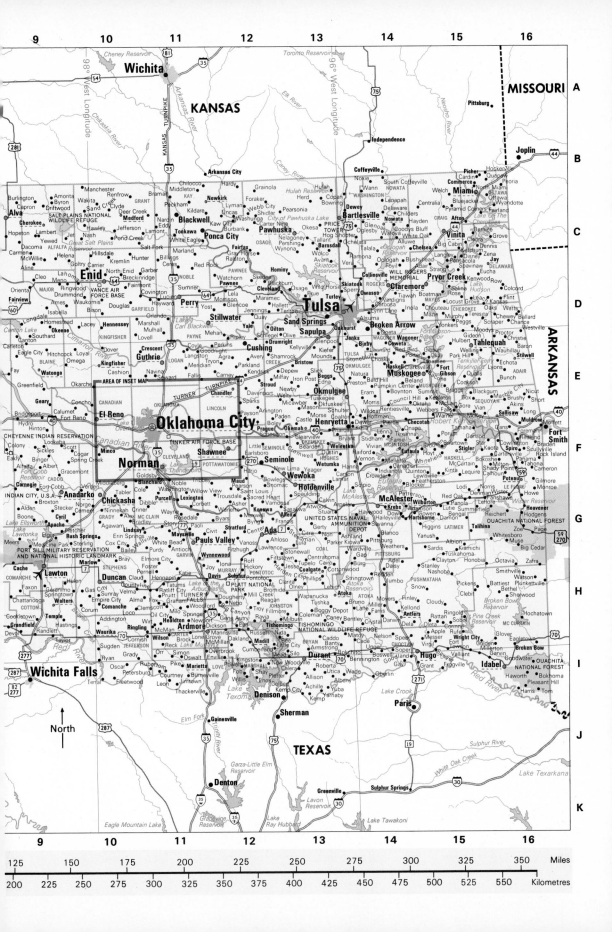

OKLAHOMA MAP INDEX

Population

2,559,253 ..Census..1970
2,328,284 ....“....1960
2,233,351 ....“....1950
2,336,434 ....“....1940
2,396,040 ....“....1930
2,028,283 ....“....1920
1,657,155 ....“....1910
790,391 ....“....1900
258,657 ....“....1890

Metropolitan Areas

Lawton 108,144
Oklahoma City ..640,889
Tulsa 476,945

Counties

Adair .....15,141..E 16
Alfalfa .....7,224..C 9
Atoka ......10,972..H 14
Beaver .....6,282..C 5
Beckham ...15,754..E 6
Blaine ....11,794..E 9
Bryan .....25,552..I 13
Caddo .....28,931..F 9
Canadian ..32,245..E 10
Carter ....37,349..I 11
Cherokee ...23,174..D 15
Choctaw ...15,141..I 14
Cimarron ...4,145..C 1
Cleveland ..81,839..F 11
Coal ......5,525..G 13
Comanche .108,144..H 8
Cotton .....6,832..H 9
Craig .....14,722..C 15
Creek .....45,532..E 12
Custer .....22,665..E 8
Delaware ..17,767..C 16
Dewey ......5,656..D 7
Ellis ......5,129..D 6
Garfield ...55,365..D 10
Garvin .....24,874..G 11
Grady .....29,354..G 10
Grant ......7,117..C 10
Greer ......7,979..G 7
Harmon .....5,136..G 6
Harper .....5,151..C 7
Haskell ....9,578..F 15
Hughes ....13,228..F 13
Jackson ....30,902..H 7
Jefferson ...7,125..I 10
Johnston ....7,870..H 12
Kay .....48,791..B 11
Kingfisher .12,857..D 10
Kiowa .....12,532..G 8
Latimer ....8,601..G 15
Le Flore ...32,137..G 16
Lincoln ....19,482..E 11
Logan .....19,645..E 11
Love ....5,637..I 12
Major ....7,529..D 9
Marshall ...7,682..I 12
Mayes .....23,302..D 15
McClain ...14,157..G 10
McCurtain .28,642..H 16
McIntosh ..12,472..F 14
Murray ....10,669..H 12
Muskogee ..59,542..E 15
Noble .....10,043..D 11
Nowata .....9,773..B 14
Okfuskee ...10,683..F 13
Oklahoma .526,805..F 11
Okmulgee ..35,358..E 13
Osage .....29,750..C 12
Ottawa .....29,800..B 16
Pawnee ....11,338..D 12
Payne .....50,654..D 11
Pittsburg ..37,521..G 14
Pontotoc ...27,867..H 12
Pottawatomie ....43,134..F 11
Pushmataha 9,385..H 14
Roger Mills .4,452..E 7
Rogers .....28,425..D 14
Seminole ...25,144..F 12
Sequoyah ...23,370..E 15
Stephens ...35,902..H 10
Texas ......16,352..C 3
Tillman ....12,901..H 8
Tulsa .....401,663..E 13
Wagoner ...22,163..D 14
Washington 42,277..B 14
Washita ....12,141..F 8
Woods .....11,920..C 8
Woodward .15,537..C 8

Cities and Towns

Achille ......382..I 13
Ada ......14,859.°G 12
Adair ....459..C 15
Adams ....C 4
Adamson ....G 14
Addington ....123..H 10
Adel ....H 14
Afton .....1,022..C 15
Agawam ....G 10
Agra ....335..E 12
Ahloso ....G 12
Albany ....I 13
Albert ....F 9
Albion ......186..G 15
Alderson* ....215..G 14
Aledo ....E 8
Alex ....492..G 10
Alfalfa ....F 9
Aline ......260..C 9
Allen ....974..G 13
Allison ....I 13
Alluwe ......116..C 14
Alma ....H 11
Alsuma ....D 14
Altus .....23,302.°H 7
Alva ......7,440.°C 8
Amber ....K 1
Ames ......227..D 9
Amorita ......63..B 9
Anadarko ..6,682.°G 9
Antioch ....G 11
Antlers ....2,685.°H 14
Apache .....1,421..G 9
Apple ....I 15
Arapaho .....531.°E 8
Arcadia ....I 3
Ardmore ...20,881.°I 11
Arkoma* ...2,098..F 16
Arlington ....E 12
Armstrong ....I 13
Arnett ......711.°D 7
Arnett ....G 6
Arpelar ....G 14
Asher ......437..G 12
Ashland ......73..G 13
Atoka .....3,346.°H 13
Atwood ....G 13
Avant ......439..C 13
Avard ......59..C 8
Avery ....E 12
Aydelotte ....J 4
Babbs ....G 8
Bacone ....E 15
Bailey ....G 10
Baker ....C 4
Bald Hill ....E 14
Balko ....C 5
Ballard ....D 16
Banner ....J 1
Banty ....I 13
Barnsdall ...1,579..C 13
Baron ....E 16
Bartlesville 29,683.°C 13
Battiest ....H 16
Bearden ....F 13
Beaver .....1,853.°C 5
Bee ....I 12
Beggs ......1,107..E 13
Beland ....E 14
Belva ....C 8
Bengal ....G 15
Bennington ...288..I 13
Bentley ....H 13
Berlin ....F 7
Bernice ......189..C 15
Bessie ......210..F 8
Bethany ...21,785..J 1
Bethel ....H 16
Bethel Acres 1,083..K 4
Big Cabin ....198..C 15
Big Cedar ....G 16
Billings ......618..C 11
Binger ......730..F 9
Bison ....D 10
Bixby ......3,973..E 14
Blackburn .....88..D 12
Blackgum ....E 15
Blackwell ...8,645..C 11
Blair ......1,114..G 7
Blanchard ...1,580..F 10
Blanco ....G 14
Blocker ....G 14
Bluejacket ....234..C 15
Boatman ....D 15
Boggy Depot ....H 13
Boise City ...1,993.°C 2
Bokchito .....607..I 13
Bokhoma ....I 16
Bokoshe ......588..F 16
Boley ......514..F 13
Boone ....G 9
Boswell ......755..I 14
Bowlegs ....F 12
Bowring ....C 13
Box ....E 15
Boynton ......522..E 14
Braden ....F 16
Bradley ......247..G 10
Braggs ......325..E 15
Braman ......295..B 11
Bray ....H 10
Breckinridge ...70..D 10
Briartown ....F 15
Bridgeport ....142..F 9
Brinkman ....7..G 7
Bristow ....4,653..E 13
Broken Arrow ...11,787..D 14
Broken Bow .2,980..I 16
Bromide ......231..H 13
Brooken ....F 15
Brooksville ....K 4
Broxton ....G 9
Bruno ....H 13
Brushy ....E 16
Bryant ......86..F 13
Buffalo .....1,579.°C 7
Bunch ....E 16
Burbank ......188..C 12
Burg ....H 14
Burlington ....165..C 9
Burmah ....E 8
Burneyville ....I 11
Burns Flat ...988..F 8
Burt ....H 8
Bushyhead ....C 14
Butler ......315..E 8
Byars ......247..G 12
Byng ....G 12
Byron ......72..C 9
Cache .....1,106..H 9
Caddo ......886..I 13
Cade ....I 14
Cairo ....H 13
Calera .....1,063..I 13
Calhoun ....F 16
Calumet ......386..E 10
Calvin ......359..G 13
Camargo ......236..D 7
Cambridge ....G 8
Cameron ......311..F 16
Camp Houston ......C 8
Canadian .....304..F 14
Caney ......200..H 13
Canton ......844..D 9
Canute ......420..F 7
Capron ......80..C 9
Cardin ....B 15
Carleton ....E 9
Carmen ......519..C 9
Carnegie ....1,723..G 9
Carney ......396..E 12
Carpenter ....F 7
Carrier ....C 10
Carson ....F 13
Carter ......311..F 7
Carter Nine ....C 12
Cartersville ....F 16
Cashion ......329..E 10
Castle ......212..F 13
Catesby ....C 6
Catoosa ......970..D 14
Cement ......892..G 10
Center ....G 12
Centrahoma ....155..H 13
Centralia ......43..C 14
Ceres ....C 11
Cestos ....D 8
Chance ....D 16
Chandler ...2,529.°E 12
Chattanooga ..302..H 9
Checotah ...3,074..F 14
Chelsea .....1,622..C 14
Cherokee ....2,119.°C 9
Chester ....D 8
Chewey ....D 16
Cheyenne .....892.°E 7
Chickasha ..14,194.°G 10
Childers ....C 14
Chilocco ....B 11
Choctaw .....4,750..J 3
Choska ....E 14
Chouteau ...1,046..D 15
Christie ....D 16
Citra ....G 13
Civit ....G 11
Claremore ...9,084.°D 14
Clarita ....H 13
Clarksville ....E 14
Claud ....H 11
Clayton ......718..H 15
Clear Lake ....C 6
Clearview ....F 13
Clebit ....H 15
Clemscott ....H 11
Cleo ......344..D 9
Cleora ....C 15
Cleveland ....2,573..D 13
Clinton ....8,513..F 8
Cloud Chief ....F 8
Cloudy ....H 15
Clyde ....C 10
Coalgate ....1,859.°H 13
Coalton ....F 14
Cogar ....F 10
Colbert ......814..I 13
Colcord ......438..D 16
Cold Springs ......G 8
Cole ....G 11
Coleman ....H 13
Collinsville ..3,009..D 14
Colony ....F 8
Comanche ...1,862..H 10
Commerce ..2,593..B 15
Concho ....E 10
Coodys Bluff ......C 14
Cookietown ....H 9
Cookson ....E 15
Cooperton ....55..G 8
Copan ......558..B 13
Corbett ....G 11
Cordell ....3,261.°F 8
Corinne ....H 15
Corn ......409..F 8
Cornish ......90..I 11
Corum ....H 10
Cottonwood ....H 13
Council High ..135..E 14
Countyline ....H 11
Courtney ....I 11
Covington ......605..D 10
Cowden ....F 8
Coweta ....2,457..E 14
Cowlington ...751..F 16
Cox City ....G 10
Coyle ......303..E 11
Crawford ....E 7
Crescent ....1,568..E 10
Criner ....G 11
Cromwell ....287..F 13
Crowder .....339..F 14
Crystal ....H 14
Cumberland ....I 12
Curtis ....D 8
Cushing ....7,529..E 12
Custer City ...486..E 8
Cyril ......1,302..G 9
Dacoma ......226..C 9
Daisy ....H 14
Dale ....J 4
Damon ....G 15
Darwin ....H 14
Davenport ....831..E 12
Davidson .....515..H 8
Davis ......2,223..H 11
Deer Creek ...203..C 11
Del City ...27,133..J 2
Dela ....H 14
Delaware ....534..C 14
Delhi ....F 7
Dempsey ....F 6
Denman ....G 15
Dennis ....C 15
Depew ......739..E 12
Devol ......129..I 9
Dewar ......933..F 14
Dewey .....3,958..C 13
Dibble ......184..G 10
Dickson ......798..I 12
Dill City ....578..F 8
Disney ......303..C 15
Dougherty ....211..H 12
Douglas ......79..D 10
Dover ....E 10
Dow ....G 14
Driftwood .....27..C 9
Drummond ...326..D 10
Drumright ..2,931..D 12
Duke ......486..H 7
Duncan ....19,718.°H 10
Durant ....11,118.°I 13
Durham ....E 6
Dustin ......502..F 13
Eagle City ....E 9
Eagletown ....I 16
Eakly ......228..F 9
Earl ....H 12
Earlsboro ....248..F 12
Echota ....E 16
Eddy ....C 11
Edmond ...16,633..I 2
Edna ....E 13
Eldorado ......737..H 7
Elgin ......840..G 9
Elk City ....7,323..F 7
Elmer ......138..H 7
Elmore City ...653..H 11
Elmwood ....C 5
El Reno ...14,510.°F 10
Empire City ....23..H 10
Enid .....44,008.°D 10
Enos ....I 12
Enville ....I 12
Eram ....E 14
Erick .....1,285..F 6
Erin Springs ....G 11
Eucha ....D 15
Eufaula ....2,355.°F 14
Eva ....C 3
Fair Oaks* ....23..D 14
Fairfax .....1,889..C 12
Fairland ......814..C 15
Fairmont ......154..D 10
Fairview ....2,894.°D 9
Fallis ......39..E 11
Fame ....F 14
Fanshawe ....199..G 15
Fargo ......262..D 7
Farris ....H 14
Faxon ......121..H 9
Fay ....E 8
Featherston ....F 14
Felt ....C 1
Fillmore ....H 13
Finley ....H 14
Fittstown ....H 12
Fitzhugh ....G 12
Fleetwood ....I 10
Fletcher ......950..G 9
Flint ....D 16
Floris ....C 5
Fob ....I 12
Foraker ......52..C 12
Forest Park ...835..J 2
Forgan ......496..C 5
Fort Cobb ....722..G 9
Fort Gibson .1,418..E 15
Fort Reno ....F 10
Fort Sill ...21,217..G 9
Fort Supply ..550..C 7
Fort Towson ..430..I 15
Foss ......150..F 8
Foster ....H 11
Fox ....H 11
Foyil ......164..C 14
Francis ......283..G 12
Franklin ....K 3
Frederick ...6,132.°H 8
Freedom ......292..C 8
Friendship ....G 8
Frogville ....I 15
Gage ......536..D 7
Gans ......238..F 16
Gap ....H 14
Garber .....1,011..D 10
Garland ....F 15
Garvin ......117..I 16
Gas City ....H 10
Gate ......151..C 6
Gay ....I 14
Geary .....1,380..E 9
Gene Autry ...120..H 12
Geronimo .....587..H 9
Gerty ......139..G 13
Gibson ....E 15
Gideon ....D 15
Gilmore ....F 16
Glencoe ......421..D 12
Glenoak ....C 14
Glenpool ....770..E 13
Glover ....I 16
Golden ....I 16
Goldsby ......298..F 11
Goltry ......282..C 9
Goodland ....I 14
Goodnight ....E 11
Goodwater ....I 16
Goodwell ...1,467..C 3
Gore ......478..E 15
Gotebo ......376..G 8
Gould ......368..G 7
Gowen ....G 14
Gracemont ...424..F 9
Grady ....I 10
Graham ....H 11
Grainola ......66..B 12
Grand Lake Towne* ......23..D 15
Grandfield ..1,524..H 8
Granite .....1,808..G 7
Grant ......273..I 14
Gray ....C 5
Gray Horse ....C 12
Grayson* .....142..F 14
Greenfield ....143..E 9
Griggs ....C 2
Grimes ....F 7
Grove .....2,000..C 16
Guthrie ....9,575.°E 11
Guymon ....7,674.°C 3
Haileyville ....928..G 14
Hall Park* ....163..F 11
Hallett ......125..D 12
Hammon ......677..E 7
Hanna ......181..F 14
Harden City ....H 12
Hardesty .....223..C 4
Hardy ......5..B 12
Harjo ....F 12
Harmon ....D 7
Harrah .....1,931..J 3
Harris ....I 16
Hartshorne .2,121..G 14
Haskell .....2,063..E 14
Hastings .....184..H 10
Hawley ....C 10
Haworth .....293..I 16
Hayden ....C 14
Hayward ....D 11
Haywood ....G 14
Headrick .....139..H 8
Healdton ...2,324..H 11
Heavener ...2,566..G 16
Helena ....769..C 9
Hennepin ....H 11
Hennessey ..2,181..D 10
Henryetta ...6,430..F 13
Herd ....C 13
Herring ....E 7
Hess ....H 7
Hester ....G 7
Hickory ......62..H 12
Higgins ....G 15
Hillsdale ......77..C 10
Hinton ......889..F 9
Hitchcock .....160..E 9
Hitchita* .....160..E 14
Hobart .....4,638.°G 8
Hochatown ....H 16
Hockerville ....B 15
Hodgens ....G 16
Hoffman .....262..F 14
Hog Shooter ....C 14
Holdenville .5,181.°G 13
Hollis .....3,150.°G 6
Hollister .....105..H 8
Homestead ....D 9
Hominy .....2,274..D 13
Honobia ....H 15
Hooker .....1,615..C 4
Hopeton ....C 8
Howe ......403..G 16
Hoyt ....F 15
Hugo ......6,585.°I 14
Hulah ....B 13
Hulbert ......505..E 15
Hulen ....H 9
Humphreys ....H 8
Hunter ......274..C 10
Hydro ......805..F 9
Idabel .....5,946.°I 16
Indiahoma ....434..H 8
Indianola ....205..F 14
Ingersoll* .....17..C 9
Inola ......948..D 14
Iona ....H 12
Iron Post ....E 13
Isabella ....D 9
Jay ......1,594.°C 16
Jefferson .....128..C 10
Jenks .....1,997..D 13
Jennings .....338..D 12
Jesse ....H 13
Jester ....G 7

Jet ....317..C 9
Jimtown ....I 11
Jones ....1,666..J 3
Joy ....H 11
Jumbo ....H 14
Kansas ....317..D 16
Katie ....H 11
Kaw City ....283..C 12
Keefeton ....E 15
Kellond ....H 14
Kellyville ....685..E 13
Kemp ....153..I 13
Kemp City ....117..I 13
Kendrick ....126..E 12
Kenefick* ....153..I 13
Kenton ....B 1
Kenwood ....D 15
Keota ....685..F 15
Ketchum ....238..C 15
Keyes ....569..C 2
Kiamichi ....G 15
Kiefer ....803..E 13
Kildare ....79..C 11
Kingfisher ..4,042.°E 10
Kingston ....710..I 12
Kinta ....247..F 15
Kiowa ....754..G 14
Knowles ....52..C 6
Komalty ....G 8
Konawa ....1,719..G 12
Krebs ....1,515..G 14
Kremlin ....200..C 10
Kusa ....F 14
Lacey ....D 10
Ladessa ....G 7
Lahoma ....299..D 10
Lake Aluma ...124..J 2
Lake Creek ....G 7
Lake Valley ....F 8
Lamar ....153..F 13
Lambert ....16..C 9
Lamont ....478..C 11
Lane ....H 14
Langley ....481..C 15
Langston ....486..E 11
Laverne ....1,373..C 6
Lawrence ....G 12
Lawton ....74,470.°H 9
Leach ....D 15
Leedey ....465..E 7
Leflore ....175..G 15
Lehigh ....296..H 13
Lela ....D 12
Lenapah ....325..C 14
Lenna ....F 14
Lenora ....D 8
Leon ....112..I 11
Leonard ....E 14
Lequire ....F 15
Lewisville ....F 15
Lexington ...1,516..G 11
Lima* ....238..F 13
Lindsay ....3,705..G 11
Little ....F 12
Little City ....80..I 12
Loco ....193..H 10
Locust Grove 1,090..D 15
Lodi ....G 15
Logan ....C 6
Lone Grove .1,240..I 11
Lone Wolf ....584..G 8
Long ....E 16
Longdale ....331..D 9
Lookeba ....165..F 9
Lookout ....B 7
Lotsee* ....16..D 14
Louis ....H 6
Loveland ....36..H 8
Lovell ....28..D 10
Loyal ....107..E 10
Lucien ....D 11
Lugert ....G 7
Lula ....G 13
Luther ....836..I 3
Lutie ....G 15
Lyman ....C 12
Lynn Lane ....D 14
Lyons ....E 16
Macomb ....41..K 4
Madill ....2,875.°I 12
Manchester ...165..B 10
Mangum ....4,066.°G 7
Manitou ....308..H 8
Mannford* ....892..D 13
Mannsville ....364..I 12
Maramec ....128..D 12
Marble City ..299..E 16
Marietta ....2,013.°I 11
Marland ....236..C 11
Marlow ....3,995..H 10
Marshall ....420..D 10
Martha ....268..G 7
Mason ....E 13
Matoy ....I 13
Maud ....1,143..F 12
Maxwell ....G 12
May ....91..C 7
Mayfield ....F 6
Maysville ...1,380..G 11
Mazie ....D 15
McAlester ..18,802.°G 14
McBride* ....44..I 12
McCurtain ....575..F 15
McKey ....F 15
McKnight ....G 6
McLain ....E 15
McLoud ....2,159..J 3
McMan ....H 11
McMillan ....I 12
McQueen ....H 7
McWillie ....C 9
Mead ....I 13
Medford ....1,304.°C 10
Medicine Park ....G 9
Meeker ....683..J 4
Meers ....G 9
Mehan ....D 12
Mellette ....F 14
Meno ....119..D 9
Meridian ....104..E 11
Messer ....I 15
Miami ....13,880.°B 15
Micawber ....E 13
Middleberg ....G 10
Middleton ....B 11
Midlothian ....I 4
Midwest City ....48,114..J 2
Milburn ....275..H 13
Milfay ....E 12
Mill Creek ....234..H 12
Miller ....H 14
Millerton ....I 15
Milo ....H 11
Milton ....F 16
Minco ....1,129..F 10
Mocane ....B 6
Moffett ....312..F 16
Monroe ....G 16
Moodys ....D 15
Moore ....18,761..K 2
Mooreland ..1,196..D 8
Moorewood ....E 7
Moravia ....F 7
Morris ....1,119..E 14
Morrison ....421..D 12
Morse ....E 13
Mounds ....766..E 13
Mountain Park 458..G 8
Mountain View ....1,110..G 8
Moyers ....H 14
Muldrow ....1,680..F 16
Mulhall ....250..D 11
Murphy ....D 15
Muse ....G 16
Muskogee ..37,331.°E 15
Mustang ...2,637..J 1
Mutual ....94..D 8
Nardin ....135..C 11
Nash ....294..C 10
Nashoba ....H 15
Natura ....E 14
Navina ....E 11
Nebo ....H 12
Nelagoney ....C 13
Nelson ....I 14
New Castle .1,271..K 2
New Liberty ....F 7
New Lima ....F 12
New Prue* ...202..D 13
New Tulsa* ....17..D 14
New Woodville ...118..I 12
Newalla ....J 3
Newby ....E 13
Newkirk ....2,173.°C 11
Newport ....H 11
Nichols Hills ....4,478..J 2
Nicoma Park 2,560..J 3
Nicut ....E 16
Nida ....I 13
Ninnekah ....G 10
Noble ....2,241..F 11
Nobscot ....E 8
Non ....G 13
Norge ....G 10
Norman ....52,117.°F 11
Norris ....G 15
North Enid ....730..D 10
North Miami ....503..B 15
Nowata ....3,679.°C 14
Noxie ....B 14
Oakhurst ....D 13
Oakland ....317..I 12
Oaks ....219..D 15
Oakwood ....129..E 8
Oberlin ....I 14
Ochelata ....330..C 13
Octavia ....H 16
Oglesby ....C 14
Oil City ....H 11
Oilton ....1,087..D 12
Okarche ....826..E 10
Okay ....419..E 15
Okeene ....1,421..D 9
Okemah ....2,913.°F 13
Okesa ....C 13
Okfuskee ....E 13
Oklahoma City ....366,481.°F 11
Okmulgee ..15,180.°E 13
Oktaha ....193..E 14
Oleta ....H 15
Olive ....D 13
Olney ....H 13
Olustee ....819..H 7
Omega ....E 9
Onapa ....F 14
Oneta ....D 14
Oologah ....458..C 14
Optima ....103..C 4
Orienta ....D 9
Orion ....D 8
Orlando ....202..D 11
Orr ....I 11
Osage ....170..D 13
Oscar ....I 10
Oswalt ....I 11
Ottawa ....B 15
Overbrook ....I 11
Owasso ....3,491..D 14
Paden ....442..F 12
Page ....G 16
Panama ....1,121..F 16
Panola ....G 15
Paoli ....480..G 11
Park Hill ....E 15
Parker ....G 13
Parkland ....E 12
Patterson ....G 15
Pauls Valley 5,769.°G 11
Pawhuska ...4,238.°C 13
Pawnee ....2,443.°D 12
Payson ....E 12
Pearson ....G 12
Pearsonia ....C 13
Peckham ....C 11
Peek ....E 7
Peggs ....82..D 15
Pensacola ....56..C 15
Peoria ....179..B 16
Perkins ....1,029..E 12
Pernell ....H 11
Perry ....5,341.°D 11
Pershing ....C 13
Petersburg ....I 11
Pharoah ....F 13
Phillips ....106..H 13
Picher ....2,363..B 15
Pickens ....H 15
Piedmont ....269..I 1
Pierce ....F 14
Pike ....I 11
Pink ....K 3
Pittsburg ....282..G 14
Plainview ....C 8
Plainview ....G 7
Platter ....I 13
Pleasant Hill ....I 16
Plunkettville ....H 16
Pocasset ....K 1
Pocola* ....1,840..F 16
Ponca City ....25,940..C 11
Pond Creek ...903..C 10
Pontotoc ....H 12
Port ....F 7
Porter ....624..E 14
Porum ....658..F 15
Poteau ....5,500.°F 16
Powell ....I 12
Prague ....1,802..F 12
Preston ....E 13
Proctor ....D 16
Prue ....D 13
Pruitt ....H 11
Pryor Creek .7,057.°D 15
Pumpkin Center ....E 14
Purcell ....4,076.°G 11
Purdy ....G 11
Putnam ....84..E 8
Pyramid Corners ....C 15
Qualls ....E 15
Quapaw ....967..B 15
Quay ....41..D 12
Quinlan ....81..D 8
Quinton ....1,262..F 15
Raiford ....F 14
Ralston ....443..C 12
Ramona ....600..C 13
Randlett ....384..I 9
Ratliff City ...250..H 11
Rattan ....H 15
Ravia ....373..H 12
Reagan ....H 12
Reck ....I 11
Red Bird ....230..E 14
Red Oak ....609..G 15
Red Rock ....233..C 11
Redden ....H 14
Redland ....F 16
Reed ....G 7
Reichert ....G 16
Renfrow ....39..B 10
Rentiesville ....96..E 14
Retrop ....F 7
Reydon ....215..E 6
Rhea ....E 8
Richland ....I 1
Ringling ....1,206..I 11
Ringold ....H 15
Ringwood ....241..D 9
Ripley ....307..D 12
Roberta ....I 13
Rock Island ....F 16
Rocky ....260..F 8
Roff ....632..H 12
Roland* ....827..F 16
Roll ....E 7
Roosevelt ....353..G 8
Rose ....D 15
Rosedale ....98..G 11
Rosston ....56..C 6
Row ....D 16
Rubottom ....I 11
Rufe ....I 15
Rush Springs 1,381..G 10
Russell ....G 7
Russett ....I 12
Ryan ....1,011..I 10
Sacred Heart ....G 12
St. Louis ....207..G 12
Salina ....1,024..D 15
Sallisaw ....4,888.°F 16
Salt Fork ....C 10
Sand Creek ....C 10
Sand Springs ..11,519..D 13
Sapulpa ...15,159.°D 13
Sardis ....G 15
Sasakwa ....321..G 13
Savanna ....948..G 14
Sawyer ....I 15
Sayre ....2,712.°F 7
Schlegel ....D 12
Schoolton ....F 13
Schulter ....F 14
Scipio ....G 14
Scott ....F 9
Scraper ....D 15
Scullin* ....9..H 12
Scullyville ....F 16
Seiling ....1,033..D 8
Selman ....C 7
Seminole ....7,878..F 12
Sentinel ....984..F 8
Seward ....E 11
Shady Point ....F 16
Shamrock ....204..E 12
Sharon ....155..D 7
Shattuck ....1,546..D 6
Shawnee ...25,075.°F 12
Shay ....I 12
Sherwood ....H 16
Shidler ....717..C 12
Short ....E 16
Shrewder ....G 7
Sickles ....F 9
Silo ....I 13
Simon ....I 11
Skedee ....117..D 12
Skiatook ....2,930..D 13
Slapout ....C 6
Slick ....171..E 13
Smith Village ..93..J 2
Smithville ....144..H 16
Snomac ....G 12
Snow ....H 15
Snyder ....1,671..H 8
Sobol ....H 15
Soper ....322..I 14
South Coffeyville ....646..B 14
Southard ....D 9
Sparks ....183..E 12
Spaulding ....G 13
Spavinaw ....470..C 15
Speer ....I 14
Spencer ....3,603..J 2
Sperry ....1,123..D 13
Spiro ....2,057..F 16
Spring Creek ....F 9
Springer ....256..H 11
Springlake Park* ....14..F 11
Stafford ....F 8
Stanley ....H 14
Star ....F 15
Stecker ....G 9
Steedman ....G 13
Stella ....K 3
Sterling ....675..G 9
Stidham ....53..F 14
Stigler ....2,347.°F 15
Stillwater ...31,126.°D 11
Stilwell ....2,134.°E 16
Stonebluff ....E 14
Stonewall ....653..G 13
Story ....G 11
Strang ....164..C 15
Stratford ....1,278..G 12
Stringtown ....397..H 13
Strong City ....40..E 7
Stroud ....2,502..E 12
Stuart ....294..G 13
Sugden ....54..I 10
Sulphur ....5,158.°H 12
Summerfield ....G 15
Summit ....E 14
Sumner ....16..D 11
Sunray ....H 10
Sweetwater ....F 6
Swink* ....88..I 15
Tabler ....G 10
Taft* ....525..E 14
Tahlequah ...9,254.°E 15
Tahona ....F 16
Talala ....163..C 14
Talihina ....1,227..G 15
Tallant ....C 13
Taloga ....363.°D 8
Tamaha ....83..F 15
Tangier ....D 7
Tatums ....H 11
Taylor ....H 10
Tecumseh ...4,451..K 4
Tegarden ....C 8
Temple ....1,354..H 9
Teresita ....D 15
Terlton ....111..D 12
Terral ....636..I 10
Texanna ....F 14
Texhoma ....921..C 3
Texola ....144..F 6
Thackerville ...257..I 11
The Village ...13,695..I 2
Thomas ....1,336..E 8
Tiawah ....D 14
Tipton ....1,206..H 8
Tishomingo .2,663.°H 12
Tom ....I 16
Tonkawa ....3,337..C 11
Tribbey ....F 12
Trousdale ....G 12
Troy ....H 12
Tryon ....301..E 12
Tullahassee ...183..E 14
Tulsa ....331,638.°D 13
Tupelo ....485..H 13
Turley ....D 13
Turpin ....C 5
Tushka ....H 13
Tuskahoma ....G 15
Tuskegee ....E 13
Tuttle ....1,640..K 1
Tyrone ....588..B 4
Uncas ....53..C 12
Unger ....I 14
Union City ....306..J 1
Utica ....I 13
Valley Brook ....2,869..J 2
Valliant ....840..I 15
Vamoosa ....G 12
Vanoss ....G 12
Velma ....611..H 10
Vera ....215..C 14
Verden ....439..G 10
Verdigris ....D 14
Vernon ....F 14
Vian ....1,131..E 15
Vici ....694..D 7
Victory ....H 7
Vinita ....5,847.°C 15
Vinson ....G 6
Virgil ....I 15
Vivian ....F 14
Wade ....I 13
Wagoner ....4,959.°D 15
Wainwright* ..135..E 14
Wakita ....426..C 10
Wallville ....G 11
Walters ....2,611.°H 9
Wanette ....303..G 12
Wann ....135..B 14
Wapanucka ...425..H 13
Wardville ....G 13
Warner ....1,217..F 15
Warr Acres .9,887..J 2
Warren ....G 8
Warwick ....146..I 4
Washington ...322..G 11
Washunga ....25..C 12
Watchorn ....D 12
Watonga ....3,696.°E 9
Watova ....C 14
Watson ....H 16
Watts ....326..D 16
Wauhillau ....E 16
Waukomis ....241..D 10
Waurika ....1,833.°I 10
Wayne ....618..G 11
Waynoka ....1,444..C 8
Weatherford .7,959..F 8
Weathers ....G 14
Webb ....E 8
Webb City ....186..C 12
Webbers Falls .485..E 15
Welch ....651..B 15
Weleetka ....1,199..F 13
Welling ....E 15
Wellston ....789..I 4
Welty ....E 13
West Siloam Springs* ....210..D 16
Westville ....934..D 16
Wetumka ....1,687..F 13
Wewoka ....5,284.°F 13
Wheeless ....C 1
White Bead ....G 11
White Eagle ....C 11
White Oak ....C 15
Whitefield ....F 15
Whitesboro ....G 16
Wilburton ...2,280.°G 15
Wild Horse ....D 13
Wildcat ....F 14
Willis ....I 12
Willow ....188..G 7
Willow View ....G 11
Wilson ....1,569..I 11
Wirt ....H 11
Wister ....927..G 16
Wolco ....C 13
Woodford ....H 11
Woodlawn Park* ....220..F 10
Woods ....J 3
Woodward ..8,710.°D 7
Wright City .1,068..I 15
Wyandotte ....297..C 16
Wye ....K 4
Wynnewood ..2,374..H 11
Wynona ....547..C 13
Yale ....1,239..D 12
Yanush ....G 15
Yarnaby ....I 13
Yeager ....107..F 13
Yewed ....C 9
Yonkers ....D 15
Yost ....D 12
Yuba ....I 13
Yukon ....8,411..J 1
Zafra ....H 16
Zena ....C 15
Zoe ....G 16

*Does not appear on the map; key shows general location.
°County seat

Source: Latest census figures (1970). Places without population figures are unincorporated areas and are not listed in census reports.

The 1970 United States census reported that Oklahoma had a population of 2,559,253 persons. The census showed that the state's population had increased 10 per cent over the 1960 figure of 2,328,284 persons.

About two-thirds of the people of Oklahoma live in urban areas. Almost half the people live in three metropolitan areas. These are, in order of size, Oklahoma City, Tulsa, and Lawton. These areas are the state's only Standard Metropolitan Statistical Areas (see METROPOLITAN AREA). For the populations of these areas, see the *Index* to the political map of Oklahoma in this article.

Oklahoma has fewer than 30 cities with populations of more than 10,000 persons. Most of these cities are in the northeast section of the state. Oklahoma City is a rapidly expanding center of industry and trade. Tulsa started as a Creek Indian village during the late 1800's. The city boomed after oil was discovered nearby in the early 1900's. Lawton serves Fort Sill, a neighboring military center. See the separate articles on the cities of Oklahoma listed in the *Related Articles* at the end of this article.

More than 95 of every 100 Oklahomans were born in the United States. Indians make up about 4 per cent of the population.

The largest religious groups in the state are Baptists, Episcopalians, Methodists, and Presbyterians. Several other religious groups have large memberships among the people of Oklahoma. These include members of the Church of Christ, the Disciples of Christ, and the Roman Catholic Church.

Bob Taylor

Harvesters Load Wheat into a trailer on a farm near Cordell. Many harvest workers own their own machinery. They work briefly on a farm, and then move to other areas as the wheat ripens.

Royce Craig, *Tulsa Tribune*

Busy Shoppers jam downtown Tulsa, Oklahoma's second largest city. Tulsa began as a Creek Indian village. The discovery of petroleum made the city a booming oil center in the early 1900's.

POPULATION

This map shows the *population density* of Oklahoma, and how it varies in different parts of the state. Population density means the average number of persons who live on each square mile.

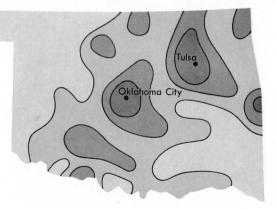

PERSONS PER
SQUARE MILE

80 to 650
40 to 80
20 to 40
1 to 20

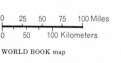

0   25   50   75   100 Miles

0   50   100 Kilometers

WORLD BOOK map

Schools. The first schools in Oklahoma were established for the Indians in the 1820's by missionaries. The Cherokee had the most advanced educational system, chiefly because of the work of one of their leaders, Sequoya. In 1821, Sequoya invented a system of writing. It was so simple that many Cherokee could learn to read and write in a few weeks. The territorial legislature first provided for schools for white children in 1890.

Oklahoma's present school system is headed by an elected superintendent of public instruction and a board of education. The U.S. government maintains 10 boarding schools to assist in the education of Indian children. By law, children between the ages of 7 and 18 must attend school. For the number of students and teachers in Oklahoma, see EDUCATION (table).

Libraries. Oklahoma has more than 100 public libraries and more than 30 college and university libraries. The first public library was founded in Guthrie in 1901. The Oklahoma Department of Libraries and the library division of the Oklahoma Historical Society are in Oklahoma City. The University of Oklahoma Library in Norman includes the DeGolyer collection on the history of science and technology, the Bass Business History collection, and the Bizzell Bible collection.

Museums. Oklahoma's museums own many fine collections on Indian history and art. The Thomas Gilcrease Institute of American History and Art in Tulsa is devoted largely to these fields. The Woolaroc Museum near Bartlesville owns one of the world's finest collections of Indian blankets. The Philbrook Art Center in Tulsa is noted for its American Indian paintings, baskets, and pottery. The Oklahoma Historical Society museum is in Oklahoma City.

The Oklahoma Science and Arts Foundation Museum in Oklahoma City features science exhibits and a collection of ivory. The Philbrook Art Center displays a number of paintings from the Italian Renaissance. The center also has collections of Chinese jade and Chinese art.

Lawton has the Museum of the Great Plains and Anadarko the Southern Plains Indian Museum and Crafts Center. Fort Sill, the United States Army Field Artillery and Missile Center near Lawton, displays unusual weapons in its artillery museum.

UNIVERSITIES AND COLLEGES

Oklahoma has 17 universities and colleges accredited by the North Central Association of Colleges and Secondary Schools. For enrollments and further information, see UNIVERSITIES AND COLLEGES (table).

Name	Location	Founded
Bethany Nazarene College	Bethany	1920
Central State College	Edmond	1890
East Central State College	Ada	1907
Langston University	Langston	1897
Northeastern State College	Tahlequah	1846
Northwestern State College	Alva	1897
Oklahoma, University of	Norman	1890
Oklahoma Baptist University	Shawnee	1910
Oklahoma Christian College	Oklahoma City	1962
Oklahoma City University	Oklahoma City	1904
Oklahoma College of Liberal Arts	Chickasha	1908
Oklahoma Panhandle State College	Goodwell	1909
Oklahoma State University	Stillwater	1890
Phillips University	Enid	1906
Southeastern State College	Durant	1909
Southwestern State College	Weatherford	1901
Tulsa, University of	Tulsa	1894

University of Oklahoma in Norman operates this building, called Sooner House, as part of the Oklahoma Center for Continuing Education. Hundreds of adult groups use the building every year for special conferences and other educational programs.

Bob Taylor

OKLAHOMA / A Visitor's Guide

Will Rogers, the famous Oklahoma cowboy humorist, once said: "There ought to be a law against anybody going to Europe until they have seen the things we have in this country." Rogers may have been thinking of some of the scenic spots in his home state. Oklahoma's attractions include beautiful natural settings, Indian villages, and striking modern buildings.

Bob Taylor

Will Rogers Statue and Museum in Claremore

--------------------- PLACES TO VISIT ---------------------

Following are brief descriptions of some of Oklahoma's many interesting places to visit.

Church of Tomorrow, in Oklahoma City, has a 2,000-seat sanctuary, an educational building, and a theater-in-the-round.

Cowboy Hall of Fame and Western Heritage Center was opened in Oklahoma City in 1965. Famous paintings and sculptures are on display.

Creek Capitol, in Okmulgee, is the building from which Creek Indians ruled their republic.

Fort Sill, a military center near Lawton, includes three national historical sites—Stone Corral, Old Guardhouse, and an artillery museum. The fort was established in 1869.

Indian City, U.S.A., near Anadarko, has authentic copies of several Indian villages. The villages resemble Plains Indian settlements of the early 1800's.

Price Tower, in Bartlesville, is a 19-story building designed by the famous architect Frank Lloyd Wright. The building features the use of many unusual materials in a unique design.

Turner Falls, near Davis, is one of Oklahoma's most scenic waterfalls. There the waters of Honey Creek tumble into a clear, deep pool.

Washita Battlefield, near Cheyenne, marks the site of an 1868 Indian fight. U.S. cavalry under General George A. Custer surprised Chief Black Kettle's camp. Custer's men killed or wounded more than 200 Cheyenne, including many women and children.

Will Rogers Memorial, in Claremore, honors the humorist. A stone ranch house, built as a museum, has exhibits about Rogers, Indians, and pioneers.

National Park and Forest. Platt National Park lies in south-central Oklahoma. The Indians thought the waters of its mineral springs had healing powers. Platt is the smallest park in the national park system. Two sections of the Ouachita National Forest lie in southeastern Oklahoma. For the area and chief features, see NATIONAL FOREST (table).

State Parks. Oklahoma has 22 state parks and several recreation areas. For information, write: Director, Division of Recreation and State Parks, Oklahoma Industrial Development and Park Department, 500 Will Rogers Building, Oklahoma City, Okla. 73105.

Bob Taylor

Turner Falls near Davis

Bob Taylor

Natural Bridge in Alabaster Caverns State Park

Church of Tomorrow in Oklahoma City

Price Tower in Bartlesville

Indian City, U.S.A., near Anadarko

ANNUAL EVENTS

Many Oklahoma towns and cities hold annual celebrations to honor "land openings" and pioneer days. Other communities have rodeos, fairs, and Indian ceremonials. Outstanding events include the celebration of the Cherokee Outlet land opening and the Oklahoma State Fair. Perry, Wakita, and other towns celebrate the opening of the Cherokee Outlet on September 16. The week-long state fair is held in late September in Oklahoma City. Other events include the following.

January-March: Midwest Boat, Sport, Travel, Vacation, and Vehicle Show in Oklahoma City (February); Redbud and Dogwood tours in eastern Oklahoma (March); Wichita Mountains Easter pageant near Lawton (Easter Sunday).

April-June: Azalea Festival in Muskogee (April); Rattlesnake roundups in Okeene, Waynoka, and Waurika (late April); '89ers Day in Guthrie (late April); Strawberry Festival in Stilwell (May); Kolache Festival in Prague (May); Sand Bass Festival in Madill on Lake Texoma (mid-June).

July-September: All Indian Baseball Tourney at Indian Hills Park in Oklahoma City (early July); Western show and rodeo in Pawhuska (late July); American Indian Exposition in Anadarko (August); Green Corn Feast in Miami (early August); Will Rogers Memorial Rodeo in Vinita (late August); State Prison Rodeo in McAlester (early September); Cherokee national holiday in Tahlequah (early September).

October-December: Tulsa State Fair in Tulsa (first week in October); Autumn Foliage tours in eastern Oklahoma (late October); National Finals Rodeo in Oklahoma City (December 5-13).

Cattle Judging at the Washita County Fair in Cordell

553

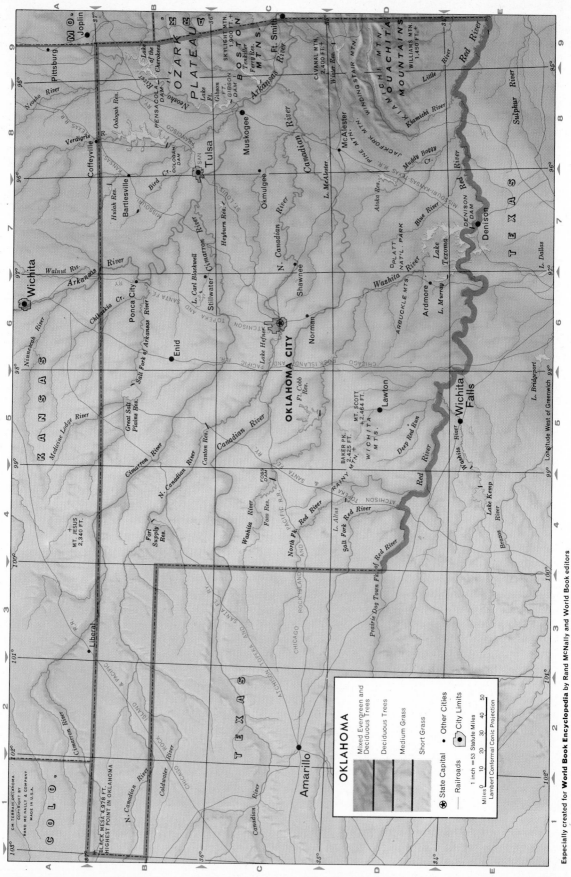

OKLAHOMA

Mixed Evergreen and
Deciduous Trees

Deciduous Trees

Medium Grass

Short Grass

⊛ State Capital   ● Other Cities
— Railroads   City Limits

1 inch = 53 Statute Miles

Miles 0 10 20 30 40 50

Lambert Conformal Conic Projection

Especially created for **World Book Encyclopedia** by Rand McNally and World Book editors

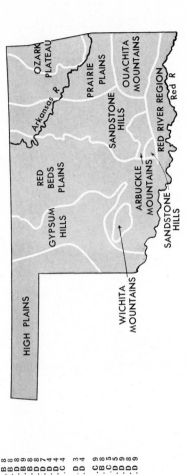
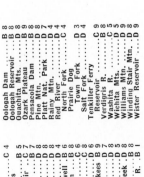

Land Regions of Oklahoma map, showing: HIGH PLAINS, GYPSUM HILLS, RED BEDS PLAINS, SANDSTONE HILLS, PRAIRIE PLAINS, OZARK PLATEAU, OUACHITA MOUNTAINS, RED RIVER REGION, ARBUCKLE MOUNTAINS, WICHITA MOUNTAINS; Arkansas R., Red R.

OKLAHOMA / The Land

Land Regions. Oklahoma has 10 main land regions: (1) the Ozark Plateau, (2) the Prairie Plains, (3) the Ouachita Mountains, (4) the Sandstone Hills, (5) the Arbuckle Mountains, (6) the Wichita Mountains, (7) the Red River Region, (8) the Red Beds Plains, (9) the Gypsum Hills, and (10) the High Plains.

The Ozark Plateau extends into northeastern Oklahoma from Missouri and Arkansas. This hilly region has many clear, swift streams, and steep-sided river valleys. The areas between the valleys are often broad and flat. Steep bluffs have been formed where streams cut into the plateau.

The Prairie Plains includes the land west and south of the Ozark Plateau. Farming and cattle ranching are the most important activities in this region. The Arkansas River Valley, east of Muskogee, produces such vegetable crops as spinach, snap beans, and carrots. Most of the state's coal and large amounts of petroleum come from this region.

The Ouachita Mountains rise in the southeastern part of the state on the border between Oklahoma and Arkansas. These mountains are a series of high sandstone ridges that form the roughest land surface in Oklahoma. The ridges run in a general east-west direction. They include Blue Bouncer, Buffalo, Jackfork, Kiamichi, Rich, and Winding Stair. The narrow valleys between the ridges have spring-fed streams. Lumbering is the region's most important industry.

The Sandstone Hills region extends south from the border with Kansas to near the Red River in southern Oklahoma. It is a region of 250- to 400-foot-high hills covered in many areas with blackjack and post oak forests. Much of the early Oklahoma oil development took place in these hills. The region still has important oil fields. Farming is also important there.

The Arbuckle Mountains are wedged into a 1,000-square-mile area in south-central Oklahoma. Millions of years ago these were tall mountains. Erosion has worn them down until they now rise only 600 or 700 feet above the surrounding plains. The erosion uncovered interesting and unusual rock formations that are often studied by geology students. The principal formations of this region include conglomerates, granite, limestone, sandstone, and shale. Ranchers use the land to raise cattle.

The Wichita Mountains are rough granite peaks in southwestern Oklahoma. The region has many small artificial lakes. These were created by damming the mountain streams to provide water for animals, and to control soil erosion. Most of the area lies within the Fort Sill Military Reservation and a federal wildlife refuge.

The Red River Region is a gently rolling prairie and forest area. Much of the soil is sandy and very fertile. Farmers in the Red River Region raise cotton, peanuts, popcorn, and vegetables.

The Red Beds Plains extend from Kansas to Texas in a wide sweep through the middle of Oklahoma. Soft red sandstone and shale lie under the soil. This gently rolling plain, Oklahoma's largest land region, slopes downward from west to east. The eastern part has forested areas and the western part is mostly grassy. The Red Beds Plains have fairly fertile soil. Farmers grow cotton and wheat in the southwestern part of the region. Oil fields have been developed in some areas.

The Gypsum Hills, west of the Red Beds Plains, extend northward to the High Plains. These hills rise between 150 and 200 feet, and are capped by layers of gypsum 15 to 20 feet thick. They are sometimes called the Glass, or Gloss, Mountains, because the gypsum sparkles like glass in the sun.

The High Plains, an area of level grassland, occupy the northwestern section. This region, which is part of

refuge occupy most of the land in the Wichita Mountains region. The mountains have many rough granite boulders.

The Highest Point in Oklahoma is Black Mesa, background, in the High Plains region. Black Mesa is 4,978 feet high.

Bob Taylor

The Wichita Mountains in southwestern Oklahoma rise from a fertile plain. Fort Sill Military Reservation and a federal wildlife

Oklahoma Industrial Development and Park Department

High Sandstone Ridges in the Ouachita Mountains region of southeastern Oklahoma form the roughest land areas in the state.

the vast Interior Plain of North America, includes Oklahoma's Panhandle. The Panhandle is the western portion of Oklahoma, a strip of land 166 miles long and 34 miles wide. The land of the High Plains rises from about 2,000 feet on the eastern edge of the region to 4,978 feet at Black Mesa, the highest point in Oklahoma. Black Mesa lies in Cimarron County in the northwestern corner of the state.

Rivers and Lakes. Oklahoma is drained by two great river systems—the Red and the Arkansas. These systems carry water from the state's rivers and streams eastward to the Gulf of Mexico. The winding Red River forms Oklahoma's southern boundary with Texas. Its main tributaries drain southern Oklahoma. These streams include the Blue, Kiamichi, Little, Mountain Fork, and Washita rivers, Cache Creek, and the North Fork of the Red River.

The Arkansas River flows through northeastern Oklahoma. Its principal tributaries flow in a broad, irregular semicircle across the entire width of the state. These include the Canadian and the Cimarron rivers. The Chikaskia, Illinois, Neosho (or Grand), Poteau, Salt Fork, and Verdigris rivers, which drain northern and eastern Oklahoma, are also important branches of the Arkansas.

Oklahoma has more than 200 man-made lakes and about 100 small natural lakes. Lake Texoma, covering 91,200 acres, is the most popular resort center. Part of it lies in Texas. Lake O' The Cherokees is in northeastern Oklahoma. It backs up the waters of the Neosho River for 65 miles. Lake Eufaula, in the east-central portion, covers more than 100,000 acres. Fort Gibson Reservoir, Greenleaf Lake, Lower Spavinaw Lake, Upper Spavinaw Lake, Tenkiller Ferry Reservoir, and Lake Wister are in eastern Oklahoma. They have popular resorts for fishing and boating. Other large lakes and reservoirs in Oklahoma include Altus, Canton, Carl Blackwell, Ellsworth, Fort Supply, Foss, Great Salt Plains, Hefner, Heyburn, Hulah, Keystone, Lawtonka, Little River, McAlester, Murray, Oologah, Overholser, and Shawnee.

OKLAHOMA/Climate

Most of Oklahoma has a warm, dry climate. Northwestern Oklahoma is cooler and drier than the southeastern part. *Precipitation* (rain, melted snow, and other forms of moisture) varies greatly throughout the state. Average precipitation ranges from 50 inches a year in the southeast to 15 inches in the western Panhandle. Snowfall ranges from about 2 inches a year in the southeast to 25 inches in the northwest. The Panhandle gets the most snow.

The average July temperature in Oklahoma is 83° F., and the average January temperature is 39° F. The state's highest temperature, 120° F., was recorded on four occasions during the summer of 1936—at Alva on July 18, at Altus on July 19 and August 12, and at Poteau on August 10. The same figure was reached at Tishomingo on July 26, 1943. The record low temperature, −27° F., was registered at two locations—at Vinita on Feb. 13, 1905, and at Watts on Jan. 18, 1930.

SEASONAL TEMPERATURES

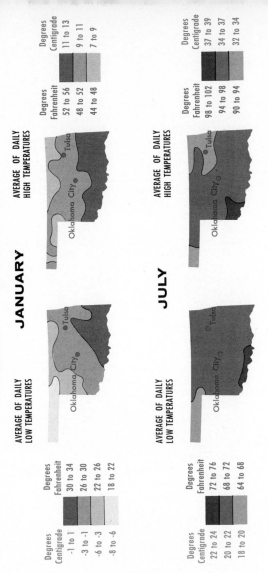

JANUARY

AVERAGE OF DAILY LOW TEMPERATURES

Degrees Centigrade	Degrees Fahrenheit
-1 to 1	30 to 34
-3 to -1	26 to 30
-6 to -3	22 to 26
-8 to -6	18 to 22

AVERAGE OF DAILY HIGH TEMPERATURES

Degrees Fahrenheit	Degrees Centigrade
52 to 56	11 to 13
48 to 52	9 to 11
44 to 48	7 to 9

JULY

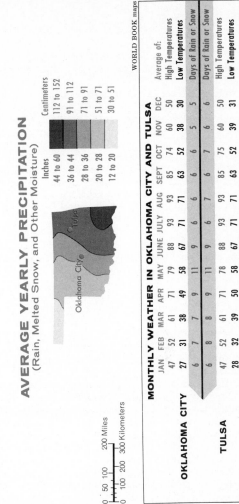

AVERAGE OF DAILY LOW TEMPERATURES

Degrees Centigrade	Degrees Fahrenheit
22 to 24	72 to 76
20 to 22	68 to 72
18 to 20	64 to 68

AVERAGE OF DAILY HIGH TEMPERATURES

Degrees Fahrenheit	Degrees Centigrade
98 to 102	37 to 39
94 to 98	34 to 37
90 to 94	32 to 34

WORLD BOOK maps

AVERAGE YEARLY PRECIPITATION
(Rain, Melted Snow, and Other Moisture)

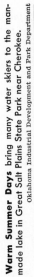

Inches	Centimeters
44 to 60	112 to 152
36 to 44	91 to 112
28 to 36	71 to 91
20 to 28	51 to 71
12 to 20	30 to 51

0 50 100 200 Miles
0 100 200 300 Kilometers

MONTHLY WEATHER IN OKLAHOMA CITY AND TULSA

		JAN	FEB	MAR	APR	MAY	JUNE	JULY	AUG	SEPT	OCT	NOV	DEC
OKLAHOMA CITY	High Temperatures	47	52	61	71	79	88	93	93	85	74	60	50
	Low Temperatures	27	31	38	49	58	67	71	71	63	52	38	30
	Days of Rain or Snow	6	7	7	9	11	9	6	6	6	6	5	5
TULSA	Days of Rain or Snow	6	8	8	9	11	9	6	7	6	7	6	6
	High Temperatures	47	52	61	71	78	88	93	93	85	75	60	50
	Low Temperatures	28	32	39	50	58	67	71	71	63	52	39	31

Temperatures are given in degrees Fahrenheit.

Source: U.S. Weather Bureau

Warm Summer Days bring many water skiers to the man-made lake in Great Salt Plains State Park near Cherokee.

Oklahoma Industrial Development and Park Department

556a

Manufacturing is Oklahoma's most important economic activity. Mining ranks second, and agriculture ranks third.

Natural Resources. Oklahoma has vast reserves of minerals and large areas of fertile soils. Its mineral wealth includes petroleum and natural gas, important fuels of today's world. Large supplies of water and a favorable climate combine with rich soils to make Oklahoma a major producer of food.

Minerals. The state's oil reserves are among the largest in the United States. Large quantities of natural gas also are present in most of the oil fields. Deposits of petroleum and natural gas have been found in 70 of Oklahoma's 77 counties.

Rich beds of coal lie in the east-central and northeastern parts of the state. Experts estimate that more than 3 billion tons of coal could be taken from the state's coal fields, which cover about 15,000 square miles.

The mountainous regions have deposits of stone and clays. Great quantities of high grade granite are found in the Wichita and Arbuckle mountains. Other minerals include copper, limestone of various kinds, glass sand, gravel, gypsum, and salt. Helium, one of the lightest gases, has been found in the natural gas of the Panhandle.

Soil varies from the fertile deposits in the river valleys to the unproductive shale and granite of the mountains. Much of the plains and grasslands area has a rich soil that produces abundant crops. Other areas have poor red clay soil.

Forests cover about 9,700,000 acres, or more than a fifth of the state's land area. The most important commercial tree is the southern pine, used for softwood lumber. Hardwood trees of commercial value include the ash, elm, hickory, oak, red gum, and walnut. The main commercial forests are in the eastern and southeastern parts of the state.

Plant Life includes the prairie grasses that provide grazing for millions of cattle. Among these grasses are bluestem, sand grass, and the shorter buffalo grass, grama, and wire grass. Other common prairie plants are mesquite and sagebrush. Dogwood and red-

bud grow in the east, central, and southern areas. The anemone, goldenrod, wild indigo, petunia, phlox, primrose, spiderwort, sunflower, verbena, and violet grow in all regions of the state.

Animal Life. Coyotes, prairie dogs, and rabbits are common on the Oklahoma plains. Animals of the forest areas include deer, minks, opossums, otters, raccoons, and gray and fox squirrels. Common birds include blue jays, crows, doves, meadow larks, mockingbirds, robins, English sparrows, starlings, and swallows.

Manufacturing provides 40 per cent of the value of goods that Oklahoma produces annually. Goods produced in the state have a *value added by manufacture* of about $1,350,000,000 a year. This figure represents the value created in products by Oklahoma's industries, not counting such manufacturing costs as materials, supplies, and fuels.

Oklahoma's leading industries, in order of value, produce nonelectrical machinery, food and food products, metal products, transportation equipment, and petroleum products.

The Tulsa and Oklahoma City areas lead in the manufacture of machinery. Blackwell, Duncan, Enid, Muskogee, and Perry also have machinery plants. Electronics and space equipment manufacturing has developed in Tulsa and Oklahoma City. These two cities also have important transportation equipment plants. Airplanes and trailers are produced in both places.

Oklahoma City is the most important food-processing center. Canneries in Muskogee and Stilwell process many kinds of vegetables. El Reno, Shawnee, and Yukon are leading centers in grain milling. Plants in many cities handle meat processing and dairy products.

Oil-refining is concentrated in the north-central and south-central regions of the state. Tulsa and Ponca City are the leading refining centers. Enid, Duncan, and Cushing also have large oil refineries. About 70 plants in the state process natural gas.

Mining in Oklahoma provides an annual income of about $1 billion, or about 30 per cent of the value of goods produced in the state. Oil is the greatest source of this income. Oklahoma has about 81,000 oil wells. They produce about 230 million barrels of crude oil a

OKLAHOMA'S PRODUCTION IN 1967

Total value of goods produced—$3,337,252,000

AGRICULTURAL PRODUCTS 29%

MANUFACTURED PRODUCTS 40%

FISH AND MINERAL PRODUCTS 31%

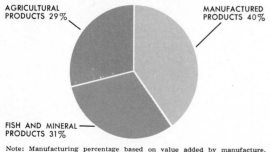

Note: Manufacturing percentage based on value added by manufacture. Other percentages based on value of production. Fish Products are less than 1 per cent.

Sources: U.S. Government statistics

OKLAHOMA'S EMPLOYMENT IN 1967

Total number of persons employed—828,800

		Number of Employees
Government	↟ ↟ ↟ ↟ ↟ ↟ ↟	170,800
Wholesale & Retail Trade	↟ ↟ ↟ ↟ ↟ ↟ ⸲	159,000
Agriculture	↟ ↟ ↟ ↟ ↟	120,800
Manufacturing	↟ ↟ ↟ ↟ ↟	116,400
Services	↟ ↟ ↟ ↟	99,700
Transportation & Public Utilities	↟ ↟	50,600
Mining	↟ ↟	42,100
Construction	↟ ⸲	34,900
Finance, Insurance & Real Estate	↟ ⸲	34,500

Source: U.S. Department of Labor

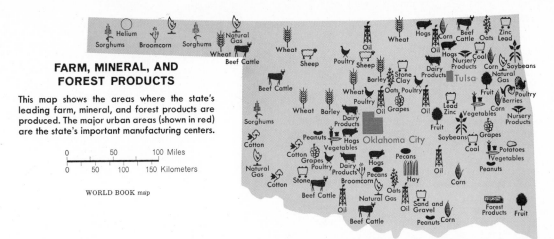

FARM, MINERAL, AND FOREST PRODUCTS

This map shows the areas where the state's leading farm, mineral, and forest products are produced. The major urban areas (shown in red) are the state's important manufacturing centers.

0   50   100 Miles

0   50   100   150 Kilometers

WORLD BOOK map

year, putting Oklahoma among the leading states in oil production. Tulsa and Oklahoma City are the state's leading oil centers, but almost every section of Oklahoma has producing wells.

Natural gas is found in many places where there is oil, and Oklahoma ranks as a leader in gas production. Most of the gas is piped to other sections of the country for use as heating and cooking fuel. Natural gas liquids, such as natural gasoline and butane, are the state's third most important mineral product.

Stone ranks high in value among Oklahoma's minerals, as do sand and gravel. Coal is also an important income producer. In the late 1960's, miners took about 800,000 tons a year from the coal beds in eastern Oklahoma. Other important mineral products include clays, copper, and gypsum.

Production of helium gas became important in the 1960's. Helium gained in value because of its use in rockets and for research. Natural gas in the Panhandle area contains a high percentage of helium. The U.S. Bureau of Mines built a large plant in Keyes to remove the helium from the natural gas. As a result, Oklahoma became one of the two leading states, with Texas, in the production of high-purity helium.

Agriculture accounts for more than a fourth of the value of goods produced in the state, or about $955,400,000 a year. The production of beef cattle is the state's leading source of agricultural income, and Oklahoma is one of the country's most important sources of

Beef Cattle feed on the rich grass of a ranch near Putnam. Beef cattle are the leading source of farm income in Oklahoma.

Bob Taylor

Mounds of Wheat cover the ground around a full grain elevator. This overflow wheat is quickly shipped to other storage areas or to flour mills. Oklahoma is a leading U.S. wheat-producing state.
Bob Taylor

Oil Derricks dot Lake Texoma, where wells pump oil from under the lake. Most parts of Oklahoma have oil wells. Thousands of miles of pipelines carry the crude oil to refineries for processing.
Bob Taylor

beef. The state has about 4 million beef cattle.

Cowboys still ride the Oklahoma range as they did in earlier days, but ranching has become a modern business. Many ranchers graze their cattle on the range for a time, and then take them to *feed lots*. A feed lot is an enclosed area where cattle are fed special feed to fatten them for market. These animals do not need to search for feed, so they gain weight more rapidly than range cattle, and bring higher prices.

Other important income from Oklahoma livestock comes from chickens, dairy products, eggs, hogs, sheep, and turkeys.

Winter wheat is the most valuable field crop for the state's farmers, and Oklahoma ranks as a leading wheat state. Vast fields of golden wheat are harvested early each summer by lines of combines. Cotton ranks second in value among Oklahoma's crops. Crops of peanuts, barley, hay, sorghum grain, and soybeans also contribute to the state's farm income. Oklahoma frequently leads the states in the production of broomcorn, from which brooms are made. Orchards in the eastern and central part of the state produce apples, peaches, pears, and pecans. Other food products include corn, spinach, strawberries, and watermelons.

Electric Power. Oklahoma uses its gas, coal, or oil to generate almost all its electricity. Less than 10 per cent is produced by water power. Most of the hydroelectric plants are in the northeast section of the state. More than four-fifths of the power is generated in privately owned plants. For Oklahoma's kilowatt-hour production, see ELECTRIC POWER (table).

Transportation. Oklahoma has more than 107,000 miles of roads and highways. About 78,000 miles are hard-surface roads. Toll highways link the major cities of Tulsa, Oklahoma City, and Lawton.

Fourteen railroads serve Oklahoma. They operate on about 5,600 miles of track in the state. Oklahoma's first railroad was the Missouri-Kansas-Texas Railroad, called "The Katy." It was built across Oklahoma to Denison, Tex., between 1870 and 1872.

Six passenger airlines serve Oklahoma. Oklahoma City and Tulsa have the major commercial airports. There are about 100 public airports and about 100 private landing fields in the state.

About 50,000 miles of pipelines carry Oklahoma's oil, natural gas, and refined products to other states. Most of the pipelines run through the central portion of the state from southwest to northeast.

Communication. Oklahoma has more than 200 weekly and more than 50 daily newspapers. The first newspaper, the *Cherokee Advocate*, was published in Tahlequah in 1844. It was printed in both English and Cherokee. Today, the largest newspapers in the state are Oklahoma City's *Daily Oklahoman*, the *Oklahoma City Times*, the *Tulsa Daily World*, and the *Tulsa Tribune*.

Station WKY in Oklahoma City, the state's first commercial radio station, went on the air in 1921. The first television stations, WKY-TV in Oklahoma City and KOTV in Tulsa, began regular broadcasts in 1949. Oklahoma has over 90 radio stations and 11 television stations.

First White Man to explore Oklahoma was Francisco Coronado in 1541. He crossed western Oklahoma in search of the legendary Seven Cities of Cibola.

The Boomers, a group of homeseekers led by David L. Payne and C. C. Carpenter, promoted Oklahoma's opening to settlement in the 1870's and 1880's.

HISTORIC OKLAHOMA

OKLAHOMA / History

Early Days. Before the white men came, bands of Indians roamed the plains of the region that now includes Oklahoma. The Indians followed the huge herds of buffalo that grazed on the grasslands. The tribes included the Arapaho, Caddo, Cheyenne, Comanche, Kiowa, Osage, Pawnee, and Wichita. See INDIAN, AMERICAN (Table of Tribes).

Europeans first reached the Oklahoma region in 1541. That year, the Spanish explorer Francisco Vásquez de Coronado led an expedition from Tiguex, N.Mex. He reached what is now Oklahoma. Later the same year, Hernando de Soto, another Spaniard, probably entered the area. Both Coronado and De Soto were searching for gold, but they found none.

In 1682, the French explorer Robert Cavelier, Sieur de la Salle, traveled down the Mississippi River. He did not reach the Oklahoma area. However, he claimed for France all the land drained by the Mississippi, including

First White Settlements in Oklahoma were at Miller Court House, Salina, and Three Forks.

First Producing Oil Well in Oklahoma was drilled in 1889 by Edward Byrd, a Kansas prospector, near Chelsea. Over 100,-000 commercial oil wells have been sunk in Oklahoma since then.

● Chelsea

● Salina

Tulsa ●

Three Forks ●

Chisholm Trail, running north from Texas through Oklahoma to Abilene, Kan., was used by millions of cattle in the 1870's.

Chisholm Trail

Linking East and West, The Butterfield stage line, a mail and passenger route across Oklahoma from St. Louis to San Francisco, opened in 1858.

★ OKLAHOMA CITY

Greatest Oklahoma Land Run was the opening of the Cherokee Outlet on Sept. 16, 1893. More than 50,000 persons staked claims the first day.

Miller Court House ●

Cherokee

Unassigned Lands

Creek

Seminole

Chickasaw

Choctaw

The Five Civilized Tribes—Cherokee, Choctaw, Creek, Chickasaw, and Seminole—received their Oklahoma lands from the federal government in the 1820's for "as long as grass shall grow and rivers run," in return for their eastern lands.

the Oklahoma region. Soon afterward, other French explorers and traders entered the Oklahoma area.

American Ownership. France claimed the Oklahoma region as part of Louisiana until 1762, when France ceded Louisiana to Spain. Napoleon regained the province for France in 1800, but he needed money to fight wars in Europe. In 1803, he sold Louisiana to the United States (see LOUISIANA PURCHASE).

Congress reorganized the administration of Louisiana several times. The section that included present-day Oklahoma was first called the District of Louisiana. In 1805, it became the Louisiana Territory. Seven years later, in 1812, the Missouri Territory was organized from the Louisiana Territory.

In 1819, the United States settled several boundary disputes with Spain. As a result, the present Oklahoma Panhandle, one of the disputed areas, was given to Spain. The rest of Oklahoma became part of the Arkansas Territory, which was created in 1819. Miller Court House (in present-day McCurtain County), Salina, and Three Forks were among the first white settlements established in Oklahoma.

The Indian Nations. After 1819, the federal government began prodding the Indian tribes in the southeastern United States to move to the Oklahoma area. The tribes—the Cherokee, Chickasaw, Choctaw, Creek, and Seminole—had lived in close contact with white men for more than a hundred years. They adopted many of the habits and customs of the whites, and became known as the Five Civilized Tribes.

At the time, Oklahoma was largely unoccupied. In 1824, to prepare the area for the Indian migration, the U.S. Army built Fort Towson and Fort Gibson. The government then forced the five tribes to give up most of their eastern lands and move west.

Between 1820 and 1842, sad processions of Indians

556e

OKLAHOMA

moved into the wooded hills and open grasslands of eastern Oklahoma. Many Indians died along the way. The Cherokee and Choctaw Indians speak of the trip as *The Trail of Tears.*

The immigrant Indians were given the right to all of present-day Oklahoma except the Panhandle. Each of the five tribes formed a nation. By treaties, the United States promised to protect the Indian nations. The government guaranteed that the Indians would own their lands "as long as grass shall grow and rivers run." Each Indian nation established its own legislature, courts, and written laws, and built its own capital. Most settlements were in the eastern part of the region, but the Indians made trips to the west to hunt buffalo.

After the first hard years, the Indians began to build schools and churches, clear land, and operate farms and ranches. They were protected from white settlement by their treaties, so the general westward movement of the pioneers passed them.

The Civil War (1861-1865) destroyed the prosperity and protection the Indians enjoyed. The Five Civilized Tribes had come from the South, and many of the Indians owned slaves. Delegations from Texas and Arkansas urged the Indians to join the Confederacy. In 1861, a Confederate military leader, Albert Pike, made treaties of alliance with some of the tribes. These tribes

Oklahoma Industrial Development and Park Department

Statue Honoring Pioneer Women stands in Ponca City. A nearby museum exhibits relics of pioneer days.

included some Plains Indians who had moved into the area. At first the Cherokee leader, Chief John Ross, tried to avoid taking sides. But the Confederates won a battle near the Cherokee border, at Wilson's Creek in Missouri, and Ross pledged the Cherokee to the South. Pike then recruited and led a brigade of Indians to fight for the South. One Cherokee, Stand Watie, became a Confederate brigadier general. Other Indians, however, fought for the Union.

After the Civil War, Congress forced the Five Civilized Tribes to give up the western part of their land because they had supported the South. Some of this land was given or sold to other Indian tribes.

The land that bordered the Indian Territory filled rapidly with settlers. Soon there was no more free or cheap land available. The whites wanted to use the fertile Indian lands. During the late 1860's, many cattlemen drove their herds across Oklahoma on their way from Texas to the Kansas railroad centers. Some cattlemen paid the Indians for grazing rights, but others did not. From 1866 to 1885, more than 6 million longhorn cattle crossed the Indian lands. The East Shawnee, West Shawnee, Chisholm, and Great Western trails were the leading routes. In 1883, an association of cattlemen leased more than 6 million acres from the Indians for five years. But the United States government declared all the leases invalid. President Benjamin Harrison ordered the white men's cattle removed in 1890.

The Great Land Rushes. "Boomers" urged the government to open the land for white settlement. The boomer leaders included C. C. Carpenter, David L. Payne, and William L. Couch. Finally the government yielded. It bought more than 3 million acres from the Creek and Seminole tribes. Authorities declared almost 1,900,000 acres in central Oklahoma open for settlement at noon, April 22, 1889. Thousands of eager settlers moved to the border to await the opening. They were held back by the army until a pistol shot signaled the opening. Then a wild race began to claim the best farms and townsites. About 50,000 people

---

———— IMPORTANT DATES IN OKLAHOMA ————

1541 Francisco Vásquez de Coronado crossed western Oklahoma in a search for gold.

1682 Robert Cavelier, Sieur de la Salle, claimed Oklahoma as part of French Louisiana.

1762 France gave Louisiana, including the Oklahoma region, to Spain.

1800 France regained Louisiana.

1803 The United States bought the Oklahoma region, except the Panhandle, as part of the Louisiana Purchase.

1819 The Oklahoma region, except the Panhandle, became part of the Territory of Arkansas.

1824 The government established Fort Gibson and Fort Towson, the region's first military posts.

1820-1842 The Five Civilized Tribes moved to Oklahoma.

1870-1872 The Missouri-Kansas-Texas railroad was built across the region.

1872 Oklahoma's first commercial coal was mined near McAlester.

1889 The United States opened part of Oklahoma to white settlement. The region's first producing oil well was drilled near Chelsea.

1890 Congress established the Territory of Oklahoma and added the Panhandle region to it.

1893 Congress established the Dawes Commission to manage the affairs of the Five Civilized Tribes. The Cherokee Outlet was opened to white settlement.

1907 Oklahoma entered the Union on November 16 as the 46th state.

1910 The state capital was moved from Guthrie to Oklahoma City.

1920 The Osage County oil fields began to produce.

1928 The Oklahoma City oil field opened.

1963 Henry Bellmon became the first Republican governor of Oklahoma.

1970 The Arkansas River Development Program was completed.

Oklahoma's Greatest Land Rush was created by the opening of the rich Cherokee Outlet on Sept. 16, 1893. Thousands of settlers poured across the border to stake claims in this 6½ million-acre area. Previously, the land had belonged to the Indians.

had moved into Oklahoma by that evening. In a single day, Guthrie and Oklahoma City became cities of 10,000 persons.

Some settlers, called Sooners, went into the area before the opening to claim the best land. To hide their early entry, many Sooners ran their horses hard on the day of the opening. Then the tired horses would be shown to the pioneers who had followed the rules, to "prove" that the owner had just arrived.

The Territory of Oklahoma was established by Congress in May, 1890, with Guthrie as the capital. The same act added the Panhandle to the territory. The Panhandle had become U.S. territory when Texas joined the Union in 1845. President Harrison appointed George W. Steele as the first territorial governor.

During the 1890's, more and more Indian tribes accepted individual *allotment* of their lands. This meant that the individual Indians, not the tribe as a whole, owned the land. The land not allotted to tribe members was opened for settlement. In some areas, settlers got their land by *run*, or land rush. Other land was distributed by a lottery.

The greatest opening occurred on Sept. 16, 1893. That day, settlement was allowed on the Cherokee Outlet, in north-central Oklahoma, and the Tonkawa and Pawnee reservations. More than 50,000 persons claimed land in the 6½ million-acre area the first day.

Progress Toward Statehood. After 1890, maps showed the Oklahoma area as the Twin Territories—Indian Territory and Oklahoma Territory. Indian Territory was the remaining land of the Five Civilized Tribes, plus a small area owned and settled by other tribes. The rest of the region was Oklahoma Territory.

White settlers now wanted the remaining Indian lands. In 1893, Congress created the Dawes Commission to bargain for the land, and to dissolve the Indian nations. Agents of the commission helped the tribes incorporate towns and prepare for citizenship. The commission divided the remaining land among members of the tribes. By 1905, commission leaders felt the Indian Territory was ready to become a state.

Leaders of the Five Civilized Tribes called a constitutional convention at Muskogee in 1905, and invited white citizens to take part. At the time, whites in the Indian Territory outnumbered the Indians five to one. The convention adopted a constitution for the proposed state of Sequoyah, and the people approved it in an election. But Congress refused to accept the area as a state. Congress wanted one state to be created from the Twin Territories. In 1906, delegates from both territories met in Guthrie to draw up a constitution.

Early Statehood. On Nov. 16, 1907, Oklahoma became the 46th state in the Union. Charles N. Haskell of Muskogee was elected the first governor. The new state had a population of 1,414,177. Guthrie was the first capital. In 1910, Oklahoma City became the capital.

Even before statehood, Oklahoma had become a center of oil production. A small well was drilled near Chelsea in 1889. The first important well was drilled at Bartlesville in 1897. Tulsa became an oil center after the Red Fork-Tulsa field was opened in 1901.

THE GOVERNORS OF OKLAHOMA		
	Party	Term
1. Charles N. Haskell	Democratic	1907-1911
2. Lee Cruce	Democratic	1911-1915
3. R. L. Williams	Democratic	1915-1919
4. James B. A. Robertson	Democratic	1919-1923
5. John C. Walton	Democratic	1923
6. Martin E. Trapp	Democratic	1923-1927
7. Henry S. Johnston	Democratic	1927-1929
8. William J. Holloway	Democratic	1929-1931
9. William H. Murray	Democratic	1931-1935
10. Ernest W. Marland	Democratic	1935-1939
11. Leon C. Phillips	Democratic	1939-1943
12. Robert S. Kerr	Democratic	1943-1947
13. Roy J. Turner	Democratic	1947-1951
14. Johnston Murray	Democratic	1951-1955
15. Raymond S. Gary	Democratic	1955-1959
16. J. Howard Edmondson	Democratic	1959-1963
17. George Nigh	Democratic	1963
18. Henry Bellmon	Republican	1963-1967
19. Dewey F. Bartlett	Republican	1967-1971
20. David Hall	Democratic	1971-

Keystone Dam on the Arkansas River near Tulsa was completed in 1964. The dam is an important part of a plan to provide flood control, hydroelectric power, recreation areas, and better navigation along the river.

But there were problems, especially among farmers. The prices of farm products were low, and many settlers found they did not have enough land to farm profitably. After the United States entered World War I in 1917, these problems disappeared in the huge demand for Oklahoma's farm and fuel products.

The 1920's. During the 1920's, many of Oklahoma's problems returned. Farm prices dropped again, and economic distress led to unrest. Secret organizations, such as the Ku-Klux Klan, stirred into action (see KU-KLUX KLAN). The Klan won many members in all parts of the state, and controlled or elected many municipal and county officials. But Governor James B. A. Robertson, who served from 1919 to 1923, fought the Klan and refused to allow any state official to join it.

In 1923, John C. Walton became governor. He was impeached for abusing his powers. The state legislature removed him from office after only 9 months and 14 days. Among other things, Walton had used the National Guard to prevent a grand jury from meeting. Lieutenant Governor Martin E. Trapp became governor and served until 1927. Trapp was a "hard roads" governor who pushed the construction of all-weather highways. Trapp also backed a law that made it illegal to wear masks at public gatherings. This law helped control the Klan. Henry S. Johnston became governor in 1927, but he, too, was impeached. After two years in office, Johnston was found guilty of incompetence and removed by the legislature. In March, 1929, Lieutenant Governor William J. Holloway became governor.

Important discoveries of oil and gas helped Oklahoma during this period. The huge Oklahoma City field was opened in 1928. It had more than 1,500 producing wells within 10 years. The Greater Seminole area led the nation in production from 1925 to 1929.

The 1930's. The campaign of 1930 was highlighted by the election as governor of one of Oklahoma's most colorful politicians, William H. "Alfalfa Bill" Murray. A former congressman, Murray appealed to the "common folks" to vote for him. After his election, Murray shut down over 3,000 flowing oil wells. The price of oil had been dropping, and Murray wanted to keep some oil off the market to force up the price. After three months, he permitted production to start again.

Oklahoma suffered many hardships during the Great Depression of the 1930's. Business was bad and farm prices were extremely low. Many banks failed and people lost their savings. The entire Great Plains region suffered a severe water shortage. Crops failed for lack of rain, and there were unusually hot summers. High winds stripped away thousands of acres of fertile topsoil, and whipped the dry dirt into massive dust storms that turned day into night. Much of the plains area became known as the *Dust Bowl* (see DUST BOWL). Many farmers left the land to try their luck elsewhere. Many miners and oil workers also left the state. Oklahoma suffered a large loss of population. See UNITED STATES, HISTORY OF (The Great Depression).

The Mid-1900's. During World War II (1939-1945), Oklahoma's major products—food and fuels—again came into great demand. Increased use of soil conservation practices helped restore many farms that had been damaged during the drought of the 1930's.

From 1943 to 1947, Governor Robert S. Kerr brought about reforms in education, state finances, and pardon and parole procedures for convicts. After his term as governor, Kerr won election to the U.S. Senate.

During the 1950's, Oklahoma's economy began to shift from an agricultural to an industrial base. Both the size and number of farms declined. Johnston Murray, the son of Alfalfa Bill Murray, became governor in 1951 and started a campaign to develop new industry in the state. His successor, Raymond S. Gary, continued Oklahoma's industrial expansion.

New industries and construction projects highlighted the state's economic progress during the 1960's. Two large electronics plants were built in Oklahoma City, and Tulsa became the site of a space equipment factory. The Federal Aviation Administration built an aeronautics center in Oklahoma City. This center trains workers for civil aviation jobs, such as that of control tower operator, and conducts research into airplane crashes. In 1963, Henry Bellmon became the state's first Republican governor. Bellmon was elected to the U.S. Senate in 1967.

Construction of a number of dams and creation of several lakes began in the mid-1900's. Some of these projects were completed in the 1960's, and the others were to be finished in the early 1970's. The man-made lakes were created to increase the state's hydroelectric power and water storage capacities.

The new dams and lakes assisted Oklahoma business and political leaders in their efforts to broaden the state's industrial activity. The state government advertised Oklahoma's abundant supplies of fuel, water, and electric power. In addition, the legislature revised the state's tax structure to attract manufacturers. As a result, Oklahoma gained new industries that do not depend on the products of its farms and mines.

Oklahoma Today is becoming increasingly industrialized. Carpet mills, plastics factories, and the manufacture of mobile homes have started to play an important role in the state's economy. The Arkansas River Development Program was completed in 1970. This $1-billion project opened the Arkansas River to navigation from the Mississippi River into Oklahoma. It provided Oklahoma with low-cost transportation for unpackaged goods.

Oklahoma faces several political and social problems in the 1970's. One challenge is to find ways to meet the increasing cost of government operations. Since

World War II, Oklahoma governors have been elected largely because they promised not to raise taxes. But many Oklahomans feel that taxes must be boosted to pay for better schools, highways, and mental health programs.

Like many other states, Oklahoma has had racial problems. During the 1960's, the state repealed laws that had segregated schools and public accommodations and had prohibited racially mixed marriages. But Negroes and Indians in Oklahoma still face problems of poverty and unequal opportunity.

W. EUGENE HOLLON, JOHN W. MORRIS, and CLARKE M. THOMAS

OKLAHOMA/*Study Aids*

Related Articles in WORLD BOOK include:

BIOGRAPHIES

Albert, Carl Bert	Rogers, Will
Chouteau (Jean P.)	Ross, John
Harris, Fred Roy	Sequoya
Harris, Roy	Tallchief, Maria
Hurley, Patrick J.	Thorpe, Jim
Monroney, A. S. Mike	Watie, Stand

CITIES

Ardmore	Muskogee	Stillwater
Enid	Norman	Tulsa
Lawton	Oklahoma City	

HISTORY

Caddo Indians	Indian Territory
Cheyenne Indians	Louisiana Purchase
Comanche Indians	Osage Indians
Five Civilized Tribes	Westward
Indian, American	Movement

PHYSICAL FEATURES

Arkansas River	Lake O' The	Pensacola Dam
Canadian River	Cherokees	Platt National
Dust Bowl	Lake Texoma	Park
Fort Supply Dam	Ozark Mountains	Red River

PRODUCTS

For Oklahoma's rank among the states in production, see the following articles:

Cattle	Horse	Nut	Petroleum
Gas	Mining	Peanut	Wheat

OTHER RELATED ARTICLES

Fort Sill	Southwestern States

Outline

I. Government
 A. Constitution
 B. Executive
 C. Legislature
 D. Courts
 E. Local Government
 F. Taxation
 G. Politics

II. People

III. Education
 A. Schools
 B. Libraries
 C. Museums

IV. A Visitor's Guide
 A. Places to Visit
 B. Annual Events

V. The Land
 A. Land Regions
 B. Rivers and Lakes

VI. Climate

VII. Economy
 A. Natural Resources
 B. Manufacturing
 C. Mining
 D. Agriculture
 E. Electric Power
 F. Transportation
 G. Communication

VIII. History

Questions

Why did Congress take land away from the Indians in the Oklahoma area after the Civil War?

What role did the Indian leader Sequoya play in the history of education in Oklahoma?

Why did a federal court order the reapportionment of the Oklahoma legislature?

What group of Indians was among Oklahoma's first permanent settlers?

What is the leading source of agricultural income in Oklahoma?

Why is Oklahoma called the *Sooner State*?

What part of Oklahoma is called the *Panhandle*?

How many of Oklahoma's 77 counties produce gas and oil?

Why is the phrase "as long as grass shall grow and rivers run" important in Oklahoma history?

Why did Oklahoma's population drop in the 1930's?

Books to Read

BAILEY, JEAN. *Cherokee Bill, Oklahoma Pacer*. Abingdon, 1952.

DALE, EDWARD E., and WARDELL, MORRIS L. *A History of Oklahoma*. Prentice-Hall, 1948.

DAVIS, RUSSELL G., and ASHABRANNER, BRENT K. *The Choctaw Code*. McGraw-Hill, 1961.

GIBSON, A. M. *Oklahoma: A Students' Guide to Localized History*. Teacher's College Press, 1965.

KEITH, HAROLD V. *Rifles for Watie*. Crowell, 1957.

MARRIOTT, ALICE L. *The Ten Grandmothers*. Univ. of Oklahoma Press, 1951. Life among the Kiowa Indians.

McREYNOLDS, EDWIN C., and others. *Oklahoma: The Story of its Past and Present*. Univ. of Oklahoma Press, 1961.

MORRIS, JOHN W., and McREYNOLDS, EDWIN C. *Historical Atlas of Oklahoma*. Univ. of Oklahoma Press, 1965.

NYE, WILBUR S. *Carbine and Lance: The Story of Old Fort Sill*. Univ. of Oklahoma Press, 1957.

RISTER, CARL C. *Oil! Titan of the Southwest*. Univ. of Oklahoma Press, 1949.

RUTH, KENT, and others, eds. *Oklahoma: A Guide to the Sooner State*. Univ. of Oklahoma Press, 1958.

SICELOFF, DAVID G. *Boy Settler in the Cherokee Strip*. Caxton, 1964.

WRIGHT, MURIEL H. *A Guide to the Indian Tribes of Oklahoma*. Univ. of Oklahoma Press, 1957.

OKLAHOMA, UNIVERSITY OF

OKLAHOMA, UNIVERSITY OF, is a state-supported coeducational school in Norman, Okla., and Oklahoma City, Okla. It has colleges of arts and sciences, fine arts, engineering, education, law, pharmacy, and business administration. In addition, there are schools of medicine and nursing, and a graduate college. Courses lead to bachelor's degrees in all fields and to master's degrees in 62 fields. Students may earn doctor's degrees in 22 fields. Oklahoma University's extension division includes correspondence courses, audio-visual education, short courses, and other services to the public. The University of Oklahoma Press publishes a quarterly review of foreign literature, called *Books Abroad*. The university was founded in 1890 by an act of territorial legislature. It was opened to students in 1892. For enrollment, see UNIVERSITIES AND COLLEGES (table).   GEORGE L. CROSS

OKLAHOMA BAPTIST UNIVERSITY is a coeducational school of arts and sciences at Shawnee, Okla. It is owned and operated by the Baptist General Convention of Oklahoma. The university grants bachelor's degrees. It was founded in 1910. For enrollment, see UNIVERSITIES AND COLLEGES (table).

OKLAHOMA CHRISTIAN COLLEGE. See UNIVERSITIES AND COLLEGES (table).

OKLAHOMA CITY, Okla. (pop. 366,481; met. area 640,889; alt. 1,195 ft.), is the capital and the largest city of the state. The city is one of the largest in area in the United States. It covers almost 650 square miles. Oklahoma City owes its importance and rapid growth to the great natural gas and oil fields nearby and the farming and livestock regions in the surrounding area.

The city lies near the geographic center of the state on the North Canadian River. It is about 185 miles south of Wichita, Kans., and about 210 miles north of Fort Worth, Tex. (see OKLAHOMA [political map]). For the monthly weather in Oklahoma City, see OKLAHOMA (Climate).

Cultural Life. Oklahoma City is the home of Oklahoma City University, the University of Oklahoma's medical school, and Oklahoma Christian College. The city has 80 elementary schools and 16 junior-senior high schools. The Oklahoma Historical Society and the National Cowboy Hall of Fame and Western Heritage Center are located there. The city has a symphony orchestra, civic ballet, art center, science and arts building, planetarium, zoo, and several libraries. The state Capitol was completed in 1917. Oklahoma City has

Oklahoma City Skyscrapers tower over the downtown business district. Development of nearby natural gas and oil resources in the 1930's hastened the city's growth.

Oklahoma City Chamber of Commerce

over 75 parks and 50 playgrounds. Its recreational facilities cover about 3,000 acres.

Industry and Trade. Oklahoma City has more than 1,000 industrial plants and wholesale houses. They include oil refineries, meat-packing establishments, flour and feed mills, machinery and ironworks, cotton compresses, cottonseed-oil mills, printing and publishing concerns, and furniture and electrical equipment factories. In recent years, the city has become an electronics center, specializing in space electronics. Nearly all the industries use natural gas, which is easily obtained in the city. The chief products traded in the city are petroleum, grain, cotton, and livestock.

Transportation. Several railway and bus lines, four transcontinental airlines, and the interstate highway system connect Oklahoma City with all parts of the United States. Oklahoma City is also an aviation center. Tinker Air Force Base is a huge supply post of the United States Air Force. It also serves as headquarters for the Oklahoma City Air Materiel Area. The Federal Aviation Administration Aeronautical Center is also located in Oklahoma City.

History. A presidential proclamation on Apr. 22, 1889, opened the site of the city to settlement. Ten thousand settlers flocked there the first day. Oklahoma City received its charter in 1891, and became the state capital in 1910. The first meat-packing plants opened the same year. Oil was discovered in 1928. Wells were drilled in residential areas of the city, and even on the grounds of the Capitol. Great industrial expansion occurred there during World War II and in the 1950's and 1960's. Oklahoma City has a council-manager form of local government.   JOHN W. MORRIS

See also OKLAHOMA (picture: The State Capitol).

OKLAHOMA CITY UNIVERSITY is a coeducational school in Oklahoma City, Okla. It is controlled by the United Methodist Church. The university has a college of arts and sciences, and schools of business, law, and music. It grants B.A., LL.B., B.M., and B.S. in Business degrees. The university was founded in 1904. For enrollment, see UNIVERSITIES AND COLLEGES (table).   JACK S. WILKES

OKLAHOMA COLLEGE OF LIBERAL ARTS is a state-supported coeducational school in Chickasha, Okla. Courses lead to bachelor's degrees in liberal arts, fine arts, and sciences. The college was founded in 1908. For enrollment, see UNIVERSITIES AND COLLEGES (table).

OKLAHOMA PANHANDLE STATE COLLEGE. See UNIVERSITIES AND COLLEGES (table).

OKLAHOMA STATE UNIVERSITY is a state-supported coeducational school in Stillwater, Okla. It has colleges of agriculture, arts and sciences, business education, engineering, home economics, veterinary medicine, and a graduate school. The university grants Associate, B.S., B.A., M.S., M.A., D.V.M., Ed.D., and Ph.D. degrees. It offers a special course in firemanship training. The Okmulgee branch offers trade courses and rehabilitation programs. The university maintains an agricultural experiment station and a state extension service. It also has Army and Air Force ROTC units.

The university colors are orange and black. Athletic teams are called *Cowboys*. The university was established in 1890, and was opened to students in 1891. For enrollment, see UNIVERSITIES AND COLLEGES (table).   OLIVER S. WILLHAM

U.S. Dept. of Agriculture
Pods of the Okra Plant

OKRA, *O kruh,* is a plant cultivated for its immature pods, which are used in stews, to thicken and flavor soup, and as a vegetable, chiefly in the southern part of the United States. The plant is an annual. It grows to a height of from 2 to 8 feet, and bears rounded, fine-lobed leaves, and greenish-yellow flowers. The pods on the plant are from 4 to 6 inches long, but sometimes exceed a foot when fully grown. The okra pods are generally cooked and canned when young and tender.

Okra is a kind of hibiscus, and is closely related to cotton. It is a native of Africa. In the southern part of the United States, where it is raised in large quantities, it is also known as *gumbo* or *okro.*

Scientific Classification. The okra belongs to the mallow family, *Malvaceae.* It is genus *Hibiscus,* species *H. esculentus.*   JOHN H. MACGILLIVRAY

ÖLAND. See SWEDEN (The Land; map).

OLAV V (1903-   ) became king of Norway in 1957 when his father, King Haakon VII, died (see HAAKON VII). Olav was born in England, and came to Norway when he was 2.

Billedsentralen, Oslo
King Olav V

He attended the Norwegian War College and Oxford University. He frequently served as regent during his father's illnesses. He was chief of Norwegian defense forces in World War II. His wife, Princess Märtha of Sweden, died in 1954.   RAYMOND E. LINDGREN

OLD AGE. See GERIATRICS; PROGERIA; SOCIAL AND REHABILITATION SERVICE; MEDICARE; LIFE (Length of Life).

OLD-AGE AND SURVIVORS INSURANCE. See SOCIAL SECURITY.

OLD-AGE PENSION. See PENSION.

OLD ARSENAL. See ARKANSAS (Places to Visit [MacArthur Park]; color map: Historic Arkansas).

OLD BAILEY is the common name for the main criminal court in London. The Old Bailey has several courts, and each one holds sessions at least four times a year. The court is located on a street called Old Bailey. This street once formed part of a *bailey* (an area between the inner and outer city walls) in medieval London.

The London city government built the Sessions House in 1550. This building became known as the Old Bailey. Persons held at nearby Newgate Prison were tried in the Old Bailey. Famous cases held there included the treason trial of judges responsible for the execution of King Charles I; the treason trial of William Joyce, who broadcast for Nazi Germany during World

Camera Press from Publix

Old Bailey, London's main criminal court, dates from 1550. The present court building, *above,* opened in 1907.

War II as *Lord Haw Haw;* and the morals trial of the author and playwright Oscar Wilde. VERNON F. SNOW

OLD BLOOD AND GUTS. See PATTON, GEORGE SMITH, JR.

OLD BULLION. See BENTON, THOMAS HART.

OLD CASCADE TUNNEL. See CASCADE TUNNEL.

OLD CATHOLIC CHURCHES are a group of Christian churches that split away from the Roman Catholic Church. The churches were formed by Roman Catholics who opposed the dogma of *papal infallibility* proclaimed at the first Vatican Council in 1870. This doctrine states that the pope is always right when he speaks as head of the church on matters of faith and morals.

The Catholics who withdrew from the Roman Catholic Church at that time established an independent church. Most of these Catholics lived in Germany, The Netherlands, Switzerland, and the Austro-Hungarian empire. The independent church formed a loose relationship with other dissenting Catholic churches under the terms of the Union of Utrecht in 1889.

Old Catholic churches generally follow Roman Catholic doctrine, although clergymen may marry. The churches encourage Bible study and conduct worship in the *vernacular* (local language). For membership in the U.S., see RELIGION (table). FRANKLIN H. LITTELL

OLD COMEDY. See DRAMA (Greek Drama).

OLD DOMINION. See VIRGINIA.

OLD DOMINION COLLEGE. See UNIVERSITIES AND COLLEGES (table).

OLD ENGLISH. See ENGLISH LANGUAGE; ENGLISH LITERATURE (The Anglo-Saxon Period).

OLD ENGLISH SHEEP DOG is best known for its long hair, "bobbed" tail, and odd, shuffling walk. Its hair hangs down over its eyes. Much brushing is required to keep the dog's long coat neat. The coat serves as excellent insulation. It is a grizzly gray or blue, often with white markings, or predominantly white, with markings. The dog stands about 22 inches high, and weighs between 50 and 65 pounds. OLGA DAKAN

See also DOG (picture: Working Dogs); SHEEP DOG.

OLD FAITHFUL. See WYOMING (color picture); YELLOWSTONE NATIONAL PARK.

OLD FUSS AND FEATHERS. See SCOTT, WINFIELD.

OLD GLORY. See DRIVER, WILLIAM.

OLD HICKORY. See JACKSON, ANDREW.

OLD IRONSIDES, locomotive. See BALDWIN, MATTHIAS WILLIAM.

OLD IRONSIDES, ship. See CONSTITUTION (ship).

OLD KING COLE. See MOTHER GOOSE.

OLD LINE STATE. See MARYLAND.

OLD MAN ELOQUENT. See ADAMS, JOHN QUINCY.

OLD MAN OF THE MOUNTAIN. See WHITE MOUNTAINS.

OLD MAN OF THE SEA was a name given to Nereus in Greek mythology. He was the son of Pontus and Gaea, and the father of the 50 Nereids (see NEREID). Nereus knew the way to the apples of the Hesperides which Hercules wanted. Hercules captured him, but Nereus changed into fire, into a lion, and then into water. At last, as Nereus, he directed Hercules to the apples.

See also HERCULES (The Twelve Labors).

Greater Boston Chamber of Commerce

The Graceful Steeple of Historic Old North Church pierces the skyline in the business district of Boston, Mass.

OLD NORTH CHURCH is the popular name for Christ Church, the oldest public building in Boston, Mass. The red-brick structure has a slender white steeple in the Christopher Wren style. Robert Newman hung the lanterns there as a signal from Paul Revere that the British were coming. The tower contains the first set of church bells in the American Colonies, cast in 1744. Storms in 1804 and 1954 toppled the spire. In 1955, the spire on the Old North Church was rebuilt to its original 190 feet. WILLIAM J. REID

See also BOSTON; REVERE, PAUL.

OLD ORCHARD BEACH. See MAINE (Land Regions).

OLD PRETENDER. See SCOTLAND (Union with England).

OLD ROUGH AND READY. See TAYLOR, ZACHARY.

OLD SLATER MILL. See RHODE ISLAND (Places to Visit; color picture).

OLD SOUTH MEETING HOUSE. See BOSTON (The Freedom Trail).

OLD SPANISH TRAIL. See SANTA FE TRAIL.

OLD SQUAW. See DUCK (Wild Ducks).

OLD STONE MILL. See RHODE ISLAND (Places to Visit).

OLD TESTAMENT is the first part of the Bible. Together with the New Testament, it forms the Scriptures that are sacred to Christians. Jews accept only the Old Testament, which they call the *Hebrew Bible*, as sacred. The word *testament* is an old word for *covenant*, or agreement. The Old Testament emphasizes the idea of a covenant between God and His people, and contains a record of their history to show how faithfully they observed this covenant.

The Bible has been called "the Book of Books" because of the tremendous influence it has exerted on mankind. For more than two thousand years, people have considered the Old Testament the word of God, and have turned to it for guidance on life's problems. Millions of persons throughout the world have found in it great religious truths and inspired ethical teachings. As a cultural treasure, the Old Testament is one of the most important sources we have for knowledge of the past. In addition, the poetry and prose of the Old Testament include some of the greatest literary masterpieces of the world.

Contents. Most Protestant and Jewish groups divide the Old Testament into 39 books. But they differ in the order they assign to the books. For a list of Old Testament books according to the King James Version of the Bible, see BIBLE (table, The Books of the Bible). Roman Catholics include the Apocryphal books of Tobit, Judith, Wisdom, Baruch, Ecclesiasticus, and I and II Maccabees in the Old Testament, bringing the number to 46 (see APOCRYPHA).

Jews divide the Old Testament into three main sections called the Torah, the Prophets, and the Writings.

The Torah consists of the books of Genesis, Exodus, Leviticus, Numbers, and Deuteronomy, and is often called the *Pentateuch* or *Five Books* of Moses (see PENTATEUCH). The Hebrew word *Torah* is usually translated as *the Law*, but a more accurate translation would be *teaching* or *guidance*. The Torah begins with an account of the creation of the world and the early traditions of man. It then concentrates on the careers of Abraham, Isaac, and Jacob, the *patriarchs* (fathers) of the Hebrew nation (see PATRIARCH). Other narratives include the story of Joseph, the history of the Israelites in Egypt, and the Exodus from Egypt under the leadership of Moses. The books of Numbers and Deuteronomy describe the experiences of the people in the desert and the death of Moses before they entered the Promised Land. Laws dealing with all phases of life are woven into the narratives. They include religious and moral teachings, ritual practices, and civil and criminal laws. Sections of the Old Testament also contain rules about health and even medical counsel.

The Prophets are divided into two parts, the Earlier Prophets and the Later Prophets. The books of Joshua, Judges, Samuel, and Kings make up the Earlier Prophets. They are often called the *historical books* because they trace the history of the Hebrew nation

National Gallery of Art, Washington, D.C., Mellon Collection

The Old Testament Story of Moses tells how Pharaoh's daughter found the infant Moses in the reeds along the Nile River. His mother hid him there after Pharaoh ordered all new-born Israelite boys killed. In his painting, *The Finding of Moses,* Paolo Veronese dressed his figures in the Venetian styles of his time.

from the time it entered Palestine until the destruction of the kingdoms of Israel and Judah (see JEWS [History]). They are included in the Prophets because they describe the lives and activities of many prophets, such as Nathan and Elijah. They also interpret the history of the Hebrews from the point of view of the prophets, who taught that man's destiny is determined by his obedience or disobedience to God's laws. The Later Prophets include the books of the three major prophets —Isaiah, Jeremiah, and Ezekiel—and of the Twelve Minor Prophets.

The Writings, or *Hagiographa,* are made up of a variety of books. Their authors include teachers, poets, and great thinkers. The Writings contain the books of Psalms, Proverbs, and Job, and the five *Megillot,* or Scrolls: Song of Solomon, Ruth, Lamentations, Ecclesiastes, and Esther. The book of Daniel and the later historical works of Ezra, Nehemiah, and Chronicles complete this section of the Old Testament.

For a fuller discussion of the contents of the Old Testament books, see the separate article on each book in THE WORLD BOOK ENCYCLOPEDIA.

Christian and Jewish groups differ in the position of importance they assign to the books of the Apocrypha.

561

Many of the books of the Apocrypha resemble those of the Old Testament in form. But the Apocryphal books were written at a later period, probably from about 200 B.C. to about A.D. 100.

Date. The Old Testament was written over a long period of time. The process was complicated because much of the material was recited or chanted out loud long before it was written down. Scholars disagree about how and when the books were actually written. But most scholars today agree that the Old Testament does contain material from the days of Moses. One of the earliest poems is the "War Song of Deborah" (Judges 5), composed about 1100 B.C. Many parts of the historical and prophetic books were written during the time of the two kingdoms of Israel and Judah. Some of the most important prophets and poets lived during the Babylonian Exile, from 587 B.C. to 538 B.C. Many traditions, laws, and historical records that had accumulated were collected and put in order at that time. The books of Psalms and the Song of Solomon were assembled after 538 B.C., when many Jews returned to Palestine. Chronicles, Ecclesiastes, Esther, and Daniel were written later. The entire Old Testament was in existence by the time of the Maccabean Wars, from 168 B.C. to 165 B.C. The Biblical manuscripts of the Dead Sea Scrolls, written about 100 years later, show that the text of the Old Testament two thousand years ago was essentially the same as it is today (see DEAD SEA SCROLLS).

Translations. The entire Old Testament was written in Hebrew, except for some chapters in the books of Daniel and Ezra and a few words in Genesis and Jeremiah. These are in Aramaic, a language much like Hebrew (see ARAMAIC).

The Old Testament was probably the first work ever translated. The books aroused great interest among peoples who could not read Hebrew. About 250 B.C., scholars living in Alexandria, Egypt, translated the Torah into Greek. This translation is called the *Septuagint* (see SEPTUAGINT). Translations of other books of the Old Testament followed. Later, the Old Testament was translated into Aramaic and Syriac (see TARGUM). The best-known Latin translation was the *Vulgate*, done by St. Jerome about A.D. 405 (see VULGATE). This translation became the official Old Testament text of the Roman Catholic Church. For a discussion of later translations of the Old Testament, see BIBLE (How the Bible Developed). ROBERT GORDIS

See also BIBLE with its list of Related Articles.

OLD WATER TOWER. See CHICAGO (color picture).

OLD WORLD is a general term applied to the Eastern Hemisphere. The Western Hemisphere is called the *New World*. The Old World includes the continents of Europe, Asia, Africa, and Australia. But the term *Old World* is often used to refer just to Europe or to European civilization. The terms Old World and New World are used in botany and zoology. For example, zoologists divide monkeys into two groups, Old World monkeys and New World monkeys. See also HEMISPHERE.

OLDFIELD, BARNEY (1877-1946), was the first man to drive an automobile at a speed of a mile a minute. His name became synonymous with speed after he did this in a much-publicized test at Indianapolis on June 15, 1903. His first racing car, the "999," was built by Henry Ford. In it, Oldfield won his first race at Detroit in 1902. In 1910, at Daytona Beach, Fla., he raced a mile at an average speed of 131 mph, which was a record at that time. BERNER ELI OLDFIELD was born in Wauseon, Ohio. PAT HARMON

See also AUTOMOBILE RACING (Automobile World Speed Records; picture).

OLDS, RANSOM ELI (1864-1950), was a pioneer automobile inventor and manufacturer. Two automobiles, the Oldsmobile and the Reo (from his initials), were named for him. In 1886, he began experimenting with steam-powered carriages in his father's machine shop in Lansing, Mich. He later made a four-wheeled steam car which he sold to a firm in India in 1893. It was the first U.S. car sold abroad.

Olds built his first gasoline-operated car in 1896. In 1899, he helped found the Olds Motor Works in Detroit, Mich. A lightweight, one-cylinder, low-cost model ($650), famous as the "curved-dash" Oldsmobile, was in volume production by 1901. Many thousands of these cars were sold by 1906. In 1904, Olds left the Olds Motor Works, and organized a company to manufacture Reo automobiles and trucks. He was president of the Reo Motor Car Company from 1904 to 1924, and later became chairman of the board.

United Press Int.
Ransom Eli Olds

Many persons consider Olds the actual founder of the automobile industry. He built the first automobile factory, and was the first manufacturer to mass-produce cars. Furthermore, the success of the Oldsmobile attracted other manufacturers into the industry, and helped to make the automobile popular with the American people.

Olds was born in Geneva, Ohio. He died Aug. 26, 1950, in Lansing, Mich. SMITH HEMPSTONE OLIVER

See also AUTOMOBILE (The Steam Car).

OLEANDER, OH lee AN der, is an ornamental flowering shrub which is valued as a house plant. The oleander sometimes grows 15 feet tall. It bears leathery lance-shaped leaves and showy roselike flowers. The two most common varieties have red and white blossoms. The oleander is native to the warm parts of Asia and to the Mediterranean region. Gardeners plant it outdoors in warm climates, but they grow it in pots and tubs in temperate regions. It is a favorite porch plant in summer.

The Oleander is a favorite indoor plant for gardeners.
J. Horace McFarland

Because all parts of the plant are poisonous to eat, children should be cautioned about eating the oleander. If the cuttings are placed in bottles of water, they will form roots in a few

Olive Fruit, *left,* turns a deep purple when ripe. An olive orchard at harvesttime, *above,* presents an attractive blend of soft gray-green colors.

J. Horace McFarland; Arthur C. Smith

weeks. Gardeners easily raise the oleander from cuttings. Then oleanders must be transplanted to moist, rich soil, where they grow well.

Scientific Classification. The oleander belongs to the dogbane family, *Apocynaceae.* It is genus *Nerium,* species *N. oleander.*   J. J. LEVISON

OLEIC ACID. See FAT.

OLEIN. See LARD.

OLEOMARGARINE. See MARGARINE.

OLEORESIN. See TREE (Tree Materials).

OLERICULTURE. See HORTICULTURE.

OLFACTORY LOBE and **OLFACTORY NERVE.** See NOSE; SMELL.

OLIBANUM. See FRANKINCENSE.

OLIGARCHY, *AHL ih GAHR kih,* is a form of government in which a small group of persons holds the ruling power. These persons rule in dictatorial fashion, without the consent of the governed. A republic may be an oligarchy if only a few persons have the right to vote (see REPUBLIC).

Most persons today do not advocate oligarchical forms of government. But many oligarchies existed in the past. Most ancient Greek city-states were classic examples of oligarchies. Another example is Venice during the Renaissance, when a small group of wealthy families controlled the city. In a broad sense, the word *oligarchy* can also be applied to some churches and to some business corporations.   WILLIAM EBENSTEIN

OLIGOCENE EPOCH. See EARTH (table: Outline of Earth History).

OLIGOPOLY. See MONOPOLY AND COMPETITION.

OLIVE, *AHL iv,* is a fruit that grows in regions near the tropics. Men grew olives even before our earliest history was written, and have grown them widely ever since. It is thought that this fruit first grew in the eastern Mediterranean basin. Hundreds of years ago it escaped from cultivation and began to grow wild all around the Mediterranean Sea. The Spaniards brought the olive to America, and it reached California in 1769.

Appearance of the Fruit and Tree. All its different parts give it an artistic appearance that men have admired for ages. Its bark and leaves are a soft gray-green, and its trunk is gnarled and uneven. Its shiny purple-black fruits are attractive.

Olive trees live longer than most other fruit trees. Some of the trees brought by the Spaniards to California are still alive. There are olive trees in Palestine which probably date back to the beginning of the Christian Era.

The olive tree has many small flowers. Most of the flowers are imperfect, and fruit cannot grow from them. They give off much pollen, and, as a rule, the wind carries the pollen from flower to flower. In all the varieties of olive, a tree can fertilize its flowers with its own pollen. In occasional seasons there is evidence that the trees benefit if they receive pollen from other trees. Most varieties do not bear large crops one season after another. There is a slack season in between. This manner of growth is called *alternate bearing.*

The olive itself is a drupe, the type of fruit which has a pit. It is apple-shaped to plum-shaped, and the ripe fruit is purple to black. The most important material in it is the olive oil. Both seed and flesh contain much oil, which makes up 15 to 30 per cent of the weight of the fresh fruit. Fresh olives have a bitter substance which makes them unpleasant to eat. The substance is largely or entirely removed when they are prepared for market.

Cultivation. Parts cut off from an olive tree will readily take root and grow into new trees. The young trees will grow in many different types of soil, but need good drainage. To produce large fruit, the grower must irrigate and prune the trees, and thin the fruit. Early harvesting partially overcomes alternate bearing. Fertilizers that add nitrogen to the soil give a larger yield.

The olive tree has remarkable powers of growing where the climate is very hot and dry. But for bearing good fruit, it needs a moderate supply of water. The fruit matures from October to January, and is injured if the temperature falls below 26° F. The tree itself is not

563

LEADING OLIVE GROWING COUNTRIES

Tons of olives grown each year. Based on a 4-year average, 1964-1967.

Italy
2,378,000 tons
⚫⚫⚫⚫⚫⚫⚫⚫⚫⚫⚫⚫⚫⚫⚫⚫⚫⚫⚫

Spain
1,635,000 tons
⚫⚫⚫⚫⚫⚫⚫⚫⚫⚫⚫⚫⚫

Greece
1,021,000 tons
⚫⚫⚫⚫⚫⚫⚫⚫

Turkey
668,000 tons
⚫⚫⚫⚫⚫

Portugal
412,000 tons
⚫⚫⚫

Tunisia
*357,000 tons
⚫⚫⚫

Morocco
*203,000 tons
⚫⚫

Algeria
*167,000 tons
⚫

Libya
119,000 tons
⚫

Syria
115,000 tons
⚫

*4-year average, 1963-1966, latest information available
Source: FAO

seriously injured until the temperature falls 10 degrees lower. The fruit needs much heat if it is to have a good quality when it matures. The air must be dry when the flowers blossom, and when the fruit begins to grow.

Harvesting and Preparation for Market. Olives abroad are grown first of all for their oil. In the United States a large part of the industry is based on preparing the fruit for eating. Oil is a side line, but American olive oil is as good as the best imported oil.

Harvesting olives requires careful handling. Farmers pick the green fruit and allow it to change color in buckets. They then haul the fruit to the processing plant in small boxes. Over long distances it is shipped in barrels of light brine. At the plant, it is fermented a short time with lactic acid. The olives are then graded and put through a machine that separates the fruit of different sizes. Next comes a lye treatment, and washing to remove the bitter substance. Then the olives are treated with air to give them all the same dark color, and are canned in brine. After canning, they are sterilized at 240° F. This treatment makes olives one of the safest of canned foods. Most of the American crop receives the California ripe-olive process, which gives a dark fruit, rich in flavor and food value. Other methods used include the Spanish green-olive process. The processed fruit can be eaten whole, or mixed with other foods to flavor them. California olives are becoming favorites.

Production. The countries bordering the Mediterranean Sea grow most of the world's olives. Italy and

Spain together produce more than half of the world output. There are about 13½ million acres of cultivated olive trees in the world, which produce about 7½ million tons of olives.

Only a few places in the United States can support the olive industry. These places lie in central and southern California. There are 32,000 acres of olive trees in California. These olive orchards produce about 44,000 tons of olives a year. The olive tree also grows in the states along the Gulf of Mexico, but it does not bear fruit there.

Scientific Classification. Olives belong to the olive family, *Oleaceae*. They are genus *Olea*, species *O. europaea*. JULIAN C. CRANE

See also FORSYTHIA; FRINGE TREE; GREECE, ANCIENT (color picture: Greek Farmers); OLIVE OIL.

OLIVE OIL is a fatty oil taken from olives. It is one of the most digestible of the edible fats. Like other fats, olive oil is a high energy food. Its chief ingredient is olein, a glycerin compound. Olive oil is used chiefly in salad dressings and as a frying fat. It is also used in soap, perfumes, and medicines.

In the manufacture of ordinary olive oil, the olives are crushed by corrugated metal rollers in brick trenches. The crushed pulp is placed in a coarsely woven fabric, and the fabric is folded over it to make a *cheese* (pulpy block) about 3 feet square and 3 inches thick. Ten or more of these cheeses are placed one above the other, with slats between them. Then pressure is applied to the cheeses.

The oil obtained by this method is filtered through woolen cloth, then allowed to settle for about 24 hours in funnel-shaped tanks. The sediment that settles to the bottom of the tank is drawn off. Then the oil is run into settling tanks lined with tin or glass. The oil stands in the tanks for two to five months. During this time, the additional sediment that settles out is drawn off several times.

The flavor of olive oil depends upon the variety of olives used, their ripeness when picked, the way they are handled, and length of time they are stored before pressing. The best oil comes from olives which are picked just after they ripen and before they turn black. If the olives are picked too green, the oil is bitter. If they are picked too ripe, the oil is rancid. The flesh of ripe olives is about half oil. When the skin is broken, a great deal of the oil comes out of the pulp. Such oil is called "virgin," or "sublime," or "first expressed" oil. It is the highest grade of olive oil. A cheap grade of olive oil is made from the cheese pulp left over after the first pressing. The cheeses are broken up, mixed with hot water and then pressed again to produce this lower-grade oil.

Most of the olive oil produced in the world comes from the Mediterranean countries. Italy and Spain combined usually produce more than half of the world olive oil production of about 1½ million tons a year. In the United States, California produces about 1,100 tons of the oil every year. LEONE RUTLEDGE CARROLL

See also OLIVE.

OLIVES, MOUNT OF. See MOUNT OF OLIVES.

OLIVET COLLEGE. See UNIVERSITIES AND COLLEGES (table).

OLIVET NAZARENE COLLEGE. See UNIVERSITIES AND COLLEGES (table).

United Press Int.

Sir Laurence Olivier

OLIVIER, *oh LIV ee ay,* **SIR LAURENCE** (1907-), is one of the leading Shakespearean actors of his time. Many regard his motion pictures of the Shakespeare plays, *Henry V* (1946), *Hamlet* (1948), and *Richard III* (1955), as screen classics.

His first Shakespearean success was on the stage in *Hamlet* at the Old Vic Theater in London in 1937. He became a managing director of the Old Vic Company in 1944. He acted with it in New York City in 1945 and toured Australia and New Zealand in 1948.

Olivier became noted for his performances in the motion pictures *Wuthering Heights* (1938) and *Rebecca* (1940), and in the plays *Oedipus Rex* (1945) and *The School for Scandal* (1948). He was born in Dorking, England, and was knighted in 1947.   RICHARD MOODY

OLMEC INDIANS developed one of the earliest high cultures in America. Their way of life flourished from about 1200 B.C. to about 100 B.C. They played an important role in the early stages of the ancient Mexican civilization. The word *Olmec,* meaning *rubber people,* comes from the Nahuatl language of the Aztec Indians. The Aztec gave the name to the people of the region along the eastern coast of Mexico, now part of the states of Veracruz and Tabasco, where they got their rubber. The name now applies to this ancient culture.

Much remains to be learned about the Olmec. But in recent years archaeologists have uncovered many remains of this ancient culture. The Olmec carved in jade and hard stone, and sometimes buried the objects. Outstanding remains include stone altars and pillars; stone heads, some 9 feet tall and weighing 15 tons; and perfectly ground concave mirrors of polished hematite. The figure of a half-human, half-jaguar creature, thought to be a god, occurs often in their art. The Olmec had some knowledge of hieroglyphic writing. An Olmec slab, with a date corresponding to 31 B.C., is considered by some historians to be America's oldest known dated work. La Venta, the site of ruins in Tabasco, was a major Olmec settlement.   GORDON F. EKHOLM

See also SCULPTURE (American Indian).

OLMEDO, JOSÉ. See LATIN-AMERICAN LITERATURE (Literature After Independence).

OLMSTED, *AHM sted,* is the family name of two American landscape architects, father and son, who greatly influenced park planning in American cities.

Frederick Law Olmsted (1822-1903) and Calvert Vaux designed New York's Central Park, the first great American park, in 1858. When he signed these plans, Olmsted placed the words *landscape architect* under his name. He was the first man to use this term. Other large park systems he designed include the grounds for the United States Capitol in Washington, D.C. (1874), the World's Columbian Exposition in Chicago (1893), and parks in many of the larger American cities. Olmsted tried to preserve the natural scenery of the area as much as possible. He tried to create a rural atmosphere in the hearts of great cities. Olmsted successfully combined beauty and function into his designs of parks.

In his early years, he traveled widely in Europe and the United States. His travels influenced him to write. His books include *Walks and Talks of an American Farmer in England* (1852), *A Journey in the Seaboard Slave States with Remarks on Their Economy* (1856), *A Journey Through Texas, with a Statistical Appendix* (1857), and *A Journey in the Back Country* (1860). Olmsted was born in Hartford, Conn., and studied at Yale University.

Frederick Law Olmsted, Jr. (1870-1957), studied landscape architecture with his father, and became a well-known landscape architect and a city planner. He served on the National Capital Park and Planning Commission in Washington, D.C., and as a professor of landscape architecture at Harvard University. He designed public parks in many American cities. Olmsted was born on Staten Island, N.Y., and was graduated from Harvard University.   ROBERT E. EVERLY

OLNEY, *AHL nih,* **RICHARD** (1835-1917), served under President Grover Cleveland as U.S. attorney general, and later as secretary of state. He was noted for breaking the Pullman strike of 1894. After the strike had tied up railroads running out of Chicago, Olney obtained an injunction against the strikers by claiming that they were interrupting the mails. Federal troops were sent in, the strike leaders were imprisoned, and the strike was broken.

In 1895, Olney vigorously upheld the Monroe Doctrine, which he believed was threatened by a boundary dispute between British Guiana (which has since been renamed Guyana) and Venezuela. He persuaded England to agree to arbitration of the matter. Olney was born in Oxford, Mass., and was graduated from Brown University.   NELSON M. BLAKE

OLYMPIA is a valley about 11 miles from Pírgos, Greece. In ancient times, religion, politics, and athletics centered at Olympia and made it important in Greek history. The Olympian games, held there every four years, were so important in Greek life that they were used as the basis for the calendar. All the buildings in Olympia were for worship or for games. The religious buildings were clustered in the *Altis* (sacred grove), which lies where the Cladeus River flows into the Alpheus River. They included the temples of Zeus and Hera, the Pelopion, the Philippeion, and the great altars.

The athletic buildings lay just outside the Altis. In the northwest corner was a gymnasium. Joining the gymnasium on the south lay the Palaestra, which was a wrestling and boxing school. On the east stood the great stadium. Southeast of the stadium was the Hippodrome, where chariot and horse races were held.

The Olympian games were prohibited in A.D. 394, and a fort was built inside the Altis. Later, earthquakes and floods covered the valley with gravel and soil. Finally, Olympia lay beneath 20 feet of earth.

In 1829, a French expedition began excavations at the temple of Zeus. The German government continued this work. Between 1875 and 1879 the entire Altis and many of the surrounding buildings were uncovered. Fragments of sculpture, coins, terra cottas, and bronzes have been found. The most important discoveries were two statues. These were the *Victory of Paeonius* (423 B.C.) and the *Hermes of Praxiteles.* Under an agreement between Germany and Greece, the originals of all discoveries remained in possession of Greece. The Germans reserved the right to take casts from sculptures, coins, or other discoveries. A museum with Olympian relics is at Olympia.   DONALD W. BRADEEN

See also OLYMPIC GAMES.

OLYMPIA, Wash. (pop. 23,111; alt. 10 ft.), is the state capital, and the gateway to southwestern Washington and the Olympic Peninsula. An important commercial port, the city lies on the southern point of Puget Sound. For location, see WASHINGTON (political map). Ocean-going ships use the harbor of Olympia to deliver petroleum products, lumber, and other goods. Beds of the delicious Olympia oyster lie in the shallow waters near Olympia. The city lists seafood processing among its major industries. Its other industries include brewing, food processing, and the manufacture of metal and lumber products. Many of the city's residents work at the state capitol. A 287-foot dome atop the Legislative Building towers over the area. See WASHINGTON (picture: State Capitol).

Fort Lewis, the largest United States Army post on the Pacific Coast, stands between Olympia and Tacoma. St. Martin's College is located in Olympia.

Homesteaders began to settle there in the 1840's. Edmund Sylvester pioneered in the development of the Olympia townsite. Olympia was named the capital city when the Washington Territory was created in 1853. The city was incorporated in 1859. It is the seat of Thurston County, and has a mayor-commissioner type of government.   HOWARD J. CRITCHFIELD

OLYMPIAD, *oh LIM pih ad.* In the Greek system of telling time, an Olympiad was the period of four years that elapsed between two successive celebrations of the Olympian, or Olympic, Games. This method of figuring time became common about 300 B.C. All events were dated from 776 B.C., the beginning of the first known Olympiad. The first year of the 195th Olympiad corresponds with the first year of Christ.

The beginning of the year of the Olympiad was determined by the first full moon after the summer solstice, the longest day of the year. This full moon fell about the first of July. Therefore, only the last six months of the first year of the 195th Olympiad corresponded to the first year of Our Lord. This method of counting time ceased about A.D. 440, after the 304th Olympiad. The Olympiads were used as measures of time by later Greek historians and other writers to refer to preceding centuries, but they were never in everyday use, as were months and years.   JOHN H. KENT

OLYMPIAS (375?-316 B.C.) was the wife of Philip II of Macedonia, and the mother of Alexander the Great. A proud and emotional woman, she influenced Alexander greatly. She told Alexander that his real father was the god Zeus-Ammon, not Philip. Olympias feared that Philip might choose another heir. Many people believe that she had Philip killed in order to ensure that Alexander would become king. After Alexander's death in 323 B.C., Olympias tried to keep the empire for her grandson, Alexander IV. She failed, and in 316 B.C. was captured by Cassander, a Macedonian prince. Olympias was eventually killed.   THOMAS W. AFRICA

See also ALEXANDER THE GREAT; PHILIP II.

The Olympic Rings, the symbol of the Olympic Games, appear on the Olympic flag. The interlocked rings are blue, yellow, black, green, and red. The colors were chosen because at least one of them appears in the flag of every nation of the world. The rings are linked together to represent the sporting friendship of the peoples of the world. For a color picture of the official Olympic flag, see FLAG (Flags of World Organizations).

OLYMPIC GAMES. Every four years, amateur athletes from nations throughout the world compete in a sports show called the Olympic Games. No other sports spectacle has a background so historic or thrilling.

Flags flutter from the top of a crowd-filled stadium. Cheers ring out as a swift runner carries a blazing torch into the arena to light the Olympic flame. The lighted torch has been brought many miles from Elis, Greece, where the games began more than 2,700 years ago. The athletes march into the stadium behind their national flags. They stand at attention and pledge to obey the rules of sportsmanship and fair play. The host nation then proclaims the opening of the Olympic Games.

Olympic events are divided into Summer and Winter games. The Summer Olympics run for about two weeks, and the Winter Olympics last 10 days. The official flag of the Olympic Games is white. At its center are five interlocking rings of blue, yellow, black, green, and red. The official motto is *Citius, Altius, Fortius,* which means *Swifter, Higher, Stronger.*

The Summer Olympics. Track events usually take the spotlight in the Summer Olympics. They include hurdles, relays, and races over various distances. Field events include the high jump, long jump, pole vault, discus throw, hammer throw, javelin throw, shot-put, and decathlon. See TRACK AND FIELD.

Athletes also compete in boxing, fencing, wrestling, gymnastics, and weight lifting. Water sports include swimming, rowing, water polo, and yachting. Horsemen take their mounts through riding events. Shooting and cycling round out the program.

The Summer Olympics sometimes also include basketball, canoeing, field hockey, judo, soccer, and volleyball. A sport must be carried on in at least 20 countries to be eligible for the Summer Olympic program. At least 12 countries must enter an event to include it on the program.

The Winter Olympics are always held in a mountainous country with plenty of snow. Mountain slopes and powdery snow are necessary for the skiing events. Skiers compete in jumping events, downhill and cross-country races, and the *slalom* (see SKIING). Speed skaters race over

olympic games

The Olympic Flame, a symbol of peace and friendship, is lit at the site of the ancient games. Runners in cross-country relays, planes, and ships carry the flame to the stadium of the host nation.

various distances. Figure skaters take part in individual and team events for men and women. Six-man teams compete in ice hockey. In the bobsledding events, two- or four-man teams pilot their sleds over icy, daredevil courses.

Olympic records are not compared from one set of games to the next in bobsledding, skiing, or figure skating. Changes in judging, differences in the condition of the snow, and variations between courses make speed and point comparisons between games unfair in these sports.

Teams. In the United States, officials choose Olympic athletes to make up the nation's team on the basis of trials held on sectional, regional, and national levels. Athletes who finish first, second, and third in the final trials earn places on the United States team.

In Great Britain and several other European countries, an athlete must not only win an elimination event, but must also meet a minimum standard. For example, an athlete would have to run the 100-meter race in 10.6 seconds to qualify for the Olympic team.

The athletes of many countries, including the United States, Great Britain, and Canada, rely on individual citizens to pay their Olympic expenses for travel, food, and lodging. However, the governments of some countries, such as Russia, pay the expenses.

Competition. The purpose of the Olympic Games is to let the great athletes of the world vie with each other in a spirit of peace and friendship. Olympic athletes pledge themselves to respect the regulations that govern them. They agree to participate as amateurs for the honor of their country and for the glory of sports. Nations do not actually compete against each other. Sports writers credit countries with points in events between teams or individuals. But this practice of ranking nation against nation is entirely unofficial. No nation ever officially "wins" the Olympics.

The International Olympic Committee sets the rules for the games and schedules the events. The Winter and Summer Olympics are governed by the same rules.

The Committee is made up of representatives of each country that takes part in the Olympic Games. The Committee chooses the places where the games are held, and appoints the judges for the games.

A country may enter only one team in each team event. Three athletes from each nation may compete in individual events. Because many athletes enter the Olympic games the number is reduced to six finalists in many events by elimination contests.

Winners of Olympic events receive gold medals. Second-place winners receive silver medals. Bronze medals go to third-place winners. The fourth-, fifth-, and sixth-place athletes receive certificates.

History. The first recorded Olympic race was held in 776 B.C. Historians believe the games were staged hundreds of years earlier, but they do not know the exact date of the first games.

The Greeks held Olympic races on the plains of Olympia, in Elis. The foot races honored Zeus, king of the Greek gods. The Eleans, who lived on the plains of Olympia, originated the Olympic festivals. Gradually, all the Greek city-states began to take part in the

Sites of the Olympic Games

YEAR	SUMMER	WINTER
1896	Athens	Not held
1900	Paris	Not held
1904	St. Louis	Not held
1908	London	Not held
1912	Stockholm	Not held
1920	Antwerp	Not held
1924	Paris	Chamonix, France
1928	Amsterdam	St. Moritz, Switzerland
1932	Los Angeles	Lake Placid, New York
1936	Berlin	Garmisch-Partenkirchen, Germany
1948	London	St. Moritz, Switzerland
1952	Helsinki	Oslo, Norway
1956	Melbourne	Cortina, Italy
1960	Rome	Squaw Valley, California
1964	Tokyo	Innsbruck, Austria
1968	Mexico City	Grenoble, France

567

⬯olympic games

The tables on these two pages list the Olympic ice hockey champions and the Olympic records in speed skating and swimming. Records for figure skating, skiing, and bobsledding are not recognized by the Olympics Committee because of the changing conditions of the snow and ice and variations in judging. The tables for these sports list the winners of the Winter Olympics held in February, 1968, in Grenoble, France.

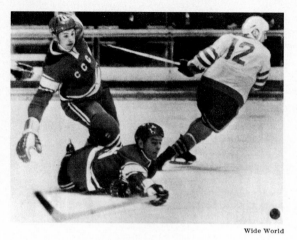

Wide World

The Russian Hockey Team won its second straight Olympic gold medal in 1968. The players in dark jerseys are Russians.

ICE HOCKEY WINNERS

Nation	Where Played	Year
Canada	Chamonix, France	1924
Canada	St. Moritz, Switzerland	1928
Canada	Lake Placid, N.Y.	1932
Great Britain	Garmisch-Partenkirchen, Germany	1936
Canada	St. Moritz, Switzerland	1948
Canada	Oslo, Norway	1952
Russia	Cortina, Italy	1956
U.S.A.	Squaw Valley, California	1960
Russia	Innsbruck, Austria	1964
Russia	Grenoble, France	1968

MEN'S SPEED SKATING

Event		Holder	Nation	Record	Where Made	Year
500	Mtrs.	Evgeny Grishin	Russia	40.2s.	Cortina	1956
1,500	Mtrs.	Cornelis Verkerk	Nether-lands	2m. 3.4s.	Grenoble	1968
5,000	Mtrs.	F. Anton Maier	Norway	7m. 22.4s.	Grenoble	1968
10,000	Mtrs.	Johnny Hoeglin	Sweden	15m. 23.6s.	Grenoble	1968

The Protopopovs of Russia won their second Olympic gold medal in pairs figure skating competition at Grenoble. Another Russian pair finished second.

Wide World

FIGURE SKATING

Event	Winner	Points	Nation
Men	Wolfgang Schwarz	1,904.1	Austria
Women	Peggy Fleming	1,970.5	U.S.A.
Pairs	Ludmilla Beloussova and Oleg Protopopov	315.2	Russia

Peggy Fleming of the U.S. decisively won the women's figure skating event in the 1968 winter games at Grenoble.

Wide World

Wide World

Nancy Greene of Canada won the women's giant slalom event at Grenoble in 1968, beating out Annie Famose of France.

WOMEN'S SKIING

Event	Winner	Time	Nation
Cross-Country			
5 Kilometers	Toini Gustafsson	16m.45.2s.	Sweden
10 Kilometers	Toini Gustafsson	36m.46.5s.	Sweden
Downhill	Olga Pall	1m.40.87s.	Austria
Giant Slalom	Nancy Greene	1m.51.97s.	Canada
Slalom	Marielle Goitschel	1m.25.86s.	France

MEN'S SKIING

Event	Winner	Time	Nation
Jump (70 meters)	Jiri Raska	216.50 pts.	Czecho-slovakia
Jump (90 meters)	Vladimir Beloussov	231.30 pts.	Russia
Nordic Combined	Franz Keller	449.04 pts.	West Germany
Cross-Country			
15 Kilometers	Harald Groen-ningen	47m.54.2s.	Norway
30 Kilometers	Franco Nones	1h.35m.39.2s.	Italy
50 Kilometers	Ole Ellefsaeter	2h.28m.45.8s.	Norway
40 Kilometer Relay	Martinsen, Tyldum, Groenningen, Ellefsaeter	2h.8m.33.5s.	Norway
Downhill	Jean-Claude Killy	1m.59.85s.	France
Giant Slalom	Jean-Claude Killy	3m.29.28s.	France
Slalom	Jean-Claude Killy	1m.39.73s.	France
Biathlon (Individual)	Magnar Solberg	1h.13m.45.9s.	Norway

BOBSLEDDING

Event	Driver	Time	Nation
2 man	Eugenio Monti	4m.41.54s.	Italy
4 man	Eugenio Monti	2m.17.39s.	Italy

Debbie Meyer of the United States won gold medals in the 200-, 400-, and 800-meter free-style swimming events of 1968.

SWIMMING

Event	Holder	Nation	Record	Where Made	Year
(Men)					
100 Meter Free Style	Michael Wenden	Australia	52.2s.	Mexico City	1968
400 Meter Free Style	Mike Burton	U.S.A.	4m.09.0s.	Mexico City	1968
1,500 Meter Free Style	Mike Burton	U.S.A.	16m.38.9s.	Mexico City	1968
200 Meter Back Stroke	Roland Matthes	E. Germany	2m.09.6s.	Mexico City	1968
200 Meter Butterfly	Kevin Berry	Australia	2m.06.6s.	Tokyo	1964
200 Meter Breast Stroke	Ian O'Brien	Australia	2m.27.8s.	Tokyo	1964
400 Meter Medley	Dick Roth	U.S.A.	4m.45.4s.	Tokyo	1964
400 Meter Medley Relay	Hickcox, McKenzie, Russell, Walsh	U.S.A.	3m.54.9s.	Mexico City	1968
400 Meter Free Style Relay	Zorn, Rerych, Spitz, Walsh	U.S.A.	3m.31.7s.	Mexico City	1968
800 Meter Free Style Relay	Clark, Saari, Ilman, Schollander	U.S.A.	7m.52.1s.	Tokyo	1964
(Women)					
100 Meter Free Style	Dawn Fraser	Australia	59.5s.	Tokyo	1964
400 Meter Free Style	Debbie Meyer	U.S.A.	4m.31.8s.	Mexico City	1968
100 Meter Back Stroke	Kaye Hall	U.S.A.	1m.06.2s.	Mexico City	1968
100 Meter Butterfly	Sharon Stouder	U.S.A.	1m.04.7s.	Tokyo	1964
200 Meter Breast Stroke	Sharon Wichman	U.S.A.	2m.44.4s.	Mexico City	1968
400 Meter Medley	Claudia Kolb	U.S.A.	5m.08.5s.	Mexico City	1968
400 Meter Free Style Relay	Barkman, Gustavson, Pedersen, Henne	U.S.A.	4m.02.5s.	Mexico City	1968
400 Meter Medley Relay	Hall, Ball, Daniels, Pedersen	U.S.A.	4m.28.3s.	Mexico City	1968

Wide World

olympic records

Al Oerter of the United States won the discus throw in 1956, 1960, 1964, and 1968. His 212-foot 6½-inch throw in 1968 broke his 1964 mark.

Wide World

Wide World

Dick Fosbury and Jim Hines of the United States won Olympic gold medals in 1968. Fosbury, *above*, using his "Fosbury Flop," high-jumped 7 feet 4¼ inches. Hines, *below*, won the 400-meter relay race and the 100-meter run.

Wide World

TRACK AND FIELD

Event	Holder	Nation	Record	Where Made	Year
(Men)					
100 Meters	Jim Hines	U.S.A.	9.9s.	Mexico City	1968
200 Meters	Tommie Smith	U.S.A.	19.8s.	Mexico City	1968
400 Meters	Lee Evans	U.S.A.	43.8s.	Mexico City	1968
800 Meters	Ralph Doubell	Australia	1m.44.3s.	Mexico City	1968
1,500 Meters	Kipchoge Keino	Kenya	3m.34.9s.	Mexico City	1968
5,000 Meters	Vladimir Kuts	Russia	13m.39.6s.	Melbourne	1956
10,000 Meters	Billy Mills	U.S.A.	28m.24.4s.	Tokyo	1964
110 Meter Hurdles	Willie Davenport, Ervin Hall	U.S.A.	13.3s.	Mexico City	1968
400 Meter Hurdles	David Hemery	Great Britain	48.1s.	Mexico City	1968
3,000 Meter Steeplechase	Gaston Roelants	Belgium	8m.30.8s.	Tokyo	1964
Marathon	Bikila Abebe	Ethiopia	2h.12m.11.2s.	Tokyo	1964
20,000 Meter Walk	Ken Matthews	Great Britain	1h.29m.34.0s.	Tokyo	1964
50,000 Meter Walk	Abdon Pamich	Italy	4h.11m.12.4s.	Tokyo	1964
High Jump	Dick Fosbury	U.S.A.	7 ft. 4¼ in.	Mexico City	1968
Long Jump	Bob Beamon	U.S.A.	29 ft. 2¼ in.	Mexico City	1968
Triple Jump	Victor Saneyev	Russia	57 ft. ¾ in.	Mexico City	1968
Pole Vault	Bob Seagren, Claus Schiprowski, Wolfgang Nordwig	U.S.A. West Germany East Germany	17 ft. 8½ in.	Mexico City	1968
Discus Throw	Al Oerter	U.S.A.	212 ft. 6½ in.	Mexico City	1968
Javelin	Yanis Lusis	Russia	295 ft. 7¼ in.	Mexico City	1968
Shot-Put	Randy Matson	U.S.A.	67 ft. 10¼ in.	Mexico City	1968
Hammer	Gyula Szivotski	Hungary	240 ft. 8 in.	Mexico City	1968
Decathlon	Bill Toomey	U.S.A.	8,193 points	Mexico City	1968
400 Meter Relay	Green, Pender, Smith, Hines	U.S.A.	38.2s.	Mexico City	1968
1,600 Meter Relay	Mathews, Freeman, James, Evans	U.S.A.	2m.56.1s.	Mexico City	1968
(Women)					
100 Meters	Wyomia Tyus	U.S.A.	11.0s.	Mexico City	1968
200 Meters	Irine Kirszenstein	Poland	22.5s.	Mexico City	1968
400 Meters	Colette Besson, Betty Cuthbert	France Australia	52.0s.	Mexico City Tokyo	1968 1964
800 Meters	Madeline Manning	U.S.A.	2m.0.9s.	Mexico City	1968
80 Meter Hurdles	Maureen Caird	Australia	10.3s.	Mexico City	1968
High Jump	Iolanda Balas	Romania	6 ft. 2¾ in.	Tokyo	1964
Javelin	Mihaela Penes	Romania	198 ft. 7½ in.	Tokyo	1964
Long Jump	Viorica Viscopoleanu	Romania	22 ft. 4½ in.	Mexico City	1968
Shot-Put	Margarita Gummel	East Germany	64 ft. 4 in.	Mexico City	1968
400 Meter Relay	Ferrell, Bailes, Netter, Tyus	U.S.A.	42.8s.	Mexico City	1968

Olympics. About 708 B.C., the Greeks added jumping, discus throwing, javelin throwing, and wrestling to the foot races. Later, they added boxing and chariot racing. Winners were crowned with wreaths of sacred olive. Criers announced their names throughout the land. Artists dedicated statues to them. Poets wrote odes to the Olympic heroes.

In the early Olympics, sacrifices of grain, wine, and lambs were made to Zeus on the first day. Solemn oaths were taken that the contests would be fairly judged and the contestants would compete as good sportsmen. The foot races usually were held first, followed by wrestling, boxing, and other events. One of the most prized contests was the pentathlon, which consisted of five tests of strength and skill. A changed form of the pentathlon is still part of the Olympics (see TRACK AND FIELD [Field Events]).

With the decline of the Greek city-states in the 300's B.C., athletes from other lands entered the Olympic Games. Gradually, the games' true purpose of glorifying the individual became lost. About A.D. 60, the Roman Emperor Nero entered the games as a contestant. Nero was a poor athlete. By competing, he lowered the Olympic standards of sportsmanship and athletic skill. The games became so corrupt that the Christian Emperor Theodosius abolished them in A.D. 394.

Fifteen hundred years passed. Then, in 1896, Baron Pierre de Coubertin of France helped organize a renewal of the Olympics in Athens. His interest in the games had been stimulated by the excavation of the ruins of the ancient Olympic stadium in 1878. Eight nations took part in the 1896 games. The marathon foot race from Marathon to Athens attracted the most interest. It was held in honor of the messenger who brought to Athens the news of the victory at Marathon, then died.

Women first competed in the modern games in 1900. The Olympic flag was used for the first time in 1920. The Winter games were added in 1924. The Olympics were not held in 1916, 1940, and 1944 because of World Wars I and II.   FRED RUSSELL

Related Articles in WORLD BOOK include:

Decathlon	Isthmian Games
Discus Throw	Marathon
Flag (color picture,	Nemean Games
Flags of World Organizations)	Olympiad
Greece, Ancient (color	Pythian Games
map, Legend and History)	Track and Field

Outline

I. The Summer Olympics
II. The Winter Olympics
III. Teams
IV. Competition
V. History

Questions

What is the purpose of the Olympic Games?
What is the smallest number of countries that can be entered to schedule an event?
Why are some records not compared from one set of games to the next?
Do U.S. athletes have to meet a minimum standard to qualify for the Olympics?
How many teams may a country enter in an Olympic event?
When did women first enter the Olympic Games?
Why can no nation "win" the Olympics?
How do athletes from the United States and Canada finance their Olympic expenses?

Bob & Ira Spring
Hikers in the Olympic Mountains pause high above the deep Hoh Valley, to view rugged Mount Olympus, *background.*

OLYMPIC MOUNTAINS are part of the Pacific Coast Range. The Olympics rise in northern Washington, south of Juan de Fuca Strait. The mountains occupy an area of about 3,500 square miles, most of which is included in Olympic National Park. Mount Olympus (7,965 feet) is the highest peak. There are over 100 small glaciers in the mountains. Forests of Sitka spruce, Douglas fir, western red cedar, and hemlock cover the lower slopes. The southwestern slopes of the Olympic Mountains receive over 140 inches of rain a year, one of the highest averages in the United States. See also OLYMPIC NATIONAL PARK.   HOWARD J. CRITCHFIELD

OLYMPIC NATIONAL PARK lies in the Olympic Peninsula of Washington, not far from Seattle and Tacoma. The tumbled, jagged peaks of the Olympic Range cover a large portion of the park, which has an area of 896,599.10 acres. The National Park Service has set aside campgrounds and winter sports facilities for tourists. The park headquarters are at Port Angeles, Wash., a resort city on the Juan de Fuca Strait.

Of special interest are the rain forests consisting mainly of Douglas fir, Sitka spruce, western hemlock, and western red cedar. These rain forests, resulting from good soil and exceptionally heavy rainfall, are almost tropical in luxuriance, with an undergrowth of vine maple, big-leaf maple, ferns, and other junglelike growth. Mosses drape the branches and tree trunks. The park is the home of the world's largest herd of Roosevelt elk, estimated at 5,000 animals. Other wildlife species include black bear, cougar, and black-tailed deer.

This wilderness of glacier-clad peaks, flower-strewn alpine meadows, turbulent streams and jewel-like lakes, and deep valleys supporting a rich forest growth, is often described as America's "last frontier." Highways penetrate only its outer fringes, but several hundred miles of trails afford the horseback rider and hiker an opportunity to visit the wilderness. Nearly 1,000 varieties of flowers grow in the park's meadows and on its mountain slopes. Some varieties, such as the *Piper bellflower,* grow nowhere else.

Part of this region was set aside as Mount Olympus National Monument by President Theodore Roosevelt in 1909. In 1938, President Franklin D. Roosevelt signed the act establishing Olympic National Park. The park was formally dedicated in 1946. The Queets Corridor and Olympic Ocean Strip were added to the park by presidential proclamation in 1953.   JAMES J. CULLINANE

OLYMPICS. See OLYMPIC GAMES.

OLYMPUS, *oh LIM pus,* is the highest mountain in Greece. It rises 9,550 feet at the eastern edge of the ridge which divides Thessaly from Macedonia. Its height and roughness made the early Greeks believe that it was the home of the gods. They believed that the 12 major gods had beautiful palaces on the many peaks of the broad summit of the mountain. The palace of Zeus was thought to be on the highest peak of all. Zeus supposedly sat there to hurl thunderbolts on all parts of the earth.

Later the Greek people came to believe that Mount Olympus was not a fit home for the gods. It was usually covered with snow and hidden behind fog and clouds. Their voyages were also showing them that Olympus was not the exact center of the world as they had thought it was. They were beginning to be able to climb the mountain, and it was not good to have the gods living too close to their worshipers. For these reasons they began to believe in an imaginary Mount Olympus that was far away in the sky.

Greek poets did much to help this new idea. Homer holds to the first idea in the *Iliad,* but in the *Odyssey* he places the gods on a far-off heavenly mountain. No one knew exactly where the new Olympus was. The gods were safe from human visitors.   CHARLOTTE E. GOODFELLOW

See also MOUNTAIN (picture chart).

OMAGUA INDIANS, *oh MAH gwah,* were a South American tribe that held power at the time of the Spanish Conquest. The Omagua lived along the western part of the Amazon River, near the borders of present-day Peru and Brazil. Few of these Indians remain.

OMAHA, *O muh haw,* Nebr. (pop. 347,328; met. area 540,142; alt. 1,040 ft.), is the largest city in Nebraska. It is also the leading cattle market and meat-packing center in the United States. The city ranks as one of the nation's leading grain markets. Its location near the center of the United States makes it a major transportation terminal. The city has a modern medical center. Offutt Air Force Base, headquarters of the Strategic Air Command, is about 5 miles from Omaha (see OFFUTT AIR FORCE BASE).

Location, Size, and Description. The city lies on the west bank of the Missouri River, across from Council Bluffs, Iowa. Omaha is about 55 miles northeast of Lincoln, Nebr., and about 500 miles southwest of Chicago. The city covers over 50 square miles. For location, see NEBRASKA (political map). For the monthly weather in Omaha, see NEBRASKA (Climate).

Cultural Life and Religion. The University of Nebraska has a campus and also its College of Medicine in Omaha. The city is the home of Creighton University, the College of St. Mary, and the Nebraska School for the Deaf. Omaha has over 160 public schools. Father Flanagan's Boys Town, the famous school for homeless boys, is west of Omaha (see BOYS TOWN).

Omaha has a symphony orchestra and a community theater. The Joslyn Art Museum, one of two museums in Omaha, is one of the leading art centers in the country. The city has a public library with several branches. The medical center has 2 schools of medicine, 6 schools of nursing, and 15 hospitals.

Omaha is the see city of the Archdiocese of Omaha of the Roman Catholic Church and of the Episcopal Diocese of Omaha. It is also area headquarters of the United Methodist and Presbyterian churches, and state headquarters of the Baptist Church.

Recreation. Omaha has about 70 parks, covering more than 3,500 acres. Fontenelle Forest, the largest unbroken tract of forest land in the state, is near the city. Almost every species of bird known in the United States can be found in the forest's bird refuge.

The Knights of Ak-Sar-Ben, one of the nation's largest civic organizations, began in Omaha in 1895. The organization, whose name is *Nebraska* spelled backwards, conducts a program of agricultural, charitable, and educational promotion. It has over 28,000 members. It sponsors the world's largest 4-H baby-beef show and the World Championship Rodeo annually.

A $6½-million city auditorium, opened in 1955, provides accommodations for many entertainment, musical, and sports events.

Industry and Trade. Food processing accounts for 65 per cent of the city's manufacturing. The city has about 20 packing plants which slaughter over 4½ million head of livestock annually. Other industries produce beverages, cereals, coffee, flour, livestock and poultry feeds, and corn, dairy, poultry, and many other food products. The city is one of the country's leading producers of frozen foods. Its 22 terminal elevators make it one of the world's chief grain markets. Omaha has one of the largest lead refineries in the world. Metal fabrication is another major industry.

Omaha is also a producer of telephone and electrical equipment. Other products include cardboard boxes, chemicals, plastics, and textiles. The city is the wholesale center of the west-central states. About 40 insurance companies have their home offices in Omaha.

Omaha stretches along the west bank of the Missouri River on the eastern border of Nebraska. The city is the leading cattle market and meat-packing center in the United States. Omaha lies in the heart of the Corn Belt, and is a leading grain market.
Omaha Chamber of Commerce

Transportation. Nine major railroads serve Omaha, making it the fourth largest railroad center in the country. Five national highways pass through Omaha, and five airlines provide air transportation. The city is a trucking center with over 200 motor carriers. Omaha is known as the *Gate City of the West.*

Government and History. Omaha adopted a commission form of government in 1912. Several years later, South Omaha, Benson, and Florence became part of the city. The mayor-council form of government was adopted in 1956. Omaha is the seat of Douglas County.

Meriwether Lewis and William Clark reached the Omaha area in 1804 while on their famous expedition to the West. The first trading post was built there around 1825. In 1846, a group of Mormons on their way to Utah established winter quarters at Florence, now a northern residential section.

In the 1850's, the Council Bluffs and Nebraska Ferry Company planned a town on the Nebraska side of the Missouri River. The Omaha Indians ceded the area to the United States government in 1854, and settlement began. The town was named after the Omaha Indians. Omaha became the capital of the Territory of Nebraska in 1855. The city was chartered in 1857, and lots were given free to settlers.

After the discovery of gold in Colorado in 1858, Omaha became the outfitting point for miners on their way west. When Nebraska became a state in 1867, the capital was transferred from Omaha to Lincoln.

The Union Pacific, first transcontinental railroad, broke ground in Omaha in 1863 to begin building the railroad west from the city. The Trans-Mississippi and International Exposition was held in Omaha in 1898 and 1899.   JAMES C. OLSON

See also NEBRASKA (color picture: Stockyards).

OMAN, *oh MAN,* is a small country on the southeastern tip of the Arabian Peninsula. It is about as big as Kansas, but it has only about one-fourth as many people as that state.

Oman is one of the hottest countries in the world. Temperatures there sometimes reach 130° F. Only a few places get more than 6 inches of rain a year. Much of the inland part of the country is desolate land where nothing grows. The border with Saudi Arabia, in the region of the *Rub' Al Khali* (Empty Quarter) desert, never has been officially agreed upon.

The country has little industry, no railroads, few roads, and only one important airport. Muscat is the capital and leading port (see MUSCAT).

Government. A *sultan* (ruler) governs the country with the aid of a five-man council he appoints. But some people living in the mountains and other inland areas

--- **FACTS IN BRIEF** ---

Capital: Muscat.

Official Language: Arabic.

Form of Government: Sultanate.

Area: 82,030 square miles. *Greatest Distances*—(north-south) 500 miles; (east-west) 400 miles. *Coastline*—about 1,200 miles.

Population: No census. *Estimated 1972 Population*—565,000; density, 7 persons to the square mile.

Chief Products: Coconuts, dates, hides, limes.

Flag: Solid red flag stands for the Moslem religion. See FLAG (color picture: Flags of Asia and the Pacific).

OMAN

support the *imam,* their Islamic religious leader, rather than the sultan. *Walis* (governors) are in charge of local government units.

People. Most of the people are Arabs who belong to the Ibadite sect of Islam. Some are members of the Sunni Moslem sect. Many Negroes, Indians, and *Baluchis* (people whose ancestors came from Baluchistan, Pakistan) live in the coastal towns. Members of the primitive Shuḥūḥ tribe occupy the Musandam Peninsula at the northern tip of the country. They live in caves and exist mainly on fish from the Gulf of Oman.

Most of the people are poor and cannot read or write. They farm or work on the large date and coconut plantations. A few are fishermen, or work for cattle and camel breeders. The people live in tents, or in houses that have mud and stone walls and flat roofs. The men wear flowing white robes and headdresses to shield them from the sun and sand. Many of them carry knives or guns. Most of the women wear long, black dresses. They also wear masks that cover most of the face to keep them from being seen by strange men.

Land. The northernmost part of the country, the barren, rocky Musandam Peninsula, is separated from the rest of the country by the Trucial States. Southeast of there, a low coastal plain stretches for about 1,000 miles along the Gulf of Oman and Arabian Sea. It rises to a plateau at 1,000 feet above sea level. Most farming is done in the fertile Al Bāṭinah area which stretches about 200 miles along the Gulf of Oman.

The mountain range of Al Ḥajar stands south of Al Bāṭinah. Mount Shām (10,400 ft.), part of Al Ḥajar, is the country's highest point. The central Aẓ Ẓāhirah plateau is dry and mostly uncultivated. The fertile Dhofar region lies in the southwest corner of the country.

Economy. Oases along the northern coast produce dates, limes, and pomegranates. Coconuts grow on the southern coast. Oman camels are bred throughout the country. The most important exports are dates and hides. Oil was discovered in the country in 1963, but production did not start until 1967.

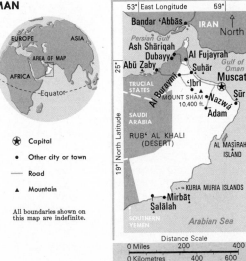

OMAN

All boundaries shown on this map are indefinite.

WORLD BOOK map

573

History. Portuguese forces captured what is now Oman in the early 1500's. But local Arabs expelled them in the mid-1600's and later took over other Portuguese possessions in East Africa. The present sultan's family came to power in 1743. In 1798, the British signed an agreement with the sultan and have maintained close relations ever since. In the 1800's, heirs to the sultanate formed Oman as it is known today.

In 1913, a newly elected imam acquired limited governing powers. The present imam headed resistance against Sultan Said bin Taimur in 1955 and 1957. When the sultan's forces defeated those of the imam in 1959, the imam fled into exile. In 1970, the sultan was overthrown by his son, Qabus bin Said. Qabus promised widespread reforms to modernize Oman.   GEORGE RENTZ

OMAR KHAYYÁM, *O mahr ky YAHM* (1050?-1123?), was a Persian poet, astronomer, and mathematician. His one long poem, *The Rubáiyát*, has brought him lasting fame. *The Rubáiyát* (meaning a collection of quatrains, or four-line rhymes) first attracted attention in 1859 when Edward FitzGerald translated about 100 of the quatrains credited to Omar Khayyám. Omar wrote with gentle melancholy about nature, regret for the fleeting sweetness of life, and the pleasure of love.

Omar Khayyám was born and educated in Nishapur (now Neyshābur, Iran). As royal astronomer, he changed the Persian calendar. He devised one that may have been more accurate than the Gregorian calendar. Omar Khayyám also wrote an Arabic book on algebra that included a classification of equations. Khayyám is an epithet probably derived from his father's trade. It means *the tentmaker.*   WALTER J. FISCHEL

See also FITZGERALD, EDWARD; RUBÁIYÁT.

OMAYYAD. See MOSLEMS (The Spread of Islam).

OMBUDSMAN, *AHM buhdz MUHN,* is a nonpartisan public official who investigates people's complaints about government officials or agencies. Most of his work involves complaints of unjust or harsh treatment of persons by police, prosecuting attorneys, or judges, and such matters as housing, taxation, voting, or welfare payments. After investigating a complaint, the ombudsman may dismiss it, with an explanation of his action. Or he may seek correction of the problem—by persuasion, by publicity, or, occasionally, by recommending prosecution.

The ombudsman idea originated in Sweden in 1809. Since World War II, it has spread, in various forms, to Japan and to several European, Commonwealth, and newly independent countries. Hawaii has a comprehensive ombudsman plan, and other states and some cities of the United States have modified plans. The idea also has gained popularity in large organizations, including corporations and universities. Its growing popularity coincides with the increasing complexities of administration and with people's need for impartial and informal handling of complaints.   HOLBERT N. CARROLL

OMDURMAN, *AHM dur MAN* (pop. 185,380; alt. 1,250 ft.), is the largest city in the Sudan. It lies on the west side of the Nile, just across the river from Khartoum. Omdurman was built in the 1880's as a model African city to replace Khartoum, which was destroyed during a war with Egypt. See SUDAN (map).

OMEGA. See ALPHA AND OMEGA.

OMEN, *O muhn,* is a sign or happening which is supposed to tell of coming events. Men used to believe that the spirits of the unseen world were always about them and controlled their lives. They thought if a person could read the signs correctly, he could learn something of the future.   WILSON D. WALLIS

See also SUPERSTITION (Foretelling the Future).

OMER. See LAG BA'OMER.

OMNIBUS BILL is a term sometimes used for a bill that includes several unrelated measures when it is put before a legislative assembly. It is used to pass several bills at once. The bill is named for an *omnibus* (bus), a vehicle that carries a number of people.

The term was first used in 1850. In that year there were a number of questions in dispute between the North and South in the Congress of the United States. Various bills had been offered dealing with slavery and the treatment of fugitive slaves. The Compromise of 1850 was proposed in an attempt to settle all these questions at once. The Compromise was denounced and jeered at as an omnibus bill.

Omnibus bills are considered bad practice. When a number of unrelated items are crowded into one bill, it is hard to give each the study it deserves. The constitutions of most states and provinces provide that a single bill shall relate to one topic only.   THOMAS A. COWAN

See also COMPROMISE OF 1850.

OMNIRANGE. See RADIO BEACON.

OMNIVORE, *AHM nih vohr,* is an animal that eats both animals and plants. The bear, the brown rat, and the opossum are examples of omnivores. See also CARNIVORE; HERBIVORE.

OMSK, *ahmsk* or *awmsk* (pop. 774,000; alt. 285 ft.), is a city in Russia. It is the gateway between European and Asiatic Russia, and lies along the railroad line that crosses Siberia. Omsk was once an outpost on the trade route to Siberia. See RUSSIA (political map).

ON-THE-JOB TRAINING. See VOCATIONS (Fields of Work).

ON THE SUBLIME. See LONGINUS.

ONA INDIANS, *OH nah,* once lived on the island of Tierra del Fuego at the southernmost tip of South America. Their way of life was one of the simplest in all America. The two main divisions of Ona were the *Selknam* and *Haush.*

The Ona hunted the guanaco, a small wild relative of the llama. They used mainly the bow and arrow for hunting and fighting. Despite severe winters, the Ona wore little clothing. They had large capes and moccasins of guanaco skins, and sometimes used leggings. But Ona men often went without clothes, even in the snow. The people made simple windbreak shelters of guanaco hides.

Every few years, several bands of Ona would meet to initiate youths into manhood. This festival was the Ona's main religious ceremony and social celebration.

The Ona numbered about 2,000 around 1875. Then sheep ranchers and gold seekers invaded the island. They killed many Ona outright, and the new diseases they brought killed others. The tribe had disappeared entirely by 1930.   CHARLES WAGLEY

See also INDIAN, AMERICAN (illustration: Ways of Life).

ONAGER, *AHN uh jer,* is the name of a fast-running animal which is a relative of the donkey. It is the *wild*

ass mentioned in the Bible, where a good description of it may be found (Job 39: 5-8). The onager travels in herds on the hot, dry plains of west-central Asia. Its color varies from cinnamon-brown in summer to yellow-brown in winter. A yellow patch covers each thigh and a broad black stripe runs along its back. The onager also has a mane, and a tuft of hair at the end of its tail. It stands about 4 feet high at the shoulders.

Scientific Classification. The onager is a member of the horse family, *Equidae*. It is genus *Equus*, species *E. onager*.

ONASSIS, ARISTOTLE SOCRATES (1906-   ), a Greek shipowner and business executive, is one of the world's wealthiest men. In 1968, he married Jacqueline Kennedy, the widow of President John F. Kennedy of the United States.

Onassis was born in Smyrna (now Izmir), Turkey, the son of a well-to-do tobacco importer. He emigrated to Argentina in 1923 after his father lost his fortune. In Buenos Aires, he became a telephone switchboard operator and later a tobacco importer. He entered the shipping business during the Great Depression of the 1930's and bought several freighters at an extremely low price. Onassis was a

Pix, Inc.
Aristotle Onassis

shrewd, daring investor and ignored the advice of many shipping experts after World War II, when he built several giant oil tankers. This venture was highly successful. In the mid-1950's, Onassis bought Olympic Airways, the only Greek domestic airline. The airline also flies to other countries.

Onassis is a citizen of both Greece and Argentina. He is a familiar figure in international high society and has entertained world leaders and celebrities on his yacht *Christina*.   LEONARD S. SILK

OÑATE, *oh NYAH tay,* **JUAN DE** (1549?-1628?), was a Spanish frontiersman and explorer. He is remembered mainly for colonizing the territory now called New Mexico, in 1598. His explorations extended from the Colorado River to the plains of Kansas. He served for a time as governor of New Mexico, but later lost favor with the Spanish government, and resigned in 1607. He was brought to trial and found guilty of having disobeyed his king. It was largely because of the work of Oñate that the city of Santa Fe was founded in 1610.

Oñate was born in Guadalajara, Mexico, the son of a Spanish settler. He married a granddaughter of Hernando Cortes.   RICHARD A. BARTLETT

ONE-CELLED ORGANISM. See PROTISTA; PROTOZOAN.

ONE-CROP FARM. See AGRICULTURE (Kinds).

ONE-STEP. See DANCING (The 1900's).

O'NEALE, MARGARET (1796-1879), caused President Andrew Jackson to reorganize his Cabinet after one of the greatest disputes in the history of Washington society. "Peggy," the daughter of a Washington innkeeper, was married to John B. Timberlake, a navy purser. She lived with her family while he was at sea. Senator John H. Eaton of Tennessee lived at the

O'Neale tavern in 1818, and became fond of Peggy. Andrew Jackson met Peggy at the tavern in 1823. Peggy's husband died at sea in 1828, and she was married to Senator Eaton on Jan. 1, 1829.

Eaton became secretary of war in 1829. Washington society refused to receive Peggy, because of her father's occupation and because of gossip about her

Brown Bros.
Margaret O'Neale

conduct with Eaton. President Jackson stood by her, despite his family's protests. Several Cabinet members resigned, and Eaton resigned in 1831. He became governor of Florida in 1834, and minister to Spain in 1836. Peggy O'Neale was born in Washington, D.C.   HELEN E. MARSHALL

ONEGA, LAKE. See LAKE ONEGA.

ONEIDA, LAKE. See LAKE ONEIDA.

ONEIDA COMMUNITY, *oh NYE duh,* a cooperative settlement in Oneida, N.Y., was founded by John Humphrey Noyes in 1848. It was probably the most extreme form of communistic experiment ever established in the United States. Its members are often called "Bible communists."

The Oneida Community began in Putney, Vt. Its members believed that perfection in life is possible through personal communion with God, and that people must share all personal possessions and live as one family. The members also believed in *complex marriage,* and everyone in the community was considered married to everyone else. Orthodox church leaders strongly objected to this practice, and forced the community to leave Putney.

In Oneida, John Humphrey Noyes set up a system of "mutual criticism." Each individual was judged by the other members of the group for the sake of personal improvement. All kinds of work were considered dignified. Women had equal rights with men, and the community raised the children.

The community flourished financially. One of the members invented a steel game trap. Factories in the community manufactured these traps, and the people became wealthy by selling them. The community also manufactured several kinds of steel chains. It used much of the money it earned from these undertakings to build factories for making silk thread and for canning.

In 1879, because of outside opposition to complex marriage, Noyes advised the community to give it up. In 1881, the Oneida Community was reorganized and incorporated as a joint-stock company that still exists. Only a few voluntary cooperative features, suggesting the original plan of the Oneida Community, now remain.   DONALD R. McCOY

ONEIDA INDIANS. See IROQUOIS INDIANS.

O'NEILL, EUGENE GLADSTONE (1888-1953), is considered America's greatest playwright. He was the first American dramatist to write tragedy consistently. Before O'Neill, most successful American plays tended to be either melodramas or sentimental comedies.

O'NEILL, EUGENE GLADSTONE

O'Neill won the Nobel prize for literature in 1936. Four of his plays won Pulitzer prizes—*Beyond the Horizon* in 1920; *Anna Christie* in 1922; *Strange Interlude* in 1928; and *Long Day's Journey into Night* in 1957, after his death.

His Life. O'Neill was born on Oct. 16, 1888, in New York City. He was the son of James O'Neill, a well-known actor. He attended Princeton University briefly in 1906, and then left school and took a variety of jobs. As a seaman, he sailed to South Africa and South America in 1910 and 1911. Many of O'Neill's plays reflect his experiences at sea. Others show his sympathy for the failures and outcasts of society he met during this time.

O'Neill was married three times, in 1909, 1918, and 1928. The first two marriages ended in divorce. O'Neill became ill with tuberculosis and entered a sanatorium in 1912. While recovering, he decided to become a playwright. In 1916, he became associated with the theater group called the Provincetown Players. The group staged his first play, *Bound East for Cardiff* (1913-1914), in 1916.

O'Neill had written most of his plays by the mid-1930's. Later in life he suffered from Parkinson's disease, a form of palsy. The disease hampered his ability to write. O'Neill died on Nov. 27, 1953.

His Plays. O'Neill's 45 plays cover a wide range of dramatic styles and subjects. They vary in length from one act, to the nine-act *Strange Interlude* (written in

Eugene O'Neill was the first important writer of tragedy in American drama. His expressionistic play *The Hairy Ape* describes how society rejects Yank, a brutal and stupid laborer. In a scene from the 1922 production, *below,* policemen beat the uncomprehending Yank.

Random House
New York Public Library, The Vandamm Collection

1926-1927) and the 11-act *Mourning Becomes Electra* (1929-1931). O'Neill wrote brutally realistic plays, including *Desire Under the Elms* (1924); expressionistic plays, including *The Hairy Ape* (1921); and satire, including *Marco Millions* (1923-1925).

O'Neill stated that his task as a playwright was to "dig at the roots of the sickness of today." He believed that science had robbed man of his faith in traditional beliefs and had not given man a new faith. Man, therefore, was left without any faith to satisfy his desire for meaning in life and to comfort him in his fear of death.

O'Neill's pessimistic view of life was influenced by the writings of German philosophers Friedrich Nietzsche and Arthur Schopenhauer and Swedish playwright August Strindberg. Modern psychology also influenced O'Neill. In *The Great God Brown* (1925), his characters wear masks to express their personalities. The characters in *Strange Interlude* speak their thoughts aloud, exposing their inner feelings. In *Days Without End* (1932-1933), two actors portray different parts of a character's personality. O'Neill used symbols in many plays. The drums in *The Emperor Jones* (1920) symbolize the primitive fears of the leading character.

Most of O'Neill's characters seek some meaning for their lives. In *Beyond the Horizon* (1918), *Anna Christie* (1920), and *Strange Interlude*, the characters turn to love to find meaning. In *Dynamo* (1928) and *Days Without End*, they turn to religion. All suffer disappointment. In *The Iceman Cometh* (1939), O'Neill's most pessimistic play, the characters in a waterfront saloon have ruined their lives. But they find meaning in their illusions about themselves. When these illusions are taken from them, they come close to despair. O'Neill says that all illusions are "pipe dreams." He seems to assert that man's only "hopeless hope" is in drink and death. But O'Neill also seems to say there is a certain admirable heroism in people who persist in living a life without hope.   HUBERT C. HEFFNER

See also AMERICAN LITERATURE (The Rise of American Drama); NATURALISM (Naturalism in Drama).

O'NEILL, SHANE. See IRELAND (The Conquest of Ireland).

ONION, *UN yun,* is a plant that belongs to the amaryllis family. It is well-known for its strong taste and odor. The odor is due to a mildly stimulating oil. This oil readily forms a vapor, which escapes into the air when onions are peeled or cut. It affects nerves in the nose connected with the eyes, and makes tears flow.

Onions first grew in Mongolia. They were raised in America as early as 1750. The leading onion-growing states are California, Colorado, Michigan, New York, Texas, and Oregon. But onions are grown in many other states and Canadian provinces. Mexico, Italy, and Spain are also noted for the size and quality of their onions.

The onion plant is a *biennial* (a plant that lives for two years). The upper part of the plant is a set of leaves growing inside each other. The lower parts of the leaves become very thick. The flowers are small and white, and grow in rounded clusters. The bulbs are enclosed in a thin papery covering made up of dried outer leaves. The onion plant has a few shallow roots.

The different kinds of onions have many different sizes, colors, and shapes. Men who trade in onions classify them as *American* (strong onions) and *foreign*

KINDS OF ONIONS

Danvers

Southport Yellow Globe

Prizetaker

Green

Bermuda

Red Globe

J. Horace McFarland

Brown Spanish

(mild onions). The strong type includes the Yellow Globe types and the flatter Ebenezer type. The home gardener can grow these from sets. These onions keep well, and they are usually eaten cooked. The foreign type are mostly Spanish and Bermuda onions. These large, mild onions are generally eaten uncooked.

Most onions that are sold in markets are raised from seeds. But home garden onions are usually raised from *sets* (very small onions that have not completed their growth). Both sets and seeds are used to produce *scallions*, a popular name for young onions that are harvested before they have developed a bulb. Onions that have lost their ability to make seeds are raised from bulbs, and are known as *multiplier onions*. Some types produce tiny bulbs, called *aerial sets*, on their seed stalks. Seeds may be sown in the field or in greenhouses. Onions need a very moist soil for good growth.

The onion thrips is one of the worst insects that attacks onions. It can be checked by spraying the young seedlings with malathion. Onion smut and maggots may be controlled by treating the seeds with arasan and aldrin.

The onion is not particularly high in vitamins or in energy value. Cooking onions takes away some food value, but it makes them more digestible and tends to remove their odor. Onions are also pickled.

Scientific Classification. Onions belong to the amaryllis family, *Amaryllidaceae*. They are genus *Allium*, species *A. cepa*.
ARTHUR J. PRATT

See also BULB; GARLIC; RAMP; SHALLOT; CHIVE.

ONOMATOPOEIA, *AHN oh MAT oh PE yuh,* is the formation of words to imitate natural sounds. The *buzz* of a bee, the *hoot* of an owl, and the *fizz* of soda water are examples of words created from the natural sound. The term comes from two Greek words meaning *to make a name.*

ONONDAGA INDIANS. See IROQUOIS INDIANS.

ONSAGER, LARS. See NOBEL PRIZES (table [1968]).

LEADING ONION-GROWING STATES
Pounds of onions grown in 1967

California
679,600,000 lbs.
🌾🌾🌾🌾🌾🌾🌾🌾🌾🌾🌾🌾🌾🌾🌾🌾🌾🌾

Texas
498,000,000 lbs.
🌾🌾🌾🌾🌾🌾🌾🌾🌾🌾🌾🌾🌾

New York
406,000,000 lbs.
🌾🌾🌾🌾🌾🌾🌾🌾🌾🌾🌾

Michigan
231,000,000 lbs.
🌾🌾🌾🌾🌾🌾

Oregon
224,000,000 lbs.
🌾🌾🌾🌾🌾🌾

Colorado
147,500,000 lbs.
🌾🌾🌾🌾

New Mexico
145,700,000 lbs.
🌾🌾🌾🌾

Source: *Vegetables—Fresh Market, 1967 Annual Summary,* U.S. Department of Agriculture

577

ONTARIO

ONTARIO, *ahn TAIR ih oh,* has more people than any other Canadian province. About a third of Canada's people live in Ontario. Ontario's manufacturing industries, its chief source of income, produce as much as those of the nine other provinces combined. Ontario ranks first among the Canadian provinces in mining and in farm income. Toronto is the capital and chief industrial center of the province. Ottawa, the capital of Canada, lies on the Ottawa River in southeastern Ontario.

Ontario has a larger area than any other province except Quebec. It reaches down between New York and Michigan, and is Canada's southernmost province. In fact, Ontario extends a little farther south than the northern boundary of California. This province also extends so far north that some of the ground beneath the surface is *permafrost* (permanently frozen ground).

The busy factories, mills, and plants of Ontario have given it the nickname *Workshop of the Nation.* Almost all the province's industries are in the warm southern region, south of Lake Nipissing. About 90 per cent of Ontario's people live there, on less than 10 per cent of the land area. The richest manufacturing section, called the *Golden Horseshoe,* curves around the western shores of Lake Ontario.

Ontario's major industry is manufacturing automobiles. Most of the province's automobile plants are in the Golden Horseshoe. Almost all the automobiles made in Canada come from there. Hamilton, a city in the Golden Horseshoe, is Canada's greatest iron and steel center. Nearby is Toronto, the chief Canadian port on the Great Lakes. The region's varied products travel from Toronto to many parts of the world by way of the St. Lawrence Seaway. Port Colborne, also part of the Golden Horseshoe, has the largest nickel-processing plant in North America.

The mines of Ontario provide about a fourth of all the minerals produced in Canada. Deposits near Sud-

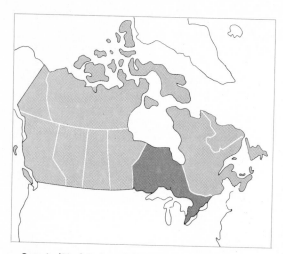

Ontario (Blue) Is Canada's Second Largest Province.

The contributors of this article are Norman L. Nicholson, Dean of the University College and Senior Professor of Geography at the University of Western Ontario; Robert F. Nielsen, Chief Editorial Writer of the Toronto Daily Star; *and John T. Saywell, Dean of the Faculty of Arts and Science and Professor of History at York University.*

Steel Mill in Hamilton

Algoma, watercolor by John Joy for the Field Enterprises Educational Corporation Collection

Wilderness near Lake Superior

bury yield more than half the western world's supply of nickel and much of its copper and platinum. The largest known uranium deposit in the world lies near Elliot Lake. No other province or state produces more gold than Ontario.

But Ontario is not only an industrial province. Its farmers provide about a third of Canada's farm products. Herds of beef and dairy cattle graze in rich pastures between Lake Huron and Lake Ontario. Tobacco flourishes along Lake Erie, and colorful orchards thrive in the famous Niagara fruit belt. Northern Ontario has thick forests that provide wood for the pulp and paper industry. Trappers catch fur-bearing animals there, and campers hunt and fish.

The province's name came from the Iroquois Indians, who lived in the region when French explorers first arrived. The word *Ontario* may mean *beautiful lake*. Or it may mean *rocks standing high* or *near the water*—referring to Niagara Falls. The thundering waters of these spectacular falls attract visitors from all parts of the world. The falls are the greatest natural source of hydroelectric power in North America.

Ontario, together with New Brunswick, Nova Scotia, and Quebec, was one of the original provinces of Canada. For the relationship of Ontario to the other provinces, see CANADA; CANADA, GOVERNMENT OF; CANADA, HISTORY OF.

─────── FACTS IN BRIEF ───────

Capital: Toronto.

Government: *Parliament*—members of the Senate, 24; members of the House of Commons, 85. *Provincial Legislature*—members of the Legislative Assembly, 117. *Counties*—43. *Districts*—11. *Voting Age*—21 years (provincial elections); 18 years (national elections).

Area: 412,582 sq. mi. (including 68,490 sq. mi. of inland water), 2nd in size among the provinces. *Greatest Distances*—(north-south) 1,075 mi.; (east-west) 1,050 mi. *Shoreline*—4,726 mi. along the Great Lakes. *Coastline*—680 mi. on Hudson and James bays.

Elevation: *Highest*—Tip Top Hill, 2,120 feet above sea level. *Lowest*—sea level at Hudson and James bays.

Population: *1966 Census*—6,960,870, first among the provinces; density, 17 persons to the square mile; distribution, 80 per cent urban, 20 per cent rural. *Estimated 1971 Population*—7,761,000.

Chief Products: *Agriculture*—cattle and calves, corn, hay, hogs, tobacco, wheat. *Fishing Industry*—herring, lake trout, perch, pickerel, pike, smelt, sturgeon, whitefish. *Manufacturing*—electrical machinery, food and food products, metal products, nonelectrical machinery, primary metals, transportation equipment. *Mining*—copper, gold, iron ore, nickel, platinum, sand and gravel, stone, uranium, zinc.

Provincial Motto: *Ut Incepit Fidelis Sic Permanet* (Loyal she began, loyal she remains).

Entered the Dominion: July 1, 1867; one of the original four provinces.

579

Lieutenant Governor of Ontario represents Queen Elizabeth in the province. He is appointed by the governor-general-in-council of Canada. The lieutenant governor's position, like that of the governor general, is largely an honorary one.

Prime Minister of Ontario is the actual head of the provincial government. The province, like the other provinces and Canada itself, has a *parliamentary* form of government. The prime minister is a member of the legislative assembly, where he is the leader of the majority party. The voters elect him as they do the other members of the assembly. He receives a salary of $16,000 a year, in addition to allowances he gets as a member of the assembly. For a list of all the prime ministers of Ontario, see the *History* section of this article.

The prime minister presides over the executive council, or cabinet. The council includes ministers chosen by the prime minister from his party's members in the legislative assembly. Each minister usually directs one or more government departments. The executive council, like the prime minister, resigns if it loses the support of a majority of the assembly.

Legislative Assembly is a one-house legislature that makes the provincial laws. It has 117 members who are elected from 117 electoral districts called *constituencies*. Their terms may last up to five years. However, the lieutenant governor, on the advice of the prime minister, may call for an election before the end of the five-year period. If he does so, all members of the assembly must run again for office.

Courts. The highest court in Ontario is the supreme court. It consists of the court of appeal and the high court of justice. The court of appeal is made up of a chief justice and nine other justices. The high court of justice, which hears major civil and criminal cases, has a chief justice and 22 other justices. The governor-general-in-council appoints all these justices, and they serve until the age of 75. He also appoints judges to county and district courts. These judges preside over

division courts as well. Provincial authorities appoint judges of magistrates' courts and juvenile courts.

Local Government. The heavily populated southern tenth of Ontario is divided into 43 counties. Nine of these counties are combined into four administrative units for purposes of government. Thus, there are 38 county governments. Each county government is headed by a council. This council consists of mayors of the cities, towns, and villages, and *reeves* of the townships. The northern nine-tenths of Ontario is made up of 11 *districts*. The provincial government administers these thinly populated areas.

Most of Ontario's cities, towns, and villages are governed by a mayor and a council, elected to terms of one or two years. Some of these municipalities have the council-manager form of government. The Municipality of Metropolitan Toronto, established in 1954, consists of the city of Toronto and five boroughs. It is governed by the metro council and metro executive chosen from the six municipal units. The council deals with such problems as highway construction, libraries, sewage disposal, traffic engineering, urban growth, water supply, and welfare.

Taxation. Taxes collected by the provincial government provide about two-thirds of its income. Most of this money comes from taxes on corporation income, gasoline, and retail sales. Ontario and Quebec are the only provinces that collect their own corporation income taxes. Other sources of Ontario's income include federal-provincial tax-sharing programs, license and permit fees, and the sale of liquor, which is under government control.

Politics. Ontario has three major political parties. They are, in order of strength, the Progressive Conservative, Liberal, and New Democratic parties. The Progressive Conservative party was formerly named the Conservative party, and today its members are usually called simply Conservatives. The New Democratic party is the youngest of Ontario's three major political

The Legislative Chamber in the main Parliament Building in Toronto has hand-carved woodwork and mahogany paneling. The legislative assembly meets in this chamber.

The Provincial Flag

Symbols of Ontario. On the coat of arms, the shield has the red and white cross of St. George, representing Ontario's ties with Great Britain. The three maple leaves are symbols of Canada. The bear above the shield stands for strength. The coat of arms was adopted in 1909. The provincial flag, adopted in 1965, has the shield of Ontario and the British Union flag.

The Provincial Coat of Arms

The Floral Emblem
White Trillium

parties. It developed partly from the old Co-operative Commonwealth Federation.

Ontario's first provincial government was a *coalition* (combination) of Liberals and Conservatives. The Liberals took full control of the government in 1871 and held it until 1905, when the Conservatives came to power. In 1919, during an economic depression, the United Farmers of Ontario took over the government. The Conservatives regained leadership in 1923 after the economy improved, but lost it to the Liberals in 1934. The Progressive Conservatives won control of the government in 1943, and have been in power ever since. An Ontario citizen must be at least 18 years of age to vote in federal elections, and at least 21 to vote in provincial elections.

Provincial Parliament Buildings are in Toronto, capital of Ontario since 1867. Earlier capitals were Newark (now Niagara-on-the-Lake, 1792-1797); York (later renamed Toronto, 1797- 1841); Kingston (capital of combined Upper and Lower Canada, 1841-1844); Montreal, Que. (1844-1849); Quebec City, Que., and Toronto, alternately (1849-1865); and Ottawa (1866-1867).

Ontario Dept. of Tourism and Information

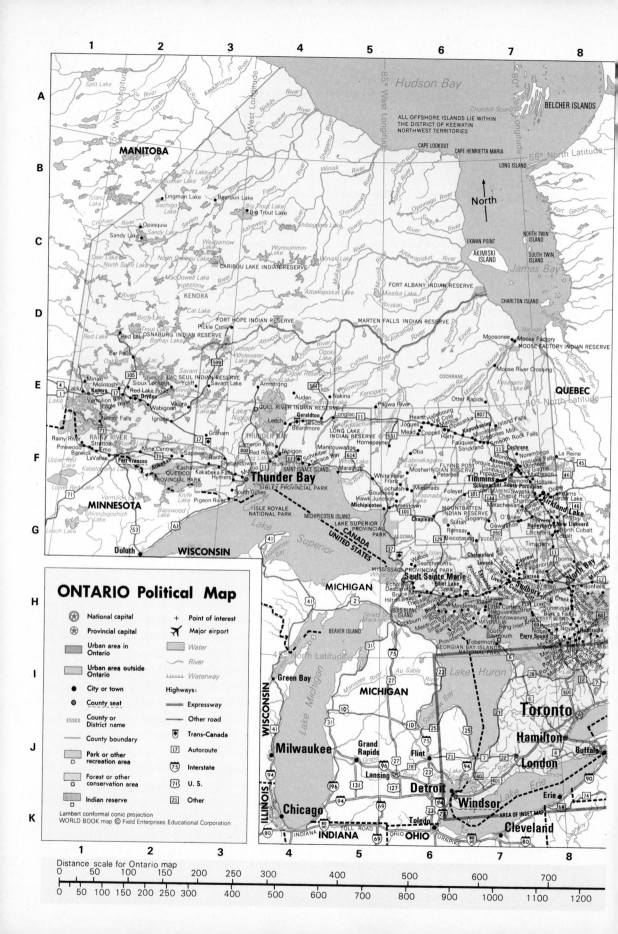

ONTARIO Political Map

Symbol	Meaning	Symbol	Meaning
National capital		+	Point of interest
Provincial capital		✈	Major airport
	Urban area in Ontario		Water
	Urban area outside Ontario		River
●	City or town		Waterway
◉	County seat		Highways:
ESSEX	County or District name		Expressway
	County boundary		Other road
	Park or other recreation area	✛	Trans-Canada
	Forest or other conservation area	17	Autoroute
	Indian reserve	75	Interstate
		71	U.S.
		21	Other

Lambert conformal conic projection
WORLD BOOK map © Field Enterprises Educational Corporation

Distance scale for Ontario map

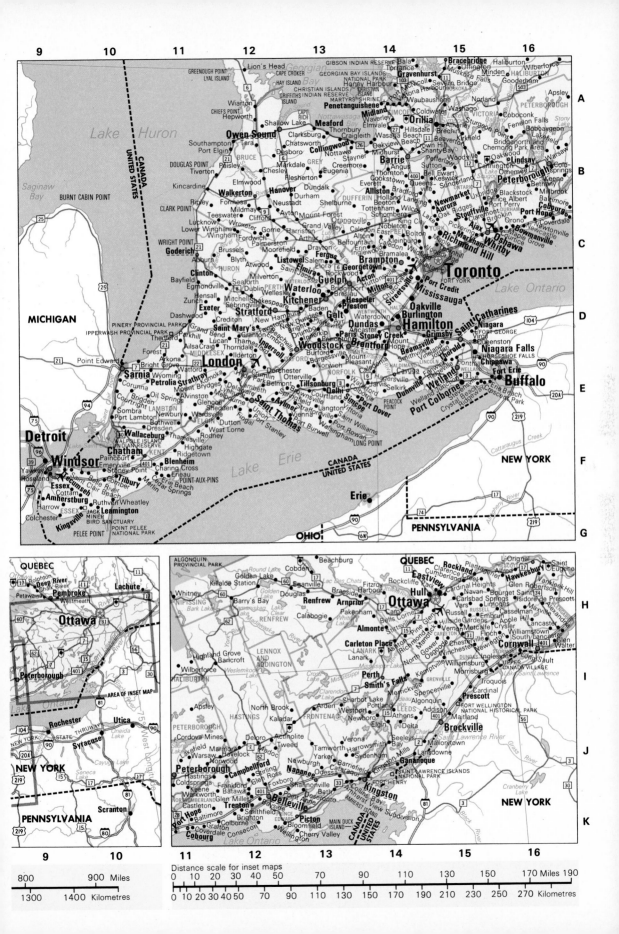

Population

7,761,000 .Estimate 1971
6,960,870 ...Census 1966
6,236,092 ......"...1961
4,597,542 ......"...1951
3,787,655 ......"...1941
3,431,683 ......"...1931
2,933,662 ......"...1921
2,527,292 ......"...1911
2,182,947 ......"...1901
2,114,321 ......"...1891
1,926,922 ......"...1881
1,620,851 ......"...1871

Metropolitan Areas

Hamilton 449,116
Kitchener 192,275
London 207,396
Ottawa 494,535
Sudbury 117,075
Toronto 2,158,496
Windsor 211,697

Counties

Brant .....90,945..E 14
Bruce .....43,085..B 12
Carleton ..407,463..I 15
Dufferin ...17,108..B 14
Dundas ....17,106..I 15
Durham ....44,549..C 16
Elgin ......61,912..F 11
Essex .....280,922..G 10
Frontenac ..97,138..J 13
Glengarry ..18,181..H 16
Grenville ...23,429..I 15
Grey ....62,592..B 13
Haldimand .30,020..E 14
Haliburton ..7,768..I 11
Halton ....140,800..D 14
Hastings ...94,127..J 12
Huron .....54,446..C 12
Kent ....96,406..F 11
Lambton ..108,236..E 11
Lanark ....41,212..I 14
Leeds ......49,129..J 14
Lennox and Addington 25,202..I 12
Lincoln ...146,099..E 15
Middlesex .249,403..E 11
Norfolk ....50,578..E 13
Northumberland .....45,074..K 11
Ontario ...170,818..B 15
Oxford .....76,018..E 13
Peel ......172,321..C 14
Perth ......60,424..D 12
Peterborough .81,959..J 11
Prescott ...27,155..H 16
Prince Edward ..21,307..K 12
Renfrew ...89,453..H 12
Russell ....21,107..H 15
Simcoe ...149,132..A 14
Stormont ...59,550..I 16
Victoria ....30,917..A 16
Waterloo .216,728..D 13
Welland ..178,818..E 15
Wellington .94,177..C 13
Wentworth 394,299..D 14
York ....2,018,019..C 15

Districts

Algoma ..113,561..G 6
Cochrane ..97,334..E 6
Kenora ....53,995..D 3
Manitoulin .10,544..H 7
Muskoka ...27,691..I 8
Nipissing ..73,533..H 11
Parry Sound 28,335..H 8
Rainy River 25,816..F 1
Sudbury ..174,102..G 7
Thunder Bay ....143,673..F 4
Timiskaming 47,154..F 7

Cities and Towns

Actinolite .....102..J 12
Acton ....4,416..C 14
Addison ....101..J 15
Ailsa Craig ....557..D 12
Ajax ....9,412..C 15
Alcona* ....733..I 8
Alexandria ..2,864..H 16
Alfred ......1,225..H 16
Algoma Mills ..80..H 6
Algonquin .....132..I 15
Alliston .....3,149..B 14
Almonte ....3,556..H 14
Alton ....450..C 14
Alvinston ......650..E 11
Amherst View Subdivision ...2,045..K 13
Amherstburg 4,641..G 9
Ancaster ....D 14
Angus ....2,265..B 14
Ansonville ..3,037..F 7
Apple Hill ....307..H 16
Apsley ....301..I 11
Arden ....233..I 13
Arkona ....409..E 11
Armstrong .....427..E 4
Arnprior .....5,693..H 14
Arthur ......1,242..C 13
Ashton ....109..I 14
Aspdin ....31..H 8
Astorville .....195..H 8
Athens ....1,002..J 14
Atherley ....341..A 15
Atikokan ....6,240..F 2
Atwood ....598..C 12
Auburn ....208..C 12
Auden ....62..E 4
Aurora .....10,425..C 15
Aylmer ......4,501..E 12
Ayr ....1,134..D 13
Ayton ....359..C 13
Azilda ....3,406..H 7
Baden ....1,041..D 13
Bala ....489..A 14
Balmertown* ...983..D 2
Balsam Creek .318..H 8
Baltimore ....223..K 11
Bancroft ....2,152..I 12
Barrie .....24,016.°B 14
Barrie Island .118..H 6
Barriefield ....323..J 14
Barry's Bay .1,388..H 12
Barwick ....126..F 1
Batawa ....692..K 12
Bath ....758..K 13
Bayfield ....464..D 11
Bayside ....1,497..K 12
Baysville ....186..I 8
Beachburg ......531..G 13
Beachville ......932..E 13
Beamsville ...3,886..D 15
Beardmore .....991..F 4
Bearskin Lake ....B 3
Beaverton ....1,242..B 15
Beeton ....998..B 14
Belfountain ....208..C 14
Bell Ewart ....327..B 15
Belle River ..2,280..F 10
Belleville ..32,785.°K 12
Bells Corners ....H 14
Belmont ....686..E 12
Bethany ....278..B 16
Big Trout Lake 54..C 3
Biscotasing ......86..G 7
Blackstock ......278..B 16
Blenheim ....3,356..F 11
Blezard Valley* ...1,090..H 7
Blind River .3,617..H 6
Bloomfield ......750..K 13
Blyth ....799..C 12
Bobcaygeon .1,251..B 16
Bolton ....2,344..C 14
Bonfield ....577..H 8
Bothwell ....820..F 11
Bourget ....744..H 16
Bowmanville 8,513..C 16
Bracebridge 3,045.°A 15
Bradford .....2,529..B 15
Braeside ....530..H 14
Bramalea ....8,846..C 14
Brampton ..36,264.°C 14
Brantford ..59,854.°D 14
Brechin ....248..B 15
Brent ....23..H 9
Breslau ....679..D 13
Bridgenorth and Chemong Park Area ......1,150..B 16
Bridgeport ..2,111..D 13
Brigden ....593..E 10
Bright ....313..D 13
Bright Grove ..773..E 11
Brighton .....2,766..K 12
Britt ....552..H 8
Brockville .19,266.°J 15
Brooklin .....1,679..C 15
Brownsville ....328..E 13
Bruce Mines ..502..H 6
Brussels ....820..C 12
Burford ....1,222..E 13
Burgessville ...256..E 13
Burk's Falls ..864..H 8
Burlington .65,941..D 14
Byng Inlet Area ....191..H 8
Cache Bay ....651..H 8
Calabogie ......360..H 13
Caledon ....260..C 14
Caledon East .673..C 14
Caledonia ...2,725..E 14
Callander ....1,148..H 8
Cameron Falls 235..F 4
Campbellford 3,445..J 12
Cannington ...1,049..B 15
Capreol ......3,092..G 7
Cardinal ......1,947..I 15
Cardinal Heights ...H 15
Carleton Place ....4,819..I 14
Carlsbad Springs .....234..H 15
Carol and Richard Park* ..721..H 7
Carp ....410..H 14
Casselman ...1,227..H 16
Castleton ......272..K 11
Cataraqui ....369..J 14
Cayuga ......1,031.°E 14
Cedar Springs 322..F 11
Chalk River .1,086..H 9
Champlain Park* ....780..H 8
Chapleau ....3,778..G 6
Chaput Hughes 912..G 8
Charing Cross 368..F 11
Charlton ....147..G 8
Chatham ..32,424.°F 11
Chatsworth ....395..B 13
Chelmsford .2,752..H 7
Cherry Valley 263..K 13
Chesley ....1,686..B 12
Chesterville .1,258..I 15
Chippawa ...3,877..E 15
Churchville ...254..C 14
Claremont ......590..C 15
Clarence Creek 470..H 15
Clarksburg ....400..B 13
Clifford ....515..C 12
Clinton ....3,280..C 12
Cobalt ....2,211..G 8
Cobden ....902..H 13
Coboconk ....490..A 16
Cobourg ...11,524.°K 11
Cochenour* ...755..D 2
Cochrane ...4,775.°F 7
Cockburn Island 6..H 6
Colborne ....385..E 13
Colborne ....1,450..K 12
Colchester ....600..G 9
Coldsprings ....K 11
Coldwater .....720..A 14
Collingwood .8,471..B 14
Collins Bay .1,054..K 13
Comber ....600..F 10
Concord* ....605..I 8
Coniston .....2,692..H 7
Connaught ....234..F 7
Consecon ....323..K 12
Cookstown ......717..B 14
Coppell ....127..F 6
Copper Cliff .3,505..H 7
Corbeil ....28..H 8
Cordova Mines 178..J 12
Cornwall ..45,766.°I 16
Corunna ......2,375..E 10
Cottam ....691..G 10
Courtice ....550..C 16
Courtland ....640..E 13
Courtright ....634..E 10
Coverdale ....671..K 11
Craigleith ....171..B 13
Crediton ....440..D 12
Creemore ....878..B 14
Creighton ....1,463..H 7
Crescent Park ......1,121..E 15
Crown Hill ...167..B 14
Crumlin ....293..E 12
Crysler ....489..H 16
Crystal Beach ....1,857..E 15
Cumberland ...537..H 15
Dashwood ......434..D 11
Deep River ...5,573..H 9
Delaware ....455..E 12
Delhi ....3,503..E 13
Deloro ....185..J 12
Delta ....369..J 14
Desbarats ......177..H 6
Desboro ....144..B 12
Deseronto ...1,836..K 13
Dobie ....242..F 8
Doon* ....547..J 8
Dorchester ...1,537..E 12
Dorset ....193..H 8
Douglas ....352..H 13
Drayton ....677..C 13
Dresden .....2,372..F 11
Drumbo ....389..D 13
Dryden ......6,732..E 2
Dublin ....326..D 12
Dundalk ....892..B 13
Dundas .....15,501..D 14
Dunnville ....5,402..E 15
Durham ......2,410..B 13
Dutton ....848..E 12
Eagle Lake ....138..H 8
Eagle River ...279..E 2
Ear Falls ......611..E 2
Earlton ....730..G 8
Eastview ...24,269..H 15
Echo Bay ....507..H 6
Eganville ....1,478..H 13
Egmondville ...420..D 12
Elgin ....286..J 14
Elk Lake ....629..G 8
Elliot Lake ..6,640..H 6
Elmira ....4,047..C 13
Elmvale .....1,031..A 14
Elmwood ....308..B 12
Elora ....1,644..C 13
Embro ....597..D 13
Embrun ......1,152..H 15
Emeryville ..1,571..F 10
Emo ....694..F 1
Englehart ...1,790..G 8
Erie Beach ....205..F 11
Erie Beach ....529..E 16
Erieau ....504..F 11
Erin ....1,195..C 14
Espanola .....5,567..H 7
Essex ....3,742..F 10
Eugenia ....82..B 13
Everett ....522..B 14
Exeter ....3,226..D 12
Falconbridge 1,097..H 7
Fauquier ......511..F 7
Fenelon Falls ......1,404..A 16
Fenwick ....722..E 15
Fergus ......4,376..C 13
Ferris West .4,338..H 8
Field ....711..H 8
Finch ....384..H 16
Fingal ....349..E 12
Fitzroy Harbour ....206..H 14
Flesherton .....514..B 13
Foleyet ....429..F 6
Fonthill .....2,790..E 15
Fordwich ....296..C 12
Forest ....2,151..E 11
Forest Hill* 23,135..J 8
Formosa ....394..B 12
Fort Erie ...9,793..E 16
Fort Frances 9,524.°F 2
Foxboro ....489..K 12
Frankford ...1,823..K 12
Franz ....142..F 5
Galt ....33,491..D 13
Gananoque ..5,237..J 14
Garson ....3,901..H 7
Gateway* ....5,590..H 8
Georgetown 11,832..C 14
Geraldton ...3,658..E 4
Glen Cairn* ..544..H 10
Glen Miller ...754..K 12
Glen Robertson 344..H 16
Glen Ross ......56..J 12
Glen Walter ..667..I 16
Glen Williams* 1,018..I 8
Glencoe ......1,185..E 11
Goderich ....6,710.°C 11
Gogama ....593..G 7
Golden Lake ..287..H 12
Gooderham ....212..A 16
Gore Bay ......693.°H 7
Gorrie ....356..C 12
Goudreau ....36..G 6
Gowganda ......283..G 7
Grafton ....349..K 11
Graham ....46..F 3
Grand Bend ..791..D 11
Grand Valley .758..C 13
Granton ....276..D 12
Gravenhurst 3,257..A 15
Gregoires Mill 169..F 7
Grimsby ......6,634..D 15
Grimsby Beach* ...3,115..J 8
Guelph .....51,377.°D 13
Guilletville* 1,102..H 7
Gwillimbury* 4,528..I 8
Hagersville ..2,169..E 14
Haileybury .3,117.°G 8
Haley Station* 180..H 9
Haliburton .....787..A 16
Hallebourg .....159..F 6
Hamilton .298,121.°J 8
Hamilton's* 1,349..H 9
Hampton* ....543..I 8
Hanmer ......3,619..H 7
Hanover .....4,665..B 12
Harriston ...1,748..C 13
Harrow ......1,941..G 9
Harrowsmith ..537..J 13
Harty ....119..F 6
Hastings ....872..J 12
Havelock ....1,224..J 12
Hawk Junction 395..G 6
Hawkesbury 9,188..H 16
Hearst ......2,882..F 6
Hensall ....934..D 12
Hepworth .....331..A 12
Hespeler ....5,381..D 13
Highgate ....421..F 11
Highland Grove 77..I 11
Hillsdale ......298..A 14
Hillside Gardens ....644..H 15
Hilton Beach .165..H 6
Holland Landing .....596..B 15
Holtyre ....458..F 8
Honey Harbour 132..A 14
Hornepayne .1,594..F 5
Hudson* ....831..E 2
Huntsville ..3,342..H 8
Hurkett ....68..F 4
Huttonsville ..421..C 14
Hyde Park ....238..E 12
Hymers ....92..F 3
Ignace ....552..F 2
Ilderton ....303..E 12
Ingersoll ....7,249..E 13
Ingleside ....816..I 16
Inglewood ......396..C 14
Innerkip ....417..D 13
Iron Bridge ...762..H 6
Iroquois ......1,141..I 15
Iroquois Falls ......1,834..F 7
Island Falls ....134..F 7
Jarvis ....824..E 14
Jellico ....188..F 4
Jogues ....138..F 6
Jordan ....210..D 15
Jumbo Gardens* .1,222..F 3
Kakabeka Falls ......346..F 3
Kaladar ....244..J 13
Kanata* ......870..H 10
Kapuskasing 12,617..F 6
Kashabowie ...127..F 3
Kearney ....316..H 8
Kearns ....478..F 8
Keene ....333..K 11
Keewatin* ..2,089..F 1
Kemptville ..2,182..I 15
Kenora ....11,295.°E 1
Keswick ....725..B 15
Killaloe Station .....825..H 12
Killarney ......442..H 7
Kincardine .2,823..B 11
King City ..2,024..C 15
Kingston ..59,004.°K 14
Kingston Mills 250..J 14
Kingsville ..3,545..G 10
Kiosk ....321..H 8
Kirkfield .....206..B 15
Kirkland Lake ....14,008..G 8
Kitchener .93,255.°D 13
Kleinburg .....296..C 15
Komoka ....544..E 12
Laclu ....63..E 1
Lakefield ...2,242..J 11
Lambeth ....3,056..E 12
Lanark ....957..I 14
Lancaster ......599..H 16
Langton ....383..E 13
Lansdowne ...498..J 14
Larder Lake 1,495..G 8
Latchford .....467..G 8
La Vallee ....70..F 1
Leamington .9,554..G 10
Leaside* ...21,250..I 8
Leitch ....F 4
Levack ......3,025..H 7
Limoges ....503..H 15
Lindsay ....12,090.°B 16
Lingman Lake .....B 2
Lion's Head ..418..A 12
Listowel ....4,526..C 13
Little Current ....1,441..H 7
Lively ......3,169..H 7
Lochalsh ....46..F 6
London ..194,416.°J 7
Long Branch* .12,980..J 8
Long Sault ...963..I 16
Longlac .....1,315..E 5
L'Orignal ...1,238.°G 16
Lower Wingham ...305..C 12
Lucan ......1,011..D 12
Lucknow ....1,096..C 12
Lyn* ....547..I 10
Lynden* ....543..J 8
Lynhurst ......370..E 12
MacTier ....844..I 8
Madoc ......1,385..J 12
Madsen* ......566..E 1
Maitland ......502..J 15
Mallorytown ..310..J 15
Malton ....C 14
Manitouwadge ...2,983..F 5
Manitowaning 356..H 7
Manotick .....387..H 15
Mansfield* ....601..H 10
Maple ....2,026..C 15
Maple Grove ..831..C 16
Marathon ...2,532..F 5
Markdale ...1,113..B 13
Markham ...7,769..C 15
Marmora ....1,331..J 12
Massey ......1,223..H 7
Matachewan ..712..G 7
Matheson .....830..F 7
Mattagami Heights* .1,690..F 7
Mattawa ....3,143..H 8
Mattice ....849..F 6
Maxville ....771..H 16
McIntosh ......117..E 2
McKellar ......131..H 8
Mead ....55..F 6
Meaford ....3,866..A 13
Melbourne ...311..E 12
Meldrum Bay ..59..H 6
Merlin ....691..F 11
Merrickville ...931..I 14
Metcalfe ......426..H 15
Michipicoten ..155..G 5
Midhurst ......251..B 14
Midland ....10,129..A 14
Mildmay ....943..C 12
Milford Bay ..204..I 8
Millbrook .....926..B 16
Milliken* ......509..I 8
Milton ....6,601.°D 14
Milverton ...1,122..D 13
Mimico* ...19,431..I 8
Minaki ....358..E 1
Mindemoya ...420..H 7
Minden ....625.°A 16
Mine Centre ...78..F 2
Missanabie ...173..F 6
Mississauga 93,492..D 15
Mitchell ....2,371..D 12
Mitchell Corners* ....549..I 8
Monkton* .....506..J 7
Monteith ......183..F 7

Toronto, Canada's second largest city, is a busy Great Lakes port and industrial center. The city has a fine natural harbor on the northwestern shore of Lake Ontario.

*Does not appear on map; key shows general location.   °County seat.   Source: Latest census (1966).

The 1966 Canadian census reported that Ontario had 6,960,870 persons. The population had increased 12 per cent over the 1961 figure of 6,236,092. By 1971, Ontario had an estimated population of 7,761,000.

The great majority of Ontarians—88 of every 100 persons—live in 8 per cent of the province's land area. This heavily populated region, the southernmost part of the province, lies south of Lake Nipissing. It includes all of Ontario's metropolitan areas except that of Sudbury. Ontario has seven Census Metropolitan Areas as defined by the Dominion Bureau of Statistics. For the names and populations of these metropolitan areas, see the *Index* to the political map of Ontario.

About four-fifths of Ontario's people live in cities and towns. Ontario has 19 cities with populations of 50,000 or more. No other province has so many large cities. Toronto, the largest city of Ontario, is second in size only to Montreal among all Canadian cities. Other large cities of Ontario, in order of size, include Hamil-

ton, Ottawa, London, Windsor, Thunder Bay, and St. Catharines. See the list of separate articles on the cities of Ontario listed in the *Related Articles* at the end of this article.

Almost 80 of every 100 Ontarians were born in Canada. The province also has large numbers of persons born in England, Germany, Italy, Poland, and Scotland. About 60 per cent of the people have English, Irish, or Scottish ancestors, and 10 per cent are of French descent. About 95,000 of the French Canadians in Ontario speak only French.

Ontario has about 50,000 Indians, more than any other province. Most of the Indians live on 170 reservations, which cover a total of over $1\frac{1}{2}$ million acres.

Roman Catholics make up the largest single religious group in Ontario. The United Church of Canada has almost as many members. Other large religious groups, in order of size, are members of the Anglican Church of Canada, Presbyterians, Baptists, and Lutherans.

POPULATION

This map shows the *population density* of Ontario, and how it varies in different parts of the province. Population density means the average number of persons who live on each square mile.

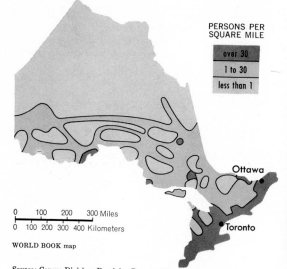

PERSONS PER SQUARE MILE

over 30
1 to 30
less than 1

Ottawa

Toronto

0   100   200   300 Miles
0 100 200 300 400 Kilometers

WORLD BOOK map

Source: Census Division, Dominion Bureau of Statistics

Miller Services

Prospectors wait their turns to file mining claims at a recorder's office. Ontario has rich deposits of nickel, gold, and uranium.

Farm Boys from Langton near Lake Erie tie tobacco leaves on a long stick. Then they hang the leaves in a barn to dry.

Don F. Smith, Miller Services

An Indian mends snowshoes in preparation for the Hudson Bay area's long, snowy winter. Most of the Indians in Ontario live on reservations.

Leavens, Photo Researchers

Carleton University's Maxwell MacOdrum Library symbolizes the modern design of the Rideau River campus. The university was established in Ottawa in 1942. A special feature is the school's Institute of Canadian Studies, founded in 1957.

Carleton University

ONTARIO /*Education*

Schools. The first *common* (elementary) schools in the Ontario region were established during the late 1780's. In 1807, the provincial government provided by law for a *grammar* (high) school in each of the province's eight districts. In 1816, the government provided for common schools throughout the province. A royal charter was granted in 1827 for a college in York (now Toronto). This college opened in 1843 as King's College, and became the University of Toronto in 1850.

Ontario's school system took its present basic form during the 1870's. All common and grammar schools became free elementary and high schools. Attendance between the ages of 6 and 16 was required by law, as it still is today. Ontario also set up provincial departments of education and university affairs headed by the minister of education, a cabinet member.

Today, Ontario has more than 4,700 public and *separate* schools. Separate schools are tax-supported schools operated by religious groups, but under control of the department of education. Individual citizens have a choice of supporting either the public schools or the separate schools with their taxes. Ontario has about 1,300 Roman Catholic separate schools. In many of these schools, French is used in all classes. Ontario, like British Columbia, offers a fifth year of high school education called *grade 13*. It is usually required for entrance to universities. For information on the number of students and teachers in Ontario, see EDUCATION (table).

Libraries. By 1867, when Ontario became one of Canada's four original provinces, it had more than 60 institutes that provided books and lectures. The Ontario Free Libraries Act of 1882 changed the institutes to public libraries. Today, Ontario has 320 public libraries, or about a third of all those in Canada. The province's libraries own more than 8,400,000 volumes.

The Toronto Public Library is the largest library system in Canada. It has more than a million volumes, including a special collection of old children's books. Scholars of Italian literature visit the University of Toronto Library to study its famous collection of early Italian plays. The Legislative and Osgoode Hall law

libraries in Toronto also own special collections. The National Library of Canada, and the libraries of the National Museum, National Research Council, Parliament, and Supreme Court of Canada are in Ottawa.

Museums. Ontario has about 40 museums. One of the world's outstanding collections of Chinese objects is owned by the Royal Ontario Museum in Toronto. This collection includes a complete tomb from the Ming dynasty. The National Museum of Canada in Ottawa houses Indian and Eskimo displays, as well as exhibits on Canadian natural history.

Ottawa's Canadian War Museum has objects from World Wars I and II on display. Articles used by Canadian pioneers during the 1800's are featured in the Historical Museum of the Twenty, in Jordan. The Huronia Museum in Midland has exhibits dealing with pioneer life of the region.

──────── **UNIVERSITIES AND COLLEGES** ────────

Ontario has 16 degree-granting universities and colleges, listed below. See the separate articles in WORLD BOOK on these institutions. For enrollments, see CANADA (table: Universities and Colleges).

Name	Location	Founded
Brock University	St. Catharines	1964
Carleton University	Ottawa	1942
Guelph, University of	Guelph	1964
Lakehead University	Thunder Bay	1948
Laurentian University	Sudbury	1960
McMaster University	Hamilton	1887
Ottawa, University of	Ottawa	1848
Queen's University at Kingston	Kingston	1841
Royal Military College of Canada	Kingston	1874
Toronto, University of	Toronto	1827
Trent University	Peterborough	1963
Waterloo, University of	Waterloo	1957
Waterloo Lutheran University	Waterloo	1911
Western Ontario, University of	London	1878
Windsor, University of	Windsor	1963
York University	Toronto	1959

Niagara Falls, with Horseshoe Falls and the Ontario Shore, *Background*, and the American Falls, *Foreground*

ONTARIO / *A Visitor's Guide*

About 18,000,000 tourists visit Ontario every year. The province's 250,000 lakes offer a variety of vacation attractions. Sparkling lakes and rushing rivers provide fine fishing and boating. Thousands of square miles of thick forests attract campers and hunters.

The sunny, southernmost resort region of the province, along Lakes Erie and Ontario, is known as *Canada's Sun Parlor*. Boat cruises take vacationers through the Thousand Islands and other islands in Ontario waters. The Kawartha and Muskoka lakes near Toronto are famous resort areas. Low, wooded hills line the shores of these lakes. The landscape becomes more rugged toward the northern and northwestern vacationlands of James Bay and Lake of the Woods. Many sportsmen fly in seaplanes to the far northern lakes. There they hunt bear, geese, moose, and other game.

PLACES TO VISIT

Following are brief descriptions of some of Ontario's many interesting places to visit.

Bell Memorial is a huge stone sculpture of Alexander Graham Bell, inventor of the telephone. It stands near the Bell Homestead, now a telephone museum, in Brantford. There, in 1874, Bell worked on his invention. In 1876, the world's first long-distance telephone call was made from the home to Bell in Paris, Ont.

Jack Miner's Waterfowl Sanctuary covers 300 acres at Kingsville. It is dedicated to the memory of the famous Ontario naturalist.

Horseshoe Falls, near the Ontario-New York border, are the largest part of Niagara Falls. They are 2,100 feet wide and 186 feet high. See NIAGARA FALLS AND NIAGARA RIVER.

Manitoulin Island in Lake Huron is probably the world's largest fresh-water island. It is 90 miles long and 5 to 30 miles wide, and covers 1,068 square miles.

Martyrs' Shrine is three miles from Midland, near the site of old Fort Sainte Marie. The fort consists of the restored ruins of a Jesuit mission established in 1639. The Iroquois Indians destroyed this mission in 1649, during their war with the Huron Indians. Nearby stands a restored Huron village of the early 1600's.

Old Forts in Ontario that have been restored include Fort Erie in Fort Erie, Fort George in Niagara-on-the-Lake, Fort Henry in Kingston, Fort Wellington in Prescott, and Fort York in Toronto.

Royal Botanical Gardens, in Hamilton, attracts garden lovers from many parts of the world. It was established in 1941.

Upper Canada Village, near Morrisburg, shows life in the Ontario region from 1784 to 1867. Some buildings were moved to the village from the area now covered by Lake St. Lawrence. Other buildings came from pioneer settlements on the road between York (now Toronto) and Montreal.

National Parks. Ontario has three national parks—Georgian Bay Islands, in Georgian Bay; Point Pelee, on the Lake Erie peninsula; and St. Lawrence Islands, on the eastern Ontario mainland and on 13 of the Thousand Islands in the St. Lawrence River. The province also has three national historic parks—Fort Malden near Amherstburg, Fort Wellington near Prescott, and Woodside near Kitchener. For the areas and chief features of these parks, see CANADA (National Parks).

Provincial Parks. Ontario has more than 80 provincial parks. Most of them provide camping facilities and waterside ramps for small boats. For information on the provincial parks of Ontario, write to Director, Parks Branch, Department of Lands and Forests, Parliament Buildings, Toronto, Ont.

Ontario's best-known annual event is probably the Stratford Shakespearean Festival, held in Stratford from June to October. Famous actors appear in the dramas of William Shakespeare. Another popular event is the Royal Canadian Henley Regatta, the oldest rowing and sculling event in North America, held in St. Catharines the last week of July. Other annual events include:

January-March: Winter Carnivals throughout the province (January through March); Canadian National Boat Show in Toronto (February); Canadian National Sportsman's Show in Toronto (March).

April-June: Blossom Week on the Niagara Peninsula (mid-May); Annual Tulip Festival in Ottawa (late May); Queen's Plate Horse Race in New Woodbine (mid-June); Annual Shaw Festival in Niagara-on-the-Lake (late June-early September); Annual Olde English Style Fortnight Festival in London (late June-mid-July).

July-September: Fish Derby in Rossport (July); Annual Six Nations Indian Pageant in Brantford (August); Rockhound Gem-boree in Bancroft (early August); Central Canada Exhibition in Ottawa (late August); Canadian National Exhibition in Toronto (August-September); Niagara Grape and Wine Festival in St. Catharines (late September).

October-December: Annual Winter Fair in Ottawa (October); Oktoberfest in Kitchener-Waterloo (October); Royal Agriculture Winter Fair in Toronto (November).

Alpha Photo Assoc.
Alexander Graham Bell Homestead in Brantford

Malak, Miller Services
Upper Canada Village near Morrisburg

Thousand Islands in the St. Lawrence River near Lake Ontario
Photographic Survey Corp. from Photo Researchers

Al Naidoff, Alpha
Fort Henry in Kingston

Land Regions. Ontario lies on a low plateau, crossed by two ranges of low hills. It has four main land regions. They are, from north to south: (1) the Hudson Bay Lowland, (2) the Canadian Shield, (3) the St. Lawrence Lowland, and (4) the Great Lakes Lowland.

The Hudson Bay Lowland curves around the southern part of Hudson Bay and extends as far south as Kesagami Lake. This flat region of northern Ontario is poorly drained, and has large *muskegs* (peat bogs). The lowland includes a narrow belt of *permafrost* (permanently frozen ground) near the Arctic.

The Canadian Shield is a vast, horseshoe-shaped region that covers almost half of Canada and part of the northern United States. This low, rocky region covers about half of Ontario. Small lakes and rivers surrounded by wooded hills attract many vacationers. The highest point in Ontario, Tip Top Hill, rises 2,120 feet in Thunder Bay District.

The Canadian Shield is rich in game, minerals, and timber. Patches of clay are scattered throughout the region. These areas were formed by the soil of ancient glacial lakes. The largest clay area, known as the clay belt, extends from the Hearst area to the Quebec border. Farmers raise a variety of crops, including grains and vegetables, in the rich clay soil. Beef and dairy cattle graze on fenced grasslands in the region. See CANADIAN SHIELD.

The St. Lawrence Lowland runs along the St. Lawrence River. In Ontario, it forms the tip of the wedge of land between the Ottawa and St. Lawrence rivers. Low hills rise above the fertile, shallow valleys. Farmers grow fruits, grains, and vegetables. Dairy farming is extensive in this region.

The Great Lakes Lowland lies along much of the Great Lakes in Canada and the United States. In Ontario, the region touches Lakes Erie, Huron, and Ontario. Great quantities of many crops are grown in the fertile gray-brown soil of the low, flat, southwestern section. These crops include corn, soybeans, tobacco, and tomatoes. The land rises gently in the northeast, where beef and dairy cattle are raised. The Niagara Escarpment, a high cliff or ridge, extends 250 miles from Manitoulin Island, through Bruce Peninsula, to Niagara Falls. The escarpment forms a natural shelter for Ontario's best fruit-growing belt. Many of Canada's largest cities and greatest industries are in the Great Lakes Lowland.

Shoreline and Coastline. Ontario's southern shores of bays, narrow inlets, and sandy beaches stretch 4,726 miles. This shoreline, including 1,888 miles of offshore island shoreline, is on Lakes Erie, Huron, Ontario, and Superior. Ontario's Manitoulin Island is the world's largest inland island. It has an area of 1,068 square miles in Lake Huron.

Oceangoing ships use the St. Lawrence Seaway to reach the Great Lakes ports of Ontario. These inland seaports include Hamilton, Port Colborne, Sarnia, Sault Ste. Marie, and Toronto. Thunder Bay on Lake Superior is the greatest wheat depot in North America. This city can store about 106,421,000 bushels of wheat for shipment. In northern Ontario, the province has a coastline of 680 miles on Hudson Bay and James Bay.

Rivers, Waterfalls, and Lakes cover a sixth of the province. A land rise separates the Ontario streams that flow into the Great Lakes from those that empty into the Ottawa River or Hudson Bay. Many lakes and rivers, some linked by canals, are important transportation routes.

Land Regions of Ontario

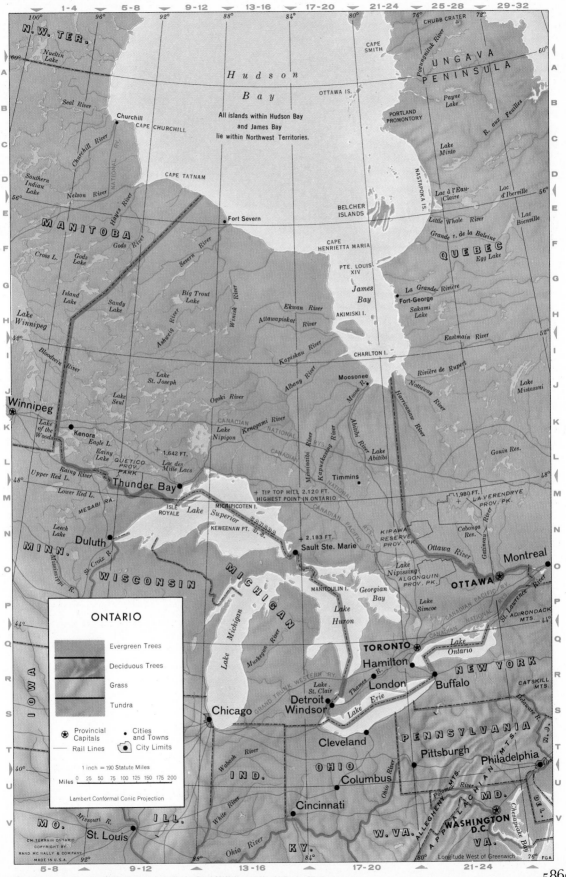

ONTARIO

Evergreen Trees

Deciduous Trees

Grass

Tundra

Provincial Capitals

Rail Lines

Cities and Towns

City Limits

1 inch = 190 Statute Miles

Miles 0 25 50 75 100 125 150 175 200

Lambert Conformal Conic Projection

N.W. TER.

Nueltin Lake

Hudson Bay

All islands within Hudson Bay and James Bay lie within Northwest Territories.

OTTAWA IS.

CHUBB CRATER

CAPE SMITH

Povungnituk River

UNGAVA PENINSULA

60°

Seal River

Churchill

CAPE CHURCHILL

Payne Lake

Lake Minto

R. aux Feuilles

PORTLAND PROMONTORY

NASTAPOKA IS.

Lac à l'Eau-Claire

Lac d'Iberville

56°

Southern Indian Lake

Nelson River

CAPE TATNAM

Fort Severn

BELCHER ISLANDS

Little Whale River

Lac Bienville

MANITOBA

Churchill River

Hayes River

Gods River

Severn River

CAPE HENRIETTA MARIA

Grande r. de la Baleine

QUEBEC

Egg Lake

Cross L.

Gods Lake

Island Lake

Big Trout Lake

Winisk River

PTE. LOUIS XIV

James Bay

La Grande Rivière

Fort-George

Sakami Lake

Lake Winnipeg

Sandy Lake

Asheweig River

Ekwan River

Attawapiskat River

AKIMISKI I.

Eastmain River

52°

Bloodvein River

Lake St. Joseph

Kapiskau River

Albany River

Moosonee

Moose R.

CHARLTON I.

Rivière de Rupert

Lake Mistassini

Winnipeg

Lake Seul

Ogoki River

Nottaway River

Harricanaw River

Gouin Res.

Kenora

Eagle L.

Rainy Lake

Lake Nipigon

CANADIAN NATIONAL RYS.

Kenogami River

Lake Abitibi

Abitibi River

Kapuskasing River

Missinaibi River

1,642 FT.

Lac des Mille Lacs

QUETICO PROV. PARK

Timmins

1,980 FT.

LA VERENDRYE PROV. PK.

48°

Upper Red L.

Rainy River

Thunder Bay

TIP TOP HILL 2,120 FT. HIGHEST POINT IN ONTARIO

KIPAWA RESERVE PROV. PK.

Cabonga Res.

Gatineau River

Lower Red L.

MESABI RA.

ISLE ROYALE

MICHIPICOTEN I.

KEWEENAW PT. U.S.

Lake Superior

CANADA

CANADIAN PACIFIC RYS.

Lake Abitibi

Ottawa River

Montreal

Leech Lake

Duluth

St. Croix R.

2,183 FT.

Sault Ste. Marie

Lake Nipissing

ALGONQUIN PROV. PK.

OTTAWA

MINN.

WISCONSIN

MICHIGAN

MANITOULIN I.

Georgian Bay

Lake Simcoe

Lake Huron

St. Lawrence River

ADIRONDACK MTS.

44°

Mississippi R.

Lake Michigan

TORONTO

Lake Ontario

NEW YORK

CATSKILL MTS.

Muskegon River

Hamilton

London

Buffalo

IOWA

Chicago

Detroit

Windsor

Lake St. Clair

Thames R.

Lake Erie

GRAND TRUNK WESTERN RY.

Cleveland

PENNSYLVANIA

Wabash River

IND.

OHIO

Pittsburgh

Philadelphia

N.J.

40°

Columbus

Ohio River

ALLEGHENY MTS.

MD.

DEL.

White River

Cincinnati

Potomac River

WASHINGTON D.C.

Chesapeake Bay

CM TERRAIN ONTARIO COPYRIGHT BY RAND McNALLY & COMPANY MADE IN U.S.A.

MO.

ILL.

Missouri R.

St. Louis

KY.

Ohio River

W. VA.

VA.

APPALACHIAN MTS.

Longitude West of Greenwich

FGA

Specially created for **World Book Encyclopedia** by Rand McNally and World Book editors

Lowlands and Swamps surround the village of Moose Factory in the Hudson Bay Lowland. The region is poorly drained and has *muskegs* (peat bogs).

Floating Logs, such as these near Kenora, are a familiar sight in the wooded Canadian Shield region. Lumbermen guide logs down rivers and lakes to sawmills farther south.

Rich, Fertile Soil makes farming an important industry around Bolton in the Great Lakes Lowland. Great quantities of many crops are grown in this region of Ontario.

The St. Lawrence River, a great natural highway for commerce, has contributed much to the growth of Ontario's economy. This waterway was enlarged during the 1950's to allow ocean vessels to reach the Great Lakes. Hydroelectric plants on the Niagara and other rivers provide Ontario with cheap power. The mighty Horseshoe Falls are formed by the Niagara River passing over the Niagara Escarpment.

The Ottawa River was part of the route of the early fur traders to Georgian Bay and the west. This river flows into the St. Lawrence River. The Ottawa drains the part of southern Ontario that does not lie in the Great Lakes basin. Other important southern rivers include the French, Grand, Thames, and Trent. The Detroit and St. Clair rivers are links between Lakes Erie and Huron. Lakes Huron and Superior are joined by the St. Marys River.

Ontario has about 250,000 lakes. Besides the Great Lakes, the largest are Lake of the Woods, Lake Abitibi, Lake Nipigon, Lake Nipissing, and Lake Seul.

Winds from the Great Lakes give southern Ontario a much milder climate than that of the rest of the province. Northern Ontario gets bitter winter cold waves that move down from the Arctic across Hudson Bay, or from the prairies to the northwest. Frost-free periods range from six or seven months in the south to about three months in the north. The highest temperature recorded in Ontario, 109° F., occurred in Stonecliffe on July 3, 1911. The lowest temperature, −73° F., was recorded in Iroquois Falls on Jan. 23, 1935.

The Great Lakes Lowland and the St. Lawrence Lowland have higher temperatures throughout the year, and longer summers, than the rest of Ontario. The average January temperature ranges from 12° F. in Ottawa to 24° F. in Windsor. The average July temperature is 69° F. in Parry Sound and 73° F. in Windsor.

The Hudson Bay Lowland and the Canadian Shield as far south as Lake Superior have long, cold winters. Summers are sunny, with hot days and cool nights. The average January temperature ranges from 12° F. in Trout Lake to −1° F. in Kapuskasing. The temperature in July averages 65° F. in Sioux Lookout and 61° F. at Trout Lake.

Southern Ontario has a yearly average of 38 inches of *precipitation* (rain, melted snow, and other forms of moisture). Rain falls fairly evenly throughout the year in this region, with no wet or dry seasons. In northern Ontario, precipitation averages 28 inches a year.

Heavy snow—more than 10 feet of it a year—falls in a region extending from London to Owen Sound and Parry Sound. Annual snowfall in the rest of the province ranges from 5 to 9 feet.

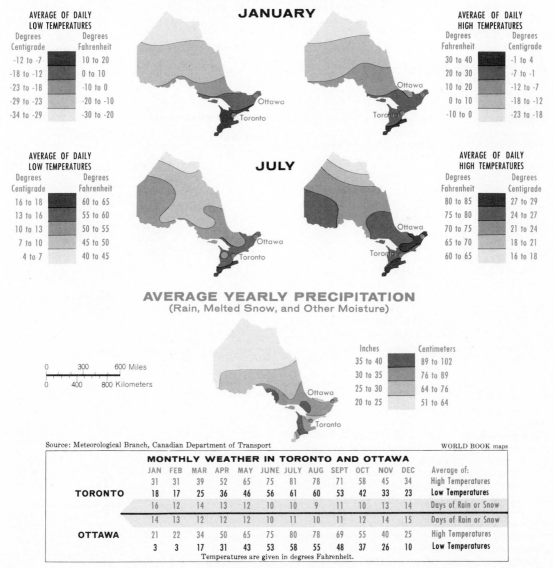

SEASONAL TEMPERATURES

JANUARY

AVERAGE OF DAILY LOW TEMPERATURES

Degrees Centigrade	Degrees Fahrenheit
-12 to -7	10 to 20
-18 to -12	0 to 10
-23 to -18	-10 to 0
-29 to -23	-20 to -10
-34 to -29	-30 to -20

AVERAGE OF DAILY HIGH TEMPERATURES

Degrees Fahrenheit	Degrees Centigrade
30 to 40	-1 to 4
20 to 30	-7 to -1
10 to 20	-12 to -7
0 to 10	-18 to -12
-10 to 0	-23 to -18

JULY

AVERAGE OF DAILY LOW TEMPERATURES

Degrees Centigrade	Degrees Fahrenheit
16 to 18	60 to 65
13 to 16	55 to 60
10 to 13	50 to 55
7 to 10	45 to 50
4 to 7	40 to 45

AVERAGE OF DAILY HIGH TEMPERATURES

Degrees Fahrenheit	Degrees Centigrade
80 to 85	27 to 29
75 to 80	24 to 27
70 to 75	21 to 24
65 to 70	18 to 21
60 to 65	16 to 18

AVERAGE YEARLY PRECIPITATION
(Rain, Melted Snow, and Other Moisture)

Inches	Centimeters
35 to 40	89 to 102
30 to 35	76 to 89
25 to 30	64 to 76
20 to 25	51 to 64

0   300   600 Miles
0   400   800 Kilometers

Source: Meteorological Branch, Canadian Department of Transport

WORLD BOOK maps

	JAN	FEB	MAR	APR	MAY	JUNE	JULY	AUG	SEPT	OCT	NOV	DEC	Average of:
MONTHLY WEATHER IN TORONTO AND OTTAWA													
TORONTO	31	31	39	52	65	75	81	78	71	58	45	34	High Temperatures
	18	17	25	36	46	56	61	60	53	42	33	23	Low Temperatures
	16	12	14	13	12	10	10	9	11	10	13	14	Days of Rain or Snow
	14	13	12	12	12	10	11	10	11	12	14	15	Days of Rain or Snow
OTTAWA	21	22	34	50	65	75	80	78	69	55	40	25	High Temperatures
	3	3	17	31	43	53	58	55	48	37	26	10	Low Temperatures

Temperatures are given in degrees Fahrenheit.

The thriving industries of Ontario make it one of the richest economic regions of North America. Among the provinces and U.S. states, Ontario is a leading producer of numerous products. Ontario leads the provinces in manufacturing, its greatest source of income, and in farming and trapping. It also ranks first in mining. Ontario is third among the provinces in forestry.

All values given in this section are in Canadian dollars. For the value of Canadian dollars in U.S. money, see MONEY (table).

Natural Resources. The valuable natural resources of Ontario have helped make the province rich. These resources include fertile soils, vast mineral deposits, great forests, much wildlife, and plentiful supplies of water.

Soil in the northern Hudson Bay Lowland consists mostly of clay, muskeg, and rock. Throughout much of the Canadian Shield, thin layers of clay and sand cover ancient rock. Near the Quebec border, glacial clays and silt cover a fertile section called the clay belt. The St. Lawrence Lowland has black loams and well-drained sands over limestone and shale. The rich sandy soils in the Great Lakes Lowland help make it one of Ontario's chief farming regions.

Minerals. Sudbury District is famous for the variety and quantity of its minerals. It is the greatest single source of Ontario's mineral wealth. More than half the western world's nickel supply and much of its platinum come from this region. Sudbury District also has large deposits of cobalt, copper, gold, and silver. In 1964, huge deposits of copper, silver, and zinc were discovered near Timmins.

Rich iron-ore deposits lie in Algoma District and near Marmora and Steep Rock Lake. In 1952, geologists discovered the western world's largest single field of uranium-bearing ore at Elliot Lake. A great field of copper and zinc was discovered in 1953 near Lake Manitouwadge.

The northern and central parts of Ontario have large gold reserves, particularly around Kirkland Lake and Porcupine. Canada's first oil field, developed in Lambton County during the 1850's, still produces about 250,000 barrels of oil annually. Southern Ontario has pools of natural gas deep in the earth. This section also has deposits of gypsum, mica, and quartz.

Rich veins of silver and cobalt are near the town of Cobalt. The James Bay area has large reserves of clay and kaolin. Deposits of lithium and columbium are found near Lake Nipigon. Other minerals found in Ontario include asbestos, calcium, salt, sand and gravel, and stone.

Forests. Ontario has about 262,000 square miles of woodlands, of which 166,000 square miles are commercially valuable. Softwoods account for about 40 per cent of the commercial forests, and hardwoods for about 15 per cent. Mixed forests of both kinds of trees make up the remainder. The provincial government owns 90 per cent of the forest land, and individuals or firms must obtain cutting licenses. In 1954, the government set aside about 87,000 square miles of forests to supply timber for pulp and paper mills.

Northern Ontario has huge forests of balsams, pines,

spruces, tamaracks, and other softwoods. Thick forests of hardwoods such as ashes, beeches, elms, maples, and walnuts once covered southern Ontario. Lumbermen cut most of the timber during the 1800's, and some sections now have second-growth trees.

Plant Life. Wild flowers are plentiful in southern Ontario. Trilliums and bloodroots blossom in spring. Autumn brings masses of asters and wild carrot blooms. The lakeside hills are thick with wild blueberry bushes. Shrubs and mosses grow in the far northern areas, where frost stays deep in the ground. Tamaracks and spruces, which grow there, do not reach their usual height in this cold, poorly drained region.

Animal Life. Moose and caribou roam the wooded northlands of Ontario. Shy white-tailed deer pause to drink from streams in the Canadian Shield. Hunters in this region often sight the tracks of black bears. Fur-bearing animals such as beavers, minks, muskrats, and otters live in northern Ontario. Rabbits and snowshoe hares are plentiful throughout the province. Birds of Ontario include ducks, geese, and ruffed grouse. The haunting cries of loons pierce the air at dusk over Ontario's lakes. Herring, perch, pike, trout, and whitefish are found in the lakes and streams.

PRODUCTION IN ONTARIO

Total yearly value of goods produced—$12,293,373,000

FISH, FORESTRY, AND TRAPPING PRODUCTS 1%

MANUFACTURED PRODUCTS 79%

MINERAL PRODUCTS 9%

AGRICULTURAL PRODUCTS 11%

Note: Manufacturing percentage based on value added by manufacture. Other percentages based on value of production.

EMPLOYMENT IN ONTARIO

Average yearly number of persons employed—2,582,197

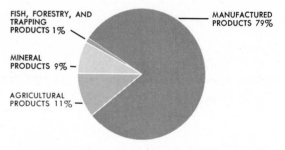

	Number of Employees
Manufacturing	806,700
Services	583,900
Wholesale & Retail Trade	369,700
Transportation, Communications & Utilities	211,900
Government & Defense	162,200
Agriculture	147,000
Construction	138,100
Finance, Insurance & Real Estate	113,400
Mining	34,500
Forestry & Fishing	14,797

Source: Dominion Bureau of Statistics

Manufacturing. Goods manufactured in Ontario have a *value added by manufacture* of about $9,733,000,-000 yearly. This figure represents the value created in products by Ontario's industries, not counting such costs as materials, supplies, and fuels.

About a third of Canada's industrial workers live in Ontario. They produce about half the country's manufactured products. The Toronto area has long been the province's major industrial area. Since 1953, the provincial government's regional development program has established factory locations in many other parts of the province.

Automobile manufacturing is Ontario's chief industry. Motor vehicles made in Brampton, Hamilton, Oakville, Oshawa, and Windsor, and near London in Talbotville account for most of Canada's production.

More than half the province's slaughtering and meat packing takes place in Toronto. The city's factories also make electrical equipment, flour and feed, hosiery and other knitted goods, and leather and rubber products. Fruit- and vegetable-canning plants, and butter and cheese factories, are scattered throughout the province.

The western world's largest papermaking machine is in Thunder Bay. Many pulp and paper mills operate in the Ottawa and Niagara Falls areas. Printing and publishing also are important, especially in Toronto.

Hamilton is Canada's leading iron and steel producer. Sault Ste. Marie and Welland are also iron and steel centers. Other Hamilton products include clothing, cotton and woolen goods, electrical equipment, farm tools, food and tobacco products, glass, and shoes.

Chemical plants in the Sarnia region produce automotive and aviation gasolines, carbon black, carbon tetrachloride, glycol, oil lubricants, and plastic resins. Canada's largest oil refinery and its only synthetic rubber factory are in Sarnia. Port Colborne has the largest nickel-processing plant in North America. Other important products manufactured in Ontario include aircraft and parts, cement, electrical machinery, industrial machines, radio and television sets and parts, and sheet-metal products.

Agriculture. Ontario's farm products have a yearly value of about $1,283,000,000. The province has about 110,000 farms. They cover one-twelfth of the province, and average 162 acres in size.

Ontario farmers earn about 70 per cent of their income from livestock. Herds of beef and dairy cattle graze on pastureland between the southeastern shores of Lake Huron to the lower western shores of Lake Ontario. Dairying is important eastward along Lake Ontario and the St. Lawrence River. Some of the finest cattle, hogs, horses, and sheep in North America come from Ontario stock farms.

Ontario's farmers raise feed crops for livestock on more than 60 per cent of their cleared land. The chief field crops include barley, beans, corn, hay, oats, potatoes, rye, soybeans, sugar beets, and wheat. Ontario's farmers also produce large quantities of butter, eggs, milk, and poultry, which are sent to markets in nearby cities.

FARM, MINERAL, AND FOREST PRODUCTS

This map shows where the leading farm, mineral, and forest products are produced. The major urban areas (shown in red) are the important manufacturing centers.

0   100   200 Miles
0   100   200   300 Kilometers
WORLD BOOK map

Grain Elevators dot the lakefront of Thunder Bay, *below.* This Lake Superior port forms the largest wheat depot in North America. From there, western grain moves east to Canadian and foreign markets.

Stage, Photo Researchers

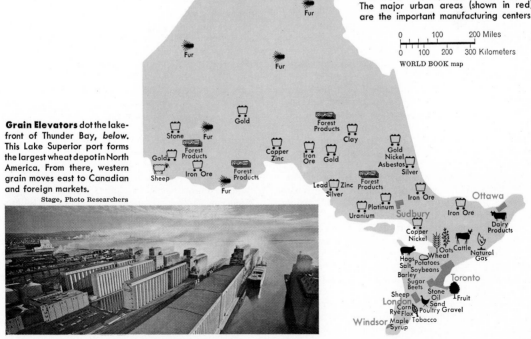

Woolen Blankets woven at textile mills in Arnprior are shipped to all parts of the world. Other leading textile cities in Ontario include Hamilton, Cornwall, Elmira, and Galt.

Harvesting Grapes. Workers pick bunches of ripe grapes from the vines. They place the grapes in boxes and load them on a wagon. Ontario is Canada's leading producer of grapes. Farmers in the Niagara fruit belt grow the famous green Niagara variety.

Malak, Miller Services; National Film Board of Canada

Other crops grow well in the rich soil of southern Ontario. Tobacco, which flourishes along Lake Erie, provides more than a tenth of Ontario's farm income. Orchards and vineyards of the famous Niagara fruit belt produce cherries, grapes, peaches, pears, plums, and other small fruits.

Maple syrup and sugar are important products. Every spring, farmers in southern Ontario tap the gray-barked maples that grow in their *sugar bush* (groves of trees, mainly sugar maples). In northern Ontario, fur farmers raise chinchillas, coypus, foxes, and minks.

Mining production in Ontario has an annual value of about $911 million. Ontario accounts for about a fourth of Canada's total mineral production, and produces about a third of its metallic minerals. Ontario leads all provinces and U.S. states in producing nickel and gold. It is a leader in uranium production.

Nickel is the most important mineral product of Ontario. Most of it comes from mines in Sudbury District. These mines also yield most of Ontario's copper and all of Canada's platinum.

The principal gold-producing areas are near Kirkland Lake, Larder Lake, and Porcupine, all in northeastern Ontario. The Kerr-Addison Mine at Larder Lake is Canada's leading gold producer. The Patricia, Pickle Crow, and Red Lake areas, in the northwestern part of Ontario, also produce gold. The Western world's largest uranium mine opened in 1952 at Elliot Lake, near Blind River. Production declined during the early 1960's because of reduced demands for uranium.

Almost half the province's iron ore comes from mines near Steep Rock Lake. Miners also dig iron ore at Capreol and Marmora, and in Algoma District north of Sault Ste. Marie. Natural gas and petroleum are

mined in southern Ontario and beneath the waters of Lake Erie. Other minerals produced in Ontario include asbestos, clay, gypsum, lime, nepheline syenite (used in making ceramics), salt, sand and gravel, and stone.

Forestry. Logs and pulpwood cut in Ontario have an annual value of about $104,643,000. Large stands of spruce trees in northern Ontario provide wood for much of the world's *newsprint* (paper used for newspapers). Lumber camps operate around Georgian Bay, along the Ottawa River, and in the region where rivers drain into Lake Superior. Lumbermen float logs of balsams, jack pines, spruces, and white pines down the rivers to sawmills farther south. Birches, maples, poplars, and other hardwoods are cut in southern Ontario.

Fishing Industry. Ontario fishermen catch about $5,995,000 worth of fish yearly. Ontario shares fishing rights with the United States in all the Great Lakes except Lake Michigan, the only one not bordering the province. Ontario also has important commercial fisheries in many other lakes and rivers. The most important fishes caught include herring, lake trout, perch, pickerel, pike, smelt, sturgeon, and whitefish. The province operates 17 fish hatcheries.

Trapping. Ontario trappers catch about $4 million worth of fur-bearing animals annually. Ontario supplies about a fourth of Canada's furs, including those produced on fur farms. The fur industry was important during the early days of the province, but the number of trappers has declined greatly. Today's trappers, operating in northern Ontario, catch mostly beavers, martens, minks, muskrats, and raccoons.

Electric Power. Hydroelectric power plants generate more than 90 per cent of Ontario's electricity. Plants operating on coal and other fuels supply the rest. The

Factory Workers assemble a truck at Chatham. Automobile and truck manufacturing is Ontario's chief industry. Ontario does about half of Canada's manufacturing.

Hydro-Electric Power Commission of Ontario, established in 1906, helped develop the province's water-power resources. This commission is now the largest publicly owned utility in Canada. Ontario and New York share the water of Niagara Falls under terms of a 1910 treaty between Canada and the United States. Ontario has about 65 hydroelectric plants, 6 fuel-electric stations, and 2 nuclear power plants. For Ontario's kilowatt-hour production, see ELECTRIC POWER (table).

Transportation. Waterways have played an important part in the history of Ontario. French explorers traveled up the Ottawa River in canoes. Early canals, particularly the Rideau and Trent systems, carried passengers and freight. The St. Lawrence Seaway, completed in 1959, brought oceangoing ships to Ontario's inland ports (see SAINT LAWRENCE SEAWAY).

During the navigation season, from mid-April to mid-December, many freighters travel between the ports of Ontario and those of the United States. Grain-carrying ships crowd the docks of Thunder Bay on Lake Superior. Ontario has 540 miles of canals, with more than a hundred locks. The largest is the 240-mile-long Trent Canal, between Trenton and Georgian Bay. The seven-mile-long Murray Canal, through the Murray Isthmus, provides the Trent system with an additional outlet to Lake Ontario.

Four major airlines serve about 80 licensed airports in Ontario. A number of government, industrial, and private airlines carry passengers and supplies to distant mining and lumbering camps in the north. The province has more than 280 landing areas, of which over half are on water.

Ontario has more than 10,000 miles of railways, about a fourth of Canada's total. About 4,000 miles of track stretch across northern Ontario. Southern Ontario, with about 6,000 miles of track, has the finest railway network in Canada. Toronto is Ontario's chief rail center. The Canadian Pacific Railway and the Canadian National Railways are the largest lines of the 12 that operate in Ontario. The province owns the Ontario Northland Railway, whose main line runs through the clay belt and the silver-mining region to James Bay.

More than 77,000 miles of highways and roads crisscross the province. Ontario has over 73,000 miles of paved highways, more than any other province. Part of the east-west Trans-Canada Highway runs across Ontario. It stretches 1,453 miles from near Hawkesbury to the Kenora area. A 510-mile expressway from Windsor to the Quebec border was opened in 1963.

Communication. Louis Roy, a Frenchman from Quebec, published the first newspaper of the Ontario region. His paper, the *Upper Canada Gazette and American Oracle*, first appeared in 1793 in Newark (now Niagara-on-the-Lake). York (now Toronto) became the capital of Ontario in 1797, and the *Gazette* moved there in 1798. It was published until 1845. Today, about 300 newspapers are published in Ontario. Nearly 50 are dailies. The *Toronto Daily Star* ranks first in circulation. Other leading dailies, in order of size, include the *Toronto Globe and Mail, Toronto Telegram, London Free Press,* the *Spectator* of Hamilton, and the *Star* of Windsor.

Station CKOC in Hamilton is Ontario's oldest radio station. It began broadcasting in 1922. The first television station, CBLT, was founded in Toronto in 1952. Today, Ontario has 92 radio stations and 19 major TV stations. A number of smaller TV stations rebroadcast programs from the major stations to distant areas.

589

Indian Days. Three major Indian groups lived in what is now Ontario when white explorers first arrived. Chippewa Indians hunted beavers and small game in the forests north and east of Lake Superior. Huron Indians lived between Lake Huron and Lake Ontario. They depended mainly on cultivated crops for food. The Chippewa and Huron feared wandering bands of Iroquois Indians, who sometimes raided their camps. The Iroquois tortured enemies who fell into their hands.

Exploration. The first white man to explore the Ontario region was Étienne Brulé of France. He was sent in 1610 by Samuel de Champlain, the founder of Quebec. In 1613, Champlain paddled up the Ottawa River. He journeyed farther south in 1615, into the Lake Huron area. Champlain found this region rich in fur-bearing animals. Young Frenchmen followed his course into the wilderness to collect pelts. They traveled deep into the forests, and traded beads and knives to the Indians in exchange for furs. During the 1620's and 1630's, other French explorers, including Brulé and Jean Nicolet, traveled farther than Champlain. They explored the Lake Superior region and pushed on into Lake Michigan and beyond. See CHAMPLAIN, SAMUEL DE.

Early Settlement. French missionaries followed the fur traders into the Ontario region. In 1639, Jesuit priests built Fort Sainte Marie as the center of a group of missions. These missions, known as Huronia, were

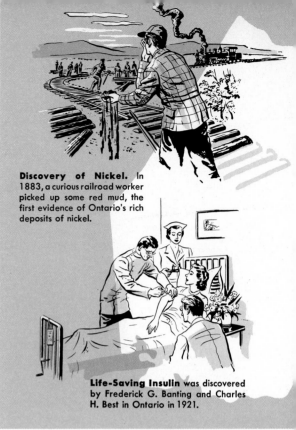

Discovery of Nickel. In 1883, a curious railroad worker picked up some red mud, the first evidence of Ontario's rich deposits of nickel.

Life-Saving Insulin was discovered by Frederick G. Banting and Charles H. Best in Ontario in 1921.

IMPORTANT DATES IN ONTARIO

1610 Étienne Brulé of France became the first white man to explore the Ontario region.

1613 Samuel de Champlain of France explored the Ottawa River area.

1639 French missionaries founded Fort Sainte Marie.

1648-1649 Indians destroyed the French missions.

1763 The Ontario region became a British possession.

1784 Loyalists settled in the Ontario region.

1791 The region became the province of Upper Canada.

1812-1814 American forces invaded Upper Canada during the War of 1812.

1837 The Rebellion of 1837-1838 began.

1867 Ontario became one of the original four provinces of the Dominion of Canada on July 1.

1883 The world's largest copper-nickel reserves were discovered at Sudbury.

1904 Ontario's automobile industry began in Windsor.

1912 The territory north of the Albany River was added to Ontario.

1945 Canada's first nuclear reactor started operating near Chalk River.

1952 The western world's largest uranium deposit was discovered at Elliot Lake.

1959 The St. Lawrence Seaway opened.

1962 Canada's first nuclear power station began operating at Rolphton.

1964 Huge deposits of copper, silver, and zinc were discovered near Timmins.

1966 The first laboratory facilities of the Sheridan Park Research Community were opened near Toronto.

1967 The nuclear power station at Douglas Point began operating.

established among the Huron Indians. Later, the Iroquois made war on the Huron and their white allies. They destroyed the missions in 1648 and 1649.

During the 1650's and 1660's, French explorers entered the region north of Lake Superior. These men included Pierre Esprit Radisson and Médard Chouart, Sieur des Groseilliers. Their explorations led to the founding of the Hudson's Bay Company in London (see HUDSON'S BAY COMPANY).

In 1763, at the end of the French and Indian War, France gave the Ontario region to Great Britain. At that time, there were only a few scattered French settlements near what are now Kingston, Niagara Falls, and Windsor. Little further settlement took place until 1784. That year, after the American Revolutionary War, persons loyal to England began arriving from the United States. About 6,000 of these United Empire Loyalists, as they were called, had arrived by 1785. They settled west of the Ottawa River. The Loyalists had lost their homes and wealth. The British government gave them food, clothing, land, livestock, and seed. About 4,000 other settlers also arrived from the United States. See UNITED EMPIRE LOYALIST.

Upper Canada. In 1791, the Ontario region became the separate province of Upper Canada. Newark (now Niagara-on-the-Lake) was the capital. The British government appointed a lieutenant-governor to govern the province. The lieutenant-governor appointed a 7-member legislative council, and the people elected a 16-member legislative assembly. Colonel John Graves Simcoe, the first lieutenant-governor, promoted road-building and expanded settlement. In 1793, Simcoe chose York (now Toronto) as the site for a new capital,

Thousands of Slaves fled from the U.S. to Ontario in the 1850's. Antislavery leader John Brown had many followers around Chatham.

Ontario's Northern Boundary was extended in 1912 from north of the Albany River to Hudson and James bays. The gray area of the map, *left*, shows Ontario from 1867 to 1912, and the light blue area shows the land added in 1912. The map on the *right* shows present-day Ontario.

The Famous Dionne Quintuplets were born at Callander in 1934.

American Forces Captured York (now Toronto), the capital of Upper Canada, during the War of 1812.

Alexander Graham Bell worked on the principle of the telephone in Brantford in 1874.

Callander

HISTORIC ONTARIO

TORONTO ★

Brantford

The Welland Canal, which opened in 1829, links the Great Lakes shipping lanes with the St. Lawrence River.

A Huge Power Plant on the Canadian side of Niagara Falls has produced electricity for Ontario since 1922.

and the government completed moving there in 1797.

Gradually, more settlers arrived, some in organized groups. Others were brought by land-development firms such as the Canada Company. These settlers were assigned farms on land owned by the companies. Many Americans who liked frontier life or wanted more land also came. Sometimes whole communities moved north. Such a group of Pennsylvania Dutch, for example, settled near what is now Kitchener. Men from the Hudson's Bay Company posts in the far north settled with their families in the southern towns. Most of these people were Scottish or English.

The War of 1812 between Great Britain and the United States began 21 years after Upper Canada was created. More than half the people of the colony were former Americans. But most of them were loyal to their new homeland. British and Canadian troops halted invading United States forces in several battles in Upper Canada. See WAR OF 1812 (Chief Battles of the War).

Early Industrial Growth. The population of Upper Canada grew rapidly during the 1820's. Towns such as Bytown (now Ottawa) became thriving centers of trade. Canals, mills and small factories, and roads were built. The Rideau, Trent, and first Welland canals date from this period. In 1825, the Erie Canal linked Lakes Erie and Ontario with New York City. Large groups of immigrants, most of them from Ireland, came after these transportation improvements were made.

Political Unrest. During the 1830's, Upper Canadians became greatly dissatisfied with their government. They elected only the legislative assembly. The real power lay with the lieutenant-governor, who was appointed by the British government. The lieutenant-governor appointed the legislative council and his cabinet. The legislative council generally represented the wealthy and powerful persons of the province. The council often blocked legislation that the people wanted and the assembly had passed. This legislation included building new roads and schools, and providing free land to settlers.

Demands for political reform were ignored by both the provincial and British governments. In 1837, William Lyon Mackenzie, a member of the assembly, and a small group of followers rebelled. British troops put down the uprising easily and quickly. Several rebels were executed, some were imprisoned, and others, including Mackenzie, fled to the United States. See RE-BELLION OF 1837-1838.

After the rebellion, the British government sent the Earl of Durham to investigate the political situation in Upper Canada. Durham urged that Upper Canada and Lower Canada (part of present-day Quebec) be united under one government. He also recommended that the government be fully responsible to the voters. In 1840, the British government passed the Act of Union. The next year, Upper and Lower Canada formed the single province of Canada. By 1849, it had gained fully responsible government. See UNION, ACT OF.

Confederation. In 1864, delegates from the province of Canada proposed a federal union of all the British provinces in eastern North America. All except Prince Edward Island and Newfoundland agreed to join the confederation. On July 1, 1867, the British North America Act created the Dominion of Canada. New Brunswick, Nova Scotia, Ontario, and Quebec became provinces in the Dominion. Ottawa was made the federal capital, and Sir John A. Macdonald of Ontario became the first prime minister of Canada. John S. Macdonald, unrelated to him, was the first prime minister of Ontario. See BRITISH NORTH AMERICA ACT.

Progress as a Province. Ontario's economy grew slowly during the depression that followed confederation. Farming increased with the development of scientific methods and the use of machinery. Ontario's pulp and paper industry began, and woodcutting expanded in the Canadian Shield. During the 1880's, construction of the Canadian Pacific Railway and extension of canals helped attract settlers to western Ontario. Manufacturing increased, but many Ontarians moved to the United States for better job opportunities.

In 1883, the world's richest copper-nickel deposits were found near Sudbury. Major mining operations did not begin until after 1892, when a practical process for separating copper and nickel was developed.

The Early 1900's. The long depression ended in 1897, and manufacturing began to increase rapidly. Cobalt became a thriving mining center after a huge silver deposit was discovered near the city in 1903. Extensive mineral exploration took place throughout the Canadian Shield. Within a few years, many valuable new mineral deposits were discovered. The region soon became one of the world's richest mining areas.

In addition to mining, the pulp and paper industry and other manufacturing activities grew to major importance. Ontario's automobile industry began in 1904. Automobile parts were ferried across the Detroit River from Detroit, Mich., and cars were assembled in Windsor. In 1906, the provincial government established the Hydro-Electric Power Commission of Ontario. This agency developed and expanded Niagara Falls and other hydroelectric sources to provide more power for the growing industries.

In 1912, Ontario's northern boundary was extended from north of the Albany River to Hudson and James bays. This action gave the province its present area. The outbreak of World War I (1914-1918) hastened Ontario's economic growth. Ontario led the provinces in the production of weapons and other military supplies.

During the 1920's, after a short depression, old cities became larger and new ones grew in number. Bush pilots flew land surveyors and prospectors to the northern forest regions, and new mines were developed. Many Finns and Scandinavians, and French Canadians from Quebec, settled there. Industrial activity, especially automobile production, continued to grow. Other important activities included the manufacture of iron and steel, and of pulp and paper. The prosperity ended with the Great Depression of the 1930's. During the 1930's, many Jewish families escaped Nazi persecution in Germany and came to southern Ontario.

The Mid-1900's. During World War II (1939-1945), Ontario's factories, farms, and mines increased production to help arm and feed the Allied armies. Later, hundreds of thousands of Europeans left their war-torn countries and came to live in Ontario. More than half of the 3 million persons who settled in Canada between 1945 and 1970 made their homes in Ontario. Ontario's population rose from about 4 million to 7½ million.

THE PRIME MINISTERS OF ONTARIO

		Party	Term
1.	John S. Macdonald	Liberal	1867-1871
2.	Edward Blake	Liberal	1871-1872
3.	Oliver Mowat	Liberal	1872-1896
4.	Arthur S. Hardy	Liberal	1896-1899
5.	George W. Ross	Liberal	1899-1905
6.	James P. Whitney	Conservative	1905-1914
7.	William H. Hearst	Conservative	1914-1919
8.	Ernest C. Drury	United Farmers of Ontario	1919-1923
9.	George H. Ferguson	Conservative	1923-1930
10.	George S. Henry	Conservative	1930-1934
11.	Mitchell F. Hepburn	Liberal	1934-1942
12.	Gordon D. Conant	Liberal	1942-1943
13.	Harry C. Nixon	Liberal	1943
14.	George A. Drew	Progressive Conservative	1943-1948
15.	Thomas L. Kennedy	Progressive Conservative	1948-1949
16.	Leslie M. Frost	Progressive Conservative	1949-1961
17.	John P. Robarts	Progressive Conservative	1961-1971
18.	William Davis	Progressive Conservative	1971-

In 1945, Canada's first nuclear reactor went into operation near Chalk River. Laboratories there worked to find ways to develop cheap nuclear power for Ontario's expanding industries. By 1960, the station had five experimental reactors and other research facilities, including an atom smasher.

Ontario experienced its greatest economic growth after World War II. By the early 1950's, manufacturing production in the province had doubled. Many mineral discoveries contributed to the economic boom. In 1952, the world's largest single uranium ore deposit was found at Elliot Lake. In 1953, prospectors discovered another huge uranium deposit near Bancroft and a rich zinc-copper field on the shore of Lake Manitouwadge.

Also during the 1950's, pipelines were laid to carry natural gas and oil to Ontario from fields in western Canada. The oil, piped to Sarnia, led to the development of that city's great refining industry. The province's iron and steel industry grew rapidly. Ontario also expanded hydroelectric stations at Niagara Falls and other sites.

In 1954, Toronto and its surrounding communities began to operate under a combined-government plan. Services for the entire area, including police protection and public transportation, are administered by the combined government. Such services as fire protection and health are handled by each community.

Ontario's economic growth continued during the 1960's. Factory production again doubled. The province's growing industries required great increases in electric power. Ontario began to make use of nuclear-power research conducted at the Chalk River reactor. Canada's first nuclear power station, at Rolphton, began operating in 1962. Its success led to the development of the nation's first full-scale nuclear station, which began operating at Douglas Point in 1967. A third nuclear plant, at Pickering, was scheduled to begin operations in 1971.

Many other research programs were started to promote Ontario's industrial growth. In 1966, the Sheridan Park Research Community, consisting of several private industries, set up the first of its multi-million dollar facilities near Toronto.

In 1964, huge deposits of copper, silver, and zinc were discovered near Timmins. An open-pit mine began operating there in 1966.

Automation caused unemployment in Ontario as machines replaced unskilled workers in factories and on farms. In 1965, the provincial and federal governments established a five-year program to fight poverty. The program included development of farmland through better land use and irrigation. Ontario also received federal aid for urban renewal in its rapidly growing cities.

Ontario Today accounts for about half of Canada's manufacturing, a third of the nation's farming, and a fourth of its mining. The province has one of the lowest unemployment rates in Canada. Manufacturing provides jobs for about a fourth of Ontario's workers. The chief industries manufacture automobiles, food products, and iron and steel. Large markets in the United States—plus access to European markets through the St. Lawrence Seaway—assure a continuing demand for Ontario's products in the 1970's.

Tourism is becoming vital to Ontario. The province's northern woods and lakes are attracting an increasing number of visitors. Private and government facilities, including a system of provincial parks and campsites, are being improved.

Ontario strongly supports progress in its schools and spends more than 40 per cent of its budget on education. From 1945 to 1970, the province combined most of its school boards, reducing the number from 5,649 to 175. In addition, 20 regional colleges of applied arts and technology have been established. They prepare students for technical and managerial jobs.

Ontario faces several problems in the 1970's. Along with rapid industrial growth have come overcrowded cities and polluted air and water. Nearly 90 per cent of Ontario's people live in the southern 10 per cent of the province. In spite of the prosperity in Ontario, poverty exists among more than 20 per cent of the population. In 1970, the provincial and federal governments extended their antipoverty program through March, 1975.

NORMAN L. NICHOLSON, ROBERT F. NIELSEN, and JOHN T. SAYWELL

ONTARIO/Study Aids

Related Articles in WORLD BOOK include:

BIOGRAPHIES

Blake, Edward
Bowell, Sir Mackenzie
Brown, George
Cartwright, Sir Richard J.
Dent, John C.
Diefenbaker, John G.
Durham, Earl of
Fleming, Sir Sandford
Gordon, Charles W.
Gould, Glenn
Hughes, Sir Samuel
Kerwin, Patrick

King, W. L. Mackenzie
Macdonald, Sir John A.
Mackenzie, Alexander
Mackenzie, William Lyon
Macmillan, Sir Ernest C.
MacPhail, Agnes C.
Massey, Vincent
Mowat, Sir Oliver
Mulock, Sir William
Pearson, Lester Bowles
Simcoe, John G.
Thomson, Tom

CITIES

Brantford
Burlington
Cornwall
Hamilton
Kingston
Kitchener
London
Niagara Falls

Oshawa
Ottawa
Peterborough
Saint Catharines
Sarnia

Sault Sainte Marie
Sudbury
Thunder Bay
Toronto
Windsor

HISTORY

Canada, History of
Fort Frontenac

Rebellion of 1837-1838
United Empire Loyalist

PHYSICAL FEATURES

Canadian Shield
Detroit River
Georgian Bay
Hudson Bay
James Bay
Lake Erie

Lake Huron
Lake of the Woods
Lake Ontario
Lake Saint Clair
Lake Superior

Manitoulin Islands
Moose River
Muskoka Lakes
Niagara Falls and Niagara River

ONTARIO, LAKE

Ottawa River	Saint Lawrence	Saint Marys River
Rainy Lake	River	Thousand Islands

PRODUCTS

For Ontario's rank in production, see:

Automobile	Forest and	Milk	Tomato
Bean	Forest Products	Paper	Turkey
Cattle	Gold	Publishing	Uranium
Cheese	Grape	Salt	Vegetable
Cherry	Iron and Steel	Silver	Wine
Copper	Maple Sugar	Tobacco	Zinc

UNIVERSITIES AND COLLEGES

Ontario's degree-granting universities and colleges have separate articles in WORLD BOOK. They are listed in a table in the *Education* section of this article.

OTHER RELATED ARTICLES

Rideau Canal	Soo Canals
Saint Lawrence Seaway	Welland Ship Canal

Outline

I. Government
- A. Lieutenant-Governor
- B. Prime Minister
- C. Legislative Assembly
- D. Courts
- E. Local Government
- F. Taxation
- G. Politics

II. People

III. Education
- A. Schools
- B. Libraries
- C. Museums

IV. A Visitor's Guide
- A. Places to Visit
- B. Annual Events

V. The Land
- A. Land Regions
- B. Shoreline and Coastline
- C. Rivers, Waterfalls, and Lakes

VI. Climate

VII. Economy
- A. Natural Resources
- B. Manufacturing
- C. Agriculture
- D. Mining
- E. Forestry
- F. Fishing Industry
- G. Trapping
- H. Electric Power
- I. Transportation
- J. Communication

VIII. History

Questions

What is Ontario's chief manufacturing activity?

Where do the great majority of Ontarians live?

How did Ontario pioneer in Canada's development of cheap nuclear power?

What is Ontario's *Golden Horseshoe?* Where is it?

What is Ontario's most famous annual event?

What caused the Rebellion of 1837-1838?

What is the major mineral product of Ontario?

How do ocean vessels reach Ontario's inland ports?

How much of Canada's manufacturing, mining, and farming does Ontario account for?

When did Ontario's greatest period of economic growth begin?

Books for Young Readers

BRAITHWAITE, MAX and LAMBERT, R. S. *We Live in Ontario.* Book Society of Canada (Aigincourt), 1957.

BURNFORD, SHEILA. *The Incredible Journey.* Little, Brown (Toronto), 1961.

CRAIG, JOHN E. *The Long Return.* McClelland (Toronto), 1959.

HOLLING, HOLLING C. *Paddle-to-the-Sea.* Allen (Toronto), 1941.

McPHEDRAN, MARIE. *Cargoes on the Great Lakes.* Macmillan (Toronto), 1952.

MEADER, STEPHEN W. *Trap-lines North: A True Story of the Canadian Woods.* McClelland (Toronto), 1946.

PINKERTON, KATHRENE. *Adventure North.* McClelland (Toronto), 1940.

REID, DOROTHY M. *Tales of Nanabozho.* Univ. of Toronto Press (Toronto), 1963.

SETON, ERNEST T. *Two Little Savages: Being the Adventures of Two Boys Who Lived as Indians and What They Learned.* Doubleday (Toronto), 1959. First published in 1903.

THOMPSON, STUART L. *Outdoor Rambles.* Longmans (Toronto), 1958.

Books for Older Readers

FOX, WILLIAM S. *The Bruce Beckons: The Story of Lake Huron's Great Peninsula.* Rev. & enl. ed. Univ. of Toronto (Toronto), 1962.

GUILLET, EDWIN C. *Early Life in Upper Canada.* Univ. of Toronto (Toronto), 1963.

JAMESON, ANNA B. *Winter Studies and Summer Rambles in Canada.* Nelson (Toronto), 1943. First published in 1838.

LANGTON, ANNE. *A Gentlewoman in Upper Canada: Journals.* Ed. by Hugh H. Langton. Clarke, Irwin, 1950.

LEACOCK, STEPHEN B. *Sunshine Sketches of a Little Town.* McClelland (Toronto), 1948.

MOODIE, SUSANNA. *Roughing It in the Bush: Or, Forest Life in Canada.* McClelland (Toronto), 1962. First published in 1852.

QUIMBY, GEORGE I. *Indian Life in the Upper Great Lakes: 11,000 B.C. to A.D. 1800.* Univ. of Toronto (Toronto), 1960.

SLATER, PATRICK. *Yellow Briar: A Story of the Irish on the Canadian Countryside.* Allen, T. (Toronto), 1933.

ONTARIO, LAKE. See LAKE ONTARIO.

ONTOLOGY. See METAPHYSICS (Branches).

ONWARD, CHRISTIAN SOLDIERS. See HYMN.

ONYX, *AHN icks,* is a term used loosely to apply to a banded marble and also to agate, a fine-grained variety of quartz (see AGATE).

Ordinary onyx of quartz or agate is dyed black and white, green and white, or red and white, and so on. *Sardonyx* is brown and white onyx. Onyx is strong and hard and takes a high polish. It is widely used in the carving of cameos and intaglios. Today, jewelers refer to dyed, single-color agate as *onyx*. When they speak simply of onyx, they mean the black stone. *Green onyx* is the same stone dyed green.

Onyx marble (Mexican onyx) is a variety of calcite marble which is found on the walls of caves. Mexican onyx shows a banding like that of agate, but it is much coarser. The colors of Mexican onyx range from white to green, red, and brown. Much of this soft onyx marble is cut into gem stones, colored with an aniline dye, then set in inexpensive native silver jewelry. The stones are brittle and not durable. Mexican onyx is also used as a decorative stone.   FREDERICK H. POUGH

See also CAMEO; GEM (color picture); SARDONYX.

OOSTENDE. See OSTEND.

OOZE is a name for the mud found on the bottom of the ocean in deep waters. One variety of this mud consists of red clay and occurs extensively on the bottom of the Pacific Ocean. Another variety is made up mostly of shells and skeletons of tiny sea organisms called *foraminifera, radiolaria,* and *diatoms.* All three are termed *plankton,* which is the name for helpless forms of life which cannot swim, but can only float in the water and drift with currents. The foraminifera make their shells from calcium carbonate contained in solution in the sea water. A type of limestone called *nummulitic limestone* is made up mostly of the shells. The hard parts of the radiolaria and diatoms usually contain silicon.

The term ooze is also used for any mud, either on the surface of the earth, or in the beds of rivers, streams, ponds, or lakes.　　　　　ELDRED D. WILSON

See also DIATOM; PLANKTON.

OPA. See PRICE CONTROL.

OPAL is a gem stone that contains a rainbow of colors. But it is made mostly of the elements of common sand, or silica. Opals may be black, brown, or white in background. But cut and polished opals reflect many colors when they are held to the light. The opal is the birthstone for the month of October.

The most prized opals are the deep-glowing black gems from New South Wales, Australia. The finest of these stones are lightened by brilliant flashes of reds and yellows in addition to greens and blues.

The opal is unique among gem stones, because it is not found in nature in the form of crystals. Instead it is found in irregular patches, often filling cavities in rocks. Gemmologists speak of an opal as a hydrated silica gel, because it contains water along with the silica. The water content makes some opals a risky buy. Many of them *check* (crack) after a long time in dry air. The checking occurs as the water in the gel dries out.

Most scientists believe the color flashes are caused by the water in the gems. Each of the different layers of silica gel in an opal has a different *index of refraction*. That is, it bends light at a different angle. The angle varies according to the amount of water the layer contains. Scientists believe that these many different bendings break up the light which strikes the stone into its various rainbow colors.

There are many different kinds of opals. They are classified according to the color of their background and the brilliance of the light rays that they reflect. Opals that give off brilliant flashes of color are *precious* opals. The black opals of New South Wales and the white opals of Europe, Queensland, and Mexico are examples of precious opals. The *girasol* is a precious opal. Its background is bluish-white with reddish reflections. The *common* opal is usually not a precious stone and shows no colors. The *fire* opal is a variety of common opal. It is a hyacinth red—often without color flashes. Other common opals may be transparent, and red, brown, green, or yellow in color. Some opals are almost colorless.

Since the beauty of the opal lies in its internal color flashes, it is never cut with facets, like a diamond. Instead, it is cut with a gently rounded convex surface.

Large opals of the world include a Hungarian opal that weighs 594 grams, now in the Museum of Natural History in Vienna. The *Roebling* opal, which was found in Nevada, is the most beautiful American opal. It is almost pitch black, with color flashes of great brilliancy. It weighs 530 grams and is on display at the United States National Museum.　　　FREDERICK H. POUGH

See also GEM (color picture).

OPAL GLASS. See GLASSWARE (Milk Glass, or Opal Glass).

OPECHANCANOUGH. See INDIAN WARS (Jamestown).

OPEN-CIRCUIT CELL. See BATTERY.

OPEN CITY is a city of a nation at war that is declared by that nation to be undefended and not used for military purposes. *Undefended* means that the city is open for the enemy to enter and occupy.

A city is declared open to avoid enemy bombardment and to preserve human life and valued art, churches, and historic sites. International agreements state the conditions for and treatment due an open city. France declared Paris an open city in June, 1940, after Germany defeated the French army.　　STEFAN T. POSSONY

OPEN-DOOR POLICY is a term used in international relations. It means that powerful countries have equal opportunities to trade with colonial, or so-called backward, countries. When countries agree to observe the Open-Door Policy in a given area, they are simply agreeing to permit their merchants and investors to trade freely in that area.

John Hay, United States secretary of state, started the idea of the Open Door in 1899. At that time, several Western powers had special interests in China. Each power was trying to get all the trading rights for itself. The U.S. secretary of state sent notes to the competing powers, asking them to maintain complete equality for all nations that wished to trade with China. The powers accepted Hay's proposal and signed treaties agreeing to observe the Open-Door Policy.

Since that time, the Open-Door Policy has been used in other areas.　　　　　　DWIGHT E. LEE

See also CHINA (Fall of the Manchus).

OPEN-END INVESTMENT COMPANY. See MUTUAL FUND.

OPEN-HEARTH FURNACE. See IRON AND STEEL (Methods of Making Steel).

OPEN HOUSING refers to the civil rights belief that a person may live wherever he chooses and can afford to live. In the United States, the federal government and many local and state governments have passed laws and regulations to protect this right. The laws prohibit discrimination in the sale and rental of housing on the basis of race, religion, or nationality. Open housing laws are sometimes referred to as *fair housing* laws or *open occupancy* laws.

The U.S. Civil Rights Act of 1968 contained the first national open housing law of the 1900's. The act prohibits discrimination in the sale or rental of about 80 per cent of all housing in the United States. It applies to all housing except (1) owner-occupied dwellings of four or fewer units, such as boarding houses; and (2) single-family houses sold or rented without the aid of a broker or realtor. In June, 1968, the Supreme Court of the United States went beyond the 1968 open housing law. The court ruled that a federal law passed in 1866 prohibits racial discrimination in the sale and rental of all property.

OPEN-PIT MINE. See IRON AND STEEL (How Iron Is Mined); MINING (Kinds of Mining; picture).

OPEN SEASON. See GAME (Game Laws).

OPEN SHOP is a term applied to any business that employs both union and nonunion workers. It is the opposite of a *closed shop*, where only union members may be employed. A union may represent the workers in an open shop if a majority of the workers belong to the union. But no one must be required to belong to the union in order to obtain employment.　　GERALD G. SOMERS

See also CLOSED SHOP.

OPENING OF THE WEST. See WESTERN FRONTIER LIFE; WESTWARD MOVEMENT.

NBC

Gian Carlo Menotti Wrote _Amahl and the Night Visitors_ for Television.

OPERA. The Latin word for "work" is _opus_. The plural of _opus_ is _opera_, meaning "works." And truly an opera is more than just a single work. It is a combination of works. It contains the orchestral and vocal music which might be heard at a symphony concert. But in addition to this, it offers the staging, the actions, and the characterizations of fine drama. An opera is a play set to music, a kind of music drama. It combines the excitement of drama with the power of music.

Forms of Opera. There are several kinds of operatic composition, and different names are used in the various countries to describe these types. _Grand opera_ is opera in which usually every word is sung. But there are exceptions, as in _Fidelio_ by Beethoven, where the dialogue, which is very important, is spoken. Even the _recitative_ parts—the speeches which are not set to a tune—are accompanied by music. _Opéra comique_ is the French name for opera in which the dialogue is spoken instead of sung. French light opera which contains much of the comic element is called _opéra bouffe_. Italian light opera

is called _opera buffa_, but in the Italian form of the light opera the dialogue is sung, not spoken.

With the exception of grand opera, these terms are little used in America. _Light opera_, or _comic opera_, is the name applied to operas in which comedy is emphasized and in which there is some spoken dialogue. Examples are Gilbert and Sullivan's _Mikado_ and Reginald de Koven's _Robin Hood_. _Operetta_ is a common name for light opera with some comedy elements, but with the romantic quality emphasized. _Blossom Time_, based on Schubert's life and using his melodies, is an example of an operetta. _The Student Prince_, a musical version of _Old Heidelberg_, is also an operetta.

Another form of musical play popular with Americans is the so-called _musical comedy_. It has elaborate scenery and showy costumes, but only a sketchy and usually farcical plot. Victor Herbert composed the music for numerous musical comedies, but many of these really deserve to be called operettas.

Development of the Opera. The ancient Greek

596

dramas had choruses and were operatic in character. But the opera as we know it today is of modern date and of Italian origin. The first opera, *Dafne*, was produced in 1597, but has since been lost. Its words were written by Rinuccini, a poet. Most of its music was composed by Jacopo Peri, one of the most celebrated musicians of his time. The orchestra consisted of four instruments— a harpsichord, a harp, a violoncello, and a lute. There was no attempt at *airs* (musical themes), and the dialogue was rendered without regular rhythm or melody. The birth of real opera came in 1600 when *Euridice*, composed by Peri and Giulio Caccini, was produced as the entertainment at a royal wedding.

In 1607 Claudio Monteverdi (1567-1643) of Milan produced his *Orfeo*. Monteverdi improved opera by adding many instruments to the orchestra, and also by giving more flow and expression to the recitative. Alessandro Scarlatti of Naples (1659-1725) wrote many beautiful melodies. He was one of the first opera composers to make the airs harmonize with the dialogue.

Opera was also making great strides in Germany, France, and England. Jean Baptiste Lully (1633?-1687) introduced the ballet in France. In England the operas of Henry Purcell (1659?-1695) showed boldness of thought and dramatic planning. But the dominating personality of the German composer Handel (1685-1759) overshadowed the influence that Purcell might have had over English music. Today Handel's operas are not often heard, because they lack dramatic power.

In the 1700's, the German composer Gluck (1714-1787) brought about reforms in operatic music. He tried to make the music, voices, and dance of his operas express the dramatic situations. His most famous works include *Alceste* and *Orfeo ed Euridice*. Gluck influenced Mozart, whose *Don Giovanni* and *The Marriage of Figaro* are among the masterpieces of German opera. Other important German operas include Beethoven's *Fidelio* and Weber's *Der Freischütz*.

The Italian style of opera flourished again in the 1800's and early 1900's. Leaders here were Rossini, Verdi, Puccini, Mascagni, and others. In Germany, Richard Wagner made an outstanding contribution to the development of opera. Every composer since has shown some trace of his remarkable influence. Wagner believed that the arts of music, action, poetry, and scenery should stand on equal footing in opera. And in the music of his operas there is a flow of many melodies which work together into one glorious, harmonious whole. His outstanding works represent the height of dramatic perfection, and are best-described by the name which he gave them—*music drama*.

Many notable operas have been produced since 1900. Among these are *Salomé* and *Der Rosenkavalier*, by Richard Strauss; *The Girl of the Golden West* and *Madame Butterfly* by Giacomo Puccini; *Pelléas et Mélisande*, by Claude Debussy; *The Medium* and *Amahl and the Night Visitors*, by Gian Carlo Menotti; *The Turn of the Screw*, by Benjamin Britten; and *Susannah*, by Carlisle Floyd.

Some of the Famous Operas

Aïda, *ah E dah*, is an Italian grand opera composed by Giuseppe Verdi (1813-1901) to celebrate the opening of the Grand Opera House at Cairo, Egypt, and the Suez Canal. It was first produced in 1871. Ismail Pasha, the khedive of Egypt, chose Verdi for this honor. Today

Aïda is one of the most popular of all operas. Its scenes are laid at Memphis and at Thebes.

The opera relates the story of the slave Aïda (soprano), daughter of the king of Ethiopia, and her lover Rhadamès (tenor), captain of the Egyptian Royal Guard. Amneris (mezzo-soprano), daughter of the Pharaoh, is also in love with Rhadamès. She plots to win the handsome young man for herself. But the lovers never falter in their mutual love, and the curtain falls upon their death song ("O terra addio"), which they sing together.

The opera contains many passages of great beauty. The triumphal march of the trumpeters in Act II is known to all music lovers. Rhadamès' aria "Celeste Aïda" ("Heavenly Aïda") is a favorite with many tenors. Another favorite is the soprano aria, "Ritorna vincitor" ("Return Victorious").

Barber of Seville is a comic grand opera of the Italian school. It was composed by Gioacchino Rossini (1792-1868) and was first produced in Rome in 1816. Its scenes are laid in Seville, Spain, in the 1600's. The story was taken from Beaumarchais' *The Barber of Seville* and it is light and sparkling throughout. Mozart's *The Marriage of Figaro*, based on another Beaumarchais comedy, concerns the same characters in other episodes.

Rossini's plot is concerned with the attempt of Count Almaviva (tenor) to woo the wealthy and beautiful Rosina (soprano). Complications appear in the form of Rosina's guardian, Dr. Bartolo (bass), who wishes to marry her himself. The Count wins the lady through the help of Figaro (baritone), a barber. Figaro's preposterous schemes create many laughs at the expense of Basilio (bass), a singing master. With all its hilarity, the opera has an excellent score.

Two of the most popular melodies of this opera occur in the first act. One is Figaro's very fast "Largo al factotum" ("Room for the Factotum"), which leaves all but the greatest singers gasping for breath. The other is Rosina's "Una voce poco fa." During the famous music lesson scene in Act II, the soprano often sings an aria of her choosing.

Boris Godunov is a tragic grand opera in Russian, composed by Modest Mussorgsky (1839-1881). It is considered Mussorgsky's masterpiece. The story is based on a play by Alexander Pushkin. The opera was first produced at the Imperial Opera House in Saint Petersburg. After Mussorgsky's death, Nikolai Rimski-Korsakov revised the long opera. Many critics believe he took out much of the opera's strength, but it is usually the revised version that is offered on the stage.

Boris Godunov centers around the mad Czar Boris of Russia, and is partly historical. The scene is Russia and Poland of 1598 to 1605. Boris (bass) is a privy councilor of the Czar Feodor. He secretly orders the czar's only son Dmitri, to be killed. When the czar dies, Boris takes the throne. In a convent, meanwhile, Gregory (tenor) learns of Dmitri's murder. He is about Dmitri's age, and so he spreads the rumor that the boy is alive. He convinces the crowds that he, Gregory, is Dmitri and starts a march to Moscow. Boris hears of this and wonders if murdered boys can come to life. The noblemen see his agitation. Boris counsels his son Theodore to be a good ruler. And then his agony is so great that he falls dead. The music

OPERA

and choruses throughout this opera are national in character and create magnificent effects.

Carmen is a French tragic grand opera founded upon Prosper Mérimée's novel of the same name. It was composed by Georges Bizet (1838-1875), and has been exceedingly popular since its first production in Paris in 1875. The scene is Seville, Spain, about 1820.

The heroine, Carmen (mezzo-soprano), is a Spanish cigarette girl of fiery temperament and wonderful fascination. Her charms win her the love of Don José (tenor), a corporal of the dragoons. José forgets honor and duty in his mad love for Carmen and joins a band of smugglers. After wrecking her lover's career, Carmen turns to a new man, the handsome and popular bull fighter Escamillo (baritone). Don José finally stabs the heartless girl to death outside the bullfighting arena. The victorious Escamillo emerges with the shouting mob to find his rival sobbing over Carmen's body.

The opera is full of color and dramatic interest, and the music is richly melodious. The famous "Toreador" song of Escamillo and the "Habanera" of Carmen are enduringly popular. Other favorites include the many stirring choruses, the overture, and the exquisite aria sung in the third act by the soprano role, Micaela.

Cavalleria Rusticana, *KAH vah lay RE ah ROO ste-KAH nah*, is a colorful one-act grand opera in Italian, composed by Pietro Mascagni (1863-1945). Its title means *Rustic Chivalry*. Its first presentation, at Rome in 1890, brought the composer from obscurity to fame. The words of the opera were written by two of Mascagni's friends. They based their work on a tale of Sicilian life by Giovanni Verga.

Turiddu (tenor), the handsome young lover of the story, goes away to the wars. While he is away, his sweetheart Lola (mezzo-soprano) marries Alfio (baritone), the village carter. When Turiddu returns, he consoles himself with a beautiful village maiden, Santuzza (soprano). But the fickle Lola soon wins back his love. In despair, Santuzza tells Lola's husband of her unhappiness. The jealous Alfio kills Turiddu in a duel with knives. At one point during the opera's single act, the stage is empty. It is during this interval that the orchestra plays the very popular "Intermezzo."

The opera has swift movement, dramatic interest, and attractive melodies throughout.

Das Rheingold was first performed at Munich in 1869. Wagner considered it a prelude to the Ring cycle of operas. The cycle opens with the theft of a treasure (the Rhinegold) which has been guarded under the Rhine River by the three Rhine-Maidens. This treasure, when fashioned into the shape of a ring, would give its owner great wealth and power. But whoever would have it must first give up love. The dwarf Alberich (baritone) gives up love and takes the treasure to Nibelheim, the land of the dwarfs (Nibelungs). At the same time, in Valhalla the god Wotan (baritone-bass) must give up the goddess of love, Freia, to the giants in order to fulfill a promise. At length the giants agree to take the Rhinegold instead. So Wotan persuades Alberich to change himself into a toad and then captures him and steals the treasure. The giant Fafner (bass) slays his own brother Fasolt (bass) and leaves with the treasures.

Daughter of the Regiment (La Fille du Régiment) is a French comic opera composed by Gaetano Donizetti (1797-1848). The opera was first given in 1840. It tells the story of an orphan girl who is adopted by a regiment in Napoleon's army. A young peasant lad falls in love with her and joins the army to win her hand.

A Ballet Scene Is Performed in Act IV of *Carmen*, Bizet's French Opera with a Spanish Setting.

Der Freischütz is a romantic German music drama by Carl Maria von Weber (1786-1826). The opera is important because it opened the way for the supreme music dramas which later came from Wagner. *Der Freischütz* was first performed at Berlin in 1821. Its title means *one who uses magic bullets*. According to legend, anyone who sold his soul to the Demon Hunter would receive seven such bullets in exchange. After using the seventh, he would have to give up his soul to the demon. He could save himself only by persuading another person to sell his soul to the demon. Then the *Freischütz*, or freeshooter, would receive seven new bullets and longer life.

The opera is laid in Bohemia, about 1750. The lovers are Max and Agathe. Agathe has promised her hand to Max if he should win a shooting contest soon to be held. Max is introduced to the demon Samiel by his friend Caspar and agrees to sell his soul for the bullets. At the contest Max aims his seventh bullet at a dove (Agathe in another shape). Agathe faints, and then Caspar is claimed by Samiel. Max is banished, but is brought back after a hermit has revived Agathe. And the two live happily ever after.

Die Götterdämmerung (Twilight of the Gods) was first given at Bayreuth in 1876. It contains the impressive "Siegfried's Rhine Journey" and "Brünnhilde's Immolation." Gunther, king of the Gibichungs, plots to win both Brünnhilde and the Ring from Siegfried. He gives Siegfried a magic potion to drink, and gets Brünnhilde away. But Siegfried must return the Ring to the Rhine-Maidens who first guarded it—only then could the curse of the Ring be lifted from earth and Valhalla. Siegfried cannot be persuaded to give up the ring. During a hunt, Siegfried is killed by Hagen, son of the dwarf Alberich. The faithful Brünnhilde builds a funeral pyre for Siegfried, then rides into it herself on her steed. When the fire has died down, the Rhine-Maidens come and take the ring. As had been foretold, Valhalla goes up in flames. Now only the power of Love remains to rule the world. This opera was the last in Wagner's Ring cycle.

Die Meistersinger (The Mastersingers) is a German music drama by Wagner. It was first performed at Munich in 1868. This opera holds a unique place in the long list of Wagner's works. It is the only opera he wrote that is based on a humorous theme. In addition it is the only one that uses actual history — the trade guild called "Die Meistersinger" (see MASTERSINGER). The music is appropriate to the theme, and is often used on the concert stage. The popular "Overture" contains the theme of the tenor's finest aria, the "Prize Song."

The story tells of the love of Sir Walter von Stolzing (tenor) for the lovely Eva (soprano). But Eva's father has promised to give her hand in marriage to the man who should win a song contest to take place soon. Walter studies to become a meistersinger, so that he can enter the contest. Nevertheless, he fails to qualify for the guild. The time of the contest arrives. Through the intervention of the cobbler Hans Sachs (bass), Walter is permitted to sing the song, "Prize Song," he has composed. He wins the contest, Eva's hand, and membership in the singer's guild.

Don Giovanni is considered one of the greatest operas ever written. It is an Italian romantic work and was composed by Wolfgang Amadeus Mozart (1756-1791). It was first performed in Prague in 1787. The opera tells the adventures of a gay lover, the nobleman Don Giovanni. The scene is laid in Seville about 1650.

The handsome Giovanni (baritone) has broken the hearts of countless girls. As the opera opens, he breaks the heart of Donna Anna (soprano) and then kills her father Don Pedro (bass) in a duel. Only Donna Elvira (soprano), whom he deserted during a previous elopement, remains true to him. Finally the lover crowns his past misdeeds by mistreating the peasant girl Zerlina (soprano), and all the angry young ladies plan vengeance. During his nightly wanderings with his servant Leporello (bass), Giovanni has invited the statue of Don Pedro to dinner. In the final scene, the statue walks into the banquet hall. The floor opens up, and flames from the underworld are seen. Then demon hands drag the evil scoundrel down to his doom.

Falstaff was the last opera composed by Giuseppe Verdi. The man who had written so many tragic operas chose to turn to comedy when he was over eighty years of age. And it turned out to be a masterpiece. Verdi based his last opera on two of Shakespeare's plays, *Merry Wives of Windsor* and *King Henry IV*. The amusing opera was first presented at Milan in 1893.

In the opera, the fat Falstaff gets himself in trouble by writing exactly the same love letters to two married women. A group of angry men are out to avenge the prank. During the hilarity that follows, Falstaff is hidden in a laundry basket and dumped into the Thames River. He is finally punished when the entire company, dressed as fairies, encounter him in a dark wood. Soon all the confusion is settled, and Falstaff agrees to behave himself in the future.

Faust, *foust,* is a tragic grand opera in French, adapted from Goethe's tragedy. It was composed by Charles Gounod (1818-1893) and first presented in Paris in 1859.

Faust (tenor) is an old man, weary of books and learning and disappointed with life. The devil, Mephistopheles (bass), appears to him and shows him a vision of the beautiful Marguerite (soprano). Faust is persuaded to sign a contract with Mephistopheles, and the old man becomes young again, giving himself up to the pleasures of youth and love. In the end, Marguerite dies in prison to the chant of a heavenly choir. Then Mephistopheles carries out the terms of the contract by dragging Faust down with him into the regions below. Other important characters are Dame Martha (alto), companion of Marguerite; the heroine's brother Valentine (baritone), who is killed by Faust in a duel; and Siebel, a friend of Valentine. The role of Siebel is usually acted by a woman, because the music for that part is written for a mezzo-soprano.

The popularity of *Faust* is due to its exquisite music. Marguerite's spinning-wheel song, "Once There Lived a King in Thule," "Jewel Song," the stirring "Soldiers' Chorus" of the fourth act, and the lovers' duet "Forever Thine" are among the favorite melodies of the opera.

Fidelio is the only opera composed by Ludwig van Beethoven (1770-1827). It is a romantic opera in German, and was first performed at Vienna in 1805. "Fidelio" and "Leonore No. 3" are two of its four overtures. The overtures are heard more often than the opera itself.

The scene is laid at a prison near Seville, Spain, in the

A Splendid Minuet Closes the First Act of Mozart's Witty yet Tragic Opera, *Don Giovanni*.

1700's. The Spanish nobleman Florestan (tenor) has been unjustly imprisoned by the governor of the prison, Pizarro (bass). Pizarro has told people that Florestan is dead. But the prisoner's faithful wife Leonore (soprano) refuses to believe this. She disguises herself as the youth Fidelio and gets work at the prison. The Minister of the Interior is soon to come to the prison to investigate reports of Florestan's death. Pizarro decides to kill the prisoner himself. Leonore intercedes. The Minister arrives just in time to prevent the killing. He frees Florestan and punishes Pizarro.

Fra Diavolo, *frah de AH voh loh*, is a French comic grand opera, composed by Daniel F. Auber (1782-1871) and first produced in Paris in 1830. The story is laid in Terracina, Italy, in the 1800's. It tells the exploits of an Italian bandit named Michele Pezza. The bandit earned the name Fra Diavolo (brother devil) because of his cruelties and because he had once been a monk.

In Auber's opera, Fra Diavolo (tenor) mingles with society as the "Marquis of San Marco" at the same time that he is directing a band of robbers under cover. A large reward has been offered for the robber's arrest. Lorenzo (tenor) hopes to win the money so that he may marry Zerlina (soprano), daughter of the innkeeper, Matteo (bass). But Zerlina's father has promised her to a rich peasant.

The opera pictures the escapades of Fra Diavolo and his followers. Finally Lorenzo is successful in capturing them and revealing the true identity of the "Marquis." Thus he wins the hand of Zerlina. This opera has long been a favorite because of its tuneful score and sparkling gaiety.

Girl of the Golden West is a sentimental grand opera in Italian, with music by Giacomo Puccini. It is founded on David Belasco's play of the same name. The opera was first presented in New York in 1910. It tells a tale of the California mining camps of 1849-1850. The hero Ramerrez (tenor) is a notorious bandit who goes by the

name of Dick Johnson. The heroine is Minnie (soprano), an attractive and spirited girl who has been running her father's barroom since his death. Minnie is loved by both the bandit and the sheriff, Jack Rance (baritone). But Minnie loves only Johnson. When the sheriff discovers Johnson's true identity, he is more anxious than ever to capture him and put him out of the way.

In the meantime, Johnson's love for Minnie has made him resolve to lead a better life. But Minnie learns who Johnson is when he is trapped in her cabin by the sheriff's men. She casts him off, but later saves his life by cheating cleverly in a poker game with Rance. Finally Rance persuades the miners to hang the outlaw. But Minnie arrives in time to save his life again, and the two lovers go away together.

Hänsel und Gretel (Hansel and Gretel) is a German opera based on the fairy tale that is familiar to children throughout the world. Its music was composed by Engelbert Humperdinck (1854-1921). The opera was first produced at Weimar in 1893, and two years later was given in English in New York.

Hansel and Gretel are the children of a poor broommaker. In the operatic version, they become lost in the woods after leaving home to hunt for strawberries. Night descends upon the forest, but the two children sleep safely, watched by their guardian angels. In the morning they see a neat little house made all of candy and surrounded by a fence of gingerbread boys and girls. Within the house lives a wicked old witch who is planning to make gingerbread of Hansel and Gretel. Finally Gretel tricks the witch into peering into the oven. Then she gives the witch a great shove into the oven. The oven falls apart, the gingerbread boys and girls come to life, and the broommaker and his wife find their children safe and sound.

Humperdinck's opera is filled with the folk songs of his country, and its melodies are hummed by adults and children everywhere. One of the best-known is the

"Children's Prayer," a duet for soprano and mezzo-soprano.

Il Trovatore, *eel TROH vah TO ray*, is a melodious romantic grand opera in the Italian style, composed by Giuseppe Verdi. It was first given in Rome in 1853.

The opera takes place in Spain in the 1400's. The lovers are the troubadour Manrico (tenor) and Duchess Leonora (soprano), lady in waiting to a princess of the House of Aragon. Manrico is a chieftain of the Prince of Biscay. Everyone believes he is the son of the gypsy Azucena (mezzo-soprano). Actually, he is the second brother of the Count di Luna, now dead. Manrico's brother is the present Count di Luna (baritone), and the villain of the story. Azucena's mother had been burned at the stake as a witch. The frenzied Azucena had then stolen the old count's son with the intention of throwing him into the flames as vengeance. Instead, she had thrown her own child. Keeping the mistake to herself, she had carried off Manrico and raised him as her son.

The opera records the efforts of the young Count di Luna to win Leonora for himself. He has thrown Manrico and Azucena into prison. Leonora finally promises to marry the Count if he will release Manrico. Then she secretly takes poison. At her lover's release, she falls dead at his feet. The Count then orders Manrico executed. Dragging the weary Azucena to the window of her prison, he bids her witness the death of her son. "You have killed your brother" cries the gypsy, and falls dead. She leaves the Count to the bitterness of remorse and futile regret.

The opera is based on a Spanish drama of the same name by Antonio Gutiérrez. The title means *The Troubadour*. The complicated story provides a setting for many dramatic melodies. Some of the best-known songs include the "Anvil Chorus," "Miserere," "Farewell to Leonora," the duet "Home to Our Mountains," and Azucena's impassioned aria "Stride la vampa" ("Fierce Flames Are Soaring").

I Pagliacci, *ee pah LYAH che*, is an Italian tragic grand opera consisting of a prologue song and two short acts. It is often presented in a double bill with *Cavalleria Rusticana*. Both the book and music were written by Ruggiero Leoncavallo (1858-1919). The opera was first produced in Milan in 1892. The opera shows a play within a play, in which the leading characters see their tragic parts become real.

The action takes place in Calabria, Italy, near the small village of Montalto. The leader of a troupe of players, Canio (tenor) suspects that his wife Nedda (soprano) is untrue to him. She really does have a lover, a villager named Silvio (baritone). In the play given by the troupe, Canio plays the part of Pagliaccio, who is jealous of his wife Columbine. Columbine is loved by Harlequin (played by Peppe, tenor). The clown Taddeo is played by Tonio.

Tonio opens the opera with the melodious baritone "Prologue," which sets the mood for the drama that follows. He tries to make love to Nedda, but she cuts his face with a whip. Tonio avenges himself by telling Canio that his wife has a lover. Canio returns from a tavern in a jealous fury. But he arrives too late to find out who the lover is. Act II shows the play-within-a-play. It comes to a tragic climax when Canio, unable to restrain himself, steps out of his part and stabs Nedda to death. Silvio springs from the audience with his dagger drawn, but Canio quickly stabs him. "The comedy is ended," exclaims the crazed Canio as the curtain falls.

Pagliacci contains one of the really superb tenor arias of all opera, the "Vesti la giubba" ("On With the Play"), sung by Canio. This aria, and indeed the entire role of Canio, is often identified with the great tenor Enrico Caruso, who demonstrated its magnificence to the fullest.

Jewels of the Madonna is a tragic grand opera in Italian which was composed by Ermanno Wolf-Ferrari (1876-1948). It was first presented in Berlin in 1911. The music of this opera is somewhat commonplace, but the story has much action and lurid emotion.

It is a tale of life in Naples, where the beautiful but wayward Maliella (soprano) lives with her foster mother Carmela (soprano). Maliella is loved by both Rafaele (baritone), leader of the secret Camorrists, and her half-brother Gennaro (tenor). The girl makes Rafaele promise to steal for her the jewels that adorn the statue of the Madonna. Then she taunts Gennaro and boasts that someone else loves her enough to steal the Madonna's jewels for her. Gennaro yields to the suggestion, and that night brings her the sacred jewels. The half-crazed Maliella accepts Gennaro's love. But the next day, she adorns herself with the jewels, and enters the hideout of the Camorrists to find Rafaele. He is angered by her confession, and horrified by her wearing the jewels, and he repulses her. Maliella rushes out to throw herself into the sea, and the heartbroken Gennaro stabs himself.

Juggler of Notre Dame (Le Jongleur) is a French opera that may be classed as a musical miracle play. The music was composed by Jules Massenet (1842-1912) and the first presentation took place in Monte Carlo in 1902. The scene is Cluny, near Paris, in the 1300's. As written, the opera has no parts for women. But the tenor role of Jean the Juggler was very effectively sung by Mary Garden (soprano).

It is a tender story of an ignorant and hungry boy whose crude songs and juggling tricks make him the butt of the market-place crowds in Cluny. While the mob is loudly singing a drinking song with Jean, the indignant prior of the monastery comes out. The crowd melts away. Jean is at first terrified. But later he is comforted by the kindly old cook, Boniface, and the cook persuades him to enter the monastery.

There Jean becomes discouraged as he sees the learning and talents of the monks and realizes his own ignorance. Boniface tells him the legend of the humble sage bush that sheltered the Christ-Child. Jean thinks over this story, and one day goes into the chapel and sings and dances before the new statue of the Virgin. As he sinks in exhaustion before the altar, the horrified monks crowd about him and prepare to seize him. Suddenly a heavenly light glows in the Virgin's face, and she smiles down on the dying boy. The monks are awed by this miracle and blend their voices in a chant. Jean cries out in ecstasy and dies, while angelic voices sing his death song.

Much of the music of the opera has a mystic quality that suits the story. The baritone song about the legend of the sage bush is especially beautiful.

La Bohème, *lah bow EM*, is an Italian grand opera

A Scene from the Italian Two-Act Opera *I Pagliacci* **Features the Tenor Giovanni Martinelli as Canio.**

composed by Giacomo Puccini (1858-1924) and first produced at Turin in 1896. Its heroine is Mimi (soprano), a beautiful girl who has tuberculosis. Mimi is loved by Rudolfo (tenor), a writer who lives in an attic studio in Paris' Latin Quarter. Rudolfo and his friends lead a carefree life in the opera, based on Henri Murger's novel, *Scènes de la Vie de Bohème (Scenes from Bohemian Life)*. Rudolfo shares his studio with Marcel the painter (baritone), Colline the philosopher (bass), and Schaunard the musician (baritone). Mimi, who lives in a near-by garret and supports herself by needlework, knocks on the attic door on Christmas Eve to seek a light for her candle. Rudolfo is alone, and the two fall in love immediately. Later the two are separated, but are finally reunited just before Mimi coughs her life away. The story is made lively by the boisterous fun of the four friends, and the quarrelsome love affair of Marcel and Musetta (soprano).

The gaiety and picturesque local color of this opera have given it undying popularity. One of its most beloved melodies is "Musetta's Waltz" from Act II. Other favorites are the tenor aria "Che gelida manina" ("Your tiny hand is frozen") and the soprano aria "Mi chiamano Mimi" ("My name is Mimi").

L'Africaine (The African Maid) is a romantic grand opera composed by Giacomo Meyerbeer (1791-1864). It was first presented at the Paris Grand Opera in 1865. The opera was originally written in French, but is now generally given in Italian. Meyerbeer looked upon this opera as his masterpiece, though others favored his *Huguenots.*

The story tells the life and loves of the explorer Vasco da Gama. The scene is the early 1500's in Lisbon, Portugal. The scene shifts to a ship at sea, and finally

to India. Circumstances separate Vasco from his true love, Inez. Later she marries Don Pedro to get Vasco freed from prison. After an eventful voyage to India, Vasco marries the native queen, Selika. Then Inez appears on the scene. She has survived a shipwreck and battle which cost the life of her husband. Selika sees the love in Vasco's eyes and lets him escape the land with Inez.

Lakmé, *LAHK MAY,* is a French romantic opera by Léo Delibes (1836-1891). It was first given at Paris in 1883. The opera is produced only when there is an outstanding coloratura soprano to sing the title role. The plot is very weak, and the whole production depends upon the singing quality of the star.

The story takes place in India, where Lakmé lives. She is the daughter of the Brahman priest, Nilakantha. Lakmé and her father are praying that the English will be driven from their land. The worshippers leave the temple garden, and a party of English tourists breaks the fence and enters. When they leave, the handsome officer Gerald remains behind. Lakmé returns, and she and Gerald fall in love.

The priest discovers the broken garden fence, and vows to discover and kill the intruder. He disguises himself as a beggar, and Lakmé as a street singer, in hope that her songs will cause the intruder to betray himself. In the market place Lakmé sings the extremely difficult "Bell Song." Nilakantha sees Gerald, and stabs him. Lakmé heals Gerald's wound and once again saves his life before she dies in his arms.

La Traviata, *lah trah VYAH tah,* is a tragic grand opera of the Italian school, composed by Giuseppe Verdi. It is based upon the story of Camille, by Alexandre Dumas the Younger. The opera was first presented in Venice in 1853. It remains a favorite year after year, chiefly because of the richly emotional melodies.

The beautiful but immoral Violetta Valery (soprano) entertains Alfred Germont (tenor) at a party in her house in Paris. When the guests retire to the ballroom, Alfred tells Violetta that he loves her and wants her to forsake the gay life she leads. She goes to live with him in a quiet country house, as she is won by the thought that an honest man really cares for her. There she is found by Giorgio Germont (baritone), Alfred's father. The old man persuades her to give up Alfred for the sake of his family. Alfred believes that Violetta has tired of him, but tries to win her back. In a gambling house he insults her by flinging a bag of money at her feet, to repay her for what she has spent on him. He is then challenged to a duel by his rival Baron Douphol (baritone). In the last act, Violetta lies in her apartment, dying. Alfred has been told of her sacrifice, and comes to beg forgiveness. In the presence of the father and son, Violetta dies, comforted by the knowledge of their affection. Act I of this opera contains one of the best-loved of coloratura arias, the brilliant "Ah, fors'e lui" ("The one of whom I dreamed"). Another favorite is in Act II, the baritone aria "Di Provenza il mar" ("Thy home in fair Provence"). The preludes to Act I and Act III are also frequently heard.

Lohengrin, *LO en grin,* is considered by many to be the finest of all romantic grand operas. The music drama is written in German, with music composed by Richard Wagner. The opera has pomp and pageantry, magic, and dramatic interest, and a lovely musical setting. It was first produced in Weimar in 1850.

The events are supposed to occur in the first half of the 900's, during the reign of Henry the Fowler, king of Germany (bass). Wagner based his opera on three legends. It tells the love story of Elsa, Duchess of Brabant (soprano), and the mysterious knight Lohengrin (tenor). The knight Telramund (baritone) has falsely accused Elsa of murdering her brother Godfrey. Lohengrin comes to the king's court clad in shining armor and borne on the river in a skiff drawn by a white swan. Lohengrin defeats Telramund and marries Elsa. In the meantime she has promised never to ask Lohengrin's name and origin. But Telramund and his sorceress wife Ortrud (mezzo-soprano or alto) persuade Elsa to break her vow. Before the assembled court Lohengrin reveals that he is the son of King Parsifal in Mountsalvat and has helped guard the Holy Grail. By the law of his order, he must now say farewell forever. But before he departs, the swan is transformed into the youth Godfrey. Ortrud's wicked spell had changed the boy into a bird. As Lohengrin's skiff disappears down the river, the girl falls lifeless.

The score has many beautiful melodies. But the most familiar are the Prelude to Act III and the "Wedding March."

Lucia di Lammermoor, *loo CHE ah dee LAHM mer MOOR,* is an Italian tragic grand opera, with music by Gaetano Donizetti. It is based on Sir Walter Scott's *The Bride of Lammermoor.* The opera was first produced in Naples in 1835, and is still very popular because of its entrancing music. The "Sextet" is probably the most famous of all operatic compositions for mixed voices.

The scenes of the opera are laid in Scotland during the late 1600's. Lucia (soprano) is loved by Sir Edgar of Ravenswood (tenor). There is a bitter feud between him and Lucia's brother Sir Henry Ashton (baritone), Lord of Lammermoor. But the suitor is willing to forget the feud for love of Lucia.

Sir Henry wishes to marry his sister to Sir Arthur Bucklaw (tenor) for financial and political reasons. He steals the letters Edgar has written to Lucia. Then he forges a new letter which would prove that Edgar is unfaithful to Lucia. The letter convinces Lucia, and she consents to marry Sir Arthur. But during the wedding festivities, Edgar enters suddenly and reveals that he has always been true to Lucia. Lucia is driven mad by grief, and kills the bridegroom. Edgar goes to the churchyard, armed for a duel with Sir Henry. While there he learns that Lucia has died, and in despair he plunges his dagger into his own heart. The mad scene which follows the announcement of Sir Arthur's murder is famous for demanding the highest skill of a coloratura soprano.

Madame Butterfly is an Italian tragic grand opera founded upon a story by the American novelist, John Luther Long. The music was composed by Giacomo Puccini, and the opera was first presented in Milan in 1904. The appeal of this beautiful opera is unvarying. The picturesque background of Japanese life, the pathetic story of the little bride, and the lovely harmonies of the score combine to give it unfailing popularity.

Madame Butterfly (soprano) is a Japanese geisha girl named Cho-Cho-San. Through the help of the marriage broker Goro (tenor), she is married to Lieutenant Pinkerton (tenor) of the United States Navy. It is springtime, and robins are nesting in the little garden overlooking the harbor of Nagasaki. After a short honeymoon, Pinkerton sails away. He promises to return when robins nest again. Butterfly's lovely aria "Un bel di vedremo" ("Some Day He'll Come") tells of her hopes. Three years later, Butterfly is visited by the American consul Sharpless (baritone). Sharpless wants to tell her that Pinkerton has married an American girl, and will soon arrive with his wife. But the words will not come. He ends by merely advising Cho-Cho-San to accept Prince Yamadori (baritone), a wealthy suitor. Then she shows Sharpless her golden-haired baby boy, and protests her undying loyalty to Pinkerton.

Butterfly's maid Suzuki (alto) comes in with news of a ship anchored in the harbor. The women read the ship's name through a telescope. Then the unhappy wife sits up all night waiting for her husband. The next day she learns about Pinkerton's marriage. She talks with his American wife, and promises her baby boy to her. Then the unhappy girl kills herself with her father's dagger. As she is dying, Pinkerton rushes in to beg forgiveness. He falls on his knees beside her, overcome with remorse.

Manon, *mah NOHN,* is a French tragic grand opera based on the novel *Manon Lescaut* by Abbé Marcel Prévost. The music is by Jules Massenet. The opera was first presented in Paris in 1884. An opera by Puccini with the same theme was produced in Turin in 1893. but Massenet's work has always been the more popular. It is brilliant in setting and full of movement.

The Banquet Scene Is a High Point in the Opera *La Traviata* by Giuseppe Verdi.

Manon (soprano) is on her way to a convent. She stops at the courtyard of an inn at Amiens, where she is to meet a cousin, Lescaut (baritone). While Lescaut is in the tavern gambling, Manon flirts with a handsome young officer, the Chevalier des Grieux (tenor).

They elope, and she lives with him for some time in luxury. When poverty threatens, she leaves Des Grieux for the rich nobleman De Brétigny (baritone). Then Manon learns that Des Grieux is consoling his grief by a life of religious devotion in the seminary of Saint Sulpice. The fickle Manon seeks him there and wins him back. Des Grieux recklessly spends all his money on Manon, and then takes to gambling. He is accused of cheating, and is saved from prison only by the intervention of his father. Manon is condemned to exile as an immoral woman. While she is waiting to be deported at the docks of Le Havre, Des Grieux comes to find her. He calls upon her to flee. But Manon is so exhausted from the hardships of prison life that she dies in his arms.

The Marriage of Figaro is an Italian comic opera by Mozart. Mozart chose the second of Beaumarchais' Figaro comedies for his story. The first was later used by Rossini for his *Barber of Seville*. Mozart conducted the first performance of his opera in Vienna in 1786. *The Marriage of Figaro* is one of the masterpieces of comic opera. Its humorous overture is especially well loved.

The rollicking story is full of plots and disguises. Figaro suspects his bride-to-be, Susanna, of being unfaithful. Count Almaviva suspects the same about his wife Rosina. The Countess is in reality faithful to her husband, while he wants to make love to Susanna.

All is confusion until explanations are made in the fourth act and everyone is restored to his rightful lover.

Martha is a romantic grand opera which was first produced in 1847. The opera is of the French type, was written by a German, Friedrich von Flotow (1812-1883), but is usually sung in English. Secondary companies often give it in Italian. *Martha* is universally loved for its amusing action and its delightful melodies.

The scene is laid in England, during the reign of Queen Anne. Lady Harriet Durham (soprano), maid-of-honor to the queen, is bored with court life. She disguises herself as a peasant girl and seeks relaxation at the village fair. She takes along her maid Nancy (alto) and an elderly but devoted admirer, Sir Tristan Mickelford (bass). Lionel (tenor) and Plunkett (bass or baritone), two young farmers who are foster brothers, come to the fair. They wish to hire someone to do their housework, and ask Lady Harriet and Nancy to take service with them. Jokingly, the girls agree to go. They discover too late that they are actually bound to service for a year.

The young farmers lead the girls away to their farmhouse, in spite of Sir Tristan's protests. They instruct "Martha" and "Julia," as the girls are called, in their household duties. Shortly after midnight, Sir Tristan helps the girls escape. Lionel becomes melancholy through the loss of his beloved Martha. Later the two brothers come upon the girls in a hunting party, and soon learn that the whole affair was a jest. Through a ring that he wears, Lionel is discovered to be the heir to the banished Count of Derby. Lady Harriet seeks a reconciliation with Lionel, but the wounded lover spurns her. She wins back his love by repeating the scene of the fair. The opera ends joyously with Lionel and "Martha" and Plunkett and "Julia" planning marriage.

The favorite air in this charming opera is "The Last Rose of Summer," sung by the soprano in the farmhouse kitchen. But Lionel's "M'Appari" ("Like a Dream") is a close second in popularity.

Mignon, ME NYAWN, is a French sentimental grand opera based upon Goethe's novel, *Wilhelm Meister*. This opera was composed by Ambroise Thomas (1811-1896), and was first produced in Paris in 1866. It has an appealing story and delicate, haunting melodies.

The chief soprano role is that of Filina, a dashing young actress. Mignon (mezzo-soprano) is a young dancing girl who travels with a band of gypsies. In the courtyard of a German inn, Mignon is rescued from the cruelty of her master by Lothario (bass), a half-crazy minstrel, and by Wilhelm Meister (tenor), a student out for adventure.

Mignon loses her heart to Wilhelm. She persuades him to let her follow him disguised as a page. Meanwhile Wilhelm becomes infatuated with Filina. At the castle of a baron, where the players are to give a performance, he tells Mignon that they must part. At the height of the performance, the unhappy Mignon expresses a wish that the castle may burn down. Lothario hears her, and sets it on fire. Wilhelm rescues Mignon from the flames, and discovers that he loves her.

Mignon suffers a long illness and Wilhelm takes her to a castle in Italy. After she recovers, she learns that she is the long-lost daughter of Lothario. The aged minstrel regains his senses and realizes that the castle is his own home. The three look forward to a life of happiness together. Some famous songs from the opera include the "Gavotte" and Mignon's aria "Know'st Thou the Land?" Filina's "Polonaise" ("I'm Fair Titania") is a favorite of coloratura sopranos.

Nibelungen Ring (The Ring of the Nibelung) by Richard Wagner is the most ambitious work undertaken by any composer of opera. *The Ring* is made up of four operas based on ancient Germanic and Scandinavian legends. All are connected by musical themes, as well as by plot. Wagner began writing his poetical drama in 1848. But he did not finish the entire cycle until twenty-six years later. In these music dramas, as in all his others, Wagner makes frequent and effective use of musical themes. Each theme is connected with a certain person, place, object, or event. When a particular subject enters into the drama, the orchestra plays the accompanying theme. Each theme is like a hint of what is to come. These little themes which are easily recognizable are called *leitmotivs* and are always associated with Wagner. And as certain climaxes appear in the drama, the hints are broadened out into magnificent anthems. Wagner's orchestral requirements were so exacting that he even invented new musical instruments especially for *The Ring*. The cycle's four operas are *Das Rheingold*, *Die Walküre*, *Siegfried*, and *Die Götterdämmerung*.

Parsifal is Wagner's last music drama. It was completed and first performed in 1882, the year before his death. The opera is religious in theme, and Wagner himself wanted it to be performed only at his theater in Bayreuth. In spite of his wishes, it was presented at the Metropolitan Opera House in New York in 1903. After the copyright expired in 1913, *Parsifal* was also

Metropolitan Opera

The Noted Italian Singer Salvatore Baccaloni appeared as Dr. Bartolo in Rossini's *Barber of Seville*. This comic bass part is of a type which is very common in Italian operas.

given elsewhere in Europe. Today some parts of this work are considered among the finest music ever composed on a religious theme. Especially notable are the "Prelude" and the "Good-Friday Spell."

The hero of the drama is Parsifal (tenor), whose name was derived from the Arabian *Fal parsi*, meaning *guileless fool*. The scene is medieval Spain, at the Castle of the Holy Grail. A group of knights live at the castle, guarding the Grail (the cup from which Jesus drank at the Last Supper) and the spear with which He was struck during the Crucifixion. The evil Klingsor, who was not allowed to guard the treasures, lives near the castle. The magician Klingsor has resolved to steal the Grail from its keepers. With the help of Kundry, a beautiful woman, he succeeds in gaining the holy spear. With it he wounds Amfortas (baritone), son of King Titurel (bass) of the holy knights. In a revelation, Amfortas learns that his wound will be healed only by a "blameless fool." Parsifal appears at that moment. After many years he obtains the spear from Klingsor and finds his way back to the castle. There he is declared the new king of the knights. He touches Amfortas' wound with the spear, and it heals.

Porgy and Bess is an American folk opera, with music composed by George Gershwin. It was based on a play, *Porgy*, by DuBose Heyward. The opera was first presented in 1935. But it did not achieve great success until 1942, when it was presented again in New York City. *Porgy and Bess* was a musical experiment of the young genius Gershwin. It is the first truly American opera, based on the tragedies and the great musical contributions of the American Negro.

The setting of the opera's three acts is a street known as Catfish Row in Charleston, S.C. All the characters

Puccini's *Madame Butterfly* Tells the Touching Story of a Japanese Woman's Love for an American Officer.

are Negroes, and the opera is usually given by an all-Negro cast. As the opera opens, Bess and the swaggering Crown are lovers. During an argument over Bess, Crown kills a man named Robbins and is forced to hide out from the police. In the confusion, Bess turns to Porgy, a crippled beggar. The two are happy together until Crown turns up again. Porgy kills Crown and is sent to jail. Upon his release, he finds that Bess has skipped off to New York with a dope peddler named Sportin' Life. As the opera closes, Porgy hitches his goat to his wagon, sings the sad aria "I'm on My Way," and starts off to find his love.

Gershwin's music exhibits beautifully the characteristics of the Negro spirituals. Among the best-known selections from *Porgy and Bess* are the lullaby "Summer Time" and the chorus "A Woman Is a Sometime Thing" from the first act; Porgy's song "I Got Plenty o' Nuttin'," the lovers' duet "Bess, You Is My Woman Now," and the amusing "It Ain't Necessarily So," sung by Sportin' Life and the chorus in Act II; and the trio "Where's My Bess?" and Porgy's final aria from Act III.

Rigoletto, RIG *oh* LET *oh,* is an Italian tragic grand opera based on Victor Hugo's *The King Amuses Himself.* It was composed by Giuseppe Verdi and was first presented in Venice in 1851. Verdi's music is among the most melodious of all operatic scores. The famous quartet, *Bella figlia dell' amore,* is known and loved throughout the world, and the tenor aria "La donna è mobile" ("Woman is fickle") is hummed on many a street. Gilda's aria "Caro nome" ("Dearest name") is forever a favorite with coloratura sopranos.

The scene of the opera is laid in and near Mantua in the 1500's. Rigoletto (baritone) is the hunchback jester to the dissipated Duke of Mantua (tenor). The

Duke has posed as a student to win the innocent love of Rigoletto's daughter Gilda (soprano). Gilda remains loyal to her lover, even after she learns of his bad qualities. Rigoletto forms a plot to kill the duke. Gilda suspects her father's plan. Dressed as a youth, she goes to the inn where the deed is to be done and substitutes herself as the victim. When Rigoletto receives a sack supposed to contain the body of the duke, he opens it, only to discover that it contains the body of his dying daughter.

Romeo and Juliet is a romantic opera based on Shakespeare's play of the same name. The opera was composed by Charles Gounod and was first given at Paris in 1867. In the opera, Juliet sings the famous "Waltz" song. The story follows Shakespeare's plot closely. Romeo and Juliet, of two rival families, are married by Friar Laurence. When all looks black for the two, the friar gives Juliet a potion to bring on a sleep like death. He sends a message to Romeo, which the lover fails to get. Romeo finds Juliet apparently dead, and drinks poison. At that moment Juliet awakens. She sees her lover dying, and takes her own life with a dagger.

Rosenkavalier is a German comic opera in three acts by Richard Strauss (1864-1949). The libretto was written by the poet Hugo von Hofmannsthal. The opera was first given in Dresden in 1911. Strauss included in the opera's music many lovely waltz melodies which have proved popular on the concert stage.

The story takes place at Vienna in the 1700's. The drunken Baron Ochs of Lerchenau is to marry the lovely Sophie Faninal. The match has been arranged by Sophie's father, and Sophie is none too happy about it. Following a custom in announcing engagements, the baron brings a silver rose to the Princess von Werden-berg. She sends her youthful lover Octavian to deliver the rose to Sophie. Immediately Sophie and Octavian fall in love. Eventually Octavian persuades Sophie's angry father that the baron is not a fit husband for her, and the two lovers are happily reunited.

Salomé, *sa LO me,* is a tragic grand opera in German, with a score by Richard Strauss. The book is by Oscar Wilde and was founded on the Biblical story of John the Baptist. The opera was first produced in Dresden in 1905. It is an example of perfect harmony between music and action. But the unpleasant theme has kept this work from becoming widely popular.

Salomé (soprano) is loved by her stepfather, Herod Antipas (tenor), the tetrarch of Judea. But her restless heart is inflamed with love for John the Baptist, called Jokanaan (baritone), whom Herod has imprisoned. But the prophet rejects the girl's love. Herod has promised Salomé that she may ask of him what she will. Her request is that she be given Jokanaan's head. The deed is done. And when Salomé exultantly caresses the head, Herod orders the guards to kill her.

Samson and Delilah is a French tragic grand opera based on the Biblical story of Samson. Its music is by Camille Saint-Saëns (1835-1921). The opera was intro-duced in Weimar in 1877. The role of Delilah is written for the mezzo-soprano or alto. Samson is the tenor.

Delilah, the daughter of the high priest of Dagon, uses all her charms to weaken the strong Samson. Sam-son has dedicated his strength to the undoing of the Philistines. Though Samson has been warned against Delilah, he cannot resist her. At length he reveals to her that his strength lies in his hair. Delilah then betrays him to the Philistines. The Philistines blind Samson, cut off his hair, and put him to work grinding at a mill.

While enemies jeer at him in the temple of Dagon, Samson prays that his strength might return to him. His prayer is answered. The great man then moves the two marble pillars that support the temple, and the building crashes down.

The music of this opera is of a high order. The cho-ruses of the first act are notable, as are Delilah's ex-quisite love song, "My Heart, At Thy Sweet Voice" in Act II, and the oriental "Bacchanale" of Act III.

Siegfried, by Richard Wagner (1813-1883), was first given at Bayreuth, Germany, in 1876. It opens in the smithy of the dwarf Mime (tenor). Mime tells the handsome Siegfried (tenor) how he raised him. After the death of Siegfried's father, his mother fled through the forest. She died in Mime's cave after giving birth to Siegfried. Now Siegfried sets out to steal the Rhinegold from the giant Fafner, who has changed himself into a dragon in order to guard it better. Only Siegfried's father's sword "Nothung" will accomplish this, but it is broken. And only the man who has never felt fear can forge it together again. Siegfried accom-plishes this, then slays the dragon Fafner. He tastes of the dragon's blood and learns the language of the birds. They warn him that Mime is plotting to steal the treas-ure from him. So the hero kills Mime. Then the birds tell him of a beautiful maiden (Brünnhilde) who sleeps surrounded by flames. Siegfried awakens Brünnhilde with a kiss, and the two find themselves in love.

Tales of Hoffmann is a French grand opera of the sentimental type, with music by Jacques Offenbach

(1819-1880). It was first produced in Paris in 1881. The story is based on three tales written by the German romantic novelist, E. T. A. Hoffmann.

In a tavern at Nuremberg, the poet Hoffmann (tenor) is drinking with a crowd of students. He proposes to tell a story about each of three women whom he has loved. This scene is the prologue.

The following three acts describe Hoffmann's adven-tures in love. Olympia, heroine of the first act, is really a beautiful mechanical doll whom Hoffmann sees through magic spectacles. The second heroine, Giulietta, is a woman of sensuous charm who first lures him on and then deserts him. The third, Antonia, is a woman of virtue who loves music. But unfortunately, she suffers from consumption and is forbidden to sing. In the end the girl is persuaded to sing, and falls dead from over-exertion.

In the epilogue, Hoffmann brings his story to an end. He declares that after love has failed there is only the intoxication of liquor left for him. Alone in the room, Hoffmann is visited by the Muse, who tells him that he still has his art.

The opera is tuneful and fantastic. The most popular melody in it is the "Barcarolle," which is sung by soprano and alto in Act II. Usually the same soprano fills the three roles of Hoffmann's loves.

Tannhäuser, *TAHN hoi zer,* with both words and music by Richard Wagner, is a very noble music drama. It is based on the stories of the 1200's of the com-peting *minnesingers,* German poet-musicians. The opera was first heard in Dresden in 1845.

Tannhäuser (tenor), a minstrel knight, spends a year of pleasure in the abode of Venus (soprano). He wearies of her spell and returns to earth. The sight of a band of pilgrims on their way to Rome stirs his conscience, and he prays for mercy before a shrine to the Virgin. Soon he is seen and recognized by a hunting party of his former friends. Tannhäuser is persuaded by Wolfram von Eschenbach (baritone) to enter the competition of minnesingers at Wartburg. Wolfram tells the young man that Elizabeth (soprano), niece of the Landgrave of Thuringia (bass), is pining in his absence. At the singing tournament, Tannhäuser sings the praises of love. The knights draw their swords to kill him when he forgets himself and pictures the sensual pleasures of love, and sings of the beauty of Venus. Elizabeth's plea saves his life. But his remorse is so great that he joins a band of pilgrims to seek forgiveness from the pope.

Tannhäuser's friend Wolfram is secretly in love with Elizabeth. One day he finds her kneeling before the shrine of the Virgin. They hear the pilgrims chanting a chorus, but their eager eyes cannot find Tannhäuser among them. In despair, Elizabeth goes weakly home to her uncle's castle. As Wolfram sorrowfully watches her go, he sings the exquisite "Hymn to the Evening Star," commending the soul of his beloved one to heaven's protection. As his song ends, he sees a weary and ragged pilgrim approaching. It is Tannhäuser, who has received no blessing from the Holy Father. Before he can hope for pardon, the barren staff in the pontiff's hand must put forth new leaves. The anguished knight calls on Venus, and she appears with all her train. A sound of funeral chant is heard. And when Wolfram tells

A Street Scene Is One Setting in *Porgy and Bess,* Gershwin's Opera of Negro Life in Charleston, S.C.

the tale of Elizabeth's devotion, Venus disappears. As Elizabeth's funeral bier is brought to them, Tannhäuser falls beside it and dies, praying for forgiveness. Just then excited pilgrims approach. They are bearing the holy staff, now covered with leaves and flowers.

Few operas have a richer score than this great work. The lofty music of the "Pilgrim's Chorus" is contrasted with the materialism of the "Venusberg Music." Throughout the opera, the score faithfully brings out the varying action.

The Flying Dutchman is a German tragic grand opera based on Heinrich Heine's poetical version of the legendary story. The opera was composed by Richard Wagner (1813-1883), and was first presented in Dresden in 1843. The scene of the opera is laid in Norway during the 1700's.

Daland (bass), a Norwegian sea captain, has anchored his ships in a harbor seven miles from his home. While waiting for a favorable wind, he is amazed at the sight of a blood-red ship with black masts which has just come into the harbor. Its captain (the Dutchman) has been condemned for his sins to sail the seas until he shall find a woman who will be true to him till death. Once in seven years he may seek her on land.

The Dutchman (baritone) persuades Daland to take him to his home. There the two discuss a marriage between the Dutchman and Daland's daughter Senta (soprano). Senta is loved by Eric (tenor). But she feels that it is her destiny to save the Dutchman from his curse, and consents to marry him. Then the Dutchman sees Eric on his knees pleading for Senta's love. The Dutchman believes Senta is unfaithful and prepares to sail away. Senta then throws herself into the sea. The ship goes down, but the lovers, clasped in each other's arms, rise from the wreckage to heaven. Thus the curse is lifted.

The best-known melody from this opera is the ever popular *Overture.*

The Huguenots, *HYOO geh notz,* is a French tragic grand opera based on the massacre of Saint Bartholomew's Day. The opera was composed by Giacomo Meyerbeer, and was first produced in Paris in 1836. The scene is laid in Paris and Touraine in August, 1572.

The great religious tragedy provides the colorful background for the story of the Huguenot nobleman, Raoul de Nangis (tenor) and Valentine (soprano), daughter of an ardent Catholic, Saint Bris. In the château of the Count de Nevers (baritone) a merry party is taking place. Raoul tells the guests how he rescued a beautiful lady from a band of students. Later, he sees the same woman, Valentine, talking to the count. Valentine has come to break her engagement with De Nevers, for she loves Raoul. But Raoul misunderstands. He refuses to marry Valentine when Queen Margaret of Valois (soprano) requests the marriage in order to bring together the Huguenot and Catholic parties.

Valentine marries De Nevers. But, later, she warns Raoul of a plot to kill him. During a fight between the followers of Raoul and of Saint Bris, Queen Margaret interrupts to tell Raoul the truth about Valentine's visit to De Nevers. Later, Raoul hides in the count's home and overhears a plot to massacre the Huguenots. When the signal bell rings, he tears himself from Valentine's arms and rushes into the fray.

As the opera is usually presented, the story ends here. But there is another act in which Raoul and Valentine are married after De Nevers has been killed. Soon after the ceremony the lovers are shot down by a band of assassins led by Saint Bris. The music and spectacular atmosphere of this opera make it extremely impressive. But it is not often heard, because it requires such a heavy cast.

608

Tosca, *TOHS kah,* is an Italian tragic grand opera composed by Giacomo Puccini. It is considered his masterpiece. It is based on a drama by Victorien Sardou. *La Tosca* had its first presentation in Rome in 1900. Brilliant music and dramatic action, keyed to a high pitch, make this an outstanding opera. Especially fine is the famous tenor aria "E lucevan le stelle" ("Stars were shining") which the hero sings just before he dies.

The scene is Rome in the year 1800. The beautiful prima donna Floria Tosca (soprano) and the painter Mario Cavaradossi (tenor) are lovers. Mario aids an escaped political prisoner, Angelotti (bass), and is arrested by the malicious chief of police, Scarpia (baritone). Scarpia persuades Tosca to come to his apartments in the Farnese Palace by saying he has news of her lover. Mario is brought into the room in chains. When he is questioned, he refuses to tell where Angelotti is. He manages to tell Tosca not to reveal anything, and is then led into an adjoining room to be tortured.

Tosca becomes distracted by sounds of anguish, and tells Scarpia that Angelotti is hidden in a well in the garden. News comes that Napoleon has triumphed over the Italian forces. When Mario taunts Scarpia and predicts his downfall, the angry chief of police orders him executed. Scarpia then tells Tosca that she may save Mario's life by giving up her honor to him. She consents, but demands safe conduct for Mario and herself from the city that night. Scarpia assures her that Mario will have to go through a mock execution, but that he will be saved for her. When Scarpia approaches Tosca with open hands, she stabs him to death.

Tosca reveals everything to Mario at the place of execution. She tells him to fall at the first shot, pretending to be dead. The squad fires, and Mario falls. Tosca rushes to him, only to find that he has been killed. She leaps from the parapet to her death when Scarpia's agents try to arrest her.

Tristan, *TRIS tan,* **and Isolde,** *ih SOLD,* is a music drama in German, with both words and music by Richard Wagner. It was first performed at Munich in 1865. Wagner based this opera on an old Celtic legend. He created a magnificent work in which words, action, and score are parts of a harmonious whole. Many consider this music drama Wagner's masterpiece.

Tristan (tenor), nephew of King Mark of Cornwall (bass), has slain Morold, brother of the king of Ireland. According to custom, he has sent Morold's head to Isolde (soprano), daughter of the Irish king, who was engaged to Morold. Tristan's own wound does not heal. Disguised as a minstrel, Tantris, he goes to Ireland to take advantage of the healing art of Isolde. She heals him, but discovers who he is through matching the splinter found in Morold's skull with the notch in the "minstrel's" sword. In spite of this, the two become lovers. Back at the court of King Mark, Tristan sings the praises of Isolde. The king is much impressed. Finally he orders Tristan to return to Ireland to ask the princess to become queen of Cornwall. Isolde is outraged that Tristan is to woo her for another, but she submits.

As the ship is nearing the Cornish shores, Isolde calls upon her servant, Bragäne (soprano), to prepare a death cup for Tristan to drink. She drinks half of the potion herself, only to discover that Bragäne has mixed a love draught. The lovers are unable to resist the magic of the cup, and meet secretly while the king is on a hunt-

ing party. One of the king's courtiers, Melot (tenor), betrays them. In the scene of their discovery he wounds Tristan. Tristan's faithful servant Kurvenal (baritone) takes him to Brittany, where he lingers close to death. In the meantime Kurvenal has sent for Isolde. When the delirious Tristan learns that her ship is in sight, he tears the bandage from his wound. Isolde arrives only to see him die. The king's forces arrive and fight their way in. King Mark tells Isolde that Bragäne has confessed to mixing the love potion. But the unhappy girl, conscious only of her lover, sinks by his body and dies. Before she dies, however, Isolde sings one of the finest of all soprano arias, the heart-searing "Liebestod" ("Love-Death"). This aria repeats themes of the stirring "Love Duet" sung by the lovers in Act II.

Valkyrie (Die Walküre), by Wagner, was first given at Munich in 1870. Siegmund the Walsung (tenor), tired after long wandering, arrives at the forest home of Sieglinde (soprano) and her hated husband Hunding (bass). He tells Sieglinde the tragic story of his life and learns that Hunding is the enemy who has pursued his family. Later that evening, Sieglinde tells Siegmund that he is to free her by drawing out a sword that has been buried in a tree. Siegmund does this easily, then he and Sieglinde flee.

The goddess Fricka has decided that Hunding must be avenged. But one of Wotan's daughters, the Valkyrie Brünnhilde, wants to save Siegmund. Wotan smashes Siegmund's sword, and Hunding kills the young man. Then Wotan kills Hunding and swears vengeance on Brünnhilde for her disobedience. Her punishment is to sleep on a rock surrounded by fire until a man comes to save her. This opera contains the "Ride of the Valkyries" and the "Magic Fire" music.   KONRAD NEUGER

Related Articles. Biographies of Opera Singers are listed in the Related Articles of the SINGING article. See also the following articles:

Aria	Libretto	Musical Comedy
Ballet	Metropolitan	Operetta
Chorus	Opera Association	Overture
La Scala	Music (History)	Singing

Outline

I. Forms of Opera
II. Development of the Opera
III. Some of the Famous Operas

Questions

What is an opera? From where does the name *opera* come?

How is light opera different from grand opera?

What was the first opera ever produced? When was it produced?

What contribution did Richard Wagner make to ideas concerning the opera?

What opera was originally written without any parts for women's voices?

What music from the opera *Lohengrin* is often played at weddings?

What date marks the beginning of real opera?

In which opera may the soprano sing an aria of her own choosing? Why?

How does a thoughtless prank form the basis for the opera *Martha*?

How long is the opera *I Pagliacci*? With what other opera is it usually presented?

How did the opera *Aïda* happen to be written? Who was its composer?

OPÉRA BOUFFE. See OPERA (Forms of Opera).
OPERA GLASS. See FIELD GLASS.
OPERATION. See SURGERY.
OPERATION BREADBASKET. See NEGRO (picture).
OPERATION DEEP FREEZE. See ANTARCTICA (International Cooperation).
OPERATION HIGH JUMP. See ANTARCTICA (American Exploration).

OPERETTA is a light, short opera. It usually has gay, lilting music and an unpretentious plot. Much of the dialogue in an operetta is spoken. Operettas are sometimes called *light operas* because both forms are musical-dramatic works that are noted for their comedy. In England, the term *comic opera* is also used. A comic opera is sometimes longer than an operetta.

In American operettas, the dialogue may be both spoken and sung. The dialogue of most Italian operettas is carried in *recitativo secco* (dry, or unaccompanied, recitative), which means that the orchestra sounds only a few chords of music to enable the singer to hold to the key. In English, German, and French operettas, most of the dialogue of the recitative is spoken.

The operetta as known today began in the 1800's. An Austrian composer, Franz von Suppé, wrote more than 150 operettas, which were highly popular in Vienna. Two of his well-known works are *The Beautiful Galatea* and *Boccaccio.* Another Austrian, Johann Strauss the Younger, wrote such world-famous operettas as *Die Fledermaus* (The Bat) and *The Gypsy Baron.* Later, Franz Lehár's *The Merry Widow* became one of the most successful operettas ever written.

Jacques Offenbach made the operetta a popular form of entertainment in France in the 1800's. Many of his works, including *Bluebeard* and *Orpheus in the Underworld,* were performed with great success in both Europe and the United States. Two Englishmen, the composer Sir Arthur Sullivan and the dramatist Sir William S. Gilbert, together wrote some of the most delightful operettas of all time. Their most popular works include *H.M.S. Pinafore, The Mikado, Patience,* and *Iolanthe.*

Sigmund Romberg and Victor Herbert were well-known American composers of operettas. Romberg's works include *The Student Prince* and *Blossom Time.* Some of the songs from Herbert's operettas have become as famous as the operettas themselves. Among them are "Kiss Me Again" from *Mlle. Modiste,* "Italian Street Song" from *Naughty Marietta,* and "Toyland" from *Babes in Toyland.* The musical comedy developed from the operettas of the 1800's and early 1900's (see MUSICAL COMEDY). RAYMOND KENDALL

OPHIR, *O fer,* was an ancient region, perhaps in southern Arabia, which was famous for the abundance and fineness of its gold. The Bible says that Solomon built ships which brought him gold, silver, gems, ivory, apes, and peacocks from Ophir (I Kings 9-10).

OPHTHALMIA, *ahf THAL mee uh,* is a name for severe diseases affecting the eye membranes. These diseases may be caused by infections, poisons, or injuries. For example, *ophthalmia neonatorum* is an infection of the eyes of newborn babies, usually caused by the germ that causes gonorrhea. *Sympathetic ophthalmia* spreads to both eyes after an injury to one eye and often leads to blindness. See also BLINDNESS (Diseases). JOHN R. McWILLIAMS

OPHTHALMOLOGY, *AHF thal MAHL uh jee,* is the field of medicine involving the diagnosis and treatment of eye diseases. An *ophthalmologist,* sometimes called an *oculist,* must have an M.D. degree and three to five years of specialized training in a hospital.

The ophthalmologist limits his medical practice to the eye. He examines the eye with special equipment and determines the degree of *refraction* in the lens of the eye. Refraction is a measurement of the eye's ability to see. If the examination shows that the patient needs glasses, the ophthalmologist gives him a prescription for them. Glasses are made by an *optician.* If the ophthalmologist discovers that an eye condition requires surgery, he performs the necessary operation to correct the condition.

By studying the retina, an ophthalmologist may discover signs of a disease of some other part of the body. For example, such diseases as diabetes, hypertension, and certain forms of anemia may involve changes in the appearance of the retina. SIDNEY LERMAN

See also SURGERY (Specialties).

OPHTHALMOSCOPE, *ahf THAL muh skohp,* is an optical instrument for examining the interior of the eye. Physicians trained to treat the eyes can make certain

Bausch & Lomb

An Ophthalmoscope is an instrument used by an eye physician (ophthalmologist) to examine the interior of a patient's eye. A prism in the ophthalmoscope focuses a beam of light from the instrument into the eye.

diagnoses by examining abnormalities of the eye's interior with the use of the ophthalmoscope. The ophthalmoscope contains an electric light and a prism to focus light on the interior of the eye. Lenses are mounted with the light and prism in the head of the instrument, which is attached to a handle containing a flashlight battery. The lenses make it possible to focus the light to provide a clear view of the interior of the eye.

The ophthalmoscope was invented by a German physicist, Hermann von Helmholtz, in 1851 (see HELMHOLTZ, HERMANN L.). Helmholtz' instrument consisted of a sandwich of three thin plates of glass mounted at a 45 degree angle on a handle. A light was placed to the side of the eye under examination. Some light passed through the glass plates, but some was reflected into the eye. The lighted inside of the eye was observed through the glass. WILLIAM L. BENEDICT

OPIATE, *O pih ayt,* is a type of drug made from or containing opium. *Morphine* and *codeine* are opiates. Most opiates put a person to sleep, and partially or completely deaden the feeling of pain. Medicines of this kind are usually classed in the larger group, *narcotics* (sleep inducers). Narcotics are addicting, and should be taken only by prescription. SOLOMON GARB

OPINION. See THOUGHT AND JUDGMENT (Judgment); PUBLIC OPINION.

OPINION POLL. See POLL OF PUBLIC OPINION.

OPIUM, *O pih um,* is a powerful narcotic drug made from the juice of poppies native to Greece and the Orient. Cultivation of these plants is illegal in the United States. Doctors consider drugs made from opium to be among the most valuable of medicines. But these drugs become a menace to a person's health and morals when they are used improperly. Opium gets its name from the Greek word *opos,* meaning *juice.*

Opium poppies are cultivated in India, Egypt, and Turkey. The poppy grows 3 to 4 feet high. All parts of the plant contain a thick, milky juice. Commercial opium comes from the juice of the unripened *capsule* (seed pod), which forms beneath the flower petals. As soon as the petals fall, workers slit the green capsule

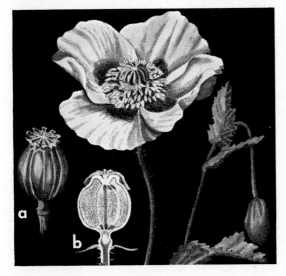

The Opium Poppy. Plant parts are (a) the ripe seed pod, and (b) a cross section of the pod showing the seeds in it.

and the juice oozes out. As the juice dries, it becomes brown and gummy. Workers gather the sticky substance, roll it into balls, and ship it to refineries. Refined opium is a white powder with a distinctive odor and a sharp, bitter taste.

Pure opium powder is rarely used in medicine. Physicians use compounds made from opium such as morphine and codeine to relieve pain, to ease convulsions, and to bring on sleep. Opium mixtures are sometimes used to control diarrhea.

Doctors always use medicines that contain opium or those that are made from it with great care because it is easy for patients to develop a craving for it. The craving may grow into a habit which the victim cannot overcome without treatment.

A person becomes addicted to opium because the drug causes a feeling of happiness and brings on wild, beautiful visions. Then, the person falls asleep or becomes half conscious. Some drug addicts eat opium or smoke it in pipes. Others inject the drug with a hypodermic needle or inhale it. See DRUG ADDICTION.

The moral and physical effects of the opium habit are similar to those produced by *morphine.* Morphine is the most important alkaloid in opium. *Laudanum,* or tincture of opium, is opium, alcohol, and water. *Paregoric,* which is often given to check intestinal fermentation, is opium, benzoic acid, and camphor. Opium and ipecac together form the drug called *Dover's powder.*

The Bureau of Narcotics and Dangerous Drugs, an agency of the United States government, administers federal laws concerning the sale and use of narcotic drugs. These drugs include opium and the various preparations made from it, such as codeine and morphine. The importation of crude narcotic drugs and the manufacture and distribution of products made from them are under strict government regulation. Doctors must state certain facts on narcotic prescriptions, and druggists must keep records of these prescriptions.

At one time, all drug addicts were imprisoned. But in 1935, the United States government opened a farm for drug addicts near Lexington, Ky. Addicts can live and work there while receiving treatment.

The Canadian government levies heavy customs duties to limit the amount of opium that can be imported. It entirely prohibits the importation of powdered opium prepared for smoking.

There is a large illegal trade in opium and the drugs made from it. "Dope" peddling is carried on in America and Europe. But the trade works the most havoc in Oriental countries where the public has not been educated against the evils of opium.

In 1917, China passed a law which made the growing of poppies unlawful. Some years later a vigorous drive was started against opium. But during World War II, Japanese invaders removed all restrictions on opium. They even set up large opium factories. In 1953, the United Nations Opium Conference adopted a memorandum designed to limit the production, export, and use of opium throughout the world. A. K. REYNOLDS

See also ANALGESIC; CODEINE; MORPHINE; PAREGORIC; POPPY.

OPIUM WAR. See CHINA (The "Unequal Treaties").

OPORTO. See PORTO.

611

Pix

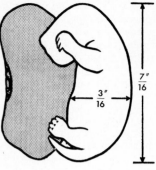

A Newborn Opossum is about the same size as a kidney bean.

7"/16

3"/16

A Teaspoon can hold from 15 to 18 newborn opossums.

A Mother Opossum carries her young on her back. Baby opossums stay in their mother's pouch for about two months after birth. They remain near the mother for several more weeks. Finally, when they can take care of themselves, they go off on their own.

OPOSSUM, *oh PAHS um,* is a furry animal that looks something like a rat. The female opossum carries its young in a pouch in its stomach. Opossums, kangaroos, and other animals that carry their young this way are called *marsupials*. Opossums are the only marsupials that are native to North America. They live in many places from Ontario south into South America and, in the United States, from New England to the state of Washington.

There are many *genera* and *species* (kinds) of opossums. Some opossums of Central and South America are as small as mice. But the *Virginia opossum,* the most common kind in the United States, grows to about the size of a house cat.

The Virginia species has rough grayish-white hair. This animal has a long snout, dark beady eyes, and big hairless ears. The Virginia opossum has a long tail that does not have much hair on it. The animal can hang upside down by wrapping its tail around the branch of a tree.

Virginia opossums have 50 teeth, more than any other North American *mammal* (milk-giving animal). Their teeth and claws are sharp. Opossum tracks are easy to recognize because the animal has long, widely separated toes.

Opossums are born in groups of from 5 to 20. At birth, an opossum is only about as big as a kidney bean. Like most other female marsupials, the female opossum has a pouch in the outer skin of its *abdomen* (lower part of its stomach). It carries its tiny babies in the pouch for about two months after birth. After leaving the pouch, the young stay near the mother for several more weeks.

Opossums hunt at night. They eat almost any kind of animal or vegetable food. When in danger, opossums lie motionless and appear to be dead. From this habit,

we say a person is "playing possum" when he pretends to be injured.　　　　　　　　　　FRANK B. GOLLEY

Scientific Classification: Opossums make up the opossum family, *Didelphidae*. The Virginia opossum is genus *Didelphis,* species *D. marsupialis.*

See also ANIMAL (color picture: Animals of the Woodlands); MARSUPIAL; YAPOK; CUSCUS.

OPPENHEIMER, J. ROBERT (1904-1967), an American physicist, became known as the man who built the atomic bomb. From 1943 to 1945, Oppenheimer directed the Los Alamos laboratory near Santa Fe, N.Mex., where the design and building of the first atomic bomb took place.

After World War II, Oppenheimer served as a leading government adviser. He was consultant to the newly formed U.S. Atomic Energy Commission (AEC), and played a key role in drafting its policies. Oppenheimer also served as a policy adviser to the U.S. Department of Defense, and helped draft the first U.S. proposals for international control of atomic energy.

In 1953, Oppenheimer's loyalty to the United States was questioned. His opposition to the development of the hydrogen bomb, together with his record of association with Communists, led to an investigation by an AEC security panel. The panel cleared Oppenheimer of all charges of disloyalty, but voted to deny him further access to official secrets. In 1963, however, the AEC awarded Oppenheimer its highest honor, the Enrico Fermi

United Press Int.

J. Robert Oppenheimer

award, for his work in the field of nuclear physics.

Oppenheimer was born in New York City. He studied theoretical physics at Harvard University, and graduated with honors in three years. From 1925 to 1929, he studied under some of Europe's leading physicists. He returned to the United States in 1929, and taught theoretical physics at the University of California and at the California Institute of Technology. Oppenheimer served as director of the Institute for Advanced Studies at Princeton University from 1947 until he retired in 1966.   RALPH E. LAPP

OPPER, FREDERICK BURR. See COMICS (History).

OPPOSITION, in astronomy, is a term which refers to the point at which the sun, the earth, and one of the outer planets from the earth are in a direct line with one another. When Mars, for example, is in line with the earth and the sun, Mars is said to be *in opposition.*

OPTIC NERVE. See EYE (The Eyeball; diagram).

OPTICAL GLASS. See GLASS (Specialty Glasses).

OPTICAL ILLUSION. As we look down a long, straight road, we see that it seems to grow narrower in the distance. Trees and telegraph poles along the road appear to grow smaller as they stretch away toward the horizon. We know that a white house looks larger than the same house painted a dark color, and that a person wearing a suit with up-and-down stripes looks thinner than he would if the stripes went crosswise. We call appearances

of this kind *optical illusions* because we know that in such cases things are not the way they appear to be.

Optical illusions of the kind described above are called "normal" illusions, because every person with normal eyesight experiences them. But an optical illusion does not occur every time we are deceived by what we see. Often we make mistakes in interpreting the impressions our eye receives. For example, many persons will read the sentence "he walked though the busy street," and never notice that the third word has no "r" in it. They *expect* to see "through" and therefore they *do* see "through." Such mistaken impressions are not optical illusions.   FRANK J. KOBLER

See also COLOR (How Color Fools the Eye); PSYCHOLOGY (picture: A Psychologist's Study of Perception); PERCEPTION (Factors Affecting Perception); MIRAGE.

OPTICAL MASER. See LASER.

OPTICAL SCANNER. See COMPUTER (Input Equipment).

OPTICIAN. See OPTOMETRY.

OPTICS, *AHP ticks,* is the branch of physics that studies light. *Physical optics* describes light and tries to explain why it acts as it does. Theories of waves and electromagnetism as they apply to light fall within this branch of optics. Another branch is *geometrical optics*, which deals

SOME COMMON OPTICAL ILLUSIONS

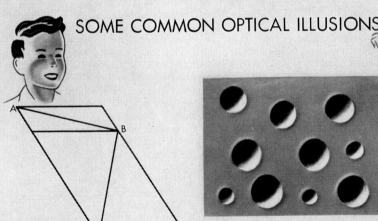

Line B-C Appears Longer than line A-B. Measure them and you will find they are the same length.

As You Look at This, the spots above appear to be depressions. But turn the book upside down and they will look like raised places.

Are You Looking Down at the top of these steps? Or are you looking up at them from below? Keep looking and watch them change from top to bottom.

Which Dish of ice cream is the larger? Wrong! They are the same size. The farthest one looks larger because it is not drawn in proper perspective.

In Time of War ships create optical illusions by means of camouflage. This makes it difficult to tell their size and shape, and the direction in which they are moving.

with reflection and refraction. It studies mirrors, lenses, and prisms, and gives the rules for these instruments. *Electrostatic electron optics* is the study of magnetic and electronic fields within an electron microscope.

Problems in optics include the speed of light, and the methods of measuring it. Optics measures brightness, and studies colors and spectra. Optics also studies the different optical instruments such as the camera, microscope, telescope, and eye. Other subjects are polarized light, interference, and diffraction.　　SAMUEL W. HARDING

Related Articles in WORLD BOOK include:

Camera	Huygens, Christian	Optometry
Color	Light	Polarized Light
Electron Microscope	Microscope	Refraction
Eye	Mirror	Spectroscope
Glasses	Newton, Sir Isaac	Telescope

OPTIMISM, *AHP tuh miz'm,* is the belief that there is much more good than evil in the world, and that the good will ultimately triumph over the evil. From Socrates to Leibniz, the greatest modern optimist, philosophers have held that evil is in the world so that men may learn to choose the good. The optimists hold that everything in nature, being the work of God, is ordered to produce the highest good; and that, since God is all wise and all powerful, this is the best possible world. The theory is the exact opposite of pessimism.

OPTIMIST INTERNATIONAL is a federation of men's service clubs in the United States and Canada. Membership is open to business and professional men. Optimists try to develop optimism as a philosophy of life. They also promote good government and civic affairs, respect for law, patriotism, friendship among all people, and service to youth.

The Optimist emblem is called a "Symbol of Service." The organization sponsors a wide range of community service projects and programs. For example, its *Respect for Law* program urges citizens to help improve law enforcement by supporting local police departments. Working with young people is another important Optimist activity. Clubs sponsor Bike Safety Week each April and Youth Appreciation Week each November. Optimists award five college scholarships annually to International Boys' Oratorical Contest winners.

Eleven Optimist clubs founded Optimist International in Louisville, Ky., in 1919. The organization now has over 100,000 members and over 3,000 clubs. Headquarters are at 4494 Lindell Boulevard, St. Louis, Mo. 63108.　　Critically reviewed by OPTIMIST INTERNATIONAL

OPTOMETRY is the practice of testing the eyes, measuring possible defects in vision, and prescribing glasses. In the United States, an *optometrist* has attended a college of optometry for four years. He must previously have attended a regular college for at least two years. He is required to have a license to practice his profession.

An optometrist has an O.D. (Doctor of Optometry) degree. He does not have an M.D. degree, and he thus differs from an *ophthalmologist,* a physician who specializes in the eye. Optometrists have no specific postgraduate training in a hospital.

The optometrist is restricted to examining the eye and measuring the behavior of its lens without the use of drugs. He may not prescribe drugs for any eye condition. Some optometrists prepare, fit, and sell glasses.

An *optician,* who has special training in optics, also prepares, fits, and sells glasses prescribed for a patient by an ophthalmologist or an optometrist.　　SIDNEY LERMAN

See also VOCATIONS (picture: Optometrists).

OPUNTIA. See CACTUS (Kinds of Cacti).

OPUS is the number given to a musical composition. It indicates the chronological position of a composition among a composer's works. An opus number is not always reliable, because it may be added at the time of publication. Opus is abbreviated *Op.*

ORACLES, *AHR uh k'ls,* in ancient Greece and Rome, were the answers given by a god to some question. The word can also mean the priest or other means by which the answer was given, or the place where the answer was given. Two well-known Greek oracles were the oracles of Apollo at Delphi and Zeus at Dodona.

The ancient Greeks and Romans believed that their gods took a personal interest in human affairs. The people asked the gods for advice. The gods were supposed to answer them through the oracles. The meanings of the answers were often difficult to understand, so special priests or priestesses interpreted the god's meaning. The people rewarded the priests and priestesses by giving them gifts.

At times, it was impossible even for the priests to know what the oracle meant. Croesus, king of Lydia, consulted the gods before he invaded Cappadocia. The oracle said that if he invaded this country he would bring ruin to an empire. Croesus thought this meant he would win, but the oracle had meant that the empire of Croesus would be ruined. And it was.

Many dishonest people pretended to be oracles. They tricked many of the worshipers and took their money.　　PADRAIC COLUM

See also CROESUS; DELPHI; DODONA; OLYMPIA.

ORAL CONTRACEPTIVE. See BIRTH CONTROL.

ORAL LAW is a body of Jewish laws, arising from interpretations and qualifications of the written law found in the Bible. These changes were made necessary by time, condition, and circumstances, and were handed down by word of mouth. They were finally put into writing in the Talmud, and helped Judaism to adjust itself to the changing science, philosophy, and sociology of new generations. After the Oral Law was codified and written, new interpretations of it in the form of commentaries arose to keep a dynamic tradition from becoming static. See also TALMUD.　　LOUIS L. MANN

ORAL MESSAGE. See FERLINGHETTI, LAWRENCE.

ORAL SURGERY. See DENTISTRY.

ORAN, *oh RAN,* or *oh RAHN* (pop. 187,390; met. area 425,875; alt. 35 ft.), is a Mediterranean Sea port in Algeria. It lies about 225 miles west of Algiers and across the sea from Cartagena, Spain. For location, see ALGERIA (color map). The city of Oran trades with cities of inland Africa and ports of southern Europe.

Oran was built by the Moors, and some of the old Moorish buildings are still standing. The city was captured by the Spaniards in 1509, by the Turks in 1708, and again by the Spaniards in 1732. Spain abandoned the city after it was destroyed in 1791 by an earthquake. In 1831, the French took possession of the ruins and rebuilt Oran into a place of importance. American forces were stationed in the city during World War II, after they invaded North Africa.　　KEITH G. MATHER

ORANGE. See COLOR.

ORANGE. The orange is the most important of all citrus fruits. It is widely used as a source of vitamin C, and can be drunk as juice or peeled and eaten.

There are two kinds of oranges, both of them closely related. The *sweet orange* is the kind commonly grown and eaten in the United States. The other kind is called the bitter, sour, Seville, or bigarade orange. The tangerine is often considered an orange. Actually, it is a citrus fruit of the *mandarin* group.

The sweet orange is thought to have come from southern China. It seems not to have reached the Mediterranean until several hundred years after the bitter orange. The bitter orange came from India, and was grown in the countries surrounding the Mediterranean Sea a thousand years after the birth of Christ. Both kinds of oranges were brought to America by the Spanish and Portuguese in the 1500's. The early Spanish settlers in Florida planted orange trees. The mission fathers of southern California planted orange trees there in the latter part of the 1700's.

The Orange Tree. The orange tree has dark green leaves that are shed gradually in spring and other periods of *growth flush* (increased growth). The white, waxy flowers appear in abundance during spring, and in scattered blooms during growth flushes. For hundreds of years orange blossoms have been considered a symbol of marriage. Honey made from orange blossoms is very good. The orange tree has long been considered one of the most beautiful trees. To the people who lived in northern Europe it was a symbol of the beauty of the sunny lands of Italy and Spain.

The orange tree grows to a height of about thirty feet. Its branches are very symmetrical and do not spread very much. The tree thrives in warm countries, and often requires irrigation. The bitter orange tree is somewhat hardier and resists cold somewhat better than the sweet orange. Both the bitter and the sweet orange resist cold better than limes or lemons.

U.S.D.A.

Washington Navel Orange Trees produce most of California's winter oranges. They were first imported from Brazil.

The Fruit of the orange is known to botanists as a *hesperidium*. It is really a special type of berry which grows only on citrus trees. The fruit has a soft central axis made of pith. Ten to fifteen segments surround the pith and contain the juice. The whole orange is enclosed in a soft rind. The *albedo* (inner part of the rind) is white and spongy. The *flavedo* (outer part) is orange-colored and is made up of small glands that contain an essential oil.

The juice of the orange contains sugars and citric acid. The spongy part of the rind contains a jelling substance called pectin. Orange juice is very high in vitamins A, B, and C, and it also contains mineral salts which are useful in the diet.

Oranges vary greatly in the number of seeds they contain. Most kinds of oranges contain many seeds. A few varieties have no seeds. Oranges are considered commercially seedless if they contain five seeds or less.

The Valencia orange is the most important late-season orange of California and Florida. Valencias account for almost half of the annual orange crop in the United States. They have a thin skin and a golden orange color, and are usually seedless.

The navel orange is really a double orange. A small second fruit that does not develop is embedded in one end of the main fruit to produce the so-called navel. All citrus fruits occasionally produce double fruits, but navel oranges do so regularly. The Washington navel

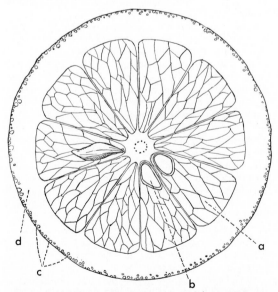

The Cross Section of an Orange shows (a) the edible part of the fruit; (b) location and cross section of the seed; (c) oil reservoirs just under the surface of the rind; and (d) the rind.

615

Fruit Sizers separate oranges into groups. Some oranges go directly to market. Others are made into juice and marmalade.

orange is normally seedless. The California navel orange is an important crop because it is harvested during the summer when Florida has no orange crop.

The *blood orange* is an interesting variation with juice that is colored by a red pigment called *anthocyanin*. It has a slightly higher iron content than other oranges. Blood oranges are more popular in Europe than in the United States.

Climatic factors cause Florida oranges and California oranges to differ. Oranges become bright orange only in regions where the night temperatures are below 50° F. during much of the ripening period. Florida oranges often require a red food-grade dye to obtain an orange color. The Florida orange is thinner-skinned, juicier, and has more sugar and less acid than California oranges. Florida oranges decay more easily and have a less attractive appearance. Green oranges from either state are often treated with ethylene gas to remove the green color and bring out the orange color.

Cultivation. Orange trees are sensitive to cold and sudden heat. If the temperature falls to 25° F., the fruit and the trees may be injured. If it falls to 20° F., injury may be severe. For this reason, the trees require a tropical or subtropical climate. In the latter, during occasional cold spells the trees are kept warm by means of orchard heaters.

While the orange tree itself grows very well in the tropics, the fruit is pale and flat in taste. For this reason its commercial culture is largely confined to the subtropics. In such areas, however, the trees are sometimes subject to sudden heat waves, which cause the young fruit to fall off. The tree is also sensitive to strong or prevailing winds. Living windbreaks are commonly used to provide wind protection.

The orange can be grown in a much wider range of climate than the lemon can, but it is not able to grow in as wide a range of climate as the grapefruit. In the United States, most oranges are grown in central and southern Florida, the lower Rio Grande Valley in Texas, and parts of Arizona and southern California.

It costs more to produce oranges in California than in Florida. The Florida rainfall is usually adequate, and irrigation is necessary only when the distribution of rainfall is irregular throughout a season. Irrigation is necessary in California and Texas. Also, labor costs are higher and crop yields are lower in California.

The orange tree is bud grafted onto the root systems of other citrus trees. The bitter orange is generally used because it is hardier and more resistant to disease than the root system of the sweet orange. But it is easily affected by a dreaded virus disease called *Tristeza*. Other kinds of rootstocks used include those of the rough lemon, sweet orange, and grapefruit. The sweet lime tree is used in Israel. The orange tree can adapt itself to many different kinds of soil. But it requires soil that is well drained and not too acid or alkaline. It also suffers if too much irrigation is given. Orange trees yield best when they are very heavily fertilized. They respond mainly to applications of nitrogen and organic matter. They sometimes respond also to applications of magnesium. To make certain that the trees get enough of these necessary elements, salts containing zinc and copper are commonly sprayed on the trees. A complete nutritional program that includes such elements as manganese, molybdenum, and boron is necessary in light, sandy soils.

To control insects and fungus diseases, the trees are sprayed with *pesticides* (pest-killers), the use of which is regulated by the federal government. In other cases, insects are controlled by introducing or aiding their enemies. Fungi which grow in the insects' bodies are sometimes sprayed on the trees. Sometimes insects which prey on harmful insects are especially raised for this purpose.

Oranges require a good deal of heat in order to ripen. Only in very hot places do oranges ripen during the fall and winter months. In cooler climates the oranges ripen in the spring or summer a year after the trees have bloomed. Therefore, in the late spring months a tree may carry ripe fruit, young green fruit, and flowers all at the same time.

Some kinds of oranges require more heat than others to ripen their fruit. Therefore, there are varieties which ripen early, others that ripen in midseason, and still others that are late in maturing. Oranges in California ripen throughout the year. Therefore, California oranges are the only ones that are commonly found in grocery stores during the summer months.

Harvesting and Marketing. Oranges are picked when the juice, sugar, and acid contents reach the levels established by state and federal laws. Most oranges are clipped off the trees in California. Workers prefer to pull Florida oranges. Oranges are usually sent to the packing house for immediate processing, unless it is necessary to color them with ethylene gas. The oranges are washed, dried, waxed, graded, and sized. They may also be color-added, stamped, and treated with a *fungicide* (fungus-killer). Most California oranges are shipped to serve as fresh fruit. As many as 80 per cent of the Florida oranges are sent to canneries that produce frozen orange concentrate.

Uses. Over three-fourths of the oranges processed in the United States are made into frozen orange juice concentrate. Other products include soft drinks, wine, and powdered instant orange juice.

LEADING ORANGE-GROWING STATES

Boxes (70 pounds) of oranges and tangerines grown in 1969

Florida ꙮꙮꙮꙮꙮꙮꙮꙮꙮꙮꙮꙮꙮꙮꙮꙮꙮꙮꙮꙮ
171,371,000 boxes

California ꙮꙮꙮꙮꙮꙮ
48,150,000 boxes

Arizona ꙮ
5,946,000 boxes

Texas ꙮ
5,786,000 boxes

Source: *Citrus Fruits, By States, 1968-69 and 1969-70,* U.S. Department of Agriculture

Various by-products of the orange include the peel, which can be candied, dried, or made into marmalade. Orange oil and pectin are other products made from the peel. It is also used in candymaking. Cannery wastes are used in the preparation of livestock feed. Orange oil is used for flavoring and perfumes.

The world production of oranges has increased greatly since World War II. It now averages about 860 million 70-pound boxes a year. The United States is the largest producer in the world. More than a fourth of the oranges grown come from the United States. Brazil, India, Israel, Italy, Japan, and Spain are other leading producers. Orange growing is also important in Algeria, Argentina, Communist China, Egypt, Greece, Morocco, Pakistan, and South Africa.

Over 90 per cent of the oranges in the United States are produced in Florida and California. The states of Arizona, Texas, and Louisiana grow the remainder. About 250,000 acres in California are planted in orange trees. The industry traditionally centered around Los Angeles, but the increased growth of cities in that area has forced the industry north and east. Nearly 300,000 acres in Florida are used for growing oranges. The Florida industry centers chiefly in central Florida. Winter Haven and Orlando are important orange growing centers. But a series of severe freezes since 1957

LEADING ORANGE-GROWING COUNTRIES

Boxes (70 pounds) of oranges and tangerines grown in 1969

United States ꙮꙮꙮꙮꙮꙮꙮꙮꙮꙮꙮꙮꙮꙮꙮꙮꙮꙮꙮꙮꙮꙮꙮ
237,028,000 boxes

Brazil ꙮꙮꙮꙮꙮꙮꙮꙮꙮ
92,374,000 boxes

Japan ꙮꙮꙮꙮꙮꙮꙮꙮ
82,264,000 boxes

Spain ꙮꙮꙮꙮꙮꙮ
57,068,000 boxes

Italy ꙮꙮꙮꙮꙮ
52,785,000 boxes

Israel ꙮꙮꙮ
30,172,000 boxes

India ꙮꙮꙮ
28,345,000 boxes

Source: *Monthly Bulletin of Agricultural Economics and Statistics,* June, 1970, FAO

caused growers to move south into newly reclaimed swamplands. About 35,000 acres in Texas are used to grow oranges.

The Bitter Orange. The bitter orange is widely grown for use as *rootstock seedlings*, on which to bud-graft sweet oranges and other citrus fruits. It also is grown for other purposes in the Mediterranean region, particularly in Spain. Bitter orange marmalade is made from it. In southern France, the flowers of the bitter orange are distilled for their perfume. Eau de Cologne is made from it, and essential oils are made from the tender buds, shoots, and leaves of the trees.

Scientific Classification. The orange tree belongs to the rue family, *Rutaceae.* The common or sweet orange is genus *Citrus,* species *C. sinensis.* The bitter orange is *C. aurantium.*　　　　　　　　　WILLIAM GRIERSON

See also FOOD, FROZEN (pictures); LEAF (picture: Kinds of Tree Leaves); TANGOR.

ORANGE, HOUSE OF. See MARY (II); WILLIAM (III) of England; WILLIAM I, PRINCE OF ORANGE.

ORANGE BOWL. See FOOTBALL (table).

ORANGE DAY. See NORTHERN IRELAND (People; picture); GREAT BRITAIN (picture).

ORANGE FREE STATE is a province of South Africa. It is a land of rolling plains and light rainfall. The province covers an area of 49,866 square miles. For location, see SOUTH AFRICA (color map).

Most of the 1,386,547 people who live in the Orange Free State are Bantus, a Negro group. They live mainly by raising livestock. More and more land is being planted in grain, especially in the eastern districts. Great deposits of gold and uranium have been discovered in the province. Bloemfontein is the capital of the Orange Free State.

Europeans first entered the area in the 1700's. About 1836, Boers from Cape Colony settled the section. The British claimed the land in 1848 and called it the Orange River Sovereignty. In 1854 it was declared independent and renamed the Orange Free State.

By 1899, disagreements between the Boers and the British led to the Boer War (1899-1902). The Boers were defeated. In 1900, the Orange Free State again became a British possession, and was known as the Orange River Colony. Ten years later, as the Orange Free State, it became a part of the Union of South Africa (now Republic of South Africa).　　　HIBBERD V. B. KLINE, JR.

See also BLOEMFONTEIN; BOER; BOER WAR; PRETORIUS.

ORANGE HAWKWEED. See DEVIL'S-PAINTBRUSH.

ORANGE RIVER is the longest river in South Africa. It was named for the princes and noblemen of the Dutch House of Orange. The Orange rises in the high eastern mountains of Lesotho, less than 200 miles west of the Indian Ocean. The river follows a winding course westward for about 1,300 miles as it cuts across the continent to empty into the South Atlantic Ocean. The upper river forms the border between the Cape of Good Hope and Orange Free State provinces. The lower river separates the Cape Province and South West Africa. The Vaal River is the largest branch of the Orange River.

Steep banks border the Orange River. For the last 200 miles of its course the river flows through almost desert country. The stream has many rapids and falls. At King George's (Aughrabies) Falls, the waters drop nearly 400 feet into a deep canyon in solid rock. These rapids and a large sand bar at the mouth of the stream, which is one mile wide, make shipping impossible. But the waters above the Great Falls are useful for many irrigation projects. See SOUTH AFRICA (color map).

In 1962, the South African government announced a 30-year development plan for the Orange River. The $630 million project includes 12 hydroelectric dams, and will irrigate 720,000 acres of land. KENNETH ROBINSON

See also VAAL RIVER.

ORANGEMEN. See WILLIAM (III).

ORANGEROOT. See GOLDENSEAL.

ORANGES, THE, are a group of cities in New Jersey. See EAST ORANGE.

ORANG-UTAN, *oh RANG oo tan,* is a large, rare ape that lives in Sumatra and Borneo. The name *orang-utan* comes from a Malay word meaning *man of the woods.* The orang-utan stands from 3 to 5 feet tall, and is covered with coarse reddish-brown hair. Male orang-utans may weigh from 150 to 200 pounds. Some males have an arm spread of 7½ feet, one of the largest of all the apes. Females are only about half as large as males. The orang-utan's arms reach to its ankles when the animal stands.

The orang-utan lives in trees, and rarely comes down to the ground. It moves carefully through the forest by climbing from branch to branch with its arms. It builds a nest in the trees to sleep in during the night. These nests are from 20 to 80 feet above the ground. The orang-utan usually eats fruits and leaves.

Orang-utans are silent, peaceful animals. Man is their main enemy. They live in groups of from two to five animals. These groups may not always stay together.

Arthur W. Ambler, National Audubon Society

Orang-Utans are powerful but peaceful apes. They use their long, strong arms to climb through branches in the forest.

Sometimes the animals travel through the forest alone.

Scientific Classification. Orang-utans belong to the anthropoid ape family, *Pongidae.* They are classified as genus *Pongo,* species *P. pygmaeus.* GEORGE B. SCHALLER

See also ANIMAL (color picture: Animals of the Tropical Forests); APE.

ORATORIO, *AWR uh TOH rih oh,* is a musical composition using soloists, chorus, and orchestra. The subject is usually taken from the Bible, but may be a theme which is not strictly sacred. Scenery and action are not used in the performance. The oratorio is named from the Oratory, or mission hall, in Rome, where from 1571 to 1594 sacred musical performances were held. These were the basis of modern oratorios. The first and most popular subject was the Passion, or suffering of Christ. Johann Sebastian Bach's *Passion According to Saint Matthew* is the most famous. The next step was the epic oratorio, of which George Frideric Handel was the greatest writer. He composed 15 grand oratorios. The *Messiah* and *Judas Maccabaeus* are the best known of these. After these came Joseph Haydn's *The Creation* and *The Seasons,* and then Felix Mendelssohn's *Elijah* and *Saint Paul.*

Oratorios of today often have a dramatic element. Outstanding examples are Sir William Walton's *Belshazzar's Feast,* Ralph Vaughan Williams' *Sancta Civitas,* and Arthur Honegger's *King David.* RAYMOND KENDALL

See also BACH (family); CHORUS; HANDEL, GEORGE FRIDERIC; OVERTURE.

ORATORS AND ORATORY. An orator is a skillful speaker who tries to influence his listeners by eloquent speeches. The art of an orator is called *oratory* or *rhetoric.* An orator follows rules of oratory. For some of the rules used today, see PUBLIC SPEAKING; DEBATE.

Beginnings. A mass of lawsuits arose when a democracy was established in Syracuse in Sicily in 466 B.C. They were brought by former exiles whose property had been seized by the tyrants. Many claims were several years old, and documentary evidence was often lacking. The claimants needed help in presenting their cases. Corax, a Sicilian Greek, was the first to supply this help, and is considered the founder of oratory. He established a system of rules for public speaking in the 460's B.C., with the aid of his pupil Tisias. He developed rules governing the organization of speech materials. He said that a speech usually should have five parts: (1) *proem* (introduction); (2) narrative; (3) arguments; (4) subsidiary remarks; and (5) summary.

Other early teachers of rhetoric include Protagoras, who developed the principles of debate; Gorgias, who emphasized style; Hippias, who was chiefly interested in the use of memory; and Lysias, who "showed how perfect elegance could be joined to plainness."

From Syracuse, the study of speechmaking spread to Athens, where the democratic form of government led to a general interest in the new art. During the 400's B.C., almost all male Athenian citizens attended the general assembly, where public policies were debated. They took part in the formulation of policies and the administration of justice. In the courts, they acted as jurors. The whole decision in each case rested with members of the jury, because there were no judges. Those who brought the charges and those who defended themselves pleaded their own cases. This led to a study of speechmaking.

Classical Orators. The first great Greek orator was Pericles. His speeches were reported by Thucydides in his famous *History of the Peloponnesian War*. Pericles' Funeral Oration is the best-known of all his speeches. The greatest Greek orator was Demosthenes. By patriotic speeches, he tried to inspire his countrymen to make Athens the leader of the Greek city-states.

The outstanding Greek writer on rhetoric was Aristotle. He defined rhetoric as "the faculty of discovering in every case the available means of persuasion." Aristotle emphasized three methods of proof: (1) *ethical* (the influence of the speaker's personality); (2) *pathetic* (the influence of the speaker's use of emotional appeal); and (3) *logical* (the influence of the use of formal principles of reasoning in proof).

Cicero holds first place among the important early Roman orators. Authorities believe that the *Rhetorica ad Herennium* was written by Cicero about 86 B.C. It states that an orator must divide his preparation of a speech into five steps. These steps are: (1) *invention* (analysis of speech situation and audience, investigation and study of subject matter, and selection of speech materials); (2) *disposition* (the arrangement of the speech materials under what we now call introduction, discussion, and conclusion); (3) *style* (the use and grouping of words to express ideas clearly, accurately, vividly, and appropriately); (4) *memory* (methods of memorizing material); and (5) *delivery* (the oral presentation).

Book I of Cicero's *De Oratore*, written about 55 B.C., develops the theme that a great orator must be a man of great learning and that the "proper concern of an orator . . . is language of power and elegance accommodated to the feelings and understandings of mankind." Book II emphasizes the importance of invention and disposition, with particular attention to court oratory. Book III deals with style and delivery. Here, Cicero shows that an orator should speak "correctly, perspicuously, elegantly, and to the purpose."

The *Institutes of Oratory* (A.D. 90) by Quintilian deals with the teaching of speechmaking and the education of orators. Even today, the *Institutes of Oratory* is one of the most comprehensive works on training speakers.

Later Orators. With the coming of Christianity, the preacher replaced the political speaker. Famous early preachers include Paul, John Chrysostom, and Augustine. Outstanding speakers for religious reform were Savonarola in the late 1400's and Martin Luther and John Calvin during the Reformation in the 1500's.

Political oratory again became important in the 1700's. During the French Revolution, Comte de Mirabeau spoke for the common people fighting royal authority.

Great Britain has produced many distinguished speakers throughout its history of parliamentary government. They include Edmund Burke, Benjamin Disraeli, William Gladstone, and Winston Churchill.

American orators include Patrick Henry, John C. Calhoun, Daniel Webster, Stephen A. Douglas, and William Jennings Bryan.   W. HAYES YEAGER

Related Articles in WORLD BOOK include:

FAMOUS AMERICAN ORATORS

Adams, John Q.	Henry, Patrick
Bryan (William J.)	Ingersoll, Robert G.
Clay, Henry	Lincoln, Abraham
Douglas, Stephen A.	Phillips, Wendell
Douglass, Frederick	Roosevelt, Franklin D.
Everett, Edward	Rutledge, John
Grady, Henry W.	Sumner, Charles
Hamilton, Alexander	Webster, Daniel

OTHER ORATORS

Aeschines	Isocrates
Burke, Edmund	Lysias
Chrysostom, Saint John	Mirabeau, Comte de
Churchill, Sir Winston	Pericles
Cicero	Pitt (family)
Demosthenes	Quintilian

ORBIT, in astronomy, is the path of any object in space whose motion is controlled by the gravitational pull of a heavier object. Astronomers call the heavier object the *primary* and the lighter object the *secondary*. The moon is a secondary that revolves in an orbit around the earth, a primary. The earth, in turn, is a secondary that travels in an orbit around the sun.

The term *orbit* is used for the path of either a natural object or a man-made object, such as a spacecraft. Early spacecraft could travel only around the earth. Today, spacecraft can move out of earth orbit and become secondaries of the moon, the sun, or another planet.

A certain speed is required before a secondary can orbit around its primary. If a secondary does not achieve *escape velocity*, the speed required to escape the gravita-

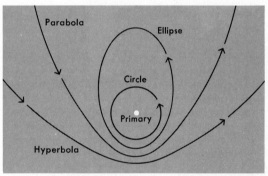

WORLD BOOK diagram

The Shape of the Orbit an object takes around a primary, such as the sun, depends on its speed in relation to the speed needed to escape from the primary. The shape may be a circle, ellipse, parabola, or hyperbola.

tional pull of its primary, its orbit is a closed curve called an *ellipse* (see ELLIPSE). The primary is not at the exact center of the ellipse, and so the secondary travels closer to the primary at some times than at others. The point in the orbit of any secondary of the earth where it is nearest the earth is called the *perigee*. The farthest point is called the *apogee*. An orbit could be a perfect circle, but truly circular orbits rarely occur.

If a secondary reaches escape velocity, its orbit becomes an open curve called a *parabola*. If a secondary moves faster than escape velocity, its orbit becomes a flatter open curve called a *hyperbola*. A spacecraft that leaves earth orbit on a trip to another planet must travel in a hyperbolic orbit. See PARABOLA; HYPERBOLA.   ERIC D. CARLSON

See also MOON (How the Moon Moves); PLANET; SPACE TRAVEL.

ORBITING OBSERVATORY. See SPACE TRAVEL (Scientific Satellites); OBSERVATORY (picture).

ORCHARD. See FRUIT; HORTICULTURE.

Orchestra Concerts draw large crowds, especially for outdoor programs of beautiful music played under the stars.

ORCHESTRA is a group of musicians playing together. They may be playing on various stringed, wind, and percussion instruments. The term *orchestra* in ancient Greek theaters meant the space between the audience and stage, which was used by the chorus. Today the word still is used to mean the musicians' space before the stage, and sometimes the whole main floor. But it is more often used to mean the musicians themselves and their instruments.

Orchestras can be of almost any size. A string orchestra contains only stringed instruments. A symphony orchestra is large and has all the instruments needed to play symphonies. An orchestra may perform alone, it may accompany voices as in an opera or oratorio, or it may play with a solo instrument as in a concerto. It also may accompany dancers in a ballet, or provide "incidental" music between acts of a play.

Television and radio have special uses for the orchestra. It may introduce and identify a program by playing a "theme song," or add to the mood of a dramatic program by playing specially written "background" music. The motion picture uses orchestras more and more for this purpose. Sometimes music furnished by an orchestra tells part of the story, or furnishes clues as to what is happening. Producers have used orchestras in all kinds of productions. As a result, millions of people have come in contact with great orchestras.

A symphony orchestra is made up mainly of stringed instruments. It also has wind and percussion instruments, but fewer of them than of strings. A *band* usually has only wind and percussion instruments. A *dance orchestra* usually has wind and percussion instruments, a piano, and perhaps a few strings.

Orchestral Instruments can be grouped under four main types—strings, wood wind, brass, and percussion. The *string section* contains first violins, second violins, violas, violoncellos, and basses. The parts played by these instruments correspond roughly to the soprano, alto, tenor, baritone, and bass voices of a chorus. The symphony orchestra usually has about ten to fifteen first violins, ten to twelve second violins, and eight to ten violas, violoncellos, and basses.

The *wood-wind section* chiefly provides different tone

The Conductor Uses Signals and Gestures to tell the musicians how he wants them to play. These four candid photographs show how conductor Eugene Ormandy looks to the orchestra at rehearsal. First he asks the violins, on his left, to play lightly and delicately. Then he tells the whole orchestra to hold a phrase. He then asks for a sharp note from the brasses. Finally he pulls deep notes from basses and brasses.

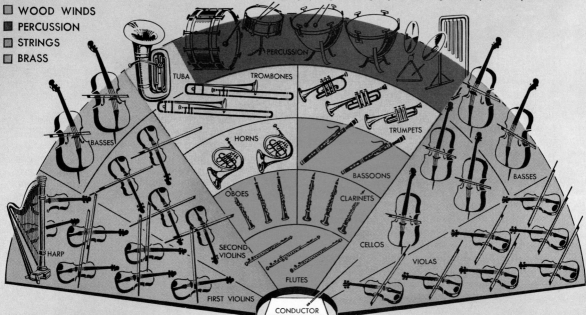

SEATING ARRANGEMENT

☐ WOOD WINDS
■ PERCUSSION
☐ STRINGS
☐ BRASS

The Conductor Chooses his own seating arrangement. Fritz Reiner had Chicago Symphony brasses grouped on the right and a piano with percussion.

TUBA

PERCUSSION

TROMBONES

TRUMPETS

BASSES

HORNS

BASSOONS

BASSES

OBOES

CLARINETS

CELLOS

HARP

SECOND VIOLINS

VIOLAS

FLUTES

FIRST VIOLINS

CONDUCTOR

One Arrangement has the violins facing the violas and cellos. The shape of the stage and the number of players influence seating arrangement.

School Orchestras are arranged to fit the number of students taking part. This orchestra has a large number of violins, but few cellos.

A **Dance Orchestra** provides music for such dances as the two-step, waltz, jitterbug, rock-and-roll, cha-cha-cha, twist, and mambo. Many dance orchestras feature singers.

Gay Claridge Orchestra

qualities. The flute, clarinet, and oboe are all high-pitched, but each has its own tone color. The flute tone is pure and velvety. The clarinet has a rich resonance in the low register and a trumpetlike tone in the high register. The oboe tone is thin, sweet, and rather shrill. The English horn is in a lower-pitch register and is more somber, or sad. Some other wood winds are the bassoon, the piccolo, and the contra bassoon.

The *brass section* also has different pitch registers. The trumpets are the soprano brass, the French horns are the alto or tenor, the trombones are the tenor, baritone, or bass, and the tuba is the true bass.

The *percussion section* gives a rhythmic background and special tone-color effects. This group includes the timpani (or kettledrums), the snare drum, the bass drum, cymbals, gongs, bells, triangle, tambourine, and many other types of rhythm instruments.

The harp is sometimes used in the orchestra, especially in the symphony orchestra. The piano is not a regular orchestral instrument, but is often used in playing modern scores.

The Conductor is one of the most important members of the orchestra. He has two main duties. He must first conduct the rehearsals, and then see that his directions are followed during the actual performance. First he must see in rehearsal that all parts are played correctly and that the important melodies and harmonies are heard distinctly. The players must understand the conductor's style, interpretation, and choice of *tempo*, or speed. Stringed-instrument players must use their bows correctly and uniformly. Wind-instrument players must tongue and slur their parts carefully.

During the concert performance, the eyes of all players are on the conductor. Before him is a "full score,"

Photo by Colin McPhee, *courtesy HiFi Review*

An **Indonesian Orchestra** includes rhythm instruments, gongs, and *gamelangs*, somewhat like our xylophones. These instruments once belonged to the orchestra that played for a royal court in Java.

which contains all players' parts. The conductor leads the musicians by means of his baton, hand gestures, facial expressions, and movements of his body. Each movement has a meaning which all players must know. Some conductors use no scores. They have memorized entire symphonies.

Learning About Orchestral Performance is simple for everyone. We can all hear the finest symphony orchestra music through radio or recordings. We can buy inexpensive miniature scores of most standard orchestral works. By following these scores, it is possible for us to *hear* the music and *see* it at the same time. With a little practice, we can easily identify the different instruments and their characteristics.

It is much more interesting to hear an actual performance by a symphony orchestra if one is familiar with the music and the score. Then, there is the added thrill of seeing the players at their work—the great body of violinists with arms and bows working in unison, the brasses and wood winds making their entrances with precision and clarity, and the conductor producing seeming magic by the slightest movements of his baton or his hands.

History. Orchestras date back to the beginning of mankind. Even primitive peoples had crude musical instruments which they probably played in orchestral groups. The result probably would not have sounded like music to us, but it was probably rhythmic. Real orchestras did not appear until bowed string instruments became common, and wind instruments were developed so that the pitch could be controlled. It was also necessary to have a system of writing music before real orchestras could fully develop.

The modern orchestra began its slow growth about three hundred years ago. The small and poorly balanced groups of the 1600's were very different from the symphony orchestra of our day. The composer Jean Baptiste Lully (1633?-1687) *scored* (arranged) much of his operatic music for stringed instruments, although he sometimes added flutes, oboes, trumpets, and drums. Lully also used bassoons. But these wind instruments did not have their own parts to play. They merely *doubled* (played along with) the string parts. Later composers, chiefly Alessandro Scarlatti (1659-1725) and Henry Purcell (1659?-1695), wrote special parts for wind instruments and included the French horn.

The orchestras of Johann Sebastian Bach (1685-1750) and George Frideric Handel (1685-1759) had two flutes, two oboes, one or two bassoons, two horns, two trumpets, drums, and strings. These orchestras were prominent in the early and middle 1700's. Christoph Willibald Gluck (1714-1787) added two clarinets and some special percussion instruments. Joseph Haydn (1732-1809) and Wolfgang Amadeus Mozart (1756-1791) enlarged the orchestra still further. During the period from about 1760 to 1800, the clarinet became a fixed part of the orchestra. At this time, a balance of stringed instruments was established in the orchestra, and improvements were made in wind instruments.

In the 1800's, the orchestra added the trombone and tuba, increased the number of horns, and enlarged the string section. Great progress was made in the manner and style of writing scores. By the end of the 1800's, the full symphony orchestra was established, with its 90 to 100 players. CHARLES B. RIGHTER

Related Articles in WORLD BOOK include:

AMERICAN CONDUCTORS

Bernstein, Leonard	Rodzinski, Artur
Damrosch (Walter)	Shaw, Robert
Fiedler, Arthur	Sousa, John P.
Gould, Morton	Stock, Frederick A.
Herbert, Victor	Stokowski, Leopold A.
Mitropoulos, Dimitri	Whiteman, Paul
Ormandy, Eugene	

BRITISH CONDUCTORS

Barbirolli, Sir John	Goossens, Sir Eugene
Beecham, Sir Thomas	Sargent, Sir Malcolm
Boult, Sir Adrian	

GERMAN CONDUCTORS

Bülow, Baron von	Klemperer, Otto
Busch, Fritz	Muck, Karl
Damrosch (Leopold)	Spohr, Louis
Furtwängler, Wilhelm	Walter, Bruno

OTHER CONDUCTORS

Ansermet, Ernest	Mahler, Gustav
Ganz, Rudolph	Monteux, Pierre
Golschmann, Vladimir	Nikisch, Arthur
Iturbi, José	Reiner, Fritz
Karajan, Herbert von	Richter, Hans
Koussevitzky, Serge	Szell, George
Kubelik (Rafael)	Toscanini, Arturo
MacMillan, Sir Ernest C.	Villa-Lobos, Heitor

OTHER RELATED ARTICLES

Band	Music
Chamber Music	Symphony
Conducting	Symphonic Poem
Instrumental Music	

ORCHESTRA BELLS imitate the effect of real bells of cast bronze. The two types of orchestra bells are tubular chimes and metal bars. The chimes are usually from one to two inches in diameter and vary in length with the pitch. They are hung from a metal frame, and are struck with heavy leather-headed mallets. Their sound is deep and resonant. The metal bars are of varying size, usually not more than half an inch in thickness, and are arranged in rows much like the piano keyboard. They are struck with a hard mallet, and produce a ringing sound, more brilliant and higher-pitched than that of the tubular, hanging chimes. CHARLES B. RIGHTER

ORCHID, *AWR kid*, is one of the most beautiful flowers in the world. More than 6,000 *species* (kinds) of wild orchids grow throughout the world. Most of these are found in tropical and subtropical lands. But many kinds are found in cool, damp woods and swamps.

Each orchid blossom has three sepals and three petals. The petals range in color from white to deep violet, and they may be speckled or streaked. One petal, called the *lip*, always has a special shape. It may be long and narrow, wide with a fringe, or shaped like a pouch. The lip of the *lady's-slipper orchid* is shaped like a pouch or slipper. This orchid grows in United States forests and swamps. Blossoms of the *butterfly orchid* of Britain look like white butterflies with red spots. Early Spaniards named the *Holy Ghost orchid*. They believed its blossoms were sacred because they looked like the holy dove that flew down at the baptism of Christ.

Each kind of orchid is fertilized by pollen carried by a particular kind of insect. The size and shape of an orchid's blossoms are suited to that insect. Special

623

ORCHIDS

A Hybrid Cattleya Orchid, developed by crossbreeding in a conservatory. Cattleyas are popular but costly as cut flowers.

Cymbidium Orchids Are Native to southeastern Asia. This handsome Cymbidium is a hybrid developed under cultivation.

Odontoglossum Orchids, native to the Andes, require a cool, moist greenhouse.

This Greenhouse Cypripedium, with its vivid spots and strange shape, is related to the pink and yellow lady's-slippers of North America.

markings on the lip guide the insect toward the nectar inside the blossom. As the insect approaches this nectar, it brushes against pollen sacs in the blossom. Some of the pollen, and even the sacs themselves, may stick to the insect and be carried to another orchid of the same species. This process assures cross-fertilization within each kind of orchid (see FLOWER [How Flowers Reproduce; illustrations]).

In cool regions, orchids grow in the ground. But in tropical lands, many kinds of orchids grow high on the branches of trees. Their tiny seeds are carried there by the wind. When a seed sprouts, the young plant sends its roots out along the branch. These roots gather in a loose mass and some of them dangle in the air. Some of these orchids have a special corklike covering on their roots that enables the root to gather moisture directly from the air.

Raising orchids is a hobby that fascinates many people. They collect beautiful orchids from many lands and often build special greenhouses to raise them. Some of these orchids require six or seven years from the planting of the seed until they produce blossoms.

Some orchids produce useful items. For example, a climbing orchid called the *vanilla vine* has pods known as *vanilla beans* that produce the vanilla flavoring used in foods and beverages. Other orchids have potato-like swellings on their roots. These swellings are dried to make *salep*, a substance that is used in medicines.

Scientific Classification. Orchids make up the orchid family, *Orchidaceae*. Lady's-slippers make up the genus *Cypripedium*. Other genera in the Americas include *Arethusa, Calypso,* and *Habenaria*.   ROBERT W. SCHERY

See also FLOWER (color pictures: Cattleya Orchid, Flowers of the Woodland [Showy Orchis, Pink Lady's-Slipper], Mountain Flowers [Calypso]); LADY'S-SLIPPER; VANILLA.

ORCUS. See PLUTO.

ORD RIVER in Western Australia is the center of a development project that includes two dams and hydroelectric power plants. The project will supply water to irrigate about 200,000 acres of land for cotton, rice, and other crops. Its power plants will supply power for the area.

The Ord River rises near Hall's Creek and flows northward for about 300 miles through the dry, sandy region in the northeast corner of Western Australia. It empties into Cambridge Gulf near Wyndham. With its tributaries, the Ord River drains about 17,000 square miles.

ORDER is a unit of scientific classification. Animals and plants are divided into seven major groups called kingdoms, phyla, classes, orders, families, genera, and species. Members of an order are more closely related than are members of a class. But members of orders are not so closely related as are members of families. See also CLASSIFICATION (table).   WILLIAM V. MAYER

ORDER, FRATERNAL. See FRATERNAL SOCIETY.

ORDER IN COUNCIL. Decrees issued by the British Crown when matters of great importance confront the nation are called Orders in Council. They get this name from the fact that they are proclaimed with the advice of the Privy Council. In 1807, Great Britain issued Orders in Council in answer to Napoleon's threat to blockade the island empire. By these orders, British ships blockaded

the European coast and kept neutral trading vessels from entering ports of Napoleonic Europe. See also CONTINENTAL SYSTEM; PRIVY COUNCIL.   BASIL D. HENNING

ORDER OF ————. Many orders are listed in THE WORLD BOOK ENCYCLOPEDIA under the key word in the names of the order, for example: DE MOLAY, ORDER OF.

ORDERED PAIR. See ALGEBRA (Functions).

ORDERS, RELIGIOUS. See RELIGIOUS LIFE.

ORDINANCE is a public law or regulation made usually by the governing body of a city, town, or village. A *resolution* of a city council is another name for an ordinance. Ordinances are usually only local in nature.

The name *ordinance* has also been given to regulations that serve as laws, but are not actually constitutions. The Ordinance of 1787 was such a regulation (see NORTHWEST ORDINANCE). *Ordinance* may also refer to a church sacrament, such as Communion.

ORDINANCE OF SECESSION. See CIVIL WAR (Secession).

ORDINANCE OF 1785. See WESTWARD MOVEMENT (Solving Frontier Problems).

ORDINANCE OF 1787. See NORTHWEST ORDINANCE.

ORDINARY. See COLONIAL LIFE IN AMERICA (Recreation).

ORDNANCE, *AWRD nunce,* is a military term used for weapons and ammunition. Most armies, navies, and air forces have ordnance departments. It is the job of the departments to design, make, repair, and distribute weapons and ammunition. The term *ordnance* also includes the tools used in the manufacture of these items.

See also AMMUNITION; WEAPON.

ORDOVICIAN PERIOD. See EARTH (table: Outline of Earth History).

ORE, *ohr,* is a mineral or a rock that contains enough of a metal to make it worth mining. Often, two or more metals can be obtained from the same ore. Ores naturally occur in beds or veins, mixed in with valueless minerals called the *gangue.*

There are two types of ores—*native metals* and *compound ores.* In *native metals,* the valuable mineral occurs as a pure metal. It is not chemically combined with other substances. Gold, silver, platinum, and copper often occur as native metals. Smelting melts the bands or lumps of pure metal out of the gangue.

In *compound ores,* the valuable metal is joined to other substances such as oxygen, sulfur, carbon, or silicon to form various chemical compounds. The ores of iron, aluminum, and tin are usually found joined with oxygen and form compounds called *oxides.* Copper, lead, zinc, silver, nickel, and mercury are found joined with sulfur and form compounds called *sulfides.* Chemical changes free the metal from the compound. Some metals are freed by electric current in a process called *electrolysis.* Other metals are dissolved out of the ore by acids in a process called *leaching.* More information on these processes is found in METALLURGY (Extractive Metallurgy).   RICHARD M. PEARL

See also MINERAL; ROCK.

ÖRE, *UH reh,* is a bronze coin used in Norway, Denmark, and Sweden. It is worth one-hundredth of a krone, or krona. See also KRONA; KRONE.

OREAD. See NYMPH.

OREGANO. See MARJORAM.

Sunset on the Oregon Coast at Cannon Beach

Ray Atkeson

Oregon (blue) ranks 10th in size among all the states, and 2nd in size among the Pacific Coast States (gray).

The contributors of this article are Jesse L. Gilmore, Associate Professor of History at Portland State University; Richard M. Highsmith, Jr., Chairman of the Department of Geography at Oregon State University; and Robert C. Notson, Publisher of The Oregonian.

——————— FACTS IN BRIEF ———————

Capital: Salem.

Government: *Congress*—U.S. senators, 2; U.S. representatives, 4. *Electoral Votes*—6. *State Legislature* (Legislative Assembly)—senators, 30; representatives, 60. *Counties* —36. *Voting Age*—21 years (state and local elections); 18 years (national elections).

Area: 96,981 square miles (including 772 square miles of inland water), 10th in size among the states. *Greatest Distances*—(east-west) 375 miles; (north-south) 295 miles. *Coastline*—296 miles.

Elevation: *Highest*—Mount Hood in Clackamas and Hood River counties, 11,245 feet above sea level. *Lowest*—sea level, along the Pacific Ocean.

Population: *1970 Census*—2,091,385; 31st among the states; density, 22 persons to the square mile; distribution, 67 per cent urban, 33 per cent rural. *1960 Census*—1,768,687.

Chief Products: *Agriculture*—beef cattle, cherries, dairy products, eggs, greenhouse and nursery products, hay, mint, onions, pears, potatoes, snap beans, strawberries, wheat. *Fishing Industry*—Dungeness crabs, salmon, shrimp, tuna. *Manufacturing*—food and food products, lumber and wood products, machinery, transportation equipment. *Mining*—clay, diatomite, gem stones, gold, mercury, nickel, peat, perlite, pumice, sand and gravel, silver, stone.

Statehood: Feb. 14, 1859, the 33rd state.

State Motto: The Union.

State Song: "Oregon, My Oregon." Words by J. A. Buchanan; music by Henry B. Murtagh.

OREGON

THE BEAVER STATE

OREGON, a Pacific Coast state, is known for its vast forests of evergreen trees. Forests cover almost half the state, and every large Oregon city has factories that make wood products. Oregon has nearly a fifth of the nation's timber, and it leads in lumber production.

The rugged beauty of Oregon's mountains, seacoast, and forest lands attracts more than 7½ million tourists a year. Hunters shoot deer and elk and other game in Oregon's wooded regions. Sportsmen enjoy fishing in sparkling lakes and rivers, and in Pacific waters.

Oregon is often called the *Pacific Wonderland* because of its outstanding natural wonders. These include Crater Lake in the Cascade Mountains, the Columbia River Gorge, Hells Canyon on the Snake River, and Oregon Caves National Monument. Mount Hood, Mount Jefferson, and other snow-covered peaks rise majestically in the Cascade Range. The Wallowas, in northeastern Oregon, also offer spectacular mountain scenery. Steep cliffs rise along much of Oregon's wave-swept coast. But parts have sandy beaches and protected harbors.

The dry lands east of the Cascade Mountains have large livestock ranches. Potatoes, sugar beets, and other vegetables grow in irrigated areas of eastern Oregon. Wheat, Oregon's most valuable crop, comes chiefly from the north-central area. Orchard fruits from Oregon's Hood and Rogue river valleys are world famous.

The mighty Columbia River forms most of the boundary between Oregon and Washington. Huge dams on the Columbia supply electric power for homes and industries. The dams also improve the river for shipping, and provide water for irrigation. The Columbia was once called the Oregon, or *Ouragan*, which means *hurricane* in French. Some authorities think that Oregon's name came from this historic name. Oregon is known as the *Beaver State*, because the region supplied thousands of beaver skins during fur-trading days.

In the early days, Oregon meant the end of the trail for many pioneers. During the 1840's and 1850's, thousands of settlers traveled by covered wagon on the Oregon Trail to the fertile farmlands of the Willamette Valley. Today, the Willamette Valley is Oregon's greatest center for trade and industry. It is also important for dairy products, flower bulbs, fruits, and vegetables. Most of Oregon's large cities are in the Willamette Valley. They include Portland, the largest city, and Salem, the state capital. Portland extends along both banks of the Willamette River near the place where the Willamette flows into the Columbia. It is an industrial city and a major seaport. More dry cargo is handled at Portland than at any other Pacific Coast port.

For the relationship of Oregon to other states in its region, see the article on PACIFIC COAST STATES.

Artist's View of Eugene

Constitution. The present state Constitution was adopted in 1857, two years before Oregon joined the Union. Constitutional amendments may be proposed by either house of the state legislature. A majority of each house must approve the amendments. The voters must then approve the proposed amendments in the next regular general election, unless the legislature orders a special election.

Constitutional amendments may also be proposed and passed directly by the people, through their powers of *initiative and referendum* (see INITIATIVE AND REFERENDUM). In addition, the Constitution may be revised by a constitutional convention called after a majority of the legislators and the voters approve.

Executive. The governor of Oregon is elected to a four-year term. He cannot serve more than 8 years during any 12-year period. The governor receives a yearly salary of $28,500. He also receives an expense allowance of $1,000 a month. The governor appoints members of many state boards and commissions. For a list of all the governors of Oregon, see the *History* section of this article.

Other top state officials include the secretary of state, attorney general, treasurer, and labor commissioner. These officials are also elected to four-year terms. The secretary of state and the treasurer cannot serve more than 8 years during any 12-year period.

Legislature of Oregon is called the *Legislative Assembly*. It consists of a Senate of 30 members and a House of Representatives of 60 members. The state is divided into 19 senatorial districts and 28 representative districts. The number of senators or representatives elected by each district depends on the population of the district. State senators serve four-year terms. Rep-

resentatives hold office for two years. The assembly meets in regular session in odd-numbered years. Sessions usually begin on the second Monday in January. The length of the session is not limited by law.

Courts. The highest court in Oregon is the state Supreme Court. It has seven justices elected to six-year terms. The court elects one of its members to serve a six-year term as chief justice. The next highest state court is the court of appeals. It has five judges who are elected to six-year terms.

Oregon is divided into 20 judicial districts. Each district has one or more circuit court judges. Circuit judges are elected to six-year terms by *nonpartisan* (no-party) ballot. A special tax court, which was created in 1961, ranks with the circuit courts. Lower courts include district courts, county courts, and justice courts.

Local Government. Oregon gives its cities and towns *home rule*. This means they have the right to choose their own form of government. Most cities with more than 5,000 persons have the council-manager form of government. Portland has a mayor and four commissioners. Most smaller cities have a mayor and a city council.

A 1958 amendment to the state Constitution extended home rule privileges to Oregon counties. However, only 4 of the state's 36 counties have taken action under this law.

A county judge and two commissioners rule on county business in most counties. A three-member board of commissioners exercises governmental power in most of the other counties. Most county judges and commissioners are elected to four-year terms.

Taxation. The state government receives most of its tax income from individual and corporation income

Entrance to Oregon's Capitol is flanked by massive marble monuments. One sculpture, *left*, honors the Lewis and Clark expedition through the Oregon region in 1805. The other sculpture, *right*, shows pioneers in a covered wagon on the Oregon Trail.

Oregon State Highway Dept.

The State Seal

The State Flag

Symbols of Oregon. On the state seal, 33 stars represent Oregon's entry into the Union as the 33rd state. The departing British man-of-war and arriving American merchant ship symbolize the end of British influence and the rise of American power. The sheaf of grain, the pickax, and the plow represent Oregon's mining and agricultural resources. The seal was adopted in 1859. The flag, adopted in 1925, has a reproduction of the seal.

taxes, gasoline taxes, and property taxes. The federal government provides about a third of the state's revenue, in the form of grants and other programs. Other sources of state revenue are inheritance taxes, gift taxes, and license taxes on motor vehicles, hunting, and fishing.

Politics. The Republican party has controlled Oregon politics during most of the state's history. Many industrial workers who settled in Oregon cities after World War II caused changes in the state's politics. In the mid-1950's, registered Democrats began to outnumber registered Republicans. The legislative districts were changed in the early 1960's. This action gave more representation to urban areas, where the Democrats have their greatest strength. But the state continued to elect Republicans to the governorship and other high state offices. For Oregon's voting record in presidential elections since 1860, see ELECTORAL COLLEGE (table).

The State Bird
Western Meadow Lark

The State Capitol in Salem was completed in 1939. It has a cylinder-shaped dome topped by a golden statue called *Pioneer.* Salem has been Oregon's capital since 1855. Earlier territorial capitals were Oregon City (1849-1851), Salem (1851-1855), and Corvallis (1855).

The State Flower
Oregon Grape

The State Tree
Douglas Fir

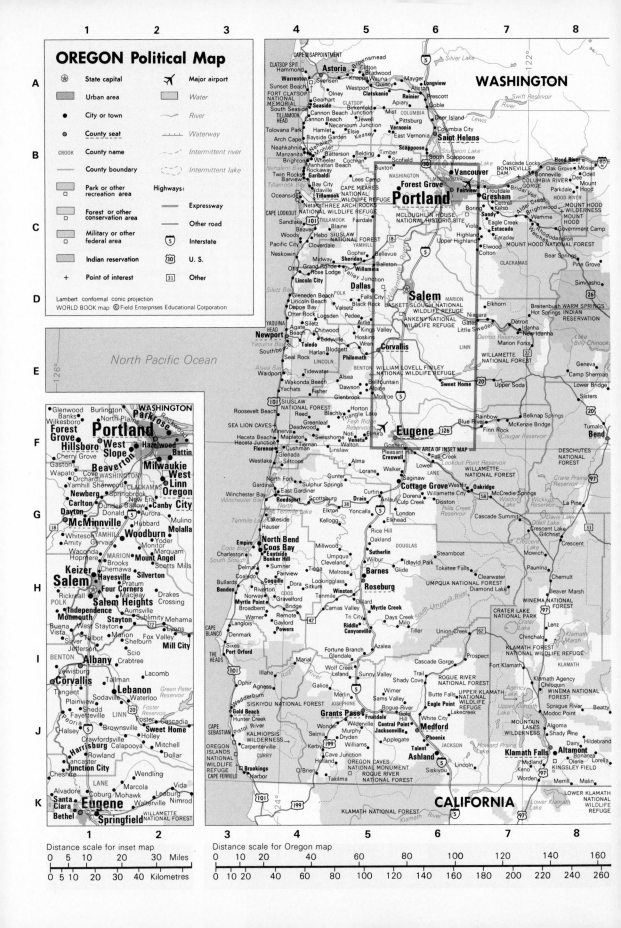

OREGON Political Map

Legend

✪	State capital	✈	Major airport
	Urban area		Water
●	City or town		River
⊙	County seat		Waterway
CROOK	County name		Intermittent river
	County boundary		Intermittent lake
	Park or other recreation area		Highways:
	Forest or other conservation area		Expressway
	Military or other federal area		Other road
	Indian reservation	⑤	Interstate
+	Point of interest	㉚	U.S.
		㉛	Other

Lambert conformal conic projection
WORLD BOOK map ©Field Enterprises Educational Corporation

North Pacific Ocean

WASHINGTON

CALIFORNIA

Distance scale for inset map
0 5 10   20   30 Miles
0 5 10 20 30 40 Kilometres

Distance scale for Oregon map
0 10 20   40   60   80   100   120   140 160 Miles
0 10 20 40 60 80 100 120 140 160 180 200 220 240 260

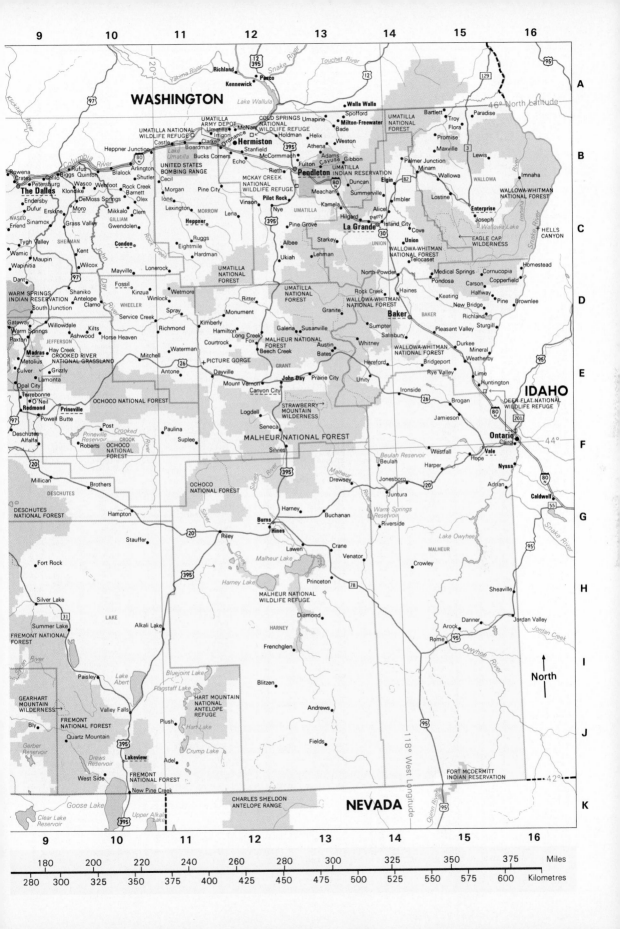

Population

2,091,385 ..Census..1970
1,768,687 ....“...1960
1,521,341 ....“...1950
1,089,684 ....“...1940
953,786 ....“...1930
783,389 ....“...1920
672,765 ....“...1910
413,536 ....“...1900
317,704 ....“...1890
174,768 ....“...1880
90,923 ....“...1870
52,465 ....“...1860
12,093 ....“...1850

Metropolitan Areas

Eugene 213,358
Portland 1,009,129
(880,675 in Ore.;
128,454 in Wash.)
Salem 186,658

Counties

Baker .....14,919..D 15
Benton ....53,776..E 5
Clackamas 166,088..D 7
Clatsop ..28,473..A 5
Columbia ..28,790..A 6
Coos ....56,515..H 4
Crook ....9,985..F 10
Curry ......13,006..J 3
Deschutes ..30,442..G 9
Douglas ....71,743..G 5
Gilliam .....2,342..C 10
Grant ....6,996..E 12
Harney .....7,215..I 12
Hood River .13,187..C 8
Jackson ....94,533..J 6
Jefferson ...8,548..E 9
Josephine ..35,746..J 5
Klamath ...50,021..I 8
Lake ....6,343..H 10
Lane .....213,358..F 6
Lincoln ....25,755..E 4
Linn ....71,914..E 6
Malheur ...23,169..G 15
Marion ....151,309..D 6
Morrow .....4,465..C 11
Multnomah 556,667..B 6
Polk ....35,349..D 5
Sherman ....2,139..C 9
Tillamook ..17,930..C 4
Umatilla ...44,923..C 13
Union ......19,377..C 14
Wallowa ....6,247..B 15
Wasco .....20,133..C 9
Washington .....157,920..B 5
Wheeler .....1,849..D 10
Yamhill ....40,213..C 5

Cities and Towns

Adams ....219..B 13
Adel ....J 11
Adrian ....G 16
Agate Beach ....D 4
Agness ....I 4
Airlie ....D 5
Albany ....18,181.°I 1
Albee ....C 12
Alder Creek ....C 7
Alfalfa ....F 9
Algoma ....J 8
Alicel ....C 14
Alkali Lake ....I 11
Allston ....A 6
Alma ....F 5
Alpine ....E 5
Alsea ....E 5
Altamont ..15,746..J 8
Alvadore ....K 1
Amity ....708..G 1
Andrews ....J 13
Anlauf ....G 5
Antelope ....51..D 9
Antone ....E 11
Apiary ....A 6
Applegate ....J 5
Arch Cape ....B 4
Arlington .....375..B 10
Arock ....I 15
Ashland ....12,342..J 6
Ashwood ....D 9
Astoria ....10,244.°A 4
Athena ....872..B 13
Aumsville .....590..H 1
Aurora ....306..G 2
Austin ....E 13
Azalea ....I 5
Bade ....B 13
Baker ....9,354.°D 14
Ballston ....D 5
Bandon .....1,832..H 3
Banks ....430..F 1
Barlow ......105..G 2
Barnes ....H 5
Barnett ....C 10
Bartlett ....A 15
Barview .....1,388..B 4
Bates ....E 13
Batterson ....B 4
Battin ....F 2
Bay City ......898..B 4
Bayside Garden ....B 4
Bear Springs ......C 8
Beatty ....J 8
Beaver ....C 4
Beaver Marsh ......H 8
Beaverton ..18,577..F 2
Beech Creek ....E 12
Belding ....B 5
Belknap Springs ...F 7
Bellevue ....C 5
Bellfountain ......E 5
Bend ......13,710.°F 8
Bethel ....K 1
Beulah ....F 14
Biggs ....B 9
Birkenfeld ....A 5
Blachly ....F 5
Black Rock ....D 5
Blaine ....C 4
Blalock ....B 10
Blitzen ....I 12
Blodgett ....E 5
Blue River ....F 7
Bly ....J 9
Boardman ....192..B 11
Bonanza ......230..J 8
Bonneville ....B 7
Boring ....C 7
Bradwood ....A 5
Breitenbush
Hot Springs ......D 7
Bridal Veil ....B 7
Bridge ....H 4
Bridgeport ....E 14
Brighton ....B 4
Brightwood ....C 7
Broadbent ....H 4
Brogan ....E 15
Brookings ...2,720..K 3
Brooks ....H 1
Brothers ....G 10
Brownlee ....D 16
Brownsmead ....A 5
Brownsville .1,034..J 1
Buchanan ....G 13
Bucks Corners .....B 12
Buena Vista ....I 1
Bullards ....H 3
Bunker Hill .1,549..H 3
Burlington ....E 1
Burns ....3,293.°G 12
Butte Falls ...358..J 6
Buxton ....B 5
Cairo ....F 16
Calapooya ....J 2
Camas Valley ......H 4
Camp Sherman ......E 8
Canby ......3,813..G 2
Cannon Beach 779..B 4
Cannon Beach
Junction ....A 4
Canyon City ..600.°E 12
Canyonville ..940..I 5
Carlton .....1,126..G 1
Carpenterville ......J 3
Carson ....D 15
Cascade Gorge .....I 6
Cascade Locks 574..B 7
Cascade Summit ....G 7
Cascadia ....J 2
Castle ....B 11
Cave Junction .415..J 4
Cayuse ....B 13
Cecil ....B 11
Celilo ....B 9
Central Point 4,004..J 6
Central Point
West* .....1,988..J 6
Charleston ....H 3
Chemawa ....H 1
Chemult ....H 8
Chenoweth* .2,329..B 9
Cherry Grove ......F 1
Cheshire ....K 1
Chiloquin .....826..I 7
Chinchalo ....I 8
Chitwood ....D 4
Clarke ....B 11
Clarno ....D 10
Clatskanie ...1,286..A 5
Clearwater ....H 7
Clem ....C 10
Cleveland ....H 5
Clifton ....A 5
Cloverdale ....C 4
Coaledo ....H 3
Coburg ....665..K 1
Cochran ....B 5
Colton ....C 7
Columbia City 537..B 6
Condon ....973.°C 10
Coos Bay ...13,466..E 3
Copperfield ....D 16
Coquille .....4,437.°H 3
Cornelius* ...1,903..C 6
Cornucopia ....D 15
Corvallis ...35,153.°E 5
Cottage
Grove .....6,004..G 5
Cottrell ....C 7
Courtrock ....E 12
Cove ....363..C 14
Cove Orchard ......F 1
Crabtree ....I 1
Crane ....G 13
Crates ....B 9
Crawfordsville .....J 1
Crescent ....G 8
Crescent Lake ......G 7
Creswell ....1,199..F 6
Crowley ....H 14
Culp Creek ....G 6
Culver ....407..E 9
Curtin ....G 5
Cushman ....F 4
Dairy ....J 8
Dallas ......6,361.°D 5
Danner ....H 15
Dant ....D 9
Dawson ....E 5
Days Creek ....H 5
Dayton ....949..G 1
Dayville ....197..E 11
Deadwood ....F 4
Dee ....B 8
Deer Island ....B 6
Delmar ....H 3
De Moss Springs ...C 9
Denmark ....I 3
Depoe Bay ....D 4
Deschutes ....F 9
Detroit ....328..D 7
Diamond ....H 13
Diamond Lake ......H 7
Dillard ....H 5
Disston ....G 6
Dollar ....J 2
Donald ....231..G 2
Dora ....H 4
Dorena ....G 6
Drain ....1,204..G 5
Drakes Crossing ....H 2
Drewsey ....22..F 13
Dryden ....J 5
Dufur ....493..C 9
Duncan ....B 13
Dundee ....588..G 1
Dunes* ....976..F 4
Durham* ......410..C 6
Durkee ....E 15
Eagle Creek ....C 7
Eagle Point .1,241..J 6
East Gardiner .....G 4
East Vernonia .....B 5
Eastside ....1,331..H 4
Echo ....479..B 12
Eddyville ....E 4
Eightmile ....C 11
Elgin ....1,375..B 14
Elkhead ....G 5
Elkhorn ....D 7
Elkton ....176..G 5
Elmira ....F 5
Elsie ....B 5
Elwood ....C 7
Endersby ....C 9
Enterprise ...1,680.°C 15
Erskine ....C 9
Estacada ....1,164..C 7
Eugene ....76,346.°F 5
Fairdale ....C 5
Fairview ....1,045..B 7
Fairview ....H 4
Falcon
Heights* ..1,389..J 8
Fall Creek ....F 6
Falls City ....745..D 5
Faraday ....C 7
Fayetteville ......J 1
Fields ....J 13
Finn Rock ....F 7
Fisher ....E 4
Flora ....B 15
Florence .....2,246..F 4
Forest Grove 8,275..B 5
Fort Klamath ......I 7
Fort Rock ....H 9
Fortune Branch ....I 5
Fossil ....511.°D 10
Foster ....J 2
Four Corners 6,199..H 1
Fox ....E 12
Fox Valley ....I 2
Frenchglen ....I 13
Friend ....C 9
Fruitdale ...2,655..J 5
Fulton ....B 13
Galena ....D 13
Galice ....I 4
Gardiner ....G 4
Garibaldi ...1,083..B 4
Gaston ....429..F 1
Gates ....250..D 7
Gateway ....D 9
Gaylord ....H 4
Gearhart ......829..A 4
Geneva ....E 8
Gervais ....746..G 1
Gibbon ....B 13
Gilchrist ....G 8
Gladstone* ..6,237..C 6
Glenada ....F 4
Glenbrook ....E 5
Glendale ......709..I 5
Gleneden Beach ....D 4
Glenwood ....F 1
Glide ....H 5
Goble ....A 6
Gold Beach .1,554.°J 3
Gold Hill .....603..J 5
Gopher ....C 5
Goshen ....F 6
Government Camp ...C 8
Grand Ronde ....D 5
Granite ....4..D 13
Grants Pass 12,455.°J 5
Grants Pass
Southwest* 3,431..J 5
Grass Valley ..153..C 9
Gravelford ....H 4
Green* ......1,612..H 5
Greenleaf ....F 4
Gresham ....9,875..C 7
Grizzly ....E 9
Gunter ....G 5
Gwendolen ....C 10
Haines ....212..D 14
Halfway ......317..D 15
Halsey ....467..J 1
Hamilton ....D 12
Hamlet ....B 5
Hammond ....500..A 4
Hampton ....G 10
Happy
Valley* ...1,392..C 7
Harbor ....K 3
Hardman ......19..C 11
Harlan ....E 4
Harney ....G 13
Harper ....F 15
Harrisburg ..1,311..J 1
Hauser ....G 3
Hay Creek ....E 9
Hayesville ...5,518..H 1
Hazelwood ....F 2
Hebo ....C 4
Heceta Beach ......F 4
Heceta Junction ...F 4
Helix ....152..B 13
Heppner ....1,429.°C 11
Heppner Junction ..B 11
Hereford ....E 14
Hermiston ...4,893..B 12
Highland ....C 7
Hildebrand ....J 8
Hilgard ....C 14
Hillsboro ...14,675.°F 1
Hines ....1,407..G 12
Holdman ....B 12
Holland ....J 5
Holley ....J 2
Homestead ....C 16
Hood River .3,991.°B 8
Hope ....F 15
Hopmere ....H 1
Horse Heaven ......D 10
Horton ....F 5
Hoskins ....D 5
Hubbard ......975..G 2
Hunter Creek ......J 3
Huntington ...507..E 15
Idanha ....382..D 7
Idaville ....B 4
Idleyld Park ....H 5
Illahe ....I 4
Imbler ....139..C 14
Imnaha ....B 16
Independ-
ence ......2,594..H 1
Ione ....355..C 11
Ironside ....E 14
Irrigon ....261..B 11
Island City ...202..C 14
Jacksonville .1,611..J 6
Jamieson ....F 15
Jefferson ......936..I 1
Jewell ....A 5
John Day ...1,566..E 12
Jonesboro ....F 14
Jordan Valley .196..H 16
Joseph ....839..C 15
Junction City 2,373..K 1
Juntura ....56..G 14
Kamela ....C 13
Keasey ....B 5
Keating ....D 15
Keizer .....11,405..H 1
Kellogg ....G 5
Kelso ....C 7
Keno ....K 7
Kent ....C 10
Kerby ....J 4
Kilts ....D 10
Kimberly ....D 11
King City* ..1,427..C 6
Kings Valley ......D 5
Kinzua ....D 11
Klamath Agency ...I 7
Klamath
Falls ....15,775.°J 8
Klondike ....B 10
Knappa ....A 5
Lacomb ....I 2
Lafayette* ....786..C 6
La Grande ..9,645.°C 14
Lake
Oswego* ..14,573..C 6
Lakecreek ....J 6
Lakeside ....G 4
Lakeview ....2,705.°J 10
Lamonta ....E 9
Lancaster ....J 1
Langlois ....I 3
La Pine ....G 8
Lawen ....G 13
Leaburg ....K 2
Lebanon ....6,636..I 1
Lebanon
South* ....2,229..E 6
Lees Camp ....B 5
Lehman ....C 13
Leland ....I 5
Lena ....C 12
Lenz ....I 8
Lewis ....B 15
Lewisburg ....I 1
Lexington .....230..C 11
Lime ....E 15
Lincoln ....K 7
Lincoln Beach .....D 4
Lincoln City 4,198..D 4
Linslaw ....F 4
Little Sweden ......D 7
Logdell ....F 12
Logsden ....D 4
London ....G 5
Lonerock ......12..D 11
Long Creek ...196..D 12
Lookingglass ....H 5
Lorane ....F 5
Lorella ....J 8
Lostine ....196..B 15
Lowell ....567..F 6
Lower Bridge ......E 8
Lyons ....645..I 2
Macleay ....H 1
Madras .....1,689.°E 9
Malin ....486..K 8
Manhattan
Beach ....B 4
Manzanita ....261..B 4
Mapleton ....F 4
Marcola ....K 1
Marial ....I 4
Marion ....I 1
Marion Forks ......E 7
Marquam ....H 2
Maupin ....428..C 9
Maxville ....B 15
May Park* ..1,466..C 14
Mayger ....A 6
Mayville ....D 10
Maywood
Park* .....1,230..C 6
McCormmach ....B 13
McCredie Springs ..G 7
McKenzie Bridge ...F 7
McMinnville 10,125.°G 1
McNary ....B 12
McNulty* ...1,017..B 6
Meacham ....C 13
Medford ...28,454.°J 6
Medford
West* ....3,919..J 6
Medical Springs ....D 15
Mehama ....I 2
Melrose ....H 5
Merlin ....J 5
Merrill ....722..K 8
Metolius ......270..E 9
Midland ....K 8
Midway ....C 5
Mikkalo ....C 10
Mill City ....1,451..I 2
Millican ....F 9
Millwood ....E 5
Milo ....I 5
Milton-Free-
water ....4,105..A 13
Milwaukie ..16,379..F 2
Minam ....B 14
Mineral ....E 15
Minerva ....F 4
Mist ....A 5
Mitchell ......196..E 10
Mitchell ....J 2
Modoc Point ....J 7
Mohawk ....K 1
Mohler ....B 4
Molalla .....2,005..G 2
Monitor ....G 2
Monmouth ..5,237..H 1
Monroe ....443..E 5
Monument ....161..D 12
Morgan ....B 11
Moro ....290.°C 9
Mosier ....217..B 8
Mount Angel 1,973..H 2
Mount Hood ....B 8
Mount Vernon .423..E 12
Mowich ....H 8
Mulino ....G 2
Murphy ....J 5
Myrtle Creek 2,733..H 5
Myrtle Creek
South* ....1,039..H 5
Myrtle Point 2,511..H 4
Neahkahnie ....B 4
Necanicum Junction B 4
Nehalem ......241..B 4
Neskowin ....C 4
Netarts ....C 4
New Bridge ....D 15
New Era ....G 2
New Idanha ....D 7
New Pine Creek ....K 10
Newberg ....6,507..G 1
Newport ....5,188.°E 4
Niagara ....D 7
Nimrod ....K 2
North Bend .8,553..G 3

North Fork	G	4
North Plains	F	1
North Powder .304	D	14
Norway	H	4
Noti	F	5
Nye	C	12
Nyssa 2,620	F	16
Oak Grove	B	8
Oakland 1,010	G	5
Oakridge 3,422	G	7
O'Brien	K	4
Oceanside	C	4
Odell	B	8
Olene	J	8
Olex	C	10
Olney	A	4
O'Neil	E	9
Ontario 6,523	F	16
Opal City	E	9
Ophir	I	3
Ordnance	B	12
Oregon City 9,176	°G	6
Otis	D	4
Otter Rock	D	4
Pacific City	C	4
Paisley 260	I	10
Palmer Junction	B	14
Paradise	A	15
Parkdale	C	8
Parkrose	F	2
Paulina	F	11
Paunina	H	8
Paxton	D	9
Pedee	D	5
Pendleton 13,197	°B	13
Peoria	J	1
Perry	C	14
Petersburg	B	9
Philomath 1,688	E	5
Phoenix 1,287	J	6
Pilot Rock 1,612	C	13
Pine	D	16
Pine City	B	12
Pine Grove	C	13
Pine Grove	C	8
Pistol River	J	3
Pittsburg	B	5
Plainview	J	1
Pleasant Hill	F	6
Pleasant Valley	D	15
Plush	J	11
Pondosa	D	15
Port Orford 1,037	I	3
Portland 382,619	°C	6
Post	F	10
Powell Butte	F	9
Powers 842	I	4
Prairie City 867	E	13
Pratum	H	1
Prescott 105	A	6
Princeton	H	13
Prineville 4,101	°E	9
Promise	B	15
Prospect	I	6
Quartz Mountain	J	9
Quincy	A	5
Quinton	B	10
Rainbow	F	7
Rainier 1,731	A	6
Redmond 3,721	E	9
Reed	F	4
Reedsport 4,039	G	4
Remote	H	4
Rhododendron	C	7
Rice Hill	G	5
Richland 133	D	15
Richmond	D	11
Richreall	H	1
Riddle 1,042	I	5
Rieth	B	12
Riley	G	12
Ritter	D	12
Riverside	G	14
Riverton	H	3
Roberts	F	9
Rock Creek	B	10
Rock Creek	D	14
Rockaway 665	B	4
Rockwood	F	2
Rogue River 841	J	5
Rome	I	15
Roosevelt Beach	F	4
Rose Lodge	D	4
Roseburg 14,461	°H	5
Rowena	B	9
Rowland	J	1
Rufus 317	B	9
Riggs	C	11
Rye Valley	E	15
Saginaw	F	5
St. Helens 6,212	°B	6
St. Paul* 347	D	6
Salem 68,296	°D	6
Salisbury	D	14
Sams Valley	J	6
Sandlake	C	4
Sandy 1,544	C	7
Santa Clara	K	1
Scappoose 1,859	B	6
Scio 447	I	1
Scofield	B	5
Scotts Mills 208	H	2
Scottsburg	G	4
Seal Rock	E	4
Seaside 4,402	A	4
Selma	J	4
Seneca	F	12
Service Creek	D	11
Shady Cove	I	6
Shady Pine	J	6
Shaniko 58	D	9
Sheaville	H	16
Shedd	I	1
Shelburn	I	1
Sheridan 1,881	C	5
Sherwood 1,396	G	1
Shutler	B	10
Siletz 596	D	4
Siltcoos	F	4
Silver Lake	H	9
Silverton 4,301	H	2
Silvies	F	12
Simnasho	D	8
Sinamox	C	9
Siskiyou	K	6
Sitkum	H	4
Sixes	I	3
Sodaville 125	J	1
South Junction	D	9
South Medford* 3,497	J	6
South Scappoose	B	6
South Seaside	A	4
Southbeach	E	4
Spofford	A	13
Sprague River	I	8
Spray 161	D	11
Springbrook	G	1
Springfield 27,047	K	1
Stanfield 891	B	12
Starkey	C	13
Stauffer	G	11
Stayton 3,170	I	2
Steamboat	H	6
Sturgill	D	16
Sublimity 634	H	2
Sulphur Springs	G	4
Summer Lake	H	9
Summerville 76	B	14
Sumner	I	1
Sumpter 120	D	14
Sunny Valley	I	5
Sunset Beach	A	4
Suplee	F	11
Susanville	D	13
Sutherlin 3,070	E	5
Suver	I	1
Svensen	A	5
Sweet Home 3,799	E	6
Swisshome	F	4
Takilma	K	4
Talbot	I	1
Talent 1,389	J	6
Tallman	I	1
Tangent	I	1
Telocaset	C	14
Tenmile	H	5
Terrebonne	E	9
The Dalles 10,423	°B	9
Tidewater	E	4
Tiernan	E	4
Tigard* 5,302	C	6
Tillamook 3,968	°C	4
Tiller	I	6
Timber	B	5
Tioga	H	4
Toketee Falls	H	6
Toledo 2,818	E	4
Tolovana Park	B	4
Trail	I	6
Tri City	H	5
Triangle Lake	F	5
Troutdale 575	B	7
Troy	A	15
Tualatin* 750	C	6
Tumalo	F	8
Turner* 846	D	6
Twin Rocks	B	4
Tygh Valley	C	9
Ukiah	C	12
Umapine	A	13
Umatilla 679	B	12
Umpqua	H	5
Union 1,531	C	14
Union Creek	I	6
Unity	D	15
Upper Highland	C	7
Upper Soda	G	7
Vale 1,448	°F	15
Valley Falls	J	10
Valley Junction	D	5
Valsetz	D	5
Venator	H	14
Veneta 1,377	F	5
Vernonia 1,643	B	5
Vida	K	2
Vinson	C	12
Viola	C	7
Waconda	H	1
Wakonda Beach	E	4
Waldport 700	E	4
Walker	B	5
Wallowa 811	B	15
Walterville	K	2
Walton	F	5
Wamic	C	9
Wapato	F	1
Wapinitia	C	9
Warm Springs	D	8
Warner	H	4
Warrenton 1,825	A	4
Wasco 412	B	9
Waterloo 186	J	2
Waterman	E	11
Wauna	A	5
Weatherby	E	15
Webfoot	B	10
Wedderburn	J	3
Welches	C	7
Wemme	C	7
Wendling	K	2
West Linn 7,091	F	2
West Side	K	10
West Slope	F	2
West Stayton	I	1
Westfall	F	15
Westfir	G	6
Westlake	F	4
Weston 660	B	13
Westport	A	5
Wetmore	D	11
Wheeler 262	B	4
White City	J	6
Whiteson	G	1
Whitney	D	14
Wilbur	H	5
Wilcox	C	10
Wilderville	J	5
Wilkesboro	F	1
Willamette City	G	6
Willamina 1,193	D	5
Williams	J	5
Willowdale	D	9
Wimer	J	5
Winchester Bay	G	4
Winlock	D	11
Winston 2,468	H	5
Wolf Creek	I	5
Wonder	J	5
Wood Village* 1,533	B	7
Woodburn 7,495	G	1
Woods	C	4
Worden	J	7
Wren	E	5
Yachats 441	E	4
Yamhill 516	G	1
Yoder	H	1
Yoncalla 675	G	5

*Does not appear on the map; key shows general location.
°County seat

Source: Latest census figures (1970). Places without population figures are unincorporated areas and are not listed in census reports.

Portland is Oregon's largest city and the industrial, commercial, and cultural center of the state. Portland lies near the intersection of the Columbia and Willamette rivers, and is Oregon's leading port. Majestic Mount Hood rises east of the city.

Oregon State Highway Dept.

Branding Cattle, as these cowboys are doing near John Day, is a familiar sight on the ranches of eastern Oregon.

Surefooted Loggers guide logs to a sawmill. Oregon's forests provide about a fifth of the nation's lumber.

POPULATION

This map shows the *population density* of Oregon, and how it varies in different parts of the state. Population density means the average number of persons who live on each square mile.

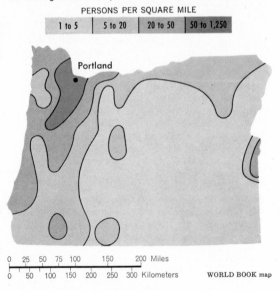

PERSONS PER SQUARE MILE

1 to 5	5 to 20	20 to 50	50 to 1,250

Portland

0   25   50   75   100   150   200 Miles
0   50   100 150 200   250   300 Kilometers   WORLD BOOK map

OREGON / *People*

The 1970 United States census reported that Oregon had 2,091,385 persons. The population had increased 18 per cent over the 1960 figure, 1,768,687.

About three-fifths of the people of Oregon live in the metropolitan areas of Portland, Eugene, and Salem. These three areas are Standard Metropolitan Statistical Areas (see METROPOLITAN AREA). For the populations of these areas, see the *Index* to the political map of Oregon.

Most of Oregon's large cities lie in the rich Willamette Valley in the northwestern part of the state. Portland, the largest city, is the commercial, industrial, and cultural center of the state. Its lovely rose gardens give it the nickname *City of Roses*. Eugene, the second largest

city, is a trading and processing center. The largest cities outside the valley are Klamath Falls in south-central Oregon, and Medford in the southwest. See the separate articles on the cities of Oregon listed in the *Related Articles* at the end of this article.

About 96 of every 100 Oregonians were born in the United States. Some trace their ancestry to settlers who came on the Oregon Trail. Most Oregonians born elsewhere came from Canada and the Scandinavian countries. A majority of Oregon's people are Protestants. But Roman Catholics form the largest religious group. Other religious groups include Baptists, Disciples of Christ, Episcopalians, Lutherans, Methodists, Mormons, and Presbyterians.

Schools. Jason Lee, a Methodist missionary, established a school for Indian children in French Prairie as early as 1834. After the Oregon Territory was organized in 1848, an act provided that income from two sections (1,280 acres) of land in each township should be set aside for educational purposes. In 1849, the territorial legislature passed laws providing for a free public school system. The first free public school opened in 1851.

Today, a state board of education heads Oregon's public school system. The governor appoints the seven board members, subject to approval by the state Senate. The superintendent of public instruction administers the school system. He is elected to a four-year term.

Children between the ages of 7 and 18 must attend school. For the number of students and teachers in Oregon, see EDUCATION (table).

Libraries. Oregon's first circulating library was organized in Oregon City in 1842. The Portland Library Association (now Multnomah County Library) was the first to serve the public on a large scale. It began in 1864 on a membership basis. Each member contributed

money to buy books. Then he could use the books without charge. This library became a free public library in 1902. Today, Oregon has over 180 public libraries and branches. The Oregon State Library provides mail-order service to citizens without local libraries. The Ashland Public Library owns a large collection of books on Shakespeare. The Astoria Public Library has a collection of Finnish language books.

Museums. The Portland Art Museum displays a large collection of paintings and sculpture. These works feature Indian art from the Northwest Coast and pre-Columbian Mexican art. The University of Oregon Museum of Art in Eugene owns the Warner Collection of Oriental Art, one of the finest in the country. The Oregon Museum of Science and Industry in Portland features demonstrations that show science at work in Oregon industries. The Oregon Historical Society in Portland has many items from pioneer days.

UNIVERSITIES AND COLLEGES

Oregon has 18 universities and colleges accredited by the Northwest Association of Secondary and Higher Schools. For enrollments and further information, see UNIVERSITIES AND COLLEGES (table).

Name	Location	Founded
Eastern Oregon College	La Grande	1929
George Fox College	Newberg	1892
Lewis and Clark College	Portland	1867
Linfield College	McMinnville	1849
Marylhurst College	Marylhurst	1930
Mount Angel College	Mount Angel	1887
Mount Angel Seminary	St. Benedict	1889
Northwest Christian College	Eugene	1895
Oregon, University of	Eugene	1872
Oregon College of Education	Monmouth	1856
Oregon State University	Corvallis	1868
Pacific University	Forest Grove	1849
Portland, University of	Portland	1901
Portland State University	Portland	1946
Reed College	Portland	1910
Southern Oregon College	Ashland	1926
Warner Pacific College	Portland	1937
Willamette University	Salem	1842

Portland Art Museum

The Portland Art Museum, established in 1892, owns one of the nation's finest collections of Indian art of the Pacific Northwest.

Reed College, in Portland, is a leader among U.S. colleges in the percentage of its students who later earn Ph.D. degrees.

Ray Atkeson

Rose Festival Parade in Portland

Timber Carnival in Albany

OREGON/A Visitor's Guide

Oregon is known for its beautiful mountain and coastal scenery. Majestic snow-covered Mount Hood towers above the Cascade Range about 50 miles east of Portland. U.S. Highway 26 skirts Mount Hood and offers close-up views of its glacier-clad slopes. U.S. Highway 101 follows the Oregon coastline for hundreds of miles. Motorists driving along this route see views of white sand dunes, coastal lakes and bays, and cliffs rising above the shore.

Oregon is a sportsman's paradise. Deer, elk, and pronghorn roam the fields and forests. Fishermen battle steelhead trout and other major game fish. Grouse, pheasant, quail, and other game birds are plentiful.

Slopes in the Cascades, Wallowas, and other Oregon mountains offer excellent skiing. Timberline, on Mount Hood, is perhaps the most famous ski area in the state. The skiing season in most areas begins in December and lasts through April.

PLACES TO VISIT

Following are brief descriptions of some of Oregon's many interesting places to visit.

Bonneville Dam, the first major dam on the Columbia River, has a series of fish ladders. In season, salmon and other fish can be seen jumping up the ladders on their way upstream to spawn.

Columbia River Gorge. Here the Columbia River cuts through the Cascade Mountains on its way to the Pacific Ocean. Colorful basalt cliffs line the deep gorge for about 60 miles between The Dalles and Troutdale. Multnomah and other waterfalls tumble into the gorge.

Picture Gorge, by the John Day Highway (U.S. 26) near Dayville, is a canyon of basalt rock named for the Indian pictures on the walls. The John Day Fossil Beds have fossils of prehistoric animals and plants.

Sea Lion Caves, on the Pacific Coast near Florence, is the winter home of hundreds of sea lions from September through spring.

National Parks and Forests Crater Lake National Park, the only national park in the state, lies in the Cascade Mountains in south-central Oregon. Crater Lake, 1,932 feet deep, rests in the basin at the top of an ancient volcano. See CRATER LAKE NATIONAL PARK.

Eleven national forests lie entirely within Oregon. They are Deschutes, Fremont, Malheur, Mount Hood,

Ochoco, Siuslaw, Umpqua, Wallowa, Whitman, Willamette, and Winema. Oregon shares Umatilla National Forest with Washington, and Klamath, Rogue River, and Siskiyou with California. In 1964, Congress set aside nine areas in Oregon's national forests as national wilderness areas, to be preserved in their natural condition. For the area and chief features of each national forest, see NATIONAL FOREST (table).

National Monuments, Memorials, and Historic Sites. Oregon Caves National Monument is in the Siskiyou Mountains of southwestern Oregon. Its limestone caverns contain beautiful stone formations. See OREGON CAVES NATIONAL MONUMENT.

Fort Clatsop National Memorial near Astoria was the site of the winter encampment of Meriwether Lewis and William Clark during their famous expedition to the region in 1805 and 1806. McLoughlin House National Historic Site in Oregon City was built by John McLoughlin, often called the *Father of Oregon.* He lived there from 1846 until his death in 1857.

State Parks. Oregon has about 190 state parks. Many of them have overnight camping and recreational facilities. For further information, write to Superintendent, State Parks and Recreation Division, Oregon Highway Department, 301 Highway Commission Building, Salem, Ore. 97310.

Shakespearean Festival in Ashland

Young Skiers Practice near Mount Hood

--- **ANNUAL EVENTS** ---

One of the most famous Oregon events is the Shakespearean Festival in Ashland, from mid-July through early September. Plays by Shakespeare are presented in an Elizabethan theater. Before showtime, "Dancing on the Green" features Shakespearean songs.

Other leading events are the Portland Rose Festival in early June and the Pendleton Round-Up and Happy Canyon Pageant in mid-September. The rose festival features a spectacular Grand Floral Parade. The four-day rodeo includes an Indian historical pageant.

Other annual events in Oregon include the following.

January-May: Ski Tournaments at Mount Ashland near Ashland, at Mount Bachelor near Bend, and at Government Camp near Mount Hood (January); Sled Dog Races in Bend and Union Creek (January-February); All Northwest Barber Shop Ballad Contest and Gay Nineties Festival in Forest Grove (late February); McKenzie River White Water Boat Parade near Springfield (mid-April); All-Indian Rodeo in Tygh Valley (mid-May); Rhododendron Festival in Florence (late May); Fleet of Flowers Memorial Service in Depoe Bay (May 30).

June-August: Strawberry Festival in Lebanon (early June); Rodeo in St. Paul (early July); World Championship Timber Carnival in Albany (early July); Buckeroo in Molalla (early July); Chief Joseph Days in Joseph (late July); Peter Britt Music and Arts Festival in Jacksonville (August); Regatta in Astoria (late August); State Fair in Salem (August-September).

September-December: Oktoberfest in Mount Angel (mid-September); Pacific International Livestock Exposition in Portland (early October); Lord's Acre Auction and Barbecue in Powell Butte (early November); Christmas Pageant in Rickreall (mid-December).

Fish Ladders at Bonneville Dam

Oregon Caves National Monument near Grants Pass

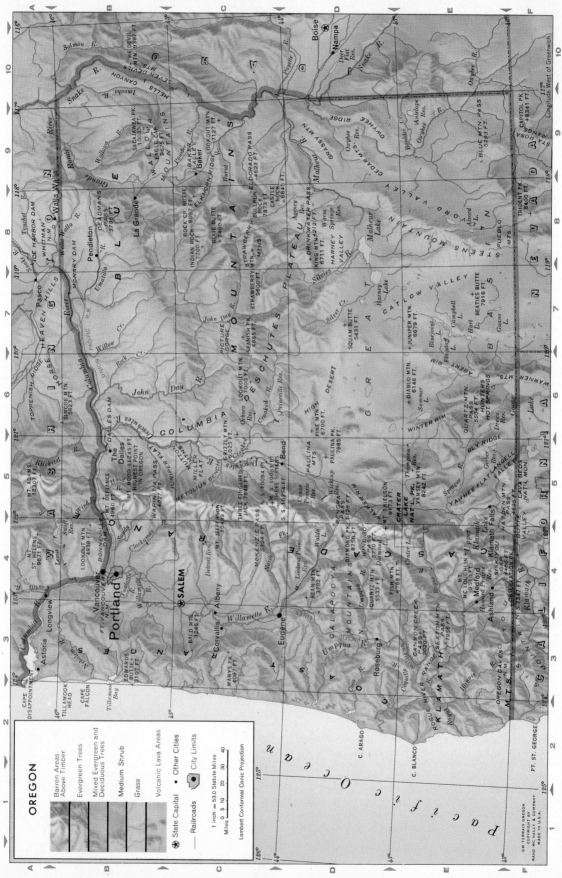

OREGON

Barren Areas
Above Timber

Evergreen Trees

Mixed Evergreen and
Deciduous Trees

Medium Shrub

Grass

Volcanic Lava Areas

⊛ State Capital
🏛 Other Cities
--- Railroads
City Limits

1 inch = 53.0 Statute Miles

Miles 0 5 10 20 30 40

Lambert Conformal Conic Projection

CM TERRAIN OREGON
COPYRIGHT BY
RAND MC NALLY & COMPANY
MADE IN U.S.A.

Especially created for **World Book Encyclopedia** by Rand McNally and World Book editors

Pacific Ocean

PT. ST. GEORGE

C. BLANCO

C. ARAGO

CAPE
DISAPPOINTMENT

TILLAMOOK
HEAD

CAPE
FALCON

Tillamook
Bay

Astoria

Longview

Vancouver
FT. VANCOUVER
N.M.

Portland

SALEM

Albany

Corvallis

Eugene

Roseburg

Ashland

Medford

Klamath Falls

The Dalles

Bend

Pendleton

Walla Walla

Pasco

La Grande

Baker

Boise

Nampa

Salmon R.

Snake R.

HE DEVIL
MTN. 9397 FT.
SEVEN DEVILS
MTS.

HELLS CANYON

EAGLE CAP
9675 FT.

SACAJAWEA PK.
10033 FT.

WALLOWA MOUNTAINS

BLUE MOUNTAINS

HIGHEST POINT
IN OREGON
MT. HOOD 11245 FT.

MT. JEFFERSON
10499 FT.

THREE SISTERS

CRATER
LAKE
NAT'L PK.

KLAMATH MOUNTAINS

SISKIYOU MOUNTAINS

OREGON CAVES
N.M.

STEENS MOUNTAIN

MALHEUR
LAKE

HARNEY
LAKE

GREAT BASIN

CATLOW VALLEY

WARNER MTS.

Columbia R.

Snake R.

Deschutes R.

John Day R.

Willamette R.

Umpqua R.

Rogue R.

Pacific Ocean

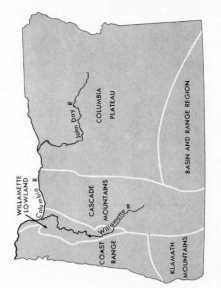

Land Regions of Oregon

OREGON / The Land

Land Regions. Oregon has six main land regions: (1) the Coast Range, (2) the Willamette Lowland, (3) the Cascade Mountains, (4) the Klamath Mountains, (5) the Columbia Plateau, and (6) the Basin and Range Region.

The Coast Range region borders the Pacific Ocean from Washington's Chehalis Valley on the north to the Klamath Mountains of Oregon on the south. The rolling Coast Ranges run parallel to the shoreline. They are the lowest of Oregon's main mountain ranges, with average elevations of less than 2,000 feet. Marys Peak, southwest of Corvallis, rises 4,097 feet and is the highest point in the region. Forests of Douglas fir, hemlock, spruce, and other evergreen trees cover much of the area.

Several valleys in the region, such as Triangle Lake Valley, are beds of ancient lakes. Many small coastal lakes were formed when the mouths of streams sank and sand dunes dammed their waters. Along much of the coast, the land rises from the sea in sheer cliffs, some of them nearly a thousand feet high. In some places, the coastal mountains rise in a series of terraces. Each terrace was once the coastline.

The Willamette Lowland is a narrow strip wedged between the Coast Ranges on the west and the Cascade Mountains on the east. The Willamette River and its branches flow north to the Columbia River. They drain the level and gently rolling farm and forest lands of the Willamette Valley. Over half the state's people live in the region. Rich soil, a favorable climate, and nearby water transportation make it the most important farming and industrial area in the state.

The Cascade Mountains region, a broad belt of rugged land crowned by volcanic peaks, includes some of the highest mountains in North America. Mount Hood, the highest peak in Oregon, rises 11,245 feet above sea level. Mount Jefferson is 10,499 feet high. Other beautiful Cascade peaks include the Three Sisters, which rises over 10,000 feet high, and Mount McLoughlin, which is 9,510 feet high.

The Klamath Mountains cover the southwestern corner of Oregon. Thick forests grow on the mountainsides and provide shelter for game animals. This region also has the state's richest mineral deposits.

The Columbia Plateau covers most of eastern Oregon and extends northeastward into Washington and Idaho.

Mountains and Rocks line the Pacific Ocean at Cannon Beach near Ecola State Park in the Coast Range.

Crater Lake fills the hollow of a dead volcano in the Cascade Mountains in southwest Oregon.

Great Wheat Fields thrive in the Columbia Plateau of eastern Oregon. This field is located in Wasco County.

Thousands of years ago, lava flowed out of cracks in the earth's crust to form the plateau. Deep canyons of the Deschutes, John Day, and other rivers cut through the plateau in north-central Oregon. The state's great wheat ranches lie in this area. Much of the so-called "plateau" in Oregon is actually rugged and mountainous. The Blue and Wallowa mountains rise in north-eastern Oregon. Rolling timberlands cover the Blue Mountain area. The Wallowa Mountains, cut by glaciers, provide spectacular scenery. The Snake River has carved the famous Hells Canyon on the Oregon-Idaho border. This great gorge lies between the Wallowa Mountains and Idaho's Seven Devils Mountains. Its depth is about 5,500 feet.

The Basin and Range Region covers part of southeastern Oregon and extends into California and other nearby states. In Oregon, the region consists of a high basin broken by occasional low mountains. The Cascade Range to the west cuts off moisture-bearing winds from the Pacific Ocean and makes much of the area a semi-desert.

Coastline. Oregon's coastline extends 296 miles along the Pacific Ocean. Much of the shore is rugged, with steep cliffs rising up from the sea. But many bays and harbors have been formed where rivers from the Coast Ranges and Klamath Mountains flow into the sea. These bays and harbors include Tillamook, Yaquina, Alsea, Winchester, and Coos.

Rivers, Waterfalls, and Lakes. The mighty Columbia River flows westward to the Pacific Ocean, forming most of the border between Oregon and Washington. The Columbia drains more than half of Oregon. The Columbia and its branch, the Willamette River, form the largest system of navigable waterways in the state. The Snake River forms much of the Oregon-Idaho border. It joins the Columbia in Washington. The Snake and its branches drain the easternmost part of Oregon. The Deschutes River travels northward through central Oregon and empties into the Columbia. The John Day River, rises in the Strawberry Mountains in eastern Oregon. It flows west and north to the Columbia and drains much of north-central Oregon.

Hundreds of streams in the Cascade Mountains rush down the slopes in rapids and waterfalls. Among the best known waterfalls in the Cascades are Benham, Pringle, Salt Creek, Steamboat, and the many falls along Silver Creek. About a dozen waterfalls, some of them over 200 feet high, tumble into the Columbia River Gorge. These waterfalls include Bridal Veil, Coopery, Elowah, Horsetail, Latourell, and Multnomah.

The Cascade Mountains region has many lakes. Crater Lake in the Cascades, 1,932 feet in depth, is the deepest lake in the United States. It lies in the *caldera* (a great basin surrounding the crater) of an extinct volcano. Wallowa Lake in the Wallowa Mountains is famous for its sparkling clear water. Most of the lakes in southeastern Oregon are shallow and salty. Some evaporate during dry seasons and leave salt deposits in the lake beds. But a few, such as Harney and Malheur, are large year-round lakes. A number of small lakes near the Oregon coast were formed when deposits of soil and sand blocked the mouths of streams and kept the streams from emptying into the ocean.

Ray Atkeson

Mild, moist winds from the Pacific Ocean greatly influence Oregon's climate. These winds give western Oregon a climate that is unusually mild for a state so far north. Temperatures near the coast average 45° F. in January and 60° F. in July. The winds rise and become cooler when they strike the Coast Ranges. Much of their moisture condenses and falls as rain. In some coastal areas, yearly *precipitation* (rain, snow, and other forms of moisture) exceeds 130 inches.

In the Willamette Valley, east of the Coast Ranges, precipitation averages about 40 inches a year. Almost all of it occurs during the cool season. As the winds rise up the western slopes of the Cascade Mountains, more of their moisture falls. Precipitation in this region averages 50 to 75 inches a year.

The winds are usually dry by the time they have crossed the Cascades. Dry winds do not keep the climate mild, as moist winds do. For this reason, eastern Oregon has relatively cold winters and hot summers. In the southeast, temperatures average 27° F. in January and 72° F. in July. Much of eastern Oregon receives only 6 to 12 inches of precipitation a year.

Oregon's record low of −54° F. occurred on Feb. 9, 1933, at Ukiah, and on Feb. 10, 1933, at Seneca. The highest temperature, 119° F., occurred at Prineville on July 29, 1898, and at Pendleton on Aug. 10, 1898.

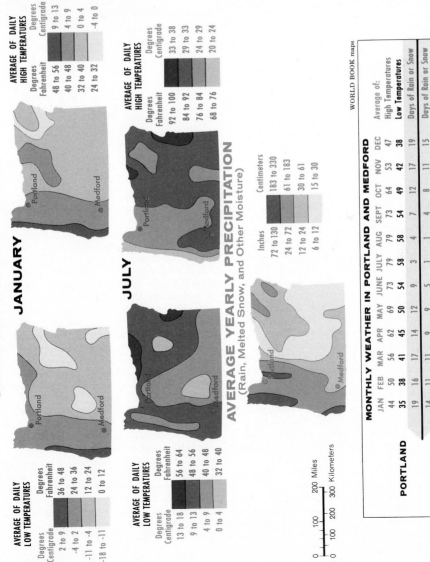

Crops and Forests flourish in the moist, mild climate of the Iowa Hills in western Oregon.

SEASONAL TEMPERATURES

JANUARY

AVERAGE OF DAILY LOW TEMPERATURES

Degrees Centigrade	Degrees Fahrenheit
2 to 9	36 to 48
-4 to 2	24 to 36
-11 to -4	12 to 24
-18 to -11	0 to 12

AVERAGE OF DAILY HIGH TEMPERATURES

Degrees Fahrenheit	Degrees Centigrade
48 to 56	9 to 13
40 to 48	4 to 9
32 to 40	0 to 4
24 to 32	-4 to 0

JULY

AVERAGE OF DAILY LOW TEMPERATURES

Degrees Centigrade	Degrees Fahrenheit
13 to 18	56 to 64
9 to 13	48 to 56
4 to 9	40 to 48
0 to 4	32 to 40

AVERAGE OF DAILY HIGH TEMPERATURES

Degrees Fahrenheit	Degrees Centigrade
92 to 100	33 to 38
84 to 92	29 to 33
76 to 84	24 to 29
68 to 76	20 to 24

AVERAGE YEARLY PRECIPITATION
(Rain, Melted Snow, and Other Moisture)

Inches	Centimeters
72 to 130	183 to 330
24 to 72	61 to 183
12 to 24	30 to 61
6 to 12	15 to 30

0   100   200 Miles
0   100   200   300 Kilometers

WORLD BOOK maps

MONTHLY WEATHER IN PORTLAND AND MEDFORD

		JAN	FEB	MAR	APR	MAY	JUNE	JULY	AUG	SEPT	OCT	NOV	DEC	Average of:
PORTLAND		44	50	56	62	69	73	79	79	74	64	53	47	High Temperatures
		35	38	41	45	50	54	58	58	54	49	42	38	Low Temperatures
		19	16	17	14	12	9	3	4	7	12	17	19	Days of Rain or Snow
MEDFORD		14	11	11	9	9	5	1	1	4	8	11	15	Days of Rain or Snow
		45	52	59	66	73	80	89	89	82	68	54	45	High Temperatures
		30	33	35	39	44	50	55	54	47	41	34	32	Low Temperatures

Temperatures are given in degrees Fahrenheit.

Source: U.S. Weather Bureau

The Cascade Mountains divide Oregon into two major economic regions. Manufacturing industries are concentrated in the Willamette Valley in western Oregon. This region also produces most of the state's dairy products, flower bulbs, fruits, and vegetables. The dry lands east of the Cascades are important for livestock and wheat production, and for vegetable production in irrigated areas.

The Hood River Valley in the north and the Rogue River Valley in the southwest are famous fruit-growing regions. Lumbering and wood-processing are important industries in the forested parts of the state.

Natural Resources. Oregon's many natural resources include huge timber reserves, small deposits of many minerals, and a plentiful water supply.

Forests. Oregon has almost a fifth of the nation's timber. Forests cover more than 30,500,000 acres, of which about 26,500,000 acres are commercial forest land. Oregon has two forest regions: (1) the Douglas fir region west of the Cascade Mountains, and (2) the ponderosa (western yellow) pine region east of the mountains.

The Douglas fir, Oregon's state tree, provides the largest amount of timber. Ponderosa pine, western hemlock, western red cedar, Sitka spruce, and several kinds of true firs also grow in the Douglas fir region. Some Douglas fir trees grow in the ponderosa pine region, as do Engelmann spruce, Idaho white pine, lodgepole pine, sugar pine, and true firs. See FIR.

Oregonians conserve their timber reserves by protecting them from fire, harmful insects, and tree diseases. Forest owners plant seedlings in areas where large trees have been cut down. They also grow trees on tree farms. These farms cover more than 5 million acres in the state.

Minerals. Deposits of bauxite (aluminum ore) have been found in northwestern Oregon. Chromite occurs in several parts of the state. The Klamath Mountains region has important deposits of nickel ore. Veins of cinnabar, from which mercury is made, lie under many parts of the state. Other metallic minerals found in Oregon include copper, gold, iron ore, lead, silver, uranium, and zinc.

Deposits of *bituminous* (soft) coal, some of them 10 feet thick, occur near Coos Bay. Some parts of the state have deposits of high-grade limestone. Clay for bricks and tiles comes from the Willamette Valley and other areas. Oregon also has deposits of asbestos, barite, diatomite, peat, perlite, pumice, semiprecious gems, and silica sand.

Water is one of Oregon's most important resources. Melted snow and winter rain from the mountains feed Oregon's rivers and provide unusually pure water for industry and home use. The Columbia River and its tributaries are important sources of water for power and irrigation.

Soils. Gray-brown soils cover the Coast Range and Klamath Mountains regions. The Willamette Lowland has deep, fertile soils. Shallow soils cover most of the eastern Cascade slopes, and the Basin and Range Region. The wheat belt of north-central Oregon has rich soils good for growing crops.

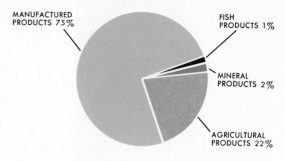

OREGON'S PRODUCTION IN 1967

Total value of goods produced—$2,737,044,000

Note: Manufacturing percentage based on value added by manufacture. Other percentages based on value of production.

Sources: U.S. Government statistics

OREGON'S EMPLOYMENT IN 1967

Total number of persons employed—720,200

		Number of Employees
Manufacturing	👤👤👤👤👤👤	171,200
Wholesale & Retail Trade	👤👤👤👤👤👤	149,700
Government	👤👤👤👤👤	123,900
Services	👤👤👤👤	98,700
Agriculture	👤👤👤	60,200
Transportation & Public Utilities	👤👤	49,100
Finance, Mining & Other	👤👤	34,000
Construction	👤👤	33,400

Source: U.S. Department of Labor

Plant Life. Many kinds of wild flowers grow in Oregon because the state has a variety of climates and elevations. Oregon is famous for its azaleas, laurels, rhododendrons, and other flowering shrubs. The state flower, the Oregon grape, grows in most parts of the state. Hardwood trees in Oregon include alder, ash, cottonwood, juniper, madroña, maple, and willow.

Animal Life. Columbian black-tailed deer and Roosevelt elk live in Oregon's mountain and coastal forests. Mule deer and Rocky Mountain elk are found east of the Cascades. Pronghorns thrive in the southeast. Small bands of mountain goats live in the Wallowa Mountains. Smaller animals found in Oregon include bobcats, beavers, coyotes, foxes, minks, muskrats, otters, and timber wolves. Seals and sea lions live along the coast in winter and early spring.

Oregon's most valuable fish for commerce is the salmon. Salmon are also caught by sportsmen. Every year, thousands of salmon leave the ocean and swim up Oregon's rivers to lay their eggs. They leap up low waterfalls and climb fish ladders to get around dams. Cod, halibut, herring, ling cod, ocean perch, rockfish, sablefish, shad, and sole live in Oregon's coastal waters.

The steelhead trout is perhaps the most prized of Oregon's many game fishes. Other fishes in Oregon's rivers and lakes include perch, striped bass, and cutthroat and rainbow trout.

Photos, Ray Atkeson

Acres of Daffodils carpet a valley near Portland. Farmers carefully tend these plants to provide flower bulbs, one of Oregon's profitable agricultural products. Similar farms throughout western Oregon grow gladiolus, iris, lily, and tulip bulbs.

Huge Logs from the thick forests of the Klamath Mountains region provide valuable timber for Oregon's lumber industry.

Manufacturing accounts for about three-fourths of the value of goods produced in Oregon each year. Products manufactured in the state have a *value added by manufacture* of about $2 billion a year. This figure represents the value added to products by Oregon's industries, not counting such costs as materials, supplies, and fuels.

Wood Processing is by far Oregon's most important manufacturing industry. Lumber and wood products have a value added by manufacture of about $775 million a year. Most cities have sawmills or plants that make wood products. Oregon leads the states in lumber production. It cuts about 8 billion board feet of lumber a year—more than a fifth of the nation's supply. Oregon produces over half of the plywood manufactured in the nation. Oregon plants produce nearly 2 million tons of pulp and nearly 2 million tons of paper a year.

Food Processing. Oregon plants process over 40 crops grown in the state. Portland, Salem, and other Willamette Valley cities have many canneries and freezing plants that pack fruits and vegetables. Several meat-processing plants also operate in the region. Canneries and freezing plants in Astoria pack a variety of fishes and shellfishes. Seafood is processed in Coos Bay, The Dalles, and other coastal and Columbia River cities.

Factories in Tillamook County produce world-famous Tillamook cheese. Large quantities of peas are processed in the Pendleton area. Sugar is made from sugar beets in Nyssa.

Other Leading Industries in Oregon produce electrical machinery, nonelectrical machinery, printed materials, and transportation equipment. Metal processing is also an important industry in Oregon. Aluminum-processing plants operate in The Dalles and Troutdale, near inexpensive hydroelectric power resources. They ship heavy materials on the Columbia River. Portland has a steel mill and metal-fabrication plants. Riddle has a large ferronickel plant, and Albany has several plants that process such metals as titanium and zirconium.

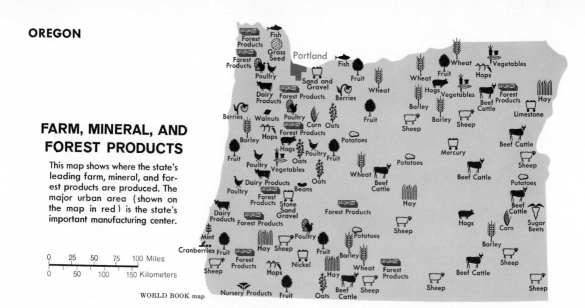

FARM, MINERAL, AND FOREST PRODUCTS

This map shows where the state's leading farm, mineral, and forest products are produced. The major urban area (shown on the map in red) is the state's important manufacturing center.

0   25   50   75   100 Miles
0   50   100   150 Kilometers

WORLD BOOK map

Bob and Ira Spring

Ray Atkeson

Yaquina Bay Harbor at Newport, *above,* exports many of Oregon's lumber products. The state has over 30,200,000 acres of trees. Oregon is divided into two forest regions. One region, west of the Cascade Mountains, has Douglas fir forests. Ponderosa pine forests grow in the other region, east of the Cascades.

Fruit Pickers Harvest Pears in the Rogue River Valley, *right.* Oregon is the country's leading producer of winter pears. Much of the state's best farmland lies in its river valleys. The Hood River Valley produces pears and apples. The Willamette River Valley is Oregon's most important vegetable-growing region.

Agriculture accounts for about $595,800,000 a year, or about a fifth of the total value of goods produced in Oregon. The state has about 39,700 farms. They average 515 acres in size.

Oregon has valuable herds of livestock, especially cattle and calves. Beef cattle are Oregon's most important farm product. They produce a yearly income of about $119 million. Most beef cattle are raised on ranges east of the Cascades. Western Oregon has large herds of dairy cattle. Dairy products are Oregon's second most important source of farm income.

Wheat is Oregon's most valuable crop. Much wheat grows in the plateau area of north-central Oregon. Hay is Oregon's second most important grain crop, followed by barley. Oregon usually produces more oats than any other state on the Pacific Coast.

Greenhouse and nursery products are another chief source of agricultural income in the state. Western Oregon is an important bulb-growing region. Farmers there grow daffodils, gladioli, irises, lilies, and tulips for bulbs. Such nursery products as shrubs and trees are also important.

Oregon leads the states in growing green snap beans. It also produces green peas, onions, and sweet corn. The Willamette Valley is the chief vegetable-growing region. Oregon farmers also grow large potato and sugar beet crops on irrigated land east of the Cascades. Oregon also produces hops, used in making beer. Marion and Josephine counties lead in hop production.

Oregon leads the states in the production of winter pears. The Hood and Rogue river valleys are famous pear-growing regions. Many Anjou, Bosc, and Comice pears from Oregon are used in gift packages. The Hood River Valley is also a center for apple production. Oregon fruit growers grow many cherries, especially in Wasco County. The western and northern counties produce peaches, plums, and prunes. Oregon ranks as a leading strawberry-producing state. Farmers in coastal areas grow cranberries. Other berries grown in Oregon include blackberries, blueberries, boysenberries, gooseberries, loganberries, and raspberries.

Oregon produces one of the nation's largest crops of nuts each year. Over 90 per cent of the nation's filbert nuts and about 3 per cent of the nation's walnuts come from Oregon.

Oregon farmers specialize in several crops that are not grown widely in many other states. For example, Oregon produces almost all the nation's seed for bent, fescue, and ryegrass, and most of the seed for common vetch, crimson clover, and merion bluegrass. These crops are grown mainly in northwestern counties. Oregon often leads the states in peppermint production.

Douglas County, in southwestern Oregon, leads in sheep raising. Sheep also graze on the eastern ranges and the Willamette Valley grasslands. Willamette Valley farmers raise most of the state's chickens. Umatilla County is the leading hog producer in Oregon. A number of fur farms operate in the state. Most of them specialize in raising mink.

Mining. Oregon mines about $67 million worth of minerals a year. Stone and sand and gravel account for about two-thirds of the value of Oregon's mineral output. These products are quarried in almost all counties. Basalt is the chief stone quarried. Oregon is the only state that produces nickel from raw ore. Other leading minerals include clay, diatomite, gem stones, gold, mercury, peat, perlite, pumice, and silver.

Fishing Industry. Oregon has an annual fish catch valued at about $16 million. Salmon, especially the Chinook and silver varieties, are Oregon's most valuable fishery product. Thousands of pounds of iced salmon are shipped from Oregon to distant markets each year. Other commercial seafoods from Oregon include Dungeness crabs, ocean perch, oysters, rockfish, sablefish, shad, shrimp, sole, steelhead trout, and tuna.

Electric Power. Huge dams and power facilities stand on the Columbia River between Oregon and Washington. These dams include Bonneville, John Day, McNary, and The Dalles. They form part of a power pool that supplies electricity to the entire Pacific Northwest. Both private and public power generating sources contribute to the pool. The pool provides about 65 per cent of Oregon's electricity.

The rest of the electric power production is generated at dams that are entirely within Oregon. These dams include Detroit and Lookout Point on the Willamette River, and smaller dams on the Clackamas, Deschutes, Klamath, Rogue, and Umpqua rivers. For Oregon's kilowatt-hour production see ELECTRIC POWER (table).

Transportation. From 1843 to the coming of the railroads in the 1860's, thousands of persons traveled the famous Oregon Trail to Oregon (see OREGON TRAIL). Today, Oregon has over 90,000 miles of roads. Railroads, including three major systems, operate on about 3,500 miles of track in the state.

Oregon has over 180 airports. The largest is Portland International Airport. Other major commercial airfields are located at Corvallis, Eugene, Klamath Falls, Medford, North Bend, and Pendleton. Portland is a major ocean port, although it is a hundred miles inland. Portland ships more dry cargo than any other West Coast port. Ocean-going ships follow a deepened channel up the Columbia and into the Willamette River to reach Portland's harbor.

Barges can travel for many miles up the Willamette beyond Portland. A series of dams and locks allows barges to travel up the Columbia to Pasco, Wash. Oregon river ports near the Columbia include Hood River, The Dalles, and Umatilla. Coastal ports include Astoria, Coos Bay, Bay City, Nehalem, Newport, Port Orford, and Tillamook.

Communication. Oregon's first newspaper, the *Oregon Spectator*, began publication at Oregon City in 1846. It is no longer published. *The Oregonian* was established in Portland in 1850 as the *Weekly Oregonian*. The *Oregon Statesman* appeared in Oregon City in 1851, and later moved to Salem. These two papers are still published today.

Other leading newspapers include the *Capital Journal* of Salem, *Eugene Register-Guard*, and *Oregon Journal* of Portland. Oregon has about 135 newspapers, including about 20 dailies. Oregon publishers also issue about 75 periodicals.

Oregon's first commercial radio station, KGW, opened in Portland in 1922. The state's first television station, KPTV, began operating in Portland in 1953. In the 1960's, Oregon had about 90 radio stations and 12 television stations.

Fort Clatsop sheltered members of the Lewis and Clark expedition during the winter of 1805-1806 after their journey across the continent.

Captain Robert Gray visited the Oregon country in 1792. He discovered the mouth of a great river which he named after his ship, the *Columbia*.

Salmon Runs take place on the Columbia River every year. For hundreds of years, Indians speared the salmon as they swam upstream to spawn.

Astoria

Astoria, founded by John Jacob Astor's fur company in 1811, marked the beginning of the settlement of Oregon.

The First U.S. Government in the Pacific Northwest was organized in 1843 at Champoeg by Oregon settlers in the Willamette Valley.

Willamette Valley Settlers, William Meek and Henderson Luelling, brought several hundred young fruit trees over the Oregon Trail from Iowa in 1847. Fruit from the valley is now world-famous.

HISTORIC OREGON

Bonneville Dam and lock, completed in 1937, made the Columbia River navigable for seagoing vessels. It provides electricity for the Portland region.

Indian Days. When the first white men entered the Oregon region, many Indian tribes lived there. The Chinook lived along the lower Columbia River, where they fished for salmon. The Clackama, Multnomah, and Tillamook tribes also made their homes in the northwest part of the region. The Bannock, Cayuse, Paiute, Umatilla, and a branch of the Nez Percé lived in the region east of the Cascade Mountains. The Klamath and the Modoc were in the south, near Oregon's present-day border with California.

Exploration and Settlement. Spanish sailors who went from Mexico to the Philippines during the 1500's and 1600's were the first white men to see the Oregon coast. Historians think that Sir Francis Drake of England touched Oregon's southern coast in 1579 while searching for an ocean route from the northern Pacific to the Atlantic. In 1778, the British sea captain James Cook discovered and named Cape Foulweather, north of Yaquina Bay. Robert Gray and other Americans landed on the Oregon coast in 1788. George Vancouver of Great Britain explored and mapped the coast in 1792. Also in 1792, Gray discovered the river which he named for his ship, the *Columbia*. The explorers Meriwether Lewis and William Clark reached the mouth of the Columbia by land in 1805. Their expedition, together with Gray's discovery of the river, gave the United States a strong claim to the Oregon region.

In the early 1800's, the Oregon region stretched from Alaska, which was claimed by Russia, to California, which was claimed by Spain. It extended eastward from the Pacific Ocean to the Rocky Mountains. Four nations—Russia, Spain, Great Britain, and the United States—claimed parts of the region. Russia based its claims on Russian explorations along the northern Pacific Coast. In treaties with Great Britain and the United States in 1824 and 1825, Russia gave up its interests south of latitude 54° 40'. In 1819, by treaty, Spain gave up its claim north of latitude 42°, Oregon's present southern boundary. Great Britain and the United States could not agree on a boundary line to separate their claims. They postponed a decision by signing a treaty in 1818 that permitted citizens of both countries to trade and settle in the region. The treaty was renewed in 1827.

John Jacob Astor, an American fur trader, began the white settlement of Oregon. He established a fur-trading post at Astoria in 1811. The Hudson's Bay Company, a powerful British trading firm, established Fort Vancouver (now Vancouver, Wash.) near the Columbia River in 1825. John McLoughlin directed the activities of the Hudson's Bay Company and ruled the region for about 20 years. He later became a U.S. citizen, and today he is known as the *Father of Oregon*.

In 1834, Methodist missionaries established the first permanent American settlement in the Willamette Valley. The first large overland migration into Oregon came in 1843. That year, about a thousand persons traveled the Oregon Trail and settled in the Willamette Valley. Hundreds of American settlers arrived each year from then on. The increasing number of settlers put pressure on the U.S. government to settle the boundary dispute with Great Britain. In 1844, James K.

IMPORTANT DATES IN OREGON

1579 Sir Francis Drake possibly touched the Oregon coast.

1792 Robert Gray discovered the Columbia River.

1805 Meriwether Lewis and William Clark reached the mouth of the Columbia.

1811 John Jacob Astor founded Astoria.

1819 A treaty between the United States and Spain fixed the present southern border of Oregon.

1843 The Willamette settlers at Champoeg organized a provisional government.

1846 A treaty made the 49th parallel the chief boundary between British and U.S. territory in the Oregon region.

1848 Oregon became a territory.

1850 Congress passed the Oregon Donation Land Law.

1859 Oregon became the 33rd state on February 14.

1877 Chief Joseph helped lead the Nez Percé Indians in a war against the white men, but finally surrendered.

1902 Oregon adopted the initiative and referendum.

1912 The state adopted woman suffrage.

1937 Bonneville Dam was completed.

1948 Oregon celebrated its territorial centennial.

1959 Oregon celebrated its statehood centennial.

1961 A freeway between Portland and Salem was finished.

1964 Heavy floods damaged western Oregon.

Polk based his campaign for the presidency partly on the claim that land south of latitude 54° 40' belonged to the United States (see FIFTY-FOUR FORTY OR FIGHT). In 1846, President Polk signed a treaty with Great Britain. This treaty fixed the 49th parallel as the chief dividing line between U.S. and British territory.

Indian Wars. In 1847, Indians massacred Marcus Whitman and 13 others, near present-day Walla Walla, Wash. (see WHITMAN, MARCUS). This massacre led to the Cayuse War of 1847, in which the Indian villages were destroyed. The Rogue River Wars of the 1850's resulted from the Indians' anger at being driven from their lands. Chief John, the Indian leader, surrendered in 1856 and was imprisoned.

One of the most spectacular Indian wars, the Modoc War, began in 1872 and lasted over a year. White settlers tried to force the Modoc Indians onto the Klamath reservation. But the Indians hid near the California border among lava beds which provided natural defenses. A small band of warriors kept more than a thousand U.S. soldiers at bay until the Indians finally surrendered.

The Nez Percé War began in 1877. Chief Joseph and other Nez Percé leaders refused to let the government move their people from the beautiful Wallowa Valley to a reservation in Idaho. Joseph retreated slowly across hundreds of miles of territory into Idaho and Montana. He hoped to wipe out the U.S. troops who pursued him. Joseph was finally captured near the Canadian border, where he surrendered. The Paiute and Bannock Indians rose against Oregon settlers in 1878, but were quickly defeated. See INDIAN WARS (In the Northwest).

Provisional and Territorial Governments. In 1843, settlers in the Willamette Valley met at Champoeg (near present-day Newberg) to organize a provisional government. A similar attempt had been made unsuc-

640g

cessfully two years before. In 1843, the settlers adopted a set of laws which were based on the laws of Iowa.

Oregon became a territory in 1848, with Oregon City as the capital. The capital was moved to Salem in 1850. Oregon's present boundaries were established in 1853, when Congress created the Washington Territory.

The Donation Land Law of 1850 spurred territorial growth and development. This law provided that any male American citizen over 18 who settled in Oregon before December, 1850, could receive 320 acres of land. His wife could also receive 320 acres. To qualify for ownership, he had to cultivate his claim for four years. From December, 1850, to December, 1855, a settler had to be at least 21 to receive land, and he got only 160 acres.

Progress as a State. Oregon joined the Union as the 33rd state on Feb. 14, 1859. Salem became the state capital. John Whiteaker, a Democrat, served as the first state governor, from 1859 to 1862.

During the Civil War (1861-1865), state volunteers protected eastern Oregon against Indian attacks. The attacks continued for 15 years after the war. Oregon's population increased rapidly after the Civil War ended. Former soldiers from both sides sought new opportunities in the West. In 1860, about 52,000 persons lived in Oregon. By 1890, over 300,000 lived there.

During the 1890's, William S. U'Ren, a political leader, began a movement for governmental reform. U'Ren favored laws that would give the voters more direct control over the state government.

The Early 1900's. In 1902, Oregon adopted the *initiative and referendum*, procedures that permit voters to take a direct part in lawmaking (see INITIATIVE AND REFERENDUM). In 1908, it adopted the *recall*, a procedure for removing undesirable officials from office. The use of these direct-government procedures became known as the *Oregon System*. Many states have passed initiative, referendum, and recall laws based on this system.

In 1912, Oregon gave women the right to vote for the first time in the state's history. Passage of the law followed a long and difficult campaign for women's rights led by Abigail Jane Scott Duniway.

During the Great Depression of the 1930's, the federal government provided money to build Bonneville Dam on the Columbia River. The dam and nearby locks supplied electric power for industry and improved the river for navigation. Owyhee Dam, completed in 1932, provided irrigation water for thousands of acres in the Owyhee and Snake river valleys.

The Mid-1900's. By 1940, Oregon's population had grown to more than a million. During World War II (1939-1945), many of the state's factories produced military equipment. Portland became a major port for shipment of supplies to Russia and to U.S. armed forces in the Pacific. The city's shipyards produced cargo vessels and warships. Thousands of people from other states came to work in Oregon defense plants, and many of them settled in the state after the war.

During the 1950's, McNary and The Dalles dams were built on the Columbia River. These dams greatly increased Oregon's supply of low-cost electric power. In 1956, pipelines brought natural gas into the state

for the first time. Both developments contributed greatly to Oregon's industrial growth. Many people began to move from rural to urban areas to take manufacturing jobs.

Important changes took place in the Oregon timber industry during the 1960's. In the past, sawdust, bark, and other logging by-products had been wasted. Now, Oregon companies began to use many of these materials to make hardboard, pulp, and other wood products. Forestry specialists discovered new uses for forest products and studied ways to conserve the state's timber reserves. The industry replanted an increasing number of trees to replace those that had been cut down.

Changes also occurred in Oregon agriculture. The state's farms became larger and more closely linked with food processing. Farmers used more and more machinery. Irrigation projects allowed farmers to grow fruits and vegetables on land that once had been too dry for any crops except grasses.

Low-cost hydroelectric power from dams on the Columbia and Willamette rivers helped Oregon's economy grow during the 1960's. Gas pipelines were extended to many parts of the state. Industries, including the manufacture of metal products and electrical and electronic machinery, grew in importance.

In the 1960's, Oregon completed a freeway system from Portland to California and finished the major part of a freeway network from Portland to Idaho. Tourism continued to grow rapidly. Millions of tourists visited Oregon to fish, hunt, ski, and swim, and to enjoy the state's scenery.

The worst floods in Oregon's history hit the state in 1964. Storms and floods caused millions of dollars of damage, killed several persons, and forced thousands from their homes.

THE GOVERNORS OF OREGON

		Party	Term
1.	John Whiteaker	Democratic	1859-1862
2.	A. C. Gibbs	Republican	1862-1866
3.	George L. Woods	Republican	1866-1870
4.	La Fayette Grover	Democratic	1870-1877
5.	Stephen F. Chadwick	Democratic	1877-1878
6.	W. W. Thayer	Democratic	1878-1882
7.	Z. F. Moody	Republican	1882-1887
8.	Sylvester Pennoyer	Democratic-Populist	1887-1895
9.	William Paine Lord	Republican	1895-1899
10.	T. T. Geer	Republican	1899-1903
11.	George E. Chamberlain	Democratic	1903-1909
12.	Frank W. Benson	Republican	1909-1910
13.	Jay Bowerman	Republican	1910-1911
14.	Oswald West	Democratic	1911-1915
15.	James Withycombe	Republican	1915-1919
16.	Ben W. Olcott	Republican	1919-1923
17.	Walter M. Pierce	Democratic	1923-1927
18.	I. L. Patterson	Republican	1927-1929
19.	A. W. Norblad	Republican	1929-1931
20.	Julius L. Meier	Independent	1931-1935
21.	Charles H. Martin	Democratic	1935-1939
22.	Charles A. Sprague	Republican	1939-1943
23.	Earl Snell	Republican	1943-1947
24.	John H. Hall	Republican	1947-1949
25.	Douglas McKay	Republican	1949-1952
26.	Paul L. Patterson	Republican	1952-1956
27.	Elmo Smith	Republican	1956-1957
28.	Robert D. Holmes	Democratic	1957-1959
29.	Mark O. Hatfield	Republican	1959-1967
30.	Tom McCall	Republican	1967-

Oregon Today faces several problems. State leaders are searching for ways to pay for the high cost of schools and other public services in the 1970's. In 1969, the legislature increased state income taxes and proposed a 3 per cent sales tax. Oregon voters rejected the sales tax.

Air and water pollution have accompanied Oregon's industrial and urban growth. Oregon citizens have become concerned with such issues as the disposal of sewage and other wastes and the public's right to use recreational facilities including beaches and lakes.

Oregon business and political leaders are seeking industries that will not harm the state's natural resources. They hope that the increasing supply of cheap water power will continue to aid Oregon's economic growth.   JESSE L. GILMORE,
RICHARD M. HIGHSMITH, JR., and ROBERT C. NOTSON

OREGON/*Study Aids*

Related Articles in WORLD BOOK include:

BIOGRAPHIES

Astor (John Jacob)	Meeker, Ezra
Graves, Morris	Morse, Wayne L.
Gray, Robert	Palmer, Joel
Lee, Jason	Parkman, Francis
McKay, Alexander	Pauling, Linus C.
McLoughlin, John	Turner, Richmond K.
McNary, Charles L.	Whitman, Marcus

CITIES

Astoria Eugene Portland Salem

HISTORY

Fifty-Four Forty or Fight	Pioneer Life in America
Indian, American	Trails of Early Days
Lewis and Clark Expedition	Western Frontier Life
Oregon Trail	Westward Movement

NATIONAL PARKS AND MONUMENTS

Crater Lake National Park	Oregon Caves National Monument

PHYSICAL FEATURES

Bonneville Dam	High Desert
Cascade Range	Mount Hood
Coast Range	Multnomah Falls
Columbia River	Owyhee Dam
Crater Lake	Snake River
Detroit Dam	Willamette River
Great Basin	

PRODUCTS

For Oregon's rank in production, see:

Cherry	Lumber	Peppermint
Forest and Forest Products	Pea	Plum
	Pear	Potato

OTHER RELATED ARTICLES

Columbia River Highway	Oregon Grape
Diatom	Pacific Coast States
Meteor (picture: Willamette Meteorite)	Pacific Northwest

Outline

I. Government
  A. Constitution D. Courts   F. Taxation
  B. Executive   E. Local Govern- G. Politics
  C. Legislature   ment
II. People
III. Education
  A. Schools   B. Libraries   C. Museums
IV. A Visitor's Guide
  A. Places to Visit   B. Annual Events
V. The Land
  A. Land Regions   C. Rivers, Waterfalls,
  B. Coastline   and Lakes
VI. Climate
VII. Economy
  A. Natural Resources   B. Manufacturing
  C. Agriculture   F. Electric Power
  D. Mining   G. Transportation
  E. Fishing Industry   H. Communication
VIII. History

Questions

What four nations once claimed parts of Oregon?
What is the deepest lake in the United States?
In what region are most of Oregon's large cities?
How did the United States obtain the Oregon region?
What are Oregon's two major forest regions?
Where does Oregon get most of its electric power?
What is Oregon's most important manufacturing industry?
How do ocean-going ships get to Portland?
Who was Chief Joseph?
What is Oregon's most valuable crop?
What changes have taken place in Oregon's lumber industry during the 1960's?

Books for Young Readers

AMERICAN HERITAGE. *Westward on the Oregon Trail.* Narrative by Marian T. Place. Harper, 1962. A well illustrated story of the pioneers making their way westward.

HAINES, FRANCIS. *Red Eagle and the Absaroka.* Caxton, 1960. A story concerning two boys tells of tribal life, with drawings illustrating tools and equipment.

LAMPMAN, EVELYN S. *Princess of Fort Vancouver.* Doubleday, 1962. The story of Eloisa McLoughlin.

LEWIS, OSCAR. *The Story of Oregon.* Garden City Books, 1957.

MCKEOWN, MARTHA F. *Come to Our Salmon Feast.* Binfords, 1959. A photographic story of Wy-am Indian rites at Celilo Falls.

NEUBERGER, RICHARD L. *The Lewis and Clark Expedition.* Random House, 1951.

SPERRY, ARMSTRONG. *River of the West.* Winston, 1952. The story of Robert Gray's trip around Cape Horn, and his discovery of the river he named the *Columbia* for his ship.

Books for Older Readers

BALDWIN, EWART M. *The Geology of Oregon.* Univ. of Oregon Coop. Bookstore, Eugene, Ore., 1959.

BROGAN, PHIL F. *East of the Cascades.* Binfords, 1964. A history of central Oregon.

BROOKS, JAMES E., ed. *The Oregon Almanac and Book of Facts, 1961-62.* Binfords, 1961.

CLARK, ELLA E. *Indian Legends of the Pacific Northwest.* Univ. of California Press, 1953.

HIGHSMITH, RICHARD M., ed. *Atlas of the Pacific Northwest Resources and Development,* 3rd ed. Oregon State Univ. Press, 1962.

LEWIS, MERIWETHER, and CLARK, WILLIAM. *Journals.* Ed. by Bernard de Voto. Houghton, 1953.

NETBOY, ANTHONY, ed. *The Pacific Northwest.* Doubleday, 1963. The chapter on Oregon was written by Stewart Holbrook.

OREGON. THE SECRETARY OF STATE. *Oregon Blue Book.* A biennial handbook of the government of Oregon.

OREGON, UNIVERSITY OF

OREGON, UNIVERSITY OF, is a state-supported co-educational school in Eugene and Portland, Ore. On the main campus in Eugene are the college of liberal arts and the schools of architecture and allied arts, business administration, community services and public affairs, education, health, physical education and recreation, journalism, law, librarianship, and music, and the graduate school. The medical and dental schools are in Portland. Programs of study lead to bachelor's, master's, and doctor's degrees. The university offers special courses in radio and television production, using university radio studios and closed-circuit television equipment. It has museums of art and of natural history. The school colors are emerald green and lemon yellow. The university was chartered in 1872 and opened to students in 1876. For enrollment, see UNIVERSITIES AND COLLEGES (table). ARTHUR S. FLEMMING

OREGON CAVES NATIONAL MONUMENT is a 480-acre area in Oregon containing the limestone caves in the Siskiyou Mountains, and a game preserve. The vast caves have unusual limestone formations created by the stream that runs through them. The area was made a national monument by President Taft in 1909. See also OREGON (color picture).

OREGON COLLEGE OF EDUCATION is a state-supported coeducational teacher's college in Monmouth, Ore. The school was founded in 1856 as Monmouth University. Its name was changed to Christian College in 1865, to Oregon Normal School in 1882, and to the present title in 1937. For enrollment, see UNIVERSITIES AND COLLEGES (table). R. E. LIEUALLEN

OREGON GRAPE. This wild plant, also called the Oregon hollygrape, is the state flower of Oregon. It grows from western Oregon through Washington into British Columbia. The Oregon grape is a low plant, and does not climb as the wild grape does. Its leaves look like those of the holly, and its wood is yellow. The clusters of dainty yellow flowers open in the early summer. The berries ripen late in the fall. They look like grapes or blueberries. The berries of this plant are often used for jelly. Despite its names, the Oregon grape is neither a grape nor a holly.

Scientific Classification. The Oregon grape belongs to the barberry family, *Berberidaceae*. It is genus *Mahonia*, species *M. nervosa*. EARL L. CORE

See also BARBERRY; OREGON (color picture: The State Flower).

OREGON LAUREL. See LAUREL.

OREGON QUESTION. See POLK, JAMES KNOX ("Oregon Fever").

OREGON STATE UNIVERSITY, in Corvallis, Ore., is a state-controlled, coeducational, land-grant school. The university emphasizes science and engineering. It offers courses in liberal arts and sciences, business, engineering, forestry, pharmacy, education, agriculture, home economics, physical education, medicine, nursing, dentistry, and medical technology. Courses lead to bachelor's, master's, doctor's, and professional degrees. The school operates an agricultural experiment station and supervises federal cooperative extension work in Oregon. There are air force, army, and navy ROTC units on the campus. The college was founded in 1868. For enrollment, see UNIVERSITIES AND COLLEGES (table). J. KENNETH MUNFORD

OREGON SYSTEM. See OREGON (History [Progress as a State]).

OREGON TERRITORY was created after the settlement in 1846 of a boundary dispute between the United States and Great Britain. It included the present states of Idaho, Oregon, and Washington and part of Montana and Wyoming. Before 1846, the Oregon Country, occupied jointly by the U.S. and Britain, included the area south of Alaska, north of California, and west of the Rocky Mountains. The 1846 settlement gave the United States the land south of the 49th parallel, except for Vancouver Island. The Oregon Country became a territory in 1848. Oregon was admitted to the Union on Feb. 14, 1859. O. O. WINTHER

Oregon State University

Oregon State University's Social Science Hall forms part of a well-landscaped quadrangle on the campus of the university in Corvallis.

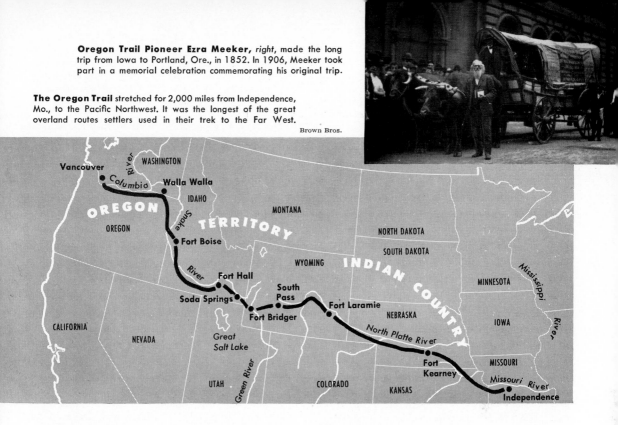

Oregon Trail Pioneer Ezra Meeker, *right*, made the long trip from Iowa to Portland, Ore., in 1852. In 1906, Meeker took part in a memorial celebration commemorating his original trip.

The Oregon Trail stretched for 2,000 miles from Independence, Mo., to the Pacific Northwest. It was the longest of the great overland routes settlers used in their trek to the Far West.

Brown Bros.

OREGON TRAIL was the longest of the great overland routes used in the westward expansion of the United States. It wound 2,000 miles through prairies and deserts and across mountains from Independence, Mo., to the Pacific Northwest. Even today, travelers can see the deeply rutted road cut by wagon wheels along sections of the trail.

Families traveling to the Oregon region usually gathered at Independence, near the Missouri River. They followed a trail which ran in a northwesterly course to Fort Kearney, Nebr. Then they traveled up the Platte River and its north branch to Fort Laramie, Wyo. From this point, they continued along the North Platte to its Sweetwater branch, and crossed through South Pass in the Rocky Mountains to the Green River Valley at Fort Bridger, Wyo. The route turned northwest to Fort Hall in the Snake River area, and on to Fort Boise, Ida. Settlers crossed the Grande Ronde Valley and the Blue Mountains to Marcus Whitman's mission at Walla Walla, Wash. Then they traveled down the Columbia River to Fort Vancouver and the Willamette Valley of Oregon.

Travel on the Oregon Trail was a severe test of strength and endurance. The journey in a covered wagon took six months. Settlers often had to cross flooded rivers, and sometimes had to contend with whirlpools in fords. Indians attacked the wagon trains, and cholera and other diseases were common. Food, water, and wood were always scarce, and the travelers often encountered contaminated water holes.

Explorers and fur traders first traced the course of the Oregon Trail. In 1805, Meriwether Lewis and William Clark traveled on a western section of the route in the region of the Snake and Columbia rivers. Traders returning from Astoria also used the trail. Benjamin Bon-

neville is credited with taking the first wagons through South Pass in the 1830's. Nathaniel J. Wyeth also led companies over the trail. John C. Frémont surveyed a portion of the route in 1842 for the United States Army.

Settlers began following the trail to Oregon about 1841. By 1843, so many were there that a provisional government was organized. The Oregon country's northern boundary was set in 1846, and the Territory of Oregon was set up in 1848.   W. TURRENTINE JACKSON

Related Articles in WORLD BOOK include:

Bridger, James	Pioneer Life (How the
Meeker, Ezra	Pioneers Traveled)
Palmer, Joel	Westward Movement (Set-
Parkman, Francis	tling the Far West)

ORELLANA, *OH ray (L)YAH nah*, **FRANCISCO DE** (1500?-1550?), was the first white man to explore the full course of the Amazon River, the longest river in South America (see AMAZON RIVER). He made the voyage in 1541, in command of about 50 men. On the journey, he saw Indian warrior women who reminded him of the Amazon warriors of Greek mythology. He called their country the *Land of the Amazons.* Orellana was born in Trujillo, Spain.   CHARLES E. NOWELL

ORESTES, *oh RES teez*, according to Greek legend, was the son of Agamemnon and Clytemnestra, rulers of Argos. When Clytemnestra killed Agamemnon on his return from Troy, Orestes was a young boy being educated away from home. He did not return to Argos until he was grown. Then, with the help of his vengeful sister Electra and a friend, Orestes killed his mother and her lover, Aegisthus. The Erinyes (Furies) punished Orestes by driving him insane. But he regained his sanity, and was acquitted of his sin.   H. LLOYD STOW

See also ELECTRA; HERMIONE; IPHIGENIA.

ORGAN. See HUMAN BODY.

643

ORGAN

ORGAN is a musical instrument in which the sound is made by wind pressure. The modern pipe organ has pipes of different shapes and sizes. The word *organ* also describes other instruments or groups of instruments that make organlike sounds.

Pipe Organ

A large pipe organ is larger and more powerful than any other musical instrument. True organ sound, produced only by a pipe organ, results from many pitches of *diapason* pipes, called the Diapason or Principal Chorus. A complete organ today may also have tones that represent varieties of flutes and trumpets, as well as those that imitate strings, wood winds, and chimes.

Size. Each pipe organ is built to fit the building where it is to be used. The smallest organ has about 370 pipes, and the largest has more than 40,000 pipes. The larger the organ, the greater the range of musical effects it can play.

The Main Parts of a pipe organ are the keyboards, the valve mechanism, the pipe assembly, the wind chest, and the blower. The player presses the keys, which carry an electrical impulse, or vibration, to the valve mechanism. This mechanism changes the electric impulse into a *pneumatic impulse* (one made by air). The air impulse opens a valve that lets air into the pipes, and produces sound. The air comes from a wind chest that is filled by a *blower* (electrically-driven fan).

The Keyboards are set in a case called a console. There are usually several rows of keys, called *manuals* because they are played with the hands. An organ may have as many as six manuals, known as: the *great organ; swell organ; choir organ; solo organ; bombarde;* and *echo organ.* A *pedal organ*, consisting of large wooden keys, lies at the base of the console. These are played with the feet. *Stop knobs* at the side of the keyboard or *stop keys* above the keyboards control the sets of pipes.

The Valve Mechanism may be built in various ways. In many organs, pressure on a key makes an electric contact below the key. The electricity opens a valve, which in turn opens a bellows. A wire on the bellows opens a valve in the air reservoir. The rush of air into a certain set of pipes sounds the desired note.

The Pipes are sometimes enclosed in a pipe chamber. Openings in the chamber have shutters which can be opened and closed for regulating the tone. A vibrating brass reed makes the tone in the *reed pipes.* The tone in the *flue pipes* comes from a vibrating column of air, like an ordinary whistle. The flue pipes are made of metal or wood. The pipes measure from $\frac{1}{2}$ inch to 32 feet long. Each organ *stop* (group of pipes) is *voiced* (built) to produce the desired tone. Each tone must be matched with the tones of all the other organ stops.

Wind Chest and Blower. Each set of pipes rests on a *wind chest.* The chest, a wooden box, has holes bored in it so that air can get into the pipes. The blower keeps the air in the box at a certain pressure. The air reservoir, between the blower and wind chest, is necessary to keep the same amount of pressure at all times.

Other Organs

The Reed Organ, better known as the *harmonium* or *melodeon,* was common in churches and homes in the late 1800's. The tone comes from one or more series of different-sized reeds like those in an accordion or harmonica. The player pumps up and down on two pedals to produce the power for air pressure. Reed organs of today usually use a suction blower for air pressure, like that in a pipe organ.

Electronic Organs, or *electrones,* are instruments that use electronic amplification to increase the volume of sound. An electronic organ has no pipes, but does have three elements in common with the pipe organ. A player may hold the tone for as long a time as desired. He may increase or decrease the sound while holding it. The electrone also has the same kind of range of tone and volume as a pipe organ.

The electronic organ's tone, always heard through loudspeakers, is different from the pipe organ tone, except in large installations. All the electronic instruments use radio tubes to amplify the sound.

The great advantage of the small electrones over a pipe organ is that they are cheaper and take less space. But they do not have the tone or volume of pipe organs.

History

Early Organs. The earliest form of organ was probably an instrument the Greeks called the *syrinx* (pipes of Pan). It consisted of a series of hollow tubes of different lengths. The player blew into or across the open upper ends of the pipes.

About 200 B.C., Ctesibius of Alexandria, an engineer, constructed an instrument which made use of water power to force air into the pipes. It was called a *hydraulus* (water organ). Byzantium (now Istanbul) became an important center of organ building in the A.D. 100's or 200's. The pneumatic air organ, with wind supplied by bellows, first developed there. Craftsmen exported organs and documents on organ building from Byzantium to Europe and the Middle East. Organs appeared in Spain in the 400's and in England about the 700's, and were probably used in churches in the 600's.

Middle Ages. Pipe organs developed slowly in the early Middle Ages. But they changed rapidly between the 1400's and 1600's, especially during the Renaissance. This growth may possibly have resulted from the development of instrumental music at this time. Many of the organ parts common today first appeared during this period. Between the 1300's and the 1800's, the Germans led the world in organ building. Famous German organ builders include Andreas Silbermann, who built the organ in the Cathedral of Strasbourg, and his brother Gottfried, who built one in the Cathedral of Freiburg.

During the 1800's, the English ranked as the most important builders. English organ builders included Charles Barker; William Hill, who built the organ of St. Peter's church in London; and Henry Willis, who rebuilt the organ of St. Paul's, London. The first American electric-action organ appeared at the Philadelphia Centennial Exposition in 1876. WILLIAM H. BARNES

Related Articles in WORLD BOOK include:

Buxtehude, Dietrich	Harmonica
Clavilux	Harmonium
Franck, César A.	Saint-Saëns, Camille
Gibbons, Orlando	Schweitzer, Albert
Hand Organ	

ORGAN-GRINDER. See HAND ORGAN (picture).

ORGAN OF CORTI. See EAR (How We Hear).

New Pipe Organs are put together and tested thoroughly at the factory. The pipes of this organ range in size from one about sixteen feet tall to one smaller than an ordinary pencil.

Electric Organs are popular as home musical instruments. They take up much less space than pipe organs, and are easier to play.

An Old-Fashioned Reed Organ makes a fine accompanying instrument on such occasions as this song session at a summer camp.

ORGAN PIPE CACTUS NATIONAL MONUMENT
is an unspoiled desert in southern Arizona. It covers
over 330,000 acres, and contains the organ pipe cactus
and other unusual forms of plant and animal life found
nowhere else in the United States. It was established as
a national monument in 1937. See also NATIONAL
PARK SYSTEM (map); CACTUS (picture).

ORGAN TRANSPLANT. See TISSUE TRANSPLANT.

ORGANDY, *AWR gun dee,* is a thin, transparent material made of fine cotton yarns. It is usually very stiff
and is often used for evening dresses, and for trimming.

ORGANIC ACID. See ACID.

ORGANIC CHEMISTRY. See CHEMISTRY.

ORGANISM, *AWR gun iz'm,* is a living individual of
any kind. Organisms are divided into two kingdoms,
plant and animal. All organisms are made up of living
material called *protoplasm,* and almost all are composed
of cells (see PROTOPLASM). Pieces of living tissue or a
live organ, such as a heart, are not organisms. An organism is a complete living unit in itself. See also CELL;
LIFE; MICROBIOLOGY.   C. BROOKE WORTH

ORGANISTS. See AMERICAN GUILD OF ORGANISTS;
ORGAN.

ORGANIZATION. See MANAGEMENT; PARLIAMENTARY PROCEDURE.

ORGANIZATION FOR ECONOMIC COOPERATION AND DEVELOPMENT. See EUROPE (Toward
European Unity); MARSHALL PLAN.

ORGANIZATION OF AFRICAN UNITY is an association of 41 independent African nations. It was
established in 1963, when the heads of 30 African
states and governments signed the Charter of African
Unity at a conference in Addis Ababa, Ethiopia.

The charter states the organization's aims: (1) to
promote the unity and solidarity of African states; (2)
to promote cooperation among African states; (3) to
defend the sovereignty and independence of African
states; (4) to remove all forms of colonialism from
Africa; and (5) to promote international cooperation.
The charter affirms the policy that African states should
not ally themselves with either the Communist or the
Western power blocs in world affairs.

The charter set up special commissions to carry out
the aims of the organization. These commissions include an economic and social commission; an educational and cultural commission; a health, sanitation,
and nutrition commission; a defense commission; and a
scientific, technical, and research commission.

The Assembly of the Heads of States and Governments is the highest authority of the organization. It
meets at least once a year. The Council of Ministers
consists of foreign ministers or other ministers appointed
by the governments of member states. It approves the
resolutions of the assembly. The council meets at least
twice a year. The Commission of Mediation, Conciliation, and Arbitration works to settle disputes between
member states. A permanent secretariat, headed by an
administrative secretary-general, is located in Addis
Ababa, the organization's headquarters.

See also AFRICA (Today).

ORGANIZATION OF AMERICAN STATES (OAS)
is an association of 23 Latin-American countries
and the United States. The OAS is a regional organi-

zation within the general framework of the United
Nations. It seeks to provide for collective self-defense,
regional cooperation, and the peaceful settlement of
controversies. The OAS charter sets forth the group's
guiding principles. These include a belief in the value of
international law, social justice, economic cooperation,
and the equality of man without distinction as to race,
nationality, or creed. The charter also states that an act
of aggression against one American nation is regarded
as an act of aggression against all the nations.

The OAS functions through several bodies. Major
policies are formed at annual sessions of the *General
Assembly.* All member nations can attend, and each has
one vote. Special *Meetings of Consultation of Ministers of
Foreign Affairs* deal with urgent problems, especially
those relating to defense or the maintenance of peace in
the Americas. The *Permanent Council,* with headquarters
in Washington, D.C., is the executive body of the
OAS. Each member nation is represented. For convenience, diplomatic representatives in Washington serve
as council members. The council supervises the *General
Secretariat,* makes plans for General Assembly sessions,
and oversees OAS administration. The secretary-general, the chief administrative officer of the OAS, is
elected to a five-year term by the General Assembly.
Specialized conferences and organizations promote
inter-American cooperation.

The Organization of American States had its early
beginning at the First International Conference of
American States, which met in Washington, D.C., in
1889 and 1890. The delegates established the Union of
American Republics, with the Commercial Bureau as
its central office. This bureau was renamed the Pan
American Union in 1910. The Pan American Union
became the General Secretariat of the OAS when it was
organized in 1948 at the ninth Pan-American Conference, held in Bogotá, Colombia. The organization's
original charter became effective in December, 1951,
and an amended charter took effect in February, 1970.

Early in 1962, the OAS voted to exclude Cuba's
Communist government from active membership. But
Cuba itself remained an OAS member even though its
government cannot participate in the organization's
activities. Later in 1962, the OAS supported a United
States *quarantine* (blockade) of Cuba to prevent delivery
of Russian shipments of missiles to the island.

Anti-American riots broke out in Panama in 1964,
and Panama ended diplomatic relations with the U.S.
The OAS helped restore these relations. Also in 1964,
the OAS voted sanctions against Cuba for aggression
in Venezuela. All the members except Mexico agreed
to boycott trade and transportation to Cuba.

In 1965, a revolt in the Dominican Republic led the
OAS to set up its first military force. Troops from six

MEMBERS OF THE OAS		
Argentina	Dominican	Nicaragua
Barbados	Republic	Panama
Bolivia	Ecuador	Paraguay
Brazil	El Salvador	Peru
Chile	Guatemala	Trinidad and
Colombia	Haiti	Tobago
Costa	Honduras	United States
Rica	Jamaica	Uruguay
Cuba	Mexico	Venezuela

Latin-American countries and the United States took part. The troops and OAS committees worked to restore order in the Dominican Republic. In 1969, the OAS acted quickly to end a five-day invasion of Honduras by troops from El Salvador. TOM B. JONES

See also LATIN AMERICA (History; picture); PAN-AMERICAN CONFERENCES.

ORGANIZED LABOR. See LABOR.

ORGANOSOL. See PLASTICS (table: Plastics Terms).

ORGANUM. See MUSIC (The Middle Ages).

ORIENT, *O ree ent,* is another name for the Asiatic countries and islands, or the East. Sometimes the term is used to mean only the eastern part of Asia, which is also called the *Far East.*

ORIENTAL EXCLUSION ACTS, a series of acts passed by Congress in 1882, 1888, and 1892, prohibited Asians from entering the United States.

Chinese first came to the United States in large numbers after the discovery of gold in California in 1848. They were well received for a time, but met hostility when they moved to large cities. Between 1864 and 1869, Chinese coolies were brought to the United States to help build the Central Pacific Railroad. In 1868, China and the United States signed the Burlingame Treaty to protect this immigration.

However, Americans accused the Chinese of unfair competition in business, of lowering wages, and of immoral and unsanitary habits. During the economic depression of the 1870's, feeling against the Chinese increased. In some instances, they were victims of mob violence. Westerners demanded that Chinese immigration be halted. Despite the treaty of 1868, Congress passed the first Oriental Exclusion Act in 1882. These laws were first intended to be only temporary, but Congress made exclusion permanent in 1902.

Japanese began coming to the United States in increasing numbers during the late 1800's. Many of them settled on the West Coast and became farmers. Their farming methods and their low living standards made competition difficult for the white farmers. California adopted laws designed to drive the Japanese from agriculture in that state. A demand for the prohibition of Japanese immigration grew.

In 1907, the "gentleman's agreement" between the United States and Japan greatly reduced immigration, but it did not satisfy the people of the West (see GENTLEMAN'S AGREEMENT). The Immigration Act of 1924 prohibited the entry of all Asiatic laborers.

During World War II, Congress repealed the laws against the Chinese. They may now enter the United States on a quota basis, and are eligible for citizenship. The Immigration and Nationality Act of 1952 extended the same privileges to other Asians, including the Japanese. HAROLD W. BRADLEY

ORIENTAL INSTITUTE. See CHICAGO, UNIVERSITY OF.

ORIENTAL RUG. See RUGS AND CARPETS.

ORIFLAMME. See FLAG (color picture: Historical Flags of the World).

ORIGAMI. See PAPERWORK, DECORATIVE.

ORIGEN, *AHR ee jen,* (185?-254?) was an early Christian philosopher and writer. He believed that all knowledge comes from God, and finds its highest and most complete expression in Christianity. He had great influence in ancient times, and was said to have written 6,000 books on religious subjects. He was born and

educated in Alexandria, Egypt. He died as a result of torture by the Roman Emperor Decius. F. A. NORWOOD

ORIGIN OF SPECIES. See DARWIN (Charles Robert); EVOLUTION (History).

ORINOCO RIVER, *ohr uh NO koh,* is the sixth longest river in South America. It has two known sources, both in the Parima highlands in Venezuela, near the boundary of Brazil. The river is about 1,700 miles long. It flows northwest to Colombia and forms the boundary between Colombia and Venezuela. Then it swings eastward. About 110 miles before it reaches the seacoast, it divides into many channels. During the rainy season, floods sometimes cover thousands of square miles. For location, see VENEZUELA (color map).

Small oceangoing vessels can sail 260 miles upstream from the mouth of the Orinoco. Ships can use the river for about 500 miles above the Maipures and Atures rapids. Ciudad Bolívar is the center of the Orinoco river trade. Steamships run between Trinidad and Ciudad Bolívar most of the year. Major branches of the Orinoco are the Casiquiare, the Meta, and the Apure. Including its branches, the Orinoco has a navigable length of 4,300 miles. MARGUERITE UTTLEY

See also RIVER (chart: Longest Rivers).

ORIOLE, *O ree ohl.* In America, orioles form a subdivision of the blackbird family. In Europe, the name oriole is given to a family of orange and black birds related to the crows. Most of the American orioles live in or near the tropics. In Jamaica, they are known as *banana birds.* Three common kinds of orioles live in southern Canada and the United States—the eastern *Baltimore oriole,* the western *Bullock's oriole,* and the more southerly *orchard oriole.* Altogether there are nine native orioles. Orioles have beautiful feathers and loud musical voices. They weave hanging nests, and help farmers by eating insects. But in some areas they eat ripening grapes. Some orioles are also called *troupials.*

Scientific Classification. The American oriole belongs to the icterid family, *Icteridae.* The Baltimore oriole is genus *Icterus,* species *I. galbula;* Bullock's oriole is *I. bullockii;* the orchard oriole, *I. spurius.* GEORGE E. HUDSON

See also BALTIMORE ORIOLE; BIRD (Building the Nest; pictures: Favorite Songbirds, Bird Nests, Birds' Eggs).

An Orchard Oriole feeds its hungry young. These orioles breed in North America and spend the winter in the Caribbean Sea area.
John H. Gerard

ORION, *oh RYE un*, was a mighty hunter in Greek mythology. He was the son of the god Poseidon (Neptune), who gave him the power to walk through the sea and on its surface (see NEPTUNE).

The goddess Artemis (Diana) fell in love with the handsome Orion. Her brother, Apollo, did not like this, and plotted to destroy Orion. One day while Orion was swimming, Apollo walked by with Artemis. Apollo challenged her to hit the target bobbing in the water. Artemis did not know that it was the head of her lover, and killed him with her arrow. Her sorrow was great. She placed Orion in the sky as a constellation.

Another story says that Artemis killed Orion because she was jealous of his attention to Aurora.   VAN JOHNSON

ORION, the Great Hunter, is a brilliant constellation that straddles the celestial equator. The red star Betelgeuse marks the right shoulder of the hunter. The star Bellatrix marks the left shoulder. The blue-white star Rigel, at the southwest corner, marks the giant's upraised left foot. Three bright stars mark the belt. A sword hilt, marked by faint stars, dangles from the belt. The Great Nebula of Orion, a mass of gases and dust, can be seen surrounding the center part of the sword. Orion faces the constellation of Taurus, the Bull, and seems to be warding off the bull's attack. He holds a club in his right hand. In his left hand, he grasps a lion's skin, which he can use as a shield.   I. M. LEVITT

See also ASTRONOMY (Skies of the Seasons); BETELGEUSE; CANIS MAJOR; RIGEL.

ORISKANY, BATTLE OF. See SAINT LEGER, BARRY.

ORITHYIA. See BOREAS.

Orion Has a Row of Three Large Stars Forming a Belt.

ORIZABA, *OHR uh ZAH buh* (pop. 69,706; alt. 4,028 ft.), is a resort and cotton-milling city in southern Mexico. It lies 65 miles southwest of Veracruz. For location, see MEXICO (political map). The city has cotton and jute mills, cigar factories, railroad-repair shops, a brewery, and a paper mill. The Spaniards founded Orizaba in the 1550's.   JOHN A. CROW

ORIZABA, or .CITLALTÉPETL (*SEE tlahl TAY peht'l*), is the highest mountain in Mexico, and the third highest in North America. It rises 18,701 feet above sea level about 30 miles northwest of the city of Orizaba. See also GEOGRAPHY (picture: The Earth as Man's Home).

ORKNEY ISLANDS lie north of the British Isles. They are separated from Scotland by the Pentland Firth, which is six miles wide. There are 67 islands in the group, and a number of rocky islets. They cover a total area of 376 square miles, and have a total coastline of about 100 miles. People live on 25 of the islands. For location, see GREAT BRITAIN (physical map).

The principal islands of the group are Mainland (Pomona), Hoy, North and South Ronaldsay, Flotta, Burray, Rousay, Shapinsay, Stronsay, Eday, Westray, and Sanday. Mainland and Hoy are hilly. The other islands lie rather low. Warm ocean currents give the islands a mild climate, and the soil is fertile.

About 17,550 persons live in the Orkneys. Most of them are of Scandinavian and Scottish descent. Agriculture and fishing are the chief occupations. The farmers grow barley, oats, turnips, and potatoes. Livestock, seafood, poultry, and eggs are exported. The Orkneys are so far north that they have scarcely any daylight in winter and scarcely any night in summer. Thousands of tourists visit the islands. Kirkwall (the capital) and Stromness are the only towns. Both are on Mainland.

In early times, a Celtic people lived on the islands, and the Norsemen often visited there. In the 900's, Norse earls settled and ruled the Orkneys. Scottish nobles replaced them in 1231, but the islands remained under the kings of Norway and Denmark. About 1468, the Orkneys were promised to Scotland as security for the dowry of Princess Margaret of Denmark, engaged to marry James III of Scotland. The dowry was never paid, and Scotland took the islands in 1472.

The islands are an important naval base. Scapa Flow, an enclosed anchorage south of Mainland, was the base of the British Grand Fleet during World War I (see SCAPA FLOW).   FREDERICK G. MARCHAM

ORLANDO. See ROLAND.

ORLANDO, Fla. (pop. 99,006; met. area 428,003; alt. 70 ft.), is a popular winter resort and the commercial center of a large fruit and truck-farming area. It lies in the heart of the Orange County lake region, with about 50 lakes within the city limits (see FLORIDA [political map]). Orlando has a U.S. naval training center and the Florida Symphony Orchestra. Walt Disney World, an amusement park and vacation center, lies 15 miles south of Orlando.

The first settlers came to this area in 1837. The city was named in honor of Orlando Reeves, a pioneer who died in an Indian battle. Orlando has a mayor-council government.   KATHRYN ABBEY HANNA

ORLANDO, *awr LAN doh*, **VITTORIO EMANUELE** (1860-1952), served as prime minister of Italy from 1917 to 1919. He took office just after the Italian Army had suffered a terrible defeat in World War I. He did much to raise Italian civilian morale and to spur Italian armed forces on to victory.

Orlando began his political career in the Italian Chamber of Deputies in 1897. Between 1903 and 1917, he held various government jobs. He led the Italian delegation to the Versailles Peace Conference in 1919. He made strong demands there for increased territory for Italy. When the Allies failed to give Italy all that Orlando wanted, he was forced to resign as prime minister.

In 1922, Orlando supported the dictator, Benito Mussolini. But he denounced him in 1925, after Mussolini's henchmen murdered a Socialist leader. Orlando helped overthrow Mussolini in 1943. Orlando was born in Palermo, Sicily. R. JOHN RATH

See also WILSON, WOODROW (picture, Landing in France).

ORLÉANS, *AWR LAY AHN* (pop. 84,289; met. area 120,000; alt. 362 ft.), is an important commercial and transportation center in France. It is the capital of the department of Loiret. Orléans is in the heart of the Château Country, a region of many large estates and *châteaux* (country houses). It lies along the Loire River, about 70 miles southwest of Paris. For location, see FRANCE (color map).

Important industries in Orléans include textiles, food-processing, tanning, distilling, and brewing. The city's factories produce clothing, candies, chocolates, liqueurs, vinegar, machinery, and pharmaceuticals.

Joan of Arc was called the *Maid of Orléans* after she led the French against the English, who besieged the city in 1429. A statue of Joan stands in the public square. Other places of historical interest in Orléans include the Cathedral of Sainte Croix, which was destroyed by the Huguenots in 1567 and rebuilt by Henry IV and his successors. Large sections of Orléans were damaged during World War II. EDWARD W. FOX

ORLÉANS, *AWR LAY AHN*, was the name of two branches of the royal French family, the houses of Valois-Orléans and Bourbon-Orléans (see BOURBON; VALOIS).

Louis (1372-1407) founded the house of Valois-Orléans. He was the second son of King Charles V, and the brother of Charles VI. Louis became duke of Orléans in 1392. He wanted to rule when Charles VI became mentally ill, but his uncle, Philip of Burgundy, ruled. Philip's son John plotted Louis' assassination.

Historical Pictures Service

Regent Philippe

Charles (1391-1465), the oldest son of Louis, was one of the greatest poets of France. His court at Blois attracted such noted poets as François Villon. Charles commanded French forces against the English in the Battle of Agincourt in 1415. He was captured and held in England until 1440. His son Louis XII was the first member of the Valois-Orléans branch to gain the throne (see LOUIS [XII]). The Duchy of Orléans was united with the crown after Louis became king.

Philippe (1640-1701), the son of Louis XIII and the only brother of Louis XIV, founded the house of Bourbon-Orléans. He became duke of Orléans in 1661.

Philippe (1674-1723), son of the founder of the Bourbon-Orléans branch, became duke of Orléans in 1701. He acted as regent of France until Louis XV came of age. He let John Law introduce a large amount of paper currency, which led to bankruptcy.

Louis Philippe Joseph (1747-1793), the grandson of Philippe, was known as Philippe Egalité (Equality). He took this name during the French Revolution to show the people that he sided with them against the nobles. He voted for the death of King Louis XVI. But Philippe and other members of the Bourbon family were arrested in 1793, and he was beheaded. He was the father of Louis Philippe (see LOUIS PHILIPPE). Ferdinand, the eldest son of King Louis Philippe, became the duke of Orléans when his father became king.

Louis Philippe Robert (1869-1926), the grandson of Ferdinand, was the last real claimant to the throne of France. He was a famous scientist, and led expeditions to the Arctic regions and to British East Africa. He was born in Twickenham, England, and was exiled from France in 1886. RICHARD M. BRACE

ORLÉANS, BATTLE OF. See ARMY (Famous Land Battles of History).

ORLICH, FRANCISCO J. See COSTA RICA (Recent Developments).

ORLON is a Du Pont Company trademark name for a widely used synthetic fiber. It can be woven or knit into fabrics. Orlon fabrics are comfortable to wear, dry quickly, and hold their shape. Orlon has a bulkiness that makes it suitable for garments such as sweaters.

Many different kinds of Orlon fibers are made to meet the needs of various materials. The fibers vary in size, brightness, softness, and the ability to absorb dyes. One fiber, Orlon Sayelle, gives fabrics elasticity and a wool-like feel.

Orlon production started in 1950 in Camden, S.C. Heavy yarns were produced there for industrial uses that required materials that resisted acids or exposure to sunlight. Manufacturers soon found that spun Orlon was excellent for wearing apparel, and fiber for knit and woven materials was produced. Textile manufacturers developed attractive, long-wearing Orlon fabrics for clothing and for upholstery and carpets.

Orlon belongs to the *acrylic* class of plastics (see PLASTICS [table, Kinds of Plastics]). Orlon acrylic fiber was discovered when Du Pont chemists found that *polyacrylonitrile*, a synthetic chemical, dissolved in certain unusual solvents. It produced a concentrated solution from which yarns could be spun.

Orlon is made from *acrylonitrile*, a chemical used as a *monomer* (basic building block). This substance is *polymerized*. In this process, the molecules of acrylonitrile join together to form long, chainlike molecules of polyacrylonitrile. Workers then dissolve the chemical in a solvent to produce a thick and sticky solution. The solution goes through machines which cast it into fibers by forcing the liquid through tiny openings called *spinnerets* into heated gas. The solvent evaporates in the gas. Machines also stretch the fibers to several times their original length to strengthen and toughen them. The Orlon is then dried and packaged in bales for shipment to textile mills. E. M. HICKS, JR.

Eugene Ormandy

NBC

ORMANDY, *AWR muhn dee,* **EUGENE** (1899-), became one of the world's best-known conductors during his long career as director of the Philadelphia Orchestra. From 1936 to 1938, Ormandy shared the direction of the orchestra with Leopold Stokowski. Ormandy became the orchestra's sole music director in 1938. His performances stress romantic and neoromantic music and emphasize fine string playing and rich orchestral tones. Under Ormandy's leadership, the orchestra has toured many countries and made a great number of recordings.

Eugene Ormandy Blau was born in Budapest, Hungary. He studied the violin with Jenö Hubay, a noted Hungarian violinist. In 1921, Ormandy went to the United States intending to make a concert tour. Instead, he became a violinist in the orchestra of the Capitol Theater in New York City. Soon he had opportunities to conduct and in 1931 he became principal conductor of the Minneapolis Symphony Orchestra. He held this position until moving to Philadelphia. Ormandy became a U.S. citizen in 1927. ROBERT C. MARSH

ORMOLU. See FURNITURE (Louis XV).

ORNAMENT. See the following articles, with their lists of Related Articles: ART AND THE ARTS; CLOTHING; GEM; JEWELRY.

ORNITHISCHIA. See DINOSAUR (Bird-Hipped).

ORNITHOLOGY, *AWR nih THAHL oh jih,* is the bird-study branch of the science of zoology. It includes the description and classification of birds, their distribution, their activities, and their economic relations to man. The activities of birds which are studied include mating, nesting, rearing of young, feeding, and migrations. Photography has been used to record the activities of birds. Recordings have been made of bird songs.

The beauty of birds, their interesting habits, and their importance to man attract both professional and amateur scientists. Many persons belong to bird clubs. The American Ornithologists' Union was established in 1883. It has headquarters at 2557 Portsmouth Ave., Toledo 13, Ohio. L. B. AREY

See also BIRD (Bird Study); AUDUBON, JOHN JAMES; AUDUBON SOCIETY, NATIONAL; BARTRAM (William).

ORNITHOPOD. See DINOSAUR (Bird-Hipped Dinosaurs).

ORNITHOPTER, *AWR nih THAHP ter,* is a machine designed to fly by flapping its wings like a bird. No one has ever built a successful ornithopter, but men have dreamed of such a vehicle since ancient times. Some small-scale models have flown. But all attempts to build man-carrying ornithopters have failed, because man has not developed materials that are light enough and strong enough for birdlike machines.

Ornithopters are classified in two ways. The first type uses various forms of wings for support in the air, and fastens the wings to the body of a man. The second type uses a cabin or cockpit to house the pilot. The wings are attached and operated from the cockpit. The English philosopher Roger Bacon suggested the idea of the ornithopter about 1250. LESLIE A. BRYAN

See also AIRPLANE (Early Experiments and Ideas); BIRD (How Birds Fly).

ORNITHOSIS. See PSITTACOSIS.

OROZCO, *oh ROHS koh,* **JOSÉ CLEMENTE** (1883-1949), was one of Mexico's best-known painters. His style was powerful, spiritual, and dramatic. His murals decorate the National Preparatory School in Mexico City and other public buildings in Mexico and the United States. Another series is at Dartmouth College. A part of his mural in the Dartmouth College Library appears in the PAINTING article. Orozco was born in Zapotlán, Jalisco, and attended the Academy of Fine Arts in Mexico City. ROBERT C. SMITH

See also FRESCO; MEXICO (picture: Palace of Justice).

José Orozco Paints a Fresco on the southwest wall of the Museum of Modern Art in New York City.

Schall, Pix

ORPHANAGE is an institution which serves as a home for children who are deprived of their parents' care. Parents sometimes abandon their children, either because of poverty or because of lack of interest in rearing the children. Or, children may be left alone when both their parents die. Most large cities in America have orphanages to take care of these children. The oldest orphanage in America is Bethesda, near Savannah, Ga. It was opened in 1740.

There are important differences between an orphanage and a foundling hospital. A foundling hospital tries to save the life of a deserted infant and then attempts to place the child in a private or public home. An orphanage takes care of a child for a number of years. By training and education, the orphanage tries to prepare the child to take care of himself. In many places, strict laws regulate the operation of orphanages and foundling hospitals. These laws generally concern the admission of children, and their care. EMORY S. BOGARDUS

See also CHILDREN, SOCIETIES FOR.

Orpheus Crossed the River Styx into Hades, the realm of Pluto. Rowing the boat is Charon, who ferried souls across the river. Orpheus stands in the center of the boat with his lyre. Orpheus went to ask that his wife Eurydice be returned to earth.

Brown Bros.

ORPHEUS, *AWR fyoos,* or *AWR fee us,* was a musician in Greek mythology. He played such lovely music on his lyre that animals, trees, and stones followed him, and rivers stopped flowing to listen. He was the son of Apollo and the Muse Calliope. He married Eurydice, and loved her dearly (see EURYDICE). When she died, he went to the Lower World to bring her back. He played his lyre and charmed Pluto and Persephone so much that they granted his request. They warned Orpheus that he must not look back at Eurydice on the way up to earth. But he glanced back too soon, and she disappeared. Because he wanted no woman but Eurydice, Orpheus angered some Thracian women, and they tore him to pieces. His head and lyre murmured sad music as they floated down the river Hebrus.   JOSEPH FONTENROSE

ORPHIC MYSTERIES. See MYSTERIES.

ORR, JOHN BOYD. See BOYD ORR, LORD.

ORREFORS, *awr uh FORSH,* Sweden (pop. 786), is famous for its crystal and glass works. It lies northwest of Kalmar, in southeastern Sweden. Orrefors glass is known for its design and its fused layers of colored and transparent glass. Orrefors glass designers include Simon Gate, Edvard Hald, Ingeborg Lundin, Nils Landberg, and Sven Palmquist.   JAMES J. ROBBINS

ORRERY. See PLANETARIUM.

ORRISROOT, *AWR is root,* is the dried, sweet-smelling *rhizome* (underground stem) of certain irises. It is used to give perfumes a scent of violets. The fragrant oil extracted from orrisroot is not so widely used as it once was, because of its high price and the availability of synthetic substitutes. But small amounts are still used in certain expensive perfumes. Orrisroot comes from three species—*Iris florentina, Iris germanica,* and *Iris pallida.* These irises are cultivated near Verona and Florence, Italy; and Grasse, France. The rhizomes are dug in the summer, and dried in the sun after the outer layer is peeled off. They yield a waxy material containing an oil that smells like violets and is used in perfumes.   PAUL Z. BEDOUKIAN

See also IRIS.

ORT. See WOMEN'S AMERICAN ORT.

ORTEGA Y GASSET, *awr TAY guh ee gah SET,* **JOSÉ** (1883-1955), a Spanish philosopher, wrote *Meditations on Quixote* (1914). This book anticipated themes that existentialist philosophers made popular more than 10 years later (see EXISTENTIALISM). His later theory of truth and his best-known work, *The Revolt of the Masses* (1930), show the influence of Friedrich Nietzsche. In *The Dehumanization of Art* (1925), Ortega discussed the tendency of modern art to rid itself of human content. He was born and taught in Madrid. Ortega lived in France, South America, and Portugal. He returned to Spain in 1949.   WALTER KAUFMANN

ORTHODONTICS, *OR thoh DAHN ticks,* is the branch of dentistry that prevents or treats irregular positions of the teeth. These positions may be caused by heredity, or by early loss of the first teeth, dietary disorders, or thumb sucking and other undesirable habits. Teeth out of position prevent a child from chewing his food properly, hurt his appearance, and may lead to cavities and gum diseases. Few children outgrow their irregularities, and most have to be treated. Dentists use a number of devices, commonly called *braces,* that move the teeth by applying gentle pressure on them. ROBERT G. KESEL

ORTHODOX, EASTERN. See EASTERN ORTHODOX CHURCHES.

ORTHOGRAPHY, *awr THAHG ruh fih,* is the art of spelling words correctly. See SPELLING.

ORTHOPEDICS is the correction of deformities of the skeletal system in persons of any age.

ORTHOPTERA, *awr THAHP tur uh,* is a large order of destructive insects. The Orthoptera include the crickets, locusts, grasshoppers, katydids, cockroaches, walking sticks, and mantids. The name *Orthoptera* comes from two Greek words meaning *straight wings.*

All members of the group have biting mouth parts, with which they bite off and chew their food. Most of them feed on plants. The mantids, and a few other Orthoptera, devour other insects.

Related Articles in WORLD BOOK include:

Cockroach	Katydid	Mole Cricket
Cricket	Leaf Insect	Mormon Cricket
Grasshopper	Locust	Walking Stick
Insect	Mantid	

ORTHORHOMBIC SYSTEM. See CRYSTAL AND CRYSTALLIZATION (Classification).

651

ORTOLAN, *AWR toh lun,* is a small bird that lives in the gardens of Europe and western Asia. It belongs to the finch family, and is about the size of an English sparrow. Its upper parts are brown, streaked with darker colors. Its ear region, throat, and rings around the eyes are lemon-yellow. Its upper breast is greenish-yellow, and the rest of the underparts are chestnut-brown. The well-known bobolink is sometimes called the *American ortolan,* as is the common sora, or sora rail.

In the spring, the ortolan breeds as far north as Lapland. When autumn draws near, it flies southward again to the Mediterranean countries. Hunters catch great numbers of ortolans, usually in nets. They feed and fatten the birds, and then kill them for eating.

Scientific Classification. The European ortolan is in the finch family, *Fringillidae.* It is genus *Emberiza,* species *E. hortulana.* HERBERT FRIEDMANN

ORURO, *oh ROO roh* (pop. 96,363; alt. 12,149 ft.), is Bolivia's second largest city (see BOLIVIA [map]). It became a flourishing silver-mining town in the 1600's and 1700's. The city has been the center of a rich tin-mining area since the late 1800's. Railroads link Oruro with mining and farming areas in other parts of Bolivia. The Technical University of Oruro operates a mine on the outskirts of the city. The people of Oruro enjoy a colorful ceremony before Ash Wednesday each year. Masked dancers move through the streets like the paraders in New Orleans' Mardi Gras. Oruro was founded in 1601. HAROLD OSBORNE

ORWELL, GEORGE, was the pen name of ERIC ARTHUR BLAIR (1903-1950), an English novelist and social critic. Orwell became famous with his novel *1984,* published in 1949. The book is a frightening portrait of a totalitarian society that punishes love, destroys privacy, and distorts truth. The grim tone of *1984* distinguishes it from Orwell's *Animal Farm* (1945), an animal fable satirizing Communism.

Paul Popper

George Orwell

Orwell was a unique combination of middle-class intellectual and working-class reformer. A strong autobiographical element runs through most of Orwell's writing, giving both his novels and essays a sense of immediacy and conviction. For example, his experiences living in poverty color *A Clergyman's Daughter* (1935). The novel attacks social injustice and ranges from the miseries and hypocrisies of the poor of middle-class background to the near-starvation of the slum-dweller. *Homage to Catalonia* (1938) is a nonfiction work based on Orwell's brief career as a soldier. In it, he describes his disillusionment with the Loyalists during the Spanish Civil War.

Orwell was born in Bengal, India, the son of an English civil servant. He attended Eton from 1917 to 1921 and served with the Indian Imperial Police in Burma from 1922 to 1927. He lived in poverty in England and Europe until the mid-1930's. FRANK W. WADSWORTH

ORYX. See ANTELOPE (Kinds of Antelope).

OSAGE INDIANS, *oh SAYJ* or *OH sayj,* once roamed through Missouri, Arkansas, and Oklahoma. Oil discoveries on their lands in the early 1900's made them the richest tribe in the United States.

In early days, the round, mat-covered houses of the Osage lay in villages, with cornfields around them. The Osage camped on the plains, and hunted buffalo when they were not busy tending their crops. They had dignified ceremonies that they believed would make the corn grow and make their warriors brave. The Osage ceded most of their land to the United States by a series of treaties between 1808 and 1870. After the tribe moved to a small reservation in Oklahoma, geologists found oil on their lands. The Bureau of Indian Affairs managed the oil leases for the tribe. Funds from the holdings were distributed among the Osage. JOHN C. EWERS

OSAGE ORANGE is a small- to medium-sized tree planted across the United States for hedges, ornamental purposes, and shade. It originally was found in Texas, Oklahoma, and Arkansas. The name refers to the Osage Indians of that region, and to the large greenish-

New York Botanical Garden
Fruit of the Osage Orange Tree Is Not Edible.

yellow fruit that looks like an orange but is inedible. The tree is also called *bodark, bois d'arc,* or *bowwood.*

The tree has a short trunk and many crooked branches. Its long, pointed leaves are a shiny dark green. It has thorny twigs and a milky, bitter sap. The pioneers planted Osage orange trees as a "living fence" around their farms before barbed wire came into use.

The yellow wood of the Osage orange is hard, strong, and durable. The Indians preferred it for their bows and war clubs. It makes good fence posts and was used for wagon wheels. A yellow dye can be made by boiling chips of the wood in water.

Scientific Classification. The Osage orange tree belongs to the mulberry family, *Moraceae.* It is genus *Maclura,* species *M. pomifera.* ELBERT L. LITTLE, JR.

OSAKA, *oh SAH kuh* (pop. 3,084,092; alt. 40 ft.), is the second largest city in Japan. Osaka has been called the *Chicago of Japan.* The city was the site of the 1970 world's fair. More than 800 bridges cross the canals, rivers, and arms of the sea that cut through Osaka. The city was badly damaged during World War II. United States servicemen are stationed at Itami Air

Base, which stands about 10 miles from Osaka. Osaka lies on the southern coast of the island of Honshu. For location, see JAPAN (political map). It has a cotton-spinning industry, metal foundries, machine shops, and potteries. See also KOBE.   HUGH BORTON

OSBORN is the family name of two American zoologists, father and son.

Henry Fairfield Osborn (1857-1935) was an authority on fossil vertebrate animals and evolution. He was best known for his studies of ancient reptiles and warm-blooded animals, or mammals. He wrote about rhinoceroses; elephants and their relatives; and *titanotheres* (creatures that once roamed the American West). His book, *From the Greeks to Darwin* (1894), treated evolution.

Osborn served as president of the American Museum of Natural History in New York City from 1908 to 1933. Under his administration, it became one of the world's largest museums. Osborn was born in Fairfield, Conn. He was graduated from Princeton University.

Fairfield Osborn (1887-1969), was an outstanding conservation leader. He became president of the New York Zoological Society in 1940 and founded the society's conservation foundation in 1948. His conservation projects included the Save the Redwoods League, the International Commission for Bird Protection, the National Audubon Society, and the Boone and Crockett Club. He was instrumental in building the Marine Aquarium at Coney Island, N.Y., which opened in 1957. Osborn was born in Princeton, N.J., and was graduated from Princeton University.   A. M. WINCHESTER

OSBORNE, JOHN JAMES (1929-   ), a British dramatist, won fame for his savage satirical attacks on British social institutions and values. Osborne's play *Look Back in Anger* (1956) was one of the most discussed plays of the 1950's. It shows the bitterness of certain young English adults over what they believe is mismanagement of most aspects of English life. The play earned Osborne the label of "angry young man." The phrase was soon applied to many English writers in the late 1950's.

Osborne also wrote *The Entertainer* (1957), *Luther* (1961), *Inadmissible Evidence* (1964), and *A Patriot for Me* (1965). Each has a central character who complains lengthily and loudly over the problems life has placed in his path. The strength of the plays lies in the complex characters, who are both sympathetic and outrageous. Osborne was born in London.   MALCOLM GOLDSTEIN

OSBORNE, THOMAS MOTT (1859-1926), was an American prison reformer. In 1913, as chairman of the New York State Commission for Prison Reform, he spent a week in prison, secretly, so he could understand and help prisoners. He served as warden of Sing Sing (N.Y.) Prison from 1914 to 1916 and of Portsmouth (N.H.) Naval Prison from 1917 to 1920. He organized the Mutual Welfare League to help prisoners rebuild their lives. He wrote *Within Prison Walls* (1914) and *Society and Prisons* (1916). Osborne was born in Auburn, N.Y. and was graduated from Harvard.   LOUIS FILLER

OSCAN, *AHS kun*, was a language used by one of the earliest known races in Italy. It was part of the Indo-European family, and was distantly related to Latin.

OSCAR. See MOTION PICTURE (table: Academy Awards).

OSCAR was the name of two kings of Sweden and Norway, father and son.

Oscar I (1799-1859) ruled as King of Norway and Sweden from 1844 until his death. He began a mild reform program for Sweden that made him popular with everyone except the upper classes. But he did not keep his early promises of major reforms, and they were not accomplished until the reign of his son, Charles XV. Oscar was born in Paris, the son of Jean Bernadotte, who became King Charles XIV John of Sweden and Norway (see BERNADOTTE, JEAN B. J.).

Oscar II (1829-1907), the third son of Oscar I, came to the throne in 1872 after the death of his brother, Charles XV. Oscar II became very popular with his people. He devoted himself to artistic interests, and supported museums and education. He wrote several books and poems. In 1905, he tried to prevent the separation of Norway and Sweden. But the Norwegian desire for independence was too strong, and Oscar had to give up the Norwegian throne in 1905. He continued as King of Sweden until his death two years later. He was born in Stockholm.   RAYMOND E. LINDGREN

OSCEOLA, *AHS ee OH luh* (1803?-1838), led the Seminole Indians in Florida in the Second Seminole War, which began in 1835. He resisted the attempts of the United States to force the Seminoles to move to the Indian Territory west of the Mississippi River. He hid his followers deep in the Florida Everglades, and inflicted a series of defeats on the American troops. In 1837, however, when invited by General Thomas Jesup to discuss peace under a flag of truce, Osceola was treacherously taken prisoner. He died soon afterward, in the Fort Moultrie prison near Charleston, S.C.

Osceola was one-quarter white. His grandfather was

Osceola led the Seminole Indians in Florida during the Second Seminole War. An American officer treacherously seized him during a truce. Osceola died in prison.

Historical Pictures Service

OSCILLATOR

Scottish. After Osceola's father died, his Indian mother married a white man named Powell. Osceola was sometimes known by this name. He took the name Osceola, or *Asi-Yaholo*, from *asi*, a black drink containing caffeine which was used in tribal ceremonies, and *Yaholo*, the long-drawn-out cry sung by the man serving this drink to the Indian braves. Osceola was born on the Tallapoosa River in Georgia, then a part of the Creek Indian territory.　　　　　E. Adamson Hoebel

See also Indian Wars. (In the South).

OSCILLATOR. See Electronics (table: Terms).

OSCILLOGRAPH, *uh SIL oh GRAF,* is a device that records the *oscillations*, or variations, of an unknown quantity against a known quantity. Usually it records changes in electrical charges. One type works by means of a current-carrying coil of wire suspended in a magnetic field, and a mirror. Variations of current in the wire cause force against the magnetic field. This twists the wire. The attached mirror deflects a beam of light that can be recorded on a moving photographic film. Another kind records oscillations by means of a *stylus*, or lightweight pen, that writes on a moving paper chart. Scientists call such permanent photographic or written records *oscillograms*.

Other oscillographs display oscillations by means of a cathode-ray tube similar to a television picture tube. Oscillographs of this type are generally known as *oscilloscopes*.　　　　　L. Arthur Hoyt III

See also Oscilloscope.

OSCILLOSCOPE, *uh SIL oh SKOHP,* is an electronic device used to observe and measure any *oscillation* (vibration) that can be changed into electricity. For example, a microphone changes the vibrations of sound waves into electrical vibrations. The oscilloscope shows these electrical vibrations on the fluorescent screen of a cathode-ray tube. This tube is similar to a television picture tube.

The oscilloscope's cathode-ray tube produces a beam of electrons. This beam passes between plates connected to electrical circuits. The vibrations to be studied are changed into an electrical voltage and are fed to these plates. These vibrations cause the voltage of the plates to vary. These variations change the direction of the electron beam so that it traces out the pattern of the

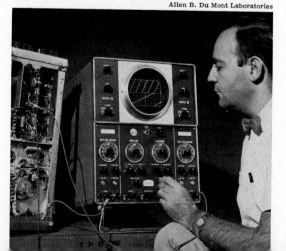

Oscilloscopes show the pattern of radio waves, sound waves, or any vibrations that can be changed into electricity. The pattern appears on a screen similar to a television screen.

Allen B. Du Mont Laboratories

vibrations as a thin line of light on the fluorescent screen of the tube. There these vibrations can be observed, measured, and photographed.　　　　　L. Arthur Hoyt III

See also Cathode Rays; Oscillograph.

OSCULUM. See Sponge (The Body of the Sponge).

O'SHAUGHNESSY DAM is a power and water-supply project. It lies on the Tuolumne River in east-central California. It supplies water and electric power for the city of San Francisco. The O'Shaughnessy Dam is built of concrete, and is 910 feet long and 430 feet high. The reservoir formed by the dam has a total capacity of 360,000 acre-feet of water. O'Shaughnessy Dam was built to a height of 344 feet in 1923, and brought to its present size in 1938. The total cost of the dam was about $10 million. The dam is named for M. M. O'Shaughnessy, former city engineer of San Francisco, who directed the original construction. At first, the project was known as Hetch Hetchy, an Indian term for the grass that grew in the valley now occupied by the reservoir.　　　　　T. W. Mermel

OSHAWA, Ont. (pop. 78,082; alt. 332 ft.), is an industrial port city in southeastern Ontario, Canada. It lies about 30 miles east of Toronto, on the bank of Lake Ontario (see Ontario [political map]). The city manufactures automobiles and other iron and steel products. It also has printing plants and woolen mills, and produces furniture, neon signs, and cement products. Oshawa was incorporated as a village in 1850, and as a city in 1924. It has a mayor-council government.

OSHKOSH, Wis. (pop. 53,221; alt. 760 ft.), once had lumbering as its only industry. Today, its factories make sashes and doors, overalls, trucks, fiber and wool twine, coffins, matches, and metal products.

Oshkosh and Appleton form a metropolitan area that has 276,891 persons. Oshkosh lies at the point where the Fox River empties into Lake Winnebago, about 85 miles northeast of Madison (see Wisconsin [political map]). Oshkosh began as a fur-trading post. It was named for a Menominee Indian chief.

The city is the home of Wisconsin State University at Oshkosh. It has a council-manager government. Oshkosh is the seat of Winnebago County.　　　　　James I. Clark

OSIER, *OH zhur,* is the name given to certain shrubs and small trees in the willow family. They grow best along streams. These willows have tough slender stems that can be used for making baskets and furniture. The coarse stems of the osier are not used for weaving, but the finer stems are peeled and bleached. The *common osier* and the *purple osier* are willows that have been brought to the United States from other parts of the world. They are cultivated for their flexible stems. One kind of dogwood is called *red-osier dogwood* because its bark resembles that of some willows. See also Willow.

Scientific Classification. Osiers belong to the willow family, *Salicaceae*. The common osier is genus *Salix*, species *S. viminalis*. The purple osier is *S. purpurea*. The red-osier dogwood is in the dogwood family, *Cornaceae*. It is genus *Cornu*, species *C. stolonifera*.　　　　　Robert W. Hoshaw

OSIRIS, *oh SI ris,* was the chief god of the underworld among the ancient Egyptians. He was worshiped in many great temples of Egypt. Osiris was the prince of the dead. He ruled the underworld of the tomb, which was populated by the souls of the dead. Every good Egyptian believed that, when he died, he himself became Osiris.

Osiris was the husband of Isis and the father of Horus

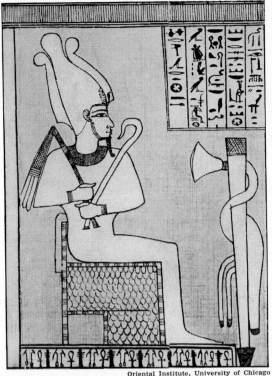

Oriental Institute, University of Chicago

Osiris, One of the Principal Gods of Egypt, is shown on his throne in the lower world, where he ruled as king. The picture appears on an old papyrus made in Egypt about 330 B.C.

(see HORUS; ISIS). His brother was Set, who represented evil (see SET). According to a tradition, Set tricked Osiris into getting into a box, and then threw it into the Nile River. Isis found the box, but Set stole the body and cut it into 14 pieces. Isis found Osiris' body and brought it back to Egypt, where Horus was born. Horus avenged Osiris' death by defeating Set and his followers. Osiris was given new life. He then ceased to be a king of this world, and became king of the underworld. Thus, the idea of resurrection became the central theme in the worship of Osiris. Osiris is often represented in art as a mummy, wearing the crown of Upper Egypt on his head.   I. J. GELB

See also ANUBIS; APIS.

OSLER, *OHS ler*, **SIR WILLIAM** (1849-1919), was a Canadian physician and one of the greatest medical teachers. His brilliant teaching and informal and genial personality had a far-reaching influence on medical progress, and on many of his students.

One of Osler's most notable contributions to medicine was the organization of a clinic at the Johns Hopkins Hospital in Baltimore, Md., along systematic lines new to the United States. He strongly favored

Sir William Osler
Culver

using "the patient for a text," and he perfected the method of teaching that encourages students to learn the practical art of medicine at the bedside. Osler once said that he would like his epitaph to read, "Here lies the man who admitted students to the wards."

He discovered the presence in the blood stream of what later were called *disks*, or *blood platelets* (see BLOOD [Parts of the Blood]). He made studies of the heart, and of typhoid fever, pneumonia, malaria, infant mortality, and other public health menaces. He helped found the National Tuberculosis Association (now the National Tuberculosis and Respiratory Disease Association) in 1904.

His Writings. Osler published *Principles and Practice of Medicine* in 1891. It is still a standard textbook in the United States. In 1897, a member of John D. Rockefeller's philanthropic staff read the book and was amazed to learn how few infectious disease germs had been discovered. This incident led to the founding of the Rockefeller Institute for Medical Research in 1901 (see ROCKEFELLER UNIVERSITY). Osler also wrote *Aequanimita* (1904), a collection of essays, *An Alabama Student* (1908), and *The Evolution of Modern Medicine* (1921).

His Life. Osler was born on July 12, 1849, at Bond Head, Ont., Canada. He was graduated from McGill University in 1872. He served at McGill from 1875 to 1884 as a lecturer in physiology and as professor of medicine. He was pathologist at Montreal General Hospital at the same time. In 1884, he became clinical professor of medicine at the University of Pennsylvania. He was appointed professor of the principles and practice of medicine at Johns Hopkins University four years later. He was also made physician-in-chief to the new hospital there. Osler went to Oxford University in 1905 as regius professor of medicine, the highest medical position in Great Britain. He became a baronet in 1911. He organized the British medical profession during World War I to meet the war emergency.   CAROLINE A. CHANDLER

OSLO, *AHZ loh* or *OHS loh* (pop. 483,196; met. area 598,515; alt. 55 ft.), is the capital and leading seaport of Norway. Until 1925, it was known as Christiania. Oslo is at the head of the great Oslo Fiord, located on the southeastern coast of Norway. It lies about 80 miles from the Skagerrak, an arm of the North Sea. For location, see NORWAY (color map). Oslo extended its city limits in 1948, and now half the city is forested land. Christiania was founded by the Danes in 1624, on the site of a town called Oslo, founded in 1047. After 300 years, the people used again the Norwegian name of Oslo.

The city is the seat of the Norwegian government. Oslo is largely a modern city. Brick and stone buildings have taken the place of older wooden ones. The Royal Palace stands severe and white in the center of the city. The Folk museum contains three famous ships which were used by the Norse Vikings of old. These ships were discovered and excavated in modern times. The museum has the *Fram*, the ship used by explorers Fridtjof Nansen and Roald Amundsen; and *Kon-Tiki*, Thor Heyerdahl's raft. A statue of Christian IV, the king who founded Christiania, stands in the market place.

The University of Oslo (The Royal Frederiks University until 1939) was founded in 1811 by a grant from King Frederik VI. About 4,000 students attend there yearly. In Frogner Park, there is a bust of Abraham

Scenic Oslo, the capital and gateway of Norway, lies at the head of the great Oslo Fiord. Steep pine-wooded hills stand on three sides of the city.

Norwegian Fishing Boats dock at the wharves in front of the Oslo Town Hall. Oslo is the leading seaport of Norway. Its harbor is ice-free throughout the year.

Norwegian Information Service; Billedsentralen

Lincoln which was given to the people of Oslo by Norwegians in North Dakota.

Oslo is a favorite center of much northern European tourist traffic. Regular passenger steamers serve the port from Hull, Newcastle, and London, from Bergen and the Norwegian coast cities, and from numerous ports of northern Europe. Electric power is furnished by plants on the Glommen River. Industry in Oslo centers in cotton and woolen mills, paper, match, and soap factories, food plants, shipyards, foundries, and machine shops. There is also a large granite paving-stone business and large ice storehouses. The chief products are timber, wood pulp, condensed milk, butter, and animal hides.

On the hills around Oslo there are sanatoriums and inns, and beautiful landscaped gardens. The Norwegians built three new theaters between World War I and World War II, and carried out various municipal improvements. Between 1912 and 1921 they spent large sums improving the harbor facilities. Vessels up to 10,000 tons can be constructed in the shipbuilding yards.

Oslo was attacked and occupied by German forces on April 9, 1940, and held until the German surrender in 1945. The city was cut off from its import and export trade and suffered as a result. Rebuilding of world trade, because of its importance to the nation's economy, was given priority after the war.   OSCAR SVARLIEN

See also NORWAY (picture, Oslo's Frogner Park).

OSMAN. See TURKEY (The Ottoman Empire).

OSMIUM, *AHZ mih um* (chemical symbol Os), is a hard metallic element. It has the greatest density of all known elements. It is twice as heavy as lead, and has a specific gravity of 22.48. It has an atomic weight of 190.2 and its atomic number is 76. Smithson Tennant discovered it in England in 1804. Osmium is refined from the same ores in which platinum is found. Some has been found in platinum mines in California and Tasmania.

The pure metal is a fine, black powder or a hard blue-gray mass. Its melting point is 4892°F., but it can vaporize before a high temperature is reached. When heated above 200°F., osmium gives off a vapor which may cause total or partial blindness. The metal is used to tip gold pen points and to make standard weights and measures. Electric-light filaments are also made of osmium. HARRISON ASHLEY SCHMITT

OSMOSIS, *ahs MOH sis*, is the passage of one fluid into another through a membrane between them. It occurs with both liquids and gases. This passage, or transfusion, results in a mixture of the two fluids. Osmosis takes place through a *semipermeable membrane*. This is a membrane which allows certain substances to pass through and keeps out others.

How Osmosis Works. The following experiment shows how osmosis works. A piece of parchment or a porous kind of cellophane is tied over one end of a glass tube. Colored sugar water is poured into the tube. The covered end of the tube is then placed in a jar of fresh water, so that the water in the jar is level with the solution in the tube. After a while the pure water will become colored, and the solution will become lighter, showing that each of the fluids is passing through the membrane. But the solution will rise in the tube, showing that the water from the jar is passing in more rapidly than the sugar solution is passing out. If the apparatus is large, enough water may push its way into the tube to raise the level in the tube 20 or 30 feet. This pressure of the water is called *osmotic pressure*. Often it is many pounds to the square inch. The mixing of water and solution will continue until the solution is the same

in the tube and in the jar. Then the liquid in the jar and that in the tube will have the same *solution pressure*.

Osmosis works because of the nature of the membrane, which is porous, and the nature of the solution. The particles of water are smaller than the dissolved particles of sugar, so the membrane lets the water through more readily than the sugar. Osmosis also works with two solutions. It depends on the concentration of the dissolved substances. The more dilute solution, which contains more water particles, passes through into the less dilute solution. Osmosis also depends on the temperature of the solutions.

A light gas, like stove gas, will also pass through a porous earthenware cup containing air. The stove gas is lighter than the air—made of smaller particles. If a tube from the cup is placed under water, air from the cup will bubble out through the water.

Importance of Osmosis. Osmosis affects many things in our daily life. Dried fruits swell when they are cooked in water, while fresh fruits shrivel when they are placed in strong sugar solutions. Meats shrink when packed in salt—their water passes out into the salt solution. Too much rain will burst cherries on a tree and ruin the crop. The water will pass through the skin of the cherry by osmosis. The principle of osmosis is used in preserving foods such as fish or pickles in brine or salt solution. The osmotic pressure of the salt solution kills the organisms which might cause decay.

In the human body, food passes into the blood by osmosis through the wall of the intestine. From the blood, it then passes into the cells by osmosis through the cell wall. Oxygen also enters the blood by osmosis, and both oxygen and carbon dioxide pass through the membranes of the lungs by this process.

Plants also depend on osmosis. Minerals dissolved in water pass from the soil to the plant through root membranes. Osmotic pressure probably helps raise the sap to the high branches of trees. LOUIS MARICK

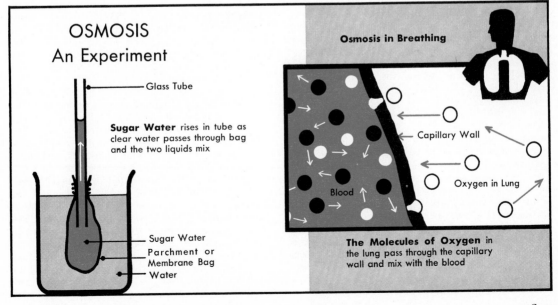

OSMOSIS
An Experiment

Glass Tube

Sugar Water rises in tube as clear water passes through bag and the two liquids mix

Sugar Water
Parchment or Membrane Bag
Water

Osmosis in Breathing

Capillary Wall

Blood

Oxygen in Lung

The Molecules of Oxygen in the lung pass through the capillary wall and mix with the blood

Ospreys plunge feet first into the water and grasp fish with the long, sharp talons on their feet. They are often called *fish hawks.*

Allan Cruickshank

OSPREY, *AHS prih,* is a large bird of prey in the hawk family. Its name comes from a Latin word which means *bonebreaker.* It is also called *fish hawk* and *fishing eagle.* The osprey lives near both fresh and salt water in almost every temperate and tropical country in the world. The American osprey breeds from northwestern Alaska to Newfoundland, and south to Lower California, western Mexico, and the Gulf States. It winters from the southern United States to northern Argentina and Paraguay.

The osprey is about 2 feet long, with a wingspread of nearly 6 feet. It is very dark brown above and has enough white on its head to resemble the bald eagle. It is white below with a few streaks of dark brown.

Ospreys usually nest in the tops of tall trees near large bodies of water. Sometimes they nest in chimney tops, on telephone pole crossbars, on ledges, in dead stumps, and even on the ground. The birds usually lay three eggs, colored whitish and spotted with shades of brown.

Ospreys feed on fish that stay close to the surface and are of little value to man. The bird hovers over the water, then sets its wings and dives feet first, hitting the water with a great splash, and often going completely under. The bird's feathers are close and firm and slightly oily, so that it can plunge into the water without becoming soaked.

Scientific Classification. The osprey belongs to the family *Accipitridae.* It is genus *Pandion,* species *P. haliaetus,* subspecies *carolinensis.*   OLIN SEWALL PETTINGILL, JR.

See also BIRD (color picture, Hunters of the Sky).

OSSICLE. See EAR (The Middle Ear).

OSSIETZKY, *AWS ee ETS kee,* **CARL VON** (1889-1938), a German journalist, won the 1935 Nobel prize for peace. He was awarded the prize after he had been sent to a Nazi concentration camp for his antimilitaristic writings. Ossietzky fought for Germany in World War I, but he later wrote articles in his weekly publication denouncing Nazi rearming. He was imprisoned as a "traitor" in 1933. He contracted tuberculosis in prison and was in a sanitarium when the Nobel award was announced. He was born in Hamburg.   ALVIN E. AUSTIN

OSSINING, N.Y. See SING SING.

OSSOLI, MARCHIONESS. See FULLER, MARGARET.

OSTEND, *aws TAHND* (pop. 56,494; alt. 10 ft.), is a Belgian city on the North Sea, about 77 miles northwest of Brussels (see BELGIUM [color map]). It is also called OOSTENDE. Only Antwerp has a larger port in Belgium. Ostend conducts an export-import business with many countries. It is the harbor for cross-channel boats from Dover, England. Ostend fishermen catch much cod and herring. Oysters are cultivated offshore. Ostend is a fashionable summer resort. Visitors enjoy its sea walk and listen to concerts in a building called the *Kursaal,* the center of social life.

Dutch, Spanish, and French troops have fought many battles for Ostend, because of its value as a port. In 1865, its fortifications were destroyed by the Belgian government, and Ostend became important for shipping. Ostend was damaged in World War I and again in World War II.   DANIEL H. THOMAS

OSTEND MANIFESTO. In 1854, the United States Secretary of State authorized three diplomats to negotiate for the purchase of Cuba by the United States. These men were James Buchanan, Minister to Great Britain, John Young Mason, Minister to France, and Pierre Soulé, Minister to Spain. They met at Ostend, Belgium, on October 18, 1854, and signed a dispatch later known as the Ostend Manifesto. It declared that if Spain would not sell Cuba, the United States would be justified in taking the island by force.

The three signers pretended to fear that a slave rebellion might turn Cuba into a disorderly Negro republic. But historians believe that they acted from the hope that Cuba might become a slave state of the United States. All United States political parties condemned the Manifesto.   JOHN D. HICKS

OSTEOLOGY, *AWS tee AHL oh jih,* is the study of the bones of man and animals. Osteologists can determine the sizes and living habits of prehistoric animals from bones. They can tell the age, sex, height, and weight of the person or animal from which the bones came. Osteology also includes the study of bone disorders and diseases. See also BONE.   IRVIN STEIN

OSTEOMYELITIS, AHS *tee oh* MY *uh* LIE *tihs*, is an inflammation of bone and *bone marrow*, the jelly-like material in the core of bones. Osteomyelitis can be caused by infection from any kind of germ, but the usual cause is a bacterium called *Staphylococcus aureus*. Infection of bone marrow may occur if a person has a compound fracture. In such a fracture, bone marrow may be exposed to the air. In some cases, the blood carries germs from a boil or from infected tonsils into the bone marrow. Symptoms of acute osteomyelitis include fever, chills, pain, and nausea. Doctors can check and cure the infection with penicillin. MARSHALL R. URIST

OSTEOPATHY, AHS *tee* AHP *uh thih*, or OSTEO-PATHIC MEDICINE, is a system of medical practice, including major surgery. Osteopathic physicians use all the medical, surgical, immunological, pharmacological, psychological, and hygienic procedures of modern medicine. They believe that health depends not only on mental condition, environment, nutrition, and sanitation, but also on proper body mechanics. Osteopathic medicine emphasizes the importance of the *musculoskeletal* system (the muscles and bones of the body and their connecting tendons and ligaments), and the interrelations of this system with other parts of the body. Osteopathic medicine deals with the influence of the musculoskeletal system on the functioning of the blood, nerves, lungs, and on the various other body systems.

Osteopathic physicians believe that disturbances of the musculoskeletal system may lead to conditions that will initiate disease processes in the body. The detection and treatment of these disturbances in the musculoskeletal system require skilled care. Osteopathic physicians treat these disturbances by *osteopathic manipulation*. This form of therapy is a distinctively osteopathic

Students of Osteopathic Medicine must complete seven years of college before spending a year as hospital interns.
American Osteopathic Assoc.

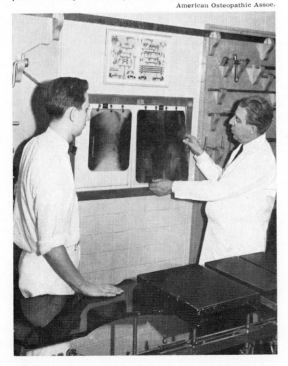

approach to the many problems of health and disease.

History. The founder of osteopathy was Andrew Taylor Still (1828-1917), who announced the basic principles of osteopathy in 1874. Still organized the first osteopathic college at Kirksville, Mo., in 1892.

The first law regulating osteopathy was passed in Vermont in 1896. There are now such laws in all the states, and in most of the provinces of Canada. In most states, graduates of recognized osteopathic schools are eligible to be licensed as physicians and surgeons.

Careers in Osteopathy. To become an osteopathic physician (D.O., or Doctor of Osteopathy), a person must complete three years of preprofessional training in an accredited college or university and four years of professional education in an approved osteopathic college. Almost all students spend an additional year as an intern in an approved osteopathic hospital.

Graduate education in osteopathic medicine, if it involves specialization, follows a distinct program carried out under the constant supervision of the profession's approving and accrediting agencies. Certification in any given specialty requires a five-year program above the internship level.

There are five approved colleges of osteopathy and surgery in the United States. These colleges are the Chicago College of Osteopathy; College of Osteopathic Medicine and Surgery, Des Moines, Iowa; Kansas City (Mo.) College of Osteopathy and Surgery; Kirksville (Mo.) College of Osteopathy and Surgery; and Philadelphia College of Osteopathy.

More than 14,000 osteopathic physicians practice in the United States. Most of them are members of the American Osteopathic Association, which has its headquarters in Chicago, Ill. The Association publishes two professional periodicals, *Journal of the American Osteopathic Association* and *D.O.* It also publishes a magazine that contains information for laymen, *Health: An Osteopathic Publication.* TRUE B. EVELETH

OSTEOSCLEROSIS, AHS *tee oh sklee* ROH *sihs*, means hardening, thickening, and increased density of bone. It may involve part of a bone, a whole bone, or the whole skeleton. The most common form of osteosclerosis occurs in children and is called *marble bones* or *osteopetrosis*. In this disease, the bones become chalky. Commonly, chalky tissue replaces the bone marrow, the tissue that makes red blood cells. As a result, the child develops severe anemia. Osteosclerosis may develop in part of a bone as the result of an infection or a tumor. MARSHALL R. URIST

ÖSTERREICH. See AUSTRIA.

OSTRACISM. See TRIBE.

OSTRAVA, AW *strah vah* (pop. 251,959; alt. 710 ft.), is the fourth largest city in Czechoslovakia. It is in northeastern Moravia, about 170 miles east of Prague. For location, see CZECHOSLOVAKIA (color map).

Ostrava is the center of the country's largest industrial area. It has been called *The Pittsburgh of Czechoslovakia* because of its great iron and steel works. There are coal mines nearby, as well as petroleum refineries and chemical plants. Ostrava is also well known for its manufacture of house-building materials, food products, wearing apparel, and furniture. The city was badly damaged during World War II. S. HARRISON THOMSON

Beth Bergman, N.A.S.

Richard Harrington, Three Lions

Ostrich Eggs are large, and usually weigh about 3 pounds each. Several ostrich hens usually lay their eggs in the same nest.

An Adult Ostrich, *left,* is the world's largest bird. It stands nearly 8 feet tall and may weigh over 300 pounds when fully grown.

A Week-Old Ostrich, *below,* has spotted down that blends with the ground, to protect the baby bird from its enemies.

Richard Harrington, Three Lions

OSTRICH, *AHS trich,* is the largest living bird. It may stand nearly 8 feet tall and weigh as much as 345 pounds. Ostriches live on the plains and deserts of Africa. The extinct moas of New Zealand, which were 10 feet tall, were the only birds taller than ostriches. The extinct elephant birds of Madagascar, which weighed about 1,000 pounds, were the only heavier birds. See ELEPHANT BIRD; MOA.

The ostrich is the only bird that has only two toes on each foot. The rhea, which is also called the *South American ostrich,* is three-toed, and it is not a true ostrich. See RHEA.

The male ostrich is a handsome bird. It has black feathers on its bulky body, with large white feathers, or plumes, on its small wings and tail. Its long, thin legs and upper neck and its small head have almost no feathers. The bare skin varies in color from pink to blue. Thick black eyelashes surround its eyes. The female is dull brown, both on its body and on its wings and tail.

The male ostrich has a strange voice. It gives a deep roar like that of a lion, but with a strange hissing sound. The ostrich cannot fly, but it is known for its speed. Its long legs can carry it in 15-foot steps at speeds up to 40 miles an hour. Its speed and its unusually good eyesight help the ostrich escape from its enemies, which are mainly lions and men. The ancient belief that

Ostrich Hide is valuable for making ladies shoes and handbags. The leather is durable, and it has an attractive quill design.

Fluffy Ostrich Feathers were popular in women's fashions before World War I. They were used to decorate hats and dresses.

the ostrich hides its head in the sand when frightened is not true. If the ostrich is exhausted and cannot run any farther, or if it must defend its nest, it kicks with its powerful legs. Its long toes, the largest of which is 7 inches long, have thick nails that become dangerous weapons when the bird is cornered.

How the Ostrich Lives. The ostrich usually eats plants, but it will eat lizards and turtles if it can find them. It also eats much sand and gravel to aid in grinding food for digestion. Ostriches drink water when they find it. But they can live for long periods of time without drinking if the plants they eat are green and moist.

Ostriches are *polygamous* (the male has more than one mate). Each *cock* (male) digs a shallow nest in sand, and from three to five *hens* (females) lay their eggs in the nest. Each hen lays as many as 10 eggs. Each egg is almost round, nearly 6 inches in diameter, and weighs about 3 pounds. The eggs are a dull yellow, and have large pores and a thick shell.

The male sits on the eggs at night. But during the day the hens share the task of keeping them warm. The eggs take five or six weeks to hatch. When a young ostrich is a month old, it can run as fast as an adult. Ostriches live up to 70 years. Few other birds have such a long lifetime.

Ostrich Farming. Hundreds of years ago, great flocks of ostriches roamed over Africa and western Asia. Arabs in western Asia hunted them for sport, and Africans took their eggs for food or killed them for feathers. But ostriches were seldom killed for food, because their flesh is tough and does not taste good.

Then in the late 1800's and the early 1900's, ostrich plumes came to be in great demand. They were used for decorating hats and clothing. Large numbers of birds were killed, and the ostrich disappeared from Asia and from much of Africa. The plumes were so expensive that it became profitable to raise ostriches in captivity. Plumes could be taken twice a year from live birds kept on ostrich farms.

Ostrich farms were established in North and South Africa, the United States, Australia, and southern Europe. Between 1914 and 1918, fashions changed

again, and the demand for ostrich plumes dropped sharply. Ostrich farming was no longer profitable. Today, about 25,000 birds are still raised in South Africa. But they are raised principally for their skins, which are made into fine quality leather.

Scientific Classification. The ostrich is in the ostrich family, *Struthionidae*. It is classified genus *Struthio*, species *S. camelus*.　　　　　　　　　　　　　R. A. PAYNTER, JR.

OSTROGOTH. See GOTH.

OSTROVSKY, ALEXANDER. See RUSSIAN LITERATURE (Early Realism).

OSTWALD, *OHST vahlt,* **WILHELM** (1853-1932), a German chemist, writer, and teacher, won the 1909 Nobel prize for chemistry. He received the award mainly for his studies in surface phenomena and speeds of chemical reactions. He wrote one of the early books on electrochemistry. His research on the oxidation of ammonia helped Germany make explosives during World War I. He was born in Riga, Latvia.　　　K. L. KAUFMAN

See also COLOR (Characteristics of Color).

OSTWALD PROCESS. See NITRIC ACID.

OSWALD, LEE HARVEY (1939-1963), was accused of assassinating President John F. Kennedy on Nov. 22, 1963, in Dallas, Tex. Two days later, while millions of television viewers looked on, Oswald was killed. He was shot to death by Dallas night-club owner Jack Ruby, while being transferred from the city jail to the county jail in Dallas. Ruby pushed through a ring of police officers to shoot Oswald down.

No one saw Oswald shoot the President. The high-powered Italian rifle said to have killed the President was traced to Oswald through a Chicago mail-order firm. Oswald worked in the Texas School Book Depository, the building from which the fatal shots were fired. A worker recalled seeing Oswald carry a long narrow package into the building the morning of the assassination. Police captured Oswald, who was armed with a revolver, in a Dallas motion picture theater about 90 minutes after the assassination.

Oswald was also charged with killing police officer J. D. Tippit. Tippit was shot to death in Dallas shortly after the President was killed. But Oswald denied killing either Tippit or the President. A presidential commission headed by Chief Justice Earl Warren investigated the case. After a 10-month investigation, the commission reported in September, 1964, that Oswald, acting alone, had killed Kennedy and Tippit.

A Dallas jury convicted Ruby of Oswald's murder in 1964. The conviction was reversed in 1966 on the grounds that the trial judge had allowed illegal testimony. A new trial was ordered, but Ruby died in 1967 before the new trial started.

Oswald was born in New Orleans. Investigators said his school and military records showed emotional difficulty. Oswald dropped out of high school at 17 and joined the U.S. Marine Corps. He was discharged in September, 1959, and went to Russia a month later. He tried to become a Russian citizen, but was turned down. He returned to the United States in 1962 with his Russian-born wife, Marina.   CAROL L. THOMPSON

See also KENNEDY, JOHN F.; WARREN REPORT.

OSWEGO, N.Y. (pop. 23,844; alt. 295 ft.), is the most eastern port on the Great Lakes. It lies at the point where the Oswego River empties into Lake Ontario (see NEW YORK [map]). Coal and other products are shipped from Oswego to Canada. Wheat and lumber are brought into the port. Oswego produces aluminum, paper products, knitted underwear, engines and boilers, matches, oil-well supplies, silk, rayon, and cotton goods.

Oswego stands on the site of the earliest English trading post on the Great Lakes. The post was founded about 1722. During and after the Revolutionary War, the British held Oswego until 1796. In 1825, the Erie Canal was extended from Buffalo to the east, and Oswego lost importance as a port. Oswego became a village in 1828, and a city in 1848. It has a mayor-council form of government.   WILLIAM E. YOUNG

OSWEGO TEA is a small horsemint plant that grows in eastern North America from Canada to Georgia. It is about 3 feet high and has small red flowers.

Scientific Classification. Oswego tea is in the mint family, *Labiatae*. It is genus *Monarda*, species *M. didyma*.

OTHELLO. See SHAKESPEARE, WILLIAM (Synopses).

OTHMAN. See TURKEY (The Ottoman Empire).

OTIS, ELISHA GRAVES (1811-1861), an American inventor, built the first elevator protected by safety devices against accidentally falling. While supervising the construction of a factory at Yonkers, N.Y., in 1852, he invented the improved elevator. Its safety device operated automatically in case the lifting rope or chain failed to hold the elevator. Otis demonstrated this safety device at the New York Fair in 1854 when he cut the lifting rope while standing on the elevator.

He also invented a steam plow in 1857, a bake oven in 1858, and a steam elevator in 1861. Otis was born on a farm near Halifax, Vt.   ROBERT P. MULTHAUF

OTIS, JAMES (1725-1783), was an American patriot and agitator against Great Britain. Otis was one of four representatives of Boston to the General Court, the provincial legislature, in 1761. There he proposed a meeting of representatives of all the colonies. His plan led to the Stamp Act Congress of 1765 (see STAMP ACT).

In 1768, Otis answered the British demand that the Massachusetts Assembly take back its plea to the colonies to fight the Townshend Acts by saying, "We are asked to rescind, are we? Let Great Britain rescind

Culver

James Otis became one of the most forceful leaders in the American colonies' struggle for independence from Great Britain.

her measures, or the colonies are lost to her forever."

The next year, as he entered the British Coffee House, Otis was attacked by British revenue officers, who resented his bitter criticism of their acts and methods. A head wound received during the attack eventually caused Otis to lose his mind. He was killed by lightning.

He was born in West Barnstable, Mass., and was graduated from Harvard in 1743. He became king's advocate-general of the vice-admiralty court at Boston in 1756. He resigned four years later when the British revived the expiring writ of assistance (see WRIT OF ASSISTANCE).   CLARENCE L. VER STEEG

OTIS ART INSTITUTE OF LOS ANGELES COUNTY. See UNIVERSITIES AND COLLEGES (table).

OTOLARYNGOLOGY. See MEDICINE (table: Kinds).

OTOLOGIST. See EAR (Care of the Ear).

OTOSCLEROSIS. See DEAFNESS (Causes of Deafness).

OTOSCOPE is an instrument that doctors use to examine the eardrum. The otoscope consists of a magnifying lens and a light powered by a battery. The light illuminates the eardrum and the lens magnifies it about six times. The otoscope makes it possible for the doctor to see changes in the eardrum resulting from infections and diseases.   NOAH D. FABRICANT

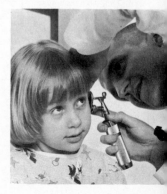

An Otoscope makes it possible for a physician to examine the eardrum of a patient.

WORLD BOOK photo by Henry Gill

662

National Film Board

Parliament Buildings in Ottawa stand on the south bank of the Ottawa River. Across the water is Hull, a Quebec industrial city.

The Ottawa Crest

OTTAWA, *AHT uh wuh*, Ontario (pop. 290,741; met. area pop. 494,535; alt. 276 ft.), is the capital and seventh largest city of Canada. It lies on gently rolling hills along the south bank of the Ottawa River in southeastern Ontario. Parks, stately government buildings, and scenic drives add beauty to the city.

The 291-foot-high Peace Tower is the first thing most travelers see as they approach Ottawa. It is part of the Parliament Buildings group which stands on Parliament Hill, the highest point overlooking the river and the city. The Canadian governor-general lives in dignified Rideau Hall, about a mile northeast of Parliament. Other places of interest to visitors include the Supreme Court of Canada Building, the National Gallery, the National Museum, the National War Memorial, and the Public Archives. See CANADA, GOVERNMENT OF (color pictures).

Ottawa was a small lumbering town when Queen Victoria chose it as the capital of United Canada in 1857. Its two chief industries are still lumbering and government. Since 1857, Ottawa has been largely replanned in keeping with its dignity as the capital.

Location, Size, and Description

Ottawa lies about 125 miles west of Montreal, Canada's largest city. It covers about 47 square miles of land along the southern bank of the Ottawa River.

The Rideau River flows through Ottawa from the south. It plunges over a 37-foot-high cliff into the Ottawa River at the northeastern end of the city. *Rideau* is the French word for *curtain*. These falls reminded early French explorers of a curtain of water. The Rideau Canal, a section of which branches off the Rideau River in the city, is an improved natural waterway running between Lake Ontario and Ottawa. It enters the Ottawa River at the eastern edge of Parliament Hill. The canal's eight Ottawa locks, arranged in "steps," drop boats about 80 feet to the river. Several docks stand where the canal and river meet. See RIDEAU CANAL.

The countryside south of Ottawa is level, fertile farm land. The Gatineau Hills rise along the north bank of the Ottawa River and merge into the Laurentian Mountains to the east. They are drained by the Gatineau River, which empties into the Ottawa opposite the falls of the Rideau. The woods, hills, and lakes of the Canadian Shield, north of the city, provide an excellent recreational area (see CANADIAN SHIELD).

Small boats and barges move up and down the Ottawa River between Montreal and Ottawa. Coming up the river to Ottawa, a traveler passes Rockcliffe Airport, operated by the Canadian Armed Forces. He then comes to the barracks of the Royal Canadian Mounted Police. Next he notices Rockcliffe Park, a wooded residential area. After he passes the Rideau Falls, he sees the graceful spires and green roofs of the Parliament buildings towering above a point that rises steeply from the river. This mass of buildings is dominated by the tall Peace Tower, topped by a lighted

663

clock and housing a *carillon*, or group of bells. Just before reaching Parliament Hill, the traveler passes under the Interprovincial Bridge, the first of three bridges crossing the Ottawa River. It connects the capital with Hull, Quebec. Many public buildings surround Parliament Hill.

Just northwest of the city, rapids and falls interrupt the flow of the Ottawa River. The river flows into Lake Deschênes west of the Chaudière Falls. The area around these falls is an industrial district, with woodworking establishments, a hydroelectric power station, and warehouses. The Chaudière Bridge crosses the river at the falls. The Champlain Bridge is a mile farther up, built above a number of islands.

Historically, Ottawa grew out of two settlements, Upper and Lower Town, lying west and east of the Rideau Canal. Residents still use these names. The principal shopping districts are Sparks Street in Upper Town, and the Byward Market, farmers' market, and Rideau Street in Lower Town. The residential areas of the city include Rockcliffe Park, New Edinburgh, and Eastview to the east; Ottawa South, the Glebe, and Alta Vista to the south; and Ottawa West, Britannia, and Westboro to the west.

The federal government adopted a decentralization policy in the mid-1940's to establish clusters of government buildings around the outskirts of the city. The laboratories of the National Research Council, for example, are in the eastern part of the city. The Queen's Printer is located in Hull, and the Dominion Bureau of Statistics occupies a site in the west end.

What to See and Do in Ottawa

Many visitors come to Ottawa during the last two weeks in May to enjoy the Canadian Tulip Festival, when thousands of bulbs are in bloom. The tulips are set in large beds on slopes near roads and streets, and dazzle passers-by with their beauty. From 1940 to 1945, Queen Juliana of The Netherlands, then a princess, lived in Ottawa while the Germans occupied her country. After returning home, she sent the festival 16,000 bulbs each year in gratitude for the city's hospitality and for the role Canadian soldiers played in freeing her people.

The annual Central Canada Exhibition takes place in late August in Lansdowne Park. It features agricultural, industrial, and scientific exhibits. The Summer Festival in Lakeside Gardens offers motion pictures, drama, music, painting, and sculpture.

Following are brief descriptions of interesting places to visit in Ottawa.

The Parliament Buildings provide the greatest tourist attraction. They consist of three sandstone buildings—the East Block, Centre Block, and West Block—forming three sides of a 35-acre quadrangle. The open side of the quadrangle faces the United States Embassy on Wellington Street.

The Prince of Wales, later King Edward VII, laid the cornerstone of the Centre Block in 1860, and workers completed the three buildings five years later. Fire destroyed most of the Centre Block in 1916. The only part saved was the eight-sided Parliamentary Library, connected to the main building by a corridor. The Centre Block was rebuilt along the same lines as the earlier structure, except that its new dimensions (470 feet by

Light gray shaded area
shows Ottawa city limits

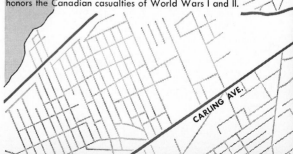

Ontario Dept. Travel & Publicity

National War Memorial on Confederation Square
honors the Canadian casualties of World Wars I and II.

Rideau Canal enters the Ottawa River through a series of eight locks.

OTTAWA RIVER

ROCKCLIFFE DR.

ROYAL CANADIAN MOUNTED POLICE BARRACKS N DIVISION

ROCKCLIFFE

HEMLOCK RD.

SAINT LAURENT BLVD.

RESIDENCE OF PRIME MINISTER

RIDEAU HALL

BEECHWOOD AVE.

MACKAY ST.

EASTVIEW

MONTREAL RD.

RIDEAU FALLS

CITY HALL

SUSSEX DR.

ROYAL CANADIAN MINT

ST. PATRICK ST.

RIDEAU ST.

HULL

INTERPROVINCIAL BRIDGE

NATIONAL WAR MEMORIAL

LOCKS

PARLIAMENT

UNIVERSITY OF OTTAWA

RIVERSIDE DR.

CHAUDIÈRE BRIDGE

FALLS

ST.

SUPREME COURT

NATIONAL GALLERY

SPARKS

DUKE ST.

LAURIER AVE.

BANK ST.

ELGIN ST.

DRIVEWAY

RIDEAU CANAL

RIDEAU RIVER

RUSSELL RD.

WELLINGTON ST.

PRESTON ST.

BRONSON AVE.

NATIONAL MUSEUM

CHAMBERLAIN AVE.

PRETORIA AVE.

N

W   E

S

EXHIBITION GROUNDS

DOW'S LAKE

Rideau Hall, the official home of the Canadian governor-general, is a limestone building erected in 1838 as a private home.

National Film Board

DOMINION OBSERVATORY

CENTRAL EXPERIMENTAL FARM

ISLAND PARK DR.

1 inch = 0.6 Statute Miles

0   ¼   ½   ¾   1

MILES

CARLETON UNIVERSITY

RIVERSIDE DR.

245 feet) were larger, and an extra story was added, making six. It reopened in 1920. Fire damaged the library in 1952, and it opened again in 1956. Its pine-lined circular reading room has over 500,000 books.

The second floor of the soaring Peace Tower of the Centre Block includes the Memorial Chamber. Its Altar of Sacrifice holds the hand-printed Books of Remembrance, including the names of over 100,000 Canadians killed in World Wars I and II. The carillon in the tower has 53 bells. The government dedicated the tower on July 1, 1927. See CARILLON (picture).

The red-carpeted Senate Chamber in the Centre Block has a gilded ceiling and colored windows. Oak partially lines the limestone walls of the chamber, which measures 85 feet long and 41 feet wide. On state occasions, the governor-general of Canada sits in a large chair under a canopy at the north end. The House of Commons Chamber also has limestone and oak walls. Hand-painted Irish linen covers the ceiling. This room is 72 feet long and 54 feet wide.

The privy council, prime minister, and department of external affairs have offices in the East Block. The secretary of state and other officials have headquarters in the West Block.

Rideau Hall, the official residence of the governor-general, is near the mouth of the Rideau River. Thomas McKay, a lumberman, built it in 1838. The Canadian government bought it in 1868 for Baron Monck, the first governor-general. This handsome gray limestone building stands in a 65-acre park. The home of the prime minister of Canada, 24 Sussex Drive, is nearby.

Other Places of Interest. The Royal Canadian Mint, which makes all of Canada's coins, stands near the Parliament Buildings. Next to the mint, the Public Archives stores records and exhibits historical documents. The nearby Canadian War Museum owns collections relating to World Wars I and II. Laurier House, the former residence of two prime ministers, has been preserved as a historical museum.

The National Museum of Canada is primarily a research museum. It features geological specimens and materials illustrating Indian and Eskimo cultures. The National Gallery moved into a new building in 1960. It specializes in Canadian and European painting.

Many tourists visit the Dominion Observatory, the Supreme Court of Canada, and the 1,300-acre Central Experimental Farm (see DOMINION OBSERVATORY). King George VI unveiled the National War Memorial in Confederation Square in 1939. Bronze figures of the armed forces march through a granite arch. Originally dedicated as a World War I memorial, it now honors the casualties of World Wars I and II.

Parkways. A magnificent system of parkways and drives helps beautify Ottawa. Drives run parallel to both sides of the Rideau Canal. The parkway system also extends across the river into the Gatineau Hills. Here, a 45-mile network of drives offers panoramic views of the Ottawa Valley from 75,000-acre Gatineau Park.

The People and Their Work

Most of Ottawa's residents trace their ancestry to Great Britain or France. The residents of Ottawa are divided almost equally between the Roman Catholic and various Protestant churches. The United Church of Canada, the Anglican Church of Canada, the Presbyterian Church, and the Baptist Church rank as the largest Protestant faiths.

Civil servants make up the largest group of workers in Ottawa. Most of them work for the Canadian government or for national agencies that have offices in Ottawa. Many others are employed by the embassies and legations of other countries.

Woodworking is the leading manufacturing industry. Ottawa has about 300 manufacturing and processing plants, including sash, door, and planing mills; food-processing plants; scientific equipment factories; and printing and bookbinding firms.

Transportation and Communication

The federal government maintains Uplands Airport south of the city as the main airfield for commercial flights. The Canadian Pacific Railway and the Canadian National Railways use the same huge terminal, Union Station. It stands in Confederation Square opposite the Château Laurier, the city's largest hotel. Water transportation no longer plays an important part in the economy of the city, although some barges still travel to Montreal on the Ottawa River. Ottawa has about 450 miles of streets. A city-owned company provides bus service within the city.

Ottawa publishers issue three daily newspapers, the English-language *Citizen* and *Journal*, and the French *Le Droit*. Three radio stations and a television station broadcast from the city.

Education

Schools. The Ottawa school system includes more than 40 public and over 60 Roman Catholic elementary schools, as well as about 10 public high schools. Elected boards, operating under policies of the provincial department of education, manage all these schools. Carleton University and the University of Ottawa are in Ottawa.

Libraries. Ottawa has a public library with several branches. The Parliamentary Library owns one of the great book collections of Canada. The government plans to construct a building for the National Library of Canada, which was founded in 1953.

Government

A board of control and a council administer the city government. A mayor and four controllers, each elected for two years, make up the board. Twenty aldermen, also elected to two-year terms, serve on the council. Most of the city's revenue comes from property taxes. The Canadian government pays an annual grant, instead of municipal taxes, on its buildings. The provincial government also pays a yearly grant toward the city's educational and general expenses.

History

Early Days. The French explorer Samuel de Champlain passed through the Ottawa region in 1613 on a visit to the Algonkian Indians farther upstream. Fur traders used the Ottawa River as a route to the west. But almost 200 years passed before anyone made a settlement in the vicinity. In 1800, Philemon Wright of Massachusetts, who had fought on the American side during the Revolutionary War, took up a large tract of land where Hull now stands. In addition to cultivating part of this grant, he established a sawmill and began the great lumbering industry of the Ottawa Valley. In 1821, Wright sold part of his property on the south side of the river to one of his employees, Nicholas Sparks.

Bytown. The real settlement of Ottawa dates from 1826, when British troops and workers, under Colonel

John By, arrived to build the Rideau Canal. The colonel bought land from Sparks, and in 1827 the community that grew up around the headquarters was named Bytown. It had a population of 1,000.

Bytown was a stormy place during its early years, with frequent conflicts between the Irish canal workers and the French-Canadian lumbermen. The lumber trade on the Ottawa River had begun in 1807, when Wright took the first raft of squared timber down to the St. Lawrence River. Bytown became a center of this trade. Sawmills and other related lumber industries sprang up. In 1850, the bustling lumber community was incorporated as a town. It became a city in 1855 with the new name of Ottawa and a population of 10,000. The word *Ottawa* comes from the name of an Algonkian tribe that once lived in the area.

Capital of Canada. United Canada had a succession of capitals after its creation in 1840. Kingston, Montreal, Toronto, and Quebec took turns while the legislature debated the question of a permanent capital. Canada referred the decision to Queen Victoria in 1857. She chose Ottawa, largely because of its beautiful setting and its remoteness from the American border. The last sessions of the legislature of United Canada took place in the newly built Parliament Buildings in 1866. The first meetings of the Dominion Parliament after confederation were held there in 1867.

City Plans. Canadians have given much thought to the beautification of Ottawa since it became the country's capital. The federal government formed a commission in 1899 to work with civic authorities toward this end. The Federal District Commission replaced the 1899 commission in 1927. In 1937, the government appointed Jacques Gréber, a French architect, to replan the center of the city and to suggest locations for government buildings. A key item in the plan is to relocate the railroad station on the southeastern outskirts of the city. This will reduce the number of railway lines entering the city, and will free valuable land in the heart of Ottawa for parks and roadways.

In 1944, parliament defined a national capital district of 900 square miles, including areas on both sides of the river. Ottawa has never been administered as a separate federal district, as is the District of Columbia in the United States. Planning is aided by yearly votes of money from parliament. But it depends on the cooperation of four municipalities in the district, as well as the provincial governments of Ontario and Quebec. The government recognized these circumstances, and replaced the 1927 commission with the National Capital Commission in 1959. It also granted additional funds to help the commission achieve its purpose. The commission received money to buy land for a green belt of parks around the city. When the project is completed in 1967, the 100th anniversary of confederation, Ottawa will be one of the best designed and most beautiful cities in North America.

Ottawa opened a new city hall in 1958. This limestone and gray plate-glass building stands on Green Island at the mouth of the Rideau River.

King George VI and Queen Elizabeth visited Ottawa in May, 1939. This was the first visit to the capital of Canada by a reigning sovereign of the British Commonwealth. Queen Elizabeth II and Prince Philip came to Ottawa in 1957 and again in 1959. D. M. L. FARR

Capital Press Service

The University of Ottawa was founded as the College of Bytown in 1848. Classes are conducted in French and English.

OTTAWA, UNIVERSITY OF, is a private coeducational school in Ottawa, Canada. It was operated by the Roman Catholic Oblate Fathers of Mary Immaculate until 1965, when it was chartered under control of an independent board of directors. Classes are conducted in French and English. The university has faculties (colleges) of arts, civil and common law, medicine, philosophy, psychology and education, pure and applied science, and social sciences. There is also a teachers college and schools of hospital administration, library science, nursing, and physical education and recreation.

The University of Ottawa was founded as the College of Bytown in 1848. It received a civil charter in 1866 and a papal charter in 1889. In 1965, its civil and papal charters were transferred to the newly founded Saint Paul University. Saint Paul University students receive degrees from the University of Ottawa. For enrollment of the University of Ottawa, see CANADA (table, Universities and Colleges). GERARD WILLIAM BOSS

OTTAWA RIVER is the chief branch of the Saint Lawrence River and one of the most important streams of Canada. For location, see QUEBEC (physical map). Great quantities of lumber float down the Ottawa from forests in the north.

The river begins in central Quebec, about 160 miles north of the city of Ottawa. It flows west to the Quebec-Ontario border, and forms the border as it flows southeastward. It ends its 696-mile course near the island of Montreal, where it empties into the Saint Lawrence River. Canada's federal government buildings stand on the Ontario side of the river. The city of Hull, on the Quebec side, faces Ottawa.

Rapids and falls along the river make it unnavigable for large ships. But the rapids and falls develop two million horsepower of electric power a year. Chaudière Falls, north of the city of Ottawa, is the largest waterfall on the river. Dams and slides for large logs have been built on the Ottawa to aid the lumber industry. Canals built along the river once aided shipping. But they are now used only for pleasure boats. The Rideau Canal system connects the Ottawa River with Lake Ontario at Kingston. The river was an early canoe route to the interior of Canada. French explorer Samuel de Champlain explored the Ottawa River during the early 1600's. J. BRIAN BIRD

OTTAWA UNIVERSITY, Kans. See UNIVERSITIES AND COLLEGES (table).

The River Otter is one of the world's best fishermen. Its thick, flexible body and webbed feet give it great speed in the water.

Hunters and trappers seeking the otter's fine fur have greatly reduced the number of river and sea otters.

OTTER, *AHT ur,* is a fur-bearing animal that spends much of its time in the water. Otters are related to the weasels and are *carnivorous* (flesh-eating) mammals. They live on all continents except Australia. They are divided into two groups, *river otters* and *sea otters.*

The *river otter* has a thick, flexible body, and a long tapering tail. Its head is large and flattened. It has strong sharp teeth, large nostrils, and small ears and eyes. Its short, stout legs have webbed toes for swimming, and sharp, curved claws. The animal is $3\frac{1}{2}$ to $4\frac{1}{2}$ feet long, including its tail. Females are usually smaller than males.

Like the beaver, the otter has two layers of fur. Its underfur is short, soft, and whitish-gray in color. Over these hairs is a covering of long, stiffer hairs, which are a rich, shining dark brown in color. Under the skin, a layer of fat covers the entire body and acts as insulation against the cold. Otters swim rapidly and dive for fish. Fish and crayfish make up their principal food, but they also eat other shellfish, snails, frogs, and insects. Otters like to play. On land, they go tobogganing by sliding down muddy slopes or icy hills. Common river otters make their homes in burrows in the banks along streams, or in caves above the ground. The river otter is one of the best swimmers of all the land mammals. It can swim under water for a quarter of a mile without coming up for air. It gives birth to one to five young —usually two or three—between February and April.

Furriers consider the pelt of river otters one of the most beautiful, durable, and valuable of North American furs. They often use it for fur coats, collars, and cuffs. They pluck the long outer hairs and dress the fur. Otters have been raised experimentally on farms.

Sea Otters live only along the Asiatic and North American coasts of the Pacific Ocean. They spend almost all their time in the water. In the water, they resemble seals, and sometimes are mistaken for them. A sea otter is 5 to 11 feet long, including its tail. A large male will weigh up to 80 pounds. Sea otters live mainly on sea urchins, clams, crabs, snails, mussels, and other shellfish. They do not eat much fish.

The sea otter's fur is valuable. It is soft, dense, and unusually fine. The fur varies in color from reddish brown to black, with silvery guard hairs. The pelt of the sea otter is as scarce as it is beautiful. A single skin has sold for as much as $1,700. During the days when China was an empire, robes used for state occasions were trimmed with sea otter fur.

Sea otters were once curious and unwary. They have been so hunted and persecuted, however, that they now are very shy and cautious. They were captured by spearing, shooting, clubbing, or with nets. Now they are given complete protection while in United States waters. They have only one offspring at a time. The young may be born during any season of the year. Chinese fishermen have taught river otters to help them in fishing. Otters are also used by fishermen in Bengal.

Scientific Classification. Otters belong to the fur bearing family, *Mustelidae.* They make up the subfamily *Lutrinae.* The common river otter of Canada, and the United States is genus *Lutra,* species *L. canadensis.* The sea otter of the Bering Sea and North Pacific Ocean is genus *Enhydra,* species *E. lutris.* E. LENDELL COCKRUM

See also ANIMAL (color picture: Animals of the Woodlands); FUR.

OTTER CREEK. See VERMONT (Rivers and Lakes).

OTTER HOUND was developed in Great Britain for the sport of hunting otter. It has a thick, rough coat, with an oily undercoat that enables it to stay in cold water for long periods. Its feet are slightly webbed, and this helps make the dog a good swimmer. The otter hound looks much like a bloodhound in size and build.

Joyce R. Wilson

The Otter Hound Is a Hardy Dog and a Good Swimmer.

But the otter hound has a longer coat and shorter ears than the bloodhound. The otter hound's color ranges from grizzled blue and white to sand, with black and tan markings. Some breeders believe the otter hound originally came from the bloodhound. Others believe its ancestors were bulldogs.   OLGA DAKAN

OTTERBEIN COLLEGE. See UNIVERSITIES AND COLLEGES (table).

OTTO. See ATTAR.

OTTO was the name of three German kings and emperors, father, son, and grandson. Their combined rule lasted from A.D. 936 to 1002.

Otto I, The Great (912-973), was the first king to become Holy Roman Emperor. He followed his father, Henry I, as king of Germany in 936. Otto's father had actually ruled only his own duchy of Saxony, but Otto tried to rule all Germany. In 951, he crossed the Alps and declared himself the king of Italy. He was forced to return to Germany when the other German princes began a series of revolts. At the same time, the Slavs in Poland and Bohemia revolted, and the Magyars, or Hungarians, invaded Germany. Otto crushed the Magyars in the battle of the Lech River in 955. The Poles and Bohemians were forced to accept his rule. Otto was able to replace most of the rebellious German princes with members of his own family. The young king of Arles, or Burgundy, also had to accept German rule. Otto then turned his attention toward Italy. He married the widow of an earlier Italian king, and defeated a rival for the throne. In 961, Otto crossed the Alps in answer to an appeal from Pope John XII to put down an uprising in Rome. For this service, Otto was crowned emperor of what was later known as the Holy Roman Empire (see HOLY ROMAN EMPIRE).

Otto II (955-983) was Holy Roman Emperor from 973 to 983. He followed his father's example and tried to keep power over Lombardy, Burgundy, Germany, and the Slavic borderlands. Otto II tried to extend his power by claiming several provinces in southern Italy. But the Greek emperor opposed his claim, and called on the Saracens for help in a war against the Germans. Otto was defeated at Cotrone in 982 and left southern Italy. He died in Rome, where he was planning another campaign.

Otto III (980-1002), was 3 years old when his father died, but he was crowned king of the Germans. His mother and grandmother ruled for him as regents. He spent his life in Italy and took little interest in ruling Germany. He tried, instead, to bring back the glories of ancient Rome. His death ended the direct line of Saxon emperors.   FRANKLIN D. SCOTT

OTTO I (1815-1867), a Bavarian prince, became the first king of Greece after it was liberated from Turkey in 1830 (see GREECE [Otto I]). Otto was an unpopular ruler. He was not Greek, and he failed to move toward the realization of the "Great Idea." This idea was to liberate all Greeks still under Turkish rule in such territories as Crete, Thessaly, and Macedonia.

Otto and the Greeks were prepared to join the Russians against the Turks during the Crimean War (1853 to 1856). Great Britain and France sent troops to Greece and prevented it. The Greeks blamed Otto and deposed him in 1862. Otto, however, was a good king who worked hard for his people. He rebuilt Athens, established the first Greek university, and refounded the town of Sparta. Otto was born in Salzburg, Austria, on June 1, 1815.   R. V. BURKS

OTTO, NIKOLAUS AUGUST. See GASOLINE ENGINE (Development of the Gasoline Engine).

OTTO THE CHILD. See BRUNSWICK (family).

OTTOMAN EMPIRE. See TURKEY (History).

OUABAIN. See POISON.

OUACHITA BAPTIST UNIVERSITY. See UNIVERSITIES AND COLLEGES (table).

OUACHITA MOUNTAINS. See ARKANSAS (Land Regions; picture, Lake Hamilton); OKLAHOMA (Land Regions).

OUACHITA RIVER, *WASH ee taw,* begins in the Ouachita Mountains of western Arkansas and flows east and then south into Louisiana. Sometimes called the *Washita,* it is about 605 miles long. The Ouachita joins the Tensas River to form the Black River about 25 miles west of Natchez. Large ships can sail about 350 miles up the river to Camden, Ark. During high water seasons, ships can sail about 70 miles farther, to Arkadelphia. For location of the Ouachita River, see SOUTHERN STATES (color map).   WALLACE E. AKIN

OUAGADOUGOU, *WAH guh DOO goo* (pop. 59,126; alt. 1,010 ft.), is the capital and commercial center of Upper Volta, a republic in western Africa. Factories there process the agricultural products grown in the surrounding region.

See also UPPER VOLTA (map; History).

OUIDA, *WEE duh* (1839-1908), was the pen name of the English novelist Marie Louise de la Ramée. *Ouida* was the way she said *Louise,* as a child. Her romantic novels show a sharp sense of the dramatic. The best known is *Under Two Flags* (1867). She also wrote children's stories, including *A Dog of Flanders* (1872) and *Two Little Wooden Shoes* (1874). Her other works include *The Silver Christ* (1894) and *Street Dust* (1901). Ouida was born in Bury St. Edmunds, England, but she lived in Italy most of her life. The first of her nearly 20 novels, *Held in Bondage,* was published in 1863. She died in Viareggio, Italy.   LIONEL STEVENSON

OUIJA BOARD. See DIVINATION.

OUISTITI. See MARMOSET.

James Purdue, NAS

The Ounce, or Snow Leopard, Has a Heavy Coat of Fur.

OUNCE is a name given to the beautiful snow leopard that is a member of the cat family. When full-grown, this animal is six feet to six feet eight inches long. The ounce's summer home is as far up as 13,000 feet in the cold Tibetan plateau of central Asia, from the Altai Mountains south to the Himalayas. During the coldest winter months, the animal goes down into the valleys as low as 6,000 feet. Its heavy hair is pale gray in color, and marked with leopardlike brown spots. Its pale color helps it to steal unnoticed over the snow. In its native rocky home, the ounce feeds on ibex, bharal, marmots, pikas, and other animals.

Scientific Classification. The ounce belongs to the cat family, *Felidae*. It is classified as genus *Felis*, species *F. uncia*.　　　　　　　　　　　ERNEST S. BOOTH

See also ANIMAL (color picture: Animals of the Mountains).

OUNCE is a measure of weight and of volume. The name comes from the Latin *uncia*, meaning a *twelfth*. In *avoirdupois* weight, the ounce is equal to one-sixteenth of a pound, or 437½ grains. In *troy* weight and *apothecaries'* weight, the ounce is equal to one-twelfth of a pound, or 480 grains. Grains are the same in all these systems. The avoirdupois ounce is a unit employed in weighing ordinary merchandise, such as foodstuffs. The troy ounce is used in weighing precious metals, and the apothecaries' ounce is employed in compounding prescriptions.

There are 16 fluid ounces to a liquid pint, which has a volume of 28.875 cubic inches. Canada uses a fluid ounce based on the Imperial gallon; this ounce is one-twentieth of a pint, equal to 34.6775 cubic inches. In compounding liquid medicines, the American pharmacist uses fluid drams, equal in volume to one-eighth of a fluid ounce.　　　　　　　　　　　PHILLIP S. JONES

See also WEIGHTS AND MEASURES.

OUR CHALET. See GIRL SCOUTS (In Other Countries).

OUR LADY OF FATIMA is the name used to describe the Virgin Mary as she reportedly appeared near Fatima, Portugal, in 1917. On May 13th of that year, three Portuguese children told of having seen a vision of a lady in a cove while tending their sheep. The children said that the lady, dressed in a white gown and veil, told them to come there on the 13th day of each month until the following October when she would tell them who she was. On October 13, she said that she was the Lady of the Rosary, and told the children to recite the rosary every day. She asked that a chapel be built in her honor.

The Roman Catholic Church erected a shrine with a basilica at Fatima. In 1932, the Church authorized devotion to Our Lady of Fatima, under the title of Our Lady of the Rosary. Since then, thousands of persons have made pilgrimages to Fatima.

OUR LADY OF THE ELMS, COLLEGE OF. See UNIVERSITIES AND COLLEGES (table).

OUR LADY OF THE LAKE COLLEGE is a liberal arts school for women at San Antonio, Tex. It is conducted by the Roman Catholic Congregation of the Sisters of Divine Providence. The Graduate School of Education and the School of Social Service are coeducational. The school was founded in 1896 as a high school and became a college in 1911. For enrollment, see UNIVERSITIES AND COLLEGES (table).　　　　　　JOHN L. MCMAHON

OURSLER, *OURZ ler,* **FULTON** (1893-1952), was an American writer and editor. He wrote *The Greatest Story Ever Told* (1949) and *The Greatest Book Ever Written* (1951). His *The Greatest Faith Ever Known* (1953) was completed by his daughter after his death. He was an editor of *Liberty* magazine from 1931 to 1942, and served as an editor of *Reader's Digest* from 1944 until 1952. He was born CHARLES FULTON OURSLER in Baltimore, Md., on Jan. 22, 1893.　　　　　　CARL NIEMEYER

OUTBOARD MOTOR is a gasoline or electric motor clamped to the stern of a small boat. It operates a vertical driving shaft to which the propeller is geared under water to propel the boat.

Gasoline outboard motors are the most frequently used type. They may have either horizontal or "V-shaped" cylinders. There may be one, two, four, or six cylinders in a gasoline outboard motor.

Outboard motors operate at high speed and deliver their full power at 4,000 revolutions per minute. Some of the smaller types are also designed for low speeds and are used by fishermen for trolling.

Electric outboard motors are less frequently used because their power comes from storage batteries that must be recharged frequently.

See also MOTORBOAT (Outboard Motorboats).

Outboard Motors can drive small boats across the water at high speeds. Their rapidly spinning propellers churn the water into a fine spray.

Wagemaker Co.

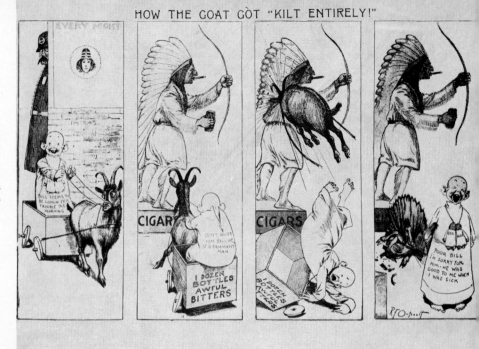

HOW THE GOAT GOT "KILT ENTIRELY!"

The Yellow Kid comic strip made Richard Outcault famous. It pictured the bald, grinning fellow in brilliant yellow dress in many humorous situations connected with events of the day in New York City.

OUTCAULT, *OWT kawlt,* **RICHARD FELTON** (1863-1928), was an American cartoonist. His "Yellow Kid" appeared in 1894. This was the first comic strip printed in color (1896), and led to the term "yellow journalism," which means a highly sensational kind of newspaper writing. Outcault had introduced the "Yellow Kid" in the *New York World.* But he accepted an enormous salary from the *New York Journal* to draw the strip for its pages. The *World* hired another artist to draw the "Yellow Kid," and the papers started a sensational rivalry. Other newspapers called them "Yellow Kid journals," later "yellow journals." Outcault was born at Lancaster, Ohio.   DICK SPENCER III

OUTDOOR EDUCATION. See CAMPING.

OUTDOOR RECREATION, BUREAU OF, is an agency of the United States government. It was established in 1962 as part of the Department of the Interior to coordinate federal recreation programs and handle long-range planning. It also provides assistance to states, encourages interstate and regional cooperation, and conducts outdoor recreation resource surveys.

OUTER MONGOLIA. See MONGOLIA.

OUTLAW. See BANDIT with its Related Articles.

OUTLINES AND OUTLINING. An outline gives the main topics, or principal ideas, of a subject. It is a writer's blueprint, or plan, for an article, a theme, or a book. It may also be used to summarize an article or a book for study, or to prepare a speech.

Formal outlines are of two kinds. The *topic outline* is a summary of topics and subtopics, or nouns and phrases, to indicate ideas. The *sentence outline* uses complete sentences for each division.

Organization. All topics of equal importance should be phrased in similar form and indented equally. The subject should be covered completely, but without too many main topics. Topic headings should be clear.

The topics and subtopics may be organized with Roman numerals (I), capital letters (A), Arabic numerals (1), and small letters (a), in that order. Use periods after the numbers and letters. If more subdivisions are needed, repeat the numbers and letters in parentheses. Do not use periods after parentheses. Always use at least two subheads. Capitalize the first letter of the first word of each topic and subtopic. Use periods after complete sentences.

A Sample Topic Outline follows.

Outline on Floods

I. **What Is a Flood?**
  A. Its Extent
  B. Its Effects
    1. Bad effects
      a. Destroys property and homes
      b. Carries off topsoil
      c. Causes injuries and deaths
    2. Good effects
      a. Creates fertile regions
      b. Transports soil
        (1) Nile Valley
        (2) Mississippi delta

II. **Kinds of Floods**
  A. River Floods
    1. Rivers that commonly overflow
      a. Mississippi-Missouri system
      b. Hwang Ho, or Yellow River
    2. Causes
      a. Too heavy rains
      b. Too fast melting of snow and ice
    3. Great floods
      a. Ohio and Indiana, 1913
      b. Mississippi, 1927
      c. Ohio and Mississippi, 1937
  B. Seacoast Floods
    1. Causes
    2. Great Floods

III. **Flood Control**
  A. Reclaiming dry, barren highlands
  B. Planting trees
  C. Building reservoirs, levees, flood walls

Examples of outlines may be found in WORLD BOOK at the ends of many articles, such as BIRD; FRANCE; OHIO; and PUBLIC SPEAKING.

669

Javanese Fishermen Use Double Outriggers on their sailing boats to keep them from capsizing in the rolling waves of coastal waters, *above*. Riding the surf in an outrigger canoe, *below*, is one of the most popular water sports in Hawaii.

Pix; United Air Lines

OUTRIGGER BOAT is a rowing boat with the oarlocks mounted on *outriggers* (brackets) which run out from the sides of the boat. By moving the oarlocks farther from the oarsman, the leverage that the oarsman puts on the oars is increased. In the United States, outriggers are rarely used except in "shells," or very light boats such as are used in college or interclub boat racing. In the Indian and Pacific oceans, an "outrigger" is a canoe with a log attached to a framework extending from one side. The log is a counterbalance and keeps the canoe from capsizing. Some outriggers can hold 30 men. See also MARQUESAS ISLANDS (picture); INDIAN OCEAN (picture).   ROBERT H. BURGESS

OUZEL. See WATER OUZEL.

OVANDO, NICOLÁS DE. See COLUMBUS, CHRISTOPHER (Columbus in Disgrace; Fourth and Last Voyage).

OVARY. See FERTILIZATION; FLOWER (The Pistils); GLAND (The Sex Glands).

OVEN. See STOVE; BREAD (How Bread Is Baked; History); COOKING (History).

Hal Harrison, National Audubon Society
The Ovenbird Conceals Its Nest on the Forest Floor.

OVENBIRD is a common American bird that belongs to the family of warblers. The ovenbird looks like a small thrush. It is about 6 inches long, and has a brownish olive-green back, dull orange crown, and a white breast spotted with black. Its song sounds like the word *teacher*, repeated several times with increasing loudness. The ovenbird is often called the *teacher bird*.

The ovenbird nests from Oklahoma to Georgia, and north to Manitoba and Labrador. Its name comes from the shape of its nest, which looks somewhat like an old-fashioned rounded oven. The ovenbird builds its nest of grasses and leaves, and carefully conceals it on the forest floor. It lays four to six white eggs, speckled with cinnamon brown. It eats mostly woodland insects.

Scientific Classification. The ovenbird belongs to the wood warbler family, *Parulidae*. It is genus *Seiurus*, species *S. aurocapillus*. GEORGE J. WALLACE

See also WARBLER.

OVERDRIVE. See TRANSMISSION (Overdrive).

OVERLAND MAIL. See PONY EXPRESS.

OVERLAPPING SET. See SET THEORY.

OVERPOPULATION. See POPULATION; BIRTH CONTROL.

OVERSEAS HIGHWAY. See FLORIDA (Transportation).

OVERTONE. See HARMONICS.

OVERTURE, *O ver tyoor*, is a musical composition written as an introduction to an opera, oratorio, or, in some cases, to a play or spoken drama. An overture may contain some of the principal themes of the main work, or it may be entirely independent. The overture may be in *sonata-allegro* (first movement) form (see SONATA). An overture to an opera compares with the first movement of a symphony. It is intended to put the listener into the proper frame of mind for what is to follow.

The musical introduction which leads to a drama is called a *dramatic overture*. Beethoven's overture to *Coriolanus* and Schubert's overture to *Rosamunde* are good examples. Other overtures are similar to symphonic poems and are written so that they may be played separately as concert pieces. These are known as *concert overtures*.

In the 1600's, the French-Italian composer Jean Baptiste Lully made the first important contribution to the development of the overture. Lully wrote short movements to be played as openings for his operas and ballets. These musical preludes became known as overtures.

In Italy, the first overture was probably written in

1607. The opera *Orfeo* by Claudio Monteverdi began with a musical overture of nine bars, played three times. Such an overture was known at that time as a *sinfonia*.

The first overture for an opera in which the music was directly related to the opera was written by Christoph Gluck, who wrote an overture to his opera *Iphigénie en Tauride*. The music of the overture prepared the listener for the opening act, which was a storm scene.

Mozart, an Austrian composer, made an important contribution to the development of the overture in 1787. He wrote an overture to his opera *Don Giovanni* that has become famous, and is played apart from the opera.

The next step in the development of the overture was made in the early 1800's by Beethoven. He wrote four overtures to his only opera, *Fidelio*. Three of them are called *Leonore* overtures, after the heroine of the story. All four contain themes from the music of the opera.

The overture reached its finest development in the preludes to the operas of Richard Wagner (1813-1883). The preludes to *Die Meistersinger*, *Lohengrin*, and *Tannhäuser* are really overtures. RAYMOND KENDALL

OVERWEIGHT. See WEIGHT CONTROL.

OVID, *AHV id* (43 B.C.-A.D. 17?), the most versatile of the Roman poets, wrote the 15-book *Metamorphoses*. It contains about 250 stories, arranged chronologically from the creation of the world to Julius Caesar. The connecting principle between the stories is that each involves some *metamorphosis* (change), such as shapeless matter changed into the world, or Julius Caesar into a star. Ovid's full name was PUBLIUS OVIDIUS NASO.

Ovid also wrote the popular *Heroides*, a series of 21 fictional letters in verse addressed by famous women of mythology to their departed husbands or lovers. Each is a pretty and dramatic story. His other love poetry includes three books of *Love Elegies*, a three-book *Art of Love*, and a verse treatise *On Cosmetics*.

The emperor Augustus banished Ovid to Tomis (now Constanţa, in Romania) on the Black Sea in A.D. 8. Augustus was interested in moral reform, and it is believed Ovid's love poetry was considered a bad influence. The exiled Ovid worked on, but never finished, the *Fasti*, a kind of religious calendar telling why certain days were festive or mournful. He also wrote two collections of poems, *Tristia* and *Letters from Pontus*, that plead for his restoration. But Ovid died in exile.

He was born in Sulmona, in northern Italy, the son of a wealthy family. He studied law, but found that everything he wrote fell naturally into verse. MOSES HADAS

See also ARETHUSA; NARCISSUS; PYRAMUS AND THISBE.

OVIPAROUS ANIMAL, *oh VIP uh rus*, is a type of animal that reproduces by laying eggs that hatch outside the parent's body. The young animals develop inside the egg. In *viviparous* animals, the young develop inside the parent until they are ready to be born. Viviparity is considered the higher method of birth, since it better protects and nourishes the young. Most vertebrates below mammals are oviparous, but there are exceptions. For example, certain sharks, lizards, and snakes bear live young. Among the mammals, the platypus is oviparous. WILLIAM C. BEAVER

OVIPOSITOR. See GRASSHOPPER; ICHNEUMON FLY.

OVULE. See FLOWER (The Pistils).

OWEN

OWEN is the family name of two social theorists, father and son.

Robert Owen (1771-1858), a Welsh-born social reformer, pioneered in cooperative movements. He tried to prove as a businessman that it was good business to think of the employees' welfare. He set up the famous New Harmony community in Indiana in 1825.

Owen was part owner and the head of the New Lanark cotton mills in Scotland in 1799. It was during the Industrial Revolution, when machines were replacing home sewing and weaving. New factories were rarely built with the comfort of the workers in mind. Wages were low, and women and children were not treated with consideration.

He organized a model community. Instead of employing children, he built schools for them. He kept his mills in good repair, and tried to take care of his laborers' needs. The success of his mills impressed many visitors.

Brown Bros.
Robert Owen

New Harmony. Owen wrote on the subject of proper social conditions, and tried to interest the British government in building "villages of cooperation." He thought these villages ought to be partly agricultural and partly industrial. He made up his mind to show they could succeed. He then set up New Harmony.

Owen believed in equal opportunity for all. His ideas in education were influenced by Johann Pestalozzi, a Swiss educator. Owen opposed mere book learning. He believed children also could be taught "correct ideas" by surrounding them with good examples.

He lost popularity by his antireligious views. Many of his associates at New Harmony refused to work. The community failed in 1827, and Owen returned to England in 1828.

Cooperatives. Owen retired from business to devote all his time to his social theories. He moved to London in 1828. There, trades unions became interested in his "villages of cooperation." In 1833, Owen organized the Grand National Consolidated Trades Union. It had more than 500,000 members. The movement tried to reorganize industry into cooperatives. The government and manufacturers opposed it, and by 1834, the union had collapsed. Owen continued to write and agitate for government aid. Although his plans were not accepted, his ideas influenced all later cooperative movements.

Owen was born in Newtown, Wales. He left school when he was 9 to work as a cotton spinner.

Robert Dale Owen (1801-1877) was a social theorist and an American legislator. He worked with his father, Robert Owen, in the New Lanark and New Harmony model communities. He edited the New Harmony *Gazette* with Frances Wright. When New Harmony collapsed in 1827, Owen moved to New York City. He and Frances Wright edited the *Free Enquirer* and tried to organize the Working Men's party in 1829 in New York.

Owen was elected to the Indiana state legislature in 1836 and served until 1838. He was a member of the U.S. House of Representatives from 1843 to 1847. He served as Minister to Naples from 1855 to 1858. Owen championed emancipation for Negro slaves, and influenced President Abraham Lincoln's views. He was a freethinker in religion, and a pioneer in advocating birth control and universal education. He was born in Glasgow, Scotland.   LOUIS FILLER

See also COOPERATIVE; NEW HARMONY; NURSERY SCHOOL; PESTALOZZI, JOHANN H.

Culver
Robert Dale Owen

Ruth Bryan Owen

OWEN, RUTH BRYAN (1885-1954), was the first American woman ever chosen to represent the United States in another country. She served as United States Minister to Denmark from 1933 to 1936.

Mrs. Owen was born in Jacksonville, Ill., the oldest daughter of the well-known statesman, William Jennings Bryan. She served as a Democrat from Florida in the U.S. House of Representatives from 1929 to 1933. She served as alternate U.S. representative to the UN General Assembly in 1949.   GEORGE M. WALLER

OWEN-STANLEY MOUNTAINS lie in the eastern part of Australian New Guinea. The highest mountain is Mount Victoria (13,363 feet). Other peaks more than 10,000 feet high include Mounts Albert Edward, Suckling, Scratchley, Yule, and Obree. Streams from the southern slopes of the Owen-Stanley Mountains flow into the Coral Sea.   JUSTUS M. VAN DER KROEF

OWENS, JESSE (1913-   ), an American Negro athlete, held world track records in sprinting, hurdling, and jumping. On one day, May 25, 1935, he set three world records and tied another. The records were in the 220-yard dash, 220-yard low hurdles, and the running broad jump. He tied the 100-yard dash record. Owens won Olympic Games championships in 1936 at Berlin in the 100-meter dash, 200-meter dash, and running broad jump. He was born in Decatur, Ala., and attended Ohio State University.   PAT HARMON

OWENS, MICHAEL JOSEPH. See BOTTLE.

OWENS LAKE. See MOJAVE.

OWENSBORO, Ky. (pop. 50,329; met. area 79,486; alt. 395 ft.), lies on the south bank of the Ohio River, 80 miles southwest of Louisville. Factories in Owensboro make radio tubes, steel, cigars, and chemicals. Owensboro was founded in 1797 as Yellow Banks, and later renamed in honor of Colonel Abraham Owens, who died in the Battle of Tippecanoe. Owensboro was incorporated in 1877, and has a council-manager government. Owensboro is the seat of Daviess County. For location, see KENTUCKY (political map).

OWL. The owl usually lives alone and hunts for food at night. It is known for its solemn appearance. The owl has been called the "night watchman of our gardens" because it eats harmful rodents at night. Although it is a bird of prey, or a bird which kills and eats other animals, the owl is a closer relative of the nighthawks, whippoorwills, and other goatsuckers than of the hawks.

Scientists have identified about 525 various kinds of owls. They live throughout the temperate, tropical, and subarctic regions of the world. Owls have been found on sea islands cut off from the mainland.

The smallest of owls is the tiny *elf owl* of the southwestern United States and western Mexico. It is hardly six inches long. The largest is the *great gray owl*, which lives in the deep woods of Canada and Alaska as far north as trees grow. It is 30 inches long, and has a wingspread of between 54 and 60 inches.

General Appearance. A person can recognize any owl at once by its large, broad head with a ruff of feathers around the eyes. This ruff is called the *facial disk*. It also covers enormous ear openings. The eyes are very large. These eyes point forward, unlike the eyes of most birds. For this reason owls can watch an object with both eyes at the same time. They have binocular vision like man. But unlike man, owls cannot move their eyes in their sockets, so they must move their heads to see a moving object. Their eyes have long lashes, and their upper eyelids close over them. Owls' eyes make them look as if they were wiser than other animals. The owl has long been a symbol of wisdom. The ancient Greeks thought it was sacred to Athena, their goddess of wisdom. Actually, geese, crows, and ravens are all smarter than owls.

Owls have short, thick bodies; strong, hooked beaks, and powerful feet with sharp claws. These are the only ways in which they resemble hawks. Some owls have tufts of feathers on their heads. The tufts are often called "ears" or "horns." Their feathers are soft and fluffy, and often make the birds seem larger than they are. The plumage is also dull, or colored so that the bird blends with its surroundings. Owls can fly fairly fast. Their fluffy feathers muffle the swishing sound that most birds make when they fly. An owl can swoop down on its prey unseen and unheard in the shadowy still night. All owls can see in the daytime, but usually not very well. A few can see well in the daytime, and hunt both by day and night. Others hunt only at night. These birds usually have extremely sensitive eyes and can see well in the dark.

Owls eat mostly mammals. The larger owls catch rabbits and squirrels, and the smaller ones catch many mice, rats, and shrews. Usually they capture their food alive, but now and then owls will pick up animals which have been recently killed along highways. Some owls will take a few birds and insects. Others have been known to fish in waters that are so shallow that the owls do not have to dive for their prey. Like the hawks, owls tear their prey into pieces when they eat it. Sometimes, if the prey is small enough, they swallow it whole. Later they throw up pellets of bones, fur, scales, and feathers which they cannot digest. These pellets can be found under their roosting places.

Owls are among the most useful birds to the farmer. They destroy harmful rodents, such as mice, rats, and

John Markham

The Barn Owl nests in old and abandoned buildings. It aids farmers by helping to keep farms free of rats and mice.

moles. But they seldom touch poultry, which are asleep and inside when owls come out to hunt.

Owls are not good nest builders. The nests are usually crude structures in hollow trees, caverns, underground burrows, barns, deserted houses, belfries, and old nests of hawks and crows. The eggs are nearly round, and are white tinged with buff or blue. There are usually three or four eggs, but some owls lay from two to twelve.

Both males and females help care for the nest. The larger owls bravely defend their nests against any intruder, including men. Sometimes they draw blood when they strike with their vicious talons. Young owls are attractive in their covering of thick white down. They are reared and fed in much the same way as young hawks. They stay in the nest longer than most birds.

Important Owls. There are two families of owls, which have certain body differences. They are the *barn owls* and the *typical owls*. There are ten species of barn owls. They live in most places except the colder regions. The *North American barn owl* ranges from the latitude of northern California and southern New England south to Central America. It is about eighteen inches long.

OWL

Sometimes it is called *monkey-faced owl* because its heart-shaped face, beady eyes, and amusing actions make it look like a monkey. It usually nests in a hollow tree, but sometimes selects a belfry or the dark places in a barn, which give it its name. Barn owls are very valuable birds. They eat many mice, rats, sparrows, blackbirds, and frogs.

Of the typical owls, the *great horned owl* lives in many places throughout North America. It is common in the heavy forests of the East and North, and among cliffs and canyons of the dry regions in the West. It grows two feet long, and is the only large owl with tufts of feathers on its head. Like other owls, it is heard more often than seen. It sounds like a barking dog in the distance—*whoo, hoo-hoo, whoo, whoo.*

The great horned owl is the only one which destroys poultry. It makes up for this destruction by keeping down the number of rabbits. This owl chooses old crow or hawk nests for its three eggs. Both males and females sit on the eggs at different times. The young cannot fly until they are 9 to 10 weeks old.

The *barred owl* lives only in the woodlands of eastern North America, from Canada south to Mexico. It is about the same size as the great horned owl, but has no ear tufts. Brownish-gray bars run across its breast and the length of its belly. This owl deserves the name hoot owl more than any other. It gives a series of eight or more loud hoots, the last one ending with an *ah: whoo, whoo, whoo, whoo—whoo, whoo, whoo, whoo-ah.*

The best known small owl is the *screech owl*. It is another woodland bird that lives in North America from the northern woodlands through Mexico. Most screech owls are about 10 inches long, and are the only small owls with ear tufts. Screech owls in the eastern United States may be either reddish or grayish.

These owls like to spend the day in hollow trees and to nest there. Sometimes they will live in a birdhouse if it has a single compartment and the opening is not less than 3 inches across. They often use the trees along the city streets and in parks. Screech owls may give no signs that they are around until night. Then they give their weird trembling calls and hollow whistles that run down the scale. Superstitious people think these sounds mean that death or disaster is near.

Screech owls eat mostly mice and other small rodents, insects, and sometimes birds. Most families have from four to six young, but sometimes there are as many as nine.

The adult male *snowy owl* is usually pure white, although it may have brown spots. It is about 20 inches long. It breeds in the Arctic and migrates in the winter, sometimes as far as the Caribbean Sea.

The *long-eared owl* is another woodland bird. In summer it ranges from southern Canada to southern California and Virginia, and in winter it flies as far south as Florida. It is about two-thirds as large as the great horned owl, with ear tufts close together and lengthwise streaks on the breast.

The *saw-whet* also lives in the woods. Its name comes from its rasping call. In the course of the year this bird makes its home from Alaska and Nova Scotia south to Mexico. It is often tame and can be captured by hand.

Two kinds of owls live in open country and hunt by day as well as night. The *short-eared owl* is about the size of the long-eared owl. It is buff colored all over with many brown streaks. The ear tufts are so short that they are not noticeable. This owl nests from the Arctic south to California, Kansas, and New Jersey. It spends the winter in the United States and south to Central America. It lives mostly on prairies, meadows, and marshes, and nests on the ground. *Burrowing owls* live in the ground in burrows like snakes and prairie dogs. They have long legs which help them move on the ground, and they can

SOME KINDS OF OWLS

Owls are good hunters. They see and hear well and can fly almost noiselessly. Most owls build their nests in hollow trees. Others nest on ledges of cliffs or in burrows in the ground. Owls are helpful to man because they eat mice, rats, and other rodent pests.

Leonard Lee Rue III, Monkmeyer

Russ Kinne, Photo Researchers

Burrowing Owl
Speotyto cunicularia
Found on plains of
Western Hemisphere
(Body length 9 inches)

Snowy Owl
Nyctea scandiaca
Found in Arctic
(Body length 20 inches)

Elf Owl
Micrathene whitneyi
Found in Southwestern United States
and Mexico
(Body length 5½ inches)

Walker, APF

see well in the daytime. They usually live near a colony of prairie dogs because these small animals are a favorite food of the burrowing owls.　OLIN SEWALL PETTINGILL, JR.

Scientific Classification. The owls in America north of Mexico belong to two families. The first is the barn owl family, *Tytonidae*. It includes the barn owl which is genus *Tyto*, species *T. alba*. The other family is the typical owl family, *Strigidae*. It includes the following:

Barred owl	*Strix varia*
Burrowing owl	*Speotyto cunicularia*
Elf owl	*Micrathene whitneyi*
Great gray owl	*Strix nebulosa*
Great horned owl	*Bubo virginianus*
Long-eared owl	*Asio otus*
Pygmy owl	*Glaucidium gnoma*
Saw-whet owl	*Aegolius acadicus*
Screech owl	*Otus asio*
Short-eared owl	*Asio flammeus*
Snowy owl	*Nyctea scandiaca*
Spotted owl	*Strix occidentalis*
Whiskered owl	*Otus trichopsis*

See also BIRD (color pictures: Hunters of the Sky, Bird Nests, Birds' Eggs).

OWNERSHIP. See ABSTRACT; TITLE.

OWYHEE DAM, *oh WYE ee,* is one of the larger concrete arch gravity dams in the world. It lies on the Owyhee River in Oregon, about 11 miles southwest of the town of Adrian, Ore., near the Idaho state line. The dam is 417 feet high and 830 feet long. It can store 1,120,000 acre-feet of water. It forms a reservoir 52 miles long which stores water for irrigating about 16,000 acres of land. This dam was built by engineers of the United States Bureau of Reclamation. It was completed in 1932 at a cost of $6,671,000.

See also DAM.

OX. Oxen include domestic cattle, water buffalo, bison, musk oxen, brahman, yak, banteng, and other members of the bovine family. Most oxen first came from Asia and Europe. The musk ox and bison are natives of North America. South America, Australia, and Madagascar have no native oxen.

Oxen have heavy bodies, long tails, and divided hoofs, and they chew their cud. Their smooth horns stand out from the side of the head, and are curved.

Domestic oxen give meat, milk, and leather. They are powerful work animals and serve as beasts of burden in some parts of the world.

Scientific Classification. The different kinds of oxen belong to the bovid family, *Bovidae*. Domestic cattle are genus *Bos*, species *B. taurus*.　DONALD F. HOFFMEISTER

Related Articles. For pictures of oxen see the articles IRRIGATION; PARAGUAY; URUGUAY. See also the following articles:

Bison	Gaur	Water Buffalo
Brahman	Kouprey	Yak
Cattle	Musk Ox	

OXALIC ACID, *ahks AL ik,* is a strong organic acid found in many vegetables and other plants. It occurs abundantly as its potassium salt in the sap of dock and other plants in the oxalis and rumex plant families. It is found in spinach, rhubarb, tomatoes, grapes, and sweet potatoes. Oxalic acid is also produced in the body. It has been known since early times.

Industry uses oxalic acid in processing textiles, bleaching straw hats, and removing paint and varnish. It is widely used in chemistry as an analytical reagent. Oxalic acid forms substances called *complexes* with various metals, especially iron. For this reason, it is also used as a rust and scale remover.

The acid is prepared commercially by heating sodium formate with sodium hydroxide. Oxalic acid can also be obtained by treating sugar with nitric acid, or by heating sawdust or other carbohydrates with sodium hydroxide.

Saw-whet Owl
Aegolius acadicus
Found from Alaska to Mexico
(Body length 8 inches)

Great Gray Owl
Strix nebulosa
Found in northern North America and Western Eurasia
(Body length 30 inches)

Ron Austing, Photo Researchers

Frank and John Craighead

OXALIS

Oxalic acid occurs as clear, colorless crystals, soluble in water. It is highly poisonous if swallowed. Its chemical formula is $(COOH)_2 \cdot 2H_2O$, and it melts at 101.5° C. (215° F.). This formula is the dihydrate form, as shown by the two water molecules. When heated to 212° F., the crystals lose the water and have the formula $(COOH)_2$ (see HYDRATE).   JOHN E. LEFFLER

See also ACID; OXALIS.

OXALIS, *AHK suh lis,* is the name of a group of plants, sometimes grown in hanging baskets, window gardens, or rock gardens. There are about 500 different kinds of oxalis. Most of the plants grow in Africa and the warm parts of America. Most kinds of oxalis grow from bulbs or tubers. They have showy flowers in various pastel colors. The leaves are shaped somewhat like clover leaves. Both leaves and flowers close up at night.

The leaves of these plants taste sour, because they contain *oxalic acid.* The acid is so named because it comes from the oxalis plant. The *wood sorrel* is a kind of oxalis that grows in the woods of North America. The leaves of some kinds of oxalis can be used in salads. Oxalis from South America have roots that can be eaten.

Scientific Classification. Oxalis belong to the wood sorrel family, *Oxalidaceae.* They form the genus *Oxalis.* The American wood sorrel is *O. montana.*   DONALD WYMAN

OXBOW LAKE. The curves of winding rivers that have been cut off from the main stream are called oxbow lakes. Such a lake is usually formed when a river changes its course to a more direct path. The river leaves deposits of earth at either end of the curve and these deposits later separate it from the main stream. Oxbow lakes are often rather shallow and may disappear after a time, usually as a result of their being filled with sediment and decayed vegetation. Many of these lakes are found along the course of the Mississippi and Connecticut rivers. There are many oxbow lakes in Louisiana, Arkansas, and Mississippi along the slow-flowing tributaries of the Mississippi River.   F. G. WALTON SMITH

OXEN. See Ox.

OXENSTIERNA, *OOK sen sher nah,* **AXEL GUSTAFSSON** (1583-1654), a Swedish statesman, was friend and adviser to King Gustavus Adolphus. His brilliance as a statesman helped the king achieve great military victories. As chancellor, Oxenstierna directed Sweden's political affairs from 1612 to his death. This period marked Sweden's greatest influence in Europe.

Oxenstierna carried out important diplomatic missions for Gustavus Adolphus during the Thirty Years' War (1618-1648), a struggle between Roman Catholics and Protestants. After Gustavus died in battle in 1632, Oxenstierna directed Sweden's foreign affairs and provided vital leadership throughout the war. From 1636 to 1644, he headed the *regency* (temporary ruling group) that ruled Sweden during Queen Christina's childhood. He was born in Fåno, Sweden.   THEODORE S. HAMEROW

OXFORD, England (pop. 109,350; alt. 235 ft.), is the seat of Oxford University. Oxford shares leadership in English education with Cambridge University. The inhabitants of Oxford are called Oxfordians or Oxonians. The city lies on the Thames River, about 50 miles northwest of London. For location, see GREAT BRITAIN (political map). Automobile factories are on the outskirts of Oxford.   FRANCIS H. HERRICK

OXFORD GROUP. See MORAL RE-ARMAMENT.

OXFORD MOVEMENT is the name given to a revival in the Church of England which began in 1833 at Oxford. A powerful sermon was preached by John Keble (1792-1866), who tried to show the people the evils that were threatening the church because of their indifference and ignorance. Two leaders joined Keble in the Oxford Movement. One was the brilliant John Henry Newman, and the other was the learned Edward B. Pusey (1800-1882). They preached and wrote for a number of years, seeking to impress on the people that the church was "more than a merely human institution; that it had privileges, sacraments, a ministry ordained by Christ; that it was a matter of the highest obligation to remain united to the Church."

They wrote a series of essays called "Tracts for the Times." These were widely read and the movement grew. But in 1841 Newman wrote a tract which was so decidedly Catholic that the Anglican bishops condemned it. In 1845, Newman joined the Roman Catholic Church, and was eventually made a cardinal.

John Keble and Edward B. Pusey continued the work of the Oxford Movement, and new leaders took it up. A notable book, called *Lux Mundi (Light of the World),* edited by Charles Gore, afterwards Bishop of Oxford, was published in 1889. It created a great stir throughout the Anglican Communion.

The Oxford Movement had great influence upon the Anglican world, including the Episcopal Church in the United States. It revived faith in the church as the divine society, not to be controlled by the state. It made the pastor's office more important. It extended the church's work among the poor in larger cities. And in general it awakened church and laity to a broader view of their power and duty.   WALTER H. STOWE

See also CHURCH OF ENGLAND; NEWMAN, JOHN HENRY CARDINAL; WILBERFORCE (Samuel).

OXFORD UNIVERSITY is the oldest university in England. It is situated at Oxford, England, about 50 miles northwest of London. There are several traditions concerning the origin of the institution. No genuine records of the existence of a school at this place before 1167 have been found. But there is record of lecturers from other European countries at Oxford as early as 1117. During 1167 or 1168 foreign students were expelled from the University of Paris when relations between England and France broke off. Many students returned to England and went to Oxford with their masters.

This early school at Oxford was a *guild,* an organization of tradesmen whose chief purpose was to control teaching by limiting the number of teachers. There is no record of the plan of university organization before 1214. Probably the masters elected one of their number as head officer and gave him the title of *chancellor.* The head of the university still bears this title. The students organized themselves into groups, much like modern college fraternities.

There are now 31 colleges and five private halls at Oxford. The three earliest of these are University College, founded in 1249 by William of Durham; Balliol College, founded by John de Baliol about 1263; and Merton College, founded in 1264. Merton is particularly interesting because it was the first college in the modern sense. Its organization became a model for all other colleges at both Oxford and Cambridge. The other colleges

Martha E. Bonham

The Tower of Magdalen College, Oxford University, Is Shown from Across the Cherwell River at Oxford, England.

include Exeter, Queen's, Magdalen (pronounced *MAWD lin*), Corpus Christi, Christ Church, Trinity, New College, and All Souls (for graduates only).

Women have been permitted to attend lectures since 1879. Since 1920, they have been admitted to full membership, and allowed to take degrees.

When the student registers, he is assigned a tutor who guides and advises him through his collegiate career. The tutor outlines the things the student is expected to know, the examinations he must pass, and the reading he must do. University instruction is almost entirely by lecture. There are no recitations or quizzes such as American colleges have. Attendance is not compulsory for lectures. It is the student's duty, guided by his tutor, to attend those that are related to his studies.

The university, and not the colleges, conducts the examinations and grants the degrees. There are two types of bachelor degrees, *pass* and *honors*. The honors degree requires more severe examinations, and may be followed by a Master of Arts degree without further examination. The university also grants the degrees of doctor of divinity, law, medicine, literature, science, music, and others. Americans are especially interested in Oxford because of the system of Rhodes scholarships for students from the United States. The scholarship entitles students to two years' residence and study at Oxford. It may be extended through a third year. Enrollment is more than 10,000. R. W. Morris

See also Bodleian Library; Rhodes Scholarship.

OXFORDSHIRE. See England (color map: The 38 Counties of England).

OXIDATION, *AHK suh DAY shun*, has two meanings in chemistry. The term originally referred to any chemical process in which a substance combines with oxygen. Today, the term also refers to the loss of electrons by a substance during a chemical reaction.

The rusting of iron is a common example of the original meaning of oxidation. In this process, iron (chemical symbol Fe) combines with oxygen to form iron oxide. Iron oxide then combines with water to form rust. Similar examples of oxidation include the decay of plant and animal matter and the formation of vinegar from cider. These oxidations take place slowly, and produce heat slowly as they proceed. Rapid oxidation, called *combustion*, produces heat fast enough to cause a flame. Methane (CH_4) is a gas that oxidizes rapidly.

Today, any process in which a substance loses electrons is also called oxidation. For example, iron atoms are oxidized in the presence of *ions* (electrically charged atoms) of copper (chemical symbol Cu). The chemical equation for this reaction is written:

$$Fe + Cu^{++} \rightarrow Fe^{++} + Cu.$$

In this reaction, each neutral iron atom loses two electrons and becomes an iron ion (Fe^{++}). This half of the complete reaction can be written:

$$Fe \rightarrow Fe^{++} + 2e^{-}.$$

Electrons released during oxidation must be captured by another substance. The process of gaining electrons is called *reduction*. In the reaction of iron and copper, electrons released by the iron atoms are captured by the copper ions. Each copper ion (Cu^{++}) captures two electrons and becomes a neutral copper atom. The re-

Electrochemical Oxidation occurs when a substance loses electrons. When an iron nail is dipped into a concentrated solution of copper sulfate, *above*, iron atoms in the nail are oxidized. Each iron atom loses two electrons and becomes an iron ion in the solution. Copper ions in the solution capture the released electrons, and become copper atoms which coat the nail.

Oxidation With Oxygen occurs when oxygen combines with another substance. In a gas flame, *above*, oxygen combines rapidly with carbon and hydrogen atoms in methane molecules, producing carbon dioxide gas and water vapor. When metal rusts, *below*, iron combines slowly with oxygen and water, forming rust.

duction half of the complete reaction can be written:

$$2e^- + Cu^{++} \rightarrow Cu.$$

One substance cannot be oxidized unless another substance is reduced. The combination of reduction and oxidation is called the *redox* process. ESMARCH S. GILREATH

Related Articles in WORLD BOOK include:

Combustion	Food (Food as Fuel)	Reduction
Corrosion	Oxidation Potential	Rust
Fire	Oxide	

OXIDATION POTENTIAL is a measure, in volts, of an element's tendency to *oxidize* (lose electrons). The symbol for oxidation potential is E°. If a chemist knows an element's oxidation potential, he can predict how the element will react with another substance. He can also tell how much voltage would be produced if the element were used to make a battery.

Chemists measure the oxidation potential of a metal by means of an electrical cell that consists of two electrodes in a solution that conducts electricity. One electrode is the metal whose potential is to be measured. The other electrode is hydrogen. In this cell, a chemical reaction takes place that produces a voltage, E°, between the electrodes. This voltage produces a flow of electrons from the hydrogen electrode to the metal, if the metal's tendency to lose electrons is less than that of hydrogen. It produces a flow of electrons in the opposite direction if the metal's tendency to lose electrons is greater than that of hydrogen. Oxidation potentials are measured at the standard conditions of 25° C. and one atmosphere of pressure (14.7 pounds per square inch).

Chemists measure the voltages produced by the test cell with a voltmeter. In the United States, a metal is assigned a positive oxidation potential (+) if electrons go from the metal to hydrogen. A metal is assigned a negative potential (−) if electrons flow from hydrogen to the metal. Scientists in other countries use a system in which the plus and minus signs are opposite those in the U.S. system. For example, the E° of iron is +0.44 in the United States and −0.44 in other countries. In both systems, the oxidation potential of hydrogen is arbitrarily assigned as zero.

E° values are used extensively in chemistry and physics. Scientists can predict the total voltage of a battery cell by adding the E° values of the chemical elements that make up the reaction. Oxidation potentials can also be used to predict whether a chemical reaction will take place. Chemical reactions take place spontaneously if the total voltage of the reacting elements is positive. F. BASOLO

See also ELECTROMOTIVE SERIES; ELECTRIC CURRENT; OXIDATION; ELECTRODE; BATTERY.

─── STANDARD OXIDATION POTENTIALS ───

Element	E° (volts)	Element	E° (volts)
Potassium	+2.92	Hydrogen	0
Magnesium	+2.37	Copper	−0.34
Aluminum	+1.66	Mercury	−0.79
Zinc	+0.76	Silver	−0.80
Iron	+0.44	Gold	−1.42

OXIDE, *AHK side*, is a chemical compound of oxygen with some other element. Oxides are commonly formed when the elements are oxidized. For example, burning the carbon present in coal or wood gives carbon dioxide (CO_2) and carbon monoxide (CO). Burning is rapid oxidation. Carbon dioxide is also formed by the slow oxidation of animal cells, and is exhaled from the lungs.

The rusting of iron is slow oxidation. Rust contains ferric oxide (Fe_2O_3).

Metallic oxides combine with water to form basic hydroxides, while nonmetallic oxides with water form oxygen acids. The oxides of sulfur and nitrogen are important because they can be used to form sulfuric and nitric acids. Nitrous oxide, a nitrogen-oxygen compound, is a common anesthetic. It is also called *laughing gas* because inhaling it makes some persons laugh.

Calcium oxide is *quicklime* (CaO). When mixed with water it forms the *slaked lime* used in whitewash and plaster. Sand, which is so important in glassmaking, is one form of *silicon dioxide*, called silica (SiO_2). Other forms are quartz, onyx, and opal.

See also MERCURIC OXIDE; NITROUS OXIDE; OXIDATION.

OXIDIZER. See ROCKET (Liquid-Fuel Rockets).

OXNAM, GARFIELD BROMLEY (1891-1963), was a bishop of the Methodist Church. He was bishop of the Washington, D.C., area from 1952 to 1960, when he retired. His books and speeches emphasized his liberal social beliefs. They favor justice for laboring people and equal rights for all classes. Bishop Oxnam's books include *Russian Impressions* (1927), *Youth and the New America* (1928), *Facing the Future Unafraid* (1944), and *Labor in Tomorrow's World* (1945).

He was ordained a Methodist minister in 1916. He taught at the Boston University of Theology from 1927 to 1928. He was president of DePauw University in Greencastle, Ind., from 1928 to 1936. He was bishop of the Omaha area from 1936 to 1940, of the Boston area from 1940 to 1944, and of the New York area from 1944 to 1952.

Oxnam became president of the Federal Council of Churches of Christ in 1944, and later chairman of its Commission to Study the Bases of a Just and Durable Peace. He was president of the Methodist Church Council of World Service and Finance in 1956, and of the Council of Bishops of the Methodist Church in 1958. He was born in Sonora, Calif. He attended the University of Southern California and Boston University, and traveled in the Far East.   L. J. TRINTERUD

Brown Bros.

G. Bromley Oxnam

OXUS RIVER. See AMU DARYA.

OXYACETYLENE. See ACETYLENE; WELDING.

OXYGEN, *AHK suh jun*, is a life-supporting gas and a chemical element. Nearly all living things need oxygen to stay alive. Oxygen combines with other chemicals in plant and animal cells to produce energy needed for life processes. Oxygen is also needed to make most fuels burn. During the burning process, oxygen combines with the fuel in a chemical reaction. Heat is released during this process.

Oxygen is one of the most plentiful chemical elements on the earth. It makes up about a fifth of the volume of air. Nitrogen makes up most of the other four-fifths. Oxygen is also found in the earth's crust and in water. This oxygen is not pure, but is combined with other

OXYGEN

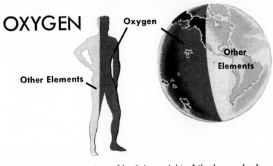

Oxygen makes up about ⅔ of the weight of the human body. The oxygen in the earth's crust weighs almost as much as all the other chemical elements put together.

elements. On the average, 100 pounds of the earth's crust contains $46\frac{1}{2}$ pounds of oxygen. Nearly half of the weight of most rocks and minerals is oxygen. Every 100 pounds of water contains about 89 pounds of oxygen. Hydrogen makes up the other 11 pounds.

How Oxygen Supports Life. Only a few kinds of living things, including certain germs, can live without *free* (chemically uncombined) oxygen. Man and the other land animals get oxygen from the air. Fish and most other water animals get dissolved oxygen from water. Free oxygen enters a man's blood stream through the lungs. It enters a fish's blood stream through the gills. The blood carries oxygen to the cells of the body. In the cells, oxygen combines with chemicals obtained from food. Energy produced during this process makes it possible for each cell to perform its function in the body. Carbon dioxide is produced in the cells as a waste product (see RESPIRATION).

Men once believed that breathing pure oxygen would lead to an early death. They incorrectly thought the body's cells would use oxygen too fast, and a person would die of exhaustion. But in certain situations, breathing pure oxygen may be necessary. For example, pilots who fly at high altitudes, where the air is too thin to supply enough oxygen, breathe from tanks of pure oxygen.

Plant cells use oxygen in much the same way that animal cells do. Plant cells also make oxygen in the process of *photosynthesis*. During this process, the cells use the energy of sunlight to make sugar from carbon dioxide and water. Oxygen is produced during photosynthesis as a by-product, and is released into the atmosphere.

Other Uses of Oxygen. Oxygen has many uses in industry. Some steel is manufactured by the *basic oxygen process*. In this process, a stream of high-pressure oxygen blasts down on melted pig iron and burns out impurities. This process can change a hundred tons of pig iron to steel in about an hour. Welders mix oxygen with fuel in their torches to produce an extremely hot flame with a temperature of about 6000° F.

Liquid oxygen, called *LOX*, is used in rockets propelled by liquid fuels. LOX burns various fuels, including kerosene and liquid hydrogen, to produce the rocket's *thrust* (pushing force). LOX is also mixed with other fuels to make explosives for blasting.

Making Oxygen. Most commercial oxygen is distilled from liquid air. During the distillation process, the nitrogen boils before the oxygen does, because nitrogen has a lower boiling point. As the nitrogen boils away,

679

the liquid air is left with a greater concentration of oxygen. Commercial oxygen is stored in steel tanks at a pressure of about 2,000 pounds per square inch, more than a hundred times the pressure of the atmosphere.

Small amounts of oxygen can be made by heating potassium chlorate. A little manganese dioxide added to the potassium chlorate speeds up oxygen formation.

History. Oxygen was discovered by two chemists working independently. They were Carl Scheele of Sweden and Joseph Priestley of England. Scheele's laboratory notes show that he prepared oxygen between 1770 and 1773 by heating various compounds, including saltpeter and mercuric oxide. But Scheele's experiments were not published until 1775. Priestley also published his experiments in 1775. He described how he prepared oxygen in 1774 by heating mercuric oxide.

Scheele called oxygen *fire air*. Priestley called it *dephlogisticated air*. In 1777, the French chemist Antoine Lavoisier named the gas *oxygen*. The word means *acid producer*. Lavoisier and others had found that oxygen is a part of several acids. Lavoisier incorrectly reasoned that oxygen is needed to make all acids. He combined the Greek words *oxys* (meaning *sharp* or *acid*) and *gignomai* (meaning *produce*) to form the French word *oxygene*. This word is *oxygen* in English.

Chemical Properties. Oxygen is a colorless, odorless, and tasteless gas. Its chemical symbol is O. Its atomic number is 8 and its atomic weight is 15.9994. Ordinary oxygen molecules are made of two oxygen atoms. Molecules made of three oxygen atoms make up the gas *ozone*, O_3. Oxygen combines with many elements, forming a class of compounds called *oxides*. The process by which oxygen combines with other elements is called *oxidation*.

Oxygen changes to a pale blue liquid when cooled to its *boiling point*, $-183.0°$ C. at atmospheric pressure. Oxygen liquefies at a higher temperature when the pressure is increased. At a pressure of 730 pounds per square inch, oxygen liquefies at $-118.8°$ C. These values are oxygen's *critical temperature and pressure*. It is impossible to liquefy oxygen at a higher temperature at any pressure. Liquid oxygen is magnetic and can be held between the poles of a strong magnet. Oxygen freezes at $-218.4°$ C.

FRANK C. ANDREWS

Related Articles in WORLD BOOK include:

Anoxia	Liquid Air	Oxygen Tent
Element, Chemical	Oxidation	Ozone
Iron and Steel (The Basic Oxygen Process)	Oxide	Welding

OXYGEN TENT is a device used in medicine for patients who require more oxygen than is normally contained in the air. There are several types of tents. The simplest tent for emergency purposes is a dome-shaped hood made of material through which oxygen cannot pass. This tent is large enough to completely cover an infant. The oxygen enters through a hose at the top.

Professional types of oxygen tents are larger and more convenient. These tents cover the entire head end of the bed. Windows of mica or some other transparent material that will not burn are provided for vision and for the convenience of nursing care. Most professional model tents have a motor-driven fan for circulating the oxygen-air mixture. Others use the oxygen pressure or the energy gained from melting ice. The oxygen-enriched air passes through a chamber filled with ice for cooling and a thermostat is used for maintaining a comfortable temperature. In some instances, the humidity is mechanically controlled and is normally kept at 50 per cent. The carbon dioxide exhaled by the patient is removed by soda lime.

Some patients feel distressed when they are shut inside an oxygen tent. An oxygen room may be preferable for such patients. Some modern tents are made of large sheets of transparent, fire-resistant material and the patient does not feel so confined in them.

The oxygen tent is used in the treatment of *anoxia* (the deficiency of oxygen supply to the tissues). It is valuable as an aid when anoxia results from such diseases as pneumonia, heart ailments, and carbon-monoxide poisoning.

HOWARD A. CARTER

See also ANOXIA; OXYGEN.

OXYGENATED WATER. See HYDROGEN PEROXIDE.

OXYHEMOGLOBIN. See HEMOGLOBIN.

OXYTOCIN. See GLAND (The Pituitary Gland).

Linde Company

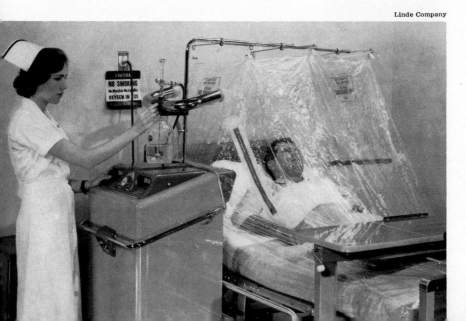

An Oxygen Tent, *left,* provides a patient with air containing more than the normal amount of oxygen. This tent covers a patient's entire bed.

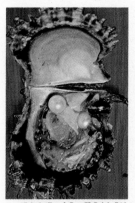

Sakata Pearl Co. (U.S.A.), Ltd.

The Pacific Pearl Oyster, *above,* has been cut to show the two gleaming jewels inside.

Young Oysters, *below,* are about as big as a needle point. They float and swim in the sea.

U.S. Dept. of Interior

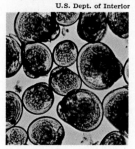

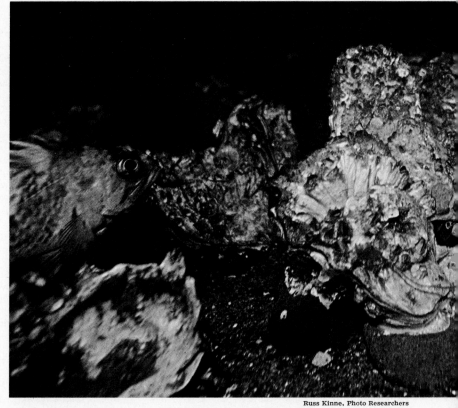

Russ Kinne, Photo Researchers

Oysters Live in Quiet Waters on the Ocean Bottom. They attach their shells to rocks or other hard objects in shallow water near the shore.

OYSTER is a sea animal with a soft body inside a hard, two-piece shell. Oysters live on the ocean bottom, mostly in inlets near shore where the water is usually quiet and not deep. They are found in many parts of the world that have a mild or warm climate.

Oysters are among man's most valuable shellfish. Oysters of the Persian Gulf and the Pacific Ocean make the pearls used as jewels. Man also uses oysters as food, and catches more oysters than any other shellfish. The United States produces about 800 million pounds of oysters a year, more than any other country.

Man has eaten oysters for thousands of years. About A.D. 43, Roman pioneers in England caught oysters along the sea coasts. In winter, they packed the animals in snow and ice, put them in cloth bags, and sent them to Rome. Fishermen of ancient Rome raised oysters on "farms" in the waters off the Italian coasts. Today, about half the oysters in the United States come from undersea farms along the Atlantic Coast.

Oysters, like clams, scallops, and some other shellfish, are called *mollusks.* Mollusks make up a major

---

R. Tucker Abbott, the contributor of this article, holds the du Pont Chair of Malacology at the Delaware Museum of Natural History and is the author of American Seashells *and* Sea Shells of the World.

---

division of the animal kingdom. For a description of other kinds of mollusks, see the WORLD BOOK article on MOLLUSK.

The Body of an Oyster

Shell. An oyster's shell is the animal's skeleton. It consists of two parts called *valves.* Oysters are often called *bivalves,* which means *two valves.* The valves are held together at one end by a hinge. One valve is deeper, larger, and thicker than the other, and the oyster's body rests in it. The second valve acts as a lid.

--- FACTS IN BRIEF ---

Names: *Male,* none; *female,* none; *young,* spat or seed oyster; *group,* bed.

Hatching Period: About 10 hours.

Number of Newborn: About 500 million a year for each oyster.

Length of Life: About 6 years.

Where Found: Mild or warm seas of the world.

Scientific Classification: Oysters used for food make up the oyster family *Ostreidae.* The oyster of the eastern North American coast is genus *Crassostrea,* species *C. virginica.* The European oyster is genus *Ostrea,* species *O. edulis.* The pearl oyster belongs to the pearl oyster family *Pteridae.* It is genus *Pinctada,* species *P. margaritifera.*

681

The oyster usually keeps the valves of its shell open just a bit. When an enemy comes near, the oyster snaps the valves shut by means of a strong muscle called an *adductor*. This muscle attaches the oyster's body to the inside of the shell. It holds the valves closed until danger has passed. An oyster can keep its shell closed for as long as several weeks.

The *mantle*, a fleshy organ, lines the inside of the shell and surrounds the body organs. It produces liquid substances that harden and form the shell. It also makes the colors that appear in the shell. The mantle adds material to the shell, so that the shell becomes larger as the oyster grows. Lines on the outside of the shell mark the additions of this material from the mantle. The inside of the shells of oysters used for food is dull white and purple. The inside of pearl oyster shells is covered with a smooth, shiny substance called *mother-of-pearl* or *nacre*. For information about how shells grow, see the WORLD BOOK article on SHELL (How Shells Are Formed).

Sometimes a grain of sand or some other object gets into the shell and rubs against the oyster's body. The mantle covers the object with thin layers of shell material, and in this way forms a pearl. Pearls used as gems come from pearl oysters, which live in tropical waters. Pearls produced by the oysters used as food have little value.

Body Organs. The oyster's soft body is a grayish mass of tissues that contain the body organs. The animal has no head. It has two pairs of W-shaped gills that look somewhat like the surface of a feather. The oyster uses its gills to breathe and also to capture food. Hairlike parts of the gills gather tiny plants and animals from the water and push them toward the oyster's mouth. The mouth is a funnel-shaped opening at the narrowest part of the body. The oyster's digestive system includes a stomach, a digestive gland, and an intestine. The oyster's heart has two chambers that pump blood throughout the animal's body. The blood carries food and oxygen to all parts of the body, and removes waste materials.

An oyster has no eyes, ears, or nose, so it cannot see, hear, or smell. However, two rows of small feelers on the edges of the mantle respond to certain changes in the oyster's surroundings. The feelers hang over the edges of the open shell, and changes in light or in chemicals in the water cause them to contract. The contracting feelers signal the powerful adductor muscle to close the shell against possible danger.

The Life of an Oyster

An oyster spends all except the first few weeks of its life in one spot on the sea bottom. It uses the shell material produced by the mantle to fasten itself to a rock or to some other object in quiet waters. The shell substance hardens, and holds the larger valve firmly in place. Most oysters live about 6 years, but some live as long as 20 years.

Young. A female oyster may produce as many as 500 million eggs a year. The yellowish eggs are so tiny that a mass of them looks somewhat like thick cream. The female lays the eggs by spraying them into the water. The *spat* (young oysters) hatch about 10 hours later. Each spat is about as big as the point of a needle, and looks somewhat like a toy top. The young oysters swim by means of hairlike growths called *cilia*. The cilia beat the water like whips and push the oysters forward. When the oysters are about 24 hours old, their shells begin to grow.

An oyster spends about the first two weeks of its life floating and swimming. During this time, the animal has a muscular "foot" that extends from its body. The foot disappears after the oyster finds a place to settle. The oyster uses its foot as a feeler to test rocks, empty shells, and other hard objects. Then it fastens itself to one of the objects. Several oysters may use the same rock as a home. They may attach themselves not only to the rock, but also to each other. Large, crowded *beds* (groups) of oysters can be found in rocky inlets along the coasts.

Young oysters grow rapidly. A month-old oyster is about the size of a pea, and a year-old oyster is about an inch in diameter. Oysters grow about an inch a year for three or four years, and then grow even more slowly for the rest of their lives. Some oysters grow as long as 12 inches.

Enemies. An oyster has many enemies, and no defense except its shell. Man is probably the oyster's greatest enemy. He catches and eats millions of oysters every year. Fish may swallow thousands of newly hatched oysters in one gulp. Crabs and other sea animals eat young oysters after crushing the soft new shells. Starfish pull the shells open with their tube feet and eat the oyster meat. Oyster-drill snails and whelks use their filelike teeth to bore holes in the shells and suck out the soft parts. A bird called the oyster catcher pries open the

THE BODY OF AN OYSTER

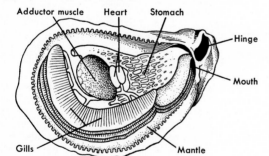

Adductor muscle   Heart   Stomach

Hinge

Mouth

Gills   Mantle

THE PARTS OF AN OYSTER SHELL

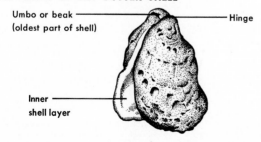

Umbo or beak
(oldest part of shell)

Hinge

Inner
shell layer

WORLD BOOK illustration by Tom Dolan

Harvesting Oysters with a dredge, oystermen watch the heavy net haul up their catch from the ocean bottom. The oysters are dumped in a pile on the ship's deck, and then are taken into port to be cleaned and packaged for market.

M. E. Warren, Photo Researchers

shells with its strong beak. Diseases caused by viruses that are harmless to man may kill millions of oysters in one year.

The Oyster Industry

Oyster Farming. Oysters are one of the most popular foods that man takes from the sea. Man's fondness for eating oysters—and his fear that they might die out—led him to raise the animals on undersea "farms."

An oyster farmer chooses an area of quiet water where the sea bottom is firm. Loose, shifting sand or deep, soft mud might cover and smother the oysters. Each farmer marks his plot with floats. He puts old shells or slabs of hardened clay called *tiles* on the sea floor. The shells and tiles provide places for the young oysters to attach them-

WHERE OYSTERS ARE FOUND

The black areas of the map show the parts of the world where edible oysters are found. The map includes oyster farm areas.

selves. The oyster farmer can buy *seed oysters* to "plant" in his farming area. The oysters grow there and are harvested when they are 2 to 4 years old and 2 to 4 inches in diameter.

Almost all the oysters that man raises for market come from oyster farms. One of the largest oyster-farming centers in the world is in the Bay of Arcachon, on the southwestern coast of France. More than 75 per cent of the oysters produced in the United States come from farms along the Atlantic Coast. The beds in American coastal waters, especially those of Chesapeake Bay, are also among the largest in the world. Oystermen fish in the waters along the Atlantic Coast from Maine to Florida, and along the Gulf Coast from Florida to Texas. They also fish along the Pacific Coast from California to Washington.

The leading oyster-producing states are Virginia, Louisiana, and Maryland. In Canada, the provinces of British Columbia and Prince Edward Island produce the most oysters. France, The Netherlands, and Italy are the largest oyster-producing countries of Europe. Japan, Australia, and New Zealand also produce many oysters.

Oyster Harvesting takes place during fall and winter in most regions. Groups of oysters in shallow waters are picked up with tongs that open and close somewhat as scissors do. Oysters in deeper waters are brought up by machines called *dredges*. The dredges are operated by hand or by steam power.

Some oysters are sold while still in their shells. Workers scrub the shells, pack the oysters in ice, and ship them to market. Most oysters are sold unshelled. Men called *shuckers* have great skill in removing the shells. A shucker places the edge of the shell on a chisel blade, which is fastened to a heavy block of wood. Then he hits the shell with a wooden hammer. The blow drives the tip of the chisel between the valves of the closed shell. The shucker then slips a knife blade into the shell and pulls it open so the valves lie flat. The adductor muscle, which attaches the body to the shell, is cut, and the soft flesh is removed, washed, and packed for shipment.

There is an old saying that oysters should be eaten only in months that have an "R" in their names. The saying once had some basis, because most oysters caught during the summer months are of poor quality. Today, with the use of modern preserving methods, oysters can be eaten safely the year round. They are caught when they are of top quality, and are canned or quick-frozen for later use. R. TUCKER ABBOTT

See also MOLLUSK; MOTHER-OF-PEARL; PEARL; SHELL.

OYSTER CATCHER is the name of a family of wading birds which live on seacoasts in most sections of the world. The name comes from the sharp-edged, chisel-shaped bill with which an oyster catcher stabs open oysters, limpets, and clams upon which it feeds.

The common oyster catcher of the United States lives on both coasts of the Americas, but usually is not seen north of New Jersey in the east, and Lower California in the west. It has smoky-brown body feathers and a black head and neck. The under parts of its body are white. The black oyster catcher lives on the Pacific

The Oyster Catcher has a long, strong bill which it uses like a chisel to open the oysters it finds along the shore.

Coast. The *sea pie* of Great Britain is the European kind of oyster catcher. Oyster catchers lay their three or four eggs among the bare pebbles.

Scientific Classification. Oyster catchers form the oyster catcher family, *Haematopodidae.* The east and west coast oyster catcher is genus *Haematopus*, species *H. palliatus;* the black is *H. bachmani;* and the European oyster catcher is *H. ostralegus.*   ALEXANDER WETMORE

OYSTER PLANT. See SALSIFY.

OZALID PROCESS is a method of producing copies of documents. The original paper is placed on a chemically treated sheet of Ozalid paper and fed into an Ozalid machine. Ultraviolet light shines through the translucent paper of the original copy and changes the chemicals on the Ozalid paper to a colorless compound. But it does not shine through the opaque lines or letters on the original copy. The Ozalid machine then develops the Ozalid paper, and the parts not struck by ultraviolet light appear, making an accurate copy.

OZARK MOUNTAINS. This range of hills extends from the southern part of Illinois, across Missouri, and into Arkansas and Oklahoma. The Ozarks rise from 1,500 feet to 2,300 feet above sea level. The highest peaks are the Boston Mountains of Arkansas.

The Ozark region has a total area of about 40,000 square miles. The hills are covered with timber and contain rich mineral deposits. Lead, coal, and iron are mined here. Marble quarrying is also carried on. One of the low plateaus in the Ozarks, known as Springfield Plain, covers about 10,000 square miles in western Missouri, northwestern Arkansas, and northeastern Oklahoma. This plateau contains good farm lands on which corn, wheat, and fruits are grown. Other prairie regions in the Ozarks provide good grazing lands.   WALLACE E. AKIN

See also MISSOURI (Land); ARKANSAS (pictures).

OZARK NATIONAL SCENIC RIVERWAYS. See NATIONAL PARK SYSTEM (Parkways and Other National Parklands).

OZARKS, COLLEGE OF THE. See UNIVERSITIES AND COLLEGES (table).

OZARKS, SCHOOL OF THE. See UNIVERSITIES AND COLLEGES (table).

OZAWA, *oh ZAH wah,* **SEIJI,** *SAY jee,* (1935-   ), is one of the outstanding symphony orchestra conductors of his time. He established his reputation with a broad range of music, including that of many modern Japanese composers.

Ozawa was born in Hoten, Japan. He left Japan for Europe in 1959 and studied with the Austrian conductor Herbert von

Seiji Ozawa

Karajan in West Berlin. There, Leonard Bernstein, conductor of the New York Philharmonic Orchestra, observed Ozawa and named him one of the orchestra's three assistant conductors for the 1961-1962 season. Bernstein recalled Ozawa as sole assistant conductor for the 1964-1965 season. From 1965 to 1969, Ozawa served as conductor of the Toronto Symphony. In 1968, he was named conductor and musical director of the San Francisco Symphony.   KEITH POLK

OZONE, *O zone,* is a form of oxygen. Its sharp odor is often noticed near electric switches and machinery, and in the air after a thunder storm. Ozone is a strong cleaning agent, because it reacts with dirt and soot. Ozone is also used to remove unpleasant odors from foods and from the air, to kill germs, and to bleach oils, fats, and textiles. It was discovered in 1840 by German chemist Christian Friedrich Schönbein.

Molecules of ordinary oxygen are made of two oxygen atoms joined tightly together. But ozone molecules have a third oxygen atom loosely attached to these two. The third atom can easily separate from the molecule and combine with other substances. As a result, ozone is a chemically active gas. Every flash of lightning converts some oxygen into ozone. The gas is also formed by electric sparks, such as those from motors.

Very high energy radiation from the sun strikes oxygen in the earth's atmosphere and converts some of it to ozone. On the average, air at ground level contains less than 1 part of ozone per million parts of air. But 15 miles above the ground there is a more concentrated layer of ozone. This layer contains only about six parts of ozone per million parts of air. But it shields the earth from much of the sun's ultraviolet light. Ultraviolet rays harm living tissues. Without this protective ozone layer, plants and animals probably could not live on the earth.

Commercial ozone is made in a machine called an *ozonizer.* In this machine, either air or oxygen blows past metal plates that are charged with high-voltage electricity. As the gas passes between these plates, some of the oxygen molecules split into atoms. These atoms then unite with oxygen molecules to form ozone molecules. The remaining oxygen molecules can be sent through the machine again.

The chemical symbol for ozone is O_3, and its molecular weight is 47.998. Concentrated ozone has a pale blue color. In strong concentrations, ozone irritates the eyes and nose and is highly poisonous. At atmospheric pressure, the gas liquefies at $-111.9°$ C. and freezes at $-193°$ C.   FRANK C. ANDREWS